① read
② class/notes
③ re-read/notes

SEVENTH EDITION

ANNOTATED INSTRUCTOR'S EDITION

Social Psychology

UNDERSTANDING HUMAN INTERACTION

ROBERT A. BARON
Rensselaer Polytechnic Institute

DONN BYRNE
University at Albany/State University of New York

Instructor's Section Prepared by

Bem P. Allen
Western Illinois University

Gene F. Smith
Western Illinois University

Allyn and Bacon

Boston ■ London ■ Toronto ■ Sydney ■ Tokyo ■ Singapore

Vice President and Publisher: Susan Badger
Editorial Assistant: Laura L. Ellingson
Cover Administrator: Linda Dickinson
Manufacturing Buyer: Megan Cochran
Editorial-Production Service: Leslie Anderson Olney
Page Layout Artist and Quark Files: DeNee Reiton Skipper
Text Designer: Melinda Grosser
Cover Designer: Design Ad Cetera

Printed in the United States of America

10 9 8 7 6 5 4 3 2 1   98 97 96 95 94 93

ISBN 0-205-15181-7

Brief Contents

Contents

Chapter One ▪ The Field of Social Psychology: How We Think About and Interact with Others 2

Chapter Two ▪ Social Perception: Understanding Others 38

Chapter Three ▪ Social Cognition: Thinking about Others and the Social World 82

Chapter Four ▪ *Attitudes: Evaluating the Social World* 126

Chapter Five ▪ *Social Identity: Self and Gender* 172

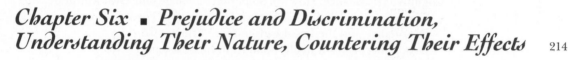

Chapter Six ▪ *Prejudice and Discrimination, Understanding Their Nature, Countering Their Effects* 214

Chapter Seven ▪ Interpersonal Attraction: Getting Acquainted, Becoming Friends 262

Chapter Eight ▪ Close Relationships: Friendship, Love, and Sexuality 304

Chapter Nine ▪ *Social Influence: Changing Others' Behavior*   348

Chapter Ten ▪ *Prosocial Behavior: Providing Help to Others* 390

Chapter Eleven ▪ *Aggression: Its Nature, Causes, and Control* 432

INSTRUCTOR'S SECTION

Chapter Twelve ▪ Groups and Individuals: The Consequences of Belonging   480

Chapter Thirteen ▪ *Social Psychology and the Individual: Population, Health, and Environmental Applications* 534

Only Baron & Byrne is as

DYNAMIC &
UP TO DATE
AS THE FIELD IT COVERS!

SOCIAL PSYCHOLOGY:
Understanding Human Interaction
Seventh Edition

Robert A. Baron
Rensselaer Polytechnic Institute
Donn Byrne
State University of New York at Albany

More students — over 1.2 million — and professors have used Baron and Byrne than any other text in the history of the field.

What makes it such an overwhelming favorite?

The authors' unparalleled commitment to making each edition the most up-to-date and innovative text available!

And the Seventh Edition continues to lead the way — with new research and extensive coverage of the dynamic changes in social psychology!

Only Baron and Byrne gives students a text that truly captures the pulse and excitement of social psychology.

And the supplements package is more comprehensive than ever! It includes a new and expanded Test Bank, an Annotated Instructor's Edition, exclusive CNN Video Series, Video Guide, Video Library, Study Guide, Transparencies and more!

Only Baron & Byrne is as
DYNAMIC & UP TO DATE
AS THE FIELD IT COVERS!

Powerful New Features Give Students the Knowledge They Need to Understand Human Interaction!

"SOCIAL DIVERSITY: A CRITICAL ANALYSIS" sections

Students can examine a wide range of issues relating to cultural and ethnic diversity in these new in-depth sections found at the end of each chapter. They discuss recent research on the differences between cultures or ethnic groups within a given society with respect to various aspects of social behavior. Students will become sensitive to the fact that practices and behaviors accepted in one society may be viewed quite differently in another.

A few key topics include ...

■ How Culture Shapes Thought: Effects of Cultural Schemas (Chapter 3)

■ Divergent Female Gender Roles in Singapore, Mexico, and among Native Americans (Chapter 5)

■ Love and Intimacy: Western Europe, South Africa, Japan, and the U.S. (Chapter 8)

■ Culture and Aggression: The Social Context of Violence (Chapter 11)

Social Diversity ▼ A Critical Analysis

Help-Seeking in Communal and Individualistic Cultures: Israel and Hong Kong

Cross-cultural comparisons often focus on societies that differ in their emphasis on individual versus communal behavior. At the individualistic extreme on the spectrum, each person strives to be a self-contained unit and seeks success and recognition on the basis of individual achievement. It's every man for himself, every woman for herself. In contrast, communal societies stress interlocking familylike connections in which individuals depend on one another, sharing

unique opportunity for such comparisons because there are both urban dwellers whose environment stresses typical Western attitudes such as self-reliance and individual achievement and kibbutz dwellers whose environment stresses egalitarian-communal ideology (see Figure 10.21).

Based on these cultural differences, Nadler predicted that those living in a kibbutz would expect to be dependent on one another and thus should be willing to seek help when it is need-

subgroups. Some high school students were placed in a situation that involved a group, while others were supposed to be working only for themselves. In other words, they were given a communal task or an individual task. Specifically, subjects worked on anagrams that were supposedly a measure of success at the university; a score would be assigned either to the person's group or to the individual. They were allowed to ask for hints on those anagrams for which they

---

and behave. Such findings suggest that gender role behavior involves expectancies that are not always carried out and that behavior may depend on the sex of the audience. Also note that despite assumptions of widespread sex differences, men and women were alike on more traits than those on which they differed.

On the topic of sex differences, firm conclusions remain elusive. We understand that you probably feel frustrated when we say that, but our statement reflects the reality of scientific research and thinking at this time. On second thought, you might prefer scientific uncertainty to the unscientific certainty that once surrounded these issues. In Great Britain in the nineteenth century, Queen Victoria became incensed at talk of the "mad, wicked folly" of women's rights "with all its attendant horrors" and let her subjects know her conclusions about sex differences. "God created men and women different—then let them remain each in their own position" (Queen Victoria, 1881).

Despite the convictions of Queen Victoria, men and women do not necessarily remain in fixed roles, as illustrated in the following **Social Diversity** section.

Social Diversity ▼ A Critical Analysis

Divergent Female Gender Roles in Singapore and Mexico, and among Native Americans

Studies of behavior in different cultures provide important evidence relevant to the question of biological versus environmental determinants of gender differences. When cultural anthropologists, social psychologists, and others find quite different behavior in different cultures, this provides evidence supporting environmental effects. Conversely, when behavior *doesn't* vary despite differences in language, race, religion, political structure, and so on, biological determinism is supported. What do such studies tell us about gender roles?

In Singapore, Yuen and Lim (1990) examined gender roles in a changing society. In this business-oriented nation ("Singapore, Inc."), the traditional Anglo-Chinese culture of achieving men and homebound women is being supplanted by

an equal-opportunity culture in which success depends primarily on merit. The researchers had male and female business administration students read three scenarios involving managers of both sexes in organizational settings. Male participants rated male business managers more positively than female managers in the first two stories. That is, the traditional gender roles of this society seemed to be operating as part of their decision-making. When an additional variable was added to the third scenario (the developmental *potential* of the managers), the business students made quite different decisions. High-potential females were viewed as favorably as high-potential males; responses to low-potential individuals were quite negative, with males at the bottom. Here the information

about managerial potential was relevant to the new, merit-based structure of Singapore, and the old gender roles were set aside. Even in this highly traditional society, men and women are beginning to alter their perception of gender in response to new cultural pressures.

In a quite different setting—the Mexican town of Morelos—change is not a factor, but Martin (1990) has found that gender roles involve elements different from those in either the old or new Singapore and from those in the United States. In some respects, gender roles resemble those found in many cultures; that is, the women are perceived as the primary caretakers, and they look after the children, cook the meals, and so forth. In other respects, gender expectancies differ quite a bit. The women of Morelos also

"INDIVIDUAL DIVERSITY" sections

Instead of dealing with individual differences in a separate chapter, they are now included throughout the text. These sections illustrate that differences are not an isolated area of study; rather, they play a role in all aspects of social behavior. Students can explore these differences, and analyze how they relate to their own personalities and their own understanding of diversity.

Chapters include material on ...

■ Showing Less Than We Really Feel: Self-Monitoring and the Suppression of Gloating in Public (Chapter 2)

■ Need for Cognition and the Nature of Social Thought (Chapter 3)

■ Personality and Obedience: Who Resists and Who Obeys? (Chapter 9)

■ The Altruistic Personality: Dispositional Factors Associated with Providing First Aid (Chapter 10)

"WORK IN PROGRESS" sections

Research in social psychology is a vital, ongoing process — and what better way to show students than by giving them actual examples!

"Work in Progress" sections in each chapter describe follow-up research to studies covered in the text. In many cases, this research, by well-known psychologists such as Bill Swann, Jennifer Crocker, Brenda Major, Sam Gaertner, and Anthony Pratkanis, is so current that is has not yet been published.

Students are challenged to participate actively in the learning process and to sharpen their critical thinking skills.

A sampling of topics includes ...

■ The Retrospective Impact of Expectations: Remembering What We Expected to Experience...But Didn't (Chapter 3)

■ Prejudice in a Multicultural High School: Testing the Common Group Identity Model in a Field Setting (Chapter 6)

■ Complaining in Close Relationships: Evidence For Some Intriguing Gender Differences (Chapter 9)

Individual Diversity

THE ALTRUISTIC PERSONALITY: DISPOSITIONAL FACTORS ASSOCIATED WITH HELPING OTHERS

Over the years, despite the demonstrated importance of situational variables, numerous investigations have suggested that some individuals are more altruistic than others. In some instances, altruistic behavior seems to be motivated by other concerns. Certain individuals, for example, have a strong *need for approval*, and they are more likely to provide help *if* they have previously received positive interpersonal feedback for this kind of behavior (Deutsch & Lamberti, 1986). Other research indicates that altruistic motives are important predictors of who will help (Clary & Orenstein, 1991) and that an individual's altruism is probably based on his or her socialization experiences (Grusec, 1991). What exactly are the components of the **altruistic personality?**

Bierhoff, Klein, and Kramp (1991) reviewed the literature and identified a

Because one's self-concept contains multiple elements, it is possible to focus on only a portion of it at any one time. For example, Showers (1992a) has provided evidence that many people store positive and negative aspects of themselves separately in memory. Thus, if the individual focuses on the negative, his or her mood and subsequent behavior will be different than if the focus is on the positive. Some individuals, however, seem to store positive and negative self-knowledge together; the result is less negative affect and higher self-esteem (Showers, 1992b). The most general conclusion is that the organization of self-evaluations affects self-esteem and mood beyond what could be predicted on the basis of simply the *amount* of positive and negative content. Additional implications of this conceptualization are currently being explored in further research.

═══ Work in Progress ═══

Compartmentalizing Self-Information: Warding Off Depression in Times of Stress

As we will discuss in chapter 13, changes in one's life (such as divorce, death of a loved one, or moving to a new location) tend to be stressful. Showers and Ryff (1993) proposed that individual differences in self-organization influence the emotional effects of such events. The basic prediction is that a well-differentiated (compartmentalized) self-concept helps control the effects of stress *if* some of the separate domains of information are *very positive* and *very important* to the individual.

Showers and Ryff based their research on a survey of 120 women aged fifty-five and older who had relocated during the past year (Ryff & Essex, 1992). Professor Showers calculated the degree of self-compartmentalization for each woman on the basis of self-ratings of the positive and negative aspects—following the move—of such domains as daily activities, health, finances, family, and friends.

Consistent with earlier laboratory findings, women who perceived *great improvement* in one or more important domains of the self (compartmentalized organization) were less depressed than women who experienced the same average level of improvement spread evenly across several domains of the self (integrative organization). Thus, high evaluative differentiation was beneficial.

Professor Showers suggests that having separate, positive aspects of the self to fall back on when stress occurs may protect the person against depression. It also appears that both styles of organization can be useful. That is, a compartmentalized organization may be most helpful if one focuses on positive domains and ignores negative domains in times of stress. An integrative organization may help the person deal with negative domains without experiencing a decrease in general self-esteem. In future research, Showers hopes to determine just how people develop the tendency to integrate or to compartmentalize evaluative information about the self.

Though the self-content on which a person focuses influences mood (Sedikides, 1992), mood also affects self-focusing behavior, and environmental factors in turn affect one's mood (Salovey, 1992). If you are in a negative mood, for example, because you have a toothache and are scheduled to visit the dentist, you are more likely to recall (focus on) negative aspects of yourself. The extent and the content of the self-focusing behavior as well as mood can affect expectations. Thus, a depressed individual who is self-focused on negative content is more pessimistic than either nondepressed individuals or

The Self: Multiple Components of One's Identity 193

Only Baron & Byrne is as
DYNAMIC &
UP TO DATE
AS THE FIELD IT COVERS!

Baron & Byrne does a Superb Job of Illustrating the Integrated Nature of Social Psychology!

"CONNECTIONS"

Students approaching a discipline for the first time often find it difficult to see how it all "fits together." Baron and Byrne makes it easy! At the beginning of each chapter, "Connections" explain how the content of the chapter is linked to topics in other chapters, and they clearly illustrate the integrated nature of social psychology.

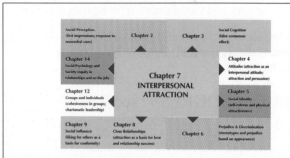

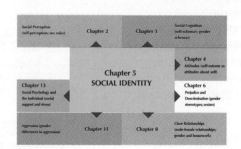

cult as it is to give a complete answer to that question, each of us spends a great deal of time and effort thinking about *ourself*—the center of each person's social universe.

We acquire our self-identity, or **self-concept**, primarily through our social interactions, and the **self** and its acquisition are matters of long-standing interest in social psychology (Higgins, 1987; Markus & Wurf, 1987; Suls & Greenwald, 1986). We will first review current knowledge about the self from the point of view of social cognition (see chapter 3). In other words, we will focus on the self in terms of its cognitive framework—a special framework that influences how we process not only social information (Klein, Loftus, & Burton, 1989) but our own motivation, emotional states, and our feelings of well-being (Van Hook & Higgins, 1988).

SELF-CONCEPT: THE CENTRAL SCHEMA

If you wanted to describe your current concept of yourself, what information would be relevant? Most people describe their physical appearance (tall, short, blond, brunette, etc.), indicate their major traits (outgoing, shy, anxious, calm, etc.), and sometimes mention their major goals and motives (to get rich, to make the world a better place, etc.). Altogether, the self-concept is a complex collection of diverse information that somehow is held together as *you*. If each of us is not just a random collection of information (like the mixed-up pieces of dozens of jigsaw puzzles), what is the "glue" that holds all of the information together in a unified self-image? For most social psychologists interested in the self, the answer lies in the concept of the *schema*, which was described in chapter 3.

THE SELF-SCHEMA AND ITS COGNITIVE EFFECTS.   A schema is an organized collection of beliefs and feelings about some aspect of the world. Each of us has a **self-schema** in which our self-knowledge is organized (Markus & Nurius, 1986). That is, the self-schema is a cognitive framework that guides the way we process information about ourselves. Self-schemas reflect all of our past self-relevant experiences; all of our current knowledge and existing memories about

Popular Features from the Previous Edition have been Updated ...

"FOCUS ON RESEARCH: CLASSIC CONTRIBUTIONS"

The classic studies described in these sections give students a solid foundation upon which to build, and show them that even the newest research has its roots in past research and theory.

"FOCUS ON RESEARCH: THE CUTTING EDGE"

These sections present important recently published research. Together with "Work in Progress" and citations throughout the text, they provide comprehensive coverage of all the latest developments in the field.

"SOCIAL PSYCHOLOGY: ON THE APPLIED SIDE"

From these sections and from additional material throughout the text, students will learn how to apply theory and research to practical problems and issues.

Focus on Research: Classic Contributions

GROUP PRESSURE: THE IRRESISTIBLE SOCIAL FORCE?

Suppose that just before an important exam, you discover that your answer to a homework problem is different from that obtained by another member of the class. How do you react? Probably with mild concern. Now imagine that you learn that a second person's answer, too, is different from yours. Moreover, to make matters worse, it agrees with the answer reported by the first person. How do you feel *now*? The chances are good that your anxiety will rise to high levels. Next you discover that a third person agrees with the other two. At this point you know that you are in big trouble. Which answer should you accept? Yours or the one obtained by your three friends? There's no time to find out, for at this moment the exam starts. Sure enough, the first question on the exam relates to this specific problem. Which answer should you choose? Can all three of your friends be wrong while you are right?

Life is filled with such dilemmas—instances in which we discover that our own judgments, actions, or conclusions are different from those reached by other persons. What do we, and others, do in such cases?

Exercise 1   The answer is provided by a series of studies conducted by Asch (1951) that are considered to be true classics in social psychology. In his research Asch asked participants to respond to a series of simple perceptual problems such as the one in Figure 9.3. On each problem they indicated which of three comparison lines matched a standard line in length. Several other persons (usually six to eight) were also present during the session; but, unknown to the real participant, all were accomplices of the experimenter. On certain occasions (twelve out of eighteen problems) the accomplices offered answers that were clearly wrong (*e.g.*, they unanimously stated that line A matched the standard ...fore the partici... e type of dilem... sons present or ...pants in Asch's ...se tested in sev... at least once. In ...o responded to ...ch errors.

Focus on Research: The Cutting Edge

RESPONDING TO AID FROM A SIBLING

Laboratory research has provided considerable support for the threatening aspects of being helped by similar others, but there has been only limited evidence about the real-life effects of being helped by someone who is actually very much like oneself. Searcy and Eisenberg (1992) obtained just such data with a sample of college students and their siblings.

Because age differences among siblings are perceived as crucial during childhood and adolescence, age tends to be equated with status even after the siblings reach adulthood. Older siblings have higher status, more power in the family, more knowledge while growing up, and so on. So when an older sibling offers help (either in childhood or in adulthood), such behavior is expected; but similar help is threatening if it comes from a younger sibling. Gender is also a crucial variable, in that older sisters tend to help siblings much more than older b...

On... that th... while ... brothe... of thei... emotio... The de... was ass... from a... in offe...

Th... emotio... esteem... help f... posed ... most t... which ... threat...

EXP...

As you ... the qu... bilities ... and se... behavi... researc... ent ex... cally se...

Moving from large-scale problems of world and national population issues, there is another area of concern that is relevant both to the population issue and to the health of individuals. As the following **Applied Side** section indicates, unwanted teenage pregnancies have been the focus of a considerable amount of research, theory, and application.

Social Psychology: On the Applied Side

CONTRACEPTIVE NEGLECT AMONG SEXUALLY ACTIVE ADOLESCENTS

Despite the many political and ideological controversies that surround issues of overpopulation and fertility control, there is much more agreement about the related problem of unwanted teenage pregnancies. That is, essentially no one argues in favor of adolescent males impregnating adolescent females when neither the potential mother nor the potential father wishes to become a parent. The only disagreement is whether to concentrate on encouraging chastity or on encouraging the use of contraception.

Primarily because the incidence of youthful premarital sexual activity continues to rise, most of the research interest in the United Sstates has centered on identifying the reasons for the nonuse of contraception among those who are sexually active. (A neglected issue is the fact that studies of teenage females who are pregnant, give birth, or contract an STD indicate that 70 percent of their male partners are over age twenty; Males, 1992.) At least 20 percent of the fifteen-year-olds in this country are sexually active (Moore, Nord, & Peterson, 1989). Despite fears of AIDS and widespread publicity about its dangers, teenage sexual activity rates continue to increase (Centers for Disease Control, 1991). Among American high school students, the increases are striking. In 1971, less than one-third of these teenagers engaged in intercourse; by 1990, 54 percent were sexually experienced, and this figure was 72 percent for high school seniors (Haber, 1993)—see Figure 13.4. However one evaluates youthful premarital sexuality, one aspect of this behavior is curiously maladaptive. For at least thirty years, the data have consistently indicated that large proportions of these couples fail to use contraceptives consistently, use ineffective methods of contraception, or avoid contraception altogether (Byrne, Kelley, & Fisher, 1993; Ingham, Woodcock, & Stenner, 1991).

With high rates of sexual intercourse and low rates of contraceptive use, the outcome is obvious. Each day in the United States, about 2,740 adolescents conceive, and this means approximately a million unplanned teenage pregnancies each year (National Center for Health Statistics, 1987). Despite high rates of abortion and miscarriage, half of these pregnancies result in the birth of an unplanned—and often unwanted—child (Brody, 1991).

For social psychologists and others, the primary questions center on why teenagers do not use contraception and what to do to change their behavior. The reasons for nonuse of contraception include lack of accurate information, widely held beliefs in subgroups of the population that conception is desirable, situational constraints on obtaining contraception, and personality dispositions that interfere with contraceptive use. Figure 13.5, p. 547, provides a summary of these factors.

Only Baron & Byrne is as
DYNAMIC & UP TO DATE
AS THE FIELD IT COVERS!

To Address Areas of Increasing Importance and Respond to Requests from Colleagues and Students ...

there are New
and Reorganized Chapters ...

■ **Social Identity: Self and Gender** (Ch. 5) This entirely new chapter delves into the multiple components of identity, including the gender-related aspects of identity. The topics of Self and Gender also receive substantial coverage throughout the book.

■ A full chapter (Ch. 10) is now devoted to **Prosocial Behavior.** Why do people voluntarily help others? This chapter discusses motivation and its implications.

■ Two chapters (Ch. 13 & 14) on **Applying Social Psychology** have been completely revised. Students will learn how to apply the theories of social psychology to health, politics, law, business, and the environment.

Personal strivings are the characteristic recurring goals that a person is trying to accomplish in his or her life. People differ in whether they strive for relatively difficult, abstract goals or relatively easy, concrete ones. Those who emphasize high-level strivings experience more psychological stress (because they can't meet their goals) but less physical illness (because their commitment increases hardiness). Those who emphasize low-level strivings experience less emotional discomfort (because they can reach their goals) but more illness (because of a lack of commitment).

TABLE 13.2 High-level versus low-level goals in life

High-Level, Abstract Strivings	Low-Level, Concrete Strivings
I want to deepen my relationship with God.	I want to look well-groomed and clean-cut.
I want to be totally honest.	I want to be funny and make others laugh.
I want to be a fun person to be around.	I want to look attentive and not bored in class.
I want to compete against myself rather than against others.	I want to be organized and neat—clean my room and make my bed.
I want to increase my knowledge of the world.	I want to work hard or at least look like I'm working hard.

Gender problems

FIGURE 5.13 As societal norms undergo change, gender roles, gender stereotypes, and gender discrimination create some degree of confusion, discomfort, and anger for many men and women.
Source: Universal Press Syndicate, February 22, 1981.

for their children. In the most important race of all, however, the major candidates for president of the United States were all men. When these individuals were asked when they expected a woman to be elected president, the typical response was that it would happen very soon, but not before 1996. Considering the fact that such a question and such an answer would have been unimaginable in the past (at least until Geraldine Ferraro was the Democratic vice-presidential candidate in 1984), perhaps this should be taken as a sign of progress beyond gender-role stereotypes. In many other nations (e.g., Israel, Great Britain, Pakistan, Nicaragua, India, Argentina, and the Phillipines), women have already served successfully in the role of chief executive (Genovese, 1993). In academia, U.S. women are still at a disadvantage with respect to doctorates granted, salaries, and professorships (Callaci, 1993).

SUPPORT FOR TRADITIONAL GENDER ROLES. In the Judeo-Christian tradition men were originally specified as the owners of their families (Wolf, 1992). In the Talmud, for example, categories of property include cattle,

plus Scores of New Topics including ...

- **Impression Management: Does It Really Work?**

- **The Costs of Thinking Too Much**

- **Genetic Factors in Attitude Formation**

- **Self-Focusing Behavior**

- **The Repulsion Hypothesis: New Findings**

- **Relationship Patterns Among Married Couples**

- **Deliberation Style and Group Decisions**

- **Effects on Health of Striving for Low-Level versus High-Level Goals**

- **and many more!**

Making a good first impression

FIGURE 2.12 Many persons believe that first impressions are very important. Because of this assumption, they try to enhance their appearance before meeting others for the first time.

ovided by several , 1981; Burnstein

l by Asch (1946). different groups person:

ly in the order in ts are followed by f the impressions e receive first (by asked to report ls exposed to the exactly what hap- son as more socia-

order was impor- aning of the ones ne was intelligent ectives within this rson was *critical* ligence. With the rson was envious as also intelligent

attitudes concerning related issues. This would be so because related issues would be linked in memory. To test this prediction, they presented several political attitudes in a row to participants. In some cases these were related (for example, *nuclear weapons freeze* followed by *nuclear test ban; right to abortion* followed by *equal rights amendment*). As shown in Figure 4.1, results offered support for the major hypothesis: Participants responded more quickly to the related attitudes than to the unrelated ones. This and other findings offer support for the view that activation of one attitude can—and often does—tend to activate related attitudes as well. This is an important point, and one to which we'll return in later sections of this chapter.

Now that we've defined attitudes and described some of their basic features, we can turn to the wealth of information about them uncovered by social psychologists. In order to provide you with a useful overview of this intriguing body of knowledge, we'll proceed as follows. First, we'll examine the process through which attitudes are *formed* or *developed*. Next, we'll consider the relationship between attitudes and behavior. This link is more complex than you might expect, so be prepared for some surprises. Third, we'll examine how attitudes are sometimes *changed* through persuasion and related processes. The word *sometimes* should be emphasized, for as we'll note in another section, changing attitudes that are important to those who hold them is far from easy. Finally, we'll consider *cognitive dissonance*—an internal state with far-reaching implications for social behavior and social thought that, surprisingly, sometimes leads individuals to change their own attitudes in the absence of external pressure to do so.

FORMING ATTITUDES: LEARNING, EXPERIENCE, AND . . . GENES?

Do babies enter the world with political preferences, racial hatreds, and the diverse preferences they will express as adults fully formed? Few of us would say yes. On the contrary, most people believe that attitudes are acquired in a gradual manner through experience. In a word, most people believe that attitudes are primarily *learned*. Social psychologists, too, accept this position. But please take note: We would be remiss if we did not call your attention to a small but growing body of evidence suggesting that genetic factors, too, may play some role in our attitudes. So, after examining the major ways in which attitudes are acquired, we'll briefly describe some of the evidence pointing to this surprising conclusion.

SOCIAL LEARNING: ACQUIRING ATTITUDES FROM OTHERS

One source of our attitudes is obvious: We acquire them from other persons through the process of **social learning**. In other words, we acquire many of our views from situations in which we interact with others or merely observe their behavior. Such social learning occurs in diverse ways, but three are most important.

CLASSICAL CONDITIONING: LEARNING BASED ON ASSOCIATION. It is a basic principle of psychology that when one stimulus regularly precedes another, the one that occurs first may soon become a signal for the one that occurs second. In other words, when the first stimulus is presented, individuals come to expect that the second will follow. As a result, they may gradually show

Forming Attitudes: Learning, Experience, and . . . Genes?   *131*

con- sh to ghts many oth- ogni- rious pre- hich nory, ons. pri- men- des, ts of one tion, d by ness,

h we orm arch face.

D

peo- mply too high. On the contrary, most of us engage in active efforts to regulate how we appear to others in order to appear in the best or most favorable light pos-

Negative impression management

FIGURE 2.13   Very few of us would behave like this character when applying for a job.
Source: NEA, Inc., 1987.

Only Baron & Byrne is as DYNAMIC & UP TO DATE

AS THE FIELD IT COVERS!

The Outstanding Supplements Package makes it Easy to Keep Your Classroom Dynamic and Exciting!

For the First Time in the Seventh Edition —

An Annotated Instructor's Edition

The Annotated Instructor's Edition (AIE) saves you time and helps you incorporate the various elements of the Supplements Package into classroom discussions. It includes all the material from the student's edition plus marginal notations throughout, and an Instructor's Section upfront.

■ Instructor's Section

by Bem Allen and Gene Smith

This section provides Chapter-At-A-Glance planning charts to help you transition to this new textbook, outlines of each chapter, learning objectives, topics for discussion, exercises, related films and videos, CNN video segments, transparencies, critical thinking/essay questions, and additional sources for lectures. It also coordinates all Study Guide materials.

■ Annotated Text

The annotations, which appear only in the Instructor's Edition, indicate the most appropriate places to use exercises and supplemental materials. Annotations include:

- CNN Video Segments
- Video Library Segments
- Discussion Questions
- Exercises
- Critical Thinking Questions/Essays
- Transparencies
- Wayne A. Lesko — Readings In Social Psychology: General, Classic, and Contemporary Selections (readings related to text topics)

Chapter-at-a-Glance

Chapter Four
Attitudes:
Evaluating the Social World

Chapter Outline	Instruction Ideas	Supplements
Introduction	Discussion Question 4	CNN Video Segment 4, *AIDS Attitudes* and Segment 5, *Times Mirror Poll—see* CNN Video Guide
I. Forming Attitudes: The Role of Learning and Experience Social Learning: Acquiring Attitudes from Others / Direct Experience: Acquiring Attitudes from Life / Genetic Factors: Some Surprising Recent Findings	Exercise 2 Discussion Question 5 Critical Thinking Question 2	
II. Attitudes and Behavior: The Essential Link Attitude Specificity / Attitude Components / Attitude Strength, Vested Interest, and the Role of Self-Awareness / Attitude Accessibility: The Force That Binds	Discussion Question 5 Critical Thinking Question 2	Reading: Lesko 11—Attitudes vs. Action
III. Persuasion: The Process of Changing Attitudes Persuasion: The Traditional Approach / Persuasion: The Cognitive Approach / The Reciprocity of Persuasion: When Attitude Change Is a Two-Way Street	Exercises 1 and 3–5 Discussion Question 3 Critical Thinking Questions 3 and 4	Readings: Lesko 10—American Values Test
IV. When Attitude Change Fails: Resistance to Persuasion Reactance: Protecting Our Pesonal Freedom / Forewarning: Prior Knowledge of Persuasive Intent / Selective Avoidance	Exercises 1 and 3–5 Discussion Question 3 Critical Thinking Questions 3 and 4	Exercises 1 and 3–5 Discussion Question 3 Critical Thinking Questions 3 and 4
V. Cognitive Dissonance: How We Sometimes Change Our Own Attitudes Dissonance and Attitude Change: The Effects of Forced Compliance / Dissonance and the Less-Leads-to-More Effect / Dissonance: Does It Really Stem from Inconsistency?	Discussion Question 1 Critical Thinking Question5	Transparencies 4.1–4.4 Reading: Lesko 12—Cognitive Dissonance in Psychotherapy

I N S T R U C T O R ' S   S E C T I O N

IS–20   Chapter Four   Attitudes: Evaluating the Social World

NEW!
CNN Video Connections in Psychology

Allyn & Bacon and Cable News Network team up to bring CNN programming right into your classroom. These segments, all related to textbook material, include fascinating and controversial topics such as ...

- ✔ AIDS Attitudes
- ✔ Self-Esteem
- ✔ The Mommy Track
- ✔ Beauty in Society
- ✔ Commuter Love
- ✔ Children and Violence
- ✔ Women Combat Pilots
- ✔ Domestic Violence
- ✔ and more!

Video Guide

Written by the authors, this handy Instructor's Video Guide summarizes each CNN segment, relates it specifically to the text discussion, and offers follow-up questions for discussion.

Video Library

An extensive selection of professionally-produced segments features Bob Baron and noted social psychologist Margaret Clark using effective dramatization to illustrate material from the text. Other video materials are also available; contact your local Allyn & Bacon Representative for details.

Allyn & Bacon
CNN™
Video
CONNECTIONS

in
Social Psychology

A User's Guide for

SOCIAL PSYCHOLOGY:
Understanding Human Interaction
Seventh Edition

by Robert A. Baron and Donn Byrne

Copyright ©1994 by Allyn & Bacon

For Additional Readings and Cross-Cultural Material, Allyn & Bacon Offers:

NEW!
Readings in Social Psychology: General, Classic, and Contemporary Selections, Second Edition
Wayne A. Lesko, Marymount University

This collection of readings gives students broad exposure to popular, contemporary and classic articles. It's organized to correspond closely with Baron and Byrne's *Social Psychology, Seventh Edition* and includes critical thinking questions for each selection.

NEW!
Social Psychology Across Cultures: Analysis and Perspectives
Peter B. Smith, University of Sussex
Michael Harris Bond, Chinese University of Hong Kong

This important new paperback supplement focuses on social psychology from a cross-cultural perspective. Drawing on numerous studies from around the world, the authors examine how the theories of social psychology apply across different cultures. Students will gain an understanding of how social processes are embedded in culture especially in areas such as intergroup behavior, negotiation, multinational enterprises, immigration, and acculturation.

Allyn & Bacon's Professional Library Includes...

C.R. Snyder and Donelson R. Forsyth's
Handbook of Social and Clinical Psychology: The Health Perspective ©1991

Marshall H. Segall, Pierre R. Dasen, John W. Berry and Ype H. Poortinga's **Human Behavior in Global Perspective: An Introduction to Cross-Cultural Psychology** ©1990

David L.Shapiro's **Forensic Psychological Assessment: An Integrative Approach** ©1991

Eldon Tunks and Anthony Bellissimo's
Behavioral Medicine: Concepts and Procedures ©1991

Robert M Liebert and Joyce Sprafkin's
The Early Window: Effects of Television on Children and Youth, Third Edition ©1988

Instructor's Section Contents

Introduction

Introduction to the Instructor's Section

We, Gene Smith and Bem Allen, are proud once again to present the ancillary package for Baron and Byrne's *Social Psychology*. The seventh edition of *Social Psychology* continues the traditions that have made the Baron and Byrne text a leader in its field for many years. As in previous editions, *Social Psychology* contains up-to-date coverage of the most relevant research. As usual, studies are related to current theory and outlined in clear and concise English.

This edition also contains new wrinkles that extend the tradition of timely responsiveness to social change. The "Social Diversity" sections are expanded to acknowledge both within-group and between-group diversity. The structure and content reflecting an increased emphasis on applied social psychology has also been enhanced in this edition. In addition, a new chapter provides increased coverage of prosocial behavior.

The Baron and Byrne Instructor's Section also represents both continuity and change. Once again we have fused the Instructor's Section and the students' Study Guide into a coordinated pedagogical unit. For example, instructions on the conduct of exercises are included in the Instructor's Section, and *materials needed by students to participate in exercises* are provided in he Study Guide. (Allyn and Bacon will provide you with a copy of the Study Guide, even if you decide not to require it.) The Instructor's Section makes special efforts to facilitate the elevated interest in critical thinking.

Overall, we have sought to help college teachers turn class sessions into occasions for whipping up enthusiasm about social psychology, rather than periods devoted solely to the tried but not necessarily so true lecture method. Specifically, we have developed an expanded film/video list that emphasizes easily acquired, interesting audiovisual supplements to the text. Each list of films/videos for a given chapter begins with reference to one of several new video segments. Each segment related to a chapter features text author

Robert A. Baron and noted social psychologist Margaret Clark discussing and illustrating chapter material with the help of some effective dramatizations. All of these segments, each about twenty minutes in length, will be available to you through your Allyn and Bacon sales representative. In addition, Allyn and Bacon is offering CNN segments, taken from actual television broadcasts, that provide students with exciting new information about human (and animal) social behavior. The technical quality of these new segments exceeds that available in most, if not all, currently available psychology videotapes.

In this version, each Instructor's Section chapter coverage begins with an outline containing all chapter headings. Space is provided for your handwritten inserts so you can use the outlines as a basis for notes to be used in class. These outlines can also be copied as transparencies and thereby provided to students during class.

As has always been the case, Learning Objectives are included to guide you and the students (the same objectives are provided in the Study Guide).

The Discussion Questions found in each chapter are designed to be user friendly. Much detail is provided, as always. We've given you extensive background information to help you lead the discussion. We've also made suggestions concerning how to start the discussion and how to avoid sensitive but irrelevant issues. We also advise you on what to expect, on the potential value of the discussion, and on how to conclude it.

The Classroom Exercises in this edition of the Instructor's Section also are designed to be easy and interesting to use. We have noted measures that have appeared in reports of research or been used effectively by psychological professionals. In tune with the new emphasis on coordination of the Instructor's Section and Study Guide, *these measures are found in the Study Guide.* Thus, if you require the Study Guide, there will be no need for you to copy and distribute materials for students to use in exercises. In almost every case you will need little or no preparation before class and can comfortably conduct the entire exercise during class. Expected results will graphically make important points for students and provide them with enjoyable in-class experiences that will cement important concepts in their memories. You are told what to do, what to expect, and how to guide students to accurate conclusions. Suggested analyses are easy and quick to do.

Critical Thinking/Essay Questions center on provoking thought rather than just promoting reproduction of information contained in the text. These questions often ask students to apply what they have learned from their readings.

As always, Sources for Lecture is a compilation of articles from popular and often nonpsychological sources that will allow you to spice up your in-class presentations. The Update section again includes new articles from social psychological and other professional sources or articles that were not covered in the text for lack of space.

The Transparencies list once again provides materials for the overhead projector that will make in-class presentations more interesting and easier to grasp.

The file of multiple choice test items is provided separately. In a tradition started last edition, items focus on inspiring students to think and reason, rather than just asking them to regurgitate back what they have studied. We believe that these items will convince you that multiple choice tests can promote critical thinking and make testing a learning experience instead of just an occasion for evaluation.

Finally, new in this edition is annotation of Instructor's Section features to help you use this section more easily and effectively. You will find references to the Baron-Clark and CNN videos provided by Allyn and Bacon in the margins of your instructor's edition. Also in the margins are notations indicating points in the text where discussion questions and exercises might be most productively inserted into in-class interactions with students concerning text materials. Critical thinking essay items are also indicated in the margins so that you can provoke thoughtfulness in students at the most appropriate points in the consideration of text materials. References to transparencies, too, have been placed in the margins.

Finally, we offer an innovation that we find exciting: Wayne A. Lesko has developed a revised book of readings, *Readings in Social Psychology, General, Classic, and Contemporary Selections,* that is coordinated with Baron and Byrne's *Social Psychology.* Should you wish to assign students additional readings that include many selections from popular sources such as *Psychology Today,* you may do so easily. Annotations in the margins of this instructor's edition indicate where each Lesko reading is most appropriately related to text materials. Students will find each of these selections "a good read" that will be particularly relevant to their lives.

Just as Baron and Byrne's *Social Psychology* is even better than before, we believe that the Instructor's Section and its coordinated materials make up the most productive ancillary package associated with any social psychology text. We expect that use of it will make life in class more interesting for both you and your students.

BEM ALLEN
GENE SMITH

INSTRUCTOR'S SECTION

Chapter-at-a-Glance

Chapter One
The Field of Social Psychology:
How We Think about and Interact with Others

Chapter Outline	Instruction Ideas	Supplements
Introduction	Exercise 2	CNN Video Segment 1: *Diversity,* *see* Video Guide
I. Social Psychology: A Working Definition Social Psychology Is Scientific Nature / Social Psychology Focuses on the Behavior of Individuals / Social Psychology Seeks to Understand the Causes of Social Behavior and Thought / Social Psychology:	Exercises 1 and 3 Critical Thinking Question 1	Reading: Lesko 2—Social Psychology and Science
II. Social Psychology: A Capsule Memoir The Early Years: Social Psychology Emerges / Social Psychology's Youth: The 1940s, 1950s, and 1960s / The 1970s and 1980s: A Maturing Field / Where Do We Go from Here? The 1990s and Beyond		
III. Answering Questions about Social Behavior and Social Thought: Research Methods in Social Psychology The Experimental Method: Knowledge through Intervention / The Correlational Method: Knowledge through Systematic Observation / Social Psychologists As Perennial Skeptics: The Importance of Replication and Multiple Methods in Social Research / The Role of Theory in Social Psychology / The Quest for Knowledge and the Rights of Individuals: Seeking a Defensible Balance	Exercises 4 and 5 Discussion Questions 1–4 Critical Thinking Questions 2–5	Transparencies 1.1–1.5 Readings: Lesko 1—The Sample with the Built-in Bias and Lesko 3—The Subjects were White and Middle Class
IV. Using this Book: A Displaced Preface		

Chapter One

The Field of Social Psychology: How We Think about and Interact with Others

Chapter Outline: Getting the Overall Picture

I. Social Psychology: A Working Definition
   A. Social Psychology Is Scientific in Nature
   B. Social Psychology Focuses on the Behavior of Individuals
   C. Social Psychology Seeks to Understand the Causes of Social Behavior and Thought
      1. The Actions and Characteristics of Others
      2. Cognitive Processes
      3. Ecological Variables
      4. Cultural Context
      5. Biological Aspects
   D. Social Psychology: Summing Up
II. Social Psychology: A Capsule Memoir
   A. The Early Years: Social Psychology Emerges
   B. Social Psychology's Youth: The 1940s, 1950s, and 1960s
   C. The 1970s and 1980s: A Maturing Field
      1. Growing Influence of a Cognitive Perspective
      2. Growing Emphasis on Application: Exporting Social Knowledge
         a. Is Justice Really Blind? Defendants' Attractiveness and the Legal Process
   D. Where Do We Go from Here? The 1980s and Beyond

   1. Cognition and Application: Growing Knowledge, Growing Sophistication
   2. The Role of Affect: Realizing That Feelings Count, Too
   3. Adoption of a Multicultural Perspective: Taking Full Account of Social Diversity
III. Answering Questions about Social Behavior and Social Thought: Research Methods in Social Psychology
   A. The Experimental Method: Knowledge through Intervention
      1. Experimentation: Its Basic Nature
      2. Successful Experimentation: Two Basic Requirements
   B. The Correlational Method: Knowledge through Systematic Observation
   C. Social Psychologists As Perennial Skeptics: The Importance of Replication and Multiple Methods in Social Research
   D. The Role of Theory in Social Psychology
      1. Meta-Analysis: Combining Results across Experiments
   E. The Quest for Knowledge and the Rights of Individuals: Seeking a Defensible Balance
IV. Using This Book: A Readers' Road Map

Learning Objectives

1. Describe "common sense" as a basis of knowledge in social psychology, and indicate why common-sense notions present a confusing picture of human social behavior.
2. What is your textbook's definition of social psychology?

3. Explain why social psychology is a "scientific field."
4. Why does the field of social psychology focus its study on the behavior of individuals?
5. Describe the five major causes of social behavior and thought: (a) the actions and characteristics of others; (b) cognitive processes; (c) ecological vari-

ables; (d) cultural context; and (e) biological aspects.

6. Compare the approaches to social psychology in the 1924 McDougall text and the 1924 text by Floyd Allport.

7. Describe the growth in social psychology through the 1930s, focusing on the contributions by Sherif and Lewin.

8. Describe contributions of the 1940s, 1950s, and 1960s, including emphases on groups, the authoritarian personality, cognitive dissonance theory, and social cognition.

9. Note the recent emphasis in social psychology on the cognitive perspective.

10. Understand the recent trend toward application in such areas as health, the legal process, and work settings.

11. Summarize ways in which defendants' personal characteristics, ethnicity, and physical attractiveness influence judgments about them.

12. What two trends, already under way, do the authors expect to continue in the 1990s and beyond?

13. What do the authors predict for this decade regarding the role of affect in social psychological theorizing?

14. Compare the assumption that the findings of social psychology are generalizable across cultures with the developing multicultural perspective.

15. Describe the basic steps involved when an investigator conducts an experiment.

16. Understand the nature of independent variables and dependent variables, drawing examples from the speed of talking/persuasion experiment.

17. Give an example illustrating the advantage of including two independent variables in the same study, namely that the results can now demonstrate an interaction between variables.

18. Why is it important that subjects be randomly assigned to groups in an experiment?

19. Explain the importance of holding factors other than the independent variable constant.

20. What are the two reasons that it is often impossible to use the experimental method to investigate a particular question?

21. Describe the procedures followed when an investigator examines a hypothesis using the correlational method.

22. Describe the major drawback that plagues the correlational method, and give examples illustrating how third variables often underlie correlational findings.

23. How do social psychologists use theories to derive testable research hypotheses?

24. Trace the steps in an investigation, from formulating a theory, to deriving a hypothesis, to testing the hypothesis, and finally reexamining the theory.

25. Why are summaries of many studies using meta-analysis preferable to summaries based on a narrative review?

26. Why do social psychologists often deceive their research subjects?

27. Describe ethical issues raised by the use of deception, and indicate how informed consent and debriefing help to decrease the dangers of deception.

Discussion Questions

1. Middlemist, Knowles, and Matter (1976) conducted a naturalistic field study to determine the degree to which invasion of one's personal space arouses stress. The researchers observed male users of a college restroom through a periscope to determine whether onset of urination and amount of time taken to complete urination would be affected by the presence of a nearby confederate. Is this an invasion of the subjects' privacy? Ask your students whether they believe this is a legitimate psychological study. (The Middlemist, Knowles, and Matter study is in the *Journal of Personality and Social Psychology, 33,* 541–546.) A later issue of *JPSP* (*35,* 120–124) has a couple of brief articles debating the ethics of the study.

2. Have one of the more verbal students in class engage in role playing. Give the student a complete description of an experiment, and have him or her tell the class how he or she would behave in the experiment; or you might have the entire class write down how they'd behave. The ideal experiment to choose is one in which the role player will behave differently from actual subjects. Possibilities include Milgram's obedience paradigm, the bystander studies, or West, Gunn, and Chernicky's "Watergate Study."

Consider, for example, a role-playing replication of the Milgram obedience study. Describe in detail the teacher's situation, and then ask the students to imagine themselves in the learner's position. Ask the students whether they would obey the experimenter's commands and ultimately deliver 450 volts. Also ask them to estimate the proportion of people in the general population that would deliver 450 volts. If you ask the above questions before your students have been exposed to the results of Milgram's research, you will find that very few expect that they would deliver 450 volts. Furthermore, the students will greatly underestimate the proportion of the population that would fully obey.

After demonstrating that students' predictions are inaccurate, discuss reasons why intuition is unable to predict behavior. Among the reasons that role playing underestimates the level of obedience are the following: (a) People don't know where their focus of attention would lie in the actual situation. Although they imagine that the victim would grab their attention, in the actual situation the experimenter may be the focus. (b) People are unable to recreate the physiological components of their reactions. (c) People can't imagine the degree to which the flow of events traps them into obedience.

You might conclude the discussion by emphasizing the necessity for empirical research using involved subjects. The two methods, role playing and involved subjects, exhibit different behavior, and a psychology that relied on subjects' introspective reports of behavior would often be in error.

3. To introduce students to the idea of experimenter bias, a discussion of the role played by the examiner giving a lie detector test might be helpful. The polygraph is, of course, a sensitive physiological recording device that measures the emotional arousal of a suspect by recording changes in galvanic skin potential. The basic assumption is that a guilty person will become emotionally aroused whenever he or she tells a lie in response to an incriminating question. However, it is probable that even innocent people become emotionally aroused when being questioned, and their arousal may well be greatest to "incriminating" questions. The person being questioned knows he or she is a suspect; thus, when the examiner asks a question such as "Where were you the night your neighbor died?", an emotional response may well be elicited, irrespective of guilt.

To correct the above problem, the examiner often determines a set of facts about the crime that only a guilty suspect would know. This relevant information is then presented to the suspect embedded in other equally plausible facts. Presumably, a guilty person will respond more strongly than an innocent person to the special meaning of the significant facts.

Even with the procedure described above, however, there is still a potential problem. The polygraph examiner and others present during the test are usually aware of the critical pieces of information. These people have usually formed a hypothesis about the guilt or innocence of the particular suspect, and they are in a position to influence the suspect's responses. Discuss with students ways in which subtle and inadvertent cues given by the examiner may influence the suspect. Is the examiner in a position analogous to that of the psychological experimenter? What might be done to prevent this kind of subtle influence?

4. Some persons have argued that some aspects of social behavior are best left unstudied. One such topic is the nature of love. Former Senator William Proxmire of Wisconsin has criticized the work of Ellen Berscheid and Elaine Hatfield (formerly Walster), saying, "Americans want to leave some things in life a mystery, and right at the top of things we don't want to know is why a man falls in love with a woman and vice versa." Are the questions of how people fall in love and how long-term relationships develop worthy of psychological study? Do the students agree with Senator Proxmire that some topics should be placed out of bounds?

5. Does the requirement of obtaining informed consent from research subjects have any effect on their behavior in an experiment? A couple of research studies have suggested that the use of informed consent forms can change subjects' behavior in significant ways. Gardner (1978) argued that the forms change behavior in environmental stressor research. Gardner's article is in the *Journal of Personality and Social Psychology* (*36*, 628-634). Second, Dill and colleagues (1982) have argued that human subjects regulations are a source of methodological artifact. Their study appears in *Personality and Social Psychology Bulletin*, (*8*, 417-425).

Classroom Exercises/Demonstrations

1. Art Lyons of Moravian College suggests a demonstration to be used on the first day of the term by faculty members teaching two sections of social psychology. Lyons suggests that the faculty member vary his or her style of dress in the two different sections and gather the students' first impressions of their professor. For example, Lyons reports in *Teaching of Psychology* (*8*(3), 173–174) that he wears a coat and tie in one section and removes them in another section. Lyons has the students rate him on several trait dimensions using a semantic differential format. He reports that discussing the results provides an excellent opportunity for active class participation and sets the stage for dealing with both methodological and conceptual issues later in the course. A discussion of the uses Lyons makes of this demonstration is found in his *Teaching of Psychology* article. Possible dimensions to be used in the ratings are as follows:

attractive	—|—|—|—|—	unattractive
intelligent	—|—|—|—|—	unintelligent
open-minded	—|—|—|—|—	closed-minded
conservative	—|—|—|—|—	liberal
talkative	—|—|—|—|—	quiet
emotional	—|—|—|—|	unemotional
self-confident	—|—|—|—|—	lacking in self-confidence

2. Chapter 1 begins by discussing the wisdom contained in everyday, commonsense knowledge. The present exercise is designed to show students that, despite the intuitive appeal of commonsense ideas, they should be careful in wholeheartedly accepting them. The exercise asks students to provide their friends with information that certain commonsense notions are true. Each student in the class should provide one friend with information stating that research has supported the idea that similar people like each other, and another friend with information that opposites attract. The friends should be asked to indicate in a sentence or two why they think the statement is true, and then they should rate the degree to which the notion is true. A sheet for your students to use in doing this exercise is found in chapter 1 of your students' Study Guide. Have the students bring their friends' ratings to class so that you can test whether both of these conflicting statements are rated to be true.

3. Have students watch newspapers or magazines for reports of research. They might watch for stories that draw erroneous conclusions about cause and effect. Or they might watch for reports that they understand better because they're taking social psychology. Encourage them to be alert for these materials, and encourage them to bring relevant articles to class.

4. Quiz the students regarding their own reactions to various field studies in social psychology. This exercise repeats the procedure of the Wilson and Donnerstein (1976) study (published in the *American Psychologist, 31*(11), 765–773). Wilson and Donnerstein read brief descriptions of actual experiments and asked subjects to rate each experiment for its ethics, its appropriateness, its legality, and so forth. The descriptions of the experiments from Wilson and Donnerstein are presented in chapter 1 of the Study Guide. Have your students answer some or all of the following questions about each of the experiments. For each question, the students should answer "yes," "no," or "not sure."

> **1.** If you discovered that you had been a subject in this experiment, would you feel that you had been harassed or annoyed?
> **2.** If you discovered that you had been a subject in this experiment, would you feel that your privacy had been invaded?
> **3.** Do you feel that such an experiment is unethical or immoral?

> **4.** Would you mind being a subject in such an experiment?
> **5.** Do you feel that psychologists should be doing such an experiment?
> **6.** Is doing such an experiment justified by its contribution to our scientific knowledge of behavior?
> **7.** Does such an experiment lower your trust in social scientists and their work?
> **8.** Do you feel that the psychologist's actions in this experiment are against the law?

5. Have students respond to the scenarios in their Study Guides in which they are asked to identify the independent and dependent variables. If you want to carry the exercise one step farther, the next thing you can do is to have them consider the following questions as a way to sharpen their metholological sophistication:

> **1.** What if the observer recording the children's aggressive acts becomes fatigued or bored during the course of the thirty-minute sessions? Would it matter that the observer's criterion as to what represents an aggressive act changed over the course of the thirty-minute sessions?
> **2.** Assume that "to avoid confusion" the researchers decide to have the actual drug administered by one psychiatric nurse and the placebo by another nurse. Is this a good idea? Why or why not?
> **3.** Some subjects in the high fear condition might choose to discontinue their participation in the experiment after hearing about the painful shocks, and ethical guidelines require that the experimenter release them. Would the experimental procedure be compromised if 15 percent of the high-fear subjects dropped out, but none of the low-fear subjects did so?
> **4.** The experimenter allowed distributed-practice subjects to "do whatever they wanted" during the two-minute rest periods, and many of them mentally rehearsed the nonsense syllables during this time. Is this a problem? If so, what changes are needed to correct for it?
> **5.** Obviously, the educator could not randomly assign the children to attend the various schools. Also, he was not allowed to decide which teachers or schools would use each technique. What problems are caused by: (1) not being able to assign children randomly to the schools? (2) having teachers "choose" which teaching technique to use?

Film Notes: A Picture Is Sometimes Worth a Thousand Words

The Case of ESP, 1985, color videocassette, 57 mins. Time-Life Video, 100 Eisenhower Drive, P.O. Box 644, Paramus, NJ 07653. This "NOVA" program explores research into extrasensory perception and claims for and against paranormal phenomena. Can serve to introduce discussions of research ethics, values, and methodology.

Inferential Statistics: Hypothesis Testing—Rats, Robots, and Roller Skates, 33877, 1975, color, 28 mins. Pennsylvania State University, Audiovisual Services, Special Services Building, University Park, PA 16802 (814-865-6314). Uses humorous sketches to explain hypothesis testing, one of the most important applications of inferential statistics. Illustrates the need for a control group and for random assignment of subjects to groups, the necessity of statistics as a way to overcome population variability, the formulation of a statistical hypothesis and the possible errors of decision that can be made, and the way in which hypotheses about the mean are tested. Produced by Robert Johnson.

Invitation to Social Psychology, 32074, 1975, color, 25 mins. Pennsylvania State University, Audiovisual Services, Special Services Building, University Park, PA 16802 (814-865-6314). Introduction to social psychology with emphasis on three questions: What is the subject matter of social psychology? What are its methods of investigation? What are some of its findings? Examples include interpersonal events in a cafeteria, reactions of bystanders on a city street, Milgram's obedience study, and Zimbardo's prison simulation. From the *Social Psychology* series. Stanley Milgram.

Methodology: The Psychologist and the Experiment, 32000, 1975, color, 30 mins. Pennsylvania State University, Audiovisual Services, Special Services Building, University Park, PA 16802 (814-865-6314). Documents research methodology used in Stanley Schachter's "fear and affiliation" experiment in social psychology and Austin Riesen's physiological experiment on visual motor coordination. Discusses independent and dependent variables, control groups, random assignment to conditions, and use of statistics in research. From the *Psychology Today* series. A CRM production.

Social Psychology, videotape, 30 mins. CRM Films, 2233 Faraday Ave., Carlsbad, CA 92008 (800-421-0833). This tape introduces the subject matter and methods of social psychology by tracing attempts to desegregate an urban school.

Social Psychology Laboratory, 33167, 1975, color, 24 mins. Pennsylvania State University, Audiovisual Services, Special Services Building, University Park, PA 16802 (814-865-6314). Introduces three experiments in social psychology to demonstrate some of the standard features of experimental methodology. Shows such experimental procedures as briefing and debriefing sessions, as well as aspects of establishing the environmental setting such as design of the laboratory, standard seating arrangements, and the type of apparatus commonly used to monitor the progress of the experiment. Experiments explore the stability of three–person groups, nonverbal communication, and interaction in problem solving. Produced for the British Open University. V. Lockwood.

Understanding Research, Number 2 in this 1990 videotape series, 30 mins. The AnnenbØrg Project, Holt, Rinehart & Winston, 1990, contact Lee Sutherlin, Marketing Manager (817-334-7632). Covers basic research techniques used in both the laboratory and in the field.

Transparencies

1.1 *Correlation versus Causation*
1.2 *Testing a Hypothesis with Correlation Method*
1.3 *Testing a Hypothesis Experimentally*

1.4 *Confounding of Variables*
1.5 *Correlation versus Causation*

Critical Thinking/Essay Questions

1 Provide a definition of social psychology and describe the essential features of the field of social psychology.
2. Summarize the basic steps that are followed when one conducts an experiment. Include in your answer a discussion of the independent and dependent variables, random assignment of subjects to groups, and the necessity of avoiding confounding.
3. Under what circumstances do social psychologists use deception methodology in their research? Is the use of deception justified?
4. Compare the experimental and correlational techniques for conducting social psychological studies. What are the advantages and disadvantages of each technique?
5. Describe the role of theory in social psychological research. What is the role of theory in explaining behavior and in predicting behavior?

Sources for Lecture

Berkowitz, L. (1971). Sex and violence—We can't have it both ways. *Psychology Today,* December, pp. 14–23. Is this a case where social scientists' values, as well as the general public's values, interfere with our ability to interpret the information found in research? Research results on both violence and pornography were similar, yet different policy decisions were advocated.

Campbell, D., & Tavris, C. (1975). The experimenting society: To find programs that work, government must measure its failures. *Psychology Today,* September, pp. 46–56. Campbell advocates using experimental methods to determine which social programs work and which ones don't.

Cornell, J. (1984). Science versus. the paranormal. *Psychology Today,* March, pp. 28–34. Why do so many people continue to believe in the paranormal despite disconfirmations? The Committee for the Scientific Investigation of the Paranormal is reviewed.

Hogan, R., & Schroeder, D. (1981). Seven biases in psychology. *Psychology Today,* July, pp. 8–10, 12, 14. Biases in psychology textbooks are reviewed. What kinds of values are being presented to students in this way?

Rubenstein, C. (1982). Psychology's fruit flies. *Psychology Today,* July, pp. 83–84. Do the college students used in so many of our experiments behave and think like other adults? This article argues that the answer may be no.

Rubin, Z. (1983). Taking deception for granted. *Psychology Today,* March, pp. 74–75. This critical overview notes that the use of deception remains at a high level among social psychologists, and it agues that the use of deception retards progress.

Update: Current Articles from Professional Sources

Anderson, C. A., & Sechler, E. S. (1986). Effects of explanation and counterexplanation on the development and use of social theories. *Journal of Personality and Social Psychology, 50,* 24–34. When subjects explained how or why two variables might be related, it increased their use of and belief in the explained relationship. A counterexplanation task eliminated this bias. Might scientists be affected by these same processes?

Hedges, L. V. (1987). How hard is hard science, how soft is soft science? The empirical cumulativeness of research. *American Psychologist, 42,* 443–455. Are research results in the behavioral sciences less replicable than results in the physical sciences? Although many say yes, the article questions this assumption. Methods for examining the consistency of research results are presented and examined.

Horvat, J. (1986). Detection of suspiciousness as a function of pleas for honesty. *Journal of Personality and Social Psychology, 50,* 921–924. This experiment reports a way to measure suspiciousness in deception experiments. Truly suspicious subjects will be found out, whereas naive subjects will be kept from falsely reporting suspiciousness.

Related Readings: The following selections from *Readings in Social Psychology: General, Classic, and Contemporary Selections,* 2nd Edition, by Wayne Lesko (Allyn and Bacon, 1993) accompany this chapter:

Huff, D. (1954). The sample with the built-in bias. Most students know that good survey research requires a random sample of respondents if the researcher is to generalize results. What students don't realize is how difficult it is to obtain a random sample. Presents interesting examples of how biases creep into the process of assembling a representative sample. (1)

Schlenker, B. (1974). Social psychology and science. Presents a defense for the scientific basis of social psychology by refuting arguments of authors who consider the social sciences to be fundamentally different from the natural sciences. (2)

Graham, S. (1992). Most of the subjects were white and middle class: Trends in published research on African Americans in selected APA journals. Research dealing with African Americans is examined in two ways. The first question is the frequency of research with African Americans as subjects. The second question is the type of research in which African Americans have been studied and whether any methological biases may be present in these studies. (3)

Chapter-at-a-Glance

Chapter Two
Social Perception:
Understanding Others

Chapter Outline	Instruction Ideas	Supplements
I. Nonverbal Communication: The Unspoken Language Nonverbal Communication: The Basic Channels / Nonverbal Behavior and Social Interaction: Self-Presentation and the Detection of Deception	Discussion Question 5, Critical Thinking Question 2	CNN Video Segment 2, *Italian Gestures* and Segment 3, *School Dress Code—see* CNN Video Guide Video: Communication
II. Attribution: Understanding the Causes of Others' Behavior Theories of Attribution: Frameworks for Understanding How We Attempt to Make Sense out of the Social World	Exercises 1, 2, 4, 5 and 6 Discussion Questions 2 and 3 Critical Thinking Questions 3 and 4	Transparencies 2.1–2.6 Video: Constructing Social Reality
III. Impression Formation and Impression Management: Combining—and Managing—Social Information Impression Formation: Some Basic Facts / Impression Management: The Fine Art of Looking Good	Exercise 3 Discussion Question 4 Critical Thinking Question 5	
Social Diversity: A Critical Analysis— Cultural and Ethnic Differences in Nonverbal Communication	Critical Thinking Question 1	Exercise 3 Discussion Question 4 Critical Thinking Question 5

Chapter Two

Social Perception: Understanding Others

Chapter Outline: Getting the Overall Picture

Learning Objectives

1. Why is it important to gauge the temporary moods and emotions of others, why do people often hide these from us, and how do we use nonverbal behaviors to determine moods and emotions? (Page 000)
2. What are the six basic emotions expressed in unique facial expressions? Does this mean we're capable of only six different facial expressions? Explain.
3. What is the relationship between electrical activity in facial muscles and simultaneous self-reports of thoughts and feelings?
4. Describe patterns of physiological activity created when subjects pose particular facial expressions.
5. How do we respond when others (a) maintain high levels of eye contact; (b) avoid eye contact; and (c) stare at us?
6. Describe patterns of emotional arousal communicated by various forms of self-touching, compare body postures of threatening versus warm ballet characters, and examine information communicated by gestures and gait.
7. How did being touched by a waitress in the Crusco and Wetzel (1984) study affect the size of customers' tips?
8. Examine gender differences and age differences in touching.
9. Consider the aspects of nonverbal behavior that a person must regulate to engage in effective self-regulation.
10. What four nonverbal cues help us to recognize that someone is lying?
11. In the Friedman and Miller-Herringer (1991) study, compare the "gloating" of subjects who were alone versus with two competitors when they received their positive feedback. How is self-monitoring related to the ability to suppress gloating?
12. Based on Jones and Davis's theory, understand why correspondent inferences occur when behavior is freely chosen, produces noncommon effects, and is low in social desirability.
13. Compare the ability of subjects in the Gilbert et al. (1992) study to categorize verbal behavior, characterize the speaker, and correct their judgments when listening to a degraded versus a normal audiotape.
14. Using Kelley's theory of attribution, distinguish between internal and external causes of behavior.
15. Compare attributions made when consensus is low, distinctiveness is low, and consistency is high with attributions made when consensus is high, distinctiveness is high, and consistency is high.
16. Give examples of how past experience may keep us from engaging in careful causal attribution, and note how unexpected events and unpleasant outcomes heighten causal attribution.
17. Explain the discounting that occurs when two possible supportive causes for a behavior are present, and the augmenting that occurs when both a supportive and an inhibitory cause are present.
18. How were ratings of female employees in the Summers (1991) study affected by whether the organization was pro- or anti-affirmative action and by the sex of the rater?
19. Describe the fundamental attribution error, along with explanations for its occurrence.
20. What is the actor-observer effect, and why does it occur?
21. Describe self-serving bias, and indicate how the study by Brown and Rogers (1991) supports the motivational explanation for self-serving bias.
22. How do self-defeating attributions contribute to depression, and how does attributional style relate to learned helplessness along with the ability to be immunized against it?
23. What is primacy? Compare Asch's "change of meaning" explanation and the more modern "loss of attention" explanation.
24. Understand the four factors that determine how much weight one gives a piece of information in forming an impression, along with the role played by person types in impression formation.
25. List tactics used in impression management.
26. Compare the effectiveness of the controlling versus the submissive interview techniques used by "applicants" in the Kacmar et al. (1993) study.
27. Summarize evidence supporting the notion that facial expressions for particular emotions are universal and that the meaning of expressions is universally recognized.
28. Describe ways in which Levenson et al. (1992) found the Minangkabau to be different from Americans in emotional expression, facial expressions, and physiological arousal.

Discussion Questions

1. How does one's name affect interpersonal judgments? You might ask the class to imagine a person named David, then to list five traits that David possesses.

Next, ask the class to imagine a person named Winthrop and have them list his traits. Do the two lists differ? Why?

Another way to approach this question is to ask the class whether they have ever felt that the names they were given implied a certain set of attributes. You might particularly seek responses from those with popular names or those with unusual names to see if they ever felt dissatisfied with their first names and why. Do we form impressions of people based on part on their names?

2.   How does one's choice of clothing affect the ratings received from others? Assuming that clothing does influence the personality attributed to a person, is this a case of biased judgment? Or is it simply rational processing of available information?

3.   Have students look for applications of attributional principles in advertising. For example, the person trying to get us to buy a product may be presented as a person who doesn't generally like the type of product. A boy may declare that he "doesn't like bran cereals," for instance. But we then see that the particular brand he tries is so extraordinarily good that it wins him over. In attributional terms, the response to the particular brand is high in distinctiveness.

Another example might be the communicator who tries to convince us that the majority of people prefer a certain brand. This time the attributional strategy is one of high consensus. Many examples of attributional strategies exist. Alert your students to be thinking in attributional terms when they see advertisements, and have them report relevant examples to the class.

4.   Discuss the basis for judging celebrities, political candidates, and the like. Do the same rules apply to interpersonal perception in a face-toface encounter and in our judgment of people we know only in the media? Would it be an advantage for a political candidate to be familiar with the social perception research? It might be interesting to design an advertising campaign, based on this research, to create a favorable impression of a candidate. Or analyze the ads employed by a candidate to determine whether the principles presented in chapter 2 are being followed.

5.   Paul Ekman has thoroughly investigated the use of gestures, voice qualities, and facial expressions as clues to whether a person is telling the truth. There is much evidence that some concealment cues are obvious to most people, while other cues that can be detected only by trained observers. For example, there are muscles located mainly in the forehead that momentarily express our sincere emotions, and that can be detected by a keen observer who knows what to look for. In total, Ekman's behavioral checklist contains twenty-two separate clues for detecting deceit.

An interesting question is the degree to which historical figures have fallen victim to deception from others. Ekman has analyzed several historical cases of deception, including the willingness of British Prime Minster Neville Chamberlain to believe Hitler in 1938 when Hitler said Germany's intentions were nonaggressive. Should a U.S. president be given lie detection training before going off to a summit with a foreign power? (Ekman's work is summarized in the book *Telling Lies* (1985), published by W. W. Norton. Included in the book is the list of twenty-two clues for detecting deceit.)

Classroom Exercises/Demonstrations

1.   This exercise asks students to read a story in which six characters appear. The story is presented in chapter 2 of your students' Study Guide. The students are instructed to rank the characters in descending order according to how responsible each is perceived to be for the woman's death. (It is possible to read or tell the story to the class, but the exercise works better if each person has his or her own copy.)

The class will tend to split evenly, with about half the class ranking the wife as most responsible and about half ranking the highwayman first. A few people will also choose other characters. A quite lively discussion can develop, in which each group supports its own choice and challenges the others. As course instructor, you should remain neutral in the debate. Rather than telling them what you believe the correct answer is, challenge them to reach their own conclusions. (The idea and materials for this exercise were provided by Jeanine Bloyd of Spoon River Junior College, Canton, Illinois.)

2.   It is relatively easy to demonstrate the difference in causal attributions made by actors and observers. Have the students obtain two subjects outside of class. One subject should respond to the list of behaviors in the Study Guide that describes actions performed by the self. The other subject should respond to the list of behaviors that describes actions performed by another person. Have the class members score the responses from the two subjects, finding the average score on the internal/external dimension for each subject, and bring the data to class. Combine the data from class members to see if you can find evidence to support the actor/observer difference.

3.   Warm versus cold is a trait dimension that has been shown to affect dramatically the impression formed of a stimulus person. This classic finding has been labeled the "central traits" effect, and a discussion of why it occurs can be found in many sources. You should prepare two lists of traits (given below), one said to be characteristic of Person A and the other characteristic of Person B. Each student in the class receives only one

list, either the A or the B list. In fact the two lists have six traits in common, and only the middle trait (warm versus cold) is different. If you are unable to prepare the list ahead of time, you can simply present them to the class on the chalkboard. Have half the class copy each list. When the "other list" is being presented, have those students who aren't supposed to see it cover their eyes. The trait lists are:

Person A	Person B
intelligent	intelligent
skillful	skillful
industrious	industrious
warm	cold
determined	determined
practical	practical
cautious	cautious

After the students have copied their respective lists, ask them to rate their stimulus person using the following six traits: (a) generous, (b) wise, (c) happy, (d) good-natured, (e) reliable, and (f) important. For each trait ask the students to make a "yes" or "no" response. You will find that the warm/cold difference will dramatically affect each of the first four traits, but not the last two traits.

4. This exercise should be done as soon as possible after students have received their test scores on an exam. The exercise asks students to explain the score they received. The prediction is that students who have done well on the exam will explain their performance internally, whereas students who have done relatively poorly will explain their performance more externally.

To find out whether this hypothesis is confirmed, the class should compute attributions to the internal factors (ability and effort) and to the external factors (the test and luck). According to self-serving bias successful people should attribute their success to the internal factors, whereas unsuccessful people should attribute their relative failure to the external factors. A questionnaire for your use is presented in chapter 2 of the Study Guide.

5. In the transparency section of this Instructor's Section three situations are presented that can be used to illustrate the basic ideas of Kelley's theory of attribution. Each example describes a behavior and then provides consensus, consistency, and distinctiveness information. At the end of each example, the student is asked to choose the best explanation of the behavior. Transparency 2.4 contains low-consensus, high-consistency, and low-distinctiveness information and should result in students making attributions to the situation (i.e., Professor Ward). Transparency 2.6 contains low-consensus, high-consistency, and high-distinctiveness information, and no simple attribution is obvious.

6. Chapter 2 of the Study Guide presents a page entitled "Applying Attribution to Everyday Situations." Students are instructed to describe the consensus, consistency, and distinctiveness information contained in each of two scenarios. Have the students respond to the scenarios outside of class (homework!); or you might provide time during class. After students have answered the questions, discuss their answers in class. Students appreciate an opportunity to determine whether they understand Kelley's theory.

Film Notes: A Picture Is Sometimes Worth a Thousand Words

Allyn and Bacon Videos

* *Constructing Social Reality* . Discusses the factors that contribute to our interpretation of reality and how understanding the psychological factors that govern our behavior may help us to become more empathic and independent members of society. (Discovering Psychology Series, On Tape #10.)
* *Communication: Social Cognition and Attribution,* videotape, 28.5 mins. To obtain this tape, consult your Allyn and Bacon sales representative. Dramatization is used to generate an exchange between Robert A. Baron and Margaret Clark concerning attributional processes and nonverbal communication.

Other Videos and Films

Communication: The Nonverbal Agenda, 32009, 1974, color, 30 mins. Pennsylvania State University, Audiovisual Services, Special Services Building, University Park,

PA 16802 (814-865-6314). Discusses the importance of being able to recognize the nonverbal messages that one receives and sends. Examples include interviews between an executive and three department heads, and a male–female encounter in a bar. Describes how communication problems between administrators, as well as manager-subordinate relationships, are worked out. From the *Behavior in Business* series. A CRM production.

I Guess I Got the Job, 21745, 1975, color, 13 mins. Pennsylvania State University, Audiovisual Services, Special Services Building, University Park, PA 16802 (814-865-6314). Two young men are interviewed for the same job. One is completely honest but shows a lack of confidence, while the other adopts interests and attitudes that he thinks will make him look good. From the *Conflict and Awareness* series.

Judging Emotional Behavior, ES-328, 24 mins. Indiana University, Audiovisual Center, Bloomington, IN

47401. Presents the emotional responses of subjects to emotion-eliciting stories. Shows the subjects first without sound, allowing the audience to judge the emotions being expressed; then shows the same sequences with narration to allow the audience to determine the accuracy of their judgments.

Kinesics, 80036, 1964, 73 mins. Pennsylvania State University, Audiovisual Services, Special Services Building, University Park, PA 16802 (814-865-6314). Filmed lecture by Raymond L. Birdwhistell of the Eastern Pennsylvania Psychiatric Institute on linguistic kinesics. Describes a system of categorizing and defining facial expressions, posturing, and gestures in terms of communicative meaning.

Nonverbal Communication, 21888, 1976, color, 22 mins. Pennsylvania State University, Audiovisual Services, Special Services Building, University Park, PA 16802 (814-865-6314). Overview of research and theory on communication through gesture, body posture, intonation, eye contact, and facial expression. Interviews with Hall on interpersonal distance, Argyle on the equilibrium theory of eye contact, Rosenthal on sex differences in the perception of nonverbal behavior, Akaret on gestures and expressions in photographs, and Eibl-Eibesfeldt on biological programming. From the *Social Psychology* series. Stanley Milgram.

Transparencies

2.1 *Correspondent Inference: When Do We Infer the Traits of Others?*
2.2 *Kelley's Theory of Causal Attribution*
2.3 *Discounting and Augmenting: Two Basic Principles of Causal Attribution*
2.4 *Low Consensus, High Consistency, and Low Distinctiveness Produce an Internal Attribution*
2.5 *High Consensus, High Consistency, and High Distinctiveness Produce an External Attribution*
2.6 *Low Consensus, High Consistency, and High Distinctiveness Present Us with Mixed Information*

Critical Thinking/Essay Questions

1. Cite evidence to support the idea that humans show universal facial expressions and that they universally recognize the meaning of facial expressions.
2. How do we know whether someone is lying to us? How skilled are we in detecting deception in others?
3. Summarize the role played by each of the following factors in determining whether we make a correspondent inference:
   a. The degree to which the person had free choice.
   b. The degree to which noncommon effects were produced by the behavior.
   c. Whether the behavior was high or low in social desirability.
4. Summarize how our attributions about someone's behavior are affected by consensus, consistency, and distinctiveness information.
5. Describe tactics used for impression management and indicate whether the tactics are likely to succeed.

Sources for Lecture

Bower, B. (1985). The face of emotion. *Science News,* July 6, *128*, pp. 12–13. Explores the idea that facial expressions cause us to experience various feelings, with particular attention to Robert Zajonc's resurrection of Waynbaum's (1906) theory. Also discusses other theorists dealing with the facial feedback issue.

Driscoll, R. (1982). Their own worst enemies. *Psychology Today,* July, pp. 45–49. Examines the messages sent by severely self-critical people.

Sadalla, E., & Burroughs, J. (1981). Profiles in eating: Sexy vegetarians and other diet-based social stereotypes. *Psychology Today,* October, pp. 51–57. Eating preferences are correlated with how people see themselves and how others see them.

Snyder, C. R. (1985). Excuses, excuses. *Psychology Today,* September, pp. 50–55. Discusses self-handicapping defensive attributions, as well as other ways that people preserve their self-image and reduce stress.

Trotter, R. J. (1983). Baby face. *Psychology Today,* August, pp. 14–20. Presents evidence that infants possess a rich repertoire of inborn emotional expressions.

Update: Current Articles from Professional Sources

Alicke, M. D., & Klotz, M. L. (1993). Social roles and social judgment: How an impression conveyed influences an impression formed. *Personality and Social Psychology Bulletin, 19*, 185–194. Subjects instructed to enact the role of introvert saw their partner as more extraverted, while those instructed to enact the role of extravert saw the partner as more introverted. Actual behavior of the partner was held constant; thus role enactment itself was the basis for the judgment of the partner.

Ambady, N., & Rosenthal, R. (1993). Half a minute: Predicting teacher evaluations from thin slices of behavior and physical attractiveness. *Journal of Personality and Social Psychology, 64*, 431–441. Very brief (thirty seconds and less) silent video clips of college teachers' nonverbal behavior significantly predicted end-of-the-semester student evaluations of teachers. These results have important implications for research on impression formation.

Bassili, J. N. (1993). Procedural efficiency and the spontaneity of trait inference. Personality and Social Psychology Bulletin, 19, 200–205. How subjects encode information about a target has been shown to be important in determination of trait inferences. Practice with various kinds of inferences influences the spontaneity of further trait inferences.

Bond, Jr., C. F., et al. (1992). Fishy-looking liars: Deception judgment from expectancy violation. Journal of *Personality and Social Psychology, 63*, 969–977. How do we determine that others are lying? This study says we perceive deception when others display behavior that violates normative expectations.

Buck, R., Losow, J. I., Murphy, M. M., & Costanzo, P. (1992). Social facilitation and inhibition of emotional expression and communication. *Journal of Personality and Social Psychology, 63*, 962–968. How accurately can we tell the type of slide viewed by another person on the basis of his/her facial expression? How is accuracy changed if the person displaying the expression is with a partner who is also viewing the slides? How is accuracy changed if the subject rating the expression is alone versus. with another rater? Buck, et al. answer these questions.

Fincham, F. D., & Bradbury, T. N. (1993). Marital satisfaction, depression, and attributions: A longitudinal analysis. *Journal of Personality and Social Psychology, 64*, 442–452. Relates attributions made by partners in a marital relationship to satisfaction in the relationship. Attributions made for negative partner behavior seem to be particularly important.

Gonzales, M. H., & Meyers, S. A. (1993). "Your mother would like me": Self-presentation in the personal ads of heterosexual and homosexual men and women. *Personality and Social Psychology Bulletin, 19*, 131–142. Researchers examined self-presentational strategies in personal ads of heterosexual and homosexual men and women and coded the ways in which attractiveness, financial security, expressiveness, sincerity, and sexual activities were mentioned. Advantages of using personal ads to understand self-presentation are discussed.

Keltner, D., Locke K. D., & Audrain, P. C. (1993). The influence of attributions on the relevance of negative feelings to personal satisfaction. *Personality and Social Psychology Bulletin, 19*, 21–29. Negative feelings caused by specific events may become incorporated into global self-judgments. We can understand the degree to which this takes place examining attributions made about the feelings.

Related Readings: The following selections from *Readings in Social Psychology: General, Classic, and Contemporary Selections,* 2nd Edition, by Wayne Lesko (Allyn and Bacon, 1993) accompany this chapter:

Sadalla, E., & Burroughs, J. (October, 1981). Profiles in eating: Sexy vegetarians and other diet-based stereotypes. Do we judge people based on what they eat? Sadalla and Burroughs found that knowing people's food preferences is sufficient to activate personality stereotypes. In addition, they found a significant correlation between food preferences and self-ratings. (4)

Kelley, H. (1950). The warm-cold variable in first impressions of persons. Students were presented with two different descriptions of a substitute instructor. Some students were told their instructor was a "rather warm" person, others that he was "rather cold." Changing this one adjective affected ratings of the instructor and behavior toward him. (5)

Etaugh, C., & Birdoes, L. (1991). Previous studies found married individuals in their forties are rated more favorably than nonmarried individuals. Etaugh and Birdoes wondered whether this tendency to rate married persons more positively would occur in other age groups as well. The article sensitizes readers to the vast array of everyday information that influences first impressions. (6)

Chapter-at-a-Glance

Chapter Three
Social Cognition:
Thinking about Others and the Social World

Chapter Outline	Instruction Ideas	Supplements
Introduction		Video: Attribution and Social Cognition
I. Heuristics: Mental Shortcuts in Social Cognition Representativeness: Judging by Resemblance / Availability: What Comes to Mind First?	Exercises 1–3 Discussion Questions 1 and 3 Critical Thinking Questions 1 and 2	
II. Basic Aspects of Social Thought: Tilts, Tendencies, and Potential Errors Dealing with INconsistent Information: Paying Attention what Doesn't Fit / Automatic Vigilance: Noticing the Negative / Motivated Skepticism: In Reaching Conclusions, How Much Information Is Enough? / Counterfactual Thinking: The Effects of Considering "What Might Have Been" / What's Mine Is Good: The Mere Ownership Effect	Discussion Question 2 Critical Thinking Question 3	Transparency 3.2 Video: Remembering and Forgetting Readings: Lesko 7—Matters of Choice Muddled by Thought and Lesko 9—Just World? Sexual Orientation and AIDS
III. Affect and Cognition: How Thought Shapes Feelings and Feelings Shape Thought The Nature of Emotion: Contrasting Views and Some Recent Advances / How Affect Influences Cognition / How Cognition Influences Affect	Critical Thinking Questions 4 and 5	Transparency 3.3 Video: Cognitive Processes Readings: Lesko 8—Determinants of Emotional State

Chapter Three

Social Cognition: Thinking About Others and the Social World

Chapter Outline: Getting the Overall Picture

Learning Objectives

1. Describe the basic nature of heuristics, indicating how they allow us to remain cognitive misers and to avoid information overload.
2. Describe the representativeness heuristic, and indicate how the representativeness heuristic sometimes leads us to commit the base-rate fallacy.
3. Describe the availability heuristic, and indicate whether ease of recall or sheer amount of information recalled is the more important factor underlying it.
4. Define the false consensus effect, and explain it in terms of both the self-enhancing hypothesis and the availability heuristic.
5. Indicate a circumstance under which the false consensus effect fails to occur.
6. Describe research that demonstrates the priming effect, along with studies of automatic priming and of self-generated primes.
7. Compare the impact of consistent versus inconsistent information on social judgments, focusing on the study by Hilton et al. (1991).

8. Describe the automatic vigilance effect, including the face-in-the-crowd effect and the study by Pratto and John (1991).

9. Describe motivated skepticism, focusing particularly on the study by Ditto and Lopez (1992).

10. Based on the research by Wilson and Schooner (1991), indicate how "thinking too much" while rating jams or rating courses lowered the accuracy of the ratings.

11. Give examples of counterfactual thinking, and indicate how people's thinking is affected by it.

12. Describe the mere ownership effect and the conditions under which it occurs.

13. Focusing on women's recollections of "symptoms" occurring during menstruation, how do people's implicit theories about stability and change influence personal memories?

14. Compare people high versus low in "need for cognition."

15. Summarize the views of emotion expressed by the Cannon-Bard theory, the James-Lange theory, and Schachter's two-factor theory.

16. Describe the facial feedback hypothesis, along with research findings relevant to the hypothesis.

17. Describe Zajonc's vascular theory of emotional efference, and summarize experimental evidence that supports the hypothesis.

18. What are the three ways in which our current affective state can influence how we process social information?

19. What is a "motivated processing strategy?"

20. Summarize research on how moods influence our processing of social information.

21. Know the five ways in which cognition influences emotional reactions, focusing on how thought suppression may lead us to think of the suppressed thought.

22. Examine strategies used to process familiar versus unfamiliar written information by Paluans and Americans in the Pritchard (1991) study.

Discussion Questions

1. Chapter 3 opens with a discussion of the notion that information overload is the basic fact of social cognition. Because we are bombarded with thousands of stimuli, it is argued, we need to be efficient in screening, sorting, and storing social information. But an alternative view is that humans simply are not very good at remembering the content of information that is presented to them. Jacoby and Hoyer (1982) had subjects view a thirty-second videotape in U.S. shopping malls and then had them answer twelve true/false questions pertaining to the videotape. Despite the facts that the videotape was viewed under ideal conditions, that the tape was of short duration, and that the testing was done immediately after viewing, only 3.5 percent of the respondents answered all twelve questions correctly. Could it be that what we remember is simply not an accurate representation of what we see? (Jacoby and Hoyer's article appears in *Journal of Marketing, 46,* 12–16.)

2. Watch the news for reports of extreme acts of behavior. Can you find evidence that news analysts overemphasize drastic cases in reporting the news? Does reporting of acts of terrorism, for instance, lead us to a distorted perception of the views of the average resident of the terrorists' home countries?

3. Describe the availability heuristic to the class. Ask students to describe instances in which they were affected by this heuristic. Make sure that you have a firm grasp of the heuristic yourself so that you are ready to respond to their examples. Next, do the same thing with the representativeness heuristic: Describe the heuristic and request students to describe instances in which they were affected by representativeness.

4. An interesting, although perhaps controversial, way to introduce the ideas of covariation and illusory correlation is to examine the relationship between homosexuality and other behaviors. A paper presented by Paul Cameron at the Midwestern Psychological Association meeting in May 1983 argued that homosexuality is disproportionately associated with murder. Cameron based his conclusion on an examination of sexually related mass murders in the United States. Another relationship that is "understood to be true" among some fire investigators (personally communicated to the author by a state arson investigator) is that arson is associated with homosexuality. Consider these examples in contrasting the difference between actual covariation and illusory correlation.

5. People have fairly detailed conceptions of the characteristics possessed by various groups. For example, we possess a well-developed schema for the elderly. One aspect of this schema is a notion that there are specific occupations appropriate for the elderly. There is evidence that some occupations are age typed. Prepare a list of occupations and ask students to rate them for the most appropriate age of a person in that occupation. What are the processes underlying judgments of age appropriateness for individual occupations? Do people use the availability heuristic; that is, do they search their memories for instances of incumbents of various ages? Do people consider the importance of various work skills? What other factors do they consider? Another

aspect of this schema is our view of how a grandmother looks and acts. Brewer, Dull, and Lui (1981) published an interesting article in the *Journal of Personality and* *Social Psychology* (*41*, 656–670) in which they explored the traits attributed to a grandmother.

Classroom Exercises/Demonstrations

The chapter summarizes a variety of biases that contaminate our thinking. A useful way to introduce this chapter is to have students experience some of these biases firsthand. The brief exercises that follow introduce some of these biases. You may want to present these to the class early in your consideration of social cognition, as some of the examples are presented in the text.

1. *The availability heuristic.* We often use ease of recall as a basis for judging the frequency of events. Just because we can more readily recall one category of events, however, does not necessarily mean that the category is more frequent. Pose the following question to the class: Does the letter *k* appear more often as the first letter of a word or as the third letter? Most people judge that *k* appears more often at the beginning of a word, but in fact *k* is three times more likely to appear as the third letter. Why the error? The reason seems to be that our relative ease of recall words beginning with k convinces us that they are also more frequent.

2. *The representativeness heuristic.* Tell the students that you have a series of thumbnail descriptions of one hundred individuals, thirty of whom are engineers and seventy of whom are lawyers. From this sample, the following description has been drawn at random: John is a thirty-nine-year-old man. He is married and has no children. A man of high ability and motivation, he promises to be quite successful in his field. He is well liked by his colleagues. What is the probability that John is a lawyer? People generally will respond to this question by saying it is fifty-fifty as to whether he is a lawyer or an engineer. What they have done is ignore the base-rate information and instead relied upon useless anecdotal information.

3. *The false consensus effect.* To illustrate this effect, you need to have students respond to some informational questions. An obvious source is exam questions. Tell the students whether they answered the particular question right or wrong. Then have them indicate the percentage of students in the class whom they believe correctly answered that particular question. For the questions they answered correctly, students should overestimate the percentage of correct responses. For the questions they answered wrong, they should underestimate the percentage.

4. Chapter 3 discusses *the self-reference effect* and summarizes it in Figure 3.18. (Figure 3.18 is reproduced as a transparency at the end of this Instructor's Section chapter.) You can have the students do an exercise that demonstrates the effect rather convincingly. The exercise can be done either in class with the instructor serving as the experimenter or outside of class with students serving as the experimenters. Half of the subjects are instructed to read a list of trait adjectives and decide whether each of the words describes themselves. The other half of the subjects reads the same list of trait adjectives and indicates whether each of the words contains an *e.* After the subjects have gone through the entire list of adjectives, they are given a surprise recall test.

You will find that people who have gone through the list deciding whether the word describes the self will recall more of the words than people who simply decide whether each word has an *e.* This is because the words related to self are processed more deeply than the other words. When I do this exercise in class I find that students are impressed by the analogy between the exercise and their own study habits. Oftentimes studying becomes an exercise of "just reading words." To learn material, a student must process it deeply; one way to accomplish this is to be able to relate it to something already well known. What is better known than the self?

A list of thirteen trait adjectives to use in conducting the exercise is found in your students' Study Guide. Two identical lists are presented on the assumption that your students may want to gather data from friends by having one person do the task under each instructional set. You can then have the students bring their data to class and combine the data to see whether you have demonstrated the self-reference effect.

Film Notes: A Picture Is Sometimes Worth a Thousand Words

Allyn and Bacon Videos

* *Cognitive Processes.* Explores the higher mental processes—reasoning, planning, and problem solving—and why the "cognitive revolution" is attracting such diverse investigators, from philosophers to computer scientists. (Discovering Psychology Series, On Tape # 5)

* *Communication: Social Cognition and Attribution,* video-tape, 28.5 mins. To obtain this tape, consult your Allyn and Bacon sales representative. Dramatization is used to generate an exchange between Robert A. Baron and Margaret Clark on the principles of social cognition.

* *Remembering and Forgetting.* A look at the complex process of memory: how images, ideas, language—even physical actions, sounds, and smells—are translated into codes, represented in memory, and retrieved when needed. (Discovering Psychology Series, On Tape #5)

Other Videos and Films

Information Processing, 31761, 1971, color, 29 mins. Pennsylvania State University, Audiovisual Services, Special Services Building, University Park, PA 16802 (814-865-6314). Psychologist Donald A. Norman and comedian David Steinberg used a cocktail party to reveal basic principles and far-reaching ramifications of human information processing. Includes short- and long-term memory, the Stroop phenomenon, mnemonics, retrieval strategies, and problem solving. From the *Psychology Today* series. A CRM production.

Judgment and Decision Making, Number 11 in this 1990 videotape series, 30 mins. The Annenborg Project, Holt, Rinehart & Winston, contact Lee Sutherlin, Marketing Manager (817-334-7632). A look at the process of making judgments and decisions, how and why people make good and bad judgments, and the psychology of risk taking.

Transparencies

3.1 *Self-Schemata and Memory*
3.2 *Mental Simulations and Sympathy for Victims*
3.3 *Mood and Social Judgments: A Field Study*
3.4 *How Cognition Sometimes Shapes Affect*

Critical Thinking/Essay Questions

1. What is the representativeness heuristic, and how is it related to the base-rate fallacy?
2. Describe the false consensus effect, and give a reason it occurs.
3. Summarize how counterfactual thinking occurs when negative outcomes follow unusual actions.
4. Describe the facial feedback hypothesis, and summarize evidence that supports the hypothesis.
5. How does our current affective state influence how we process social information?

Sources for Lecture

Allman, W. F. (1985). Staying alive in the 20th century. *Science '85,* October, pp. 34–41. Compares how the experts' assessments of various risks in everyday life are related to the assessment of the general public. Provides excellent examples of the irrationality of human thought.

Langer, E. J. (1982). Automated lives. *Psychology Today,* April, pp. 60–71. Langer discusses the tendency to engage in "mindlessness"—to do things and to make decisions without really thinking.

LeBrecque, M. (1980). On making sounder judgments. *Psychology Today,* June, pp. 32–42. Provides a review of some common errors in human thinking and offers guidelines for minimizing such errors.

Offir, C. W. (1975). Floundering in fallacy: Seven quick ways to kid yourself. *Psychology Today,* April, pp. 66–68. Discusses common fallacies in human thinking.

Update: Current Articles from Professional Sources

Rubin, D. C. (1975). The subtle deceiver: Recalling your past. *Psychology Today,* September, pp. 38–46. Our ability to remember the past details of our lives is hampered by our present lives and our beliefs about ourselves.

Slovic, P., Fischhoff, B., & Lichtenstein, S. (1980). Risky assumptions. *Psychology Today,* June, pp. 44–48. Presents examples of how errors in human thinking get us into trouble. Focuses especially on the over-confidence and vividness effects.

Bourgeois, M. J., Horowitz, I. A., & Lee, L. F. Effects of technicality and access to trial transcripts on verdicts and information processing in a civil trial. *Personality and Social Psychology Bulletin, 19,* 220–227. How do jurors deal with information that is too complex? By falling back on simplifying, heuristic devices. The study examined jurors' use of a readily available counterfactual heuristic when highly technical evidence was presented. Access to trial transcripts and blocking use of the heuristic led jurors to process information more systematically.

Bugental, D. B., et al. (1993). Social cognitions as organizers of autonomic and affective responses to social challenge. *Journal of Personality and Social Psychology, 64,* 94–103. Researchers presented computer-simulated children who behaved responsively or unresponsively on a computer game. Women raters first filled out a "Parent Attribution Test" to measure where they perceived the locus of control to reside. The researchers studied how these women responded autonomically and affectively to these "children."

MacLeod, C., & Campbell, L. (1992). Memory accessibility and probability judgments: An experimental evaluation of the availability heuristic. *Journal of Personality and Social Psychology, 63,* 890–902. Procedures that reduce the latency of response for past events also are found to increase subjects' estimates of future probability.

Riemann, R., & Angleitner, A. (1993). Inferring interpersonal traits from behavior: Act prototypicality vs. conceptual similarity of trait concepts. *Journal of Personality and Social Psychology, 63,* 356–364. Subjects were presented with six fictitious persons about whom they had to make trait ratings. Two models of the process underlying these trait ratings are investigated.

Showers, C. (1992). Evaluatively integrative thinking about characteristics of the self. *Personality and Social Psychology Bulletin, 18,* 719–729. A comparison was made of persons who think of themselves by clustering positive and negative information in "separate packages" versus persons who tend to integrate positive and negative information together. Persons who generated evaluatively integrated information had higher self-esteem.

Slugoski, B. R., Shields, H. A., & Dawson, K. A. (1993) Relation of conditional reasoning to heuristic processing. *Personality and Social Psychology Bulletin, 19,* 158–166. Two main factors that seem to be involved in reasoning were discovered. The factors correspond to an availability and a representativeness dimension.

Wegner, D. M., & Erber, R. (1992). The hyperaccessibility of suppressed thoughts. *Journal of Personality and Social Psychology, 63,* 903–912. Subjects who try to suppress thinking about a target word end up having greater access to the word. Thoughts we try to eliminate from attention remain remarkably near the surface and ready to return to consciousness with minimal prompting.

Related Readings: The following selections from *Readings in Social Psychology: General, Classic, and Contemporary Selections,* 2nd Edition, by Wayne Lesko (Allyn and Bacon, 1993) accompany this chapter:

Gladwell, M. (March 4, 1991). Matters of choice muddled by thought. People asked to analyze their decisions tend to act differently, often for the worse. Gladwell considers cases where "thinking too much" interferes with decision making. There are, he asserts, decisions where nonverbal intuition is "correct" and where verbal reasoning hinders the quality of decision. Research-based examples are provided. (7)

Schachter, S., & Singer, J. (1962). Cognitive, social, and physiological determinants of emotional state. The question of what determines subjective emotional states is addressed. "Emotion" is partly due to physiological arousal, but without a cognitive label to attach to the arousal, the authors argued that no specific emotion will be experienced. (8)

Anderson, V. (1992) For whom is this world just? Sexual orientation and AIDS. When bad things happen, the "just world" hypothesis says we have a cognitive need to blame the victim. Anderson uses this hypothesis to explain our tendency to blame gay men who contract the AIDS virus more than we blame heterosexual men who do so. (9)

Chapter-at-a-Glance

Chapter Four
Attitudes:
Evaluating the Social World

Chapter Outline	Instruction Ideas	Supplements
Introduction	Discussion Question 4	CNN Video Segment 4, *AIDS Attitudes* and Segment 5, *Times Mirror Poll—see* CNN Video Guide
I. Forming Attitudes: The Role of Learning and Experience Social Learning: Acquiring Attitudes from Others / Direct Experience: Acquiring Attitudes from Life / Genetic Factors: Some Surprising Recent Findings	Exercise 2 Discussion Question 5 Critical Thinking Question 2	
II. Attitudes and Behavior: The Essential Link Attitude Specificity / Attitude Components / Attitude Strength, Vested Interest, and the Role of Self-Awareness / Attitude Accessibility: The Force That Binds	Discussion Question 5 Critical Thinking Question 2	Reading: Lesko 11—Attitudes vs. Action
III. Persuasion: The Process of Changing Attitudes Persuasion: The Traditional Approach / Persuasion: The Cognitive Approach / The Reciprocity of Persuasion: When Attitude Change Is a Two-Way Street	Exercises 1 and 3–5 Discussion Question 3 Critical Thinking Questions 3 and 4	Readings: Lesko 10—American Values Test
IV. When Attitude Change Fails: Resistance to Persuasion Reactance: Protecting Our Pesonal Freedom / Forewarning: Prior Knowledge of Persuasive Intent / Selective Avoidance	Exercises 1 and 3–5 Discussion Question 3 Critical Thinking Questions 3 and 4	Exercises 1 and 3–5 Discussion Question 3 Critical Thinking Questions 3 and 4
V. Cognitive Dissonance: How We Sometimes Change Our Own Attitudes Dissonance and Attitude Change: The Effects of Forced Compliance / Dissonance and the Less-Leads-to-More Effect / Dissonance: Does It Really Stem from Inconsistency?	Discussion Question 1 Critical Thinking Question 5	Transparencies 4.1–4.4 Reading: Lesko 12—Cognitive Dissonance in Psychotherapy

Chapter Four

Attitudes: Evaluating the Social World

Chapter Outline: Getting the Overall Picture

Learning Objectives

1. Examine the various aspects of the textbook's definition of "attitude."
2. Explain the procedure used by Judd, Drake, Downing, and Krosnick (1991) to demonstrate that activation of a particular attitude can cause activation of other, related attitudes.
3. Describe evidence to support the idea that attitudes can be formed via classical conditioning.
4. How did Krosnick and his colleagues demonstrate subliminal conditioning of attitudes, and how do these results relate to the demand characteristics argument?

5. Explain how particular attitudes can be strengthened or weakened via instrumental conditioning.

6. Describe the role played by modeling in the transmission of attitudes.

7. In what ways do attitudes acquired through direct experience differ from attitudes acquired in other ways?

8. What conclusion regarding the attitude-behavior relationship was supported by the LaPiere (1934) study and the Wicker (1969) review?

9. Indicate how the study by Newcomb, Rabow, and Hernandez (1992) supports the conclusion that specific attitudes are better predictors of overt behaviors than more general attitudes.

10. Describe circumstances under which behavior is determined by the affective component of attitudes and circumstances where it is determined by the cognitive component of attitudes.

11. Why are attitudes acquired through direct experience better predictors of behavior than attitudes acquired through observation?

12. Based on the study by Sivacek and Crano (1982), describe how having a vested interest increases the strength of the attitude-behavior link.

13. Explain how self-awareness is related to the attitude-behavior relationship and indicate why.

14. How is attitude accessibility related to the attitude-to-behavior link?

15. Indicate how research by Bargh, Chaiken, Govender, and Pratto (1992) provides support for the automatic attitude activation model.

16. Know the eight conclusions reached by researchers dealing with how sources, messages, and the audience affect the persuasion process.

17. Compare the assumptions of the traditional versus the cognitive approach to persuasion.

18. Contrast how persuasion takes place on the central route versus the peripheral route, according to the elaboration likelihood model.

19. Describe research findings that can be understood in terms of the elaboration likelihood model, especially the study by Roskos-Evoldsen and Fazio (1992).

20. Compare the cognitive analysis engaged in by persons who are personally involved in issues versus that engaged in by persons who are uninvolved.

21. Why do high self-monitors process messages from attractive sources carefully, while processing messages from expert sources less carefully?

22. Describe the study by Hutton and Baumeister (1992), indicating how it supports the idea that self-awareness heightens the impact of persuasive messages, particularly when the message is convincing.

23. Examine the idea that different attitude objects serve different functions for the holder, and compare the type of ad preferred for utilitarian versus self-identity products in the Shavitt (1990) study.

24. Describe how reciprocity produced public attitude change in the experiment by Cialdini, Green, and Rusch (1992), and indicate conditions necessary for private attitude change to also occur.

25. How does the notion of "reactance" explain the fact that we often show negative attitude change when faced with hard-sell persuasion attempts?

26. Why are we better able to resist persuasive messages when they are preceded by forewarning of persuasive intent?

27. Describe the roles played by selective avoidance and selective exposure in helping us to resist persuasion.

28. Summarize evidence from Tyler and Schuller (1991) to support the hypothesis that people remain open to attitude change throughout life.

29. What is cognitive dissonance, how is it produced in the forced compliance situation, and what strategies do people use to get rid of such dissonance?

30. Describe how strong attitudes and behavioral commitment are produced by feelings of hypocrisy, and be sure to understand the applications of this technique to safe sex and water conservation.

31. Describe research that demonstrates the less-leads-to-more effect and indicate the three conditions necessary for this effect.

32. Compare the view that dissonance stems from inconsistency with the view that it stems from feeling responsible for negative outcomes.

33. Indicate how cultural and ethnic factors influence sexual attitudes, and summarize differences in sexual attitudes in the United States by comparing (1) whites versus. blacks and (2) Hispanics versus non-Hispanic white Americans.

Discussion Questions

1. As an alternative to dissonance theory, Charles Kiesler has proposed that the reason we change our attitudes in the direction of counterattitudinal behaviors is that we become committed when we perform an action. Whereas dissonance theory is concerned only with the effects created by our counterattitudinal behaviors, Kiesler has proposed that acting in a manner consistent with what we believe can also have important consequences for our attitudes. Dissonance theory considers attitude-consistent actions irrelevant because they do not arouse any dissonance. Kiesler's ideas are presented in a 1971 book, *The Psychology of Commitment,* (Academic Press).

As in dissonance theory, Kiesler has proposed that only some kinds of behavioral acts will result in a person's becoming committed. Some of the factors determining one's degree of commitment are as follows:

1. *The explicitness of the behavior.* Publicly expressing an opinion is a stronger commitment than expressing your views to a stranger.
2. *The importance of the behavior.* Expressing an opinion to someone important is a stronger commitment than expressing your views to a stranger.
3. *The degree of irrevocability.* Expressing an opinion in a written statement is a stronger commitment than expressing your views orally.
4. *Number of actions.* Expressing an opinion over and over again is a stronger commitment than expressing it only once.
5. *Degree of volition.* Expressing an opinion of your own free will is a stronger commitment than expressing it because someone makes you do it.
6. *Effort.* Going to a lot of trouble to express an opinion is a stronger commitment than expressing it easily.

2. Have the students write down their attitudes on some important topic, and also have them list the people and experiences that contributed to the development of this attitude. You may want to direct their thinking toward some important issue, such as homosexuality, abortion, or racial prejudice, so that the entire class will be thinking about the same issue. After the students have made their lists, introduce the factors that social psychologists have concluded to be important in attitude formation. Do the students have examples of classical conditioning, instrumental conditioning, modeling, and direct experience that they can relate to the class discussion?

3. Analyze the credibility of current political figures. This is especially relevant in a presidential election year. Analyze the contribution of expertise, attractiveness, similarity, trustworthiness, and so on. What is the basis for attributing each of these characteristics to a political figure?

4. A time-consuming but potentially valuable exercise is to have the class construct an attitude questionnaire. During one class period have the students write a set of items relevant to a particular topic. A large number of items (perhaps one hundred) is needed. Next, select the best forty or so items and have the students ascertain their friends' attitudes on these items. Determine which items best discriminate between people who are above or below average on the measured attitude. (The topic should be one that is interesting to students. Allow them to choose the topic from among women's rights, fraternities, raising tuition, or any other issue that is important to them.)

5. Lewittes and Simmons published an article in 1975 suggesting that we often engage in impression management when performing a sexually motivated behavior. They suggest that one reason people say one thing and do another is that they sometimes must do things in public that they consider embarrassing. For example, some people find it embarrassing to buy contraceptives at the pharmacy counter. Likewise, college students buying *Playboy*, *Penthouse*, and similar magazines at a university bookstore show discomfort. Lewittes and Simmons found that those buying magazines such as *Playboy* purchased more additional items, such as other magazines or candy, and more often asked for a bag for their purchases. Finally, a Dallas cable television franchise conducted a survey to find out what kinds of services people wanted and didn't want. Adult programming was rated very low in the survey, but 60 percent of the subscribers signed up for the adult channel. When asked to make public statements for the survey, most disapproved the sex and nudity of the adult channel; when they could privately sign up for it, most did so. (Lewittes and Simmons's article appears in the *Journal of Social Psychology*, *96*, 39–44.)

Classroom Exercises/Demonstrations

1. Ryckman and Sherman (1974) asked college students to rate the trustworthiness of members of a variety of occupations on a scale of 1 to 4; a rating of 1 meant most trustworthy, while a rating of 4 meant least trustworthy. Your students can repeat the procedure conducted by Ryckman and Sherman (published in *Journal of Applied Social Psychology*, *4*, 351–364). Having rated these occupations, ask the students to explain the basis of their judgments. What characteristics do they associate with trustworthiness? What is the reason for some occupations being rated low in trustworthiness? The occupations to be rated are found in chapter 4 of your students' Study Guide.

2. Make a list of buildings on your campus. Have the students rate these buildings on two different dimensions, once for likability and once for familiarity or how often they've been there. Each of these ratings can be done on a five-point scale. Gather up the ratings and determine their degree of correlation. Is there support for the frequency of exposure/liking hypothesis? Do students report liking those buildings with which they are most familiar?

3. Have students bring in advertisements from newspapers and magazines so that you can analyze the techniques of persuasion being used in them. In a 1985 article in *Teaching of Psychology* (*12*[1], 42–43), Vivian Makosky suggests there are three major persuasion techniques that can be identified in this way. In addition, she suggests several variations on the exercise. One variation is to compare the appeals made in men's magazines with those in wo.nen's magazines. Another variation is to compare the appeals in *Vogue* with those in *Family Circle*. Still another variation is to analyze what it is that turns people off in certain ads. Whatever avenue you choose, it is clear that advertising is a rich source of material for testing hypotheses on attitude change.

4. Chapter 4 presents a detailed discussion of the difference between the central and the peripheral route to persuasion. Have students describe examples of television ads that use the two routes. The ads using the central route are presented directly to the viewer, whereas ads using the peripheral route are embedded in distraction. Can the students come up with examples of these types of ads? Are those using the central route based on better arguments than those using the peripheral route?

5. Chapter 4 looks at differences between high self-monitors and low self-monitors in terms of the type of communicator that appeals to each. The Self-Monitoring Scale, authored by Mark Snyder is presented in chapter 5 of the Study Guide. An interesting extension of the exercise presented in chapter 5 is to see whether you can replicate the attitudinal effect; that is, to see whether high self-monitors really are more influenced by a source's attractiveness, whereas low self-monitors are more affected by the expertise of the source. Prepare a persuasive appeal and vary the source of the message. Half the time it should come from an expert, half from a nonexpert. Half the time it should come from an attractive communicator, half from a less attractive source. Can you replicate the self-monitoring effect?

Film Notes: A Picture Is Sometimes Worth a Thousand Words

Persuasion Box, I-306, film, 21 mins. Audiovisual Services, Western Illinois University, Macomb, IL 61455 (309-298-2417). This film shows how attitudes are changed in everyday life; special emphasis is given to the language of persuasions in advertising and in the mass media.

The Psychology of Mass Persuasion, 727-GK, 35 mm. filmstrip with accompanying audio cassette, 39 mins. Human Relations Media, 175 Tompkins Avenue, Pleasantville, NY 10570. Provides an analysis of mass persuasion in modern society. Looks at who the mass persuaders are and the techniques they use.

Social Animal, 3-I56, 1963, 29 mins. Audiovisual Services, Western Illinois University, Macomb, IL 61455 (309-298-2417). One of the topics covered is the classic experiment by Festinger and Carlsmith (1959) showing the consequences of publicly stating something contrary to one's belief. Cognitive dissonance interpretation is presented.

Social Psychology, 31762, 1971, color, 33 mins. Pennsylvania State University, Audiovisual Services, Special Services Building, University Park, PA 16802 (814-865-6314). Documentary footage of the busing of black children to previously all-white schools in a middle-class suburb is used to explain the social comparison theory, how attitudes are formed and changed, and the nature of racial prejudice. Commentary by psychologists Kenneth B. Clark, Thomas Pettigrew, David Sears, and Thomas Cottle. From the *Psychology Today* series. A CRM production.

Transparencies

4.1 *Cognitive Dissonance Theory in a Nutshell*
4.2 *The Forced Compliance Paradigm for Studying the Effects of Engaging in Attitude–Discrepant Behavior*

4.3 *Dissonance: The Price of Inconsistency*
4.4 *Rewards and Forced-Compliance: Why "Less" Sometimes Leads to "More"*

Critical Thinking/Essay Questions

1. Describe evidence in support of the idea that attitudes can be formed via classical conditioning.
2. Describe an attitude-change program that would not only change targets' attitudes but would also cause the target to behave consistently with the newly formed attitudes.
3. compare the traditional approach to persuasion and the cognitive perspective

4. If your professor reads your term paper "on the central route", how will your grade be determiend? If your professor reads your term paper "on the peripheral route", how will your grade be determined?
5. Describe the less-leads-to-more effect, and indicate the three conditions necessary for the effect to occur.

Sources for Lecture

Ball-Rokeach, S. J., Rokeach, M., and Grube, J. W. The great American values test. *Psychology Today,* November 1984, pp. 34–41. Can television alter basic beliefs? An experimental TV program aired one night in 1979 set out to find an answer.

Benson, P. L. Religion on capitol hill: How beliefs affect voting behavior in the U.S. Congress. *Psychology Today,* December 1981, pp. 47–57. An interesting examination of the attitude-behavior relationship.

Diamond, E. and Bates, S. The political pitch. *Psychology Today,* November 1984, pp. 23–32. A discussion of the problems and pitfalls of political advertising and political commercials.

Kipnis, D. and Schmidt, S. The language of persuasion. *Psychology Today,* April 1985, pp. 40–46. This article examines whether one should use a "hard" or a "soft" persuasion strategy. The answer is that it depends on some omther variables.

Poindexter, J. Shaping the consumer. *Psychology Today,* May 1983, pp. 64–68. Describes how companies unobtrusively monitor consumers' purchases and use the information to tailor commercial messages to consumer habits.

Poindexter, J. Voices of authority. *Psychology Today,* August 1983, pp. 53–61. Lee Iacocca and omther chief exec utives of U.S. corporations seem to be succeeding as communicators in advertising. This article examines why.

Update: Current Articles from Professional Sources

Blasovich, J., Ernst, J. M., Tomaka, J., Kelsey, R. M., Salomon, K. L., & Fazio, R. H. (1993). Attitude accessibility as a moderator of autonomic reactivity during decision making. *Journal of Personality and Social Psychology, 64,* 165–176. Researchers explored the hypothesis that accessibility of an attitude from memory determines the power of the attitude. Attitudes toward abstract paintings were made accessible via rehearsal. The study compared decision making for paintings with accessible and less-accessible attitudes and measured autonomic reactivity.

Breckler, S. J., & Fried, H. S. (1993). On knowing what you like and liking what you smell: Attitudes depend on the form in which the object is represented. *Personality and Social Psychology Bulletin, 19,* 228–240. How is one's attitude toward "blue" different when one rates the word "blue" versus rating an actual blue-colored patch. Research suggests that the form in which an attitude object is presented has an impact on responses. This study compares odors presented descriptively versus odors as scratch-and-sniff patches.

Coleman, L. M., Beale, R., & Mills, C. (1993). Identifying targets of communication styles: An exploratory study. *Personality and Social Psychology Bulletin, 19,* 213–219. Do speakers communicate in distinguishably different ways when speaking to a child, a foreign adult, a mentally retarded adult, or a normally intelligent native speaker? Judges were asked to identify listeners on the basis of audiovisual clips of speakers. Child listeners and normal native adults were most readily identified. Implications are discussed.

DeBono, K. G., & Klein, C. (1993). Source expertise and persuasion: The moderating role of recipient dogmatism. *Personality and Social Psychology Bulletin, 19,* 167–173. Individuals high and low in dogmatism read a counterattitudinal message from either an expert or a nonexpert source who supported the position with either strong or weak arguments. Low-dogmatic individuals tended to be persuaded by the strength of the arguments regardless of the source. High dogmatic individuals were persuaded by the strength of the arguments when the source was a nonexpert but were equally persuaded by strong or weak arguments when the source was an expert.

Miller, A. G., McHoskey, J. W., Bane, C. M., & Dowd, T. G. (1993). The attitude polarization phenomenon: Role of response measure, attitude extremity, and behavioral consequences of reported attitude change. *Journal of Personality and Social Psychology, 64,* 561–574. Subjects holding extreme attitudes assimilated an essay on capital punishment by showing polarization. The hypothesis that polarized persons would subsequently write particularly strong essays on the topic was not supported.

Peterson, B. E., Doty, R. M., & Winter, D. G. (1993) Authoritarianism and attitudes toward contemporary social issues. *Personality and Social Psychology Bulletin, 19,* 174–184. The authors show that authoritarianism is applicable to understanding attitudes on many important issues of the 1990s. Attitudes about AIDS, drug use, the environment, child abuse, the trade deficit, political changes in the former Soviet Union, and so forth are all shown to be related to authoritarianism.

Pyszczynski, T., Greenberg, J., Solomon, S., Sideris, J., & Stubing, M. J. (1993). Emotional expression and the reduction of motivated cognitive bias: Evidence from cognitive dissonance and distancing from victims' paradigms. *Journal of Personality and Social Psychology, 64,* 177–186. Study 1 determined that writing a counterattitudinal essay and then expressing tension produced by doing so reduces the extent of dissonance-reducing attitude change. Study 2 found that expressing fear of cancer reduced defensive distancing from cancer patients. Implications for the role of affect in defense are discussed.

Related Readings: The following selections from *Readings in Social Psychology: General, Classic, and Contemporary Selections,* 2nd Edition, by Wayne Lesko (Allyn and Bacon, 1993) accompany this chapter:

Ball-Rokeach, S., Rokeach, M., & Grube, J. (November, 1984). The great American values test. These researchers conducted an unusual experiment in which subjects in Washington state watched a television program that prodded viewers to accept basic American values. Evidence showed that two to three months later, viewers' attitudes and behaviors were still influenced by the program. (10)

LaPiere, R. (1934). Social forces: Attitudes versus actions. This study is often cited as an example of research showing the inconsistency between what people say they would do and what they actually do. Written responses from various establishments indicated an unwillingness to serve Chinese customers, and yet a Chinese couple was rarely refused service. Raises interesting theoretical questions and also provides historical perspective on prejudice and discrimination in the United States. (11)

Axsom, D. (1989). Cognitive dissonance and behavior change in psychotherapy. The effort justification hypothesis is examined in an applied setting. Do we undergo greater behavior change in psychotherapy when we anticipate the therapy will require considerable effort on our part? Two studies, one with snake phobics and the other with speech anxious subjects, suggest effort facilitates behavior change under certain conditions. (12)

Chapter-at-a-Glance

Chapter Five
Social Identity:
Self and Gender

Chapter Outline	Instruction Ideas	Supplements
Introduction		CNN Video Segment 6: *Self-Esteem Commission* and Segment 7, *Mommy Track—see* Video Guide Transparency 12.2 *see* Video Guide
I. The Self: Multiple Components of One's Identity Self-Concept: The Central Schema / Self-Esteem: Attitudes about Oneself / Self-Efficacy: Differential Expectations of Competence / Self-Monitoring Behavior: Emphasis on Internal versus External Factors / Self-Focusing: The Relative Importance of Self	Exercises 1–3 Discussion Questions 1–4 Critical Thinking Question 1, 2	Transparencies 12.1, 12.3–12.5 Video: The Self Reading: Lesko 13—Many Me's of the Self-Monitor and Lesko 15—Self-concept from High School to College
II. Gender: Maleness or Femaleness as a Crucial Aspect of Identity Biological Determinants of Sex / Gender Identity and Stereotypes Based on Gender / Behaving in Ways Consistent with Gender Roles / Differences between Males and Females Sex, Gender, or Both?	Critical Thinking Questions 3–5	Video: Self and Gender Reading: Lesko 14—Measurement of Androgyny

Chapter Five

Social Identity: Self and Gender

Chapter Outline: Getting the Overall Picture

I. The Self: Multiple Components of One's Identity
  A. Self-Concept: The Central Schema
  B. Self-Esteem: Attitudes about Oneself
    1. The Discrepancy between Self and Ideal Self
    2. The Consequences of Negative Self-Evaluations
    3. Self-Esteem As a Dispositional Variable
    4. Situational Influences on Self-Esteem
    5. Measuring Self-Esteem
  C. Self-Efficacy: Differential Expectations of Competence
    1. Self-Efficacy and Performance
    2. Factors That Influence Self-Efficacy
    3. Self-Efficacy in Social Situations
    4. Factors that Influence Self-Efficacy
    5. The Role of Self-Efficacy in Snake Phobia
  D. Self-Monitoring Behavior: Emphasis on Internal versus External Factors
    1. Measuring Self-Monitoring Behavior
    2. Correlates of Self-Monitoring Behavior
    3. Self-Monitoring As a Factor in Interpersonal Behavior
  E. Self-Focusing: The Relative Importance of Self
    1. Self-Focusing As a Trait, or at Least a Tendency
    2. Situational Influences on Self-Focusing
    3. Compartmentalizing Self-Information: Warding Off Depression in Times of Stress

II. Gender: Maleness or Femaleness As a Crucial Aspect of Identity
  A. Biological Determinants of Sex
    1. We Begin with Either an XX or an XY Chromosome
    2. What Is the Effect of Having an XY versus an XX Chromosome?
  B. Gender Identity and Stereotypes Based on Gender
    1. Developing a Gender Identity
    2. Theories of Gender Identity
  C. Bem's Sex Role Inventory: Differences in Adherence to Typical Masculine or Feminine Roles
  D. Behaving in Ways Consistent with Gender Roles
    1. Support for Traditional Gender Roles
    2. Effects of Gender Roles in the Home
    3. Gender as the Criterion for Selection
  E. Differences between Males and Females: Sex, Gender, or Both?
    1. Testosterone Level and Male Behavior
    2. Interpersonal Behavior
    3. Self-Perception
    4. Explaining Sex Differences in Personality
  F. Justification, Control, and Self-Blame
  G. Divergent Female Gender Roles in Singapore and Mexico, and among Native Americans

Learning Objectives

1. What is self-esteem, and how is discrepancy between self and ideal self related to self-esteem?
2. Describe two ways in which a person experiencing a large self-discrepancy can elevate self-esteem.
3. Consider the view that self-esteem is a trait and examine early experiences that are related to low self-esteem.
4. Understand the view that self-esteem is influenced by immediate situational events.

5. Describe the Collective Self-Esteem Scale, indicate how it was developed, and understand the four components of Collective Self-Esteem.
6. Define self-efficacy, noting that it tends to be situation-specific and does not usually generalize.
7. How is self-efficacy related to endurance, academic success among professors, and test-writing performance by students?
8. How are social self-efficacy and social anxiety related?

9. Compare the attributions made in the face of negative feedback by high-self-efficacy persons versus low-self-efficacy persons.

10. How are feelings of self-efficacy affected by direct experience, social comparison, and positive feedback?

11. What role does self-efficacy play in helping persons in therapy to overcome a snake phobia?

12. Describe high and low self-monitors (including the two views of high self-monitors), and discuss the Self-Monitoring Scale.

13. Compare high and low self-monitors on each of the following: (a) type of ad they prefer; (b) degree of behavioral consistency; (c) confidence expressed in their own decisions; (d) first- versus third-person speech patterns; (e) basis for choosing a companion; and (f) overall mental health.

14. Understand differences between persons who are self-focused and those who are not.

15. How do the following circumstances affect self-focusing: (a) instructions; (b) a mirror; (c) familiar versus unfamiliar surroundings?

16. Consider the biological bases of sex differentiation, including XX versus XY chromosomes and prenatal developmental processes.

17. Describe stages in children's development of gender identity, and indicate how gender development is accounted for by each of these theories: (a) psychoanalytic theory; (b) cognitive-developmental theory; (c) social learning theory; and (d) gender schema theory.

18. Describe the Bem Sex Role Inventory (BSRI), and indicate characteristics of persons who are masculine, feminine, androgynous, and undifferentiated.

19. Consider how gender roles affect the following: (a) the workplace; (b) the home; (c) self-esteem and self-evaluation; (d) politics.

20. In what ways do children's books and television provide support for traditional gender roles?

21. Examine sex differences in aggressiveness, and compare biological and social training explanations for these differences.

22. Based on the study by Brown et al., what role do familiarity and training play in producing displays of visual dominance?

23. Describe ways in which the interpersonal behavior of men and women differ and ways in which concern with appearance impacts women.

24. Examine ways in which men and women's self-reports differ and ways in which conclusions by male and female observers differ, and indicate how these findings relate to the four models of sex differences.

25. How did gender roles affect the ratings given men and women in the study by Yuen and Lim (1990), and why did information about "potential" wipe out the gender difference?

26. Examine implications of diverse gender role behaviors found in Morelos, Mexico, and among Native Americans.

Discussion Questions

1. Personality theorists and social psychologists often disagree on the relative importance of traits versus situations as determinants of behavior. Personality theorists examine the impact of individual differences on behavior and expect that different persons will behave differently from each other. Social psychologists, on the other hand, examine effects created by the situation and expect that most persons in a particular situation will behave the same way. Who is correct, the personality theorist or the social psychologist?

To examine this question, consider a characteristic such as shyness. Ask students to consider what it means to be shy. Is shyness simply a personality trait, with some people being very shy and others being less shy? Or is shyness a common response to certain situations, with most people becoming shy if the situation is "right"?

Another characteristic to consider is friendliness. What are the manifestations of "friendly" behavior? Ask students to describe the behavior of a friendly, outgoing person versus an unfriendly, introverted person. Next, compare the "friendliness" of persons who are at work, at a party, or in class. Which is a better basis for predict-ing the person's behavior, *who* the person is or *where* the person is? After pondering this question, students will probably be surprised at the degree to which behavior is determined by situations.

2. The previous discussion question oversimplifies the personality versus situation issue. The best conclusion is undoubtedly that *both* personality and the situation are important. Who you are typically interacts with where you are to produce behavior. The interactionist position is implicitly supported in chapter 5 of the text, since several aspects of the self are discussed first as trait features and then as situationally determined features. Self-esteem, self-efficacy, and self-focusing are all discussed in this way. In chapter 7, the text also approaches affiliation from both perspectives, discussing "need for affiliation" as a disposition and then discussing it as a "response to external events."

3. Measures of self-esteem generally involve asking people to make an evaluation of themselves by responding to statements such as "On the whole, I am satisfied with myself." Most measures assume that self-esteem is relatively stable; that is, some people feel good about themselves most of the time, whereas others rate themselves quite negatively a good part of the time. Positive self-esteem is generally considered good, the mark of a psychologically healthy person; low self-esteem, on the other hand, is considered bad, the mark of an unhealthy person.

An interesting question to examine is the degree to which positive self-esteem involves overestimating the positive aspects of our self. People who claim to have unrealistic positive aspects generally will score higher on self-esteem scales. Likewise, those who admit to negative aspects will score lower. A study by Roth, C. R. Snyder, and Pace (1986) suggests that one way we enhance self-esteem is, in fact, to overestimate positive aspects of our selves. When subjects were asked to respond to items that were positive but too good to be true for most people, a surprising number of people endorsed them. Furthermore, the people who were most likely to endorse the unrealistic positive items were also likely to score high on a test of self-esteem. (An example of a too-good-to-be-true item is "I am always courteous, even to disagreeable people.") The question to ponder with your students is the degree to which positive self-esteem rests on a realistic view of oneself, and the degree to which self-esteem is enhanced by unrealistic positive views. The article by Roth et al. is published in the *Journal of Personality and Social Psychology, 51,* pages 867–874.

4. There are many features of the self that one can evaluate quickly and easily by comparing one's standing on the characteristic to some objective criterion. Height, weight, and eye color are examples. On the other hand, many facets of the self cannot be measured by any objective standard and instead can be evaluated only by comparison of oneself with other people. Leon Festinger

(1954) developed his classic social comparison theory to explain the circumstances under which we seek out other people as a means of evaluating ourselves.

Joanne Wood (1989) has done a recent review of research and theory in this area and has identified three reasons people use social comparison. The first reason is *self-evaluation.* To get an accurate evaluation of our own ability in some area, we generally choose to compare ourselves to people whose abilities are similar to our own. High school ball players don't try to evaluate themselves by comparison to major leaguers or to Little Leaguers, but instead compare themselves to someone who plays at the same level they do. Gender is another relevant factor in choosing a comparison, with people preferring a same-sexed comparison partner.

A second reason people engage in social comparison is *self-improvement.* People who are particularly achievement oriented or competitive are likely to compare themselves with others who are somewhat better on the relevant dimension, although otherwise similar. It's as if the person says, "If someone like me can do it, then I can too!"

The third reason for social comparison, according to Wood, is *self-enhancement.* When a person needs to improve his/her self-esteem, it is likely that a comparison person who is worse off than the person will be chosen. If we do not have a relevant comparison in our personal experience, we may fabricate an imaginary comparison or simply generalize about others who are worse off. When people enter the hospital, for example, they generally feel sorry for themselves; but they usually manage to find a comparison other who is worse off and thereby feel better about their own circumstances.

Wood's article on social comparison is in *Psychological Bulletin, 106,* pages 231–248.

Classroom Exercises/Demonstrations

1. Mark Snyder's Self-Monitoring Scale, found in chapter 5 of your students' Study Guides, is perhaps the fastest-growing personality test in the United States. A large number of research articles relating self-monitoring to a variety of social behaviors have been published since the scale first appeared in 1974. The scale seems to relate to everything, including dating preferences, responses to ads, and attitude-behavior consistency. Students enjoy finding out whether they are high or low in self-monitoring, both as a way to learn about themselves and as a way to appreciate the text material on self-monitoring. Most people are "satisfied" with their own score on this test, and thus some students may be willing to share their score with other class members. The scale is quite easy to score; the score is simply the number of statements for which the respondent made

the high-self-monitoring choice. The high-self-monitoring choice for each item is as follows: 1.f; 2.f; 3.f;4.f; 5.t; 6.t; 7.t; 8.t; 9.f; 10.t; 11.t; 12.f; 13.t; 14.f; 15.t; 16.t; 17.f; 18.t; 19.t; 20.f; 21.f; 22.f; 23.f; 24.t; 25.t.

2. In chapter 3 of the previous edition of the Baron and Byrne text, the authors considered the "self-reference effect." This is a robust phenomenon that can be demonstrated quite readily in a classroom demonstration. The exercise can be done either in class with the instructor serving as the experimenter or outside of class with students recruiting friends to serve as the subjects. Subjects are presented with a list of trait adjectives and are required to respond to each trait word on the list. Half of the subjects are instructed to read the trait list and decide if each word describes themselves. The other half of the subjects are told to read the list and decide

whether each word is long. After the subjects have gone through the entire list of adjectives, they are given a surprise recall test to determine how many of the adjectives they can remember.

Subjects who previously determined whether each word "described themselves" will recall more of the words than subjects who simply had to decide whether the words were long. This occurs because subjects who relate the words to themselves process them more deeply than subjects who respond simply to a physical characteristic of the words. A list of thirteen trait words words to use in doing the exercise is as follows: aggressive, intelligent, friendly, superstitious, quiet, sentimental, bold, athletic, persistent, trusting, sensitive, energetic, shy.

3. How does what happens to you influence how you view yourself? Have students fill out the log sheet in chapter 5 of their Study Guides. If students do the exercise described there, they will gain insight and self-understanding. The exercise provides personal informa-

tion on the interplay between self-view (personality) and situational determinants ("what happens to you"). Students simply follow the straightforward instructions accompanying the sheet. The easiest way to score the words is to assign a positive or negative valence to each word, depending on how favorable or unfavorable it is, and then an overall valence, according to whether positive or negative valences are more frequent. Also, a positive or negative valence could be assigned to each description of "what happened to you." The descriptions should be done first for a block of about ten days (have students make copies of the log sheet). Then they can be scored and the possible correspondence between the two ratings can be observed. More objective ratings occur if students place code numbers on their log sheets and have fellow students score the words and "happenings" blind. (A 1983 book by Allen and Potkay entitled *Adjective Generation Technique* and published by Irvington Press deals more formally with the issues raised in this exercise.)

Film Notes: A Picture Is Sometimes Worth a Thousand Words

Allyn and Bacon Videos

* *The Self.* How psychologists systematically study the origins of self-identity and self-esteem, social determinants of self-conceptions, and the emotional and motivational consequences of beliefs about oneself. (Discovering Psychology series, On Tape #8.)
* *Self and Gender.* The ways in which males and females are similar and different, and how sex roles reflect social values and psychological knowledge. (Discovering Psychology series, On Tape #9.)

Other Videos and Films

A Day in the Life of Jonathon Mole, film, 30 mins. CRM/McGraw-Hill Films, 110 Fifteenth Street, Del Mar, CA 92014. Graphically depicts how personal characteristics and social circumstances interplay to produce a bigoted personality.

Evaluating Personality, videotape, 30 mins. Insight Media, 121 W. 85th Street, New York, NY 10024-4401 (800-233-9910). This tape investigates various personality evaluation methods.

Personality, film, 25 mins. CRM/McGraw-Hill Films, 110 Fifteenth Street, Del Mar, CA 92014. A college student's personality is analyzed according to traditional trait-personality notions.

Shyness: Reasons and Remedies, videotape, 30 mins. Insight Media, 121 W. 85th Street, New York, NY 10024-4401 (800-233-9910). This video studies the causes of shyness and how it affects our personal and social well-being.

Transparencies

Critical Thinking/Essay Questions

1. In what ways is self-esteem influenced by situational events. Give specific examples.
2. Describe a high and a low self-monitor. Indicate two specific ways in which these two personality types are different from each other and explain the difference in terms of self-monitoring processes.
3. Compare biological and social learning explanations for the sex difference that is typically found between men and women in aggressiveness.
4. Describe a masculine, a feminine, an androgynous, and an undifferentiated person.
5. In what ways do children's books and television provide support for traditional gender roles?

Sources for Lecture

Fischman, J. (1987). Getting Tough. *Psychology Today,* December, pp. 26–28. The personality characteristic of "hardiness" grew out of the 1970s research linking sickness to emotional stress. Perhaps hardiness is a buffer against life's stresses and the illness they cause.

Horn, J. (1986). Measuring a man by the company he keeps. *Psychology Today,* March, p. 12. Mark Snyder, Ellen Berscheid, and Peter Glick asked high and low self-monitors what kind of information they wanted about potential dates. The lows went for personality information and the highs for physical attractiveness profiles.

Roberts, M. (1988). School yard menace. *Psychology Today,* February, pp. 52–56. Is bullying a personality trait? Or does the school yard bring out meanness in children? Bullies are usually boys and usually come from families that neglect, reject, or abuse, or that create a climate of violence.

Trotter, R. J. (1987). Stop blaming yourself. *Psychology Today,* February, pp. 31–39. The title says it! People whose explanatory style reflects learned helplessness blame thenselves and suffer health consequences because of it.

Update: Current Articles from Professional Sources

Baumeister, R. F., Heatherton, T. F., and Tice, D. M. (1993). When ego threats lead to self-regulation failure: Negative consequences of high self-esteem. *Journal of Personality and Social Psychology, 64,* 141–156. People with high self-esteem often make inflated assessments and predictions about themselves, which carries the risk that they'll make commitments that exceed their capabilities. Setting goals beyond their capabilities was found for high self-esteem subjects under conditions of high ego threat.

Brown, J. D., & Mankowski, T. A. (1993). Self-esteem, mood, and self-evaluation: Changes in mood and the way you see you. *Journal of Personality and Social Psychology, 64,* 421–430. How does a change in mood affect how people evaluate themselves? Self-evaluations among high-self-esteem people are not much affected by their moods, but self-evaluations of low-self-esteem persons are more prone to fluctuate.

Crocker, J., Cornwell, T. K., & Major, B. (1993). The stigma of overweight: Affective consequences of attributional ambiguity. *Journal of Personality and Social Psychology, 64,* 60–70. The low self-esteem of overweight persons is examined. Overweight women received either positive or negative feedback from a male evaluator. Overweight women who received negative feedback attributed the feedback to their weight and did not blame the evaluator. This pattern of attribution produced negative mood in these women. Implications for weight-loss programs and psychotherapy for the overweight are considered.

Greenberg, J., et al. (1992). Why do people need self-esteem? Converging evidence that self-esteem serves an anxiety-buffering function. *Journal of Personality and Social Psychology, 63,* 913–922. This study examined how people responded to such events as a video portraying vivid images of death and anticipated painful shock. It was hypothesized that increasing self-esteem would reduce anxiety. Both success and positive personality feedback reduced physiological arousal in the face of a threat.

Jacobs, J. E., & Eccles, J. S. (1993). The impact of mothers' gender-role stereotypic beliefs on mothers' and children's ability perceptions. *Journal of Personality and Social Psychology, 63,* 932–944. The researchers examined the relationships among mothers' gender stereotypic beliefs, their perceptions of their children's abilities, and their children's self perceptions. Abilities in math, sports, and social domains were examined, and mothers' beliefs clearly influenced perceptions.

James, K. (1993). Conceptualizing self with in-group stereotypes: Context and esteem precursors. *Personality and Social Psychology Bulletin, 19,* 117–121. Female subjects had their attention focused either on their own unique characteristics or on their gender-group conceptions. Masculinity and femininity scores from the BSRI were obtained as dependent measures. How subjects' responses were affected by their focus of attention depended on their self esteem.

Spence, J. T. (1993). Gender-related traits and gender ideology: Evidence for a multifactorial theory. *Journal of Personality and Social Psychology, 64,* 624–635. College students were given two measures of gender-related personality traits, the Bem Sex Role Inventory and the Personal Attributes Questionnaire. The study examined relationships between these and other measures to test various conceptualizations of gender.

Stoppard, J. M., & Gruchy, C. D. (1993). Gender, context, and expression of positive emotion. *Personality and Social Psychology Bulletin, 19,* 143–150. Subjects read a scene in which the main character either did or did not express positive emotion toward the self or another person. After imagining themselves as the main character, subjects rated how others would respond if they behaved as depicted.

Findings indicate interesting ways in which norms for expression of positive emotion are gender differentiated.

Related Readings: The following selections from *Readings in Social Psychology: General, Classic, and Contemporary Selections,* 2nd Edition, by Wayne Lesko (Allyn and Bacon, 1993) accompany this chapter:

Snyder, M. (March, 1980). The many me's of the self-monitor. Snyder compares the actions of high and low self-monitors on a variety of behavioral dimensions. High self-monitors, for instance, are skilled in managing the impressions they make on others. Several other characteristics are also explored. (13)

Bem, S. (1974). Bem describes the development of her sex-role inventory. The characteristics of masculine, feminine, and androgynous persons are summarized. Especially highlighted are the characteristics of androgyny. (14)

Hesse-Biber, S., & Marino, M. (1991). From high school to college: Changes in women's self-concept and its relationship to eating problems. Researchers studied changes in self-concepts as young women went from high school to college. Measures of self-concepts were obtained on three occasions: (1) senior year in high school; (2) sophomore year in college; and (3) senior year in college. Self-concept seems to be at a low during the sophomore year. The relationship to eating disorders is examined. (15)

Chapter-at-a-Glance

Chapter Six
Prejudice and Discrimination:
Understanding Their Nature, Countering Their Effects

Chapter Outline	Instruction Ideas	Supplements
Introduction	Exercise 1	*CNN Video Segment 8:Working Women Woes*, Segment 9, *Female Bias*, and Segment 10, *Beauty in Society* *see* Video Guide
I. Prejudice and Discrimination: What They Are and How They Differ Prejudice: Choosing Whom to Hate / Discrimination: Prejudice in ActionSumming Up	Discussion Question 3 Critical Thinking Question 1–3	Transparencies 6.1, 6.2, 6.6 Video: Prejudice
II. The Origins of Prejudice: Contrasting Perspectives Direct Intergroup Conflict: Competition As a Source of Prejudice / Social Categorization As a Basis for Prejudice: The Us-versus-Them Effect and the "Ultimate" Attribution Error / Early Experience: The Role of Social Learning / Cognitive Sources of Prejudice: Stereotypes, Illusory Correlations, and Outgroup Homogenieity	Critical Thinking Questions 4–8	Transparencies 6.6, 30 Readings: Lesko 17—Experiments in Group Conflict
III. Challenging Prejudice: Potentially Beneficial Steps Breaking the Cycle of Prejudice: On Learning *Not* to Hate / Direct Intergroup contact: The Potential Benefits of Acquaintance / Recategorization: Redrawing the Boundary Between "Us" and "Them" / Cognitive Interventions: when Stereotypes Shatter—Or At Least Become Less Compelling	Discussion Questions 1, 4 Critical Thinking Question 9	Transparency 6.6
IV. Prejudice Based on Gender: Its Nature and Effects Gender Stereotypes: The Cognitive Core of Prejudice toward Females / Discrimination against Females: Subtle but Often Deadly / Sexual Harassment: When Discrimination Takes a Sleazy Turn	Exercises 2 and 4 Discussion Question 3 Critical Thinking Question 10	Video: Sex and Gender Readings: Lesko 16—Chill in the College Classroom and Lesko 18—Detecting and Labeling Prejudice
IV. Social Diversity: A Critical Analysis—The Effects of Prejudice: Racial Identification Among African Americans	Exercise 3 Discussion Question 2 Critical Thinking Question 11	

Prejudice and Discrimination: Understanding Their Nature, Countering Their Effects

Chapter Outline: Getting the Overall Picture

Learning Objectives

1. Be able to review prejudice and discrimination in the past and at present and tell what forms has it taken. (Page 000)
2. Learn the definition of prejudice, how attitudes of this kind function as schemata, how they relate to social cognition, how they relate to heuristics, and how prejudice is a reflection of the limits of the cognitive system.
3. Be able to define discrimination and indicate its degrees of severity both here and abroad.
4. Learn some examples of "subtle forms of prejudice," the answer to "What is tokenism?," how tokensim affected subjects in Chacko's (1982) study (women in management), and the negative effects of tokenism.
5. Consider "reverse discrimination" and how is it reflected in the study by Chidester (1986; conversation with microphones and headphones); outline the Fajardo (1985) study (evaluations of black and white students' essays); and show when reverse discrimination is most likely.
6. Address the conflict between the development of more positive attitudes toward targets of prejudice and lingering negative feelings by understanding the procedure and results of the Devine et al. (1991) study of low- and high-prejudiced persons' orientation to gays and African-Americans.
7. Learn the principles of realistic conflict theory: How do they relate to the escalation of opposition between one group and the next? Indicate how the Hovland and Sears (1940) study demonstrates this theory.
8. Know the procedure of the Robber's Cave study, how competition created animosity between the groups of boys, and how "superordinate goals" destroyed the ill feelings.
9. Appreciate how the us-versus-them orientation leads to prejudice as a "natural" part of the formation of even arbitrarily constructed groups for competition against other groups, and how the us-versus-them effect can be overcome.
10. Outline the "social learning" theory of prejudice and the role of social norms, and discuss how the media play a role in the social learning of prejudice.
11. Learn what constitutes a stereotype, how it affects the information to which we attend, how we interpret and remember that information, and how is it self-confirming.
12. Know the procedures of the Bodenhausen (1988) study of how stereotypes affect juror bias and how the time at which information-activating stereotypes was introduced affected results.
13. Appreciate when and under what circumstances stereotypes are activated and applied by reference to the Gilbert and Hixon (1991) study employing a white and an Asian experimenter and how busyness affected stereotyping and the application of stereotypes.
14. Understand the definition of "illusory correlation," its role in prejudice, the conditions that negate the harmful influence of illusory correlations, and the procedures and results in Strossner, Hamilton, and Mackie's (1992) study of the effect of "being in a mood" on illusory correlation.
15. Learn the significance of the perception that outgroups are homogeneous and ingroups are differentiated, and how this tendency relates to cross-race facial identification and to stereotype maintenance.
16. How much hope exists that parents will work to lessen prejudice in their children? Indicate how Harris et al. (1992) examined the way prejudice can negatively affect prejudiced people, how the boys in their study experienced less enjoyment of their task and poor social outcomes due to their negative expectations, and why knowledge of these outcomes might deter parents from teaching bigotry to their children.
17. What are the three reasons that contact between minority and majority persons should decrease prejudice in the latter? What are the six conditions that must be met if contact is to work to reduce prejudice?
18. Learn why us-versus-them disappeared from an Italian city, and how this same phenomenon was shown in the Gaertner and colleagues (1989) study (subjects assigned to three-person teams for competition).
19. Learn how attribute-driven, as opposed to category-driven, processing might lessen stereotyping; how outcome-biased inferences can affect prejudice; how the Mackie et al. study (1992) showed that whether a majority of liberal or conservative groups voted for a liberal measure affected outcome interpretation greatly, depending on whether the issue passed or not; and how this bias can help reduce prejudice in real life.
20. Explore how the stereotypes of women are like those attributed to other groups. Explain why women are typically confined to low-paying jobs; be able to show that the answer lies in part in lower expectations of women based on stereotypes of them (refer to Van Vianen and Willemsen [1992]). Indicate for whom the masculine-feminine dimension is important for hiring, men or women.
21. Learn how job discrimination against women has become subtle, and survey the role of expectations,

self-confidence, withholding of credit, and negative reactions to female leaders in this subtle bias. Describe how Butler and Geis (1990) showed the bias against female leaders in terms of nonverbal cues. What is sexual harassment, and how common is it on the job?

22. Learn the definition of Eurocentricism, how it applies to the study of prejudice, the results of the orginal Kenneth Clark doll studies, criticisms of those studies, and their possible relation to African-Americans' senses of identity.

23. List the three key aspects of racial identification among African-Americans and tell how the experience of racial prejudice figures in the manifestation of identity in African-Americans according to Sanders Thompson (1990).

Discussion Questions

1. During World War II dehumanization promoted vicious hatred between Japanese and Americans. The Japanese thought that Americans were less than human, and we regarded them in the same way. As a result we unconstitutionally imprisoned and harassed hundreds of thousands of American citizens of Japanese descent, and they starved and tortured to death several thousand American POWs.

The final scene of perhaps the greatest antiwar film, *Paths of Glory* with Kirk Douglas, can help students understand the role of dehumanizing the targets of bias in the promotion of prejudice against them. In that scene, battle-weary World War I French soldiers are gathered at a night club awaiting the entertainment for the evening. Finally the proprietor emerges from back-stage with a youthful German woman in tow. The soldiers roar in laughter as she cowers at the sight of them. Derisive comments about her reverberate around the room. Much to their delight, she is terrorized. As the men drink up, the proprietor forces the woman to sing. Her halting whisper of a voice causes the soldiers to jeer even louder. In response, her utterances increase in volume. Slowly the soldiers come to realize that she is singing a sentimental song familiar to them. The noise begins to subside and one or two soldiers start to sing along with the woman. Instantly she is transformed from daughter of the German beast to human being. Soon all the men are singing along, and many are crying. When the soldiers and a representative of the enemy join together in song, they are able to appreciate the tragedy of their common circumstances and, in turn, one another's humanity. *Paths of Glory* can be rented from many videotape stores (or they can find it for you; if not, your audiovisual people probably can). Play that last scene for the students and ask them why the soldiers initially reacted so violently to a harmless non-combatant only to join her suddenly in a show of tender emotions. Point out the implications for perceptions of homogeneity of the outgroup and for the effect of a joint enterprise on dissolution of those perceptions. Help them understand why it is so easy to hate people who are regarded as less than human and so difficult to hate those same people once their humanity is appreciated.

2. "Cultural diversity" is becoming a catchphrase on many campuses. Why? Sometime during the next century, the many U.S. ethnic groups of non-European heritage will total more people than the current U.S. majority, just as non-Russians outnumbered Russians in the former Soviet Union. As in the former Soviet Union, extraordinary diversity will characterize the United States. We need to understand diversity better than the Soviets did, or we could suffer their fate: fragmentation of the country. You could start on the light side by showing students how common gestures vary in meaning from culture to culture (see Sources for Lecture for a reference). Tapping the head means "I'm thinking" in Argentina and Peru, but elsewhere it means "He's crazy." Have the students imagine using this gesture in the presence of the wrong audience. The forearm jerk, one hand on the hollow of an elbow joint causing the clenched fist of the other hand to thrust upward about eyeball high, means "——— you" in Mediterranean countries and in the United States but is a sign of appreciation equivalent to a wolf whistle in England. Placing the thumb under the index finger and thrusting the thumb upward, palm outward is an obscene gesture in some European and Mediterranean countries, but in Brazil and Venezuela is such a good-luck symbol that it is reproduced in the form of paper-weights and golden amulets worn around the neck. Imagine using these gestures in the wrong place! How about the "impudent third finger?" Since the time of the Romans it has meant much the same around the world.

But how about some less-trivial and more-meaningful cultural differences in our own country? If we learned about these differences, we could avoid some conflicts and appreciate the fact that some distasteful behaviors—from the majority American point of view—are not so bad once understood. For example, consider the old African saw "If you throw a rock into a pack of dogs, the one that yelps is the one that was hit." Knowing this proverb helps to understand why a black person who says "Whites are racists"—but doesn't mean all whites—is suspicious of a white person who responds with denial. To many white Americans, two people who are vehemently yelling at each other are getting ready to fight; to many black Americans, the two are just "woofing" (as long as they continue, everything is fine). If you start a discussion on racism in your class, black students, who are usually taught it is good to air emotions, will likely want to argue things out. White students, however, typically learn it is embarrassing to express strong emotions publicly and will probably clam up. Little wonder it may go badly . . . unless the two opposite tendencies are discussed first.

Other examples include the observation that whereas some Anglos will march up to the boss and ask for a raise, some Hispanics who are equally loyal and hardworking will wait to be given the raise, because they believe the boss is supposed to reward their loyalty spontaneously. A Japanese boss will not chastise an errant employee in front of his or her peers—it would cause the employee to lose face and reflect badly on the peers. An American boss, however, will not hesitate to dress down an employee in front of peers. (Neither will the Japanese boss, if he or she and the employees have had several drinks together after work!) We "ground" naughty children in their rooms; the Japanese put them outside. Use these and other examples provided by yourself or students as a basis for a discussion on cultural diversity. But be cautious: Students must learn to approach people from different cultural backgrounds as unique individuals, while bearing cultural differences in mind so that misunderstandings are avoided. Trying to "learn" someone else's culture can be counterproductive: Stereotypes are what is likely to be learned.

3. If smooth relations between one cultural group and another, as well as between men and women, are to characterize the future, we must learn to monitor the assumptions behind what we say. The following examples (which may or may not expand on what you already know) can serve to illustrate unfortunate assumptions. College and university administrators are sometimes heard to say, "We are looking for *qualified minority* [or women] faculty." The phrase "qualified minority" implies that most "minority" academics are not qualified and that therefore one must search hard for the few qualified ones. The word "minority" may also be offensive, because it lumps all the diverse U.S. ethnic groups together as if they were the same. Different cultural groups are very proud of their unique identities. Even the word "Hispanic" is problematic, because of the great diversity among the groups that are classed under this label. "Latino" seems better—most Americans who speak Spanish are from South or Central America—but excludes women ("Latina").

Referring to "natural ability" as an explanation of why members of certain groups are disproportionately represented among the most successful in a certain field can be less than flattering (e.g., blacks in sports and Asians in high-tech areas). It implies that these successful people didn't have to do anything to succeed except show up, an affront to their perception that they have had to work very hard, probably harder than others. Referring to women or members of certain ethnic groups as "hired through our affirmative action program" can be insulting. It implies that these individuals were less qualified than others who were candidates for the same job. In fact, the spirit of affirmative action is, "All other things being equal, consider ethnic identification or gender when deciding whom to hire." Businesses would be cutting their own throats if they hired less-qualified people instead of acting according to that spirit.

Calling on women or members of certain ethnic groups to "tell us what your people think" can be upsetting. For groups as large as "women" or "blacks," for example, no one member can represent all the others, because great diversity exists *within* any large group. If you throw out these examples, and/or other similar ones, it is likely that women and members of different cultural groups in your class will provide many more. The result could be a very enlightening discussion.

4. One of the Instructor's Section authors (Allen) teaches a multicultural course in which there tends to be a relatively equal representation of European-American and African-American students. (There are few other "minority" students.) Many of the European-American students come to the class not believing African-Americans' claims that they are victims of discrimination. That they are skeptical is not entirely because of their own prejudices. In part, it is due to the fact that most have never been victimized themselves. Having little or no personal insight into discrimination, they are unable to see the often subtle kinds of discrimination that African-Americans experience. By the end of the class, however, the European-Americans' term papers and in-class comments reflect a different point of view. They have gotten to know the African-American students in the class—almost every class is dominated by a lively discussion—and have opened their ears and their minds to their black classmates' personal experiences with discrimination.

During the course of the semester, the white students have learned how some of their African-American classmates have been repeatedly stopped for no apparent reason and body-searched by police who, finding nothing, then release them. They hear that African-American students are routinely followed by store detectives, ignored by clerks, and assumed to lack the money to pay for merchandise. They learn that black classmates routinely field racial epithets hurled by whites. Many European-Americans leave the class believing that discrimination is an everyday part of African-Americans' lives. If you talk to your African-American, Hispanic, Asian, or other students of color before having a session on discrimination, they may be willing to disclose instances of discrimination that would be edifying to

European-American students. After consultation with students of color, one way to approach the discussion is simply to ask all students, "How many of you have been followed by store detectives?" "Been repeatedly body-searched by police?" and so forth. Looking around the room will make it plain who is most likely to be a target of discrimination. Ask some of the students to describe their experiences. Some insight may be gained by all, as students of color may be amazed at the amazement of European-American students.

Classroom Exercises/Demonstrations

1. The following is a set of excerpts from a questionnaire on racism that was actually distributed in the classrooms of the Ann Arbor, Michigan, high schools. The results, expressed in numbers that represent percentages, are printed with each item. (A duplicate without the percentages is found in the corresponding Study Guide chapter.) The questionnaire has been altered slightly to be more appropriate to college students. You could give it to your students and compile their answers as percentages (number of students who answered in a certain way divided by total students present). Students will likely be fascinated to find out how their answers differed from those of younger people who attend high schools that have been fraught with racial conflict (see Sources for Lecture for the reference to this work).

Is There Racism at This School?

This is an anonymous survey written by students. Circle or mark *all* relevant responses—remember there is no one right answer. Any comments are encouraged. This is not a test. The survey will probably take about fifteen to twenty minutes.

1. Here are some definitions of racism; check those that you agree with and leave blank those you disagree with.

   88 Racism is when people aren't given or allowed equal opportunities because of their racial or ethnic background (for example, black, Asian, Jewish, white, Hispanic, Arab etc.).

   56 Racism is whenever people are discriminated against.

   79 Racism is when people are segregated according to which racial or ethnic background they are from.

   82 Racism is when people hate, dislike, or fear other people because of their racial or ethnic background.

   80 Racism is something that degrades, demoralizes, or hurts people because they are from a certain racial or ethnic group.

   13 Other: Please write your own definition _____

2. Is there racism at your school? Yes(*85*) No(*6*) Other(*9*)

   If yes. . . .

   a. In your school how is racism shown? (Check all that apply.)

62	Ethnic slurs	*29*	Threats against a person
64	Offensive remarks	*21*	Threats against a group
22	Physical assault	*31*	Exclusion
38	Physical intimidation	*54*	Social segregation
64	Mocking stereotypes	*7*	Other (be specific): _____

   b. How do you know about racist incidents at your school? (Check all that apply.)

31	You've been in the incident	*56*	You witnessed an incident
57	Someone told you of one	*8*	I know of no racist incidents at my school
47	Rumors	*10*	Other: _____

3. To what extent do you feel racism to be a serious problem in your school? (Rate on a scale of 1 to 5 with "1" = very serious, and "5" = not a problem at all.) Circle your choice. 1(*6*) 2(*21*) 3 (*39*) 4(*24*) 5(*7*)

4. What causes racism? (Check all that apply.)

40	Feelings of inadequacy	*68*	Ignorance	*56*	Past experiences
45	Peer pressure	*75*	Upbringing	*28*	Media
70	Stereotypes	*51*	Fear	*6*	Other _____

5. Check the words or symbols you think are racist.

54	swastika	*93*	"nigger"	*34*	"skinhead"
75	"Jap" (Japanese)	*64*	"JAP" (Jewish)	*74*	"white boy"
80	"chink"				

6. If you think some social groups are racially segregated, is it because (check if you agree; leave blank those you disagree with):

- 63   People come from different backgrounds
- 45   People stay with friends from their own neighborhoods
- 57   People have racist feelings
- 39   People from the same race or ethnic group have more in common
- 16   Other (please explain):_____
- 8   I don't think social groups are racially segregated

7. Have you ever seen racism in any of these forms? (Check if yes, leave blank if no.)

- 25   Discrimination in textbooks
- 31   Faculty ignoring or singling out minority students
- 22   Faculty being more negative to minority students
- 10   Faculty presenting class material in a discriminatory way
- 21   Not enough minority faculty members
- 11   Other: _____

8. Do you think that minority students discriminate against whites? (Circle one,)

Yes (*72*)   No(*5*)   I don't know (*15*)

9. Do you and your friends discuss racism?

Yes(*65*)   No(*26*)

10. Do you hold racist feelings?

Yes (*23*)   No(*49*)   Other(*10*) (Explain "other.") _____

    The following questions are completely *optional*. The reason they are asked is not to be personal, but to find out if certain groups of people feel more or less strongly about racism. (82% answered these questions)

Sex: Male / Female

Year in school: 1st,   2nd,   3rd   4th,   5th

What is your racial identity? (Ex. black, Caucasian) _____

What is your ethnic identity? (Ex. Italian, Jewish) _____

Reprinted with the permission of Shael Polakow-Suransky

---

2. Have your students complete the simple "gender makes a difference" and "race makes a difference" scales found in the Study Guide chapter corresponding to this one. One of the Instructor's Section authors has found that students' responses pile up in the middle-to-little-difference end of the race scale. Students have trouble seeing that race affects their reactions. Gender, however, is another matter. Students' responses tend to pile up at the "gender makes a difference" end of the scale. If your students react the same way, ask them why it is relatively obvious to them that they act differently to people of different gender. (If they show a very different pattern, write or call us; we'll be curious and will help with the interpretation.) Some of the answers you will get will relate to courtship. Men and women, maybe especially young, single ones, are heavily invested in appearing attractive to the opposite gender. It also may seem important to reaffirm one's own gender identity when confronting the opposite gender. But why the necessity of these reactions? Does it have to be this way? Perhaps you can lead your students to consider the possibility that one's first reactions to a stranger should be founded on appreciation of that person's unique, human characteristics, regardless of gender.

If you have more than one social psychology section, results might be interestingly different for the two classes if these two scales were given to one of your classes before and one after they read the text material and participated in relevant classroom events. Alternatively, one of your classes might complete the scales under the additional instruction "Respond to these scales according to what you think should be the case, rather than what is the case," while the other class got no instruction or were told to "respond to these scales according to what really is the case, not what should be." Any of these procedures could lead to fruitful exchanges.

3. As your text author points out, prejudice, and particularly stereotypes, have been assessed from the perspective of European-Americans (whites). Every European-American "knows" the stereotypes of African-Americans, but what are the stereotypes of whites? On those rare occasions when stereotypes of European-Americans have been assessed, it has usually been from their own perspective. It might be interesting to consider the stereotypes of whites from African-Americans' perspective. Ask students anonymously to write down five words to describe "blacks" and five words to describe "whites." (You may need the cooperation of colleagues who teach other classes if you have few African-Americans in your class.) Compile a list of words used by at least 5 percent of European-American students in their descriptions of African-Americans and a similar list for self-descriptions.

Do the same for the words used by African-Americans. Now compare the two lists describing African-Americans and the two describing European-Americans. Do European-Americans agree with African-Americans on the stereotyped words applicable to African-Americans? Ask the same question about words used by the two groups to describe European-Americans. Then compare your lists with the lists, printed after this exercise, that are taken from some actual research. These lists are also reproduced as transparencies 6.7 and 6.8.

You will undoubtedly find that each group's stereotypes of themselves are different from those attributed by the other group. You may also find that African-Americans "know" European-Americans better than the latter know the former: There is more agreement between the two groups on the stereotyped words applicable to European-Americans than on the stereotypes of African-Americans. If such is the case, how do students explain it?

TABLE 1: Agreements and Disagreements about European-Americans
(European-American % listed first)

Words used by about the same % of each sample	Words used at different % by the samples	Words in one sample, but in < 5% of the other
inventive (18,12)*	prejudiced (10,27)*	egotistical (7,0)
competitive (19,18)	corrupt (6,27)	free (6,0)
independent (12,14)		happy (6,0)
friendly (15,14)		kind (6,0)
arrogant (15,14)		jealous (<5,14)
conceited (7,9)		powerful (<5,14)
smart (32,27)		wealthy (<5,14)
greedy (19,27)		mean (<5,18)
		humorous (12,<5)
		lazy (12,<5)
*Chi Sqr. did not approach significance	*Chi Sqr. significant at least at the .035 level	intelligent (10,<5)
		rich (10,<5)

TABLE 2: Agreements and Disagreements about African-Americans
(African-American % listed first)

Words used by about the same % of each sample	Words used at different % by the samples	Words in one sample, but in < 5% of the other
corrupt (9,11)*	smart (36,9)*	oppressed (18, <5)
arrogant (14,10)	independent (27,10)	proud (14, <5)
	athletic (14,40)	competitive (14,<5)
	friendly (23,11)	beautiful (14,0)
	strong (18,6)	determined (9,0)
		educated (9,0)
		religious (9,0)
		intelligent (9,<5)
		inventive (9,<5)
		loud (<5,25)
		humorous (<5,21)
		funny (<5,10)
		mean (<5,9)
		prejudiced (<5, 7)
		musical (<5,7)
		poor (<5,6)
		moody (0,6)
*Chi Sqrs. did not approach significance	*Chi Sqrs. significant at .001 to .077 level	fast (0,6)
		obnoxious (0,7)

4. How do women fare as leaders? Let's see. Divide your class into approximately equal groups, with each group not to exceed five members. Make sure that the number of females in each group is proportional to their number in the class. Appoint males as leaders for half of the groups and females as leaders for the remaining groups. As a first order of business, have each member complete a "map" of the first name and seating position of each person so that group members' names can be learned (maps are included in the Study Guide chapter corresponding to this one). Give each group a social psychology topic to discuss from among those found in currently assigned chapters. Have members gain recognition from the leader before they speak, and instruct leaders

to make a brief comment about each speaker's contribution. Allow at least fifteen minutes of discussion. If you don't normally have class discussion of this sort, indicate that you are "trying a new learning technique."

After the discussions, have each member vote for the "member who made the greatest contribution to the discussion." There is a suggestion in the literature that you will find leaders getting the most votes, but male leaders doing better than female leaders (see Butler & Geis in the text's references). Or you may find that female leaders do no better than rank-and-file members, whereas such is not true for male leaders.

Film Notes: A Picture Is Sometimes Worth a Thousand Words

Allyn and Bacon Videos

* *Sex and Gender.* This video covers the ways in which males and females are similar and different and shows how sex roles reflect social values and psychological knowledge. (On Tape #9.)
* *Prejudice,* video, 28.5 mins. To obtain this videotape, consult your Allyn and Bacon sales representative. Robert A. Baron and Margaret Clark use dramatizations as a point of departure for a discussion on prejudice.

Other Videos and Films

From Dr. J. Q. Adams's *Dealing with Diversity* one-hour videotapes on multicultural studies (order Classes 6, 20, and 23 from Television Services, Governors State University, University Park, IL 60466):

Class 6—Race: The World's Most Dangerous Myth. Professor Jerry Hirsch, behavioral geneticist at the University of Illinois, comments on notions of "race," and studio guest Professor Bem Allen talks about race and IQ. Different methods of classifying humans by race are also considered, and students respond to a Racial Quotient Questionnaire.

Class 20—Sexual Orientation Issues in the U.S.: Part 1. Stereotypes about homosexuality, difficulties of gays and lesbians in establishing open relationships, homophobia, and violence against gays and lesbians are considered by studio guests Jovita Baber and Vernon Huls of the Illinois Gay and Lesbian Task Force.

Class 23—Hate Group in the U.S. Studio guest Arthur Jones of the America First Committee, a former American Nazi and continuing white supremacy advocate, generates quite a reaction from African-American students when, among other

insults, he refers to blacks as "retards." Dr. Adams, who is African-American, responds with such equanimity and intellectual sophistication that Jones is at times left speechless.

What's the Difference Being Different?, 19511 (video) or #1949 (film), 19 mins. Research Press, Box 3177, Dept. K, Champaign, IL 61821 (217-352-3273). This video or film shows what multicultural education is all about as it goes inside an exciting program in the Nashville schools.

Perceiving and Believing, PB130, video. Insight Media, 121 W. 85th Street, New York, NY 10024-4401 (800-233-9910). Ed Asner hosts a show that features dramatic and comic vignettes showing the error of referring to others as "them." Simplistic perceptions and unfair prejudgments are also considered.

Prejudice: The Eye of the Storm, PB22, video, 25 mins. Insight Media, 121 W 85th Street, New York, NY 10024-4401 (800-233-9910). Also inquire at Indiana University (see below). This winner of the Peabody Award depicts the classic schoolroom demonstration: Students are divided into blue-eyed and brown-eyed groups, and one group is declared "inferior" and treated accordingly.

Racism in America, FC-1919, video, 26 mins. Films for the Humanities and Sciences, Inc., P.O. Box 2053, Princeton, NJ 08543 (800-257-5126). Graphic depictions of the resurgence of bigotry and racially motivated acts of violence and vandalism.

The Asianization of America, FC-1912, video, 52 mins. Films for the Humanities and Sciences, Inc., P.O. Box 2053, Princeton, NJ 08543 (800-257-5126). Asians are the nation's fastest-growing group. Stereotypes have been changing: Love/hate, then condescension, has given way to admiration and jealousy. This tape looks at where it will lead.

Sex Role Development, ESC-1303, film, 30 mins. Indiana University, Audiovisual Center, Bloomington, IN

47401. Considers the influence that sex roles and stereotypes have on people's lives, the way people learn those stereotypes, and new models for behavior.

Fable of He and She, CSC-2561, film, 15 mins. Indiana University, Audiovisual Center, Bloomington, IN 47401. Cartoon characters portray sex stereotypes and in so doing show the absurdities to which we all may be driven by these stereotypes.

Transparencies

6.1 *A Theory of the Relationship between Racism and Prejudice*
6.2 *Methods of Measuring Prejudice*
6.3 *Theories of Prejudice*
6.4 *The Tendency to View Outgroups As More Homogeneous*

Than Ingroups: Empirical Evidence
6.5 *Intergroup Contact: How It Exerts Its Effects*
6.6 *Male and Female Executives: The Stereotype That Failed*
6.7 *Agreements and Disagreements about African-Americans*
6.8 *Agreements and Disagreements about European-Americans*

Critical Thinking/Essay Questions

1. Thoroughly describe the relationship between prejudice and discrimination. Under what real-life circumstances will prejudice be expressed in discrimination? Not expressed?
2. How do prejudiced attitudes "color" most of what a bigoted person says and does? Give examples from your own experience, including at least one that involves a subtle form of prejudice.
3. Discuss tokenism and "reverse discrimination." Give an example of each from your experience. Tell how both can have benefits and drawbacks for "token" individuals and targets of reverse discrimination.
4. List the principles of realistic conflict theory, then illustrate two of them with examples from your experience.
5. Outline the procedure of the Robber's Cave experiment. How were us-versus-them and social competition illustrated by the experiment's results?
6. Use social learning theory as a framework for examining how stereotypes are formed and can become self-fulfilling. Briefly indicate how "illusory correlation" contributes to stereotypes that would bias jurors in a murder trial where the defendant is African-American.
7. Pick some group to which you belong and describe the variety of traits that members possess. Do the

same for some group to which you do not belong. Look at the differences between the descriptions. What do they illustrate?
8. Examine and resolve the dilemma that busyness helps to prevent the activation of stereotypes but that once stereotypes are activated, busyness increases their use.
9. Choose some habitually conflicting groups and design a way to get them to work together and think differently about each other. (Hint: think of the Italian city study and of the Robber's Cave experiment.)
10. Give some real-life examples of valued traits that are assigned to men and devalued traits that are assigned to women. If you were president of a company, what could you do to redistribute those trait assignments across your female and male employees?
11. Being targets of prejudice and discrimination increases African-Americans' sense of racial identity. Will knowledge of that link help European-Americans reduce their own prejudices? Hint: What kind of insight will European-Americans experience if they become convinced that African-Americans are showing increased racial identity?

Sources for Lecture

Axtell, R. G. (Ed.). (1985). *Do's and taboos around the world*, New York: Wiley. Axtell compiled this fascinating collection of cultural misunderstandings for the Parker Pen Company to help their international staff avoid blunders. It contains many practical examples of the

need to appreciate cultural diversity.
Beyond Hate with Bill Moyers, PBS, May 13, 1991. (Order by title; $5.00 from Journal Graphics, Inc., 1535 Grant Street, Denver, CO 80203.) Bill Moyers takes a long and chilling look at hate. White Aryan Resistance representatives, Jimmy Carter, David Duke, Tom

Metzger, neo-Nazis, Elie Wiesel, Skinheads, Professor Jerome Kagan, Morris Dees, and John Kenneth Galbraith are among those interviewed.

Dreyfous, L. (1991, August 4). "Jungle Fever" focuses attention on interracial families. Associated Press, *Peoria Journal Star*, p. D7. Spike Lee's movie gets people talking about interracial marriages, which increased from 50,000 to 200,000 from 1970 to 1990. Is the increase in interracial marriages (still a tiny percent of marriages) a sign that racism is dying a slow death?

Gregor, T. (1979). Short people. *Natural History, 88,* 14. If you have suspected that short people are objects of prejudice, you're right, especially if you live in the tropical forest of central Brazil.

Polakow-Suransky, S. & Ulaby, N. (1990, April). Students take action to combat racism. *Phi Delta Kappan, 71,* 601–606. This paper chronicles the study of high school students' prejudices—the study that used the questionnaire found in Discussion Questions (question 1) above. It shows that students can do something constructive about racism.

Primetime Live, ABC News, September 26, 1991. (Transcript #212; $5.00 from Journal Graphics, Inc., 1535 Grant Street, Denver, CO 80203.) Correspondent Diane Sawyer follows two young professionals, one African-American and the other European-American, as they examine subtle racism by prowling the department-store corridors, apartment rentals, and employment application beat.

The differential treatment of the two men shocks the white man and angers the difficult-to-perturb black man.

Smart-Grosvenor, V. (1983, June). Obsessed with "racial purity." *Ms.* An obscure Louisiana law, probably dating to the days of slavery, still requires that citizens be classified by race. Suzie Guillory Phipps, who thought she was white, discovered she was "colored" when applying for a passport. To make an ugly situation worse, she fought the classification in the courts. Her husband commented, "Hell, she ain't a nigger."

Toch, T. & Davis, J. (1990, April 23). Separate but equal all over again. *U.S. News and World Report*, pp. 37-38. Deja vu. Even in 1990, Louisiana still had not desegregated its colleges and universities. This case shows that segregation is still very much alive and well.

Trouble at the Top (1991, June 17). *(U.S. News and World Report,* pp. 38–48. Vivid depiction of the "glass ceiling" confronting women in the workplace. Women are shown to be behind in salary in almost every profession; this is true for college professors, elementary teachers, nurses, and waiters, among many others.

Webb, J. (1990, December 14). Car dealers cheat blacks and women. Associated Press, *Peoria Journal Star,* p. A14. Ian Ayres, a Northwestern University law professor, conducted a study that showed women in general and blacks in particular are considered "suckers" by auto dealers, who charge them more.

Update: Current Articles from Professional Sources

Brush, S. G. (1991, September/October). Women in science and engineering. *American Scientist, 79,* 404–419. Examines the observation that women are still seriously underrepresented in the sciences and engineering and have made little progress in the preceding five years. The author concludes that women are "leaking out of the science and engineering pipeline" because those who wish to hire them are not providing adequate incentives, working conditions, and opportunities for promotion. Women are embracing other career opportunities and will not reconsider science and engineering until barriers such as rewards, promotion opportunities, and conflicts with family life are removed.

Crocker, J., Cornwell, B., & Major, B. (1993). The stigma of overweight: Affective consequences of attributional ambiguity. *Journal of Personality and Social Psychology, 64,* 60–70. When can bigoted people display their prejudice and get away with it, not even experiencing the scorn of the victim? If the victim is an overweight woman, she blames her weight for

the negative feedback provided by insensitive others, not those others.

Duckitt, John. (1992). Psychology and prejudice: A historical analysis and integrative framework. *American Psychologists, 47,* 1182-1193. Duckitt, a South African psychologist, does an excellent job of tracing the history of our (Western, primarily U.S.) orientation to the study of prejudice. He ends with a reasonable suggestion concerning how psychologists might integrate the various historical themes in the study of prejudice.

Levinson, W., Tolle, S. W., Lewis, C. (1989, November 30). Women in academic medicine. *New England Journal of Medicine, 321,* (22), 1511–11516. The authors, all physicians and two out three women, conclude that it is possible, but difficult, for women to pursue careers in academic medicine. Most women academics interviewed believed that motherhood slowed their progress.

Monteith, M. J., Devine, P. G., & Zuwerink, J. R. (1993). Self-directed versus other-directed affect as a consequence of prejudice-related discrepancies. *Journal of Personality and Social Psychology, 64,* 198–210. Low-prejudiced subjects, regardless of the type of response, experienced negative *self-directed* affect when they transgressed against their nonprejudiced standards regarding gays. High-prejudiced subjects also had negative affect when they trangressed against their nonprejudiced standards for relatively controllable and unacceptable prejudiced responses, but they directed the affect *toward others.*

Ross, S. I., & Jackson, J. M. (1991). Teachers' expectations for black males' and black females' academic achievement. *Personality and Social Psychology Bulletin, 17,* 78–72. Teachers predicted the academic performance of black male and female fourth-grade students from twelve case histories. Even when students had equivalent qualities, teachers consistently held more negative expectations for black males. Lowest expectations were for independent, nonsubmissive black males, who were least preferred as future pupils.

Related Readings: The following selections from *Readings in Social Psychology: General, Classic, and Contemporary Selections,* 2nd Edition, by Wayne Lesko (Allyn and Bacon, 1993) accompany this chapter:

Allen, B. P., & Niss, J. E. (1990). A chill in the college classroom. The authors placed video cameras in professors' classes to record their interactions with students. Among other results they found that males were more rewarded than females and that professors used a warmer voice tone when addressing white compared to black students. (16)

Sherif, M. (1956). Experiments in group conflict. Here are the details of Sherif and colleagues' famous camp study, which is featured in the text. (17)

Baron, R. S., Burgess, M. L., & Kao, C. F. (1991). Detecting and labeling prejudice: Do female perpetrators go undetected? Yes they do. If the perpetrator of a sexist act against a female is a female, it is less likely to be labeled "sexist." (18)

Chapter-at-a-Glance

Chapter Seven
Interpersonal Attraction:
Getting Acquainted, Becoming Friends

Chapter Outline	Instruction Ideas	Supplements
Introduction	Exercise 3 Discussion Questions 2 and 4	CNN Video Segment 11: *Toiletries /Isreal*, Segment 12, *Fashion Diet*, and Segment 13, *Roommate Matching—see CNN* Video Guide
I. When Strangers Meet: Proximity and Emotions Physical Factors Control Contact, and Contact Leads to Liking / Affect:	Exercise 1 Discussion Question 2 Critical Thinking Questions 1 and 2	Transparency 7.1
II. Becoming Acquainted: The Need to Affiliate and Reactions to Observable Characteristics Affiliation Need: Individual Differences and External Events / Responding to Observable Characteristics	Exercise 2 Discussion Question 5 Critical Thinking Questions 3 and 5	Readings: Lesko 19—The Eye of the Beholder and Lesko 21—Exchange Theory in Interracial Dating
III. Becoming Friends: Similarity and Reciprocity Similarity: We Like Those Most Like Ourselves / Reciprocity: Mutual Liking	Exercises 4 and 5 Critical Thinking Question 4	Reading: Lesko 20—Attraction and Attitude Similarity

Chapter Seven

Interpersonal Attraction: Getting Acquainted, Becoming Friends

Chapter Outline: Getting the Overall Picture

I. When Strangers Meet: Proximity and Emotions
  A. Physical Factors Control Contact, and Contact Leads to Liking
    1. Residential Propinquity and Marriage
    2. The Power of Propinquity
    3. Why Does Propinquity Lead to Attraction?
    4. Subliminal Repeated Exposures: Misattribution and Manipulation
  B. Affect: Emotions and Attraction
    1. Affect As the Basis of Attraction
    2. Social Interaction As the Source of Affect
    3. Why Does Affect Influence Attraction?
II. Becoming Acquainted: The Need to Affiliate and Reactions to Observable Characteristics
  A. Affiliation Need: Individual Differences and External Events
    1. Dispositional Differences in Affiliation Need
    2. Social Skills Can Help or Hinder Affiliation
    3. External Events Can Arouse Affiliation Needs
  B. Responding to Observable Characteristics
    1. The Effects of Superficial Characteristics

    2. Is Behavior Ever Related to Observable Characteristics?
    3. Attracted by Attractiveness
      a. Appearance Anxiety, Interpersonal Behavior, and Weight
    4. The Matching Hypothesis: Seeking an Equally Attractive Partner
      a. When Roommates Are Mismatched in Attractiveness
    5. What, Exactly, Determines Attractiveness?
III. Becoming Friends: Similarity and Reciprocity
  A. Similarity: We Like Those Most Like Ourselves
    1. Similar Attitudes, Dissimilar Attitudes, and Attraction
    2. The Repulsion Hypothesis: Are Similar Attitudes Irrelevant?
    3. Why Do We Care about the Attitudes of Others?
    4. Other Kinds of Similarity Influence Attraction, Too
  B. Reciprocity: Mutual Liking
  C. Status and Attraction in Japan and the United States

Learning Objectives

1. Describe how propinquity affects: (a) whom one marries; (b) friendship formation in dormitories and in other residential environments.
2. How is friendship formation in classrooms affected by where individuals are seated?
3. According to Zajonc, what is the process by which repeated exposure increases our attraction to a particular stimulus?
4. Describe the method used by Moreland and Beach (1992) to demonstrate the effect of repeated exposure in a college classroom.

5. What two conditions often cause propinquity to produce a decrease rather than an increase in liking?
6. Describe the impact of affect on attraction, including affect caused by music, radio news, humidity, movies, and the moods of others.
7. Indicate how opening lines arouse affect, and describe how this affect influences subsequent liking.
8. Give examples in which attraction is influenced simply by a person's being associated with good or

bad feelings, and interpret the examples in terms of the reinforcement-affect model.

9. Describe the need for affiliation and friendship motivation, and be familiar with Hill's four affiliative motives.

10. How do birth order, transition from high school to college, and interpersonal strategies relate to a person's social skill?

11. When does our need for social comparison cause affiliation, when does our need for information cause affiliation, and what hospital patients want to be alone?

12. How do we exclude "unsuitable" persons as potential friends through the process of cognitive disregard?

13. Describe how body type, youthfulness, behavioral cues, and impression making influence judgments.

14. In what ways are responses to individuals determined by their obesity and their clothing? Describe research demonstrating that being obese or wearing particular types of clothing causes changes in individuals.

15. Examine ways in which attractive individuals are rated differently than less-attractive individuals.

16. What characteristics are related to appearance anxiety?

17. In what ways do attractive individuals actually differ from less-attractive individuals, and what differences simply represent inaccurate stereotypes?

18. Describe the matching hypothesis, and indicate how we respond to obvious mismatches according to equity theory.

19. Compare responses of attractive and less-attractive roommates when roommates are mismatched in attractiveness.

20. What is "attractive" according to each of the following: (a) the two-type view of Cunningham; (b) computer-generated composites; (c) desirable body features; and (d) the situationally determined view?

21. Compare the degree of attraction to someone who agrees with you on 2 out of 4 topics versus on 50 out of 100 topics. How would this be affected by whether you were high in empathy or not?

22. Explain the role of similar and dissimilar attitudes in creating the similarity-attraction effect, according to Rosenbaum's repulsion hypothesis.

23. Examine the false consensus effect, and indicate its relationship to Rosenbaum's repulsion hypothesis.

24. Indicate how each of the following supports the original hypothesis that similarity is the basis of liking: (a) Smeaton, Byrne, and Murnen (1989); (b) Singh and Tan (1992); and (c) Smeaton et al. (1992).

25. How do each of the following account for our response to attitude agreement/disagreement by others: (a) balance theory; (b) consensual validation; and (c) genetic similarity?

26. Describe how our behavior toward an individual is affected by the receipt of a positive evaluation from him/her.

27. Compare the horizontal orientation of American workers and the vertical orientation of Japanese workers.

Discussion Questions

1. The romantic ideal, the notion that people should marry on the basis of their being "in love," is perhaps more firmly established in the United States than in any other country in the world. Parents still have a great deal to say about the choice of a marriage partner in many countries, and in some cultures it is even the case that parents arrange marriages. An interesting question is the degree to which parents and their children would agree as to the appropriateness of a particular potential mate. Who is in a better position to make a rational choice of a marriage partner—parents or their children? In what ways will their choices be different? Before you begin the discussion, have students indicate their agreement or disagreement with the following statement: "One should not marry against the serious advice of one's parents."

2. Ask students to think of their best friend and to describe how they became friends. Then ask them to describe generally what it is that causes them to choose others as friends. Compare the students' reports to the theories presented in the text. Do they mention propinquity, conditioned emotional responses, similarity, physical attractiveness, reciprocal evaluations, and so on? Are the same factors important early as well as later in a relationship?

3. Researchers disagree about whether love is just an extreme form of liking or whether love and liking are qualitatively different emotions. Zick Rubin distinguishes between liking and loving and has developed separate scales to measure each. Similarly, there is the commonly made distinction between passionate love and companionate love. A good source to read for background information is the book *Liking, Loving and Relating* by Hendrick and Hendrick, published in 1983 by Brooks/Cole. This is the kind of question on which most people have an opinion, so it's important for you to be familiar with the conclusions reached by the experts.

4. Lee has proposed a typology of love that includes six major styles of loving. The styles of loving proposed by Lee (1977) are as follows:

Eros: Loving someone primarily because of his or her physical appearance. The Eros lover searches for a person whose physical appearance matches his or her ideal physical type.

Ludus: Playful love. The Ludus lover does not commit to a single relationship but prefers to play the field.

Storage: Loving someone as a result of a slowly developing attachment to that person. The Storge lover moves slowly, carefully, without great passion, to a lasting commitment.

Mania: Intense romantic love. The Mania lover is jealous, thinks intensely and excessively about his or her beloved, and needs repeated reassurance that he or she is loved in return.

Agape: Altruistic love. Given without expectation of getting anything in return; gentle, caring, and dutiful.

Pragma: Selecting the "right" person. The Pragma lover looks for someone who has the "right" education, religion, job, and so on.

Lee's typology is presented in an article in *Personality and Social Psychology Bulletin* (*3*, 173–182). A 1986 article on Lee's typology by the Hendricks is presented in the "Update" section below. Included in the 1986 article is a scale for measuring each of the six types.

5. Does equity theory predict one's level of satisfaction with an intimate relationship? Some theorists have argued that a love relationship in which a partner is concerned about his or her own outcome is flawed. These theorists contend that true love means that the person is concerned only with what they can *give* the partner, not with what they can *get* from the relationship. On the other hand, equity theorists have maintained that in intimate relationships, just as in other human relationships, people are driven by a desire for equity. Chapter 7 of the Study Guide provides a series of questions for students to assess the degree to which they feel they are being equitably treated in a relationship.

Although a "pure reward" theory might argue that the more one gets for oneself from a relationship, the greater the satisfaction, this doesn't seem to be the case. Instead the most satisfied are those who feel equitably treated. Does your class agree with the equity theory prediction?

Classroom Exercises/Demonstrations

1. An exercise that students can carry out in their everyday environment is to construct a friendship map of their dormitory floor. The map should be a summary of who is friends with whom. If several students construct maps of their own floors, it would be instructive to combine the information to determine the probability of friendship as a function of propinquity. Are the students surprised to learn how much impact propinquity has on their friendship developments?

2. The text discusses recent work by Craig Hill that proposes that four basic motives underlie the disposition to be affiliative. Hill has developed the Interpersonal Orientation Scale to measure the four motives. The scale is presented in your students' Study Guide in chapter 7 with permission of Craig A. Hill. You are encouraged to have your students find out how they stand on each of the four motives.

The items for each of the four subscales on the Interpersonal Orientation Scale are as follows:

Items on the Emotional Support Subscale: 1, 4, 9, 15, 17, 23

Items on the Attention Subscale: 5, 8, 16, 19, 21, 22

Items on the Positive Stimulation Subscale: 3, 6, 10, 11, 13, 20, 24, 25, 26

Items on the Social Comparison Subscale: 2, 7, 12, 14, 18

To compute scores for each subscale, first convert the alphabetic letters on the scales to numeric values: A = 1, B = 2, C = 3, D = 4, E = 5. Then add the numeric values together for the items listed for each subscale.

3. Some theorists have discussed a phenomenon they call *romanticism.* Romanticism tends to have two components. One is a belief that "love will conquer all" and the other is that one should marry for love. In chapter 7 of the Study Guide you will find examples of statements used to assess people's degree of romanticism. For each of the five statements, the respondent should indicate his or her degree of agreement. Determine scores by adding up the responses. Before the responses are added, items 1 and 3 should be reversed (i.e., agreement with items 2, 4, and 5 indicates a romantic attitude, whereas disagreement with items 1 and 3 indicates a romantic attitude). What are the consequences of a belief in romanticism?

4. This exercise is designed to test the hypothesis that similarity and attraction are related. The text devotes much attention to the similarity-attraction hypothesis. This exercise provides very reliable data and generally serves as an interesting introduction to the chapter.

An Adjective Checklist for use in the exercise is presented in chapter 7 of the Study Guide. Students are instructed to go through the list of adjectives three times. First, they should go through the list and check those adjectives that describe themselves. Second, they should think of their best friends and check the adjectives that apply. Finally, in the third column they should check the adjectives that apply to a person they know, but with whom they could never be friends.

After the students have completed the checklist, have them count the number of traits in common between self and friend. A trait in common occurs whenever a trait is checked for both self and friend, or whenever a trait is unchecked for both. Likewise, have them count the number of traits in common between self and nonfriend. You will find that students have more in common with their friends than with their nonfriends.

5. Jeffrey Simpson of Texas A & M has published a survey in *Teaching of Psychology* (*15*[1], 31–33) that assesses past dating behavior and willingness to change partners, both of which are components of commitment to relationships. The dating survey is found in the Study Guide. On the basis of their responses to the survey, students are placed into one of three categories. Students who answer "yes" to the first question on the survey (i.e., those who are dating one person exclusively) are referred to as "exclusive daters." Students who answer "no" to the first question but "yes" to the third one (i.e., those who are not dating one person exclusively but who have dated at least two people in the past year) are referred to as "multiple daters." Those who respond "no" to both questions because they are married or because they do not date cannot provide data for classroom analysis. (Simpson found, however, that only 15 to 20 percent of undergraduates enrolled in daytime cours-es typically fall into this third category. Even though these students cannot provide data for the exercise themselves, they still find the exercise to be interesting and valuable.)

Once students have completed the dating survey, the next step is to find out whether commitment in dating relationships is related to the widely studied individual difference dimension of self-monitoring. Two studies published by Snyder and Simpson (1984) in *Journal of Personality and Social Psychology* (*47*, 1281–1291) found that high self-monitors typically adopt an uncommitted orientation to dating relationships, whereas low self-monitors tend to adopt a committed one. The Self-Monitoring Scale is found in chapter 5 of the Study Guide. After students have completed and scored the Self-Monitoring Scale, determine whether you have replicated the self-monitoring results of Snyder and Simpson. Create four columns on the chalkboard, one for each of the following groups: High self-monitors/exclusive daters; high self-monitors/multiple daters; low self-monitors/exclusive daters; and low self-monitors/multiple daters. Two comparisons are especially suggested. First, using only exclusive daters, compare the number of months in the relationship for high and low self-monitors. The expectation is that low self-monitors will remain in relationships longer. Second, using only multiple daters, compare the number of partners for high and low self-monitors. The expectation is that high self-monitors will report a higher number of partners. Detailed suggestions regarding how to analyze and present the data to your class is found in the *Teaching of Psychology* article mentioned above.

Film Notes: A Picture Is Sometimes Worth a Thousand Words

Are We Still Going to the Movies? 21730, 1974, color, 14 mins. Pennsylvania State University, Audiovisual Services, Special Services Building, University Park, PA 16802 (814-865-6314). A young couple's relationship is suffering as a result of their disagreement on the amount of sexual involvement to have with each other. Intended to provoke discussion of premarital sexuality and sex roles. From the *Conflict and Awareness* series. Produced by Tom Lazarus.

Beauty Knows No Pain, 31910, 1973, color, 25 mins. Pennsylvania State University, Audiovisual Services, Special Services Building, University Park, PA 16802 (814-865-6314). Coeds aspiring to join the Kilgore College majorettes submit to the ordeal of training and testing. Reactions of both winners and losers show the value that the "Rangerette" ideal holds for them. Produced by Elliott Erwitt.

Divorce: For Better or for Worse, Parts 1 and 2, 50423, 1976, color, 51 mins. Pennsylvania State University, Audiovisual Services, Special Services Building, University Park, PA 16802 (814-865-6314). Divorce is "a kind of death," according to one of the narrators, a form of saying good-bye that entails grief and restructuring of lives and that touches most of us in some way. Film focuses on actual case histories of the divorced and divorcing to show the emotional and financial toll, the need for legal reform, and the need for stricter regulation of counselors and therapists. From the ABC News "Closeup" series.

Kinds of Love, NET 2037, 29 mins. Audiovisual Center, Indiana University, Bloomington, IN 47401. Interviews with Father Thurston David and Erich Fromm address misconceptions about love, the relationship between sexuality and love, and love as a religious virtue.

Love and Sex (from Phil Donahue's "The Human Animal" series), EC-1132, VHS or Beta videotape, color, 52 mins. Falling in love, having sex, making babies—these are easy. Understanding human sexuality is much harder. Phil Donahue takes viewers on an odyssey showing women at a male strip club and a gay rights march, a hospital room where an unwed teenage mother is giving birth, and classrooms where teachers and parents are trying to help teenagers come to grips with their sexual selves. Love, monogamy, hetero- and homosexuality are among the topics covered by Donahue, by consultants Dr. William Masters of the Masters & Johnson Institute and Dr. June Reinisch of the Kinsey Institute, and by Donahue's best resource, ordinary people.

Love Tapes, MVCS-1034, 1980 videocassette, 30 mins. Pennsylvania State University, Audiovisual Services, Special Services Building, University Park, PA 16802 (814-865-6314). A series of three-minute statements by people from all walks of life who can-

didly record their feelings about love against background music of their own choosing. Included are Darrell, a black college student, afraid of love; Darlene, unloved as a child, who finds that men treat her callously; Rose, in her eighties, recalling her changing needs; and Frieda, a disabled professor, who struggles for self-worth. The tapes were recorded as part of an experimental video art project that involved the installation of video recording equipment in museums and other public places. Produced by Wendy Clarke.

Morning After, 1983, color, 17 mins. Filmmakers Library, Inc., 133 E. 58th Street, New York, NY 10022. Shows the vulnerability of a seemingly cool, sophisticated man to the breakup of a long-term relationship.

Transparencies

7.1 *The Reinforcement-Affect Model of Attraction*

7.2 *The Three-Factor Theory of Passionate Love*

Critical Thinking/Essay Questions

1. Summarize the effect that propinquity has on interpersonal attraction.
2. Describe findings that show how interpersonal liking is influenced by mood induced by situational events. How does the reinforcement-affect model account for these results?
3. Compare relationships in which partners are

matched versus mismatched in physical attractiveness.

4. Explain how the repulsion hypothesis accounts for the fact that we are more attracted to similar than to dissimilar others.
5. Explain how the dispositional need for affiliation is related to the acquaintance process.

Sources for Lecture

Cash, T. F., & Janda, L. H. (1984). In the eye of the beholder. *Psychology Today*, December, pp. 46–52. Attractive women are preferred for dates, friendships, and jobs. On the job, however, women are perceived more positively if they do not look too feminine.

Davis, K. E. (1985). Near and dear: Friendship and love compared. *Psychology Today*, February, pp. 22–30. Friendship and love have much in common, but there are two additional clusters of factors that are typical of love: a "passion cluster" and a "caring cluster."

Fischer, C. (1983). The friendship cure-all. *Psychology Today*, January, pp. 74–78. The California State Department of Mental Health conducted an advertising campaign to convince people to develop their social relationships. This article takes a critical look at the campaign.

Hamburger, A. C. (1988). Beauty quest. *Psychology Today*, May, pp. 29–32. The authors note that cosmetic surgery to improve looks and figures is more common than ever before. What can people expect after undergoing such surgery? Oftentimes, people expect too much.

Lynn, M., & Shurgot, B. A. Responses to lonely hearts advertisements: Effects of reported physical attractiveness, physique, and coloration. *Personality and Social Psychology Bulletin, 10*(3), 349–357. Lynn and Shurgot analyzed personal ads, the lonely hearts classifieds, that appeared in a Columbus, Ohio, monthly. They tabulated the number of responses to each ad to determine what characteristics were most appealing to potential romantic partners.

Meer, J. (1985). The dating game: Ladies' choice. *Psychology Today*, March, p. 16. How a woman can ask for a date and not be seen as making a sexual

Rubenstein, C. (1983). Love and romance: A *Psychology Today* reader survey. *Psychology Today*, February, pp. 60–64. A questionnaire surveys the current status of love and romance.

Trotter, R. J. (1986). The three phases of love. *Psychology Today*, September, pp. 46–54. Summary of Sternberg's three-sided theory of love. The components? Commitment, intimacy, and passion.

Update: Current Articles from Professional Sources

Baumeister, R. F., Wotman, S. R., & Stillwell, A. M. Unrequited love: On heartbreak, anger, guilt, scriptlessness, and humiliation. *Journal of Personality and Social Psychology, 64,* 377–394. Unreciprocated romantic attraction is explored through comparison of narrative accounts of would-be lovers and rejectors. Judgments and attributions made by both are examined.

Forgas, J. P. (1993). On making sense of odd couples: Mood effects on the perception of mismatched relationships. *Personality and Social Psychology Bulletin, 19,* 59–70. Subjects made judgments about couples who were either well-matched or ill-matched for physical attractiveness. Mood of the subjects making the judgments was also varied. Mood had a greater influence on judgments of ill-matched couples than it did on judgments of well-matched couples.

Kenrick, D. T., Montello, D. R., Gutierres, S. E., & Trost, M. R. (1993). Effects of physical attractiveness on affect and perceptual judgments: When social comparison overrides social reinforcement. *Personality and Social Psychology Bulletin, 19,* 195–199. Researchers recorded subjects' responses to photos of attractive individuals. Sometimes attractive photo sequences were interrupted by an average face, sometimes not. Results were different for same- and opposite-sex sequences, but results suggest that one's cognitive appraisal of physical attractiveness and one's affective reaction to it operate independently.

Kurdek, L. A. (1993). Predicting marital dissolution: A 5-year prospective study of newlywed couples. *Journal of Personality and Social Psychology, 64,* 221–242. Four approaches were examined for their ability to predict which newlywed couples would remain together and which would part. Factors examined include demographics, personality traits, interdependence, discrepancies in traits, and conflict-resolution styles.

Zebrowitz, L. A., Olson, K., & Hoffman, K. (1993). Stability of babyfacedness and attractiveness across the lifespan. *Journal of Personality and Social Psychology, 64,* 453–466. Changes in babyfacedness and attractiveness as a function of age were examined. A distinction was drawn between differential stability, structural stability, and absolute stability in facial appearance, with relatively low levels of stability generally being found.

Chapter-at-a-Glance

Chapter Eight:
Close Relationships: Friendship, Love, and Sexuality

Chapter Outline	Instruction Ideas	Supplements
I. Interdependent Relationships: Moving Beyond Casual Friendship Relatives, Friends, and Lovers / What Is This Thing Called Love? / Loneliness: The Absence of a Close Relationship	Exercises 1 and 4 Discussion Questions 3 and 4 Critical Thinking Questions 1–5	CNN Video Segment 14, *Parents/Grandparents,* Segment 15, *Commuter Love,* Segment 16, *Marriage Survey—see* CNN Video Guide Transparencies 8.2, 8.4 Video: Friendship Readings: Lesko 23—Measurement of Romantic Love and Lesko 24—The Social Stigma of Loneliness
II. Sexually Intimate Relationships Premarital Sexuality / Marriage	Exercise 3 Discussion Question 1 Critical Thinking Questions 6 and 7	Transparencies 8.1, 8.5
III. Troubled Relationships: Problems, Solutions, Failures Problems in Relationships, and Possible Solutions / When Relationships Break Up: From Dissatisfaction to Dissolution	Exercise 2 Discussion Question 2 Critical Thinking Questions 8–11	Transparencies 8.3, 8.6
Social Diversity: A Critical Analysis— Love and Intimacy: Western Europe, South Africa, Japan, and the U.S.		Reading: Lesko 22—Getting at the Heart of a Jealous Heart

Chapter Eight

Close Relationships: Friendship, Love, and Sexuality

Chapter Outline: Getting the Overall Picture

I. Interdependent Relationships: Moving beyond Casual Friendships
  A. Relatives, Friends, and Lovers
    1. Close Relatives
    2. Close Friends
    3. Romantic Relationships
    4. When Relationships Are Too Close, Experimental Closeness, and Pregnancy
  B. What Is This Thing Called Love?
    1. Passionate Love
    2. Evolution versus
    3. Other Varieties of Love
  C. Loneliness: The Absence of a Close Relationship
    1. Measuring Loneliness
    2. Loneliness in Childhood
    3. Interpersonal Skills and Loneliness
    4. Doing Something to Relieve Loneliness
II. Physically Intimate Relationships
  A. Premarital Sexuality
    1. New Sexual Patterns
    2. Sociosexuality: Choosing a Romantic Partner
    3. Is Sexual Behavior Becoming Less Permissive?
    4. Does Premarital Sexuality Affect Subsequent Marriages?
    5. Dating As a Unique Relationship

  B. Marriage
    1. Similarity and Marriage
    2. Relationship Patterns among Young Married Couples
    3. Sexuality and Parenthood
    4. Is Marriage Less Fun Than It Used to Be?
III. Troubled Relationships: Problems, Solutions, Failures
  A. Problems in Relationships, and Possible Solutions
    1. Problems of Conflict in Male-Female Interactions
    2. Discovering Dissimilarities
    3. Boredom
    4. Positive versus Negative Communications between Partners
    5. Jealousy: A Special Threat
  B. When Relationships Break Up: From Dissatisfaction to Dissolution
    1. Differences between Friendships and Intimate Relationships
    2. Responding to Relationship Problems
    3. Breakup and Divorce
    4. The Aftereffects of Relationship Failure
    5. Sometimes, Offspring "Break Up" with Their Parents
IV. Love and Intimacy: Western Europe, South Africa, Japan, and the United States

Learning Objectives

1. Learn the most common element in close relationships, examine sibling relationships and explain how they change over time, indicate the two components of love for parents, tell how parent-child relationships affect the child's adult relationships, and indicate where children of stepfamilies spend much of their time.

2. Examine the traits of close friendships. Who is most content, friends or lovers? What did Berscheid et al. (1989) ask subjects to disclose about their close relationships? How does love differ from other close relationships, and what is the

role of initial closeness?

3. Learn whether love begins with friendship and what initiates love and friendship relationships. Understand the difference between passionate love and sexual desire, the traits of passionate love, what mutual gazing can do, the validity of our notion that love should precede marriage, the role of genetic similarity, and what men and women look for in potential spouses.

4. Indicate the age preferences of men and women, what Kenrick and Keefe (1992) found when they "advertised" in the lonely hearts column, whether there are U.S./African differences in love, and the explanations of gender differences in age preference that are alternatives to the genetic hypothesis.

5. Explain whether arousal, regardless of its source, leads to sexual attraction. Compare compassionate and companionate love, indicate what other varieties of love are proposed by Hendrick and his colleagues, and outline Sternberg's (1986, 1989) triangular model of love.

6. Define loneliness. Indicate what aspects of loneliness have been studied, how it is measured, what the measure is related to, what a lonely young person is like, what skills he or she lacks, when loneliness is at a peak, and what serious condition may accompany this peak.

7. Outline the lonely person's communication style and the cynicism that accompanies it. What strategies do lonely people resort to in the hope of easing loneliness? What is the cognitive style of lonely people, and how can cognitive therapy help them?

8. What was the sexual revolution? Indicate when it occurred and how it has affected attitudes. Tell whether gender differences in sexual behavior are strong, and how, now a days, emotions figure into gender differences in sexuality.

9. Explain sociosexuality and how the sexes differ on it. What is "fitness" versus "investment," and how do these factors relate to choice of a spouse? Understand Simpson and Gangestad's (1991, 1992) results using the Sociosexual Orientation Inventory (SOI), the two factors that relate to scoring high or low on the SOI, and the role of genetics in these considerations.

10. Learn the motivations for and reactions to engaging in "free sex" during the "revolution," including gender differences. Discuss the parental/peer conflict regarding "free sex" and its effects on young people (Moore & Rosenthal, 1991), and tell how mother/father differences affect youths' sexual behavior.

11. Appreciate the implications of the teen pregnancy epidemic, especially regarding the abortion debate; the relative threat of gonorrhea, chlamydia, genital herpes, and HIV/AIDS; how the latter relates to homophobia; for whom the "revolution" has continued and for whom it has ended with the HIV scare; and how premarital sexuality affects subsequent marriages.

12. How widespread is the desire to marry? What is the myth of the single-parent household? What did Caspi, Herbener, and Ozer (1992) find regarding the similarity between spouses, and what was discovered in their twenty-year follow-up of married couples? Describe Johnson et al.'s (1992) four types of couples, and how one type produces the most children.

13. Outline the course of sexual intercourse frequency as marriages age; how children affect sex; what has happened to the link between marriage and happiness; and how gender figures in, especially in regard to women's increased economic freedom and the "modern husband's" expectation of his wife.

14. Describe the basic conflicts/problems that predict trouble for marriages. Define "relationship awareness," list Buss's (1989a) husband/wife conflicts in marriage and his genetic explanation of them, and indicate who provokes conflict. Tell what spouses discover, once they are married, about their assumptions of mutual similarity, and discuss marital boredom and its cure.

15. Chart how courtship behavior fades to marital indifference and how satisfied and dissatisfied couples interact. What are the three reasons we tend to be meaner to lovers than to strangers, and what is the simple solution to this problem?

16. Describe jealousy, what accompanies it, and what it does to self-esteem. Outline how it differs among cultures and between genders. What do deliberate efforts to provoke jealousy do to marriages?

17. List Levinger's (1980) stages in a relationship. Contrast friendship and romantic relationships. Describe the Rusbult groups' (1983, 1990) ways to end a relationship. Indicate who uses which way, and consider under what conditions solving problems may be likely.

18. Learn about the "dependence model of breakups," the divorce rate and when divorce happens, the effect of divorce on ex-spouses and children, and the effects of remarriage.

19. Describe the spread of the "love" concept, how much love is valued in Japan and Germany relative to here, Japanese gender expectations, and the difference conceptions of love in the United States and France (with attention to gender differences).

20. Indicate the factors upon which Ting-Toomey's (1991) research concentrated and how the variation of U.S., French, and Japanese people along the individualism-collectivism continuum affects love factors.

Discussion Questions

1. "Prenuptial agreements" have become familiar to the public since several famous media stars revealed that they sought to avoid large settlements in the event of divorce by drawing up marriage-dissolution papers before their vows were taken. A related phenomenon may be the wave of the future: marriage contracts; see A. K. Shulman, A marriage agreement, in A. Jaggar and D. Rothenberg (Eds.), *Feminist frameworks* (pp. 311–315), New York: McGraw-Hill. One of the components of such a contract might be division of labor: Who will do what housework and which child-care duties. Prime the students with this information. Then give each student, say, twenty minutes to write up what would be an ideal contract from his or her point of view. Next, have students indicate the aspects of marriage they have covered in their contracts and put them on the board (e.g., sexual fidelity, allocation of house space, provisions for continuation of hobbies and interests, etc.). After having determined what aspects are included in students' contracts, ask students to provide examples of provisions they have included in their contracts that relate to these aspects. (Tell them they are not obliged to reveal sensitive information.) A lively discussion should ensue.

2. The fact that chance may play a role in whom one marries may be unsettling to students. They are apt to think that someone is predestined to be their "one and only" or that they will carefully sort through candidate partners to find the one that suits them best. In fact, as Albert Bandura pointed out some time ago (*American Psychologist*, 1982, 37, 747–755), pure chance will in great part determine whom one marries. Ask several students to indicate how their parents came to know each other well enough to end up married. Put the examples up on the board until you have several that involve pure chance (e.g., "My dad was driving home from a business meeting and had a car wreck. He spent several weeks in a hospital outside a small town he had never heard of before. My mother was his nurse, and six months later, they were married"). Now point these examples of chance out to students. Be ready for arguments about the difference between chance and destiny!

3. How do parents figure into a romantic relationship? There is a thing called the "Romeo and Juliet effect": Interference by parents may actually drive lovers closer together (see Driscoll et al., 1972, *Journal of Personality and Social Psychology, 24,* 1–10). Ask students to indicate their direct and indirect experience with parental interference in romantic relationships. Determine whether there is a pattern fitting the Romeo and Juliet effect. If you refer only to cases of interference that occurred *before* marriage, you will probably find support for the effect. If you do, identify the effect and inform students that their experience confirms it. If you do not, students will be interested in the observation that their experience is an exception to the Romeo and Juliet "rule." In any case, it will be informative to have students speculate concerning why parental interference tore apart, bonded together, or had no effect on the romantic relationships in their experience. (E.g., if increased closeness occurred, did the parties involved misattribute the arousal due to parental meddling to love?)

4. To get at "what's a friend?", it is helpful to discover what is not a friend. Have students discuss each of the following, indicating the nature of each and telling why each is not "true friendship"; then end the discussion by concluding what is true friendship. Non–true friendships: acquaintance (passersby, co-workers, schoolmates); neighbors; confederates (two people engaged in some joint enterprise in which a symbiotic relationship exists, but who have little connection outside of the pursuit—e.g., robbing banks, selling cars, working for the homeless); pals (people with some activity in common, such as beer buddies, horse-lovers, or shopping companions); close kin; convenience friends (people who trade babysitting chores, borrow from one another, share rides to work); and people in a mentor relationship (where a usually older person shows the ropes to an up-and-coming neophyte; e.g., a full professor and a new assistant professor).

Classroom Exercises/Demonstrations

1. According to *Psychology Today* surveys, it is young people—adolescents and young adults—not elderly people who are the loneliest. And loneliness is a personality trait that matters: As indicated in the text, it is related to important issues such as health. Get your young people to open up about the issue. You could begin by having them indicate "what it is like to be lonely." An exercise included in the Study Guide chapter 8 can help.

Students could do the Robert Weiss exercise in class before an exchange of experiences begins. After the exercise and any student testimonials, ask students why young people are the most lonely. Relate loneliness to shyness and introversion. Have students come up with solutions to the problem.

2. Is the sexual revolution over? As the text indicates, probably not. However, it may have changed its charac-

ter. Have students answer several questions anonymously; better have them do so outside of class and bring results to you in identical sealed envelopes. (1) At what age did you first become sexually active? (2) Currently, how many times a month do you have some form of sex with some person (or with different persons)? (3) If you are sexually active, do you have a single partner to whom you are committed, or do you have sex with several people? (4) If you have a single partner with whom you exclusively have sex, why is that? Love for the partner? Fear of sexual disease? Practicality (for example, convenience of living together)? Other (indicate)? (5) Do you currently use protection against pregnancy most of the times you have sex? (6) Do you currently take precautions against disease—for example, use a condom—most of the times you have sex?

Simply tally the numbers; compute averages when the questions call for a number or frequencies for questions that can be scored "yes" or "no." Display this data for the students in class. What do the numbers say? The sexual revolution may be said to be "still on" for students if they start young and currently practice sex at least a few times a month, on average. But has it

changed its character? The revolution has taken a turn if students tend to have single rather than multiple partners. Is love the main reason for single partners? Do students take precautions against disease and pregnancy? Discuss the students impressions of how the revolution may have changed.

3. Consider ideal friendship by using the "Rate Your Friendship" scale found in the Study Guide. Have students imagine an ideal friend, then complete the scale with that friend in mind. The goal is to score as high as is possible. The higher the score, the more students have grasped the qualities of true friendship.

The Rate Your Friendship scale is a test of quality of friendship. Have students count the left-most scale as an 8, then number to the right so that the right-most point is 1. Next, for each scale item, have the students write down the value of the scale points that they have checked. Finally, have them add their scale scores over the ten scales. If they score 70–80, their grasp of the qualities of friendship is very good. Those who score 10–20 have a poor grasp. Scores in the range of 60–70 and 30–20 may also be interpreted as high and low, respectively.

Film Notes: A Picture Is Sometimes Worth a Thousand Words

Allyn and Bacon Video

* *Friendship,* video, 28.5 mins. To obtain this tape, see your Allyn and Bacon representative. A dramatization leads Robert A. Baron and Margaret Clark to an in-depth discussion of friendship, especially as it differs for men and women.

Other Videos and Films

Love and Sex, FC1132, video, 52 mins. Films for the Humanities & Sciences, P.O. Box 2053, Princeton, NJ 08543 (800-257-5126). This is possibly the best of Phil Donohue's excellent "The Human Animal" series. Love and sex and their joys and heartbreaks are covered in poignant fashion.

The Sexual Brain, EC1738, video, 28 mins. Films for the Humanities & Sciences, P.O. Box 2053, Princeton, NJ 08543 (800-257-5126). The battle of the sexes that sometimes ends in marriage, sometimes in friendship, and sometimes in mutual rejection starts with the brain. This tape ends with questions about the structural and reproductive roots of the differences between the sexes.

Are We Still Going to the Movies?, 21730, film, 14 mins. Pennsylvania State University, Audiovisual Services, Special Services Building, University Park, PA 16802

(814-865-6314). A young couple's relationship is suffering as a result of their disagreement on amount of sexual involvement.

Love Tapes, MVCS-1034, video, 30 mins. Pennsylvania State University, Audiovisual Services, Special Services Building, University Park, PA 16802 (814-865-6314). An interesting and varied sample of people talk candidly about their experiences with love.

Divorce: For Better or for Worse, Parts 1 & 2, 50423, film, 51 mins. Pennsylvania State University, Audiovisual Services, Special Services Building, University Park, PA 16802 (814-865-6314). Focuses on actual case histories of divorced and divorcing couples and on the emotional as well as financial toll that divorce exacts.

Morning After, film, 17 mins. Filmmakers Library, Inc., 133 E. 58th Street, New York, NY 10022. Shows the vulnerability of a seemingly cool, sophisticated man to the breakup of a long-term relationship.

Kinds of Love, Net 2037, film, 29 mins. Audiovisual Center, Indiana University, Bloomington, IN 47401. Misconceptions about love, the relationship between sexuality and love, and love as a religious virtue are discussed in interviews with Father Thurston David and Erich Fromm..

Transparencies

8.1 *Reinforcement-Affect Theory: How Some Relationships May Start*

8.2 *An Unromantic Explanation of Passionate Love*

8.3 *Levinger's Theory That Relationships Pass through Five Stages from Beginning to End*

8.4 *Sternberg's "Triangular Model of Love"*

8.5 *Relationships among Findings in the Lauers' Study of 351 Married Couples*

8.6 *Behaviors That upset Men versus Behaviors That Upset Women*

Critical Thinking/Essay Questions

1. Consider the Berscheid, Snyder, and Omoto (1989) study of close relations among college students. What kind of relationship was closest for these students, and what kind lasted longest? Was there a gender difference in perceived closeness of closest relationships?

2. Contrast friendship and romantic love. What does each have that the other lacks? Also contrast romantic love in general with the more specific variety, passionate love.

3. Contrast Sternberg's triangular model with the Hendricks' "basicl Love styles" approach. Could you collapse them into one model?

4. Are there alternatives to the text explanations of why older men prefer younger women as potential partners? Describe one of them.

5. Indicate how the stage is set for loneliness during childhood. What are lonely people like in terms of traits and social behavior, and what can be done to change them in a way that is likely to lessen loneliness?

6. Some say the sexual revolution has come and gone. What was beneficial about it, and what was detrimental? Contrast the "revolution" period with today's orientation to sexual matters.

7. Describe the way marriage has changed since the early 1970s. How have men and women's views of marriage changed in different directions? What must be shared among spouses in the future if the trend toward marital problems is to be halted?

8. Paint a picture of a jealous person. What will that individual's characteristics be? How does jealousy vary around the world? What aspects of the jealous person will be most in need of change?

9. What happens when boredom sets in during the course of a marriage? What makes it happen, and how can it be corrected?

10. What are the factors that cause dissimilarities to arise during marriage, and can the development of negative attributions be short-circuited?

11. Examine divorce and remarriage. How likely is divorce? Is divorce more or less likely in a second marriage than in a first? Indicate a major effect of divorce on children.

Sources for Lecture

Bower, B. (1991, October 21). Darwin's minds: Psychologists probe the descent of the human psyche. *Science News, 140,* 232–234. Award-winning science writer tracks the progress of evolutionary explanations of human behavior. Considers sexual attractiveness as well as sex differences in mating preferences and in jealousy.

Budiansky, S. (1987, May 4). All by your lonesome. *U.S. News and World Report,* p. 71. Summarizes research on what it is like to be isolated.

Fuhr, J. (1987). Standardization of divorce mediation. *Conciliation-Courts-Review, 25,* 65–68. Mediation between spouses can sometimes stop divorce before it is final. If not, it can lead to more manageable agreements. This article concentrates on the child custody aspect of divorce settlement.

Mainardi, P. (1992, May-June). The politics of housework. *Ms.,* pp. 40–41. Examines men's excuses for not helping out more.

Roberts, M. (1988, March). Be all that you can be. *Psychology Today,* pp. 28–29. This article indicates which, among the several self-improvement methods available, really may help lonely people develop the kinds of skills that allow success in general and social success in particular.

Tan, N-T. (1988, Spring). Developing and testing a family mediation assessment instrument. *Mediation Quarterly,* pp. 53–68. An instrument to assess couples who present themselves for mediation reveals some dimensions that are important to the mediation process.

Tavris, C. (1988, November). Coping with jealousy. *Psychology Today,* p. 302. Carol Tavris is well known for her theorizing about anger and has also turned

Update: Current Articles from Professional Sources

her attention to jealousy. Here she provides useful information about coping with jealousy.

Bradbury, T. N., & Fincham, F. D. (1992). Attributions and behavior in marital interaction. *Journal of Personality and Social Psychology, 63,* 613–628. Spouses were asked to report their marital quality, to make attributions for marital difficulties, and to engage in problem solving. Spouses' maladaptive attributions were related to less-effective problem-solving behaviors, particularly among wives, as well as to higher rates of negative behavior and, for wives, to increased tendencies to reciprocate negative partner behavior.

Cantor, N., Acker, M., & Cook-Flannagan, C. (1992). Conflict and preoccupation in the intimacy life task. *Journal of Personality and Social Psychology, 63,* 644–655. A study of sorority women's pursuit of romantic intimacy. For those in a serious relationship, conflict was associated with romantic satisfaction, but also with a narrow focus on communion in the relationship. For those dating casually, conflict was associated with the perceived difficulty and dissatisfaction of the intimacy task.

Gootman, J. M., & Levenson, R. W. (1992). Marital processes predictive of later dissolution: Behavior, physiology, and health. *Journal of Personality and Social Psychology, 63,* 221–233. Based on conversations between spouses at two different times, researchers classified married couples as "regulated" (showing a balance of positive and negative interaction) and "nonregulated." Compared with regulated couples, nonregulated couples had more severe marital problems at time one, poorer health at time two, more negative ratings of interactions, more negative and less positive emotional expression, greater defensiveness, and greater risk of dissolution.

Kurdek, L. A. (1993). Predicting marital dissolution. A 5-year prospective longitudinal study of newlywed couples. *Journal of Personality and Social Psychology, 64,* 221-242. Through five annual assessments, researchers studied 222 couples, 64 of which dissolved their marriages. Husbands and wives who would dissolve their marriages showed a greater decline in interdependence scores and had greater increases in discrepancies on interdependence variables than did husbands and wives in stable marriages.

Sedikides, C., Olsen, N., & Reis, H. T. (1993). Relationships as natural categories. *Journal of Personality and Social Psychology, 64,* 71–82. To show that people organize social information around relationship categories, investigators informed some subjects about targets grouped as four married couples; other subjects were informed about targets but were not told whom targets were married to. As expected, the first set of subjects did organize information about targets around couple categories more than the second set. We tend to see married couples as a unit.

Related Readings: The following selections from *Readings in Social Psychology: General, Classic, and Contemporary Selections,* 2nd Edition, by Wayne Lesko (Allyn & Bacon, 1993) accompany this chapter:

Adams, V. (1980). Getting at the heart of the jealous heart. This *Psychology Today* article begins by showing that jealousy is common and then addresses such questions as "What is jealousy? (Different from envy?)," "Who gets jealous?," "Who is most jealous, he or she?," and what cultures are associated with the most jealousy?" (22)

Rubin, Z. (1970). Measurement of romantic love. Covers Rubin's now-classic research on the development of a love scale. The scale proved valid in that high scorers spent more time gazing into one another's eyes than low scorers. (23)

Lau, S., & Gruen, G. E. (1992). The social stigma of loneliness: Effect of target person's and perceiver's sex. Are lonely people subject to negative feedback from others, implying they lack social skills, as the text indicates? Yes. They are liked less; seen as more passive; and rated as weaker, less attractive, and less sincere. (24)

Chapter-at-a-Glance

Chapter Nine
Social Influence:
Changing Others' Behavior

Chapter Outline	Instruction Ideas	Supplements
Introduction	Critical Thinking Question 1	CNN Video Segment 17: *Dress Code* and Segment 18, *Movie Stereotypes* *see* CNN Video Guide, Video: Power of the Situation
I. Conformity: Group Influence in Action Factors Affecting Conformity: Cohesiveness, Grup Size, and Social Support / The Bases of Conformity: Why We Often Choose to "Go Along" / The Need for Individuation and the Need for Control: Why, Sometimes, We Choose *Not* To Go Along / Minority Influence: One More Reason Why the Majority Doesn't Always Rule	Exercise 1 Discussion Question 3 Critical Thinking Questions 2, 3, 5, 6	Transparencies 9.1, 9.5 Video: Power of the Situation
II. Compliance: To Ask—Sometimes— Is To Receive Ingratiation: Liking As a Basis for Influence / Multiple Requests: Two Steps to Compliance Sweetening the Deal: the "That's Not All!' Technique / Complaints: Griping One's Way to Compliance	Exercises 2 and 4 Discussion Questions 3 and 4 Critical Thinking Questions 7–11	Transparencies 9.3, 9.6
III. Obedience: Social Influence by Demand Destructive Obedience: Some Basic Findings / Destructive Obedience: Why Does It Occur? / Destructive Obedience: Resisting Its Effects	Exercise 3 Discussion Question 1 Critical Thinking Questions 10	Transparency 9.4 Readings: Lesko 25—Education of a Torturer, Lesko 26—Behavioral Study of Obedience and Lesko 27— Understanding Behavior in the Milgram Experiment
Social Diversity: A Critical Analysis— Gender Differences and Conformity: The Vanishing Myth of Female Submissiveness	Critical Thinking Question #	Transparency 9.2

Chapter Nine

Social Influence: Changing Others' Behavior

Chapter Outline: Getting the Overall Picture

I. Conformity: Group Influence in Action
  A. Group Pressure: The Irresistible Social Force?
  B. Factors Affecting Conformity: Cohesiveness, Group Size, and Social Support
    1. Cohesiveness and Conformity: Accepting Influence from Those We Like
    2. Conformity and Group Size: Why "More" Isn't Always "Better" with Respect to Social Influence
    3. The Effects of Support from Others: When Having an Ally Helps
  C. The Bases of Conformity: Why We Often Choose to "Go Along"
    1. The Desire to Be Liked: Normative Social Influence
    2. The Desire to Be Right: Informational Social Influence
  D. The Need for Individuation and the Need for Control: Why, Sometimes, We Choose *Not* to Go Along
    1. Resisting Implicit Social Pressure: Threats to Personal Control in Everyday Interactions
  E. Minority Influence: One More Reason Why the Majority Doesn't Always Rule
II. Compliance: To Ask—Sometimes—Is to Receive
  A. Ingratiation: Liking As a Basis for Influence

  B. Multiple Requests: Two Steps to Compliance
    1. The Foot in the Door: Small Request First, Large Request Second
    2. The Door in the Face: Large Request First, Small Request Second
    3. Comparing the Foot-in-the-Door and Door-in-the-Face Tactics: The Role of Source Legitimacy
  C. Sweetening the Deal: The "That's Not All!" Technique
  D. Complaining: Griping One's Way to Compliance
    1. Complaining in Close Relationships: Evidence for Some Intriguing Gender Differences
  E. Social Influence in Everyday Life: Which Tactics Do People Use Most, When Do They Use Them, and with What Effect?
III. Obedience: Social Influence by Demand
  A. Destructive Obedience: Some Basic Findings
    1. Personality and Obedience: Who Resists and Who Obeys?
  B. Destructive Obedience: Why Does It Occur?
  C. Destructive Obedience: Resisting Its Effects
IV. Gender Differences and Conformity: The Vanishing Myth of Female Submissiveness

---

Learning Objectives

1. Define "social influence," "conformity," and "obedience." Learn how social norms play a role in conformity, and appreciate how conformity prevents social chaos—but is sometimes not necessarily helpful.

2. Describe Asch's experimental method for studying conformity. What percent of his subjects conformed at least once, and what percent not at all?

3. Discuss the importance of cohesiveness in determining whether group members will conform and how Crandall's (1988) study of sorority members and binge eating shows the effects of cohesiveness.

4. What happens when individuals exposed to group pressure begin to expect collusion? Understand the Social Influence Model (SIM), which explains the relationship between number of influence sources and number of targets.

5. Explain why and under what conditions having an ally when one is in the minority helps in resisting conformity pressure.

6. How do "normative social influence" and "informational social influence" help explain our tendency to "go along"? What is the role of information diffusion as revealed in the Weenig & Midden (1991) study of an energy conservation program?

7. Explain the roles of the need for uniqueness and the desire for control in the tendency sometimes to disagree with the group and how Burger (1987) experimentally illustrated the effects of desire for control.

8. Identify figures in history who had unanimous majorities against them, but doggedly stuck with their unusual ideas anyway. Outline the four "rules" that a minority must follow if it is successfully going to influence the majority, and indicate how minorities provoke increased deep thinking.

9. Define ingratiation and explain the "target-directed," "self-enhancement," "self-depreciation," and "self-disclosure" methods of getting others to comply. Indicate when flattery can backfire. Analyze the Godfrey, Jones, and Lord (1986) videotape study concerning the success rate of ingratiation attempts, and indicate how well ingratiation tactics work in applied contexts.

10. Understand what the "foot-in-the-door" method entails and the conditions under which it is likely to work or not. What are the two prominent explanations of why the method works, and what evidence supports their efficacy? How does developmental stage affect effectiveness of this method (Eisenberg, Cialdini, et al., 1987).

11. Know what goes into the "door-in-the-face" technique and the two explanations of why it works.

12. Discuss whether one of the two major compliance techniques has an advantage over the other. How do the time interval between requests, whether the two requests are made by the same or different persons, and the perceived legitimacy of the requester influence the effectiveness of the two methods differently?

13. Explain how "that's not all!" works by outlining the procedure and results of Burger's (1986) cookie-cupcake sale study, and indicate when TNA works and when it fails.

14. Explain the influential effects of complaints by reference to the study by Alicke, Braun, Glor, Klots, Magee, and Siegle (1992). List the categories of complaints discovered in this study, and indicate how well complaining works.

15. Describe Yukl and Falbe's (1990) results when they asked almost two hundred people what influence tactics they tended to use, and discuss whether the answers were different when another sample was asked what tactics were used on them. Consider the relative effectiveness of person-based versus position-based tactics.

16. Know the basic procedure that Stanley Milgram used to study obedience, what Milgram found in his most representative study and in the variations of it, the three primary reasons why people obey, and the four avenues to resistance.

17. Learn the roles of authoritarianism, locus of control, and religion in obedience.

18. Discuss the three prominent ways that obedience is explained, the importance of uniforms, and the four sources of resistance to obedience.

19. Consider early studies' results concerning gender differences in conformity. How did "knowledge of appropriate behavior" explain why one gender conformed more than the other in early studies (Sistrunk & McDavid, 1971)? Have times changed?

20. Know why the presumed status of women may be the reason some studies have shown more conformity by them, how Maupin and Fisher (1989) demonstrated the effect of equality or female superiority in early performance on changes in later opinion responses, and how the proportion of females in a group affect each gender's participation.

Discussion Questions

1. One day in class, begin arbitrarily to reseat class members. Giving no reason, curtly order some students to sit on the front row and others to sit in the back, some on the aisle and some in the center portion. Reshuffle again, until someone asks "Why?" Discuss what was going through subjects' minds as they were arbitrarily pushed and pulled about and why they complied. Was it thoughtless obedience? "To save you embarrassment?" To save themselves embarrassment by avoiding the question "Why?" Some hypothesis about your (the instructor's) reasons? Or responses to pres-

sure that seemed to be exerted by students who were obeying quickly and efficiently?

More generally, ask students what instructor characteristics and aspects of peer behavior led to initial obedience. Also, ask students under what circumstances might all or most of them refuse rather immediately or continue to obey without asking why. (One of our former colleagues, a behavior modification expert, ordered opposite-sexed students signed up for a weight-loss/B-mod class to disrobe in preparation for a weigh-in. They began to comply so quickly and in such large numbers that the colleague had trouble stopping them with assurances that it was just a joke!)

2. Begin a lecture talking in an unusually low voice approaching a whisper. Tape the session without students' knowledge by placing a tape recorder where you can see it but the students cannot—e.g., in an open attache case. Elicit questions and comments from class members. Subtly record the tape counter points at which given students' voices are recorded; also record the counter number when you terminate the taped session. As the lecture continues, slowly begin to raise your voice until it goes well above its normal level, again asking for questions and comments.

First, ask students if they were aware of anything unusual. Play the tape. Before revealing what is reflected on the tape, ask students if they are, at this point, aware of conforming to subtle pressure applied by you. Some will say yes; then ask them to indicate the form of their conformity. If they have trouble, cue them by making reference to your voice amplitude. Pick out a few students you have on the tape and ask each if he or she showed conformity. If a given one denies it, play the tape back for her or him. Now you are ready to talk about the sometimes unconscious nature of conformity. Playing the very beginning and the very ending of the tape will make your point and stimulate further discussion.

3. A class discussion of the ethical implications associated with the various "sales techniques" should be enlightening. Methods such as "door in the face" and "foot in the door" could be considered legal confidence games. The the way to avoid being duped by these methods is to understand at a commonsense level how the methods' users deceive us.

Just what are the deceptions involved with such methods? The answers come from a "real-life" understanding of the theoretical explanations for why these methods work. By probing students for "off-the-top-of-the-head" explanations, you can cause them to arrive at the theories.

For example, in regard to the "foot-in-the-door" technique, if a student says something like "He [the requester] is getting me to grant a small request so I'll look at myself and think 'I must be a pretty good person to help somebody out like this,'" point out the implications for self-perception. If another exclaims, "After I grant the first small request and she [the requester]

heaps lavish praise on me, she will expect that I'll get addicted to granting requests; then, zap, the big one comes," point out how this statement fits the "positive view of helping" explanation.

Use a similar strategy for "foot in the door." By probing for everyday explanations that fit the relevant theories, you will allow your students to gain a firsthand appreciation of sales techniques. More important, this level of awareness will allow them to resist these methods.

4. Have students discuss subtle methods of ingratiation, such as "encouraging other people to talk about themselves." Salespeople use these methods as well. Cue students concerning the "talk about self" method by asking, "If you wanted to get someone to feel good about themselves in your presence so you would get credit you could use at request time, but wanted to be sure that you didn't look like a flatterer, what could you do to pump up the person's ego?" If students don't come to the "let them talk about themselves" method right away, give a clue: "What would asking them questions about themselves do?"

Pointing out feelings in common with a client is a favorite example: On a hot and humid day, salesperson says to client, "Gee, I feel hot and sticky today. How about you, Mr. Mark?" You might cue this technique by asking students, "What social rule have you learned so far in this course that is a powerful cause of people liking each other?" The answer you are looking for is, of course, similarity. When some student identifies "similarity" one way or another—it's okay to expand on what they say a bit—ask students how they would establish similarity during a conversation with the "mark." Move them in the direction of pointing out trivial similarities—"so you're a Midwesterner too!"—that they can easily establish prior to a request. Have students think of additional methods of ingratiation. Include ones that backfire—for example, pointing out too many of one's negative traits during a self-disclosure session designed to make one look humble, or slavishly conforming to the mark's opinions.

This exercise may cause students to become conscious of their own, probably unconscious, attempts to manipulate others, and of their occasional victimization. To make sure they learn to protect themselves and avoid exploitive behavior, be sure to lead them in poking fun at these underhanded methods.

Classroom Exercises/Demonstrations

1. Before getting into the conformity material—and also before students read about it—tell your students that you would like to replicate an experiment on "aesthetics." You are interested in comparing results

obtained from former students enrolled in this class during a previous semester with those produced by your present students. Have them turn to the the Study Guide chapter 9 where they will find a set of numbered symbols grouped in 10 different sets. For each set, labeled A–J, pick one symbol at random (give the number of the column in which it is found) and tell students that it is the one picked as most interesting and intriguing by at least 80 percent of former students. (Be sure to note which you picked for each set.) Then ask the students to pick the symbol they think is the most interesting and intriguing, and circle it. Do this for all 10 sets. Then ask students to exchange sheets and to score each other's sheets. Beginning with set A, call out the "previous students' favorite" that you actually picked at random and tell them to circle the letter for the set (A) if the students whose sheets they are scoring made the same choice as the "previous students." Do the same for sets B–J. Then collect the sheets and count the number of sheets that have at least 6 of the 10 letters circled.

After explaining that actually the symbols were picked at random—you invented the other class's responses, and there is no evidence that any of the symbols are more interesting and intriguing than the others—you can report to the class the percentage of students who "agreed" with the phantom "previous students'" responses (number of students "agreeing" at least 6 out of 10 times divided by total number of students).

You may expect that at least 33 percent of students will have "gone along" in a majority of the ten cases. Explain to them how the "previous students" were "exerting pressure on them" to make the same choices as they supposedly made. Ask them for reflections, and be ready to entertain the subject of deception in social psychological experiments. (You may have to explain that telling the absolute truth and asking them to "pretend that some other students had made the [actually random] responses" would have generated attempts to appear uninfluenceable, rather than genuine responses on their part.)

2. Dr. Vivian Parker Makosky has identified three basic appeals used in advertising (in *Teaching of Psychology, 12*, February 1985, pp. 42–43). A straightforward and, according to her experience, fascinating demonstration for students involves locating magazine ads that represent examples of each kind of appeal, or combinations of them. The first of these appeals is "the appeal to or creation of needs." It is based on four of the needs in Maslow's hierarchy. Examples include "Aren't you hungry for Burger King now?" (physiological needs); "Get a piece of the rock" (safety and security needs); "Brush your breath with Dentine" (belongingness and love needs); and "When E. F. Hutton speaks . . ." (self-esteem and status needs). (Appeals to Maslow's cognitive, aesthetic, and self-actualization needs are much less common.)

The second group are "social and prestige suggestion" appeals—buy it because all kinds of people do. Examples include the "Pepsi generation" ad, the

Wrigley's Spearmint Gum ad, and other ads "featuring lots of people, in different types of clothes and/or settings, often of different ages and races . . ." (p. 43). Examples of "prestige suggestion" appeals—buy it because famous people do—are Michael Jordan for Wheaties, Michael J. Fox for Pepsi, and various famous athletes for light beer.

The third kind of appeal is "loaded words and images." "This technique is the most subtle because it is not what is said so much as how it is said, or what you are seeing while it is being said" (p. 43). Examples include ads with attractive, athletic people touting snacks like Snickers candy bars; the use of buzzwords such as "natural" for beauty products or foods, or "light" in order to make all kinds of foods seem dietetic; and the use of "images" associated with products, such as Harvey's Bristol Cream sherry as a symbol of the sophisticated life-style, BMW the emblem of wealth and status, or Ford (or Chevy) trucks the epitome of masculine good times.

Because the three categories of appeals each have subcategories, it is possible, and productive, to divide the class into groups, each to bring to class examples of some subcategory. The groups can then discuss their example ads in class, pick the best illustrative ads for their subcategory, decide why these ads are appropriate examples of their subcategory, and report to the class on their conclusions. Other questions for groups to consider: What kinds of ads appeal to men and what kinds to women? What kinds of ads may be true "turn-ons," and what kinds may actually backfire? What kinds of ads are most effective for what kinds of products? What kinds of ads are most effective for which age groups?

Or let them have some fun while they learn à la *Crazy People* with Dudley Moore, a movie about truth in advertising ("buy Metamucil, it will help you go to the toilet"; "your fear of flying may be valid . . . fly with us . . . more of our passengers arrive alive than any other airline"; "buy Volvo, it's boxy but it's good"). Have students rewrite some ads to bring their hidden appeals up front. Examples: "Buy a Whopper, it will fill you up and you won't be hungry for a long time." "Buy Coca Cola, because almost all cola drinkers do (except those who drink Pepsi)." "Buy Imperial 'Light' margarine so you won't be fat." "Buy a BMW so people will think you are rich, sporty, and sexy." "Eat Wheaties so you can be more like Michael Jordan."

3. Before getting into Milgram's research, briefly describe his basic study to students. A description like that in the book is adequate. Alternatively, show them one segment from Milgram's film (see the film list below) involving one subject in the standard experiment. In either case, don't reveal the proportion who obeyed. Rather, have students estimate how many out of 100 would obey, and whether they personally would

obey. (Let "obey" be defined as "go all the way to the last switch, the 450-volt switch".) The Study Guide contains the needed response sheet.

Ask students to indicate whether they had previously heard of or read about Milgram's work. Separate the responses into those who have heard of the Milgram research and those who have not. For both groups, determine students' estimates of how many people out of 100 will obey and compare to 65 percent. You will almost certainly find that students think that fewer than 65 percent of others would obey and that an even smaller proportion of themselves would obey, regardless of group. Students with prior information should come closer to estimating correctly the proportion of others who would obey, but such knowledge should not affect their estimates of their own behavior very much. (Predicted results are based on an instructor's use of this demonstration.)

4. Illustrate the "two-feet-in-the-door" technique. In one of your classes, pass out index cards. Ask students to write their phone numbers on the cards and place them in a receptacle by the door as they leave if they are willing to "donate two out-of-class hours of your time to a colleague's research project . . . unfortunately, there is no compensation".) In your social psychology class, ask your students to stay beyond class time, "just a couple of minutes," to help you with your research. After class, simply write a phone number on the board and indicate a time to call that is convenient to you or your assistant. Make sure that this process only takes a couple of minutes.

To those who call, ask whether they are willing to "donate two out-of-class hours of your time to a colleague's research project . . . unfortunately, there is no compensation." Compare the number of cards you collected with the number of affirmative answers from the social psychology students who called. The number of students who volunteer to participate in the two-hour out-of-class "research" should be greater for the social psychology class "sucked in" by compliance to the prior small requests for "two minutes after class" and the time it takes to make a phone call than for those in the other class who were given only the larger request for two out-of-class hours. Revelation of results and explanation of the "foot-in-the-door" technique should generate lively classroom discussion.

Film Notes: A Picture Is Sometimes Worth a Thousand Words

Allyn and Bacon Videos

Conformity, video, 28.5 mins. To obtain this video, consult your Allyn and Bacon sales representative. Robert A. Baron and Margaret Clark use dramatizations as points of departure for a discussion of conformity and other forms of social influence.

The Power of the Situation, 30 mins.; On Tape #10 of the series available through your Allyn and Bacon representative. This video tells how social psychologists attempt to understand human behavior within its broader social context, and how beliefs and behavior can be influenced and manipulated by other people and subtle situational forces.

Other Videos and Films

Obedience, U-60027, film, 50 mins. University of Iowa, Audiovisual, Iowa City, IA 52242. Perhaps the most significant media presentation ever produced about social psychology. Filmed excerpts from Milgram's actual obedience research contain an element of suspense, several surprises, and a nearly profound conclusion.

Conformity and Independence, 21885, film, 23 mins. Pennsylvania State University, Audiovisual Services, Special Services Building, University Park, PA 16802 (814-865-6314). Includes much in only twenty-three minutes: Sherif's experiments on norm formation, Asch's conformity research, Milgram's experiment on "action conformity," and some prominent theorists discussing their ideas.

Group Pressures, film, 25 mins. University Films of Canada, 7 Hyden Street, Suite 305, Toronto, Ontario, Canada M4Y 2P2. This film on laboratory and field research on conformity includes Asch's work.

Transparencies

Critical Thinking/Essay Questions

1. Give some everyday examples of conformity. Include some that are beneficial, some that are not, and at least one that involves conformity by a large majority.

2. Indicate some factors that promote group cohesiveness. When group cohesiveness is high, is the discrepancy between public compliance and private compliance likely to be great or small?

3. Explain why directing influence attempts to several targets instead of just one lowers the impact of those attempts. When one is in the minority, as the number of allies one has increases, what happens to one's impact on others?

4. Discuss the reasons why females have been seen as more conformist and the reasons why that perception is incorrect. As females gain in status within a group, what happens to usual assumptions about their degree of influenceability?

5. Contrast "normative social influence" and "informational social influence" by providing real-life examples of each.

6. Describe some famous people in history—other than those included in the text—who constituted minorities of one regarding some important issue. Be sure that at least one of them was a person who sought to be unique—to separate him- or herself from the majority—and that one exerted influence without creating obvious behavioral change during his or her own time.

7. Come up with a scheme to ingratiate yourself with a "boss"—a scheme different from those discussed in the book.

8. Contrast the foot-in-the-door and door-in-the-face techniques. Also, provide at least one real-life example for each that illustrates when each would likely fail.

9. Indicate how the "That's not all!" (TNA) method overlaps with the "door" techniques and is different from them.

10. Describe how you would alter the basic Milgram obedience procedure in order to lower obedience to near zero. The smaller the change you make and still have a good argument for near-zero obedience, the better your answer.

Sources for Lecture

Cookson, P., & Rersell, C. The price of privilege. (1986, March). *Psychology Today*, pp. 31–35. Money may be a rich child's ticket into an elite prep school, but once there, the child must often buy acceptance and success at the price of stifling conformity.

Cooper, M., & Soley, L. C. (1990, February-March). All the right sources. *Mother Jones*, pp. 20–26/45–48. Are the news media evenhanded and unbiased or, as many suspect, subtly designed to infuse the public mind with the points of view that are favored by whoever happens to be in power? A two-year study found that the "experts" typically interviewed by the major networks were more often spokes*men* for the status quo than unbiased analysts.

Nissani, M. (1990). A cognitive reinterpretation of Stanley Milgram's observations of obedience to authority. *American Psychologist, 45,* 1384–1385. This short "cognitive reinterpretation" asserts that Milgram's subjects, to be disobedient, would have had to undergo a "conceptual shift." Supposedly, they obeyed because they "knew" that nothing bad would happen and they believed in the morality of the experimenter. Only a shift from this position would allow disobedience.

Pines, M. (1981, May). Unlearning blind obedience in German schools. *Psychology Today.* Have the German people learned from the lessons of World War II? According to this 1981 article, the answer seemed to be yes.

Remley, A. (1988, October). From obedience to independence: Parents used to raise their children to be dutiful. *Psychology Today*, p. 54. The times have changed. Now parents are raising their children to be self-reliant, rather than obedient._

Sheridan, C., & King, R. (1974). Obedience to authority with an authentic victim. *Proceedings of the American Psychological Association Convention,* 165–166. What happens when a learner is actually shocked? Who obeys the most, males or females? See this paper for the answers.

Update: Current Articles from Professional Sources

Bond, C. F., Omar, A., Pitre, U., Lashley, B. R., Skaggs, L. M., & Kirk, C. T. (1992) Fishy-looking liars: Deception judgment from expectancy violation. *Journal of Personality and Social Psychology, 63,* 669–677. One of the ways that people attempt to influence other people is through lying to them. Subjects in the United States and in India viewed people describing acquaintances while performing weird behavior such as arm raising and staring. In both countries subjects inferred lying from weird behavior. That is, if people act weird when telling us something, we are apt to infer that they are lying to us.

Buck, R., Losow, J. I., Murphy, M. M., & Costanzo, P. (1992). Social facilitation and inhibition of emotional expression and communication. *Journal of Personality and Social Psychology, 63,* 962–968. Senders viewed provocative slides (e.g., with sexual content), and their video-recorded reactions constituted messages to receivers. Accuracy of receivers' guesses about slide content was a function of who was present during sending. When senders had a stranger present during recordings, accuracy of guessing slide content was inhibited. Friends, however, had a facilitory effect for some slides and an inhibitory effect for others.

Dillard, J. P. (1991). The current status of research on sequential-request compliance technique. *Personality and Social Psychology Bulletin, 17,* 283–288. Compares recent meta-analyses of foot-in-the-door research and door-in-the-face research, then tries to build a theoretical perspective that accounts for both.

Petty, R. E., Schumann, D. W., Richman, S. A., & Strathman, A. J. (1993). Positive mood and persuasion: Different roles for affect under high- and low-elaboration conditions. *Journal of Personality and Social Psychology, 64,* 5–20. Yes, positive mood tends to generate positive attitudes in the context of persuasive attempts, but the path through which it works can be Byzantine. If subjects do not have the opportunity to elaborate on thoughts associated with the persuasive attempt, the path is direct: Positive mood generates positive attitudes. If they can elaborate, the path is through positive thoughts created in the process of elaboration.

Prentice, D. A., & Miller, D. T. (1993). Pluralistic ignorance and alcohol use on campus: Some consequences of misperceiving the social norm. *Journal of Personality and Social Psychology, 64,* 243–256. "Pluralistic ignorance" is when everyone believes that everyone else believes something or other, but no one really does. In this case, students believed that the average student was relatively comfortable with campus alcohol practices compared with themselves. Male students shifted their attitudes about alcohol use in the direction of the position they mistakenly believed that other students held. That is, they were conforming to a norm that didn't exist.

Reno, R. R., Cialdini, R. B., & Kallgren, C. A. (1993). The transituational influence of social norms. *Journal of Personality and Social Psychology, 64,* 104–112. Two kinds of norms were investigated: descriptive norms specifying what is typically done in the setting, and injunctive norms specifying what is typically approved by society. The injunctive norm "It's wrong to litter" had more general impact: It suppressed littering in both clean and littered environments, and it worked in the setting where the norm was evoked as well as in a different setting.

Related Readings: The following selections from *Readings in Social Psychology: General, Classic, and Contemporary Selections,* 2nd Edition, by Wayne Lesko (Allyn & Bacon, 1993) accompany this chapter:

Gibson, J., & Haritor-Fatouros, M. (1986). The education of a torturer. This article begins by pondering the age-old question of whether people who torture and kill do so because they are monsters, ordinary people "just following orders," or the products of special training. The authors choose the latter and illustrate by an analysis of Greek torturers. (25)

Milgram, S. (1963). Behavioral study of obedience. This is the classic paper by Milgram on his research. It is certainly one of the most important research publications in the history of psychology. (26)

Blass, T. (1991). Understanding behavior in the Milgram obedience experiment: The role of personality, situations, and their interactions. Dr. Blass has become the current-day expert on Milgram's experiments and their implications, including for the Holocaust (see this article's reference list). Here Blass covers *situational* determinants of obedience in those experiments, resurrects *personality* variables as a factor, and concludes that the interaction of the two provides the most complete account. (27)

Chapter-at-a-Glance

Chapter Ten
Prosocial Behavior:
Providing Help to Others

Chapter Outline	Instruction Ideas	Supplements
Introduction	Exercise 1	CNN Video Segment 19: *Brooklyn Murders* and Segment 2, *Hurricane Volunteers, see* CNN Video Guide
I. Responding to an Emergency Bystander "Apathy" versus Diffusion of Responsibility / Providing or Not Providing Help: Five Necessary Cognitive Steps	Exercise 2 Discussion Questions 1 and 2 Critical Thinking Questions 1, 2, 8	Transparencies 10.1, 10.3, 10.6 Video: Helping and Prosocial Behavior Readings: Lesko 28—Who Will Help in a Crisis and Lesko 29—From Jerusalem to Jericho
II. Internal and External Factors that Influence Altruistic Behavior Role Models: Providing Helpful Cues / Emotions: Effects of Positive versus Negative Mood	Exercise 3 Discussion Question 3 Critical Thinking Questions 3, 4, 6, 9, 10	Transparency 10.5
III. Explanations of Prosocial Behavior Empathy-Altruism Theory: Unselfish Helping / Egoistic Theory: Helping Others Reduces Uncomfortable Feelings / Empathic Joy: An Alternative Egoistic Th eory / Genetic Selfishness: Helping Similar Others	Exercise 4 Discussion Question 4 Critical Thinking Questions 5 and 7	Transparency 10.2 Readings: Lesko 30—Noncompliance with Persuasive Appeals

Chapter Ten

Prosocial Behavior: Providing Help to Others

Chapter Outline: Getting the Overall Picture

I. Response to an Emergency: What Do Bystanders Do?
  A. Bystander "Apathy" versus Diffusion of Responsibility
  B. Providing or Not Providing Help: Five Necessary Cognitive Steps
    1. Attending to the Emergency
    2. Perceiving That an Emergency Exists
    3. Is It My Responsibility to Help?
    4. How to Help? Knowing What to do
    5. Deciding to Help
II. The Altruistic Personality: Dispositional Factors Associated with Helping Others
III. Internal and External Factors That Influence Altruistic Behavior
  A. Role Models: Providing Helpful Cues
  B. Emotions: Effects of Positive versus Negative Moods
    1. Positive Emotions
    2. Negative Emotions

C. AIDS Volunteerism: Motivation, Helping Experiences, and Consequences
D. Who Needs Help? Characteristics of the Victim
    1. Victim Responsibility
    2. Attraction
E. Who Asks for Help and How Does it Feel to be Helped?
    1. Asking for Help
    2. Reactions Being Helped
    3. Responding to Aid from a Sibling
IV. Explanations of Prosocial Behavior
  A. Empathy-Altruism Theory: Unselfish Helping
  B. Egoistic Theory: Helping Others Reduces Uncomfortable Feelings
  C. Empathic Joy: An Alternative Egoistic Theory
  D. Genetic Selfishness: Helping Similar Others
V. Help-seeking in Communal and Individualistic Cultures: Israel and Hong Kong
  A. Help-Seeking by Immigrants from the United States and the Soviet Union

Learning Objectives

1. Learn what "prosocial behavior" and "altruism" mean, and how these terms apply to the Texas Tower and Kitty Genovese cases. (Page 000)
2. Discuss "diffusion of responsibility." How is it a better explanation than "bystander apathy" for cases of failure to help? Appreciate how the "seizure" study demonstrates the "bystander effect" and how Lang's (1987) study defines six responses to an emergency that indicate a finer-graded continuum of helping than "helped" or "didn't help."
3. Learn the five steps to helping posed by Darley and Latane (1970). Why did seminary students fail to notice something unusual on their way to a talk on the Good Samaritan?

4. Explain the role of "potentially looking foolish" in failure to see a situation as an emergency, how ambiguity and "social comparison" play a role in assessment of a situation as an emergency, how "pluralistic ignorance" helps to explain the results of the "smoke study," and the roles of ambiguity and social acceptability in responses to the "lovers' quarrel" study (Shotland & Strau, 1976).
5. Show that the Schwartz and Gottlieb (1980) study demonstrates how perceived responsibility of the bystander contributes to helping, and indicate how competency influences whether or not one proceeds to help (Cramer et al., 1988].
6. Discuss the role of knowing the other bystanders in

whether observers of an emergency proceed to help, and explain why people who have been drinking alcohol are more likely to help.

7. List the components of the "altruistic personality" and the five basic measures upon which helpers at the scene of an automobile accident scored higher in the study by Bierhoff, Klein, and Kramp (1991).

8. Learn how altruistic role models affect observers' help rate. How does a nonhelpful model inhibit others' helping, and what happened to help rates when children watched shows like "Lassie" (Sprafkin et al., 1975) or "Sesame Street" (Forge & Phemister, 1987)?

9. Discuss the kinds of events that put people in an emotional state that increases their likelihood of helping. What is the exception to the rule that positive emotional states increase helping?

10. Tell when negative emotional states decrease helping and when they increase helping. (Hint: What are the three conditions in which negative mood is associated with helping?) Indicate the impact on helping of focusing on a negative mood or of focusing on victims of an emergency.

11. List the steps to helping AIDS victims and the tasks helpers can perform. What are the five motivations that lead to helping AIDS victims (Snyder & Omoto, 1992), and what are some motivations that inhibit helping AIDS victims?

12. Explain how a victim's responsibility for her or his plight can influence bystanders' help rate, the role of "repression" and "sensitization" in Thornton's (1992) study focusing on a young woman who was open to blame for her own rape, and the importance of attraction to the victim.

13. Indicate how shyness, similarity to the potential helper, and feelings of competency affect willingness to ask for help; how being helped affects the victim's self-esteem and future self-help; and the importance of liking the helper.

14. Appreciate Searcy and Eisenberg's (1992) hypothesis concerning how being helped by a younger or older male or female sibling affects the person helped. Be able to rank the possible combinations of gender and age of sibling helpers in terms of most to least threatening to those helped.

15. Outline what Doherty et al. (1990) found regarding attribution of motive for helping by the helper and by observers. Explain Batson's view that the development of empathic concern is crucial to altruism, discuss the general procedure of the studies by the Batson group that tested their theory of empathic altruism, and explain how subjects reacted when empathy was high versus low and escape was easy versus difficult.

16. Discuss the "negative state relief" hypothesis that Cialdini and colleagues invoked to explain helping. Why did Cialdini and colleagues (1987) indicate that the co-occurrence of sadness and empathy supported their theory, and how did the Batson group counter the Cialdini group's claim regarding co-occurrence?

17. Show how the "empathic joy" notion posed by Smith and colleagues (1989) explains the "helper's high" and the observation that positive affect accompanies helping, even when the helper is required to provide help.

18. Learn how feedback concerning the positive effects of helping may resolve the conflict between "empathic joy" and "altruistic" explanations of helping (Smith, Keating, & Shotland, 1989). What role does the victim's refusal to accept help play in resolving the "empathic joy"/"altruism" controversy (Cheuk & Rosen, 1992)?

19. Explain the evolutionary/sociobiological terms "selection," "the selfish gene," "maximizing inclusive fitness," "fitness," and "genetic selfishness." Tell why Rushton claims (1989a) we seek a similar spouse; indicate whether Rushton can answer the question, "How do we perceive that a candidate for help is similar?"; and outline criticisms of Rushton (concerning whether superficial similarities mean genetic similarity, and questioning the accuracy of "story telling").

20. Appreciate the difference between a "communal" and an "individualistic" culture. What did Nadler (1986) find regarding help seeking among kibbutz dwellers compared to city dwellers in Israel, and how does a communal versus an individualistic orientation explain different behaviors on the part of city versus kibbutz inhabitants during an anagram task?

21. Discuss Shek and Cheung's (1990) findings regarding uniformity or diversity in communal versus individualistic behavior of Hong Kong residents, define "locus of coping" and indicate how it relates to communal versus individualistic behavior, and explore these researchers' conclusions concerning differences within and between cultures on help-related orientation.

Discussion Questions

1. In 1904, industrialist Andrew Carnegie founded the Carnegie Hero Fund with an endowment of $5 million. The purpose of the fund is to reward heroes who risk their own lives in efforts to save the lives of others.

Since 1904 more than 63,000 people have been nominated for heroism awards, but only 7,313 (about 11 percent) have been chosen to receive them. Of those chosen for awards, 91 percent have been males. Each recipient is awarded $2,500, accompanied by a bronze medal inscribed with the New Testament verse: "Greater love hath no man than this, that a man lay down his life for his friends." More than 1,500 Carnegie heroes, or roughly 21 percent, have died performing their rescues, the most common cause being drownings or fires. In these cases additional monetary compensation is often provided in the form of pensions for beneficiaries, funeral expenses, and scholarships for surviving dependents.

Candidates are excluded from awards if they are obligated to act because of their occupation, such as fire fighter or lifeguard. A person who rescues a family member is also excluded, unless the rescuer is severely injured or killed. A candidate is not excluded for failing to save the person's life; the awards are for those who risk their *own* lives in an effort to save others.

Discuss the issue of heroism with the class. In conjunction with the discussion, watch the news for actions that are described as "heroic." Students respond positively to current examples. Ask the students to define *heroism,* and get them to list the criteria they would use to grant Carnegie awards. Finally, compare the definition of *hero* with the text's definition of *prosocial behavior.*

2. Who is more likely to help others in need, an urban dweller or a person who lives in a small town? Where is a person more likely to be helped, in the city or in the country?

Most of the social psychological research indicates that small-town residents are more likely than city dwellers to help. The kinds of help studied have varied considerably, including such actions as helping people who called the wrong phone number, giving back overpayments to customers, mailing lost letters, buying greeting cards from the Multiple Sclerosis Society, helping to pick up dropped envelopes, and correcting inaccurate directions. If you want to read on this topic, studies by Amato (1983) in the *Journal of Personality and Social Psychology* (*45,* 571–586) and by Korte and Kerr (1975) in the *Journal of Social Psychology* (*95,* 183–184) would be helpful. In any case, you can relate the kinds of help-needed situations that are likely to occur in real life (e.g., car has flat tire, person passes out, auto breaks down, someone needs change) so that students have a knowledge sufficient for discussion.

Having primed students with this information, you can ask them to relate their experiences of helping, being helped, or watching others being helped or not. As our university has a mix of urban and rural students,

we are always able to get reports from students that are interesting and illuminating to other students and allow an urban/rural comparison. You will probably also get a variety of reports, and enough from both urban and rural students, to compare helping behavior in the country and the city.

3. The research conducted by social psychologists has generally dealt with helping that occurs in response to an immediate, short-term need. Researchers create a "victim" and systematically vary aspects of the situation to determine their impact on helping. A logical question is whether the results of these short-term studies adequately explain long-term helping, particularly long-term helping carried out despite great danger and cost to the helper. An example is the behavior of persons who hid Jews from the Nazis in occupied countries during World War II. To have been caught in this humanitarian effort could have resulted in death for the helper. Is this type of long-term, carefully planned altruism caused by different factors than the help that occurs in short-term emergency situations? Have students speculate on how the psychological dynamics may be different for these extraordinary helpers. Here individuals know that helping on one occasion will increase rather than decrease the likelihood of future requests for help from victims. In fact, help on the first occasion commits the helper to supplying aid for an indefinite period of time, exactly the opposite of the usual short-term help circumstance. Also ask students how well these long-term helpers, whose lives are continually at risk, fit the egotistic/self-serving theories of helping.

4. Focus on those theories that claim people help because there is always something in it for them—distress reduction, self-esteem enhancement, and so forth. Generate a debate among students: Is there any such thing as altruism untainted by self-centered need fulfillment? Start the debate by asking if there is anyone who is willing to argue that the reason people help is to get something out of it. Ask if some other person will take the other side: argue that people can and do help others solely to benefit them, not for personal gain at any level of abstraction. If you can induce these two volunteers to debate, other students will surely break in to support or challenge one debater or the other.

1. In chapter 10 of your students' Study Guide you will find descriptions of several situations that may or may not show prosocial behavior. Have the students respond to these items individually and then poll the class to

Classroom Exercises/Demonstrations

find out how many students considered each item to be prosocial. You will find that there is considerable disagreement whether most of the situations represent prosocial behavior. Go through the items one at a time, asking students who indicated that the situation was not

prosocial behavior to explain why. The ensuing discussion should help students to develop a better idea of the meaning of prosocial behavior, and also to appreciate the difficulty of determining underlying motivation for behavior.

2. Rushton et al. (1981) devised a scale to measure helpfulness in which subjects provide an estimate of the frequency with which they have performed various concrete helping acts. The Self-Report Altruism Scale, found in chapter 10 of the Study Guide, is a twenty-one-item scale requiring respondents to estimate the number of times they have performed such acts as making change for another, donating blood, holding the door open for someone, and so forth. Have the students respond to the scale anonymously, then score it by adding the responses to the twenty-one items. Display the average (or median) reported performance of each prosocial behavior included on the scale. Do the students as a whole show social desirability (all tend to show high levels of helpfulness)? If so, talk about their sincere perceptions of being helpful and the fact of nonhelpfulness in real-life settings when, among other considerations, there are meaningful consequences to helping. To some degree the students will show more of an inclination to help in terms of some items than others. Ask them to explain why helping is more likely in some situations than in others.

3. Consider offering students extra points applicable to final grades if they will go out into the real world and create help-needed situations. Be cautious about what they propose to do. Have them run all proposals by you before they are allowed to execute them. There are many simple scenarios that can be enacted. For example, have them volunteer to collect money for some real organization (of course, they would get prior permission from the organization). They could collect while dressed up as they would be to attend church or go to a sales job. Then have them dress very casually and conduct the same collection. Does the amount of money collected differ across the two conditions? Another possibility is to leave an auto's lights on and doors open in a variety of settings. In what kinds of settings do passers-by stop, open a door, and turn out the lights, thus preserving the battery? Or students could ask for directions while well dressed or dressed like a "street person." Perhaps some African-American and some European-American students could panhandle at the same sites on alternate days and compare results. How about the tone of the help request? Students could enter some local government office asking for information that should be available, using either a polite voice or a cold and subtly demanding tone. Students might find it interesting to make requests of local offices identifying themselves either as students or as nonstudents. There are a variety of interesting alternatives.

4. Demonstrate that children can learn prosocial behavior by observing a model. If yours is a fairly large, urban college or university class, you will have students with children aged two to five. Have one of them bring a child to class. Stage a help-needed situation. Perhaps, in front of the class (or in private, if you can arrange a videotaping session outside of class), have one adult drop something, such as a stack of small paperback books. The child's parent would then help pick up the books. The scene may have to be repeated, even several times (if an audience is present, warn them in advance not to laugh). Will the child join in the task of picking up the books? Alternatively, for extra credit, have a student go into a local preschool and stage a similar scene. The school may be glad to have the student teach prosocial behavior to its pupils. Results could be reported back to the class.

Film Notes: A Picture Is Sometimes Worth a Thousand Words

Allyn and Bacon Videos

* *Helping and Prosocial Behavior,* videotape, 28.5 mins. To obtain this tape, consult your Allyn and Bacon sales representative. Using dramatizations as a stimulus, Robert A. Baron and Margaret Clark discuss the mechanisms behind helping or not helping.

Other Videos and Films

Aspects of Behavior, color film also available on video, 30 mins. CRM Films, 2233 Faraday Avenue, Carlsbad, CA 92008 (800-421-0833). The social psychology section is about ten minutes. This film includes an excellent portrayal of the smoke-filled room study by Latane and Darley. Interviews with Latane and Darley on the bystander effect and with Milgram on city living are also included.

Invitation to Social Psychology, color film, portion on helping approximately 5 mins. Harper & Row Media, 10 E. 53rd Street, New York, NY 10022. John Darley and Bibb Latane discuss bystander apathy.

Social Modification of Organically Motivated Behavior, silent, 12 mins. Indiana University, Audiovisual Center, Bloomington, IN 47401. Hungry rats display both altruistic and competitive behavior.

When Will People Help? The Social Psychology of Bystander Intervention, 25 mins. Harcourt, Brace, & Jovanovich, 757 Third Avenue, New York, NY 10017. Daryl Bem is narrator for reenactments of some of the early Latane and Darley studies, including the smoke-filled room study and the seizure study.

Transparencies

10.1 *Good Samaritan Road Map*
10.2 *Helping As a Function of Empathy and Empathic Arousal*
10.3 *Six Levels of Helpfulness–Unhelpfulness*
10.4 *Components of the Altruistic Personality*
10.5 *Motivations Underlying AIDS Volunteerism*

Critical Thinking/Essay Questions

1. Discuss why "bystander apathy" was so readily accepted by the press and the public when cases of failure to help began to appear regularly in the media. Why are we so pessimistic?

2. Examine the "five steps to helping." Are these all that are needed? Can you add some? If not, consolidate the five steps into just three.

3. Indicate the essential qualities of the victim that would maximize her/his likelihood of being helped. What are the traits that would greatly lower the probability a person would get help in an emergency?

4. Construct three scenarios where help is needed. Be sure to make them quite different from each other. Outline how successful help requests would have to differ for the three situations.

5. Argue either for the "pure altruism" point of view (people help for selfless reasons) or for one of the theories that asserts that people help because there is "something in it for them."

6. Think up some help-needed situations in which positive mood would facilitate helping and some in which negative mood would be facilitative. Be sure to tell how these situations are different in such a way that one kind of mood or the other is facilitative.

7. Become a sociobiologist and argue that people help in order to "promote their genes." Exactly who will be helped if this theory is sound? In what situations will they be helped? In what ways will they be helped?

8. Paint a picture of the altruistic personality. What would be the essential characteristic of a person who would reliably help others who suffer emergencies?

9. Make some suggestions concerning how to motivate people to volunteer for work with AIDS victims. How would you reassure them? How would you convince them that their help is vitally important?

10. Imagine you have some preschool children in your charge. Map out a strategy to teach them to be helpers. Of course, you will have to show them when help is needed and what help is appropriate and possible for them to carry out. Tell how role models would be useful and how children's natural empathic responses (e.g., if one child cries, others will follow suit) might be called into play.

Sources for Lecture

Devore, I., & Morris, S. (1977). The science of genetic self-interest. *Psychology Today,* February, pp. 42–51, 84–88. Describes the selfishness "built into our genes" from a sociobiological point of view.

Fogelman, E., & Weiner, V. L. (1985). The few, the brave, the noble. *Psychology Today,* August, pp. 60–65. During World War II some people risked their lives to save Jews from Nazis. Why? Some were motivated by deep moral values, whereas others were motivated by personal attachments or identification with the victim.

Kohn, A. (1988). Beyond selfishness. *Psychology Today,* October, pp. 34–38. We start helping others early in life, though we're not always consistent. What makes us helpful sometimes and sometimes not?

Luks, A. (1988). Helper's high. *Psychology Today,* October, pp. 39–42. The author asserts that people feel physically and emotionally good when they help others. In the same manner that running promotes inner calm, helping is said to promote good health.

Pines, M. (1979). Good Samaritans at age two? *Psychology Today,* June, pp. 66–77. Examines altruistic behavior in very young children. Some babies as young as one are capable of comforting others who are in pain or are crying. More sophisticated behaviors are demonstrated before age three.

Shotland, R. L. (1985). When bystanders just stand by. *Psychology Today,* June, pp. 50–55. The author reviews the literature on personal and situational factors that determine whether a bystander will help a crime victim.

Update: Current Articles from Professional Sources

Clark, M. S. (Ed.). (1991). *Prosocial behavior* in the series *Review of personality and social psychology.* Newbury Park, CA: Sage Publications. Review of prosocial behavior research. Features chapters by some of the major contributors to the area, including Daniel Batson, Mark Snyder, Arie Nadler, Peter Salovey, Sam Gaertner, John Dovidio, Jane Piliavin, and John M. Darley.

Collins, W. A., & Kuczaj, S. A. (1991). *Developmental psychology.* New York: MacMillan. Contains an unusually complete and readable section on prosocial behavior in children.

Corey, G., Corey, M. S., & Callanan, P. (1993). *Issues and ethics in the helping professions.* Pacific Grove, CA: Brooks/Cole. Three practicing help professionals relate their experiences with moral and ethical issues endemic to the health professions. People needing help are vulnerable and can be wounded easily. This book tells how to avoid doing more harm than good.

Corey, M. S., & Corey, G. (1993). *Becoming a helper.* Pacific Grove, CA: Brooks/Cole. Two noted help professionals tell how to become an effective helper. Covers the dos and don'ts of aiding various people in need (e.g., AIDS patients) and avoiding "burnout."

Eisenberg, N. (1992). *The caring child.* Cambridge, MA: Harvard University Press. Provides as near a complete understanding of the motivations behind prosocial behaviors in children and how these motives develop and are elicited in various situations as is currently available.

Krebs, D. L., Denton, K. L., Vermeulen, S. C., Carpendale, J. I., & Bush, A. (1991). Structural flexibility of moral judgment. *Journal of Personality and Social Psychology, 61,* 1012–1023. Thirty men and thirty women responded to two of the dilemmas in Kohlberg's Moral Judgment Interview and to a prosocial dilemma as well as an impaired-driving dilemma. Half of them responded to the prosocial and impaired-driving dilemmas from the perspective of a hypothetical character, and half responded from their own perspective. No sex or perspective differences in moral maturity were observed. Subjects scored highest on Kohlberg's dilemmas, intermediate on the prosocial dilemma, and lowest on the impaired-driving dilemma.

Related Readings: The following selections from *Readings in Social Psychology: General, Classic, and Contemporary Selections,* 2nd Edition, by Wayne Lesko (Allyn and Bacon, 1993) accompany this chapter:

Darley, J. M., & Latane, B. (1968). When will people help in a crisis? The authors describe their classic work on the bystander effect and examine the steps an intervener must go through in order to explain when help will be given. (28)

Darley, J. M., & Batson, D. (1973). "From Jerusalem to Jericho": A study of situational and dispositional variables in helping behavior. Seminary students, some of them on their way to give a talk on the "good Samaritan," encountered a shabbily dressed person slumped by the wayside. Religious and personality variables, and whether they were to give a talk or not, failed to predict helping. (29)

Ferrari, J. R., & Leippe, M. R. (1992). Noncompliance with persuasive apppeals for a prosocial, altruistic act: blood donating. Most people can't be persuaded to give blood (only an average of about 13 percent gave in these studies). Yet the ones who do give are low on responsibility denial. (30)

Chapter-at-a-Glance

Chapter Eleven
Aggression:
Its Nature, Causes, and Control

Chapter Outline	Instruction Ideas	Supplements
Introduction	Exercise 3	CNN Video Segment 21: *Private Arsenals,* Segment 22, *Children and Violence,* Segment 23, *Women Combat Plots,* Segment 24, *Domestic Violence* *see CNN* Video Guide
I. Theoretical Perspectives on Agression: In Search of the Roots of Violence Aggression As an Innate Tendency / Aggression As an Elicited Drive: The Motive to Harm or Injure Others / Aggression As a Reaction to Aversive Events: The Role of Negative Affect Aggression As Learned Social Behavior	Exercise 1 and 3 Critical Thinking Question 1	Reading: Lesko 2—Social Psychology and Science
II. Social Determinants of Aggression: How Others' Actions, or Our Understanding of Them, Influence Aggression Frustration: Why Not Getting What You Want (and What You Expect) Can Sometimes Lead to Aggression / Direct Provocation: When Aggression Breeds Aggression / Exposure to Media Violence: The Effects of Witnessing Aggression / Heightened Arousal: Emotion, Cognition, and Aggression / Sexual Arousal and Aggression: Are Love and Hate Really Two Sides of the Same Behavioral Coin? / The Effects of Violent Pornography: Aggressive Actions, Hardened Attitudes / Alcohol and Aggression: A Potentially—But Not Necessarily—Dangerous Mix	Exercises 1 and 2 Discussion Questions 1 and 4 Critical Thinking Questions 2–7	Transparencies 11.1, 11.3, 11.4, 11.6 Readings: Lesko 31—Why Violent Toys Are Good for Kids and Lesko 32— Transmission of Aggression
III. Personal Causes of Aggression The Type A Behavior Pattern / Perceiving Evil Intent in Others: Hostile Attributional Bias / Shame-Proneness and Aggression: From Self-Rejection to Hostility and Anger / Gender Differences in Aggression: Are They Real?	Exercise 4 Discussion Question 2 Critical Thinking Questions 8 and 10	
IV. The Prevention and Control of Aggression: Some Useful Techniques Punishment: An Effective Deterrent to Violence? / Catharsis: Does Getting It Out of Your System Really Help? / Cognitive Interventions: The Role of Apologies and Accounts / Other Techniques for Reducing Aggression: Nonaggressive Models, Training in Social Skills, and Incompatible Responses	Discussion Question 3 Critical Thinking Questions 9 and 10	Transparencies 11.3 Readings: Lesko 33—The Control of Aggression

Chapter Eleven

Aggression: Its Nature, Causes, and Control

Chapter Outline: Getting the Overall Picture

Learning Objectives

1. Discuss instinct theory and relate it to "sociobiology." Indicate the problems with these points of view, and outline "drive theories" as well as the related "frustration-aggression hypothesis." (page 000)

2. Learn the "cognitive neoassociationist" view, examine the "social learning" position, learn how culture determines the forms of aggression, and describe the content of three orientations to aggression.

3. How has aggression been studied with Arnold Buss's "aggression machine," and how is Stuart Taylor's method different? What are the criticisms of these methods?

4. Outline the "frustration-aggression" hypothesis; its limitations; the role of unexplained, illegitimate frustration; and Buss's belief concerning why frustration doesn't always lead to aggression.

5. Learn the role of direct provocation in generating aggression, what actions provoke aggression, the roles of reciprocity and intentionality in provocation, and how mitigating circumstances impact the likelihood of aggression after provocation.

6. How do the early and later laboratory studies, field studies—including interviews with moviegoers—and long-term follow-ups of children exposed to TV violence support the assertion "media exposure increases violent tendencies"?

7. Consider whether the presence of "aggressive cues" (guns) influences aggressiveness, the evidence for and against an affirmative answer to this question, the four avenues through which the media influence aggressiveness, and how the study of "interest in seeing violent films" (Langely et al., 1992) supports the "priming effect."

8. In what state is "excitation transfer" maximal, and how does emotional arousal affect aggressiveness? How does Zillmann's two-factor theory of "excitation transfer" explain the effects of "heightened arousal"?

9. Learn about the effect of cognition on arousal, how Zillmann and Cantor (1976) show the influence of mitigating circumstances on the relationship between these factors, and how arousal affects cognition.

10. Differentiate between the effects of mild and strong sexual arousal, and examine Zillmann's two-phase model for explaining sexual arousal effects. What is "violent pornography"? Indicate two ways it can predispose people to violence, and examine the Demare, Briere, and Lipa (1988) investigation of tendency to rape and inclination to watch depictions of violence against women.

11. How does being drunk affect aggressiveness, both in real life and in the lab? Discuss how Taylor and Sears's (1988) procedures helped them show that alcohol makes people more subject to social influence but allows continued cognitive monitoring. Outline the effects of alcohol in nonthreatening situations and when a helpless victim is present.

12. Compare Type A's to Type B's regarding aggression. Contrast A drivers to B drivers (Evans et al., 1987); indicate how "hostile attributional bias" affects aggressiveness, in particular in children at play and in adolescents in a maximum security prison; and in the latter case, compare effects for reactive and proactive aggression (Dodge et al., 1990).

13. Differentiate shame and guilt, and tell how shame affects subsequent aggression. Describe what Tangney et al. (1992) found when they measured shame-proneness along with irritability, anger, and tendency to be aggressive, and indicate what makes shame-prone people be aggressive.

14. Indicate the extent of gender difference in aggressiveness. What kinds of aggressive acts does one gender shows more than the other? What did Bjorkqvist et al. (1992) find regarding gender differences in kinds of aggression as a function of age? Discuss whether gender differences are due to biology or culture.

15. Examine the role of testosterone in aggression, what Gladue (1991) found in a study of aggressiveness in gay and straight males and females as a function of testosterone levels, and whether any biologically determined proneness to aggression in males means they *must* be more aggressive.

16. List the conditions that must be met if punishment is to deter aggression successfully. Are these conditions commonly met? Does cathartic activity work to lessen aggression? Does catharsis through vicarious aggression (for example, watching a violent movie) lessen aggression? Does catharsis through attacks on inanimate objects or through verbal aggression lessen aggression?

17. Indicate the effectiveness of apologies and excuses offered by offenders in reducing aggression against them. Outline the effects of nonaggressive models on observers' aggression, and tell how a lack of basic social skills affects aggressiveness.

18. Examine the results of Schneider's (1991) study of social skills training for conduct-disordered children. Describe "incompatible responses" and how they interfere with aggressiveness.

19. Learn how the microculture explains the greater violence of one Mexican village compared to an almost identical neighboring village, and how stereotyping regarding aggressiveness affects relations between two highly similar Italian villages.

20. Outline the results of Kaufman et al.'s (1990) study comparing aggressiveness of Anglo and Hispanic children who were frustrated by minority status.

Contrast Japanese and Israeli customs regarding the expression of aggression in and outside the family.

Discussion Questions

1. A popular movie starring Jody Foster was based on an actual incident involving gang rape. In the actual case, four men raped a twenty-one-year-old mother of two for 120 agonizing minutes while fellow patrons at a New Bedford, Massachusetts, bar cheered the attackers and taunted the victim. No one helped the victim, but two men were accused of assisting the rapists.

At first there was sympathy for the victim. About 2,500 to 4,000 people joined a candlelight procession in protest of the outrage, and a local women's group began organizing a rape crisis center and sensitivity training for police officers. Letters arrived containing expressions of understanding and money for the victim. But then the local mood grew into something different. Although her identity was unknown, callers to a local talk show claimed that the victim was actually a prostitute who "got what she deserved."

There are at least two potentially interesting topics for discussion here. First, the label "prostitute" suggests the victim was looking for sex and, thus, got what she was seeking. That is, rape is a sexual act. If rape is sexual, then some women might be seen as getting what they were looking for. But what if rape is assumed to be an act of violence? Would any reasonable person assert that there are women who go forth seeking to be humiliated, beaten, and dehumanized?

Second, the attribution of "prostitute" to the victim can be viewed as supporting the "just world hypothesis." In the just world, you get what you deserve and deserve what you get (see the writings of psychologist Melvin J. Lerner). By believing in the "just world," New Bedford citizens could reason that "a bad thing happened to the rape victim, because she is a bad and careless person; I'm good and careful and thus need not worry." In this second case, discussion could center on how belief in the "just world" promotes violence by destroying sympathy for victims of aggression.

2. Discuss the multitude of ways that parents teach aggression to their children. Besides what is implied by information in the text, consider subtle methods such as permitting aggressive acts and thus tacitly approving of aggression. Also, consider the subtle ways parents communicate that aggression is appropriate for male children, but not for female children.

3. Discuss methods of controlling aggression in addition to those included in the text. For example, imagine a parent recoiling with horror at discovering his or her two children mutually masturbating. Would people aggress very often if every time they did, witnesses reacted with similar repugnance? What would happen if people stopped patronizing violent movies and clicked off their TVs when violent programs were scheduled? What if football and hockey game attendance dropped dramatically? What if public figures were as roundly condemned and as thoroughly ruined for acts like punching a photographer as were some members of the British royalty for their sexual escapades?

4. During the late 1980s several appalling incidents occurred on the highways of California. July 30: A teenager motorist was shot dead while driving away from an argument involving his passenger. The death brought fifty California police agencies onto the freeways in a show of force. August 3: Between June 18 and August 3 there had been sixteen shooting incidents on the nation's highways. Ninety percent of the shootings had involved handguns. On August 3, in Sun Valley, a tanker truck was hit by gunfire coming from occupants of a green Chevy panelvan. Soon after the tanker incident, a motorist ran afoul of the van and received gunfire. Another van was the source of gunfire in a separate occurrence. Still later, a motorist reported drawing fire from a van with tinted windows.

These actual incidents further illustrate the authors' point that something about being behind the wheel brings out aggression in drivers. Philip Zimbardo's theory of deindividuation suggests that the driver and passengers of one vehicle constitute an antagonistic group in opposition to drivers and passengers of other vehicles. Further, tinted windows, enclosed vans, and sunglasses make occupants of different vehicles anonymous to one another. Add the arousal that comes from driving under congested and competitive conditions, the noise of the crowded freeway, fatigue after a day's work (most shooting incidents have been in the afternoon), and the presence of alcohol in the systems of some drivers, and all the ingredients for aggression on the highway are in the mix. Describe the above incidents to students and ask them if they know of others. Then ask them to come up with the conditions, listed above, that contribute to aggression on the highway. Finally, offer them the opportunity to suggest ways to avoid aggression among motorists.

Classroom Exercises/Demonstrations

1. Under the guise of conducting an "impression formation" demonstration, have each class member stand up in front of the class and present name, home town, major, and favorite hobbies to other students. For each presentation, have other students write a few lines on scratch paper giving their impression of the speaker. On each sheet of notes have students identify themselves and the speakers by name. A few days later, pass back a few "impressions of you" to each student, implying that the choices of impressions were random. Among the bits of feedback each student receives will be a contrived description with the name of a collaborator from among class members. For half the students, the bogus "impression" will be very positive, and for the others very negative. Collect these from students at the end of class so they can't compare notes. Some time later announce that in the interest of studying persuasive communication a student has volunteered to read a paper just completed for a communications class. Have the collaborator, whose name was on the bogus positive or negative impression received by each student, give his or her name and read the paper as a persuasive attempt. Students should then "evaluate" the communicator with the favorability scale presented in the Study Guide chapter 11. You can just sum over agreement scores for each student and compare mean agreement for the positive and negative groups (just calculate the two means and display them or compare them with a simple t-test). Separating the evaluations of the communicator by students given a positive "impression" by him or her from those by students given a negative "impression" will allow you to demonstrate how provocation can lead to aggression expressed in the form of negative evaluations.

2. Consider the appreciation of "mitigating circumstances" in alleviating the need to respond to others' aggressive acts. After all, aggression is often a response to someone else's hostile acts. For the class in which this exercise is to be done, recruit a student you know reasonably well. On test day, have the student come up during a test to complain about items, using moderate amplitude of voice tone. At the end of the test, have the student slam her or his test down and stomp out of the room, complaining loudly about the "unfair items" and unreasonable professor as he or she departs. Exclaim, "Wonder what's wrong with him (or her)?"

Next class, have students respond to the Understanding Aggression Form. (It might be a good idea to have the student who attacked your test be absent on the day the form is completed, at least until the exercise is over.) The form, found in the Study Guide, is designed to create insights concerning mitigating circumstances. Have the class use the form to analyze the angry student's reactions to the test. Tally the results up on the board under the categories used on the form: (1) reasons for the aggression relating to the target of aggression (you, the instructor, in this case); (2) reasons relating to the aggressor's relationships with people other than the target; (3) reasons relating to the aggressor's feelings about himself or herself and his or her skills and efforts. Use a representative sampling of responses in each category; otherwise there will be too many reactions to write on the board and too much for students to appreciate. When the total picture is displayed on the board, step back and say, "Here are three possible categories of reasons for the student's behavior toward me after the last test. If you knew that I had decided to retaliate against the student in some way—I may scold the student the next time I see him/her—which category would you guess that I had assumed contains the real reasons for the student's behavior?" Students should tend to choose the reasons in category 1. If they don't, you may ask questions like, "Why would I retaliate if I knew that the student's aggression had nothing to do with me; it was caused by a quarrel with a lover?" (or "test anxiety"; or "lack of self-confidence"). The point is to show students that targets of aggression are unlikely to resort to aggression themselves if they know that the person who has attacked them has done so for reasons unrelated to them.

3. Psychologist Ludy T. Benjamin of Texas A&M University has devised a method for providing insightful answers to the question, "What is aggression?" (See Benjamin [1985], Defining aggression . . . *Teaching of Psychology, 12,* 40–42.) The method allows students to define aggression for themselves through an ingenious exercise. On a list of twenty-five statements, students simply anonymously check all statements that they believe indicate aggressive acts (form included in the Study Guide). Then have them pass in their lists of statements, shuffle them, and redistribute them to the class. (With this procedure students don't necessarily call out their own responses and can thereby avoid embarrassment.) For each statement get a show of hands as to how many students thought the statement indicated aggression. Write on the board only those statements that at least 80 percent saw as indicating aggression or that 20 percent or fewer saw as indicating aggression (number of hands divided by the number of students present). Now you can take up issues such as "does aggression involve harm to living versus nonliving things?" (items 9 and 23); "accident versus intention?" (8, 11); "actual damage versus no physical damage?" (10, 13, 18); "self-defense?" (3, 13, 14); "duty or job responsibility?" (3, 4, 19, 20, 22); "predation and instinctual behavior?" (1, 2, 25) "survival?" (1, 6, 16); "acts involving animals other than humans?" (7, 16, 17, 18); "covert acts?" (11, 14); "inaction?" (12, 15); "self-

injury?" (24); and "killing for sport?" (17, 25).

4. The entire constellation of Type A behavior was once thought to put Type A people at risk for health problems. More currently, however, Type A behavior in and of itself is not believed to be the factor that puts its possessors at risk. Rather, the problem is a single trait that is part of the constellation of Type A traits: hostility. Psychiatrist Redford Williams of Duke University has developed a measure of hostility that may predict health problems (included in the Study Guide). Have students complete his questionnaire anonymously. Those who answer two out of three questions with "often" or "always" may consider themselves at risk. They may also be people so prone to hostile orientation to others that they are in danger of in some way harming important people in their lives and destroying social relations with them.

You could simply collect the questionnaires and tally the number of students who show destructive levels of hostility. This should provide a benchmark so that other students could evaluate how they stand relative to other students. Then have them respond to Williams's "Twelve Steps to a More Trusting (and healthy) Heart," also in the Study Guide. Students could check all those statements that represent steps they feel confident they could take. This second part of the exercise will sensitize students concerning how to avoid hostility and reassure those who scored "at risk" for health and social relations problems that they have a way to deal with their hostility.

Film Notes: A Picture Is Sometimes Worth a Thousand Words

Allyn and Bacon Video

* *Aggression*, video, 28.5 mins. To obtain this tape, see your Allyn and Bacon sales representative. Robert A. Baron, an expert on the topic, and Margaret Clark use dramatizations as a basis for a discussion on aggression.

Other Videos and Films

Black on Black Violence, FC1932, video, 26 mins. Films for the Humanities & Sciences, Inc., P.O. Box 2053, Princeton, NJ 08543 (800-257-5126). An American black male has a 1 in 29 chance of being murdered; for white men, the odds are 1 in 186. This video explores the reasons for the difference.

Rape: An Act of Hate, FC1055, video, 30 mins. Films for the Humanities & Sciences, Inc. P.O. Box 2053, Princeton, NJ 08543 (800-257-5126). Veronica Hamel of "Hill Street Blues" seeks to determine why people rape and to help potential victims protect themselves.

Sexual Harassment: From 9 to 5, FC1711, video, 26 mins. Films for the Humanities & Sciences, Inc., P.O. Box 2053, Princeton, NJ 08543 (800-257-5126). The motivations for sexual harassment and rape have much in common. In this video, some men of the business world couldn't understand that "no!" meant "no!" until they were sued. How employees are taught the difference between romance, harassment, and sexual extortion is a major feature.

Violence in the Family, PB81, video, 55 mins. Insight Media, 121 W. 85th Street, New York, NY 10024-4401 (800-233-9910). Those who don't believe that violence starts at home (literally) will be convinced by this video.

Human Aggression, film, 22 mins. Associated Films, Inc., 512 Burlington Avenue, La Grange, IL 60525 (312-352-3377). This film features several well-known aggression researchers and some other public figures. Activities of an actual youth gang provide the opener.

The Question of Violence, CS-1942, film, 59 mins. (two reels). Indiana University, Audiovisual Center, Bloomington, IN 47401. The social, historical, and psychological factors that seem to underlie violence in modern life are the subject of this film.

Aggression or Love? ESC-1055, film, 24 mins. Indiana University, Audiovisual Center, Bloomington, IN 47401. Examines the possible biological and evolutionary roots of aggressive behavior. Raises the question, "Can love cure aggression?"

Sexual Assault, three videos, 30 mins. each. NETCHE Videotape Library, P.O. Box 83111, Lincoln, Nebraska 68501. Three tapes explore rape from the point of view of the victim, the assailant, and the police officer, respectively.

Transparencies

11.1 *What Is Sexual Harassment?*
11.2 *Theoretical Conceptions of Aggression*
11.3 *Aggression: Causes and Cures*
11.4 *Media Violence: Mechanisms Underlying the Effects*

11.5 *Aggression According to the Neoassociationists*
11.6 *The Effects of Violent and Nonviolent Pornography on Males' Aggression toward Females*

Critical Thinking/Essay Questions

1. Contrast Freud's view of aggression, the notion of "fighting instinct," sociobiological theory, the drive notion, aggression as a response to aversive events, and aggression as a learned social behavior. Which view do you anticipate will be most supported in the remainder of the chapter?

2. Discuss the teacher-learner method of studying aggression, indicating the controversies that surround it. Can you devise a better way to study aggression?

3. What is wrong with the idea that "frustration" is a major "cause" of aggression? Indicate why the "direct provocation" notion provides a better account of why aggression occurs.

4. List the kinds of studies that have been used to investigate the possible effects of media presentations on aggression, and provide an example of each. Given that the media do affect aggressiveness, why does this happen?

5. Consider Zillmann's ideas about "excitation transfer" and how they may explain the process by which a chain of events involving "heighten arousal" may or may not end up in increased aggressiveness.

6. Use Zillmann's "two-factor" theory to explain how sexual arousal influences aggressiveness. How does violent pornography compare with nonviolent pornography in its effects on males' aggressiveness toward females?

7. Explore how alcohol affects aggressiveness. How does alcohol affect the brain in ways that will produce heightened aggression? How does social pressure to increase aggressiveness influence the difference between alcohol and no-alcohol conditions in an aggression experiment? Does alcohol always increase aggression?

8. Explain how Type A's and Type B's differ in general and in terms of the level and kinds of aggression they show. How do Type A drivers differ from Type B drivers?

9. Discuss the reasons why punishment and catharsis are quite limited as means of lessening aggression. How could each be made less limited?

10. Explore the question of gender differences in aggressiveness. Try to decide whether more biological or more cultural explanations provide better accounts of the differences.

11. Indicate the merits of apologies, nonaggressive models, social training, mitigating circumstances, and incompatible responses as means of reducing or controlling aggression.

Sources for Lecture

Bower, B. (1991, November 30). Females show strong capacity for aggression. *Science News*, p. 359. Anthropological work in the Israeli kibbutz, ethnographic work among female gangs in Mexico, and psychological investigations in Finland support the assertion that females are more aggressive than we assume, and maybe not such second-class aggressors compared to males as we have thought.

Horn, J. (1985) Fighting migraines with the Force. *Psychology Today*, November, p. 74. Type A–like boys who are described as "brightest," "head of the class," and "most athletic" have numerous problems. They are likely to be highly aggressive and some report migraine headaches. But, alas, biofeedback doesn't work with these high-strung kids. However, conjuring up the Jedi ritual allows them to relax. May the Force be with them.

Steele, C. (1986). What happens when you drink too much? *Psychology Today*, January 1986, pp. 48–52. Drinking makes people's responses more extreme. Compared to sober people, drinkers were more aggressive, looked at sexual slides longer, gambled more, disclosed more about themselves, and took greater risks.

Stone, R. (1992, October 9). HHS "violence initiative" caught in a crossfire. *Science, 258,* 212–213. If there were a link between genes and violent crime, shouldn't scientists be free to investigate it, even if the genes at fault were found to be concentrated in a particular race? Would the discovery of such genes lead to "rounding up" people with the genes, even if they weren't violent? Such questions haunt the new violence initiative of Health and Human Services.

Taubes, G. (1992, October 9). Violence epidemiologists test the hazards of gun ownership. *Science, 258,* 213–215. Arthur Kellerman, among others, is arguing that, in effect, the trigger does pull the finger. His work and that of others is showing that the presence of guns, especially in the home, contributes to violent behavior.

"20/20" (ABC News Transcript for 9/17/1991 show) "Battered women" and "Women and violence" (order for $5 from Journal Graphics, Inc., 1535 Grant Street, Denver, CO 80230). This transcript graphically portrays the plight of battered women, whose pleas for help are too often ignored until it is too late. It also examines the lives of women imprisoned for killing their abusive male partners and asks, "Should they be set free?"

Ubell, E. (1990, February 11). The deadly emotions. *Parade*, pp. 4–6. This article supports the notion that hostile people's hostility is worse for them than for their victims, but sounds an optimistic note: Formerly hostile people can learn to be laid-back.

Update: Current Articles from Professional Sources

Buss, A. R., & Perry, M. (1992). The aggression questionnaire. *Journal of Personality and Social Psychology, 63*, 452–459. Buss, one of the early investigators of aggression, and Perry have developed a new aggression questionnaire that they show to be both valid and reliable.

Gentry, J., & Eron, L. D. (1993). American Psychological Association Commission on violence and youth. *American Psychologist, 48*, 89. These authors introduce a series of articles on youth violence and how it might be controlled.

Hutton, H. E., Miner, M. H., Blades, J. R., & Langfeldt, V. C. (1992). Ethnic differences on the MMPI Overcontrolled-Hostility Scale. *Journal of Personality Assessment, 58*, 260–268. Although race, with African-Americans scoring higher than European-Americans, was the only predictor of scale scores, an examination of clinical histories and criminal records indicated that actual descriptors of overcontrolled aggressors were unrelated to scale scores. Thus, African-American patients are more likely to be incorrectly labeled as overcontrolled-hostile personalities.

Lore, R. K., & Schultz, L. A. (1993). Control of human aggression. *American Psychologist, 48*, 16–25. Lore and Schultz argue that both humans and other animals have aggression-inhibitory mechanisms that are equally as potent as any tendency to aggress. Aggression, therefore, is not inevitable; it can be suppressed when it is in our interest to do so.

Malamuth, N. M., Sockloskie, R. J., Koss, M. P., & Tanaka, J. S. (1991). Characteristics of aggressors against women: Testing a model using a national sample of college students. *Journal of Consulting and Clinical Psychology, 59*, 670-681. These researchers found that high sexual promiscuity coupled with high-hostile masculinity yielded aggression against women.

McFarland, S. G., Ageyev, V. S., & Abalkina-Paap, M. A. (1992). Authoritarianism in the former Soviet Union. *Journal of Personality and Social Psychology, 63*, 1004–1010. Studies in the former Soviet Union show that authoritarianism is associated with support of military aggression among the populace.

Reifman, A. S., Larrick, R. P., & Fein, S. (1991). Temper and temperature on the diamond: The heat-aggression relationship in major league baseball. *Personality and Social Psychology Bulletin, 17*, 580–585. Major league pitchers follow the linear heat-aggression curve closely: The hotter it is, the more likely they are to aggress against batters by hitting them.

Related Readings: The following selections from *Readings in Social Psychology: General, Classic, and Contemporary Selections,* 2nd Edition, by Wayne Lesko (Allyn and Bacon, 1993) accompany this chapter:

Skoler, G. (1989). Why violent toys are good for kids. Yes, you read it correctly. This journalist believes, in contradiction to the "aggressive cues" notion, that violent toys are good for kids. Parents inhibit their use for reasons of parental hangups, not for the benefit of the kids. (31)

Bandura, A., Ross, D. & Ross, S. (1961). Transmission of aggression through imitation of aggressive models. This classic study shows how it is all too easy for children to learn aggression from models. (32)

Baron, R. A. (1983). The control of human aggression: An optimistic perspective. Your text author Baron tells why there is considerable hope that aggression can be controlled. (33)

Chapter-at-a-Glance

Chapter Twelve
Groups and Individuals:
The Consequences of Belonging

Chapter Outline	Instruction Ideas	Supplements
I. Groups: Their Nature Group Formation: Why Do People Join? / How Groups Function: Roles, Status, Norms, and Cohesiveness	Exercise 1 Discussion Questions	CNN Video Segment 25, *Executive Women*, Segment 26, *Death from Karoshi*, Segment 27, *Japanese Productivity*—see CNN Video Guide Reading: Lesko 35—Effect of Threat Upon Interpersonal Bargaining
II. Groups and Task Performance: The Benefits—and Costs—of Working with Others Social Facilitation: Performance in the Presence of Others / Groups Versus Individuals: Which Has the Edge in Task / Social Loafing: Letting Others Do the Work in Group Tasks / Social Facilitation and Social Loafing: Two Sides of the Same Coin?	Discussion Questions 1–3 Critical Thinking Questions 1 and 2	Transparencies 12.1, 12,2
III. Decision Making by Groups: How It Occurs, The Outcomes It Yields, and the Pitfalls It Faces The Decision-Making Process: How Groups Move toward Consensus / The Nature of Group Decisions: Moderation or Polarization? / Decision Making by Groups: Some Potential Pitfalls	Exercises 2 and 3 Critical Thinking Questions 3 and 4	Readings: Lesko 34—Groupthink, Lesko 35—Space Shuttle Challenger and Groupthink
IV. Leadership: Its Nature and Impact in Groups The Trait Approach: Are Leaders Born or Made? / Gender Differences in Leadership: Do Male and Female Leaders Differ? / Leader Effectiveness: Two Influential Views / Transformational Leadership: Leadership through Vision and Charisma	Exercise 4 Critical Thinking Question 5	Transparency 12.3 Video: Decision Making and Leadership

Chapter Twelve

Groups and Individuals: The Consequences of Belonging

Chapter Outline: Getting the Overall Picture

Learning Objectives

1. List the five reasons people join groups.
2. Describe the differentiation of function that occurs within groups when members fulfill different roles.
3. Indicate how role conflict and constraints imposed by roles can be detrimental to group functioning.
4. In the Worchel and Shackelford (1991) study, understand when assigning specific roles caused positive reactions and when it caused negative reactions.
5. Describe how the prestige of various roles is reflected in status differences, and also indicate how prescriptive and proscriptive norms affect group members' behavior.
6. Define cohesiveness and list factors that contribute to group cohesiveness. Is cohesiveness always a positive factor for the group?
7. How did Zajonc's drive theory resolve the early "puzzle" created by the fact that performance is sometimes improved by an audience and sometimes impaired?
8. Describe research findings regarding the evaluation apprehension hypothesis, indicating which are consistent and which are inconsistent with the hypothesis.
9. Describe research findings that support the distraction-conflict theory, and indicate the two advantages enjoyed by the theory.
10. Examine advantages gained by having a group work on a task, and also look at the costs of doing so.
11. Compare individual versus group performance on additive, compensatory, disjunctive, and conjunctive tasks, and indicate how performance is affected by group size.
12. Describe "social loafing" in the clapping and cheering study done by Latane et al.
13. Understand the four techniques that can be used to reduce social loafing.
14. What is social compensation, and what are the three reasons why group members might try to compensate?
15. In the social compensation research by Williams and Karau (1991), summarize the impact of whether people worked alone or in groups, whether the partner's loafing was due to low effort or low ability, and whether the task was important or not.
16. How is performance affected by efficacy expectancy and outcome expectancy? When will people work hard and when will they slack off?
17. In the research by Sanna (1992), describe conditions where social facilitation occurred and conditions where social loafing occurred.
18. Summarize the four social decision schemes used by groups to make decisions, and indicate when majority-wins and truth-wins rules are used.
19. How are decisions affected by straw polls and by whether the deliberation style is verdict-driven or evidence-driven?
20. What was the surprising finding of Stoner in his early study comparing individual and group decisions?
21. Compare the risky shift and group polarization phenomena.
22. Describe how the following theories account for the occurrence of group polarization: (a) social comparison; (b) persuasive arguments; and (c) social decision schemes.
23. What are the characteristics of groupthink, why is groupthink especially likely in cohesive groups, and what three steps can be taken to avoid its occurrence?
24. Why does the apparent advantage of pooling resources often fail to be effective in group discussions?
25. On the basis of the Stasser and Stewart (1992) experiment, describe the circumstances under which groups fully discuss unshared information.
26. Summarize advantages and disadvantages of having decision-making groups communicate electronically versus face to face.
27. Why has the "great person theory" of leadership traditionally been rejected? Review recent evidence that leaders' traits *do* matter.
28. What did Eagly and Johnson (1990) find regarding sex differences on the following leadership dimensions: (a) showing consideration versus initiating structure; (b) participative versus autocratic decision style?
29. According to Fiedler's contingency theory, what determines whether a leader will be successful in helping a group achieve its goals?

    a. Contrast low-LPC leaders and high-LPC leaders.
    b. What three factors make situations favorable for leaders?
    c. Under what conditions are high-LPC leaders more effective?
    d. Under what conditions are low-LPC leaders more effective?

30. Using Vroom and Yetton's normative theory, indicate conditions where the preferred leadership style is: (a) autocratic; (b) participative.
31. What four adjustments are suggested to make Vroom and Yetton's normative theory more accurate?
32. Describe the characteristics of transformational leaders.
33. Describe these differences between Americans and Asians: (a) styles of business leaders; (b) individualistic versus collectivistic tendencies.

Discussion Questions

1. Students who are sports fans are well aware of the home court advantage in competitive sports. Playing at home is generally correlated with winning. Greer (1983) studied the performance of basketball players at Illinois and at Kansas State to determine the impact of noisy fan demonstrations on performance. Greer found that turnovers and scoring favored the home team regardless of crowd noise. The factor most affected by crowd noise was the number of fouls called against the visiting team. For fifteen seconds following noisy crowd demonstrations, the number of fouls called against the visiting team increased. Perhaps some of your students would like to replicate Greer's phenomenon. (Greer's research is found in *Social Psychology Quarterly, 46,* 252–261.)

2. Research by Jackson and Padgett (1982) has suggested evidence for a social loafing effect in songs written by John Lennon and Paul McCartney of the Beatles. The social loafing effect hypothesis was that the songs cowritten by Lennon and McCartney would be of lower quality than the songs written by either of them alone. Jackson and Padgett concluded that there is evidence of a social loafing effect, but only for those songs written after 1967. (For a full explanation, consult the research reported in the *Personality and Social Psychology Bulletin, 88,* 672–677.)

3. Challenge students to come up with examples of tasks that are additive, compensatory, disjunctive, and conjunctive. A way to help them understand the nature of these types of tasks is to have them produce illustrative examples.

4. Ask the students to report on their experience in extracurricular activity groups. The students might comment on such things as the emergence of leadership in the group, polarization effects, social loafing, and social facilitation. Also, you might encourage the students to attend a meeting of a group of which they are not currently members so that they can observe the group's functioning. By observing a group of which they are not a member, students may be better able to gain insight into the group. Encourage the students to write down their impressions of the group and to share them with the other class members.

5. Before peace talks for ending the Vietnam War could get under way in earnest, negotiators had to settle the issue of what shape the negotiating table would be. Negotiators for the United States and South Vietnam wanted to present the appearance of a two-sided negotiation, whereas the North Vietnamese wanted the appearance that four equal parties were negotiating— the Americans, the South Vietnamese, the North Vietnamese, and the National Liberation Front. The United States considered the National Liberation Front to be sponsored by North Vietnam and thus not an independent party. The final compromise, reached after eight months of negotiating, involved a round table without dividing lines. Sometimes the roles people play in a group are determined by structural factors, such as seating pattern.

Classroom Exercises/Demonstrations

1. One topic discussed in chapter 12 is the notion of what constitutes a group. One way to get students thinking about this question is to present them with several situations and have them determine whether the people described there are a group or simply a collection of individuals. Several situations of this type are presented in chapter 12 of the Study Guide. In addition to their yes/no responses, have students write down the reasons for their decisions. Afterward, you can determine the number of students who thought each situation described a group and ask them to discuss their judgments. The text's definition of a group is as follows: "two or more interacting persons who share common goals, have a stable relationship, are somehow interdependent, and perceive that they are in fact part of a group." Do the students' judgments support the text's definition?

2. This exercise not only demonstrates the nature of polarization effects but gives students a chance to interact with fellow students in a small-group setting.

Students respond twice to each of six items from the Choice Dilemmas Questionnaire (CDQ), one time on their own and the second time after a three-minute discussion. Before the class period, the instructor should prepare enough copies of the CDQ for each student in the class to have one copy. (The six CDQ items are presented in chapter 12 of the Study Guide.) Read the following instructions to the class before the exercise is begun:

> On the page(s) that I have given you, you will find descriptions of situations that might occur in everyday life. In each situation a person is faced with a choice between two courses of action. The person can continue his or her present course of action, or the person can embark on a new, more adventurous course. Your task is to decide how certain you would want to be before you would advise the person to try the new course of action.

For each situation, your task is to indicate the minimum probability of success that you would demand before recommending that the person attempt the new course of action. Note that you are not asked to indicate what the chances of success would actually *be*; rather, you are asked to indicate the smallest chance of success that you would accept and still advise the person to go ahead and try the new course of action. If you say one in ten, you are telling the person to try the new course of action even if there is only one chance in ten of succeeding. On the other hand, if you say nine in ten, you are telling the person to try the new course of action only if very sure of succeeding.

Read each situation carefully before giving your judgment. Try to place yourself in the position of the person in each situation and then indicate the smallest chance of success that you would accept and still advise the person to try the new course of action.

After everyone in the class has finished responding, the students should divide up into discussion groups of four or five persons. Groups are instructed that their task is to spend three minutes discussing the Alan situation (i.e., the first CDQ situation). Tell them that at the end of three minutes you will interrupt to ask them to write down their response to the Alan situation. You should emphasize to them the importance of keeping an open mind and of considering all points of view during the discussion. After the three-minute discussion, ask each person again to write down on his or her questionnaire the minimum probability of success that he or she would demand.

After completing the first situation, the groups should discuss the next situation for three minutes. At the end of the three minutes, again ask people to respond to the item. After the groups have completed their six discussions, ask each group to prepare a summary of their data. For each situation, have them obtain a prediscussion and a postdiscussion sum. They should add together the responses of each group member so that it can be determined whether their group changed in a risky direction, changed in a cautious direction, or stayed the same. It is expected that groups will show a risky shift on the Peter, Henry, and George situations. It is expected that groups will show a cautious shift on the Betty and Mark/Susan situations. The Alan situation produces somewhat ambivalent results, although risky shifts are more prevalent than cautious shifts. These predictions are based on the assumption that groups cause shifts in the direction of the initial response tendencies of the group members.

3. Gary Stasser of Miami (Ohio) University has provided a task for illustrating the vagaries of collective information exchange en route to a collective judgment. The task uses standard playing cards and requires that a group decide whether there are more black or red cards in an oversized deck constructed from two or more standard decks. Of course, the experimenter or instructor can control which color is more frequent in the deck as well as the degree to which the more prevalent color dominates. The procedure involves dealing a set number of cards (eleven works well, but this can be varied to simulate high- versus low-information conditions) to each member of a group. Then, as an analog of obtaining prediscussion preferences in typical group decision-making exercises, each member privately chooses either red or black as their judgment (guess) based on the information in their own hands. Ratings of certainty of judgment and a record of the actual contents of their hands are also obtained for later purposes. After these private responses are obtained, the group "discusses" by members playing, in turn, cards face up on the table. Play is continued in round-robin fashion until about fifteen cards are displayed on the table. (The number of cards played can be varied to simulate short or long discussions.) After the predetermined number of cards is played, "discussion" is stopped and the group, without further revelation of the contents of their individual hands, reaches a collective judgment based on their pooled information (i.e., the cards on the table). Of course, the cards that individuals retain in their hands can still influence their individual judgments and, thus, their votes or stated preferences in reaching the group's decision.

Even though the task is simple and the "discussion" mechanical, it does capture some of the dynamics of information exchange. First, members must actively decide what kind of information they are going to share. Second, as in most group discussions, not all of the information available to members is shared. Third, the task is cooperative, in that the collective goal is to reach the correct or best decision.

There are many kinds of data that one can quickly summarize from this task. For example, one can compare members' certainty of judgment before and after "discussion"; rated certainty is typically higher afterward, suggesting that individuals feel that they have benefited from the information exchange and are able to make a better judgment as a result. One can also compare the groups' decisions with reality. It is educational to point out in this context that whereas this task allows one to judge the correctness of the decisions, many real-life contexts do not.

The outcome that generates the most class discussion is usually the comparison of what cards are played with the cards in members' hands. Almost without exception, the color that is dominant in the hands before discussion is overrepresented on the table. For example, suppose there are five members who are dealt the following hands:

	Member				
	A	B	C	D	E
Number of red cards	6	4	6	3	5
Number of black cards	5	7	5	8	6

Three of the five members' hands favor black; and, summing across members' hands, we see that thirty-one (56 percent) of the fifty-five cards dealt are black. A typical outcome is that 70 to 80 percent of the cards played on the table will be black in the above case, and the group (as well as individual members) will end up confidently concluding black (which may or may not be right).

Such a result illustrates the tendency for shared information to overrepresent the biases that may exist in members' information before discussion. Moreover, it is instructive to ask members how they decided what to play. They often say, "I played the color that I had the most of," or, "I played the color that I thought was most likely to be correct." Members who find themselves in the "minority" (e.g., members A and C in the above example) often say, "I played red at first because I had more of those, but when others seemed to be favoring black, I decided that they could be right and didn't want to mislead the group—so I started playing black." There are many manipulations one can implement using this task. Thus, it lends itself to illustrating research methods in addition to examining some of the dynamics of information exchange. It requires few materials and is easily explained to participants. Moreover, groups can be run through several trials by using different decks. (Thanks to Gary Stasser for providing this exercise.)

4. What attributes do people perceive to be important in today's political leaders? A way to begin a discussion of the topic is to have students rate the list of characteristics found in chapter 12 of the Study Guide. The rating students should make is how much they believe these attributes are needed in today's leaders.

Film Notes: A Picture Is Sometimes Worth a Thousand Words

Allyn and Bacon Video

Group Decision Making and Leadership, videotape, 28.5 mins. To obtain this tape, consult your Allyn and Bacon sales representative. After examining a business group's discussion concerning whom to hire, Robert A. Baron and Margaret Clark get inside the workings of group decision making.

Other Videos and Films

Diagnosing Group Operation, 1961, 30 mins. Audiovisual Services, Kent State University, Kent, OH 44242. An analysis of group functions using Bale's categories.

Dynamics of Leadership, 5 films from 1961, 30 mins. each. Audiovisual Services, Kent State University, Kent, OH 44242. The five films analyze group structure, operations, communication, and leadership.

Experimental Studies in Social Climates of Groups, 32519, 1953, 30 mins. Pennsylvania State University, Audiovisual Services, Special Services Building, University Park, PA 16802 (814-865-6314). Classic study by Kurt Lewin in which a hidden camera observes three boys' clubs operated under autocratic, democratic, and laissez-faire principles. Shows how boys react when conditions of leadership are changed to another method. K. Lewin, R. Lippitt, and R. White.

Four More Days, color, 32 mins. New York University Film Library, 26 Washington Place, New York, NY 10003. The film presents the prisoner-guard experiment by Philip Zimbardo.

Group Dynamics: Groupthink, 21762, 1973, color, 22 mins. Pennsylvania State University, Audiovisual Services, Special Services Building, University Park, PA 16802 (814-865-6314). Presents the eight symptoms of groupthink as proposed by Dr. Irving L. Janis in his book *Victims of Groupthink*. Offers examples of group decision making processes that influenced historical events such as Pearl Harbor, the Korean War, and the Bay of Pigs, and describes how effective leadership can prevent a decision-making group from falling into groupthink. From the *Behavior in Business* series. A CRM production.

Individual Motivation and Behavior, 30531, 1963, 30 mins. Pennsylvania State University, Audiovisual Services, Special Services Building, University Park, PA 16802 (814-865-6314). Why do people join groups, and why do some members block or dominate group action? Professor Knowles offers comments before and after practical demonstration and discusses the motivation of each person who participates in the demonstration. One person wants to go home, another hates arguments, another wants everyone to like him, and one believes that others are trying to dominate him. From the *Dynamics of Leadership* series. Produced by NET.

Leadership: Style or Circumstance?, 32006, 1974, color, 30 mins. Pennsylvania State University, Audiovisual Services, Special Services Building, University Park, PA 16802 (814-865-6314). Considers the difference between Fiedler's relation-oriented and task-oriented leadership styles. Interviews with presidents of Baskin-Robbins and Deluxe General, Inc., show that each style can be effective and that it is important to gear leadership training programs to the specific group to be led or to the task to be accomplished. From the *Behavior in Business* series. A CRM production.

Problem Solving Strategies: The Synthetics Approach, 1980, color film, 27 mins. Also available on videotape. CRM Films, 2233 Faraday Avenue, Carlsbad, CA 92008. Shows several strategies for improving the quality of group problem solving.

Social Group, videotape, 30 mins. Western Illinois University Television Services, Macomb, IL 61455 (309-298-1880). From the *Understanding Human Behavior* series, this entry explores how social groups form and function.

Transparencies

12.1 *The Drive Theory of Social Facilitation*
12.2 *The Distraction-Conflict Theory of Social Facilitation*

12.3 *Contingency Model of Leadership Effectiveness*

Critical Thinking/Essay Questions

1. Summarize the assumptions underlying Zajonc's drive theory of social facilitation, the predictions the theory makes about behavior, and the conclusions drawn from research findings.
2. Compare the performances of individuals and groups on additive, compensatory, disjunctive, and conjunctive tasks.
3. Compare the exchange of shared versus unshared information in a group.
4. Describe the group polarization effect. Compare the explanations for group polarization put forth by the social comparison theory and by the persuasive arguments theory.
5. Describe one of the text's theories of leadership, and summarize evidence supporting and contradicting this view.

Sources for Lecture

Burrows, W. E. (1982). Cockpit encounters. *Psychology Today*, November, pp. 43–47. What makes for efficient task performance by the small group working in the cockpit to fly an airplane?

Ciulla, J. B. (1986). Corporate leadership: Try a little tenderness. *Psychology Today*, March, pp. 70, 75. Reviews of five recent books, all of which essentially take the view that the feared, powerful, Machiavellian leader has been replaced by a problem solver who empowers his or her followers.

Fiedler, F. A. (1969). Style or circumstance: The leadership enigma. *Psychology Today*, March, pp. 38–43. Fiedler's leadership theory states that both personal style and the situation are important in determining the leader's success. He examines task-oriented and relationship-oriented styles and discusses the conditions under which each is effective.

Fiedler, F. A. (1987). When to lead, when to stand back. *Psychology Today*, September, pp. 26–27. Here Fiedler probes directive and nondirective leadership styles and also looks at the role played by leader intelligence.

Goleman, D. (1985). Following the leader: Sometimes it's folly to go along with the boss. *Science 85*, October, pp. 18–20. How could E. F. Hutton continue its practice of illegally overdrawing its bank accounts without someone blowing the whistle? Goleman explains in terms of groupthink.

Hall, J. (1971). Decisions, decisions, decisions. *Psychology Today*, November, pp. 51–54, 86–88. Group decisions *can* be superior to those of individuals. The achievement of satisfactory group solutions is explored.

Latane, B., Williams, K., & Harkins, S. (1979). *Psychology Today*, October, pp. 104–106, 110. Again, the people who did the work tell us about it! These authors review their research on social loafing and question the value of working as a team in a group.

Markes, M. L. (1986). The question of quality circles. *Psychology Today*, March, pp. 36–46. The basic feature of "quality circle" programs is that small groups of people who perform similar work meet on a regular basis to analyze work problems and propose solutions to them. The article analyzes their success.

McCall, W. M., & Lombardao, M. M. (1983). What makes a top executive? *Psychology Today*, February, pp. 26–31. Two behavioral scientists from a leading think tank map the pitfalls along the corridor to the executive suite.

McCullough, D. (1983). Mama's boys. *Psychology Today,* March, pp. 32–38. Many famous historic leaders adored their mothers and were adored in return. Is the mother-son relationship crucial to leaders?

Update: Current Articles from Professional Sources

Baron, J., & Jurney, J. (1993). Norms against voting for coerced reform. *Journal of Personality and Social Psychology, 64,* 347–355. Some reforms, such as the passing of a prohibitive law or a binding agreement to solve a social dilemma, involve coercion. This study found that subjects responded to hypothetical coerced reforms with a lack of support, even though they acknowledged the reforms would improve matters. Ways in which subjects justify their resistance are examined.

Malloy, T. E., & Janowski, C. L. (1993). Perceptions and metaperceptions of leadership: Components, accuracy, and dispositional correlates. *Personality and Social Psychology Bulletin, 18,* 700–708. Mixed-sex problem-solving groups showed considerable agreement as to who their leaders were. Most of the variance (91 percent) in judgments of leadership was explained by quantity of speaking, quality of ideas, and friendliness. Leaders generally held accurate perceptions of how they were viewed. The study also explored the impact of gender and stereotypic masculine and feminine traits.

Paulus, P. B., Dzindolet, M. T., Poletes, G., & Camacho, L. M. (1993). Perception of performance in group brainstorming: The illusion of group productivity. *Personality and Social Psychology Bulletin, 19,* 78–89. When brainstorming in groups, people produce fewer ideas than when brainstorming alone. People continue to believe they are more productive in groups, however. The basis for this illusion of group productivity is explored.

Prentice, D. A., & Miller, D. T. (1993). Pluralistic ignorance and alcohol use on campus. *Journal of Personality and Social Psychology, 64,* 243–256. Students were found to be generally uncomfortable with campus alcohol practices but believed others did not share their discomfort. Over the course of a semester, male students increasingly shifted toward the perceived norm, with students who perceived themselves deviant from the norm feeling alienated from campus culture.

Reno, R. R., Cialdini, R. B., & Kallgren, C. A. (1993). The transsituational influence of social norms. *Journal of Personality and Social Psychology, 64,* 104–112. Explores ways to increase compliance to social norms against littering. Considers the effectiveness of two types of norms: Descriptive norms specify what is typically done in a given situation, whereas injunctive norms specify what is typically approved. Focusing on injunctive norms produced stronger behavioral effects.

Related Readings: The following selections from *Readings in Social Psychology: General, Classic, and Contemporary Selections,* 2nd Edition, by Wayne Lesko (Allyn and Bacon, 1993) accompany this chapter:

Janis, I. (1973). Groupthink. Janis himself discusses his well-known work on groupthink. The symptoms of groupthink are highlighted, with excellent examples of each symptom. (34)

Deutsch, M., & Krauss, R. (1960). The effect of threat upon interpersonal bargaining. A laboratory bargaining paradigm is used to study the effect of being able to threaten one's partner on interpersonal bargaining. Threat is shown to have negative effects. The findings suggest a rethinking of the use of threat and power in real-world negotiations. (35)

Moorhead, G., Ference, R., & Neck, C. (1991). Group decision fiascoes continue: Space shuttle Challenger and a revised groupthink framework. Analysis of the situation surrounding the decision to launch the space shuttle Challenger in 1986 is analyzed in terms of groupthink. Presents a revised framework proposing that time and leadership style moderate the manner in which group characteristics produce groupthink. (36)

Chapter-at-a-Glance

Chapter Thirteen
Social Psychology and the Individual:
Population, Health and Environmental Applications

Chapter Outline	Instruction Ideas	Supplements
I. Population Psychology: Unlimited Growth Versus Stabilization Overpopulation? Limitations on the Earth's Resources / Zero Population Growth: Decreasing the Birth Rate	Discussion Question 3 Critical Thinking Questions 1 and 2	CNN Video Segment 28, *People Bomb,* Segment 29, *Stress Management,* Segment 30, *Blood Pressure,* Segment 30, *Noisy City—see* CNN Video Guide Reading: Lesko 38—Territorial Rights and the Good Neighbor
II. Health Psychology: Maintaining Good Health, Responding to Illness Accepting Health-Relevant Information / Stress and Illness / Responding to Health Problems / Medical Care As a Source of Problems	Exercises 4 and 5 Discussion Question 5 Critical Thinking Questions 3, 8, 10	Transparencies 13.3, 13.4, 13.6 Video: Health Mind, and Behavior Readings: Lesko 37—Private Passions and Public Health and Lesko 39—Life Changes in Coping with Three Mile Island
III. Environmental Psychology: Effects of Environmental Factors on Behavior and Effect of Human Behavior on the Environment How the Environment Affects Human Behavior / How Human Behavior Affects the Environment	Exercises 1–3 Discussion Questions 1, 2, 4 Critical Thinking Questions 4–6	Transparencies 13.1, 13.2, 13.5
Social Diversity: A Critical Analysis— Differences in Smoking Behavior: Gender, Race, Ethnic Group, and Nationality	Critical Thinking Questions 7 and 9	

Chapter Thirteen

Social Psychology and the Individual: Population, Health, and Environmental Applications

Chapter Outline: Getting the Overall Picture

I. Population Psychology: Unlimited Growth versus Stabilization
   A. Overpopulation? Limitations of the Earth's Resources
      1. The Surprising Reality of Population Growth
      2. Why Exponential Growth Comes As a Surprise
   B. Zero Population Growth: Decreasing the Birth Rate
      1. India and China: Attempts to Control Fertility
      2. Voluntary Changes Based on the Decisions of Individuals
   C. Contraceptive Neglect among Sexually Active Adolescents
II. Health Psychology: Maintaining Good Health, Responding to Illness
   A. Accepting Health-Relevant Information
      1. Personal Relevance versus Threatening or Beneficial Self-Interest
   B. Stress and Illness
      1. The Effects of Stress
      2. Reducing the Harmful Effects of Stress
      3. How Personality Dispositions Affect Health
      4. Health Effects of Self-Concealment versus Self-Reporting

C. Responding to Health Problems
   1. Attending to Symptoms: You Have to Notice That Something Is Wrong
   2. Deciding What Is Wrong
   3. Taking Action
D. Medical Care As a Source of Problems
   1. Patient-Doctor Interactions
   2. Coping with Diagnosis and Treatment
   3. Avoiding Emotion Leads to Illness
III. Environmental Psychology: Effects of Environmental Factors on Behavior and Effects of Human Behavior on the Environment
   A. How the Environment Affects Human Behavior
      1. Noise: Loud and Unpredictable
      2. Temperature and Behavior
      3. Air Pollution
      4. Electrical Ions in the Atmosphere
      5. Viral Infections: The Ultimate Revenge of the Tropical Rain Forests?
   B. How Human Behavior Affects the Environment
      1. The Greenhouse Effect: A Warmer, Wetter World
      2. Garbage, Litter, and Other Waste Products
      3. Encouraging People to Recycle
IV. Differences in Smoking Behavior: Gender, Race, Ethnic Group, and Nationality

Learning Objectives

1. Define the phrase "applied psychology" and learn the historical growth pattern of the world's population. (Page 000)
2. Explain the phenomena of arithmetic progression and geometric progression as related to exponential growth and to population curves, and relate

these to the "secret of the Persian chess board."
3. What are the two reasons why we are surprised at exponential growth?
4. Compare the scenarios envisioned by "optimists" versus "pessimists" as to how population growth will eventually end.

5. Appreciate the difference between the ways that China and India have approached their population problems. Has India been too timid or China too harsh regarding growth curtailment? Outline how contraception and abortion have played a role in China's efforts to reduce population.

6. Discuss what countries have succeeded in voluntary fertility reduction. Does the United States have plenty of room for population expansion? List the sources of our population expansion in the future and the "violations of the Constitution" and principles of humanity that would be involved in curbing our population increases.

7. Describe how informational deficits, situational constraints in obtaining contraceptives, and personality dispositions contribute to the failure of sexually active adolescents to use contraception. Indicate the quality or nature of the information that teens should be supplied, and suggest what personality factors need to be altered for teens to avoid unplanned pregnancies.

8. Define "health psychology" and "stress." indicate how work load relates to stress, tell whether we can just add up the sources of stress to arrive at a stress "score," and indicate how "psychoneuroimmunology" approaches understanding the effects of stress.

9. Learn about the effects of "fitness" and "hardiness" on health; how these factors, along with exercise, figure into the ability of students to withstand stress (Roth et al., 1989); how neuroticism and sense of control affect coping with stress; and the Compas et al. (1991) two-step process for responding to threat.

10. Discuss how "locus of control" relates to health, what Emmoms (1992) found regarding hardiness and negative affect in his study of high- and low-level strivings among undergraduates and older married couples, and optimism's effects on health and recovery from heart surgery.

11. What component of the Type A personality relates to coronary problems? Describe what Goleman (1992) had subjects do in order to study their heart-pumping efficiency. Is childhood too early for health intervention?

12. Examine the mechanism by which social support helps people avoid health and injury problems. How does self-concealment contribute to health problems? Who had fewer physical symptoms in the weeks after writing about either trivial events or traumatic ones (Greenberg & Stone, 1992)?

13. Consider people who are the "worried well," the role of "priming" and mood in attention to symptoms, the dangers of "mislabeling" one's symptoms, and four factors that enter into people's decisions about the meaning of symptoms.

14. Describe ways in which communications between patients and medical personnel can go awry, how they can be improved, and how nonverbal skills of physicians as well as their orientation to framing information can influence communications.

15. Learn the strategies that patients can adopt to help them cope with the stresses of diagnosis and treatment. How does the perception of personal control affect recovery from medical treatment, and can modern computer technology increase personal control?

16. Explain how "dry runs" and exposure to already-treated patients can better prepare children and adults for medical procedures.

17. Describe "environmental psychology," "technophobia," and their relation to environmental stress. Indicate how loud and unpredictable noise affects us, along with how we may cope with it, and consider how exposure to chronic noise affects children and adults.

18. Appreciate the many effects of heat on behavior; the reactions of victims of chronic pollution; the affective and interpersonal effects of pollution, especially cigarette smoke; and the effects of "atmospheric electricity" on human behavior.

19. Learn how Preston (1992) explained the appearance of "the most deadly virus" since HIV and rabies and how easily forms of this new virus develop and spread. What is Preston's argument for preservation of the rain forests?

20. Explain how the "greenhouse effect" has come to be, how it may affect the world in the future, what gases contribute to it, where they come from, and how we can reduce these gases.

21. Learn what kinds of "prompts" are more helpful than others in getting people to stop littering. Do litter lotteries work? Does motivation to recycle needs a boost? Waht are the effects of rewards for turning in bottles? Understand how Kahle and Beatty (1987) demonstrated that recycling attitude change followed behavior change.

22. Outline the change in smoking habits around the world, the present death toll from smoking, how U.S. ethnic groups differ in smoking behavior, rea-

Discussion Questions

sons for quitting, and the role of family and peer pressure in smoking.

1. People seem rather unaware that they themselves

contribute to pollution. Have students list all of the cases they can think of where a typical person contributes to pollution (e.g., driving an automobile, drinking out of cans, using nonbiodegradable wrappings such as plastic). Consider substitute behaviors that would lower individual pollution. Pay special attention to easy avenues to nonpolluting behaviors.

2. The notion of "radiation phobia" raises some important issues. So long as people lump all things nuclear together and find them all to be "bad," some benefits of nuclear physics will be retarded and progress toward eliminating the truly threatening applications will be slow. There are positive outcomes of nuclear physics. For example, Rosalyn S. Yalow won a Nobel Prize for the development of radioimmunoassay, a technique that involves treating biologic substances with radiation so that the presence of certain immunological entities can be detected. It is estimated that this technique has saved many thousands of lives and that the numbers will eventually reach the millions. Yalow can now be seen on TV in antismoking ads. She is one of those who point out that cigarettes are much more dangerous than nuclear power plants. (Incidentally, radon, as she has indicated, would not be such a significant threat if its effects did not combine with cigarette smoking: The great majority of radon-related deaths are among smokers.) The use of radiation to preserve foods almost indefinitely is another example of potential positive uses of radiation. Not only do people seem to think that all things nuclear are "bad," they seem to think that they are equally bad.

If students need to know that all things nuclear are not bad, they also need to know that some products of nuclear physics are worse than others. Take nuclear power plants compared to nuclear weapons facilities as an example. Nuclear power plants are relatively well regulated. Prior to Chernobyl—and another Soviet nuclear plant disaster to which they later admitted—there have been few deaths worldwide directly attributable to power plant radiation exposure. In the United States the number is very small. By contrast, nuclear weapons facilities are relatively poorly regulated and have apparently been associated with numerous deaths (see the readings sections at the end of this chapter). Yet the antinuke people have spent as much time protesting in front of power plants as they have in front of weapons facilities. A thing to watch for in the future is continued lack of disasters associated with nuclear power plants and a possible trillion-dollar cleanup scandal associated with nuclear weapons facilities (the savings and loan fiasco may pale by comparison).

Armed with this information, you might start the discussion with "is there anything good about the application of nuclear physics?" Then guide students to understanding that some things nuclear are more threatening than others and that some may be positive. If students can appreciate that nuclear weapons are the real threat, they may act. (As of this writing, the United States–Russian nuclear disarmament pact is signed but not implemented, because the former Soviet states have not all signed.) Consider this discussion an exercise in critical thinking.

3. Abortion is becoming an option for population control worldwide. It is an explosive issue that you may well wish to avoid. Nevertheless, you are guaranteed a lively discussion if you bring up the topic. The problem is avoiding offense. If there was just some way to satisfy people on both sides of the issue. . . . Maybe there is.

Carl Sagan and Ann Druyan have attempted to develop a strategy that allows choice and at the same time is "pro-life" (see Sources for Lecture). You will need to read their article; but, to get a glimpse of it, consider a world in which contraception was widely and conscientiously used. In such a world, people would be exercising their choice to decide when or whether they would have children. At the same time, because conception would be avoided, the issue of killing the embryo or fetus would not arise. To start this discussion, begin with the question posed in the title of the Sagan-Druyan article: "Is it possible to be pro-life and pro-choice?" To avoid problems, you may want to work very hard to keep your point of view out of the discussion. Consider acting as a facilitator and moderator. You probably should guide students in the direction of considering birth control; as you know, however, even endorsement of contraception can be offensive. Rather than endorsing it, consider raising it as an issue and refer to the text authors' point that the world's population could conceivably become so great that human life itself could not be sustained. This is tricky business, but you could do some real good if you tackle this issue.

4. What can we do about the greenhouse effect? First students need to understand what causes it. Start this discussion after students have read the book, or hope that some students will have the needed information before hand. Or provide it yourself. Here is a short summary. CO_2, methane, chlorofluorocarbons (CFCs), nitrous oxides, and other gases form a blanket around the earth, letting light through but trapping heat much like a greenhouse. So far, CO_2 is the major contributor; methane and CFCs are increasing fast as are nitrous oxides. (As you recall, CFCs also deplete the ozone layer, thereby increasing ultraviolet-B with accompanying increases in the probability of skin cancer, cataracts, and the destruction of plankton—the beginning of the food chain in the world's oceans.) Excess CO_2 results primarily from the burning of fossil fuels such as oil, gasoline, and coal. Nitrous oxides also are emitted from the burning of fossil fuels and come from certain fertilizers. Excess methane comes from forest fires, landfills, rice paddies, and the digestive tracts of ruminant animals such as cattle. CFCs are found in aerosols that propel the contents of spray cans and in solvents that are used to clean computer components (microchips and circuit boards), as well as in refrigerants and foams.

Equipped with this information, students are ready to suggest ways they can contribute to reductions in greenhouse gases. Encouraging the planting of trees—and the preservation of existing trees—to help in the uptake of CO_2 is a way to reduce CO_2. Also we can drive less—carpool and take public transportation—and demand that our politicians seek regulations that ensure cleaner burning of coal and oil. Nitrous oxides will also be reduced thereby. We can decrease methane by demanding tighter control of landfills and by eating less of the red meat that comes from cattle (then there will be less cattle). Aerosols have declined because of regulation. This observation suggests that we can do more to reduce CFCs. We can demand that other solvents be used to clean computer components (there are some available). We can also reduce CFCs by decreasing our dependency on air conditioners and refrigerators. Finally, we can demand the use of containers made of materials other than Styrofoam, perhaps of recycled paper. Here is a chance to empower students by helping them pinpoint actions they can take to save the environment.

5. Some degree of stress is a fact of life for everyone (well, almost everyone). The first step in dealing with stress is to identify its sources. Have students talk about what aspects of college life "stress them out" the most. You may even want to tally these sources on the board, keeping a count of which ones are experienced by how many students. Knowing that others have the same kinds of problems helps students feel less odd and unusual. That knowledge alone lowers anxiety, a first step toward dealing successfully with stress.

Next, have students suggest how they deal with the various sources of stress, or the stress itself. When the problems are personal, it is surprising how the simplest solutions fail to occur to even the brightest of people. (An example of an easy solution: "When my roommate bugs me, I leave the room for a couple of hours. It works every time.") You may even want to have the students vote on which coping method mentioned in conjunction with a given source of stress is the most effective. Consensus can be a powerful determinant of beliefs, and when people believe strongly enough in a method, they will often make it work.

Classroom Exercises/Demonstrations

1. "In every life, a little rain must fall." Are temperature, ozone level, and ion content the only weather factors that affect social behavior? How about precipitation or lack thereof (a sunny day)? On a beautiful, sunny day have students generate five words to describe themselves. Have them do the same on a rainy day as well as on two "average" (partly cloudy) days. Students can "score" each other's words to show that a little sunshine can make a difference in how people describe themselves. Simply have them exchange descriptions and place positive signs (+) by words that are favorable and negative signs (-) by unfavorable words. (Don't score words that are neither favorable nor unfavorable.) Consider a description favorable if it has more positive than negative signs. Favorable descriptions should be more prominent on beautiful, sunny days, and unfavorable descriptions on days when it is raining or overcast.

In class, ask students why they described themselves in the way they did on assigned days. Point out the precipitation factor in weather as a determinant of descriptions. It should be the case that "beautiful days make for beautiful descriptions": We actually like ourselves better when our spirits are raised by a beautiful day.

2. The late Milton Rokeach's value conflict test might be altered to fit the case of pollution. Give the students the value scale—found in the Study Guide chapter 13—and ask them to rank the items from 1 (most important) to 18 (least important). Then compare the mean ranks of items substituted for "equality" and "freedom" in positions 6 and 8 from the top. Perhaps your students will find a clean environment for future generations more important than freedom to exploit the environment now. Whether or not they do, it will be interesting to discover how environmental issues stack up against the more personal issues found on the scale. Ask them to volunteer which three items they ranked highest. The information they provide may inspire some students to ask others why they ranked issues such as "an exciting life" or "a sense of accomplishment" above "a clean environment in the future."

3. According to psychologist Paul Slovic (see *Science*, *236*, April 17, 1987, pp. 280–285), a key to understanding risks and reacting appropriately to them is to assess them accurately. Unfortunately, certain risks, called dread risks, are quite resistant to accurate assessment: They are unfamiliar, involve fears of catastrophic future events and fatal consequences, and are perceived to be uncontrollable precursors of disaster. All of these characteristics of dread risks are reinforced by the media. In view of these characteristics, one can see why dread risks are inaccurately assessed: What is mysterious is especially frightening, and what is terribly fearful seems highly likely to occur. Thus, students can be expected to overestimate the incidence of dread risks relative to other risks.

Test this hypothesis, with regard to diseases, by asking students to guess the annual number of cases of each of several diseases, using the incidence of syphilis as a benchmark. AIDS fits the dread risk criteria and should be greatly overestimated, relative to other diseases. Students can provide their responses on a form found in the Study Guide. It is similar to Table 1 below, except that all statistics are missing except for syphilis. (Table based on information in *Morbidity and Mortality Weekly Report,* Vol. 39, No. 19, May 18, 1990.)

TABLE 1: Number of Cases of Various Diseases Accumulated during the First 19 Weeks of 1990

Measles	7216
Rabies (humans)	0
Gonorrhea	239,884
AIDS	16,056
Botulism (contamination of food)	1
Tetanus	20
Syphilis	*17,539*
Tuberculosis	7,141
Leprosy	59
Typhoid fever	128

4. What are the life events that generate the most stress? As it turns out, most such events involve close relationships, an observation that may be news to many students. To help them home in on events that may cause stress—the necessary first step in avoiding health-threatening stressors—have students examine the Holmes & Rahe Social Readjustment Scale (1967, *Journal of Psychosomatic Research, 11,* 213–218).

After they explore the scale thoroughly—it is included in the Study Guide—ask the students to find the top five most stressful events and rank them, giving a rank of 1 to the most stressful event. Then instruct them to locate the bottom five, giving a rank of 43 to the least stressful, a rank of 42 to the next least stressful, and so on. After the ranking is done, reveal the entire ranking by use of Table 2 below (from Allen [1990] *Personal adjustment,* Brooks/Cole, used with permission). Have them comment on the degree to which their rankings have approximated the actual rankings based on a 100-point scale (marriage was the standard, set at 50). Keep them going until it is clear to them that close personal relationships are the major source of the most stressful events.

TABLE 2: The Social Readjustment Scale

Events	Score	Rank	Events	Score	Rank
Death of a spouse	100	1	Change in responsibilities at work	29	23
Divorce	73	2	Son or daughter leaving home	29	23
Marital separation	65	3	Trouble with in-laws	29	23
Jail term	63	4.5	Outstanding personal achievement	28	25
Death of close family member	63	4.5	Spouse begins or stops work	26	26.5
Personal injury or illness	53	6	Beginning or end of school	26	26.5
Marriage	50	7	Change in living conditions	25	28
Getting fired from job	47	8	Revision of personal habits	24	29
Marital reconciliation	45	9.5	Trouble with boss	23	30
Retirement	45	9.5	Change in work hours or conditions	20	32
Change in health of family member	44	11	Change in residence	20	32
Pregnancy	40	12	Change in schools	20	32
Sex difficulties	39	14	Change in recreation	19	34.5
Gain of new family member	39	14	Change in church activities	39	14
Business readjustment	39	14	Change in social activities	18	36
Change in financial state	38	16	Small mortgage or loan	17	37
Death of close friend	37	17	Change in sleeping habits	16	38
Change to different line of work	36	18	Change in number of family get-togethers	15	39.5
Change in number of arguments with spouse	35	19	Change in eating habits	15	39.5
High mortgage	31	20	Vacation	13	41
Foreclosure of mortgage or loan	30	21	Christmas	12	42
			Minor violation of Law	11	43

5. Students are likely to be plagued with misconceptions concerning which physical diseases are the most danger to them. There is much one can do about health hazards, but people often waste effort by focusing on the wrong dangers. For example, cardiovascular disease is by far the biggest killer of North Americans, and there is much one can do to avoid these disorders (e.g., exercise and diet control). Cancer, a much more feared category of disorders, kills only about half as many as cardiovascular disease but may also be less controllable through behavioral intervention. If students see the two disease categories as equivalent in likelihood of cutting their lives short and equivalent in terms of possibilities for prevention, they may assume there is little they can do to save themselves. Have them consider the following list of disorders (Table 3) without numbers or ranks, reproduced in the Study Guide. (Table from Allen [1990] *Personal adjustment*, Brooks/Cole, used with permission.)

With "accidents" as the benchmark—its number alone is included in the Study Guide version—students could estimate the annual number of deaths attributed to each source and/or rank the top five killers, giving a rank of 1 to the most deadly. Then reveal to them what really are the big five killers. Finally, elicit comments until it is obvious that most of the top five are preventable with appropriate behavioral interventions. Time permitting, you may want to ask the students what social psychological methods might be used to get people moving in the direction of prevention. Methods for preventing smoking among youth and some ethnic groups are particularly relevant here.

TABLE 3: Actual U. S. Fatalities and Ranks for Several Diseases and for Accidents

Disease (or accidents)	Fatalities	Rank
Smallpox	0	
Tuberculosis	3,690	
Accidents	93,990	4
Stroke	147,390	3
Diabetes	38,950	
Cancer	465,440	2
Infectious hepatitis	677	
Heart disease	763,380	1
Syphilis	410	
Chronic lung disease	75,220	5
Measles	5	

Film Notes: A Picture Is Sometimes Worth a Thousand Words

Allyn and Bacon Video

* *Health, Mind, and Behavior*, This Allyn and Bacon video discusses how research is forcing a profound rethinking of the relationship between the mind and the traditional model. (On Tape #12.)

Other Videos and Films

Environment, NSC-1299, color, 16 mins. Indiana University, Audiovisual Center, Bloomington, IN 47401. This film outlines current environmental problems.

People by the Billions, GS-910, 28 mins. Indiana University, Audiovisual Center, Bloomington, IN 47401. Examines the current population explosion, considers past remedies for overpopulation, and suggests two methods to deal with the present problem.

The Price of Pollution, color video, 60 mins. NETCHE Videotape Library, P.O. Box 83111, Lincoln, Nebraska 68501. Famed environmentalist Barry Commoner discusses the wages of our sin, pollution.

The City and the Self, 50324, color, 52 mins. Pennsylvania State University, Audiovisual Services, Special Services Building, University Park, PA 16802 (814-865-6314). Study of human relations in the city based on psychological concepts formulated by Stanley Milgram. Examines city dwellers' perceptions of their cities and their behavior in created situations.

Noise: The New Pollutant, 31321, 30 mins. Pennsylvania State University, Audiovisual Services, Special Services Building, University Park, PA 16802 (814-865-6314). Illustrates the harmful effects of prolonged exposure to high levels of noise.

Stress Reduction: Strategies That Work, PB124, video, 30 mins. Insight Media, 121 W. 85th Street, New York, NY 10024 (800-233-9910; 212-721-6316). Presents the latest information on beating the stress that is associated with certain personalities.

Health and Lifestyles: Positive Approaches to Well-Being, film, 28 mins. Iowa Films, Media Library, University of Iowa, Iowa City, IA 52242. This film is designed to motivate viewers to take responsibility for their own health by making informed decisions.

Heart Attack: Prevention, film, 19 mins. Iowa Films, Media Library, University of Iowa, Iowa City, IA 52242. Presents a case study of the personality traits and lifestyle factors that make a person a prime candidate for coronary heart disease.

Transparencies

13.1 *Environmental Behavior Can Be Changed by Legislation*

13.2 *Three Gases Contributing to the Greenhouse Effect*

13.3 *Hardiness, Fitness, and Health*

13.4 *Decisions and Choices to Make When the Symptoms of Illness Develop*

13.5 *Concerns about Technological Hazards: The Public versus the Experts* (Table 13.4)

13.6 *High-Level versus Low-Level Goals in Life* (Table 13.2)

Critical Thinking/Essay Questions

1. Explain the grand vizier's "geometric progression." Can you think of any reasons that it might not apply to population explosion in the future?
2. Indicate how some of the controversies in the United States concerning methods of birth control may spread to other countries.
3. Can you think of any personal dispositions, other than those covered in the text, that may affect the health of those who have them?
4. List and discuss current environmental problems. What means would you suggest to mobilize people to do something about these problems?
5. Design a program to induce citizens to take action against litter. Trace the sequence of events that proceeds from legislation to behavior change to attitude change with regard to antilitter behavior.
6. Indicate how noise affects health, academic functioning, and social relations. What kind of noise is the most damaging?
7. Trace the psychological effects of air pollution, including that produced by smokers. What are the interpersonal problems involved with controlling "passive smoking"?
8. Cigarette companies are currently targeting African-Americans in ad campaigns to increase cigarette sales. What are the ethical issues involved here? What other promotion targets the same group?
9. Analyze yourself. What personal dispositions, behaviors, or concealments may affect your health?

Sources for Lecture

Abas, F. (1989, December). Rocky Flats: a big mistake from day one. *Bulletin of the Atomic Scientists*, pp. 19–24. Denver is downwind from the most infamous of several frightening nuclear weapons plants. The Rocky Flats story is a tale of things to come: We will have to face a multibillion-dollar cleanup during the later 1990s and early 2000s.

Carey, J., & Silberner, J. (1987, August, 17). Fending off the leading killers. *U.S. News and World Report*, pp. 56–65. A cogent summary of what one can do to save one's own life—a testimonial to the role of behavior in health. The end of the article is a "heart health" test.

Ehrlich, P., & Ehrlich, A. (1986, April). World population crisis. *Bulletin of the Atomic Scientists*, pp. 13–19. Two world-famous biologists present shocking statistics concerning the present and future population crises. They state that the birth of a baby in the United States is 200 times more disastrous than a birth in a third-world country, because an American baby will live to consume so much more.

Fackelmann, K. A. (1991, November 30). Many doctors would shun AIDS patients. *Science News, 140,* 356. Talk about doctor-patient communication problems . . . some physicians say they would not communicate with, or get near, AIDS patients.

Kunz, A. (1989, December). Highest disregard. *Mother Jones*, pp. 33–36, 44–48. Scientist Sherwood Rowland succeeded in convincing politicians and business figures that spray can propellants were destroying the ozone layer. Now he is battling the electronics industry over their use of solvents that destroy the ozone layer. So far he has made little headway.

Morbidity and Mortality Weekly Report. (1992, July 31). Trends in ischemic heart disease mortality 41 (No. 30), 548–549 and 555. Heart disease due to reduction of the blood supply (therefore oxygen) to the heart muscle, leading to muscle destruction, is the leading cause of death in the United States This article indicates that European-American men lead in death rate from this disease, followed by African-American men. Women, black and white, are far behind and show similar rates. All groups are displaying declines over time, but African-American women are leveling off, perhaps to increase in the future.

Revkin, A. C. (1988, October). Endless summer: Living with the greenhouse effect. *Discover*, pp. 50–61. This comprehensive and highly readable article maps out (literally) where and how the greenhouse gases will wreak their effects. Also contains information concerning sources of the effect and how it might be short-circuited.

Sagan, C., & Druyan, A. (1990, April 22). Is it possible to be pro-life and pro-choice? *Parade*, pp. 4–8. The answer is yes according to this famous scientist and wife Druyan, an activist who marshals the forces of science for the good of people.

Siegel, P. Z., et al. (1991, December). Behavioral risk factor surveillance, 1986–1990. *Morbidity and Mortality Weekly Report, 40.* This report looks at a number of behavioral factors in health: lack of leisure-time physical activity, sedentary lifestyle, smoking, overweight, binge alcohol consumption, drinking and driving, and safety belt nonuse.

Slovic, P., Flynn, J. H., & Layman, M. (1991, December 13). Perceived risk, trust, and politics of nuclear waste. *Science, 254,* 1603–1607. Slovic and colleagues show how disposal of high-level radioactive waste has been impeded by "dread risk" fears of the public based on their perceptions of mishandling of nuclear weapons waste and lingering mistrust of everything nuclear. Turning around public perceptions will not be easy.

Update: Current Articles from Professional Sources

Baradell, J. G., & Klein, K. (1993). Relationship of life stress and body consciousness to hypervigilant decision making. *Journal of Personality and Social Psychology, 64,* 267–273. Private body consciousness (PBC) was related to decision making on an analogies task. There is little relationship between life stress and decision quality or strategies for low PBCs, but for high-PBC people increasing life stress was associated with poorer performance and the use of hypervigilant strategies.

Cohen, S., Tyrrell, D. A. J., & Smith, A. P. (1993). Negative life events, perceived stress, negative affect, and susceptibility to the common cold. *Journal of Personality and Social Psychology, 64,* 131–140. Subjects completed a questionnaire on stressful life events, perceived stress, and negative affect and then were exposed to a cold virus. High scores on each of the three scales were associated with higher risk of developing a cold. The relationship between events and illness, however, was mediated by a different biologic process than that between perceived stress and illness or negative affect and illness.

Freudenburg, W. R., & Pastor, S. K. (1992). NIMBYs and LULUs: Stalking the syndromes. *Journal of Social Issues, 48,* 39–61. Three main perceptions of the public's responses to technological risks are examined: views of the public as ignorant/irrational, selfish, and prudent. The first perception is deemed unsupported; analysis of the second two involves differences between citizens and specialists. The authors offer still another viewpoint.

Hallman, W. K., & Wandersman, A. (1992). Attribution of responsibility and individual and collective coping with environmental threats. *Journal of Social Issues, 48,* 101–118. Summarizes the many sources of stress that often accompany environmental threats, individual and collective strategies for coping with environmental threats, and the efficacy of these strategies. Some of the problems with measuring coping strategies and with gauging their success are discussed.

Liberman, A., & Chaiken, S. (1992). Defensive processing of personally relevant health messages. *Personality and Social Psychology Bulletin, 18,* 669–679. Following exposure to either a low- or a high-threat message, subjects for whom the message was high in relevance were less likely to believe in the threat. Processing measures suggested that high-relevance subjects processed threatening parts of both messages in a biased fashion.

Mendolia, M., & Kleck, R. E. (1993). Effects of talking about a stressful event on arousal: Does what we talk about make a difference? *Journal of Personality and Social Psychology, 64,* 283–292. Subjects talked about their emotional reactions to a stressful stimulus or about facts relating to it. Those in the emotional reaction condition showed stronger autonomic arousal during the talk phase, but a lesser reaction and more positive affect upon a second exposure to the stimulus.

Thompson, S. C., Sobolew-Shubin, A., Galbraith, M. E., Schwankovsky, L., & Cruzen, D. (1993). Maintaining perceptions of control: Finding perceived control in low-control circumstances. *Journal of Personality and Social Psychology, 64,* 293–304. Cancer patients' perceptions of personal control were related to coping with stress. Those with greater perceptions of control were less depressed. More important than control of the course of the disease was control of daily emotional reactions and physical symptoms.

Vaughan, E., & Seifert, M. (1992). Variability in the framing of risk issues. *Journal of Social Issues, 48,* 119–135. Variability in framing risk issues can exacerbate conflict, leading to differences among people as to which perspectives are judged legitimate or valid, what solutions are seen as reasonable, and what type of information is seen as useful or relevant.

Related Readings: The following selections from *Readings in Social Psychology: General, Classic, and Contemporary Selections,* 2nd Edition, by Wayne Lesko (Allyn and Bacon, 1993) accompany this chapter:

Krajick, K. (1988). Private passions and public health. Users of AIDS testing centers and medical personnel react to AIDS testing. (37)

Sommer, R., & Becker, F. D. (1969). Territorial defense and the good neighbor. Use of markers to defend space in public areas varies as a function of area density. Neighbors are important for legitimizing space ownership. (38)

Prince-Embury, S., & Rooney, J.F. (1991). Life stage differences in resident coping with restart of the Three Mile Island nuclear generating facility. Younger and older residents of the Three Mile Island area react differently to the restart of the nuclear generating plants. (39)

Chapter-at-a-Glance

Chapter Fourteen
Social Psychology and Society:
Local, Political, and Organizational Applications

Chapter Outline	Instruction Ideas	Supplements
I. Social Psychology and the Legal System Before the Case Goes to Court: Police Interrogation and Pretrial Publicity / The Testimony of Eyewitnesses / Actions of Attorneys and of the Judge: Effects on the Verdict / Characteristics of Defendants and Jurors	Exercises 2 and 3 Discussion Questions 1 and 3 Critical Thinking Questions 1–3	CNN Video Segment 32, Japanese Employees, Segment 33, Japanese Work Ethic, Segment 34: Kennedy-Smith Trial, Segment 35: Great Speeches, Segment 37: The Smell of Success—see CNN Video Guide Transparencies 14.1, 14.3 Readings: Lesko 40—Juries on Trial and Lesko 42—The Discrediting Effect of Eyewitness Testimony
II. Social Psychology and Politics: Attitudes, Liking and Leadership Political Attitudes and Behavior / Voting for the Candidate You Like / Voting for the Candidate Who Appears to Be a Leader	Exercise 1 Discussion Question 2 Critical Thinking Questions 4 and 7	Transparency 14.2 Video: Group Decision Making and Leadership
III. Social Psychology in Work Settings: Job Satisfaction, Work Motivation, and Conflict Work-Related Attitudes: Their Nature, Measurement, and Effects / Work Motivation: Getting People to Do Their Best / Conflict in Work Settings: A Social Psychological Perspective	Exercise 4 Discussion Question 4 Critical Thinking Questions 8–10	Transparency 14.4, 14.5 Readings: Lesko 41—One More Time: How Do You Motivate Employees?
Social Diversity: A Critical Analysis— Voter Rights and Voter Apathy: Effects of Class, Race, and Age in the United States and United Kingdom	Exercises 5 Critical Thinking Questions 6	

Chapter Fourteen

Social Psychology and Society: Legal, Political, and Organizational Applications

Chapter Outline: Getting the Overall Picture

Learning Objectives

1. What are "leading questions," how do they affect trust and expectations of the witness, and how do they affect knowledgeable and naive subjects differently (Smith & Elsworth, 1987)?

2. Learn about the negative effects of media and pretrial publicity. What did Moran and Cutler (1991) find concerning the relationship between potential jurors' pretrial knowledge and the blame they placed on the accused?

3. Outline the evidence concerning accuracy and identification in eyewitness testimony, the effects of witnesses' confidence, and the amount of detail they report. What factors affect witnesses' accuracy, and what practices may improve witness accuracy?

4. What three findings did Olczak, Kaplan, and Penrod (1991) report concerning attorneys' and students' reactions to traits of potential and actual jurors? When should the defense present its opening statement for best effect? And when are attorneys most biased in addressing hostile or friendly witnesses?

5. Learn how judges influence juries and about "hanging" versus "lenient" judges. Tell how a mild or radical "jury nullification rights" statement by a judge affected mock jurors' judgments about an alleged rape by a black or a white man (Horowitz, 1988).

6. Outline the three defendant and three plaintiff behaviors and how they affected judgment outcomes in the Thomas and Parpal (1987) study. Understand how gender and subjective judgments play a role and, in the Wells (1992) study, how the presentation of statistical evidence affected the outcome of Mrs. Prob's case.

7. How did physical attractiveness affect the outcome of a case of sexual harassment where the attractiveness of the plaintiff and of the defendant varied (Castellow, Wuensch, & Moore, 1990)? And who is more likely to be judged guilty, a male or a female assailant (Cruse & Leigh, 1987)?

8. Learn how defendants' race and ethnicity affect their outcomes in court, with attention to "death" verdicts, and how leniency bias figures in the "death" verdict.

9. What do "liberal" and "conservative" really mean? Outline what Newcomb (1943) and colleagues found in a study of political attitudes at Bennington College in 1939 and in their 1960s and 1980s follow-ups of the same subjects.

10. Indicate whether it is the media or its target (you and I) that is politically biased; where political propaganda is most evident in the media; and what two criteria we use in deciding who we'll vote for, as well as what effects can be assigned to self-monitoring and repeated exposure to candidates.

11. Learn the roles of affect and optimism associated with candidates; how candidates deal with controversial issues; and how physical attractiveness (with gender thrown in), height, similarity to us, and name affect orientation to candidates.

12. List the valued traits associated with "leadership." What predicts presidential greatness? What is a general personality trait found in political leaders? How does masculinity/femininity figure into leadership along with self-confidence and honesty?

13. List and describe Simonton's (1988) five presidential leadership styles. When does "transformational leadership" become important?

14. Define job satisfaction (JS). Indicate why jobs are so important to us, tell how JS is measured and how optimism and pessimism affect it, list the two classes of factors that affect JS, and explain the roles of a reward system, participation in decisions, and perceived quality of supervision.

15. What percentage of the variation in JS may be attributable to genetic factors? Outline criticisms of the Arvey et al. (1989) genetic study of JS and the findings of Keller and her colleagues' (1992) investigation into genetic influences on a factor related to JS.

16. Learn the strength of the relationship between JS and job performance, and discuss some aspects of job performance that may be strongly related to JS. Consider the relationship between absenteeism and voluntary turnover and JS.

17. What are the three conditions associated with "expectancy theory"? How does "goal setting theory" differ from expectancy theory? What are the "guidelines" that go with this theory? What does "equity theory" focus on, and what are the factors that determine whether one is being treated fairly?

18. Explain the kind of bias that colors our perceptions of our inputs and outputs, list the three ways that people can deal with feelings of being treated unfairly, and indicate how Greenberg's (1989) subjects dealt with "fairness feelings" when they received a 6 percent pay cut.

19. Indicate how Greenberg (1990) investigated unfair treatment in three plants and how theft played a role in the study. Tell how feelings of inequity affected major-league baseball players.

20. Learn whether cooperation or conflict characterizes interactions in organizations. Give examples of "organizational causes" of conflict and of "interpersonal factors" in conflict, with attention to "faulty attributions"; then review procedures and results of Baron's (1988) study, in which a demanding negotiator either claimed to have been ordered to be unyielding or appeared to be unyielding as a personal inclination.

21. Indicate the value of bargaining and summarize three bargaining strategies. What is the "incompatibility error," and how does it impede "logrolling?" Indicate some steps toward preventing misperceptions, outline the "win-lose" and "win-win" approaches to negotiation, identify the advantages of "superordinate goals" and "incompatible respons-es," and tell what Baron (1990) found when angered subjects experienced positive feelings.

22. What did Fife-Schaw and Breakwell (1990) find regarding why U.K. citizens fail to vote , and why did Pereta (1992) argue that efforts to entice voters to the polls at the last minute are misguided?

Discussion Questions

1. "Why could shipwrecked lawyers safely swim past sharks, while others were eaten alive?" Answer: "Professional courtesy." "How can you tell the difference between road-killed lawyers and equally unfortunate animals?" Answer: "Tire skid-marks in front of the animals." "How many lawyers could you cram into a typical underground nuclear test site?" Answer: "Not nearly enough."

These are just a few examples of popular "lawyer" jokes. You and your students probably know many more (you could ask them). Despite this apparent malice toward legal counselors, TV is full of "lawyer shows" promoting positive images of the law profession, and they are well watched. Why this ambivalence? Have the students talk about it. Maybe we "hate" lawyers because they control so much of our lives. On the other hand, perhaps we "love" them because of the power they possess as manifested in the megabucks they make and their ability to shape what happens in our society.

2. Tapes or films of the famous John F. Kennedy–Richard M. Nixon TV debate of 1960 are readily available. (If your college doesn't have a copy, your audiovisual people can probably borrow it from another college.) Play as much of the debate as you think is necessary to give students the flavor of each candidate's strategy, appearance, manner, and orientation to the facts. In the eye of the viewing public, Kennedy was the clear winner. In terms of getting facts straight and speaking to the issues, some experts on debate saw Nixon as the winner. Get the students to indicate who they thought won and why. Most will likely say that Kennedy won. Their reasons will be various, but call attention to those reasons that relate to JFK's handsome looks and cool demeanor. Perhaps you can also get them to notice that he spoke in generalities more than did Nixon, who was often quite factual. In contrast, Nixon's upper lip was, as usual, sweating, and he looked pale, unhealthy, and nervous. Being substantive didn't pay off, but looking good and in charge did. Note the implications of this debate for the importance of optimism, attractiveness, apparent leadership ability, charisma, and saying "what people want to hear" rather than speaking about substantive issues.

3. The death penalty is supported by a majority of Americans but remains controversial. Whatever you feel about it personally, you can preside over a productive discussion of it. Nobel Prize winning organization Amnesty International is conducting an international campaign to abolish the death penalty. They argue that the death penalty does not deter murder (often a crime of passion that is not preceded by any thoughts of future consequences); that it is more costly than keeping murderers in prison for life (special housing inflates costs, but the legal costs of appeals balloon the costs of capital punishment the most); and—among other concerns—that it is discriminatory. Even beyond the fact that all-white juries have sent many blacks to death row, the U.S. Supreme Court has acknowledged the observation that people who kill white persons are significantly more likely to get the death penalty; that is, blacks killing whites and whites killings whites get the ultimate penalty, not those who kill blacks.

The counterarguments include the view that only legally sanctioned execution will ensure murderers don't end up on the streets again (too many murders are released after only short stays in prison); that consideration of victims and their families dictates that murders should be executed (family anguish ends only with execution); and that the deterrence value of execution has not been properly tested, because the death penalty has been too rarely meted out (few convicted murderers end up on death row, and few of those on death row are executed).

Let students hash out these arguments in class; prompt them if they forget some of the points made above. Then raise the critical question: What can social psychologists do to help resolve these issues? For example, can it be shown in the lab that all-white juries are "more likely to hang" a black person accused of murder, especially if the victim is white? Can studies be designed to show that penalties for resorting to violence deter the use of violence? (For example, during an aggression experiment in which subjects can shock someone who has offended them, will a relatively severe penalty for using shock deter its use?)

4. What primarily occupies people's time and thoughts on the job: concern and involvement in job-related tasks, or interpersonal events? We know of many cases where most energy is expended on interpersonal conflict and/or socializing (positive interpersonal events). Most of your students will have held jobs at one time or another; many will be currently employed. Have them talk about where the balance of interpersonal versus job-related cognitive and emotional energies lies. Many of them may be surprised to discover, upon reflection, that

they and others are spending an inordinate amount of time on non-job-related matters. Have them speculate about how to reduce interpersonal conflict on the job so that more time and energy can be devoted to efficient job performance, an outcome that will increase job satisfaction.

Classroom Exercises/Demonstrations

1. Hold an election to convince students that attractive candidates are most likely to win when other factors are held constant. Find a copy of a yearbook that is old enough so your students won't recognize the photos, but recent enough so that photos won't reflect out-of-style clothes and hair. Look through it until you find a block of photos that are all posed the same (seniors will probably work). Next, pick out the most attractive three males and three females you can find. Then pick out the most unattractive three males and three females. Copy the pages containing these twelve photos on transparency plastic and cut the twelve photos from their surrounds. Now check with colleagues to be sure that the final product reflects the appropriate attractiveness differences. These are your twelve "candidates" for a hypothetical student government presidential election. Next list a half dozen innocuous campus issues. (Example: The student fee for parking should not be further increased; faculty should be required to return tests within five class days of the test administration; faculty should be required to provide example essay questions at the beginning of each semester; students should be allowed two unpenalized absences per class per semester; the administration should notify students about discussions of tuition increases before they begin deliberating; 10 percent of faculty raises should be based on student ratings of faculty effectiveness.)

Select three of the issue positions (pro or con) and assign them to one of the attractive "candidates." Assign the same positions on the same issues to a candidate of the same gender from among the unattractive photos. Repeat this process until you have six matched pairs, each consisting of one attractive and one unattractive photo, both of the same gender, and each espousing the same positions on the same issues. Now you are ready for the "election." Randomly assign the names on the ballot included in the chapter 14 Study Guide to the photos—with the restriction that gender-appropriate names be assigned. Then present the transparencies of the photos in random order, mentioning the name and positions on the issues associated with each photo. Have the students take notes on each candidate and then "vote" by marking the ballot in the Study Guide. The simplest method is to have them vote for one candidate, collect the ballots, and see who received the

most votes (very likely one of the attractive candidates). To be more sure of obtaining the expected result—attractive candidates receive more votes—have the students rank-order the candidates, giving a rank of 1 to the most favored candidate, a 2 to the next most favored, etc. Then take the mean of ranks (or take median ranks if the distribution dictates) for "attractive" and "unattractive" candidates separately. Viewing these average ranks may be enough, but you may also want to perform a test of differences in average ranks, with "attractive" and "unattractive" being the conditions.

2. Judges' instructions to members of the jury may have great impact on jury decisions, as noted in the text. To illustrate this point, divide the class into "jury panels" of about six people (four, if the class is small; eight to twelve if the class is large). Then read the following case to all students: "Robert Edward Farness stands accused of killing a fellow patron at a local bar. Eyewitness testimony indicates that Farness was talking to a woman, for whom he had provided a drink, when the victim approached and began attempting to convince the woman that she should leave Farness and accompany him. Farness and the victim began to shout at one another; it was clear from what they were yelling that they knew one another and had had conflicts before. At the height of the argument, Farness was heard to shout, "I told you I'd kill you if you bullied me again!" At that point the victim broke off the neck of a beer bottle and began to thrust the jagged edge at Farness. Farness grabbed a chair, swing it at the victim, and dislodged the broken bottle from the victim's grasp. Witnesses testified that Farness then continued to bludgeon the victim with the chair, even after it was clear that he was no longer in danger. By the time Farness was restrained, the victim was so badly injured he died on the way to the hospital."

Next, give half the groups (juries) a written copy of the following "judge's instruction to the jury": "You are instructed that, should you find the accused guilty, you must provide a sentence of life in prison without parole." Give this instruction to the remaining groups: "You are instructed that, should you find the accused guilty, you may provide a sentence ranging from a minimum of ten years in prison—parole considered after five years—to a maximum of life in prison without parole." Now have the "juries" deliberate for twenty minutes or so and return a "guilty" or "not guilty" decision. Ask them to reach a unanimous decision, if they can, but to record the outcome of each vote they take before the final vote (require at least three votes). You should find that, at the minimum, "juries" given the first instruction have more difficulty reaching a decision, as reflected in more and closer votes. Chances are you will also find that "guilty" decisions are less frequent with the first instruction than with the second. Ballots are provided in the Study Guide.

3. Have the class select a jury. Some volunteers can act as potential jurors and others as attorneys (half for the prosecution and half for the defense) who pose screening questions. Allow each attorney to address ten questions to the potential jurors. Record the questions. After each attorney has posed her or his questions, have all indicate up to ten traits they considerd critically important in jurors and were therefore trying to assess through their questions.

Next make a copy of Transparency 14.3 (Table 14.1) and, on it, tally the frequency with which attorneys used each of the traits listed in the table. (You could do separate tallies for prosecutors and defense attorneys.) Also tally the number of times questions similar to each of those in the table were asked by attorneys. Finally, make a transparency of your tallies so that you can present it to the class. Did students follow the practices of real attorneys? Have your "attorneys" indicate why they did or did not endorse the traits or questions contained in

Transparency 14.3. Maybe they can conclude that some of their questions and traits make more sense than those more typically endorsed by real attorneys.

4. Do different job satisfaction questionnaires yield similar results? The question may be answered for students if you have them complete the questionnaires in transparency 14.5 (Table 14.4).. Make copies from the transparency master (14.5) and distribute to students. To put scores on the same scale, score the JDI answers as follows: Routine 1, Satisfactory 3, Good 5; Dead-end job 1, Few promotions 3, Good opportunity for promotion 5. Average the scores for each student for each scale separately. These average scores can then be fed into a T-test for paired observations. Discuss why scores on the two tests turned out differently or not as a function of whether the tests measure different factors.

5. Why don't people in Western democracies vote? Because it is a touchy subject, ask students to indicate anonymously whether or not they voted in the most recent presidential election and, if not, why not. Present the voting record (percentage of students who voted) to the class and ask whether some students would like to indicate why they did not vote. In addition to (or instead of) this process, you could indicate categories of reasons why students did not vote; for example, "one vote doesn't matter," "one person can't change the system," "politicians are disgusting," and so on. In this way students' anonymity could be preserved. Ask class members to rebut these arguments against voting. A lively interchange should result.

Film Notes: A Picture Is Sometimes Worth a Thousand Words

Allyn and Bacon Video

* *Group Decision Making and Leadership,* video, 28.5 mins. See your Allyn and Bacon Representative to learn how you may obtain this tape. Robert A. Baron and Margaret Clark discuss issues of leadership that are relevant to politics and business.

Other Videos and Films

Political Marketing: The Selling of America's Candidates, videotape, 34 mins. Television Services, Western Illinois University, Macomb, IL 61455 (309-298-1880). Illustrates the principles of marketing that have been used to sell political candidates in past presidential elections. This one does double duty: politics and business.

Sexual Harassment on the Job, videotape, 28 mins. Films for the Humanities & Sciences, Inc., P.O. Box 2053, Princeton, NJ 08543-2053 (800-257-5126). Over 70 percent of working women experience pressure to

exchange favors for advancement or continued employment. Susan Meyers defines the problem and how to solve it.

The Death Penalty, FC-1938, video, 26 mins. Films for the Humanities & Sciences, Inc., P.O. Box 2053, Princeton, NJ 08543-2053 (800-257-5126). Argues that new evidence suggests that death sentences are imposed arbitrarily and that little evidence exists to support the contention that the death penalty is a deterrent to murder.

Crime & Human Nature, FC-1327, video, 26 mins. Films for the Humanities & Sciences, Inc., P.O. Box 2053, Princeton, NJ 08543-2053 (800-257-5126). Anthropologist Ashley Montague and other experts join Phil Donahue in addressing issues that relate to the structure of our current laws.

Twelve Angry Men, commercial video (1957, United Artists) available for rental at many video stores, 95 mins. This film is perhaps the most respected attempt by Hollywood to look behind the dynamics of jury deliberation. It is outstanding.

Justice on Trial, 1977, film, 49 mins. CRM/McGraw-Hill Films, 110 Fifteenth Street, Del Mar, CA 92014. Interviews with top authorities on how disparities in sentencing have put the very concept of justice on trial.

Fidelity of Report, 11439, film, 6 mins. Pennsylvania State University, Audiovisual Services, Special Services Building, University Park, PA 16802 (814-865-6314). Watch a robbery and see how witnesses describe it.

Transparencies

14.1 *Unfair Punishment: Different Sets of Biases*
14.2 *The Bennington Experience: Liberals for a Lifetime* (Table 14.2)
14.3 *What Do Attorneys Seek in Selecting a Jury?* (Table 14.1)
14.4 *Equity and Inequity in Social Exchange*
14.5 *Questionnaires for Measuring Job Satisfaction* (Table 14.4)

Critical Thinking/Essay Questions

1. Discuss aspects of the judicial process where lawyers think they have a solid understanding of underlying dynamics but where the evidence says otherwise.
2. Indicate the implications of the finding that individuals who kill whites are more likely to end up on death row.
3. If judges can be divided up into "hanging" and "soft on crime" categories, what does that say about their objectivity?
4. Why did Bill Clinton win in 1992? Discuss those of his characteristics that fit the typical mold of the desirable president and those that do not. Do our perceptions of what makes a desirable candidate and admired president, as described in the text, fit Clinton well?
5. Argue that you are different than other people: You vote on the issues, not on the appearance of the candidate, her or his ability to dodge controversial issues, or his or her ability to *look* like a leader. Be sure to eliminate the latter three considerations from those matters that you weigh in selecting who to vote for.
6. Can you defend not voting? Build as convincing an argument as you can.
7. Write a brief description of an optimal strategy for an unknown politician to use to get elected to the U.S. Senate. Be sure to include factors such as a possible name change, optimism/pessimism, appearance similarity to voters, charisma, and leadership style.
8. Construct your own job satisfaction test. Come up with ten items that you think would adequately assess job satisfaction. Be sure to include the factors involved in job satisfaction that are included in the text.
9. Pretend that you are the boss. How would you go about motivating employees? Set up a ten-point program that would translate into high worker morale and high productivity.
10. What are the kinds of interpersonal conflicts that you would expect to develop in a typical job context? Choose from department store clerks, assembly line workers, or auto sales personnel—or some other, if you have intimate knowledge of it. Be sure to include relevant conflicts that are covered in the text.

Sources for Lecture

Ellsworth, P. (1985, July). Juries on trial. *Psychology Today,* pp. 44–46. A 1968 case is used to introduce the issue of "death-qualified" juries. The relationship between social psychological research and court cases since then is discussed.

Kaplan, S. M. (1985, July). Death, so say we all. *Psychology Today,* pp. 48–53. The author describes the emotional turmoil experienced by jurors who sat through a lengthy and traumatic trial that resulted in a death-sentence recommendation.

Mahoney, H. (1987, September). When the law is not enough. *Ms,* p. 85. Judges can make some horrible mistakes, beyond misinstructing or otherwise biasing a jury. In this case a young woman's plea for protection from her husband was ignored by a judge who told her to "act as an adult." She was subsequently murdered by the husband.

INSTRUCTOR'S SECTION

Update: Current Articles from Professional Sources

Allen, B. P. (1994). *Personality theories*. Needham Heights, MA: Allyn and Bacon. Sections on Albert Bandura summarize his work on self-efficacy and work efficiency. Material on George Kelly provides an overview of personal construct principles applicable to personnel and product evaluation.

Azzi, A. E. (1992). Procedural justice and the allocation of power in intergroup relations: Studies in the United States and South Africa. *Personality and Social Psychology Bulletin, 18,* 736–747. This study examined proportionality versus equality principles in the allocation of political power and other resources between majorities and minorities. Subjects from the United States and South Africa were more likely to divide a procedural resource (political power) equally between two simulated ethnic groups differing in size when led to identify with a minority than a majority. Equality was also more salient to members of real ethnic minorities than to members of ethnic majorities.

Brockner, J., Wiensenfeld, B. M., Reed, T., Grover, S., & Martin, C. (1993). Interactive effect of job content and context on the reactions of layoff survivors. *Journal of Personality and Social Psychology, 64,* 187–197. Field and lab studies examined the determinants of survivors' (people who survive their companies' layoffs) reactions to job layoffs. Change in perceived job quality was strongly and positively related to survivors' organizational and task commitment when the layoffs were seen as fair.

Hafer, C., & Olson, J. M. (1993). Beliefs in a Just World, discontent, and assertive actions by working women. *Personality and Social Psychology Bulletin, 19,* 30–38. Researchers assessed working women's Belief in the Just World (BJW; what you get is what you got coming) along with personal discontent, group discontent, self-directed behavior, and group-directed behavior. Those high on BJW reported less group discontent than those low. High BJWs showed fewer self- and group-directed behaviors.

Related Readings: The following selections are from *Readings in Social Psychology: General, Classic, and Contemporary Selections,* 2nd Edition, by Wayne Lesko (Allyn and Bacon, 1993) accompany this chapter:

Ellsworth, P. (1985). Juries on trial. This article written for a popular audience examines the biases to which juries are prone. (40)

Herzberg, F. (1987). One more time: How do you motivate employees? The author examines the usual methods of motivating employees, finds them wanting, and then concludes that providing employees with challenging work for which they can take responsibility is the only way to instill motivation. (41)

Kennedy, T. D., & Haygood, R. C. (1992). The discrediting effect of eyewitness testimony. In 1974 Elizabeth Loftus, the first to find fault with eyewitnesses, reported that it was not possible to shake jurors from their faith in eyewitnesses. These authors beg to differ. (42)

INSTRUCTOR'S SECTION

SOCIAL PSYCHOLOGY

Social Psychology

UNDERSTANDING HUMAN INTERACTION

ROBERT A. BARON

Rensselaer Polytechnic Institute

DONN BYRNE

University at Albany/State University of New York

Allyn and Bacon

Boston ▪ London ▪ Toronto ▪ Sydney ▪ Tokyo ▪ Singapore

To my mother Ruth, the kindest heart of all. R.A.B

To Rebecka, Lindsey, Robin, and Keven. D.B.

Vice President and Publisher: Susan Badger
Editorial Assistant: Laura L. Ellingson
Cover Administrator: Linda Dickinson
Manufacturing Buyer: Megan Cochran
Editorial-Production Service: Leslie Anderson Olney
Page Layout Artist and Quark Files: DeNee Reiton Skipper
Text Designer: Melinda Grosser
Cover Designer: Design Ad Cetera

Photo Credits

Chapter One: 1.2a, Rokuo Kawakami/The Image Bank. 1.2b, David de Lossy/The Image Bank. 1.3a, Janeart, Ltd,/The Image Bank. 1.3b, Frank Riteman/Stock, Boston. 1.4, Mark Burnett/Stock, Boston. 1.6, Jeff Greenburg/The Picture Cube. *Chapter Two:* 2.2a, Carol Lee/The Picture Cube. 2.2b, C. J. Allen/Stock, Boston. 2.2c, Sarah Putnam/The Picture Cube. 2.2d, Lynn McLaren/The Picture Cube. 2.2e, Ellis Harwig/The Picture Cube. 2.2f, Dag Sundberg/The Image Bank. 2.6a, Focus on Sports. 2.6b, The Bettmann Archive. 2.10 Eunice Harris/The Picture Cube. 2.12, Don Smetzer/Tony Stone Worldwide. 2.14a, Nicolas Foster/The Image Bank. 2.14b, Ron Bowman/Uniphoto. 2.16 Copyright Paul Ekman 1972.

(Photo credits continue on page 630, which constitutes an extension of the copyright page.)

Baron, Robert A.
    Social psychology : understanding human interaction / Robert A. Baron, Donn Byrne. —
7th edition.
        p.   cm.
    Includes bibliographical references and index.
    ISBN 0-205-14883-2
    1. Social psychology. I. Byrne, Donn Erwin. II. Title
    HM251,B437 1993
302—dc20

Printed in the United States of America

10   9   8   7   6   5   4   3   2   1   98   97   96   95   94   93

ISBN 0-205-14883-2

Contents

Chapter Three ■ *Social Cognition: Thinking about Others and the Social World*   82

Chapter Six ▪ *Prejudice and Discrimination, Understanding Their Nature, Countering Their Effects* 214

Chapter Seven ▪ *Interpersonal Attraction: Getting Acquainted, Becoming Friends*   262

Chapter Eight ▪ *Close Relationships: Friendship, Love, and Sexuality*   304

Chapter Nine ▪ Social Influence: Changing Others' Behavior   348

Chapter Twelve ▪ *Groups and Individuals:*
The Consequences of Belonging   480

Chapter Thirteen ■ *Social Psychology and the Individual: Population, Health, and Environmental Applications* 534

Chapter Fourteen ▪ Social Psychology and Society: Legal, Political, and Organizational Applications 580

Preface:
On Not *Growing Old Gracefully*

People must grow older with the passing years—that's a basic fact of life. But there's no compelling reason why textbooks have to do the same! Books, we contend, don't have to grow older along with their authors. They don't have to move, by gradual degrees, from an energetic youth to a stodgy middle-age. On the contrary, it's our firm conviction that books can come as close as any human endeavor to attaining the mystical fountain of youth: If their authors are willing to expend the needed effort, they can stay as young, resilient, and dynamic as the field they represent. This new edition represents our best efforts to translate these beliefs into concrete action. In preparing it, we have done everything in our power to keep this book truly young—in close touch with ever-changing panorama of social psychology, and *out* of the trap of the do-it-the-same-as-before mentality that causes many excellent texts to grow increasingly stale.

In order to meet these basic goals, we have made many major changes in the new edition. In fact, in some ways, this seventh edition represents the most extensive revision of the book to date. The most important of these changes are summarized below.

SPECIAL FEATURES NEW TO THE SEVENTH EDITION

This edition includes several new features that, we believe, will add significantly to its usefulness.

New *Social Diversity: A Critical Analysis* sections: Social psychology is increasingly concerned with a wide range of issues relating to cultural and ethnic diversity. To take account of this fact, we have added special *Social Diversity* sections to each chapter. These sections review recent research and findings concerned with differences between various cultures or differences between ethnic groups within a given society. They are tied to chapter content, and help illustrate an important new trend in social psychology. A few examples:

> Cultural and Ethnic Differences in Nonverbal Communication: On the Universality of Facial Expressions (Chapter 2)
> How Culture Shapes Thought: Effects of Cultural Schemas (Chapter 3)
> Divergent Female Gender Roles in Singapore, Mexico, and among Native Americans (Chapter 5)
> The Effects of Prejudice: Racial Identification Among African-Americans (Chapter 6)
> Status and Attraction in Japan and the United States (Chapter 7)
> Love and Intimacy: Western Europe, South Africa, Japan, and the U.S. (Chapter 8)
> Gender Differences and Conformity: The Vanishing Myth of Female Submissiveness (Chapter 9)
> Culture and Aggression: The Social Context of Violence (Chapter 11)
> Differences in Smoking Behavior: Gender, Race, Ethnic Groups, and Nationality (Chapter 13)

New *Individual Diversity* sections: Instead of treating personality or individual differences in a single chapter, we now include sections dealing with these topics throughout the text. These new sections describe recent research dealing with important individual differences. Since they appear in all chapters, these sections help illustrate the fact that such differences are not an isolated area of study in social psychology; rather, they are taken into account by social psychologists in their efforts to understand virtually all aspects of social behavior and social thought. Some samples include:

Showing Less Than We Really Feel: Self-Monitoring and the Suppression of Gloating in Public (Chapter 2)

Need for Cognition and the Nature of Social Thought (Chapter 3)

Discrimination With—and Without—Compunction: Contrasting Reactions of Low and High Prejudiced Persons to Discrepancies Between Their Internal Standards and Their Overt Behavior (Chapter 4)

Bem's Sex Role Inventory: Differences in Adherence to Typical Masculine or Feminine Roles (Chapter 5)

Sociosexuality: Choosing a Romantic Partner (Chapter 8)

Personality and Obedience: Who Resists and Who Obeys? (Chapter 9)

The Altruistic Personality: Dispositional Factors Associated with Providing First Aid (Chapter 10)

The Altruistic Personality: Dispositional Factors Associated with Providing First Aid (Chapter 10)

Connections: This new feature appears at the start of each chapter. It indicates how the content of a given chapter is linked to the content of other chapters in the book. This feature is designed to illustrate the truly *integrated* nature of social psychology by calling attention to the existence of important links between various areas of the field and the diverse lines of research.

New *Work in Progress* sections: In a sense, this may be the most important new feature of the book, and the one most reflective of the theme stated in the title of this Preface. These sections, which appear in all chapters, describe follow-up research to studies described in regular sections of the text. Thus, they truly represent the *cutting edge* of research in social psychology. In fact, the work described in such sections is so new, that in many cases it has not yet been published! *Work in Progress* sections illustrate the fact that research in social psychology is never finished: it is a perpetually ongoing process that yields important new information in a continuous manner. If there is one feature of the text that illustrates our commitment to keeping this book forever young—constantly in touch with new developments in the field—this is it. A few examples:

Where Politics and the Fundamental Attribution Error Meet: Shifts in Our Explanations for Why The Winner Won (Chapter 2)

The Retrospective Impact of Expectations: Remembering What We Expected to Experience . . . But Didn't (Chapter 3)

Subliminal Conditioning of Attitudes: Conscious Thought or Unconscious Association? (Chapter 4)

Compartmentalizing Self-Information: Warding Off Depression in Times of Stress (Chapter 5)

Prejudice in a Multicultural High School: Testing the Common Group Identity Model in a Field Setting (Chapter 6)

Appearance Anxiety, Interpersonal Behavior, and Weight (Chapter 7)

Dating as a Unique Relationship (Chapter 8)

Complaining in Close Relationships: Evidence For Some Intriguing Gender Differences (Chapter 9)

Practical Implications of Research on Volunteerism (Chapter 10)

Where Hormones and Personality Meet: Effects of Testosterone and Type A
Behavior Pattern on Aggression By Males (Chapter 11)
How Groups Overcome the Tendency to Discuss Shared Information: The
Role of Expectations and Strategic Processing (Chapter 12)
How Did Bill Clinton Win the 1992 Presidential Election (Chapter 14)

NEW AND REORGANIZED CHAPTERS

In order to reflect emerging areas of theory and research, this edition contains
several new or totally reorganized chapters:

Chapter 5: Social Identity: Self and Gender. This is an **entirely new** chapter,
prepared specifically for the new edition. It covers two major topics that are currently receiving a great deal of attention in social psychology and is a timely addition to the book.

Chapter 10: Prosocial Behavior: Providing Help to Others. In the previous edition, Prosocial Behavior was combined with other topics (cooperation and conflict).
Now, in response to reviewer and user comments, it receives full chapter coverage.

**Chapters 13 and 14: Social Psychology and the Individual: Population. Health
and Environmental Applications,** and **Social Psychology and Society: Legal, Political
and Organizational Applications.** These two chapters replace three chapters in the
previous edition. (Reviewers and users suggested this change.) Coverage of applications of social psychology to **health, politics,** and **law** have been increased, while
applications to population issues has been added as a new section. Coverage of
applications to business and environmental issues have been somewhat reduced.

COVERAGE OF NEW TOPICS AND LINES OF RESEARCH

In addition to the changes described above, we have updated virtually every section of the text. As a result, scores of new topics are covered in this edition. A partial listing of these topics includes:

Social Psychologists as Perennial Skeptics: The Importance of Replication
and Multiple Methods in Social Research (Chapter 1)
Self-Monitoring and the Regulation of Nonverbal Cues (Chapter 2)
Attentional Resources and Trait Attribution (Chapter 2)
Attributions and Affirmative Action (Chapter 2)
Impression Management: Does It Really Work? (Chapter 2)
Automatic Vigilance (Chapter 3)
Motivated Skepticism (Chapter 3)
The Mere Ownership Effect (Chapter 3)
The Costs of Thinking Too Much (Chapter 3)
How Culture shapes Thought: Effects of Cultural Schemas (Chapter 3)
Genetic Factors in Attitude Formation (Chapter 4)
Subliminal Conditioning of Attitudes (Chapter 4)
Individual Differences and the Elaboration Likelihood Model (Chapter 4)
Hypocrisy and the Alteration of Social Attitudes (Chapter 4)
The Reciprocity of Persuasion: When Attitude Change Is a Two-Way Street
(Chapter 4)
Social Identity (Chapter 5)
Gender Identity and Gender Roles (Chapter 5)
Self-Focusing Behavior (Chapter 5)
Prejudice With and Without Pangs of Conscience (Chapter 6)
Automatic Activation of Stereotypes (Chapter 6)
Affective States and Illusory Correlations (Chapter 6)

Outcome-Biased Inferences and Stereotypes (Chapter 6)
Sexual Harassment (Chapter 6)
Racial Identification Among African-Americans (Chapter 6)
Residential Propinquity and Marriage (Chapter 7)
Subliminal Repeated Exposure (Chapter 7)
Infants' Preference for Attractive Adults (Chapter 7)
The Repulsion Hypothesis: New Findings (Chapter 7)
Relationships Among Siblings (Chapter 8)
Adolescents' Love of Their Parents (Chapter 8)
Effects of External Pressures on Lovestyles (Chapter 8)
Hopelessness as a Result of Loneliness (Chapter 8)
Relationship Patterns Among Married Couples (Chapter 8)
Why People Are Rude to Intimate Partners (Chapter 8)
Effects of Mother-Infant Attachment Styles on Adult Relationships (Chapter 8)
Complaining as a Technique of Social Influence (Chapter 9)
Personality and Obedience: Who Resists and Who Obeys? (Chapter 9)
The Altruistic Personality (Chapter 10)
AIDS Volunteerism (Chapter 10)
Defense Mechanisms and Blaming the Victim (Chapter 10)
Reactions to Being Helped by a Sibling (Chapter 10)
The Hostile Attributional Bias and Aggression (Chapter 11)
Gender Differences in Aggression: The Potential Role of Hormones (Chapter 11)
Shame-Proneness and Aggression: Self Rejection and Aggression (Chapter 11)
Groups and Negotiation: Are Two Heads Better Than One? (Chapter 12)
Social Compensation: Making Up For Lack of Effort by Others (Chapter 12)
Deliberation Style and Group Decisions (Chapter 12)
Electronic Communication: A Plus in Group Decisions? (Chapter 12)
Transformational Leadership: Leadership Through Vision (Chapter 12)
Situational and Dispositional Influences on Teenage Pregnancy (Chapter 13)
Effects on Health of Striving for Low-Level versus High-Level Goals
    (Chapter 13)
Self-Concealment as a Determining of Anxiety, Depression, and Physical
    Symptoms (Chapter 13)
Multiple Effects of the Destruction of Tropical Rain Forests (Chapter 13)
Effect of Gender, Race, Ethnic Group, and Nationality on Smoking (Chapter 13)
Effects of Pretrial Publicity on Judicial Decisions (Chapter 14)
Effects of Cognitive Processing on Liability Decisions (Chapter 14)
Attractiveness of Plaintiff and Defendant in Sexual Harassment Cases
    (Chapter 14)
Variables Determining Presidential Greatness (Chapter 14)
The Possible Role of Genetic Factors in Job Satisfaction (Chapter 14)
Perceived Fairness (Equity) and Work Motivation (Chapter 14)
Attributions and Conflict in Organizations (Chapter 14)

CONTINUITY IN THE FACE OF CHANGE: WHAT—FOR GOOD REASONS—REMAINS THE SAME

As the preceding comments suggest, change has indeed been a dominant theme of this revision: new features, new topics, new chapters—all are sprinkled liberally throughout the book. This does not imply, however, that *everything* is new. On the contrary, we have had the same basic vision of what a useful social psychology text should be like for almost twenty-five years, and have not departed from it in this new edition. Key aspects of this perspective, which lies at the very heart of the book, include:

A Reader-Friendly Approach: As in the past, we have made vigorous efforts to make the book as interesting and appealing to students as possible. To us, this implies many concrete steps, such as, writing in language students can understand, including a wide variety of reader aids (chapter outlines, detailed summaries, glossaries), and carefully selecting and designing all illustrations. Suffice it to say that we have retained the approach and features students have liked in *Social Psychology* for more than twenty years.

Several Special Features: In addition to the *new* special features described above, this revision retains several features present in previous editions:

FOCUS ON RESEARCH: CLASSIC CONTRIBUTIONS. These sections describe classic studies in social psychology. they help illustrate the foundations of modern social psychology, and call attention to the fact that even what is newest has important roots in past research and theory.

FOCUS ON RESEARCH: THE CUTTING EDGE. These sections describe recently published research in social psychology—research that, in our view, is especially interesting or important.

SOCIAL PSYCHOLOGY: ON THE APPLIED SIDE. These sections describe applications of the findings of principles of social psychology to practical problems and issues.

(Please note, however, that *virtually of these sections, are new;* they are not merely repeats from the previous edition.)

A Broad Eclectic Approach to the Field: As in past editions, we have adopted a "Let 1,000 Flowers Bloom!" approach to presenting social psychology. In essence, we let the field speak for itself, rather than attempting to impose our own views or preferences on it.

In sum, while this new edition does indeed constitute a major revision, it maintains continuity, in important respects, with the previous six editions.

SUPPLEMENTS

All good texts should be supported by a complete package of ancillary materials, both for the student and the instructor. This book provides ample aid for both. For the student, we offer a *Study Guide* written by Bem Allen and Gene Smith. It gives students practice with short answers, definitions, matching, multiple choice, and completion questions.

For instructors, we offer an annotated instructor's edition with bound-in teaching notes, transparencies, test bank, computerized test bank, a reader by Wayne Lesko, a new set of CNN video programs linked to topics in the text, a video library, as well as custom-published ancillaries. Please feel free to contact your Allyn and Bacon sales representative for more information on all of these, as well as related titles.

SOME CONCLUDING COMMENTS—AND A LOOK AHEAD

Not many texts survive into a seventh edition, so we certainly feel honored by the support and acceptance our book has attained during the past twenty years. Indeed, it has been used by many more students than any other textbook in the history of social psychology. Yet, despite so many years of revisions, refinements, and—we hope—improvements, we realize that this is one process that is never complete. *Yes,* we have spared no effort in our attempt to improve the book. But we realize, nonetheless, that it can certainly be enhanced still further in many different ways. For this reason, we earnestly invite your comments, advice, and guidance. If there's something you feel can be improved, please—*let us know!* Write, call, fax, or send an E-mail message; the format certainly doesn't matter. What *does* matter, is this: **We will appreciate your input, and we really will listen!** Thanks in advance for your help.

About the Authors

ROBERT A. BARON is currently Professor of Psychology and Professor of Management at Rensselaer Polytechnic Institute. A Fellow of the APA since 1978, he received his Ph.D. from the University of Iowa (1968). Professor Baron has held faculty appointments at the University of South Carolina, Purdue University, the University of Minnesota, University of Texas, University of Washington, and Princeton University. He has received numerous awards for teaching excellence at these institutions. Professor Baron has also been a visiting Fellow at the University of Oxford (England). He served as a Program Director at the National Science Foundation from 1979 to 1981. Professor Baron has published more than ninety articles in professional journals and twenty-three invited chapters. He has served on the editorial boards of numerous journals (e.g., *Journal of Personality and Social Psychology, Journal of Applied Social Psychology*), and is currently an associate editor for *Aggressive Behavior.* He is the author or co-author of twenty-five books, including *Human Aggression, Psychology,* and *Behavior in Organizations.* He holds a U.S. patent for an invention designed to improve the physical environment of living and working spaces through air filtration and noise control. At present, Professor Baron's major research interests focus on applying the principles and findings of social psychology to behavior in work settings (e.g., the causes and management of organizational conflict; impact of the physical environment on task performance and productivity). Professor Baron is a long-time runner; his hobbies include woodworking, music, and enjoying fine food.

DONN BYRNE holds the rank of Distinguished Professor of Psychology and is the Director of the Social-Personality Program at the University at Albany, State University of New York. He received the Ph.D. degree in 1958 from Stanford University and has held academic positions at the California State University at San Francisco, the University of Texas, and Purdue University as well as visiting professorships at the University of Hawaii and Stanford University. A past president of the Midwestern Psychological Association and of the Society for the Scientific Study of Sex, he is a Fellow of the Society for Personality and Social Psychology, Society for the Psychological Study of Social Issues, and the Society for the Scientific Study of Sex; he is a Charter Fellow of the American Psychological Society. He has authored fifteen books, thirty-one invited chapters, one hundred and thirty-seven articles in professional journals, plus twenty-two additional publications such as book reviews and brief notes. He directed the doctoral work of forty-two Ph.D.s as well as that of several current graduate students at Albany. He has served on the Editorial Boards of *Experimental Social Psychology, Journal of Applied Social Psychology, Sociometry, Journal of Sex Research, Journal of Personality, Interamerican Journal of Psychology, Journal of Research in Personality, Psychological Monographs, Social Behavior and Personality: An International Journal,* and *Review of Personality and Social Psychology.* He was invited to deliver a G. Stanley Hall lecture at the 1981 meeting of the American Psychological Association in Los Angeles and a State of the Science address at the 1981 meeting of the Society for the Scientific Study of Sex in New York City. He was an invited participant in Surgeon General Koop's Workshop on Pornography and Health in 1986, and received the Excellence in Research Award from the University at Albany in 1987 and the Distinguished Scientific Achievement Award from the Society for the Scientific Study of Sex in 1989. His current research interests include interpersonal attraction and the prediction of sexually coercive behavior. In his leisure time he enjoys fiction, the theatre, and working on landscaping projects such as the construction of a walkway at his home.

Acknowledgements: Some Words of Thanks

Writing is a solitary task, best performed alone. Converting authors' words into a finished book, however, requires the efforts and assistance of many persons. In preparing this text, we have been aided by a large number of dedicated, talented people. We can't possibly thank all of them here, but we do wish to express our appreciation to those whose help has been most valuable.

First, our sincere thanks to the colleagues listed below, who read and commented on various portions of the manuscript:

Bem P. Allen
Western Illinois University

Galen V. Bodenhausen
Michigan State University

Nyla R. Branscombe
University of Kansas

Clive M. Davis
Syracuse University

Tamara J. Ferguson
Utah State University

Grace Galliano
Kennesaw State College

Joan A. W. Linsenmeier
Northwestern University

Angela Lipsitz
Northern Kentucky University

David Lundgren
University of Cincinnati

Laura Sidorowicz
Nassau Community College

Richard Moreland
University of Pittsburgh

Ralph Erber
DePaul University

Cyndy Nordstrom
Illinois State University

Gene Smith
Western Illinois University

Kathryn Kelley
SUNY—Albany

Jacqueline Pope-Tarrence
Western Kentucky University

Janet B. Ruscher
Tulane University

Robert Seaton
College of DuPage

Dean Keith Simonton
University of California, Davis

Linda Skitka
Southern Illinois University

Gail Williamson
University of Georgia

Frank Wong
Hofstra University

In addition, of course, we are indebted to the many colleagues who kindly completed our preliminary survey; to a large degree, data from that survey guided the entire revision process. Professor Grace Galliano, Kennesaw State College; Professor Barry Gillen, Old Dominion University; Professor John Harvey, University of Iowa; Professor Joan Linsenmeier, Northwestern University; Professor Angela Lipsitz, Northern Kentucky University; Professor Sandy Maxedon, Angelo State University; Professor Lynn McCutcheon, Northern Virginia Community College; Professor Peter McDonald, North Georgia College; Professor Richard Moreland, University of Pittsburgh; Professor Bradley C. Olson, Northern Michigan University; Professor Jack Powell, University of Hartford; Professor Richard Reardon, University of Oklahoma; Profesor Gail Williamson, University of Georgia; Professor Frank Wong, Hofstra University; Professor Robert Ahlering, Central Missouri State University; Professor Anne Baumgardner, Michigan State University; Profesor Galen Bodenhausen, Michigan State University; Professor Lisa Bohan, California State University—Sacramento; Professor Nyla Branscombe, University of Kansas; Professor R. D. Clark, Flroida State University; Professor Thomas Cooley, Worcester State College; Professor Thomas Crawford, University of California—Irvine; Professor James Dabbs, Georgia State University; Professor James Davis, University of Illinois; Professor William C. Davis, Texas Southmost College; Professor Roberta DeWick, University of Tennessee; Professor James Driscoll, University of Louisville; Professor Robert Fitzsimmons, Central Connecticut State University; Professor Rachel Foster, Central Michigan University; Professor Gail Futoran, Texas Tech University.

Also, we would like to recognize our Sixth Edition Reviewers.

Second, our sincere thanks to Matthew Hogben for his help with the **Social Diversity** sections, with the Test Bank, with preparing a draft of one chapter, and with the reference list. His dedication and diligence were obvious from start to finish, and we truly appreciate his help.

Third, we are very grateful to the colleagues who provided input for the new **Work in Progress** sections. Their willingness to take time out from their busy schedules to discuss their most recent research with us, and to provide us with preprints, manuscripts, and letters describing this work was invaluable, and we wish to offer our thanks to all these gracious colleagues here: Mark D. Alicke, Art Aron, Elliot Aronson, Paul C. Bernhardt, Robert F. Bornstein, Bob Bringle, Jerry M. Burger, Wilbur Castellow, Shelley Chaiken, Jennifer Crocker, Jim Dabbs, Peter H. Ditto, Robert Emmons, Kenneth L. Dion, Karen K. Dion, Sam L. Gaertner, Daniel T. Gilbert, Brian AS. Gladue, Jon A. Krosnick, Akiva Liberman, Stewart J. H. McCann, Diane L. Mackie, Brenda Major, Gary Moran, Ari Nadler, Anthony Pratkanis, Carol D. Ryff, Barry H. Schneider, Sharon Shavitt, Carolin Showers, Mark Snyder, Garold Stasser, Bill Swann, Leigh Thompson, and Tim D. Wilson.

Fourth, we wish to thank what we might well describe as our "Secret Weapon"—Susan Badger, our editor at Allyn & Bacon and Vice President and Publisher. She is truly an outstanding person, and we (and this book) have profited from her expertise, good judgment, and commitment to the project at every step along the way.

Fifth, our sincere thanks to our Project Manager, Leslie Olney. She oversaw many key aspects of production, and we were indeed fortunate to have her, with her many talents, as part of the team.

Sixth, our thanks to Jay Howland for her very careful and constructive copyediting. No author looks forward to seeing all those red marks and little yellow slips on their work. But in this case, the extra work was well worth the effort, since it certainly helped improve the manuscript.

Seventh, our thanks to several other persons who contributed to various aspects of the production: to Rose Corbett Gordon for diligent photo research; to Melinda Grosser for a bright and inviting design; to DeNee Reiton Skipper and Karla Grinnell for page makeup and composition; and to Linda Dickenson for a striking cover.

Eighth, our thanks to the following colleagues for providing reprints and preprints of their work—Gary Moran, J. Phillipe Rushton, David Buss, Bill Fisher, Vincent Jeffries—and to many others; for their aid in a variety of ways too numerous to mention here.

Finally, we wish to thank Gene Smith and Bem Allen for their outstanding work on the Instructor's Section, and for their help in preparing the Study guide.

To all these truly outstanding people, and to many others, our warm personal thanks!

SOCIAL PSYCHOLOGY

The Field of Social Psychology:
How We Think about and
Interact with Others

Special Sections

Rodeos; barbecues; the Rio Grande River; cowboys and campfires; those were the images that filled my imagination. It was the spring of 1974, and I had just accepted a visiting appointment at the University of Texas. My wife and I were busy with the chores of packing, and one task was to sell our car. We had decided that since we were going to live in a larger town with a much warmer climate, we needed a bigger car with better air conditioning. So I ran an ad for our Toyota Corona in the local newspaper. In the past, I had had good luck starting such ads with the phrase "For Sale by Purdue Professor"; I adopted the same strategy once again.

Much to my delight, a potential buyer arrived the next day. I showed him our Toyota and extolled its many virtues. He liked the car very much and, after a short test drive, said, "Okay, I'll take it." I was happy—but confused. Did this mean that he was willing to pay the full asking price? "You mean that you want to buy it?" I stammered lamely. "Yes," he replied. "That was $950 you were asking, right?" Now I was really mixed up. Yes, I *had* asked for $950 in the ad, but that was $200 more than I actually hoped to get. What should I do? Here was someone willing to pay me more than I thought the car was actually worth! I struggled with my conscience for a moment, and then surrendered to my better instincts: "Look," I said with some embarrassment, "are you sure you want to pay that much? To be honest, I was really willing to take less. I don't think it's worth $950. How about $800?"

Now it was *his* turn to look bewildered. And was it my imagination, or did he actually take a step backward, away from me? He thought for a moment and then, pulling at his ear, asked: "What's wrong with it? If you're willing to drop the price, it must have some problem you haven't mentioned."

"No, really," I protested. "There's no problem. It's just that I expected you to bargain with me."

Now I was sure: He *was* backing away. "Well, I don't know . . ." he said uncertainly. "I guess I'd better have it checked by my mechanic. . . ." My feelings were hurt. Here I was, trying to do him a favor, and all I was getting in return was mistrust and suspicion. What a world! But I knew the car was okay, so I agreed. His mechanic gave it a thorough inspection and then nodded his approval. The next day my buyer returned with a check for $800 and drove the car away. But I could tell from the look on his face that he still had doubts and that he didn't trust me. When I described these events to my wife, she didn't seem surprised at all. "Naturally

he was suspicious," she commented. "People around here aren't used to bargaining like you are. So when you offered to lower the price, he figured you were trying to pull a fast one."

"But it was just the opposite!" I protested vehemently. "I lowered the price because I was trying to be fair. Well, that'll teach me. I try to do the right thing, and all that happens is that I'm treated like some kind of tricky used car salesman. I just can't figure people out!"

"Well, you're the psychologist," my wife reminded me, laughing. "If *you* can't, then who can?"

And that insightful comment provides a very good start for this book, because in essence, that is precisely what it is all about: *people.* More specifically, it is a text about people interacting with, and thinking about, others—the *social side* of our existence as human beings. In our opinion, this is truly a fascinating topic, partly for the following reason: *other people often play a crucial role in our lives.* At different times and in different contexts, other people are the source of many of our most satisfying forms of pleasure (love, praise, help) and many of our most important forms of pain (rejection, criticism, embarrassment). So it is not at all surprising that we spend a great deal of our time interacting with others, thinking about them, and trying to understand them (see Figure 1.1).

The incident presented above (which really happened) provides a good introduction to our powerful concern with the social side of life. Consider my plight when the potential buyer agreed to pay the full price. He was not behaving according to my expectations—my *script* for this social interaction, as social psychologists would term it (Fiske & Taylor, 1991). I expected him to bargain; instead, he offered me the full asking price. Why? What should I do? Informal rules (*norms*) governing buyer-seller exchanges suggest that if a buyer makes an offer acceptable to a seller, then the seller should agree. But this is where my sense of fairness—*equity,* in the terminology of social psychology—came into play (Greenberg, 1990). I felt that the car was worth less than he offered; how could I sell it to him for more? In addition, I was concerned about another issue. Remember: My ad began, "For Sale by Purdue Professor." Was he

Chapter 1
THE FIELD OF SOCIAL PSYCHOLOGY

▼

This chapter is connected to all other chapters, since it introduces
the field and basic methods of research in social psychology.

offering me the full price because of the positive *stereotype* that professors are
totally honest and trustworthy? If so, wouldn't it be wrong for me to take
advantage of this belief by accepting the full asking price?

The buyer, too, had lots to consider in this unusual situation. Why was I
offering to sell the car for less than he had offered? Talk about violating expectations or social norms! Sellers are not supposed to lower the price of an item
without being asked—and certainly not to a figure lower than that offered by
the buyer. What was I up to? No wonder he became suspicious; my actions
must have seemed totally weird to him. So, while I was busy trying to figure out
what to do, the buyer was facing several dilemmas and puzzles of his own.

You're innocent until proved guilty, Mr. Throgmorton
. . . although I don't think I've ever seen beadier eyes.

 **The social side of life:
Why it's so important**

FIGURE 1.1 We spend much of
our time interacting with others,
thinking about them, or trying to
understand them.
Source: The Wall Street Journal, 8
March 1988.

Admittedly, this situation is a somewhat unusual one. But the key point it illustrates is true across a very wide range of contexts: *our social relations with others constitute a very important part of our lives.* Consequently, we *do* spend a lot of time and effort thinking about others, trying to understand them, and trying to extract basic principles concerning social behavior—principles that can help us predict others' actions in our future dealings with them. In these efforts we are often guided by what many people call "common sense"—the collective knowledge of our own society concerning social relations. Such knowledge is informal in nature and is based partly upon casual observation of human behavior in social situations, and partly on the writings of poets, philosophers, novelists, and playwrights who have written about human social relations for thousands of years. "Commonsense" knowledge is highly appealing and often seems to capture essential truths about social behavior. Consider the following well-known sayings: "Love looks with the heart, not with the eyes"; "Misery loves company"; "Birds of a feather flock together."

Exercise 2

Yet, in many respects, such *informal knowledge* offers a somewhat confusing picture of human social behavior. For example, common sense suggests that prolonged separation can strengthen bonds of affection: "Absence makes the heart grow fonder." At the same time, though, it warns us that separation can weaken such bonds: "Out of sight, out of mind." Which is correct? Can both be right? The "wisdom of the ages" offers no clear-cut answers.

This is a small sample of the questions that are currently being studied by social psychologists, and that we'll address in this text.

TABLE 1.1 The Breadth of Social Psychology

Question	Chapter in Which It Is Covered
How can we tell when another person is lying	Chapter 2
What techniques do individuals use to "look good" to others—to manage the impressions they make upon them?	Chapter 2
Do we pay more attention to negative information about others than to positive information about them? And if so, why?	Chapter 3
Can our attitudes be changed by stimuli we don't consciously notice?	Chapter 4
Why do some individuals have positive self-evaluations (high self-esteem) while others are much lower in this regard?	Chapter 5
Do affirmative action policies influence perceptions of the qualifications of minority group members?	Chapter 6
What specific characteristics make people physically attractive?	Chapter 7
What is jealousy? What are its major causes? Effects?	Chapter 8
Do people complain in order to get their own way?	Chapter 9
Are people less likely or more likely to offer help to others when they are part of a crowd than when they are alone?	Chapter 10
Does alcohol consumption lead to increased aggression?	Chapter 11
Are optimists really more resistant to the harmful effects of stress than pessimists?	Chapter 12
What are charismatic leaders? What characteristics make them so successful in influencing their followers?	Chapter 13
How do people react when they conclude that they've been treated unfairly, either by another person or by an organization?	Chapter 14

How, then, can we obtain more conclusive—and accurate—information about this topic? How, in short, can we replace speculation, intuition, and insightful guesses with something more definitive? One compelling answer is provided by the field of **social psychology**. And the answer is as follows: *Accurate and useful information about even the most complex aspects of social behavior and social thought can be acquired through the use of basic methods of science.* In short, social psychologists suggest that our understanding of the ways in which we think about and interact with others can be greatly enhanced if we replace the informal methods used by poets, philosophers, playwrights, and novelists with the more systematic methods that have proved invaluable in other fields of science.

From the perspective of the 1990s, this assertion may strike you as quite obvious. After all, if scientific methods have worked so well in illuminating other aspects of the natural world, why not apply them to social behavior as well? You may be surprised to learn, therefore, that a science-oriented field of social psychology did not emerge until well into the present century and that it has flourished primarily during the past four or five decades. Despite its recent appearance, however, social psychology has already made impressive progress. Perhaps the breadth and potential value of the information it yields are best suggested by a list like the one in Table 1.1. Please note that the questions in the table represent only a small sample of the many topics currently being studied by social psychologists. The field is currently so diverse and so far-ranging in scope that no single list could possibly represent all of the topics it considers.

We trust that the list in Table 1.1 has whetted your appetite for more information about social behavior and social thought. If so, please be patient. We will consider all of the topics listed in the table—plus many others—in later chapters. Before doing so, however, we want to provide you with some background information. The reason for this is straightforward: Research findings indicate that people have a much better chance of understanding, retaining, and using new information if they are first provided with a framework for holding it. With this thought in mind, we will use the remainder of this chapter for completing three preliminary tasks.

Exercise 3

First, we will present a formal *definition* of social psychology—what it is and what it seeks to accomplish. This knowledge will help orient you to the field and give you an overview of what it is all about. Second, we will offer a brief overview of social psychology's *history*—how it began, how it developed, where it is today, and where, we believe, it may be going in the future. This information will assist you in understanding why social psychologists choose to study certain topics and why they approach these in specific ways. Third, we will examine some of the methods used by social psychologists to answer intriguing questions. A working knowledge of these *research methods* will help you to understand later discussions of specific research projects and will also assist you in comprehending how the body of knowledge that constitutes modern social psychology has been obtained.

SOCIAL PSYCHOLOGY: A WORKING DEFINITION

Offering a formal definition of almost any field is a complex task. In the case of social psychology, this complexity is increased by two factors: (1) the field's great diversity, and (2) its rapid rate of change. Despite the broad sweep of topics they choose to study, though, most social psychologists seem to focus the bulk of their attention on one central task: Understanding how and why

Critical Thinking Question 1

individuals behave, think, and feel as they do in situations involving other persons. Taking this central focus into account, our working definition of social psychology is as follows: *Social psychology is the scientific field that seeks to understand the nature and causes of individual behavior and thought in social situations.* In other words, social psychology seeks to understand how we think about and interact with others. We will now clarify several aspects and implications of this definition.

SOCIAL PSYCHOLOGY IS SCIENTIFIC IN NATURE

Reading (2): Lesko, Social Psychology and Science

In the minds of many persons, the term *science* refers primarily to fields such as chemistry, physics, and biology. Such persons may find somewhat puzzling our view that social psychology, too, is scientific. How can a field that seeks to investigate the nature of love, the causes of aggression, and everything in between be scientific in the same sense as astronomy, biochemistry, or geophysics? The answer is surprisingly simple. In reality, the term *science* does not refer to a select group of highly advanced fields. Rather, it refers to a general set of methods—techniques that can be used to study a wide range of topics. In deciding whether a given field is or is not scientific, therefore, the crucial question is: *Does it make use of scientific procedures?* To the extent that it does, it can be viewed as scientific in orientation. To the extent that it does not, it can be identified as falling outside the realm of science.

What are these techniques and procedures? We'll describe them in detail in a later section. Here, we'll merely note that they involve efforts to gather systematic information about issues or processes of interest, plus an attitude of skepticism. It is a basic premise of science that *all* assertions about the natural world should be tested, retested, and tested again before they are accepted as accurate. For example, consider the assertion by Ralph Waldo Emerson that "Beauty is the mark God sets on virtue"—the suggestion, in essence, that people who are beautiful possess other virtues as well. Is this true? According to basic rules of science, we can tell only by subjecting this idea to careful, systematic research. (In fact, such research has been conducted, and we'll examine it in chapter 7.) In contrast, fields that are not generally regarded as scientific in nature make assertions about the natural world, and about people, that are *not* subjected to careful tests. In such fields the intuition, beliefs, and special skills of practitioners are considered to be sufficient (see Figure 1.2).

So, is social psychology scientific? Our reply is, definitely *yes*. Although the topics that social psychologists study are very different from those in the physical or biological sciences, the methods they employ are similar in nature and orientation. For this reason, it makes good sense to describe social psychology as basically scientific in nature.

SOCIAL PSYCHOLOGY FOCUSES ON THE BEHAVIOR OF INDIVIDUALS

Societies differ widely in terms of their expectations concerning courtship and marriage; yet it is still individuals who fall in—and out of—love. Similarly, societies vary greatly in terms of their overall level of bigotry; but it is still individuals who hold stereotypes about specific groups, experience negative feelings toward them, or seek to exclude them from jobs, neighborhoods, or schools. In short, social behavior and social thought rest, ultimately, with individuals. Given this basic fact, social psychologists have chosen to focus most of their attention on the actions and thoughts of individuals in social situations. They

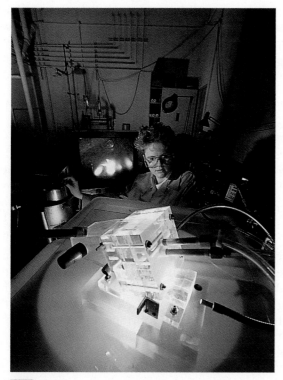

 Science versus nonscience: Different methods, different values

FIGURE 1.2   In fields such as social psychology, data are gathered systematically and all hypotheses are carefully tested before being accepted as accurate. In nonscientific fields, in contrast, hypotheses and assertions are accepted at face value in the absence of any systematic tests of their accuracy.

realize, of course, that such behaviors always occur against a backdrop of, and are influenced by, sociocultural factors. Social psychologists' major interest, however, lies in understanding the factors that shape the actions and thoughts of individual human beings within social settings.

SOCIAL PSYCHOLOGY SEEKS TO UNDERSTAND THE CAUSES OF SOCIAL BEHAVIOR AND THOUGHT

In a key sense, the heading of this section states the most central aspect of our definition, the very core of our field. What it means is that social psychologists are principally concerned with understanding the wide range of conditions that shape the social behavior and thought of individuals—their actions, feelings, beliefs, memories, and inferences—with respect to other persons. Obviously, a huge number of different factors play a role in this regard. It is also clear, however, that most factors affecting social interaction fall into five major categories: (1) *the actions and characteristics of others*; (2) basic *cognitive processes* such as memory and reasoning—processes that underlie our thoughts, beliefs, ideas, and judgments about others; (3) *ecological variables*—direct and indirect influences of the physical environment; (4) the *cultural context* in which social behavior and thought occur; and (5) *biological aspects* of our nature and genetic inheritance that are relevant to social behavior. Perhaps a few words about each of these categories will help clarify their essential nature.

THE ACTIONS AND CHARACTERISTICS OF OTHERS.   Consider the following incidents:

Exercise 1

One second after the traffic light turns green, the driver behind you begins to honk her horn angrily.

Your professor praises a paper you wrote, describing it to the entire class as the best one he's read in several years.

At the beach, a very attractive person on a nearby blanket catches your eye and smiles at you in a very enticing manner.

Will these actions by others have any impact upon your behavior and thought? Absolutely! So it is clear that often we are strongly affected by the actions of other persons.

Now, be honest: Have you ever felt uneasy in the presence of a handicapped person? Do you ever behave differently toward elderly people than toward young ones? Toward persons belonging to various racial and ethnic groups? Toward persons higher in status than yourself (e.g., your boss) than toward persons lower in status (e.g., children)? Your answer to some of these questions is probably yes, for we are often strongly affected by the visible characteristics and appearance of others.

COGNITIVE PROCESSES.   Do you remember the used car anecdote at the start of this chapter? If so, ask yourself again how the buyer interpreted my offer to sell the car for less than he had proposed. What thoughts passed through his mind? In all probability, one thing he did was compare this incident with others in which he had purchased an item from someone else. In other words, he drew on *memories* of past, related situations. In addition, he probably generated a list of possible motives for my offer and examined the likelihood that each of these was accurate. Then, after making such *judgments*, he considered various alternative actions. He could withdraw his offer and leave, ask to have the car inspected, pay me the lower price on the spot, or possibly refer me to a psychologist for personal counseling! Whatever precise thoughts went through his mind, it is clear that basic cognitive processes such as memory, reasoning, and judgment all played a role. Social psychologists are well aware of the importance of such cognitive processes and realize that they must be taken into careful account in our efforts to understand many aspects of human social behavior (Fiske & Taylor, 1991).

ECOLOGICAL VARIABLES: IMPACT OF THE PHYSICAL ENVIRONMENT. Are people more prone to wild, impulsive behavior during the full moon than at other times (Rotton & Kelly, 1985)? Do we become more irritable and aggressive when the weather is hot and steamy than when it is cool and comfortable? Does exposure to high levels of noise, polluted air, or excessive levels of crowding have any impact on our social behavior or performance of various tasks? Research findings indicate that the physical environment does indeed influence our feelings, thoughts, and behavior, so ecological variables certainly fall within the realm of modern social psychology (Baron, in press; Bell, et al., 1990). And indeed, we'll consider their impact in chapter 13.

CULTURAL CONTEXT. Social behavior, it is important to note, does *not* occur in a cultural vacuum. On the contrary, it is often strongly affected by cultural norms (social rules concerning how people should behave in specific situations), membership in various groups, and shifting societal values. Whom should people marry? How many children should they have? Should they keep their emotional reactions to themselves or demonstrate them openly? How close should they stand to others when talking to them? (See Figure 1.3.) Is it appropriate to offer gifts to public officials in order to obtain their favorable action on various requests? These are only a small sampling of the aspects of social behavior that can be—and regularly are—influenced by cultural factors. By *culture* we simply mean the organized system of shared meanings, perceptions, and beliefs held by persons belonging to some group (Smith & Bond, 1993).

As you already know, cultures differ greatly, so actions and beliefs considered fully appropriate in one culture may be deemed strange or unacceptable in another. For example, offering gifts to public officials is viewed as entirely appropriate in many cultures; indeed, such payments are expected by the officials, who count them as a regular part of their income. In contrast, in other cultures such payments are labeled *bribes* and are viewed not only as unacceptable but as illegal. Clearly, then, efforts to understand social behavior must take careful account of cultural factors. If they do not, they stand the very real chance of being what one prominent researcher described as *experiments in a vacuum* (Tajfel, 1982)—studies that tell us little about social behavior under real-life conditions and in real-life settings. As we'll note below, attention to the effects of cultural factors is an increasingly important trend in modern

 Cultural factors influence social behavior

FIGURE 1.3 The distance between two people holding a conversation varies across different cultures. In some (left photo), a distance of four to five feet is considered appropriate. In others (right photo), a much smaller distance is preferred.

social psychology, as our field endeavors to take account of the increasing cultural diversity that is a hallmark of the late twentieth century. In fact, diversity will be a major theme of this book, and one to which we will return in every chapter.

BIOLOGICAL ASPECTS.   Is social behavior influenced by biological processes and by genetic factors? Ten years ago most social psychologists would have answered no, at least to the genetic factors part of this question. Now, however, the pendulum of scientific opinion has swung in the other direction, and many believe that our preferences, behaviors, emotional reactions, and even cognitive abilities are affected to some extent by our biological inheritance (Buss, 1990; Nisbett, 1990). The view that biological and genetic factors play an important role in social behavior has, perhaps, been most dramatically stated by the field of **sociobiology**, a discipline suggesting that many aspects of social behavior are the result of evolutionary processes in which patterns of behavior that contribute to reproduction (to getting one's genes into the next generation) are strengthened and spread throughout a population. From the sociobiological perspective, in essence, we all exist primarily to serve our genes—to ensure that our genetic material is passed on to as many offspring as possible (Barkow, 1989; Wilson, 1975). And this basic assumption is used to explain many aspects of social behavior. For example, sociobiologists would argue that if we find specific physical features attractive in potential romantic partners (e.g., a smooth skin, lustrous hair), this is because such features are associated with good health and thus with high reproductive capacity. In short, we like them because doing so increases our chances of passing our genes to future children.

While many social psychologists accept the view that biological and genetic factors can play some role in social behavior, they seriously question several of the basic assumptions of sociobiology (Brewer, 1990; Cantor, 1990). For example, they reject the view that behaviors or characteristics that are affected by genetic factors cannot be altered. On the contrary, even strong genetic predispositions or preferences can be changed. For example, at the present time, millions of persons choose voluntarily to restrict their intake of foods high in cholesterol, despite the fact that we have a strong genetically determined predisposition to find such foods very tasty. Similarly, persons with vision defects—which are in large part genetically determined—readily overcome such problems by means of corrective lenses. In short, the fact that biological factors may play a role in social behavior in no way implies that such tendencies cannot be altered.

Similarly, social psychologists reject the implicit assumption that because they are the result of a long evolutionary process, tendencies in social behavior that currently exist *should* exist. In a sense, this is akin to arguing that people should make no efforts to protect themselves against diseases or parasites, since these are a natural part of the evolutionary world! On the contrary, social psychologists argue that the mere fact that some tendency or form of behavior exists is *not* a strong argument that it should exist. Human beings, after all, modify the world around them in many ways; why should they not also choose to change their own behavior?

These and other objections to the basic assumptions of sociobiology have led social psychologists who wish to study the role of biological and genetic factors in social behavior to propose another name for their field: **evolutionary social psychology** (Buss, 1990). This term suggests that social behavior is indeed affected by natural selection; tendencies toward behaviors that are most adaptive from the point of view of survival often increase in strength over time within a given population. But it also recognizes the fact that such tendencies are definitely not set in stone. On the contrary, they can—and do— change in response to shifting environmental and social conditions, and they can even be altered or overridden by cognitive processes. We will comment on the role of genetic factors in various forms of social behavior at several points in later chapters.

SOCIAL PSYCHOLOGY: SUMMING UP

To conclude: Social psychology focuses mainly on understanding the causes of social behavior and social thought—on identifying factors that shape our feelings, behavior, and thought in social situations. It seeks to accomplish this goal through the use of scientific methods, and it takes careful note of the fact that social behavior and thought are influenced by a wide range of social, cognitive, environmental, cultural, and biological factors.

The remainder of this text is devoted to summarizing some of the key findings of social psychology. This information is fascinating and we're certain you will find it of interest. But please be warned: It is also full of surprises and will challenge many of your current ideas about people and relations between them. It is probably safe to predict that after exposure to our field, you'll never think about social relations in quite the same way as before. If you value such change and look forward to gaining new insights—as we're confident you do—please read on.

SOCIAL PSYCHOLOGY: A CAPSULE MEMOIR

When, precisely, did social psychology begin? This question is difficult to answer, for speculation about social behavior stretches back to ancient times (Allport, 1985). Any attempt to present a complete survey of the historical roots of social psychology would quickly bog us down in endless lists of names and dates. Because we definitely wish to avoid that pitfall, this discussion will be quite limited in scope. We will focus mainly on the emergence of social psychology as an independent field, its growth in recent decades, where it stands now, and where we believe it will move next.

THE EARLY YEARS: SOCIAL PSYCHOLOGY EMERGES

Few fields of science mark their beginnings with formal ribbon-cutting ceremonies. Instead they develop gradually, as growing numbers of scientists become interested in specific topics or develop new methods for studying existing ones. This pattern certainly applies to social psychology. No bottles of champagne were uncorked to mark its entry on the scene, so it is difficult to choose a specific date for its official launching. Perhaps the years between 1908 and 1924 qualify as the period during which social psychology first appeared as an independent entity. In each of these years, an important text containing the words *social psychology* in its title was published. The first, by William McDougall (1908), was based largely on the view that social behavior stems from innate tendencies or *instincts*. As we have just seen, many modern social psychologists are willing to entertain the notion that genetic factors play a role in some aspects of social behavior. Most, however, reject the idea of fixed, unchanging instincts as an important cause of social behavior. Thus, it is clear that the field had not assumed its modern perspective with McDougall's book.

The second volume, by Floyd Allport (1924), is a different story. That book is much closer—surprisingly close, given the date of its publication—to the modern orientation of the field. Allport argued that social behavior stems from many different factors, including the presence of other persons and their specific actions. Further, his book emphasized the value of experimentation and contained discussions of actual research that had already been conducted on such topics as conformity, the ability to recognize the emotions of others from their facial expressions, and the impact of audiences on task performance. Because all these topics have been studied by social psychologists in recent years, the following conclusion seems justified: by the middle of the Roaring Twenties, social psychology had appeared and had begun to focus on many of the issues and topics it still studies today.

The two decades following publication of Allport's text were marked by rapid growth. New issues were studied, and systematic methods for investigating them were devised and polished. Important milestones in the development of the field during this period include research by two of its founders—Muzafer Sherif and Kurt Lewin. Sherif (1935) studied the nature and impact of *social norms*—rules indicating how individuals ought to behave—and so contributed many insights to our understanding of pressures toward *conformity*. Lewin and his colleagues (Lewin, Lippitt, & White, 1939) carried out revealing research on the nature of leadership and related group processes. Quite apart from this research, Lewin's influence on social psychology was profound, since many of his students went on to become very prominent in the field. Their names (e.g., Leon Festinger, Harold Kelley, Morton Deutsch, Stanley Schachter, John Thibaut) will feature prominently in later sections of this text.

In short, by the close of the 1930s, social psychology was an active, growing field that had already contributed much to our knowledge of human social behavior.

SOCIAL PSYCHOLOGY'S YOUTH: THE 1940S, 1950S, AND 1960S

After a pause resulting from World War II, social psychology continued its growth during the late 1940s and the 1950s. During this period, the field expanded its scope in several directions. Social psychologists focused attention on the influence that groups and group membership exert on individual behavior (Forsyth, 1991). And they examined the link between various personality traits and social behavior—in, for example, noted research on the *authoritarian personality*—a cluster of traits that predispose individuals toward acceptance of extreme political ideologies such as Nazism (Adorno, et al., 1959; see Figure 1.4, p. 15).

One of the significant events of this period was development of the theory of **cognitive dissonance** (Festinger, 1957). This theory proposed that human beings dislike inconsistency and will strive to reduce it. Specifically, the theory argues that people seek to eliminate inconsistency between their attitudes or inconsistency between their attitudes and their behavior. While this theory may strike you as being quite sensible, it actually leads to many unexpected

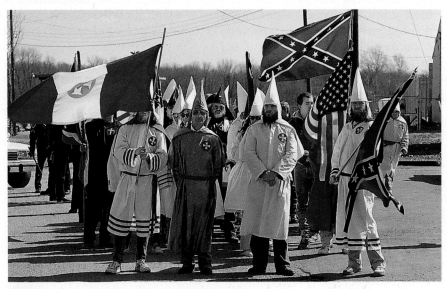

 Extremists: Do they share certain traits?

FIGURE 1.4 Research conducted by social psychologists identified a number of characteristics that appear to be shared by members of a wide variety of extremist hate groups.

predictions. For example, the theory suggests that offering individuals small rewards for stating views they don't really hold is often more effective in getting them to change these opinions than offering them larger rewards for the same actions—a principle sometimes described as the *less-leads-to-more effect*. Festinger's theory captured the interest of many social psychologists and remained a major topic of research for several decades. (We will examine it in detail in chapter 4.)

In an important sense the 1960s can be viewed as the time when social psychology fully came of age. During this turbulent decade of rapid social change, the number of social psychologists rose dramatically, and the field expanded to include practically every aspect of social interaction you might imagine. So many lines of research either began or developed during these years that it would be impossible to list them all here. Suffice it to say that the scope of social psychology virtually exploded during this period.

THE 1970S AND 1980S: A MATURING FIELD

The rapid pace of change did not slacken during the 1970s; if anything, it accelerated. Many lines of study begun during the 1960s were expanded. Several new topics rose to prominence or were studied from a new perspective. Among the most important of these were *attribution* (How do we infer the causes behind others' behavior?); *gender differences* and *sex discrimination* (To what extent does the behavior of women and men actually differ in various situations? What are the adverse effects on women of negative stereotypes concerning their supposed traits?); and *environmental psychology* (What is the impact of the physical environment—factors such as noise, heat, crowding, and air pollution—on social behavior?).

In addition, two larger-scale trends took shape in and expanded during the 1980s. Since these trends are of great significance to our understanding of modern social psychology, we will describe them here.

GROWING INFLUENCE OF A COGNITIVE PERSPECTIVE.   As noted earlier, social psychologists have long realized that cognitive factors—attitudes, beliefs, values, inferences—play a key role in social behavior. Starting in the late 1970s, however, interest in such topics took an important new form. At this time many social psychologists concluded that our understanding of virtually all aspects of social behavior could be greatly enhanced by attention to the cognitive processes that underlie them (e.g., Wyer & Srull, 1988). This approach involves, briefly, efforts to apply to many aspects of social thought and social behavior basic knowledge about such issues as (1) how memory operates, (2) how reasoning occurs, and (3) how new information is integrated into existing mental frameworks. To cite just one example, efforts have been made to understand the nature and impact of stereotypes in relation to certain aspects of memory (tendencies to recall only certain types of information) and aspects of social reasoning that can lead us to false conclusions about others (Hamilton, Sherman, & Ruvolo, 1990). The results of research conducted within this perspective have been impressive. Major insights into many aspects of social behavior have been gained, and new issues previously overlooked (e.g., the impact of current moods on social thought and vice versa; Stroessner, Hamilton, & Mackie, 1992) have been brought into sharp focus. We will discuss such research in chapters 2, 3, and 4.

GROWING EMPHASIS ON APPLICATION: EXPORTING SOCIAL KNOWLEDGE.   The 1970s and 1980s were also marked by a second major trend in social psychology: growing concern with the *application* of social knowledge. An increasing number of social psychologists have turned their attention to questions concerning *personal health* (e.g., What factors help individuals resist the adverse impact of stress? Are certain life-styles or personal characteristics linked to coronary disease?); the *legal process* (e.g., How valid is eyewitness testimony? What information is most influential in shaping the decisions of jurors?); and many aspects of behavior in *work settings* (e.g., What factors lead individuals to feel they are being treated unfairly by their companies? Do personal factors like applicants' appearance influence the outcomes of job interviews?). Whatever its specific focus, such research attempts to apply the findings and principles of social psychology to the solution of practical problems. This theme is certainly not new in our field; Kurt Lewin, one of its founders, once remarked, "There's nothing as practical as a good theory," by which he meant that theories of social behavior and thought developed through systematic research often turn out to be extremely useful in solving practical problems. There seems little doubt, however, that interest in applying the knowledge of social psychology to practical issues has increased in recent years, with many beneficial results. We will examine this work in detail in chapters 13 and 14, and we will also highlight it throughout the text in special **On the Applied Side** sections such as the one that follows.

IS JUSTICE REALLY BLIND? DEFENDANTS' ATTRACTIVENESS AND THE LEGAL PROCESS

Justice, we would all like to believe, is blind: When individuals stand before a court, accused of a crime, they should be judged solely on the basis of available evidence—*not* on the basis of their appearance or ethnic background. Many studies conducted by social psychologists indicate, however, that defendants' personal characteristics *do* seem to matter. Females tend to receive more lenient sentences than males (Cruse & Leigh, 1987). Members of ethnic minorities in the United States tend to be convicted and assigned harsher punishments than members of the majority (Stewart, 1980). Perhaps even more unsettling, attractive defendants are acquitted more often than unattractive ones (Michelini & Snodgrass, 1980) and, when found guilty, receive lighter sentences (Stewart, 1985; Esses & Webster, 1988). Does this mean that our legal system is seriously flawed? Before jumping to this conclusion, it is important to note that most of the studies mentioned above were laboratory simulations, in which students were the participants and the crimes were imaginary ones. Are similar effects found in actual courtrooms?

A study conducted by Downs and Lyons (1991) suggests that they are, at least under certain circumstances. In this investigation, courtroom records for over 2,000 women and men arrested for various misdemeanors and felonies (less serious and more serious crimes, respectively) were examined. In particular, the fines or bail set for these persons by judges were recorded. To determine whether these amounts were influenced by the physical attractiveness of the defendants, police officers *not* involved in the original arrests rated the defendants' attractiveness when these people first appeared before a judge. Ratings were made on a simple five-point scale ranging from 1 (lowest attractiveness) to 5 (highest attractiveness). Since the defendants differed in terms of gender and ethnic background, male and female police officers of varying ethnic backgrounds performed the ratings. Because the defendants appeared before the judges soon after their arrests, they had no opportunity substantially to alter their appearance. In many legal proceedings, attorneys take active steps to assure that their clients appear as clean and attractive as possible.

Results indicated that for the more serious crimes (felonies), defendants' attractiveness exerted no significant effect upon the magnitude of the bail or fines set by the judges. For the less-serious misdemeanors, however, such effects *were* observed. The more attractive the defendants, the lower the fines or bail they received. In other words, judges were more lenient toward attractive defendants than toward unattractive ones (see Figure 1.5, p. 18.).

Other research (Stewart, 1980, 1985) indicates that defendants' attractiveness does not influence decisions concerning their guilt or innocence but does influence the magnitude of the sentences they receive. The findings reported by Downs and Lyons are consistent with these conclusions, since fines or bail are set only after it has been determined that defendants are, in fact, guilty.

The practical implications of such research are clear—and somewhat disturbing. It appears that justice is actually far from blind and that judges' decisions are regularly influenced by the way defendants look, quite apart from evidence pertaining to their case. This suggests, in turn, that judges should be

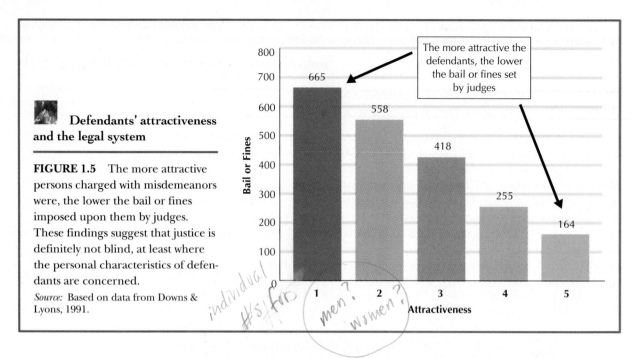

Defendants' attractiveness and the legal system

FIGURE 1.5 The more attractive persons charged with misdemeanors were, the lower the bail or fines imposed upon them by judges. These findings suggest that justice is definitely not blind, at least where the personal characteristics of defendants are concerned.

Source: Based on data from Downs & Lyons, 1991.

The more attractive the defendants, the lower the bail or fines set by judges

made aware of such effects, and that other efforts should be undertaken to help minimize the impact of this potential form of bias.

In any case, as you can readily see, research on effects of defendants' attractiveness provides a very vivid example of the way in which social psychology can help to clarify issues of great practical significance.

WHERE DO WE GO FROM HERE? THE 1990S AND BEYOND

Earlier we noted that *diversity* is a prime characteristic of social psychology. Given this fact, predictions about the future of the field are uncertain to say the least. Still, at the risk of being proven wrong by future events, we wish to offer the following guesses about how social psychology will change in the coming decades.

COGNITION AND APPLICATION: GROWING KNOWLEDGE, GROWING SOPHISTICATION. The first of our predictions is the one on firmest ground: The two major trends described above—growing influence of a cognitive perspective and increasing interest in application—will continue. Knowledge about cognitive processes (memory, reasoning, inference) is accumulating very quickly. It seems only natural that social psychologists will use that knowledge in their efforts to understand social behavior and especially social thought. Such work has already yielded valuable results, and we are confident it will continue to do so in the decades ahead.

Similarly, we predict that interest in applying the principles and findings of social psychology will also continue. Increased concern with application appears to be a natural outgrowth of increasing maturity in almost any field. Thus, as social psychology advances, efforts to apply its growing knowledge to practical issues will continue and perhaps expand.

THE ROLE OF AFFECT: REALIZING THAT FEELINGS COUNT, TOO. It is a basic law of physics that actions produce opposite reactions of comparable scope. In a sense, the same principle seems to apply to the growing emphasis on cognition in social psychology. Partly in response to the increasing interest in various aspects of social thought, many researchers have called for renewed focus on the impact of the emotional side of our existence (Schwarz, 1990). As a result, much recent research has sought to examine the impact of *affective states*—relatively mild and short-lived changes in our current moods or feelings (Forgas, 1991; Isen & Baron, 1991; Schwarz, 1991). Not surprisingly, the findings of these investigations suggest that affect is indeed an important determinant of many forms of social behavior, ranging from helping on the one hand, through aggression and conflict on the other (e.g., Isen, 1987). In addition, a growing volume of research has focused on complex interactions between affect and cognition—how feelings shape thought and how thought shapes feelings (Schwarz, 1990). We'll examine this relationship in detail in chapter 3. For the moment, we'll merely note that in our opinion, research on the role of affect in social behavior and social thought will continue, and perhaps accelerate, during the next decade.

ADOPTION OF A MULTICULTURAL PERSPECTIVE: TAKING FULL ACCOUNT OF SOCIAL DIVERSITY.   When I (Bob Baron) was in high school, I received an unusual present from my uncle: a book that provided an introduction to the United States for Europeans planning to visit this country for the first time. In retrospect, one section was of special interest. It stated that the population of the United States was "about 90 percent of European descent." How the world has changed since the late 1950s when the book was written! At the present time, the population of the United States is far more diverse than this book suggested. Consider California, the most populous state. At present, only 57 percent of its population is of European descent, and projections indicate that by the year 2000 no single group will be in the majority. And for the United States as a whole, it is projected that by the year 2050 merely 53 percent of the population will be of European descent. Such statistics indicate that multicultural diversity is a fact of life in the United States in the late twentieth century. And similar trends are present in many other countries as well. Large-scale migration is occurring in many areas, and international trade and international travel are certainly on the rise. The result: the days of relative cultural isolation are fast coming to a close (see Figure 1.6).

Multicultural diversity: A fact of life in the late twentieth century

FIGURE 1.6   In the United States and many other countries, *cultural diversity* has increased rapidly. Social psychology is currently studying this diversity and the impact of cultural and ethnic factors upon social behavior.

What is the impact of such diversity on social psychology? In our view the effects are both pronounced and far-reaching. For various historical reasons (among them the movement of many European social psychologists to the United States prior to and immediately after World War II), a large majority of practicing social psychologists live and work in North America. Because of this fact, a large proportion of all research in social psychology has been conducted here. This raises an important question: Can the findings of these studies be generalized to other cultures? In other words, are the principles established in U.S. research applicable to people all around the world? As noted recently by Smith and Bond (1993), this is an open question. Most social psychologists have assumed that the findings of their research *are* generalizable across cultures, largely because the processes they study are ones operating among human beings everywhere. Is prejudice different in Asia or Africa than in North America? Do pressures toward conformity—and reactions to them—differ in South America, the Middle East, and Europe? Most social psychologists have assumed that the answer to such questions is *no,* that these processes are essentially identical everywhere. Now, however, there is growing realization that this is not necessarily so (Smith & Bond, 1993). Many social psychologists now believe that cultural factors and forces are so powerful that they can influence even the most basic aspects of social behavior. In addition, it is increasingly apparent that cultural differences are an important topic in their own right and should receive careful attention in social psychological research. Why do persons from different cultures react in contrasting ways to various situations? What factors in their cultures are responsible for these differences? A growing number of social psychologists believe that studying such issues may help clarify which aspects of social behavior are universal among human beings and which are products of cultural factors.

For all these reasons social psychology has moved toward a **multicultural perspective**—a focus on multicultural diversity—in recent years; and it is our prediction that this trend will continue in the years ahead. To take account of this development, in every chapter we will highlight research dealing with cultural diversity and its effects in special sections titled **Social Diversity**. These sections describe intriguing differences in social behavior or social thought between various cultural or ethnic groups. They reflect our belief that interest in such differences—and in their roots—is a rising trend in social psychology.

Those, then, are our predictions. Will they prove to be accurate? Only time and the course of future events will tell. Regardless of their fate, however, there is one additional prediction we are willing to make with great confidence: No matter how social psychology changes in the years ahead, it will remain an active, vital field—one with an impressive potential for contributing to human welfare.

ANSWERING QUESTIONS ABOUT SOCIAL BEHAVIOR AND SOCIAL THOUGHT: RESEARCH METHODS IN SOCIAL PSYCHOLOGY

By now you should have a basic grasp of (1) what social psychology is; (2) how it developed; and (3) where, perhaps, it is headed. With that information in place, it is appropriate for us to turn to another essential issue: How do social psychologists attempt to answer questions about social behavior and social thought? How, in short, do they seek to expand our knowledge of these basic topics? To provide you with a useful overview of this process, we will touch on three related issues. First, we will describe two key *methods of research in social psychology*. Next, we will examine the role of *theory* in such research. Finally, we will consider some of the complex *ethical issues* that arise in social psychological research and that, to a degree, are unique to such research.

THE EXPERIMENTAL METHOD:
KNOWLEDGE THROUGH INTERVENTION

If a large sample of social psychologists were asked to name the method of research they most prefer, most would probably reply with the term **experimentation**. Unfortunately, our past experience suggests that many persons view experimentation as being somewhat mysterious and complex. In fact, that is far from the case. In its essential logic experimentation is surprisingly simple. To help you understand its use in social psychological research, we will first describe the basic nature of experimentation and then comment on two conditions that are essential for its successful use.

EXPERIMENTATION: ITS BASIC NATURE.   A researcher who decides to employ the experimental method generally begins with a clear-cut goal: to determine whether (and to what extent) a specific factor (variable) influences some aspect of social behavior. To find out, the researcher then (1) systematically varies the presence or strength of this factor, and (2) tries to determine whether those variations have any impact on the aspect of social behavior or social thought under investigation. The central idea behind these procedures is this: If the factor varied does exert such effects, individuals exposed to different amounts (levels) of the factor should show different patterns of behavior. Exposure to a small amount of the factor should result in one level or pattern of behavior, exposure to a larger amount should result in another pattern, and so on.

Critical Thinking
Question 2

Generally, the factor systematically varied by the researcher is termed the **independent variable**, while the aspect of behavior studied is termed the **dependent variable**. In a simple experiment, then, subjects in different groups are exposed to contrasting levels of the independent variable (e.g., low, moderate, high). The researcher then carefully examines and compares the behavior of these persons to determine whether it does in fact vary with different levels of the independent variable. If it does—and if two other conditions described below are also met—the researcher can tentatively conclude that the independent variable does indeed affect the aspect of behavior or cognition being studied.

Discussion Question 2

Perhaps a concrete example will help you to form a clearer picture of this process. Let's consider an experiment designed to examine the *hypothesis* (an as yet unverified suggestion) that the faster people talk (at least up to a point), the more persuasive they are. In such research, the independent variable would be the speed at which would-be persuaders speak and the dependent variable would be some measure of the attitudes or preferences held by the persons the persuaders are trying to influence. For example, such a study might involve delivery of a speech designed to alter the attitudes of audience members toward a particular issue—let's say, attitudes toward legislation that will place strict controls on the release of chemicals that deplete the earth's ozone layer. For argument's sake, imagine that the audience consists of executives from air-conditioning companies—businesses that use vast amounts of

Exercise 5

Transparency 1.3

the chemicals to be regulated. It is probably safe to assume, therefore, that they will be initially opposed to the legislation. How would the experiment proceed? A basic strategy would be to expose several different groups of participants to the same persuasive message while systematically varying the speed at which it is delivered. Thus, one group of subjects would be exposed to the message presented at a slow rate of speech (about 150 words per minute). A second group would hear the same message presented at an average rate of speech (about 170 words per minute). A third group would hear the message delivered at a very fast pace (190 words per minute).

After all groups heard the speech, the dependent variable—some measure of the audience members' attitudes toward the legislation—would be collected. For example, participants might be asked to indicate the extent to which they favored the proposed law by circling one number on a scale such as the one shown in the top part of Table 1.2. Alternatively, they might be asked to indicate the extent to which they agreed or disagreed with the speaker (see Table 1.2).

If rate of speech does affect persuasion, then we might obtain a pattern of results such as those shown in Figure 1.7. As this figure indicates, the faster the persuader speaks, the more favorable are the attitudes of audience members toward the legislation. We must assume, by the way, that subjects in the three groups do not differ with respect to their attitudes prior to hearing the persuasive message. If they do, serious complications can occur in terms of interpreting any results that are obtained. (Actually, several studies have been conducted to investigate the relationship between speed of speech and persuasion. Some have yielded a pattern of findings precisely like those in Figure 1.7; Miller et al., 1976; Woodall & Burgoon, 1984. However, other research—to which we'll return in chapter 4—indicates that fast talkers are *not* always more persuasive than slower ones; Smith & Shaffer, 1991.)

Items such as these could be used to measure the success of would-be persuaders in changing others' attitudes.

TABLE 1.2   Measuring reactions to a persuasive message

To what extent do you favor legislation designed to limit the release into the atmosphere of chemicals that damage the earth's protective ozone layer? (Please circle one number.)

Strongly Opposed						Favor
1	2	3	4	5	6	7

To what extent do you agree with the views expressed by the speaker? (Check one.)
_____ Strongly disagree
_____ Disagree
_____ Neither agree nor disagree
_____ Agree
_____ Strongly agree

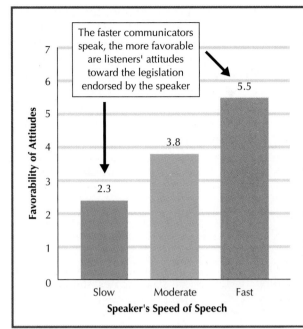

The faster communicators speak, the more favorable are listeners' attitudes toward the legislation endorsed by the speaker

Experimentation: A simple example

FIGURE 1.7   In the experiment illustrated here, groups listen to persuasive appeals delivered by a communicator who speaks at a slow, moderate, or fast rate. Results indicate that the faster the communicator speaks, the more favorable are listeners' attitudes toward the speaker's message. These findings suggest that speed of speech is one factor affecting persuasion.

At this point we should note that the example just presented describes an extremely simple case—the simplest type of experiment social psychologists ever conduct. In many instances researchers wish to examine the impact of several independent variables at once. For example, in the study just described, they might want to consider not only the speed at which a persuader speaks but the quality of her or his arguments as well. If this were the case, then a second variable—the extent to which the arguments presented by the speaker are well-reasoned and convincing—might be added to the study. When two or more variables are included in an experiment, a larger amount of information about the topic of interest can usually be obtained. In real social situations, after all, our behavior and thought are usually influenced by many different factors acting concurrently, not simply by one factor. Even more important, potential **interactions** between variables can be examined—that is, we can determine whether the impact of one independent variable is affected in some manner by one or more other variables. For example, in the experiment described above we might find that fast talkers are more persuasive, but only when their arguments are quite convincing. When their arguments are weak, the opposite may be true: People who talk at a fast pace may actually be less persuasive than ones who talk more slowly (see Figure 1.8, p. 24).

SUCCESSFUL EXPERIMENTATION: TWO BASIC REQUIREMENTS. Earlier it was noted that before we can conclude that an independent variable has affected some form of behavior, two important conditions must be met. And a basic understanding of these conditions is essential for evaluating the usefulness of any experiment.

The first condition involves what is usually termed the **random assignment of subjects to groups**. According to this principle, each person taking part in a study must have an equal chance of being exposed to each level of the inde-

Reading: (1): Lesko, The Sample with the Built-in Bias

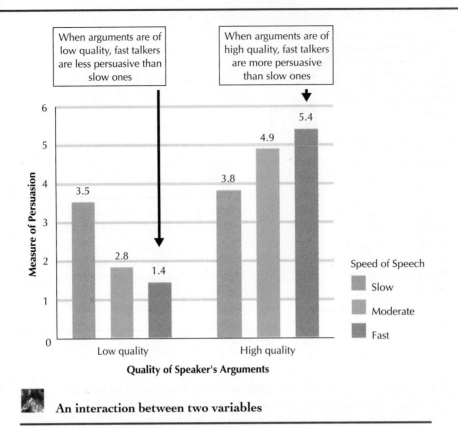

When arguments are of low quality, fast talkers are less persuasive than slow ones

When arguments are of high quality, fast talkers are more persuasive than slow ones

Speed of Speech

Slow

Moderate

Fast

Measure of Persuasion

3.5

2.8

1.4

3.8

4.9

5.4

Low quality

High quality

Quality of Speaker's Arguments

An interaction between two variables

FIGURE 1.8   Two independent variables are systematically manipulated: speakers' rate of speech and the quality of her or his arguments. Results indicate that when the quality of arguments is high, the faster the speaker talks, the greater the extent to which listeners are persuaded. In contrast, when the quality of arguments is low, the faster the speaker talks, the less the extent to which listeners are persuaded. This constitutes an *interaction* between the two variables.

pendent variable. The reason for this rule is simple: If subjects are *not* randomly assigned to each group, it may prove impossible to determine whether differences in their behavior in the study stem from differences they brought with them, from the impact of the independent variable, or from both. For instance, continuing with our study of speed of speech and persuasion, imagine participants in the study are drawn from two different sources: first-year law students and a group of high school dropouts enrolled in a special course designed to equip them with basic vocational skills. Now imagine that because of purely logistical factors (such as differences in the two groups' schedules), most of the participants exposed to the slow talker are law students, while most of the people exposed to the fast talker are high school dropouts. Suppose that results indicate that participants exposed to the fast talker show much more agreement with the views expressed than participants exposed to the slow talker. What can we conclude? Not much, because it is entirely possible that this difference stems from the different mixes of participants in the two experimental conditions: In the slow-talker condition, 75 percent of the participants are law students and 25 percent are high school dropouts, while in the fast-talker condition the opposite is true. Since law students may be somewhat harder to persuade than high school dropouts (see chapter 4), we can't really tell why these results occurred. Did they derive from differences in the persuader's rate of speech? From different proportions of the two groups of participants in each condition? Both factors? It's impossible to tell. To avoid such problems, it is crucial that all subjects have an equal chance of being assigned to different experimental groups (treatment).

Transparency 1.4
Discussion Question 3

The second condition referred to above may be stated as follows: Insofar as possible, all other factors that might also affect participants' behavior, aside from the independent variable, must be held constant. To see why this is so, consider what would happen if, in the study on speed of speech and persuasion, different speakers were used in each condition. Further, imagine that one of these speakers—the fast talker—had a beautiful English accent (an accent many Americans find very pleasant). Now assume that participants express greatest agreement with this speaker. What is the cause of this result? The fact that the speaker talked rapidly? Her accent? Both factors? Obviously, it is impossible to tell. In this situation, the independent variable of interest (speed of speech) is "confounded" with another variable—whether the speakers have an accent—that is not really part of the research. When such **confounding** occurs, it is impossible to determine the precise cause of any differences among the various groups in an experiment. The result: The findings are largely uninterpretable.

In the case we have just described, confounding between variables is relatively easy to spot. Often, though, it enters in more subtle ways. For this reason, researchers wishing to conduct successful experiments must always be on guard against it. Only when confounding is prevented can the results of an experiment be interpreted with confidence.

THE CORRELATIONAL METHOD: KNOWLEDGE THROUGH SYSTEMATIC OBSERVATION

Earlier we noted that experimentation is usually the preferred method of research in social psychology. (We'll see why below.) Sometimes, though, experimentation simply cannot be used. There are two reasons why this may be so. First, systematic variation in some factor of interest may be beyond an experimenter's control. Imagine, for example, that a researcher believes that panic in the stock market often stems from certain kinds of statements by the president and by the head of the Federal Reserve Board. Obviously, the researcher cannot arrange for these persons to make such statements in order to observe the effects. The actions of the president and other high government officials are outside her or his control.

Transparency 1.2

Second, ethical constraints may prevent a researcher from conducting what might otherwise be a feasible experiment. In other words, it might be possible to vary some factor of interest, but doing so would violate ethical standards accepted by scientists or society generally. For example, imagine that somehow a researcher *could* induce the president and the head of the Federal Reserve Board to make statements calculated to trigger a wild panic on Wall Street. Clearly, doing so would be unethical. After all, what gives this researcher the

Discussion Question 4

right to expose millions of persons to financial or psychological harm? Similarly, and perhaps a bit more realistically, suppose that a social psychologist had reason to suspect that certain kinds of beliefs about one's romantic partner are especially damaging to long-term relationships. Could this researcher try to induce such beliefs among one group of couples but not among another in order to determine whether divorces and other breakups were more common in the first group than in the second? Obviously not, for in conducting such a study, the researcher would endanger the happiness and well-being of the unknowing participants.

Faced with such difficulties, social psychologists often adopt an alternative research technique known as the **correlational method**. In this approach, researchers make no efforts to change one or more variables in order to observe the effects of these changes on some other variable. Instead, they merely observe naturally occurring changes in the variables of interest to learn if changes in one are associated with changes in the other. Such associations are known as *correlations,* and the stronger the association, the higher the correlation. (Correlations range from –1.00 to +1.00, and the greater the departure from 0.00, the stronger the relationship between the variables in question. Thus, a correlation of –.80 indicates a stronger relationship between two variables than a correlation of +.40.)

Transparency 5

To illustrate the correlational method, let's return, once again, to our study of speed of speech and persuasion. A researcher wishing to examine this issue by means of the correlational method might proceed as follows. First, she or he would measure the speed of speech of many would-be persuaders in a wide range of contexts (politics, sales, and so on). In each of these contexts, the researcher would also obtain some measure of the success of the would-be persuaders—for example, the percentage of votes each candidate receives, the amount of merchandise each salesperson moves. If fast talkers are more persuasive than slow talkers, results might indicate that these two variables are positively correlated: The faster candidates and salespersons speak, the greater their success.

The correlational method offers several useful advantages. For one thing, it can be used to study behavior in many real-life settings. For another, it is often highly efficient and can yield a large amount of interesting data in a short time. Moreover, it can be extended to include many different variables at once. Thus, in the study described above, information on the physical attractiveness, age, height, and gender of the political candidates and salespersons might be obtained. Through a statistical procedure known as *regression analysis,* the extent to which each of these variables is related to—and therefore predicts—success in politics and sales could then be determined.

Critical Thinking
Question 4

Transparency 1.1

Unfortunately, however, the correlational method suffers from one major drawback that greatly lessens its appeal to social psychologists. *In contrast to experimentation, the findings it yields are often somewhat uncertain with respect to cause-and-effect relationships.* The fact that changes in one variable are accompanied by changes in another in no way guarantees that a causal link exists between them—that changes in the first caused changes in the second. Rather, in many cases, the fact that two variables tend to rise or fall together simply reflects the fact that both are caused by a third variable. For example, suppose that a researcher finds that the faster politicians talk, the higher the percentage of votes they receive. Does this mean that speed of speech causes voters to prefer certain candidates? Perhaps. But it may also be that fast-talking candidates know more about the issues than slower-talking ones. If this is the case, then the

All of the correlations listed here have actually been observed. However, none indicates that the two factors involved are causally linked. Can you determine what third factor makes each pair of factors seem to be related to one another? (Answers appear below.)

TABLE 1.3 Examples of correlations that don't imply causation

Observed Correlation	Possible Underlying Cause
1. The more people weigh, the higher their salaries.	1. ~~↑age – ↑weight – ↑experience,~~ ∴ ↑$$
2. The greater the number of storks nesting on roofs in Northern Europe, the greater the number of births nine months later.	2. ~~cold weather → ↑birds nesting →~~ more people inside → ↑sex.
3. The greater the degree of crowding in cities, the higher their crime rates.	3. ~~related to poverty~~

Answers

1. Weight and earnings both increase with age and experience.
2. Cold weather makes roofs an attractive place to nest, and also causes people to remain indoors—where they engage in activities that increase births!
3. Crowding and crime are both related to poverty.

relationship between speed of speech and the outcome of elections is somewhat spurious. In fact both speed and success as a candidate are related to a third factor—knowledge of the issues. Perhaps this key point can be clarified by a few additional examples of correlations that do not indicate causation. These are listed in Table 1.3. Can you identify the third factors that may underlie the relationships shown in the table?

By now the main point should be clear. The existence of even a strong correlation between two factors should not be interpreted as a definite indication that they are causally linked. Such conclusions are justified only in the presence of additional, confirming evidence.

SOCIAL PSYCHOLOGISTS AS PERENNIAL SKEPTICS: THE IMPORTANCE OF REPLICATION AND MULTIPLE METHODS IN SOCIAL RESEARCH

Let's return once again to the research question we have addressed several times already: *Are fast talkers more persuasive than slow ones?* Suppose that we conducted a very careful experiment—one in which participants were randomly assigned to conditions and one in which the only conceivable difference between these two conditions was the speed with which the would-be persuader spoke. Further, imagine that the study yielded highly significant results: Participants exposed to the fast talker expressed much greater agreement with the views of this person than those exposed to the slow talker. On the basis of these results, can we conclude that our *hypothesis* has been confirmed—that fast talkers are indeed more persuasive than slow talkers?

While it is tempting to answer yes, most social psychologists would take a somewhat different stand. They'd agree that we were off to a good start and that initial findings were indeed consistent with the hypothesis. However, before concluding that this hypothesis represents *truth*—an accurate description of the social world—they would require additional proof. Social psychologists would require that you, and perhaps many other investigators too, *confirm* these results in subsequent studies. In other words, they'd insist that the initial findings be *replicated* over and over again before they'd accept these findings as fully valid. Further, they'd insist that such confirmations employ a wide range of methods, and that they be conducted in naturalistic field settings as well as the laboratory. Only if the findings of such additional research confirmed the initial ones would they accept them with confidence.

And here is where a serious rub enters the picture: Only rarely do the results of social psychological research yield totally consistent findings. A more common pattern is for some studies to offer support for a given hypothesis while others fail to offer such support. Why is this the case? In part because of the efforts of researchers to test various hypotheses under different conditions, in different settings, and using different methods. Such procedures are necessary to establish the *generality* of any findings—to assure that they apply to a wide range of persons and in many different contexts. But they also increase the likelihood that the various studies conducted will yield different—and sometimes inconsistent—results.

INTERPRETING DIVERSE RESULTS: SEARCHING FOR AN OVERALL PATTERN.   As we have already noted, a lack of total consistency in research findings seems to be the natural state of affairs in social psychology. Given the richness and complexity of the issues explored in social psychology (recall Table 1.1), this is hardly surprising. But this lack of total consistency in research findings does raise some troubling practical issues. For example, imagine that over the years, fifty different experiments were conducted to study the effects of speed of speech on persuasion. Of these, thirty-five yielded results like the ones described earlier: The faster people talk, the greater their success in influencing others. However, ten reported exactly the opposite findings: The faster people talk, the less their success as persuaders. And five reported no difference in persuasiveness between slow and fast talkers. What can we conclude? And how would we go about reaching such a judgment? In the past, the answer involved reviewing all the existing evidence and then, on the basis of what can be described only as insight and judgment, reaching some conclusion about the meaning of these diverse results. Such *narrative reviews*, as they have sometimes been termed (Beaman, 1991; Cooper & Lemke, 1991) were certainly more than simple box scores, in which the most frequently occurring findings were assumed to be the more accurate ones. But they did rest on the judgments of individual researchers—and this, of course, left them open to potential sources of error.

META-ANALYSIS: A SUPERIOR METHOD FOR COMBINING RESULTS ACROSS EXPERIMENTS.   More recently, a better means of dealing with such situations—for combining the results of independent studies in order to reach conclusions about the topics they investigate—has been developed. This technique is known as **meta-analysis**, and it has recently gained increasing popularity among social psychologists (e.g., Dillard, 1991; Johnson, 1991). In actual use, meta-analysis involves complex statistical procedures far beyond the scope of this discussion. In essence, however, these procedures simply combine the results of many different studies in order to estimate the *direction* and *size* of the effects of independent variables that have been investigated in numerous experiments. For example, a meta-analysis on the results of the fifty studies on speed of speech and persuasion would combine the findings of all of these investigations in order to determine whether, across all fifty, the speed variable has any effect. Further, such a meta-analysis would indicate the relative size of such effects, should they be found to exist.

Is meta-analysis superior to the kind of narrative reviews conducted in the past? A careful comparison of the two types of reviews by Beaman (1991) indicates that they are. For example, Beaman found that meta-analytic reviews are much more likely than narrative reviews to indicate how studies were selected for inclusion in the review, to give the direction and magnitude of effects uncovered, and to address theory (see Figure 1.9). On the other hand, meta-

Meta-analysis: Some key advantages

FIGURE 1.9   As shown here, meta-analysis offers important advantages over narrative reviews.
Source: Based on data from Beaman, 1991.

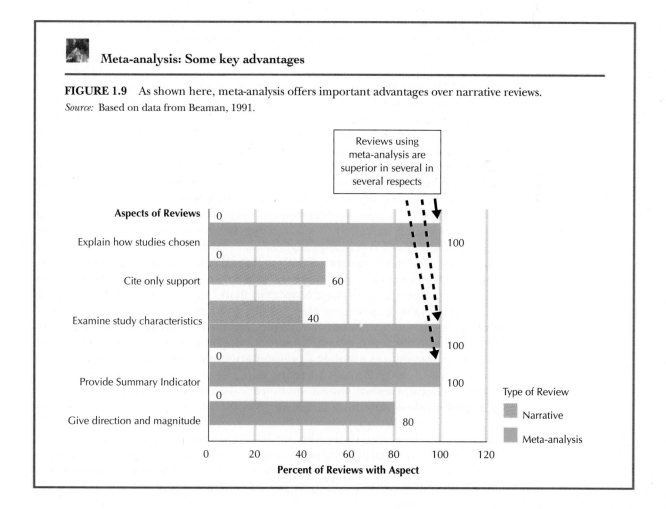

analytic reviews are *less* likely than narrative reviews to include only studies with positive results.

In sum, meta-analysis is an important tool for understanding the results of social psychological research, and so for understanding social behavior and social cognition. Throughout this text, therefore, we will refer to reviews of existing literature based on this procedure whenever possible. As noted by Myers (1991), meta-analytic reviews can help counteract our tendency to be unduly influenced by the results of one or a few studies that are especially interesting or ingenious, since such reviews combine the findings of many studies by statistical formula.

THE ROLE OF THEORY IN SOCIAL PSYCHOLOGY

Critical Thinking
Question 5

Over the years, the students in our classes have often asked: "How do social psychologists come up with such interesting ideas for their research?" As you can probably guess, there is no simple answer. Some research projects are suggested by informal observation of the social world around us. Social psychologists take note of some puzzling aspect of social behavior or social thought and plan investigations to increase their understanding of that aspect. On other occasions, the idea for a research project is suggested by the findings of an earlier study. Successful experiments in social psychology do not simply answer questions; they often raise new ones as well. Perhaps the most important basis for research in social psychology, however, is formal **theories**.

In simple terms, theories represent efforts by scientists in any field to answer the question *Why?* Theories involve attempts to understand precisely why certain events or processes occur as they do. Thus, theories go beyond mere observation or description of aspects of social behavior; they seek to *explain* them as well. The development of comprehensive, accurate theories is a primary goal of all science (Howard, 1985; Popper, 1959), and social psychology is no exception. Accordingly, a great deal of research in our field is concerned with efforts to construct, test, and refine theoretical frameworks. But what, precisely, are theories, and how are they used in social psychological research? Perhaps the best way to answer is through a concrete example.

Imagine that a social psychologist is interested in the following question: When people are in a good mood, are they more willing or less willing to take risks? Common sense seems to suggest that people who are feeling good will be high rollers and take more or larger risks. On examining existing evidence, however, the researcher finds a mixed pattern of results. In some studies people in a good mood did take greater risks than those in a more neutral mood, but in others the opposite was true. What's going on here? How can being in a positive mood both enhance and reduce risk taking? On the basis of current knowledge about the effects of mood on behavior and cognition, the researcher begins to formulate a preliminary theory. Perhaps people in a good mood seek to maintain this pleasant state. Thus, if taking risks helps them reach that goal, they will indeed be more willing to take risks than people in a neutral mood. If, in contrast, taking risks threatens the persistence of their positive feelings, the opposite may be true: People in a good mood will actually take smaller risks than those who are in a more neutral state. The researcher now predicts (primarily on the basis of previous evidence and existing theories) that the key factor may be the potential for actual loss. If people in a good mood believe that taking risks can lead to substantial losses, they will refrain from such behavior. If, instead, they view the potential for losses as minor or nonexistent, then being in a good mood may make them feel expansive and so increase their risk-taking tendencies.

In sum, the social psychologist now has a preliminary theory concerning the effect of mood on risk taking. In older fields of science such as physics or chemistry, theories are often stated as mathematical equations. In social psychology, however, they are usually phrased as verbal statements or assertions such as those above. Regardless of how they are expressed, theories consist of two main parts: (1) several basic concepts (in our example, risk taking, mood, potential losses); and (2) statements concerning relationships among these concepts ("Being in a good mood will increase risk taking when potential losses from such risks are small but will reduce risk taking when potential losses are large.")

Formulation of a theory is just the first step in a continuing process, however. Only theories that have been carefully tested and confirmed are useful; so in social psychology, as in all other fields of science, after a theory is proposed, several procedures normally follow. First, predictions are derived from the theory. These predictions are formulated in accordance with basic principles of logic and are known as *hypotheses.* For example, one hypothesis from the theory of mood and risk taking described above is as follows: People who have just received some kind of good news (and so are in a good mood) will be more likely to purchase a lottery ticket than people who have not received good news. (This would be the case because the only loss associated with taking that kind of risk is not winning, and lottery tickets are relatively inexpensive.)

Next, hypotheses are tested in actual research. If they are confirmed, confidence in the accuracy of the theory is increased. If, instead, such predictions are disconfirmed, confidence in the theory is weakened. Then the theory may be altered so as to generate new predictions. These are subjected to test, and the process continues. If the modified predictions are confirmed, confidence in the revised theory is increased; if they are disconfirmed, the theory may be modified again or, ultimately, rejected. Figure 1.10 on p. 32 summarizes this process.

Please note, by the way, that theories are useful from a scientific point of view only to the extent that they lead to *testable* predictions. If a theory fails to generate hypotheses that can be examined in actual research, it cannot be viewed as scientific in nature.

THE QUEST FOR KNOWLEDGE AND THE RIGHTS OF INDIVIDUALS: SEEKING A DEFENSIBLE BALANCE

In their use of experimentation and systematic observation, and in their reliance on comprehensive theories, social psychologists do not differ from researchers in many other fields. One technique, however, does seem to be unique to research in social psychology: **deception.** Basically, this technique involves efforts by researchers to withhold or conceal information about the purposes of a study from the persons who participate in it. The reason for using this procedure is simple: Many social psychologists believe that if participants know the true purposes of an investigation, their behavior will be changed by that knowledge. The research itself will then have little chance of providing useful information.

On the face of it, this is a reasonable belief. For example, imagine that in a study designed to examine the effects of physical attractiveness on first impressions, participants are informed of this purpose. Will they now react differently to a highly attractive stranger than they would have in the absence of this

Discussion Question 1

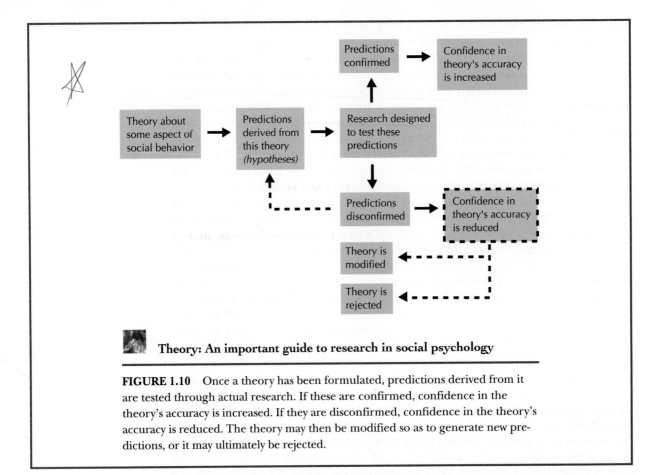

Theory: An important guide to research in social psychology

FIGURE 1.10 Once a theory has been formulated, predictions derived from it are tested through actual research. If these are confirmed, confidence in the theory's accuracy is increased. If they are disconfirmed, confidence in the theory's accuracy is reduced. The theory may then be modified so as to generate new predictions, or it may ultimately be rejected.

information? Perhaps, for now, they may lean over backwards to avoid evaluating the attractive person in a favorable manner, to prove that *they* are not affected by a stranger's outward appearance.

Exercise 4 Because of such considerations, many social psychologists feel that deception—at least on a temporary basis—is essential for their research (Suls & Rosnow, 1988). The adoption of this technique is not, however, without its costs. Deceiving research participants or withholding information from them, no matter how justified, raises important ethical issues.

First, it is possible that at least some persons exposed to deception will resent having been led astray. They may then adopt a negative attitude toward social research generally. Second, deception, even when temporary, may result in some type of harm to the persons exposed to it (Kelman, 1967). They may experience discomfort, stress, or negative shifts in self-esteem. Finally, there is the very real question of whether scientists committed to the search for knowledge should place themselves in the position of deceiving persons kind enough to assist them in this undertaking.

Critical Thinking
Question 3 In short, the use of deception does pose something of a dilemma to social psychologists. On the one hand, it seems essential to their research. On the other, its use raises serious problems. How can this issue be resolved? At pre-

sent, opinion remains divided. Some of our colleagues feel that deception, no matter how useful, is inappropriate and should be abandoned. Yet many others (perhaps a large majority) believe that temporary deception *is* acceptable, provided that certain safeguards are adopted (Baron, 1981). The most important of these are **informed consent** and thorough **debriefing**. (Both procedures, by the way, are required by ethical standards published by the American Psychological Association.)

Informed consent involves providing research participants with as full as possible a description of the procedures to be followed *prior to* their decision to take part in a study. By following this principle, researchers ensure that subjects know what they are getting into and what they will be asked to do before making a commitment to participate. In contrast, debriefing *follows* each experimental session. It consists of providing participants with a full explanation of all major aspects of a study, including its true goals and an explanation of the need for temporary deception. The guiding principle is that research participants should leave in at least as favorable or positive a state as when they arrived.

Fortunately, a growing body of evidence indicates that together, informed consent and thorough debriefing can eliminate—or at least substantially reduce—the potential dangers of deception (Smith & Richardson, 1985). For example, most subjects report that they view temporary deception as acceptable and do not resent its use (Rogers, 1980). And thorough debriefing does appear to eliminate many negative effects experienced by subjects as a result of temporary deception (Smith & Richardson, 1985). Still, it is unwise to take the safety or appropriateness of deception for granted (Rubin, 1985). Rather, it appears that the guiding principles for all researchers planning to use this procedure in their studies should be these: (1) Use deception only when it is absolutely essential to do so—when no other means for conducting a study exist; (2) always proceed with great caution; and (3) make certain that the rights, safety, and welfare of research participants come first, ahead of all other considerations.

USING THIS BOOK: A READERS' ROAD MAP

Before concluding this introduction to the field of social psychology, we'd like to comment briefly on several features of this text. Much of this information is also contained in the Preface, but since many readers seem to skip authors' prefaces, we thought it would be useful to repeat some information here. First, please note that we've taken several steps to make our text easier and more convenient for you to use. Each chapter begins with an outline of the major topics covered and ends with a detailed summary. Key terms are printed in **boldface type** and are defined in a glossary at the end of the chapter. Because figures and charts contained in original research reports are often quite complex, every graph and table in this text has been specially created for it. In addition, all graphs contain special labels designed to call your attention to the key findings presented (see Figure 1.11 on p. 34 for an example). We think that you'll find all of these illustrations easy to read and—more importantly—that they'll contribute to your understanding of social psychology.

Second, we want to note that we've included several distinct types of special sections throughout the text. None of these interrupt the flow of text mate-

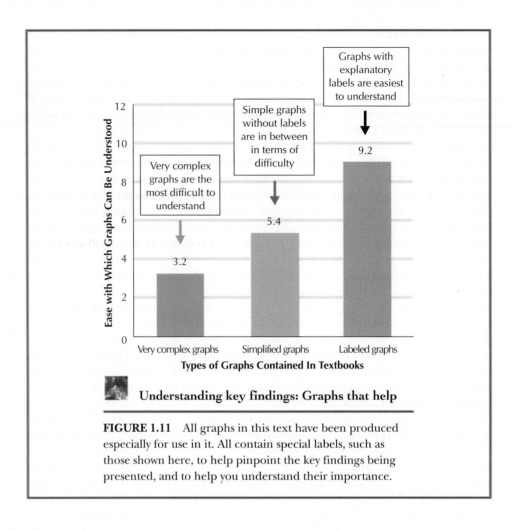

Understanding key findings: Graphs that help

FIGURE 1.11 All graphs in this text have been produced especially for use in it. All contain special labels, such as those shown here, to help pinpoint the key findings being presented, and to help you understand their importance.

rials; rather, they are presented at natural breaks in content. All are designed to highlight information we feel is especially important and interesting.

The first type of special insert is called **Focus on Research** and describes specific studies performed by social psychologists. These sections appear in two forms: (1) those subtitled *Classic Contributions,* which describe studies now widely viewed as classics in the field, and (2) those subtitled *The Cutting Edge,* which focus on projects carried out at what we feel are the frontiers of knowledge in social psychology.

The second type of special section is titled **Social Psychology: On the Applied Side**. These sections highlight the practical implications of social psychology—ways in which its knowledge and principles can contribute to the solution of a wide range of practical problems.

A third type of special section occurs near the end of each chapter and is titled **Social Diversity: A Critical Analysis**. These sections represent the growing *multicultural perspective* within social psychology. Thus, they present information concerning differences between ethnic groups within a given society, or differences across various cultures. For example, one such section (see chapter 2) examines cultural differences in the use of nonverbal cues—facial expressions, eye contact, and posture. Another (see chapter 11) explores possible explanations for the very large differences in incidence of violent crimes in different countries. **Social Diversity** sections are closely linked to the content of the chapters in which they occur, and seek to examine key aspects of social behavior and social thought from a multicultural perspective.

While ethnic and cultural groups certainly differ, so, too, do individuals *within* any given group. To take account of this important fact, we have also included special sections entitled **Individual Diversity**. These sections describe recent research and findings concerned with the role of individual differences in various forms of social behavior.

Finally, from time to time, we present special sections labeled **Work in Progress**. These are included for two reasons: (1) to report very recent follow-ups to specific studies, and (2) to illustrate the fact that research in social psychology is never complete. On the contrary, it is an ongoing process in which each investigation leads naturally to others and in which the number of intriguing questions remaining to be answered *increases* rather than decreases over time.

TO SUM UP: It is our hope that together, these features of our text will help to enhance your first encounter with social psychology. We also hope that they will help us to communicate to you our own excitement with the field, for despite the fact that between us we have more than fifty-five years of combined teaching and research experience in social psychology, we still find it as fascinating as—perhaps even *more* fascinating than—ever. To the extent we succeed in these tasks, and only to that extent, will we conclude that as authors, teachers, and representatives of social psychology, we have succeeded.

Summary and Review

The Nature of Social Psychology

Social psychology is the scientific field that seeks to understand the nature and causes of individual behavior in social situations. It uses scientific methods to obtain new information about how we interact with and think about other persons.

The Development of Social Psychology

Speculation about social behavior and thought has continued since antiquity; a science-oriented field of social psychology, however, emerged only during the present century. Once established it grew rapidly and currently investigates every conceivable aspect of social behavior and social thought.

Two recent trends in the field have involved the growing influence of a *cognitive perspective*—efforts to apply knowledge about cognitive processes to the task of understanding social behavior—and an increasing emphasis on *apply-*ing the principles and findings of social psychology to a wide range of practical problems.

We predict that these trends will continue in the future and that, in addition, social psychology will also adopt a *multicultural perspective* that both studies and takes careful account of ethnic and cultural factors as determinants of social behavior.

Research Methods in Social Psychology

In conducting their research, social psychologists often employ *experimentation* and the *correlational method*. Experimentation involves procedures in which researchers systematically vary one or more factors (variables) to examine the impact of such changes on one or more aspects of social behavior or thought. The correlational method involves careful observation and measurement of two or more variables to determine whether changes in one are accompanied by changes in the other.

In choosing the topics of their research and in planning specific studies, social psychologists are often guided by formal *theories*. These are logical frameworks that seek to explain various aspects of social behavior and thought. Predictions from a theory are tested in research. If they are confirmed, confidence in the accuracy of the theory is increased. If they are disconfirmed, such confidence is reduced.

To compare the findings of many studies on a given topic, social psychologists often use a statistical procedure known as *meta-analysis*. Meta-analyses indicate the extent to which specific variables exert similar effects across many different studies, and also provide estimates of the magnitude of such effects. Meta-analysis is superior in several respects to *narrative reviews,* in which the findings of many studies are compared without the aid of statistical procedures.

Social psychologists often withhold information about the purpose of their studies from the persons participating in them. Such temporary *deception* is deemed necessary because knowledge of the hypotheses behind an experiment may alter participants' behavior. Although the use of deception raises important ethical issues, most social psychologists believe that it is permissible, provided that proper safeguards such as *informed consent* and *thorough debriefing* are adopted.

Key Terms

Cognitive Dissonance An unpleasant state that occurs when individuals discover inconsistencies between two of their attitudes or between their attitudes and their behavior.

Confirmation Bias A tendency on the part of human beings to seek support or confirmation for their beliefs. Scientists must always be on guard against such tendencies. If they are not, they may overlook data that are inconsistent with theories they support and at the same time may emphasize data that *are* consistent with such frameworks.

Confounding Confusion that occurs when factors other than the independent variable in an experiment vary across the experimental conditions. When confounding occurs, it is impossible to determine whether results stem from the effects of the independent variable or from the other variables.

Correlational Method A method of research in which a scientist systematically observes and measures two or more variables to determine whether changes in one are accompanied by changes in the other.

Debriefing Procedures at the conclusion of a research session in which participants are given full information about the nature of the research and the hypothesis or hypotheses under investigation.

Deception A technique whereby researchers withhold information about the purposes or procedures of a study from persons participating in it. Deception is used in situations in which information about such matters might be expected to change subjects' behavior, thus invalidating the results of the research.

Dependent Variable The variable that is measured in an experiment. In social psychology, the dependent variable is some aspect of social behavior or social thought.

Evolutionary Social Psychology A newly emerging area of research that seeks to understand the potential role of genetic factors in various aspects of social behavior.

Experimentation A method of research in which one factor (the independent variable) is systematically changed to determine whether such variations affect a second factor (the dependent variable).

Independent Variable The variable that is systematically varied by the researcher in an experiment.

Informed Consent A procedure by which subjects are told in advance about the activities they will perform during an experiment. The subjects then take part in the study only if they are willing to engage in such activities.

Interactions (between variables) Instances in which the effects of one variable are influenced by the effects of one or more other variables.

Multicultural Perspective Focus on understanding the cultural and ethnic factors that influence social behavior and which contribute to differences in social behavior or social thought between various ethnic and cultural groups.

Meta-analysis A statistical technique for combining data from independent studies in order to determine whether specific variables (or interactions between variables) have significant effects across these studies.

Random Assignment of Subjects to Groups A basic requirement for conducting valid experiments. According to this principle, research participants must have an equal chance of being exposed to each level of the independent variable.

Social Psychology The scientific field that seeks to understand the nature and causes of individual behavior and thought in social situations.

Sociobiology A field that contends that many forms of behavior can be understood within the context of efforts by organisms to pass their genes on to the next generation.

Theories Efforts by scientists in any field to answer the question *Why?* Theories involve attempts to understand precisely why certain events or processes occur as they do.

For More Information

Jackson, J. M. (1988). *Social psychology, past and present: An integrative orientation.* Hillsdale, NJ: Erlbaum.

A thoughtful overview of the roots and development of social psychology. The book is organized around major themes in social psychological research and emphasizes the fact that modern social psychology has important intellectual roots in several different fields.

Jones, E. E. (1985). Major developments in social psychology during the past five decades. In G. Lindzey & E. Aronson (Eds.), *Handbook of social psychology* (Vol. 1). New York: Random House.

In this chapter an eminent social psychologist describes what he perceives to be the major trends in theory and research in social psychology during the past fifty years. After reading this summary, you'll have a very good idea of how social psychology emerged as an independent field and how it then developed.

Social Perception:
Understanding Others

Robert Delaunay

Special Sections

"The dean will see you now," said the kindly gray-haired woman behind the desk. And with that she rose, announced me to the dean, and ushered me inside. I had heard that deans' offices were often plush, but this one was downright luxurious. The carpet was thick, and the furniture was elegant. The dean's desk—which was made out of some beautiful kind of wood I did not recognize—was twice the size of mine, and the whole room was suffused with a soft glow cast by the tasteful curtains of the floor-to-ceiling window. "A class act," I thought to myself. The dean greeted me graciously and waved me to a deep, comfortable chair. My colleagues had told me that she was impressive, and they were right. Her smile was warm and friendly, but intelligence literally shone from her eyes. I didn't know much about women's clothing, but I could tell at a glance that her suit was expensive and that it fit her perfectly. Basically, she looked as though she could have stepped out of the pages of an elegant fashion magazine. I was glad that I had worn my best sport jacket and put on my new silk tie.

"How are you enjoying your stay?" she began. I was spending my sabbatical at another university and had made an appointment with the dean simply to express my gratitude for all the hospitality I had received.

"Very much," I said. "In fact, that's the main reason I'm here today. I understand that you approved my appointment and that you also got me that great office. What a view! I just wanted to meet you and let you know how much I appreciate it."

"Oh, it's a pleasure," the dean responded with a smile. "We're glad to have you with us." She walked over to the desk and picked up a beautiful leather folder containing papers. "I can see from your CV that you're from Purdue," she continued. "That's a fine university. In fact, I have some very good friends there." And then she proceeded to list several world-famous professors whose names I had heard, but whom I didn't know personally.

After this, our conversation ranged over many different topics; the dean asked me about my research interests, where I was living, and how I liked Seattle (where this university was located). She seemed quite interested in my answers and quickly put me at ease. But all the time we were speaking, I had the distinct impression that there was a question in her eyes—that there was something she wanted to know that we were not discussing. I lost track of time, but obviously the

dean didn't, because precisely at the end of my scheduled half hour, she began to wind things up. I wasn't sure exactly how she did it, but somehow she began to send me subtle signals that our conversation was drawing to a close. As I shook her hand and prepared to leave, I was more certain than ever: There *was* a question in her eyes. But what was it? I hadn't a clue.

Later that day my friend Tom asked me how the meeting had gone. "Pretty well," I answered. "And you were right; she really *is* impressive."

"Oh, she's a smooth one, all right," Tom said with a chuckle. "And quick, too. She doesn't miss a thing." He added a question: "Did she get you to sit in the big red armchair?"

"Yeah, come to think of it, she did."

"Naturally," Tom commented. "It's so soft that it practically lulls you to sleep. Also, the chair opposite is higher, so that she's kind of looking down at you while you speak. What a move!"

I thought for a moment and realized that Tom was right. Then,

thinking out loud, I remarked: "You know, one thing puzzles me. I kind of had the feeling that she was wondering about something the whole time I was there. What could it be?"

"Oh, I can tell you," Tom replied with confidence. "She was wondering about *what the heck you wanted!*"

"What do you mean? I didn't want anything. I only went there to say thanks. That's what I told her."

"Sure, but I know our dean. She wouldn't buy that. She operates on the assumption that *everyone* who comes to see her wants something. No wonder she looked a little puzzled. You were probably the first person in there in weeks—maybe months—who didn't bring a shopping list along."

I could see in a flash that Tom was right. "So that's it," I said. "I knew something was going on, but I couldn't quite put my finger on it."

"Well, I'll bet you tomorrow's lunch that she asks some discreet questions about you in the next few days. Someone who doesn't want anything—that must have *really* shaken her up!"

Admit it. Other persons are often puzzling. They say and do things we don't expect, have motives we don't understand, and seem to see the world through eyes very different from our own. Yet, because they play such a key role in our lives, the mystery of other people is one we can't afford to leave unsolved. Accordingly, we often engage in efforts to understand others—to gain insight into their intentions, traits, and motives. Like the dean in the incident described above, we try to figure out what other persons are really like, why they do and say the things they do. Then, on the basis of that knowledge, we try to determine the best ways of interacting with them. The process through which

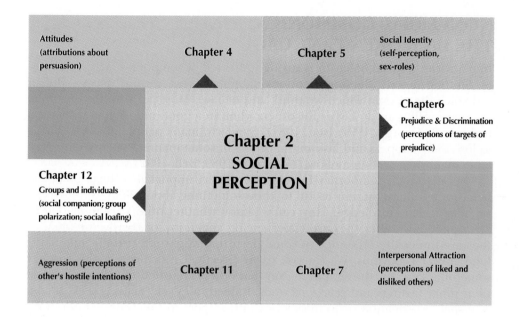

| Attitudes (attributions about persuasion) | Chapter 4 | Chapter 5 | Social Identity (self-perception, sex-roles) |

Chapter6
Prejudice & Discrimination (perceptions of targets of prejudice)

**Chapter 2
SOCIAL
PERCEPTION**

Chapter 12
Groups and individuals (social companion; group polarization; social loafing)

Aggression (perceptions of other's hostile intentions)

Chapter 11

Chapter 7

Interpersonal Attraction (perceptions of liked and disliked others)

we seek such information is known as **social perception**, and it has long been a central topic of research in social psychology.

While our efforts to understand the persons around us take many different forms, two aspects of this process seem to be most important. First, we try to understand other persons' current feelings, moods, and emotions—how they are feeling here and now. Such information is often provided by *nonverbal cues* from their facial expressions, eye contact, body posture, and movements. Second, we attempt to understand the more lasting causes behind others' actions—their traits, motives, and intentions. Information relating to this second task is acquired through *attribution*—a complex process in which we observe others' behavior and then attempt to *infer* the causes behind it from various clues (Kelley, 1972). This process was readily apparent in the dean's puzzlement over why I had come to see her: What did I want? What was I trying to accomplish? These are the kinds of questions that probably crossed her mind during our meeting.

Because nonverbal communication and attribution are basic aspects of social perception, we will consider them in detail in this chapter. They are not the entire story where social perception is concerned, however. In addition, social perception frequently involves efforts to form unified *impressions* of other persons. When we interact with others—and especially when we do so for the first time—we try to combine diverse information about them (for example, information about their appearance, their words, and their actions) into a consistent overall impression. Common sense suggests that such *first impressions* are very important; and, as we'll soon see, research findings tend to confirm this widespread belief. The other side of the coin, of course, involves efforts on *our* part to make favorable impressions on others—a process known as *impression management.* I certainly attempted to make a good impression on the dean by wearing my best clothes, being early for my appointment, and so on. And, of course, her efforts at impression management were apparent in the elegance of her office and her dress, and in her casual mention of her acquaintance with some of the most famous people at my home university. Because *impression formation* and *impression management* are important aspects of social perception, we'll consider these topics, too.

NONVERBAL COMMUNICATION: THE UNSPOKEN LANGUAGE

In many cases, social behavior is strongly affected by temporary factors or causes. Shifting moods, fleeting emotions, fatigue, illness, various drugs—all can influence the ways in which we think and behave. Most persons, for example, are more willing to do favors for others when in a good mood than when in a bad mood (George, 1991; Isen, 1987). Similarly, many people are more likely to lose their tempers and lash out at others in some manner when feeling irritable than when feeling mellow (Anderson, 1989; Bell, 1992).

Because such temporary factors often exert important effects on social behavior and thought, it is useful to know something about them. But how can we obtain such knowledge? How can we know whether others are in a good or a bad mood; whether they are experiencing anger, joy, or sorrow; or whether they are under the influence of some drug that might affect their judgment? One answer is obvious: We can ask them directly. Unfortunately, this strategy sometimes fails, for the simple reason that others are often unwilling to reveal their inner feelings and reactions to us. Indeed, they may actively seek to conceal such information or to mislead us with respect to their current emotions (DePaulo, 1992). Their reasons for doing so are often good ones. For example, a saleswoman who reveals her own aversion to products favored by potential customers will probably obtain few orders. A diplomat who reveals his or her true feelings to opponents may be less effective as a negotiator than one who conceals such reactions.

In situations such as these, when others actively attempt to conceal their true feelings or preferences from us, it is not necessary to give up in despair. On the contrary, we can often still obtain revealing information about their inner feelings and reactions by paying careful attention to their *nonverbal behaviors*—changes in facial expressions, eye contact, posture, body movements, and other expressive actions. As noted by DePaulo (1992), such behavior is relatively *irrepressible*—that is, difficult to control—so even when others *try* to conceal their inner feelings, these often leak out in many ways through nonverbal cues. So, in an important sense, nonverbal behaviors constitute a silent but eloquent language (see Figure 2.1). For this reason, the meanings they convey and our efforts to interpret these, are often described by the term **nonverbal communication**. Such communication is very complex, and it has been studied from many different perspectives. Here, however, we will focus on two major issues: (1) What are the basic channels through which nonverbal communication takes place? And (2) what is the role of nonverbal communication in social perception and ongoing social interaction?

NONVERBAL COMMUNICATION: THE BASIC CHANNELS

Think for a moment: Do you act differently when you are feeling elated and at times when you are down in the dumps? The answer seems obvious: of course. People do behave differently when they are experiencing sharply contrasting emotional states. But precisely how do they differ? What aspects of their behavior reveal their varying inner feelings or reactions? This is a basic question with respect to nonverbal communication—perhaps the most basic question one can ask. For this reason, it has been the subject of careful research attention for several decades. The findings of that research have identified the *basic channels* of nonverbal communication—those aspects of our behavior that

Nonverbal communication in action

FIGURE 2.1   Individuals often communicate important information to others without the use of words, through *nonverbal* cues.

Source: King Features Syndicate, Inc.

transmit key information about our inner emotional and affective states. These seem to involve *facial expressions, eye contact, body movements and posture, and touching.*

UNMASKING THE FACE: FACIAL EXPRESSIONS AS CLUES TO OTHERS' EMOTIONS.   More than two thousand years ago, the Roman orator Cicero stated: "The face is the image of the soul." By this he meant that human feelings and emotions are often reflected on the face and can be read there in specific expressions. Modern research suggests that Cicero—and many other observers of human behavior—were correct in this belief: It *is* possible to learn much about others' current moods and feelings from their facial expressions. In fact, it appears that six different basic emotions are represented clearly, and from a very early age, on the human face: anger, fear, sadness, disgust, happiness, and surprise (Ekman, in press; Izard, 1991; see Figure 2.2, p. 44). Please note: This in no way implies that human beings are capable of demonstrating only six different facial expressions. On the contrary, emotions occur in many combinations (for example, anger along with fear, surprise with happiness). Further, each of these reactions can vary greatly in strength. Thus, while there seem to be only a small number of basic themes in facial expressions, the number of variations on these themes is large.

But do facial expressions really reflect individuals' underlying emotions? After all, as we'll note in more detail later, most persons learn to regulate their facial expressions so that they smile, frown, or show surprise only in situations defined by their particular culture as appropriate for such expressions (DePaulo, 1992). What evidence indicates that facial expressions are closely linked to underlying emotional states and so can serve—at least part of the time—as accurate guides to these reactions? Many lines of research address this issue, but two seem to be most revealing.

In the first, researchers record electrical activity in various facial muscles associated with distinct facial expressions—while participants describe experiences associated with a wide range of emotions (e.g., Cacioppo et al., 1988). The same persons are then shown videotapes of their own faces and asked to

Basic facial expressions

FIGURE 2.2 Facial expressions such as these provide valuable information about others' emotional states. Can you identify the emotion shown on each face.?

Answers are: The emotion shown, top, left to right are anger; fear; sadness; at bottom, left to right are disgust; happiness; and surprise.

indicate what they were thinking, feeling, or imagining at various times. When these self-reports are related to electrical activity in facial muscles at those times, revealing patterns emerge. For example, certain muscles show maximal electrical activity at times when participants report feeling sad, while different muscles show maximal electrical activity at times when participants report feeling happy. So underlying emotional experiences do seem to be closely linked to facial expressions.

A second line of research on the relationship between facial expressions and underlying emotional experiences adopts a different approach (e.g., Levenson, Ekman, & Friesen, 1990; Levenson et al., 1992). In these studies individuals are asked to move various parts of their faces so as to produce configurations resembling certain facial expressions. For example, they are asked to wrinkle their nose while letting their mouth open (an expression resembling that of disgust) or to crease their brow (as in a frown). Note that participants are *not* told to demonstrate happiness, anger, fear, and so on; they are merely asked to move parts of their faces in very specific ways. While they move various facial muscles, a wide range of physiological reactions, such as heart rate, finger temperature, respiration, and skin conductance, are recorded. Finally, participants also report on any emotional experiences, thoughts, or memories they experience while moving their facial muscles. Results indicate that different posed facial expressions are accompanied by changes in patterns of physiological activity. For example, the facial expression of fear is associated with high heart rate and short respiratory periods (short intervals between breaths), while facial expressions of happiness are associated with longer respiratory periods and lower heart rate. In addition—and this is a key finding—the more closely the facial expressions shown by participants resemble those associated with specific emotions, the greater the tendency of participants to report experiencing those same emotions.

In sum, it appears that the link between emotional experiences and certain aspects of facial expressions is a real and basic one. When individuals experience various emotions, electrical activity in specific facial muscles increases, and when they move these muscles into the patterns of specific facial expressions, they show distinctive shifts in physiological reactions *and* report experiencing the emotions in question. (See Figure 2.3 for an overview of this evidence.) On the basis of such findings, it seems reasonable to conclude that unless individuals deliberately seek to override the links between emotions and facial expressions, they will, as DePaulo (1992, p. 205) notes, usually ". . . wear their emotions on their faces." We will return to efforts to control or manage facial expressions below, in a discussion of the role of nonverbal cues in efforts at deception. And we'll examine another important issue relating to facial expressions—the question of whether such expressions are universal among all human beings—in the **Social Diversity** section at the end of this chapter.

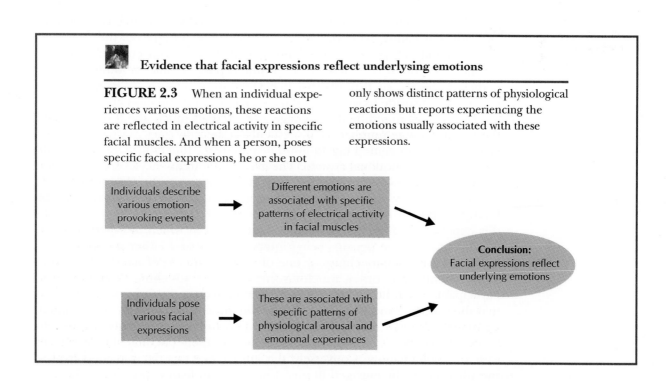

Evidence that facial expressions reflect underlysing emotions

FIGURE 2.3 When an individual experiences various emotions, these reactions are reflected in electrical activity in specific facial muscles. And when a person, poses specific facial expressions, he or she not only shows distinct patterns of physiological reactions but reports experiencing the emotions usually associated with these expressions.

Individuals describe various emotion-provoking events → Different emotions are associated with specific patterns of electrical activity in facial muscles →

Individuals pose various facial expressions → These are associated with specific patterns of physiological arousal and emotional experiences →

Conclusion: Facial expressions reflect underlying emotions

GAZES AND STARES: THE LANGUAGE OF THE EYES.   Have you ever had a conversation with someone wearing mirror-lensed glasses? If so, you know that this can be an uncomfortable situation. Since you can't see the other person's eyes, you are uncertain about how she or he is reacting. Taking note of the importance of cues provided by others' eyes, ancient poets often described the eyes as "windows to the soul." In one important sense, they were right: We do often learn much about others' feelings from their eyes. For example, we interpret a high level of gazing from another as a sign of liking or friendliness (Kleinke, 1986). In contrast, if others avoid eye contact with us, we may conclude that they are unfriendly, don't like us, or are simply shy (Zimabardo, 1977).

While a high level of eye contact from others is usually interpreted as a sign of liking or positive feelings, there is one important exception to this general rule. If another person gazes at us continuously and maintains such contact regardless of any actions we perform, she or he can be said to be **staring**. A stare is often interpreted as a sign of anger or hostility—consider the phrase *a cold stare*—and most people attempt to minimize their exposure to this particular kind of nonverbal communication when possible (Ellsworth & Carlsmith, 1973). Thus, they may quickly terminate social interaction with someone who stares at them; they may even leave the scene (Greenbaum & Rosenfield, 1978). Given these facts, it is clear that staring is one form of nonverbal behavior that should be used with great caution in most situations.

BODY LANGUAGE: GESTURES, POSTURE, AND MOVEMENTS.   Try this simple demonstration:

First, try to remember some incident that made you angry—the angrier the better. Think about it for about a minute.

Now try to remember another incident—one that made you feel sad—again, the sadder the better.

Compare your behavior in the two contexts. Did you change your posture or move your hands, arms, or legs as your thoughts shifted from the first event to the second? The chances are good that you did, for our current moods or emotions are often reflected in the position, posture, and movement of our bodies. Together, such nonverbal behaviors are termed **body language**, and they too can provide us with several useful kinds of information about others.

First, as just noted, body language often reveals much about others' emotional states. Large numbers of movements—especially ones in which one part of the body does something to another part (e.g., touching, scratching, rubbing)—suggest emotional arousal. The greater the frequency of such behavior, the higher the level of arousal or nervousness seems to be (Harrigan, 1985; Knapp, 1978). The specific movements made, too, can be revealing. A study by Harrigan and her colleagues (Harrigan, et al., 1991) is especially revealing. In this experiment participants watched videotapes in which one person interviewed another. The persons being interviewed showed either no body movements involving self-touching, or one of several patterns of hand activity: one hand touching the other, touching their nose, or touching their own arm. Participants rated the interviewees on several dimensions, and results indicated that the specific hand movements made did affect these ratings. For example, an interviewee was rated as most calm when he or she engaged in no self-touching movements, less calm with nose or hand self-touching, and least calm with arm self-touching. Conversely, the interviewee was rated as most expressive when he or she engaged in nose touching, but least expressive in the control (no movement) condition. These and related findings indicate that it is not only the total amount of movement that provides information on others' feelings or traits; the pattern and nature of such movement matters too.

Larger patterns of movement, involving the whole body, can also be informative. Such phrases as "he adopted a *threatening posture*" and "she greeted him with *open arms*" suggest that different body orientations or postures can be suggestive of contrasting emotional reactions; and, in fact, recent research by Aronoff, Woike, and Hyman (1992) confirms this possibility. To study the effects of body posture or movement on social perception, these investigators adopted an ingenious approach—one indicative of the high level of ingenuity shown by social psychologists in selecting research methods. First they identified characters in classical ballet known to play dangerous or threatening roles (for example, Macbeth, the Angel of Death, Lizzie Borden) or warm, sympathetic roles (Juliet, Romeo). Then they carefully examined samples of dancing by these characters in actual ballets to see if they adopted different kinds of postures. In particular, Aronoff and his colleagues measured the extent to which poses by the characters were diagonal or angular versus rounded, the percentage of time in which the characters showed a rounded arm versus angled-arm pattern, and the percentage of time they engaged in rounded versus angled movements (see Figure 2.4).

 Rounded and angular body postures

FIGURE 2.4 Recent evidence indicates that rounded body postures communicate friendliness and warmth while angular body postures communicate threat or hostility.

Source: Based on information in Aronoff, Woike, & Hyman, 1992.

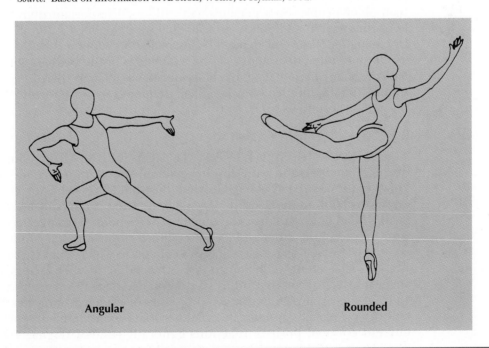

Angular   **Rounded**

Results provided clear support for the hypothesis that the two groups of characters (threatening versus warm) would indeed show contrasting body postures and movements. The threatening characters used diagonal poses nearly three times as often as the warm characters. In contrast, the warm characters engaged in rounded poses almost four times as often as the threatening characters. Of course, it is important to note that the postures shown by the dancers were carefully posed ones; thus, there is no guarantee that the same results would be obtained with respect to real-life (nonposed) postures. Still, when combined with other research conducted by Aronoff et al. (1992), these findings suggest that large-scale body movements or postures can sometimes serve as an important source of information about others' emotions and traits.

Finally, we should add that more specific information about others' feelings is often provided by gestures. These fall into several different categories, but perhaps the most important are *emblems*—body movements carrying highly specific meanings in specific cultures. For example, in several countries, holding one's hand with the thumb pointing up is a sign of "Okay." Similarly, seizing one's nose between the thumb and index finger is a sign of displeasure or disgust. Emblems vary greatly from culture to culture, but every human society seems to have at least some signals of this type for greetings, departures, insults, and the description of various physical states.

Another category of gestures important in nonverbal communication are the *hand gestures* that accompany conversational speech. Such gestures are used for emphasis or clarification and occur quite frequently during face-to-face conversations. Existing evidence indicates that they can aid comprehension of spoken messages, although only to a relatively minor degree (Graham & Argyle, 1975; Krauss, Morrel-Samuels, & Colasante, 1991).

Even **gait**—the manner in which individuals walk—can serve as an important source of nonverbal information about others. Research by Montepare and Zebrowitz-McArthur (1988) indicates that gait changes with age. Younger people walk with more hip sway, knee bending, loose-jointedness, and bounce than older people. So a person's gait can be an important nonverbal cue to her or his age. In addition, it appears that we rate persons showing a youthful gait as higher on several characteristics, including happiness and power.

In sum, there does appear to be a language of the body—a set of nonverbal cues that communicate much about others' feelings, reactions, and traits. And we draw upon such body language frequently in our efforts to understand the people around us.

TOUCHING: THE MOST INTIMATE NONVERBAL CUE. Suppose that during a conversation with another person, she or he touched you briefly. How would you react? What information would this behavior convey? The answer to both questions is, it depends. And what it depends upon is several factors relating to who does the touching (a friend or a stranger, a member of your own or of the other gender); the nature of this physical contact (brief or prolonged, gentle or rough); and the context in which it takes place (a business or social setting, a doctor's office). Depending on such factors, touch can suggest affection, sexual interest, dominance, caring, or even aggression. Despite such complexities, a growing body of evidence indicates that when one person touches another in a manner that is considered acceptable in the current context, positive reactions generally result (Alagna, Whitcher, &

Fisher, 1979; Smith, Gier, & Willis, 1982). This fact is clearly illustrated by an ingenious study carried out by Crusco and Wetzel (1984). These investigators enlisted the aid of waitresses working in two restaurants, who agreed to treat customers in one of three distinct ways when giving them their change: They either refrained from touching these persons in any manner, touched them briefly on the hand, or touched them for a longer period of time on the shoulder. The investigators assessed the effects of these treatments by examining the size of the tips left by the patrons. Results were clear: Both a brief touch on the hand (about one-half second) and a longer touch on the shoulder (one to one and a half seconds) significantly increased tipping over the no-touch control condition. Thus, consistent with previous findings, being touched in an innocuous, nonthreatening way seemed to generate positive rather than negative reactions among recipients. Please note: touching does not always produce such effects. If it is perceived as a status or power play, or if it is too prolonged, or too intimate in a context where such intimacy is not warranted, touching may evoke anxiety, anger, and other negative reactions.

Gender differences in touching: Who touches whom, and when? While touching is strongly affected by social context and by cultural rules dictating who can touch whom and when, another aspect to physical touching deserves careful attention: gender differences in this form of nonverbal activity. An early and frequently cited study on this issue by Henley (1973) reported that in public places males are more likely to touch females than vice versa. More recent research, however, suggests that the relationship between gender and touching is more complex than this (e.g., Stier & Hall, 1984). In greetings and leave-takings, gender differences in touching do not seem to occur (Major, Schmidlin, & Williams, 1990). And age appears to be an important determinant of who touches whom.

The clearest evidence to date on the effects of age on touching is that reported by Hall and Veccia (1991). These researchers observed touching between thousands of persons in a wide range of public places—shopping malls, movie lines, hotel lobbies, airports. The researchers recorded instances of touching with the hand and with other body parts, as well as the age of the people involved. (This ranged from the teens through middle age.) They observed several interesting sex differences. For example, across all ages, males tended to use "arm-around" touching more frequently than females, while females more often used "arms-linked" touching. Overall, however, there was no difference between the sexes in frequency of touching: Females touched males about as frequently as males touched females. Striking gender differences *were* observed, however, when age was taken into account. Among young couples, males touched females far more often than females touched males. This disparity decreased with age, however, until, among older couples, females touched males far more often than males touched females (see Figure 2.5, p. 50).

What is the reason for this reversal with increasing age? One possibility mentioned by Hall and Veccia (1991) is that among younger persons (especially teenagers) relationships are not yet well established; and in such relationships, sex roles encourage visible gestures of possessiveness by males. As relationships develop, however, sex roles may require more gestures of possessiveness by females. Whatever the explanation for the age reversal observed by Hall and Veccia, it is interesting to note that across all ages there is no overall differ-

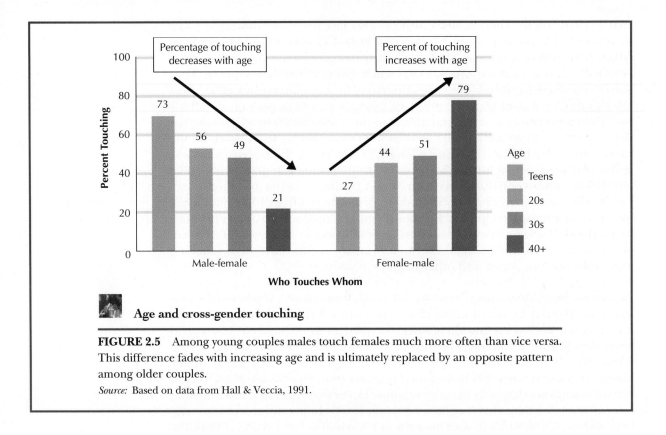

Age and cross-gender touching

FIGURE 2.5   Among young couples males touch females much more often than vice versa. This difference fades with increasing age and is ultimately replaced by an opposite pattern among older couples.

Source: Based on data from Hall & Veccia, 1991.

ence in touching between males and females. This is just one example of a supposed gender difference that tends to disappear on systematic closer observation; we'll meet many others in this book, especially in chapters 5 and 6.

NONVERBAL BEHAVIOR AND SOCIAL INTERACTION: SELF-PRESENTATION AND THE DETECTION OF DECEPTION

Video: Communication The Nonverbal Agenda

Because they are an important source of information about others, nonverbal cues play a role in several forms of social interaction. One of the most important of these is the process of **self-presentation** (Schlenker & Weigold, 1989). Self-presentation involves efforts to regulate one's own behavior in order to create a particular (usually favorable) impression on others (Jones & Pittman, 1982). As we'll see in a later section on **impression management,** a closely related process, people use many different tactics to accomplish this goal—to place themselves in a favorable light in social situations. And one self-presentational tactic, as noted recently by DePaulo (1992), is the use of nonverbal cues. If you have ever (1) pretended to be surprised by a "surprise" you knew was coming, (2) smiled or otherwise pretended to like someone or something when in fact you did not, or (3) tried to refrain from showing amusement when another person fell down or looked foolish in some other way, you are already familiar with the use of nonverbal cues for purposes of self-presentation. In these and many other situations, we attempt to manage our facial expressions, eye contact with others, body movements, and other nonverbal cues in order to convey a desired impression. Needless to say, there are large differences in the extent to which individuals can accomplish this task. Attractive persons tend to be better at this task than unattractive ones (DePaulo et al., 1988); females tend to be more effective at it than males (Hall, 1984); and most people tend to get somewhat better at it as they grow older (Saarni, 1988). In addition, certain personal characteristics play a role in nonverbal self-presentation. For example, persons high in *expressiveness*—the tendency to show strong and clear nonverbal cues—are often better at such self-presentation than those who are low in expressiveness (e.g., Tucker & Riggio, 1988). We'll consider another trait related to the use of nonverbal cues in the **Individual Diversity** section on p. 52.

Critical Thinking Question 2

Another aspect of social behavior in which nonverbal cues play an important role is the *detection of deception*—efforts to determine when others are being truthful or when they are lying. Research on this topic suggests that in attempting to perform this crucial task, we rely heavily on nonverbal cues. Moreover, many such cues enable us to be at least moderately successful in recognizing deception when it occurs (e.g., DePaulo, 1992; DePaulo, Stone, & Lassiter, 1985; Ekman, 1985). Several nonverbal cues seem especially helpful in this regard.

First, we rely on **microexpressions**—fleeting facial expressions lasting only a few tenths of a second. Such reactions appear on the face very quickly after an emotion-provoking event and are difficult to suppress (Ekman, 1985). As a result, they can be quite revealing about the feelings and emotions others are actually experiencing.

Second, we rely on what have been termed *interchannel discrepancies* (e.g., DePaulo et al., 1985). These are inconsistencies between nonverbal cues from different basic channels; they result from the fact that persons who are lying find it difficult to control all aspects of their nonverbal behavior simultaneously. For example, a negotiator who is lying to an opponent may succeed in maintaining an expression of open honesty on his face and may also succeed in preserving a high level of eye contact with the opponent. At the same time, however, he may engage in postural shifts or body movements that alert the opponent that something else is going on.

Third, we rely on changes in the nonverbal characteristics of people's speech. When people lie, the pitch of their voices often rises (Zuckerman DePaulo, & Rosenthal, 1981) and they often speak more slowly and with less fluency. In addition, they engage in more *sentence repairs*—instances in which they start a sentence, interrupt it, and then start again (Stiff et al., 1989).

Discussion Question 2

Finally, deception is often revealed in various aspects of eye contact. Liars blink more frequently and often show more dilated pupils than persons telling the truth. They may also show an unusually low level of eye contact or—paradoxically—an unusually high one, as they attempt to feign honesty by looking others right in the eye (Kleinke, 1986).

Through careful attention to these nonverbal cues, we can often tell when others are lying. Our performance in this respect is far from perfect—skillful liars do often succeed in deceiving us. But their task is made much more difficult by our ability to read, interpret, and use a wide range of nonverbal cues.

As noted earlier, people attempt to regulate their nonverbal behavior for reasons other than lying. How do they seek to accomplish such regulation? And what traits or characteristics help them to succeed? For information on these issues, please see the **Individual Diversity** section on p. 52.

SHOWING LESS THAN WE REALLY FEEL: SELF-MONITORING AND THE SUPPRESSION OF GLOATING IN PUBLIC

After winning the gold medal for men's figure skating in the 1988 Winter Olympics, Brian Boitano was universally described by the press as a "grand and classy champion." Why was he singled out for so much praise? One clue is provided by descriptions of his behavior while receiving his award. Eyewitnesses described Boitano as standing *stone-faced* next to the runner-up (and long-term rival), Brian Orser, as he received his medal. In commenting on his own behavior, Boitano noted: "I had to hold back. My facial expression could only make him feel worse. I was not going to gloat."

There is an important message in this incident for understanding nonverbal communication and its role in social behavior. There are many situations in which individuals seek to control or manage their facial expressions and other nonverbal cues, not to deceive others, but rather because culturally determined *display rules* indicate that it is inappropriate to demonstrate certain emotions publicly. Winning athletes are not supposed to gloat over their own victories and the defeat of opponents, while losers are supposed to smile and be gracious—and not show envy (see Figure 2.6); physicians should not show

Suppressing facial expressions

FIGURE 2.6   Persons such as athletes or beauty contest winners who defeat their rivals are supposed to suppress facial expressions of joy on such occasions (left photo). Similarly, persons who lose in these situations are supposed to suppress expressions of anger or envy (right photo).

horror when examining patients; children should not smile when being scolded by parents; these are just a few of the situations in which good control over one's nonverbal behavior is advantageous (DePaulo, 1992).

The fact that nearly everyone attempts to regulate his or her own nonverbal behavior on some occasions, however, does not imply that all persons will attain equal success. On the contrary, it is clear that in this respect large individual differences exist—and influence social interaction. Are there personal traits or characteristics that contribute to (or at least predict) effectiveness in self-regulation? Research by Friedman and Miller-Herringer (1991) suggests that there are.

On the basis of previous findings, these investigators predicted that several characteristics would play such a role. Here, we'll focus primarily on one that has received growing attention from social psychologists: **self-monitoring** (Snyder, 1987). Self-monitoring refers to a cluster of characteristics closely related to the ability to adapt one's behavior to current social situations. Persons high in self-monitoring might be described as *social chameleons*—they can readily adjust their social behavior to the demands of a given situation. In contrast, a person low in self-monitoring tends to show a higher degree of consistency: He or she is the same person across a wide range of situations. Friedman and Miller-Herringer (1991) predicted that persons high in self-monitoring would be more successful than persons low in self-monitoring in concealing their true emotions in situations where it was inappropriate to show them.

To study this possibility, they arranged for participants low or high in self-monitoring to receive positive feedback indicating that they had done very well on a problem-solving task. Participants received this feedback both while alone and when in the presence of two other persons (actually assistants of the experimenters). In both cases the three persons were, presumably, competing against each other. In the *alone* condition they could not see one another, while in the *social* condition they could. Friedman and Miller-Herringer reasoned that participants would attempt to suppress signs of happiness and joy (gloating) in the social condition, and results offered strong support for this prediction. When a group of raters watched videotapes of participants' faces while they received news of their victories, they did indeed show stronger signs of happiness in the alone than in the social condition. Of even greater interest, self-monitoring was significantly related to participants' success in managing their facial expressions. When they were in the presence of their opponent (in the social condition), high self-monitors showed fewer outward signs of happiness and made fewer victory gestures than low self-monitors. Instead, high self-monitors engaged in such actions as twisting their mouth to one side and biting their lips, presumably, to prevent themselves from smiling and so demonstrating their glee at winning. Are high self-monitors better able to regulate their facial reactions than low self-monitors, or are they simply more highly motivated to do so? At the moment, we can't tell. But it is clear that high self-monitors did a better job of managing their own facial expressions.

In sum, it appears that high self-monitors are better able than low self-monitors to suppress outward signs of their emotional reactions under conditions where it is inappropriate that these be revealed. In this and other ways, they gain an important edge with respect to nonverbal communication, and so also with respect to social interaction generally.

ATTRIBUTION: UNDERSTANDING THE CAUSES OF OTHERS' BEHAVIOR

Exercise 1 Accurate knowledge about others' current moods or feelings can be useful in many ways. Yet where social perception is concerned, this knowledge is often only the first step. In addition, we usually want to know more—to understand others' lasting traits and to know the causes behind their behavior—why they have acted as they have. The process through which we seek such information is known as **attribution**. More formally, attribution refers to our efforts to understand the causes behind others' behavior and, on some occasions, the causes behind *our* behavior, too. Attribution has been a topic of major interest in social psychology for several decades (e.g., Graham & Folkes, 1990; Heider, 1958; Jones, 1990).

THEORIES OF ATTRIBUTION: FRAMEWORKS FOR UNDERSTANDING HOW WE ATTEMPT TO MAKE SENSE OUT OF THE SOCIAL WORLD

Video: Constructing Social Reality*

Transparency 2.1 Because attribution is complex, many theories have been proposed to explain its operation (e.g., Gilbert, Pelham, & Srull, 1988; Trope, 1986). Here, we will focus on two that have been especially influential, plus recent efforts to extend and refine them.

FROM ACTS TO DISPOSITIONS: USING OTHERS' BEHAVIOR AS A GUIDE TO THEIR LASTING TRAITS.   The first of these theories—Jones and Davis's (1965) theory of **correspondent inference**—asks how we use information about others' behavior as a basis for inferring that they possess various traits or characteristics. In other words, the theory is concerned with how we decide, on the basis of others' overt actions, that they possess specific traits or dispositions that they carry with them from situation to situation and that remain fairly stable over time.

At first glance this might seem to be a trivially simple task. Others' behavior provides us with a rich source on which to draw, so if we observe it carefully, we should be able to learn a lot about them. Up to a point this is true. The task is complicated, however, by the following fact: Often, individuals act in certain ways not because doing so reflects their own traits or preferences, but rather because external factors leave them little choice. For example, imagine that you observe a clerk refusing to accept a customer's personal check. Does this mean that the clerk is suspicious of strangers? Not necessarily. She may merely be obeying strict company rules concerning payment for merchandise. She may actually be a very trusting person who experiences great embarrassment in such instances. In situations such as this—which are extremely common—using others' behavior as a guide to their lasting traits or motives can be quite misleading.

How do we cope with such complications? According to Jones and Davis's theory (Jones & Davis, 1965; Jones & McGillis, 1976), we accomplish this difficult task by focusing our attention on certain types of actions—those most likely to prove informative.

Critical Thinking Question 3 First, we consider only behaviors that seem to have been freely chosen. We tend to ignore or at least discount behaviors that were somehow forced on the person in question. Second, we pay careful attention to actions that produce what Jones and Davis term **noncommon effects**—outcomes that can be achieved by one specific action, but not by others. The advantage offered by focusing on noncommon effects can be readily demonstrated.

Imagine that one of your casual friends has just gotten engaged. Her future spouse is extremely handsome, has a great personality, is wildly in love with your friend, and is very rich. Why did she agree to marry him?

Obviously, it's difficult to tell. There are so many good reasons that you can't choose among them. Now, in contrast, imagine that your friend's fiance is very attractive but that he is known to be painfully boring and irritating and treats your friend with great indifference; also, that he has no visible means of support and intends to live on your friend's savings. Does your friend's decision to marry this person tell you anything about her personal characteristics? Now, it does; in fact, you can probably assume that she places great weight on physical attractiveness in potential lovers. So, as you can see, we can usually learn more about others from actions or decisions on their part that yield non-common effects than from ones that do not.

Finally, Jones and Davis suggest that we also pay greater attention to actions by others that are low in *social desirability* than to actions that are high on this dimension. In other words, we learn more about others' traits or characteristics from actions they perform that are somehow out of the ordinary than from actions that are very much like those performed by most other persons. For example, if you watched the sales clerk mentioned above operate the register or wrap customers' packages, you would not learn much about her as a unique individual. These actions are basically part of her job. But if you saw her urging a customer to visit another store where some item was cheaper, you would learn something of interest: Such behavior is definitely *not* part of her regular duties.

In sum, according to the theory proposed by Jones and Davis, we are most likely to conclude that others' behavior reflects their stable traits (i.e., we are likely to reach accurate or *correspondent inferences* about them) when that behavior (1) occurs by choice; (2) yields distinctive, noncommon effects; and (3) is low in social desirability.

ATTENTIONAL RESOURCES AND TRAIT ATTRIBUTION: WHAT WE SOMETIMES LEARN FROM OBSCURE BEHAVIOR. The theory proposed by Jones and Davis offers a useful framework for understanding how we use others' behavior to identify their key traits. However, recent research has extended the theory in several ways. Perhaps the most important of these approaches this important aspect of attribution from the perspective of *conscious attentional resources*. As we'll see in more detail in chapter 3, modern conceptions of social thought generally assume that as human beings we have limited cognitive resources—limited capacity to process information from the social world around us (e.g., Gilbert & Osborne, 1989). Thus, if we devote attention to one cognitive task, we have less remaining for other tasks.

Gilbert, Pelham, and Krull (1988) have applied this basic principle to the topic of how we infer others' traits. They suggest that this process involves three basic parts: *categorization* of the behavior of a person—deciding what the behavior is about; *characterization* of the actor in terms of specific traits—deciding what traits he or she possesses; and *correction* of such trait inferences on the basis of information about the situation in which the behavior has taken place. For example, if we see a motorist behaving meekly toward a state trooper, we may correct our tendency to infer that he is a meek person because we know there are strong situational constraints on his behavior: acting belligerently toward state troopers can be harmful to one's health!

Gilbert and his colleagues note that generally we have sufficient cognitive resources available to us to engage in the correction stage; generally others' behavior is fairly easy to categorize and we have lots of specific trait labels available. But in some cases, they note, others' behavior is *obscure*—it is difficult to tell precisely what they are doing. In such cases, Gilbert, Pelham, and Krull (1988) suggest, the extra effort we must devote to categorizing others' behavior may interfere with our ability to draw accurate inferences about their underlying traits.

Direct evidence for these proposals has recently been reported by Gilbert et al., (1992). In this investigation female participants listened to tape recordings of a "dating game" in which a woman asked a man a series of questions. The woman's comments suggested very clearly either that she preferred a man with a traditional sex role orientation (e.g., one who would ask her out) or that she like a nontraditional sex role orientation (e.g., a man who liked being asked out by women). In both cases, the man's answers were consistent with the woman's preferences. Under these conditions, Gilbert and his associates proposed, listeners would normally carry out the *correction* phase noted above: They would realize that the man was trying to please the woman and would be reluctant to assume that his answers were a true reflection of his own sex role preferences. But what would happen if his behavior were somehow obscured so that it was hard to observe? Under these conditions, the researchers predicted, subjects would have to devote cognitive resources to the task of categorizing the behavior. As a result, they might be tempted to conclude that the man's answers were a true reflection of his views.

To test this possibility, the researchers presented the audiotape in one of two forms: a normal version, in which the man's answers were easy to understand, and a *degraded* version, in which lots of noise was present on the tape. Because of the noise participants had to listen very carefully in order to under-

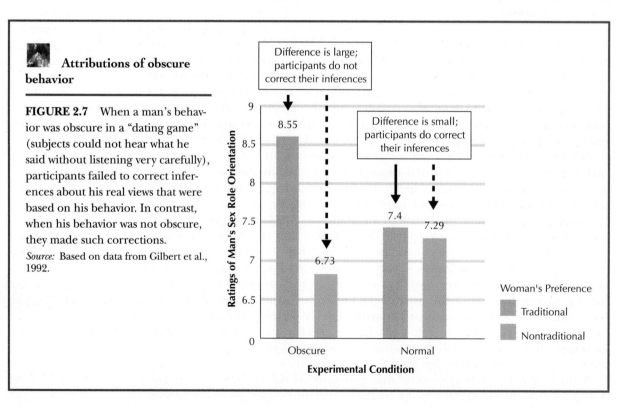

Attributions of obscure behavior

FIGURE 2.7 When a man's behavior was obscure in a "dating game" (subjects could not hear what he said without listening very carefully), participants failed to correct inferences about his real views that were based on his behavior. In contrast, when his behavior was not obscure, they made such corrections.

Source: Based on data from Gilbert et al., 1992.

stand the man's answers. After hearing one of these tapes, subjects rated the man's true sex role attitudes. Gilbert and his colleagues predicted that subjects would be more likely to assume that his statements accurately reflected his views when his answers were obscured (the degraded tape); and, as shown in Figure 2.7, this is precisely what happened. In other words, when subjects had to listen very carefully to understand the man's answers, they were more likely to infer his views, and traits, from his actions. These findings suggest that in cases where others' behavior is obscure, the effort we devote to answering the question *What?* (What are they doing or saying?) may make it more difficult for us to answer the question *Why?* (What does their behavior tell us about their traits?) Or, to put it another way, when some activity drains our attentional resources, we become less able to carry out the *correction* phase with respect to trait inferences.

Work in Progress

Countering the Effects of Attentional Load: Automatizing the Correction Stage of Trait Inferences

Research findings reported by Gilbert and his colleagues suggest that when we try to form accurate inferences about others' traits while busy with some other task that drains our cognitive resources, we may be prone to make errors. In particular, we may fail to correct for the impact of situational factors and so tend to perceive their behavior as stemming from dispositional factors, such as individual traits, more than is actually justified. But is this always the case? Gilbert and Booker (1993) reason that sometimes such "slippage" in our trait inferences can be avoided. In particular, this may be true when we have had plenty of practice in making a particular kind of correction—in taking account of situational factors. Under these conditions, they believe, the correction stage may become *automatized*, and errors in trait inference will not necessarily occur.

To test these predictions Gilbert and Booker are currently conducting a study. In the first part of the study, some participants—those in a *practice condition*—will watch videotapes in which female strangers behave anxiously. In some tapes these persons will discuss anxiety-provoking topics (e.g., their sexual fantasies), while in others they will discuss more mundane topics. When asked to rate the level of anxiety shown by these persons, Gilbert and Booker predict that participants will take account of the situation. Thus, they will rate the women who discussed anxiety-provoking topics as being less anxious than those who discuss mundane topics. In contrast, par-

ticipants in a *no practice* condition will not watch these tapes; thus, they will have no practice in making this particular kind of correction.

In the second part of the study, both groups will watch more videotapes showing anxious-looking female targets who, again, will discuss either anxiety-provoking or mundane topics. This time, however, the participants will view the tapes while rehearsing an eight-digit number—a task that absorbs considerable attention. The major prediction is that under these conditions, participants in the no-practice condition will fail to perform the correction stage very well: They will rate the women in the tapes as equally anxious regardless of whether the topics the women discussed are anxiety-provoking or mundane. In contrast, those in the practice condition will *not* be subject to these errors: They will rate the women who discuss anxiety-provoking topics as being less anxious. In other words, their practice in making this kind of correction will improve their performance and allow them to correct for situational factors.

The data are currently being collected, so the findings aren't in. But if they do turn out as Gilbert and Booker predict, they will suggest that we are not doomed to errors where the correction phase of attributions is concerned. On the contrary, this may be one more case in which the right kind of practice can make us, if not perfect, at least a great deal better.

KELLEY'S THEORY OF CAUSAL ATTRIBUTIONS: HOW WE ANSWER THE QUESTION *WHY?*   Consider the following events:

Transparency 2.2

You receive a much lower grade on an exam than you were expecting.

Your roommate refuses to lend you a small amount of money, even though he has often done so in the past.

You phone one of your friends repeatedly and leave messages on her answering machine, but she never returns your call.

What question would arise in your mind in each of these situations? The answer is clear: *Why?* You would want to know *why* your grade was so low, *why* your roommate refused to lend you the money, and *why* your friend wouldn't return your calls. In countless life situations, this is the central attributional task we face. We want to know why other people have acted as they have, or why events have turned out in a particular way. Do you remember the used car incident described at the beginning of chapter 1? This was a situation in which the basic attributional question *Why?* arose: The buyer wanted to know why I suggested selling the car for less than he had offered. Such knowledge is crucial, for only if we understand the causes behind others' actions can we adjust our own actions accordingly and hope to make sense out of the social world. Obviously, the number of specific causes behind others' behavior is large. To make the task more manageable, therefore, we often begin with a preliminary question: Did others' behavior stem mainly from *internal* causes (their own characteristics, motives, intentions); mainly from *external* causes (some aspect of the social or physical world); or from a combination of the two? For example, you might wonder whether you received a lower grade than expected because you didn't study enough (an internal cause), because the questions were difficult and tricky (an external cause), or, perhaps, because of both factors. Similarly, you might wonder whether your friend hasn't returned your calls because her machine is malfunctioning (an external cause) or because she is upset with you for some reason (an internal cause). Revealing insights into how we carry out this initial attributional task are provided by a theory proposed by Kelley (Kelley, 1972; Kelley & Michela, 1980).

Discussion Question 3

According to Kelley, in our attempts to answer the question *Why* about others' behavior, we focus on information relating to three major dimensions. First, we consider **consensus**—the extent to which others react to some stimulus or event in the same manner as the person we are considering. The higher the proportion of other people who react in the same way, the higher the consensus. Second, we consider **consistency**—the extent to which the person in whose behavior we are interested reacts to the stimulus or event in the same way on other occasions. In other words, consistency relates to the extent to which the person's behavior is unvarying over time. And third, we examine **distinctiveness**—the extent to which the person reacts in the same manner to other, different stimuli or events. (Please don't confuse consistency and distinctiveness. Consistency refers to similar reactions to a given stimulus or event *at different times*. Distinctiveness refers to similar reactions to *different stimuli or events*. If an individual reacts in the same way to a wide range of stimuli, distinctiveness is said be *low*.)

Exercise 5

Transparency 2.4

Critical Thinking Question 4

Kelley's theory suggests that we are most likely to attribute another's behavior to *internal* causes under conditions in which consensus and distinctiveness are low, but consistency is high. In contrast, we are most likely to attribute another's behavior to *external* causes under conditions in which consensus, consistency, and distinctiveness are all high. Finally, we usually attribute

Transparency 2.5
Transparency 2.6

behavior to a combination of these factors under conditions in which consensus is low but consistency and distinctiveness are high. Perhaps a concrete example will help illustrate the reasonable nature of these suggestions.

Imagine that during important negotiations, one side makes an offer to the other. Upon receiving the offer, the leader of the opposing team loses his temper, shouts angrily about the offer being insulting, and stalks off, thus bringing the discussion to a halt. Why has he acted this way—because of internal causes or because of external causes? In other words, is the recipient a person with a bad temper who often blows his stack in social situations? Or was the offer really so low as to be anger-provoking? According to Kelley's theory, your decision (as an outside observer of this scene) would depend on information relating to the three factors mentioned above. First, assume that the following conditions prevail:

1. No other negotiator is angered by the offer (*consensus is low*).
2. You have seen this negotiator lose his temper during other sessions in response to this kind of offer (*consistency is high*).
3. You have seen this negotiator lose his temper in response to other, different stimuli too (*distinctiveness is low*).

In this case Kelley's theory suggests that the negotiator lost his temper because of internal causes: He is a person with a short fuse (see the upper portion of Figure 2.8).

Now, in contrast, assume that the following conditions hold:

1. Several other negotiators also express anger at the offer (*consensus is high*).
2. You have seen this negotiator lose his temper during other negotiating sessions in response to this kind of offer (*consistency is high*).
3. You have *not* seen him lose his temper in other contexts (*distinctiveness is high*).

Here, you would probably attribute his behavior to external causes—the offer really *was* an unreasonable one (refer to the lower portion of Figure 2.8, p. 60).

Exercise 6

As we noted earlier, Kelley's theory is reasonable; and it seems applicable to a wide range of social situations. Further, basic aspects of the theory have been confirmed by the results of many different studies (e.g., Harvey & Weary, 1989; McArthur, 1972). We should note, though, that research on the theory also suggests the need for certain modifications. Some of these are described below.

WHEN DO WE ENGAGE IN CAUSAL ATTRIBUTION? THE PATH OF LEAST RESISTANCE STRIKES AGAIN. The kind of causal analysis described by Kelley requires considerable effort. Paying close enough attention to others' behavior to gather information about consensus, consistency, and distinctiveness can be quite difficult. Given this fact, it is not surprising to learn that people tend to avoid such cognitive work whenever they can. Often, they are all too ready to jump to quick and easy conclusions about the causes behind others' actions (Lupfer, Clark, & Hutcherson, 1990). They can do this because they know from past experience that certain kinds of behavior generally stem from internal factors, while other kinds usually derive from external ones (Hansen, 1980). For example, most people believe that success is generally the result of ability and effort—two internal causes. Thus, when they encounter someone who is experiencing success they quickly assume that this

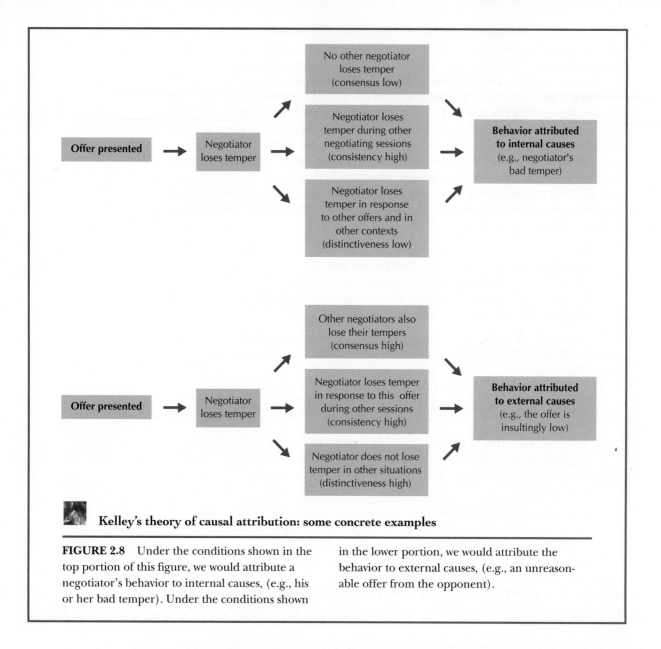

Kelley's theory of causal attribution: some concrete examples

FIGURE 2.8 Under the conditions shown in the top portion of this figure, we would attribute a negotiator's behavior to internal causes, (e.g., his or her bad temper). Under the conditions shown in the lower portion, we would attribute the behavior to external causes, (e.g., an unreasonable offer from the opponent).

outcome derives from one or both of these internal causes. In contrast, most people assume that laughing or being amused is largely the result of external causes—exposure to a funny image or situation. Thus, when they see another person laughing, they tend to assume that she or he is doing so because of external causes.

So, precisely when does the kind of careful analysis described by Kelley occur? Primarily under two conditions: (1) when people are confronted with unexpected events (ones they cannot readily explain in terms of what they already know about a specific situation or person, or about people generally); and (2) when they encounter unpleasant outcomes or events. In sum, Kelley's theory appears to be an accurate description of causal attribution *when such attribution occurs.* It may not describe people's behavior in many situations, though, because they simply don't want to bother.

AUGMENTING AND DISCOUNTING: MULTIPLE POTENTIAL CAUSES. Transparency 2.3
Suppose that you see one of your neighbors shouting angrily at her child.
What would you conclude about the causes of this behavior? One possibility is
that she has a bad temper and is a poor parent who will soon harm her child
psychologically. But now, imagine that you learn that she was shouting at her
child because he ran out in front of traffic on a busy street. Would you remain
convinced that your neighbor was an irritable, bad-tempered parent? Probably
not. You now realize that there are at least two possible causes for her behavior: a bad temper and a dangerous action by the child. This example illustrates
the **discounting principle** (sometimes called the *subtraction rule*), which suggests that we reduce (discount) the importance of any potential cause of
another person's behavior to the extent that other potential causes also exist.

Now imagine a somewhat different situation: You see your neighbor shouting angrily at her child, but this time a minister from her church is also present. Now what will you conclude? Almost certainly, that she is indeed a person
with a bad temper. After all, she is shouting at her child in front of someone
who might be expected to disapprove of such actions. This example illustrates
a second attributional principle—the **augmenting principle**, which suggests
that when a factor that might facilitate a given behavior and a factor that
might inhibit it are both present and the behavior actually occurs, we assign
added weight to the facilitative factor. We do so because that factor has succeeded in producing the behavior even in the face of an important inhibitory
barrier.

A growing body of evidence suggests that both augmenting and discounting play an important role in attribution, especially when we can't observe others' actions over extended periods of time or in several situations (i.e., when
information about consistency and distinctiveness is lacking). Thus, both augmenting and dicounting should be taken into account when we apply Kelley's
theory.

For an unsettling but timely illustration of the effects of augmenting and
discounting, please see the **Cutting Edge** section below.

Focus on Research: The Cutting Edge

AUGMENTING, DISCOUNTING, AND AFFIRMATIVE ACTION: ATTRIBUTIONS ABOUT THE CAUSES OF WOMEN'S PROMOTIONS

Affirmative action—this is definitely a loaded phrase in the United States in the
1990s. It implies that it is not enough for schools, businesses, and other organizations merely to eliminate barriers that previously excluded persons belonging
to various groups. Instead, *active* efforts to hire and promote these persons are
required. While the debate over affirmative action will certainly continue for
many years to come, it is clear that in combination with other policies and legislation, affirmative action has already produced major changes in society. The
proportions of doctors, lawyers, professors, managers, and other professionals
who are women or members of minority groups have risen significantly. Similar
trends have occurred at many other occupational levels, and in many other
areas of society as well.

Does this mean that affirmative action is an unmixed blessing? Unfortunately, there is growing evidence in social psychological research that it is not. Even when affirmative action programs succeed in their stated goals, they may have some unexpected, negative side effects. First, it appears that persons who obtain employment or promotions on the basis of affirmative action sometimes suffer reductions in self-esteem (Chacko, 1982). They may feel that they obtained an outcome or benefit they didn't really deserve, and this can be disconcerting. Second, such persons may also find that their performance and qualifications are evaluated negatively by others (Heilman & Herlihy, 1984). Others tend to attribute their achievements not to hard work or talent but to external factors (affirmative action policies) that literally guaranteed their success. Perhaps the clearest evidence for such effects has been reported by Summers (1991). This researcher presented male and female participants with information about the performance and qualifications of a woman who had recently been promoted by her company. This information was ambiguous; it was not clear whether she actually deserved this recognition. Half of the participants learned that she had been promoted in a company that favored affirmative action and worked hard to implement it, while the others learned that she had been promoted in a company that was against affirmative action and had strongly resisted it. After reading this information, participants rated the woman's qualifications for her new job on a number of dimensions.

Results indicated that the woman was rated as more qualified when her company was anti–affirmative action than when it was pro–affirmative action. This suggests that *augmenting* played a role in subjects' evaluations. After all, if a woman was promoted even in an organization that was against affirmative action, she *must* be good! An even more important finding, however, is represented in Figure 2.9. For men, whether the woman's organization was pro– or anti–affirmative action had little influence on their evaluations; they tended to

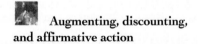

Augmenting, discounting, and affirmative action

FIGURE 2.9   Men rated the qualifications of a woman who had just been promoted fairly low regardless of whether her company was pro– or anti–affirmative action. In contrast, women rated the woman's qualifications very high if her company was anti–affirmative action. Thus, they showed *augmenting* under these conditions.

Source: Based on data from Summers, 1991.

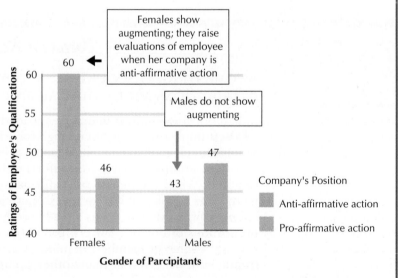

rate her quite low in both cases. For women, however, this factor was very important. When the woman's organization was anti–affirmative action, strong augmenting occurred: Female subjects rated her as highly qualified for her new job. In contrast, when her organization was pro–affirmative action, females behaved liked males and seemed to *discount* (down-rate) the manager's qualifications.

These findings suggest that attributional processes play an important role in reactions to affirmative action programs. Further, they point to one practical implication: Companies that implement such programs should avoid placing strong emphasis on their role in individual personnel decisions. When they do, such companies run the risk that other employees will perceive the persons who benefit from the program as unqualified—that discounting will occur. Where affirmative action in workplaces is concerned, therefore, organizations must carefully consider what they say about such programs as well as what they actually do with respect to them.

ATTRIBUTION: SOME BASIC SOURCES OF BIAS

Our discussion of attribution so far seems to imply that it is a highly rational process in which individuals seeking to identify the causes of others' behavior follow orderly cognitive steps. In general, this is so. We should note, however, that attribution is also subject to several forms of bias—tendencies that can lead us into serious errors concerning the causes of others' behavior. Several of these errors are described below.

THE FUNDAMENTAL ATTRIBUTION ERROR: OVERESTIMATING THE ROLE OF DISPOSITIONAL CAUSES. Imagine that you witness the following scene. A man arrives at a meeting forty minutes late. On entering, he drops his notes all over the floor. While he is trying to pick them up, his glasses fall off and break. Later he spills coffee all over the desk. How would you explain these events? The chances are good that you would reach conclusions such as these: This person is disorganized, clumsy, and generally incompetent. Are such attributions accurate? Perhaps. But it is also possible that the man was late because of unavoidable delays at the airport, dropped his notes because they were printed on very slick paper, and spilled the coffee because the cup was too hot to hold. That you would be less likely to consider such potential causes reflects what is often termed the **fundamental attribution error**—our strong tendency to explain others' actions in terms of dispositional (internal) rather than situational (external) causes. In short, we tend to perceive others as acting as they do because they are "that kind of person," rather than because of the many situational factors that may have affected their behavior.

This tendency to overemphasize dispositional causes while underestimating the impact of situational ones seems to arise from the fact that when we observe another person's behavior, we tend to focus on his or her actions; the context in which these occur often fades into the background. As a result, the potential impact of situational causes receives less attention. A second possibility is that we do notice such situational factors but tend to assign them insufficient weight (Gilbert & Jones, 1986).

Discussion Question 2

Whatever the basis for the fundamental attribution error, it has important implications. For example, it suggests that even if individuals are made aware of the situational forces that adversely affect disadvantaged groups in a society (e.g., poor diet, shattered family life), they may still perceive these persons as "bad" and responsible for their own plight. In such cases, the fundamental attribution error can have serious social consequences.

Interestingly, growing evidence suggests that while our tendency to attribute others' actions to dispositional causes is robust, it weakens over time (e.g., Burger, 1986; Frank & Gilovich, 1989). In other words, while we tend to attribute others' actions to internal causes soon after it has occurred, we take greater and greater account of situational (external) causes as time passes. This kind of shift in attributions is illustrated very clearly in research conducted by Burger (1991). In several studies, he asked participants to listen to a speech given by a stranger. Participants were told that the person had no choice but to take the position he had—this was required. Despite this fact, however, when participants were asked to rate the speaker's true attitude immediately after hearing the speech, they tended to believe that what the speaker said reflected his actual views; in other words, they ignored the situational causes and made internal attributions ("If he said it, that's what he believes"). Other participants, however, asked to rate the speaker's true attitudes one week *after* hearing the speech, did not show the same pattern—they did not attribute the speaker's comments to his true attitudes. Apparently the fundamental attribution error decreases over time because the accessibility of personal information diminishes more rapidly than the accessibility of situational information (Burger, 1991).

Work in Progress

Where Politics and the Fundamental Attribution Error Meet: Shifts in Our Explanations for Why the Winner Won

Shifts in our attributions over relatively short periods of time in laboratory studies is one thing; shifts in attributions over long periods and for real-life events would be quite another. Do these actually occur? Does our tendency to attribute others' actions to internal causes decrease with time under natural conditions?

Research conducted recently by Burger and Pavelich (1993) suggests that they do. In an ingenious follow-up to the earlier work by Burger (1991), this study analyzed people's explanations for the outcomes of presidential elections occurring between 1968 and 1984 in the United States. The researchers examined articles and columns appearing on the editorial pages of major newspapers (e.g., the *New York Times, Wall Street Journal,* and *Christian Science Monitor*) within five days of presidential elections and again two or three years

after each election. They analyzed the content of these sources to determine whether the outcomes were attributed to personal characteristics of one or both candidates, or to circumstances surrounding the election or actions by people outside the candidates' control. An example of personal causes is: "Mondale made the outcome worse by the ineptitude of his campaign." An example of situational causes is: "The shadows of Watergate . . . cleared the way for Carter's climb to the presidency." Results were clear: Within a few days of the elections, nearly two-thirds of the explanations for the outcome were personal. Two or three years later, however, this opposite was true: Two-thirds of the explanations referred to situational factors. So, over time, the fundamental attribution error was totally reversed. Interestingly, a follow-up study, in which researchers interviewed voters immediately after an election and one year later, showed that this shift toward more situational explanations over time occurred primarily among persons whose candidate lost. Apparently, persons who voted for the winning candidate maintained their tendency to explain the victory in personal terms. Since the winner was their personal choice, this is hardly surprising.

In sum, it appears that our attributions do often shift over time, and that as a result the tendency to explain others' actions in terms of internal causes may fade with the passing weeks or months. When such shifts lead us to more accurate conclusions about why others behaved as they did, of course, these changes may be beneficial ones.

THE ACTOR-OBSERVER EFFECT: YOU FELL; I WAS PUSHED.   Another and closely related type of attributional bias can be readily illustrated. Imagine that while walking along the street, you see someone stumble and fall down. How would you explain this behavior? Probably in terms of internal characteristics. You might assume that the person is clumsy. Now, suppose the same thing happens to you; would you explain your own behavior in the same terms? Probably not. Instead, you might well assume that you tripped because of situational causes—wet pavement, slippery shoes, and so on.

This tendency to attribute our own behavior to external or situational causes, but that of others to internal ones, is known as the **actor-observer effect** (Jones & Nisbett, 1971) and has been observed in many different studies (e.g., Frank & Gilovich, 1989). It seems to stem in part from the fact that we are quite aware of the situational factors affecting our own actions but, as outside observers, are less aware of such factors when we turn our attention to the actions of others. Thus, we tend to perceive our own behavior as arising largely from situational causes but the behavior of others as deriving mainly from their traits or dispositions.

Exercise 2

THE SELF-SERVING BIAS: "I CAN DO NO WRONG, BUT YOU CAN DO NO RIGHT."   Suppose that you write a term paper for one of your courses. When you get it back you find the following comment on the first page: "An *excellent* paper—one of the best I've read in years. A++." To what will you attribute this success? If you are like most people, the chances are good that you will explain your success in terms of internal causes—your high level of talent, the tremendous amount of effort you invested in writing the paper, and so on.

Now, in contrast, imagine that when you get your paper back, this comment is written on it: "Horrible paper—one of the worst I've read in years. D–." How will you interpret *this* outcome? In all likelihood, you will be sorely tempted to focus mainly on external (situational) factors—the difficulty of the task, your professor's unreasonable standards, and so on.

This tendency to attribute positive outcomes to internal causes but negative ones to external factors is known as the **self-serving bias,** and it appears to be both general in its occurrence and powerful in its effects (Brown & Rogers, 1991; Miller & Ross, 1975).

Exercise 4

Why does this "tilt" in our attributions occur? Several possibilities have been suggested, but most of these can be classified into two categories: cognitive and motivational explanations. The cognitive model suggests that the self-serving bias stems primarily from certain tendencies in the way we process social information (Ross, 1977). Specifically, it suggests that we attribute positive outcomes to internal causes but negative ones to external causes because we expect to succeed and we have a stronger tendency to attribute expected outcomes to internal causes than to external causes. In contrast, the motivational explanation suggests that the self-serving bias stems from our need to protect and enhance our self-esteem, or the related desire to look good in the eyes of others (Greenberg, Pyszczynski, & Solomon, 1982). While both cognitive and motivational factors may well play a role in this type of attributional error, recent evidence offers support for the latter. For example, consider a study conducted by Brown and Rogers (1991).

These researchers reasoned that arousal may play an important role in the self-serving bias. Failure experiences induce a negative state of arousal; attributing failure to external causes beyond one's control can help reduce such arousal. In contrast, success generates positive arousal that can be maintained by attributing such outcomes to internal causes. If this reasoning is correct, then it would be expected that the stronger the arousal individuals experience in response to success or failure, the stronger their tendency to demonstrate the self-serving bias. To test this prediction, Brown and Rogers provided individuals with bogus feedback suggesting either that they had done extremely well on a complex task (success condition), or extremely poorly (failure condition). Their skin conductance—one measure of physiological arousal—was

 The self-serving bias: Some potential implications

FIGURE 2.10   Why do many people assume that wealthy people do not deserve the riches they possess? One possibility involves operation of the self-serving bias. This attributional error leads us to assume that our own positive outcomes stem largely from internal causes (e.g., our own talent), while those of others stem from external causes (e.g, luck, special privilege).

monitored continuously while they performed the task and received the feedback. Finally, at the end of the session, participants rated the extent to which their task performance was due to ability and effort (internal causes), as well as to task difficulty and luck (external causes). Results offered support for the major prediction—at least with respect to failure: Individuals who experienced high levels of arousal attributed their poor performance to their own ability to a lesser degree than individuals who experienced lower levels of arousal. For subjects in the success condition, levels of arousal had little impact upon attributions. This latter finding is not surprising, since the motivational model emphasizes the role of the self-serving bias in protecting or enhancing self-esteem following negative outcomes.

Whatever the precise origins of the self-serving bias, it can be the cause of much interpersonal friction. For example, it often leads persons who work together on a joint task to perceive that *they*, not their partners, have made the major contributions. Similarly, it leads individuals to perceive that while their own successes stem from internal causes and are well deserved, the successes of others stem from external factors and are less appropriate (see Figure 2.10). Also, because of the self-serving bias, many persons tend to perceive negative actions on their part as reasonable and excusable, but identical actions on the part of others as irrational and inexcusable (Baumeister, Stillwell, & Wotman, 1990). Thus, the self-serving bias is clearly one type of attributional error with serious implications for interpersonal relations.

Can basic knowledge about attributions and their role in social behavior and social thought be put to practical use? For a discussion of this issue, please see the **On the Applied Side** section below.

Social Psychology: On the Applied Side

ATTRIBUTION THEORY TO THE RESCUE: OVERCOMING DEPRESSION AND DEFEATING LEARNED HELPLESSNESS

Kurt Lewin, one of the founders of modern social psychology, often remarked: "There's nothing as practical as a good theory." By this he meant that once we have obtained scientific understanding of some aspect of social behavior, we can put this knowledge to practical use. Where attribution theory is concerned, this has truly been the case. As basic knowledge about attribution processes has grown, so too has the range of practical problems to which such information has been applied. Indeed, attribution theory has served as a useful framework for understanding issues and topics as diverse as the causes of marital dissatisfaction (e.g., Holtzworth-Munroe & Jacobson, 1985), the nature of interpersonal conflict (Baron, 1990), and techniques for improving poor grades in college and substandard performance on the job (Brockner & Guare, 1983; Wilson & Linville, 1982). Perhaps the most intriguing applications of attribution theory to date, however, have involved efforts to apply such frameworks to understanding—and alleviating—two serious personal problems: *depression* and what psychologists term *learned helplessness*.

Depression is the most common psychological disorder. In fact, estimates indicate that at any given time more than 10 percent of the general population is suffering from this problem to some degree (Alloy et al., 1990). Although many factors play a role in depression, one that has received increasing attention in recent years is what might be termed a *self-defeating* pattern of attributions. In contrast to most people, who show the self-serving bias described earlier, depressed individuals tend to adopt an opposite pattern. They attribute negative outcomes to lasting internal causes such as their own traits or lack of ability, but attribute positive outcomes to temporary, external causes such as blind good luck or special favors from others. As a result, such persons come to perceive that they have little or no control over what happens to them—that they are mere chips in the winds of unpredictable fate. Little wonder that they become depressed and tend to give up on life! Fortunately, several forms of therapy that seek to change such attributions—and the ways in which depressed people think about themselves and others generally—have been developed and put to effective use (Abramson, Metalsky, & Alloy, 1990). These new forms of therapy do not mention repressed urges, inner conflicts, or traumatic events early in life, but they do work. Indeed, they appear to be at least as effective as—perhaps more so than—older and more traditional forms of treatment for depression. Since attribution theory provides the basis for these innovative forms of treatment, it has certainly proven very useful in this respect.

A second personal problem to which attribution theory has been successfully applied involves what psychologists describe as *learned helplessness*. This term refers to the negative effects of being exposed to uncontrollable negative events—ones that individuals are powerless to prevent or terminate (Seligman, 1975). After exposure to such conditions, individuals seem literally to give up: They come to believe that nothing they do matters much, and as a result they experience strong negative feelings (for example, feelings of hopelessness) and sharp drops in motivation. Perhaps worst of all, since they assume that events are outside their control, they never bother to find out that what they do *can* make a difference in many situations. Thus, as the name of this effect suggests, they learn to feel helpless in a wide range of situations—even ones where outcomes *are* under their control.

What does attribution have to do with learned helplessness? According to several researchers (e.g., Peterson & Seligman, 1984), quite a lot. It appears that individuals' *attributional style*—the extent to which they tend to attribute negative outcomes to stable, internal causes (such as their own traits) versus specific external causes—may determine both their susceptibility to learned helplessness and the extent to which they can be protected against its occurrence by exposure to situations in which they *can* control negative events. Evidence for this conclusion has recently been provided by Ramirez, Maldonado, and Martos (1992).

These researchers exposed students at a university in Spain to a task known to induce learned helplessness; in this task, subjects tried to choose the correct stimulus in pairs of stimuli. They were told that when they failed to choose the correct response, they would be exposed to a loud, irritating noise. But in fact they could not avoid the noise; there were no correct answers. Before performing this task, some subjects worked on a different task in which performance *was* under their control; this task was designed to protect or "immunize" them against the effects of the later helplessness experience. Among these immunized participants, some were known to have an external attributional style—they generally attributed negative outcomes to external causes. In contrast, others had an internal attributional style—they generally attributed negative outcomes to internal causes. In a third phase of the study, all participants performed a task in which their performance *was* under their

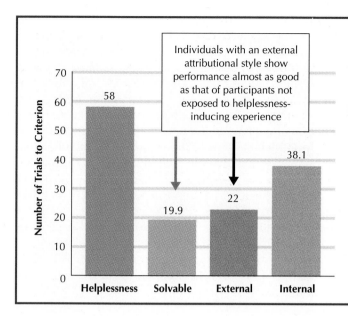

Attributional style and learned helplessness

FIGURE 2.11 Immunization against learned helplessness was more effective for individuals with an *external attributional style*—a tendency to attribute negative outcomes to external causes, than for individuals with an *internal attributional style*—a tendency to attribute negative outcomes to internal causes.

Source: Based on data from Ramirez, Maldonado, & Martos, 1992.

control. Participants in a control group were never exposed to helplessness-inducing conditions; they worked only on solvable tasks.

Results indicated that the immunization procedures worked, but mainly for participants with an external attributional style. Such persons did as well on the final task as those in the control condition. In contrast, immunized participants with an internal attributional style performed more like those in the helplessness group who had never had an immunizing experience (see Figure 2.11).

These findings indicate that attributions do indeed play an important role in learned helplessness. Moreover, they suggest that altering individuals' attributional style, so that they attribute negative outcomes to external causes, can lessen their susceptibility to feelings of helplessness. Given the devastating effects that learned helplessness can exert upon individuals' careers, personal relationships, and psychological health, this is another instance in which insights gained from attribution theory have contributed measurably to practical efforts to enhance human welfare.

IMPRESSION FORMATION AND IMPRESSION MANAGEMENT: COMBINING—AND MANAGING—SOCIAL INFORMATION

First impressions, it is widely held, are very important. Most of us assume that the initial impressions we make on others will shape the course of our future dealings with them in crucial ways. Further, we believe that such impressions may quite be resistant to change, even in the face of later contradictory information. It is for these reasons that most people prepare very carefully for first dates, job interviews, and other situations in which they will meet others for the first time (see Figure 2.12, p. 70). Are these commonsense assumptions

Making a good first impression

FIGURE 2.12 Many persons believe that first impressions are very important. Because of this assumption, they try to enhance their appearance before meeting others for the first time.

Exercise 3 about the nature of first impressions accurate? The answer provided by several decades of research is at least a qualified *yes* (e.g., Anderson, 1981; Burnstein & Schul, 1982; Wyer, 1988).

The first systematic research on this issue was performed by Asch (1946). He used a straightforward procedure in which subjects in two different groups were given one of the following descriptions of a hypothetical person:

intelligent-industrious-impulsive-critical-stubborn-envious

envious-stubborn-critical-impulsive-industrious-intelligent

Obviously, the two lists are identical in content; they differ only in the order in which the adjectives are presented. In the first list, positive traits are followed by negative ones, while in the second list, the opposite is true. If the impressions we form of others are more strongly affected by information we receive first (by information with *primacy*), then we might expect that when asked to report their overall impression of the hypothetical person, individuals exposed to the first list would report more favorable reactions. In fact, that is exactly what happened. Subjects who read the first list rated the imaginary person as more sociable, humorous, and happy than those who read the second list.

Why did these differences occur? Asch suggested that the order was important because the first adjectives subjects read changed the meaning of the ones they read later. With the first list, having learned that someone was intelligent and industrious, they interpreted the later, more negative adjectives within this favorable context. Thus, the fact that the hypothetical person was *critical* implied that this person made good use of his or her intelligence. With the second list, in contrast, having learned that the imaginary person was envious and stubborn, subjects interpreted the fact that she or he was also intelligent as suggestive of calculating shrewdness.

A more modern interpretation of Asch's findings—and one based on what we now know about social thought—suggests that these "primacy effects" occur because once we have some initial information at our disposal, we just don't bother to pay a lot of attention to additional input. After all, we already have enough information to form an impression, so why deal with any more? As we'll see in more detail in chapter 3, this tendency to minimize the amount of cognitive work we do when thinking about others is a strong one and plays a key role in many forms of social thought (Fiske & Taylor, 1991).

IMPRESSION FORMATION: SOME BASIC FACTS

Asch's research was, of course, only the beginning where the study of first impressions is concerned. Social psychologists have examined this topic for decades, and in an increasingly sophisticated manner. This research suggests that in forming impressions of others, we seem to combine available information about them into a kind of cognitive weighted average. In other words, we combine this information, with each piece being weighted by various factors that determine its importance (Anderson, 1981). What are the factors that influence the relative weight we place on various pieces of information about others? Among the most important of these are: (1) the source of the input—information from sources we trust or admire is weighted more heavily than information from sources we distrust (Rosenbaum & Levin, 1969); (2) whether the information is positive or negative in nature—we tend to weight negative information about others more heavily than positive information, perhaps because it is more novel or distinctive (Fiske, 1980; Mellers, Richards, & Birnbaum, 1992; see chapter 3); (3) the extent to which the information describes behavior or traits that are atypical or extreme—the more unusual it is, the greater the weight we place on it (please refer to our discussion of trait inferences above); and finally, as Asch found, (4) we often assign greater weight to information we receive first (information with primacy) than to information we receive later.

Perhaps a concrete example will help illustrate these points. Imagine that you accept a blind date. Prior to the date, you receive conflicting opinions of the person you are going to meet from a close friend and from someone you hardly know. Clearly, information from your friend will probably weigh more heavily in your developing impression. If the information provided by the casual acquaintance is negative, however, while that provided by your friend is positive, the negative information may have a stronger impact. (We'll examine why this may be the case in chapter 3.) When you meet your blind date, the first thing this person does is compliment you. Later your date says some annoying things. Still, she or he started out on the right foot, so your impression remains relatively favorable. During the course of the evening, you discover that your date likes pizza and finds most college textbooks (except this one, of course) dull and dry. These are typical reactions, so they don't influence your developing impression very much. When you learn that your date carries a miniature camera and is taking clandestine photos of the night's events, however, *this* information does have a big impact on your impression; after all, this is highly unusual behavior among the persons you know.

Discussion Question 4

IMPRESSION FORMATION: A COGNITIVE APPROACH.   Before concluding, it's important to emphasize the fact that in recent years our conceptions of the nature of impression formation and the ways in which it unfolds have been strongly influenced by advances in the field of *social cognition*—the area of social psychology that focuses on how we think about other persons and process information about them (e.g., Fiske & Taylor, 1991). Since we'll consider many different aspects of social cognition in chapter 3, we merely wish to mention this topic here and to note that it has provided important insights into impression formation (e.g., Higgins & Bargh, 1987). In particular, many findings in the field of social cognition indicate that initial meetings with others—when the impression formation process starts—do not occur in a cognitive vacuum. On the contrary, mental frameworks representing our previous experience in many social situations and with a wide range of persons are present. These frameworks, often known as *schemas*, can strongly influence which information about others we notice, how such input is entered into memory, and what later judgments or evaluations we make about these persons. Because of such preexisting cognitive frameworks, we don't seem to focus primarily on information about others' specific traits, or even on basic dimensions along which all persons can be placed (e.g., Anderson & Sedikides, 1991). Instead, we often focus on what might be termed *person types*—sets of traits that past experience tells us tend to cluster together. For example, one such cluster might be labeled *extroverted*; it includes such traits as ambition, enthusiasm, energy, outgoingness, confidence. Another could be described by the term *aggressive;* it includes such traits as domineeringness, possessiveness, aggressiveness, a tendency to dominate.

In sum, impression formation is a complex cognitive process in which we combine information about others with existing cognitive frameworks to form unified, overall impressions. The task itself often seems effortless, but research by social psychologists indicates that there is a lot going on beneath the surface.

IMPRESSION MANAGEMENT: THE FINE ART OF LOOKING GOOD

The desire to make a favorable impression on others is a strong one. Few people would behave like the character shown in Figure 2.13; the stakes are simply too high. On the contrary, most of us engage in active efforts to regulate how we appear to others in order to appear in the best or most favorable light pos-

 Negative impression management

FIGURE 2.13 Very few of us would behave like this character when applying for a job.
Source: NEA, Inc., 1987.

sible. This process is known as **impression management,** and considerable evidence indicates that persons who can perform it successfully gain important advantages in many social settings (Schlenker, 1980; Luginbuhl & Palmer, 1991). But what tactics do individuals use to create favorable impressions on others? And which of these are most successful? These are the issues we'll consider next.

IMPRESSION MANAGEMENT: BASIC TACTICS.   As your own experience probably suggests, impression management takes many different forms and involves a wide range of specific tactics. First, and perhaps most obviously, individuals wishing to make a good impression on others often attempt to alter their own appearance in specific ways. For example, they dress in ways that they believe will be evaluated favorably by others. Such tactics appear to succeed. It has been found, for example, that when women dress in a professional manner (business suit or dress, subdued jewelry), they are evaluated more favorably for management positions than when they dress in a more traditionally feminine manner (dresses with patterns, large jewelry; Forsythe, Drake, & Cox, 1985). Many other aspects of personal appearance, too, are involved in efforts at impression management, including hair styles, cosmetics, and even eyeglasses (e.g., Baron, 1989; Harris, 1991). Most of these efforts to improve personal appearance may smack of vanity, but they are not potentially dangerous to the persons who use them. One effort to enhance personal appearance, however—developing a suntan—*is* quite dangerous. Many young men and women find moderate levels of suntan in others to be attractive, so millions of people expose themselves to ultraviolet light, either from the sun or from artificial sources, to attain this look (Broadstock, Borland, & Gason, 1991). Unfortunately, such radiation is known to be a major cause of skin cancer; the costs of enhancing one's appearance in this manner can be very high (see Figure 2.14, p. 74).

Other tactics of impression management involve what are sometimes described as *other-enhancement*—efforts to induce favorable reactions in target persons by specific actions toward them. Among the most important of these tactics are *flattery*—heaping undeserved praise on target persons; expressing agreement with their views; showing a high degree of interest in them (hanging on their every word); and demonstrating high levels of liking or approval for them either verbally or nonverbally. An additional tactic involves doing favors—favors smaller than the ones the person engaging in impression management wants in return. Finally, recent evidence indicates that individuals sometimes ask for advice or feedback from others as a means of gaining their approval (Morrison & Bies, 1991). Many people find it flattering to be asked for such aid, and this can lead them to form favorable impressions of the person seeking the assistance.

Critical Thinking
Question 5

IMPRESSION MANAGEMENT: DOES IT SUCCEED?   Now for one key question where impression management is concerned: Does it work? Can individuals take steps that actually enhance the impressions they make on others? While there is no simple answer to this question, a growing body of evidence suggests that if used with skill and care, the tactics listed above can indeed be helpful—at least to the persons who use them (Godfrey, Jones, & Lord, 1986)! For example, consider a recent study by Kacmar, Delery, and Ferris (1993).

The potential costs of enhancing one's appearance

FIGURE 2.14 Because many people find a moderate degree of suntan attractive, millions of persons expose themselves to potential harm in an effort to attain this look.

These researchers examined the impact of impression management in an important applied setting: job interviews. Obviously, job applicants want to make the best impression possible on interviewers in order to increase their chances of being hired. On the other hand, interviewers want to avoid being unduly influenced by such techniques; after all, their task is to choose the most qualified applicants—*not* the ones most skilled at impression management. Previous studies had indicated that applicants who engage in several different impression management tactics do generally receive higher ratings from interviewers than those who do not (Gilmore & Ferris, 1989); so Kacmar and her colleagues attempted to carry this research one step farther by comparing two different types of impression management tactics. The first type included efforts by the applicant to direct the course of the interview and to focus attention on herself or himself. Kacmar et al. (1993) labeled such tactics *controlling* and included in this category such actions as claiming responsibility for positive events in one's background and building up one's own past performance. The second type of tactic involved efforts by the applicant to focus the conversation on the interviewer. Such *submissive* techniques included flattering the interviewer, agreeing with her or his opinions, and offering to do small favors for this person.

Kacmar and her associates trained assistants to engage in these two different styles of impression management, and then had them employ one style or the other during simulated interviews conducted by participants in the study. After the interviews were over, participants rated the "applicants" on various dimensions and indicated whether they would recommend hiring them. Because the interview situation is one that seems to call for controlling behavior by applicants, Kacmar and her colleagues predicted that applicants would receive higher ratings when they used the controlling rather than the submissive tactics. As shown in Figure 2.15, this prediction was confirmed. Similarly, the applicants received a job offer much more often when they used the controlling than when they used the submissive impression management tactics. Please note: These findings do not imply that controlling tactics will be more effective in all contexts. They do, however, appear to succeed where job interviews are concerned.

These findings and those of several other studies (e.g., Godfrey, Jones, & Lord, 1986) indicate that impression management tactics do often succeed in enhancing the appeal of persons who use them. Given this fact, should *you* learn to use them? The answer, of course, depends on the extent to which you feel comfortable with trying to gain an edge over others by enhancing your image and likability. Social psychology can study impression management and find out which tactics are most successful; but the decision to put these procedures to actual use is an ethical one centering more on personal values than on the findings of scientific research.

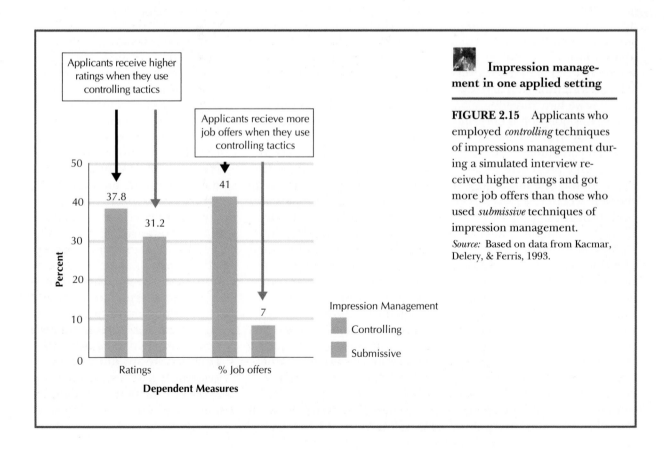

Impression management in one applied setting

FIGURE 2.15 Applicants who employed *controlling* techniques of impressions management during a simulated interview received higher ratings and got more job offers than those who used *submissive* techniques of impression management.

Source: Based on data from Kacmar, Delery, & Ferris, 1993.

Cultural and Ethnic Differences in Nonverbal Communication: On the Universality of Facial Expressions

Critical Thinking
Question 1

In chapter 1 we noted that social psychologists generally assume that the findings of their research are universal—that they apply to all human beings in all cultures and perhaps across time (Smith & Bond, 1993). This is a comforting assumption, for it suggests that the findings of social psychology are on a par with those of physics, chemistry, and other sciences; after all, no one suggests that the laws of physics operate any differently in Asia than in South America, or that they were different fifty years ago than they are now. Is this premise about the generalizability of social psychology justified? *Is* social behavior universal across cultures and across time? As we have already noted, this question is currently receiving growing attention in social psychology.

And the process of social perception is one major area of the field where this issue has been brought sharply into focus. For example, numerous studies have examined the question of whether attribution operates in the same manner across different cultures (e.g., Maas & Volpato, 1989). The aspect of social perception that has received most attention from a multicultural perspective, however, is nonverbal communication. And here one question seems to have been the subject of more research

activity than any other: How universal across various cultures are facial expressions?

Evidence that the Link Between Emotions and Facial Expressions Is Universal

Suppose that you traveled to a remote part of the world and visited a group of people who had never before met an outsider. Would their facial expressions in various situations resemble your own? In other words, would they smile when they encountered events that made them happy, frown when exposed to conditions that made them worried, and so on? Further, would you be able to recognize these distinct expressions as readily as those shown by persons belonging to your own culture? The answer to both questions appears to be yes. People living in widely separated geographic areas do seem to demonstrate similar facial expressions in similar emotion-provoking situations, and these can be readily—and accurately—recognized by persons from outside their own ethnic or cultural group (Ekman, 1989). Perhaps the most convincing evidence for such conclusions is provided by a series of studies conducted by Ekman and Friesen (1975).

These researchers traveled to isolated areas of New Guinea

and asked persons living there to imagine various emotion-provoking events—for example, your friend has come for a visit and you are happy; you find a dead animal that has been lying in the hot sun for several days, and it smells very bad. Then these subjects were asked to show by facial expressions how they would feel in each case. As you can see from Figure 2.16, their expressions were very similar to ones you might show yourself in these situations. It appears that when experiencing basic emotions, human beings all over the world tend to show highly similar facial expressions. Certainly these are not identical—different cultures have contrasting *display rules* indicating when and how various emotions should be expressed, and these can alter facial expressions considerably. When such rules don't intervene, however, the link between specific emotions and discrete facial expressions is quite universal.

But what about perceptions of such expressions; are these also universal? In other words, is a smile interpreted as a sign of happiness everywhere? Again, the answer seems to be yes. Look again at Figure 2.16. Do you have any difficulty in recognizing the expressions shown by the person in these photos? Almost certainly you do not, despite the fact that he comes from a different culture and a distant geographical location. Systematic research confirms this: When individuals living in widely separated countries are shown photos of strangers demonstrating anger, fear, happiness, sadness, surprise, and disgust, they are quite accurate in identifying these emotions (e.g., Ekman, 1973). Thus, it appears that facial expressions do communicate the same basic messages across diverse cultures around the world.

Evidence for Cultural Differences in the Emotion–to–Facial Expression Link

The fact that facial expressions are quite universal in our species suggests that in contrast to spoken language, nonverbal cues do not require an interpreter. This is comforting both from the point of view of the generalizability of social psychology's findings and, more importantly, from the perspective of enhanced communication between diverse ethnic and cultural groups. It does *not* imply, however, that cultural differences in facial expressions do not exist, or that the linkages between emotions and facial expressions are identical in all cultures. On the contrary, there is intriguing evidence for the existence of such differences. Consider a recent cross-cultural study conducted by Levenson et al. (1992).

These researchers investigated the facial expressions and underlying emotional experiences of a cultural

 Facial expressions: Much the same around the world

FIGURE 2.16   The man shown here lives in an isolated part of New Guinea. When asked to imagine various emotion-provoking events and show how he would feel, he demonstrated these facial expressions. The fact that these are very similar to facial expressions you would show when performing the same task provides evidence for the view that facial expressions are indeed universal. (The emotions shown are—in clockwise order—happiness, sadness, anger, and disgust.)

Source: From Ekman & Friesen, 1975, p. 27; by permission of the authors.

group named the Minang-kabau who live in West Sumatra (part of Indonesia). In the Minangkabau culture the internal aspects of emotion—the subjective feelings we experience as individuals—are viewed as less important than is true in many other cultures. Instead, the Minang-kabau emphasize the external aspects of emotion, such as the effects of emotional expression on interpersonal relations. Thus, members of this culture are trained as children to mask strong negative emotions, especially anger, to a much greater degree than persons in Western cultures. This reflects the Minangkabau's belief that expression of such emotions is disturbing to normal social relations.

To study the role of these cultural factors in emotion and facial expressions, Levenson and his colleagues asked young Minangkabau males to show various facial expressions—ones usually identified as reflecting happiness, sadness, disgust, fear, and anger.

The participants' physiological reactions were recorded as they showed each expression; and, in addition, participants reported on whether and to what extent they experienced various emotions as they produced these facial expressions. Because of the Minangkabau's cultural constraints against expressing strong emotions, it was predicted that they might have more difficulty in demonstrating these emotions than Americans; this prediction was confirmed. In addition, it was predicted that they would show weaker physiological arousal and would also report experiencing weaker emotions than Americans when showing each facial expression. These predictions, too, were supported. However, it is important to note that the *patterns* of physiological reactions shown by members of both cultures when demonstrating various facial expressions were highly similar. Differences between the cultures were mainly ones of intensity, not ones reflecting different patterns of subjective

or physiological reactions to various facial expressions.

In sum, it appears that regardless of where they live, human beings tend to show specific facial expressions at times when they experience certain emotions. Further, these expressions are readily recognized by persons from other cultures as reflecting specific emotional states. However, important differences do exist between cultures with respect to *display rules*—beliefs about when, and to what degree, various emotions should be expressed. Moreover, these cultural differences are reflected in emotional reactions and subjective experiences as well as facial expressions. In answer to the questions with which we began, therefore, we can conclude that yes, certain aspects of facial expressions are quite universal. But cultural factors affect even this very basic aspect of social perception and should not be overlooked.

Summary and Review

Nonverbal Communication

Social perception is the process through which we attempt to understand other persons. To obtain information about the temporary causes of behavior (e.g., others' emotions or feelings) we focus on *nonverbal cues*. These are provided by others' facial expressions, eye contact, body posture or movements, and touching. Nonverbal behavior plays an important role in social interaction. It is often used for purposes of *self-presentation*—to create a particular impression on others. In addition, through the use of nonverbal cues, we can often recognize when others are attempting to deceive us. Persons high in *self-monitoring* are more successful than persons low in self-monitoring in concealing their true emotions in situations where it is inappropriate to reveal these.

Attribution: Understanding the Causes of Others' Behavior

Knowledge about the lasting causes of others' behavior is acquired through attribution. In this process, we infer others' traits, motives, and intentions from observation of their behavior; and we focus on the aspects of their behavior that are most likely to be revealing in this respect. In order to determine whether others' behavior stems mainly from internal or external causes, we focus on information relating to consensus, consistency, and distinctiveness. We engage in careful causal analysis only under certain circumstances, however—for example, when others behave in unexpected ways. Attributions are affected by discounting—a tendency to discount one potential cause of behavior when others are also present—and by augmenting—a tendency to emphasize the importance of factors that might cause a specific behavior when the behavior occurs despite the presence of factors that might inhibit it. Augmenting and discounting seem to play a role in reactions to persons who gain promotions or other benefits through affirmative action programs. Attribution is subject to several forms of bias or error, including the fundamental attribution error, the actor-observer effect, and the self-serving bias. Attribution theory has been put to practical use in several contexts, particularly in devising effective treatments for depression and learned helplessness.

Impression Formation and Impression Management

Common sense is correct in suggesting that first impressions are important. We form such impressions by combining available information about others, with each piece of information weighted in terms of its importance. Individuals engage in many tactics to make favorable impressions on others. Together, these are known as tactics of *impression management*. These include efforts to improve one's personal appearance and various forms of *other-enhancement*; for example, flattery and agreeing with others' views. Impression management often succeeds in its goals.

Social Diversity: The Universality of Facial Expressions

Existing evidence indicates that facial expressions of emotion are relatively universal. When exposed to emotion-provoking events, people from different cultures show similar expressions—ones readily recognizable to persons from outside their own culture. Cultural differences in the expression of emotions do exist, however, and often influence the nature and intensity of the facial expressions shown by individuals in various situations.

Key Terms

Actor-observer-effect The tendency to attribute our own behavior mainly to situational causes but the behavior of others mainly to internal (dispositional) causes.

Attribution The process through which we seek to identify the causes of others' behavior and so gain knowledge of their stable traits and dispositions.

Augmenting principle The tendency to attach greater importance to a potential cause of behavior if the behavior occurs despite the presence of other, inhibitory causes.

Body language Cues provided by the position, posture, and movement of people's bodies or body parts.

Consensus The extent to which actions by one person are also shown by others.

Consistency The extent to which an individual responds to a given stimulus or situation in the same way on different occasions (i.e., across time).

Correspondent inference (theory of) A theory describing how we use others' behavior as a basis for inferring their stable dispositions.

Discounting principle The tendency to attach less importance to one potential cause of some behavior when other potential causes are also present.

Distinctiveness The extent to which an individual responds in a similar manner to different stimuli or different situations.

Emblems Gestures with specific meanings within specific cultures.

Fundamental attribution error The tendency to overestimate the impact of dispositional (internal) causes on others' behavior.

Gait The characteristic way in which a person walks.

Impression Management See *self-presentation*.

Microexpression Brief and incomplete facial expressions that occur on individuals' faces very quickly after exposure to a specific stimulus and before active processes can be used to conceal them.

Noncommon effects Effects produced by a particular cause that could not be produced by any other apparent cause.

Nonverbal communication Communication between individuals that does not involve the content of spoken words. It consists instead of an unspoken language of facial expressions, eye contact, and body language.

Self-monitoring A personality trait involving the ability to manage one's own nonverbal cues and change one's behavior in order to make favorable impressions on others, together with sensitivity to others' reactions.

Self-presentation Techniques designed to create a favorable impression of oneself in others (target persons).

Self-serving bias The tendency to attribute positive outcomes in one's own life to internal causes (e.g., one's own traits or characteristics) but negative outcomes or events to external causes (e.g., chance, task difficulty).

Social perception The process through which we seek to know and understand other persons.

Staring A form of eye contact in which one person continues to gaze steadily at another regardless of what the recipient does.

For More Information

Harvey, J. H., & Weary, G. (Eds.) (1985). *Attribution: Basic issues and applications*. San Diego: Academic Press.

This collection of chapters, each prepared by an expert researcher, discusses major theories of attribution, recent research findings, and how knowledge about this key aspect of social perception has been applied to many practical problems.

Ross, M., & Fletcher, G. J. O. (1985). Attribution and social perception. IN G. Lindzey and E. Aronson (Eds.), *Handbook of social psychology*. New York: Random House.

A comprehensive discussion of many aspects of social perception. While the chapter is intended mainly for professional social psychologists, it is clearly written and contains a great deal of interesting information.

Siegman, A. W., & Feldstein, S. (Eds.) (1987). *Nonverbal behavior and communication.* Hillsdale, NJ: Erlbaum.

Contains chapters on various aspects of nonverbal communication prepared by experts on this topic. Included are truly fascinating discussions of body movement and gestures, nonverbal aspects of speech, and the ways in which nonverbal cues regulate conversations and even group processes. This is an excellent source to consult if you'd like to know more about nonverbal communication.

Social Cognition: Thinking about Others and the Social World

Interior with Girl Reading (1905 - 1906) by Pierre Matisse

It was a snowy January evening in 1978. My wife and I had just finished dinner in a Hungarian restaurant and were about to head home. The meal had been delicious, and we were both in high spirits as I approached the edge of the road. It had snowed a lot during the past few days, so there were large piles on either side. I looked both ways and, since there seemed to be nothing coming, started to pull out. Suddenly, there it was: a Volkswagen beetle hurtling toward us at breakneck speed. I tried to stop, but it was too late, and we felt a rocking motion as my front bumper grazed the passing little car. We pulled over immediately. At first I couldn't see the other vehicle. Then I realized that it had skidded across the road and was partially buried in a large snowbank. I rushed over to see if the other driver was okay. As he opened the door to get out, I detected a strong smell of alcohol. He was a pretty rough-looking character with a thick black beard and what seemed to be a wild look in his eye. When I asked him if he was all right, I discovered that he didn't speak English; he just stood there muttering in some foreign language and shaking his head. "One of *those*," I found myself thinking. "A drunk; we're lucky to be alive!" And as such thoughts raced through my mind, I found my attitude toward this stranger hardening. "Just wait till the police get here," I thought. "I'll blame him for the whole thing— it's just what he deserves!"

Soon, a state trooper *did* arrive. Although he didn't say anything specific, I could tell that the officer had quickly sized up the other driver in the same way I had. In fact, just before leaving he remarked: "Don't worry. We're going to give this character an alcohol test when we get him back to the station. People like that ought to be kept off the roads!"

Our car had practically no damage—just a small dent on the bumper—but the right side of the other car was a mess. Still, I didn't feel sorry for the other driver. No, I didn't care about *his* car; only

mine seemed to matter. I was very attached to our old Dodge; why, it was practically a member of the family! For several days after the accident, in fact, I repeatedly tortured myself with the thought that this was the first time we had gone to that restaurant; if only I had listened to my wife, who wanted to eat at one of our regular places instead. If I hadn't insisted on trying something new, the accident would never have happened.

About a week later I received several major surprises. First, I learned that the other driver had passed the alcohol test: He *wasn't* drunk. In fact, my insurance agent told me, the smell of alcohol came from a Christmas present, an

expensive bottle of brandy, that had been broken by another package in the trunk. The other driver's rough appearance, too, was misleading. He was actually a famous scientist from Eastern Europe, not the potentially dangerous drifter I had assumed. (I should have known; the piles of books and scientific journals on the back seat of his car were a dead giveaway.) Finally, I learned that he wasn't speeding. The accident had occurred simply because he couldn't see me over the snowdrifts, just as I couldn't see *him*. So, it seemed, I had jumped to several false and unfounded conclusions at once.

Thinking about others, and about the social world in general, is one of life's major tasks. Like the little girl in Figure 3.1, we want to understand the people around us—to know why they do and say the things they do. And frequently, we must make various kinds of judgments about them: Do we like them or dislike them? Do they like or dislike *us*? Are they someone with whom we want to work—or to live? Are they suited for certain roles or jobs? Are they someone we can rely on, or do they change their beliefs and allegiances as often as they change their clothes? These are only a few of the many questions we ask—and seek to answer—about others.

In order to unravel such mysteries and to make judgments about others, we must somehow notice, sort, remember, and use a wealth of social information. As you probably know from your own experience, the task of doing so is anything but simple. The raw materials for social thought are all around us, all the time. Thus, even when making relatively simple judgments about others, we have a truly vast array of potential input at our disposal. We know what people look like, what they've said at various times, and how they have acted in different situations (e.g., Stangor et al., 1992). We have expectations about them and can compare their current words or deeds to these personal predictions (Hilton, Klein, & von Hippel, 1991). Finally, we have feelings about them, and these too enter into the picture. How, then, do we use all this information in

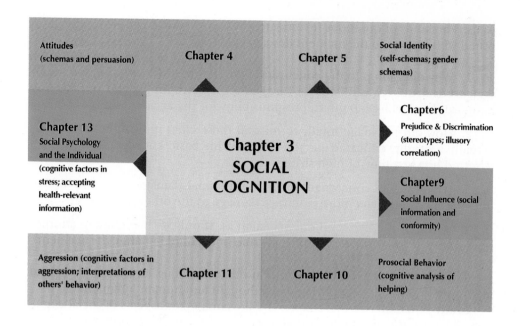

Attitudes (schemas and persuasion)	**Chapter 4**	**Chapter 5**	Social Identity (self-schemas; gender schemas)

Chapter 13
Social Psychology and the Individual (cognitive factors in stress; accepting health-relevant information)

**Chapter 3
SOCIAL
COGNITION**

Chapter 6
Prejudice & Discrimination (stereotypes; illusory correlation)

Chapter 9
Social Influence (social information and conformity)

Aggression (cognitive factors in aggression; interpretations of others' behavior)

Chapter 11

Chapter 10

Prosocial Behavior (cognitive analysis of helping)

our attempts to understand others and the social world? In other words, what is the nature of *social thought* (or **social cognition** as it is often termed), how does it proceed, and what factors affect it? Efforts to investigate these questions constitute a major theme of modern social psychology (e.g., Fiske & Taylor, 1991; Forgas, 1991a; Miller, Turnbull, & McFarland, 1990; Ross, 1989). A very large volume of current research focuses on precisely how we notice, interpret, remember, and then use the wealth of social information available

Video: Attribution and Social Cognition

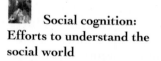 **Social cognition:
Efforts to understand the
social world**

FIGURE 3.1   Like the little girl in this cartoon, we often expend considerable effort in attempts to understand various aspects of the social world.

Source: The New Yorker

"Why does she want to go back to Kansas, where everything is in black-and-white?"

to us. The kinds of questions investigated in such research can be readily illustrated with respect to the incident described above:

1. Why did I jump to the conclusion that the other driver was a potentially dangerous drunk? Was it because I *wanted* to perceive him in this unflattering light—and so feel free to pin full responsibility for the accident on him?

2. How did I manage totally to miss all those clues indicating that he was actually a bright, educated person—even if his basic knowledge of English deserted him at a time of high stress?

3. Why was I so concerned about the minimal damage to my car but so unconcerned about the more extensive damage to the other driver's car?

4. Why did "if only . . ." thoughts (such as "If only we had gone to another restaurant . . .") play such an important role in my thinking after the accident?

As we'll see, research on social cognition offers revealing answers to these and many other questions concerning social thought and human judgment.

In the remainder of this chapter, we'll examine key aspects of social cognition. First, we'll consider several shortcuts and strategies people use to help them in their attempts to make sense out of the social world. While these strategies often succeed in simplifying social cognition and in reducing the effort it requires, their ultimate impact is highly similar to that of other types of shortcuts: Sometimes they lead us astray and cause more problems than they solve. Second, we'll examine several tendencies or "tilts" in social thought, tendencies that cause us to pay more attention to some kinds of input than to others and therefore to reach conclusions that are different, and often less accurate, than might otherwise be the case. Included here are seemingly strong tendencies to discount information inconsistent with our initial beliefs or conclusions and to assign extra weight to negative information about others when making social judgments (e.g., Ditto & Lopez, 1992; Pratto & John, 1991). Finally, we will examine the complex interplay between **affect**—our current feelings or moods—and *cognition*. As we'll soon note, this relationship is indeed a two-way street, with feelings influencing cognition, and cognition in turn shaping affect. Please note: Another key aspect of social cognition—our efforts to understand *ourselves*—will be discussed in detail in chapter 5.

HEURISTICS: MENTAL SHORTCUTS IN SOCIAL COGNITION

People, it is often noted, prefer the path of least resistance. In other words, when faced with a task, they select the approach that will allow them to reach their goal with the least amount of effort. As we mentioned in our discussion of causal attribution (see chapter 2), this preference applies to cognitive as well as to physical work. In fact, it is a guiding principle of social cognition. All things being equal, most of us will do the least amount of mental work we can get away with in most situations (e.g., Fiske & Taylor, 1991). In other words, we are usually unwilling to expend more than the minimum amount of cognitive effort required in a given situation. Of course, this is not always true. There are situations in which individuals willingly engage in complex and effortful forms of social thought (e.g., Tetlock & Boettger, 1989). This is more likely to be the exception than the rule, however; usually we seek to minimize cognitive effort whenever feasible.

This fact points to the following conclusion: In many cases people adopt Discussion Question 1 strategies designed to reduce cognitive effort and to decrease the possibility of **information overload**—having to deal with more information than they can handle. To be successful, such strategies must have two properties. First, they must provide a quick and simple way of dealing with large amounts of social information. Second, they must *work*—they must be reasonably accurate much of the time.

While many potential shortcuts for reducing mental effort exist, the ones that have received most attention with respect to social cognition are **heuristics**—simple decision-making rules we often use to make inferences or draw conclusions quickly and easily. To understand how heuristics work, consider an analogy. Suppose you want to estimate the dimensions of a room but don't have a tape measure. What will you do? One possibility is to pace off its length and width by placing one foot almost exactly in front of the other. Since the distance from the heel to the toe of an adult's foot is approximately twelve inches, you will be able to get rough estimates of the room's dimensions through this "quick-and-dirty" method.

In a similar manner, we make use of many different mental heuristics in our efforts to think about and use social information. Two of these that are used frequently in everyday life are known as *representativeness* and *availability*.

REPRESENTATIVENESS: JUDGING BY RESEMBLANCE

Imagine that you have just met your next-door neighbor for the first time. On the basis of a brief conversation with her, you determine that she is very neat in her habits, has a good vocabulary, reads many books, is somewhat shy, and dresses conservatively. Later you realize that she never mentioned what she does for a living. Is she a business executive, a librarian, a waitress, an attorney, or a dancer? One quick way of making a guess is to compare her with other members of each of these occupations; simply ask yourself how well she resembles persons you have met in each of these fields. If you proceed in this fashion, you may well conclude that she is a librarian. After all, her traits seem to resemble the traits many people associate with librarians more closely than the traits of dancers, attorneys, or waitresses. In this instance, you would be using the **representativeness heuristic**. In other words, you would make your judgment on the basis of a relatively simple rule: *The more similar an individual is to "typical" members of a given group, the more likely he or she is to also belong to that group.*

Are such judgments likely to be accurate? Since membership in particular groups affects the behavior and mannerisms of the persons in them (see our discussion of this topic in chapter 12), and since individuals are attracted to specific groups because they share various interests or characteristics with the group's members, the representativeness heuristic *is* often accurate. As you probably know from your experience, however, there are exceptions to this general rule. Some librarians are extroverted and lead exciting social lives; some dancers are shy and read lots of books. And some professors (believe it or not) climb mountains, practice sky-diving, and even run for political office in their spare time (see Figure 3.2, p. 88). Because of such exceptions, the representativeness heuristic, although useful, can lead to serious errors in at least some instances. In addition, and perhaps more importantly, reliance on this heuristic can lead us to overlook other types of information that could potentially be very useful. The most important type is information relating to *base rates*—the frequency with which some event or pattern occurs in the general population. The tendency to overlook such information when relying on the representativeness heuristic was illustrated some years ago by a famous study carried out by Tversky and Kahneman (1973).

Participants in this study were told that an imaginary person named Jack had been selected from a group of one hundred men. They were then asked to guess the probability that Jack was an engineer. Some participants were told that thirty of the one hundred men were engineers (thus, the base rate for engineers was 30 percent). Others were told that seventy of the men were engineers. Half of the subjects received no further information. The other half, however, also received a personal description of Jack that either resembled the common stereotype of engineers (e.g., they are practical, like to work with numbers, etc.) or did not. When participants in the study received only information relating to base rates, their estimates of the likelihood that Jack was an engineer reflected this information: They thought it more likely that Jack was an engineer when the base rate was 70 percent than when it was 30 percent. However, when they received personal information about Jack, they tended to ignore this important information. They made their estimates primarily on the basis of whether Jack seemed to resemble their stereotype of an engineer. In

 The representativeness heuristic in action

FIGURE 3.2 Do you find it surprising that the persons shown here are Hewlett-Packard employees? If so, this may result in part from the operation of the *representativeness heuristic*—our tendency to assume that the more similar an individual is to "typical" members of a given group, the more likely it is that she or he belongs to that group.

sum, subjects tended to overlook a valuable form of information and to operate in terms of representativeness alone. This tendency to ignore useful base rate information is known as the **base rate fallacy**.

AVAILABILITY: WHAT COMES TO MIND FIRST?

Which is more common—words that start with the letter *k* (e.g., king) or words with *k* as the third letter (e.g., awkward)? Tversky and Kahneman (1982) put this question to more than one hundred people. Their findings were revealing. In English there are more than twice as many words with *k* in third place as there are with *k* in first place. Yet despite this fact, a majority of the subjects guessed incorrectly: They assumed that there were more words beginning with *k*. Why was this the case? In part, because of their use of another heuristic— **availability**. According to this heuristic, the easier it is to bring instances of some group or category to mind, the more prevalent or important these are judged to be. This heuristic, too, makes good sense: After all, events or objects that are common *are* usually easier to think of than ones that are less common, because we have had more experience with them. But relying on availability in making such judgments can also lead to errors, such as the one involving words with the letter *k*. As another example, consider the case of a professor who is grading students on the basis of class participation. As she assigns grades, she thinks: "Hm . . . let's see . . . how often did Jose participate? Did he speak up more than Laurel?" Does the ease with which she can recall each student's comments reflect the actual frequency with which the students contributed? Not necessarily. Perhaps she is more likely to remember comments that were made very forcefully, with lots of conviction. To the extent this is so, she may assign higher grades to those students who express themselves with greatest conviction—not necessarily to those who have participated most.

Do we actually rely on the availability heuristic in making judgments about the social world—or about ourselves? While research findings such as those reported by Tversky and Kahneman (1973) and other researchers (Grabielcik & Fazio, 1984) suggest that we do, there is a complication in the picture. When information is easy to remember, we may recall more of it than when it is difficult to remember. Thus, we may judge easy-to-remember information as more frequent or likely to occur for this reason—not simply because of our subjective feeling that it is easy to bring to mind. While this seems like a very logical possibility, research conducted by Schwarz and his colleagues (Schwarz et al., 1991) provides convincing evidence that the availability heuristic does indeed operate through our subjective feelings concerning the ease with which information can be brought to mind.

To disentangle these two factors—ease of recall and amount of information remembered—Schwarz and his coworkers asked female students at a German university to remember either six or twelve situations in which they had behaved assertively and felt at ease or six or twelve examples of situations in which they had behaved unassertively and felt insecure. Previous research had indicated that students could readily remember eight or nine behaviors in these categories but found it very difficult to remember ten or more. After completing the task, participants were asked to rate themselves in terms of assertiveness. Schwarz et al. (1991) reasoned that if the ease with which information is recalled is important, then participants would rate themselves as more assertive or more unassertive when asked to recall only six examples of each type of behavior than when asked to remember twelve examples. In con-

Exercise 1

Discussion Question 2

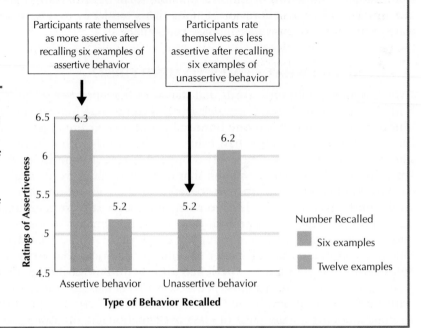

The availability heuristic and ease of recall

FIGURE 3.3 Individuals rated themselves as more assertive or less assertive when asked to recall six examples of assertive or unassertive behaviors than when asked to recall twelve examples of each type of behavior. These findings indicate that the ease with which information can be brought to mind plays a key role in the impact of such information on subsequent judgments.

Source: Based on data from Schwarz et al., 1991.

trast, if it is the amount of information remembered that is crucial the opposite should be true: Those asked to remember twelve examples of assertive or unassertive behavior would rate themselves as more assertive (or unassertive) than those asked to remember only six.

As you can see from Figure 3.3, results offered support for the view that it is ease of recall that is crucial, not the amount of information remembered. Participants rated themselves as more assertive when asked to recall only six examples of assertive behavior and as less assertive when asked to recall only six examples of unassertive behavior. These results were confirmed in two follow-up studies. So it appears that the ease with which information can be brought to mind is indeed one mental shortcut people frequently use when making social judgments. Information that can be brought to mind readily *is* judged to be more frequent or likely than information that is harder to bring to mind. In short, in making social judgments, it is not only what we remember that's important; the ease or difficulty with which we remember it is crucial too.

THE FALSE CONSENSUS EFFECT: AVAILABILITY AND THE TENDENCY TO ASSUME THAT OTHERS THINK AS WE DO. Be honest: on a scale ranging from 1 (Strongly Opposed) to 7 (Strongly in Favor), what is your view about permitting persons with an openly homosexual life-style to join the nation's military forces? Now, out of one hundred other students, how many do you think share your view, whatever it is? (That is, how many are on the same side of the neutral point on this scale [4] as yourself?) If you are like most people, the number you indicated is higher than what would be revealed by an actual survey. In other words, you assume that people agree with you to a greater extent than they actually do. This is known as the **false consensus effect**, and it has been observed in many different contexts. For example, in one study high school boys who smoked estimated that 51 percent of their fellow male students smoked, but nonsmoking boys estimated that only 38 percent smoked (Sherman, Presson, & Chassin, 1984). In a similar manner, students tend to overestimate the proportion of other students who agree with their attitudes about drugs, abortion, seat belt use, university policies, politics, and even Ritz crackers (Nisbett & Kunda, 1985; Suls, Wan, & Sanders, 1988). In short, the false consensus effect is quite common (although in an absolute sense, it is not very large).

Critical Thinking
Question 2

Exercise 3

What is the basis for this tendency to assume that others think as we do? Two factors seem to play a role. First, most people want to believe that others agree with them, because this enhances their confidence that their own actions, judgments, or lifestyles are normal or appropriate (Marks & Miller, 1987; Sherman, Presson, & Chassin, 1984). In other words, the false consensus effect serves as a self-enhancing function.

Second, this tendency seems to stem, at least in part, from reliance on the availability heuristic. This can occur two distinct ways. Some people, at least, find it easier to notice and later remember instances in which others agreed with them than instances in which they disagreed. As a result of such distortion in processing social information, people find it easier to bring instances of agreement to mind. Then they perceive these instances as more frequent than instances of disagreement. Alternatively, since most of us tend to choose as friends and associates others who share our views (see our discussion of attraction in chapter 7), we are actually exposed to many instances of agreement. This, too, leads to higher availability for agreement than disagreement and contributes to the occurrence of the false consensus effect.

We should note, by the way, that while the false consensus effect is common, it is far from universal. It is comforting to assume that others share our attitudes and, perhaps, even our undesirable attributes (such as the inability to resist rich desserts). However, for highly desirable attributes, people may be motivated to perceive themselves as unique (e.g., Goethals, 1986; Suls & Wan, 1987). Thus, when the desire to stand out from the crowd in some positive way is stronger than the desire to be similar to others, the false consensus effect may fail to occur (Campbell, 1986).

PRIMING: SOME EFFECTS OF INCREASED AVAILABILITY.   During the first year of medical school, many students experience what is known as the "medical student syndrome." They begin to suspect that they (or their friends or families) are suffering from serious illnesses. An ordinary headache, for example, may cause such students to wonder if they have a brain tumor. A mild sore throat may result in anxiety over the possibility that some rare but fatal type of infection has begun. What accounts for these effects? Two factors seem crucial. First, the students are exposed to descriptions of diseases day after day in their classes and assigned readings. As a result, such information is high in availability. Thus, when a mild symptom occurs, it is readily brought to mind, with the result that the students tend to imagine the worst about their current health!

Such effects are termed **priming**. Specifically, priming involves any stimuli that heighten the availability of certain types or categories of information so that they can be readily brought to mind. Many instances of priming occur in everyday life. For example, after watching an especially frightening horror movie, many persons react strongly to stimuli that would previously have had little impact upon them ("What's that dark shape at the end of the driveway?" "What's that creak on the stairs?"; see Figure 3.4).

Heuristics: Mental Shortcuts in Social Cognition

 Priming in action

FIGURE 3.4 After seeing a frightening horror movie, many persons react with fear to stimuli that might fail to evoke such reactions in the absence of such *priming* (i.e., at times when they have *not* recently seen such a scary film.

Similarly, after viewing a television show filled with sexual remarks and content, some persons, at least, are more likely to perceive innocuous remarks or gestures by others as come-ons than might otherwise be true.

The occurrence of priming effects has been demonstrated in many different studies (e.g., Higgins & King, 1981; Wyer & Srull, 1980). For example, in one of the earliest experiments on this topic (Higgins, Rohles, & Jones, 1977), participants were shown lists of positive traits (e.g., adventurous, independent) or negative traits (e.g., reckless). Then, in what they thought was a separate task, they were asked to form an impression of an imaginary person. They formed these impressions on the basis of descriptions of his behavior that were either relevant to the previously viewed traits (e.g., sailing across the Atlantic, climbing mountains) or unrelated to them. Results indicated that subjects' impressions of the imaginary character were indeed affected by the trait words, but only when these were relevant to the descriptions of his behavior. Thus, participants' impressions were more favorable if they had previously seen relevant positive traits (e.g., adventurous) than if they had previously seen relevant negative ones (e.g., reckless). In short, their social judgments were affected by priming—by words that had activated different aspects or categories of their memories.

More recent research on priming suggests that it is a pervasive phenomenon. In fact, it seems to occur even when individuals are unaware of the priming stimuli—an effect known as **automatic priming** (e.g., Bargh & Pietromonaco, 1982). For example, in one intriguing study on this topic (Erdley & D'Agostino, 1989), words relating to the trait of honesty (words such as honorable, truthful, sincere) were flashed on a screen so briefly that participants were not aware of them. In contrast, participants in a control group were exposed to words unrelated to this trait (words such as what, little, many, number). After this experience, individuals in both groups read a description of an imaginary person—a narrative that described her in ambiguous terms. Finally, they rated this imaginary person in several trait dimensions, some of which were related to honesty. As automatic priming predicts, those exposed to the honesty-related words rated her higher on these trait dimensions than those exposed to the neutral words.

Perhaps even more surprising is the fact that in many situations, we seem to generate our own *primes*. Apparently, this happens when we receive information about another person and, on the basis of this input, infer that she or he possesses certain traits. These *spontaneous trait inferences*, in turn, act as primes, influencing our subsequent judgments about this person with respect to the primed trait dimension. Direct evidence for such effects has recently been reported by Moskowitz and Roman (1992). These researchers asked participants to read five sentences about a fictitious person and either (1) to memorize these sentences, or (2) to form an impression about this person. Within each of these conditions, the sentences implied that the stranger was stubborn and conceited, persistent and confident; or (in a control condition) none of these.

After completing this task, participants read a paragraph describing a person named Donald—a paragraph specifically designed to be ambiguous concerning the extent to which Donald was stubborn, conceited, persistent, or confident. Finally, participants rated Donald on these trait dimensions. Moskowitz and Roman (1992) reasoned that persons asked to memorize the sentences would generate spontaneous trait inferences and that these would serve as primes. In contrast, persons asked to form an impression would form conscious inferences about him; these would not act as primes. Thus, it was predicted that participants asked to memorize the sentences would rate

 Self-generated primes

FIGURE 3.5 Individuals who memorized sentences suggesting that a stranger possessed certain traits later rated him as higher in these traits than persons who read the same sentences and did not memorize them but were asked to form an impression of the stranger.

These findidngs suggest that when we make inferences about others' traits, these inferences can serve as *primes*, which then influence our later social judgments.

Source: Based on data from Moskowitz & Roman, 1992.

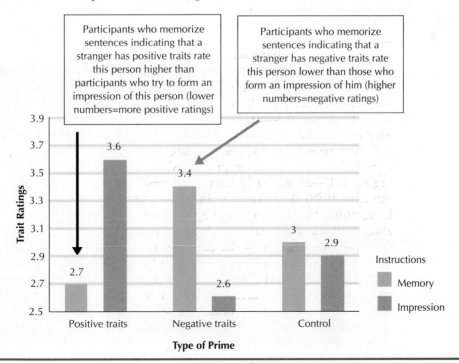

Donald higher on the various traits than those asked to form an impression of him. Remember: The description of Donald was quite ambiguous, so any effects of spontaneously generated primes would be visible in these ratings. As shown by Figure 3.5, p. 93, results offered support for these predictions. Participants in the memory condition did indeed rate Donald higher on positive traits (persistent, confident) and higher on negative traits (stubborn, conceited) than those in the impression formation group.

In sum, priming seems to be a basic fact of social thought. External events and conditions increase the availability in memory of specific types of information. Such heightened availability, in turn, strongly influences our social judgments. And on some occasions our spontaneous inferences about others' traits seem to serve the same function: Once they are formed, they increase the availability of specific kinds of information and so shape our social judgments. In such cases, social cognition can indeed be described as following a self-directed route.

BASIC ASPECTS OF SOCIAL THOUGHT: TILTS, TENDENCIES, AND POTENTIAL ERRORS

Human beings are definitely not computers. While we can *imagine* a person who reasons in a perfectly logical manner and rarely (if ever) makes errors, we are unlikely ever to meet one—unless it is Mr. Spock of "Star Trek" fame (see Figure 3.6). Being human, we are fallible—highly fallible—where the cognitive side of life is concerned. Social thought is certainly no exception to this rule. In fact, our efforts to understand others and make sense out of the social world are subject to a wide range of biases and tendencies which together can, and sometimes do, lead us into serious error. In this section we'll consider several of these imperfections of social cognition (e.g., Fiske & Taylor, 1991; Srull & Wyer, 1989). As you'll soon see, these tendencies are as intriguing as they are potentially disturbing.

The only totally logical being in existence?

FIGURE 3.6 While Mr. Spock (of "Star Trek") appears to be totally logical, the rest of us, as mere human beings, can't hope to match his performance where social thought is concerned.

Before turning to them, however, we should carefully emphasize the following point: While these aspects of social thought do sometimes result in errors, they are also, in key respects, quite adaptive. They help us to focus on the kinds of information that are usually most informative, and they reduce the overall effort required for understanding our social world. So, as is true of virtually every important aspect of human behavior, these tendencies cut both ways and can be beneficial as well as detrimental. Having said that, we'll turn without further delay to several key aspects of social thought.

DEALING WITH INCONSISTENT INFORMATION: PAYING ATTENTION TO WHAT DOESN'T FIT

Imagine the following situation: You are watching an evening talk show on television. The guests are not especially interesting, so you are also leafing through a magazine at the same time. One of the guests is Madonna, the rock star, and you only half listen as she makes a number of fairly extreme—but for her, not very surprising—comments about life, love, and money. Then, in a quiet voice, she says something totally unexpected: She has decided that she has earned enough money for one lifetime and is going to retire and devote most of her time to helping charities. You drop the magazine you are holding and stare in disbelief. Can you believe your ears? Did she really say such a thing?

Returning to reality from this flight of fantasy, your reactions in this situation are readily understandable. In general, we tend to pay much more attention to information that is *unexpected*—information that is somehow *inconsistent* with our expectations—than to information that is expected or consistent. Thus, a statement by Madonna that she had lost her interest in money would literally leap out at you, demanding close and careful scrutiny.

This tendency to pay greater attention to information inconsistent with our expectations than to information consistent with them is an important and basic aspect of social cognition. It is apparent in a wide range of contexts (e.g., Belmore & Hubbard, 1987; Srull & Wyer, 1989). And it has important effects, for the greater the amount of attention we pay to information, the better its chance of entering into long-term memory and the greater its potential for influencing our later social judgments (Fiske & Neuberg, 1990). Clear evidence for this strong tendency to allocate much of our attention to inconsistent and unexpected information is provided by an experiment conducted by Hilton, Klein, and von Hippel (1991).

These researchers used an ingenious technique borrowed from cognitive psychology to compare the attention-seizing capacity of consistent and inconsistent information. This technique, known as *dichotic listening*, involves presenting different information to a listener's two ears. Since individuals can't process information from both sources simultaneously, they tend to switch back and forth, paying attention first to information reaching them through one ear, and then to the other. If they can later remember more information presented to one ear than to the other, this is taken as evidence that participants devoted more attention to that source of input.

Adapting these procedures to the study of social cognition, Hilton and his colleagues (1991) asked participants to listen to the responses of two children to a test of intellectual performance. Information about each child's response was presented to one ear and information about the other child's performance was presented to the other ear. One of the children (the control) performed at a constant level, answering 60 percent of the questions correctly throughout the session. The other child (the target) showed one of two contrasting patterns: Either he started out very well (90 percent of the first ten items were correct) and then showed a sharp drop in performance (30 percent of the next ten items were correct), or the opposite (30 percent correct followed by 90 percent correct). To create expectations concerning this child's performance, participants were informed either that he came from an advantaged background and was an exceptional student or that he came from a disadvantaged background and was a very poor student.

Hilton, Klein, and von Hippel (1991) predicted that participants would pay more attention to information inconsistent with their expectations than to information consistent with them. To test this prediction, they asked participants to indicate how many questions each child answered correctly, and how many each child answered correctly on the first and last ten questions. As shown in Figure 3.7, results agreed with the hypothesis. When the target child's initial performance was good, individuals who expected him to do poorly were more accurate in reporting how many questions he answered correctly than those who expected him to do well. In contrast, when the target child's initial performance was poor, those who expected him to do well were more accurate than those who expected him to do poorly. Another prediction involved ratings of the target child's abilities. The greater the attention paid to his performance, presumably, the greater the extent to which ratings would reflect his actual performance. Since the target child's overall performance on the test was moderate (60 percent correct), the researchers predicted that participants would rate him more moderately when his initial performance was *in*consistent with their expectations than when it was consistent. This is because they would pay more attention to the child's actual performance when it was inconsistent with their expectations. This prediction, too, was confirmed.

These results, and those of many other studies, indicate that individuals do often allocate more of their attention to actions by others that don't fit with

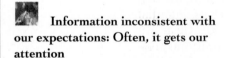 **Information inconsistent with our expectations: Often, it gets our attention**

FIGURE 3.7 Individuals who received different information in their two ears tended to pay greater attention to input that was inconsistent with their expectations than to information that was consistent with their expectations. As a result, they were more accurate in later reporting this inconsistent information.

Source: Based on data from Hilton, Klein, & von Hippel, 1991.

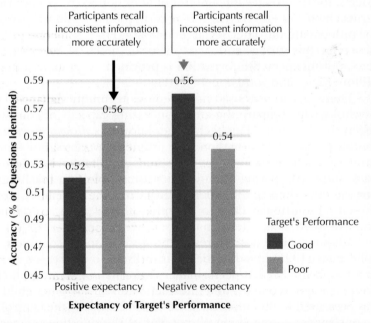

their expectations than to actions by others that do match such expectations. But please note: the fact that we pay more attention to inconsistent than consistent information doesn't necessarily imply that the latter is more influential in shaping our views or perceptions. On the contrary, although we readily *notice* information inconsistent with our expectations, we often tend to discount it or downplay it. For example, imagine that you saw a news photo of Saddam Hussein kissing a baby. This information is unexpected, so you might pay careful attention to it. But would it be likely to change your views about this dictator? Probably not. On the contrary, you'd be more likely to interpret it in a manner that would allow you to explain it away. For example, you might reason that Saddam is simply using the baby for propaganda—as a good photo opportunity. So, the fact that we often pay careful attention to inconsistent information does not mean that such information is necessarily more influential in shaping our views.

AUTOMATIC VIGILANCE: NOTICING THE NEGATIVE

Read the following information about someone named Joan:

> *Joan is a junior at State U.—a biology major with an A– grade point average. She hopes to enter medical school after graduation. She is a warm and genial person, so her friends think that she'll make a great doctor. Joan's hobby is music, and she has a large collection of CDs. She works part time to help pay for her education and to cover the insurance on her car, which is high because of several speeding tickets. Joan grew up in a medium-sized city and has one brother, Jason, who is a senior in high school. She is fairly neat and easy-going, so she never has any trouble getting roommates and is currently living with three other women at her college.*

Quick: What piece of information stands out most when you think about Joan? If you said "those speeding tickets," you are in good company, because in general, we seem to pay more attention to negative information about others than to positive information about them. In fact, it is reasonable to say that we are *exquisitely sensitive* to negative social information. If another person smiles at us twenty times during a conversation but frowns once, it is the frown that gets our attention. If one of our friends describes someone to us and mentions twenty positive things about this individual but one negative thing, *this* is the thing on which we focus and the one about which we are most likely to seek further input. So strong is this tendency to pay attention to negative information that some researchers describe it as **automatic vigilance**—a powerful tendency to pay attention to undesirable information or stimuli (e.g., Shiffrin, 1988).

In an important sense, this is eminently reasonable. After all, negative information may alert us to potential danger, and it is crucial that we recognize it—and respond to it—as quickly as possible (Pratto & John, 1991). But of course, since attentional capacity is limited, when we direct attention to negative social information we run the risk of overlooking or ignoring other valuable forms of input. As is true with all *tilts* in social perception or social cognition, therefore, it is possible for automatic vigilance to cause us difficulties.

How strong is this tendency to focus on negative social information? A growing body of evidence suggests that it is powerful indeed. For example, consider a phenomenon known as the *face-in-the-crowd effect* (Hansen & Hansen, 1988): We are especially sensitive to negative facial expressions on the part of others—so sensitive that we can pick out the angry face in a crowd very

The face-in-the-crowd effect

FIGURE 3.8 Look at these pictures for a brief time. Did any face stand out from the others? If you are like most people, you noticed the angry face. Research findings suggest that we are strongly programmed to pay attention to negative or potentially threatening information, and an angry face in a crowd of smiling ones certainly stands out in this manner. *Source:* Hansen & Hansen, 1988.

quickly (see Figure 3.8). This effect is demonstrated very clearly by research conducted by Hansen and Hansen (1988). These researchers showed participants photos of crowds (nine faces) in which all the individuals but one had the same expression. In one condition all the faces were happy except one: It was angry. In another, all the faces were angry except one: It was smiling. Finally, in a third condition, all crowd members showed a neutral expression except for one who was either smiling or frowning. How quickly could people find the face that was different? Results were clear: An angry face in a happy crowd was identified most quickly of all. A happy face in an angry crowd, in contrast, was recognized more slowly. These findings suggest that we are strongly programmed—by either our past experience, genetic factors, or both—to notice negative facial expressions on the part of others. Since others' anger poses greater potential danger than others' happiness, this finding is hardly surprising. On the contrary, it would be surprising if we were *not* especially sensitive to such input.

An ingenious study conducted by Pratto and John (1991) provides additional evidence for the automatic vigilance effect These researchers showed participants eighty trait adjectives ranging from very desirable (kind, sincere, talented) to very undesirable (sadistic, mean, hostile). The words were printed in different colors, and participants were asked to name the color in which each word appeared as quickly as possible. Their voices triggered an electronic circuit, so very precise measures of their reaction times could be obtained.

Pratto and John (1991) reasoned that the more negative the meaning of the words, the greater would be participants' attention to them, and so the slower their reaction time. (This would be the case because while paying attention to the words' meanings, the participants could not respond as quickly to the colors.)Results confirmed this prediction. In a follow-up study, the same researchers asked participants to remember as many of the words they had seen as possible. It was predicted that if participants paid more attention to the undesirable words, they would remember more of these. This was actually the case. In fact, participants remembered twice as many undesirable words (2.6) as desirable words (1.3).

So it appears that where social information is concerned, we are indeed especially sensitive to negative input. And since the information to which we pay most attention often exerts the strongest effects on our social thought and our judgments about others, basic research on this aspect of social cognition helps explain why, as we noted in chapter 2, making a favorable first impression on others can be so important.

MOTIVATED SKEPTICISM: IN REACHING CONCLUSIONS, HOW MUCH INFORMATION IS ENOUGH?

Suppose that the time for national elections is drawing near. There are two candidates for president and although you haven't made up your mind, you are leaning toward one of them. One evening you tune in a debate between the two candidates—a debate in which both persons try to clarify their positions on various issues. How much information *consistent* with your own views will it take for you to make up your mind that you will in fact vote for the candidate you already prefer? And how does this compare with the amount of information it would require to make you change your initial preference and decide to vote for the other candidate—the one you initially did not prefer? If you think about this situation for a moment, you will probably realize that since you already have a preference for the first candidate, it won't take much to move you firmly into her or his camp: A relatively small amount of information will probably do the trick. But what about the other candidate? Clearly, this person will have to say a lot of things with which you agree before you reverse your initial preference and decide to vote for her or him.

This situation illustrates another basic and important principle of social cognition: In general, we are skeptical about information that is inconsistent with our initial preferences but quite open to information that supports these views. Put another way, we examine information that supports our preferred conclusions much less carefully (and less skeptically) than information that is inconsistent with our preferred conclusions—with what we *want* to believe or decide.

Evidence for the operation of this tendency, sometimes termed **motivated skepticism,** is provided by the findings of many different studies (e.g., Ditto et al., 1988; Kruglanski, 1990). Several studies conducted by Ditto and Lopez (1992) provide an especially clear illustration of this principle in operation. In the first of these investigations, the researchers asked female college students to evaluate information about two potential partners with whom they would later work in order to choose the one who was more intelligent. Some of this information related to the likableness of the two potential partners. In one condition (the *no preference* condition), both were described as likable. In another (the *preference* condition), one person was described as being pleasant and likable, while the other (the target person) was described as unpleasant and rude. Additional information related to the performance of each of these persons on a short test related to intelligence. This information was contained on index cards and participants were told to turn these over one at a time in order to see how each of the two potential partners did on this test. They were further instructed to stop as soon as they felt they had enough information to reach a decision as to which of the two potential partners was more intelligent. Performance information indicated that one potential partner had done very well while the other had done quite poorly.

Since participants would have to work with one of these persons, it was assumed that they would start with a preference for the partner described as being very likable. Thus, when this partner performed very well on the test, information about her performance would be consistent with this preference. In contrast, when she performed poorly on the test—less well than the rude potential partner—performance information would be *inconsistent* with this initial preference. On the basis of previous research on motivated skepticism, Ditto and Lopez (1992) predicted that participants would require less information to conclude that the dislikable target person was less intelligent—a conclusion consistent with their initial preference—than to conclude that this person was *more* intelligent—a conclusion inconsistent with their initial preference. As shown in Figure 3.9, this is precisely what happened. Participants turned over fewer cards before indicating that they had enough information to reach a decision when the dislikable target performed poorly than when this person performed well. Also as expected, there was no difference in the amount of information participants required to reach a decision in the no preference condition, when both potential partners were described as being likable.

These findings indicate that we do indeed set different criteria for reaching decisions consistent or inconsistent with our initial preferences. We require relatively little supporting information to arrive at the conclusions we *want* to reach, but a great deal of disconfirming information to arrive at conclusions opposite to our initial inclinations. This does not mean, of course, that we *never* acknowledge the accuracy or usefulness of information contrary to our preferences; clearly, we do accept such input in some instances. But in general, we do seem to possess several kinds of *cognitive filters* that make it more difficult for such information to enter into our social thought and to shape our conclusions. Motivated skepticism is one of these filters. When it operates, the answer to the question "How much information is enough for reaching a decision?" is "That depends on how closely it matches our preferences."

Evidence for motivated skepticism

FIGURE 3.9 Participants required less information to reach conclusions that were consistent with their initial preferences than to reach conclusions that were inconsistent with their initial preferences. Thus, they required less information to conclude that a dislikable person was less intelligent than to conclude that this person was more intelligent than the other person.

Source: Based on data from Ditto & Lopez, 1992.

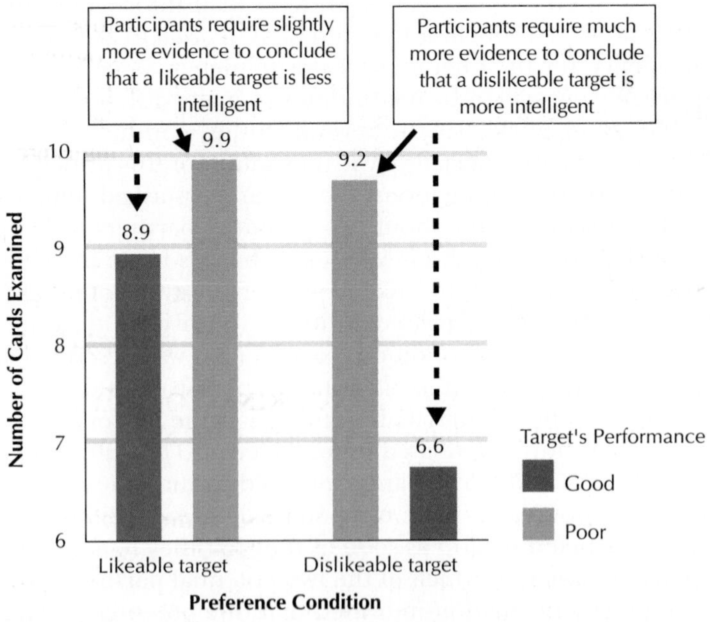

Participants require slightly more evidence to conclude that a likeable target is less intelligent

Participants require much more evidence to conclude that a dislikeable target is more intelligent

Number of Cards Examined

8.9 9.9 9.2 6.6

Target's Performance
Good
Poor

Likeable target   Dislikeable target
Preference Condition

The Upside *of Motivated Skepticism: Thinking More Deeply about Preference-Inconsistent Than Preference-Consistent Information*

Research on motivated skepticism and related topics indicates that we have a strong tendency to reject information that is inconsistent with our preferences. But there is also growing evidence for the conclusion that sometimes we tend to think more deeply or effortfully about such information than about information that serves to confirm our preferences or beliefs. True, on some occasions we simply choose to ignore or deny the unwanted information. But at other times we may focus upon it and process it very carefully.

Ditto and his colleagues are now conducting several studies to examine this hypothesis. Specifically, these researchers predict that individuals will sometimes process preference-inconsistent information more carefully than information that tends to confirm their preferences. In one study designed to test this prediction (Ditto & Skoblesk, 1993), participants are being exposed to arguments that either support or refute their initial views on various issues. Some of these arguments are strong and convincing, while others are weak and uncon-

vincing. If people process information that is inconsistent with their preferences more carefully than information that is consistent, it follows that argument strength will be most important when the arguments are *contrary* to the participants' beliefs. Under these conditions the participants will be convinced to a greater degree by the strong, high-quality arguments than by the weak, low-quality ones. This fits with the informal observation that only good arguments can convince us of something we don't want to believe.

In contrast, when the information in the arguments is consistent with participants' beliefs, argument strength or quality will be relatively unimportant: Both weak and strong arguments will prove quite convincing. After all, we often view any argument that supports our views as a good one! To the extent Ditto and Skoblesk obtain findings consistent with these predictions, evidence for the view that motivated skepticism has an *upside,* in terms of more careful processing of important information, will be provided.

Heuristics, motivated skepticism, automatic vigilance—all these aspects of social cognition can be viewed as efforts to hold our cognitive effort to a minimum, to help us do the least possible amount of cognitive work. Is this adaptive? Or would engaging in more social thought be beneficial? For some surprising evidence on this question, please see the **Cutting Edge** section below.

THE POTENTIAL COSTS OF THINKING TOO MUCH: JUSTIFICATION FOR OUR TENDENCY TO ACT LIKE COGNITIVE MISERS

When I was a teenager, my friends and I sometimes said to each other: "Don't think too much, it'll hurt your head!" While we meant this phrase to refer to the target's supposedly limited cognitive capacity, research findings suggest that there may actually be a grain of truth in this suggestion: Too much thinking *can*, sometimes, be a negative thing. How can this be so? Isn't it important to think—and think carefully—about the problems and decisions we confront in daily life? In many cases, it certainly is. But in some instances, it seems, thinking too deeply about such questions as why we feel or react the way we do can be confusing and even counterproductive.

Tantalizing hints to the effect that thinking too much—introspecting too carefully or completely—can reduce the quality of our judgments or decisions are provided by the results of many different studies. For example, when individuals try to verbalize their memories for nonverbal stimuli such as faces (for example, by describing them), their ability to recognize these stimuli actually decreases relative to persons who don't engage in such efforts (Schooler & Engstler-Schooler, 1990). Similarly, when individuals try to identify the causes of their attitudes, they often find this task confusing; further, consistency between their attitudes and their behavior may be reduced by such activities (e.g., Wilson, 1990).

Perhaps the most surprising evidence for the potential downside of thinking too much, however, is that provided by Wilson and Schooler (1991) in a series of related studies. In one of these experiments, college students were asked to sample and rate several strawberry jams. Half were simply asked to taste the jams and rate them; the others were asked to analyze their reactions—to indicate why they felt the way they did about each jam. Wilson & Schooler (1991) reasoned that when individuals engage in such introspection, the reasons they bring to mind may simply be the ones that are most accessible and salient—the easiest to remember or put into words. However, these may *not* be the most important factors in their judgments. As a result, they may be misled by the reasons they report, and may make less accurate or valid judgments.

To determine if this is actually the case, Wilson and Schooler (1991) compared the judgments made by the two groups of participants (those who analyzed the reasons for their ratings of the jams and those who did not) with ratings by experts—people who make their living comparing various products. Results were clear: Participants who simply rated the jams agreed much more closely with the reactions of the experts than participants who tried to report their reasons for their reactions to the various jams.

In a follow-up study, college students were asked to read course descriptions and student evaluations of these courses, and then to indicate the likelihood that they would take these courses themselves. Some students (the control group) merely rated the courses while others were asked either (1) to analyze the reasons they might want or not want to take each course (the *reasons* condition), or (2) to stop and think about each piece of information on each course as they read it and to rate the extent to which it made them more or less likely to take the course (the *rate all information* condition). Information on actual course enrollments indicated that students in the two "think" conditions were less likely to preregister for and then to actually take the highly rated courses than those in the control condition (see Figure 3.10). Thus, in this case, thinking too much seemed to interfere with a real and important decision.

Why did this occur? Wilson and Schooler (1991) suggest that it may have stemmed from the fact that students in the *reasons* and *rate all information* conditions evaluated the courses on many different dimensions. And considering many different dimensions, past research suggests, causes individuals to moderate their evaluations. Thus, for these students, the highly rated and poorly rated courses may have seemed more similar to each other than was true for

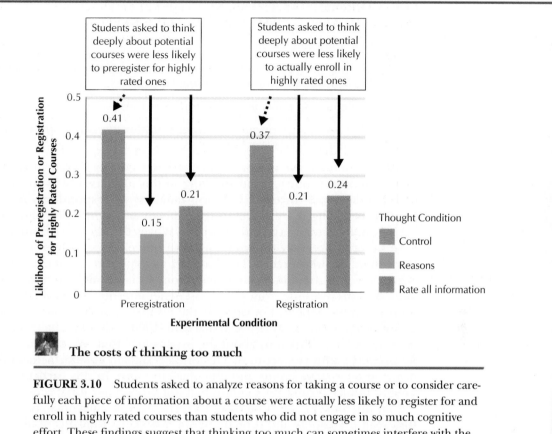

The costs of thinking too much

FIGURE 3.10 Students asked to analyze reasons for taking a course or to consider carefully each piece of information about a course were actually less likely to register for and enroll in highly rated courses than students who did not engage in so much cognitive effort. These findings suggest that thinking too much can sometimes interfere with the accuracy of our judgments.

Source: Based on data from Wilson & Schooler, 1991.

those in the control condition, who were not asked to think so deeply during this task.

In short, it appears that on some occasions, too much thinking can get us into serious cognitive trouble. While this idea may seem strange at first blush, it is not very far from the kind of experience most persons have had while learning to perform a wide range of skilled actions—everything from swinging a golf club to playing a musical instrument. During such activities, thinking too much about what one is doing can be greatly disruptive. Wilson and Schooler's (1991) findings explore effects in the sphere of conscious decisions and judgments, but similar principles may be operating, at least to an extent, in both cases. Taking the available evidence into account, then, the best advice we might offer concerning thinking may be this: "By all means, *think*–it is usually good for your cognitive health. But try to remember that even where such a beneficial activity as thought is concerned, there can sometimes be too much of a good thing."

COUNTERFACTUAL THINKING: THE EFFECTS OF CONSIDERING "WHAT MIGHT HAVE BEEN"

Imagine the following events:

Ms. Caution never picks up hitchhikers. Yesterday, however, she gave a stranger a ride. He repaid her kindness by robbing her.

Now, in contrast, consider the following events:

Ms. Risk frequently picks up hitchhikers. Yesterday, she gave a stranger a ride. He repaid her kindness by robbing her.

Which of these two persons will experience greater regret? If you answered "Ms. Caution, of course," your thinking in this instance is very much like that of other persons. An overwhelming majority of respondents identify Ms. Caution as feeling more regretful (Kahneman & Miller, 1986). Yet, take a step back from the situation and think again: Why is this the case? Both individuals have suffered precisely the same negative outcome: They have been robbed. Why, then, do we perceive Ms. Caution as experiencing more regret? The answer involves some intriguing facts about social thought and the judgments and reactions resulting from it. In most general terms, it appears that our reactions to events depend not only on the events themselves but on what these events bring to mind (Miller & McFarland, 1990). When we have some experience, we do not think only about the experience itself. We also engage in *mental simulation* with respect to it. This often results in **counterfactual thinking**—bringing alternative events and outcomes to mind. In this particular instance, we may think, "If only Ms. Caution had not broken her usual rule against picking up hitchhikers, she'd be okay." Alternatively, we may imagine that "If Ms. Risk read the papers and thought about how dangerous it is to pick up hitchhikers, she might act differently." (By the way, I engaged in precisely this kind of counterfactual thinking after my automobile accident. I kept thinking, "If only we had gone to the other restaurant where we usually eat, the accident would never have happened!")

But why, precisely, does such counterfactual thinking lead us to believe that Ms. Caution will experience more regret? In part, because it is easier to imagine alternatives to unusual behavior, such as Ms. Caution's picking up the hitchhiker, than it is to imagine alternatives to usual, normal behavior (e.g., Ms. Risk's picking up the hitchhiker). So, we conclude that Ms. Caution experienced more regret because it is easier to imagine her acting in a different way—sticking to her rule—than it is to imagine Ms. Risk acting differently. After all, Ms. Risk always picks up hitchhikers; it was just her bad luck that it finally caught up with her. (Another way to put this is to note that, in a sense, she has been asking for trouble all along—and finally found it.)

Critical Thinking
Question 3

Transparency 3.2

This reasoning leads to the interesting prediction that negative outcomes that follow unusual behavior (behavior that elicits mental simulations that are primarily *dissimilar* to it) will generate more sympathy than ones that follow usual behavior (behavior that elicits mental simulations that are primarily *similar* to it). Precisely such effects have been demonstrated in many recent studies (Kahneman & Tversky, 1982). For example, in one such investigation, Miller and McFarland (1986) asked subjects to read a description of a victim of a crime to determine how much money he should receive as compensation for his injuries. All subjects read about a male victim who lost the use of his right arm as the result of a gunshot wound that occurred when he walked in on a robbery in a neighborhood convenience store. One group of subjects (the *nor-*

mal behavior condition) learned that on the night he was shot, the victim had gone to a store he visited frequently. Another group (the *abnormal behavior* condition) learned that he had gone, for a change of pace, to a store he rarely visited. (Please note: In this context "abnormal" merely means unusual.) After reading the descriptions, all subjects indicated how much (from no money to $1 million) the victim should receive in compensation. As predicted, subjects assigned greater compensation to the victim when his wound occurred at a store he rarely visited than when it occurred at a store he visited frequently. In other words, when subjects could readily imagine alternative events (e.g., the man did not visit this store and was not wounded), they felt more sympathy for him and awarded him larger compensation.

More recent evidence indicates that the effects of counterfactual thinking extend to evaluations of the persons responsible for negative outcomes as well as to the victims of such unfortunate events. In research on this possibility, Macrae (1992) had two groups of college students read different versions of an incident in which a young woman got food poisoning after eating in a restaurant. In one condition the restaurant was one she regularly visited. In the other it was described as her first visit to this particular restaurant—in other words, her behavior in going there was unusual. Participants were then asked to indicate how much compensation the victim should receive and how large a fine the restaurant should pay for its negligence. As shown in Figure 3.11, both the recommended compensation and the fines were larger in the unusual behavior condition than in the usual behavior condition. Similar results were obtained in a follow-up study describing an incident in which a young woman was injured by scaffolding that fell from a building while she was walking to work. Again participants recommended that she receive greater compensation and that the construction firm should pay a larger fine when her route past the building was an unusual one than when it was usual.

Reading (9): Lesko, *For Whom Is This World Just? Sexual Orientation and AIDS*

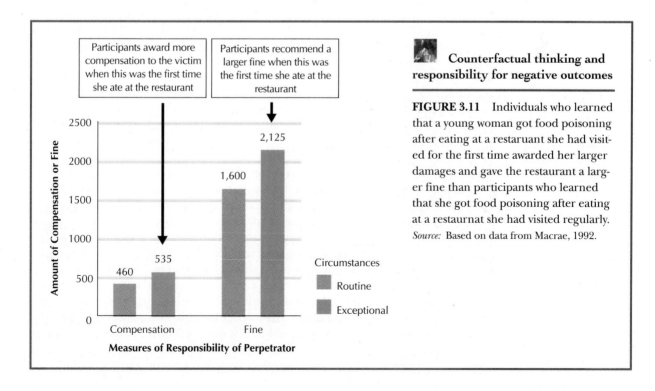

Counterfactual thinking and responsibility for negative outcomes

FIGURE 3.11 Individuals who learned that a young woman got food poisoning after eating at a restaruant she had visited for the first time awarded her larger damages and gave the restaurant a larger fine than participants who learned that she got food poisoning after eating at a restaurnat she had visited regularly. *Source:* Based on data from Macrae, 1992.

As you can see, counterfactual thinking is closely related to the availability heuristic. The ease with which individuals can imagine alternative events ("What might have been") depends, to some extent, on how available alternative outcomes are. The more readily such alternatives can be brought to mind, the stronger our reactions to the present situation.

In addition, other research findings suggest that counterfactual thinking is also closely related to judgments of causality (e.g., Wells & Gavanski, 1989). (Recall our discussion of *attribution* in chapter 2.) In particular, it appears that an event will be perceived as causing an outcome to the extent that individuals can readily imagine changes in that event that would undo the outcome. For example, returning to the holdup story above, imagine that on the night in question, only one store had a holdup, the store the man chose to visit. How important was his decision as to which store to visit? Most of us would say "Very important." This is because if he had visited the other store, he would not have been shot, so we can readily imagine changes that would lead to other outcomes. But now imagine that on the night in question both stores had holdups. Now how important was his choice of store as a cause of his being shot? Most people tend to rate the choice as less important, since he might well have been shot no matter where he went on that violent and dangerous evening, and it is harder to imagine events that would undo the harm he experienced.

Whatever the precise mechanisms involved, it is clear that our reasoning about the causes of various events, and our judgments or decisions about these events, can be strongly influenced by counterfactual thinking—by our thoughts about "what might have been."

WHAT'S MINE IS GOOD: THE MERE OWNERSHIP EFFECT

A well-known saying contends that "We are what we eat." A variation of this expression, however, might well state: "We are what we *own.*" In other words, for most of us, part of our personal identity is reflected in our possessions. We buy various products not just because we like or need them, but because owning them makes some statement about us, and generally a positive one: We are bold, intelligent, sensitive, discerning, and so on, because we own and use some product. Advertisers, of course, actively seek to encourage this association between specific items and a positive social image (see Figure 3.12).

If our self-image, and possibly certain aspects of our self-esteem, are linked to our possessions, then an intriguing possibility follows logically: In general, we should tend to evaluate objects we own more favorably than other, equivalent objects that we don't own. This is so because, in a sense, we think of objects we own as extensions of our selves (Fridlund, in press).

Research conducted recently by Beggan (1992) offers clear support for this reasoning. In an initial study on the **mere ownership effect**—the tendency to evaluate objects we own more favorably than objects we don't own—Beggan (1992) asked female college students to evaluate a number of different inexpensive objects—a key ring, plastic combs, an address book, peanut brittle, and so on. One of the objects in this assortment was a drink insulator, a plastic tube designed to hold beverage cans and keep them cold, and in one experimental group (the *ownership* condition), participants were told by the researcher that they would receive this object as a gift; thus, they learned that they owned it before evaluating it and the other objects. In a *control* condition, in contrast, they were not given this object as a gift. Finally, in a *mood control* condition included to determine whether merely receiving a gift would elevate

If you could drive
one car to your high school reunion,
this would be it.

As you swing into your alma mater in a beautiful new Jaguar XJS convertible, you can almost see the heads turn as your classmates ask, "Isn't that...?"

A fantasy? It doesn't have to be. This year's XJS is priced almost $10,000 less than last year's. And it's absolutely the best XJS we've ever built, with the exhilarating performance of a newly available 219-horsepower AJ6 engine, newly available four-speed automatic transmission, and optional five-speed manual transmission. That's on top of features like Connolly leather, walnut fascia and trim, a driver side air bag, ABS brakes, and a remote entry system.

This year's XJS also reflects the hundreds of meaningful improvements in quality Jaguar has made over the past two and a half years. Today, our commitment to quality can be compared to that of any other luxury marque on the road, which is why we confidently offer a four-year, 50,000-mile Royal Charter Care warranty.

Call 1-800-4-JAGUAR for the name of your nearest Jaguar dealer. Even if a reunion is not soon on the horizon, there are many other fantasies this car is waiting to fulfill.

JAGUAR

Enhancing one's image through possessions

FIGURE 3.12   Many ads suggest that individuals can enhance their image by owning certain items.

ratings of all the objects, participants were given an item that was not included in the group of items they later rated—a plastic key-holder. Participants then rated each object in terms of its attractiveness, value, and quality of design. Results strongly indicated the occurrence of a mere ownership effect: Participants who received the drink insulator as a gift rated it significantly higher than those in the other two conditions, who did not own this object.

These findings indicated that owning an object does indeed enhance evaluations of it. But do such effects actually stem from the fact that people seek to enhance their social image through positive assessments of their possessions? To find out, Beggan (1992) conducted another study in which participants' desire to engage in such self-enhancement was either strengthened or weakened before they were given an object as a gift. Beggan reasoned that if the mere ownership effect stems from the motive for self-enhancement, conditions that enhance individuals' self-image will weaken this effect while conditions that reduce their self-image will increase the effect. To test the accuracy of this reasoning, participants first worked on a complex task and received feedback suggesting either that they had done very well (the *success* condition) or that they had done quite poorly (the *failure* condition). After receiving one of these two forms of feedback, they either received or did not receive the drink insulator as a gift.

It was predicted that when their self-image had been threatened by a failure experience, participants would show a strong mere ownership effect: They would evaluate the gift object more favorably when they owned it than when they did not. In contrast, when their self-image had been enhanced, their motivation to engage in self-enhancement would be reduced, and the mere ownership effect would be weaker. This is precisely what happened. In fact, in the success condition the mere ownership effect vanished completely and participants actually rated the item *less* favorably when they owned it than when they did not.

So it appears that our possessions *are* often linked to our self-image, and that as a result of such links, our evaluations of possessions may be enhanced. In such cases physical objects take on a special social significance and become, in an important sense, grist for the mill of our social thought.

Do people differ in the extent to which they engage in social cognition? And if so, what are the effects of such differences? For information on these questions, please see the **Individual Diversity** section below.

Individual Diversity

Need for Cognition and the Nature of Social Thought

Everyone thinks about other people; given their importance in our lives, it could hardly be otherwise. But as you probably know from your own experience, some people engage in a lot more of this activity than others. Some spend a great deal of time thinking about why other people do what they do and, what emotions they are feeling, and trying to predict how they will act in the future. In contrast, others show relatively little interest in these matters. Similarly, some people invest a lot of cognitive effort in trying to understand *themselves*, while for others such introspection is a rare event. Do individual differences in the tendency to engage in social thought have any effects upon the nature of social cognition itself? Lassiter and his colleagues suggest that they may (e.g., Lassiter, Briggs, & Bowman, 1991; Lassiter, Briggs, & Slaw, 1991). Specifically, these researchers contend that individual differences in what is often termed the **need for cognition**—the desire to think about and increase one's understanding of various events—have important implications for several aspects of social cognition.

Take, for example, the tendency to try to explain unexpected or inconsistent events. Presumably, persons high in the need for cognition would be more likely to engage in causal social thought about such events than persons low in the need for cognition. In other words, they would be more likely to think about possible explanations for unexpected events. As a result, of course, they would then be more likely to remember the events than persons low in the need for cognition (e.g., Srull, Lichtenstein, & Rothbart, 1985).

Direct evidence for such differences has been obtained in research conducted by Lassiter, Briggs, and Slaw (1991). These researchers asked college students to read descriptions of an imaginary person named Lou. The descriptions, which consisted of lists of traits, portrayed Lou either as a friendly person (gregarious, sincere, warm, outgoing) or as a hostile individual (unsociable, cold, phony, alienated). After reading these descriptions, participants received information about Lou's behavior in the form of sixteen sentences describing his actions. Twelve of these behaviors were consistent with the initial impression created by the adjectives, while four were inconsistent. An example of information inconsistent with the friendliness impression was "Lou criticized citizens of other countries." An example of a sentence inconsistent with the hostility impression was "Lou invited the charity collector to stay for dinner."

After examining this information, participants rated Lou on several dimensions. Then they were asked to write down any and all thoughts they had about Lou while reading the sentences about his behavior. These thoughts were then coded by an assistant as *explanatory*—they expressed an attempt to explain some aspect of Lou's behavior (e.g., "Maybe he was in a bad mood") —or as *nonexplanatory*—they did not seek to explain his behavior. Participants in the study had previously completed a measure of the need for cognition, so it was now possible to compare the thoughts listed by persons high in this need and by those low in this need. The major prediction, of course, was that persons high in need for cognition would report having more explanatory thoughts than those low in need for cognition. As shown in Figure 3.13, this is what happened. Further, there was no difference in the number of nonexplanatory thoughts reported by persons high and low in need for cognition. Thus, the key difference between them seemed to involve contrasting tendencies to seek to explain the inconsistencies in Lou's behavior.

Additional findings from a follow-up study indicated that persons high in need for cognition also remembered more inconsistent information concerning Lou's behavior than persons low in need for cognition. Further, it was their greater tendency to engage in causal thinking about Lou that accounted for this difference.

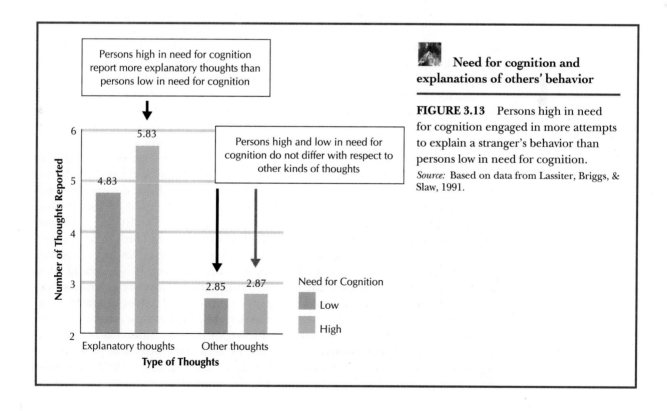

Need for cognition and explanations of others' behavior

FIGURE 3.13 Persons high in need for cognition engaged in more attempts to explain a stranger's behavior than persons low in need for cognition.

Source: Based on data from Lassiter, Briggs, & Slaw, 1991.

In sum, it appears that the need for cognition—individual differences in the tendency to think about and to seek to understand events—is an important dimension where social cognition is concerned (Lassiter, Briggs, & Bowman, 1991). All things being equal, the greater the effort people are willing to invest in social thought, the broader the knowledge base for their social judgments. Does this imply that persons high in need for cognition are also generally more accurate in their thinking and their judgments? Direct evidence on this issue is not yet available. However, given the fact that many errors in social judgments stem, at least in part, from our strong tendency to take the path of least resistance, it seems reasonable to predict that in this task, as in many others, extra effort often pays off.

AFFECT AND COGNITION: HOW THOUGHT SHAPES FEELINGS AND FEELINGS SHAPE THOUGHT

Imagine the following situation: You are sitting in your room studying when your thoughts turn to something that happened earlier in the week. You have a lab partner in one of your courses, and the two of you are working together on an important project. You made an appointment to meet at the library to go over your plans for the project, but your partner wasn't there at the agreed-upon time. You waited for him with mounting impatience for almost thirty minutes. Just when you were about to give up, he finally showed up. When you expressed your annoyance at his being so late, he muttered a weak excuse about losing track of the time. When you stated that that was no reason to be so late, he actually got mad at *you* and threatened to leave. Since the project is very important, you bit your tongue and went on with the meeting. But now, as you think about this incident, you feel yourself getting angry all over again. Just who the heck does he think he is, anyway? What colossal nerve!

Video: Cognitive Processes*

Situations such as this one suggest that cognitive processes—our current thoughts as well as memories we bring to mind (and perhaps ones of which we are not directly conscious)—frequently exert strong effects upon our emotional states (Isen, 1987; Schwarz, 1990). Indeed, such internally generated factors seem to trigger emotional reactions that are fully as intense as those produced by external causes (e.g., events we experience, the words or deeds of others). Social psychologists are well aware of such effects and have devoted careful attention to them. More frequently, however, they have focused on the reverse: The impact of emotions on various aspects of social thought (e.g., Forgas, 1991b). Since much of this work has dealt with the effects of mild, temporary shifts in feelings rather than with those of intense and long-lasting emotions, the term *affect* seems more suitable than the term emotion in describing such work (Isen, 1987). Thus, we'll use this term throughout most of this discussion.

Research on the influence of affect on cognition has yielded many intriguing results (e.g., Isen & Baron, 1991; Schwarz, 1991). It is now clear that even very mild shifts in individuals' current feelings can alter aspects of cognition. Before turning to such evidence, however, we'll first consider several contrasting views concerning the nature of emotion (e.g., Ekman, 1992) and one intriguing explanation for how even mild shifts in affect can influence social cognition.

THE NATURE OF EMOTION: CONTRASTING VIEWS AND SOME RECENT ADVANCES

Feelings are a central part of everyday life, so over the centuries, many different views about the nature of emotions have been offered. Within psychology, however, three approaches have received most attention. The first, often known as the **Cannon-Bard theory**, is the commonsense perspective. It suggests that when we are exposed to emotion-provoking (emotion-eliciting) events or stimuli, we quickly experience *both* the physiological signs of emotion and the subjective experiences we label as fear, anger, joy, and so on. In other words, both types of reaction occur concurrently and stem from the same eliciting events. For example, imagine that one day, you switched on the radio and learned that you had just won the lottery. Your pulse and blood pressure would leap to high levels, and you would quickly be swept by waves of surprise and intense elation.

In contrast, the **James-Lange theory** proposes that our subjective emotional experiences are actually the *result* of our relatively automatic physiological reactions to various events. According to this view, we experience anger, fear, joy, or sorrow *because* we become aware of a racing heart, tears streaming down our face, and so on. Returning to the lottery example, the James-Lange theory suggests that you would experience elation *because* you quickly feel (and become aware of) all the physiological signs of this emotion. As James himself noted in another example, if you see a bear while in the woods, you begin to run. Then you experience fear because of the feelings of intense arousal produced by this activity.

A third view—Schachter's **two-factor theory**—suggests that any form of arousal, whatever its source, initiates a search for the causes of these feelings. The causes we then identify play a key role in determining the label we place on our arousal, and so in the emotion we experience. Thus, if we feel aroused in the presence of an attractive person, we may label our arousal as "love" or "attraction." If we feel aroused after a near miss in traffic, we label it as "fear" or perhaps "anger" (toward the other driver, who was clearly at fault!). In short, we perceive ourselves to be experiencing the emotion that external cues suggest we *should* be feeling (see Figure 3.14). This is an intriguing view, and one that is supported by the findings of many studies (e.g., Reisenzein, 1983).

Reading (8): Lesko, Cognitive, Social, and Physiological Determinants of Emotional State

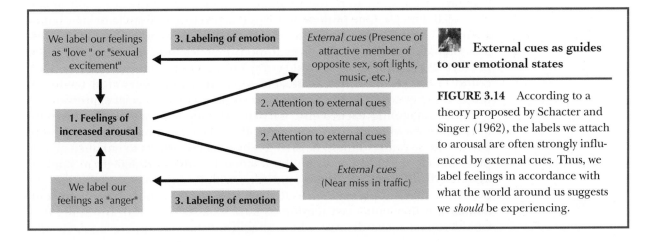

External cues as guides to our emotional states

FIGURE 3.14 According to a theory proposed by Schacter and Singer (1962), the labels we attach to arousal are often strongly influenced by external cues. Thus, we label feelings in accordance with what the world around us suggests we *should* be experiencing.

We should note, however, that the process described by Schachter and Singer seems to occur in cases where our level of arousal is relatively low. Intense feelings of arousal seem to be aversive (negative) in and of themselves, and are interpreted as such regardless of the situation (e.g., Marshall & Zimbardo, 1979).

Which of these views is most accurate? As we'll note in chapter 5, the results of many studies offer support for the view proposed by Schachter and Singer, so it is clear that cognitive and situational factors do play a role in our subjective emotional reactions (e.g., Olson & Ross, 1988). Over the years, however, even more attention has been directed to the task of determining whether the Cannon-Bard or the James-Lange view is more accurate. Until recently, the weight of existing evidence seemed to favor the commonsense Cannon-Bard approach: Emotion-provoking events produce both physiological arousal and the subjective experiences we label as emotions. More recently, however, the pendulum has swung in the opposite direction, with an increasing amount of evidence providing support for some form of the James-Lange theory. For example, research conducted with highly sophisticated equipment indicates that different emotions are indeed associated with different patterns of physiological activity. Not only do anger and sorrow *feel* different, they are reflected in somewhat different patterns of brain activity and in contrasting patterns of activity in various facial muscles (e.g., Ekman, Davidson, & Friesen, 1990; Izard, 1992). Perhaps the most dramatic evidence for the suggestion that we experience various emotions because of bodily changes is provided by studies that have tested the "facial feedback hypothesis" (e.g., Matsumoto, 1987).

Critical Thinking
Question 4

THE FACIAL FEEDBACK HYPOTHESIS: DO WE FEEL WHAT WE SHOW?

The **facial feedback hypothesis** suggests that changes in our facial expressions sometimes *produce* changes in our emotional experiences rather than merely reflect them. In other words, if we smile, we feel happy; if we frown, we feel sad, and so on. Two versions of this hypothesis exist. The *strong* version suggests that facial expressions are sufficient to induce emotional reactions. In contrast, the *weak* version suggests that facial expressions merely intensify (or reduce) such reactions. While there are many complexities in testing this hypothesis, the results of several studies offer support for its accuracy.

In one such study, McCanne and Anderson (1987) asked female participants to imagine positive and negative events (e.g., "You inherit a million dollars"; "You lose a really close friendship"). While imagining these events, participants in the study were told to either enhance or suppress tension in certain facial muscles. One of these muscles is active when we smile or view happy scenes. The other is active when we frown or view unhappy scenes. Measurements of electrical activity in both muscles indicated that after a few practice trials, most subjects could carry out this task quite successfully. They could enhance or suppress muscle tension when instructed to do so. Moreover, they could do this without any visible change in facial expressions.

After imagining each scene, participants rated their emotional experiences in terms of enjoyment or distress. If the facial feedback hypothesis were correct, these ratings should be affected by subjects' efforts to enhance or suppress muscle tension. For example, if subjects enhanced activity in muscles associated with smiling, they would report more enjoyment of the positive events. If they suppressed such activity, they would report less enjoyment. Similarly, if they enhanced tension in muscles associated with frowning, they would report more distress when imagining the unhappy events. Results

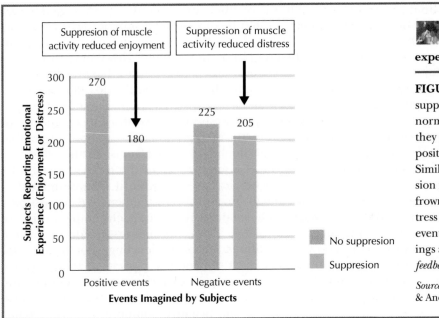

FIGURE 3.15 When participants suppressed tension in muscles normally active during smiling, they reported less enjoyment of positive events they imagined. Similarly, if they suppressed tension in muscles active during frowning, they reported less distress in response to negative events they imagined. These findings are consistent with the *facial feedback hypothesis.*

Source: Based on data from McCanne & Anderson, 1987.

offered partial support for these predictions. As shown in Figure 3.15, participants did report less enjoyment of the positive events when they suppressed activity in the appropriate muscle. In addition, they showed a slight tendency to report less distress to the negative events when they suppressed the muscle involved in frowning. Interestingly, subjects also reported less ability to imagine and experience scenes of both types when suppressing activity in their facial muscles.

These findings suggest that there may be a substantial grain of truth in the James-Lange theory and modern views related to it (e.g., Zajonc, Murphy, & Inglehart, 1989). Subjective emotional experiences do often arise directly in reaction to specific external stimuli, as the Cannon-Bard view suggests. However, they can also be generated by changes in (and awareness of) our own bodily states—even, it appears, by changes in our current facial expressions (Strack, Martin, & Stepper, 1988).

While research on the facial feedback hypothesis offers support for this contention, it does not, by itself, explain *how* such effects may occur. In other words, such research does not indicate the mechanism through which changes in facial expressions may influence affective states. Fortunately, this perplexing issue has recently been addressed by Zajonc and his colleagues in the **vascular theory of emotion** (Zajonc, Murphy, & Inglehart, 1989).

THE VASCULAR THEORY OF EMOTION: HOW FACIAL EXPRESSIONS INFLUENCE AFFECT.   Consider the following phrases: *hot-headed, boiling mad, hot under the collar.* All refer to anger, and all describe it in terms relating to temperature: When we are angry, we feel hot. As we'll note in later chapters, this relationship may operate in the other direction, too: When people are exposed to uncomfortably high temperatures, they often *become* more irritable and aggressive (e.g., Anderson, 1989). This suggestion of a link between unpleasant warmth and negative emotions raises an intriguing question: Are positive and negative feelings (affect) somehow related to changes in the temperature of the brain? Such a possibility has recently been suggested by Zajonc, Murphy, and Inglehart (1989) in a modern version of the **vascular theory of emotional efference**. (We say "modern" because an early version of this theory was proposed by Waynbaum [1907] more than eighty years ago.)

Zajonc and his colleagues suggest that changes in facial expressions influence the vascular system of the head—the arteries and veins that serve the brain. Specifically, they propose that facial expressions can enhance or restrict cooling of the venous blood supply of the brain in two ways: mechanically, by pressing on these veins; and indirectly, by regulating the amount of air that enters the nasal cavities and so cools the blood in such veins. Further, they suggest that such changes can produce slight changes in the temperature of the brain and, in this manner, neurochemical events within it that are related to positive and negative feelings. Small drops in brain temperature are assumed to generate positive feelings, while small increases in such temperatures are assumed to generate negative feelings. These predictions are derived from, and consistent with, several observations. For example, congestion of the nasal passages during common colds restricts the cooling capacity of the nasal passages. And at such times, most people report experiencing considerable discomfort. Similarly, when individuals' noses are packed with gauze during medical procedures, they often report strong negative emotions, including panic (Vig, 1985). Such evidence, however, is indirect and far from convincing. Much more conclusive support for the vascular theory has been reported by Zajonc and his colleagues (1989) in a series of carefully conducted studies. In one of these investigations, students were asked to repeat seven different vowel sounds (e.g., *i, e, o, a, ah*) over and over again. While they repeated them, readings of the temperature at two separate points on their foreheads (previously found to be related to internal brain temperature) were recorded. After repeating the vowels, subjects were asked to rate their liking for them and to indicate whether saying these vowels put them in a good or bad mood. Results were striking. A vowel sound known to restrict the entry of air into the nasal passages (*u*, a sound common in German but not in English) raised forehead temperature and also received the most negative ratings. In contrast, two vowels known to expand nasal air access (*ee* and/or *ah*) lowered forehead temperature and received the most positive evaluations.

In an even more provocative study, Zajonc et al. (1989) asked subjects to breathe air that was either at approximately room temperature (22.2° C, approximately 72° F); relatively warm (32.2° C, approximately 90° F); or relatively cool (18.9° C, approximately 66° F). Subjects were told that the air they breathed contained mild scents, and that their task was to rate these scents. In fact, only the room-temperature air contained any scent. (A mild odor of the spice oregano was introduced in this condition.) Subjects' forehead temperatures were measured as they sniffed the air, and after doing so, they rated the supposed scents on several dimensions (liking, familiarity, pleasantness). Results again offered support for the vascular theory. As expected, the warm air raised forehead temperature, and the cool air reduced it. More important, subjects reported liking the cool scentless air more than the warm scentless air. The air containing a mild aroma of oregano was rated in between.

These findings and other results reported by Zajonc, Murphy, and Inglehart (1989) offer support for the vascular theory of emotional efference. This theory, in turn, suggests a mechanism through which facial expressions may influence affective states. Apparently, several expressions can change the temperature of the blood supply serving the brain, and so the temperature of the brain itself. These shifts, in turn, seem to influence neurochemical events that play a role in the occurrence of positive and negative feelings. We should hasten to add that many details remain to be determined, and that the data reported by Zajonc and his colleagues, valuable as it is, should certainly not be viewed as definitive. On the contrary, additional evidence is clearly needed before this theory can be accepted as verified. Further, there is no suggestion in the vascular theory that changes in brain temperature are the only, or even the most important, source of positive and negative affect.

Such reservations aside, the vascular theory does offer some intriguing benefits. For example, it helps explain why, as noted in chapter 2, facial expressions are so universal in form and in meaning around the globe. If such expressions are linked to affective states through shifts in brain temperature and associated neurochemical events, then it would be surprising if they were *not* universal.

In sum, the vascular theory suggests that important, if subtle, links exist between face and brain. Certainly our facial expressions often reflect our current emotions and affective states. However, the relationship may operate in the other direction as well so that what we feel really *is* influenced by the expressions we show to the outside world.

HOW AFFECT INFLUENCES COGNITION

Does being in a positive or negative mood influence the way we think? Informal observation suggests that this is indeed the case. As one old song puts it, when we are happy, "We see the world through rose-colored glasses"—everything takes on a positive tinge. And most people are aware of the fact that they think differently when feeling happy than when they are depressed. For example, when we are experiencing positive feelings (affect), difficult tasks or situations seem easier to perform or deal with than when we are experiencing negative feelings. Are these subjective impressions correct? Growing evidence suggests that they are—that our current affective states do indeed have important effects on how we process social information.

Critical Thjinking
Question 5

First, it has been found that affective states influence the perception of ambiguous stimuli. In general, a person perceives (and evaluates) these more favorably when he or she is experiencing positive affect than when experiencing negative affect (see Figure 3.16, p. 116; Fiske & Neuberg, 1990; Isen & Shalker, 1982). For example, when asked to interview applicants whose qualifications for a job are ambiguous, research subjects assign higher ratings to these persons when they are in a positive mood (e.g., they have just received favorable feedback or won a small prize) than when they are in a negative mood (e.g., they have just received negative feedback; Baron, 1987). Interestingly, such effects are strongest when the qualifications of the applicants are truly ambiguous: They are neither highly qualified nor clearly unqualified for the job. When qualifications are very good or very bad, the effects of mood on this kind of decision are greatly reduced (Baron, 1993).

Second, positive and negative affect exert a strong influence upon memory (Isen, 1987). In general, information consistent with our current mood is easier to remember than information that is inconsistent with it. Moreover, mood seems to exert such effects both at the time of *encoding* (when information is first entered into memory) and at the time of *retrieval* (when such information is recalled; e.g., Forgas, 1991; Forgas & Bower, 1988). Positive and negative affect have also been found to influence the way in which information is

Moods and social judgment

"We're shorthanded this week, Sneedby.
We've got three agents out with a good mood!"

FIGURE 3.16 Being in a good mood may lead to behavior and judgments inconsistent with the duties of a tax-collector!
Source: North America Syndicate. Inc. 1990.

organized in memory. Persons experiencing positive affect seem to include a wider range of information within various memory categories than persons in a neutral or negative mood (Isen & Daubman, 1984). Those experiencing positive affect provide more unusual associates to neutral words and rate objects that are not very typical of a given category as more representative of it than persons who are not in a positive mood. (For example, they rate the word *elevator* as more representative of the category *vehicle* than persons in a negative mood; Baron, Rea, & Daniels, 1992; Isen et al., 1985).

Finally, there is some indication that persons in a good mood are more creative. At least, they are more successful in performing tasks involving creative problem solving (searching for novel approaches, exploring new uses for familiar objects) than persons in a neutral mood (Isen, Daubman, & Nowicki, 1987).

So, a large body of evidence indicates that affective states do indeed influence many aspects of social cognition. The question then arises: How do positive and negative moods exert such effects? Research on this important issue has begun only recently. However, one intriguing framework for understanding the impact of moods on cognition has been proposed by Forgas (1991a). According to Forgas, an individual can use any one of several different strategies to process social information. One of these is a *direct access strategy,* when preexisting judgments are simply retrieved from memory and applied to the present situation. For example, if I already have a very positive view of persons from England, when I meet one I can apply this judgment directly and can conclude with little effort that I will probably like this individual too. We have already considered another processing strategy—one based on the use of *heuristics.* Here, we adopt mental rules of thumb to minimize the amount of effort required in making the judgment. The most important strategy from the point of view of understanding the role of affect in cognition, however, is what Forgas describes as a **motivated processing strategy**. Here, our preexisting goals lead to a selective search for and use of information. In other words, we seek certain types of information because we wish to reach certain conclusions.

What is the relationship of our affective states to such motivated processing? Forgas suggests that when we are in a positive mood, we are motivated to maintain these feelings. Thus, we may avoid any form of hard cognitive work, since this might interfere with our positive affect. In contrast, when we are in a negative mood, motivated processing designed to help eliminate these feelings may occur. In such cases, we will engage in a selective search for information designed to enhance our feelings and may recall such information more accurately. At the same time, however, we may also adopt other strategies, such as making global judgments of others that are consistent with our desire to eliminate negative feelings.

Forgas (1991b) has recently tested these predictions in an integrated series of studies. In these experiments, participants were first put in a good or bad mood by watching films: either scenes from a highly successful comedy series or a film that showed a mother dying of cancer. (Those in a neutral control condition saw no mood-influencing film.) Then participants were given the task of choosing the most suitable future partner either for themselves or for another person from a group of eight potential candidates. To select the best candidate, participants examined index cards containing information about these persons. Some of the information related to task competence (e.g., intelligence, performance on previous projects), while other information related to personal characteristics and likability. Participants were told that they could examine the index cards in any order they wished. They were also asked to rate the usefulness of the information contained on each card in terms of making their decisions.

The researchers gathered many different measures of participants' strategies for processing this social information about the potential partners. Together, however, these measures indicated that mood exerted strong effects upon these strategies. For example, it was found that as expected, those in a bad mood tended to focus on their partner's interpersonal qualities, presumably so that they could choose a pleasant partner who would help them feel better (see Figure 3.17). In contrast, those in a good mood concentrated on information about potential partners' task competence. Also as predicted,

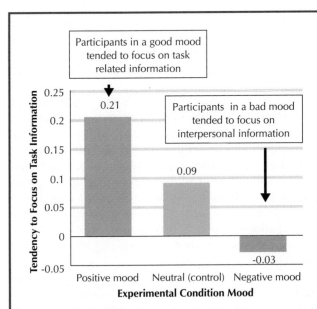

 Mood and motivated processing

FIGURE 3.17 Persons in a negative mood focused on information about potential partners' interpersonal qualities. In contrast, those in a positive mood concentrated on information about potential partners' task competence.

Source: Based on data from Forgas, 1991b.

both of these tendencies were stronger when individuals chose a partner for themselves rather than for another person. Similarly, those in a negative mood were more likely to adopt a global, "overall impression" strategy for choosing a partner than those in a good mood. This is consistent with the view that persons in a bad mood will be more strongly motivated to find a rewarding partner; hence they rely on global impressions of others rather than on comparing their traits one by one.

These findings, and those of other investigations (Schwartz & Bless, 1991) indicate that our current moods often influence the way in which we process social information. Since these processing strategies, in turn, shape the decisions we make and the judgments we reach, it is clear that affective states play a key role in social cognition and also in many aspects of our relations with other persons.

HOW COGNITION INFLUENCES AFFECT

Most research on the relationship between affect and cognition has focused on how feelings influence thought. However, there is also compelling evidence for the reverse—the impact of cognition on affect. We have already mentioned one aspect of this relationship in our earlier discussion of the two-factor theory of emotion proposed by Schachter and Singer (1962). As you may recall, their theory suggests that often we don't know our own feelings or attitudes directly. Rather, since these internal reactions are often somewhat ambiguous, we look outward—at our own behavior or at other aspects of the external world—for clues about our feelings' essential nature. In such cases, the emotions or feelings we experience are strongly determined by the interpretation or cognitive labels we select. (Please recall that such effects are most likely to occur when levels of arousal or other internal reactions are mild. When they are intense, these feelings may be perceived as unpleasant regardless of the situational context.)

A second way in which cognition can affect emotions is through the activation of *schemas*, or cognitive frameworks, containing a strong affective component. For example, if we label an individual as belonging to some group, the schema for this social category may suggest what traits he or she probably possesses. In addition, it may also tell us how we *feel* about such persons. Thus, activation of a strong racial, ethnic, or religious schema or stereotype may exert powerful effects upon our current feelings or moods (please refer to our discussion of stereotypes in chapter 6.)

Third, our thoughts can often influence our reactions to emotion-provoking events by determining how we interpret or appraise the events. For example, imagine that while you are standing in line outside a theater, a woman bumps up against you. Will you react with anger? This depends strongly on your interpretation of her act. If you conclude that she is trying to push ahead of you, you may become angry, even perhaps push back! If, instead, you conclude that she merely tripped over an irregularity in the sidewalk, you probably won't experience such feelings or take defensive action. As we'll note in chapter 11, growing evidence suggests that our interpretations of provocative actions by others often play a key role in our emotional reactions to them, and in our tendencies to behave aggressively (Zillmann, 1988).

A fourth way in which cognition influences affect involves the impact of *expectancies* upon our reactions and judgments. Growing evidence indicates that when individuals hold expectations about how they will react to a new event or stimulus, these expectations shape their perceptions of, and feelings about, the event or stimulus when they actually encounter it (e.g., Wilson et al., 1989). Many instances of such effects are visible in everyday life. For example, when people expect that they will dislike a new food, they often show visible signs of displeasure even before they put it into their mouths. Conversely, when people expect to enjoy a film, joke, or story, they are very likely to do so, even if they might have had weaker positive reactions in the absence of such expectations. Indeed, it appears that in many cases, expectations can play a stronger role in shaping reactions to a stimulus or event than characteristics of the stimulus or event themselves. For example, in one study on these effects, Wilson and his colleagues (Wilson et al., 1989) showed participants two sets of cartoons. Those in the first set were known (from previous ratings) to be very funny, while those in the second set were known to be less funny. Before seeing the second set of cartoons, some participants were told that they were lucky: They were going to see very funny cartoons. The others were not given such expectations. When the participants later rated the second group of cartoons, those given the positive expectations rated them as much funnier than participants not given such expectations. Thus, their reactions were indeed strongly influenced by their expectancies about how they would react.

Work in Progress

The Retrospective Impact of Expectations: Remembering What We Expected to Experience . . . but Didn't

That expectations influence our experiences is hardly surprising. We have all encountered situations in which it is clear that our reactions were strongly shaped by our expectations. But what about the impact of expectations after the fact? In other words, can expectations also shape our memories of events so that we recall them as more (or less) pleasant than they actually were? Wilson has extended his research on the role of expectations in order to find out. In an ingenious study on this issue, Wilson and Klaaren (1992) phoned some persons who had signed up to participate in a study and told them that it was great fun and that other people enjoyed it a lot. Other participants were not given these positive expectations.

When they actually arrived for their appointments, all the participants watched a classic Charlie Chaplin movie (*The Immigrant*). Half watched the movie under pleasant conditions; they sat in comfortable chairs. The remainder watched the film under unpleasant conditions: They sat in uncomfortable chairs and were required to keep their chin on a headrest—a position that made viewing

the television screen on which the movie was shown very awkward. Not surprisingly, both expectations and actual viewing conditions influenced participants' current reactions to the film. Those who expected to enjoy it rated it higher than those who did not, and those who watched under pleasant conditions rated it higher than those who saw it under unpleasant conditions.

Wilson and Klaaren, however, were also interested in what would happen with the passage of time. When asked to take part in the study again, would expectations or actual viewing conditions be more important in determining participants' decisions? To find out, three to four weeks later they phoned persons who had taken part in the study and asked if they'd be willing to repeat the study exactly as before, with one exception: They would see a different film. Results were clear: Expectations predominated. Those who had expected to enjoy the film were significantly more likely to volunteer again, regardless of actual conditions while watching the film. And these conditions, in and of themselves, had no appreciable effect on rate of volunteering. As Wilson and Klaaren put it (1992, p. 22): *"Affective expectations may take on a life of their own in our memories, overriding, at least to some extent, the objective experiences we have."* Of course, such effects will not always occur: If the discrepancy between expectations and reality is truly large, people may reexamine and alter their expectations. Still, within broad limits, it appears that not only do we experience, affectively, what we expect to experience; we also tend to *remember* what we expected to experience rather than our actual experiences themselves.

Finally, an important link between cognition and affect or emotion is suggested by our reactions in situations where we try our best to suppress certain thoughts. Such experiences are far from rare. Almost everyone has tried to eject amusing thoughts or images from their minds in situations where they are supposed to remain serious; and when feeling unhappy or depressed, most persons try to push from consciousness the thoughts that lie behind these reactions. Findings reported by Wegner and his colleagues (e.g., Wegner et al., 1990; Wenzlaff, Wegner, & Klein, 1991) suggest that such efforts at thought suppression may promote the establishment of links or associations between the suppressed thoughts and various moods. This is the case because people use thoughts about their feelings to distract their own attention from the thoughts they are trying to suppress. As a result, mood itself may become a cue or stimulus for the suppressed thoughts so that they return more strongly when a person is in the same mood once again than when he or she is in a different mood. Further, the link or association between suppressed thoughts and moods works both ways, so later, if a person thinks of the suppressed thoughts, the initial mood will be reinstated (see Figure 13.18).

Such effects have been convincingly demonstrated by Wenzlaff, Wegner, and Klein (1991) in a study where participants were first asked either to think

 Mood and suppression thoughts

FIGURE 3.18 Efforts at thought suppression may promote the development of links or associations between the suppressed thoughts and current moods. As a result, suppressed thoughts may return more strongly when individuals are in the same mood once again than when they are in a different mood. Similarly, when suppressed thoughts occur, they may tend to trigger the mood that prevailed when efforts to suppress them took place.

Source: Based on suggestions by Wenzlaff, Wegner, & Klein, 1991.

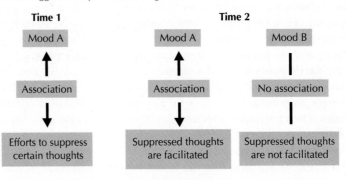

about a white bear or to suppress such thoughts. While performing these tasks, the participants listened to music previously shown to put people in a positive or negative mood. Later, all participants were asked to think about a white bear and to write down their thoughts while doing so. At this time they also rated their mood. As predicted, those who previously tried to suppress thoughts about a white bear in the presence of music that put them in a positive mood now reported experiencing more positive affect than those who tried to suppress such thoughts in the presence of music that put them in a negative mood.

When are people most likely to try to suppress various thoughts? Primarily, Wenzlaff, Wegner, and Klein (1991) contend, when they are in a negative state—when they are depressed, anxious, or inhibited. If this is true, then negative moods may be more likely than positive moods to become associated with specific suppressed thoughts. As a result, mild negative feelings may be more likely to trigger specific thoughts that increase negative affect than mild positive feelings are to trigger thoughts that increase positive feelings. This may be one reason why it is generally easier for individuals to think themselves into depression and unhappiness than to think themselves into a happy state. Such links between suppressed thoughts and moods, therefore, may be one more reason why (as we noted on pp. 101–102) it is sometimes potentially harmful to think too much!

Social Diversity ▼ A Critical Analysis

How Culture Shapes Thought: Effects of Cultural Schemas

One key finding of research on social cognition is this: Our thoughts about the social world are definitely *not* a mixture of random ideas and knowledge. On the contrary, information we have acquired through experience is organized into cognitive structures known as **schemas** (e.g., Fiske & Taylor, 1991; Wyer & Srull, 1984). In a sense, schemas can be thought of as "mental scaffolds"—cognitive structures that hold and organize information. Schemas are important because once they are formed, they exert powerful effects on what aspects of the social world get our attention; what information gets entered into memory (usually, information consistent with schemas); and what is later retrieved from memory

storage. In these respects they play a key role in our understanding of other persons, ourselves, and the social world generally.

Since schemas develop out of experience, it seems likely that many of these structures are influenced by, and related to, specific cultures. Persons growing up in diverse cultures have contrasting experiences in many spheres of life. As a result, their schemas for everything from friendships and roles within the family to religious activities and courtship may differ greatly. And if these schemas differ, it can be argued, so too may various aspects of social thought and social behavior related to them. This possibility has recently become an important

topic of research in several different fields—anthropology and sociology as well as social psychology (e.g., Shore, 1991). The findings of such investigations indicate that culturally based schemas do indeed affect many aspects of social thought and social behavior. An especially revealing example of such research has recently been reported by Pritchard (1991).

Pritchard reasoned that because of the existence of cultural schemas, individuals would find it easier to read and comprehend culturally familiar information than culturally unfamiliar information. Moreover, this would be the case because individuals would use somewhat different processes in reading and comprehending these two kinds of material. To test this prediction, Pritchard (1991) asked high school students in the United States and in Palau (a small Pacific island nation) to read letters written by a woman to her sister, in which the writer described events surrounding a typical funeral. Since funerals differ greatly in the United States and Palau, it was anticipated that participants would find the letter about their own culture more comprehensible than the one about the other culture. But would they use different strategies in processing these two types of information? To address this intriguing issue, Pritchard asked participants to report on what they were doing and what they were thinking as they read the passages. Red dots were placed at specific points in the letters, and participants were instructed to stop when they reached these and to explain what was happening, what they were thinking about as they read it, and what they did as they read. Their responses were then carefully coded. On the basis of this coding, five distinct categories of processing strategies were derived: (1) *developing awareness*—participants' growing awareness of their progress and of problems they were encountering; (2) *accepting ambiguity*—participants' realization that they should not abandon their attempts to understand the text even if they were experiencing current difficulties; (3) *establishing intrasentential ties*—attempts to develop understanding of the sentence they were currently reading; (4) *intersentential ties*—efforts to relate one sentence to other

portions of the passage; (5) *background knowledge*—participants' attempts to build their understanding of the passages by drawing on some aspect of their background knowledge. In addition, after reading the letters, participants were asked to retell what they had read; in this way their memory for the information contained in each letter was assessed. Finally, the extent to which participants attempted to relate a given sentence to different portions of the text or to personal experiences was also coded.

Results indicated that individuals from the two cultures did use different processing strategies in reading culturally familiar and unfamiliar passages. For example, they used strategies relating to developing awareness and establishing intrasentential links more often with the unfamiliar than with the familiar materials. In contrast, and as might be expected, they used the strategy of relying on background knowledge much more often with the culturally familiar than with the unfamiliar passage.

Persons from the two cultures also differed in several ways with respect to the strategies they used. First, Americans used a wider range of strategies than the Palauans. In addition, the Americans reported using such strategies as developing awareness, accepting ambiguity, and using background information more than Palauans (see Figure 3.19). In terms of accuracy of recall for the passages (retelling), results were very clear: Individuals were much more successful in recalling information from the culturally familiar than from the unfamiliar passages. Finally, sig-

nificant results were also obtained in terms of *connections*—the extent to which participants tried to relate one part of the letters to other parts or to their own experiences. When reading culturally unfamiliar passages, a large majority of Americans (87 percent) followed a sequence of identifying the meaning of a sentence, then relating it to personal experience, and finally making a concluding statement. In contrast, a large majority of Palauans (84 percent) did *not* make a concluding statement. Similar differences did not emerge with respect to culturally familiar passages.

In sum, individuals from both cultures did use different strategies in processing written information that was culturally familiar or culturally unfamiliar to them. In addition, Americans and Palauans differed in several interesting ways with respect to this task. As Pritchard (1991, p. 289) notes, Americans used a wider range of strategies and adopted strategies that required somewhat greater flexibility than did Palauans—for example, they showed greater acceptance of ambiguities. Given that Palauan culture discourages risk-taking behavior, these differences appear to be consistent with differences between the two cultures. The fact that Palauans were less likely to make connections when reading culturally unfamiliar materials may reflect the fact that they come from a much more homogeneous culture and so have less well-developed schemas for dealing with input from other cultural groups than Americans, whose culture is ethnically diverse.

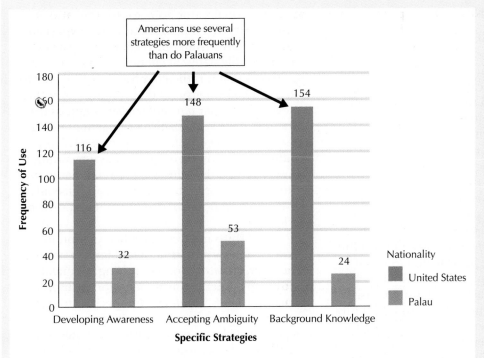

Cultural schemas and information processing

FIGURE 3.19 For understanding written passages describing a funeral, Americans reported using some strategies to a greater extent than persons from the Pacific Ocean nation of Palau. These differences may reflect contrasting cultural schemas for such events. *Source:* Based on data from Pritchard, 1991.

Taken together, these findings and those of related studies (e.g., Lipson, 1983) indicate that cultural schemas do indeed influence several aspects of social thought. These results have practical implications for enhancing the educational process. The greater the knowledge base—and therefore schemas—individuals have about a given topic prior to reading about it, the easier it is for them to understand the information. Thus, increased familiarity with diverse cultures might well enhance the comprehension of many types of reading material for children living in a culturally diverse society such as the United States. Thus, the impact of cultural schemas provides one more compelling reason for taking full account of cultural diversity in our efforts to educate our children.

Summary and Review

Heuristics As Mental Short-cuts

Social Cognition consists of the processes through which we notice, interpret, remember, and later use information about the social world. In order to minimize the effort required for these complex tasks, individuals often use mental short-cuts. Some of these involve the use of *heuristics*—mental rules of thumb that permit rapid decisions about various stimuli. For example, people may judge the frequency of a stimulus in terms of *representativeness*—the extent to which it is similar to other, related stimuli. Another important heuristic is *availability*—the ease with which information can be brought to mind. Recent evidence indicates that the greater such ease, the stronger the impact of the information on our judgments. *Priming* involves procedures that increase the availability of specific information in consciousness. External conditions can serve as primes, but in many cases we generate our own primes on the basis of our inferences about others' traits.

Basic Aspects of Social Thought

Unlike Mr. Spock of "Star Trek" fame, we are *not* entirely logical or accurate our social thought. Rather, our social cognition is subject to a number of tendencies that can sometimes reduce its accuracy. First, we tend to pay more attention to information inconsistent with our expectations or beliefs than to information that is consistent with them. Second, we tend to notice, and emphasize, negative social information. So strong is this tendency that it is sometimes described by *automatic vigilance*—our seemingly automatic tendency to pay attention to negative input. A third important tendency in our social thought is *motivated skepticism*. This refers to the fact that we need more information to reach conclusions inconsistent with our initial preferences than we do to reach conclusions consistent with these preferences. Interestingly, thinking too much can sometimes interfere with the accuracy of our judgments and conclusions.

We often imagine the opposite of what has actually happened—a process known as *counterfactual thinking*. Such thinking leads us to have more sympathy for persons who suffer negative outcomes after unusual behavior than after typical behavior. Similarly, we assign greater responsibility and blame to those who have caused negative outcomes if they occur under unusual circumstances—that is, we can readily imagine how such outcomes might *not* have occurred. Finally, we tend to evaluate objects we own more favorably than ones we don't own. In such cases, social cognition seem to involve objects rather than other persons.

Affect and Cognition

Sharply contrasting views of the nature of emotions have been proposed. The *Cannon-Bard theory* suggests that emotion-provoking stimuli evoke both physiological reactions and subjective emotional states. In contrast, the *James-Lange theory* suggests that emotional experiences stem primarily from our recognition of changes in our bodily states. Schachter's *two-factor theory* proposes that it is the cognitive label we attach to physiological arousal that is crucial. Another view, the *vascular theory of emotion*, suggests that changes in affect (positive or negative feelings) can be produced by facial expressions. These influence airflow through the nasal passages, and so indirectly influence brain temperature. Small rises in brain temperature produce negative affect, while small drops generate positive affect.

Mild shifts in affect have been found to influence interpretation of ambiguous stimuli, memory, creative problem solving, risk taking, and many other forms of behavior. In addition, current moods influence the specific strategies we adopt for processing social information. Cognition also influences our affective states. The emotions we experience are determined, at least in part, by the labels we attach to arousing events; and our emotional reactions to provocative actions by others depend, in part, on our interpretation of the causes behind these actions. Finally, if we expect to like or dislike some stimulus or event, our affective reactions to it will usually be consistent with such expectations.

Social Diversity: How Culture Shapes Thought

As a result of contrasting life experiences, individuals in various cultures develop different *cultural schemas* relating to various activities or relationships. Growing evidence indicates that such schemas can influence their perceptions of many social events, and even the strategies they use in attempting to read written passages. In general, individuals find it easier to understand information that is culturally familiar than information that is culturally unfamiliar.

Key Terms

Affect Temporary and relatively mild feelings, or moods.

Automatic priming Occurs when stimuli of which individuals are not consciously aware alter the availability of various types or categories of information in memory.

Automatic vigilance The strong tendency to pay attention to undesirable or negative information

Availability heuristic A strategy for making judgments on the basis of how easily specific kinds of information can be brought to mind. Information that can be readily remembered is viewed as more prevalent or important than information that cannot be readily remembered.

Base rate fallacy The tendency to ignore or underuse information relating to base rates—the relative frequency with which conditions, events, or stimuli actually occur.

Cannon-Bard theory A theory of emotion suggesting that various stimuli elicit both physiological reactions and the subjective reactions we label as emotions.

Counterfactual thinking The tendency to evaluate events by thinking about alternatives to them (e.g. "What might have been"). The more readily such alternative events or outcomes come to mind, the stronger our reactions to the events that actually occurred.

Facial feedback hypothesis The suggestion that changes in facial expression can induce shifts in emotions or affective states.

False consensus effect The tendency to assume that others behave or think as we do to a greater extent than is actually true.

Heuristics Rules or principles that allow individuals to make social judgments rapidly and with reduced effort.

Information overload Instances in which our ability to process information is exceeded.

James-Lange theory A theory of emotion contending that emotional experiences result from our perceptions of shifts in bodily states. For example, according to this theory, we become fearful because of awareness of such physiological reactions as increased heartbeat, shortness of breath, and so on.

Motivated Skepticism The tendency to be skeptical about information that is inconsistent with our views or beliefs.

Mere ownership effect The tendency to evaluate objects we own more favorably than comparable objects we don't own.

Need for Cognition The desire to think about and increase one's understanding of various events.

Priming Occurs when stimuli or events increase the availability of specific types of information in memory.

Representativeness heuristic A strategy for making judgments based on the extent to which current stimuli or events resemble ones we view as being typical.

Schemas Organized collections of beliefs and feelings about some aspect of the world. Schemas operate like mental scaffolds, providing structure for the interpretation and organization of new information we encounter.

Social cognition The manner in which individuals interpret, analyze, remember, and use information about the social world; a major area of research in social psychology.

Two-factor theory A theory of emotion suggesting that in many cases we interpret our emotional states in terms of external cues. That is, we sometimes experience the emotions that our inspection of the world around us suggests we *should* be experiencing.

Vascular theory of emotion (or *of emotional efference*) A theory suggesting that positive and negative affect stem, at least in part, from changes in the pattern of blood flow to the brain and resulting increases or decreases in brain temperature.

For More Information

Forgas, J. P. (Ed.). (1991). *Emotion and social judgments*. Elmsford, NY: Pergamon Press.

    Chapters in this volume deal with the complex relationship between affect and cognition. In particular experts in this field carefully examine the many ways in which our feelings can influence our social judgments.

Fiske, S. T., & Taylor, S. E. (1991). *Social cognition* (2nd ed.). New York: McGraw-Hill.

    A clear and thorough review of research on social cognition. Many basic aspects of our thinking about others (e.g., attribution, memory for social information) are examined in an insightful manner.

Kahneman, D., Slovic, P., & Tversky, A. (Eds.). (1982). *Judgment under uncertainty: Heuristics and biases*. Cambridge, England: Cambridge University Press.

    A collection of articles and chapters focused on heuristics, biases, and fallacies. If you want to learn more about the ways in which we make use of mental shortcuts and err in our efforts to understand the social world, this is must reading.

Chapter FOUR

Attitudes: Evaluating the Social World

Forming Attitudes: Learning, Experience, and . . . Genes?

Social Learning: Acquiring Attitudes from Others Direct Experience: Acquiring Attitudes from Life / Genetic Factors: Some Surprising Recent Findings

Attitudes and Behavior: The Essential Link

Attitude Specificity / Attitude Components / Attitude Strength, Vested Interest, and the Role of Self-Awareness / Attitude Accessibility: The Force That Binds

Persuasion: The Process of Changing Attitudes

Persuasion: The Traditional Approach / Persuasion: The Cognitive Approach / The Reciprocity of Persuasion: When Attitude Change Is a Two-Way Street

When Attitude Change Fails: Resistance to Persuasion

Reactance: Protecting Our Personal Freedom / Forewarning: Prior Knowledge of Persuasive Intent / Selective Avoidance

Cognitive Dissonance: How We Sometimes Change Our Own Attitudes

Dissonance and Attitude Change: The Effects of Forced Compliance / Dissonance and the Less-Leads-to-More Effect / Dissonance: Does It Really Stem from Inconsistency?

SOCIAL DIVERSITY ▼ A Critical Analysis
Sexual Attitudes: Some Cultural and Ethnic Differences

Special Sections

WORK IN PROGRESS—Subliminal Conditioning of Attitudes: Conscious Thought or Unconscious Association?

INDIVIDUAL DIVERSITY—Individual Differences and the Elaboration Likelihood Model: Self-Monitoring and Self-Awareness

WORK IN PROGRESS—Attitude Functions and the Processing of Persuasive Appeals: When Communicator Attractiveness Does, and Does Not, Matter

FOCUS ON RESEARCH: THE CUTTING EDGE—Age and Attitude Change: Are We Open to Experience throughout Life?

SOCIAL PSYCHOLOGY: ON THE APPLIED SIDE—Putting Dissonance to Use: Hypocrisy and the Alteration of Societally Important Attitudes

It was the fall of 1972, and the presidential campaign was really heating up. I had always considered myself a Democrat, but now I faced a real dilemma. The Democratic candidate was George McGovern, a senator from South Dakota, and the more I listened to his speeches, the more uneasy I became about his candidacy. The biggest issue for me was his plan for a "negative income tax." McGovern favored massive new government programs and wanted to pay for them by doubling the taxes on people he described as "the fortunate few." When he began his campaign, he identified these people as ones with yearly incomes of $50,000 or more; but over the course of the summer, he dropped this figure first to $30,000, then to $20,000, and finally to a mere $15,000. Even in 1972, that was not a very high income; in fact, it was lower than my own salary as an associate professor. So, for personal reasons, I had serious doubts about McGovern.

But when I considered his opponent—Richard Nixon—I became even more uneasy. I had come to despise Nixon during the 1950s when he was vice president. During that period, he was widely known as "Tricky Dick," and this title seemed to fit him to a T. Even the best makeup experts couldn't prevent him from looking shifty-eyed. And my memories of his ugly Red-baiting tactics were still vivid. Yet, even though I had voted *against* him in 1968 (Hubert Humphrey was my choice), I had to admit that Nixon had been a fairly effective president. And the platform on which he was now running sounded more reasonable to me, in several respects, than McGovern's. A balanced budget, no new taxes, a speedy end to the Vietnam war—all these views were closer to my own positions than the ones expressed by his Democratic opponent.

What should I do? I knew that most of my friends were going to vote for McGovern. Yet the polls indicated that millions of Democrats planned to desert the party and vote for Nixon. I finally made my decision on the weekend just before the election. My wife and I were at a party when, predictably, the subject of the election arose. Opinion was divided, but most people present seemed to prefer McGovern. The most outspoken of these was Joe Grunebaum, a sociologist well known for his extreme left-wing views.

"Voting for Nixon," Joe pronounced with obvious disdain, "would be like voting for the Czar! Anyone who'd believe a word from that liar probably also believes in the Tooth Fairy.

McGovern's right. We've got to soak the rich!"

As usual, I was disturbed by Joe's extreme views. I considered myself to be moderately liberal, but I couldn't stomach Joe or his ideas. So, realizing what would probably follow, I protested. "Come on, Joe. You call people earning $15,000 a year rich? To me, they're just middle class. Why punish them? What have they done?"

This mild comment was enough to really get Joe going. He turned on me with the wrath that only true fanatics can muster. "Look what we have here," he snarled, sarcasm dripping from every word. "A defender of special privilege. 'Don't make me pay; it'll cramp my bourgeois life-style.' Ugh! You and people like you make me sick!"

"But Joe," I objected. "Try to be reasonable. Who's talking about special privilege? I'm only saying that people in the middle class already pay their share. A lot of them simply can't afford any more."

"Just listen to him!" was Joe's reply. "They're all the same. *They* get on board, and the first thing they want to do is pull up the lad-

der. What about all those people who don't have your fancy degree or your nice little suburban house? How should we get rid of 'em—gas 'em, shoot 'em, or what?"

Now *I* was getting angry. "I never said anything like that. I don't want to turn my back on anyone. I just think that there has to be a better solution than squeezing people in the middle. Remember, they're really the backbone of the country!"

Our conversation continued for a while; but gradually most of the people who had gathered around to listen drifted off, and the episode ended. Later that night, while we were driving home, my wife rebuked me.

"Why do you get into arguments with Joe? You know you can't win and he only gets you upset."

"Yeah, you're right," I agreed, "but sometimes I can't help it. Everyone else was just standing there, letting him get away with those stupid remarks. I just couldn't bear it. Anyway, I'll tell you one thing: I finally know who I'm voting for on Tuesday, and it sure isn't McGovern. If Joe Grunebaum is *for* him, then I'll be darned if I'll give him *my* vote!"

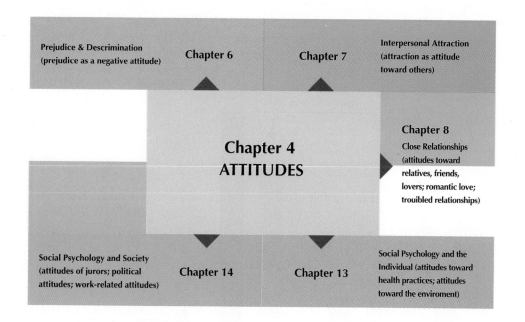

Did the fact that Joe Grunebaum was strongly pro-McGovern really push me over the line—albeit reluctantly—into the Nixon camp? Why was I reluctant to vote for McGovern even though I considered myself to be a Democrat and disliked Nixon so strongly? And why was making this choice so difficult and unpleasant for me in the first place? Many social psychologists would suggest that in order to answer these questions—and truly to understand what was happening in this situation—it would be necessary to consider my *attitudes*. They would note that I was reluctant to vote for McGovern because of my *negative attitude* toward his new income tax plan, and would add that I was equally hesitant to vote for Nixon because of my strong *negative attitude* toward him as an individual. The fact that this situation was so uncomfortable for me, too, could be explained in terms of attitudes: After all, it involved a head-on clash between different attitudes that I held concurrently. How could I, a Democrat, vote for a Republican—especially one I disliked so much? Yet how could I vote for a Democrat whose views were contrary to my own?

Attitudes have long been a central topic in the field of social psychology, and for good reason: They shape both our social perceptions and our social behavior (Pratkanis, Breckler, & Greenwald, 1989). But what, precisely, are they? Many different definitions have been suggested, but recently there has been growing consensus among social psychologists that attitudes involve *associations between attitude objects (virtually any aspects of the social world) and evaluations of those objects* (Fazio, 1989). More simply, many researchers believe that attitudes can be viewed as *evaluations of various objects that are stored in memory* (Judd et al., 1991). Returning to the incident above, my attitude toward Nixon involved an evaluation of him—in this case, extreme dislike—plus a link or association between Nixon and this evaluation. Whenever I encountered an image of Nixon, his name in a newspaper or magazine, this evaluation was retrieved from memory. And once present in my consciousness, it colored my perceptions and exerted a directing influence on my social behavior—in this case, my tendency to vote for or against him.

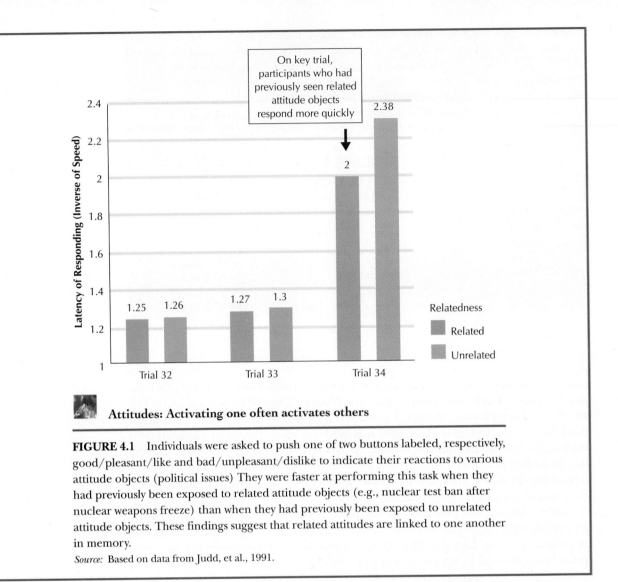

On key trial, participants who had previously seen related attitude objects respond more quickly

Attitudes: Activating one often activates others

FIGURE 4.1 Individuals were asked to push one of two buttons labeled, respectively, good/pleasant/like and bad/unpleasant/dislike to indicate their reactions to various attitude objects (political issues) They were faster at performing this task when they had previously been exposed to related attitude objects (e.g., nuclear test ban after nuclear weapons freeze) than when they had previously been exposed to unrelated attitude objects. These findings suggest that related attitudes are linked to one another in memory.
Source: Based on data from Judd, et al., 1991.

The same basic principles apply to any other attitude object—any aspect of the social world that is the focus of an attitude. Thus, my negative attitude toward McGovern's income tax plan involved my evaluation of this plan (strongly negative) together with the tendency for this evaluation to be retrieved from memory and brought into conscious thought whenever the plan, or perhaps related topics, was mentioned (Judd & Krosnick, 1989).

One additional, and important, point: Attitudes definitely do *not* exist in isolation. Rather, they are linked to one another in memory. Thus, activation of one attitude can lead to activation of other, related attitudes. This fact is demonstrated very clearly in research conducted by Judd et al. (1991). These investigators showed participants the names of various things (e.g., football teams, rock stars, political issues) on a computer screen. As each item was presented, participants were asked to push one of two buttons; one of these was labeled *good/pleasant/like* and the other was labeled *bad/unpleasant/dislike.* The length of time that elapsed before they pushed one of these buttons was recorded. Judd and his colleagues reasoned that exposure to various political issues would activate attitudes toward these issues *and*, to some degree, other attitudes concerning related issues. This would be so because related issues would be linked in memory. To test this prediction, they presented several political attitudes in a row to participants. In some cases these were related (for example, *nuclear weapons freeze* followed by *nuclear test ban; right to abortion* followed by *equal rights amendment*). As shown in Figure 4.1, results offered support for the major hypothesis: Participants responded more quickly to the related attitudes than to the unrelated ones. This and other findings offer support for the view that activation of one attitude can—and often does—tend to activate related attitudes as well. This is an important point, and one to which we'll return in later sections of this chapter.

Now that we've defined attitudes and described some of their basic features, we can turn to the wealth of information about them uncovered by social psychologists. In order to provide you with a useful overview of this intriguing body of knowledge, we'll proceed as follows. First, we'll examine the process through which attitudes are *formed* or *developed*. Next, we'll consider the relationship between attitudes and behavior. This link is more complex than you might expect, so be prepared for some surprises. Third, we'll examine how attitudes are sometimes *changed* through persuasion and related processes. The word *sometimes* should be emphasized, for as we'll note in another section, changing attitudes that are important to those who hold them is far from easy. Finally, we'll consider *cognitive dissonance*—an internal state with far-reaching implications for social behavior and social thought that, surprisingly, sometimes leads individuals to change their own attitudes in the absence of external pressure to do so.

Discussion Question 4

FORMING ATTITUDES: LEARNING, EXPERIENCE, AND . . . GENES?

Do babies enter the world with political preferences, racial hatreds, and the diverse preferences they will express as adults fully formed? Few of us would say yes. On the contrary, most people believe that attitudes are acquired in a gradual manner through experience. In a word, most people believe that attitudes are primarily *learned*. Social psychologists, too, accept this position. But please take note: We would be remiss if we did not call your attention to a small but growing body of evidence suggesting that genetic factors, too, may play some role in our attitudes. So, after examining the major ways in which attitudes are acquired, we'll briefly describe some of the evidence pointing to this surprising conclusion.

SOCIAL LEARNING: ACQUIRING ATTITUDES FROM OTHERS

One source of our attitudes is obvious: We acquire them from other persons through the process of **social learning**. In other words, we acquire many of our views from situations in which we interact with others or merely observe their behavior. Such social learning occurs in diverse ways, but three are most important.

CLASSICAL CONDITIONING: LEARNING BASED ON ASSOCIATION.   It is a basic principle of psychology that when one stimulus regularly precedes another, the one that occurs first may soon become a signal for the one that occurs second. In other words, when the first stimulus is presented, individuals come to expect that the second will follow. As a result, they may gradually show

Critical Thinking Question 1

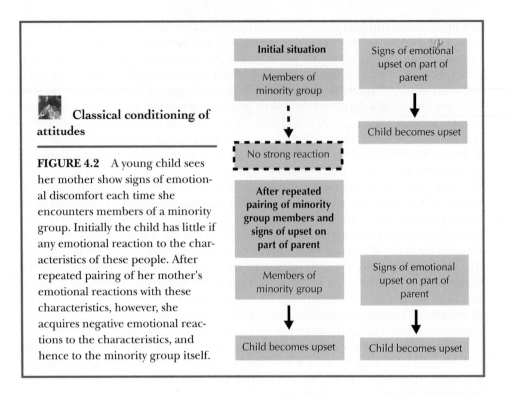

Classical conditioning of attitudes

FIGURE 4.2 A young child sees her mother show signs of emotional discomfort each time she encounters members of a minority group. Initially the child has little if any emotional reaction to the characteristics of these people. After repeated pairing of her mother's emotional reactions with these characteristics, however, she acquires negative emotional reactions to the characteristics, and hence to the minority group itself.

the same kind of reactions to the first stimulus as they do to the second, especially if the second stimulus is one that induces fairly strong reactions when encountered. Consider, for example, someone whose shower emits a low hum just before the hot water runs out and turns into an icy stream. At first he may show little reaction to the hum. After it is followed by freezing water on several occasions, though, he may well experience strong emotional arousal (fear!) when it occurs. After all, it is a signal for what will soon follow—something quite unpleasant.

What does this process—known as **classical conditioning**—have to do with attitudes and their formation? Potentially, quite a bit. Many studies indicate that when initially neutral words are paired with stimuli that elicit strong negative reactions—electric shocks, harsh sounds—the neutral words acquire the capacity to elicit favorable or unfavorable reactions (e.g., Staats & Staats, 1958; Staats, Staats, & Crawford, 1962). Since evaluative reactions lie at the very core of attitudes, these findings suggest that attitudes toward initially neutral stimuli can be acquired through classical conditioning. To see how this process might work under real-life conditions, imagine the following situation. A young child sees her mother frown and show other signs of displeasure each time the mother encounters members of a particular minority group. At first the child is quite neutral toward members of this group and their identifiable characteristics (skin color, style of dress, accent). Repeated pairing of these characteristics with her mother's negative emotional reactions, however, produces classical conditioning: Gradually the child comes to react negatively to these visible stimuli, and so to the minority group itself (see Figure 4.2). We'll consider such attitudes in more detail in chapter 5, in our discussion of *prejudice*.

Until recently, the primary evidence for the occurrence of this process was provided by the kind of studies described above—ones in which neutral words (for example, the names of imaginary groups of people) were paired with various emotion-provoking stimuli. Unfortunately, the results of such studies are far from conclusive, because it is possible that the persons who participated in them expressed favorable or unfavorable attitudes to these words because they guessed that this was what the experimenter hoped to find—an effect often termed **demand characteristics**. This interpretation is supported by the finding that in such studies, only individuals who were aware of the link between neutral words and the occurrence of positive or negative events showed the conditioning effect (Page & Kahle, 1976). A recent study, however, provides more convincing evidence for the role of classical conditioning in the formation of attitudes.

Evidence for the subliminal conditioning of attitudes. Krosnick, Betz, Jussim, and Lynn (1992) showed college students photos of a stranger engaged in routine daily activities: walking into her apartment, shopping in a grocery store, sitting in a restaurant. Each photo was shown for two seconds. Immediately before these photos were presented, participants in two groups were also exposed to photos previously demonsrated to produce either positive or negative feelings. Among the photos that produced positive feelings were ones of a bridal couple, people playing cards and laughing, and smiling friends playing rugby. Photos that produced negative feelings included a bloody shark, a werewolf, and open-heart surgery. These affect-inducing photos were presented for *very brief periods*—less than a tenth of a second. In fact, they were shown so briefly that participants could not even tell whether they were words or photos. Thus, they were presented *subliminally*—below the threshold for conscious awareness of their contents. After viewing these stimuli, participants were asked to indicate their attitudes toward the person shown in the photos and to rate this person on a variety of trait dimensions (unfriendly/friendly, cruel/kind, unselfish/selfish, considerate/thoughtless).

Krosnick and his colleagues reasoned that under these conditions, subjects would not be able to guess the purpose of the study, so demand characteristics would not operate. Thus, if subjects' attitudes were influenced by the affect-inducing slides, this would provide strong evidence for the classical conditioning of attitudes. As you can see from Figure 4.3, these effects were actually

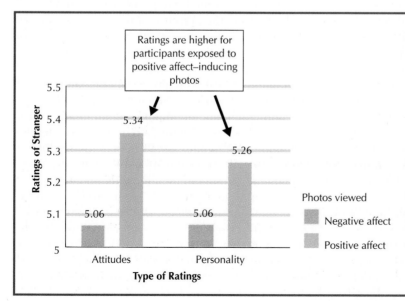

Ratings are higher for participants exposed to positive affect–inducing photos

Photos viewed

Negative affect

Positive affect

Subliminal conditioning of attitudes

FIGURE 4.3 Individuals saw affect-inducing photos for very brief periods of time immediately before viewing photos of a stranger engaged in normal life activities. Although the affect-inducing photos were shown so briefly that participants in the study could not report their contents, exposure to these photos affected ratings of the stranger. These findings provide evidence for the subliminal conditioning of attitudes.

Source: Based on data from Krosnick et al., 1992.

obtained. Subjects exposed to the positive affect–inducing scenes reported significantly more positive attitudes, and rated the target person more favorably on trait dimensions, than those exposed to the negative affect–inducing scenes. In short, findings provided evidence for the **subliminal conditioning** of attitudes.

These results help explain why some attitudes—including various forms of racial and ethnic prejudice—are so resistant to efforts to change them. If these attitudes are developed through classical conditioning in a largely unconscious manner (as in the example of the child and mother presented earlier), then it is not at all surprising that rational arguments against such views are unsuccessful in altering them. After all, they are based primarily on emotional reactions acquired through conditioning. To the extent this is so, then other approaches may be more effective in countering such attitudes. We'll return to some of these in chapter 6.

Work in Progress

Subliminal Conditioning of Attitudes: Conscious Thought or Unconscious Association?

The research conducted by Krosnick and his colleagues (1992) indicates that stimuli we can't recognize or identify can sometimes shape our attitudes. But it does not answer definitively the question of *why* such effects occur. One possibility is that this kind of conditioning involves an associative process occurring totally outside of conscious awareness: Positive or negative feelings associated with subliminal stimuli become linked with attitude objects such as the person evaluated in Krosnick et al.'s research. Conscious thought about these attitude objects is unnecessary. Another possibility is that we misattribute consciously experienced affect. For example, a participant exposed to the pleasant subliminal stimuli might have reasoned: "I have pleasant feelings as I see photos of this woman going about her daily activities. I guess there must be something about her that I like." Which of these interpretations is correct?

A recent investigation conducted by Betz and Krosnick (1993) suggests that the interpretation in terms of unconscious associations may be more accurate.

In this study, affect-arousing stimuli (photos or words) were shown to participants immediately before scenes of a woman performing everyday activities (reading a book, talking on the telephone, and so on). The photos or words were presented for varying durations ranging from 8.5 milliseconds up to 127.5 milliseconds. Two sets of trials were conducted. During the first, participants were asked whether the briefly flashed stimuli were pleasant or unpleasant. During the second set of trials, they were asked whether a brief stimulus had preceded each scene of a woman performing her daily activities (this was true on only some of the trials) and, if so, whether these stimuli were words or photographs.

Results indicated that participants could indeed detect the presence of the affect-inducing words and photos even at very brief durations: They did better than would be expected by chance even at exposures of 8.5 milliseconds and 14.5 milliseconds, and substantially better than this for exposures greater than 14.5 milliseconds. The key question, however, was this: Could they detect the *affective tone* of the stimuli even at these brief levels of exposure? The answer appeared to be *no*. In short, recognition of the affective tone of the briefly flashed stimuli took longer than simple detection of their presence. These findings imply that subliminal conditioning effects do *not* involve conscious recognition of the affective tone of such stimuli. Rather, since participants can recognize the presence of subliminal stimuli *before* they can identify their nature or affective tone, such conditioning seems to be based on a process of association occurring outside conscious awareness.

These findings, by the way, have important implications for the relationship between affect and cognition. It has frequently been argued that affective reactions to various stimuli may precede clear cognitions about them (e.g., Zajonc, 1984). For example, as Zajonc (1980) put it, a rabbit must experience fear, and run, before it has clearly identified a nearby movement in the bushes as a snake; waiting to consider the attributes of snakes or the probability of an attack is likely to prove fatal! The findings obtained by Betz and Krosnick (1993),

however, suggest that the rabbit may run *before* it experiences any affective reaction; fear, in fact, may *follow* the rabbit's initial perception of the nearby movement. We should hasten to add that the relationship between affect and cognition is very complex. No single experiment can clarify all aspects of this important issue. Still, it does seem that we can sometimes detect, and react to, potentially affect-inducing stimuli without experiencing conscious affective reactions. In such cases, at least, cognition—or at least perception—may precede clear-cut affective responses.

INSTRUMENTAL CONDITIONING: LEARNING TO STATE THE "RIGHT" VIEWS.   Have you ever heard a three-year-old state, with great conviction, that she is a Republican or a Democrat? Or that Fords (Hondas) are superior to Chevrolets (Mazdas)? Children of this age have little comprehension of what these statements mean. Yet they make them all the same. Why? The answer is obvious: They have been praised or rewarded in various ways by their parents for stating such views. As we're sure you know, behaviors that are followed by positive outcomes are strengthened and tend to be repeated. In contrast, behaviors that are followed by negative outcomes are weakened, or at least suppressed. Thus, a second way in which attitudes are acquired from others is through the process of **instrumental conditioning**. By rewarding their children with smiles, agreement, or approval for stating the "right" views—the ones they themselves favor—parents and other adults play an active role in shaping their offspring's attitudes. It is for this reason that until they reach their teen years, most youngsters express political, religious, and social views highly similar to those held by their families. Given the power of positive reinforcement to influence behavior, it would be surprising if they did not.

Discussion Question 2

MODELING: LEARNING BY EXAMPLE.   A third process through which attitudes are formed can operate even when parents have no desire to transmit specific views to their children. This third process involves **modeling**—in which individuals acquire new forms of behavior merely through observing the actions of others. It is often said that "little pitchers have big ears," and where attitude formation is concerned, this is certainly true. In many cases children hear their parents say things not intended for their ears, or observe their parents engaging in actions the parents tell them not to perform. For example, mothers and fathers who smoke often warn their children against such behavior, even as they light up a cigarette. Similarly, parents may warn their children against the dangers of alcohol, but then throw parties at which people drink until they become tipsy—or worse. What message do children acquire from such instances? The evidence is clear: That they should do as their parents *do*, not as they *say*.

DIRECT EXPERIENCE: ACQUIRING ATTITUDES FROM LIFE

While we often acquire attitudes from others through social learning, we also form such reactions through direct personal experience. For example, how do you know that you like or dislike various foods? Probably because you have tasted them. How do you know that you like or dislike different kinds of music? Again, because you have heard them and found that you enjoyed some types but found others unappealing. Of course, this is not always the case. Sometimes people merely *assume* that they will react negatively to various experiences and so avoid actually having them. For example, many people recoil at the thought of eating squid or octopus, without ever having tasted these foods. They assume that they won't like them, and they may be totally surprised if, gathering their courage, they do try them and find that such foods are delicious.

Exercise 2   Interestingly, research findings suggest that attitudes formed through direct experience with attitude objects are stronger in several respects than the kind of "anticipated" attitudes just described or attitudes borrowed from others (Fazio & Zanna, 1981). For example, individuals who form their attitudes about an object through direct experience with it have been shown to respond more quickly when asked to express their reactions to the object than individuals who form such attitudes indirectly (by watching someone else eat some food or engage in other activities; Fazio et al., 1982). Quick responses of this type are usually interpreted as a sign of attitude strength. In addition, attitudes stemming from direct experience are held more confidently and are more resistant to change than attitudes formed through indirect experience (Wu & Shaffer, 1987).

In sum, attitudes resulting from direct experience tend to be stronger in several respects than ones resulting from vicarious experiences. One practical message in such findings is clear: If you hold strong attitudes about some aspect of the social world and want someone else to share them, you should arrange for this person to have direct experience with the attitude object. In the absence of such experience, his or her attitudes will probably be only pale reflections of your own more passionate views.

GENETIC FACTORS: SOME SURPRISING RECENT FINDINGS

Can we inherit our attitudes—or, at least, a propensity to develop certain attitudes about various topics or issues? At first glance, most people—and most social psychologists—would answer with an emphatic *no*. While we readily believe that genetic factors can shape our height, eye color, and other physical characteristics, the idea that such factors might also influence our thinking—including our preferences and our views—seems strange to say the least. Yet if we remember that thought occurs within the brain and that brain structure, like every other part of our physical being, is certainly influenced by genetic factors, the idea of genetic influences on attitudes becomes, perhaps, a little easier to imagine. And in fact, direct empirical evidence for such influences has been obtained in several recent studies (Arvey et al., 1989; Keller et al., 1992).

Most of this evidence involves comparisons between identical (monozygotic) and nonidentical (dizygotic) twins. Since identical twins share the same genetic inheritance, while nonidentical twins do not, higher correlations between the attitudes of the identical twins would suggest that genetic factors play a role in shaping such attitudes. This is precisely what has been found: The attitudes of identical twins *do* correlate more highly than those of nonidentical twins (e.g., Waller et al., 1990). Additional studies have examined the attitudes of twin pairs (both identical and nonidentical) who were separated very early in life. Even though such twins were raised in very different environments, their attitudes still correlate more highly than the attitudes of nonidentical twins or unrelated persons (Waller et al., 1990). It is also important to note that such findings have been obtained for several different kinds of attitudes, ranging from interest in religious occupations and religious activities through job satisfaction (Arvey et al., 1989).

Needless to add, twin research, like research employing any methodology, can be questioned on several grounds. For example, twins are an unusual group, so results obtained with them may not generalize to other groups of people. Similarly, even when separated early in life, twins may be assigned by adoption agencies to similar environments; this could falsely inflate the apparent role of genetic factors in social attitudes. Still, given the many safeguards and controls built into these studies, it is hard to ignore their findings. To the extent the results they report are confirmed in additional research, we will be left with the rather startling conclusion that some of our attitudes, like many aspects of our physical appearance, are influenced—at least to a degree—by propensities inherited from our parents. (Please see chapter 14 for further discussion of this topic.)

ATTITUDES AND BEHAVIOR: THE ESSENTIAL LINK

Do attitudes shape behavior? Your first answer is likely to be, "Of course." After all, you can remember many incidents in which your own actions were strongly shaped by your opinions. You may be surprised to learn, therefore, that until quite recently, evidence concerning the strength of the link between attitudes and behavior was far from conclusive. Many studies seemed to suggest that this relationship was sometimes more apparent than real. For example, in a classic study on this topic, LaPiere (1934) toured the United States with a young Chinese couple, stopping at more than 250 hotels, motels, and restaurants. In all that time, he and his friends were refused service only once. When LaPiere wrote to the same businesses several months later and asked whether they would serve Chinese patrons, however, *fully 92 percent reported that they would not!* (Remember, this was 1934—a time when it was not unusual for people to admit openly to strong racial or ethnic prejudice.)

Reading: Lesko (11), *Special Forces: Attitudes vs. Actions*

To make matters worse, about twenty-five years ago, one social psychologist (Wicker, 1969) reviewed all the evidence existing at that time on the link between attitudes and behavior and came to an unsettling conclusion: Attitudes and behavior are at best only weakly related, and often there is virtually no relationship between them. Social psychologists were stunned. Had they been wasting their time by studying the nature of attitudes and various means of changing them?

Discussion Question 5

The answer that has emerged from systematic research conducted during the past two decades is a definite *no*. Attitudes and behavior, it appears, *are* often closely linked. This is not always the case, and the relationship between them is far more complex than common sense would suggest. In general, though, attitudes do predict many forms of social behavior across a wide range of contexts. In the remainder of this discussion, we will focus on various factors that determine the strength of the crucial attitude-to-behavior link.

Critical Thinking Question 2

ATTITUDE SPECIFICITY

Consider two of your own attitudes. Suppose, for example, that you like catsup on your hamburger (a specific attitude) and that you oppose racial discrimination (a more general attitude). Which attitude will be more strongly related to your actual behavior? If you like catsup, the odds are very high that you will put it on virtually every hamburger you eat. Thus, your behavior in such situations is highly predictable from your attitude. But now consider your opposition to racial discrimination. Probably you don't take every opportunity to protest such discrimination—you don't participate in every demonstration or sign every petition relating to this important issue. As a result, your actions can't be predicted very accurately from your general attitude about discrimination, or at least, not as accurately as your use of catsup on hamburgers. So, while you probably feel that opposing racial discrimination is a far more important issue than the use of catsup, your specific attitude toward catsup may well be a better predictor of your overt actions than your more general attitude about racial discrimination.

A concrete, and persuasive, illustration of the greater power of specific than general attitudes to predict behavior is provided by a study conducted by Newcomb, Rabow, and Hernandez (1992). They asked students in three different countries (the United States, Britain, and Sweden) to express both general and specific attitudes about nuclear war. General attitudes related to the view that war is unacceptable, while specific attitudes involved more specific reactions to nuclear weapons, nuclear war, and even nuclear power plants. Participants also reported on the extent to which they had engaged in activist behaviors relating to nuclear issues—whether they had joined a group, given money, written a letter to a newspaper, or signed a petition relating to these issues. As predicted, specific attitudes concerning nuclear war and nuclear issues were much better predictors of activist behaviors than more general attitudes; this was true in all three countries. These findings, and those of many other studies, indicate that specific attitudes are indeed better predictors of overt behavior than more general attitudes.

ATTITUDE COMPONENTS

You love pizza. Just the thought of one—hot, bubbling, crusty—brings a smile to your lips. You also have several thoughts about why you love it so much: You know that it tastes good, is really quite nourishing, and is both filling and inexpensive. In short, your attitude toward pizza involves both feelings (an affective or evaluative component) and various forms of knowledge (a cognitive component). Which of these components exerts a stronger impact on your behavior and is a better predictor of it? Probably your feelings—especially when you are hungry.

Now consider a situation in which you must choose between two college courses. One sounds more interesting than the other, but you know that the duller-sounding course will count toward your degree requirements. Again, your attitude toward these courses involves both affective and cognitive components. Which component will play a more important role in your choice? Here, it seems reasonable to predict that the cognitive component will predominate.

These examples help illustrate another key point about the attitude-behavior relationship: The various components of attitudes are not always highly consistent. For example, the affective component may be very positive—you are in love!—while the cognitive component is not so favorable—you have doubts about the future of the relationship. More to the point, when the components are inconsistent, one of them may be more closely related to specific forms of behavior than the other (Millar & Tesser, 1989); and it is this more closely related component that is the best predictor of behavior. Thus, when you are in the presence of the object of your affections, being in love (the affective or evaluative component) may predict your actions to a greater degree than the doubts about the future of your relationship (the cognitive component). In contrast, when you are apart from this person, the cognitive component may be a better predictor of your behavior.

ATTITUDE STRENGTH, VESTED INTEREST, AND THE ROLE OF SELF-AWARENESS

Obviously, strong attitudes predict behavior better than weak ones. There are several less-obvious factors related to attitude strength, however. One of these is direct experience. Earlier, we noted that attitudes formed through direct personal experience are often stronger than ones acquired through observation. It is not surprising, then, that attitudes of the first type are generally stronger predictors of behavior than attitudes of the latter type (Fazio et al., 1982).

A second factor is the extent to which individuals have a **vested interest** in the attitude object. When we say that someone has a vested interest, we mean that the event or issue in question has a strong effect on the person's life. Having a vested interest increases the strength of the attitude-behavior link. This fact is demonstrated quite clearly in a study conducted by Sivacek and Crano (1982). They contacted students and pretended to solicit their help in campaigning against a proposed state law that would raise the legal drinking age from eighteen to twenty. Nearly all students were opposed to the law, regardless of their own age. Some of them, however, had a vested interest—the ones young enough so that passage of the law would prevent them from drinking legally in the years immediately ahead. Students who were a little older had no vested interest; even if the law passed, they would already be over twenty by the time it took effect. Which group do you think agreed to campaign against the law? The younger students, of course. The older ones, while equally opposed to it in principle, lacked any vested interest. Thus, their attitudes were not as accurate a predictor of their overt behavior.

A third factor determining the strength of the attitude-behavior link involves *self-awareness*. This refers to the extent to which individuals focus on their own attitudes and actions—a state that can be induced even by such simple actions as gazing into a mirror (see Figure 4.4, p. 140). Growing evidence indicates that heightened self-awareness increases the degree of consistency between privately held attitudes and overt behavior (e.g. Hutton, & Baumeister, 1992; Pryor et al., 1977). There are two reasons why this is so: (1) Self-awareness increases our access to our own attitudes—we can report them more accurately when our self-awareness is heightened than when it is not. Obviously, the more readily we can bring attitudes to mind, the greater the possibility that they will affect our behavior. (2) In situations where overt behaviors are required, self-awareness can bring specific attitudes more sharply into focus, thus enabling them to guide the actions that follow. Enhancing self-awareness,

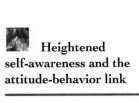 **Heightened self-awareness and the attitude-behavior link**

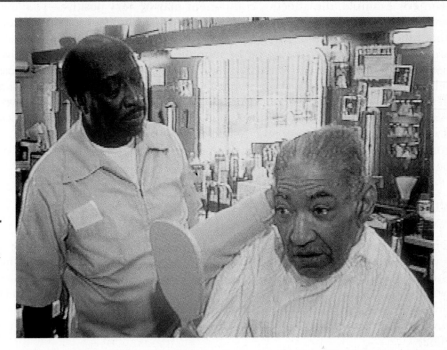

FIGURE 4.4 Growing evidence suggests that when individuals experience heightened self-awareness, the link between their attitudes and their overt behavior is strengthened.

it appears, is akin to saying to someone: "Before you act, stop for a moment and think about who you are and what you believe to be true. In light of these thoughts, what course of action should you take?" Such reflection makes it more likely that behavior will follow from existing attitudes and less likely that it will be determined by situational factors. The result? The link between attitudes and overt behavior is strengthened.

ATTITUDE ACCESSIBILITY: THE FORCE THAT BINDS

In our discussion of social cognition (chapter 3), we called attention to the concept of *availability*—the ease with which specific information can be brought to mind. A similar concept is useful in understanding the relationship between attitudes and behavior: **attitude accessibility**. This refers to the ease with which specific attitudes can be recalled from memory and brought into consciousness, where they can influence and guide behavior. According to the *attitude accessibility model* proposed by Fazio (1989), such accessibility plays a key role in the attitude-to-behavior link. This model suggests that in an initial step, attitudes are *activated*—retrieved from memory by presentation of the attitude object or some other stimulus. Once activated, attitudes influence perception of the attitude object and of the situation in which it is encountered. These perceptions, in turn, then influence subsequent behavior toward the attitude object (see Figure 4.5 for an overview of the model).

But what determines whether specific attitudes are activated? The attitude accessibility model proposes that *associative strength*—the strength of the association in memory between an attitude object and its evaluation—is crucial. The stronger this association, the more readily is an attitude activated and the stronger its effects on subsequent behavior. Having said this, we should note that recent evidence indicates that in fact many attitudes are activated in a seemingly automatic manner by the attitude objects to which they refer. This *automatic attitude activation effect* is compellingly illustrated by research performed by Bargh et al. (1992).

These researchers presented to participants the names of various attitude objects (e.g., beer, cake, crime, divorce, gift, recession, taxes) on a computer screen for a brief period of time. Soon afterward, an adjective appeared on the screen. Participants' task was to indicate whether the adjective was good or bad in meaning by pushing one of two buttons labeled *good* or *bad*. Some of these adjectives had a positive meaning (beautiful, excellent, magnificent), while others had a negative meaning (dreadful, painful, miserable, hideous). The researchers reasoned that presentation of each attitude object would automatically elicit the matching attitude. If this was of the same valence as the adjective shown (for example, both were positive), then they predicted that subjects' speed in reporting whether the adjective was good or bad would be enhanced. If the attitude was different in valence from the adjective, however, the opposite effect would occur: Speed would be reduced. This is precisely what occurred. Moreover, in contrast to findings of earlier research (e.g., Fazio et al., 1986), this was true for relatively weak attitudes (ones relatively low in accessibility) as well as for relatively strong ones (attitudes high in accessibility). So, in short, it appears that many attitudes are activated in a seemingly automatic manner by the attitude objects to which they refer. And once activated, of course, they are present in consciousness to guide overt actions. Why, then, are some attitudes better predictors of behavior than others? The answer may involve the fact that although many attitudes are activated in an automatic fashion, the intensity of such activation may vary greatly. Thus, the presence of a hot, bubbling pizza may activate your attitude toward pizza in a powerful fashion; coming across a newspaper article about the budget deficit may activate your attitude toward the deficit to a much weaker degree.

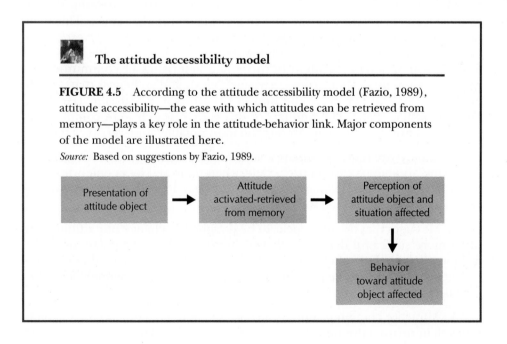

The attitude accessibility model

FIGURE 4.5 According to the attitude accessibility model (Fazio, 1989), attitude accessibility—the ease with which attitudes can be retrieved from memory—plays a key role in the attitude-behavior link. Major components of the model are illustrated here.

Source: Based on suggestions by Fazio, 1989.

Presentation of attitude object → Attitude activated-retrieved from memory → Perception of attitude object and situation affected → Behavior toward attitude object affected

Regardless of the precise mechanisms involved, one key point seems clear: Attitude accessibility plays an important role in the attitude-to-behavior link. Moreover, this concept allows us to tie together seemingly diverse factors and findings about this crucial link. Attitude strength, specificity, vested interest, and even self-awareness can all be understood in terms of their relationship to attitude accessibility. In each case, the kinds of attitudes that have been found to be closely related to behavior are the ones that would probably be most accessible—for example, strong, specific, and personally relevant ones (Krosnick, 1989). Thus, as the attitude accessibility model suggests (Fazio, 1989), attitude accessibility may indeed be crucial to understanding why attitudes sometimes predict behavior accurately and why sometimes they do not.

PERSUASION: THE PROCESS OF CHANGING ATTITUDES

How many times during the past twenty-four hours has someone, or some organization, tried to change your attitudes? If you stop and think for a moment you may be surprised at the result, for it is clear that every day we are bombarded with countless efforts of this type. Newspaper and magazine ads, radio and television commercials, political speeches, appeals from charitable organizations—the list seems almost endless (see Figure 4.6). To what extent are such attempts at **persuasion** successful? And what factors determine whether they succeed or fail? It is to these issues that we turn next.

PERSUASION: THE TRADITIONAL APPROACH

In most cases, efforts at persuasion involve the following elements: Some *source* directs some type of message (*communication*) to those whose attitudes she or he wishes to change (the *audience*). Taking note of this fact, much early research on persuasion focused on these key elements, addressing various aspects of the question: *Who* says *what* to *whom* and with what effect? This traditional approach to persuasion is sometimes known as the *Yale Approach,* since much early research within this framework was conducted at Yale University. Such research sought to identify those characteristics of communicators (sources), communications (persuasive messages), and audiences that, together, would serve to maximize the impact of efforts at persuasion (Hovland, Janis, & Kelley, 1953). The findings of this early research were complex and not always entirely consistent. Among the most notable, however, were these:

Reading: Lesko (10), The Great American Values Test

1. Experts are more persuasive than nonexperts (Hovland & Weiss, 1951). The same arguments carry more weight when delivered by people who seem to know what they are talking about and to have all the facts than when they are made by people lacking such expertise.

2. Messages that do not appear to be designed to change our attitudes are often more successful than ones that seem intended to manipulate us in this fashion (Walster & Festinger, 1962). In other words, we usually don't trust—and generally refuse to be influenced by—persons who deliberately set out to persuade us.

Exercise 1 **3.** Attractive communicators (sources) are more effective in changing attitudes than unattractive ones (Kiesler & Kiesler, 1969). This is one reason why

 Efforts at persuasion: A common theme of modern life

FIGURE 4.6   Each day we are exposed to many attempts to alter our attitudes.

politicians devote so much effort to the task of enhancing their personal appeal to voters. (Please refer to our discussion of *impression management* in chapter 2.)

4. People are sometimes more susceptible to persuasion when they are distracted by some extraneous event than when they are paying full attention to what is being said (Allyn & Festinger, 1961). This is one reason why political candidates often arrange for "spontaneous" demonstrations during their speeches: The distraction generated among audience members may enhance their acceptance of the speaker's points.

5. Individuals relatively low in self-esteem are often easier to persuade than those high in self-esteem (Janis, 1954). Lacking in self-confidence, low-self-esteem persons are more susceptible to social influence from others.

6. When an audience holds attitudes contrary to those of a would-be persuader, it is often more effective for the communicator to adopt a *two-sided* *approach,* in which both sides of the argument are presented, than a *one-sided approach.* Apparently, strongly supporting one side of an issue while acknowledging that the other side has a few good points in its favor serves to disarm audiences and makes it harder for them to resist the source's major conclusions.

Discussion Question 3

7. People who speak rapidly are generally more persuasive than persons who speak more slowly (Miller et al., 1976). This idea is contrary to the popular view that people distrust fast-talking salespersons and politicians. One reason rapid speech is more persuasive is that it seems to convey the impression that the communicator knows what she or he is talking about.

8. Persuasion can be enhanced by messages that arouse strong emotions (especially fear) in the audience, particularly when the message provides specific recommendations about how a change in attitudes or behavior will prevent the negative consequences described in the fear-provoking message (Leventhal, Singer, & Jones, 1965). Such fear-based appeals seem to be especially effective in changing health-related attitudes and behavior (Robberson & Rogers, 1988).

At this point we should insert a note of caution: While most of these findings have withstood the test of time and appear to be accurate, some have been modified, to a degree, by more recent evidence. For example, while fast talkers are often more persuasive than slow ones, recent findings indicate that this is true only when the speakers present views different from those held by their audience (Smith & Shaffer, 1991). When they present views consistent with those of their audience, fast talkers may actually be less persuasive, in part because the speed of their speech prevents listeners from thinking about and elaborating the message while it is being presented. Similarly, persons low in self-esteem are not always easier to persuade than those high in self-esteem (Baumeister & Covington, 1985). Indeed, it appears that people high in self-esteem are often persuaded, but simply don't want to admit it! Such exceptions aside, the findings reported above represent useful generalizations about persuasion, and form an important part of our knowledge about this process.

PERSUASION: THE COGNITIVE APPROACH

Critical Thinking Question 3

The traditional approach to understanding persuasion has certainly been useful; it provided a wealth of information about the "when" and "how" of persuasion—when such attitude change is most likely to occur and how, in practical terms, it can be produced. This approach was less helpful, however, with respect to the *why* of persuasion: it did not provide an equal number of insights into the question of why people change their attitudes in response to persuasive messages.

This issue has been brought into sharp focus in a more modern approach to understanding the nature of persuasion known as the **cognitive perspective** (Petty & Cacioppo, 1986). The cognitive perspective asks not *Who says what to whom and with what effect?* but *What cognitive processes determine when someone is actually persuaded?* In other words, this newer perspective focuses on what many researchers term a *cognitive response analysis*—efforts to understand (1) what people think about when they are exposed to persuasive appeals; and (2) how these thoughts and relevant cognitive processes determine whether, and to what extent, people experience attitude change (Petty, Ostrom, & Brock, 1981).

THE ELABORATION LIKELIHOOD MODEL: TWO ROUTES TO PERSUA-
SION.   What happens when individuals receive a persuasive message?
According to Petty and Cacioppo (1986), they think about it, the arguments it
makes, and (perhaps) the arguments it has left out. It is these thoughts—not
the message itself—that then lead either to attitude change or to resistance.

Critical Thinking
Question 4

But how does persuasion actually occur? According to the **elaboration likelihood model** (ELM), two different routes are possible, reflecting contrasting
amounts of cognitive effort on the part of message recipients. When persuasive
messages deal with issues that are important or personally relevant to recipients, the recipients are likely to devote careful attention to the message and
the arguments it contains. In that case, persuasion occurs through what is
known as the **central route**. Here, such activities as evaluating the strength or
rationality of the argument and deciding whether its content agrees or dis-
agrees with current beliefs tend to occur. When messages are processed via this
central route, attitude change will occur only to the extent that the arguments
presented are convincing and that the facts marshaled on their behalf are
strong ones.

Exercise 4

In contrast, when messages deal with issues that are relatively unimportant
and not personally relevant to recipients, persuasion occurs through what is
known as the **peripheral route**. Here, little cognitive work is performed, and
attitude change, when it occurs, involves a seemingly automatic response to
persuasion cues—information relating to the source's prestige, credibility, or
likability, or to the style and form of the message she or he presents. Attitude
change is more likely to occur through the peripheral route when audience
members are distracted and can't engage in a careful analysis of the speaker's
message (e.g., Petty, Wells, & Brock, 1976). Figure 4.7 presents an overview of
the ELM model and the two routes to persuasion it describes.

     The elaboration likelihood model

FIGURE 4.7   According to the *elaboration likelihood model,* persuasion can occur in either of two distinct ways. Individuals can engage in careful, systematic processing of the information contained in persuasive messages, in which case persuasion occurs through the *central route* (upper pathway). Alternatively, individuals may respond largely to *persuasion cues* (such as information about the source's credibility, status, or likability). In this case persuasion occurs through the *peripheral route* (lower pathway).
Source: Based on suggestions by Petty & Cacioppo, 1986.

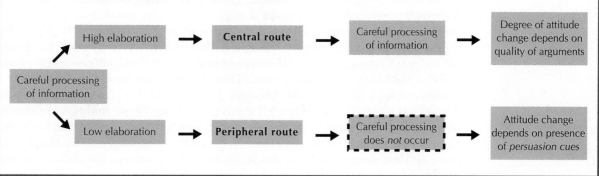

At this point, it is important to note that a persuasive message may be relevant or important to us for several reasons. As Johnson and Eagly (1989) state, we may find such messages personally involving because they are relevant to our basic values or because they are related to important outcomes. Research findings suggest that in the former case, involving persuasive messages will indeed activate careful cognitive processing; but we will engage in this processing primarily to bolster and support our current attitudes—*not* to weigh or evaluate carefully the information the messages contain. Thus, even when we find a message important or personally involving, we will not necessarily enter the central route and think systematically about its content.

The elaboration likelihood model appears to be of considerable value in several respects. Perhaps most important, it helps explain, in modern cognitive terms, the impact of many variables found, in earlier research, to affect persuasion. For example, it helps explain why individuals who are distracted by events or stimuli unrelated to a persuasive message may be influenced by the message to a greater degree than those who are not. Such distraction may prevent individuals from engaging in careful analysis of the communication—from entering the central route. Thus, they may be more readily persuaded by relatively weak arguments, or may respond to persuasion cues such as the communicator's attractiveness (DeBono, 1992). Similarly, consider the effect of likability of the source. Many studies indicate that persuasive messages from sources we like are more effective in producing persuasion than identical messages from sources we dislike, or even from those toward whom we have neutral feelings (Kiesler & Kiesler, 1969). The ELM model explains this finding in the following manner: The greater our liking for the sources of persuasive messages, the stronger our motivation to process this information. And then, assuming the message contains convincing arguments, the greater the extent to which we will be persuaded by it. Direct evidence for this reasoning has recently been provided by a study conducted by Roskos-Ewoldsen and Fazio (1992).

These researchers exposed participants to a persuasive message that advocated the banning of aerosol cans. This message contained several convincing arguments (the chemical propellant in aerosol cans is destructive to the earth's ozone layer; aerosol spray cans are dangerous because they can explode if they become too hot). In a control condition, this message was not attributed to any particular source. In two other conditions, in contrast, it was attributed to Jacques Cousteau—an individual toward whom most people report relatively positive attitudes. Instead of attempting to vary participants' liking toward Jacques Cousteau, the researchers adopted a different strategy: They varied the number of times the participants rated him on various dimensions. In a *low accessibility* condition, participants rated Cousteau on only one dimension: unlikable/likable. In a high accessibility condition, in contrast, they rated him on five different dimensions (e.g., deceptive/trustworthy, unpleasant/pleasant, unlikable/likable). The researchers reasoned that liking for Jacques Cousteau would be more accessible in the high accessibility group than in the low accessibility group. Thus, participants would express greater agreement with his persuasive message in this condition. As shown in Figure 4.8, results offered clear support for this prediction. These findings are consistent with the elaboration likelihood model, which would suggest that individuals will exert more cognitive effort in processing messages from liked than from disliked sources or, as in this study, from liked sources for whom such liking has been made more accessible.

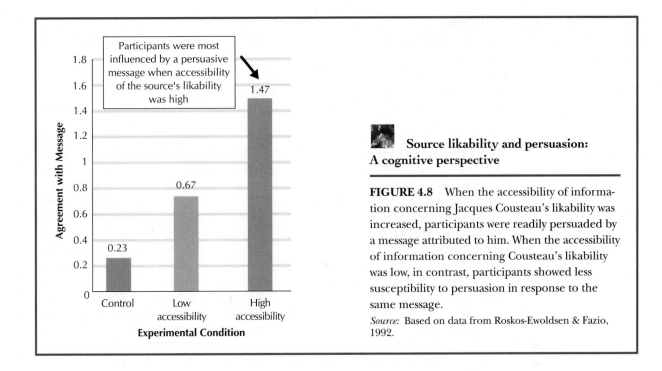

FIGURE 4.8 When the accessibility of information concerning Jacques Cousteau's likability was increased, participants were readily persuaded by a message attributed to him. When the accessibility of information concerning Cousteau's likability was low, in contrast, participants showed less susceptibility to persuasion in response to the same message.

Source: Based on data from Roskos-Ewoldsen & Fazio, 1992.

THE HEURISTIC MODEL OF PERSUASION. A closely related view of persuasion is the **heuristic model** proposed by Chaiken (1987). As we hope you'll recall from chapter 3, heuristics are mental shortcuts—rules of thumb we find useful in processing social information. Chaiken suggests that when a situation is personally involving (e.g., when it deals with attitudes important to the people in question), systematic processing of input occurs. Thus, individuals engage in the kind of careful cognitive analysis described above with respect to the central route to persuasion. In contrast, when personal involvement is low, individuals rely on various heuristics to determine whether or not to change their attitudes. For example, they are persuaded more by expert than by nonexpert and more by likable than by nonlikable sources, by a greater rather than a smaller number of arguments, and by arguments bolstered by the presence of statistics than by arguments not supported in this manner (e.g., Chaiken, 1980; Eagly & Chaiken, 1984). So, again, persuasion can occur through either of two mechanisms, depending on the circumstances involved. This model, too, has been supported by the findings of several different studies (e.g., Axsom, Yates, & Chaiken, 1987).

In sum, both the ELM and the heuristic model offer important insights into persuasion. Both help explain *how* persuasive messages induce attitude change, and both call attention to the fact that persuasion can occur along either of two distinctly different routes. Clearly, such models constitute a marked advance in our understanding of this important process.

Do individuals differ in the ease with which they can be persuaded? And are such differences related to the ways in which they process the information contained in persuasive appeals? For information on this issue, please see the **Individual Diversity** section on the next page.

Exercise 3

INDIVIDUAL DIFFERENCES AND THE ELABORATION LIKELIHOOD MODEL: SELF-MONITORING AND SELF-AWARENESS

As we have just seen, modern theories of persuasion emphasize the role of cognitive processes occurring at the time individuals are exposed to persuasive messages. According to these theories, whether recipients of such messages are persuaded depends, to an important extent, on whether they engage in careful, systematic analysis of the messages or, instead, tend to accept them in a less critical—and less effortful—manner. But what determines whether individuals adopt the central or the peripheral mode of processing? As we have already noted, this depends to an important extent upon the importance and relevance of the issues in question: In general, we are more likely to engage in careful processing of such input when these issues are personally important or relevant than when they are not. Growing evidence indicates, however, that the amount of cognitive efforts individuals expend in processing persuasive messages may also have a good deal to do with their personal characteristics. In other words, because of their own predispositions, individuals may find some issues or types of situation more involving than others.

Exercise 5

One characteristic that appears to play an important role in this respect is **self-monitoring** (Snyder, 1987). As we noted in chapter 2, self-monitoring refers to a cluster of characteristics closely related to the ability to adapt one's behavior to current social situations. Persons high in self-monitoring might be described as social chameleons—they can readily adjust their social behavior to the demands of a given situation. In contrast, low self-monitors tend to show a higher degree of consistency: They are very much the same person across a wide range of situations. Persons high in self-monitoring are also more concerned with making a good impression on others than those low in self-monitoring. Given these characteristics, it seems reasonable to predict that high self-monitors will find situations in which they receive communications from *attractive* sources to be especially involving and will engage in careful processing of messages from such sources. In contrast, they will not find situations in which they receive persuasive messages from *expert* sources to be highly involving, and will tend to process such input through the peripheral route. The opposite may be true of low self-monitors: Such persons would process appeals from expert communicators more carefully than appeals from attractive ones. These predictions have been examined in several recent studies, and they have generally been confirmed (DeBono & Harnish, 1988). So self-monitoring does appear to be one important characteristic that determines whether individuals engage in central or peripheral processing of persuasive messages.

Another characteristic that may play such a role is *self-awareness* (Carver & Scheier, 1981). As we noted earlier, this refers to the extent to which individuals focus on their own attitudes and their own behavior—in a sense, the degree to which they become the object of their own social perception. Individuals differ in the extent to which they are self-aware, and it seems reasonable to suggest that the higher their self-awareness, the more likely they are to respond with careful processing to persuasive messages dealing with issues they find important. While direct evidence for this prediction is lacking, a recent study by Hutton and Baumeister (1992) provides some support for its accuracy.

These researchers did not measure self-awareness as a stable individual difference; rather, they attempted to induce relatively high or low levels of self-awareness among participants in their studies. They reasoned that when self-awareness was heightened, participants would process persuasive messages dealing with important issues very carefully—more carefully than they would when self-awareness was lower. Thus, persons for whom self-awareness had been heightened would be persuaded by convincing messages to a greater extent than those for whom self-awareness had *not* been heightened, but would be persuaded by weak, unconvincing messages to a lesser extent.

To test these predictions, the researchers exposed participants to essays advocating a tuition increase. One of these contained very convincing arguments in favor of the increase—it suggested that this was necessary to attract higher-quality faculty and to enhance the university's research facilities. The other message contained unconvincing arguments—it indicated that the extra funds were needed for landscaping and for new carpeting in the hallways. Participants expressed their attitudes toward the tuition increase both before and after receiving one of these messages. In order to vary their level of self-awareness, half of the participants read the essays and expressed their attitudes in the presence of a mirror, a procedure known to increase self-awareness. For the others, the mirror was not present.

As shown in Figure 4.9, results offered support for the view that level of self-awareness would affect persuasion. Among participants for whom self-awareness had been heightened, the convincing essay produced significantly more attitude change than the unconvincing essay. Among those for whom self-awareness had *not* been heightened, in contrast, there was no difference in the degree of persuasion produced.

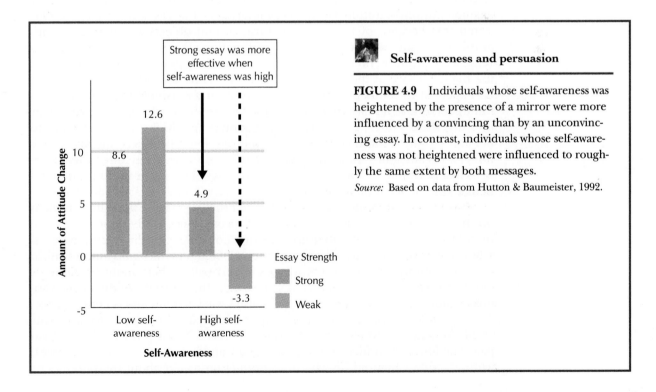

Self-awareness and persuasion

FIGURE 4.9 Individuals whose self-awareness was heightened by the presence of a mirror were more influenced by a convincing than by an unconvincing essay. In contrast, individuals whose self-awareness was not heightened were influenced to roughly the same extent by both messages.

Source: Based on data from Hutton & Baumeister, 1992.

While this study did not measure individual differences in self-awareness directly, other research indicates that stable differences along this dimension exist, and that they influence behavior in a manner similar to that of situational variations in self-awareness such as the one used here (e.g., Carver & Scheier, 1981; Scheier & Carver, 1992). Taking such evidence and the findings reported by Hutton and Baumeister (1992) into account, it seems reasonable to suggest that self-awareness is another individual difference factor with important implications for the process of persuasion.

ATTITUDE FUNCTION, ATTITUDE OBJECT, AND PERSUASION. At several points in this chapter, we have noted that attitudes can serve any of several different functions for the persons who hold them. Often, attitudes help the attitude-holders to organize and interpret diverse sets of information (*knowledge function*). They also permit individuals to express their central values or beliefs (*self-expression* or *self-identity function*). And attitudes sometimes help their holders to maintain or enhance their self-esteem (*self-esteem function*) by, for example, comparing themselves favorably with other persons or groups.

The functions served by attitudes are important from the point of view of a cognitive analysis of persuasion. Persuasive messages containing information relevant to specific attitudes—and, especially, information relevant to the functions served by those attitudes—will be processed differently (perhaps more carefully) from persuasive messages that do not contain such information. To the extent this is true, the precise conditions required for successful persuasion should vary with the functions served by various attitudes.

Convincing evidence for a relationship between attitude function and persuasion has been gathered in several different studies (Shavitt, 1989). For example, in one carefully conducted experiment on this issue, Shavitt (1990) noted that because of their basic nature, certain objects are associated with attitudes serving primarily one kind of function. For example, some objects (e.g., air conditioners) serve primarily a *utilitarian function*—people buy and use them because of the rewards they provide. Thus, attitudes about them can be expected to focus on this function. In contrast, other objects (e.g., perfume) serve a *social identity function*—they permit individuals to express their identity, their values, or the reference groups to which they would like to belong. To put it more concretely, people buy some products, like air conditioners, because they enjoy the comfort these provide. They buy other products, like perfume, at least in part because these allow them to transmit a particular kind of personal image.

Given such differences, Shavitt reasoned that persuasive appeals that focus on the appropriate attitude function for a given object will be more successful than those that focus on other attitude functions. Specifically, persuasive messages that emphasize the features of a product should be more successful in changing attitudes about air conditioners and coffee than about perfume or greeting cards. In contrast, persuasive messages that emphasize the image various products yield should be more persuasive for perfume and greeting cards.

To test these predictions, Shavitt exposed female participants to four pairs of ads—one ad about each of two brands of each of four products. In each ad pair, one focused on features (e.g., the flavor and aroma of a brand of coffee), while the other focused on what the product indicated about the purchaser's taste and values (e.g., how use of a brand of coffee would indicate to others one's good judgment). Results offered strong support for the major hypothesis. For the utilitarian products (air conditioners, coffee), participants strongly preferred the brands that had been promoted by ads that focused on their features. For the self-identity products (perfume, greeting cards), however, participants strongly preferred the brands that had been promoted on the basis of their snob appeal. In short, the persuasive appeals whose content matched the function of the product (and hence attitudes about it) were more effective than those whose content did not. These findings indicate that where persuasion is concerned, the functions served by attitudes are an important factor to consider. Messages that draw a bead on these functions may be processed more carefully, and so exert greater impact, than ones that do not.

Work in Progress

Attitude Functions and the Processing of Persuasive Appeals: When Communicator Attractiveness Does, and Does Not, Matter

Shavitt and her colleagues (e.g., Shavitt, Swan, & Lowrey, 1993) have recently extended research on attitude function and persuasion to consider an intriguing variable: the *attractiveness* of persons who endorse a given product in advertisements. They reasoned that the impact of this variable on acceptance of an advertisement, and on evaluation of the product or service the ad recommends, would depend on the attitude function operating at the time the ad was received. To test this prediction, they exposed individuals to ads for a new restaurant. The persons in the ad who endorsed the restaurant were either highly attractive or average in appearance, and the restaurant was either one that was about to open locally (high involvement) or one that was located in a distant state (low involvement). Participants were also exposed to "priming" information designed to induce one of two contrasting motives: *simple sensory gratification* or *enhancing their own social image*. To induce these different motives, the researchers had participants complete brief questionnaires that asked them how good or bad they felt after various sensory experiences (e.g., eating microwave popcorn, smelling fresh air), or to what extent various activities would make a good impression on others (e.g., wearing a Rolex watch, serving imported beer).

Shavitt and her colleagues reasoned that when sensory gratification had been primed, evaluations of the restaurant would serve a *utilitarian* function. Thus, attractiveness of the endorsers shown in the ad would serve as a *peripheral* cue and would influence these evaluations only under low involvement (when the restaurant was not a local one). In contrast, when social image had been primed, evaluating the restaurant would serve a *social identity* function. In that case, attractiveness of the endorsers would be more *central* to evaluating the restaurant and would affect evaluations primarily when involvement was high. Results offered support for these predictions. When participants focused on the restaurant's food, highly attractive endorsers produced more favorable evaluations of the restaurant in the *low involvement* condition but not in the *high involvement* condition. In contrast, when participants focused on the effect of the restaurant on their image, attractive endorsers produced more favorable evaluations in the high involvement condition but not in the low involvement condition.

These results serve to extend the findings reported earlier by Shavitt (1989, 1990) by indicating that there is a close and important relationship between the functions served by attitudes and the way in which information relating to attitudes is processed. The motives to which attitudes are linked, in short, can strongly determine people's reactions to persuasive appeals designed to change these attitudes.

THE RECIPROCITY OF PERSUASION:
WHEN ATTITUDE CHANGE IS A TWO-WAY STREET

Where social behavior is concerned, *reciprocity* appears to be the guiding principle. With few exceptions, we like others who like us, cooperate with others who cooperate with us, help others who help us, and aggress against others who treat us in a harsh fashion (e.g., Cialdini, 1988). Given the strength and generality of this principle, it seems reasonable to suggest that reciprocity may play a role in attitude change too, and recent evidence suggests very clearly that this is indeed the case. In other words, we tend to change our attitudes—or at least our public expression of them—in response to persuasion from others who have previously changed *their* views in response to our own efforts at persuasion. Perhaps the most impressive demonstration of such effects is provided by research conducted recently by Cialdini and his colleagues (Cialdini, Green, & Rusch, 1992).

In order to determine whether reciprocity plays an important role in persuasion, these researchers conducted a study in which participants first expressed their views on two proposals: comprehensive senior examinations at their university and an increase in the legal drinking age. Then participants were asked to prepare three arguments supporting their opinions on the drinking age proposal. After doing so, each participant discussed these arguments with another person, who was actually an assistant of the researchers. When the discussion was complete, the assistant indicated that he or she was either strongly influenced by the participant's views (the *yield* condition) or not influenced by them (the *resist* condition). The assistant did this by pointing to a large chart on the wall with a scale of positions ranging from "disagree totally with proposal" to "agree totally with proposal." In the yield condition the assistant indicated that he or she had shifted 20 points toward the participant's view on the basis of the participant's comments, while in the resist condition the assistant indicated no change in position at all. In a third, *control* condition no discussion between the two persons took place. Following these procedures, the assistant then presented his or her views on the comprehensive exam issue, and finally, participants indicated their current attitudes on this issue both publicly and in private. An additional aspect of the study involved the relevance of the exam proposal to participants; this was varied by information indicating either that the exams would be instituted next year (high relevance) or in ten years (low relevance).

As shown in Figure 4.10, results offered strong support for the operation of reciprocity with respect to public reports of persuasion. Participants in the *yield* condition showed much more movement toward the assistant's position than those in the *control* or *resist* conditions. Moreover, this was true regardless of whether topic relevance was high or low. Private attitudes, however, did *not* show the reciprocity effect. Participants demonstrated relatively little shift in their privately expressed views regardless of the assistant's prior actions. Thus, it appeared that reciprocity operated only with respect to public reports of persuasion—not with respect to actual persuasion itself.

In a follow-up study, however, Cialdini and his coworkers demonstrated that private attitude change *could* be influenced by reciprocity. They reasoned that if the arguments presented by the assistant were very convincing ones, then participants would attribute their tendency to match the assistant's persuasion not to reciprocity but to the strength of these arguments. In other words, they would have an out; they could alter their attitudes in a reciprocal

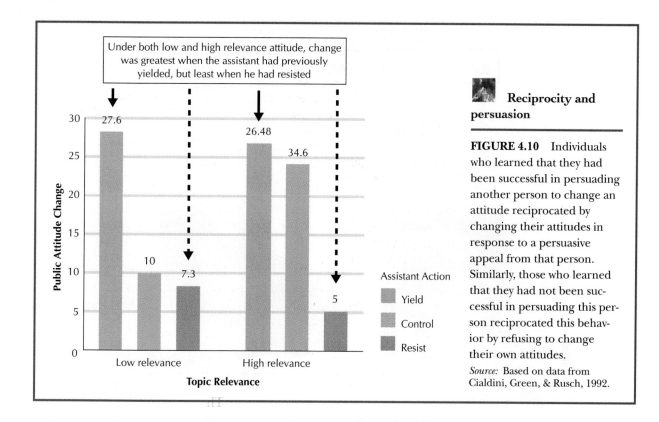

Under both low and high relevance attitude, change was greatest when the assistant had previously yielded, but least when he had resisted

Reciprocity and persuasion

FIGURE 4.10 Individuals who learned that they had been successful in persuading another person to change an attitude reciprocated by changing their attitudes in response to a persuasive appeal from that person. Similarly, those who learned that they had not been successful in persuading this person reciprocated this behavior by refusing to change their own attitudes.
Source: Based on data from Cialdini, Green, & Rusch, 1992.

fashion without admitting to themselves that they were changing in order to follow the principle of reciprocity. Results offered support for this prediction. Under conditions where the assistant's arguments were cogent ones, participants in the yield condition showed the greatest shift in private attitudes while those in the resist condition showed the least change in this regard.

In sum, it appears that our tendency to reciprocate the treatment we have received from others plays a role in persuasion, just as it does in many other forms of social behavior and social thought. The greater the extent to which others have yielded to our efforts at persuasion, the greater our tendency to yield to theirs; and this may involve shifts in our private attitudes as well as in our publicly stated views. In a sense, then, our powerful tendency toward social reciprocity offers would-be persuaders yet another potentially effective path toward their ultimate goal: changing others' attitudes.

WHEN ATTITUDE CHANGE FAILS: RESISTANCE TO PERSUASION

Given the frequency with which we are exposed to persuasive messages, one point is clear: If we changed our attitudes in response to even a small fraction of these messages, we would soon be in a sorrowful state. Our views on a wide range of issues would change from day to day or even from hour to hour; and, reflecting this fact, our behavior too would show a strange pattern of shifts and reversals. Obviously, this does not happen. Despite all the charm, charisma, and expertise would-be persuaders can muster, our attitudes remain remark-

 Resistance to persuasion: One reason why it's high

FIGURE 4.11 Like this character, we often tune out on persuasive appeals and hence are not influenced by them to any appreciable degree.
Source: The New Yorker.

ably stable. Rather than being pushovers where persuasion is concerned, we are a tough sell and, like the character in Figure 4.11, can withstand even powerful efforts to change our attitudes. Why? What factors provide us with such impressive ability to resist? We will now describe several of these.

REACTANCE: PROTECTING OUR PERSONAL FREEDOM

Do you recall how I reacted (in the chapter-opening story) to Grunebaum's obnoxious attempts at persuasion by deciding to do exactly the *opposite* of what he wanted? This is an example of what social psychologists term **reactance**— the negative reactions we experience when we conclude that someone is trying to limit our personal freedom by getting us to do what *they* want us to do. Research findings suggest that in such situations we often change our attitudes (or behavior) in a direction exactly *opposite* to that being urged on us—an effect known as **negative attitude change** (Brehm, 1966; Rhodewalt & Davison, 1983). Indeed, so strong is the desire to resist excessive influence that in some cases individuals shift away from a view someone is advocating even if it is one they would otherwise normally accept!

The existence of reactance is one principal reason why hard-sell attempts at persuasion often fail. When individuals perceive such appeals as direct threats to their personal freedom (or to their image of being a free and independent human being), they are strongly motivated to resist. And such resistance, in turn, virtually guarantees that many would-be persuaders are doomed to fail.

FOREWARNING: PRIOR KNOWLEDGE OF PERSUASIVE INTENT

On many occasions when we receive a persuasive message, we know full well that it is designed to change our views. Indeed, situations in which a communicator manages to catch us completely unprepared are quite rare. Does such advance knowledge or **forewarning** of persuasive intent help us to resist? Research evidence suggests that it does (e.g., Cialdini & Petty, 1979; Petty & Cacioppo, 1981). When we know that a speech, taped message, or written appeal is designed to alter our views, we are often less likely to be affected by it than if we do not possess such knowledge. The basis for such beneficial effects seems to lie in the impact that forewarning has on key cognitive processes. When we receive a persuasive message, especially one contrary to our current views, we often formulate *counterarguments* against it. Knowing about the content of such a message in advance provides us with extra time in which to prepare our defenses. In addition, forewarning also provides us with more time in which to recall relevant facts and information from memory—facts that may prove useful in refuting a persuasive message (Wood, 1982). Such effects are more likely to occur with respect to attitudes we consider to be important (Krosnick, 1989), but they occur to a smaller degree even for attitudes we view as fairly trivial. For these reasons, to be forewarned *is* to be forearmed where persuasion is concerned.

SELECTIVE AVOIDANCE

Still another way in which we resist attempts at persuasion is through **selective avoidance,** a tendency to direct our attention away from information that challenges our existing attitudes. In the context of social cognition (see chapter 3), selective avoidance is one of the ways in which attitudes (a type of schema) guide the processing of new information. For example, consider the act of television viewing. People do not simply sit in front of the tube and absorb whatever the media decide to dish out. Instead, they change channels, push the mute button, or cognitively tune out when confronted with information contrary to their existing views. The opposite effect occurs as well: When we encounter information that supports our views we tend to give it increased attention. We stop changing channels and listen carefully. Together, these tendencies to ignore or avoid information that contradicts our attitudes while actively seeking information consistent with them constitute the two sides of *selective exposure*—deliberate efforts to obtain information that supports our views. Through this mechanism, we often protect our current attitudes against persuasion and assure that they remain largely intact for long periods of time.

To conclude: because of the operation of reactance, forewarning, and selective avoidance, our ability to resist persuasion is considerable. Of course, attitude change *does* occur in some cases; to deny that it does would be to suggest that all forms of advertising, propaganda, and political campaigning are worthless (see Figure 4.12, p.156). But the opposite conclusion—that we are helpless pawns in the hands of all-powerful persuaders—is equally false.

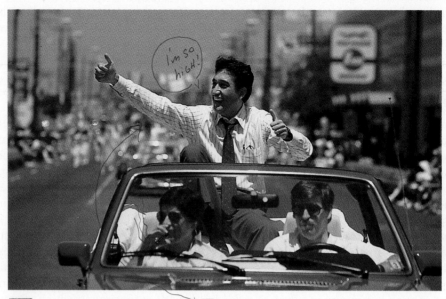

Resistance to persuasion: High, but not perfect

FIGURE 4.12 While our ability to resist efforts at persuasion is high, it is far from perfect. Thus, activities such as those shown here, of San Antonio Mayor Cisneros, *can* sometimes succeed in changing our attitudes.

Resisting persuasion is an ancient human art, and recent political events around the globe (e.g., the demise of communism in Eastern Europe and the former Soviet Union) suggest that it is alive and well as we approach the twenty-first century.

Are attitudes easier to influence at some times of life than at others? Are we equally open to change throughout the lifespan? For information on this intriguing question, please see the **Cutting Edge** below.

Focus on Research: The Cutting Edge

AGE AND ATTITUDE CHANGE: ARE WE OPEN TO CHANGE THROUGHOUT LIFE?

"Set in their ways," "Rigid," "Closed-minded." We hate to admit it, but when we ask students in our classes to list the characteristics of middle-aged people (which some define as "anyone over thirty"!), these are some of the adjectives they offer. Such descriptions suggest that once people reach a specific age (or age range), their capacity for change diminishes—they become "locked in," so to speak. Applied to the realm of attitude change, this view suggests that during our youth our attitudes are flexible and can readily be changed. Afterwards, however, they become relatively fixed and are more difficult to alter.

Is this view—sometimes known as the *impressionable years hypothesis*—really true? Are our attitudes more open to change when we are young, and less so later in life? Or, as a competing view known as the *openness to experience hypothesis* suggests, do we remain equally open to such change throughout life? Evidence on this issue is somewhat mixed (e.g., Krosnick & Alwin, 1989). Sophisticated research conducted by Tyler and Schuller (1991), however, points to the optimistic conclusion that in fact we remain open to attitude change throughout life.

In order to gather evidence on this issue, Tyler and Schuller (1991) phoned almost sixteen hundred people living in the Chicago metropolitan area and asked them to answer several questions concerning their obligation to obey the decisions of judges or police officers and their support for these authorities. In addition, they asked these people to describe any experiences they had had with judges or police officers during the past year. One year later the researchers phoned again a randomly selected sample of the same persons (more than eight hundred of them) and asked the same questions. Participants were classified into four age groups: 18–25, 26–35, 36–50, and 51–95.

Results offered several kinds of support for continued openness to attitude change throughout life. First, it was found that in all four age groups, participants' attitudes toward judges and police officers were affected by recent experiences with these authorities. Moreover, if anything, the magnitude of such effects was somewhat *greater* for older than for younger persons. Second, it was found that while attitudes prior to recent experiences with judges or police officers predicted current attitudes, there were no differences among the various age groups in this respect. In other words, older persons were not locked into stable attitudes that were resistant to change in the face of experiences that might be expected to shift them. Finally, among persons who had had recent experiences with the police or judges, current attitudes were less strongly influenced by previous attitudes than was true for persons who did not have such experiences—and again, this was true regardless of age.

That these findings were not specific to attitudes regarding law enforcement authorities is suggested by an additional study conducted by Tyler and Schuller (1991). In that investigation, attitudes toward government agencies were measured. Again, it was found that these were strongly affected by recent experiences and that the impact of such experiences on attitudes was about equal for people of various ages (18–25, 26–35, 36–45, and 46–60).

Taken as a whole these findings, and related research on attitude change throughout the lifespan (Alwin, Cohen, & Newcomb, 1991), points to a fairly optimistic conclusion: Contrary to popular belief, attitude change in response to life experiences is possible over the entire lifespan. Thus, at least where this kind of change is concerned, age definitely does not seem to equal rigidity.

COGNITIVE DISSONANCE: HOW WE SOMETIMES CHANGE OUR OWN ATTITUDES

Imagine the following situation: You have always been in favor of affirmative action (special programs for hiring and promoting members of minority groups and women). Now, however, you learn that because of this policy one of your friends has been passed over for promotion, even though your friend has more experience and better qualifications than a minority candidate who

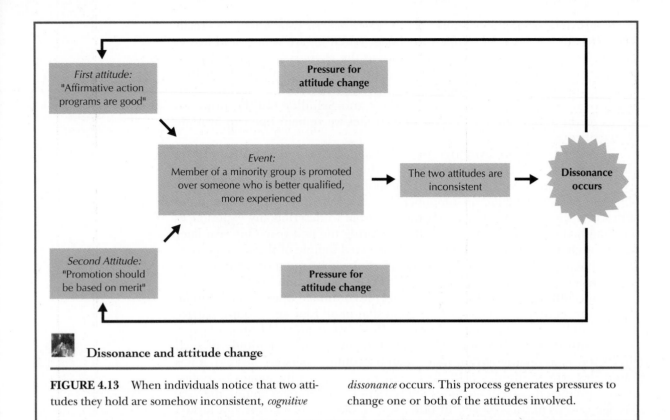

Dissonance and attitude change

FIGURE 4.13 When individuals notice that two attitudes they hold are somehow inconsistent, *cognitive* *dissonance* occurs. This process generates pressures to change one or both of the attitudes involved.

was promoted. While you are in favor of affirmative action, you also believe that people should be promoted on the basis of merit. How do you feel? If you are like most people, you find this situation disturbing. After all, you have come face to face with the fact that two of your attitudes are inconsistent—they just don't seem to fit together.

Reading: Lesko (12), *Cognitive Dissonance and Behavior Change in Psychotherapy*

In the terminology of social psychology, you would be experiencing a state known as **cognitive dissonance** (Festinger, 1957). This is the feeling, usually unpleasant, that arises when we discover inconsistency between two of our attitudes or between our attitudes and our behavior. We have already illustrated inconsistency between two attitudes in the example above, in which favorable attitudes toward affirmative action ran smack up against attitudes toward promotion on the basis of merit (see Figure 4.13). And there are many other causes of dissonance as well. It occurs whenever individuals must choose between two attractive alternatives, for rejecting one job, school, or lover in favor of another is inconsistent with the positive features of the rejected option. Most relevant to our present discussion, though, is the fact that dissonance is generated whenever individuals say things they don't mean or behave in ways that are inconsistent with their underlying attitudes or values. In such cases, the dissonance produced can have a startling effect: It can lead the people involved to change their attitudes so that these more closely reflect their words and deeds. In other words, saying or doing things that are inconsistent with their own attitudes sometimes causes people to change the attitudes themselves.

Transparency 4.1 How can this be so? Read on.

DISSONANCE AND ATTITUDE CHANGE: THE EFFECTS OF FORCED COMPLIANCE

There are many occasions in everyday life when we must say or do things Transparency 4.4 inconsistent with our real attitudes. For example, your friend buys a new car and proudly asks you how you like it. You have just read an article indicating that this model is such a lemon that the manufacturer puts a free ten-pound bag of sugar in the trunk. But what do you say? Probably something like "Nice, really nice." Similarly, imagine that at an important meeting your boss turns to you and asks your opinion of her new plan. Since you value your relationship with her (and your job!) you praise the plan, even though you realize it has serious problems. In these and countless other situations, our actions and our attitudes are inconsistent. What happens in these situations, which social psychologists describe as involving *forced compliance*? (This term derives from the fact that in such incidents we are forced by circumstances to say or do things contrary to our real views.)

Since dissonance is an unpleasant state, people who experience it are Transparency 4.2 motivated to reduce it. So something has to give (change). Several possibilities exist. First, individuals can change their attitudes so that these are now consistent with their behavior. For example, you may convince yourself that this is the right car for your friend or that your boss's plan is actually better than you thought. To the extent you do, you would experience the self-generated attitude change referred to in the title of this section.

Second—and this option is somewhat harder—individuals experiencing dissonance can change their cognitions about their own behavior. Thus, you might tell yourself that supporting your boss's views at meetings is an important part of your job. Thus, doing so is quite consistent with your attitudes.

Third, dissonance can be reduced by acquiring *new information*—information that *is* consistent with the attitudes or actions that, at first blush, seem inconsistent. For example, people who smoke cigarettes usually know that this is harmful to their health. They often try to reduce the dissonance produced by such counterattitudinal behavior by eagerly seeking evidence that smoking is truly not all *that* bad. They read reports of studies suggesting that smoking has few ill effects (ignoring the fact that these studies are sponsored by large tobacco companies). And they repeatedly remind themselves about Uncle Hal, who lived to be ninety-eight despite the fact that he smoked more than two packs a day.

Fourth, dissonance can be reduced by minimizing the importance of the inconsistency. For instance, in the incident involving affirmative action, you might convince yourself that this particular promotion is relatively unimportant since your friend plans to leave the company soon anyway.

In which of these ways do people actually seek to reduce dissonance? The answer is simple: in the way that is least effortful. In this, as in most other situations, we follow the path of least resistance and seek to reduce dissonance by changing whatever is easiest to change. Since it requires effort to change cognitions about our own actions, acquire new information, or minimize the importance of outcomes that really *are* important, the easiest route may well be to change our own attitudes. This, in essence, is why saying or doing things inconsistent with our attitudes sometimes leads us to change them.

Can *forced compliance* be put to practical, beneficial use? In other words, can it be used to change attitudes and behavior in ways that help both individuals and society? For a discussion of such possibilities, please see the **Applied Side** section that follows.

Social Psychology: On the Applied Side

PUTTING DISSONANCE TO USE: HYPOCRISY AND THE ALTERATION OF SOCIETALLY IMPORTANT ATTITUDES

While many efforts to alter our attitudes stem from what might be viewed as selfish motives—the desire to sell us some product or to win our vote—others derive from much more socially beneficial motives. Public service organizations often attempt to sway individuals' attitudes with respect to various health practices such as smoking, "safe sex," and avoiding too much sun. Similarly, organizations concerned with protecting the environment try to change people's attitudes and behavior with respect to energy conservation, proenvironmental legislation, recycling, and related matters. Most of the procedures used for such purposes are fairly traditional in nature; they seek to expose target groups to information about the costs or dangers of their current practices and the benefits of changing to the recommended ones. Unfortunately, mounting evidence indicates that such appeals are only moderately effective at best (e.g., Aronson & O'Leary, 1983). As we noted earlier, human beings are very adept at resisting efforts at persuasion; and when these are aimed at deeply entrenched attitudes and habits, the chances of much success are practically nil. Are there more effective procedures for inducing changes in individuals' attitudes that are beneficial both to them and to society as a whole? Recent research by Aronson and his colleagues (e.g., Aronson, 1993; Aronson, Fried, & Stone, 1991) suggests that there are, and that among these, techniques based on dissonance theory may be especially helpful.

Transparency 4.3

At first glance, it might seem that *forced compliance* would be one of these procedures. Forced compliance, however, involves somehow inducing people to say or do something they don't believe. Where attitudes relating to personal health practices and the environment are concerned, however, most individuals already agree with the positions recommended by health, public service, and environmental organizations. They already believe that smoking is harmful to their health, that "safe sex" (use of condoms) is the best practice, that chemicals contained in many aerosol cans damage the earth's ozone layer. How can dissonance be used to produce even stronger acceptance of such beliefs and commitment to acting upon them? Aronson and his colleagues suggest an intriguing technique—one based on inducing feelings of *hypocrisy* among the recipients of persuasive appeals. Briefly, this technique involves (1) inducing people to encourage others to engage in various recommended, socially beneficial actions, and (2) reminding them that sometimes they have failed to engage in such actions themselves. Under these conditions, people are reminded that they do not always practice what they preach. This generates dissonance, because being a hypocrite is inconsistent with their own, largely positive self-image. The result: They change both their attitudes and their behavior so as to be less hypocritical—to actually practice what they preach.

This technique has already been applied to several different topics. For example, in one study focused on AIDS prevention, Aronson, Fried, and Stone (1991) asked participants to write and deliver speeches advocating "safe sex" (use of condoms in all sexual encounters) and to make videotapes of these speeches. Half were then reminded that they had sometimes failed to follow this practice in their own behavior. As expected, persons in this condition (who experienced feelings of hypocrisy) later expressed stronger intentions to use condoms than subjects in the other groups. In a follow-up study (Stone et al., 1992) it was found that fully 83 percent of the subjects in this condition actually purchased condoms when these were offered to them at a large discount; this percentage was much higher than that in the other conditions of the study.

Perhaps an even more intriguing illustration of the potential benefits of dissonance induction in changing important social attitudes is provided by a study conducted by Dickerson et al., (1992). This project was conducted in California, where, because of population growth and drought, water conservation is a crucial issue. To determine whether the kind of hypocrisy manipulation described above could be helpful in encouraging favorable attitudes toward such conservation, and actions that actually conserve water, the researchers approached female swimmers on a college campus who were about to enter the shower room. One group (in the *commitment-only* condition) was asked to sign a flyer, reading, "Please conserve water. Take shorter showers. Turn showers off while soaping up. IF I CAN DO IT, SO CAN YOU!" A second group (*mindfulness-only*) was asked to answer questions about their own showering activities (e.g., "When showering, do you always turn off the water while soaping up or shampooing?"). These questions were designed to remind participants of their own past failures to conserve water. A third group (*hypocrisy*) was asked both to answer the questions *and* to sign the flyer; they were expected to experience the strongest feelings of hypocrisy. Finally, a fourth (control) group was not asked to perform either function.

A female experimenter was present in the shower room and actually timed the length of the showers taken by participants and, whether they turned the water off while soaping up and shampooing. It was predicted that those in the hypocrisy condition would take the shortest showers and be more likely to turn

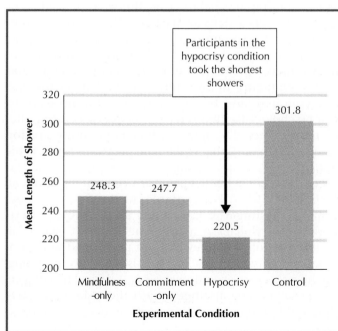

 Hypocrisy and attitude change

FIGURE 4.14 Individuals who both signed a form urging others to conserve water and were also made aware of their own past failure to follow this advice (*hypocrisy* condition) actually took shorter showers than individuals who engaged in only one of these actions or neither.
Source: Based on data from Dickerson et al., 1992.

off the water. As shown in Figure 4.14, p. 161, the first of these predictions was confirmed: Subjects in the hypocrisy condition did in fact take the shortest showers. With respect to turning off the shower, all three experimental groups were more likely to engage in such behavior than those in the control condition. Dickerson and her colleagues suggest that this may have been the case because participants in all three groups experienced feelings of hypocrisy to some degree. While these may have been strongest in the hypocrisy group, they were not sufficiently stronger to produce differences in this aspect of shower-related activities.

The results of this study, plus several others, indicate that dissonance can indeed be an effective technique for changing attitudes and behavior. Moreover, it is not necessary for individuals to engage in counterattitudinal actions for such effects to occur; merely being reminded of attitudes they hold and their own failure to live up to them can be effective. In short, individuals can change their own attitudes by saying and doing things they believe, as well as by saying or doing things they *don't* believe.

DISSONANCE AND THE LESS-LEADS-TO-MORE EFFECT

Critical Thinking
Question 5

Social psychologists generally agree that the forced compliance effect is a fact: When individuals say or do things they don't believe, they often experience a need to bring their attitudes into line with these actions. There is one complication in this process we have not yet considered, however: How strong are the reasons for engaging in counterattitudinal actions? If these reasons are quite strong, little or no dissonance will be generated. After all, if the last person to disagree with your boss publicly was fired on the spot, you would have strong grounds for praising the boss's plan even if you don't like it. Similarly, if you expect your friend to give you a lift to school in his new car every morning, you have strong reasons for praising, not belittling it. But what if good, convincing reasons for engaging in such actions are lacking? Under these conditions, dissonance will be stronger, for you must confront the fact that you said or did something you didn't believe *even though you had no strong or clear basis for doing so*. In short, dissonance theory points to the unexpected prediction that the weaker the reasons for engaging in counterattitudinal behavior, the stronger the dissonance generated, and hence the greater the pressure to change these views. Social psychologists often refer to this paradoxical prediction as the **less-leads-to-more effect**: The more inducements there are for engaging in attitude-discrepant behavior, the weaker the pressures toward attitude change (see Figure 4.15).

Surprising as it may seem, this effect has been confirmed in many different studies (e.g., Riess & Schlenker, 1977). For example, in the first and most famous of these experiments (Festinger & Carlsmith, 1959), subjects were offered either a small reward (one dollar) or a large one (twenty dollars) for telling another person that some dull tasks they had just performed were very interesting. (One of the tasks consisted of placing spools on a tray, dumping them out, and repeating the process over and over again.) After engaging in this attitude-discrepant behavior (telling another subject the tasks were interesting when they knew full well that they were not), participants were asked to indicate their own liking for the tasks. As predicted by the less-leads-to-more effect, subjects actually reported greater liking for the dull tasks when they had received the small reward than when they had received the large one.

While this and several other studies lend support to predictions based on dissonance theory, we should note that the less-leads-to-more effect occurs only under certain conditions (Sogin & Pallak, 1976). First, it occurs only in situations in which people believe that they have a choice as to whether or not to perform the attitude-discrepant behavior. Second, small rewards lead to greater attitude change than large ones do only when people believe that they were personally responsible for both the chosen course of action and any negative effects produced (Goethals, Cooper, & Naficy, 1979). And third, the less-leads-to-more effect does not occur when people view the payment they receive as a bribe rather than well-deserved pay for services rendered. These and related findings suggest that there are significant limits on the impact of forced compliance. Still, we should note that often the conditions just outlined do exist—often people do have (or think they have) freedom of action. And they frequently accept responsibility for their own behavior, even when doing so produces negative consequences. As a result, the strategy of offering others just barely enough reward to induce them to say or do things contrary to their beliefs can often be effective in inducing attitude change—and self-generated change at that.

THE LESS-LEADS-TO-MORE EFFECT REVISITED: INFERRED VALUES AND INDUCED COMPLIANCE.   As we noted above, the less-leads-to-more effect was first predicted by dissonance theory and has often been studied within this context. More recent research on compliance, however, suggests it may also

 The less-leads-to-more effect

FIGURE 4.15   Dissonance theory suggests that the weaker the reasons individuals have for engaging in attitude-discrepant behavior, the greater the dissonance they will experience and the stronger the pressure to actually alter these views.
Source: The New Yorker.

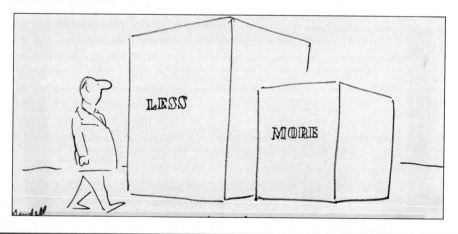

stem from a simpler and even more basic mechanism involving attributions. To see how this mechanism operates, consider the following events.

Imagine that someone offers to hire you to perform an unspecified job. This person says that she or he will pay you $100 to do the job and that the job will take only ten minutes of your time. Choose a number from one to seven to indicate how difficult, dangerous, or embarrassing you think the job is (1 = not very difficult or dangerous; 7 = very difficult or dangerous). Next, imagine that the same person offers you $5 to perform this job. Rate the job on the same scale once again. Did your ratings differ in the two instances? In all likelihood they did, for generally we assume that the more someone is willing to pay us for doing something, the more demanding or risky it must be. In short, we infer the nature or value of the task from the pay associated with it.

Turning this relationship between price and value around, assume that someone offers to sell you a painting for $10,000. How famous or talented is the artist? Now, imagine that you are offered the same painting for only $100; how famous or talented is the artist under these conditions? Once again, your ratings will probably differ, and this too will reflect the fact that you inferred value from price: The higher the price, the more famous or talented the artist.

What does all this have to do with forced compliance? According to Freedman, Cunningham, and Krismer (1992), quite a lot. These researchers argue that the less-leads-to-more effect may stem, at least in part, from the kind of attributions or inferences we have just described. In other words, they suggest that the reason people who engage in counterattitudinal behavior sometimes change their attitudes *more* when they have received a small reward than a large one is this: The large reward suggests that the counterattitudinal behavior is difficult or unpopular, while the small reward suggests that this behavior is easy or popular. Since people are more likely to change their attitudes toward popular views than unpopular ones, it is not surprising that greater attitude change occurs in the context of a small reward.

To test this explanation—which Freedman et al. describe as *inferred value theory*—the researchers performed a series of closely related studies. In one, college students were asked to rate the stressfulness and painfulness of a hypothetical experiment for which participants would be paid either $25 or $100 for serving as subjects. Results were clear: They rated the experiment as more stressful and painful in the $100 than in the $25 condition. Similar findings were also obtained when participants were asked to rate the extent to which a child would enjoy a new food under two different conditions: When her father offered her no incentive for eating it or when he offered her a large incentive (extra dessert). As expected, participants assumed that the girl would enjoy the food more in the low-incentive than in the high-incentive condition.

In a follow-up study Freedman et al. (1992) attempted to determine whether these effects will occur even when individuals have no choice about performing the action in question. Dissonance theory suggests that the less-leads-to-more effect will occur only when free choice about engaging in attitude-discrepant behavior exists. In contrast, inferred value theory suggests that having such choice is *not* necessary. To obtain evidence on this prediction, the researchers told students that a study in which they were participating involved either memory for rhythms or memory for words. They were then informed that they had been assigned to the rhythm task—they had no choice in this matter. Then they were reminded of the fact that because they were participating in the study as part of a course requirement, they would not be paid for their time. However, they were also told either that other participants, who were volunteers,

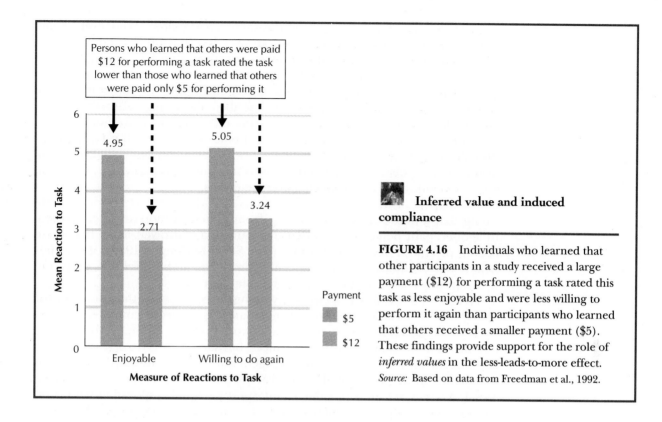

Persons who learned that others were paid $12 for performing a task rated the task lower than those who learned that others were paid only $5 for performing it

Mean Reaction to Task

4.95

5.05

2.71

3.24

Payment

$5

$12

Enjoyable   Willing to do again

Measure of Reactions to Task

Inferred value and induced compliance

FIGURE 4.16 Individuals who learned that other participants in a study received a large payment ($12) for performing a task rated this task as less enjoyable and were less willing to perform it again than participants who learned that others received a smaller payment ($5). These findings provide support for the role of *inferred values* in the less-leads-to-more effect.
Source: Based on data from Freedman et al., 1992.

received $12 for being in the study or that others received $5 for being in the study. Participants were then asked to rate the enjoyableness of the rhythm task and how willing they were to perform it again. As inferred value theory predicts, those in the high-incentive group (who had heard about the $12 fee) rated it as less enjoyable and were less willing to perform it again than those in the low-incentive group ($5) (see Figure 4.16).

In sum, it appears that when we are paid for engaging in some activity or when we must pay for some object or experience, we use the amounts involved as a basis for inferring the value of the objects or the difficulty of the tasks. And these inferences, in turn, can strongly affect our attitudes about the activities or objects in question. This may be one important reason why when we engage in actions discrepant with our attitudes, the smaller the inducement for doing so, the greater our tendency to change these attitudes.

DISSONANCE: DOES IT REALLY STEM FROM INCONSISTENCY?

Ever since the concept of cognitive dissonance was first developed in the 1950s, social psychologists have assumed *inconsistency* to be its most basic feature. It has been reasoned that people dislike inconsistency and strive to reduce it when it arises. More recently, however, Cooper and his colleagues (Cooper & Fazio, 1984; Cooper & Scher, 1992) have offered a contrasting interpretation of dissonance. This theory suggests that inconsistency is *not* the essential ingredient in dissonance. Rather, dissonance—and the motivation to reduce it—stems primarily from feelings of responsibility for negative events

Discussion Question 1

or outcomes. The reasoning behind this theory is as follows. Whenever people notice that they have brought about an aversive (harmful) event, they are motivated to determine whether they were responsible for this outcome or whether, perhaps, it stemmed from factors beyond their control. If they conclude that they were indeed personally responsible for the outcome, dissonance is generated, and all the effects described above (e.g., efforts to reduce it) then follow. Sometimes, of course, saying or doing things we don't believe can produce negative outcomes and so generate dissonance. But Cooper and his colleagues argue that attitude-discrepant behavior is not necessary for the occurrence of dissonance. What *is* essential, they maintain, is that people accept responsibility for producing aversive events.

In support of this view, Cooper and his coworkers point to evidence indicating that attitude change can follow from either attitude-consistent or attitude-discrepant behavior, provided the individuals involved learn that these actions produced negative outcomes (e.g., Scher & Cooper, 1989). When they believe that attitude-discrepant behaviors produced no harmful effects, in contrast, attitude change occurs to a much lesser degree.

While such evidence seems convincing, it is our view that the case for changing our basic conception of dissonance is far from complete. Recent research does call attention to several factors that may influence dissonance and the attitude change it often produces, but such research does not seem to account for all the intriguing findings generated in studies that have defined dissonance in the traditional, inconsistency-based manner (e.g., Baumeister, 1986). Further, it seems possible to interpret personal responsibility for aversive outcomes within the context of traditional dissonance theory. Most persons, after all, have a relatively positive self-image; discovering that they personally have been responsible for causing negative outcomes is in a sense inconsistent with that image. Accordingly, attitude change in such cases may stem, at least in part, from inconsistency.

Until such complexities are fully resolved, we believe it is reasonable to continue to view dissonance as deriving from and centering on the effects of inconsistency (e.g., Aronson, 1993). To repeat: When people discover that their various attitudes or their attitudes and behaviors don't fit neatly together, they may experience considerable pressure for change. And one of the important things that may give way in such contexts is their attitudes.

Social Diversity ▼ *A Critical Analysis*

Sexual Attitudes: Some Cultural and Ethnic Differences

As we note frequently throughout this book, *cultural factors* play an important role in social behavior and social thought. As a result, actions, ideas, and attitudes considered fully appropriate and "normal" in one culture or group may be viewed as shocking or bizarre in another (Smith & Bond, 1993). Such differences are apparent in many areas of human life, ranging from patterns of work and leisure to family relationships, but perhaps they are most dramatic in respect to sexuality (Kelley & Byrne, 1992).

Given that sexual behavior is, at least to some extent, biologically determined, it might be expected that cultural differences in this area would be relatively small—

that they would represent variations on an essentially similar underlying theme. In fact, this is not the case. Cultural and ethnic groups differ greatly—sometimes tremendously—in their **sexual attitudes**: their beliefs about, and evaluations of, various aspects of human sexuality. Here, we'll consider some of the differences in sexual attitudes that have been observed across different cultures and between ethnic groups living in multicultural societies.

Cultural Differences in Sexual Attitudes

In what ways do sexual attitudes differ among cultures? The answer is simple: Name almost any aspect of human sexuality and cultural differences will emerge. Is kissing an appropriate and stimulating activity? In Western nations it is, but among the Thonga of South Africa, it is viewed as a slightly repulsive activity. Should males fondle and kiss their partners' breasts during lovemaking? In Western cultures attitudes toward such activities are quite positive; but in many other cultures in Asia and Africa, oral contact with the female breast is viewed as improper—primarily because breasts are closely associated with the nursing of children. Is female virginity before marriage important ? At one time it was considered crucial throughout the Western world; in recent decades, however, attitudes concerning virginity have changed drastically, and it is no longer viewed as so important in most Western cultures (Kelley & Byrne, 1992).

In a similar manner, cultures differ tremendously in their atti-

Sexual attitudes, beliefs, and practices vary tremendously from culture to culture.

TABLE 4.1   Cultural variation in sexual practices and beliefs

Belief or Practice	Cultures in Which It Occurs
Sexual intercourse with a virgin is dangerous	Siberia; the Kagaba of South America
Intercourse causes menstruation to begin	Various societies, including the Murngin of Australia; Tepoztecans of Mexico
Ritual sexual acts are associated with agriculture	Native American Indian groups and ancient Sumerians of the Middle East
During foreplay, female bites off pieces of males eyebrow	Apinaye of Brazil
Sight of a navel is viewed as sexually arousing, so this part of body must always be covered in public	Samoans
As part of marriage ceremony, groom is insulted by bride's family and vice versa	Gusli in Kenya

tudes concerning various sexual practices, homosexuality, age at which first sexual encounters should occur, extramarital sexual relations, and many other topics. Table 4.1 summarizes some cultural differences in attitudes that you will probably find surprising.

Ethnic Differences in Sexual Attitudes

Multicultural societies such as the United States were once thought to be *melting pots*, in which ethnic and racial groups would intermingle and lose their unique identities. In fact, this appears to be true only to a limited degree. Various groups tend to retain their identities and often live in ethnically homogeneous communities—sometimes by choice, sometimes as a result

of discriminatory housing policies (see chapter 5). What results, therefore, is more like a mixed cultural *salad* in which various ingredients remain distinct rather than a uniform cultural soup.

Because ethnic groups retain their individual identities, the possibility exists that they will also demonstrate contrasting sexual attitudes. And in fact research evidence indicates that such differences do exist. They tend to be much smaller than commonly held stereotypes suggest, however (Belcastro, 1985). To illustrate this point, let's consider sexual differences between various ethnic or racial groups in the United States.

Do African-Americans and whites in the United States differ in this respect? Research on this topic has revealed some differ-

Hispanic-Americans: Stereotypes versus reality

FIGURE 4.17 Contrary to popular stereotypes, Americans of Hispanic descent express more conservative sexual attitudes and engage in less sexual activity than Americans of European descent.

Source: Based on data from Padilla & O'Grady, 1983.)

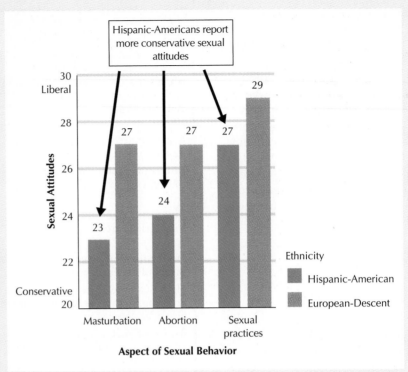

ences in sexual attitudes. In general, blacks hold slightly more permissive views about some sexual matters than those of whites (Wilson, 1986). For example, blacks report having engaged in premarital intercourse more frequently than whites and at an earlier age. They also report having extramarital affairs slightly more frequently than whites. And in general they report more positive attitudes about sexuality and about the open expression of sexual needs than whites (Wilson, 1986; Weinberg & Williams, 1988). On the other hand, blacks and whites report very similar attitudes with respect to masturbation, oral sex, and homosexuality (Wilson, 1986); both groups are less accepting of these practices than they are of other forms of sexual

behavior (Robinson & Calhoun, 1983).

Next, let's consider possible differences between persons of Hispanic (i.e., Latin American) descent and those of European descent. (The terms *white* and *black* are inappropriate here because persons of Hispanic descent can belong to either group.) Stereotypes held by European-decended white American suggest that Hispanic-Americans are more sexually active and promiscuous than other persons; but in fact, Hispanic college students actually express more conservative sexual attitudes and engage in sexual activities less frequently than persons of European descent (Padilla & O'Grady, 1983; see Figure 4.17). Other research indicates that because their culture

stresses dependence, obedience, and virginity, Puerto Rican women sometimes experience ambivalence over their sexuality and may be somewhat inhibited in sexual expressiveness (Bergos, Diaz, & Volands, 1988). Similarly, males who find that they cannot live up to the cultural tradition of *machismo*—being tough, dominant, and sexually aggressive—may feel inadequate and develop negative attitudes about their own sexuality (Bergos, Diaz, & Volands, 1988). Considerable change appears to be occurring in the sexual attitudes of Hispanic-Americans, however, and attitudes of women toward sexuality, abortion, and family planning are much more diverse than they were in the recent past. Similar changes appear to be occurring among many other ethnic groups in the United States, including persons of Asian descent (e.g., Ng & Lao, 1990).

In sum, attitudes toward various aspects of sexual behavior do indeed differ among cultures and across ethnic and racial groups within multicultural societies. Given the powerful impact of culture on social behavior and the tendency for cultural beliefs and values to persist over time, it seems likely that some of these differences will endure for many years to come. Others, however, may tend to fade in response to growing contact among cultures and the increased movement of news, information, and entertainment media around the globe.

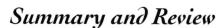

Summary and Review

The Nature and Formation of Attitudes

Attitudes are enduring mental representations of features of the social or physical world. These representations include evaluations of "attitude objects" plus information pertaining to them. Attitudes are acquired through experience and exert a directive influence on subsequent behavior. Attitudes can be acquired indirectly, from other persons, through *social learning.* This process involves three basic forms of learning: classical conditioning, instrumental conditioning, and modeling. Recent evidence indicates that *subliminal conditioning* of attitudes is also possible and may play a role in their development. Attitudes can also be acquired directly, through personal experience.

Attitudes and Behavior

Attitudes are related to behavior, but this relationship is far from simple. Specific attitudes predict behavior better than general ones. Similarly, strong attitudes, or ones in which people have a *vested interest,* are better predictors of behavior than weak or irrelevant ones. The cognitive component of attitudes predicts certain types of behavior (e.g., career decisions) better than the affective component. The opposite is true for other forms of behavior (e.g., romantic involvements). Most, if not all, of these effects can be understood in terms of *attitude accessibility*—the ease with which various attitudes can be retrieved from memory.

Persuasion

Persuasion is the process of changing attitudes through the presentation of various types of information. The *traditional view* of persuasion focused on identifying crucial characteristics of communicators, communications, and audiences. A newer *cognitive approach* focuses on the cognitive processes that underlie persuasion. Two important cognitive models of persuasion are the *elaboration likelihood model (ELM)* and the *heuristic model.* Both suggest that persuasion can occur either (1) through careful processing of attitude-relevant information, or (2) in a relatively automatic manner in response to various persuasion cues (e.g., cues relating to the expertise or likableness of would-be persuaders). Personal characteristics such as *self-monitoring* and *self-awareness* play a role in determining which of these two forms of persuasion actually occurs in a given situation. The principle of *reciprocity* plays a role in persuasion. The greater the extent to which others have yielded to our efforts at persuasion, the greater our tendency to yield to their efforts in this respect.

Resistance to Persuasion

Several factors play a role in our strong ability to resist persuasion. These include *reactance* (efforts to protect or restore personal freedom), *forewarning* (advance knowledge of persuasive intent on the part of others), and *selective avoidance* of information inconsistent with our attitudes. Contrary to popular belief, it appears that we remain open to changing our attitudes throughout life.

Cognitive Dissonance: Changing Our Own Attitudes

When individuals discover inconsistency between two attitudes they hold or between their attitudes and their behaviors, they experience *cognitive dissonance*. Dissonance motivates persons experiencing it to attempt to reduce it. When individuals say or do things inconsistent with their attitudes, they may seek to reduce the dissonance generated by changing these attitudes. The fewer good reasons they have for engaging in attitude-discrepant behavior, the greater the dissonance and the stronger the pressure for change—the *less-leads-to-more effect*. Individuals also experience dissonance when they experience feelings of *hypocrisy*—for example, when they realize that they don't always follow the recommendations they make to others concerning socially beneficial behaviors. Interestingly, recent findings suggest that the less-leads-to-more effect may stem, at least in part, from attributions suggesting that actions for which individuals receive large rewards are more valuable or difficult than those for which they receive small rewards.

Social Diversity: Cultural and Ethnic Differences in Sexual Attitudes

Large cultural differences exist with respect to sexual attitudes. These differences range from attitudes about specific sexual practices (e.g., kissing) to attitudes concerning broader issues such as virginity and homosexuality. Within multicultural societies such as the United States, some differences in sexual attitudes exist across ethnic and racial groups. However, these differences tend to be smaller than commonly held stereotypes suggest.

Key Terms

Attitude Accessibility The ease with which specific attitudes can be remembered and brought into consciousness.

Attitudes Mental representations of features of the social or physical world (including evaluations of those features) that are stored in memory.

Central Route (to persuasion) Attitude change resulting from systematic processing of information presented in persuasive messages.

Classical Conditioning A basic form of learning in which one stimulus, initially neutral, acquires the capacity to evoke reactions through repeated pairing with another stimulus. In a sense, one stimulus becomes a signal for the presentation or occurrence of the other.

Cognitive Dissonance An internal state that results when individuals notice inconsistency between two or more of their own attitudes or between their attitudes and their behavior.

Cognitive Perspective (on persuasion) An approach that attempts to understand persuasion by identifying the cognitive processes that play a role in its occurrence.

Demand Characteristics Cues that reveal the hypothesis or purpose of an experiment to participants. In the context of such information, participants may decide to "help" the researcher, by confirming the hypothesis, or may hinder the researcher by behaving in a manner opposite to the hypothesis.

Elaboration Likelihood Model (of persuasion) A theory suggesting that persuasion can occur in either of two distinct ways, differing in the amount of cognitive effort or elaboration they require.

Forewarning Advance knowledge that one is about to become the target of an attempt at persuasion. Forewarning often increases resistance to the persuasion that follows.

Heuristic Model (of persuasion) A theory suggesting that persuasion can occur either through careful cognitive analysis of persuasive messages or through the operation of simple *heuristics*—for example, the sense that we should accept influence from experts more readily than from nonexperts.

Instrumental Conditioning A basic form of learning in which responses that lead to positive outcomes or permit avoidance of negative outcomes are strengthened.

Less-Leads-to-More Effect The fact that offering individuals small rewards for engaging in counterattitudinal behavior often produces more dissonance, and so more attitude change, than offering them larger rewards.

Modeling A basic form of learning in which individuals acquire new forms of behavior through observing others.

Negative Attitude Change Attitude change in a direction opposite to that recommended in a persuasive communication.

Peripheral Route (to persuasion) Attitude change that occurs in response to persuasion cues—information concerning the expertise or status of would-be persuaders.

Persuasion The process through which one or more persons attempt to alter the attitudes of one or more others.

Reactance Negative reactions to perceived threats to one's personal freedom. Reactance often increases resistance to persuasion.

Selective Avoidance A tendency to direct one's attention away from information that challenges existing attitudes. Such avoidance increases resistance to persuasion.

Self-Monitoring A personality characteristic involving individual differences with respect to willingness to change one's behavior to match various situations, awareness of one's effects on others, and the ability to regulate one's nonverbal cues and other factors that influence others' impressions.

Sexual Attitudes Attitudes toward various aspects of human sexuality.

Social Learning The process of acquiring new forms of behavior (including attitudes) by observing or interacting with others.

Subliminal Conditioning (of attitudes) Classical conditioning of attitudes by exposure to stimuli that are below the threshold of conscious awareness.

Vested interest The extent to which an event or issue has a strong effect upon the life of a person holding an attitude about it.

For More Information

Eagly, A., & Chaiken, S. (1993). *The psychology of attitudes*. San Diego, CA: Harcourt Brace & Jovanovich.

> This book provides a comprehensive review of the vast existing literature on attitudes. Written by two expert researchers, it contains much valuable information about the nature of attitudes, how they can be changed, and their effects on behavior.

Pratkanis, A. K., Breckler, S. J., and Greenwald, A. G. (Eds.) (1989). *Attitude structure and function*. Hillsdale, NJ: Erlbaum.

> An examination of a wide range of information on attitudes. Each chapter has been prepared by expert researchers. A must for anyone interested in the nature and function of attitudes.

Rajecki, D. W. (1989). *Attitudes* (2nd ed.). Sunderland, MA: Sinauer Associates.

> A very broad introduction to current knowledge about attitudes. Covers a wide range of topics, from methods of attitude research through attitude change through group discussions. All in all, an interesting and valuable text.

Social Identity: Self and Gender

Special Sections

While the two of us waited for her school bus one morning, my ten-year-old daughter asked me, "Have you ever wanted to be a girl?" I wasn't sure whether she was really asking for my evaluation of males versus females, for reassurance that it was okay for her to want to be a boy, for confirmation that girls were superior to boys or vice versa, or for something else entirely. So I simply tried to give her an honest answer—"No, I don't think so. I already know what it's like to be a boy, and I wouldn't want to try something new."

She seemed satisfied enough and went on to another topic. I continued to think about the question, though, after she had boarded the bus and was on her way to school. *Had* I ever wanted to be a girl? In the dim, distant, sexist days of my youth, I probably considered girls much luckier than boys and so envied them their future. That is, a girl didn't have to get a job or risk getting drafted. She could just get married, stay home every day, and do whatever she wanted. Even with such biased misconceptions, I didn't really want to change places with the opposite sex—and probably for the same general reason I had given my daughter: because I would have been afraid to try something new.

I believe the basic reason for such hesitation is not a matter of anatomical differences between the sexes, but the fact that for each of us the concept of who we are includes details of gender-based roles and expectations. Gender identity is probably even stronger than other aspects of our identities. Consider other, related questions my daughter could have asked. Have you ever wanted to be an Indonesian, a sixteenth-century explorer, a druid, a movie star? I might be tempted for a moment by the last one, but not really. The same reason applies to such choices as to my disinterest in a miraculous sex change—I don't know how to assume those identities and don't want to lose my present self in order to adopt a new one.

It also occurs to me that in movies, books, and plays, the theme of a changed identity comes up over and over again, and the new identity is usually a source of problems (and, for the observer, amuse-ment). Think of stories in which two people who look alike switch places (*The Prince and the Pauper* and *The Parent Trap*), stories of mysterious changes in a person's sex (*Prelude to a Kiss*), and stories of someone of one age inhabiting a body of a different age (*Big*).

Perhaps one of the reasons that such changes are intriguing to all of us is that we are unable to avoid undergoing identity changes in our lives. That is, we change from child to teenager to young adult to middle-aged adult to senior citizen. People sometimes regret looking in the mirror and reminding themselves that they are no longer seventeen. Beyond aging, we also are likely to take on such new identities as spouse, parent, and grandparent as well as all of the elements associated with whatever occupation we settle on.

So who I am and who you are is in part the solid combination of the various aspects of what we call self, but some of those details undergo change as we grow older and move through various roles in life.

Getting back to my daughter, what exactly did she want to know? I inquired about that a few days later, reminding her of that early-morning question. As is often the case, her basic question had noth-ing to do with anything I had imagined. She was curious about Michael Jackson's increasingly feminine look and wondered whether most males wanted to be females. She couldn't find any boys who wanted to be girls. Her final conclusion, much like mine, was that, with the exception of Michael Jackson, most people simply do not want to be someone new.

" wash your face and drive me to Formansan"

Transparency 12.2 For each of us, our **social identity** is extremely important in defining who we are, what we do, and how we evaluate ourselves (Brewer, 1991; Deaux, 1993). Our social identity combines our self-concept and the various groupings of people with which we identify—including sex, race, religion, political affilia-tion, age, occupation, and so on. In this chapter we will discuss two of the major components of social identity. First, we will describe some of the cru-cial elements of the *self*, including self-concept, self-esteem, self-efficacy, self-monitoring behavior, and self-focusing. Second, we turn to *gender* and the dif-ference between the biological determinants of sex and the primarily social determinants of gender identity, gender roles, and the way in which these attributes influence behavior.

THE SELF: MULTIPLE COMPONENTS OF ONE'S IDENTITY

You meet someone for the first time, and that person asks, "Who are you?" What is your reply? You might give your name or possibly list some important aspects of who you are—nationality, occupation, religion, or whatever. As diffi-

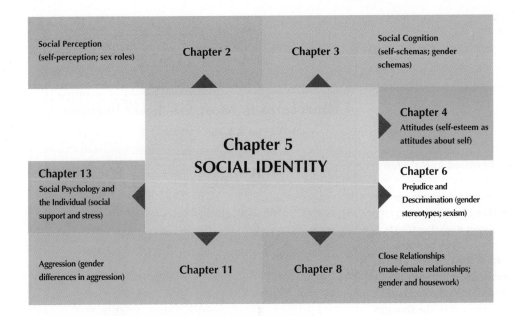

cult as it is to give a complete answer to that question, each of us spends a great deal of time and effort thinking about *ourself*—the center of each person's social universe.

We acquire our self-identity, or **self-concept,** primarily through our social interactions, and the **self** and its acquisition are matters of long-standing interest in social psychology (Higgins, 1987; Markus & Wurf, 1987; Suls & Greenwald, 1986). We will first review current knowledge about the self from the point of view of social cognition (see chapter 3). In other words, we will focus on the self in terms of its cognitive framework—a special framework that influences how we process not only social information (Klein, Loftus, & Burton, 1989) but our own motivation, emotional states, and our feelings of well-being (Van Hook & Higgins, 1988).

SELF-CONCEPT: THE CENTRAL SCHEMA

If you wanted to describe your current concept of yourself, what information would be relevant? Most people describe their physical appearance (tall, short, blond, brunette, etc.), indicate their major traits (outgoing, shy, anxious, calm, etc.), and sometimes mention their major goals and motives (to get rich, to make the world a better place, etc.). Altogether, the self-concept is a complex collection of diverse information that somehow is held together as *you*. If each of us is not just a random collection of information (like the mixed-up pieces of dozens of jigsaw puzzles), what is the "glue" that holds all of the information together in a unified self-image? For most social psychologists interested in the self, the answer lies in the concept of the *schema,* which was described in chapter 3.

THE SELF-SCHEMA AND ITS COGNITIVE EFFECTS.   A schema is an organized collection of beliefs and feelings about some aspect of the world. Each of us has a **self-schema** in which our self-knowledge is organized (Markus & Nurius, 1986). That is, the self-schema is a cognitive framework that guides the way we process information about ourselves. Self-schemas reflect all of our past self-relevant experiences; all of our current knowledge and existing memories about

Self-schema: Organized knowledge relevant to oneself

FIGURE 5.1 The *self-schema* consists of the organized knowledge relevant to each individual's self. Attention is more likely to be focused on self-relevant information than on any other type of information, and self-relevant information is more readily entered into memory and more easily recalled, as suggested by the thought processes of this rhinoceros.

Source: The New Yorker, February 8, 1988, p. 36.

ourselves; and our conception of what we were like in the past, what we are like now, and what we may be like in the future. A person's self-schema is the sum of everything that individual knows or can imagine about herself or himself.

If the self is the center of our social universe and if our self-schemas are well developed, it follows that we should do a better job of processing information that is relevant to ourselves than any other kind of information. Self-relevant information should be more likely to capture our attention, to be entered into memory, and to be recalled (Higgins & Bargh, 1987), as suggested in Figure 5.1. These hypotheses have been confirmed in studies of memory in which words deliberately made relevant to self ("Does this word describe you?") were later recalled more easily than words not made relevant ("Is this word printed in big letters?"). This tendency for information related to the self to be most readily processed and remembered is known as the **self-reference effect**.

Though the self-reference effect has been firmly established experimentally, think for a minute about *why* it should occur. What is it about relating information to the self that enhances our ability to process it effectively? Experiments by Klein, Loftus, and their colleagues (e.g., Klein, Loftus, & Burton, 1989) offer valuable insights. For example, in an important study Klein and Loftus (1988) reasoned that recall of self-relevant information might be facilitated in one of two ways—each of which has been shown to enhance memory. First, self-relevance encourages what is termed *elaborative processing*—the tendency to think about the meaning of words or events. Second, self-relevance might facilitate *categorical processing*—the tendency to place stimuli in specific categories. To determine whether the self-relevance effect rests on either (or both) of these mechanisms, Klein and Loftus presented each of three different groups of subjects with a list of thirty words. The words on each list were either related to one another (Canada, Mexico, France, etc.; jazz, opera, rock, etc.) or unrelated to one another (aspirin, library, boat, etc.). The first group was told to think of a definition of each word (the *elaboration* task). The second group was told to place each word in one of five categories—things associated with a day by the sea, for example— (the *categorization* task). The third group was asked to indicate whether each word brought to mind an important personal experience (the *self-reference* task). After completing its task, each group was given a surprise recall task— "Write down as many of the words as you can remember."

Klein and Loftus predicted that for the unrelated words, the categorical processing task would be especially helpful for memory, because without such processing, relations among the words would not be readily apparent. In contrast, for the related words, the elaborative processing task would be helpful; because the relations were already obvious, but thinking about definitions would add something extra. Klein and Loftus reasoned that if the self-reference effect was based on elaborative processing, the self-reference task and the elaborative processing task would have the same effect on memory (each would enhance performance on the list of related words). If, however, the self-reference effect was based on categorical processing, the self-reference task and the categorical processing task would have the same effect on memory (each would enhance performance on the unrelated words). The results were clear in that the self-reference task had both effects. For the unrelated words, the recall performance of the self-reference group was equal to that of the categorization group; for the related words, performance was equal for the self-reference group and the elaboration group. In summary, the ability to process information related to the self more readily than other information seems to derive from two powerful mechanisms. We think about such information more deeply than we do about other information, and we categorize it more effectively. Both mechanisms underlie the self-reference effect, making it easier to recall self-relevant information (see Figure 5.2).

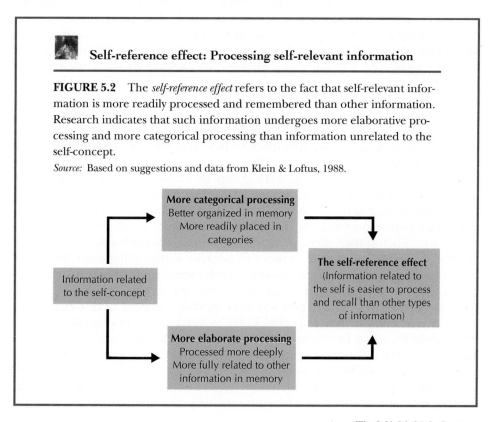

Self-reference effect: Processing self-relevant information

FIGURE 5.2   The *self-reference effect* refers to the fact that self-relevant information is more readily processed and remembered than other information. Research indicates that such information undergoes more elaborative processing and more categorical processing than information unrelated to the self-concept.

Source: Based on suggestions and data from Klein & Loftus, 1988.

More categorical processing
Better organized in memory
More readily placed in categories

Information related to the self-concept

The self-reference effect
(Information related to the self is easier to process and recall than other types of information)

More elaborate processing
Processed more deeply
More fully related to other information in memory

FOR EACH PERSON, MANY SELVES ARE POTENTIALLY POSSIBLE. When people speak about themselves, they often assume stability and the absence of change. Despite this, most of us realize that we can and do change. You are not the same person you were ten years ago, and you can safely assume that ten years from now you will not be exactly the same person you are today. Your daydreaming fantasies are likely to involve how you might change once you get out of school, get married, enter a career, make more money, or move to a new location. So, along with a self-concept, we are each somewhat aware of other, **possible selves**, as well.

Markus and her colleagues (e.g., Markus & Nurius, 1986) contend that each person's self-concept at any given time is actually only a *working self-concept* that is open to change in response to new experiences, new feedback, and new self-relevant information. We also actively imagine and sometimes take steps to bring about alternate selves by getting in better shape physically, learning to play the piano, changing our hair styles, and so forth. We can also imagine alternate selves that are less desirable—ourselves gaining weight, losing our friends, developing lung disease, and so forth.

Alternative possible selves affect us in several ways (Markus & Nurius, 1986). First, they affect motivation, because an image of a future self acts as an incentive to work hard, study, exercise, stop smoking, save money, and so on, so that you can become a college graduate, an attorney, a businessperson, a homeowner, or whatever seems an ideal goal to you. Second, there is sometimes a discrepancy between self-perceptions and the way others perceive us. We see ourselves as we are *and* as we hope to become; other people are likely to see only the current self. Third, discrepancies between how we are and how we would like to be can be painful and emotionally upsetting (Van Hook & Higgins, 1988). Fourth, individual differences arise, in that some people (optimists) envision positive self-changes in the future while others (pessimists) view their future selves in negative terms.

The concept of possible selves has led to some interesting research. In one such study Porter, Markus, and Nurius (1984) asked thirty individuals who were the victims of a major crisis in their lives (death of someone close to them, a critical illness, etc.) to describe their current selves and possible future selves. Those who reported having recovered from the crisis and those who had not recovered were found to describe similar current selves—they were fearful, resentful, and depressed, and felt a loss of control. The two groups differed, however, in their imagined future selves. The recovered group described future selves that were happy, confident, secure, optimistic, and involved with many friends; while the poor-recovery group envisioned future selves that were unpopular, unimportant, weak, depressed, and prone to failure.

In considering possible selves ("What do you want to be when you grow up?"), one person may imagine many alternatives while another considers only a very limited number. According to Niedenthal, Setterlund, and Wherry (1992), the more limited the number of possible selves, the greater the affective response—positive *or* negative—to any informational feedback about one's ability to become a particular self. For example, if you are considering twenty possible careers, finding that you are not especially talented in one of them is not very upsetting. If your only goal in life is wrapped up in one career possibility, however, it may be devastating to you to learn that you lack the necessary ability. In research designed to test this proposal, the investigators assessed *possible self-concept complexity* (number of aspects or categories of one's possible self). Participants then received success or failure feedback relevant to their goals—science skills for premed students, artistic creativity for art majors, future marital happiness for females in introductory psychology. As hypothesized, the more alternative possible selves an individual considered, the less positive the emotional response to success feedback and the less negative the response to failure feedback. (In a similar way, the more complex a person's present self-concept, the less is the affective response to feedback relevant to present goals.) It appears that it is emotionally beneficial to consider multiple alternatives for one's future *and* for one's present.

The realization that individuals have many possible selves in addition to their current working self-concepts presents a more complicated, but probably more accurate picture of how human beings conceive of themselves.

SELF-ESTEEM: ATTITUDES ABOUT ONESELF

We have just seen how people differ in describing their future selves in optimistic versus pessimistic terms. They also differ in describing their current selves in positive or negative terms. **Self-esteem** refers to the self-evaluations each individual makes. A person expressing *high self-esteem* believes himself or herself to be fundamentally good, capable, and worthy; *low self-esteem* is a view of oneself as useless, inept, and unworthy. The opinions expressed by others probably help shape these attitudes, and outsiders' opinions may sometimes bring about changes in one's self-esteem. Self-evaluations are also affected by the characteristics of others with whom we compare ourselves (Brown et al., 1992). With respect to people in general or those with whom we are not psychologically close, our self-views become more positive when we identify something *deficient* or *inadequate* about another person—a contrast effect. Thus, comparing oneself with someone who is worse off (downward comparison) results in a more positive mood and higher self-esteem (Reis, Gerrard, & Gibbons, 1993). When we feel psychologically close to another person, self-appraisals become more positive when we identify something *exceptionally good* about that person—an assimilation effect (Brown et al., 1992).

At any given time, of course, self-esteem refers to one's own evaluations of oneself rather than to the reactions or characteristics of others (see Figure 5.3). A large body of research has concentrated on this concept, because it is a

Low self-esteem affects feelings and behavior

FIGURE 5.3 A person's attitude about himself or herself is also known as *self-esteem*. As suggested here, low self-esteem is associated with unhappiness and interpersonal difficulties.

central and pervasive aspect of the self, influencing behavior even when esteem does not seem to be especially relevant to what is going on at the time (Greenwald, Bellazza, & Banaji, 1988).

THE DISCREPANCY BETWEEN SELF AND IDEAL SELF.   The difference between a person's perception of how he or she is and how that person believes he or she *should be* is known as **self–ideal discrepancy**. The less discrepancy between one's self and one's ideal self, the higher one's self-esteem.

Consider a situation in which you find a wallet containing $100 lying on the sidewalk. We all know the right thing to do, and ideally your behavior will match that standard; if you return the wallet, you will probably feel proud of yourself and evaluate yourself highly, experiencing high self-esteem. But the money may look very tempting, and you may decide to keep it. If so, any guilt about not doing the right thing and not living up to your ideals will result in a negative self-evaluation.

Transparency 12.1 THE CONSEQUENCES OF NEGATIVE SELF-EVALUATIONS.   Research has consistently shown that having positive self-regard is generally beneficial, provided that it is not carried to extremes. For example, people with high self-esteem tend to be less lonely than those whose self-esteem is low (see chapter 8), suggesting that a positive self-evaluation is associated with good social skills (Olmstead et al., 1991). In addition, the lower an individual's self-esteem, the more depressed that person feels (Pillow, West, & Reich, 1991). These effects of low self-esteem are shown in Figure 5.4.

There are a few situations, however, in which high self-esteem causes problems. At times, those with high self-esteem are *too* confident and optimistic about their ability, and they fail to live up to their expectancies. Such overconfidence is most likely to occur when the person's ability is threatened. To

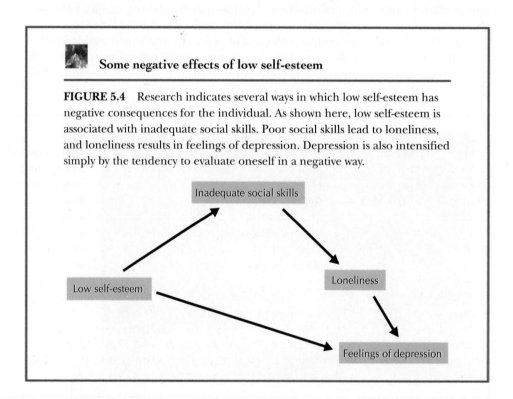

Some negative effects of low self-esteem

FIGURE 5.4   Research indicates several ways in which low self-esteem has negative consequences for the individual. As shown here, low self-esteem is associated with inadequate social skills. Poor social skills lead to loneliness, and loneliness results in feelings of depression. Depression is also intensified simply by the tendency to evaluate oneself in a negative way.

Inadequate social skills

Low self-esteem

Loneliness

Feelings of depression

determine how such processes operate, Baumeister, Heatherton, and Tice (1993) used a video game in which players have to steer an airplane as quickly as possible past hot-air balloons, trees, and other obstacles; time is lost whenever an obstacle is hit. After learning and practicing the game, each participant was given one last chance to reach a specific criterion score. Success would pay $2, but each player had the option of setting a higher speed goal and winning an extra dollar for each second faster than that; failure to reach the higher goal resulted in a loss of all the winnings. Half of the subjects were given this basic task, and those with low and high self-esteem won approximately the same amount of money (about $1.35). Half of the subjects were placed under threat by being told, "Now, if you are worried that you might choke under pressure or if you don't think you have what it takes to beat the target, then you might want to play it safe and just go for the two dollars. But it's up to you." In response to this threat, those with high self-esteem set overly high goals and showed a drop in performance, ending with an average winning of 25 cents. Those with low self-esteem actually performed better than before when threatened and won an average of about $3. This and follow-up experiments indicated that egotism causes those high in self-esteem to overreact to threat, setting goals that they cannot reach.

Other research indicates that depression is not just a matter of low self-esteem; it is also related to *variable self-esteem*. That is, those whose self-esteem frequently goes up or down in response to changes in the situation are the ones most likely to become depressed (Roberts & Monroe, 1992). The explanation is that anyone whose self-esteem is strongly affected by each minor occurrence has feelings of self-worth that are based on less stable sources than is true for those whose self-esteem remains at a fairly constant level.

Anyone who has felt lonely and depressed is likely to agree that these are unsatisfactory conditions. What can be done? Within the framework of self-discrepancy theories, self-esteem can be elevated either by changing behavior to match one's ideals or by lowering ideal standards to match more closely one's actual behavior. This may sound strange, but consider the people who set impossibly high standards for themselves. If, for example, you wish to be perfect in all that you do, never making mistakes and being liked by everyone you meet, these are almost certainly unreasonable goals, and your self-evaluation will be unnecessarily low. The best way to raise self-esteem in this context is to lower your expectations about what you want to be.

Is it common to adjust ideal standards in order to protect self-esteem? Most people are, in fact, attuned to do just this. Students who receive a favorable outcome—such as a good test score—are likely to internalize the result and take credit for being intelligent or for working hard (Burke, Hunt, & Bickford, 1985). An unfavorable outcome is more likely to be attributed to external factors (such as "the room was too hot" or "the instructor was unfair"). If this point seems familiar, it is because in chapter 2 we discussed taking credit for favorable outcomes and looking elsewhere for the cause of unfavorable events as attributional biases. Many common attributional biases serve to protect self-esteem.

If self-esteem represents the characteristic evaluation an individual makes, it would seem to be an internal *trait* or dispositional variable. If self-esteem can be raised or lowered in response to the evaluations of others, it would seem to be a temporary *state* that fluctuates with changes in the external situation. In fact, both trait and state concepts of self-esteem are accurate, and in the following section we will discuss research consistent with each.

SELF-ESTEEM AS A DISPOSITIONAL VARIABLE.   When self-esteem is conceptualized as a trait, it is measured along a positive-negative dimension that indicates where the person falls in relation to others. Dispositional self-esteem does not indicate a totally unchanging characteristic set in concrete but rather a general tendency to evaluate oneself in a relatively consistent way at different times and in many different situations. If your dispositional self-esteem is higher than the person sitting next to you, you probably feel better about yourself than he or she does—both today and next month, both after doing well on an exam and after doing poorly.

Most studies of trait self-esteem concentrate on environmental factors that bring about individual differences. Childhood experiences can be especially important, because children's self-concepts are in the process of being formed. For example, Felson (1989) found that children tend to evaluate themselves in part on the basis of how they think their parents evaluate them. A classic example is that of a child whose parents divorce; self-blame follows when the child makes the false assumption that one parent is leaving because the child did something wrong (see Figure 5.5, p. 183). Such childhood misperceptions may underlie the Kaplan and Pokorny (1971) finding that negative childhood events—having a parent enter a mental hospital, divorce, remarry, or die—are associated with low general self-esteem as an adult.

Data that require a more complicated explanation indicate that middle-born children have significantly lower self-esteem than first or last-born children (Kidwell, 1982). One suggestion is that the youngest child tends to receive the most parental affection and first-borns tend to be allowed the most freedom of action, leaving the middle-born offspring feeling unloved and mistrusted.

In contrast to the long-lasting effects of early experiences on dispositional self-esteem, situational effects in later life are likely to be temporary.

SITUATIONAL INFLUENCES ON SELF-ESTEEM.   Have you ever felt elated after something very positive happened to you, or really down in the dumps after an especially negative experience? If so, you know that your mood was affected, and very possibly your feelings about yourself as well. One explanation is that the emotionally relevant outcome of an immediate event commands more of our attention than long-term factors, so self-esteem may shift up or down. As a result, a temporary change in mood leads to an equally temporary change in self-esteem (Esses, 1989). Those who are already low in self-esteem are especially vulnerable to the effects of negative moods (Brown & Mankowski, 1993). These situationally based effects wear off in time, and one's self-esteem returns to its more customary level.

Self-esteem can be raised rather easily in an experimental setting; all researchers have to do is provide fake feedback indicating that an individual did well on a "personality test" (Greenberg et al., 1992). On the basis of what is known as the *terror management theory of self-esteem* (Solomon, Greenberg, & Pyszczynski, 1991), experimenters hypothesized that self-esteem acts to reduce anxiety. After having their self-esteem raised by the feedback (or, for the control group, *not* raised), participants were shown either a threatening video about ways to die or a nonthreatening, neutral video. The death video raised the anxiety of participants in the control group, but not those whose self-esteem had been raised. Later research with individuals expecting to receive a painful electric shock also found that increased self-esteem resulted in less anxiety. One explanation for these findings is that high self-esteem has a

Negative childhood events can result in low self-esteem

FIGURE 5.5 Research indicates that a variety of negative childhood events ranging from parental divorce and remarriage to the death of a parent can result in low self-esteem in adulthood. One reason seems to be the tendency for the child to assume that parents blame him or her for the problem and that they dislike the child as a consequence; the child then adopts this perceived negative evaluation as a self-evaluation.

"buffering" function that protects the person against the anxiety that threat can cause.

Social identity and its consequences also influence self-esteem, as was shown in research by Hirt et al. (1992). Among sports fans, one aspect of social identity involves identification with a specific team or teams. Hirt and his colleagues reasoned that the success or failure of a fan's team would affect the self-esteem of the fan. In one experiment, one group of Indiana University basketball fans watched Bobby Knight's Hoosiers in a winning game while another group saw the team lose. (A control group watched a Division II basketball game between schools irrelevant to Indiana fans: South Dakota State versus Jacksonville State.) Self-esteem was found to become more positive after an I.U. victory and more negative after the team lost; no such effects were found in the control group. In addition, the changes in the fans' self-esteem influenced their mood, their estimates of the team's future success, and their estimates of their own future performance in tasks involving mental and social skills. Considering that this study involved identification with a basketball team rather than the individual's gender, race, religion, or any other central aspect of self, these findings provide clear indications of the importance of social identity in our lives.

MEASURING SELF-ESTEEM.   If you need to assess someone's self-esteem, the simplest way is to ask whether that person feels good or bad about himself or herself. Other people do not always tell you how they really feel, however, so more subtle methods may be necessary. One possibility is to pay attention to others' behavior to determine whether they seem to be self-positive or self-negative. For example, when you observe Hamlet deliberating on whether or not to end his troubled life, it seems a safe guess that his self-esteem is low. Even overt behavior may be deceptive, however. If you see someone sitting quietly and looking out the window of a bus, train, or plane, you probably have no clue as to whether that individual's self-esteem is high or low.

The general solution chosen by psychologists is to utilize a scale to measure self-esteem—a series of statements to which the person responds. Each response is scored, and the total score provides an indication of general, or "global," self-esteem. A recent example of such a measure is the **Collective Self-Esteem Scale**. This test specifically treats the concept of self within a social framework by measuring feelings about the social groups to which the individual belongs (Luhtanen & Crocker, 1992). The goal is to measure self-esteem as related to *social identity* rather than *personal identity*. This test contains sixteen items selected to assess self-esteem in public and private situations. The items deal with how subjects feel about the social groups to which they belong, how they feel about their contributions to those groups, how others evaluate the groups, and how important the memberships are to their identity.

How were the items selected? As is often the case, new scales are developed to measure what earlier scales such as that of Rosenberg (1965) already measure, but with the goal of doing so more precisely and more specifically. The initial measures of self-esteem usually contained a mixture of items dealing with many aspects of behavior; those items that correlated with one another were retained to measure the general construct. For example, Butler and Haigh (1954) developed a measure with one hundred positive and negative self-statements involving such attributes as poise, intelligence, sexual attractiveness, hopelessness, hostility, and unreliability. With the Collective Self-Esteem Scale, the investigators focused on a more limited aspect of behavior and used statements believed to measure self-esteem with respect to membership in social groups. Statistical analysis revealed that four different components (or factors) are measured by this new scale, as shown in Table 5.1, and scores on this test correlate with Rosenberg's measure of self-esteem.

Presumably, other specific aspects of social identity could be measured in the same general way. For example, items such as "I often regret that I belong

The *Collective Self-Esteem Scale* measures a specific aspect of self-esteem: the way an individual evaluates his or her membership in social groups. This scale consists of four components, and sample scale items are shown for each component.

TABLE 5.1 Components of collective self-esteem

The Collective Self-Esteem Scale

Membership Component	Private Component	Public Component	Identity Component
I feel I don't have much to offer to the social groups I belong to.	I often regret that I belong to some of the social groups I do.	Overall, my social groups are considered good by others.	The social groups I belong to are an important reflection of who I am.
I am a worthy member of the social groups I belong to.	I feel good about the social groups I belong to.	Most people consider my social groups, on the average, to be more ineffective than other social groups.	Overall, my group memberships have very little to do with how I feel about myself.

Source: Based on information in Luhtanen & Crocker, 1992.

to some of the social groups I do" could be rewritten as "I often regret that I am a male (or, a Canadian, Catholic, homosexual, or Irish-American). This kind of approach can potentially extend what we know about various aspects of self-esteem.

SELF-EFFICACY: DIFFERENTIAL EXPECTATIONS OF COMPETENCE

Self-efficacy is the component of the self-concept that deals with one's perceived abilities and competencies to deal with a given task (Bandura, 1977). Self-efficacy is often confused with self-esteem, perhaps because when one feels a lack of self-efficacy, low self-esteem is likely to follow. The difference is that self-efficacy is much more dependent on the specific situation than is self-esteem.

Further, feelings of self-efficacy do not usually generalize from one situation to another (unless the two situations are *very* similar). An example is provided by Burger and Palmer (1992), who studied university students just after they had experienced the 1989 earthquake in California. Immediately after the event, students reported feeling vulnerable to natural disasters and unable to cope with them. That is, their self-efficacy was low in this specific context. In other aspects of their lives (such as school performance), feelings of vulnerability and inability to cope were unaffected.

People seem to be able to distance themselves from areas of low self-efficacy so that their overall self-esteem remains unaffected. For example, you may be great in math but a hopelessly clumsy tennis player. You can easily define math and your self-efficacy in that subject as important aspects of yourself while perceiving tennis as something that is irrelevant in your life. In effect, you don't care that you are incompetent at tennis. So, despite a lack of self-efficacy in certain situations, it is possible to maintain a self-image that is favorable overall.

SELF-EFFICACY AND PERFORMANCE.   Self-efficacy is highly relevant in settings that involve physical and academic task performance. Feelings of self-efficacy can lead to better performance, independently of the person's ability.

Gould and Weiss (1981) found that people high in self-efficacy are able to last longer than low-efficacy individuals in exercise involving physical endurance. Bandura and his colleagues (1988) were able to show that physical performance lasts longer because high self-efficacy stimulates the body to produce *endogenous opioids,* which function as natural painkillers.

Among professors, self-efficacy is one of the predictors of academic success—along with the job involvement component of the Type A personality that is discussed in chapters 11 and 13 (Taylor et al., 1984). As outlined in Figure 5.6, p. 186, these two dispositional characteristics lead to behaviors (goal setting and involvement in multiple projects) that result in professional recognition (productivity and citations of their work); recognition, in turn, leads to academic success as defined by rank and salary.

Transparency 12.4

In a group of college students, Tuckman and Sexton (1990) examined the relationship between self-efficacy and the ability to write test questions for a class; those high in efficacy wrote better questions than those who were low. The students were also asked to predict how well they would do at this task. Those with high self-efficacy tended to outperform their expectations, while those with low self-efficacy didn't live up to their expectancies. It appears that high self-efficacy can boost performance, while low self-efficacy hinders it.

Transparency 12.5

Discussion Question 3

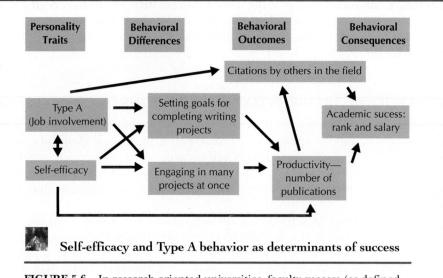

Personality Traits	Behavioral Differences	Behavioral Outcomes	Behavioral Consequences

Citations by others in the field

Type A (Job involvement)

Setting goals for completing writing projects

Self-efficacy

Engaging in many projects at once

Productivity—number of publications

Academic sucess: rank and salary

Self-efficacy and Type A behavior as determinants of success

FIGURE 5.6 In research-oriented universities, faculty success (as defined by rank and salary) is found to be determined in part by such dispositional variables as self-efficacy and the job involvement component of Type A behavior. Faculty members who are high in self-efficacy and job involvement tend to set goals and engage in many projects simultaneously. These behaviors lead to their work being published and being cited by others. Productivity and citations, in turn, lead to academic success.

Self-efficacy is almost always beneficial. For example, patients high in self-efficacy adapt better to illness and disorders such as rheumatoid arthritis (Schiaffino & Revenson, 1992).

SELF-EFFICACY IN SOCIAL SITUATIONS.   So far we have discussed the effects of self-efficacy on performing specific and tangible tasks. Social situations can also be viewed as tasks involving the ability to conduct oneself in an appropriate manner. As you might expect, those with low social self-efficacy experience high levels of social anxiety (Jennings, 1985; Morris, 1985). These negative feelings, in turn, lead the individual to avoid social situations. As a result, there is little opportunity to learn new and better social skills. It is also true that levels of self-efficacy differ in different social situations. One undergraduate may perform very comfortably in a party setting but be a bundle of nerves when asked to talk in front of a class; another student may show exactly the opposite pattern.

People with low social self-efficacy make different attributions than do high-efficacy individuals about the outcomes of social interactions, as shown by Alden (1986). This experimenter found that feedback inconsistent with a person's perceptions of his or her social abilities was interpreted as externally caused. For example, when someone with high social self-efficacy received negative feedback after a social exchange, the unfavorable outcome was attributed not to deficient social skills but to something about the situation. Negative feedback for those low in social self-efficacy, however, was interpreted in terms of lack of ability. You can think of these results as involving self-schemas relevant to social self-efficacy; when information fails to fit our schema, we reinterpret it to *make* it fit.

FACTORS THAT INFLUENCE SELF-EFFICACY.   Feelings of self-efficacy can be changed. A psychology major who originally feels confident about being able to cope with the statistical requirements of this field may later decide that his or her skills simply don't include data analysis. Conversely, a friendly and informative statistics course can raise a student's level of understanding and feelings of efficacy in this area. In effect, the student will find that previously incomprehensible material has become understandable; the situation thus can be mastered through direct, successful experience (Bandura, 1986).

Discussion Question 2

Social comparison (see chapter 7) can also affect self-efficacy (Bandura, 1986). For example, when a person does well on a task relative to the performance of other people, the perception of self-efficacy rises. A more direct social influence occurs when someone who is believable convinces you that your performance is good. In studies of *bogus feedback,* another person inflates or deflates one's feedback about task performance (Bandura, 1986). This is most effective in a situation in which the person has no prior conceptions about his or her abilities. When a child ties a shoelace for the first time, an adult who praises or criticizes the performance can have a major impact on feelings of self-efficacy involving this skill.

Discussion Question 4

Self-efficacy can also be raised whenever a person's success in a given activity is clearly defined and available for recall. In various sports, coaches often exhort their teams by invoking images of outstanding performances and the fruits of success. The strong image of the desired behavior can increase an athlete's feelings of self-efficacy and hence improve performance. In the former Soviet Union, sports psychologists went a step farther and showed athletes videotapes of their best performances, sometimes edited to make the performance look better than it had actually been (Feltz, 1982). Again, self-efficacy and performance improved.

In the following **Classic Contributions** section, we describe an early application of the concept of self-efficacy in research designed to reduce fear of snakes.

Focus on Research: The Classic Contributions

THE ROLE OF SELF-EFFICACY IN SNAKE PHOBIA

Albert Bandura originated the concept of self-efficacy and proposed that it was applicable to a wide variety of situations, including therapy. Bandura and his colleagues performed a series of experiments that dealt with phobias. The goal was to show that a single cognitive mechanism, self-efficacy, was the underlying factor in defensive reactions such as phobia. Further, it was hypothesized that all forms of behavioral therapy strengthen self-efficacy—thus procedures that reduced a phobia should also raise self-efficacy.

To test this idea, Bandura and Adams (1977) recruited snake-phobic individuals through newspaper ads and determined their perceptions of self-efficacy in situations involving a snake, as in Figure 5.7, p. 188. The participants

 **Snake phobia: Fear, arousal, and low self-efficacy**

FIGURE 5.7   The role of self-efficacy in phobias was shown in a series of investigations by Bandura. A phobic individual responds to certain cues (such as snakes) with fear, physiological arousal, and feelings of low self-efficacy in being able to deal with the situation. After the individual undergoes behavior therapy based on systematic desensitization, the fear and arousal decrease in the presence of the feared stimulus, and feelings of self-efficacy increase.

included individuals who were sufficiently afraid of snakes that they could not engage in gardening or play golf; one person was even afraid to use the toilet after reading about a snake that had been flushed into the sewer system. As expected, efficacy was low—these fearful volunteers had little or no confidence in their ability to cope with a snake under any circumstances. The next step was a process of **systematic desensitization** in which the participants were gradually taught over a series of trials to relax in the presence of snake cues such as photographs, toy snakes, a small snake in a glass cage, and so on. After becoming desensitized, these individuals were tested on a series of twenty-nine different tasks involving a red-tiled boa constrictor. The tasks ranged from low threat (observing the snake from a distance through glass) to high threat (letting the snake slither across one's lap). The desensitization process was a success in that all subjects were eventually able to come in contact with the snake without discomfort. The experimenters were also able to verify the hypothesis that as the phobia was overcome, feelings of self-efficacy increased.

Another aspect of this experiment dealt with the amount of physiological arousal experienced by the participants while they were performing the twenty-nine snake-related tasks. The decrease in phobic behavior was accompanied by a decrease in physiological arousal as well as an increase in self-efficacy. Bandura hypthesized that arousal is a source of information relevant to both cognitive and emotional processes. That is, the awareness of decreased arousal informs the individual that he or she is performing well with the feared object, and this information increases self-efficacy.

Bandura and Adams also tested the generalization of the increases in self-efficacy and found that they did not transfer to other situations, such as social interactions. Once again, we see that self-efficacy is situation-specific.

In subsequent research the same principles were successfully applied to other snake-phobic individuals as well as to some whose phobias involved spiders and still others who were *agoraphobic*—afraid of open spaces (Bandura, Adams, & Hardy, 1980; Bandura, Reese, & Adams, 1982).

SELF-MONITORING BEHAVIOR: EMPHASIS ON INTERNAL VERSUS EXTERNAL FACTORS

Snyder and his colleagues have identified **self-monitoring behavior** as still another important component of the self (Gangestad & Snyder, 1985; Snyder & Ickes, 1985). Self-monitoring refers to the degree to which individuals regulate their behavior on the basis of the external situation and the reactions of others (high self-monitors) or on the basis of internal factors such as their own beliefs, attitudes, and interests (low self-monitors).

Exercise 1

In the original formulation of self-monitoring, it was assumed that high self-monitors engage in role-playing in an attempt to behave so as to receive positive evaluations from others. Thus, high self-monitoring was described as a useful characteristic for people such as politicians, salespeople, and performers, who wish to please those with whom they interact. More recently, Schwalbe (1991) proposed that the high self-monitoring behavior of some individuals is based not on skillfully tuned role-playing in response to the reactions of other people but on relatively permanent images or "scripts" assumed to be appropriate in a given situation. For example, a college student may always be outgoing and amusing with those his own age and always quiet and shy with older individuals—regardless of how others are actually responding to his behavior. This theory suggests two types of high self-monitors—those guided by the audience and those guided by assumptions about what to do in particular situations, irrespective of any specific audience reaction.

MEASURING SELF-MONITORING BEHAVIOR.   The first measuring device for this construct was the **Self-Monitoring Scale** developed by Snyder (1974). This test requires the respondent to express agreement or disagreement with a series of statements that reflect either emplasis on internal reasons to act or a tendency to be guided by external cues. Examples of these items are shown in Table 5.2, p. 190.

Though various criticisms and modifications of the Self-Monitoring Scale have been offered (Beauvois & Le Poultier, 1986; Briggs & Cheek, 1988; Montag & Levin, 1990), there is considerable evidence supporting the validity of the original measure. For example, Lippa and Donaldson (1990) conducted a field study in which Snyder's test was used. Students first responded to a computer program asking them to list the primary people with whom they interacted, the situations in which the interactions took place, and their characteristic behavior in such situations. Then they completed the Self-Monitoring Scale, and—over a ten-day period—they kept a detailed behavioral diary. Scores on the scale were found to predict the consistency of their behav-

On Snyder's *Self-Monitoring Scale,* respondents answer each item by indicating whether it is true or false with respect to themselves. On the sample items presented here, high self-monitors would tend to agree with the first two and to disagree with the second two.

TABLE 5.2   Measuring self-monitoring behavior

Items from the Self-Monitoring Scale

When I am uncertain how to act in social situations, I look to the behavior of others for cues.

In different situations and with different people, I often act like very different persons.

My behavior is usually an expression of my true inner feelings, attitudes, and beliefs.

I would not change my opinions (or the way I do things) to please someone else or to win their favor.

Source: Based on information in Snyder, 1974.

ior as indicated on the computer program and in the diaries. That is, high self-monitors were responsive to specific situations and audiences, and low self-monitors behaved in consistent ways regardless of the situation. Other research also indicates that low self-monitors vary less from situation to situation than high self-monitors (Koestner, Bernieri, & Zuckerman, 1992).

Critical Thinking Question 2

CORRELATES OF SELF-MONITORING BEHAVIOR. The differential attention paid to situation versus self is even reflected in how individuals react to advertising. Some ads emphasize information about quality and intrinsic rewards, while others emphasize image and extrinsic rewards—as shown in Figure 5.8, p. 191. DeBono and Packer (1991) found that high self-monitors rated advertised products more positively and perceived them as more self-relevant after seeing an image-based ad ("Heineken—you're moving up"). Low self-monitors liked the products better and perceived them as more self-relevant after seeing a quality-based ad ("Heineken—you can taste the difference"). The distinction seems to be based on whether one is concerned about the product making a good impression on others or about liking the product oneself.

Reading: Lesko (13), The Many Me's of the Self-Monitor

Because high self-monitors are especially concerned about public approval, Cutler and Wolfe (1989) proposed that these individuals would express more confidence in their decisions in order to be liked more. Examples of such behavior can be found in politics. Politicians who waver in their opinions or qualify their beliefs are perceived as having low confidence in their decisions and as being deficient as leaders (see chapter 14). In the 1992 presidential election, H. Ross Perot lost many of his supporters when he entered the primaries, then dropped out of the race, then changed his mind a second time by reentering the contest. In their research Cutler and Wolfe found that, indeed, high self-monitoring, as hypothesized, was linked to being confident about one's decisions. Interestingly enough, this confidence was unrelated to the accuracy of the decisions!

SELF-MONITORING AS A FACTOR IN INTERPERSONAL BEHAVIOR. High self-monitors would be expected to pay attention to others and low self-monitors to pay attention to themselves. These hypothesized differences do occur, even in speech patterns. Ickes, Reidhead, and Patterson (1986) discovered that low self-monitors were more likely than high self-monitors to speak in the first person (I, me, my, mine, etc.). High self-monitors were relatively more likely to speak in the third person (he, she, her, his, their, etc.). Such differences suggest that high self-monitors are more attentive to and concerned with the actions and reactions of others, while low self-monitors are more concerned with themselves.

These differences in attention are also reflected in the interpersonal choices people make. High self-monitors tend to select a companion (for example, a tennis partner) on the basis of how well the other person performs; low self-monitors are more likely to choose a companion on the basis of how much they like the other person (Snyder, Gangestad, & Simpson, 1983). Why? The explanation is based on an emphasis on the situation (I want to *play tennis* with

 Advertising: Quality versus image

FIGURE 5.8 Studies of self-monitoring behavior indicate that high self-monitors rate an advertised product more positively when the ad stresses image and what other people will think if the consumer purchases it. Low self-monitors rate a product more positively when the ad stresses quality and information about how the consumer will benefit from it.

you) versus an emphasis on personal feelings about the other person (I want to play tennis with *you*). The results of this and other investigations (Snyder & Simpson, 1984) provide evidence that low self-monitors are more committed to individuals while high self-monitors are more committed to situations.

Some of these findings may suggest that low self-monitors are better adjusted than those who score high on this dimension. For example, people tend to believe that consistency across situations is preferable to inconsistency (Beauvois & Dubois, 1988). Research indicates, however, that individuals who score between the two extremes are less maladjusted than those on the two ends of the spectrum (Miller & Thayer, 1989). Compared to people whose scores fall in the middle of the dimension, neuroticism was greater among high self-monitors (whose behavior fluctuates with the situation) *and* low self-monitors (whose behavior is unvarying, regardless of the situation).

SELF-FOCUSING: THE RELATIVE IMPORTANCE OF SELF

So far we have examined several aspects of the self, including the way one's self-esteem and feelings of self-efficacy are affected by situational factors and also the way these elements of the self (along with self-monitoring tendencies) influence behavior. We now examine the self in a slightly different way. **Self-focusing** refers to the centrality of an individual's sense of self. The extent to which you are self-focused is indicated by the degree to which your attention is directed inward towards yourself as opposed to outward toward the environment (Fiske & Taylor, 1991).

Self-focusing is tied to memory and cognition. You can focus on yourself only if you can recall relevant past events and process relevant current information. Klein, Loftus, and Burton (1989) have identified two areas of memory involving self-focusing. Self-focus affects the accuracy of biographical recall (how well you can retrieve factual information about yourself) and the complexity of self-descriptive judgments (Dixon & Baumeister, 1991). If you were asked "are you happy with your social life?", would you answer the same way as if you were asked "are you unhappy with your social life?" In other words, does the wording (framing) of the question lead you to focus on specific positive versus negative aspects of yourself? Kunda et al. (1993) find that one's memory and one's working self-conception *are* affected by such questions, but only if one's self-knowledge contains both positive and negative elements. For example, if your social life were totally positive, the wording of a question about it would be irrelevant.

In addition, a brief period of self-focusing improves self-insight, in that research participants who are instructed to think briefly about themselves are better able to make accurate assessments of social feedback than those not given such an opportunity (Hixon & Swann, 1993). We will now describe how these processes operate.

SELF-FOCUSING AS A TRAIT, OR AT LEAST A TENDENCY.   Duval and Wicklund (1972) suggested that a person who is high in self-focusing (or self-awareness) either acts to reduce any discrepancies between his or her self-concept and actual behavior or avoids situations in which such discrepancies occur. In both instances, behavior is influenced by whether or not attention is focused on the self (Carver & Scheier, 1981). As with self-monitoring behavior, those whose self-focus is strong would be expected to show consistent behavior across situations, while a weak self-focus would be associated with behavior that changed as the situation changed.

Because one's self-concept contains multiple elements, it is possible to focus on only a portion of it at any one time. For example, Showers (1992a) has provided evidence that many people store positive and negative aspects of themselves separately in memory. Thus, if the individual focuses on the negative, his or her mood and subsequent behavior will be different than if the focus is on the positive. Some individuals, however, seem to store positive and negative self-knowledge together; the result is less negative affect and higher self-esteem (Showers, 1992b). The most general conclusion is that the organization of self-evaluations affects self-esteem and mood beyond what could be predicted on the basis of simply the *amount* of positive and negative content. Additional implications of this conceptualization are currently being explored in further research.

Work in Progress

Compartmentalizing Self-Information: Warding Off Depression in Times of Stress

As we will discuss in chapter 13, changes in one's life (such as divorce, death of a loved one, or moving to a new location) tend to be stressful. Showers and Ryff (1993) proposed that individual differences in self-organization influence the emotional effects of such events. The basic prediction is that a well-differentiated (compartmentalized) self-concept helps control the effects of stress *if* some of the separate domains of information are *very positive* and *very important* to the individual.

Showers and Ryff based their research on a survey of 120 women aged fifty-five and older who had relocated during the past year (Ryff & Essex, 1992). Professor Showers calculated the degree of self-compartmentalization for each woman on the basis of self-ratings of the positive and negative aspects—following the move—of such domains as daily activities, health, finances, family, and friends.

Consistent with earlier laboratory findings, women who perceived *great improvement* in one or more important domains of the self (compartmentalized organization) were less depressed than women who experienced the same average level of improvement spread evenly across several domains of the self (integrative organization). Thus, high evaluative differentiation was beneficial.

Professor Showers suggests that having separate, positive aspects of the self to fall back on when stress occurs may protect the person against depression. It also appears that both styles of organization can be useful. That is, a compartmentalized organization may be most helpful if one focuses on positive domains and ignores negative domains in times of stress. An integrative organization may help the person deal with negative domains without experiencing a decrease in general self-esteem. In future research, Showers hopes to determine just how people develop the tendency to integrate or to compartmentalize evaluative information about the self.

Though the self-content on which a person focuses influences mood (Sedikides, 1992), mood also affects self-focusing behavior, and environmental factors in turn affect one's mood (Salovey, 1992). If you are in a negative mood, for example, because you have a toothache and are scheduled to visit the dentist, you are more likely to recall (focus on) negative aspects of your self. The extent and the content of the self-focusing behavior as well as mood can affect expectations. Thus, a depressed individual who is self-focused on negative content is more pessimistic than either nondepressed individuals or

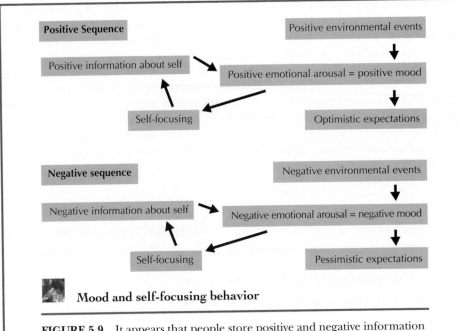

Positive Sequence

Positive environmental events

Positive information about self

Positive emotional arousal = positive mood

Self-focusing

Optimistic expectations

Negative sequence

Negative environmental events

Negative information about self

Negative emotional arousal = negative mood

Self-focusing

Pessimistic expectations

Mood and self-focusing behavior

FIGURE 5.9 It appears that people store positive and negative information about themselves separately in memory. The diagram illustrates the relationships among positive versus negative self-information, self-focusing, mood arousal, and optimistic versus pessimistic expectations. Thus, outside events can affect one's mood, mood can affect whether one focuses on negative or positive self-information, and information plus mood can affect expectations.

Exercise 2   other depressed individuals who are *not* self-focused on negative content. Figure 5.9 presents examples of how these factors are interrelated.

Though little research has been done to determine why some people are more self-focused than others, Ullman (1987) examined some of the developmental aspects of this behavior. He found that young children tend to define themselves to others in terms of external characteristics (age, sex, etc.). As adolescents grow older, they concentrate more on defining themselves to others in terms of their "true" selves (personal qualities, etc.). Thus, from childhood to adolescence, self-focusing increases.

SITUATIONAL INFLUENCES ON SELF-FOCUSING.   Though the tendency to be relatively self-focused or not reflects the trait aspects of focusing, no one is *uniformly* self-focused or situation-focused. People can even be induced to focus on themselves through simple instructions (Johnson, 1987). That is, you can direct where your attention is focused—right now, think about your most unpleasant characteristics. You can do that, or you can think about (recall) the most pleasant ones. In addition, external cues, such as the presence of a mirror, act to increase self-focusing.

In everyday behavior self-awareness is not always a conscious process (Epstein, 1983), so we may not notice how much self-focusing is occurring in a given situation. In general, if you are in a familiar, comfortable situation, you pay less attention to the environment and more attention to yourself. If the situation is unfamiliar and threatening, environmental cues become all-important. Think of the difference between driving along a familiar road in daylight and navigating an unfamiliar road on a rainy night. Self-focusing in the first situation is common, but in the second situation it could be fatal.

In some circumstances, self-focusing and the situation can have reciprocal effects. Strentz and Auerbach (1988) studied FBI agents in training who took part in a realistic simulated abduction in which they were assigned the role of hostages for four days. The trainees were abducted from an FBI van by staff members dressed like Middle Eastern terrorists. The abductors fired their guns (using blanks), and the van's driver and his assistant broke concealed blood bags as they dropped to the ground, apparently murdered. A few of the trainees thought that real terrorists had interrupted the exercise with an actual kidnapping. The trainees were handcuffed, a pillowcase was placed on each person's head, and they were driven to a secret location. Before the abduction began, some of the trainees were told to concentrate on their emotional state (self-focusing) during the experience; some were told to concentrate on the events (situation-focusing); and still others received no instructions. Those who focused on themselves reported the least anxiety and emotional distress, and observers rated their behaviors as showing less distress than the situation-focused or no-instruction groups. In addition, the self-focused individuals were found to seek more social support (see chapter 13) during the abduction than those in the other two conditions, as shown in Figure 5.10. Social support was measured on a Ways of Coping checklist, on which the participants indicated their behavior with respect to such items as "talked to someone to find our about the situation" and "talked to someone about how I was feeling" (Folkman & Lazarus, 1980; Vitaliano, 1985). Presumably, in an extremely unpleasant situation, self-focusing results in additional emotional awareness and hence the need for interpersonal contact and communication.

Exercise 3

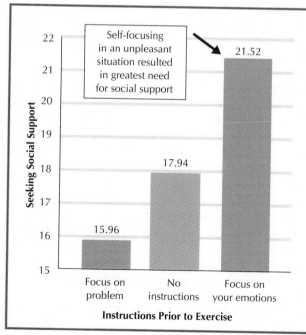

Self-focusing in an unpleasant situation resulted in greatest need for social support

21.52

17.94

15.96

Seeking Social Support

Focus on problem | No instructions | Focus on your emotions

Instructions Prior to Exercise

Self-focusing — seeking social support

FIGURE 5.10   FBI trainees took part in a four-day exercise in which they played the role of abducted hostages. Some were instructed to focus on their emotional state and some on the situation, while some were given no instructions. In this very unpleasant situation, self-focusing on emotions led to increased emotional awareness and the need to seek social support.
Source: Based on data in Strentz & Auerbach, 1988.

GENDER: MALENESS OR FEMALENESS AS A CRUCIAL ASPECT OF IDENTITY

We have been discussing social identity from the standpoint of individuals in terms of various processes of the self. As suggested at the very beginning of this chapter, however, each of us defines himself or herself in large part on the basis of various cultural subgroups, including race, nationality, religion, occupation, age, and so forth. In most societies the most central of these subgroupings, and a primary determinant of social identity, is maleness or femaleness.

The terms **sex** and **gender** are often used interchangeably. In our discussion, however, we will define *sex* in terms of biological factors, the anatomical and physiological differences that are genetically determined and present at birth. *Gender* will refer to essentially everything else associated with one's sex in a given society, including the roles, actions, preferences, and other attributes that are—or that the society assumes to be—typical of women or men.

BIOLOGICAL DETERMINANTS OF SEX

Before getting to the social psychological aspects of gender differences, we first consider the basic biological differences that define the two sexes.

WE BEGIN WITH EITHER AN *XX* OR AN *XY* CHROMOSOME.   The initial determination of who becomes a male and who a female is based on differences at the chromosomal level. A **chromosome** is a string of deoxyribonucleic acid (DNA) that contains genetic information. Human beings possess forty-six chromosomes (in twenty-three pairs) containing the blueprints that orchestrate our development in terms of species, sex, skin color, hair texture, eye color, body build, and many other aspects of our physical being.

One of the chromosome pairs determines the biological sex of each person. The mother contributes an X chromosome to this pair, and the father contributes either an X or a Y chromosome. If the offspring receives an X from each parent, her sex is female. If the offspring receives an X from the mother and a Y from the father, his sex is male (see Figure 5.11, p. 197). Thus, the father's chromosome determines the sex of the child. This is ironic because historically, in many cultures, the woman received praise (or, more often, blame) for producing offspring of a given sex.

Theoretically, the chance of inheriting a Y chromosome is 50 percent, but data indicate that in the United States about 105 males are born for every 100 females. There are, nevertheless, more females than males (about 51 percent to 49 percent), because males are more susceptible than females to virtually every kind of disease; they also die at a higher rate and an earlier age (Chester-Taxin, 1993). This relative fragility among males is in part a function of having a Y chromosome, which does not have as many genes as an X chromosome. This means that a male does not have a duplicate of every gene that is present on his X chromosome, while a female does. As a result some inherited diseases (such as *hemophilia*) occur only in males. Animal research has also suggested that after puberty males may be weakened by the task of continually producing sperm. Another explanation for these differences between men and women in health and longevity is that women take better care of themselves physically.

WHAT IS THE EFFECT OF HAVING AN *XY* VERSUS AN *XX* CHROMOSOME?   At conception and for a time afterward, future males and females are identical except that the former have a Y chromosome instead of two X's.

Chromosomes determine one's sex at conception

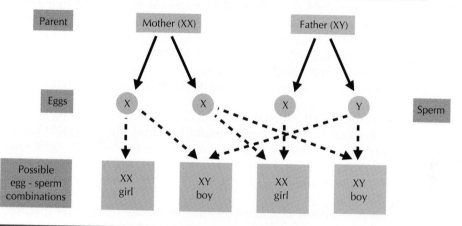

FIGURE 5.11 Each egg produced by females contains an X chromosome; males produce sperm of which about half contain an X and half contain a Y chromosome. The sex of the offspring is determined at conception. When a sperm carrying an X chromosome penetrates an egg, the result is an embryonic cell containing an XX combination, and a female has been conceived. When a sperm carrying a Y chromosome penetrates an egg, the result is an embryonic cell containing an XY combination, and a male has been conceived.

It appears that genes on the Y chromosome direct such fetal processes as the formation of testes in males (Page et al., 1987). The testicles and ovaries each develop from sexually undifferentiated gonadal tissue; when there is an XX pair, ovaries develop, while an XY pair results in testes.

As human fetal development continues, the different hormones produced by these structures influence other physical characteristics. There is an immediate effect on genital structure and the prostate gland and a delayed effect (at puberty) on such factors as facial hair, breasts, and a prominent Adam's apple—each of which differentiates males from females (Gooren & Cohen-Kettenis, 1991).

The primary question of interest to social psychologists is whether the sexes differ in other ways; and, if so, are the differences based on genetic determination or on conditions imposed by cultural beliefs and attitudes?

GENDER IDENTITY AND STEREOTYPES BASED ON GENDER

An individual's **gender identity** refers to the sex that the person associates with herself or himself. Most often, biological sex and gender identity match. It is possible, though much less common, for a person to be of one sex but to identify with the opposite gender—an identification known as *transsexualism.*

DEVELOPING A GENDER IDENTITY.   Adults generally react to a newborn's sex as an all-important defining characteristic. They want to know and to inform others of the baby's sex, they quickly provide a boy name or a girl name, select pink versus blue clothing, decorate the infant's room in a suitably masculine or feminine style, and begin the process of selecting "sex-appropriate" toys and wearing apparel.

Young children, meanwhile, are not ordinarily aware of either their sex or their gender until they are about age two. At this point they can identify themselves in terms of "girl" or "boy," though it is likely that these are simply labels supplied by parents or older siblings. Small children tend to be extremely self-centered and to assume that everyone else is like themselves physically, attitudinally, and perceptually (Piaget, 1965). Between the ages of four and seven, children acquire the principles of **gender consistency**. They come to the realization that gender is a basic attribute of an individual that remains the same over time and is unaffected by external factors like hair length or clothing style (Kelley & Byrne, 1992). It is sometimes upsetting and sometimes amusing to children (and to many adults as well) when there is a mismatch between such external factors and gender identity. For example, Johnny Cash sings of "A Boy Named Sue"—the name a father gives his son to ensure that the boy would be teased and have to fight and thus learn to defend himself.

Video: *Self and Gender**

THEORIES OF GENDER IDENTITY.   What accounts for differences between males and females beyond anatomical and physiological details? Historically, this question was not even raised, because male-female behavioral and attitudinal differences were assumed to constitute a biological given. Today, for a variety of reasons, many researchers argue that most of the differences are acquired.

Bem (1984) described four major theories of gender identity, two of which involve primarily social concepts. In *psychoanalytic theory*, Freud in 1933 proposed that a child comes to perceive himself or herself as having a specific gender through identification with the same-sex parent. This identification provides an acceptable resolution of the problems caused by the child's desire to possess the opposite-sex parent (Freud, 1963).

Cognitive-developmental theory assumes that gender identification results from cognitive development. Once children identify themselves as masculine or feminine, they then learn to identify the "appropriate" roles that are consistent with the chosen gender. Thus, **sex-typing** occurs when the child learns what it means to be a male or a female in a given culture.

Critical Thinking
Question 3
Social learning theory suggests that children observe their parents and learn to match certain behaviors with each parent. Over time, the child begins to generalize these matched behaviors to other people and to assume causality between the behaviors and gender—"Mommy wears a dress because she's a girl" or "Daddy wears a tie because he's a boy." Children also receive approval and support for engaging in gender-appropriate behavior but encounter disapproval for engaging in gender-inappropriate behavior. Consider the possible response of parents to a little girl who wants a doll for her birthday versus their response to a little boy who expresses the same wish. On the basis of observation and differential reinforcement, children learn to behave in gender-typed ways and to identify with one or the other gender.

Bem's (1983) own views combine social learning and cognitive developmental theories: *Gender schema theory* suggests that children have a "generalized readiness" to organize information about the self based on cultural definitions of sex-appropriate behavior (Bem, 1984).

Whatever the best explanation, children in the United States are found to have learned gender stereotypes by the time they reach the sixth grade (Carter & McCloskey, 1984). They identify behaviors in terms of gender suitability and

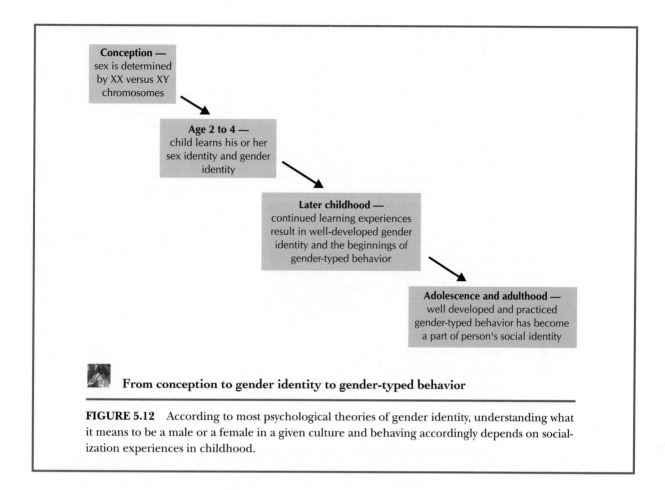

From conception to gender identity to gender-typed behavior

FIGURE 5.12 According to most psychological theories of gender identity, understanding what it means to be a male or a female in a given culture and behaving accordingly depends on socialization experiences in childhood.

express willingness to avoid or punish those who engage in out-of-role behavior. Figure 5.12 outlines the stages of development of gender identity.

Bem developed a measure of the extent to which individuals identify with the culturally defined norms of gender-typed (or sex-typed) behavior, as described in the following **Individual Diversity** section.

Individual Diversity

BEM'S SEX ROLE INVENTORY: DIFFERENCES IN ADHERENCE TO TYPICAL MASCULINE OR FEMININE ROLES

Given the importance of gender stereotypes in our everyday lives, social psychologists became interested in identifying such characteristics more specifically and in determining how they influence behavior. Sharon Bem was studying traits, and she became curious about how certain characteristics came to be considered typical of females, while others were considered typical of males. She also noted that despite these widely held perceptions, not all males

Reading: Lesko (14), *Bem Describes the Development of Her Sex-Role Inventory*

and females behaved according to the gender role assigned by society. The first task was to identify precisely the content of **sex-role stereotypes** and then to study the effects of individual differences in adherence to these stereotypes—**sex-role behavior.** Incidentally, in the terminology of this chapter, we would have used the terms gender-role stereotypes and gender-role behavior.

Bem (1974) made lists of the traits that seemed to be perceived as different for males and females, and this eventually developed into a measure known as the **Bem Sex Role Inventory** (**BSRI**). This test consists of a long list of characteristics to which one is asked to agree or disagree as to whether each trait applies to oneself. These characteristics were originally selected because they were rated as being more desirable for one sex than the other.

The gender differences identified by Bem in the 1970s appear to have changed very little in the 1980s and 1990s. Martin (1987) administered portions of the BSRI to a large group of research participants in Canada and asked them to estimate the percentage of North American adult males and adult females characterized by each trait. As summarized in Table 5.3, there was widespread agreement as to which characteristics applied to men and which to women. Men were believed to possess more leadership ability and to be more assertive, dominant, forceful, and so on than women. Women were believed to be more gentle, tender, compassionate, warm, and so on than men. Even when researchers limit participants to characterizing only *intelligent* males and females, the two genders are perceived differently. Intelligent women are described as being high in social skills while intelligent men are

On the *Bem Sex Role Inventory,* people in our culture perceive some characteristics as more masculine than feminine and some as more feminine than masculine. Individuals who respond to the scale indicate which items are and are not characteristic of them. People tend to adopt sex roles (gender roles) that are traditionally masculine, traditionally feminine, both (androgynous), or neither (undifferentiated).

TABLE 5.3 Male versus female role characteristics

Male Characteristics	Female Characteristics
leadership abilities	gentle
assertive	tender
dominant	compassionate
strong personality	warm
forceful	sympathetic
aggressive	sensitive
willing to take a stand	soothes hurt feelings
independent	affectionate
willing to take risks	understanding
defends beliefs	loves children

Source: Based on data in Martin, 1987.

perceived as being high in cognitive skills (Raty & Snellman, 1992). Chapter 6 discusses the potential effects of gender stereotypes along with the role they play in prejudice and discrimination.

In the scale itself, one-third of the items consist of traits perceived to be masculine and one-third feminine; the remaining third are neutral items. Respondents can accept or reject as many items as they wish as being self-descriptive. Each masculine trait that is endorsed earns points on the masculinity dimension and each feminine trait that is endorsed earns points on the femininity dimension.

Bem defines a sex-typed individual as one who scores high on either the masculine or the feminine dimension and low on the other. In describing themselves, high-self-esteem women are less tied to traditional gender stereotypes than low-self-esteem women. When, however, those with high self-esteem are induced to focus on gender issues (e.g., through writing an essay on how men and women think differently), they move closer to the stereotypes (James, 1993). If the person responding to the inventory scores high on both masculinity and femininity, he or she is said to be androgynous. **Androgyny** refers to the tendency to describe oneself as behaving in ways typical of both gender roles, and this is considered by some to be the preferred orientation—though that characterization remains controversial (Kelley & Byrne, 1992). A fourth category consists of individuals who endorse almost none of the items, and they are labeled *undifferentiated* with respect to gender roles.

Critical Thinking
Question 4

A great deal of research has focused on identifying the ways in which these different gender-related roles influence behavior. Many of the findings indicate the positive aspects of androgyny. For example, compared to those who endorse primarily masculine or feminine roles, androgynous men and women are liked better (Major, Carnevale, & Deaux, 1981); are better adjusted (Orlofsky & O'Heron, 1987); are more adaptable to various situational demands (Prager & Bailey, 1985); are more comfortable with their sexuality (Garcia, 1982); and are more satisfied interpersonally (Rosenzweig & Daley, 1989). In a marriage, when both partners are androgynous, marital satisfaction is higher than for spouses who represent any other combination (Zammichieli, Gilroy, & Sherman, 1988).

Other findings focus on the fact that males who express the masculine gender role tend to be more violent and aggressive than those who endorse other roles (Finn, 1986). On the other hand, a benefit for both women and men of being either masculine or androgynous is that these characteristics are associated with higher self-esteem than is found among those who are feminine or undifferentiated (Lau, 1989).

Altogether, the BSRI provides a way to identify gender stereotypes and to investigate the effects of adopting gender roles that fit or fail to fit these stereotypes.

BEHAVING IN WAYS CONSISTENT WITH GENDER ROLES

Once people learn to associate specific characteristics with their gender, they tend to behave in ways consistent with the stereotypes. Thus, **gender roles** represent the extension of stereotypes into actual activities deemed suitable for one or the other gender (Chatterjee & McCarrey, 1991).

Critical Thinking
Question 5

As discussed in chapter 6, the job market is one place where gender roles were especially visible in the past. To some extent, societal expectations about appropriate gender-based behaviors have influenced men and women to respond differently in the work context. To examine sex differences in response to occupational possibilities, Subich et al. (1986) presented undergraduates with information about three relatively unfamiliar occupations (administrative assistant, information analyst, and traffic coordinator). The participants were asked to indicate their interest in these occupations and the factors influencing their responses. Men expressed more interest in the novel jobs than women, had a higher expectation of success, and placed much more importance on salary. Women, in contrast, tended to emphasize whether the job would be personally satisfying to them.

However their perceptions and expectations may differ from those of men, women are now "full-scale participants in the world of work" (Norwood, 1992, p. 102). It is no longer as socially acceptable (or legal) to refuse anyone employment on the basis of his or her sex; nevertheless, some role restrictions based on sex still operate in the labor market (Kelley & Streeter, 1992). Evidence of the devaluation of feminine roles is provided by the finding that specific professions are perceived as less and less prestigious as the percentage of women in those professions increases (Johnson, 1991). As Figure 5.13, p. 203, suggests, the ongoing changes in our society with respect to stereotypes and gender discrimination remain a source of confusion and discomfort when men and women interact.

EFFECTS OF GENDER ROLES IN THE HOME.   One obvious place in which gender roles operate is in home life. Even when both partners are employed in demanding and high-paying jobs, work at home is most often divided along gender lines (see chapter 8). Men are likely to take out the garbage and perform the bulk of the "yard work," while women are more likely to engage in housecleaning, cooking, and child care. Altogether, women do more work at home than men, even if they are androgynous (Gunter & Gunter, 1991). Only those androgynous men with a high sense of responsibility perform their share of household tasks. Apparently, freedom from traditional gender roles ends somewhere short of the kitchen sink.

Despite the inequities of housework, women who are employed in an outside job are found to be higher in self-esteem, less anxious, and in better physical health than full-time homemakers (Coleman & Antonucci, 1983). When the quality of such employment is low, however, psychological distress is common unless the woman's husband and/or children provide considerable support (Barnett, Marshall, & Singer, 1992).

GENDER AS THE CRITERION FOR SELECTION.   When women are assigned a task and told that gender was the primary criterion for their being chosen, they evaluate their performance as less adequate than women who are told that the assignment was based on merit (Turner, Pratkanis, & Hardaway, 1991). This effect occurs regardless of whether the task is one typically viewed as masculine or feminine.

In politics, 1992 was declared to be the year of the woman in the United States. Many women won in races for the Senate and the House of Representatives. President Clinton appointed several women to high positions in his administration (see Figure 5.14, p. 204), though sexism slipped back in when only women nominees came under fire for hiring illegal aliens to care

Gender problems

FIGURE 5.13 As societal norms undergo change, gender roles, gender stereotypes, and gender discrimination create some degree of confusion, discomfort, and anger for many men and women.
Source: Universal Press Syndicate, February 22, 1981.

for their children. In the most important race of all, however, the major candidates for president of the United States were all men. When these individuals were asked when they expected a woman to be elected president, the typical response was that it would happen very soon, but not before 1996. Considering the fact that such a question and such an answer would have been unimaginable in the past (at least until Geraldine Ferraro was the Democratic vice-presidential candidate in 1984), perhaps this should be taken as a sign of progress beyond gender-role stereotypes. In many other nations (e.g., Israel, Great Britain, Pakistan, Nicaragua, India, Argentina, and the Phillipines), women have already served successfully in the role of chief executive (Genovese, 1993). In academia, U.S. women are still at a disadvantage with respect to doctorates granted, salaries, and professorships (Callaci, 1993).

SUPPORT FOR TRADITIONAL GENDER ROLES.   In the Judeo-Christian tradition men were originally specified as the owners of their families (Wolf, 1992). In the Talmud, for example, categories of property include cattle, women, and slaves. In the New Testament, Ephesians (5:22–24) instructs married women as follows: "Wives, be subject to your husbands as you are to the Lord. For the husband is the head of the wife just as Christ is the head of the Church." In a number of realms, traditional gender roles continue to be taught and—sometimes subtly—supported. For example, males and females are most often portrayed in children's books and stories in stereotypical ways (McArthur & Eisen, 1976; Weitzman et al., 1972) in which men and boys play more active roles while women and girls either tag along or need to be rescued. Think of such classics as *Snow White,* in which the heroine is saved from murder by the huntsman, goes into a frenzy of housecleaning for the dwarfs, is too dense to avoid the poisoned apple, is preserved in a glass case by the seven little men, and is eventually brought back to life by a kiss from the handsome prince. More recently, efforts have been made to locate and publish stories with brave and intelligent heroines who fight when necessary, rescue male victims, and otherwise engage in nontraditional feminine behavior (Phelps, 1981). Further, experiments indicate that after reading stories with reversed-role characters, third- and fourth-graders raise their expectations about what females can accomplish (Scott & Feldman-Summers, 1979).

Studies of prime-time television, soap operas, and even "Sesame Street" reveal that typical gender roles are portrayed more frequently than not (Helman & Bookspan, 1992; Manes & Melynk, 1974). Presumably, such depictions appeal to the majority of viewers.

TV advertising also tends to portray boys and girls (as well as men and women) in a very traditional fashion. Boys play with guns and trucks, girls with dolls and toy household appliances. Men engage in active sports, drink beer, and sometimes appreciate the food cooked by the wife or her skill at getting clothes both clean and soft. Women shop, clean, cook, and are grateful for the crumbs of masculine appreciation.

The year of the woman in politics?

FIGURE 5.14 During the election campaign, 1992 became known as the "year of the woman" because of the large number of successful female candidates. Later, the women appointed to various high positions in Clinton's administration added to the impression that women were playing increasingly important roles in governing the United States. How long do you think it will be before a woman is elected to the presidency?

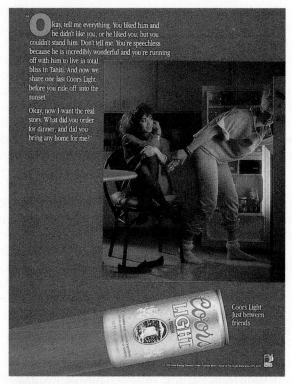

 Perpetuating traditional gender roles

FIGURE 5.15   From childhood on we are exposed to presentations in which men and women are characterized in traditional, stereotyped ways. However, the ads here examplify the changing attitudes by presenting two activities that are not commonly linked to the man or women shown.

Nevertheless, as shown in Figure 5.15, the stories and the TV programs and the advertising are gradually changing, as are gender-related attitudes and behaviors in everyday life.

DIFFERENCES BETWEEN MALES AND FEMALES: SEX, GENDER, OR BOTH?

Studies of gender identity clearly indicate the effect of social influences on the details of how maleness and femaleness are defined. Studies of varying social groups (see, for example, the following section on social diversity) also provide evidence that the characteristics associated with each sex can vary when cultural influences are different. Nevertheless, such findings do not rule out the possibility of some built-in, genetically controlled behavioral and/or psychological differences between the sexes. Both research evidence and everyday experience indicate that there *are* differences between males and females. The question is whether these differences are based on biology, social learning, or a combination of the two (Eagly & Steffen, 1986). In addition to the material to be presented here, explanations for sex differences in aggression will be discussed in chapter 11.

INTERPERSONAL BEHAVIOR.   In many instances sex differences are found in the way people interact with others. For example, women are more likely than men to share rewards (Major & Deaux, 1982) or to deprive themselves in order to help someone else (Leventhal & Anderson, 1970).

In managerial roles, women tend to get things done by means of leadership styles characterized as *connective* and *interactive*. That is, women prefer collaboration, consultation, and negotiation rather than the more masculine tradition of competition, individual achievement, and demands (Lipman-Blumen, 1988; Rosener, 1990). Other research indicates that these gender differences are related to the person's self-esteem (Josephs, Markus, & Tafarodi, 1992). For men self-esteem is linked to individual personal achievements, while for women self-esteem is a function of interpersonal attachments to specific others.

It seems reasonable to explain these male-female differences in terms of different expectancies learned as parts of one's gender role rather than in terms of biology (Major & Adams, 1983). For example, a history of social pressure to accept second place in assertive and aggressive situations may be the reason that women are less likely than men to emphasize masculine behavioral styles (Nadkarni, Lundgren, & Burlew, 1991).

A different explanation for these sex differences is found, however, in studies of the effects of testosterone levels on behavior. Beyond its limited effect on sexual activity, the hormone testosterone strongly affects the tendency to dominate and control. Among our ancient ancestors, the production of testosterone was useful in increasing the odds of male reproduction in that the most combative and dominant individuals could subdue rival males *and* the desired female sexual target. Today the remnants of these primitive tendencies can be seen in the competitive, dominant, and sometimes aggressive actions of males compared to females. Differences in testosterone production among men also affect their behavior; high levels of this hormone are associated with choosing dominant and controlling occupations such as trial lawyer, actor, and politician, as well as with turning to violent crime (Dabbs, 1992).

Altogether, then, many of the behaviors that differentiate males and females seem to be based on higher testosterone levels in males. In addition, individual differences among males in hormone levels also seem to account for behavioral differences, as will be discussed further in the following **Work in Progress** section.

Work in Progress

Testosterone Level and Male Behavior

Professor Dabbs (1993) and his colleagues are actively investigating how testosterone affects behavior *and* how behavior affects testosterone level among such diverse groups as convicted criminals, ministers, skinheads, and sports fans.

One general conclusion is that testosterone has a significant effect on antisocial behavior, but that both personality and social variables can moderate antisocial tendencies and hold them in check. The primary action of this hormone is on dominance,

and there are many ways to dominate others. Among college males, for example, high testosterone is related to sociability, and those with high hormone levels attend more parties than those with low levels. These high-testosterone males, appear not to be genuinely friendly, and they smile less in their yearbook photographs. Testosterone is also related to cognitive style, in that high levels are associated with low verbal skills and high spatial abilities. Dabbs speculates that this pattern may be useful in physical competition; for example, men in combat could be at an advantage if they have good spatial skills but don't think much about what they're doing.

Behavioral effects on testosterone are also found. You may remember our earlier description of research indicating the effect of winning and losing on the self-esteem of basketball fans. Bernhardt and Dabbs (1993) report that testosterone rises among male basketball fans whose team has just won. They propose that this occurs because of an increase in the feelings of status that a person gets from association with winners—the *basking in reflected glory* effect. In addition, *before a contest* both athletes and interested male fans also show a rise in testosterone. Fans seems to be vicariously engaged in the competitive activity: before, during, and after. These hormonal changes may explain why fans sometimes riot after their team is highly successful.

In future research, Dabbs and his coworkers are planning to explore the effects of various kinds of success and failure experiences on testosterone level and on the verbal and spatial skills of both sexes.

SELF-PERCEPTION.   Similarly, sex differences exist in self-perception. Women are more likely than men to attach great importance to their overall body image (Pliner, Chaiken, & Flett, 1990); to be dissatisfied with their bodies (Heinberg & Thompson, 1992); to develop eating disorders (Forston & Stanton, 1992; Hamilton, Falconer, & Greenberg, 1992); and to become depressed (Strickland, 1992). Consider the special emphasis our society places on the physical attractiveness of women in general and on specific features such as breast size (Thompson & Tantleff, 1992). One consequence is that women are vulnerable on issues related to appearance; for example, depressed women become more depressed when told that they weigh more than they think they do (Mori & Morey, 1991).

Women also seem to accept masculine reactions to feminine obesity as being their own fault. Crocker, Cornwell, and Major (1993) point out that overt expressions of most negative stereotypes are explained away by the victim as indicating prejudice on the part of the evaluator. Interestingly enough, however, when a male gives negative social feedback to an overweight female (little interest in dating her), she tends to attribute his reaction to her weight (self-blame) rather than to his prejudice, and she subsequently feels bad about herself rather than angry at him. The reason for this self-blame is being explored in subsequent research, as described in the following **Work in Progress** section.

Work in Progress

Justification, Control, and Self-Blame

A basic question raised by the reaction of overweight women to rejection is *why* they should blame themselves. Professors Crocker and Major propose two primary possibilities (Crocker, 1993).

One explanation is that these women believe that the negative reactions to their apperance are *justified*. That is, there is no justification for rejecting a friendship on the basis of skin color; in contrast, romantic relationships are based in part on physical attraction. As a result, if overweight individuals are unattractive, it is "justifiable" to reject them as dates. This proposal leads to the hypothesis that an overweight woman rejected as a potential work partner would believe that such a reaction was less justified than rejection in the dating situation, and this prediction was confirmed (Crocker & Major, 1993).

A related explanation is based on *controllability*. Skin color is not under one's control, whereas weight is. So, if being overweight leads to rejection and if the weight is under one's control, negative reactions from others are basically one's own fault. A study is currently under way among overweight and normal-weight undergraduates to determine their beliefs about the controllability of weight and to examine the effects of overweight on self-esteem, depression, and satisfaction with one's life.

These investigations support the general conclusion (Crocker & Major, 1991) that stigmatized individuals who believe that negative outcomes based on their stigma are unjustifiable could be expected to react with anger and high self-esteem; their subsequent behavior would include attempts to fight back at the injustice of the negative outcome. On the other hand, stigmatized individuals who believe that negative outcomes are based on controllable stigma and are justifiable could be expected to react with depression and low self-esteem; their subsequent behavior could involve either hopelessness or attempts to bring about personal change.

Female concern with weight also seems to be associated with seemingly unrelated health risks. According to psychiatrist Susan Fiester at the National Institutes of Health, the possibility of weight gain is sufficiently important to women that they have more difficulty than men in giving up smoking. Women become more upset than men about temporary weight gains when they quit, and they respond by going back to cigarettes (Anstett, 1992).

As suggested in Figure 5.16, physical attractiveness and youth are especially emphasized when people evaluate women—women are rated as less feminine as they grow older, while aging men are not rated as less masculine (Deutsch, Zalenski, & Clark, 1986); though attractiveness ratings decrease with age for both sexes (Zebrowitz, Olson, & Hoffman, 1993). Nevertheless, compare the number of gray-haired males versus gray-haired females you see anchoring television news broadcasts.

Women tend to outperform men in social skills (Margalit & Eysenck, 1990), but it makes sense that the ability to avoid angry interactions and to compromise are of special value to those who have been denied access to power and who have learned not to be assertive and aggressive. Once again,

Societal emphasis on female youthfulness and attractiveness

FIGURE 5.16 When people evaluate women, they place much more emphasis on youth and physical attractiveness than when they evaluate men. Thus, aging men can be perceived as masculine, while aging women are less likely to be perceived as feminine.

observed sex differences can be explained (or explained away) on the basis of differences in what males and females learn and in different expectations about how they should behave.

There is obviously no final answer to the reason for sex differences, but the following **Cutting Edge** section describes additional research designed to identify how and why males and females differ.

Focus on Research: The Cutting Edge

EXPLAINING SEX DIFFERENCES IN PERSONALITY

Feingold (1992) contrasted biological and environmental explanations of sex differences in behavior and presented four models that are widely accepted. The basic *biological model* assumes that many sex differences are innate and are based on differences between the genes on the X and Y chromosomes or on hormonal differences created by the action of those genes (Zuckerman, 1991). The *sociocultural model* proposes that wide-ranging social and cultural factors exert pressure on males and females to behave differently (Eagly & Wood, 1991). The *expectancy model* is similar, but emphasizes cultural influences on perceptions about the sexes that create different expectancies; those who conform to gender expectancies are rewarded, and those who do not comply are punished (Deaux & Major, 1987). The *artifact model* suggests that sexual stereotypes influence what we believe about ourselves (creating self-held beliefs) but not necessarily what we do (Feingold, 1990).

Feingold (1992) focused on two areas of personality research in which sex differences have commonly been reported—personality inventories on which the participants make self-ratings, and experiments in which the participants rate another person (an experimental accomplice). Note that if the artifact model is correct, greater sex differences would be expected in self-reports than in ratings by outside observers.

An analysis of the findings of a great many investigations revealed a number of consistent sex differences in self-reports. Women, for example, describe themselves as more anxious, gregarious, trusting, and nurturing than men. Men describe themselves as more assertive than women. No sex differences were found for a number of characteristics—for example, impulsiveness, activity level, creativity, and orderliness. But the findings in the studies in which the ratings were made by others are somewhat different from the self-reports. Male observers agree that females are more gregarious, but female observers rate other women lower on this dimension than men do. Men also perceive women as less anxious than women do. Female observers, on the other hand, perceive males as more assertive than other men do. Clearly, what people say about themselves and how their behavior is perceived by others are not the same—and clearly, men and women differ in their perceptions of the two sexes.

As in other research, these findings provide some support for both biological and environmental models. For example, over the past generation, both self-reports and ratings by observers consistently indicate that women are more gregarious than men, findings that are at least consistent with the biological model. Environmental models provide a more reasonable explanation of findings that the sexes differ more in self-reports than in observed behavior and that males and females differ in their *perceptions* of how men and women feel and behave. Such findings suggest that gender role behavior involves expectancies that are not always carried out and that behavior may depend on the sex of the audience. Also note that despite assumptions of widespread sex differences, men and women were alike on more traits than those on which they differed.

On the topic of sex differences, firm conclusions remain elusive. We understand that you probably feel frustrated when we say that, but our statement reflects the reality of scientific research and thinking at this time. On second thought, you might prefer scientific uncertainty to the unscientific certainty that once surrounded these issues. In Great Britain in the nineteenth century, Queen Victoria became incensed at talk of the "mad, wicked folly" of women's rights "with all its attendant horrors" and let her subjects know her conclusions about sex differences. "God created men and women different—then let them remain each in their own position" (Queen Victoria, 1881).

Despite the convictions of Queen Victoria, men and women do not necessarily remain in fixed roles, as illustrated in the following **Social Diversity** section.

Social Diversity ▼ A Critical Analysis

Divergent Female Gender Roles in Singapore and Mexico, and among Native Americans

Studies of behavior in different cultures provide important evidence relevant to the question of biological versus environmental determinants of gender differences. When cultural anthropologists, social psychologists, and others find quite different behavior in different cultures, this provides evidence supporting environmental effects. Conversely, when behavior *doesn't* vary despite differences in language, race, religion, political structure, and so on, biological determinism is supported. What do such studies tell us about gender roles?

In Singapore, Yuen and Lim (1990) examined gender roles in a changing society. In this business-oriented nation ("Singapore, Inc."), the traditional Anglo-Chinese culture of achieving men and homebound women is being supplanted by

an equal-opportunity culture in which success depends primarily on merit. The researchers had male and female business administration students read three scenarios involving managers of both sexes in organizational settings. Male participants rated male managers more positively than female managers in the first two stories. That is, the traditional gender roles of this society seemed to be operating as part of their decision-making. When an additional variable was added to the third scenario (the developmental *potential* of the managers), the business students made quite different decisions. High-potential females were viewed as favorably as high-potential males; responses to low-potential individuals were quite negative, with males at the bottom. Here the information

about managerial potential was relevant to the new, merit-based structure of Singapore, and the old gender roles were set aside. Even in this highly traditional society, men and women are beginning to alter their perception of gender in response to new cultural pressures.

In a quite different setting—the Mexican town of Morelos—change is not a factor, but Martin (1990) has found that gender roles involve elements different from those in either the old or new Singapore and from those in the United States. In some respects, gender roles resemble those found in many cultures; that is, the women are perceived as the primary caretakers, and they look after the children, cook the meals, and so forth. In other respects, gender expectancies differ quite a bit. The women of Morelos also serve as the community's protesters, particularly if the complaints involve inadequate services or official corruption. Martin suggests that some of these assertive actions could be interpreted as extensions and variations of the traditional caretaker role. That is, the women are taking care of and nurturing the community as a whole by ensuring that services are carried out. The protests against corruption are viewed as a modification of another gender role, that of the pure woman who is like the Virgin Mary; purity leads to abhorrence of corruption. However one explains it, taking to the streets and angrily protesting government wrongs is unlike the behavior of either most American or most Singaporean women.

Examples of still different gender behavior is provided by many Native American cultures (La Fromboise, Heyle, & Ozer, 1990), as shown in Figure 5.17. Among the gender roles women fulfilled that were unlike those in other societies were those of primary educators and historians in many tribes. An even more dramatic gender role difference can be seen in the "warrior women"

 Cultural differences in gender roles

FIGURE 5.17 When data from other cultures indicate that women can and do engage in behavior that is not part of our conception of the female gender role, it suggests that whatever biological determinants of sex differences there may (or may not) be, situational factors can modify, eliminate, or even reverse them.

of groups such as the Cheyenne, Blackfeet, and Pawnee; these women played active combat roles for centuries. In the United States today, however, the possibility of women volunteering for this kind of assignment is still a matter of heated controversy.

The general point, of course, is that female behavior that seemed natural and God-given to Queen Victoria can take quite different forms in different cultures. At the very least, such studies tell us that any inborn tendencies for females to be meek, submissive, and unassertive homemakers can be overcome and outweighed by cultural demands for quite different behavior.

Summary and Review

Social identity refers to an individual's self-definition. It includes the many facets of one's self-concept and identification with various categories of people defined in terms of sex, race, religion, political affiliation, age, occupation, and so on.

Aspects of the Self-Concept
As Part of One's Social Identity

A person's *self-concept* is defined as a *schema*—an organized collection of beliefs and feelings about everything relating to that individual's self-knowledge. Such schemas guide the way we process self-relevant information. In addition to our current self, we can and do imagine a variety of *possible selves* we could be. *Self-esteem* refers to self-evaluation—the attitude a person has about himself or herself. Positive self-esteem occurs when there is minimal difference between an individual's ideal and his or her current behavior, and most evidence indicates that a positive self-evaluation is a beneficial attribute. *Self-efficacy* is the aspect of self that involves a person's perceived abilities and competencies to deal with specific tasks. Feelings of self-efficacy lead to better task performance on the job, in school, in interpersonal situations, and in dealing with fears. *Self-monitoring behavior* refers to whether a person regulates his or her behavior in response to the external situation and the reactions of others (high self-monitors) or on the basis of internal factors (low self-monitors). High self-monitoring is associated with a positive response to image-based advertising, low behavioral consistency across situations, and interpersonal preferences based on the activity at hand rather than on feelings about the other individual. *Self-focusing* refers to the extent to which one's attention is directed inward toward the self or outward toward the environment.

Biological and Cultural Determinants of Sex and Gender

We define *sex* as the basic biological differentiation of males and females. *Gender* refers to the roles, actions, preferences, and other attributes associated with a given sex. Sex is determined at conception by the presence of an X chromosome from each parent (creating a girl) or an X from the mother and a Y from the father (creating a boy). *Gender identity* is formed when a child identifies himself or herself as belonging to a specific sex, and many of the details of this identity are clearly influenced by cultural practices and beliefs. An issue that has been a continuing source of controversy in the study of gender is the extent to which gender differences are based on the biological factors that differentiate the sexes or on experiential factors involving culture, cognitive development, modeling, and differential reinforcement. Whatever the determinants, the end result is *sex-typing*, which occurs when individuals understand what it means to be a male or a female in a given culture. Bem has shown that *gender roles* can be masculine, feminine, androgynous, or undifferentiated; such roles and the stereotypes associated with them have influenced many aspects of behavior, including job opportunities and the division of household labor. Studies of sex differences usually indicate that females have better social skills than males and that women are more concerned than men about body image.

Social Diversity: Wide Variations in Female Gender Roles

When cross-cultural differences in gender roles are found, this provides evidence that learning experiences can outweigh genetic influences in determining how men and women behave. In Singapore the traditional role of submissive female homemaker is being replaced by the image of the able, business-oriented, achieving female. In Mexico many traditional female behaviors (cooking, childcare) occur along with the role of politically active protester against government inefficiency and/or corruption. Among Native American women, the female gender role has included nontraditional elements ranging from tribal historian to warrior.

Key Terms

Androgyny On Bem's test, the characteristic of those whose responses include elements consistent with both the traditional masculine and the traditional feminine gender roles.

Bem Sex Role Inventory (BSRI) Bem's test to measure the extent to which an individual adopts a traditional masculine gender role, a traditional feminine gender role, a mixture of the two (androgyny), or neither (undifferentiated).

Chromosome A string of deoxyribonucleic acid (DNA) that contains genetic information, the blueprint that determines the physical development of an organism.

Collective Self-Esteem Scale A measure of self-esteem linked to the person's membership in social groups.

Gender All of the attributes, behaviors, personality characteristics, and expectancies associated with one's sex in a given society.

Gender Consistency The perception that gender is a basic, enduring attribute of each individual. Children come to a realization of gender consistency between the ages of four and seven.

Gender Identity The sex that a person associates with himself or herself. For most, but not all, individuals, this matches the person's biological sex.

Special Sections

My wife Sandra has a kind heart (how else could she have put up with me all these years?), so it didn't surprise me when she told me that she had decided to volunteer for a local organization that helped recent immigrants adjust to their new lives in the United States. All four of my grandparents were immigrants, so I found the idea of helping these newcomers learn English and the intricate ins and outs of American culture very appealing. When my wife told me about the way the organization operated, I was even more pleased. She explained that it didn't simply turn volunteers loose on new arrivals; rather, it required that the volunteers undergo extensive training designed to increase their sensitivity to cultural differences.

On the night of the first training session, she returned home brimming with enthusiasm. "It's really going to be fun," she said. "These people need help badly, and I'm going to enjoy working with someone from a different culture." The night of the second session, however, was very different. She was visibly upset. "What's wrong?" I asked. "Didn't the session go well?" Sandra was very pale—a sure sign that she was angry—so I wasn't surprised by her answer:

"I'm so mad I don't even want to talk about it! I'll tell you later." And she stormed out of the room.

Later that evening she did calm down, and she described her experience to me.

"We were doing an exercise about stereotypes and how people can have them without even knowing it."

"Sounds good to me," I commented. "Like it or not, stereotypes are a fact of life, so hitting 'em head on like that is a good idea."

"Sure, sure," Sandra said, "but listen to what that instructor did. Oooh! It makes me so mad!"

"Calm down and tell me already!" I interjected.

"Okay. She began by asking the class to describe people from different countries—you know, England, France, China . . . We all called out words like 'polite' for the English, 'romantic' for the French . . ."

"That makes sense," I said. "It's the kind of thing that helps people realize that they do have preconceived ideas about others. Why did that bother you?"

"It didn't!" Sandra exclaimed. "It's what she did next. After we finished that, she went to the board and wrote the names of different sections of the country—New England, Midwest, West, South. She added New York, too, even though it's a state. Then she asked us for words describing people from each area."

"So what happened then?" I asked with puzzlement.

"The words for New England were all pretty positive, just as you'd expect. People said things like 'neat,' 'hard-working,' stuff like that. The same was true for what they said about Midwesterners. They called them 'friendly,' 'open,' and 'honest.' But they stuck in a few negative words, too, like 'unsophisticated' and 'dull.'"

"Naturally," the social psychologist in me remarked. "You know what stereotypes are like. They're usually not all good or all bad."

"Right," Sandra agreed, "but then the instructor got to the South, and she was so offensive that I almost got up and left."

Now I knew what was coming. My wife was born and raised in a small town in South Carolina, and one thing that often made her angry was the negative stereotype people in other parts of the country seemed to hold about Southerners. We had encountered such views in Seattle, in Minneapolis—and now, it appeared, in upstate New York, too.

"First of all, practically everything people came up with was negative: 'slow-moving,' 'bigoted,' 'stupid'— stuff like that. But to make it worse, she even managed to twist the few positive words into something bad. One woman said 'beauty-contest winners.' She picked up on that and asked if it didn't make us think of things like 'dumb blonde' and 'bubble-headed bimbo.' And when *I* said 'polite,' she answered, 'Right—like in phony.' I could have hit her."

"Did you tell her that you were from South Carolina?" I asked.

"No, I didn't," Sandra answered. "I wasn't going to give her the satisfaction."

"But if you had, that would have changed everything."

"Sure. They would have all kept quiet and not said what they really thought. No, I wanted to hear it. It's just what I've always said, these so-called liberals in the Northeast are the *real* phonies. They're more bigoted than anyone!"

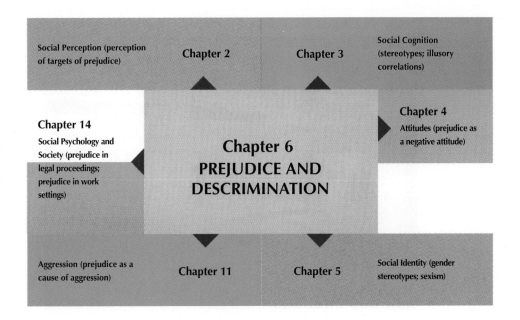

Social Perception (perception of targets of prejudice)

Chapter 2

Chapter 3

Social Cognition (stereotypes; illusory correlations)

Chapter 14

Social Psychology and Society (prejudice in legal proceedings; prejudice in work settings)

Chapter 4

Attitudes (prejudice as a negative attitude)

**Chapter 6
PREJUDICE AND
DESCRIMINATION**

Aggression (prejudice as a cause of aggression)

Chapter 11

Chapter 5

Social Identity (gender stereotypes; sexism)

Despite her negative experience that night, my wife did complete the training and did serve as a volunteer for several months. She worked with a woman from Korea who spoke virtually no English, and they soon became good friends. All in all, what started out so badly turned into a very satisfying experience. But none of this changed the fact that on that night in May, my wife came eyeball to eyeball with the ugly face of prejudice. No, it wasn't the kind of racial, ethnic, or religious hatred that fills the evening news with frightening scenes such as the one shown in Figure 6.1, p. 218. But it *was* prejudice all the same, and an upsetting experience for her.

What, precisely, is *prejudice,* and how does it differ from another term with which we are also, unfortunately, too familiar—*discrimination?* What factors contribute to the existence of prejudice and discrimination? And perhaps even more important, how can these negative forces in human society be reduced? Given the great diversity of the human species, plus the fact that contact among people of different racial, ethnic, and national backgrounds is increasing, these are vital questions and ones with which we surely must grapple in the mid-1990s. In fact, it does not seem too extreme to suggest that overcoming prejudice and discrimination is one of the most crucial tasks confronting humanity today. The alternative—permitting them to exist unchecked—seems to condemn us to an ever-rising tide of hatred and violence. If nothing else, then, social psychology's commitment to understanding, and combating, prejudice and discrimination seems more timely than ever.

A quick review of human history indicates that prejudice and discrimination have always, alas, been part of human society. At first glance, therefore, it is tempting to assume that everything that could be learned about these topics was probably uncovered long ago. In fact, nothing could be farther from the truth. Despite the best efforts of philosophers, poets, historians, and others, the nature and causes of prejudice remained unclear until very recent times. This picture has changed—and changed radically—as social psychologists have applied the increasingly sophisticated methods and concepts of their field to

Prejudice: Its ultimate effects

FIGURE 6.1 When prejudice is intense, it can lead to violent—and tragic—actions such as the L.A. Riot in 1992.

this subject. The result, we believe, has been nothing short of a series of major breakthroughs in our understanding of the psychological foundations of prejudice—its cognitive, social, and interpersonal roots (Devine, 1989; Dovidio & Gaertner, 1993). To provide you with an overview of this valuable information, our discussion of prejudice will proceed as follows.

First, we'll examine the nature of both prejudice and discrimination, indicating what these concepts are and how they differ. Second, we will consider the causes of prejudice and discrimination—why they occur and what makes them so intense and so persistent. Third, we'll explore various strategies for reducing prejudice and discrimination. Finally, because it has been the subject of an especially large amount of research attention and because it influences the lives of more than half of all human beings, we will focus on the nature and impact of one particular form of prejudice—that based on gender (sexism).

Exercise 1

PREJUDICE AND DISCRIMINATION: WHAT THEY ARE AND HOW THEY DIFFER

In everyday speech, the terms *prejudice* and *discrimination* are used interchangeably. Are they really the same? Most social psychologists draw a clear distinction between them. **Prejudice** refers to a special type of *attitude*—generally, a negative one—toward the members of some social group. In contrast, **discrimination** refers to negative *actions* toward those individuals. Since this is an important difference, let's consider it more closely.

PREJUDICE: CHOOSING WHOM TO HATE

We'll begin with a more precise definition: *Prejudice is an attitude (usually negative) toward the members of some group, based solely on their membership in that group.*

Video: *Prejudice** In other words, a person who is prejudiced toward some social group tends to evaluate its members in a specific manner (usually negatively) merely because they belong to that group. Their individual traits or behavior play little role; they are disliked (or, in a few cases, liked) simply because they belong to a specific social group (see Figure 6.2).

When prejudice is defined as a special type of attitude, two important implications follow. First, as we noted in chapters 3 and 4, attitudes often function as *schemas*—cognitive frameworks for organizing, interpreting, and recalling information (Fiske & Taylor, 1991). Thus, individuals who are prejudiced toward particular groups tend to process information about these groups differently from the way they process information about other groups. Information consistent with their prejudiced views often receives more attention, is rehearsed more frequently, and, as a result, tends to be remembered more accurately than information that is not consistent with these views (Bodenhausen, 1988; Judd, Ryan, & Park, 1991). To the extent that this happens, prejudice becomes a kind of closed cognitive loop, and, in the absence of truly dramatic experiences that refute its accuracy, it can only grow stronger over time.

Second, if prejudice is a special kind of attitude, then it may involve more than negative evaluations of the groups toward whom it is directed. In addition, it may involve negative feelings or emotions on the part of prejudiced persons when they are in the presence of, or merely thinking about, members of the groups they dislike (Stephan & Stephan, 1988). Prejudice may also involve beliefs and expectations about members of these groups—specifically, **stereotypes** suggesting that all members of these groups demonstrate certain characteristics and behave in certain ways. Finally, it may involve tendencies to

Transparency 6.1

 Prejudice as blanket condemnation or rejection

FIGURE 6.2 Prejudice leads those who hold it to reject the members of some group simply because they belong to that group.
Source: The New Yorker, 1980.

"Well, sir, then I take it you would vote for any cat in preference to a capable dog."

act in negative ways—or intentions of doing so—toward those who are the object of prejudice.

One additional point: When most people think about prejudice, they tend to focus on its emotional or evaluative aspects. They emphasize the strong negative feelings and irrational hatreds that so often characterize racial, ethnic, or religious prejudice. Such reactions are important and play a key role in many forms of prejudice. Yet it is crucial to note that prejudice also is related to, and involves, certain aspects of *social cognition*—the ways in which we notice, store, process, recall, and then use information about others. Because we have only limited capacity to perform these complex tasks (Gilbert & Hixon, 1991), we often adopt various cognitive shortcuts in our efforts to make sense out of the social world (Fiske, 1989). We described several of these shortcuts in chapter 3 and as you may recall, they *do* help to reduce cognitive effort. However, they can also lead us to draw false conclusions about others (Schaller, 1992): to place them in convenient, if inaccurate categories, and to rely on existing cognitive frameworks (schemas, memories) rather than attempting to adjust these to reflect social reality more accurately (Devine, 1989). For example, once we hold negative stereotypes about members of a specific social group, we tend to evaluate persons belonging to this group unfavorably on dimensions relating to these stereotypes *simply because they belong to this group* (e.g., Bodenhausen, 1990). Because of these and related tendencies, prejudice is often as much a reflection of the limits and operation of our cognitive processes as it is of deep-seated hatred, strong emotions, and rampant ill will. We will return to this point in more detail below, but please try to keep it in mind as you read the pages that follow.

DISCRIMINATION: PREJUDICE IN ACTION

Transparency 6.2

Attitudes, we noted in chapter 4, are not always reflected in overt action—far from it. Prejudice is definitely no exception to this rule. In many cases, persons holding negative attitudes toward the members of various groups cannot express these views directly. Laws, social pressure, fear of retaliation—all serve to deter them from putting their prejudiced views into open practice. In other instances, however, such restraining forces are absent. Then the negative beliefs, feelings, and behavioral tendencies referred to above may find expression in overt actions. Such *discrimination* (or *discriminatory behaviors*) can take many forms. At relatively mild levels it involves simple avoidance—prejudiced persons simply avoid or minimize contact with the objects of their dislike. While such discrimination may seem relatively benign, it can sometimes have serious consequences for its victims. For example, recent studies indicate that sizable proportions of health-care professionals (physicians, nurses, hospital workers) report spending less time with AIDS patients than with people suffering from other illnesses (Gordin et al., 1987, Hunter & Ross, 1991). Clearly, such discrimination can add to the pain and the suffering of the victims.

Critical Thinking
Question 1

At stronger levels, discrimination can produce exclusion from jobs, educational opportunities, or neighborhoods. Finally, in the most extreme cases, prejudice leads to overt forms of aggression against its targets. Anyone who has watched scenes of racial and ethnic violence on the evening news—whether they come from the former Yugoslavia or the streets of American cities—is familiar with these frightening expressions of prejudice.

SUBTLE FORMS OF DISCRIMINATION: PREJUDICE IN DISGUISE.

Bigots, like other persons, prefer to have their cake and eat it, too. They prefer, if possible, to harm the targets of their prejudice without any cost to themselves. How can they accomplish this goal? One answer involves the use of *subtle forms of discrimination*—ones that permit their users to conceal the underlying negative views from which they stem. Several of these subtle forms exist, ranging from heaping excessive praise on even minimal accomplishments (the implication being that good performance by members of some group is surprising; Gaertner & Dovidio, 1986), to displaying unfriendly nonverbal behavior (e.g., standing slightly too far away, failing to make appropriate eye contact; Neuberg, 1989). In this discussion, however, we'll focus on two that seem to be most common: *tokenism* and *reverse discrimination*.

Tokenism: Small benefits, high costs.   Imagine that you are hired for a job you really wanted and at a higher starting salary than you expected. At first, you are happy about your good fortune. Now assume that one day you learn that you got the job mainly because you belong to a specific group—one whose members the company must hire in order to avoid legal actions by a government agency charged with the task of eliminating discrimination in the workplace. How will you react? In all probability, you will be upset. After all, few persons enjoy discovering that they are a victim of **tokenism**: that they have been hired solely as a token member of a racial, ethnic, or religious group rather than on the basis of their qualifications. Direct evidence of such negative reactions to tokenism in work settings has been reported in several studies. For example, in one study, Chacko (1982) found that among women holding management-level jobs, the greater the extent to which they felt they had been hired purely because of their gender, the lower their satisfaction with their jobs. Similarly, other findings indicate that persons who are hired or promoted because of their gender, race, or ethnic identity may actually receive lower performance ratings from others in their company (Heilman & Herlihy, 1984). This is not surprising, since others tend to attribute the achievements of these persons to the special hiring or promotion factors rather than to hard work or talent. Finally, in a study we reviewed in chapter 2, Summers (1991) found that women whose promotions are attributed to the influence of affirmative action policies (policies that encourage the hiring and promotion of women and minorities) are often seen as less qualified by others than women whose promotions are attributed to their own hard work and talent.

We should hasten to note that tokenism occurs in many other contexts as well. More generally, it takes the form of trivial positive actions toward the targets of prejudice that are then used as an excuse or justification for later discrimination. "Don't bother me," prejudiced persons who have engaged in tokenism seem to say; "Haven't I done enough for those people already?" (e.g., Dutton & Lake, 1973; Rosenfield et al., 1982). Wherever it occurs, tokenism seems to have at least two negative effects. On the one hand, it lets prejudiced people off the hook; they can point to tokenistic actions as public proof that they are not really bigoted or that they have followed the letter if not the spirit of antidiscrimination laws. On the other hand, it can be damaging to the self-esteem and confidence of the targets of prejudice, including those few persons who are selected as tokens or who receive minimal aid. Clearly, then, tokenism is one subtle form of discrimination worth preventing.

Critical Thinking
Question 3

TOKENISM

Reverse discrimination: Giving with one hand, taking with the other.   A second type of subtle discrimination occurs in situations in which persons holding at least some degree of prejudice toward the members of a social group lean over backward to treat those group members favorably—more favorably than they would were the individuals not members of that particular group. Such **reverse discrimination** effects have been observed in several contexts. For example, Chidester (1986) had white students engage in a brief get-acquainted conversation with a stranger who was described as being either African-American or white. (The conversation took place through microphones and headphones.) When participants in the study later evaluated their partners in this conversation, they reported more favorable reactions when the unseen person was supposedly black than when she or he was supposedly white. (In fact, all participants were white; only subjects' beliefs about the race of their partner were varied.) Unless one assumes that the white participants actually held more favorable views of blacks than of members of their own race, these findings point to the occurrence of "lean over backward" reactions among participants.

Discussion Question 3

At first glance such behavior may not seem to fit our definition of discrimination. After all, it yields positive rather than negative outcomes for its victims. On one level, this is certainly true; people exposed to reverse discrimination do receive raises, promotions, and other benefits. But on another level, such favorable treatment may prove harmful, especially over the long run. A clear illustration of the potential damage stemming from reverse discrimination is provided by a study conducted by Fajardo (1985).

Transparency 6.6

In this investigation, several white teachers were asked to grade essays prepared in advance and deliberately written so as to be poor, moderate, or excellent in quality. Information attached to the essays indicated that they were written by either white or African-American students. If reverse discrimination existed, it would be expected that the teachers would rate the essays more favorably when they were supposedly prepared by black rather than by white students. Results indicated that this is precisely what happened. Moreover, the tendency of white teachers to favor black students was strongest under conditions where the essays were of moderate quality; in other words, when there was greatest uncertainty as to the rating students should receive.

In real life, as you can readily see, assigning favorable ratings to mediocre work by black students can indeed help them in the short run. But it can also set them up for later problems. It may lead some students, at least, to conclude that they are doing better in school than they actually are and to become over confident about the likelihood of future success. The anguish that follows when these hopes are dashed can be devastating. Similarly, reverse discrimination may be a subtle (and perhaps largely unconscious) tactic on the part of teachers for minimizing close contact with minority students. Students who receive consistently high grades don't need special help, so by assigning inflated evaluations to minority students' work, teachers can avoid working closely with them. In these and other ways, reverse discrimination can be as harmful as the more obvious forms of discrimination it sometimes replaces.

How do individuals feel when they engage in discrimination—subtle or otherwise? And do such reactions differ for persons who are low or high in prejudice? For discussion of these issues, please see the **Individual Diversity** section that follows.

Individual Diversity

DISCRIMINATION WITH—AND WITHOUT—COMPUNCTION: CONTRASTING REACTIONS OF LOW- AND HIGH-PREJUDICED PERSONS TO DISCREPANCIES BETWEEN THEIR INTERNAL STANDARDS AND THEIR OVERT BEHAVIOR

Most people realize that there is sometimes a gap between their overt actions—how they actually behave in a given situation—and their views about how they *should* act in that situation. Indeed, as we noted in chapter 4, noticing such discrepancies is often a first step on the road toward attitude change. This is because generally, people find discrepancies between their overt actions and their internal standards disturbing, and therefore feel internal pressure (dissonance or related states) to close these gaps.

Such discrepancies raise important questions with respect to prejudice and discrimination. Many persons in the United States and elsewhere have struggled vigorously to overcome prejudices they acquired as children. As a result of doing so, they now accept egalitarian principles and would state, if asked, that they are no longer prejudiced toward various groups (e.g., African-Americans, Jews, women). Yet they find that at some level, negative feelings about these groups persist. For example, consider the following (Pettigrew, 1987, p. 20):

> Many Southerners have confessed to me . . . that even though in their minds they no longer feel prejudice toward Blacks they still feel squeamish when they shake hands with a Black. These feelings are left over from what they learned . . . as children.

How do individuals react to such ambivalence? And does the nature of such reactions differ with the intensity of their prejudice? These and related questions have been investigated by Devine and her colleagues (Devine et al., 1991) in a series of enlightening studies.

Critical Thinking
Question 2

In these investigations Devine and her colleagues asked college students identified as low, moderate, or high in prejudice toward various groups (i.e., blacks, homosexuals) to indicate how they believed they *should* feel in various situations involving contact with these groups and how they actually *would* feel in these situations. For example, participants were asked to indicate how they should feel when a black person boarded a bus and sat next to them and how they actually would feel in that situation. Similarly, they were asked how they should feel and how they actually would feel about having dinner with a gay individual. In addition, participants were asked to indicate their current feelings about how well their actual responses (their *would* ratings) matched their personal standards (their *should* ratings). They did this by rating their feelings on a number of different dimensions. Some of these dimensions reflected *compunction*, (angry at myself, guilty, embarrassed, disappointed with myself). Other dimensions reflected more global discomfort (negative, concerned, frustrated, tense, anxious).

Results indicated that, as expected, highly prejudiced persons held internal standards that permitted more open expression of such prejudice—greater discrimination toward blacks or homosexuals. Further, persons low in prejudice reported that their personal standards regarding behavior in situations where they came into contact with targets of discrimination were highly internalized—these standards were very important to them, and they felt strong obligations to behave consistently with them. In contrast, highly prejudiced persons did not report such well-defined or internalized personal standards and reported weaker felt obligations to behave in accordance with them.

Perhaps the most important—and revealing—findings of the study concerned the affective (emotional) reactions of persons high and low in prejudice to observed discrepancies between their own behavior and their internal standards. Devine and her colleagues (1991) expected that persons low in prejudice would react negatively to such discrepancies and, in particular, that they would respond to these gaps with feelings of *compunction*—guilt and shame over failing to meet their own standards. In contrast, persons high in prejudice would report weaker reactions of this type, although they might report equally strong feelings of general discomfort. As shown in Figure 6.3, these predictions were strongly confirmed. Persons low and moderate in prejudice did experience stronger feelings of guilt and shame when there was a sizable gap between their actual behavior and internal standards than when the discrepancy was smaller. Among highly prejudiced persons, in contrast, large

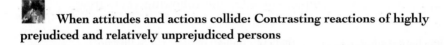

When attitudes and actions collide: Contrasting reactions of highly prejudiced and relatively unprejudiced persons

FIGURE 6.3   Individuals low or moderate in prejudice reported experiencing strong feelings of *compunction*—shame or guilt—when their attitudes concerning tolerant, unprejudiced behavior failed to find expression in their actions. In contrast, persons high in prejudice reported experiencing weaker reactions of this sort.
Source: Based on data from Devine et al., 1991.

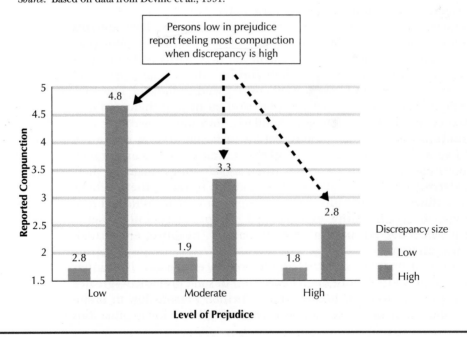

discrepancies did not produce significantly more compunction than small discrepancies. In other words, highly prejudiced persons did not feel guilty about experiencing negative reactions toward blacks and gays; low prejudiced persons did.

These findings have important implications for understanding the nature of prejudice, and especially for understanding how individuals attempt to deal with—and eliminate—prejudices they acquired early in life. One view (Dovidio & Gaertner, 1993) suggests that when people embrace egalitarian beliefs but continue to experience negative feelings toward specific social groups, they cope with such ambivalence by excluding such feelings from consciousness. The results obtained by Devine et al. (1991) indicate, in contrast, that such persons remain aware of these feelings, and—if they have truly adopted an unprejudiced perspective—are made uneasy by them. The feelings of compunction (guilt, shame, self-criticism) they experience may then serve as an important force for further change in the direction of reduced prejudice. In sum, the findings of this research provide evidence for the view that where prejudice is concerned, change *is* possible: People who wish to eliminate racist, sexist, and other prejudiced attitudes from their thinking can succeed in doing so. Indeed, recognition of the fact that they are still far from perfect in this respect and that gaps remain between their egalitarian attitudes and certain aspects of their behavior may be just the psychological nudge they need to keep them on the road toward unprejudiced beliefs and standards.

THE ORIGINS OF PREJUDICE: CONTRASTING PERSPECTIVES

That prejudice exists is all too obvious. The question of *why* it occurs, however, is more complex. Why do so many people hold negative views about the members of specific social groups? What factors or conditions foster such reactions and lead to their persistence? Many different answers to these questions have been proposed. Here, we will consider several views that have proved most influential.

Transparency 6.6

DIRECT INTERGROUP CONFLICT: COMPETITION AS A SOURCE OF PREJUDICE

It is an axiom of life that the things people value most—good jobs, nice homes, high status—are always in short supply. There's never quite enough to go around. This fact serves as the foundation for what is perhaps the oldest explanation of prejudice—**realistic conflict theory** (e.g., Bobo, 1983). According to this view, prejudice stems from competition among social groups over valued commodities or opportunities. In short, prejudice develops out of the struggle over jobs, adequate housing, good schools, and other desirable outcomes. The theory further suggests that as such competition continues, the members of the groups involved come to view each other in increasingly negative terms (White, 1977). They label one another as "enemies," view their own group as morally superior, and draw the boundaries between themselves and their opponents ever more firmly. The result, of course, is that what starts out as simple competition relatively free from hatred gradually develops into full-scale emotion-laden prejudice (refer to Figure 6.4, p. 226).

Critical Thinking Question 4

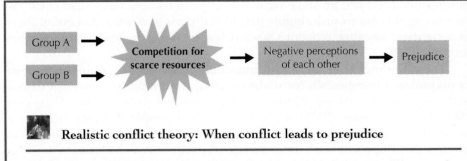

Realistic conflict theory: When conflict leads to prejudice

FIGURE 6.4 According to *realistic conflict theory*, competition between social groups for scarce resources can lead each side to view the other in increasingly negative terms. If the process continues, they may ultimately form strong prejudices toward one another.

Evidence from several different studies seems to confirm the occurrence of this process: As competition persists, the individuals or groups involved come to perceive each other in increasingly negative ways. Even worse, such competition often leads to direct and open conflict. Perhaps the most dramatic evidence for this process is provided by a classic study in social psychology conducted by Hovland and Sears (1940). These researchers examined the relationship between the number of lynchings of blacks in fourteen states in the American South and two indexes of economic conditions: farm value of cotton and acre value of cotton. (Cotton was the most important crop in the South at that time.) Their data covered a forty-nine-year period, and results were clear: The more negative economic conditions were, the greater the incidence of this atrocious type of violence.

These findings have often been interpreted as suggesting that under adverse economic conditions, competition for increasingly scarce economic resources increases. Such competition in turn increases prejudice toward groups other than one's own (in this case, prejudice on the part of whites toward blacks) and so increases the incidence of prejudice-driven violence. Interestingly, a reanalysis of Hovland and Sears's data using the more sophisticated statistical techniques available today and a more accurate measure of economic conditions has confirmed these results (Hepworth & West, 1988). Thus, it appears that increased competition between groups during periods of economic decline may indeed be one of the factors contributing to prejudice and resulting violence.

While direct conflict between racial or ethnic groups may indeed sometimes contribute to the development of strong prejudice between them (e.g., Bobo, 1983), it is important to note that this process appears to occur primarily with respect to *group conflict*—perceived threats to one group's interest by another group. When, instead, threats to individual interests are considered, there is little support for the view that conflict leads inevitably to prejudice. For example, Sears and his colleagues (e.g., Sears & Allen, 1984; Sears & Kinder, 1985) found that whites whose self-interests are threatened by forced busing—those with children in public schools—are *not* more prejudiced against blacks or more opposed to such busing than whites whose self-interests are not threatened by busing (whites without school-age children, whites whose children attend private schools). These and related findings indicate that it is primarily perceived conflict between *groups*, not individuals, that leads to intergroup prejudice. Since there are many situations in which individuals perceive that their group's interests are being threatened by members of some other group, however, it seems likely that intergroup conflict plays a role in prejudice in some instances.

For additional evidence concerning the impact of intergroup conflict on prejudice, please see the **Classic Contributions** section below.

Focus on Research: Classic Contributions

CONFLICT AND PREJUDICE IN A SUMMER CAMP: THE ROBBER'S CAVE EXPERIMENT

It was the mid-1950s, and in America Eisenhower was president, the economy was humming along, and—at least for the moment—domestic tranquillity prevailed. Yet even then social psychologists were deeply concerned with the topic of prejudice. To acquire new insights into prejudice, Sherif and his colleagues (1961) decided to conduct an intriguing project. Their study involved sending eleven-year-old boys to a special summer camp in a remote area where, free from external influences, the nature of conflict and its role in prejudice could be carefully observed.

When the boys arrived at the camp (named *The Robber's Cave*), they were divided in two separate groups and assigned to different cabins located quite far apart (see Figure 6.5). For one week, the campers in each group lived and played together, engaging in such enjoyable activities as hiking, swimming,

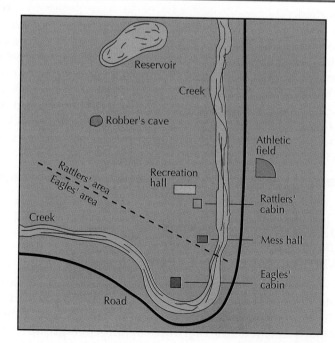

 Setting for the Robber's Cave experiment

FIGURE 6.5 The summer camp represented here served as the site of the famous Robber's Cave experiment. Note the distance between the cabins of the two opposing groups (Rattlers and Eagles) and division of the camp into two separate territories.

Source: Based on information in Sherif et al., 1961.

and other sports. During this initial phase, the boys quickly developed strong attachments to their own groups. They chose names for their teams (the Rattlers and the Eagles), stenciled them onto their shorts, and made up separate flags with their groups' symbols on them.

Reading: Lesko (17), *Experiments in Group Conflict*

At this point the second phase of the study began. The boys in both groups were told that they would now engage in a series of competitions. The winning team would receive a trophy, and its members would earn prizes (pocket knives and medals). Since these were prizes the boys strongly desired, the stage was set for intense competition. Would such conflict generate prejudice? The answer was quick in coming. As the boys competed, the tension between the groups rose. At first it was limited to verbal insults, teasing, and name-calling. Soon, though, it escalated into more direct acts—for example, the Eagles burned the Rattlers' flag. The next day the Rattlers struck back by attacking the rival group's cabin, overturning beds, tearing out mosquito netting, and seizing personal property. Such actions continued until the researchers intervened to prevent serious trouble. At the same time the two groups voiced increasingly negative views of each other. They labeled their opponents "bums" and "cowards," while heaping praise on their own group at every turn. In short, after only two weeks of conflict, the groups showed all the key components of strong prejudice toward each other.

Fortunately, the story (and the research project) had a happy ending. In the study's final phase, Sherif and his colleagues attempted to reduce the negative reactions described above. Merely increasing the amount of contact between the groups failed to accomplish this goal; indeed, it seemed to fan the flames of anger. But when conditions were altered so that the groups found it necessary to work together to reach *superordinate goals*—ones they both desired—dramatic changes occurred. After the boys worked together to restore their water supply (previously sabotaged by the researchers), pooled their funds to rent a movie, and jointly repaired a broken-down truck, tensions between the groups largely vanished. In fact, after six days of such experiences, the boundaries between the groups virtually dissolved, and many cross-group friendships were established.

It is important to note that there are major limitations to this research. The study took place over a relatively short period; the camp setting was a special one; all participants were boys; and, perhaps most important, the boys were quite homogeneous in background—they did not belong to distinctly different social groups. Despite these restrictions, however, the findings reported by Sherif and his colleagues are compelling. They offer a chilling picture of how what starts out as rational competition over scarce resources can quickly escalate into full-scale conflict, which then in turn fosters accompanying strong, negative attitudes.

SOCIAL CATEGORIZATION AS A BASIS FOR PREJUDICE: THE US-VERSUS-THEM EFFECT AND THE "ULTIMATE" ATTRIBUTION ERROR

Critical Thinking Question 5

A second perspective on the origins of prejudice begins with a basic fact: People generally divide the social world around them into two distinct categories—*us* and *them*. In short, they view other persons as belonging to either their own group (usually termed the **ingroup**) or another group (the

outgroup). Such distinctions are based on many dimensions, including race, religion, sex, age, ethnicity, occupation, and income, to name just a few.

If the process of dividing the social world into "us" and "them"—**social categorization**—stopped there, it would have little bearing on prejudice. Unfortunately, however, it does not. Sharply contrasting feelings and beliefs are usually attached to members of one's ingroup and members of various outgroups. Persons in the former ("us") category are viewed in favorable terms, while those in the latter ("them") category are perceived more negatively. Outgroup members are assumed to possess more undesirable traits, are perceived as being more alike (i.e., more homogeneous) than members of the ingroup, and are often strongly disliked (Judd, Ryan, & Park, 1991; Linville, Fischer, & Salovey, 1989; Schaller & Maas, 1989). The ingroup-outgroup distinction also affects *attribution*—the ways in which we explain the actions of persons belonging to these two categories. Specifically, we tend to attribute desirable behaviors by members of our ingroups to stable, internal causes (e.g., their admirable traits), but attribute desirable behaviors by members of outgroups to transitory factors or to external causes. For example, when asked to explain why students from one university in Hong Kong tend to receive better starting jobs than those from another university, students at the favored school attributed their success to better preparation. Those at the school whose graduates received less desirable jobs attributed this outcome to better personal connections on the part of students at the other school (Hewstone, Bond, & Wan, 1983). Similar results have been observed in many other contexts (e.g., Hewstone & Jaspars, 1982): In each instance, individuals made more favorable and flattering attributions about members of their ingroup than about members of various outgroups. One noted researcher describes this tendency as the **ultimate attribution error**, since it carries the self-serving bias that we described in chapter 2 into the arena of intergroup relations—with potentially devastating effects.

That strong tendencies exist to divide the social world into these contrasting groups has been demonstrated in many studies (e.g., Stephan, 1985; Tajfel, 1982; Turner et al., 1987). In these investigations, participants generally expressed more negative attitudes toward members of outgroups and treated them less favorably than members of their own group. Further, these patterns held true even when these categories were purely arbitrary and had no existence beyond the experiment, and when the persons involved never met face to face. On the other side of the coin, growing evidence indicates that when individuals shift the boundaries of this *us-versus-them* distinction so that persons previously on the "wrong" side of the ingroup-outgroup boundary are now viewed as being inside, prejudice toward them tends to disappear as well (Gaertner et al., 1989). Together, these findings indicate that in some settings, prejudice may well stem from a basic aspect of the way in which we think about the social world: a strong tendency to perceive others as belonging either to our own group or to some other group—outsiders.

But why, precisely, is this the case? What happens when we define others as different that leads us to view them in biased and mainly negative ways? An intriguing answer has been provided by Tajfel and his colleagues (e.g., Tajfel, 1982). These investigators suggests that individuals seek to enhance their self-esteem by becoming identified with specific social groups. This tactic can succeed, however, only to the extent that the persons involved perceive their groups as somehow superior to other, competing groups. Since all individuals are subject to the same forces, the final result is inevitable: Each group seeks to

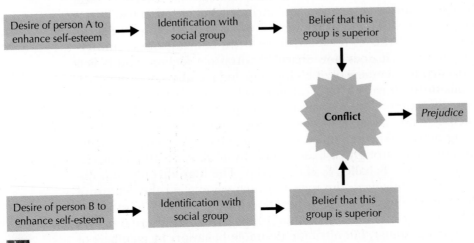

One explanation of why social categorization sometimes leads to prejudice

FIGURE 6.6 According to Tajfel (1982), prejudice sometimes arises out of *social competition*. This process reflects the desire of individuals to enhance their self-esteem by identifying with groups they view as desirable or superior. Since the members of many groups have the same desire, conflict between them occurs. Prejudice then follows from this clash of social perceptions.

Source: Based on suggestions by Tajfel, 1982.

view itself as somehow better than its rivals, and prejudice arises out of this clash of social perceptions (see Figure 6.6).

Support for the accuracy of these suggestions has been obtained in several experiments (e.g., Meindl & Lerner, 1985). Thus, it appears that our tendency to divide the social world into two opposing camps often plays a role in the development of important forms of prejudice.

EARLY EXPERIENCE: THE ROLE OF SOCIAL LEARNING

A third explanation for prejudice is one you will not find surprising: it suggests that prejudice is *learned* and that it develops in much the same manner, and through the same basic processes, as other attitudes (refer to our discussion in chapter 4). According to this **social learning view,** children acquire negative attitudes toward various social groups because they hear such views expressed by parents, friends, teachers, and others and because they are directly rewarded (with love, praise, and approval) for adopting them. In addition to direct observation of others, *social norms*—rules within a given group suggesting what actions or attitudes are appropriate—are also important (Pettigrew, 1969). As we will see in chapter 9, most persons choose to conform to most social norms of groups to which they belong. The development and expression of prejudice toward others often stems from this tendency.

While persons with whom children have direct contact are central both in social learning and in pressures toward adhering to social norms, the mass media, too, are important. Until quite recently members of racial and ethnic minorities were shown infrequently in movies or on television. Further, when they did appear, they were usually cast in low-status or comic roles. Given repeated exposure to such materials for years or even decades, it is not at all surprising that many children came to believe that the members of these groups must be inferior. After all, why else would they always be shown in this manner?

The situation has changed greatly in recent years in the United States and elsewhere. Members of various racial and ethnic minorities now appear more frequently and are shown in a more favorable manner than was true in the past. Whether these shifts will contribute to reduced prejudice remains uncertain, but at least they constitute a few steps in the appropriate (counter-prejudicial) direction.

COGNITIVE SOURCES OF PREJUDICE: STEREOTYPES, ILLUSORY CORRELATIONS, AND OUTGROUP HOMOGENEITY

A fourth source of prejudice is in some ways the most unsettling of all. As we noted earlier, it involves the possibility that prejudice stems, at least in part, from basic aspects of *social cognition*—how we think about other persons. We will now consider several forms of evidence pointing to this conclusion.

Critical Thinking Question 6

STEREOTYPES: WHAT THEY ARE AND HOW THEY OPERATE.   Consider the following groups: Afro-Americans, Asian-Americans, homosexuals, Jews. Suppose you were asked to list the traits most characteristic of each. Would you experience much difficulty? Probably you would not. You would be able to construct quite easily a list of traits for each group. Moreover, you could do this *even for groups with which you have had limited personal contact.* Why? The reason involves the existence and operation of **stereotypes**. As we saw in chapter 3, these are cognitive frameworks consisting of knowledge and beliefs about specific social groups. As noted by Judd, Ryan, and Park (1991), stereotypes involve generalizations about the typical or "modal" characteristics of members of various social groups. That is, they suggest that all members of such groups possess certain traits, at least to a degree. Once a stereotype is activated, these traits come readily to mind; hence the ease with which you could construct the lists described above (Higgins & Bargh, 1987).

Like other cognitive frameworks or *schemas,* stereotypes exert strong effects on the ways in which we process social information. For example, information relevant to a particular stereotype is processed more quickly than information unrelated to it (Dovidio, Evans, & Tyler, 1986). Similarly, stereotypes lead the persons holding them to pay attention to specific types of information—usually, information consistent with the stereotypes. Alternatively, if information inconsistent with a stereotype does manage to enter consciousness, we may actively refute it, perhaps by recalling facts and information that *are* consistent with the stereotype (O'Sullivan & Durso, 1984). Stereotypes also determine what we remember—usually, again, information that is consistent with these frameworks.

Now consider the relevance of such effects to prejudice. Once an individual has acquired a stereotype about some social group, she or he tends to notice information that fits readily into this cognitive framework and to remember "facts" that are consistent with it more readily than "facts" that are inconsistent with it. As a result, the stereotype becomes, to a large degree, self-confirming. Even exceptions to it make it stronger, for they simply induce the person in question to bring more supporting information to mind (see Figure 6.7, p. 232).

Evidence for the ways in which stereotypes influence (we might actually say *bias*) social thought has been provided by many different studies (e.g., Brewer,

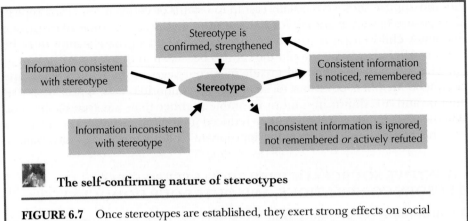

The self-confirming nature of stereotypes

FIGURE 6.7 Once stereotypes are established, they exert strong effects on social thought. Information consistent with stereotypes is noticed and remembered more readily than information inconsistent with these cognitive frameworks. As a result, stereotypes become largely self-confirming, and even exceptions to them serve to increase their strength.

1989; Fiske & Neuberg, 1990). Research performed by Bodenhausen (1988) provides an especially clear illustration. Bodenhausen asked students to play the role of jurors in an imaginary court case. Some participants received information designed to activate a negative stereotype toward Hispanics—the defendant was named Carlos Ramirez, and he came from Albuquerque, New Mexico. Others received more neutral information, unrelated to existing stereotypes—the defendant was named Robert Johnson and came from Dayton, Ohio. Half the participants learned the defendant's name before receiving evidence about the case, while the others learned his name only after reading the evidence. Bodenhausen suggested that the impact of stereotypes on subsequent social judgments and behavior derives from the fact that stereotypes bias the processing of information received after their activation. Specifically, he suggested that stereotypes change recipients' interpretation of such information, cause them to devote more effort to processing stereotype-consistent than stereotype-inconsistent information, or both.

After learning the defendant's name and reading information about the case, participants in all conditions rated the likelihood that he was guilty. Bodenhausen predicted that the defendant would be rated as more guilty when he had an ethnic name, but only when participants learned the name *before* reviewing the evidence. Results offered clear support for this prediction. Additional evidence, gathered in a follow-up study, indicated that stereotypes seem to affect the processing of social information by increasing the amount of attention and rehearsal directed to stereotype-consistent input.

Stereotypes: Are they automatic? These findings and related evidence (e.g., Wyer, 1988) suggest that stereotypes do indeed lead to biased processing of social information. Once they are activated, it appears, we tend to focus on input consistent with them while ignoring other, contradictory information. As noted earlier, this leads to a situation in which stereotypes become largely self-confirming in nature and continued prejudice is assured. Stereotypes can exert such effects only when they are activated, however. A key question, therefore, is this: Precisely *when* are stereotypes activated and applied? Until recently it was widely assumed that stereotypes are activated in an automatic fashion whenever we encounter members of the groups to whom they apply (e.g., Brewer, 1989; Devine, 1989). Recent evidence suggests, however, that this is not always the case. On the contrary, it appears that several factors can strongly determine whether, and to what extent, stereotypes become active and can then influence social thought (Bargh, 1989). Perhaps the clearest evidence on this issue has been reported by Gilbert and Hixon (1991).

Critical Thinking
Question 8

These researchers reasoned that activation of stereotypes requires cognitive resources. As we have noted repeatedly in this book, such resources are quite limited. Thus, it seems possible that when we are busy with other cognitive tasks, stereotypes will be harder to activate than would otherwise be the case. On the other hand, once they *are* activated, they provide shortcuts for our thinking about others. Thus, once stereotypes are active, being busy with other cognitive tasks may increase our tendency to use them.

To test these possibilities, Gilbert and Hixon (1991) conducted two different studies. In the first, participants were asked to perform a word fragment completion task in which they were offered fragments such as S__Y and S__ORT. These fragments were presented on a videotape by two different female assistants, one of whom was white and the other of Asian descent. Activation of the stereotype for Asian-Americans was measured in terms of the number of fragments completed with stereotype-related words; for example, S__Y = shy, S__ORT = short, POLI__E = polite. To vary participants' cognitive busyness while they worked on this task, half were asked to rehearse an eight-digit number while watching the videotapes; the others were not. If being busy with other tasks prevents activation of stereotypes, then participants who rehearsed the number should provide fewer stereotypic completions than those who did not. As shown in Figure 6.8, this is precisely what happened. So it appeared that when cognitive resources are occupied by a difficult task, the likelihood that stereotypes will be activated is reduced.

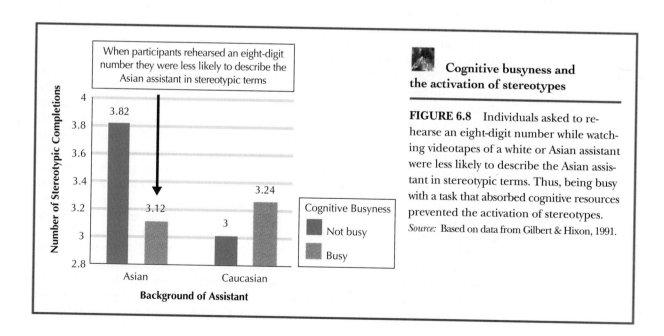

Cognitive busyness and the activation of stereotypes

FIGURE 6.8 Individuals asked to rehearse an eight-digit number while watching videotapes of a white or Asian assistant were less likely to describe the Asian assistant in stereotypic terms. Thus, being busy with a task that absorbed cognitive resources prevented the activation of stereotypes. *Source:* Based on data from Gilbert & Hixon, 1991.

In a follow-up study, Gilbert and Hixon (1991) examined the related hypothesis that once stereotypes have been activated, cognitive busyness will actually *increase* the likelihood that they will be applied. To test this possibility, they repeated the procedures of the first study but added an additional task: After finishing the word fragment task, participants also rated the assistant shown on the videotape on several dimensions related to the stereotype for Asians. The investigators varied cognitive busyness during this part of the study by having some participants perform a complex visual search task in which they had to count the number of times the letter *T* followed the letter *U* on a computer screen. It was predicted that if being occupied with other tasks increases the use of stereotypes, then participants who performed the visual search task would rate the Asian assistant in a more stereotypical fashion. This prediction, too, was confirmed.

Together, the findings reported by Gilbert and Hixon (1991) suggest that the activation of stereotypes, and their subsequent impact upon our social thought, are not inevitable. If we are busy with other tasks, they may fail to emerge, and our thinking may be relatively free of their biasing influence. Once they are activated, however, their impact on our social thought may be profound. What do these findings mean with respect to prejudice? One implication is quite encouraging: Social interaction is a complex and absorbing task. Thus, when individuals from different backgrounds who hold stereotypes about each other meet, the very fact that they must interact may help to prevent activation of stereotypes. This may be one reason why face-to-face contact helps to weaken stereotypes and associated prejudice. (We'll return to this topic in more detail on p. 242).

ILLUSORY CORRELATIONS: PERCEIVING RELATIONSHIPS THAT AREN'T THERE. Consider the following set of information: (1) There are one thousand members of Group A but only one hundred members of Group B; (2) One hundred members of Group A were arrested by the police last year, and ten members of Group B were arrested. Suppose you were asked to evaluate the criminal tendencies of these two groups: Would your ratings of them differ? Your first answer is probably "Of course not—why should they?" After all, the rate of criminal behavior is equal in the two groups (10 percent in both cases). Yet a large body of evidence suggests that you might actually assign a less-favorable rating to Group B (Hamilton & Sherman, 1989; Mullen & Johnson, 1990). Why? The answer seems to involve what social psychologists term *distinctiveness-based illusory correlations*, or, more simply, **illusory correlations**: perceived relationships between two variables when in fact none exists. In this case, you might perceive a correlation between membership in one of these groups and the tendency to commit criminal acts. Illusory correlations seem to stem, at least in part, from the fact that infrequent events are highly distinctive; thus, when two relatively infrequent events occur together, we tend to perceive that they are linked (correlated). Being arrested and belonging to Group B are both relatively infrequent events, so we perceive a stronger correlation between them than we do between being arrested and belonging to Group A (which is ten times as large).

What do illusory correlations have to do with prejudice? A great deal. For example, in the United States, whites outnumber African-Americans by approximately nine to one. Even in the mid 1990s, violent crimes are still relatively rare occurrences (except for persons living in devastated areas of major cities). Thus, when whites read or hear about a violent crime committed by an

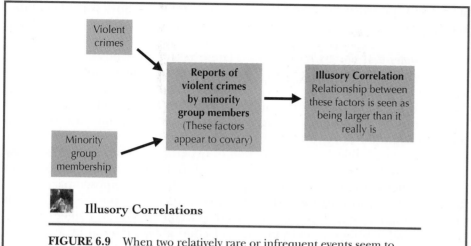

Illusory Correlations

FIGURE 6.9 When two relatively rare or infrequent events seem to covary, they are often perceived as being correlated to a greater extent than is actually the case; this is an *illusory correlation*. In the example shown here, an illusory correlation between race and violent crime results from the fact that for many white persons both such crimes and minority group members are relatively infrequent (and therefore distinctive) phenomena. Hence, many whites perceive these two factors as more closely linked than they really are.

African-American, two relatively infrequent stimuli co-occur. As a result, an illusory correlation suggesting a strong link between race and violent behavior may emerge. Please note: We are not suggesting that no such relationship exists. In the United States, members of some minority groups do commit a higher proportion of violent crimes than would be predicted solely on the basis of their numbers in the total population. Illusory correlations, however, lead many persons to assume that this relationship between racial or ethnic identity and violence is even *higher* than it is actually is. Further, illusory correlations also lead people to ignore the many factors that may be responsible for such relationships and that have nothing whatsoever to do with race or ethnic background (e.g., poverty, growing up in a highly violent environment, and so on; please see Figure 6.9).

Are illusory correlations inevitable? In other words, do the workings of our own cognitive systems condemn us to perceive relationships between variables that don't really exist? Research findings offer a relatively optimistic answer (Schaller & Maas, 1989). First, it appears that illusory correlations can be reduced or prevented by conditions that promote thorough and extensive processing of social information (Sanbonmatsu, Shavitt, & Sherman, 1991). For example, if individuals are encouraged to take account of the relative size of various groups as well as the frequency with which their members perform various actions, the tendency to perceive group membership and such actions as correlated is reduced. Similarly, and perhaps somewhat paradoxically, illusory correlations can be reduced by factors or conditions that occupy individuals' cognitive resources and prevent them from noticing differential frequencies for various events (e.g., the frequency with which members of various social groups engage in specific forms of behavior). A very clear illustration of this latter fact is provided by research conducted recently by Stroessner, Hamilton, and Mackie (1992).

Affective states and illusory correlations.   These researchers noted that affective states—positive and negative moods—often seem to reduce careful or systematic information processing (e.g., Bless et al., 1990; Mackie & Worth, 1989). Apparently, being in a positive or negative mood brings pleasant or unpleasant associations to mind, and dealing with this information may interfere with ongoing cognitive activity. If this is indeed the case, Stroessner and his colleagues reasoned, then persons induced to experience either positive or negative affect might be less likely to fall prey to illusory correlations than persons in a more neutral mood. To test this prediction they first exposed participants in their research to videotapes designed to put them in a positive, neutral, or negative mood. Positive affect was induced by a tape of a funny comedian; negative by a video about an extreme case of child abuse; neutral by a National Geographic program about a dormant volcano.

After watching these tapes, participants read sentences describing the behaviors of persons belonging to two imaginary social groups, Group A and Group B. Some of these behaviors were desirable (e.g., a member of Group A lent his neighbor some gardening tools), while others were undesirable (e.g., a member of Group B ran a red light). There were twice as many sentences about people in Group A, but for both groups, the proportion of desirable and undesirable behaviors was identical—a two-to-one ratio. After receiving this information, participants in the study were asked to indicate how much they liked the two groups and to estimate the frequency of desirable and undesirable behaviors performed by members of these groups.

It was predicted that subjects in the neutral mood condition would show illusory correlations to a greater extent than those in the positive and negative mood conditions. Results offered several forms of support for this prediction. First, participants in the neutral mood condition reported liking members of Group A significantly more than Group B; similar effects did *not* occur for persons in the positive and negative mood conditions. Second, participants in the neutral mood condition perceived stronger relationships between group membership and the frequency of desirable and undesirable behaviors than those in the positive and negative mood conditions.

Additional findings indicated that these results stemmed primarily from cognitive rather than motivational factors. A cognitive interpretation suggests that positive and negative moods reduce the occurrence of illusory correlations because affective states reduce attentional resources. A motivational interpretation, in contrast, suggests that positive affect will lead to reduced processing—since a good mood signals a satisfactory state of affairs and no need for further cognitive effort. In contrast, a negative mood signals the need for further processing in order to eliminate unpleasant thoughts or to gain a sense of control over a potentially harmful event (Schwarz, 1990). If the motivational interpretation were correct, then it would be expected that subjects in a positive mood would be less accurate than those in a neutral mood in estimating the frequency of desirable and undesirable behaviors by the two groups. In contrast, persons in a negative mood might be more accurate. But the cognitive interpretation predicts that both positive and negative moods will reduce accuracy. This is precisely what was found: Participants in the positive and negative groups were less accurate than those in the neutral condition (see Figure 6.10).

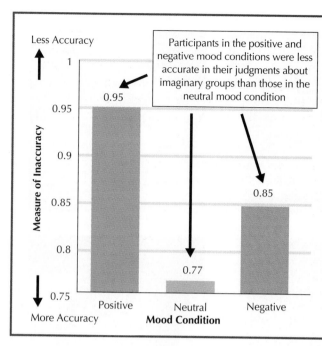

Participants in the positive and negative mood conditions were less accurate in their judgments about imaginary groups than those in the neutral mood condition

Affect and illusory correlation: Evidence for a cognitive interpretation

FIGURE 6.10 Individuals induced to experience a positive mood and those induced to experience a negative mood were less accurate than those in a neutral mood in estimating the frequency of desirable and undesirable behaviors by members of two imaginary groups. These findings offer support for the view that affective states reduce the magnitude of illusory correlations by absorbing cognitive resources.

Source: Based on data from Stroessner, Hamilton, & Mackie, 1992

In sum, it appears that illusory correlations are most likely to occur when individuals have a moderate amount of cognitive resources at their disposal for processing information about different social groups. When they direct very careful attention to such information, the tendency to perceive illusory correlations decreases. And when they are distracted or have relatively few cognitive resources available, the strength or likelihood of illusory correlations is also reduced. Unfortunately, individuals often appear to function at that critical moderate level: They pay just sufficient attention to information from the news media and other sources to form erroneous perceptions of the social world. Thus, illusory correlations appear to be quite common and may contribute to the persistence of negative stereotypes in many real-life contexts.

INGROUP DIFFERENTIATION, OUTGROUP HOMOGENEITY: "THEY'RE ALL THE SAME"—OR ARE THEY?   One remark people with a strong prejudice toward some group often make goes something like this: "You know what *they're* like; they're all the same." What such comments imply, of course, is that the members of some outgroup are much more similar to one another (i.e., are more homogeneous) than the members of one's own ingroup. This tendency to perceive persons belonging to groups other than one's own as all alike is known as the **illusion of outgroup homogeneity** (Linville et al., 1989). The mirror image of this tendency is known as the **ingroup differentiation hypothesis**—the view that we tend to perceive members of our own groups as showing much larger differences from one another than those of other groups.

Existence of the illusion of outgroup homogeneity has been demonstrated in many different contexts. For example, individuals tend to perceive persons older or younger than themselves as more similar to one another in terms of personal traits than persons in their own age group—an intriguing type of "generation gap" (Linville et al., 1989). Perhaps the most chilling example of

Transparency 6.4

Cross-racial facial identification: The illusion of outgroup homogeneity strikes again

FIGURE 6.11 Look at the photos shown here. If you are Asian, would you find it easier to recognize the strangers in the top row than those in the bottom row? If you are white, would the reverse be true?

A large body of research evidence suggests that in fact most people find it easier to recognize strangers from their own racial or ethnic group.

such outgroup homogeneity effects, however, appears in the context of *cross-racial facial identification*—the tendency for persons belonging to one racial group to be more accurate in recognizing the faces of strangers from their own group than strangers from another racial group (e.g., Bothwell, Brigham, & Malpass, 1989; see Figure 6.11). In the United States this tendency has been observed among both blacks and whites, although it appears to be somewhat stronger among whites (Anthony, Cooper, & Mullen, 1992).

Critical Thinking
Question 7

Taking account of existing evidence, it seems clear that a strong tendency does exist to perceive members of outgroups as more homogeneous than members of our own ingroup. Since it is reasonable to assume that in reality, all groups of human beings are equally diverse in their traits and behaviors, this implies that we are probably more accurate in making judgments about members of our own group than about members of various outgroups. And in fact this prediction, too, has been confirmed (Judd, Ryan, & Park, 1991).

Unfortunately, the tendency to perceive persons belonging to groups other than our own as "all alike" is yet another force operating to maintain the existence of stereotypes. After all, if we are convinced that members of outgroups show little variability with respect to important traits, why should we take the trouble to deal with them as individuals? It is much easier to conclude that we already know what they are like—and, given the negative nature of most stereotypes, this picture is usually not a favorable one. Little wonder, then, that persons belonging to different racial, ethnic, and religious groups rarely seek increased contact with each other. On the contrary, as we have noted before, they often go out of their way to minimize such contact. And this, in turn, helps assure that each group remains secluded in its own social world, insulated from change by a comforting—if dangerous—blanket of prejudice.

CHALLENGING PREJUDICE: POTENTIALLY BENEFICIAL STEPS

Whatever the specific origins of prejudice, there can be no doubt about the following point: Prejudice is a brutal, negative force in human society. Wherever and whenever it occurs, it is a drain on precious human resources. So reducing prejudice and countering its effects are important tasks—and especially crucial at a time when world population exceeds 5.5 billion and the potential harm stemming from irrational hatred is greater than ever before. Do any effective strategies for accomplishing these goals—for lessening the impact of prejudice—exist? Fortunately, they do; and while they cannot totally eliminate prejudice or discrimination, these strategies *can* make a substantial dent in the problem. Several of these tactics will now be reviewed.

BREAKING THE CYCLE OF PREJUDICE: ON LEARNING *NOT* TO HATE

Are children born with prejudices firmly in place? Or do they acquire these through experiences at home, in school, and elsewhere? At present, it would be difficult to find someone willing to support the first view, for a vast body of knowledge on human development indicates that bigots are definitely made, not born. Children acquire prejudice and related reactions from their parents, other adults, and their peers. Given this fact, one useful technique for reducing prejudice follows logically: Somehow we must discourage parents and other adults who serve as models for children from providing training in bigotry, and must encourage them instead to help children develop more positive views about others.

Having stated this principle, we must now admit that putting it into practice is anything but simple. How can we induce parents who are themselves highly prejudiced to encourage unbiased, prodiversity views among their children? One possibility involves calling parents' attention to their own prejudiced views. As we noted at the start of this chapter, few persons are willing to describe themselves as prejudiced; instead, they view their own negative attitudes toward various groups as entirely justified. A key initial step, therefore, is somehow convincing parents that the problem exists. Once they come face to face with their own prejudices, many do seem willing to modify their words and their behavior. True, some extreme fanatics actually want to turn their children into hate-filled copies of themselves. Most people, however, recognize that we live in a world of increasing ethnic and racial diversity, and realize that this environment requires a higher degree of tolerance than ever before.

Adding to the weight of these arguments is a growing body of evidence indicating that prejudice harms those who hold prejudiced views as well as its victims (Dovidio & Gaertner, 1993; Jussim, 1991). Persons who are prejudiced, it appears, live in a world filled with fear, worry, and anger—much of it of their own creation. They fear attack from presumably dangerous social groups, they worry about the economic and health risks stemming from contact with such groups, and they experience anger and other emotional turmoil over what they view as unjustified incursions by these groups into *their* neighborhoods, schools, or offices. Even at less intense levels, however, prejudice can exert negative effects on those who hold it. For example, consider a study conducted by Harris et al., (1992).

These researchers were interested in studying the impact of negative expectancies about others—expectancies closely related to certain types of prejudice—on children's social interactions. To investigate this topic, they arranged for pairs of boys in third through sixth grade, who were previously unacquainted, to play together on two different tasks. Half of the boys in the study had previously been diagnosed as being *hyperactive*, and half were normal. Before the interaction began, half of the boys were told—independently of their partner's actual behavior—that their partner had a special problem: He disrupted the class, talked when he shouldn't, and got into trouble a lot. The remainder were not provided with this information.

One of the tasks on which the boys worked involved building a design with Legos (plastic blocks); the other was more competitive in nature and involved coloring two pictures of a dinosaur with only one set of crayons. The boys' behavior during these interactions was videotaped and later rated by two trained observers on several different dimensions, such as friendliness, giving commands, and offering plans or suggestions. In addition, the boys also reported on their own feelings and reactions to the tasks.

Results indicated that, as expected, boys whose partners had been led to believe that they had a behavioral problem enjoyed the task less, rated their own performance as poorer, and took less credit for success than boys whose partners had *not* been led to believe they had such a problem. Thus, as has been found in many previous studies (e.g., Snyder & Swann, 1978), negative expectations, which are often part of prejudiced reactions, did adversely affect the targets of such expectations. This is sometimes known as the *self-fulfilling prophecy*; when others hold—and communicate—negative expectations about us, this may undermine our confidence or self-esteem and so lead us to act in ways that tend to confirm these expectancies. Needless to say, self-fulfilling prophecies can exert damaging effects on the targets of prejudice.

Another, and perhaps even more interesting, aspect of the findings obtained by Harris et al. (1991) involved the effects of such expectancies on the boys who had held them—those who had been told that their partners were hyperactive. As shown in Figure 6.12, they enjoyed the tasks less, worked less hard on them, talked less, liked their partners less, and were less friendly toward their partners than boys not given these expectations. In sum, the persons who held negative expectancies, too, were adversely affected by them. These and other findings strongly suggest that in many situations prejudice is definitely a two-edged sword: It harms its intended victims, but it exacts significant costs from the holders of prejudice, too. Educating parents about these effects may indeed cause them to think twice before indoctrinating their children with their own prejudiced views.

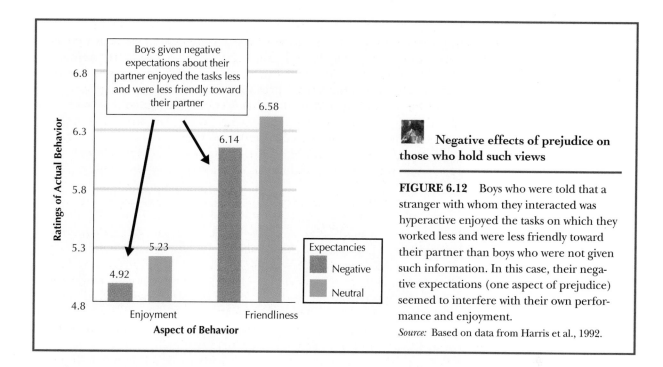

Boys given negative expectations about their partner enjoyed the tasks less and were less friendly toward their partner

Expectancies
Negative
Neutral

Enjoyment — Friendliness

Aspect of Behavior

Ratings of Actual Behavior

Negative effects of prejudice on those who hold such views

FIGURE 6.12   Boys who were told that a stranger with whom they interacted was hyperactive enjoyed the tasks on which they worked less and were less friendly toward their partner than boys who were not given such information. In this case, their negative expectations (one aspect of prejudice) seemed to interfere with their own performance and enjoyment.

Source: Based on data from Harris et al., 1992.

Please note: We don't wish to imply that holding prejudiced views, or derogating the members of outgroups, produces mainly negative effects on prejudiced persons. If that were so, prejudice would probably not constitute a major social problem. In fact, as suggested by Tajfel (1982), derogating outgroup members may help the persons who engage in such actions to establish a positive social identity. A growing body of empirical findings (e.g., Branscombe & Wann, 1993) indicates that when prejudiced persons derogate outgroup members, they sometimes experience a boost in self-esteem. So there are indeed some rewards for engaging in such behavior. The trick, it would seem, is to convince parents that the potential harm more than offsets any temporary benefits resulting from prejudiced views or actions.

DIRECT INTERGROUP CONTACT: THE POTENTIAL BENEFITS OF ACQUAINTANCE

At the present time many American cities resemble a donut in one respect: A disintegrating and crime-ridden core inhabited primarily by minority groups (the social hole, so to speak) is surrounded by relatively affluent suburbs inhabited primarily by whites and minority group members who have managed to escape, both economically and socially, from the despair of the inner city ghettos (see Figure 6.13, p. 242). Needless to say, contact between these different regions—and the people living in them—is minimal.

Discussion Question 4

This state of affairs raises an intriguing question: Can prejudice be reduced by somehow increasing the degree of contact between different groups? The idea that it can is known as the **contact hypothesis**, and there are several good reasons for predicting that such a strategy might prove effective (Pettigrew, 1981). First, increased contact between persons from different

Racial and ethnic isolation in the United States

FIGURE 6.13 Many large American cities show the pattern represented here. A disintegrating inner core populated mainly by minority groups is surrounded by affluent, and largely white, suburbs.

groups can lead to growing recognition of similarities between them. As we will see in chapter 7, perceived similarity can generate enhanced mutual attraction. Second, while stereotypes are resistant to change, they *can* be altered when sufficient information inconsistent with them is encountered. Increased contact between persons from different social groups may provide such information. Third, increased contact may help counter the illusion of outgroup homogeneity described earlier. For these reasons it seems possible that direct intergroup contact may be one effective means of combating prejudice. Is it? Existing evidence suggests that it is, but only under certain conditions (Cook, 1985).

First, the groups interacting must be roughly equal in social, economic, or task-related status. If they differ sharply in such respects, communication may be difficult and prejudice can actually be increased by contact. Second, the contact situation must involve cooperation and interdependence so that the groups work toward shared goals (as in the Robber's Cave experiment described earlier). Third, contact between the groups must be informal so that they can get to know one another as individuals. Fourth, contact must occur in a setting in which existing norms favor group equality. Fifth, the groups must interact in ways that permit disconfirmation of negative stereotyped beliefs about one another. And sixth, the persons involved must view one another as typical of their respective groups; only then will they generalize their pleasant contacts to other persons or situations (Wilder, 1984).

Transparency 6.5

When contact between initially hostile groups occurs under these conditions, prejudice between them does seem to decrease (Cook, 1985; Riordan, 1978). Such effects have been observed in the United States, where increased contact between African-Americans and whites has been found to reduce prejudice between them (Aronson, Bridgeman, & Geffner, 1978), and in many other nations as well. For example, increased school contact between Jews of Middle Eastern origin and Jews of European or American origin tends to reduce ingroup bias among Israeli soldiers (Schwarzwald, Amir, & Crain, 1992).

On the basis of these findings, it seems reasonable to suggest that when used with care, direct group contact can be an effective tool for combating cross-group hostility and prejudice. When people get to know one another, it seems, many of the anxieties, stereotypes, and false perceptions that have previously kept them apart seem to melt in the warmth of new friendships. Or, to put it another way, when stereotypes and other preconceived notions about others collide with social reality, it is sometimes reality that carries the day. As Schwarzwald et al. (1992, p. 366) put it: ". . . despite the strong social and psychological forces working to maintain the vicious circle of prejudice, change can be induced and preserved over time. Interethnic contact can alter the character of later interethnic relations."

RECATEGORIZATION: REDRAWING
THE BOUNDARY BETWEEN "US" AND "THEM"

In the town of Siena, Italy, different neighborhoods (wards) form tight-knit groups. Residents identify strongly with these groups, which date back to the Middle Ages, and proudly display the symbol of their ward (e.g., a turtle, a seashell, a falcon; see Figure 6.14, p. 244). Once a year, the various neighborhoods engage in a citywide horse race, and the struggle for victory in this event is fierce. For many days prior to the event, crowds of young people from the various neighborhoods gather in the streets to taunt one another. These sessions often become so intense that violent fights erupt, sometimes with tragic consequences. During the race itself almost any action that might bring victory is acceptable, so jockeys frequently use tactics that would be banned on most racetracks throughout the world.

Critical Thinking
Question 9

To an outsider these events seem puzzling. Siena is a small city, and the persons involved all speak the same language, share the same culture, and practice the same religion. Yet because they choose to divide their social world into competing groups, hostility and conflict between them run high. But now consider what happens when sports teams from Siena play against teams from other Italian cities. During such events, neighborhood distinctions disappear and all Sienese join together in rooting for *their* teams, which represent the

Discussion Question 1

 The us-versus-them effect

FIGURE 6.14   When neighborhoods within Siena (a small Italian city) compete against one another in a yearly horse race, each neighborhood perceives itself as *us* and the other neighborhood as *them*. Sometimes the competition becomes so intense that it leads to violent outbursts in which many persons are injured.

entire city of Siena. What has happened? In terms of the principles discussed in this chapter, the citizens of Siena have shifted the location of the boundary between "us" and "them." At the time of the citywide horse race, this boundary falls between neighborhoods. When their city competes with other towns, however, the boundary is moved outward and falls between Siena and these rivals.

Such shifts in the boundary between "us" and "them" are a common part of social life. Many of us have had the experience of rooting for our school's team when it plays against teams from other schools but of forgetting such distinctions and rooting for our city's or our state's team when it competes in a wider arena. Can this kind of boundary shift or **recategorization** be used to reduce prejudice in other contexts? Research by Gaertner and his colleagues (1989) indicates that it can. In these studies, groups of six participants first worked on a task in separate three-person teams. This was done to establish a firm *us-them* boundary between the teams. Then, in a second phase of the research, the same individuals worked on the same tasks again, but under one of several contrasting conditions. Some groups of participants continued to work as two separate teams, others worked as separate individuals (i.e., each worked alone), and still others worked together as a single six-person group. Finally, the groups rated one another on various dimensions. Gaertner and his colleagues (1989) reasoned that the experience of working either as individuals or as part of a single group would shift the us-them boundary so as to include persons who were originally members of the competing three-person team; thus, prejudice toward these persons would decrease in these conditions relative to that expressed in the condition where the boundary between these teams was maintained. Results offered strong support for this prediction.

Can this principle of recategorization (or, in the case of people working as individuals, *de*categorization) be put to practical use? Gaertner and his colleagues believe that it can, and have formulated a theoretical model—the **common ingroup identity model**—to explain how this might be so. According to this model, when various factors (e.g., perceptions of a shared fate, cultural norms stressing egalitarian values) lead individuals belonging to different groups to view themselves as members of a single social entity, attitudes toward former outgroup members become more positive. These favorable attitudes then promote increased positive contacts between members of the two previously separate groups. Such contact, in turn, reduces intergroup bias still further. In short, weakening or eliminating initial us-them boundaries starts a process that carries the persons involved toward major reductions in prejudice and hostility.

How can this process be launched? The results of a study by Gaertner et al. (1990) suggest that one factor that can get it started is "cooperative interaction" among members of the two initially distinct groups. In this investigation, two separate three-person groups were created and then brought into contact with each other under two different conditions. In the *cooperative interaction* condition, they worked together toward common goals and expected to share the same outcomes. In the *no cooperative interaction* condition, in contrast, they merely listened to the other group's discussion and did not work together in a cooperative manner. As expected, cooperative interaction increased the tendency of the two groups to perceive themselves as one entity. Moreover, cooperative interaction also reduced feelings of bias toward the former outgroup (that is, the other group). These findings and those of other research (e.g., Brewer et al., 1987; Vanbeselaere, 1987) suggest that strategies based on shifting individuals' perceived boundaries so as to include a wider range of persons inside the us-them boundary offers a very promising approach to the reduction of prejudice.

Work in Progress

Prejudice in a Multicultural High School: Testing the Common Ingroup Identity Model in a Field Setting

While the research conducted by Gaertner and his colleagues provides strong support for the common ingroup identity model, this research does suffer from one obvious drawback: It used short-lived, artificially created groups. How does the model fare when tested under more natural conditions? To find out, Gaertner et al. (1993) have recently conducted follow-up research in a multicultural high school in the United States. Students in the school came from many different ethnic back-

grounds—African-American, Chinese, Hispanic, Japanese, Korean, Vietnamese, and Caucasian. More than thirteen hundred students in the school completed a survey designed to measure their perceptions of conditions shown in previous research to influence the effects of increased contact with persons from other groups (e.g., equal status, cooperative interdependence, norms supportive of friendly intergroup contact). Other items on the survey measured students' perceptions of the extent to which the student body at the school was a single group, consisted of distinct groups, or was composed of separate individuals. Finally, students also completed items designed to measure their feelings toward both their ingroup and various outgroups.

Results offered strong support for the model. First, as predicted, perceptions of cooperative interdependence between students from different groups were positively related to the students' belief that the student body was a single group. Similarly, the extent to which the students felt as though they belonged to one group was significantly related to positive feelings toward outgroup members. Finally, the stronger the students' feelings of interdependence, the smaller the difference between their feelings toward ingroup and outgroup members. In sum, as the model predicts, the greater the extent to which students at the school felt that they belonged to a single cooperative group, the lower their feelings of intergroup bias. When combined with the results of systematic laboratory studies, these findings suggest that efforts to induce persons belonging to different groups to engage in *recategorization*—to shift the boundary between "us" and "them" so as to include persons previously excluded—can be an important first step toward the reduction of many forms of prejudice.

COGNITIVE INTERVENTIONS: WHEN STEREOTYPES SHATTER—OR AT LEAST BECOME LESS COMPELLING

Throughout this chapter, we have noted that stereotypes play an important role in prejudice. The tendency to think about others in terms of their membership in various groups or categories (*category-driven processing*) appears to be a key factor in the occurrence and persistence of several forms of prejudice (Fiske, 1989). If this is so, then interventions designed to reduce the impact of stereotypes may prove highly effective in reducing prejudice and discrimination. How can this goal be accomplished? Several techniques have been suggested.

First, and most directly, the impact of stereotypes can be reduced by encouraging individuals to think carefully about others—to pay attention to their unique characteristics rather than their membership in various groups. Recent findings indicate that such *attribute-driven processing* can be encouraged even by such simple procedures as informing individuals that their own outcomes or rewards in a situation will be affected by another's performance, or telling them that it is very important to be accurate in forming an impression of another person. Under these conditions individuals are motivated to be accurate, and this reduces their tendency to rely on stereotypes (Erber & Fiske, 1984; Neuberg, 1989).

Second, and more surprising, the impact of stereotypes can sometimes be reduced by techniques based on principles of attribution (see our discussion of this topic in chapter 2). These techniques can be viewed as fighting fire with fire, since they employ certain tilts or forms of bias in our attributions to push us out of stereotypical patterns of thinking. A compelling illustration of such procedures is provided by research conducted by Mackie et al. (1992).

These investigators noted that often we base inferences about others' characteristics on their outcomes, even if these outcomes were actually constrained by external events and are really not a firm basis for reaching such inferences. For example, consider a situation in which an individual scores 70 on an exam. Suppose that 65 is passing; how would you rate this person's motivation and intelligence? Now, instead, imagine that 75 is passing; would your ratings be any different? A large body of evidence indicates that you might well rate the person higher in intelligence and motivation in the first instance than in the second, despite the fact that her or his performance is identical. If you did, this would be an example of *outcome-biased inferences* (Allison, Worth, & King, 1990): Your inferences about this person's characteristics were strongly affected by the nature of the outcomes, quite apart from actual performance.

What does this have to do with prejudice, and specifically with countering the impact of stereotypes? Mackie and her colleagues reasoned as follows. Relying on outcomes in inferring others' traits may sometimes lead us to form *counterstereotypic inferences* about them. To the extent we do, our tendency to rely on stereotypes may actually be reduced. In order to test this prediction, Mackie et al. (1992) conducted a study in which participants learned that a conservative or a liberal political group (the Young Republicans or Young Democrats) had taken a vote on a liberal social measure (university-sponsored distribution of birth control devices on campus). In both organizations, a slight majority (57 percent) of the membership had voted in favor of this action. In one condition, however, bylaws of each group required a 65 percent majority for passage, while in another condition only a 50 percent majority was required. Since 57 percent of the membership of each group voted for the measure, it failed in the first condition, but passed in the second. After receiving this information, each subject rated the group about which he or she had read in terms of how liberal or conservative group members were. Participants also indicated how much the group's liberal or conservative attitudes had changed in the past year.

Mackie and her colleagues reasoned that because of our tendency to rely very heavily on outcomes, participants would perceive both groups as more liberal (i.e., less conservative) when the measure passed than when it failed, despite the fact that in both cases, it was supported by 57 percent of the members. Further, the researchers predicted that participants would also perceive greater change in both groups' views when the measure passed than when it failed. As shown in Figure 6.15, results agreed with these predictions.

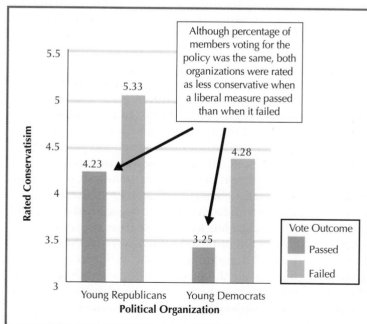

When attributions can serve to reduce prejudice

FIGURE 6.15 Individuals learned that 57 percent of the members of a conservative or a liberal political group had voted in favor of a liberal policy. Some were told that because only a simple majority was required for passage, the policy was approved; others learned that a 65 percent vote was required for passage, so it had failed. Surprisingly, participants in the study rated each organization as less conservative in the former case. These findings suggest that one form of attributional bias (outcome-biased inferences) can operate to reduce the impact of stereotypes, and hence, to reduce certain forms of prejudice.

Source: Based on data from Mackie et al., 1992.

Participants rated the Young Republicans as being less conservative when the liberal measure passed than when it failed, despite the fact that 57 percent of the members supported this action in both cases. And the same pattern occurred for ratings of the Young Democrats: They, too, were rated as less conservative when the liberal measure passed than when it failed. In addition, participants perceived greater change in each group when the outcome of the vote was discrepant with their existing stereotypes; that is, they perceived greater change in the Young Republicans when this measure failed.

These findings have important implications for efforts to reduce prejudice, and especially for the impact of *affirmative action* programs. These programs are designed to improve the outcomes of various disadvantaged groups. To the extent that such outcomes improve, perceptions of the characteristics of these groups, too, may shift. Outcome-biased inference may lead to the perception that group members are higher in talent, motivation, and intelligence than existing stereotypes suggest. Thus, while stereotypes are often self-confirming, a change in the outcomes actually experienced by stereotyped groups may serve to undermine these stereotypes—and hence to weaken prejudice against them. In essence, one form of cognitive bias (outcome-biased attributions) may serve to counter another, with beneficial consequences for society.

Work in Progress

Countering the Benefits of Outcome-Biased Inferences: Why Affirmative Action Programs Often Fail to Weaken Prevailing Steretoypes

As noted above, the findings reported by Mackie and her colleagues (e.g., Mackie et al., 1992) suggest that on some occasions, affirmative action programs can help to weaken existing stereotypes. Specifically, because of our tendency to infer others' traits from their outcomes, some observers may come to view members of minority groups who are hired, promoted, or admitted to various schools through affirmative action programs as more talented and hard-working than they previously believed. Unfortunately, however, there is a potential rub in this process. When we pay careful attention to the environmental constraints that influence others' outcomes, we are less likely to use such outcomes as a basis for inferring their traits. And, unfortunately, the publicity directed to many affirmative action programs may produce just this effect. Specifically, such publicity may call people's attention to the possiblity that different criteria are applied to different groups—that, for example, standards

for promotion or admission to various schools are lower for minority group members than for other persons. Then the tendency to use such favorable outcomes as a basis for inferring that these persons possess positive traits may be reduced.

Evidence for precisely such effects has recently been obtained by Mackie and her students (Mackie et al., 1993). In their study they informed white participants that science fair teams from two elementary schools performed equally well. However, because the two schools had different performance standards (different criteria for allowing teams to go to the science fair), teams from one school qualified to attend the science fair while those from the other school did not. Participants were further informed that students at one of the schools were black while those at the other were white. When asked to rate the intelligence of the teams, participants showed no tendency toward outcome-biased inferences: They did *not* rate the teams that qualified as more intelligent than those who did not. Moreover, this was true regardless of which school (the one with black students or the one with white students) benefited from the contrasting criteria. These findings suggest that when participants' attention was drawn to the contrasting criteria, they processed information about the teams carefully and did not tend to base inferences about the students' intelligence on their outcomes. Unfortunately, public attention to affirmative action programs may produce the same effects and so may tend to counter the potential value of such programs in countering existing stereotypes. To the extent this is true, a very startling conclusion is suggested: From the point of view of reducing racial, ethnic, or gender stereotypes, the less publicity given to such programs, the better!

PREJUDICE BASED ON GENDER: ITS NATURE AND EFFECTS

Exercise 2

More than half of the world's population is female. Yet, despite this fact, in many cultures females have been treated as though they were a minority group. They have been excluded from economic and political power; they have been the subject of strong negative stereotypes; and they have faced overt discrimination in many spheres of life—work settings, higher education, government. In the mid-1990s this situation appears to be changing in at least some countries. Overt discriminatory practices have been banned by legislation in many nations, and there has been at least some weakening of **sexism**, or negative gender-based stereotypes, about women. Yet such progress has been spotty at best (Steinberg & Shapiro, 1982). Prejudice and open discrimination against females have decreased noticeably in some countries and regions, while in others there has been virtually no change in centuries-old patterns of restriction and bias (see Kanekar, Kolsawala, & Nazareth, 1988; see Figure 6.16, p. 250). Because prejudice based on gender affects more individuals than any other single kind (more than half the human race!) and because it produces negative outcomes for males as well as females, we will consider it here in detail.

Video: *Sex and Gender**

GENDER STEREOTYPES: THE COGNITIVE CORE OF PREJUDICE TOWARD FEMALES

Females have often been the object of strong, persistent stereotypes. To an extent, so have males: They too are perceived as being "all alike" in their possession of certain traits—and woe to the male in many cultures who fails to live up to the sterotypical image. By and large, however, stereotypes about females are more negative in content than those about males. For example, in many cultures males are assumed to possess such desirable traits as *decisiveness, forcefulness, confidence, ambition,* and *rationality.* In contrast, the corresponding assumptions about females include less-desirable traits such as *passivity, submissiveness, indecisiveness, emotionality,* and *dependence* (Deaux & Lewis, 1984). Some positive characteristics, too, are included—such as warmth, nurturance, sensitivity, and understanding. Overall, however, the traits assigned to females are less desirable and less suited for many valued roles (e.g., leadership, authority) than the traits assigned to males (Heilman, Martell, & Simon, 1988).

 Opportunities for women: A spotty worldwide pattern

FIGURE 6.16 In some nations women have gained increasing equality and opportunity in recent decades. In others, however, age-old patterns of prejudice and restriction remain intact.

Are such **gender stereotypes** accurate? Do men and women really differ in the ways these stereotypes suggest? This question is complex, for such differences between the sexes, even if observed, may be more a reflection of the impact of stereotypes and their self-confirming nature than of basic differences between men and women. Existing evidence, however, points to the general conclusion that where differences between the sexes are concerned, common sense—and gender stereotypes—overstate the case. Males and females do indeed differ in some respects; for example, males tend to be more aggressive than females (Baron & Richardson, 1994), and the two sexes often use different techniques for influencing others (Carli, 1989). Overall though, the number and magnitude of such differences is far less than prevailing stereotypes suggest.

Do persistent, and largely negative, gender stereotypes have detrimental effects on females? For evidence that they do, please see the **Applied Side** section that follows.

NEGATIVE EFFECTS OF GENDER STEREOTYPES: WHY, OFTEN, MEN GET THE JOBS

Stereotypes do not exist in a social vacuum. On the contrary, they exert powerful effects on judgments and evaluations of the persons to whom they are applied. Gender stereotypes are no exception—they influence the perceptions and behavior of large numbers of persons. In the case of females, the impact of such stereotypes is largely negative. Such effects are visible in many areas of life, but perhaps they are most unsettling with respect to jobs and the world of work. A growing body of evidence suggests that when selecting applicants for various jobs—and especially for relatively high-level ones—organizations seek a good match: They want to hire the people whose characteristics resemble most closely those that they view as necessary for effective performance. This is a reasonable point of view, but, in the context of gender stereotypes, it turns out to be highly damaging to females.

What traits are assumed to be necessary for success in high-level jobs? In general, it appears, ones closer to the content of male gender stereotypes than to the content of female gender stereotypes. Leaders, most people believe, should be bold, assertive, tough, and decisive—all traits traditionally viewed as masculine in nature. In contrast, few persons want or expect leaders to be kind, sensitive, emotional, and nurturant. To the extent females are subject to traditional gender stereotypes, then, they face a difficult uphill struggle in efforts to launch and advance their careers.

Evidence for the negative impact of gender stereotypes on females in work settings has been obtained in many studies (e.g., Heilman & Martell, 1986; Heilman, Martell, & Simon, 1988). These experiments have repeatedly found that females are perceived as less suited for high-level jobs than males, primarily because they are viewed as possessing the traits required for successful performance of these jobs to a lesser extent than males.

While such findings are unsettling, much of this research used *simulation* procedures in which college students or others played the role of job interviewers or other persons charged with the task of choosing among applicants. A study by Van Vianen and Willemsen (1992), however, examined the effects of gender stereotypes on the decisions of actual members of employment selection boards.

These individuals (some of whom were female and some male) had the responsibility of interviewing applicants for high-level scientific and technical jobs at a university in the Netherlands. They completed two questionnaires: one on which they rated the attributes of ideal candidates and another on which they rated the perceived qualities of each actual job applicant. Ratings on both questionnaires involved traits previously found to be part of masculine and feminine gender stereotypes. For example, positive traits that were part of the masculine gender stereotype included *daring, forceful, logical, confident;* negative traits included *aggressive, arrogant, dominant, reckless.* Positive traits on the feminine gender stereotype included *understanding, sociable, spontaneous, warm, gentle;* negative traits included *dependent, dreamy, changeable, affected.*

Critical Thinking
Question 10

Exercise 4

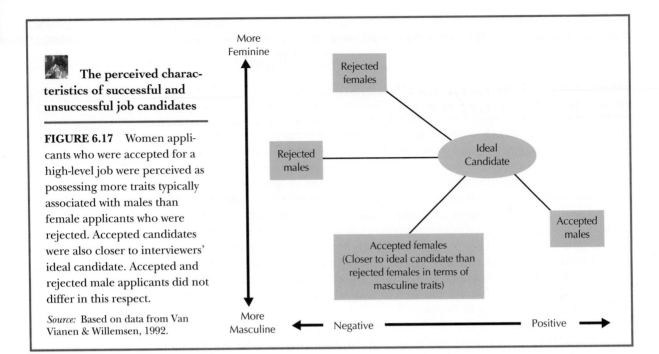

The perceived characteristics of successful and unsuccessful job candidates

FIGURE 6.17 Women applicants who were accepted for a high-level job were perceived as possessing more traits typically associated with males than female applicants who were rejected. Accepted candidates were also closer to interviewers' ideal candidate. Accepted and rejected male applicants did not differ in this respect.

Source: Based on data from Van Vianen & Willemsen, 1992.

Results provided strong support for the view that these gender stereotypes play a role both in conceptions of ideal job candidates and in the actual selection of applicants. First, descriptions of the ideal candidate provided by the interviewers included mainly traits present in the masculine gender stereotype. This implies that in the eyes of these interviewers, the traits required for success in these high-level jobs were primarily ones typically attributed to males. Second, the candidates they recommended for the job were rated as possessing masculine attributes to a greater extent than candidates they rejected. Third, as shown in Figure 6.17, accepted and rejected female candidates differed significantly in terms of their perceived possession of masculine traits: Accepted females were much closer to the description of the "ideal candidate" than rejected ones, and of course the ideal candidate was described largely in masculine terms. In contrast, rejected and accepted males did not differ significantly in perceived possession of masculine traits.

Fortunately, it appears that the impact of gender stereotypes can be reduced when clear evidence of a woman's ability or competence is provided to interviewers (Heilman, Martell, & Simon, 1988). Nevertheless, the findings reported by Van Vianen and Willemsen (1992) and other researchers suggest that in many instances persistent gender stereotypes can—and do—exert negative effects on the prospects and outcomes of working females.

DISCRIMINATION AGAINST FEMALES: SUBTLE BUT OFTEN DEADLY

In the mid-1990s, overt discrimination on the basis of sex has been made illegal by legislation in many countries. As a result, it is much more difficult for businesses, schools, and social organizations to reject applicants for jobs or admission simply because they are female (or male). Despite this fact, females continue to occupy a relatively disadvantaged position in most societies in certain respects. They are concentrated in low-paying, low-status jobs, and their average salary remains lower than that for males. Why is this the case? One possibility is that sufficient time has not yet elapsed for women to receive the full benefits of legal and social changes that occurred during the 1970s and 1980s. Another possibility—one supported by considerable research evidence—is that while overt barriers to female advancement have largely disappeared, other, more subtle forces continue to operate against women in many contexts. We'll now review several of these.

Discussion Question 3

THE ROLE OF EXPECTATIONS.   One factor impeding the progress of females involves their own expectations. In general, women seem to hold lower expectations about their careers than men. They expect to receive lower starting and peak salaries (Jackson, Gardner, & Sullivan, 1992; Major & Konar, 1984). And they view lower salaries for females as being somehow fair (Jackson & Grabski, 1988). Why do females hold these lower expectations? The findings of recent studies (e.g., Jackson, Gardner, & Sullivan, 1992) indicate that several factors play a role.

First, females expect to take more time out from work (for example, for child rearing); this tends to lower their expectations for peak career salaries. Second, women seem to place less importance on job outcomes generally, including salary, than men. To the extent this is the case, they may find lower pay relatively acceptable. Third, women realize that females do generally earn less than males. Thus, their lower expectations may simply reflect their recognition of current reality and its likely impact upon their own salaries. Fourth, women tend to compare themselves with other disadvantaged group members (other females, minority groups) rather than with relatively advantaged males (Crocker & Major, 1989). To the extent they do, it is not surprising that their expectations are relatively low. Finally, and according to recent findings perhaps most important, women view less pay as being fair both with respect to starting salaries and peak salaries (Jackson et al., 1992). In other words, they view relatively low levels of pay as more fair than males do. Whatever the specific basis for women's lower salary expectations, it is a fact of life that, in general, people tend to get what they expect. Thus, females' lower expectations with respect to such outcomes may be one important factor operating against them in many organizations.

Reading Lesko (16), *A Chill in the College Classroom*

THE ROLE OF SELF-CONFIDENCE.   Confidence, it is often said, is the single best predictor of success. People who expect to succeed often do; those who expect to fail find that prediction confirmed. Unfortunately, women tend to express lower self-confidence than men in many achievement-related situations. That they have not yet attained full equality with men in many work settings, therefore, may stem, at least in part, from this factor (McCarty, 1986).

WITHHOLDING CREDIT WHERE CREDIT IS DUE: ATTRIBUTIONS ABOUT MALE AND FEMALE ACHIEVEMENT.   A third factor that tends to operate against females in many contexts involves differences in attributions concerning successful performance by males and females. Several studies suggest that some persons, at least, tend to attribute success by males to internal factors such as effort or ability, while attributing similar performance by females to external causes such as luck or an easy task (Deaux, 1982; Nieva &

Gutek, 1981). The effects of this tendency can be devastating for females. If a man succeeds at some task, it is assumed that he has worked hard or that he possesses a high level of ability. If a female attains the same level of performance, in contrast, it is assumed that she lucked out, that she had extra help, or that the task itself wasn't very hard. Since important rewards like raises and promotions often depend on such evaluations (performance appraisals), these tendencies clearly operate against achievement by females in many work settings. Fortunately, they do not seem to occur in all contexts. When the attention of the persons making the evaluations is directed firmly to the actual performance of those being judged, such bias may vanish (Izraeli, Izraeli, & Eden, 1985). At other times, however, these tendencies may persist and exert negative effects on the careers of deserving female employees.

NEGATIVE REACTIONS TO FEMALE LEADERS: THE HIDDEN MESSAGE OF NONVERBAL CUES. Suppose you stopped a hundred people on the street and asked them the following question: "Can women be successful leaders?" In the mid-1990s most people would probably reply "Of course." And some might go on to name famous female leaders such as Margaret Thatcher (former prime minister of Great Britain). But stop and consider. Do such comments reflect people's real views? Or would many of these same persons actually react differently to male and female leaders when they meet them? A study conducted by Butler and Geis (1990) points to the latter conclusion.

These researchers reasoned that even at present many people—women as well as men—find leadership by females unexpected: It just doesn't seem to fit with prevailing gender stereotypes. Since violations of expectations often induce negative affect, Butler and Geis (1990) predicted that many persons will demonstrate such negative reactions to female leaders in their nonverbal cues—through facial expressions of displeasure or rejection.

To determine if this is actually the case, Butler and Geis observed the facial expressions of male and female participants while interacting with male and female assistants specially trained to act as leaders during a group discussion. Results were clear: Female leaders did receive more negative nonverbal cues from other members of the group than male leaders. Moreover, male leaders also received more positive nonverbal cues per minute than did female leaders. Disturbingly, these findings emerged even though subjects strongly denied any bias against females. The fact that they still showed contrasting facial reactions to identical actions by female and male leaders points to the existence of yet another subtle, but potentially damaging, barrier to equal achievement by females.

SEXUAL HARASSMENT: WHEN DISCRIMINATION TAKES A SLEAZY TURN

Reading: Lesko (18), *Detecting and Labeling Prejudice* All of the factors we have considered so far in this discussion are relatively subtle in nature. Another type of workplace discrimination against females, however, is far more obvious—and objectionable: **sexual harassment**. While this term is still being defined by society and the courts, it generally refers to uninvited and unwanted sexual advances, propositions, comments, or discussions. In the workplace such harassment ranges from very extreme forms, such as demands for sexual favors that are linked to keeping one's job or gaining a promotion, through milder (but still unacceptable) forms, such as posting offensive pinups and staring at portions of coworkers' anatomy. Regardless of the form it takes, women are much more frequently the victim of sexual harassment than men; hence, it can be viewed as a form of discrimination that impacts primarily on females.

Unfortunately, sexual harassment is all too common in many work settings. For example, in one recent poll, fully 30 percent of employed women indicated that they had been the object of such harassment on at least one occasion. And fully 50 percent of the men polled indicated that at some time in the past, they had said or done something at work that could be perceived by a female as constituting sexual harassment (Kolbert, 1991). The magnitude of the problem is suggested by the fact that only a small proportion of instances of sexual harassment are ever reported: Less than 10 percent of women who have experienced such treatment indicate that they reported it to the appropriate person in their company (Strom, 1991).

Fortunately, recognition of this problem has increased dramatically in the United States and elsewhere, partly as a result of the sexual harassment charges brought by Professor Anita Hill against Justice Clarence Thomas when he was being reviewed by the United States Senate Judiciary Committee for a seat on the Supreme Court (see Figure 6.18). Such recognition has been matched by concrete actions on the part of many organizations. They have announced clear policies against sexual harassment, indicating that it will not

 Sexual harassment as a political issue

FIGURE 6.18 Professor Anita Hill brought charges of sexual harassment against Clarence Thomas, a nominee for the United States Supreme Court. While the charges were never proven and Justice Thomas was ultimately appointed to the court, this situation made sexual harassment a topic of national interest in the United States.

be tolerated, and have established mechanisms for hearing complaints and potential penalties for persons who are found to have engaged in such actions. It is hoped that these steps will help to lessen the frequency of sexual harassment in the future. At present, however, it is clear that it remains a serious problem for females, and one society can certainly not ignore.

Discussion Question 2

Social Diversity ▼ A Critical Analysis

The Effects of Prejudice: Racial Identification among African-Americans

Eurocentric; this is definitely a loaded term in America in the mid-1990s. It refers to the view that American culture, because of its strong roots in Europe, perceives the world through a lens of European history and European values. For example, Columbus is said to have *discovered* America, as though the millions of people who lived in North and South America were floating in limbo until they were brought into contact—much to their sorrow!—with European civilization. Similarly, the many contributions to the development of the United States by persons not of European descent were largely ignored in most history texts until the past few years.

In a sense, the term *Eurocentric* also seems to apply, at least to a degree, to the study of prejudice and discrimination. Most theorizing and research on these topics has focused, at least in the United States, on prejudice *by* the European-descended majority *toward* other groups in American society. Certainly, it has been the prejudice of white Americans that has inflicted pain, suffering, and deprivation on other groups—Native

Americans, African-Americans, Hispanic-Americans, to name just a few. But in recent years it has become apparent that it is equally important to investigate the reactions of these other groups to prejudice. How have the targets of majority prejudice coped with such treatment? What has it done to their self-concept, their self-esteem, and their identification with their own group? These are the kinds of questions that have been raised with increasing frequency in systematic research.

We should hasten to add that research on the reactions of minority group members to prejudice is not new in social psychology. On the contrary, classic investigations by Kenneth Clark (Clark & Clark, 1947) examined the possibility that black children develop negative attitudes toward themselves and their own group as a result of exposure to racial prejudice. In these investigations Clark found that many black children preferred to play with a white doll rather than a black doll. Moreover, the children also described the white doll as nicer, as more attractive, and as looking more like themselves than the black doll. The

validity of these findings has been called into question, however, on several important grounds (e.g., McMillan, 1988). For example, the fact that many black children chose the white doll may have stemmed from the fact that at the time these studies were conducted, black dolls were actually less well made than white dolls. Thus, the black children were simply making a rational choice between two toys, not providing evidence for a negative attitude toward their own group. Similarly, they may have chosen the white doll because they thought this is what the researchers wanted them to do—because of *demand characteristics.*

In view of such potential flaws, many researchers have concluded that these early studies actually tell us very little about minority group members' reactions to prejudice or about their feelings of racial identity. It is at this point, fortunately, that more recent, and more sophisticated research enters the picture. During the past decade a growing number of studies have examined prejudice from the perspective of the persons who are its targets. Since much of this work has focused on such reactions among African-Americans, we will concentrate on this topic. Investigation of the reactions of other minority groups is equally important, however, and is currently proceeding.

Racial Identification of African-Americans: A Theoretical Model

One crucial effect of exposure to racial prejudice seems obvious: heightened **racial identification.** When others exclude you from their schools, offices, and neighborhoods, assume that you possess stereotyped traits, and describe your physical characteristics in negative terms, one obvious effect is to make you, as an individual, conscious of your own membership in a specific racial group. That this is part of the experience of many African-Americans is apparent (e.g., Asante, 1980; Williams, 1976). But what, precisely, does racial identification involve? Is it an all-or-nothing process in which individuals conclude that they belong to a particular racial group and to no other? Modern conceptions of racial identification, based on careful research with African-Americans, suggest that this is not so (Hilliard, 1985). In what is perhaps the most influential current model of this process, Sanders Thompson (1988, 1991) suggests that racial identification of African-Americans involves three key aspects: *physical, psychological,* and *sociocultural* components.

The physical component refers to a sense of acceptance and comfort with the physical attributes of blacks (skin color, hair texture, etc.). The psychological component refers to the individual's sense of concern for and commitment to the racial group. Group pride and feelings of group membership and responsibility are central to this aspect of racial identity. Finally, the sociocultural aspect refers to the individual's attitudes toward cultural, social, and economic issues. These include expressions of cultural heritage, as well as attitudes concerning the economic and political advancement of African-Americans. According to Sanders Thompson (1990, 1991), all three are essential components of an individual's racial identification (see Figure 6.19).

Exercise 3

Factors Affecting Racial Identity: The Key Role of Life Experiences

If racial identification is not an all-or-nothing state, a reasonable question to ask about it is this: What factors influence the development of such identification? In other words, what factors determine the extent to which individuals develop the physical, psychological, and/or sociocultural reactions described above? Clearly, it might be possible for a given individual to develop some aspects of racial identification but not others. For example, she or he might be comfortable with the physical features of African-Americans (in fact, recent evidence suggests that such satisfaction exists for many African-Americans; Bond & Cash, 1992). Concurrently, though, the same

 Racial identification: Basic components

FIGURE 6.19 According to a model proposed by Sanders Thompson (1990, 1991), racial identification involves three major components: physical, psychological, and sociocultural.

Source: Based on suggestions by Sanders Thompson, 1990, 1991.

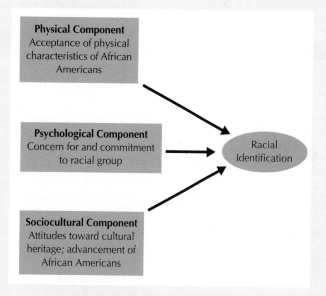

person might feel little attachment to black culture and little concern over the economic or political opportunities of other blacks. If individuals can vary in the extent to which they demonstrate these different components of racial identification, then perhaps each component is affected by somewhat different factors. A well-conducted study by Sanders Thompson (1991) provides revealing evidence on this issue.

Through interviews and a questionnaire, Sanders Thompson obtained information from almost two hundred African-Americans concerning numerous variables she felt might influence racial identification. She included demographic variables (age, income, level of education, etc.) and variables relating to a wide range of social factors, such as when and to what extent respondents had personally experienced racism, whether there had been conflict within respondents' families relating to skin color or social class, and the extent to which respondents interacted with white Americans (the proportion of whites in their neighborhood and school, their experience with interracial dating, etc.). Additional items were designed to assess the physical, psychological, and sociocultural components of racial identification.

Results indicated that by far the most important predictor of all three aspects of racial identification was the extent to which respondents had personal experience with racial prejudice. The greater such experience, the stronger their racial identification. In general, demographic factors such as age, income, and education were less important (although they did seem to play a role in the psychological aspect of racial identification). Not surprisingly, conflicts within one's own family related to skin color or social class significantly predicted physical racial identification.

What do these findings mean? For one thing, that exposure to white prejudice is a key factor in the development of a strong sense of racial identification among African-Americans. Such experiences seem to drive home the fact that blacks are viewed as different—as a definite outgroup—by the majority. And this in turn leads many African-Americans to identify strongly with their own group. Such identification can then serve as a crucial source of personal strength and support for the individuals involved (White & Parham, 1990). So, in one crucial respect, majority prejudice may have somewhat paradoxical—and largely unintended—effects: It can actually serve to strengthen the sense of group cohesion and the personal convictions of many African-Americans, thus enhancing their ability to resist. Of course, heightened racial identification among African Americans—or any other group in a culturally diverse society—is not an unmixed blessing. The ultimate goal in such a society is a high degree of tolerance and cooperation, *not* a series of groups fortified inside their own cultures. Still, if strong racial identification among African-Americans boosts their pride and self-esteem, the benefits may well outweigh any potential harm.

Critical Thinking Question 11

Summary and Review

The Nature of Prejudice and Discrimination

Prejudice is a negative attitude toward the members of some social group that is based solely on their membership in that group. *Discrimination* refers to harmful actions directed toward the persons or groups who are the targets of prejudice. Discrimination can be overt, ranging from relatively mild forms such as avoidance or exclusion to physical violence. However, it often occurs in more subtle forms such as *tokenism* or *reverse discrimination*. Highly prejudiced persons experience relatively little guilt or shame when they engage in discriminatory behavior toward the targets of their prejudice.

Origins of Prejudice

Several contrasting views have been offered concerning the origins of prejudice. The *realistic conflict* view suggests that prejudice stems from competition for scarce resources between social groups. A second theory, *social categorization,* suggests that prejudice stems from our strong tendencies to divide the social world into two camps, "us" and "them." A third perspective calls attention to the role of early experience, in which children acquire prejudiced attitudes from parents, teachers, friends, and others.

Much recent evidence supports the view that prejudice stems from certain aspects of *social cognition*—the way in which we think about others and the social world. *Stereotypes,* cognitive frameworks involving generalizations about the typical characteristics of members of social groups, play an especially important role in this regard. Once stereotypes are activated, they exert profound effects on social thought. Other aspects of social cognition that play a role in prejudice include *illusory correlations*—perceptions of stronger relationships between unusual or distinctive events than actually exist—and the illusion of *outgroup homogeneity,* which involves the tendency to perceive lower variability in the behavior of outgroup members than in the behavior of persons belonging to our own social group.

Strategies for Reducing Prejudice

One way to reduce prejudice is to encourage parents and others to transmit tolerant rather than prejudiced attitudes to children. *Direct intergroup contact* also seems to be helpful in this respect, provided that the contact occurs under appropriate conditions. Another useful technique involves somehow inducing individuals to shift the boundary between "us" and "them" so that former outgroup members are included in the ingroup. Cognitive interventions, such as inducing individuals to think about others in terms of their individual attributes rather than in terms of stereotypes, and inducing them to form *counterstereotypic inferences,* can also be effective in reducing prejudice.

Prejudice Based on Gender

Sexism, prejudice based on gender, involves acceptance of *gender stereotypes* suggesting that all males and all females share certain traits that distinguish them from each other. Overt discrimination against females is illegal in many nations, but several subtle forces continue to operate against female achievement in many contexts. These include lower expectations and lower self-confidence on the part of females, a tendency on the part of some persons to attribute success by females to external causes, and negative reactions to female leaders. Another, and more blatant, form of discrimination against females is *sexual harassment,* unwanted and uninvited sexual advances, propositions, or comments.

Social Diversity: Racial Identification among African-Americans

Since the mid-1980s a growing number of studies have examined the effects of prejudice from the perspective of those who are its targets. Much of this work has focused on the reactions to prejudice of African-Americans. Modern theories of *racial identification* propose that such identification consists of several distinct components, including *physical, psychological,* and *sociocultural identification.* While these are influenced by demographic variables (age, income, education), racial identification appears to be most strongly affected by personal experiences with racial prejudice.

Key Terms

Common Ingroup Identity Model A theory suggesting that to the extent individuals in different groups view themselves as members of a single social entity, positive contacts between groups will increase and intergroup bias will be reduced.

Contact Hypothesis The view that increased contact between members of various social groups can be effective in reducing prejudice between them. Such efforts seem to succeed only when contact takes place under specific, favorable conditions.

Discrimination Negative behaviors directed toward members of social groups who are the object of prejudice.

Gender Stereotypes Stereotypes concerning the traits supposedly possessed by females and males, traits that distinguish the two genders from each other.

Illusion of Outgroup Homogeneity The tendency to perceive members of outgroups as more similar to one another (less variable) than the members of one's own ingroup.

Illusory Correlations Perceptions of stronger associations between variables than actually exist. Illusory correlations come about because each variable is a distinctive event and the co-occurrence of such events is readily entered into and retrieved from memory.

Ingroup The social group to which an individual perceives herself or himself as belonging ("us").

Ingroup Differentiation Hypothesis The view that individuals perceive greater variability among members of their ingroup than they do among members of various outgroups.

Outgroup Any group other than the one to which individuals perceive themselves as belonging ("them").

Prejudice Negative attitudes toward the members of specific social groups.

Racial Identification The process through which individuals (especially those belonging to minority groups) acquire identification with their own racial group. Current models of racial identification suggest that it involves physical, psychological, and sociocultural components.

Realistic Conflict Theory The view that prejudice sometimes stems from direct competition among social groups over scarce and valued resources.

Recategorization Shift in the boundary between an individual's ingroup ("us") and some outgroup ("them"). As a result of such recategorization, persons formerly viewed as outgroup members may now be viewed as belonging to the ingroup.

Reverse Discrimination The tendency to evaluate or treat persons belonging to other groups (especially ones that are the object of strong ethnic or racial prejudice) more favorably than members of one's own group.

Sexism Prejudice based on gender.

Sexual Harassment Unwanted and uninvited sexual contact, propositions, or comments; often occurs in work settings.

Social Categorization Our tendency to divide the social world into two separate categories: our ingroup ("us") and various outgroups ("them").

Social Learning View (of prejudice) The view that prejudice is learned—acquired through direct and vicarious experience—in much the same manner as other attitudes.

Stereotypes Beliefs to the effect that all members of specific social groups share certain traits or characteristics. Stereotypes are cognitive frameworks that strongly influence the processing of incoming social information.

Tokenism Instances in which individuals, businesses, educational institutions, and so on perform trivial positive actions for members of outgroups toward whom they feel strong prejudice. Such tokenistic behaviors are then used as an excuse for refusing more substantive beneficial actions for these groups.

For More Information

J. F. Dovido & S. L. Gaertner (Eds.). (1986). *Prejudice, discrimination, and racism.* Orlando, FL: Academic Press.

Contains chapters prepared by various experts on the topics of prejudice and discrimination. Several call attention to the fact that racial prejudice has not actually decreased of disappeared in recent years—it has simply shifted into more subtle forms.

Knopke, H., Norrell, & Rogers, R. (Eds.). (1993). *Opening Doors: An appraisal of race relations in contemporary America.* Tuscaloosa: University of Alabama Press.

A valuable overview of the current state of race relations in the United States. Chapters by social psychologists who have studied racial prejudice in their research provide valuable insights on this important and timely topic.

Shaver, P., & Hendrick, C. (Eds.). (1987). *Sex and gender.* Newbury Park, CA: Sage.

A collection of chapters by experts on gender, sex roles, and sexism. The discussions of gender development are especially interesting. A valuable source to consult if you'd like to know more about these topics.

Stephan, W. G. (1985). Intergroup relations. In G. Lindzey and E. Aronson (Eds.), *Handbook of social psychology* (Vol. 2 599–658). New York: Random House.

A very thorough review of current knowledge about intergroup relations. Carefully examines many processes that play a role in the development of prejudice as well as several techniques for combating prejudice and discrimination.

Interpersonal Attraction: Getting Acquainted, Becoming Friends

When Strangers Meet: Proximity and Emotions

Physical Factors Control Contact, and Contact Leads to Liking / Affect: Emotions and Attraction

Becoming Acquainted: The Need to Affiliate and Reactions to Observable Characteristics

Affiliation Need: Individual Differences and External Events / Responding to Observable Characteristics

Becoming Friends: Similarity and Reciprocity

Similarity: We Like Those Most Like Ourselves / Reciprocity: Mutual Liking

SOCIAL DIVERSITY ▼ A Critical Analysis
Status and Attraction in Japan and the United States

Special Sections

FOCUS ON RESEARCH: CLASSIC CONTRIBUTIONS—Residential Propinquity and Marriage

WORK IN PROGRESS—Subliminal Repeated Exposure: Misattribution and Manipulation

WORK IN PROGRESS—Appearance Anxiety, Interpersonal Behavior, and Weight

SOCIAL PSYCHOLOGY—ON THE APPLIED SIDE—When Roommates Are Mismatched in Attractiveness

FOCUS ON RESEARCH: THE CUTTING EDGE—
The Repulsion Hypothesis: Are Similar Attitudes Irrelevant?

I lived away from home for the first time when I entered college. Because I was the only male from my high school in the entire university, it was necessary to start from scratch to make new friends. I had never thought about how that process works, and no one had ever offered any advice concerning how to go about it.

The men's freshman dormitory was five stories high, and each floor consisted of two wings (east and west) that were separated by a large central staircase. Rooms were assigned on a random basis, and the first person I met, in a corner room of 2-East, was my new roommate. Within about twenty minutes it was clear that Jay and I had nothing in common. In fact, during the first few weeks we grew to dislike one another intensely. It was more or less impossible to change rooms and roommates, so my college life was off to a great start—I was surrounded by thousands of people I didn't know and sharing a room with one person I knew and couldn't stand. What next?

Early in the first quarter, I recognized one of the other students in my French class—Will—as someone who also lived on 2-East, and we talked from time to time before and after class. I was naive enough to be surprised to learn that part of his childhood and early adolescence had been spent in a relocation camp where Japanese-

Americans living on the West Coast were confined during World War II.

One evening Will came to my room with a question about our French assignment, and Jay was as unpleasant to my Japanese acquaintance as he ordinarily was to me. So, from then on, I began going to Will's room whenever we had something to talk about. There I met his two roommates, and I found that I had a lot in common with one of them. Directly across the hall from their room three other guys roomed, and they often came over to talk to Will and his roommate, and that's how we met. One other person in the dorm who lived on the third floor became part of the group because he and one of the 2-E freshmen had met the previous summer.

For whatever reasons, this small collection of strangers became friends—eating together in the cafeteria, going to football games, driving to nearby cities to see movies, illegally and often foolishly drinking too much beer, double and triple dating, and so forth.

At the time, I knew nothing about psychology; even if I had, research on interpersonal attraction (how people become acquainted and what determines liking and disliking) hardly existed. Nevertheless, one aspect of these newfound friendships seemed remarkable to me. We came to know one another almost by chance, based on room assignments on a particular wing of a particular floor of a dormitory, taking the same section of introductory French, meeting someone because he had previous contact with a neighbor. I also

noticed that each of us had roommates who did *not* become part of this group—they, even Jay, formed their own groups of friends.

Another striking aspect of these relationships emerged much later; several of us remained in contact throughout college and afterward, even though we entered different fields and lived in different parts of the country. In fact, after more decades than I care to count, three of us (and our respective wives) still correspond at Christmas and still get together whenever we find ourselves on the same coast. A couple of years may go by between meetings, but we seem to be as comfortable interacting and to have as much fun together as we did in our first year of college.

When I entered graduate school in psychology, I was required to conduct a research project. For some reason I turned to the question of how students in a classroom become acquainted. My own early college friendships (described above) suggested to me that external, physical factors such as room assignments often bring people together in the first place. These meetings may then lead to friendship, to indifference, or even to dislike. I discovered that a few psychologists had already studied such factors, and that the term used to describe the effect of physical proximity on attraction was *propinquity*. As we will discuss in this chapter, much of the social psychological research on attraction has dealt (and still deals) with identifying the details of how people become acquainted and attempts to explain just why we come to like or to dislike our fellow human beings (Byrne, 1992).

As you go about your everyday life at school, work, or elsewhere, you interact with others. Of the multitude of people with whom you come into brief contact, only a few become known to you by name. In addition, you evaluate each of them in various positive and negative ways. This very human tendency to evaluate almost everything and everybody was discussed in chapter 4 in

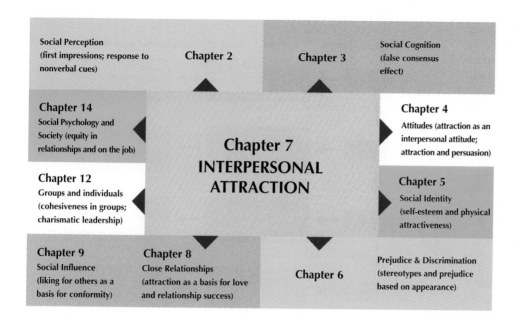

Social Perception
(first impressions; response to nonverbal cues)

Chapter 2

Chapter 3

Social Cognition
(false consensus effect)

Chapter 14
Social Psychology and Society (equity in relationships and on the job)

Chapter 12
Groups and individuals (cohesiveness in groups; charismatic leadership)

Chapter 7
INTERPERSONAL ATTRACTION

Chapter 4
Attitudes (attraction as an interpersonal attitude; attraction and persuasion)

Chapter 5
Social Identity (self-esteem and physical attractiveness)

Chapter 9
Social Influence (liking for others as a basis for conformity)

Chapter 8
Close Relationships (attraction as a basis for love and relationship success)

Chapter 6

Prejudice & Discrimination (stereotypes and prejudice based on appearance)

terms of the *attitudes* we form about the people, objects, and events that we encounter.

Discussion Question 2

Exercise 3

Discussion Question 4

The study of **interpersonal attraction** focuses on our attitudes about other people. At the beginning stages of a relationship, these attitudes fall along a dimension ranging from strong liking to equally strong dislike (see Figure 7.1, p. 266). Further extremes on this dimension can occur when some additional factors are present to create love (see chapter 8) or hate (see chapter 11). In the present chapter, we will describe the initial steps involved in establishing relationships. We will first show how most interpersonal contacts are controlled by factors that are only indirectly related to the characteristics of the people involved. Most of the individuals we meet happen to come into close *physical proximity* with us because of such impersonal environmental determinants as the location of seats in a classroom, rooms in a dormitory, or desks in an office. Because of where we sit or live or work, we see some people repeatedly. There are others just a few feet away in the same class, dorm, or office with whom we may never come in contact. The likelihood that proximity will lead to a positive versus a negative relationship is based in part on each person's *emotional state*. We tend to like others when our emotions are positive and to dislike others when our emotions are negative, regardless of the reason for feeling good or feeling bad. Even though the physical setting fosters contact and positive feelings facilitate positive evaluations, two people will progress toward getting to know one another only if they are sufficiently motivated to *affiliate*—that is, only if they feel the need to establish a relationship. Each individual is also influenced in positive and negative ways by attitudes and beliefs about the *external characteristics* of the other person (physical attractiveness, accent, skin color, height, clothing style, and so forth). Once interaction begins, interpersonal attraction is strongly determined by the extent to which the two people discover that they are *similar* in various attitudes, beliefs, values, and interests. Such relationships become even more positive if each person is able to communicate his or her *positive evaluations* of the other, either in words or in actions.

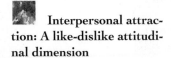 **Interpersonal attraction: A like-dislike attitudinal dimension**

FIGURE 7.1 *Interpersonal attraction* refers to the evaluation one person makes of another. In the earliest stages of a relationship, evaluations are made along an attitudinal dimension that ranges from strong liking at the positive extreme to strong dislike at the negative extreme. Most attraction research involves the attempt to identify the factors responsible for our feelings of like and dislike as well as the creation of formulations that attempt to explain these reactions.

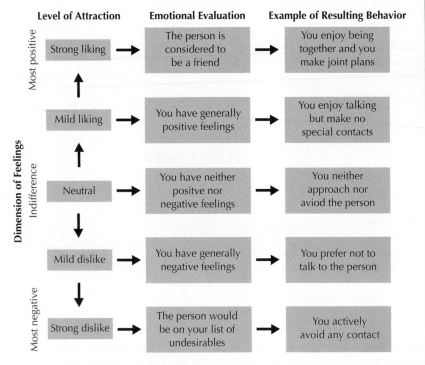

WHEN STRANGERS MEET: PROXIMITY AND EMOTIONS

There are five and a half billion people living on our planet. Each one of us interacts with only a very small percentage of the total group; nevertheless, it would be possible to know thousands of people. In fact, however, we tend to form close relationships with a quite limited number of individuals. During the last half of this century, social psychologists have been actively attempting to identify the basis we each use to narrow our social world to a manageable number of acquaintances—and to determine what factors lead us to like some of these individuals and dislike others. At the earliest stage, two people are likely to become acquainted if they are brought into contact through simple physical proximity, or **propinquity,** and if each is experiencing positive rather than negative **affect** at the time.

PHYSICAL FACTORS CONTROL CONTACT, AND CONTACT LEADS TO LIKING

As illustrated at the beginning of the chapter, friendships often begin because of a series of unplanned encounters that are controlled by the physical details of the immediate environment. On the basis of these casual, accidental contacts, each person begins to recognize the other. At this point it is common for people to exchange greetings when they see one another and to exchange remarks about the weather or whatever. This positive response to a familiar face can be observed even among infants. They are, for example, more likely to smile when exposed to a photograph of someone they have seen before than in response to a stranger's picture (Brooks-Gunn & Lewis, 1981).

The first empirical data suggesting a propinquity effect were provided by sociological studies in the 1930s, as we point out in the following **Classic Contributions** section.

Focus on Research: Classic Contributions

RESIDENTIAL PROPINQUITY AND MARRIAGE

Long before social psychologists began investigating propinquity, sociologists discovered a correlational relationship between where people live and whom they marry. In other words, in a given city love and marriage didn't represent random pairings of males and females; one of the primary factors bringing two people together was found to be the location of their respective residences.

Bossard (1932) obtained official records for the first 5,000 marriages performed in Philadelphia in 1931. He determined the addresses of each bride and groom prior to their wedding and, using a map, tabulated the number of city blocks separating the premarital addresses of each couple. As shown in Figure 7.2, 34 percent of the pairs lived within five blocks of one another before they married, and more than half (54 percent) lived within a twenty-

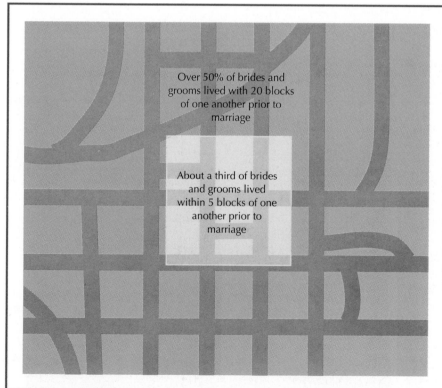

Marrying the boy or girl "next door"

FIGURE 7.2 Beginning in the 1930s, studies of marriages revealed that *propinquity* is associated with the likelihood of two people becoming husband and wife. Of all marriages in the cities studied, about a third of the brides and grooms lived within five blocks of one another before they were wed, and slightly more than half lived within twenty blocks of one another.

block radius. More generally, it was found that as the distance between their residences increased, the probability of marriage between a man and a woman decreased.

Before considering possible alternative explanations of this finding, you should first know that it was quickly replicated in a different city (New Haven)—based on nearly 1,000 marriages in 1931—and the results were almost identical (Davie & Reeves, 1939).

These early investigators realized that the location of residences may not have been the crucial factor that led to relationships and marriage. That is, city neighborhoods are often segregated on the basis of social class, race, religion, or ethnic divisions. If so, couples might meet and marry not because of the proximity between residences, but because they belonged to the same religious denomination, for example. Was proximity the important variable? That question could be resolved only by studies of settings in which living quarters were assigned without respect to class, race, or other demographic variables.

Such conditions were met in three dormitory studies in the 1940s (Evans & Wilson, 1949; Lundberg & Beazley, 1948; Lundberg, Hertzler, & Dickson, 1949) and in two married student housing studies in the 1950s (Caplow & Forman, 1950; Festinger, Schachter, & Back, 1950). In each instance, propinquity was clearly found to determine who becomes acquainted and who becomes friends. For example, in college dormitories, two-thirds of the friendships occur on the same floor, and most of the remaining friendships involve students on adjacent floors rather than farther away. Among married students, couples also were found to become acquainted on the basis of physical factors. Exercise 1 For example, in rows of apartments (see Figure 7.3), couples were very likely

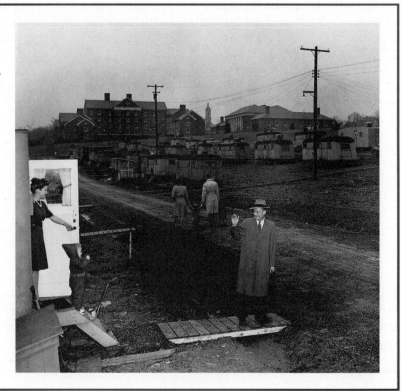

Propinquity and friendship among married students

FIGURE 7.3   Shortly after World War II, when many married veterans entered college, housing units were built for these couples. Studies of the friendship patterns that formed among such couples revealed that physical proximity was the major determinant of who became friends. For example, if the apartment entrances were no more than 22 feet apart, the couples were very likely to become acquainted. If the entrances were 88 (or more) feet apart, the couples were very *unlikely* to become acquainted.
Source: Festinger et al., 1950.

to become acquainted if they lived within 22 feet of one another and very unlikely to become acquainted if they lived more than 88 feet apart (Festinger et al., 1950).

Though these early studies were not totally conclusive, together they represent strong evidence that people become acquainted in part because of physical proximity. Continuing research over the following decades supported this conclusion. In addition, these seemingly simple findings have led to important applied implications and intriguing theoretical implications.

THE POWER OF PROPINQUITY.   The generality of the propinquity effect is shown by its extension to friendship patterns in such diverse populations as urban residents in a housing project for the elderly (Nahemow & Lawton, 1975) and young suburban families in a housing development (Whyte, 1956). It seems to be a general truth that the closer two people live, the better their chance of becoming close friends (Ebbesen, Kjos, & Konecni, 1976). When residential propinquity brings blacks and whites together in a nonconfrontational atmosphere, prejudice decreases (Deutsch & Collins, 1951).

Classroom investigations permit more precise study of such effects, because seats can be assigned and the amount of contact in this setting is limited to specific days and times. Once again, classroom friendships are clearly determined by where each person is seated. Those sitting side by side are most likely to become acquainted. When students are seated alphabetically, friendships form between those whose last names begin with the same or a nearby letter (Segal, 1974). This may not seem important until you consider the fact that you may meet some of your friends (and perhaps even your future spouse) simply because of an instructor's seating chart. For example, a couple who donated a large sum of money to a New York university in 1990 told a reporter that they met in an economics class at that institution during the 1930s because they were seated in alphabetical order—Edward George met and married Frances Gildea.

Among other implications, those given a corner seat or a seat on the end of a row make fewer friends (Maisonneuve, Palmade, & Fourment, 1952). So, the total number of friends you make in a class depends in part on where you sit. If you have someone sitting on your right and someone on your left, you are likely to make two friends, whereas a seat on the end of a row yields the likelihood of only one new friend (Byrne & Buehler, 1955). Further, if the instructor changes seat assignments once or twice during the semester, each student becomes acquainted with additional classmates (Byrne, 1961).

WHY DOES PROPINQUITY LEAD TO ATTRACTION?   To some extent, we are affected by propinquity because we tend to avoid strangers unless we are forced to come in contact because of where we live, where we are seated in a classroom, and so forth. But there is another, more basic, reason. As Zajonc (1968) and his colleagues have reported, **repeated exposure** to a new stimulus (frequent contact with that stimulus) leads to a more and more positive evaluation of the stimulus—as long as the initial reaction is not an extremely negative one. Whether the stimulus is a drawing, a word in an unknown foreign language, a new product being advertised, a political candidate, or a stranger, the greater the exposure, the more positive the response (Moreland & Zajonc, 1982). Perhaps in part because of the repeated exposure effect, even a letter of

Critical Thinking Question 1

Discussion Question 2

the alphabet that occurs in one's own name is perceived to be more attractive than a letter not in one's name (Nuttin, 1987). The general idea is that we respond with at least mild discomfort to anything or anyone new. With repeated exposure we become desensitized, anxiety decreases, and that which was *new* becomes *familiar*.

Interestingly, the repeated exposure effect is stronger when the stimulus is *not* consciously perceived than when the individual is aware of it (Bornstein & D'Agostino, 1992). When, for example, the stimulus is repeatedly presented at a rapid speed, the subject is unaware of having seen it but afterwards rates it more favorably than stimuli repeatedly presented at a normal speed. Among the questions raised by this intriguing finding are: (1) Why should the exposure effect be less when the stimulus is clearly perceived than when it is not? And (2) can this technique be used in commercial and political advertising to manipulate consumers and voters without their awareness? Both issues are explored in the following **Work in Progress** section.

Work in Progress

Subliminal Repeated Exposure: Misattribution and Manipulation

In attempting to explain why *subliminal* (below the threshold of awareness) repeated exposure is more effective than *supraliminal* (above the awareness threshold) repeated exposure, Professor Bornstein (1992, 1993) has proposed an attributional model. He suggests that a subliminal stimulus becomes increasingly familiar to the viewer with repeated presentations, though the person is not aware of these exposures. When asked to rate the stimulus later, the viewer is actually familiar with it and misattributes familiarity as indicating liking. Under ordinary viewing conditions, by contrast, the viewer obviously can recognize the stimulus and tends to attribute familiarity to the repeated exposures rather than to liking.

On the basis of this model, Bornstein and his colleagues hypothesized that if research participants were told that they had been exposed to a stimulus, the subliminal effects would decrease. To test this hypothesis, the researchers showed participants photographs subliminally and afterward asked them to rate how much they liked the photos; they also asked participants to rate unfamiliar photographs. Some participants were informed of the previous exposures, and these individuals showed significantly weaker subliminal exposure effects than did uninformed participants. In other words, when a person realizes why the stimuli are familiar, he or she is less apt to misattribute familiarity as liking.

Research is currently under way to test the model in a different way. These tests use supraliminal repeated exposure along with procedures designed to decrease the participants' ability to attribute familiarity to repeated exposure—for example, distractor tasks, presentation of irrelevant stimuli, and longer delays between exposure and ratings. The initial results are promising in indicating an *increase* in the supraliminal repeated exposure effect, presumably because—once again—familiarity is attributed to liking (Bornstein, 1993).

Because subliminal exposure to stimuli that cannot be recalled or recognized affects attitudes and behavior, this raises the somewhat threatening possibility that the technique could be used to influence consumers or voters. Bornstein (1989, 1993) argues that it is not clear that similar results can be obtained in real-world settings and that technical obstacles in today's TV and film media prevent presentations at the required brief exposure speeds. Also, if such efforts to deceive the public were revealed, the backlash against the manufacturer or the political candidate would be extremely negative. As a result, any devious plan to use subliminal advertising may well be forestalled by the risks of public outrage.

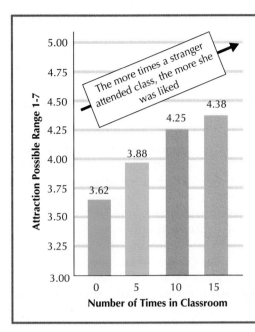

Classroom contacts and attraction

FIGURE 7.4 When female experimental assistants pretended to be students and sat quietly in a large college classroom without interacting with the professor or with fellow students, the attraction of the class members toward each assistant increased as the number of days of her class attendance increased. Attraction was least toward the assistant who never attended the class and greatest toward the individual who attended the class fifteen times.
Source: Based on data from Moreland & Beach, 1992.

In a test of how repeated exposure operates in a college classroom, Moreland and Beach (1992) found that as the number of exposures to a fellow student increases, the greater the attraction toward that person. At the end of a semester, these researchers asked students in a large college course to evaluate four different female classmates (actually, experimental assistants). One of these women never attended the class, one attended four times, one ten times, and one fifteen times. To control for other variables that might influence attraction, the experimenters selected assistants who were similar in appearance, and they instructed the assistants not to interact with any of the actual students, in or out of class. As shown in Figure 7.4, attraction toward these strangers increased as the number of classroom exposures increased; thus, the effect of repeated exposure was clearly evident.

Note that propinquity is not 100 percent effective in fostering attraction. Remember Jay, my freshman roommate? Repeated exposure to a stranger who behaves in an unpleasant fashion leads to more and more dislike (Swap, 1977). Even a stranger who is not unpleasant can be evaluated negatively if propinquity involves interference with your need for **privacy**: your need to limit others' knowledge of your personal life (Larson & Bell, 1988). Sometimes you prefer to be by yourself rather than with another person—no matter who that person is. At such times, too much propinquity can be aversive. This is one reason that those who live in close physical proximity (sailors on submarine duty, siblings sharing a bedroom, and even some married couples) may come to feel less and less attraction over time rather than more and more.

AFFECT: EMOTIONS AND ATTRACTION

Humans experience and express emotions throughout their daily lives, and these emotions strongly affect perception, cognition, learning, motivation, decision making—and attraction (Erber, 1991; Forgas, 1993a, 1993b; Zajonc & McIntosh, 1992). Even two-year-old children are accurate in identifying faces and voices as reflecting happiness, sadness, and anger (Stifter & Fox, 1987). As you'll recall from chapter 3, psychologists often use the term **affect** in referring to emotions or feelings. A person's emotional state can most concisely be described as falling along a positive–negative (or pleasant–unpleasant) dimension (McIntyre et al., 1991; Russell, Weiss, & Mendelsohn, 1989). Within these broad categories, more specific emotions can also be distinguished; the basic elements of negative affect, for example, seem to consist of fear, hostility, guilt, and sadness (Watson & Clark, 1992).

AFFECT AS THE BASIS OF ATTRACTION.   A great many experiments have established that positive feelings lead to liking, while negative feelings lead to dislike. So anything that arouses positive versus negative affect influences attraction. Music is an example. We know that music has a powerful effect on emotions and on behavior. For example, slow-tempo music played in a grocery store results in increased sales, presumably because shoppers relax, walk slowly, and consider a greater number of products (Milliman, 1982). In contrast, fast-tempo music speeds up behavior; if it is played while people eat, they respond with more bites per minute (Roballey et al., 1985). See Figure 7.5. Besides tempo, music also can arouse positive versus negative feelings. In an attraction experiment, female college students were asked to rate male strangers depicted in photographs. While they engaged in this task, the experimenter played pleasant music (rock), unpleasant music (avant-garde classical), or no music (May & Hamilton, 1980). Compared to the no-music condition, students listening to rock music liked the strangers better and even thought they were more physically attractive; the opposite was true for those listening to avant-garde tapes.

In a similar way, when emotions are manipulated by such situational variables as good versus bad news on the radio (Kaplan, 1981), happy versus sad movies (Gouaux, 1971), or pleasant room lighting (Baron, Rea, & Daniels, 1992), positive affect results in liking others and negative in disliking them.

Music influences our emotions and our overt behavior

FIGURE 7.5   Music affects how we feel and what we do in many situations. For example, when grocery stores play background music with a slow tempo, shoppers go down the aisles more slowly and purchase more items. Also, music that has an effect on emotions influences attraction responses. People like strangers more when listening to music they like, while they like strangers less when disliked music is playing.

Sometimes the affect is created by the affective state of the other person; that is, happy or sad moods can prove to be contagious (Goleman, 1991; Hsee, Hatfield, & Chemtob, 1992; Sullins, 1991). This may explain in part why depressed people are rated negatively by others (Holowaty, Pliner, & Flett, 1990). Also, people tend to laugh and smile when they hear laughter, even if they don't know what is funny (Provine, 1992). When emotional contagion was studied in public settings such as shopping centers and grocery stores, it was found that when an experimental assistant smiled at a stranger, that person was very likely to smile back. When the assistant frowned, however, this did not elicit a frown (Hinsz & Tomhave, 1991). In other words, "Smile and the world smiles with you; frown and you frown alone." The investigators also noted sex differences in that women were more likely to smile back than were men, and strangers of both sexes were more likely to return the smile of a female than of a male.

Whatever the source of an individual's emotional state, happy feelings lead to liking, but if that person feels unhappy, he or she likes other people less well (Swallow & Kuiper, 1987) and evaluates them in negative terms (Shapiro, 1988). And emotions influence interpersonal behavior as well as attraction responses (Clark & Watson, 1988). Cunningham (1988) induced happy or sad feelings in male subjects (some saw movies and others received false evaluations), then sent the subjects to a waiting room in which a female confederate was seated. The males in a positive mood communicated with the female stranger more and disclosed more about themselves than did those in a negative mood.

SOCIAL INTERACTION AS THE SOURCE OF AFFECT.   Though it is true that a person's affective state (regardless of its origin) influences attraction, social interaction itself often arouses emotions. As a general rule, social interactions are most likely to arouse positive affect (McIntyre, Watson, & Cunningham, 1990). If, however, you met someone for the first time and he or she said something that was insulting or demeaning or represented an attempt to tease you, the resulting negative emotion would lead you to dislike that person, especially if the remark was perceived as hostile and caused you pain (Farina, Wheeler, & Mehta, 1991; Shapiro, Baumeister, & Kessler, 1991). In contrast, a compliment would probably lead to positive feelings and liking (Downey & Damhave, 1991).

What happens when a male and female come in contact for the first time, and one of them wants to initiate a conversation? What might the person say? Kleinke, Meeker, and Staneski (1986) studied the "opening lines" people use and their effect on others. Many people (especially men) try to be amusing by saying something cute or flippant, hoping to elicit positive feelings and to be liked; an example is, "Hi. I'm easy, are you?" Most often the affective response is negative—the opposite of what was intended. A more positive response is likely when the opening line is either innocuous ("Where are you from?") or direct ("Hi. I'm a little embarrassed about this, but I'd like to get to know you."). Other examples of liked and disliked opening lines from this research are shown in Table 7.1, p. 274.

The relationship between types of opening lines and attraction was shown in subsequent research, in which subjects watched videotapes showing a man or a woman approach an opposite-sex stranger with one of the three categories of opening lines (Kleinke & Dean, 1990). Attraction toward the person using the opening line tended to be highest after a direct statement and lowest

In a social situation, how one initiates a conversation with someone of the opposite sex is crucial in creating a favorable first impression. Research indicates that the best strategy is to avoid cute/flippant remarks and stick with innocuous or direct opening lines. Women are somewhat more negative than men in evaluating a stranger's clumsy attempts to be amusing.

TABLE 7.1 Making a good first impression: Say something cute, innocuous, or direct?

Setting	Most-Preferred Opening Lines	Least-Preferred Opening Lines
General	Hi.	Your place or mine?
Bar	Do you want to dance?	Bet I can outdrink you.
Restaurant	I haven't been here before. What's good on the menu?	I bet the cherry pie jubilee isn't as sweet as you are.
Supermarket	Can I help you to the car with those things?	Do you really eat that junk?
Laundromat	Want to go have a beer or cup of coffee while we're waiting?	Those are some nice undies you have there.
Beach	Want to play frisbee?	Let me see your strap marks.

Source: Based on data from Kleinke, Meeker, & Staneski, 1986.

after a cute/flippant one, as shown in Figure 7.6. Parallel results were obtained when experimental accomplices used such lines in a singles bar; the person on whom the line was used evaluated the speaker afterward (Cunningham, 1989).

Transparency 7.1 WHY DOES AFFECT INFLUENCE ATTRACTION? Many investigators have concluded that a simple process underlies the relationship between emotions and liking. According to the **reinforcement-affect model** (Clore & Byrne, 1974), we like anyone or anything that makes us feel good and dislike whoever

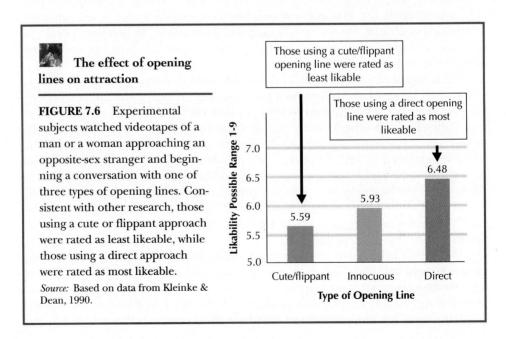

The effect of opening lines on attraction

FIGURE 7.6 Experimental subjects watched videotapes of a man or a woman approaching an opposite-sex stranger and beginning a conversation with one of three types of opening lines. Consistent with other research, those using a cute or flippant approach were rated as least likeable, while those using a direct approach were rated as most likeable.
Source: Based on data from Kleinke & Dean, 1990.

Those using a cute/flippant opening line were rated as least likable

Those using a direct opening line were rated as most likeable

or whatever makes us feel bad. The role of affect in this process is all-important. Critical Thinking Question 2 The role of reinforcement is less obvious, however. As shown in Figure 7.7, we react not only to the person or event *responsible* for arousing our emotions but also to anyone or anything simply *associated* with those feelings. For example, you view a funny movie, feel happy, and like the movie; if someone is with you at the time, you associate that person with your positive emotions and like him or her. This conditioning process is often the basis on which we form our likes and dislikes (Byrne & Clore, 1970).

As we discussed in chapter 4, there is ample evidence that attitudes can be acquired through classical conditioning when the attitude object is paired with a stimulus that evokes negative affect or with one that evokes positive affect. In the Krosnick et al. (1992) experiment on subliminal conditioning that was described, researchers conditioned attitudes toward a female stranger by pairing her pictures with either pleasant or unpleasant pictures that were present-

 The reinforcement-affect model: Emotions determine attraction

FIGURE 7.7   According to the *reinforcement-affect model,* likes and dislikes are based on the arousal of positive versus negative feelings. We like any rewarding person, thing, or event because they create positive emotions. We dislike any punishing person, thing, or event because they create negative emotions. When someone else happens to be present at the time (even though not responsible for the emotions), he or she becomes associated with the positive or negative feelings. Thus, on the basis of simple classical conditioning, we like anyone who is associated with positive emotions and dislike anyone associated with negative emotions.

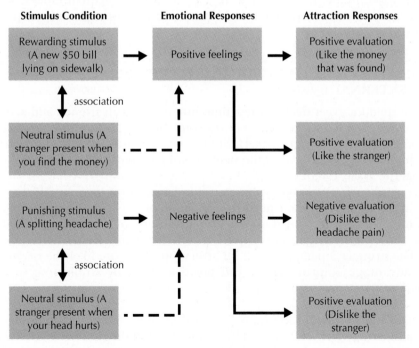

ed at speeds so rapid that the participants were unaware of them. In addition to providing new evidence consistent with the reinforcement-affect model, these investigators were able to show that it is possible to like or dislike someone—and to hold positive or negative beliefs about them—without having any realization of the basis for these reactions. It seems probable that in our everyday lives we develop some of our interpersonal likes and dislikes on the basis of just such associations; we're not always sure just why we "like Jill and dislike Jack."

Conditioning of affective responses has been studied in a somewhat different context by Rozin, Millman, and Nemeroff (1986). These investigators point out that even brief contact between a neutral object and something that arouses positive or negative feelings leads to a transfer of the emotional response to the neutral object. For example, a laundered shirt that had been worn by a disliked person was rated as less desirable than a laundered shirt that had been worn by a liked person. Even though the shirts did not actually differ, one elicited a positive evaluative response and the other a negative response on the basis of learned associations.

BECOMING ACQUAINTED: THE NEED TO AFFILIATE AND REACTIONS TO OBSERVABLE CHARACTERISTICS

If two people are brought into repeated contact by propinquity and if both experience relatively positive affect, they are at a transition point. They may simply remain superficial acquaintances who nod and perhaps say hello when they happen to see one another. Another possibility is that they may begin to converse from time to time, learn each other's names, and begin to exchange information about themselves, thus becoming close acquaintances. Which alternative is chosen depends on two factors—*affiliative needs* and reactions to *observable characteristics*.

AFFILIATION NEED: INDIVIDUAL DIFFERENCES AND EXTERNAL EVENTS

People spend a great deal of their time interacting with friends and acquaintances (see Figure 7.8), perhaps because our species has found it beneficial to behave in this way (Wright, 1984). Studies of chimpanzees and monkeys provide interesting evidence that the need to affiliate may be based on biological factors (de Waal, 1989).

Beyond such proposed evolutionary underpinnings, people differ a great deal in the strength of their **need for affiliation** or need for interpersonal relationships. Those whose need is weak prefer to spend much of their time alone, while those with a strong need prefer to interact with others whenever possible. The stronger a person's need for affiliation, the more likely he or she is to take advantage of propinquity and positive affect by attempting to move toward a close acquaintanceship.

DISPOSITIONAL DIFFERENCES IN AFFILIATION NEED.   Beginning with the pioneering work of Murray (1938/1961), psychologists have constructed various tests to measure individual differences in the need to affiliate and have

Affiliation is a major aspect of human behavior

FIGURE 7.8 Most of us spend a large portion of our free time interacting with people we know and like. Affiliation is one of the basic human needs. Individuals differ in the strength of their need to affiliate, and this motive is also affected by various external events.

conducted research to determine how such differences influence behavior. The tests used most are in the form of questionnaires. A typical finding is that males high in affiliation need are more self-confident and spend more time talking to attractive females than is true for males whose need to affiliate is low (Crouse & Mehrabian, 1977). Affiliation motivation is also positively related to the frequency of letter writing and the desire to be with other people rather than alone (McAdams & Constantian, 1983).

Much of the current research on affiliation has emphasized the existence of different varieties of motivation. McAdams and Losoff (1984), for example, focus on **friendship motivation,** the need to establish warm interpersonal relationships. Children whose friendship motivation is strong are found to know a great deal about their friends, to form stable relationships, and to be perceived by their teachers as friendly, affectionate, cooperative, happy, and popular.

There are, however, other reasons to affiliate, and Hill (1987) suggests that four basic motives may be involved. He proposes that affiliation is based on *social comparison* (the need to reduce uncertainty), *positive stimulation* (the need for interesting, lively contact with others), *emotional support* (the need for companionship when problems arise), and *attention* (the need for praise and admiration). Table 7.2, p. 278, provides examples of items that measure each of these motives. A person's score on each dimension indicates the type of situation in which he or she is most likely to engage in affiliative behavior.

Exercise 2

SOCIAL SKILLS CAN HELP OR HINDER AFFILIATION.   Beyond motivational differences, people also vary in how well they deal with interpersonal situations. Socially skilled individuals are friendly, possess high self-esteem, seldom react angrily, and find it easy to make conversation (Reisman, 1984). Those who are least skilled tend to be unfriendly, have low self-esteem, frequently become angry, and consider casual conversation to be a difficult task.

What is the explanation for differences in social skill? Birth order plays a role. Compared with firstborns, those with older siblings are better able to

The Interpersonal Orientation Scale measures the types of motivation that underlie the need for affiliation. Shown are sample items based on four quite different reasons for seeking the company of others, together with college situations in which they might be likely to occur.

TABLE 7.2 Different aspects of the need for affiliation

Type of Need	Sample Test Items That Measure the Need	Typical Situation
Social Comparison	When I am not certain about how well I am doing at something, I usually like to be around others so I can compare myself to them.	When class papers are returned to students.
Positive Stimulation	Just being around others and finding out about them is one of the most interesting things I can think of doing.	After several hours of studying in the library.
Emotional Support	One of my greatest sources of comfort when things get rough is being with other people.	After receiving a very low grade on an exam.
Attention	I like to be around people when I can be the center of attention.	When the opportunity arises to make the class laugh.

Source: Based on information in Hill, 1987.

master social situations (Ickes & Turner, 1983). Presumably such children have learned how to deal with older brothers and sisters. For the same reason, those with an older sibling of the opposite sex are able to interact more easily than other people with acquaintances of the opposite sex. We first learn how to interact with peers by interacting with the family members who are closest to us in age. These contacts with siblings are apparently crucial in that they provide the opportunity for social interactions, exposure to older models who possess social skills, and feedback on one's own skillful or unskillful social behavior.

Once an individual reaches college age, the ability or inability to deal well with others is well established. When a person enters a new social setting—such as college—social skills assume critical importance. During the first weeks and months among strangers, differences in the need to affiliate and differences in ability to make friends become obvious. The transition from familiar relationships in one's high school to a totally new situation can result in disappointment and unhappiness if the need to affiliate is strong but social skills are lacking (Arkin, Lake, & Baumgardner, 1986). Many college students have to meet strangers and establish friendships for the first time since entering elementary school, and this task can cause anxiety and emotional disruption.

Langston and Cantor (1989) studied the interpersonal successes and failures of students over a period of time to find out why some do well socially while others do not. These investigators proposed the model shown in Figure 7.9 to describe the crucial variables. Students who succeeded interpersonally differed from those who failed interpersonally in how they perceived the task of meeting new people and in the strategy they used when interacting with others. Specifically, unskilled individuals appraised the situation negatively and experienced anxiety. This *social anxiety* leads to cognitive distortions (for example, assuming that you are disliked by others) and feelings of depression (Johnson, Johnson, & Petzel, 1992). In response to their negative perceptions of the situation, unskilled individuals developed social strategies that were restrained and conservative—striving to reveal very little about themselves. For most people social anxiety and awkwardness are reduced by attempts to find out about another person (Leary, Kowalski, & Bergen, 1988). When socially unskilled students ask questions about another person's experiences and attitudes, however, they are too fearful to communicate anything meaningful about themselves (Thorne, 1987). This tendency to hold back and play it safe makes a negative impression on others. Other students, who were successful interpersonally, felt it was an interesting challenge to make new friends, and they felt comfortable in letting the other person know as much as possible about themselves. This friendly, open, outgoing strategy is a useful one in establishing friendships.

EXTERNAL EVENTS CAN AROUSE AFFILIATION NEEDS.   Though people differ in their need to interact with others, external events can also arouse this motive. You have probably been in certain situations in which total strangers began to talk to one another: the stress of a flood, the excitement of a special event such as Mardi Gras, or some other out-of-the-ordinary occurrence. Humphriss (1989) described the aftereffects of a California earthquake—the dreadful destruction of property served to unite neighbors and create friendly feelings. Even in New York City, when a snowstorm left commuters and visitors with no way to get out, those who were stranded "swapped life stories and passed around pictures of their children as snow swirled down upon the metropolitan area" (Daley, 1983, p. 1). As suggested in the cartoon in Figure 7.10, p. 280, "An emergency makes things different."

The psychological basis of these affiliative reactions was first identified by Schachter (1959) in his investigations of the effect of fear on affiliation. In an experimental setting, many of the subjects who had been told that they would soon receive painful electric shocks preferred waiting with other subjects rather than remaining alone. When they expected a nonfrightening experience, subjects preferred to wait alone or expressed no preference. Why should fear or anxiety increase the motivation to affiliate?

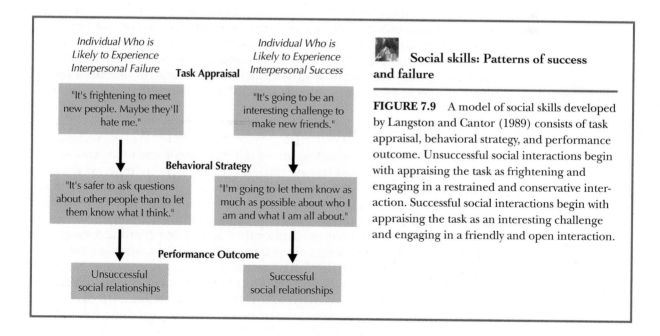

Social skills: Patterns of success and failure

FIGURE 7.9   A model of social skills developed by Langston and Cantor (1989) consists of task appraisal, behavioral strategy, and performance outcome. Unsuccessful social interactions begin with appraising the task as frightening and engaging in a restrained and conservative interaction. Successful social interactions begin with appraising the task as an interesting challenge and engaging in a friendly and open interaction.

 Emergencies can bring people together

FIGURE 7.10 It is frequently observed that emergency situations such as power failures and natural disasters can motivate people to affiliate, to help one another, and to experience camaraderie. As the cartoon character notes, "Just for a while today . . . everyone cared about everyone else."
Source: Universal Press Syndicate, February 6, 1988.

The explanation is that we seek out others—even strangers—in order to talk about what is going on, to compare perceptions, and to decide what to do (Morris et al., 1976). This behavior is an example of the **social comparison process**, the general tendency to evaluate what we think and do by comparing our reactions with those of others, thus reducing uncertainty and anxiety. A positive emotional atmosphere can occur even in very upsetting situations, because there is an opportunity to share the experience with others and to engage in novel activity (Byrne, 1991).

A related phenomenon does not rest on social comparison or sharing a novel experience: Sometimes there is the possibility of obtaining information about a frightening upcoming event by interacting with someone who has already gone through it and therefore knows the score. For example, in a medical setting those facing surgery prefer having a roommate who has already undergone the same operation (Kulik & Mahler, 1989).

RESPONDING TO OBSERVABLE CHARACTERISTICS

Even though we realize that "beauty is only skin deep" and that most stereotypes are incorrect, most of us nevertheless react to those we meet on the basis of *positive* stereotypes about physical attractiveness (Albright, Kenny, & Malloy, 1988) and *negative* stereotypes about physical defects (Fichten & Amsel, 1986), as well as with a multitude of specific prejudices. For example, we are apt to evaluate people on the basis of whether they appear old (Perdue & Gurtman, 1990), whether they wear eyeglasses (Terry & Macy, 1991), what kind of clothing they wear (Bushman, 1988; Cahoon & Edmonds, 1989), and how well groomed they are (Mack & Rainey, 1990). These judgments—along with those based on such variables as skin color, sex, height, and accent—are likely to be worthless in making accurate behavioral predictions, as we indicated in the discussion of prejudice in chapter 6. Much of the research on the effects of observable characteristics has concentrated on **physical attractiveness,** but we will first describe how several other physical attributes influence attraction.

THE EFFECTS OF SUPERFICIAL CHARACTERISTICS.   It is surprisingly commonplace for people to express like or dislike toward a stranger simply because of some irrelevant aspect of that person's outward appearance. Attention to overt characteristics is part of a general screening process known as **cognitive disregard.** According to Rodin (1987), we deal with strangers by first excluding all who strike us at first glance as "unsuitable" as acquaintances. Anyone placed in that category becomes "invisible" and is no longer an object of attention; subsequently, he or she is not even remembered. Undergraduates, for example, are found to disregard anyone who is elderly or middle-aged; middle-aged individuals disregard those who are young; and males disregard unattractive females. After we decide who doesn't count, we find out more about those who remain in order to decide whom we like. Engaging in cognitive disregard is an efficient way of eliminating anyone who we feel would not be acceptable as an acquaintance or a friend. The problem with such behavior is that evaluations based on observable characteristics are unfair, and they prevent us from ever getting to know some people who might have become our good friends.

Among the many physical characteristics that influence interpersonal reactions is physique. Both men and women stereotype strangers on this basis. Ryckman and his colleagues (1989) provided subjects with information about *somatotypes,* or body types. This once-popular system classifies people into three major groups; as shown in Figure 7.11, p. 282, *endomorphs* are round and fat, *mesomorphs* are muscular, and *ectomorphs* are thin and angular (Sheldon, Stevens, & Tucker, 1940). When asked to describe the personalities of people who fit each of the physical types, subjects tended to agree. Subjects generally perceived endomorphs as ugly, sloppy, sad, dirty, and slow. They described mesomorphs as not very kind or intelligent, but as having many friends and being healthy, brave, and attractive. And they assumed ectomorphs to be average on most traits, but they were perceived as being fearful, intelligent, and neat. Keep in mind that there is no evidence at all that fat people are sloppy, muscular people stupid, or thin people fearful.

Other physical attributes also evoke stereotypes. Research shows that people perceive adults who look or sound very young as being weak, naive, incompetent, warm, and honest (Berry & Brownlow, 1989; Berry & Zebrowitz-McArthur, 1988; Montepare & Zebrowitz-McArthur, 1987). Though these perceptions tend to be almost totally inaccurate, they continue to influence first impressions and interpersonal attraction.

In addition to physical appearance, *behavioral cues* also influence judgments in equally unfair ways. People react more positively to those whose walking style seems youthful, for example, than to those whose gaits are perceived as elderly, regardless of the person's actual age or sex (Montepare & Zebrowitz-McArthur, 1988). Emotional expressiveness and extroverted behavior create a positive first impression (Friedman, Riggio, & Casella, 1988). It is commonly found that males who behave in a dominant way are liked better than those who behave submissively (Sadalla, Kenrick, & Vershure, 1987). Thus, there is a preference for a male who gestures a lot, has a strong tennis serve, and is competitive and authoritative as opposed to one who looks down, nods his head in agreement, and plays tennis for fun rather than to win. Female dominance, in contrast, does not affect attraction one way or the other.

 Stereotypes about physique: Responding to somatotypes

FIGURE 7.11 Sheldon's classification of people according to body type provides little or no predictive power, but stereotypes about physique persist. Ryckman et al. (1989) found that endomorphs are perceived as sloppy, sad, and dirty; mesomorphs as popular and brave; and ectomorphs as fearful, intelligent, and neat.

Sometimes overt behavior is easily altered, and most people try to act so as to create a good impression. A common example: Both men and women tend to eat less in the presence of someone of the opposite sex than when they are alone or with a same-sex companion (Pliner & Chaiken, 1990). The reason is that overeating is perceived as unattractive in general and specifically as unfeminine for women (Mori, Chaiken, & Pliner, 1987).

IS BEHAVIOR EVER RELATED TO OBSERVABLE CHARACTERISTICS? Is it possible that behavior *is* sometimes predictable on the basis of the kind of overt cues we have been discussing? In a few instances, there is a relationship. We know that a physical characteristic such as obesity tends to be associated with negative evaluations (Harris, Harris, & Bochner, 1982; Larkin & Pines, 1982); one result of such evaluations is that obese individuals may face more than their share of social rejection. As a consequence, social self-esteem may be low and social anxiety high. These psychological reactions, in turn, may cause those who are overweight to deal with social situations less well than those without this stigma. Miller et al. (1990) tested this hypothesis by having obese and nonobese women engage in telephone conversations with college students who were unaware of how much they weighed or how they looked. Afterward, even without having seen them, the students rated the obese women as less likeable, less socially skilled, and less physically attractive than those who were not overweight. Keep in mind that these findings are correla-

vocal attractiveness; the more attractive a person's voice, the more positive the ratings of that individual's personality traits (Zuckerman & Driver, 1989). For male undergraduates, the more attractive a female stranger, the more sexually desirable she is judged to be and the better she is rated as a potential date and potential spouse (G. Smeaton, personal communication, 1990).

Most of the studies of physical appearance have concentrated on late adolescents or young adults of dating age, but the effect is by no means limited to this group. Even newborn infants are assumed to have more positive characteristics—such as sociability—if they are attractive rather than unattractive (Karraker, Vogel, & Evans, 1987).

Not only do adults prefer pretty babies, but—more surprisingly—babies prefer pretty adults. To determine how infants respond to attractiveness, Langlois, Roggman, and Rieser-Danner (1990) observed how the appearance of a female stranger affected the reactions of a large number of twelve-month-olds. The researchers varied the stranger's attractiveness by having her wear an attractive or an unattractive theatrical mask that was molded to her face. The stranger entered the experimental room where a mother and infant were interacting. She wore one of the two masks, but to avoid the possibility of her behaving differently when she was made to look attractive or unattractive, she was not told which mask had been placed on her face. She talked briefly to the mother and then to the baby. At this point she began interacting with the infant—playing with toys, picking the baby up, and so forth. The scene was videotaped for later observation of the infant's responses.

As predicted, babies responded differently in the attractive and the unattractive condition. As shown in Figure 7.14, these very young boys and girls showed more positive affect and more involvement in their play activity

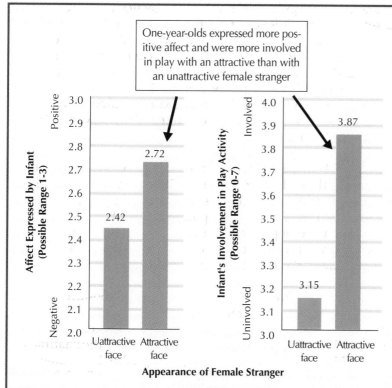

One-year-olds expressed more positive affect and were more involved in play with an attractive than with an unattractive female stranger

Infants respond to the attractiveness of adults

FIGURE 7.14 The physical attractiveness of an adult female stranger was found to affect how infants reacted to her. One-year-olds expressed more positive affect and became more involved in playing with a female stranger when she wore an attractive mask than when she wore an unattractive mask. The positive response to physical attractiveness clearly begins early in our lives.

Source: Based on data in Langlois, Roggman, & Rieser-Danner, 1990.

(accepting toys, vocalizing) when interacting with an attractive than with an unattractive stranger. Follow-up research (Langlois et al., 1991) indicated that infants also spend more time playing with an attractive than with an unattractive doll; and that their preference for an attractive adult face generalizes across faces differing in race, gender, and age. It appears that our tendency to respond positively to physical attractiveness is either learned *very* early in our lives or based on genetically determined preferences for attractive versus unattractive facial features.

At the opposite age extreme, research results indicate that people assume attractiveness among adults aged sixty to ninety-three to be indicative of desirable personality traits (Johnson & Pittenger, 1984). Relative attractiveness remains stable over the years (Pittenger, Mark, & Johnson, 1989), and the bias favoring those with a pleasing appearance operates from birth to old age.

Given the pervasive effects of attractiveness, it follows that many people may worry about their appearance. Dion, Dion, and Keelan (1990) developed a scale to measure **appearance anxiety,** defined as apprehension concerning one's physical appearance and the evaluations made by others. Subjects indicate their agreement or disagreement with a series of statements such as "I enjoy looking at myself in the mirror" and "I feel that most of my friends are more physically attractive than myself." Among college students, women indicate more appearance anxiety than men, and high scores on this test are associated with experiencing social anxiety, feeling unattractive in childhood, and having had fewer dates in high school. In recent research, described in the following **Work in Progress** section, appearance anxiety has been found to predict behavioral differences in specific social situations and to be relevant to some of the issues discussed in chapter 5.

Work in Progress

Appearance Anxiety, Interpersonal Behavior, and Weight

Currently, Professors Dion and Dion are actively exploring additional aspects of appearance anxiety (Dion, 1993). They proposed, for example, that anxiety about one's appearance would cause one to feel uncomfortable in interacting face to face with an attractive member of the opposite sex. On the basis of scores on the Appearance Anxiety Scale, the researchers selected high- and low-anxiety students to take part in a study supposedly dealing with "interpersonal communication." An attractive opposite-sex research assistant interviewed each participant and asked such innocuous questions as "What is your major?" The interview was video-taped, and judges (who did not know the appearance anxiety scores of the participants) rated the apparent comfort/discomfort of these individuals during the interaction. Women—but not men— high in appearance anxiety were rated by the judges as behaving in ways suggesting they were uncomfortable while being interviewed.

In research that is consistent with findings reported in chapter 5, the Dions found that overweight women scored higher in appearance anxiety than women whose weight was normal or below average—and also higher than men, including overweight men. Thus, women who depart from the expected standards of physical appearance with respect to weight are most anxious about how they look.

Additional work, now in progress, is designed to test the hypothesis that, among women, appearance anxiety is associated with depression. The general theoretical assumption is that concern about appearance is more closely tied to self-esteem for women than for men. As a result, when women perceive themselves (accurately or inaccurately) to be unattractive, their self-esteem drops and their depression rises.

A few negative attributes are associated with being attractive. Many people believe that beautiful women are more vain and materialistic than unattractive ones (Cash & Duncan, 1984). Attractiveness is a plus for males running for political office, but not for female candidates (Sigelman et al., 1986), possibly because elected officials are not "supposed" to be feminine. Though attractiveness is believed to lead to success, people often assume that the resulting good fortune is undeserved and simply based on looks (Kalick, 1988).

Beyond the assumptions people make about those who are physically attractive, is there any evidence that attractiveness is actually related to specific characteristics? Most of the characteristics attributed to attractive people represent inaccurate stereotypes (Feingold, 1992a). For example, there is a general stereotype that "what is beautiful is good," and one supposed correlate of physical attractiveness is intelligence (Dion, Berscheid, & Walster, 1972). Even though experimental subjects rate essays written by attractive students more positively than those written by unattractive ones (Cash & Trimer, 1984), there is in fact no relationship between attractiveness and college grade point average (Baugh & Parry, 1991).

Some of the other stereotypes seem to be true, however. Probably because people respond favorably to anyone who is good looking, attractive men and women learn to interact well with those of the opposite sex, and they have more dates than their less-attractive peers (Reis, Nezlek, & Wheeler, 1980). Similarly, a study of fifth-graders found attractive students to be more popular and less aggressive than unattractive kids (Johnstone, Frame, & Bouman, 1992). Altogether, good interpersonal skills appear to be associated with ratings of attractiveness (O'Grady, 1989).

You might assume that being attractive would increase an individual's self-esteem, but the two characteristics are unrelated (Kenealy et al., 1991). A possible reason that good-looking people don't necessarily evaluate themselves highly, is that when you are very attractive, you tend to believe that others value you only for your appearance (Major, Carrington, & Carnevale, 1984).

Critical Thinking
Question 3

*matching hypothesis
romantic partners pair off
on the basis of being similar
in physical attractiveness*

THE MATCHING HYPOTHESIS: SEEKING AN EQUALLY ATTRACTIVE PARTNER.   Despite the fact that most of us like those who are most attractive, men and women who are seeking actual relationships often fear being rejected by someone more attractive than themselves (Bernstein et al., 1983). Also, they themselves are likely to reject anyone less attractive than they are. As a result— the **matching hypothesis** states—romantic partners tend to pair off on the basis of being *similar* in physical attractiveness (Berscheid et al., 1971; Kalick & Hamilton, 1986). See Figure 7.15, p. 288. This tendency affects not only who dates whom, but also the choice of a marriage partner (Price & Vandenberg, 1979; Zajonc et al., 1987).

Matching does not occur 100 percent of the time, of course, and mismatches sometimes are observed. When people perceive an extreme appearance discrepancy between partners, it apparently makes them uncomfortable. When Forgas (1993) asked research participants to evaluate couples on the basis of their pictures, pairs similar in attractiveness (matched) were rated more positively—with respect to ability, likability, and quality of the relationship—than the couples dissimilar in attractiveness (mismatched). These differences in evaluation were intensified by the observer's mood. Participants who were first shown a comedy film rated the matched couples even more positively, and those who were first shown a film about death from cancer rated the mismatched couples even more negatively.

The matching hypothesis: Selecting a similar partner

FIGURE 7.15 Research indicates that the *matching hypothesis* is correct. People tend to choose friends, lovers, and spouses who are similar to themselves in physical attractiveness.

Reading: Lesko (21), *Exchange Theory in Interracial Dating*

Outsiders also seek to explain why the two people are together; a common response is to assume that the less attractive individual must be rich, powerful, wise, sexy, or famous to make up for his or her "deficiencies" in appearance. In effect, this assumption utilizes *equity theory* (see chapter 14), which proposes that people strongly prefer fairness in their relationships.

Discussion Question 5

Matching for attractiveness also occurs in same-sex friendships (Cash & Derlega, 1978), and this tendency is actually stronger for men than for women (McKillip & Reidel, 1983). In addition, a person's perceived attractiveness is affected by the appearance of his or her friends. If, for example, you become friends with someone less attractive than yourself, you are perceived as less good looking than if your friend is as attractive or more attractive than yourself (Wedell, Parducci, & Geiselman, 1987).

If we select friends in part on the basis of similarity in physical attractiveness, what happens when we are forced to be with someone who is either more attractive or less attractive than ourselves? To find out, see the following **On the Applied Side** section.

WHEN ROOMMATES ARE MISMATCHED IN ATTRACTIVENESS

Most of the research on attraction focuses on the variables that influence liking in an experimental setting (for example, we prefer attractive to unattractive strangers) or the variables that influence our choice of real-life friends (for example, we prefer companions who are like ourselves in attractiveness). It can quite reasonably be argued that such preferences are unreasonable and unfair. If so, with a little prodding, perhaps people should be gently forced to interact with others regardless of attractiveness and to establish relationships with others who happen to be more or less attractive than themselves. What is the outcome when this is done?

One setting in which attractiveness is regularly ignored is in dormitories during the assignment of college roommates. Many institutions use a random system in order to be as fair as possible. One result is that roommates can turn out to be relatively similar or dissimilar in attractiveness. Does it matter? In two studies of college freshmen, Carli, Ganley, and Pierce-Otay (1991) determined the attractiveness and similarity of attractiveness of same-sex roommates who had been randomly assigned to share a room. The investigators then questioned each individual privately about his or her evaluation of the roommate.

The results consistently indicated that the more similar the two individuals were in attractiveness, the more satisfied each person felt with the relationship and the more likely he or she was to request the same roommate for the following year.

When college roommates differ in their attractiveness, dissatisfaction arises, primarily for the more attractive of the two individuals. The better-looking person feels that his or her less-attractive roommate has a negative effect on outside relationships.

TABLE 7.3   Mismatched roommates: Who is more dissatisfied?

Perceptions of Students Who Believe They Are Less Attractive Than Their Roommates

I envy my roommate.

My roommate is helpful in introducing me to other people.

I would like to be more like my roommate.

Perceptions of Students Who Believe They Are More Attractive Than Their Roommates

My roommate is an obstacle to my social life.

My outside friends probably would not like my roommate.

It would be a good idea to have a different roommate next year.

Source: Based on data from Carli, Ganley, & Pierce-Otay, 1991.

The investigators further analyzed the data on dissatisfied individuals to determine whether the problem was simply dissimilarity or whether being the more- or the less-attractive member of a dissimilar pair caused the dissatisfaction. The data clearly indicated that dissimilarity led to dissatisfaction only for those who were more attractive than their roommates—not for those who were less attractive. To discover exactly why this was so, the researchers conducted a follow-up study.

In this second study, using a different group of freshmen, Carli et al. (1991) identified some of the specific problems involved when roommates are dissimilar in attractiveness. As can be seen in Table 7.3, the less-attractive member of the pair indicated envy of his or her attractive roommate, desire to be like that person, and gratitude for that individual's help in meeting people. The more attractive (and more dissatisfied) roommates, in contrast, complained about interference with their social life, reported that their friends rejected their roommates, and planned to end the association.

These findings provide a great deal of insight as to why the matching hypothesis operates in same-sex friendships and also why it is difficult to modify such preferences. In effect, those who are most attractive don't want to be held back socially by being associated with someone less attractive than themselves. Given this situation, do you feel that the reactions of the attractive roommates were fair or unfair? What would happen if dormitories decided that roommates should be relatively similar in attractiveness? Could, or should, anything be done to bring about changes in prejudice and discrimination against people who are seen as unattractive?

WHAT, EXACTLY, DETERMINES ATTRACTIVENESS?   In a given place at a given time, people agree fairly well about who is attractive and who is not (Banner, 1983); but it seems to be difficult to specify precisely what cues people utilize to evaluate attractiveness.

One way to answer the question is to identify attractive people and then determine what they have in common. Cunningham (1986) asked male undergraduates at a U. S. university to examine pictures of young women and to rate their attractiveness. Two facial types were perceived as most attractive. The highest-rated women either had childlike features (large, widely spaced eyes and a small nose and chin) or "mature" features (prominent cheekbones, narrow cheeks, high eyebrows, large pupils, and a big smile). These same two facial types were seen as attractive regardless of whether the women were white, black, or Oriental. Further, the specific stereotypes about attractiveness differ with these two types of features. A person (male or female) with an attractive, babyish face is perceived as more honest, warm, and sincere than average (Berry, 1991); but an attractive, mature face does not elicit such perceptions.

In a quite different approach to understanding attractiveness, Langlois and Roggman (1990) reduced photographs of men and women to a series of digits, then produced computer-generated composite faces. They found for both sexes that composite faces were rated as more attractive than most of the individual faces that made up the composites. Further, the more faces that went into the computer image, the more attractive the resulting face. Much like Goldilocks, we seem to prefer noses that are not too large or too small, eyebrows that are not too wide or too narrow, chins that are not too sharp or too rounded—in other words, "just right." The investigators concluded that, for most people, an attractive face is simply an average face.

Other aspects of attractiveness in women include medium-size breasts (Kleinke & Staneski, 1980) and a slim figure (Franzoi & Herzog, 1987). Attractiveness in men is associated with having slim legs and waist, broad shoulders, and small buttocks (Lavrakas, 1975) and also with being tall (Eisenberg et al., 1984; Lynn & Shurgot, 1984).

Most women prefer to date taller men, while most men prefer to date shorter women. This height preference in dating choice is actually stronger for women reacting to men than for men reacting to women (Pierce, 1992); but actual dating frequency is related to height only for women (Sheppard & Strathman, 1989), perhaps because most dates are initiated by males. In any event, within the normal height range, the less tall women are, the more they are preferred as dating partners, the more dates they have, and the more they are perceived as attractive.

Still other research suggests that judgments of attractiveness vary with the situation. Specifically, some evidence indicates that when Mickey Gilley sings of bars in which "the girls all get prettier at closing time," he may be accurate in describing the customers' perceptions (Nida & Koon, 1983; Pennebaker et al., 1979). See Figure 7.16. In a study of evening patrons at a college bar, Gladue and Delaney (1990) asked them to rate same- and opposite-sex fellow drinkers at 9:00, 10:30, and midnight. Those of the opposite sex were rated as more attractive by both men and women as closing time approached.

Boys and girls all get prettier at closing time

FIGURE 7.16 As the lyrics of a country and western song suggest, situational factors affect perceptions of the attractiveness of the opposite sex. When time is running out and the possible choices for the evening are becoming more limited, potential partners appear to be increasingly attractive.

BECOMING FRIENDS: SIMILARITY AND RECIPROCITY

As we have seen, once two people are brought together by physical proximity, the probability that they will like each other and establish some kind of relationship is increased if each is (1) in a positive emotional state, (2) motivated by affiliative needs, and (3) favorably impressed by the appearance and other observable characteristics of the other. Further steps toward a closer relationship depend on the two individuals' beginning to communicate and on the content of that communication (Byrne, 1992). The development of a friendship rests on the discovery of various kinds of *similarity* and on the indication of *reciprocal positive evaluations*.

SIMILARITY: WE LIKE THOSE MOST LIKE OURSELVES

Over twenty centuries ago, Aristotle described the nature of friendship and hypothesized that people who agree with one another become friends, while those with dissimilar attitudes do not. As the gentleman in Figure 7.17 indi-

Similar attitudes are preferred to dissimilar attitudes

FIGURE 7.17 As centuries of observation and decades of research have shown, attitude similarity is an important component of interpersonal attraction. As the man in the cartoon indicates, most people don't even want to hear about views different from their own.
Source: The *New Yorker*, March 18, 1985, p. 46.

"No, I would not welcome a contrasting point of view."

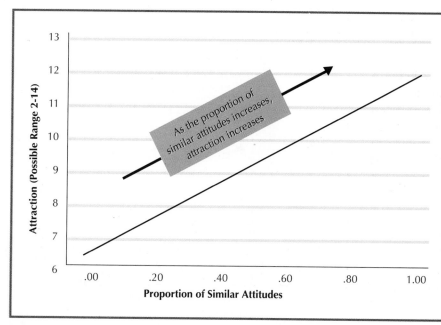

The linear relationship between proportion of similar attitudes and attraction

FIGURE 7.18 The relationship between attraction and proportion of similar attitudes is found among people differing in age, social class, and the culture in which they live. As shown here, attraction increases in a linear fashion as the proportion of similar attitudes increases.

cates, **attitude similarity** is acceptable in conversation—but not a different point of view. In books and movies opposites may attract, but in real life birds of a feather flock together. As tennis pro Bjorn Borg said of his new wife, "She's a great woman. She's just like me" (Milestones, 1989).

SIMILAR ATTITUDES, DISSIMILAR ATTITUDES, AND ATTRACTION.   The association between attitude similarity and attraction was first documented in correlational studies such as Schiller's (1932) investigation of married couples; eventually laboratory experiments (beginning with Schachter, 1951) established a cause-and-effect relationship. That is, the expression of a similar attitude, belief, or value results in liking, while dissimilar statements result in dislike. These effects hold true across age groups ranging from elementary school children to the elderly, across socioeconomic levels, and across cultures as different as those of India, Japan, Korea, Mexico, Singapore, and the United States.

When people interact, their conversation often involves the expression of their attitudes about whatever topics come up—school, music, television shows, politics, religion, and so on. As people talk, each person indicates his or her likes and dislikes (Hatfield & Rapson, 1992; Kent, Davis, & Shapiro, 1981). Research has shown that each individual in the interaction reponds to the other on the basis of the **proportion of similar attitudes** that are expressed. For example, we are equally attracted to someone who has views like our own on two of the four topics we discuss or on fifty of the one hundred topics we discuss; the proportion is .50 in each instance. The higher the proportion of similar attitudes, the greater the liking. This relationship is sufficiently strong and universal that it is possible to express it in mathematical terms as a linear function, as shown in Figure 7.18 (Byrne & Nelson, 1965).

Attempts to identify dispositional differences in response to attitude similarity/dissimilarity have most often been unsuccessful. In some instances, however, individual diversity does occur. For example, Grover and Brockner (1989) hypothesized that people high in empathy would be more sensitive to the views of others and thus more responsive to similarity or dissimilarity than

Reading: Lesko (20)
Attraction and Attitude Similarity

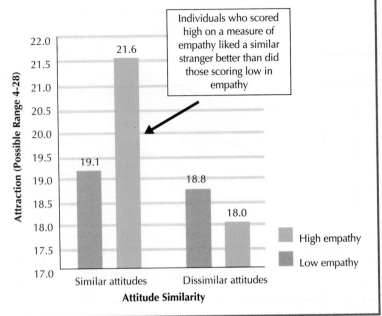

The effect of empathy on response to similarity/dissimilarity

FIGURE 7.19 Though almost everyone likes attitudinally similar others in preference to those with dissimilar attitudes, individuals vary in how strongly they are affected by the views of others. When subjects are divided into those scoring high and low on the dispositional characteristic of *empathy*, those high in empathy respond more positively to a similar stranger than do those low in empathy.

Source: Based on data from Grover & Brockner, 1989.

would people low in empathy. When subjects who differed in level of empathy responded to an attitudinally similar or dissimilar stranger, the high-empathy individuals responded more strongly than the low-empathy individuals, especially when the stranger was similar (see Figure 7.19).

Many social psychologists and sociologists have concluded that the similarity-attraction effect is an extremely solid and reliable one. For example, Cappella and Palmer (1990, p. 161) state that, "perhaps the most well known and well established finding in the study of interpersonal relations is that attitude similarity creates attraction." Nevertheless, several critics have questioned one or more aspects of the concept. A leading critic who has generated both theoretical controversy and empirical research is Rosenbaum (1986). He made a surprising proposal: Similar attitudes have *no* effect on attraction (see special section below). Sunnafrank (1992) indicated that attitude similarity between partners may have little effect on relationships, and Bochner (1991) went even farther by claiming that the attitude similarity–attraction relationship is "dead." As Duck and Barnes (1992) point out, however, the similarity–attraction relationship is like an inverted *Titanic;* everyone thinks it should sink, but it remains afloat. We will describe a portion of this conceptual battle in the **Cutting Edge** section that follows.

Focus on Research: The Cutting Edge

THE REPULSION HYPOTHESIS: ARE SIMILAR ATTITUDES IRRELEVANT?

Critical Thinking Question 4

Rosenbaum's (1986) **repulsion hypothesis** states that similar attitudes are essentially irrelevant in the attraction process—only *dissimilar* attitudes play a role.

According to this view, people initially respond to strangers with liking; this positive response shifts in a negative direction only when and if dissimilar attitudes are expressed. In other words, we aren't attracted to a select few; we are simply repulsed by certain people. In support of this proposition, Rosenbaum reported evidence indicating that similar attitudes did not *increase* attraction above the level found in a "no-information control condition," while dissimilar attitudes did *decrease* attraction when compared to the control condition.

The key element in this research was clearly the addition of a particular kind of control condition. For example, subjects are shown a photograph of a fellow college student and asked how much they like or dislike this person. Their attraction toward the stranger is as great as that of other subjects who see the photograph *plus* information that the person holds attitudes similar to their own. The photograph plus *dissimilar* attitudes, however, results in significantly less attraction. Why the difference? Is Rosenbaum correct?

A major problem with a no-information condition is that it is impossible to create (Byrne, Clore, & Smeaton, 1986). There is a general human tendency to assume that others share our opinions (Dawes, 1989; Marasch, 1992; Marks, Graham, & Hansen, 1992)—a phenomenon known as the *false consensus effect* (see chapter 3). The yearbook photographs used by Rosenbaum show fellow college students who can be assumed to be roughly similar to the subject in intellectual ability and educational goals, cues that add to the false consensus effect (Marks & Miller, 1982). Adding information about attitude similarity doesn't affect attraction because the stranger is already assumed to be similar and likeable.

But the counterargument is that such reasoning simply proves that Rosenbaum is correct. That is, we initially like almost everyone, because we assume they are similar; only dissimilarity can function to lower our evaluation of a person. Partially consistent with the repulsion hypothesis is Chapman's (1992) finding that dissimilar attitudes have a greater effect on attraction than similar ones. Other experiments, however, lead us to a slightly more complicated conclusion.

First, Smeaton, Byrne, and Murnen (1989) conducted an investigation in which the number of dissimilar attitudes was held constant (in each condition, the stranger disagreed on eight items) while the number of similar attitudes varied (the stranger agreed on either 0, 28, or 62 items). The repulsion hypothesis predicts no differences across conditions (because only similar attitudes were varied)—but the results supported the similarity hypothesis, in that attraction increased as the proportion of similar attitudes increased. Obviously, similar attitudes *do* have an effect on attraction, so that element in the repulsion hypothesis is incorrect.

Second, Singh and Tan (1992) used Rosenbaum's "no-information" control group—supposedly a stranger who was a same-sex first-year student at the subjects' university. Each subject indicated his or her attraction toward that person *and* guessed how the stranger would respond to a series of attitude items. In the control group, assumed similarity was high (73 percent) and so was attraction. When subjects were then given attitude information about the stranger, those informed of no agreement and 50 percent agreement liked the stranger less (as predicted by both the repulsion hypothesis *and* the proportion hypothesis), while those informed of 100 percent agreement liked the stranger more (as predicted by the original formulation based on proportion)—see Figure 7.20. Attraction decreases more in the totally dissimilar group than it increases in the totally similar group because 0 percent similarity

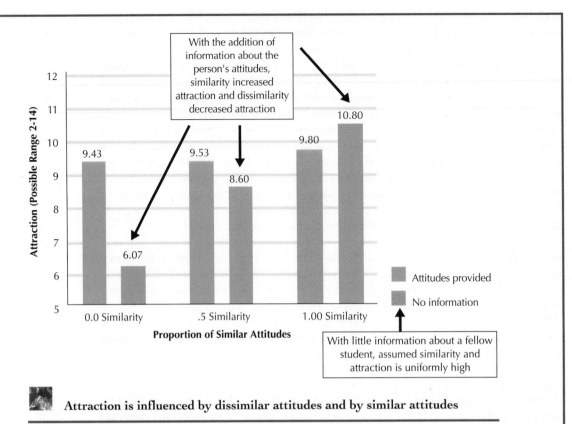

With the addition of information about the person's attitudes, similarity increased attraction and dissimilarity decreased attraction

9.43

9.53

8.60

6.07

9.80

10.80

Attraction (Possible Range 2-14)

0.0 Similarity   .5 Similarity   1.00 Similarity

Proportion of Similar Attitudes

Attitudes provided

No information

With little information about a fellow student, assumed similarity and attraction is uniformly high

Attraction is influenced by dissimilar attitudes and by similar attitudes

FIGURE 7.20   When college students were asked to make judgments about a fellow student, they assumed that the other person held attitudes similar to their own (The *false consensus effect*) and they liked him or her. When they were then provided with information about the other person's attitudes, attraction decreased in response to dissimilar attitudes and increased in response to similar attitudes.

Source: Based on data from Singh & Tan, 1992.

is more discrepant from the assumed similarity of 73 percent than is 100 percent similarity.

Third, Smeaton et al. (1992) were able to show that under certain circumstances similar attitudes actually have a greater effect than dissimilar ones. Though most of us assume that others agree with us on most issues (the false consensus effect), there are *specific issues* on which each of us feels that we hold a minority position—the **false uniqueness effect** (McFarland & Miller, 1990). Strangers are assumed to disagree with us on such topics; when they surprise us by agreeing, attraction goes up. When they respond by disagreeing as we expected, there is little or no effect on attraction. In other words, the effects are exactly the opposite from those predicted by the repulsion hypothesis.

The conclusion seems to be that attraction *is* a function of proportion of similar attitudes, but assumptions about similarity can modify how people respond. It is basically a matter of how much a stranger's attitudes deviate from what is expected. The greater the deviation (either more dissimilarity or more similarity than one's expectation), the greater the effect on attraction.

WHY DO WE CARE ABOUT THE ATTITUDES OF OTHERS? Three possible explanations have been offered as to why people respond emotionally to the similar and dissimilar attitudes expressed by others.

The oldest formulation, **balance theory** (Hummert, Crockett, & Kemper, 1990), rests on the concept that humans organize their likes and dislikes in a symmetrical way. **Balance** exists when two people like each other and agree about some topic (Newcomb, 1961). When they like each other and disagree, however, an unpleasant state of **imbalance** is created (Orive, 1988). Each person attempts to restore balance through such means as changing attitudes, convincing the other person to change attitudes, or reducing liking. When two people dislike each other, they are in a state of **nonbalance** and don't care whether they agree or disagree.

While balance theory leads to a number of interesting predictions about how people will respond to agreement and disagreement, it really doesn't explain *why* such information is important. As a result, many theorists have taken the question a step farther; they have suggested that attitudes are important because we turn to other people to obtain **consensual validation** of our views about the world through a social comparison process (Festinger, 1954; Goethals, 1986). According to this theory, when someone agrees with you, the agreement validates your views—provides "evidence" that you are correct. You are pleased to discover that you have sound judgment, are intelligent, have good taste, and so forth. Not surprisingly, you like the person who makes you feel good about yourself. Disagreement has just the opposite effect; perhaps you have faulty judgment, are not too bright, and have poor taste. Such information makes you feel bad about yourself, and you dislike the other person. If this conceptualization is correct, it means that when we sound out others on their views, we are not really seeking evidence; we simply want to identify others who agree with us. One example of this process occurs when people complain about something or about someone to their acquaintances; they are not usually attempting to solve a problem but simply to find someone who will express sympathy and agree that their complaint is a just one (Alicke et al., 1992).

More recently, a third possible explanation (also discussed in chapter 10) has been offered by Rushton (1989). He hypothesizes that people use attitude similarity, among other cues, to detect those who are genetically similar to themselves. Friends, for example, exceed chance in their similarity on such genetically determined characteristics as blood type and Rh factor. If you like someone who is similar to you, become friends, and provide that person assistance when it is needed, you are unconsciously helping to ensure that genes like your own will be protected and eventually transmitted to the next generation. For this reason, we are each biologically programmed to attend to and respond positively to similarity of all kinds. As will be pointed out in the following chapter, choosing a similar mate is even more crucial as a way to protect your portion of the gene pool.

OTHER KINDS OF SIMILARITY INFLUENCE ATTRACTION, TOO. For most characteristics that have been investigated, similarity results in liking and friendship (Griffin & Sparks, 1990). Though **complementarity** is often proposed as a contrast to similarity (dominant people should like submissive ones, etc.), research seeking this kind of attraction effect has generally been unsuccessful (Nowicki & Manheim, 1991). Complementary pairs of workers *are*

Exercise 4

found to perform tasks better than noncomplementary pairs (Estroff & Nowicki, 1992), however. Despite the overall research support for similarity, we can each come up with examples of pairs of friends or even spouses who are dissimilar in a variety of ways. Then we nod and say, "Opposites attract." Though research has not confirmed this common observation, perhaps it is partially true. That is, if two people are *very* similar with respect to 95 percent of their attitudes, values, beliefs, and interests, it is *possible* that differences on a few other characteristics are perceived as interesting or intriguing—if nothing else, it gives them something to talk about. Such examples of minor dissimilarities in the context of major similarities may account for the persistence and popularity of the complementarity hypothesis in our culture.

Exercise 5   Examples of similarity factors associated with liking include age (Ellis, Rogoff, & Cramer, 1981); religion and race (Kandel, 1978); skills (Tesser, Campbell, & Smith, 1984); smoking, drinking, and engaging in premarital sex (Rodgers, Billy, & Udry, 1984); using marijuana (Eisenman, 1985); experiencing the same emotions (Alliger & Williams, 1991); being a morning versus an evening person (Watts, 1982); and many different personality dispositions (Morell, Twillman, & Sullaway, 1989; Rosenblatt & Greenberg, 1988; Smith, 1989). Also, the more two people interact, the more similar they become in personality (Blankenship et al., 1984; Funder & Colvin, 1988), including self-concept (Deutsch et al., 1991) and ideal-self concept (LaPrelle et al., 1990).

One advantage of having friends who are similar to ourselves is that we are able to communicate better with them than with strangers (Fussell & Krauss, 1989).

RECIPROCITY: MUTUAL LIKING

Once two people discover areas of similarity, a friendship is likely to develop. One additional step is crucial, however. Each individual must indicate that the other person is liked and evaluated positively (Condon & Crano, 1988). Almost everyone is pleased to receive such feedback and very upset to receive negative evaluations (Coleman, Jussim, & Abraham, 1987). Often, even an inaccurate positive evaluation (Swann et al., 1987) or an obvious attempt at flattery (Drachman, DeCarufel, & Insko, 1978) is well received. Individuals also differ in the kind of evaluations they want from others. People with positive self-concepts (see chapter 5) are most inclined to want positive evaluations from others; in contrast, those with negative self-concepts sometimes respond well to accurate negative appraisals (Swann, Stein-Seroussi, & Giesler, 1992). It appears that some people primarily want to be praised, while others feel a stronger need to be correct about their negative self-evaluations.

Though mutual liking can easily be expressed in words, the first signs are often nonverbal (see the discussion of nonverbal cues in chapter 2). For example, when a woman converses with a man while maintaining eye contact and leaning toward him, he often interprets her behavior (sometimes incorrectly) as an indication that she likes him, and so he may be attracted to her (Gold, Ryckman, & Mosley, 1984).

When the evaluation is verbalized, there is much less ambiguity about its meaning, and there is an immediate effect on interpersonal behavior. In one experiment, some subjects were led to believe that they were liked by a stranger and others to believe that they were disliked (Curtis & Miller, 1986). When each subject then engaged in a ten-minute discussion with someone

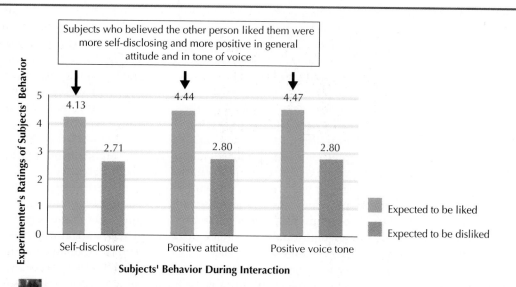

Experimenter's Ratings of Subjects' Behavior

Subjects who believed the other person liked them were more self-disclosing and more positive in general attitude and in tone of voice

Self-disclosure: 4.13, 2.71
Positive attitude: 4.44, 2.80
Positive voice tone: 4.47, 2.80

■ Expected to be liked
■ Expected to be disliked

Subjects' Behavior During Interaction

If you believe another person likes you, your positive behavior leads to your actually being liked

FIGURE 7.21   Reciprocal liking is a vital element in the formation of a relationship. In an experiment, subjects who had been led to believe that another subject liked them engaged in more self-disclosure, expressed more positive attitudes, spoke in more positive tones, and were liked more than subjects who had been led to believe that another subject disliked them.
Source: Based on data from Curtis & Miller, 1986.

supposed to be that stranger (actually, just another subject), behavior was strongly influenced by whether a positive or a negative evaluation had been given. As shown in Figure 7.21, those who had received positive feedback and thus expected to be liked made more eye contact, spoke in a warmer tone, and were more self-disclosing than those who expected to be disliked. One result in the positive condition was greater reciprocal liking afterward.

Social Diversity ▼ A Critical Analysis

Status and Attraction in Japan and the United States

Social psychologists assume that the same general principles that determine attraction in the United States, Canada, and Western Europe are also operative in quite different cultures. That is, regardless of who the individuals are and where they live, basic factors such as propinquity, affect, and similarity should be equally relevant to interpersonal attraction. Nevertheless, some specific factors can have quite different effects in different cultures. For example, a model dinner guest who belches loudly at the end of the meal is likely to evoke negative affect in the United States (as showing rudeness or lack of refinement), but the same behavior evokes positive affect in Saudi Arabia (as a sign that the man enjoyed the food).

Another example of different affective responses to the same stimulus involves *status.* Research indicates that in a social setting Americans respond negatively to status differences, but Japanese do not.

If you could choose the people with whom to spend your working hours, who would they be? Given the findings related to similarity and attraction, it is a good bet that you would decide to spend your time with people similar to yourself. For example, you might feel more comfortable with fellow workers who held jobs about like your own. How would you feel about being with someone who held a position superior to yours—one with more power and higher status? Nakao (1987) proposed that workers in the United States and Japan would differ in their preferences.

In the United States the concept of equality is stressed in our constitution, in our educational system, and in everyday life. There is even a tendency to deny or to minimize the importance of differences in social class,

power, or economic power. Bosses dress casually and play baseball with employees at company picnics. Candidates for political office attempt to demonstrate that they are just like the average person when they drop by the neighborhood bar to drink a beer, listen to the music, and eat pretzels. Most employees and voters realize that such behavior is only a charade, but blatant displays indicating superior wealth, education, or power make us uncomfortable and create negative feelings. By and large, Americans seem to be attracted to and to feel comfortable with those most like themselves; this tendency is sometimes labled a *horizontal orientation.*

Nakao (1987) points out that studies of Japanese culture more often indicate a *vertical orientation,* in which status is recognized and valued. One implication is that Japanese citizens can be expected to seek out and desire to be with those of superior status in order to curry favor, use them as role models, and be in a position to improve their own status.

To examine possible cultural differences, the investigator compared a group of male

employees in one department of a newspaper in Fullerton, California, and another group of males working in one department of a telecommunication company in Tokyo. The two groups were similar in age range, in education, and in the kind of work they did.

Members of each department were asked to rank everyone there (including themselves) as to how much power they held in the organization. The investigator also asked each employee to imagine that a new branch office was being opened where he would be transferred, and to rank everyone else with respect to whom he would prefer as coworkers in the new location.

The employees responded quite differently in the two countries. In the United States, subjects indicated the greatest attraction toward others who were most similar in status to themselves. In Japan, they indicated the greatest attraction toward those higher in status than themselves. Clearly, then, some aspects of the attraction process are not universal but are influenced or modified by cultural values.

Summary and Review

Our attitudes about other people range from strong liking to strong dislike, and research on *interpersonal attraction* focuses on the factors that determine these attitudes.

Proximity and Emotions

Friendships often begin on the basis of unplanned encounters that are controlled by the physical

details of the environment. When neighborhoods, dormitory assignments, or classroom seating arrangements bring people into regular contact, they are likely to become acquainted. Thus, proximity (or *propinquity*) leads to repeated exposure, which results in familiarity and the increased likelihood of friendly interaction.

A basic determinant of attraction is *affect,* or one's emotional state during an interpersonal interaction. Positive affect results in liking while negative affect causes dislike, whether the other person is responsible for the emotion or not. We learn to associate our emotional state with anyone who is present at the time, and attraction is sometimes a function of emotional conditioning.

Need for Affiliation and Stereotypes Based on Observable Characteristics

A relationship is most likely to form if two people are each motivated to affiliate. People differ in the dispositional variable known as *need for affiliation*, and the strength of this motive determines attraction-related behaviors. In addition, several specific underlying motives—such as the need for emotional support and the need for attention—provide different reasons for seeking relationships. Beyond motivation, people need good social skills in order to engage in successful affiliative behavior. Not only dispositions but external events involving stress or excitement can act as powerful motivators of affiliation, in that people seek out others with whom to engage in social comparison and information-gathering interactions.

Initial attraction or avoidance is often based on responses to stereotypes associated with the *observable characteristics* of others—race, sex, age, height, physique, accent, clothing, and so forth. Among the most pervasive of these characteristics is *physical attractiveness*. There is a generally positive response to both males and females who are attractive, and people tend to select others approximately as attractive as themselves (according to the *matching hypothesis*) as friends, dates, and marriage partners. Despite many positive stereotypes based on attractiveness, good

looks seem to be related only to good interpersonal skills. Perceptions of attractiveness are based not only on physical characteristics such as height but on special situational determinants such as the approach of closing time at a bar.

Similarity and Reciprocity

Observers of human behavior since before the time of Christ have noted that *attitude similarity* is associated with liking and attitude dissimilarity with negative responses. Research in the latter half of this century established a precise linear relationship between attraction and proportion of similar attitudes. Because we tend to assume that others agree with us (the false consensus effect), initial attraction to a stranger tends to be high, and subsequent attraction is a function of how far the person's actual attitudes deviate from our expectations. Also, similarity in many aspects of behavior and appearance is found to be positively related to attraction. Explanations of the similarity effect include balance theory, the need for consensual validation, and the sociobiological importance of genetic similarity.

A final, and crucial, variable in friendship formation is the expression of mutual liking (reciprocity) either in words or in nonverbal behavior.

Social Diversity: Status and Attraction

Though many aspects of the attraction process are found to be universal, cultural influences can lead to specific differences. For example, employees in the United States prefer coworkers of equal status and power; in Japan, the preference is for coworkers of higher status and power.

Key Terms

Affect Emotions or feelings.

Appearance Anxiety Apprehension or worry about the adequacy of one's physical appearance and about how others evaluate it.

Attitude Similarity The extent to which two individuals share the same attitudes about a series of topics.

Balance In Newcomb's theory, the plesant emotional state that results when two people

like each other and agree about a topic of discussion.

Balance Theory A cognitively oriented theory of the relationships among an individual's liking for another person, his or her attitude about a given topic, and the other person's perceived attitude about that same topic.

Cognitive Disregard Part of the screening process whereby some of the people we meet are excluded from further consideration as possible acquaintances or friends on the basis of our reaction to one or more of their observable characteristics. We pay little attention to those we exclude from consideration, and we tend to forget them.

Complementarity Possession of different but complementary traits. The complementarity hypothesis suggests that people with complementary traits should like one another; For example, a dominant person should be attracted to a submissive one. There is, however, very little empirical support for this appealing idea.

Consensual Validation The "validation" of one's views about any aspect of the world that one perceives on finding that someone else holds the same views.

False Uniqueness Effect The tendency to believe (often incorrectly) that most people hold views unlike one's own about specific issues.

Friendship Motivation The motive to establish warm and friendly interpersonal relationships.

Imbalance In Newcomb's theory, the unpleasant emotional state that results when two people like each other but disagree about a topic of discussion. Each is motivated to change some element in the interaction (the actual or perceived attitude of one of the individuals or the feeling of attraction) in order to achieve balance or nonbalance.

Interpersonal Attraction The degree to which we like other individuals. Interpersonal attraction varies along a dimension ranging from strong liking on one extreme to strong dislike on the other.

Matching Hypothesis The proposal that individuals with approximately equal social assets (such as physical attractiveness) select one another as friends, lovers, and/or spouses.

Need for Affiliation The motive to seek interpersonal relationships.

Nonbalance In Newcomb's theory, the indifferent emotional state that results when two people dislike each other and don't care whether they agree or disagree about a topic of discussion.

Physical Attractiveness The combination of facial features, physique, and grooming that is perceived as aesthetically appealing by members of a given culture at a given time period.

Privacy The need to limit how much other people know about one's past, present, or future activities.

Propinquity Physical proximity. As propinquity between two individuals increases, the probability of their coming in contact increases. Repeated interpersonal exposure leads to increased familiarity, and familiarity generally leads to a positive evaluative response.

Proportion of Similar Attitudes The number of topics on which two individuals hold the same views in relation to the total number of topics on which they compare their views. Expressed as a percentage or proportion: the number of topics on which there is agreement divided by the total number of total topics discussed.

Reinforcement-Affect Model A theory proposing that positive versus negative evaluations are based on positive versus negative emotions. The evaluations are directed at the person who is *responsible* for the emotions or (through classical conditioning) *simply associated* with the arousal.

Repeated Exposure Frequent contact with a stimulus. According to Zajonc's theory of repeated exposure, as the number of contacts with any neutral or mildly positive stimulus increases, the evaluation of that stimulus becomes increasingly positive.

Repulsion Hypothesis Rosenbaum's proposal that attraction is not enhanced by similar attitudes; instead, people initially respond positively to others but are repulsed by the discovery of dissimilar attitudes.

Social Comparison Process The tendency to evaluate one's abilities, accomplishments, views, actions, appearance, beliefs, and other attributes by comparing them with those of other relevant people.

For More Information

Blieszner, R., & Adams, R. G. (1992). *Adult friendship*. Newbury Park, CA: Sage.

A theoretical model of adult friendships plus an historical view of this aspect of human relationships along with coverage of current research on friendship. The authors discuss the roles of similarity and other determinants and point out the phases through which relationships progress.

Derlega, V. J., & Winstead, B. A. (Eds.). (1986). *Friendship and social interaction*. New York: Springer-Verlag.

Authors from various fields discuss friendship. Included are such topics as friendship formation, the importance of friendship in our lives, and the effects of sex and social situations on friendship functioning.

Erwin, P. (1993). *Friendship and peer relations in children*. Chichester, England: Wiley.

This book focuses on peer relationships among young children and discusses social and cognitive processes in terms of the effect of childhood friendships on later development.

Hatfield, E., & Sprecher, S. (1986). *Mirror, mirror . . . The importance of looks in everyday life*. Albany, NY: SUNY Press.

A well-written and extremely interesting summary of research dealing with the effects of physical attractiveness on interpersonal relationships. The scientific literature is well covered, and the findings are illustrated throughout with anecdotes, photographs, and drawings that consistently enliven the presentation.

Nardi, P. M. (Ed.) (1992). *Men's Friendships*. Newbury Park, CA: Sage.

A series of contributors provide chapters that cover many aspects of male friendship patterns. Included are discussions of men's power, networking, self-disclosure, friendships with women, gay relationships, and cross-cultural comparisons focused on Native American, Asian-American, and African-American men.

Close Relationships:
Friendship, Love, and Sexuality

Interdependent Relationships: Moving beyond Casual Friendships

Relatives, Friends, and Lovers / What Is This Thing Called Love? / Loneliness: The Absence of a Close Relationship

Physically Intimate Relationships

Premarital Sexuality / Marriage

Troubled Relationships: Problems, Solutions, Failures

Problems in Relationships, and Possible Solutions / When Relationships Break Up: From Dissatisfaction to Dissolution

SOCIAL DIVERSITY ▼ A Critical Analysis
Love and Intimacy: Western Europe, South Africa, Japan, and the United States

---

Special Sections:

WORK IN PROGRESS—When Relationships Are Too Close, Experimental Closeness, and Pregnancy

FOCUS ON RESEARCH: THE CUTTING EDGE—Evolution versus Culture: Sex Differences in the Preferred Age of a Sex Partner

INDIVIDUAL DIVERSITY—Sociosexuality: Choosing a Romantic Partner

WORK IN PROGRESS—Dating As a Unique Relationship

SOCIAL PSYCHOLOGY: ON THE APPLIED SIDE—Positive versus Negative Communications between Partners

WORK IN PROGRESS—Sometimes, Offspring "Break Up" with Their Parents

During my sophomore year at college, I received a telephone call one Friday evening from Mark. He had driven home for the weekend to be with a longtime friend, Lisa; but his erotic plans had been disrupted by the unexpected visit of one of Lisa's aunts and her cousin, Mamie. The two cousins wanted to spend Saturday in San Francisco, and Mark asked if I could join them as a blind date for Mamie. I had a paper to write and guessed that Mamie probably looked like President Eisenhower's wife. Nevertheless, because Mark was a nice guy and a good friend in many ways, I agreed to go. One lost Saturday wouldn't kill me.

The next morning, when Mark's car pulled up, I greeted Mark and Lisa, and then noticed a beautiful blonde in the back seat. She looked up with a dazzling smile and said "Hi." This was definitely not Mamie Eisenhower, but I tried not to look surprised.

I had never really been in love, and I was sure that "love at first sight" happened only in the movies. During the next hour, though, as we drove north up the peninsula, it happened to me. This was it—a dream come true. She was attractive, sweet, easy to talk to, and fun, and I felt as if I had known her all of my life.

The rest of that day was something of a blur. Everything was perfect. We talked and laughed and bought our lunch at a sidewalk stand on

Fisherman's Wharf. We ate, walked along the boat docks, and browsed in the souvenir shops. Mamie and I held hands and seemed to float through that beautiful spring day. It was like being part of a commercial that shows lovers running through fields of wildflowers, as seen through a soft-focus lens—with music in the background.

And then there really was music, because we spent the rest of the afternoon at a free band concert in Golden Gate Park. Mamie and I sat very close, and I can still smell her perfume when I hear songs like "A Stranger in Paradise."

Late in the afternoon, the fog began to drift in from the Pacific, chilling the spring air. We drove south out of the city and back to the campus. When we reached my dormitory, Mamie got out of the car to say goodbye, and we clung to each other and kissed until Mark honked good naturedly for us to break it up. My heart sank as the three of them drove away. I didn't want Mamie to leave; I wanted to spend the rest of my life with her. Over the following weeks, I thought of little else. I wanted to make love to her, live with her, marry her, have children, grow old together.

We exchanged letters for a month or two and talked on the phone a few times, but we never saw each other again. Our letters and telephone conversations soon made it clear that we didn't have much in common; our "love" and the magic of that day in the city quickly faded. In fact, I confess that I'm not sure her name was Mamie. It was the same as some first lady, but I've completely forgotten her real name and wouldn't recognize her if we passed on the street. I'm sure that my name and face were, for her, equally forgettable.

How could an otherwise sensible young college student fall madly in love with someone he had just met and knew nothing about? About two decades after I fell in and out of love with "Mamie," psychologists began studying just such behavior. As you will discover in the remainder of this chapter, we are still attempting to understand love and many other aspects of interpersonal relationships.

For most people, close relationships constitute a crucial aspect of their lives. Despite changes in our society and widespread changes in various attitudes and values, most of us believe that an ideal life includes interacting with cherished relatives, having close friends, falling in love, getting married, and becoming parents. We are all aware, after exposure to films and novels as well as to real-life experiences, that relatives often don't get along, friendships fade, and love can turn to hate. Sometimes close relationships cause more pain than joy. Still, despite negative examples all around us, we tend to maintain our hopes about what relationships can and should be. We don't expect our own personal relationships to be anything like those expressed by Hagar's wife in Figure 8.1.

Social psychologists, as well as other behavioral scientists, are focusing more and more attention on the study of close relationships (Duck & Barnes, 1992; Hatfield & Rapson, 1992a, 1993; Morgan & White, 1993; Werner, Altman, & Brown, 1992)—mostly among heterosexuals, but increasingly among gays and lesbians as well (Schullo & Alperson, 1984). Given the importance of family, friendship, love, and marriage to most people, what makes

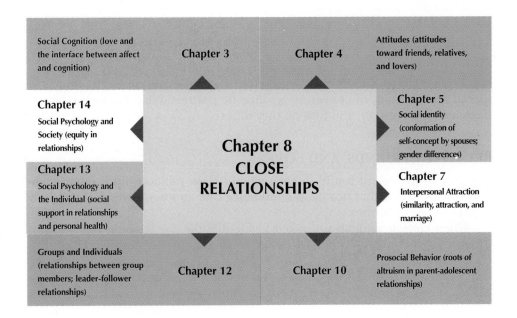

close relationships thrive, and how can such relationships lead to problems? In the following pages, we will share with you what has been learned about the factors associated with interpersonal success and failure.

We will first describe three varieties of *interdependent relationships,* discuss several varieties of *love,* and then outline the phenomenon of *loneliness* that results when such relationships are not formed or when they fail. Next we turn our attention to how *physically intimate relationships* (both *premarital* and *marital*) are established and maintained. We'll also consider *troubled relationships* and examine how *problems* arise and the effects of *dissolution.*

The effect of marriage on romantic love

FIGURE 8.1 Most of us expect to fall in love and get married, and most of us do exactly that. Though examples of fading love and unhappy marriages are common, few of us ever expect to feel the way Hagar's wife does here.

Source: King Features Syndicate, Inc., March 8, 1983.

INTERDEPENDENT RELATIONSHIPS: MOVING BEYOND CASUAL FRIENDSHIPS

Close relationships, including close same-sex friendships, are not the same as casual friendships. Closeness can develop in our ties to family members, to special friends, and, of course, to a romantic partner. What do such relationships have in common, and how do they differ?

RELATIVES, FRIENDS, AND LOVERS

The common element found in each type of close relationship is **interdependence.** This means that two people influence one another's lives and regularly engage in joint activities.

When college students are asked to identify the *one person* in the world to whom they feel most close, they describe one of three types of relationship (Berscheid, Snyder, & Omoto, 1989). Some (14 percent) specify a family member, 36 percent identify a friend, and almost half (47 percent) name a romantic partner. The remaining 3 percent mention someone else, such as a fellow worker.

CLOSE RELATIVES.   Though family relationships are important during a large portion of our lives, surprisingly little research has focused on this kind of interpersonal closeness.

There are some exceptions, such as several recent studies of sibling relationships. The great majority of children (about 80 percent) grow up with siblings, and interactions with siblings clearly provide a way to learn and practice interpersonal skills (Dunn, 1992). Brothers and sisters often experience a mixture of love and hate, closeness and rivalry; and these mixed feelings recur throughout one's life, because friendships, love affairs, and marriages tend to evoke the reactions originally associated with siblings (Klagsbrun, 1992).

Siblings interact differently at different ages; most siblings are close in childhood but then grow apart in adolescence and young adulthood. By middle age about 80 percent again establish positive relationships, while 10 percent express hostility and another 10 percent feel only indifference. Closeness in adulthood is more likely if siblings are no more than five years apart in age; both sister-sister and brother-sister pairs tend to be closer than brother-brother pairs (Rosenthal, 1992).

Another important, and often neglected, relationship is that between parents and their offspring, especially in adolescence and afterward. No matter how close parents feel toward a baby or a young child, they are often apprehensive when these same young people approach puberty. Parents fear being rejected and hated by rebellious teenagers; but most adolescents report very positive feelings about their parents, though they are naturally less close and dependent than they were in childhood (Galambos, 1992).

Jeffries (1987, 1990, 1993) has also pursued the question of the love adolescents feel for their parents. Based on the writings of St. Thomas Aquinas, Jeffries's model suggests that love for one's parents consists of two basic components: *attraction* and *virtue.* Each component in turn consists of five factors, as shown in Figure 8.2. To the extent that feelings of attraction and virtuous behaviors occur, adolescents also feel loved by their parents, experience happiness and satisfaction with this relationship, indicate high self-esteem, trust other people, and behave in an altruistic way (see chapter 10). This and other studies provide evidence that positive parent-child relationships are of vital

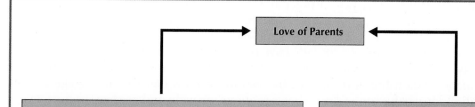

The building blocks of parental love

FIGURE 8.2   In studying adolescents and the love they feel for their parents, Jeffries concluded that this kind of love is built on two basic components—attraction toward one's parents and personal virtue. Those who like their parents and are themselves virtuous are able to experience parental love and to treat their mothers and fathers lovingly.

Source: Based on concepts presented by Jeffries, 1987, 1990, 1993.

---

importance to the success of subsequent interpersonal relationships. We will return to this topic later in the chapter.

Another aspect of family relationships was studied by Kennedy (1991), who asked young adults to describe their interactions with and feelings about their grandparents. These subjects reported feeling close to at least one of their grandparents (most often the grandmother)—a person they enjoyed being with, who loved them and expressed special interest in them, and made them feel relaxed, comfortable, and proud. When parents divorce and re-marry, the children are more likely to spend a great deal of time with their grandparents. Especially among African-Americans, grandparents may assume the role of substitute or surrogate parents.

CLOSE FRIENDS.   **Close friends,** compared with casual friends, spend more time together, interact in more varied situations, are more likely to exclude others from the relationship, and provide more emotional support to each other (Hays, 1989). One result is that friends are more accurate than non-friends in inferring what the other person is thinking and feeling (Stinson & Ickes, 1992). The continued interaction of two close friends results in increas-ingly accurate descriptions of each other's personality (Paulhus & Bruce, 1992). A casual friend is often someone who is "fun to be with," while close friends are valued for such qualities as generosity, sensitivity, and honesty (Urbanski, 1992).

Video: Friendship*

When close same-sex friendships are compared with opposite-sex romantic relationships, other specific characteristics emerge (Winn, Crawford, & Fischer, 1991). Surprisingly, pairs of friends report more contentment and

Discussion Question 4

commitment than do dating partners. Both friends and dates respond to inequity with anger, but friendships are less likely to include feelings of guilt.

In adolescence, friendships tend to be more intimate than in childhood, and such friendships generally have positive effects on the individuals involved (Berndt, 1992). Among friends of the same or of the opposite sex, an "intimate relationship" means that the two individuals feel free to engage in self-disclosing behavior, express their emotions, provide and receive support, experience trust, engage in physical contact, and feel relaxed with one another (Monsour, 1992; Planalp & Benson, 1992).

ROMANTIC RELATIONSHIPS.   Much of the research has concentrated on male-female romantic relationships (Fletcher & Kininmonth, 1992). For most individuals, the partner in such relationships is perceived as the one person to whom they feel most close (Berscheid et al., 1989). To measure closeness and its effect on relationship success, Berscheid and her colleagues developed the **Relationship Closeness Inventory.** Those taking the test are asked to indicate how much time they spent with their partner in the past week and what they did. For example, the two individuals might have watched TV together, frequented a bar, talked on the phone, or made love. Other questions ask the subject to indicate the extent to which the other person influences his or her thoughts, feelings, and behavior—for example, with respect to socializing, spending money, or planning a career. Men and women report equal degrees of closeness.

Do all relationships end? Ties with relatives and friends tend to continue or to fade away gradually as people grow less interested in one another. Romance, however, tends either to endure or to fall apart amid emotional turmoil. Using the Relationship Closeness Inventory, researchers were able to predict which romantic relationships would last and which would not (Berscheid et al., 1989). Data gathered over a nine-month period indicated that couples who remained together were those whose original closeness

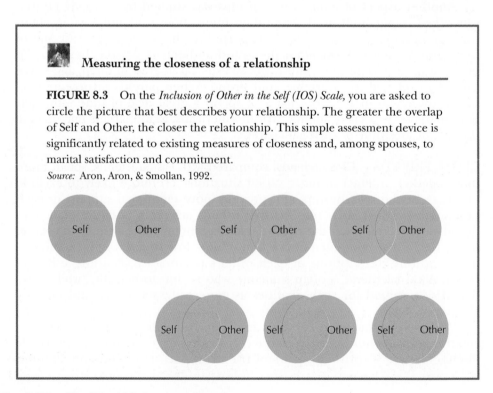

Measuring the closeness of a relationship

FIGURE 8.3   On the *Inclusion of Other in the Self (IOS) Scale,* you are asked to circle the picture that best describes your relationship. The greater the overlap of Self and Other, the closer the relationship. This simple assessment device is significantly related to existing measures of closeness and, among spouses, to marital satisfaction and commitment.
Source: Aron, Aron, & Smollan, 1992.

scores were highest. Couples whose relationship lasted between three and six months had the next-highest scores, and pairs who broke up during the first three months had the lowest scores.

An alternative way to measure closeness was developed by Aron, Aron, and Smollan (1992). As shown in Figure 8.3, the **Inclusion of Other in the Self (IOS) Scale** consists of a series of circles labeled "self" and "other." At one extreme the two circles don't overlap at all; at the other extreme they overlap almost completely. The person taking the test is asked to select whichever drawing best describes his or her current relationship. It is assumed that as closeness increases, the person chooses the circles with increased overlap. Among a large group of undergraduates, this relatively simple measure was found to correlate significantly with the Relationship Closeness Inventory and with a measure of positive emotions toward the partner. In a follow-up study conducted three months later, the IOS was also found to predict whether a relationship had continued or had ended. Additional research discovered that this scale is associated with marital satisfaction, with commitment to a relationship, and even with attraction to a stranger in a laboratory experiment designed to increase closeness (self-disclosing or pretending to be romantic partners). It seems that the IOS is a very promising way to assess relationship closeness.

Closeness in a relationship is ordinarily considered to be a positive characteristic; but recent research (discussed in the following **Work in Progress** section) indicates that, for some, there can be too much closeness.

Work in Progress

When Relationships Are Too Close, Experimental Closeness, and Pregnancy

The IOS Scale has been studied in several new investigations by Aron (1993) and his colleagues.

One area of interest is the possibility that the overlapping circles of the IOS diagram sometimes represent a loss of individuality. That is, two people can be so close to one another that their personalities "merge" or "fuse." Most people find such closeness to be pleasant, but some (more often women than men) perceive the relationship as causing a "loss of self." It is obviously threatening to feel that one's identity has blended with that of someone else—and disappeared.

In an attempt to discover "how close is too close?" Aron asks research participants to indicate the *ideal* level of closeness for them; he then determines how they react when that level is exceeded. In a laboratory setting, strangers spend between forty-five minutes and an hour and a half carrying out a self-disclosure task that results in the exchange of more and more intimate details about themselves. This interaction is found to induce in

each participant an IOS closeness response that lies at about the 40th percentile of the closeness felt in that person's closest ongoing relationship. In these experimental relationships, the degree of closeness depends on the task in which the participants engage, on whether the participants are instructed to avoid unwanted intimacy, and on such dispositional factors as attachment style. Few of these relationships become closer than each person's ideal level, but excessive closeness is expected to elicit negative feelings.

Related research by Rebecca Turner and Nancy Adams deals with the closeness experienced by pregnant women with their unborn offspring. This unique relationship combines the physical and psychological merging of two individuals. These investigators propose that some women experience an expansion of self during pregnancy. Can you think of other relationships in which the IOS Scale might be used to determine perceptions of acceptable and unacceptable levels of closeness?

We will now take a more detailed look at just what is meant by romance and love.

WHAT IS THIS THING CALLED LOVE?

Reading: Lesko (23), *Measurement of Romantic Love*

Love has long been a familiar theme in our songs, stories, and everyday lives, and a poll of 1,000 American adults reveals that 75 percent of the men and 70 percent of the women say that they are now "in love" (Vox pop, 1993). What does this mean? One suggestion is that a friendship between a man and a woman is transformed into *love* when the two individuals begin to perceive themselves as potential sexual partners. As we shall see, over two decades of social psychological research indicates that love is sometimes less sensible and less straightforward than that.

Critical Thinking Question 1

Critical Thinking Question 2

PASSIONATE LOVE.   Aron et al. (1989) point out that many people fall in love, but that there is no analogous experience of "falling in friendship." As we saw in chapter 7, propinquity and similarity are major determinants of friendship. Love, in contrast, is much more likely to be precipitated by desirable aspects of the other person, such as an attractive appearance, pleasing personality, and reciprocal liking. It is even possible to experience love toward someone who doesn't love you—*unrequited love.* The most common instances involve loving someone in your immediate environment who fails to respond and longing for a past partner who is no longer interested. Bringle and Winnick (1992), with a sample of over 400 respondents, found that most (60 percent) had experienced unrequited love at least once during the previous two years. In such situations, both individuals experience emotional distress (Baumeister, Wotman, & Stillwell, 1993). Those who are rejected as lovers respond with a decrease in self-esteem, and they believe that they were misled. Those who reject a would-be lover perceive that person as intrusive and annoying, but they still feel guilty about hurting him or her.

Discussion Question 3

Transparency 8.2

In any event, romance often begins as a sudden, intense, all-consuming response to another person. Phrases such as *falling head over heels in love* imply that love is an accident—something like slipping on a banana peel (Solomon, 1981). This kind of interpersonal response is labeled **passionate love** (Hatfield, 1988), one of several varieties of love that have been identified. A person experiencing passionate love tends to be preoccupied with his or her partner—and to perceive the love object as being perfect. Responses include sexual attraction, physiological arousal, the desire to be in constant contact, despair at the thought of the relationship ending, and the intense need to be loved in return. This emotional response can be measured by a test called the Passionate Love Scale (Hatfield & Sprecher, 1986). Some of the test items are shown in Table 8.1, and you may notice that passionate love (like attitudes) combines cognitive, emotional, and behavioral elements.

Under the "right" conditions, passionate love can arise suddenly and without warning, possibly accompanied by the secretion of neurochemicals that produce feelings of excitement and happiness (Toufexis, 1993). Even a brief contact with a stranger can sometimes lead to love at first sight (Averill & Boothroyd, 1977). When two opposite-sex strangers in a laboratory experiment are simply asked to gaze into each other's eyes for two minutes, they are likely to report feelings of passionate love for each other (Kellerman, Lewis, & Laird, 1989). What is the explanation for this seemingly irrational response?

Three conditions are required for passionate love to occur (Hatfield & Walster, 1981), as summarized in Figure 8.4, p. 314. First, you must learn what love is and develop the expectation that it will happen to you (Dion & Dion, 1988). Beginning in early childhood, most of us are exposed to the idea that people fall in love and get married. Think of *Snow White* and *Cinderella*. Though it has long been assumed that romantic love was invented in medieval Europe, some psychologists, historians, and anthropologists have recently become convinced that it is a universal phenomenon (Gray, 1993; Hatfield & Rapson, 1992b). One explanation of the origin of love is based on evolutionary theorizing (Fisher, 1992). It is assumed that about four or five million years ago, when people began to stand on two legs and forage for food to be carried back to a safe place, adequate child care and survival were most likely if there was male-female bonding. That is, males could venture forth to seek food, and females could remain safe and take care of their offspring; but—the couple had to like and trust one another. Reproductive success was enhanced by the development of brain chemistry that led to love and hence to bonding. In relatively modern times, this natural response has often been repressed and hidden by the customs and practices of a given culture. For example, while most Americans (87 percent) believe today that love is crucial to a good marriage, such beliefs are much less widely held elsewhere—in Russia and in India, for

---

Hatfield and Sprecher (1986) developed the *Passionate Love Scale* to measure the intense emotional reactions that are characteristic of this kind of love. Those taking the test are also informed that other terms for this feeling are infatuation, lovesickness, and obsessive love. The sample items shown here constitute only a portion of the total scale.

TABLE 8.1   The Passionate Love Scale

Please think of the person whom you love most passionately *right now*. If you are not in love right now, please think of the last person you loved passionately. If you have never been in love, think of the person whom you came closest to caring for in that way.

1. I would feel deep despair if _____ left me.
2. Sometimes I feel I can't control my thoughts; they are obsessively on _____ .
3. I feel happy when I am doing something to make _____ happy.
4. I would rather be with _____ than anyone else.
5. I'd get jealous if I thought _____ were falling in love with someone else.
6. I yearn to know all about _____.
7. I want _____—physically, emotionally, mentally.
8. I have an endless appetite for affection from _____.
9. For me, _____ is the perfect romantic partner.
10. I sense my body responding when _____ touches me.
11. _____ always seems to be on my mind.
12. I want _____ to know me—my thoughts, my fears, and my hopes.
13. I eagerly look for signs indicating _____'s desire for me.
14. I get extremely depressed when things don't go right in my relationship with _____.

Responses to each item are made along the following scale:

Not at all true			Moderately true			Definitely true		
1	2	3	4	5	6	7	8	9

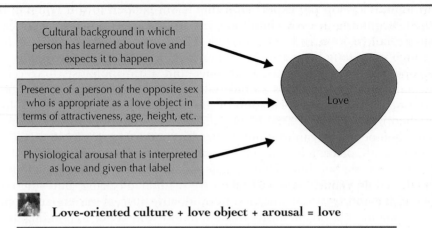

Cultural background in which person has learned about love and expects it to happen	
Presence of a person of the opposite sex who is appropriate as a love object in terms of attractiveness, age, height, etc.	Love
Physiological arousal that is interpreted as love and given that label	

Love-oriented culture + love object + arousal = love

FIGURE 8.4 According to the three-factor theory of passionate love developed by Elaine Hatfield and Ellen Berscheid, love is likely to occur when three conditions are met. If you live in a culture that teaches you what love is, meet someone who is an appropriate love object, and are physiologically aroused, you may very well interpret your aroused state as indicating love. This process underlies the behavior that has led to such familiar phrases as "love at first sight," "love is blind," and "head over heels in love." Sadly enough, passionate love is not likely to last, and enduring love requires a more realistic foundation.

example. Fisher's prediction is that cultural changes will lead to more and more expressions of love because it is a natural, biological aspect of the relationship between men and women.

The second condition required for the occurrence of passionate love is the presence of an appropriate target person with whom one can fall in love. Social learning theorists propose that we have been taught by parents, movies, books, songs, and peers to seek an attractive partner of the opposite sex—someone similar to ourselves in most respects. Thus, we base our romantic choices on culturally prescribed criteria.

In contrast, evolutionary theory hypothesizes that love objects are chosen on the basis of maximizing reproductive success. From this perspective, an appropriate love object is one who will be able to reproduce and to care and/or provide for the offspring (Buss, 1988), and similarity is desirable because it improves the odds for the continued existence of one's personal corner of the gene pool (Rushton, 1989, 1990; Rushton & Nicholson, 1988).

The third requirement for passionate love is that a state of emotional arousal occur while the love object is present. As described in chapter 3, Schachter's theory of emotion suggests that we use external cues to tell us which emotional labels to apply when we are physiologically aroused. If arousal occurs in the presence of an attractive person of the opposite sex, attraction, romantic feelings, and sexual desire often result. When the arousal involves such states as fear (Dutton & Aron, 1974) or frustration and anger (Driscoll, Davis, & Lipetz, 1972), "passionate love" is simply a misattribution. When the arousal involves sexual excitement (Istvan, Griffitt, & Weidner, 1983), love may be a more accurate label for one's aroused state. As Hatfield and Rapson (1987) point out, *passionate love* may not be very different from *sexual desire*. Perhaps we say "I love you" because that is more socially acceptable than saying "I want to have sex with you."

Further implications of evolutionary factors for mate selection are explored in the following **Cutting Edge** section.

Focus on Research: The Cutting Edge

EVOLUTION VERSUS CULTURE: SEX DIFFERENCES IN THE PREFERRED AGE OF A SEX PARTNER

Normative data and everyday observation indicate consistently that the role of age in mate selection differs for males and females. That is, men tend to prefer partners younger than themselves while women select older partners (Bolig, Stein, & McKenry, 1984), as shown in Figure 8.5. Why?

 May-December romances: Why older men and younger women?

FIGURE 8.5 Everyday observation plus a great deal of systematic data indicate that when there are marked age discrepancies in intimate relationships, the man is likely to be older than the woman. Why? Different theoretical camps agree that the phenomenon exists, but they offer different explanations. Some theorists propose a genetic basis resting on differential reproductive strategies; others emphasize cultural factors in societies where men have greater economic and political power than women. No one has devised a conclusive way to test the comparative accuracy of these contrasting views.

One theoretical possibility is that these preferences reflect sex differences in our inherited reproductive strategies (Kenrick & Keefe, 1992). Because men can reproduce throughout their adult lives while women are limited to the years between puberty and menopause, men are most attracted to women of childbearing age. Over the span of human existence, men who were attracted to prepubescent girls or to postmenopausal women would obviously not be as successful in reproducing and passing on their genes to successive generations as would men who were attracted to women of childbearing age. For a woman, on the other hand, reproductive success would be maximized by attraction to a male past the age of puberty who also would be willing and able to stay around to help feed and protect his mate and their offspring. The hypothesis is that natural selection resulted in women who are attracted to strong men possessing adequate resources and abilities (Feingold, 1992; Kenrick et al., 1990). Such sweeping assumptions cannot be directly tested, but investigators can gather data that are at least consistent with the model. For example, in a cross-cultural study of mate preferences throughout the world, Buss (1989b) found that females place the highest value on cues that indicate a male's *resource acquisition* (earning capacity, industriousness, maturity, etc.), while males most value cues indicating a female's *reproductive capacity* (youth, health, and attractiveness). These sex differences are summarized in Figure 8.6.

In their brief lifetimes, prehistoric males could be expected to have better and better skills such as hunting and toolmaking as they grew older, and to have had time to acquire substantial material resources (Kenrick & Keefe, 1992; Mealey, 1985). As a result of these evolutionary pressures over the millennia, the evolutionary hypothesis suggests, men and women today should be

Heterosexual attraction: Men and women differ

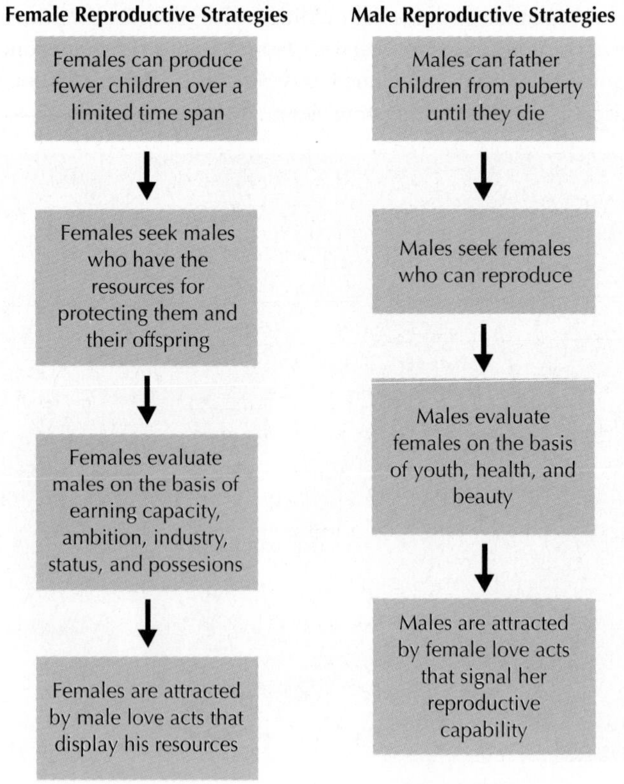

FIGURE 8.6 Evolutionary considerations suggest that natural selection has produced males who are attracted to fertile females; females have been most reproductively successful if they seek males who possess sufficient resources to protect them and their offspring. These different strategies used by our distant ancestors may explain today's sex differences in attraction.

Source: Based on suggestions in Buss, 1988.

Female Reproductive Strategies

Females can produce fewer children over a limited time span

↓

Females seek males who have the resources for protecting them and their offspring

↓

Females evaluate males on the basis of earning capacity, ambition, industry, status, and possesions

↓

Females are attracted by male love acts that display his resources

Male Reproductive Strategies

Males can father children from puberty until they die

↓

Males seek females who can reproduce

↓

Males evaluate females on the basis of youth, health, and beauty

↓

Males are attracted by female love acts that signal her reproductive capability

biologically programmed to differ in their age preferences, not on a conscious basis, but in response to genetic determinants.

To test the proposition that age preferences represent a general characteristic that differentiates men and women, Kenrick and Keefe (1992) collected several types of data. In "lonely hearts" advertisements in a singles newspaper in Arizona, women (regardless of their age) were found to seek partners either slightly younger than themselves or eight to eleven years older. In contrast, men in their twenties advertise for partners either slightly older or slightly younger; but from their mid-forties on, men clearly prefer younger women. These same age preferences also were found to occur in actual marriages based on data gathered in Seattle and Phoenix. The investigators found the same pattern in marriage data from the 1920s, in advertisements appearing in Germany, Holland, and India, and in marriage data on a small island in the Philippines from 1913 through the 1930s. Harpending (1992) presents very similar data for married and unmarried sex partners in a southern African society. It seems, then, that as men age they seek younger and younger partners while women are consistently attracted to partners older than themselves. Further, this trend holds across quite different cultures and over most decades of the twentieth century.

Critical Thinking Question 4

These various findings are quite impressive and quite consistent with an evolutionary perspective. It is also possible, however, to explain these findings on the basis of totally different factors.

One alternative explanation comes from social psychologists who utilize *equity theory* to explain mate selection. That is, potential partners seek an equitable "bargain" when they form a relationship (Clark & Reis, 1988; Wallen, 1992). Most societies today are patriarchal; males (especially older males) are therefore most likely to hold positions of power and to control monetary resources (Stephan, 1992; Wiederman & Allgeier, 1992). In effect, male material resources are traded in the marketplace for the female resources of youth and beauty. As men's status goes up (with respect to occupational prestige and wealth), the physical attractiveness of their wives is found to increase (Buss, 1987; Russell, 1992). Both sexes are simply seeking status symbols. A successful man with an attractive woman is an indication of status for each of them—an equitable exchange.

This nonevolutionary perspective also implies that male-female choices need not represent reproductive needs. That is, women may well desire wealth and prestige for reasons other than protecting offspring. Also, our culture conveys the message that women aged approximately eighteen to twenty-nine are the most attractive; as a result, men of all ages simply prefer partners of this age (Broude, 1992; Dupre, 1992). Note that men in this age range also are especially attractive to those with the inclination and the resources to establish intimate relationships (for example, older gay men or financially successful heterosexual women). From this perspective, all of the findings across cultures and across time simply reflect the ability of relatively wealthy males to attract young, attractive, and relatively less wealthy female partners. If these same sex differences in age preferences were found in a matriarchal culture in which women held the economic and political power, evolutionary theory would be strongly supported; a reverse finding would, however, be consistent with equity theory (Byrne & Kelley, 1992).

Whatever the eventual explanation, the central findings are clear. Romantic attraction is determined in part by the youth of women and the material success of men.

Passionate love: How long does it last?

FIGURE 8.7 Couples who fall in love usually believe that their relationship will last forever and that they will live happily ever after. In this cartoon, Momma predicts a much shorter time span.
Source: Creators Syndicate, Inc., September 30, 1990.

OTHER VARIETIES OF LOVE.   Despite—or because of—its intensity, passionate love is not long-lasting, as Momma suggests in Figure 8.7. Fortunately, there are other kinds of love that *can* be sustained over time.

Exercise 4

Companionate love involves not the dazzling and dizzying emotional state of passionate love but "the affection we feel for those with whom our lives are deeply entwined" (Hatfield, 1988, p. 205). Companionate love represents a very close friendship in which two people are attracted, have much in common, care about each other's well-being, and express reciprocal liking and respect (Caspi & Herbener, 1990). Clearly, this kind of love can be expected to lead to a satisfactory long-term relationship more often than does passionate love; but companionate love does not lead to romantic songs and stories.

Some theorists (Borrello & Thompson, 1990; Hendrick & Hendrick, 1986; Lasswell & Lobsenz, 1980) propose that in addition to passionate and companionate love, there are four additional varieties or "love styles." Table 8.2 presents the elements of this six-part model of love along with examples of test items that have been designed to measure each type. Research based on this model has found that men score higher than women in both passionate (Eros) and game-playing (Ludus) love. *Storge* is the ancient Greek word for loving affection, and females score higher than males in these friendly relationships as well as in logical (Pragma) and possessive (Mania) love (Hendrick et al., 1984). As you might guess on the basis of chapter 7, romantic partners tend to be similar to one another in the kind of love they express (Hendrick, Hendrick, & Adler, 1988). Game-playing love seems to be the least satisfactory type, in that it leads to relationship dissatisfaction and failure. Those who favor a game-playing approach to love tend to be concerned primarily with themselves and their own autonomy and self-fulfillment (Dion & Dion, 1991).

While the six-part model of love is based on personality differences, Jacobs (1992) proposed that emotional states or external pressures may also lead us to different kinds of love. He developed a questionnaire to identify the "facilitators" of romance in terms of these six love styles. The research participants were college students, and they described four different kinds of motivation for falling in love: *distress* (loneliness, anxiety, low self-esteem); the need to *enhance self-identity* (wanting someone who could be helpful in developing one's artistic, intellectual, or professional skills); *aging and social pressures* (the sense that others are romantically involved and one's social clock is ticking); and *sexual desire* (physiological arousal). As predicted, each of these facilitators of love was associated with a specific love style, as shown in Figure 8.8, p. 320. Jacobs suggested that different facilitators probably lead to the selection of quite different kinds of partners.

Still another conceptualization of love describes it as consisting of three basic components: Sternberg's (1986, 1988) **triangular model of love**. The first component is **intimacy**—the closeness two people feel and the strength of the bond holding them together. Partners high in intimacy are concerned with each other's welfare and happiness, and they value, like, count on, and under-

---

Hendrick and Hendrick (1986) have proposed six distinct varieties of love. These include passionate and companionate (friendship) love but add four other possibilities. This table indicates the six "love styles" and presents sample items from a scale designed to measure each of them. People differ in the kind of love they feel, so the question of love style is a crucial issue for a couple attempting to work out a relationship that is satisfying to both.

TABLE 8.2 How do I love thee? Six possible ways

Basic Love Styles		Sample Test Item
Eros:	Passionate Love	My lover and I were attracted to each other immediately after we first met.
Storge:	Friendship Love	Love is really a deep friendship, not a mysterious, mystical emotion.
Ludus:	Game-Playing Love	I have sometimes had to keep two of my lovers from finding out about each other.
Mania:	Possessive Love	I cannot relax if I suspect that my lover is with someone else.
Pragma:	Logical Love	It is best to love someone with a similar background.
Agape:	Selfless Love	I would rather suffer myself than let my lover suffer.

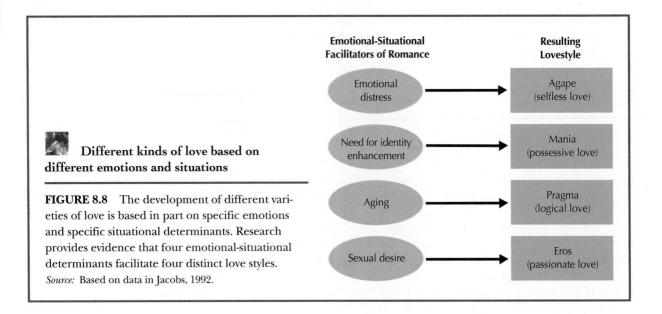

Different kinds of love based on different emotions and situations

FIGURE 8.8 The development of different varieties of love is based in part on specific emotions and specific situational determinants. Research provides evidence that four emotional-situational determinants facilitate four distinct love styles.
Source: Based on data in Jacobs, 1992.

Transparency 8.4

stand one another. The second component, **passion,** is based on romance, physical attraction, and sexual intimacy. The third component, **decision/commitment**, represents cognitive factors such as the decision that one is in love and the commitment to maintain a loving relationship. These three components and their various combinations are depicted in Figure 8.9, p. 321. Also shown are representations of love differing in intensity and in degree of balance of the three components. If passion is the primary component, the relationship tends to be short-lived; intimacy and commitment are essential to a lasting relationship.

Critical Thinking
Question 3

LONELINESS: THE ABSENCE OF A CLOSE RELATIONSHIP

Exercise 1

Though most of us place a high value on establishing relationships, some people have difficulty in doing so. In addition, it is not unusual to find oneself without a relationship as the result of the departure or death of a partner. In either instance, the result can be **loneliness:** the unfulfilled desire to engage in close interpersonal relationships (Peplau & Perlman, 1982). Research on this topic has concentrated on the consequences of loneliness, the reasons for being lonely, and ways to overcome loneliness (Marangoni & Ickes, 1989).

 A triangular model of love

FIGURE 8.9 Robert Sternberg conceptualizes love as a triangle with three basic components: intimacy, passion, and decision/commitment. Love can be based on any one of these alone, on combinations of any two components, or on all three. (A) There are seven quite different types of relationships, depending on which components are combined. (B) The shape of the triangle indicates the extent to which the three components are balanced. (C) The size of the triangle represents the emotional intensity of love for any one individual. (See page 321.)

Source: Adapted from Sternberg, 1986, 1988.

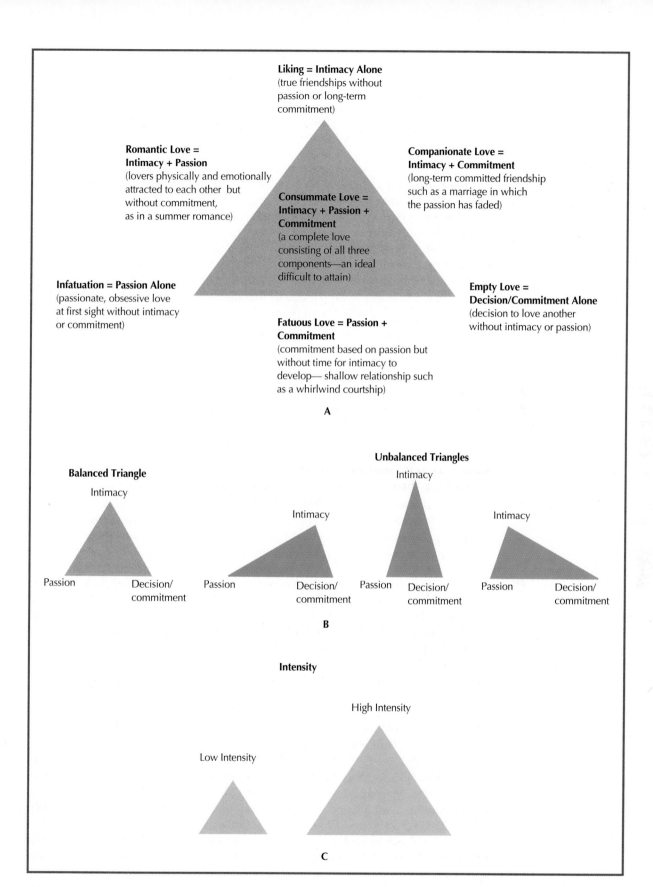

Liking = Intimacy Alone
(true friendships without passion or long-term commitment)

Romantic Love = Intimacy + Passion
(lovers physically and emotionally attracted to each other but without commitment, as in a summer romance)

Companionate Love = Intimacy + Commitment
(long-term committed friendship such as a marriage in which the passion has faded)

Consummate Love = Intimacy + Passion + Commitment
(a complete love consisting of all three components—an ideal difficult to attain)

Infatuation = Passion Alone
(passionate, obsessive love at first sight without intimacy or commitment)

Empty Love = Decision/Commitment Alone
(decision to love another without intimacy or passion)

Fatuous Love = Passion + Commitment
(commitment based on passion but without time for intimacy to develop— shallow relationship such as a whirlwind courtship)

A

Balanced Triangle

Intimacy

Passion   Decision/commitment

Unbalanced Triangles

Intimacy

Passion   Decision/commitment

Intimacy

Passion   Decision/commitment

Intimacy

Passion   Decision/commitment

B

Intensity

Low Intensity

High Intensity

C

Reading: Lesko (24),
*The Social Stigma of
Loneliness*

MEASURING LONELINESS.   The **UCLA Loneliness Scale** is a personality test constructed to assess individual differences in the experience of loneliness (Russell, Peplau, & Cutrona, 1980). Subjects are asked to respond along a scale ranging from "never" to "often" on items such as "I feel left out" and "I have a lot in common with the people around me." A person who feels lonely is likely to indicate *often* in response to the first item, *never* in response to the second.

In samples of American, Puerto Rican, and Portuguese adolescents, high scores on the UCLA Loneliness Scale are found to be associated with feelings of depression, anxiety, dissatisfaction, unhappiness, and shyness (Jones, Carpenter, & Quintana, 1985; Neto, 1992). Lonely individuals are also disliked by others and evaluated negatively on characteristics such as adjustment, achievement, strength, attractiveness, and sincerity (Lau & Gruen, 1992; Rotenberg & Kmill, 1992). As you might expect, someone who feels lonely reports spending leisure time alone, seldom engages in social activities such as dating, and has only casual friends or acquaintances (Berg & McQuinn, 1989; Williams & Solano, 1983). Lonely individuals don't have a network of friends (R. A. Bell, 1991).

LONELINESS IN CHILDHOOD.   Young people commonly go through periods of loneliness. For example, one's parents or a close friend's parents may move to a new location, making it necessary to start over again in establishing close relationships. The situation is usually temporary, and such experiences do not cause adult loneliness.

In contrast to these short-term situational experiences of loneliness, a more serious, long-lasting problem develops when children fail to learn appropriate social skills (Rubin, 1982). It is rare for any of us to be taught the best way to make and keep friends, to make others feel comfortable, to manage disagreements, and to be sensitive to the feelings of others. A child's parents or older siblings may serve as good role models; in other instances, children develop good skills by accident. But if a child fails to learn appropriate ways to interact, he or she is likely to react inappropriately. For example, interpersonal failures can lead to aggressive behavior or to withdrawal and loneliness.

Critical Thinking 5   Studies of preschool children have revealed four patterns of interpersonal relationships. Some children are very popular; some are average in the number and warmth of their relationships; other youngsters are ignored; and a few are actively rejected. Those in the latter two categories are the ones most likely to be lonely and to require help in changing their style of interacting with peers (Johnson, Poteat, & Ironsmith, 1991). Without such intervention, interpersonal inadequacies tend to remain as consistent problems from the preschool years through adulthood (Asendorpf, 1992).

INTERPERSONAL SKILLS AND LONELINESS.   Adolescence is a peak time for loneliness (Brennan, 1982). Young people are involved in the process of separating themselves from their parents and forming outside relationships. If this interpersonal effort fails, loneliness results. The person feels alienated from parents, teachers, and peers. Among the worst possible consequences is **hopelessness,** a feeling of despair that is potentially associated with suicide (Page, 1991). Again, good interpersonal skills are crucial.

Socially unskilled teenagers or adults are unaware of how best to deal with other people, and as a consequence they fail to do the right things. The interactions of a socially unskilled person with a stranger are characterized by few references to the other person, failure to follow up on topics introduced by that individual, and an absence of questions that indicate interest (Jones, Hobbs, & Hockenbury, 1982). Those who are lonely also tend to disclose very little about themselves, or to make inappropriate disclosures (Solano, Barren, & Parish, 1982).

Such interpersonal behaviors drive potential friends away, and these experiences result in expectations of interpersonal failure, along with cynicism, pessimism, and the belief that one's life is uncontrollable (Davis et al., 1992). Romantic relationships are especially troublesome, and loneliness is associated with the belief that friendship, love, and marriage are relatively unimportant and doomed to fail (B. Bell, 1991).

DOING SOMETHING TO RELIEVE LONELINESS.   Unless a major effort is made to improve interpersonal interactions, loneliness will not magically go away. Lonely individuals tend to retreat into wish-fulfilling fantasies, become absorbed in their occupations, or turn to alcohol and drugs (Revenson, 1981). Some rely on music as a substitute for interpersonal relationships, but songs of separation, heartache, and sadness actually increase feelings of loneliness (Davis & Kraus, 1989). Because these coping strategies only make things worse, what is the solution? Two successful techniques, often used together, are **cognitive therapy** and **social skills training.**

The cognitions of lonely and nonlonely people are found to differ. The *self-schema* of a lonely individual brings about selective attention to negative information involving himself or herself, thus confirming and strengthening an already negative self-concept (Frankel & Prentice-Dunn, 1990). Cognitive therapy is designed to alter such cognitions, especially with respect to social situations. If, for example, a man perceives himself as dull and boring, a therapist may be able to convince him that this self-perception is incorrect or to help him give up his false belief that only witty and exciting people can make friends. If a woman reacts to social situations as stressful because she feels others are always evaluating her (Asendorpf, 1989), she can learn that she really isn't the center of everyone else's attention.

Such changes in cognitions need to be accompanied by behavioral changes. Those who are lonely not only lack appropriate social skills, they also are anxious about not possessing these skills (Solano & Koester, 1989). One form of social skills training is to expose a lonely individual to interpersonally successful role models on videotape. The person can also practice social skills in a nonthreatening situation and view the results on tape. Specific interactions (such as initiating a conversation) can be prescribed and rehearsed. Sometimes the needed skills are very specific—how to speak easily on the telephone, give compliments, or improve one's physical appearance.

The effects of these efforts can be remarkable, even in a short period of time (Young, 1982). Once a lonely person thinks about social situations in a new way, learns how best to interact with others, and changes his or her interpersonal style, the resulting interpersonal successes can eliminate loneliness.

PHYSICALLY INTIMATE RELATIONSHIPS

Physical intimacy is a central factor in romantic relationships. As we have made clear, friendships and romantic partnerships are based on many elements unrelated to sex. Nevertheless, the increased acceptance of premarital sexuality, the increased frequency of cohabitation, and the importance of marital sexuality suggest that it is vital to know how sex affects romantic relationships.

PREMARITAL SEXUALITY

Despite centuries of formal disapproval of premarital sex, the second half of the twentieth century has witnessed widespread changes in sexual attitudes and behavior. Social psychologists now consider sexual interactions as an integral aspect of interpersonal relationships (Kelley & Harvan, 1993).

NEW SEXUAL PATTERNS.   Attitudes about sex and sexual behavior underwent dramatic alterations during the second half of the twentieth century, especially in Western Europe, Canada, and the United States. Surveys before and during this period provide evidence of a steady and consistent shift toward permissiveness with respect not only to premarital sexual relationships but to specific practices such as oral sex. In the 1960s these changes were characterized as the beginning of a "sexual revolution." As an interesting commentary on cultural differences, analogous changes did not begin in China until about 1988. The attitudinal changes there have met with governmental disapproval that takes such forms as the banning of all written, audio, and visual material that describes any kind of sexual behavior; the arrest of those who produce it; and the execution of those who sell it (Pan, 1993).

Critical Thinking
Question 6
In the Western world, attitudinal changes were also accompanied by behavioral changes. Before about 1950, the typical finding was that most men engaged in sex prior to marriage while most women did not (Kinsey, Pomeroy, & Martin, 1948; Kinsey et al., 1953). Traditionally, men satisfied their lustful desires with prostitutes or "loose" nonprofessionals. Despite current views of the 1950s as a time of sexual innocence, premarital sex among dating couples became much more common during that decade (Coontz, 1992). By the early 1980s, females were as likely as males to engage in premarital intercourse (Clement, Schmidt, & Kruse, 1984). One of the few sex differences still reported is that adolescent males have a larger number of sex partners than adolescent females (Traeen, Lewin, & Sundet, 1992). Sex has become an expected and accepted part of relationships. In one study of college couples, only 17 percent reported not having engaged in intercourse (Christopher & Cate, 1985). Sexual intimacy began on the first date for 7 percent of these couples, and soon after for 76 percent. In the 1990s men still play the traditional role as initiators of sexual activity, but women today are as likely to respond positively to such initiations as men are (O'Sullivan & Byers, 1992).

Transparency 8.1
Studies of university students indicate that most men and women approve of premarital intercourse in a serious relationship, and both sexes stress the importance of being loved and needed (Carroll, Volk, & Hyde, 1985). The major sex difference is that 85 percent of U.S. college women (compared to 40 percent of college men) express the belief that emotional involvement should be a prerequisite for sex all or almost all of the time. Consistent with these belief differences, twice as many males (84 percent) as females (42 percent) report having had sexual relations without being at all emotionally involved. Very similar findings are reported in Australia (McCabe, 1987). Within an ongoing sexual relationship (among both married and unmarried couples), these differences are also reflected in what men and women desire. Women want their partners to express more love and intimacy, while men want their partners to engage in more arousing and more varied sexual activities (Hatfield et al., 1989).

Despite these consistent sex differences, it is obvious that some men stress involvement and commitment, while some women believe that uncommitted, casual sex is quite acceptable. The effect of individual differences in beliefs about sexual relationships is described in the following **Individual Diversity** section.

SOCIOSEXUALITY:
CHOOSING A ROMANTIC PARTNER

On what basis are people attracted to a particular kind of romantic partner? Is the attraction primarily a sexual one, or is it based on the desire to form a close, loving relationship? In part, the answer is based on individual differences in a specific personality disposition. Simpson and Gangestad (1991, 1992) have identified a dimension known as **sociosexuality.** At one extreme of this dimension are individuals of both sexes who have an *unrestricted sociosexual orientation,* a willingness to engage in sexual interactions with partners even in the absence of closeness, commitment, or emotional bonding. At the other extreme are men and women who have a *restricted sociosexual orientation;* for them, a sexual relationship must be based on feeling close, committed, and emotionally bonded. An unrestricted orientation is more characteristic of males than of females, but both extremes are found in both sexes.

Simpson and Gangestad explain these differences in evolutionary terms, focusing on two alternative reproductive strategies. As discussed previously, our ancestors were most likely to be represented genetically in future generations if they selected a mate with whom there was an emotional bond—commitment and a willingness to care for offspring—*and* who exhibited "fitness"—the ability to reproduce and the possession of material resources.

Exercise 3

Simpson and Gangestad point out that it would be difficult for every individual to find a mate who was both committed and fit; as a result, some men and some women may have focused on fitness while others focused on a mate's emotional bonding and willingness to invest in offspring. These different strategies chosen by our ancestors have resulted in individual differences in today's sociosexual orientations—some people are relatively unrestricted (as the result of having ancestors who focused on fitness), while some are restricted (as the result of having ancestors who focused on commitment). Either choice enhanced reproductive success, but modern sex differences suggest that males who stressed fitness had a slight advantage over those stressing commitment, while females who stressed commitment had a slight advantage over those stressing fitness.

The **Sociosexual Orientation Inventory (SOI)** is a test constructed to measure individual differences in restrictiveness. Subjects are asked to indicate the number of different sexual partners they have had in the past year, the number of partners they expect to have in the next five years, the number of times they have had sex with someone just once ("one-night stands"), and the frequency of having sexual fantasies involving someone other than their current partner. Other questions deal with attitudes about casual, uncommitted sex in items such as "I can imagine myself being comfortable and enjoying casual sex with different partners." Responses to these various questions are combined to yield a total score; the higher the score, the more unrestricted the individual's sociosexual orientation.

Research with this test indicates that compared to restricted individuals, unrestricted persons engage in sex earlier in a relationship, require less love and closeness, and are more likely to be involved with two or more partners simultaneously. These orientation differences are unrelated to sex drive, sexual satisfaction, or sex guilt and anxiety.

Getting back to the original question, do those who differ in sociosexuality also differ in the kind of romantic partner to whom they are attracted? It was predicted that unrestricted individuals would respond to fitness cues and prefer an attractive, sexy partner, while those with a restricted orientation would respond to commitment cues and prefer a partner on the basis of relevant personal characteristics.

Several investigations have provided support for these hypothesized relationships; Figure 8.10 summarizes the findings. It seems clear that restricted

 Restricted versus unrestricted sociosexuality

FIGURE 8.10 Sociosexuality is a personality dimension ranging from restricted to unrestricted extremes. Individuals with an unrestricted orientation (the majority of whom are male) are willing to engage in casual sex with partners in the absence of closeness, commitment, or emotional bonding. Those with a restricted orientation (the majority of whom are female) feel strongly that sexual interactions are appropriate only when there *is* closeness, commitment, and love. As indicated in this figure, research findings indicate that sociosexually restricted and unrestricted individuals—regardless of their sex—differ in their romantic preferences and bases of attraction, and in the characteristics of their actual partners.

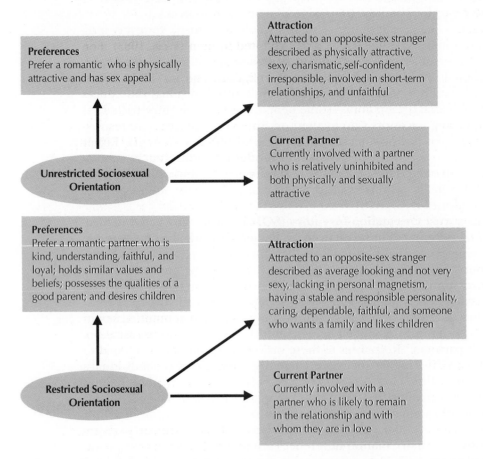

and unrestricted individuals would like to have, express a preference for, and actually become involved with romantic partners who differ in attributes involving commitment and parental investment (someone who is kind, affectionate, responsible, loyal, and faithful) versus reproductive fitness (someone who is physically attractive, sexy, and socially visible).

Note that the model is a speculative one. As Simpson and Gangestad make clear, while individual differences in sociosexuality *do* influence interpersonal preferences, they may or may not reflect genetic differences in reproductive strategies. Perhaps, for example, men and women differ because they are responding to different role models provided by our culture. Also, men are directly and indirectly encouraged to "play around," but women are encouraged to be selective. In any event, the findings indicate an important personality attribute that is consistently associated with differences in interpersonal preferences.

IS SEXUAL BEHAVIOR BECOMING LESS PERMISSIVE?   Even in the late 1970s and early 1980s, there were warning signs suggesting that totally permissive sexuality did not necessarily solve all the problems associated with love and relationships. For example, some people reported engaging in sex primarily in response to a partner's insistence, peer pressure, or a general belief that only abnormal people abstained from sex (DeLamater, 1981). Women, especially, reported feeling guilty, anxious, and exploited by men (Weis, 1983). For both sexes, there was often a conflict between their sexual behavior and the values expressed by their parents and by their religions. Those with the greatest amount of sexual experience were often perceived by their peers as relatively unsuitable marriage partners (Istvan & Griffitt, 1980).

A major source of emotional conflict has been the perception of young people that their parents are relatively negative and their peers relatively positive about sexual matters (Moore & Rosenthal, 1991). In a study of over one thousand undergraduates aged seventeen to twenty, the subjects described their parents as holding sexually conservative attitudes and as being unlikely to discuss sexual precautions beyond advocating total avoidance of sex. By contrast, the subjects described their peers as sexually liberal and slightly more likely to discuss how to avoid conception and disease. Some of the specific findings are shown in Figure 8.11, p. 328. Many of the perceived parental and peer views were found to predict the subjects' own risky sexual behavior (for example, never using a condom for vaginal or anal sex). Males who took the most risks lived away from home and described their parents as holding liberal attitudes about sex. Surprisingly, risk was greater when their mothers encouraged and their friends discussed precautions; only when their fathers discussed sexual precautions was their behavior less risky. Female risk-taking was also related to living away from home and their parents' liberal sexual attitudes; in addition, having sexually liberal friends was associated with more risky behavior. Female risk-taking was less if their friends discussed and provided practical help with respect to precautions.

Beyond various negative reactions to sexual activity, two different negative aspects of intimacy have become matters of increasing concern in the 1980s and 1990s: unwanted pregnancy and **sexually transmissible disease (STD).**

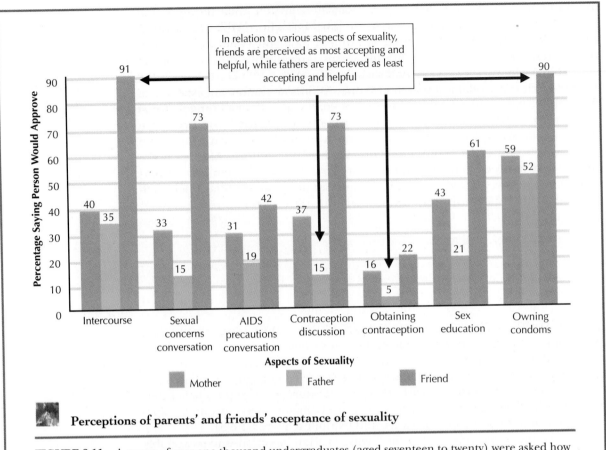

In relation to various aspects of sexuality, friends are perceived as most accepting and helpful, while fathers are perceived as least accepting and helpful

Perceptions of parents' and friends' acceptance of sexuality

FIGURE 8.11 A group of over one thousand undergraduates (aged seventeen to twenty) were asked how their parents and friends would probably respond to various aspects of sexuality. Generally, friends are perceived as much more permissive, accepting, and helpful than parents. Also, fathers are perceived as less permissive, accepting, and helpful than mothers.

Source: Based on data in Moore & Rosenthal, 1991.

Unintended pregnancies constituted the first negative consequence of the new sexual freedom. A surprisingly large proportion of sexually active teenagers and young adults failed to use effective contraceptives or used them inconsistently; as a result, since the late 1970s, over a million unwanted pregnancies occur each year in the United States alone (Byrne, Kelley, & Fisher, 1993). According to the National Center for Health Statistics (1987), approximately 2,740 adolescent pregnancies begin each day. The problem first became acute in the early 1950s, when the teenage birthrate rose to all-time highs. One "solution" was a rapid rise in teenage marriages, many of which ended in divorce within ten years; the other solution was for young women to remain single, give birth secretly, and then give up the baby. Between 1944 and 1955 there was an 80 percent increase in the number of unwed mothers choosing adoption for their babies (Coontz, 1992). Today most youthful pregnancies end in abortion, and both "pro-life" and "pro-choice" proponents agree that this is an unsatisfactory solution. When these unwanted offspring are carried to term, the data indicate an array of negative outcomes including physical, emotional, and economic difficulties for the children, their mothers, and sometimes their fathers (Byrne et al., 1993; Marsiglio, 1987; McCarthy & Radish, 1982). This *teenage pregnancy epidemic* has become a continuing source of distress for individuals and for society.

The second negative consequence of the changes in sexual practices is the increased possibility of contracting a sexually transmissible disease. Despite the existence of effective antibiotics, infections such as **gonorrhea** and **chlamydia** continue to occur at high frequencies. In recent years, fears of STD have been greatly enhanced by the appearance of two viral diseases for which no cure is yet available. The less serious one, **genital herpes,** is characterized by periodic outbreaks of painful blisters on the genitals and other parts of the body. About 10 percent of the American population is infected, and about 500,000 new cases are reported annually (Connell, 1983).

A more serious threat became widely known in the early 1980s: the spread of **human immunodeficiency virus (HIV)** infection, which leads to **acquired immune deficiency syndrome (AIDS).** This disease involves a breakdown of the body's immune system, resulting in death. Research at the Harvard School of Public Health indicates that more cases of AIDS will develop between 1993 and 1995 than in the first eleven years after the disease was identified (Darkness with . . . , 1992). As of September 1992, there were 242,000 confirmed cases of AIDS in the United States, and 160,000 of these patients had died; the U.S. Centers for Disease Control and Prevention estimate that by 1995, 330,000 Americans will have died (AIDS will claim . . . , 1993). Worldwide, over half a million victims have died (Living Memorial, 1992).

Though there is yet no cure for HIV infection or its deadly aftermath, intervention techniques have been successful in changing behavior and thus reducing the risk of disease (Fisher & Fisher, 1992; Fisher & Fisher, 1993).

Individuals who are diagnosed as having an HIV infection understandably report feeling depressed and anxious, but they also feel stigmatized, especially if their condition is public knowledge (Crandall & Coleman, 1992). Because a large proportion of those with AIDS in the United States are homosexual men, people who hold negative attitudes about homosexuality also are negative about interacting with or protecting the rights of the victims of this disease (Ambrosio & Sheehan, 1991).

Unwanted pregnancies and incurable diseases might have been expected to curtail premarital sexuality. It is true that some changes have been reported. For example, in the 1980s college women showed an increase in sex guilt (Gerrard, 1986); and the percentage of young couples using condoms the first time they had intercourse rose from 48 percent at the beginning of the 1980s to 65 percent by the end of the 1980s (Forrest & Singh, 1990). The greatest behavioral changes (safer sexual practices and fewer partners) have, however, been confined to specific groups having the highest risk for HIV infections, such as gay men and prostitutes (Ehrhardt, Yingling, & Warne, 1991).

In contrast, current data indicate that young heterosexuals are maintaining the premarital sexual practices that began at midcentury. Despite the dangers and fears, the proportion of sexually active adolescents increased 7.4 percent between 1970 and 1988, and a third of that increase occurred between 1985 and 1988 (Centers for Disease Control, 1991). One out of five fifteen-year-olds is sexually experienced (Moore, Nord, & Peterson, 1989), and a study of almost 1,500 students enrolled in the sixth through the twelfth grades found that two out of five are sexually active (Brown, 1991). By age nineteen, most relationships involve sexual intimacy.

Marriage rate unaffected by premarital sexuality

FIGURE 8.12 Marriage has retained its popularity for the vast majority of people in our society, despite changes in sexual attitudes and practices. People are equally likely to marry regardless of whether or not they have been sexually active prior to marriage and regardless of whether or not they have lived together.

DOES PREMARITAL SEXUALITY AFFECT SUBSEQUENT MARRIAGES? Despite the hopes of those who view sexual freedom as a panacea and the fears of those who view sexual freedom as immoral and socially destructive, couples who engage in premarital intercourse, including those who live together, are as likely to marry as are those who remain chaste (see Figure 8.12). Further, marital success is unrelated to the sexual histories of the partners (Markman, 1981; Newcomb, 1979).

MARRIAGE

Discussion Question 1

Before, during, and after the sexual revolution, marriage continued to be the primary interpersonal goal of most young people. More than 90 percent of those who are eighteen years of age say that they expect to marry. These expectations are accurate, in that most people actually do get married. By the time they reach their mid-forties or fifties, more than 90 percent of the population is or has been married (Thornton & Freedman, 1982). And, despite fears of the decline of the nuclear family and the realities of death, separation, and divorce, two-parent families are still much more common than one-parent families. Among all U.S. households with children, 78 percent still contain both a father and a mother (Kondracke, 1992). One of life's greatest challenges, however, is in finding happiness in this relationship and in discovering how to avoid breaking up.

Critical Thinking
Question 7

SIMILARITY AND MARRIAGE.   As we indicated in chapter 7, similarity plays a key role in attraction and in the development of relationships. It has also been established in studies dating back to the beginning of this century that married couples are similar in their attitudes, values, interests, and other attributes (e.g., Pearson & Lee, 1903; Schuster & Elderton, 1906).

While we know that similarity leads to attraction, it has also been proposed that the shared experiences within a long-term relationship would result in even greater similarity over time. The question of whether spouses become more similar over the years was answered by Caspi, Herbener, and Ozer (1992). Data were available on more than 150 couples whose values and attitudes were measured before their weddings and then again after twenty years of marriage. The measure of values dealt with their basic interests in theoretical, economic, aesthetic, political, and religious issues. The attitude items concentrated on marital issues such as premarital sex, infidelity, engaging in the same recreational activities, and how best to structure daily interactions with one another and with offspring. As expected, husbands and wives showed greater than chance similarity at the time they were engaged and also after two decades as a married couple. There was, however, *no* change in the degree of similarity over time. Similarity was maintained, but it neither increased nor decreased.

There is one type of similarity that leads to a rather odd outcome. As we indicated in chapter 5, people are motivated to confirm their self-concepts in responding to self-relevant information. In interpersonal relationships, confirmation is also important, so a person seeks a marital partner who shares his or her perception of self (Swann, Hixon, & De La Ronde, 1992). For example, if you evaluate many aspects of yourself positively, you want a spouse who also thinks highly of you. What happens, however, when your self-concept is negative? Swann and his colleagues reasoned that anyone with a negative self-concept would want a partner who viewed him or her negatively. To test this proposition, they recruited married couples (ranging in age from seventeen to seventy-eight) at a horse ranch and at a shopping mall. These husbands and wives were given self-concept tests and a questionnaire about their marriage. As you might expect, those with a positive self-concept were more committed to partners who evaluated them positively than to partners expressing negative views. As predicted, however, those with negative self-concepts were most committed to partners who thought badly of them. The investigators point out that even people who evaluate themselves negatively like *positive* feedback, especially from relative strangers. Nevertheless, these same individuals are disturbed to receive positive feedback from a spouse, because that person is supposed "to know better."

In other long-term relationships, would you expect people to prefer partners who provide feedback that verifies and validates their self-perceptions or partners who provide consistently positive feedback? The following **Work in Progress** provides an answer to that question.

Work in Progress

Dating As a Unique Relationship

Swann (1993) and his colleagues have recently examined various relationships to determine whether people prefer being with those who validate their self-concepts (self-verifying feedback) or with those who provide complimentary evaluations (positivity feedback).

As was true for married couples, college roommates and college friends also want verification from their regular companions. In effect, your conception of yourself is validated, confirmed, and reinforced when someone knows you well enough to understand both your best and your worst characteristics.

A question raised by Swann, De La Ronde, and Hixon (1993) is whether dating partners are somehow different. These investigators proposed that in dating or courtship, two people are not usually committed to one another; rather, they are "test driving" a number of potentially acceptable models. Each individual is also looking for acceptance. At the courtship stage of a relationship, then, people want to like and be liked, and each tends to praise the other person and hopes to be praised in return. If this analysis is correct, dating partners will be most concerned about being liked—receiving positive feedback—and not with self-verification.

Swann and his associates thus predicted that dating partners would prefer positivity while married partners preferred verification, and this is precisely what they found. These differential preferences held equally for men and women, regardless of age or the length of time they had known one another.

A very important implication of these findings is that the goals of courtship are different from those of marriage. As a consequence, courtship may be a very poor way to select a marriage partner, especially for anyone with a negative self-concept.

RELATIONSHIP PATTERNS AMONG YOUNG MARRIED COUPLES. We realize that not all marriages are alike, but exactly how do relationships differ? A study of the everyday lives of husbands and wives who had been married about two years revealed four distinct types of relationship (Johnson et al., 1992). The researchers interviewed spouses separately and asked them about the details of just how they engaged in household tasks, leisure pursuits, interactions, conflicts, and conversations. Four marital patterns emerged, as described in Figure 8.13: Symmetrical, parallel, differentiated, and reversed.

Transparency 8.5

Symmetrical marriages were found to be the most common type (about two out of five couples), with both working outside the home, spouses holding egalitarian beliefs about sex roles and dividing household labor in ways not based on traditional sex typing, and husbands and wives spending very little leisure time together. About one marriage in four is *parallel,* consisting of what was once the most typical relationship, in which the husband is the primary wage earner, housework is divided along sex-typed lines, and men and women go their separate ways to engage in leisure activities—he to his friends and she to her relatives. *Differentiated* couples (about one out of five) both work (though the husband is more involved in his job), divide the household work along traditional lines, and spend their leisure time together equally involved with friends and relatives. The smallest group (one out of ten) consists of relationships that are *reversed*—primarily because of the husband's unemployment. The wife is involved in her job, the household duties show little or no sex typing, the couple is highly companionate, and the husband is more involved than the wife with friends and relatives.

Despite obvious differences in employment patterns, division of household labor, and how they spend their leisure time, those in each group are equally satisfied with their marriages. They differ considerably, though, in parenthood. Both the parallel and differentiated couples are very likely to have children (77.8 and 71.4 percent); in contrast, 50 percent of those in reversed relationships and only 35.7 percent of those in symmetrical marriages are parents.

SEXUALITY AND PARENTHOOD. Surveys of married partners consistently indicate that the frequency of sexual interactions decreases over time. Udry (1980) reports, for example, that the greatest decline occurs during the first

Type of Marriage	Characteristics of Marriage
Symmetrical 42%	Husband and wife both have jobs Household tasks are not sex-typed Sex role ideology is egalitarian Spouses spend little leisure time together 35.7% have children
Parallel 27%	Husband is primary wage earner Housework is divided in sex-typed way Spouses spend little time together Husband spends time with friends Wife spends time with relatives 77.8% have children
Differentiated 21%	Both work; husbands job emphasized Housework is divided in sex-typed way Spouses spend most leisure time together and are equally involved with friends and relatives 71.4% have children
Reversed 10%	Wife is invovled with outside job Household jobs are not sex-typed Relationship is highly companionate Husbands spend time with friends and relatives 50% have children

 Four types of marriages

FIGURE 8.13 A study of the daily lives of couples who had been married about two years revealed four quite different types of relationship. These couples differed with respect to outside jobs, handling of household tasks, leisure time activities, and probability of having offspring. These very different patterns of married life were not, however, related to marital satisfaction.

Source: Based on data in Johnson et al., 1992.

four years of marriage, with rates dropping from over 11 acts of intercourse every four weeks to fewer than 7.5.

Parenthood is a mixed blessing. Both mothers and fathers say that they enjoy being parents (Feldman & Nash, 1984). Even so, their relationship in general and their sexual relationship specifically tend to show stresses and strains in response to parenthood, particularly if real-life outcomes fail to match their expectations. (Hackel & Ruble, 1992).

Having children also changes how parents spend leisure time, especially for men. After becoming fathers men engage in fewer independent activities and in more disliked activities chosen by their wives (Crawford & Huston, 1993).

IS MARRIAGE LESS FUN THAN IT USED TO BE? A consistent finding in survey research over many decades has been that those who are married report being happier than those who never married or who are divorced, separated, or widowed. In recent years, however, the association between marriage and happiness has become weaker among both men and women. Married couples still are more content with life than single individuals, but the difference is smaller now than in the past (Glenn & Weaver, 1988). The data also indicate that those who have never married, especially males, now report being happier than unmarried men did in previous years. In contrast, comparisons of married women now and in the past indicate a decrease in happiness (see Figure 8.14, p. 334). Why are single men happier and married women less happy

 Happiness and marriage: Some sex differences

FIGURE 8.14   Over the years surveys have found that those who are married report being happier than those who are not, but the difference between the two groups has decreased significantly. One reason for the change is that married women are less happy now than in the past, possibly because of the conflicting demands of being a wife, mother, and jobholder. Single men are happier today, possibly because sexual partners are easily available outside of marriage.

today than they used to be?

For men, the answer seems to lie in the previous discussion of changes in attitudes about premarital sex. Sexual relationships among unmarried partners are now common (Reed & Weinberg, 1984). As a result, sexual interactions are generally available to single men. For women, the answer may lie in their increased economic freedom; opportunities can mean financial independence for women *and* the potential for conflict between a woman's career aspirations and her desire to take care of her children (Batista & Berte, 1992). In addition, married women between the ages of twenty and forty-nine report much greater feelings of loneliness than men do, and they say it is because they feel misunderstood, unneeded, and uninteresting (Tornstam, 1992).

Men are generally accepting of the idea that their wives can work and bring home an extra paycheck (Newman & Cochrane, 1987). Problems arise, however, in different male-female expectations about what else the wife should do (Beckwith, 1992). Women who work outside the home quite reasonably believe that housework (and power) should be shared equally in the relationship (Weeks & Gage, 1984), but women do more than their share (Nyquist et al., 1985). Both men and women are happier with the marriage if they perceive themselves as controlling who carries out specific household and child-care duties (Madden, 1987).

A major task for many couples is finding ways to adjust to the demands of a two-career family (Gilbert, 1993). An extensive longitudinal study of the effect on marriage of wives' working patterns was undertaken by Helson and Roberts (1992), who obtained data from sixty-three married couples at three time periods—when the wives' average age was twenty-one, twenty-seven, and forty-three. By the time of the last testing, five recurring themes had emerged in the relationships. In each couple, interestingly, the man's personality was found to play the major role in determining the woman's work history and the success of the marriage. The five themes are summarized in Table 8.3.

Among couples who fit the *clash/career* and *dual career* themes, the wives spent a great deal of time working, and they had achieved considerable status on the job by age forty-three. These working wives rejected the role of homemaker, and tensions were characteristic of these marriages. In the clash/career marriages, the husbands were forceful, and early divorces were common. Among dual career couples (in which the husband was not forceful), there was considerable irritability, tension, and resentment, but the relationships endured.

Those who fit the *clash/intimacy* theme revealed little tension; the wife

In a study of spouses that followed sixty-three marriages for over two decades, five distinct themes emerged with respect to the effects of the husband's personality on the wife's occupational activities and on the success of the marriage.

TABLE 8.3   Five marital themes: Husband's personality and wife's career

Theme	Some Typical Characteristics
Clash/Career	Aggressive, macho husband tries to restrict wife's occupational activities after childbirth.
	Differences between husband and wife lead to separation or divorce about age 30.
Dual Career	Husband supports wife's ambitious career—financially, intellectually, or by actually participating in it.
	Husband is active father; both husband and wife want independence and control.
	Wife's career involvement may eventually lead to divorce, but not until about age 40.
Clash/Intimacy	After children enter school, husband doesn't satisfy wife's need for intimacy or excitement.
	Couples often divorce around age 30, but wife goes on to new relationship, not to a career.
Busy Husband	Husband involved in high-status career.
	Husband too busy and too self-absorbed to give wife as much attention as she wants.
	Wife seeks employment to avoid being dependent.
	Marriage tends to last until around age 40.
Accommodative	Husband has modest career, and wife pursues equally modest occupational goals after children are in school.
	Wife enjoys her job, but family needs come first.

Source: Based on information in Helson & Roberts, 1992.

adopted the homemaker role and did volunteer work, and the husband was relaxed, sociable, and responsible. In the *busy husband* marriages, marital tension resulted from the wife's resentment of the husband and her perception that she was not getting enough affection; the husband felt she wanted too much affection. In the *accommodative* marriages, the husband was not forceful, neither partner showed individuality, and the wife's status level at work was low.

These different themes are clearly relevant to the following section of this chapter—because among these couples, *all* of the early divorces took place in the clash/career and clash/intimacy marriages, whereas *no* divorces occurred in the busy husband or accommodative marriages.

TROUBLED RELATIONSHIPS: PROBLEMS, SOLUTIONS, FAILURES

What happens to turn a loving, romantic relationship into one filled with unhappiness and even hate? Some problems are universal. For example, by their very nature, intimate relationships create conflicts in each partner—between the desire for independence and the desire for closeness, between the need to be open and honest and the need for privacy, between the comfort of predictability and the excitement of the unexpected (Baxter, 1990).

Some problems are brought on by what one of the partners does or what the other partner believes that he or she has done; an example is jealousy (Johnson & Rusbult, 1989). Whatever the problem, solutions may be possible, but couples differ in how well they deal with them. In this section, we will explore some major sources of conflict, possible ways to prevent or resolve problems, and some of the consequences of a broken relationship.

PROBLEMS IN RELATIONSHIPS, AND POSSIBLE SOLUTIONS

At some point in most relationships, passionate love begins to fade, and each individual must face the reality of spending his or her life with someone who is less than perfect. People who believe they are ideally suited for one another can discover that there are negative as well as positive elements in the relationship. Studies of married couples indicate that most report having disagreements regularly (from more than once a week to monthly), while only 1.2 percent say they *never* have disagreements (McGonagle, Kessler, & Schilling, 1992).

Relationship awareness occurs when at least one member of the pair begins to think about how the two of them interact and to compare and contrast their respective roles. Such awareness is more characteristic of women than of men, but marital satisfaction is greater when husbands *do* talk about the relationship (Acitelli, 1992; Harrell, 1990). We will now examine some of the specifics that lead to conflict and dissatisfaction.

SOURCES OF CONFLICT IN MALE-FEMALE INTERACTIONS. Some behaviors are equally upsetting to both sexes (for example, unfaithfulness), while others are more annoying to one sex than to the other. Buss (1989a) asked several hundred men and women to describe the source of their conflicts with a romantic partner. Generally, women become upset if their partners are not loving and gently protective, while men become upset if their partners reject them sexually or ignore them.

Transparency 8.6

It should be noted that some people are more likely than others to behave in ways that cause a partner to be angry and upset. For example, individuals who are characteristically disagreeable, emotionally unstable, and/or unperceptive are most likely to evoke conflict (Buss, 1991). Also, those who characteristically fear being exploited in interpersonal relationships have greater difficulty in establishing and maintaining them (Cotterell, Eisenberger, & Speicher, 1992).

Discussion Question 2

DISCOVERING DISSIMILARITIES.   When partners belatedly realize that they are dissimilar in some of their attitudes, values, and preferences, negative feelings often arise. One of the problems with passionate love is that the overpowering emotional state in which "love is blind" makes it difficult or impossible to pay attention to such seemingly irrelevant details as the other person's similarities and dissimilarities to oneself. One obvious solution is for two individuals to know as much as possible about one another early in the relationship (Byrne & Murnen, 1988).

Critical Thinking Question 10

Some dissimilarities do not occur until *after* the couple is married, and thus are difficult to anticipate or avoid. For example, one of the partners may change his or her religious views, political beliefs, drinking behavior, or sexual preferences while the other does not. If so, initial similarity changes into dissimilarity (Levinger, 1988). Consider a situation in which a man marries a woman who plans to be a homemaker but who later decides to pursue a career. Her newfound interest in a life outside of the home can be a source of annoyance to her husband (Nicola & Hawkes, 1986).

Still other dissimilarities are hard to avoid because they are not relevant to a dating couple or even to the early stages of marriage. Two people may easily fail to discover (until too late) that they differ in long-range plans about saving money versus spending it, in beliefs about how best to raise children, or in concerns about health and hygiene. When their differences become apparent, marital dissatisfaction can increase.

Transparency 8.3

BOREDOM.   For some, a long-term relationship becomes a source of distress because it is boring. Many dating couples report breaking up simply because they became bored with one another (Hill, Rubin, & Peplau, 1976).

Critical Thinking Question 9

As Skinner (1986) pointed out, boredom is a major problem in our lives, but it has seldom been investigated. Married couples especially are likely to develop unchanging routines in their daily interactions, sexual and otherwise, and only gradually realize that they are in a rut. For some, this regularity and predictability is a positive feature. For others, it can be unpleasant; and then each attributes the problem to the other person, which causes marital dissatisfaction (Fincham & Bradbury, 1992, 1993).

When boredom arises, it can sometimes be overcome if the couple seeks new stimulation in the form of vacations, joint educational efforts, unfamilar dining experiences, new hobbies they can share, new sexual practices, and so on. The alternative—continuing to do the same things in the same way—can easily lead to dissatisfaction.

Though much of the research on marriage focuses on problems, it is helpful to remember that as many marriages succeed as fail. Some of the secrets of

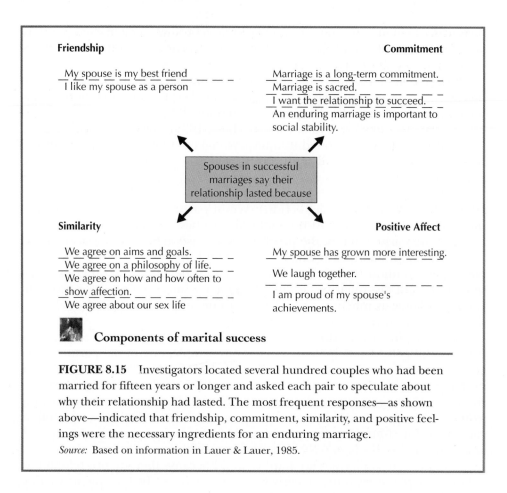

Friendship

My spouse is my best friend
I like my spouse as a person

Commitment

Marriage is a long-term commitment.
Marriage is sacred.
I want the relationship to succeed.
An enduring marriage is important to social stability.

Spouses in successful marriages say their relationship lasted because

Similarity

We agree on aims and goals.
We agree on a philosophy of life.
We agree on how and how often to show affection.
We agree about our sex life

Positive Affect

My spouse has grown more interesting.

We laugh together.

I am proud of my spouse's achievements.

Components of marital success

FIGURE 8.15 Investigators located several hundred couples who had been married for fifteen years or longer and asked each pair to speculate about why their relationship had lasted. The most frequent responses—as shown above—indicated that friendship, commitment, similarity, and positive feelings were the necessary ingredients for an enduring marriage.
Source: Based on information in Lauer & Lauer, 1985.

success were identified by Lauer and Lauer (1985) through a study of 351 couples who had been married fifteen years or longer. When the investigators asked these couples to explain why their marriages lasted, the most common responses (shown in Figure 8.15) stressed friendship, commitment, similarity, and positive affect.

A major cause of negative affect in a relationship occurs when unpleasant words and deeds begin to replace pleasant ones. In the following **Applied Side** section, we describe such interactions and suggest ways to alter them.

Social Psychology: On the Applied Side

POSITIVE VERSUS NEGATIVE COMMUNICATIONS BETWEEN PARTNERS

One of the oddest and most self-defeating aspects of a long-term relationship occurs when partners shift from providing one another with positive evaluations to words and deeds that indicate negative evaluations. As suggested in Figure 8.16, this kind of shift is characteristic of unsuccessful relationships.

Dating couples and newlyweds frequently express their positive feelings about one another. They make an effort to be together, they hold hands, they repeatedly demonstrate their love, they say kind things, they help each other, and they make it obvious that each finds the other socially and sexually desirable. Over time, however, quite different expressions of feeling occur. It is easy enough to think (or say), "I don't have to tell you I love you; I married you, didn't I?" Other indications of love can also fade away, as in "You don't bring me flowers anymore."

As dissatisfaction increases, negative interactions become more frequent (Margolin, John, & O'Brien, 1989). For one thing, some individuals make maladaptive attributions ("it's all his fault" or "it's all her fault") about the cause of any disagreement or difficulty. In an unhappy couple, instead of trying to solve problems, each person expresses negative evaluations and blames the other (Bradbury & Fincham, 1992). Videotapes of the interchanges of satisfied and dissatisfied couples indicate much higher rates of negative verbal and nonverbal behavior among those whose marriages are in trouble (Halford & Sanders, 1990).

Miller (1991) notes how puzzling this new pattern of behavior really is:

> . . . why is it that some of our most hateful, caustic, and abusive interactions take place with those we say we love? Why is it that intimacy seems to give us a license to treat people in sarcastic, critical, and cruel ways that we reluctantly use with total strangers?
>
> Even in happy marriages, spouses are characteristically meaner to each other than to mere acquaintances or friends. . . . (p.63)

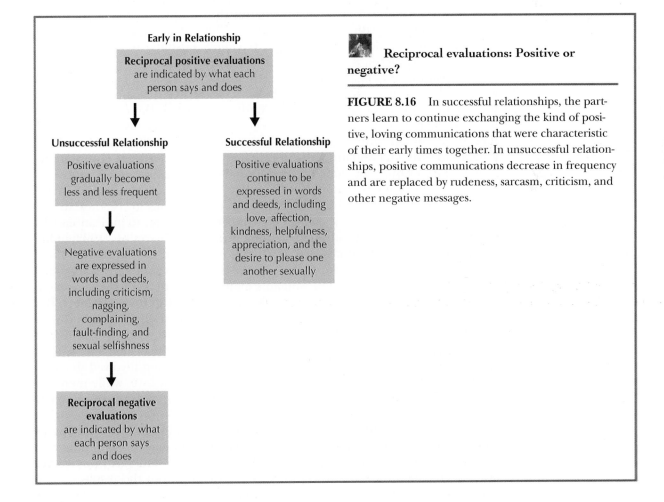

Reciprocal evaluations: Positive or negative?

FIGURE 8.16 In successful relationships, the partners learn to continue exchanging the kind of positive, loving communications that were characteristic of their early times together. In unsuccessful relationships, positive communications decrease in frequency and are replaced by rudeness, sarcasm, criticism, and other negative messages.

Miller (1991) suggests that we become rude and impolite to intimate partners for three reasons. (1) In an intimate relationship there is more *opportunity* to discover a mate's many trivial imperfections than in other relationships, in part because each person feels confident of being accepted by the partner, feels less need for impression management, and so relaxes and becomes "himself" or "herself." (2) When the other person's flaws become apparent, *misplaced expectations* lead each spouse naively to assume that the other will change for the better; it is frustrating and annoying when change doesn't occur—and it usually doesn't. (3) It is easy enough to stop complimenting and rewarding a partner because of *lack of motivation*. It requires less effort and less thought to be selfish and impolite than to be socially skillful and thoughtful. We save that for others.

The solution is seemingly simple—people need to be aware of this deadly danger in intimate relationships, to be realistic, and to be as nice and as polite to an intimate partner as to strangers, acquaintances, and friends. Though behaving in this way appears to require special effort, it would seem to be well worth it.

Exercise 2

JEALOUSY: A SPECIAL THREAT.   The possibility of attraction toward someone new is a common problem in relationships, and **jealousy** is the usual response of one's partner (White & Mullen, 1990). Among the negative emotions aroused by jealousy are suspicion, rejection, hostility, and anger (Smith, Kim, & Parrott, 1988).

Critical Thinking
Question 8

Jealousy endangers a relationship. An individual who is low in self-esteem is most likely to become jealous (Salovey & Rodin, 1991), and jealousy also precipitates a decrease in self-esteem (Mathes, Adams, & Davies, 1985). Much like passionate love in reverse, jealousy elicits a flood of all-consuming negative thoughts, feelings, and behaviors (Pines & Aronson, 1983). Cultures differ greatly, however, in evaluating what it is that gives rise to jealousy. For example, if one's partner hugs someone of the opposite sex, this causes much more sexual jealousy in Hungary than in the United States (Buunk & Hupka, 1987).

Men and women also differ; men become more jealous in response to sexual infidelity, while women's jealousy is stronger in response to indications of a partner's emotional commitment to someone else (Buss et al., 1992). One explanation is an evolutionary one. If a man's mate is intimate with other men, any offspring she has may not be his—thus, a woman's infidelity is a genetic threat to a man. If, however, a woman's mate is intimate with other women, this is no genetic threat to the woman, because her children are still hers. But her well-being *is* threatened if her mate becomes emotionally involved with another woman, because his commitment may shift to a new relationship. Oddly consistent with this sex difference is the way in which men and women justify engaging in an extramarital relationship. For women involved in extramarital affairs, sex outside of marriage is justified only by love, while men feel that sexual pleasure and variety constitute sufficient justification (Glass & Wright, 1992).

Some people deliberately try to make their partners jealous as a way to gain attention and to strengthen the relationship. They may flirt with others or talk about former lovers (White, 1980). Among college students, these tactics are used by one in three women and one in five men, but the result is more likely to damage the relationship than to help it.

WHEN RELATIONSHIPS BREAK UP:
FROM DISSATISFACTION TO DISSOLUTION

Levinger (1980) describes relationships as passing through five possible stages: initial attraction, building, continuation, and—for some—deterioration and ending. Social psychologists have become increasingly interested in understanding the last two stages in this process.

DIFFERENCES BETWEEN FRIENDSHIPS AND INTIMATE RELATION-SHIPS. Friendships often fade away quietly when friends move to new locations or develop new interests (Rose, 1984). When love is involved, however, it is very difficult to drift apart peacefully. Instead, painful emotions are aroused, feelings are hurt, and anger can become intense.

Romantic relationships don't end easily because they involve the investment of one's time, the exchange of powerful rewards, and commitment (Simpson, 1987). If an acceptable substitute is readily available, the loss of a partner is less traumatic than when one is simply cast adrift (Jemmott, Ashby, & Lindenfeld, 1989).

RESPONDING TO RELATIONSHIP PROBLEMS. Rusbult and Zembrodt (1983) point out that individuals respond to an unhappy partnership either actively or passively. An active response involves either ending the relationship ("exit") or working to improve it ("voice"). Passively, a person can simply wait for improvement to occur ("loyalty") or wait for further deterioration ("neglect"). These alternate choices are shown in Figure 8.17.

 Alternative responses to a troubled relationship

FIGURE 8.17 When a relationship is beginning to fail, the partners can respond in either an *active* or a *passive* way. Either way, a partner can take a positive or a negative approach. Assuming the best, a partner can work actively to improve the situation or wait passively in the hope that improvement will simply occur. Assuming the worst, a partner can actively end the relationship or passively wait for it to fall apart. If the relationship is not hopeless, the most adaptive response is an active, positive one. *Source:* Based on suggestions by Rusbult & Zembrodt, 1983.

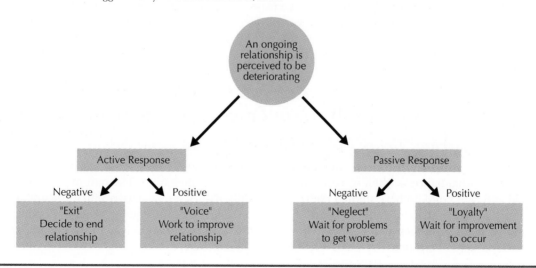

Among diverse couples (college students, older couples, and gays and lesbians), a consistent finding is that men and women whose self-esteem is high respond to relationship failure by exiting, while those with low self-esteem engage in passive neglect (Rusbult, Morrow, & Johnson, 1990).

Once deterioration begins, a breakup becomes very likely. Sometimes the only reasonable solution is for each member of the pair to start over again with someone else. Actively solving the problems and maintaining the relationship is likely only if three factors are present: a high level of *satisfaction of various needs* on the part of each person, *commitment* to the relationship based on past investment of time and effort in building the relationship, and the *absence of alternative lovers* (Rusbult, 1983; Simpson, 1987). More generally, the **dependence model of breakups** proposes that the decision whether to break up or to continue a relationship is related to an individual's degree of dependence on that relationship (Drigotas & Rusbult, 1992). Even a bad relationship may satisfy important needs that can't be met with alternate partners.

BREAKUP AND DIVORCE.   About 2.4 million American couples marry each year; during the same time period, another 1.2 million are divorced, most often during the second to sixth years of marriage (Glick, 1983). We have already discussed some of the factors that make relationships more or less likely to fail. Some additional predictors of divorce will be described here.

Observations of three different infant-mother attachment styles led Hazan and Shaver (1990) to propose that adults follow these same three patterns in forming relationships. Briefly, the three styles are *avoidant* (discomfort about intimacy and getting close, mistrust of others); *anxious-ambivalent* (perception of partner as too distant, unloving, and likely to leave); and *secure* (readiness to get close, comfort about depending on the partner, absence of worry about partner's leaving). Of these three attachment styles, only the secure style is likely to enable individuals to form long-lasting, committed, satisfying relationships (Shaver & Brennan, 1992). Research indicates that self-reports of cold or inconsistent relationships with one's parents are associated with later avoidant and/or anxious-ambivalent romantic attachments, whereas parental relationships described as warm are associated with secure romantic attachments (Bringle & Bagby, 1992).

Though lack of closeness in perceived parental attachment style seems to be an important predictor of troubled intimate relationships, we need to know more about how such factors operate in other kinds of relationship disruptions, as described in the following **Work in Progress** section.

Work in Progress

Sometimes, Offspring "Break Up" with Their Parents

In recent research, Bringle (1993) examines family attachments and what happens when these are disrupted. He and Kim Franklin have studied the reports of offspring who have, as adults, experienced estrangement from their parents. Such estrangement occurs when some degree of tension or conflict lasts over a long time and finally ends in emotional alienation. The parent and his or her adult offspring may have no further contact, or the contact may be infrequent and emotionally distant. In several respects, this situation resembles the end of a marriage.

Parent-offspring breakups may occur after the gradual deterioration of the relationship, or they may occur suddenly. As in the Bringle and Bagby (1992) study of romantic relationships, reactions to becoming estranged from parents can range from satisfaction and relief to anger and rage. Some offspring have no regrets, some later reconcile, and some even feel that the relationship improved as a result of this experience.

Remember that attachment research is based either on studies of infants and their mothers or on what adults report about their childhood attachment. An important—and difficult—next step is to tie such findings together. For example, do cold parents (as identified by researchers) have children who in fact grow up to have avoidant romantic relationships and to become estranged from their mother or father? Similarly, do warm parents have children who grow up to form secure romantic attachments and maintain close parental ties? The general theoretical model is based on such continuities, but more empirical links are needed before we can feel confident about drawing conclusions.

What else is related to marital success and failure? Kurdek (1993) obtained data from 222 newlywed couples each year for five years. Over that period, 64 of the couples dissolved their marriages. Several demographic and psychological factors were found to predict marital outcome. For example, marital dissolution was associated with low income, low educational level of the wife, a previous divorce for either partner, neuroticism, unrealistic expectations about the relationship, and a brief courtship. Also associated with marital failure were dissimilarities in spouses' need for independence, in the value they placed on attachment, and in their motives for marriage. These and other factors (each present at the time of the marriage) permitted a fairly accurate prediction of which couples would and would not remain married. Such findings suggest the possibility that couples planning marriage might find it valuable to be interviewed, tested, and informed of the likelihood that their marriage would last.

Still other research indicates a genetic factor involved in the probability of divorce. Comparing groups of identical and fraternal twins, McGue and Lykken (1992) discovered that divorce can be predicted in part by genetics. For example, consider the following situations. Two individuals who each have an identical twin sibling decide to marry; if both of their twin siblings are divorced and if both sets of parents are divorced, the predicted divorce rate for this couple is 77.5 percent. For this same couple, if both of their twin siblings are not divorced and neither set of parents is divorced, the predicted divorce rate is 5.3 percent. The suggested explanation for this powerful effect is that inherited personality differences account for differential marital success.

Note also that poverty exerts a major influence on marital success and failure. According to the U.S. Census Bureau, over a two-year period, families (both white and black) below the poverty level were twice as likely to break up as couples above the poverty level (Pear, 1993). Other background characteristics making divorce more likely include failure to complete college, unstable employment, getting married before age twenty, and experiencing an out-of-wedlock pregnancy (McGue & Lykken, 1992).

THE AFTEREFFECTS OF RELATIONSHIP FAILURE.   Both men and women suffer emotionally when a marriage fails, and those who do not remar-

Critical Thinking
Question 11

ry are likely to experience loneliness, depression, and lasting feelings of anger (Fischman, 1986). Most divorced individuals do remarry, especially males. In the United States, over two million people have been married three or more times, and that number is rapidly rising (Brody, Neubaum, & Forehand, 1988).

More than one-third of all U.S. children undergo the divorce of their parents (Bumpass, 1984). Children of a broken marriage suffer more than their parents, and they frequently respond with very negative feelings, lowered self-esteem, anxiety, and feelings of powerlessness; social and academic problems also tend to develop (Guidubaldi, Perry, & Nastasi, 1987; Slater & Calhoun, 1988).

Reasding: Lesko, (22), Getting at the Heart of the Jealous Heart

Research on relationships can help people make better decisions about entering romantic partnerships and provide needed information about how to maintain such relationships.

Despite the seeming universality of love, its specific expression is modified by specific cultures, as we'll discuss in the following **Social Diversity** section.

Social Diversity ▼ *A Critical Analysis*

Love and Intimacy: Western Europe, South Africa, Japan, and the United States

What are some of the cultural variations in how individuals express love and intimacy?

Cultural Variations in Love

A study of college students in Germany, Japan, and the United States found differences with respect to the students' attitudes about romantic love (Simmons, vom Kolke, & Shimizu, 1986). Among both men and women, researchers found that Japanese students placed much less value on romantic love than did students in the two Western nations. Unlike their Western counterparts, Japanese believe in male chivalry and in a dependent female role for women. Further, in Japan being in love seems to have primarily negative connotations—being in a dazed state and feeling jealous. Also, Japanese students expect marriage to bring disillusionment. American and German students were alike in most respects, but

German students held the most passionate view of romance.

Other research compared the love styles of French and American college students (Murstein, Merighi, & Vyse, 1991), using the measure described earlier in Table 8.2. Americans were much more likely to endorse friendship love than were the French, possibly because of the prevalence of co-educational school experiences and repeated interactions between the sexes. American men were higher on passionate love than those in France; this may reflect cultural differences, in that privacy and self-control are important in France, while Americans tend to be more open, "letting it all hang out." French women were higher on selfless love than were American women, and the authors suggested that the high proportion of Catholics in the French sample might explain this. That is, unlike the other types, selfless love better expresses a religious

view involving self-sacrifice and giving.

Expressing Intimacy

Ting-Toomey (1991) points out that all interpersonal relationships are culture-bound to some extent, and she has proposed that we each learn how to express intimacy to a romantic partner in ways that are acceptable in a given society. Her research concentrated on love commitment (perceived interdependence in a relationship), disclosure maintenance (communication about the relationship), ambivalence (expressed uncertainties about the relationship), and conflict (overt arguments and disagreements).

According to Ting-Toomey's hypothesis, behavior in intimate relationships was expected to differ as a function of cultural *individualism/collectivism*. In an individualist society the focus is on the nuclear family, while a collectivist society has a communal

In a cross-cultural study of college students, it was predicted that various kinds of expressive behavior in intimate relationships would occur more strongly as cultural individualism increased. The United States (high individualism), France (intermediate individualism), and Japan (low individualism) were compared. The expected relationships were found for expressions of love commitment, disclosure (communication), and ambivalence about the relationship. But the expression of conflict in relationships was equally high in the United States and Japan, and lowest in France.

TABLE 8.4 Cultural individualism/collectivism and behavior in intimate relationships

Behavior in Intimate Relationships	Culture Type		
	Individualist (U.S.)	Intermediate (France)	Collectivist (Japan)
Love commitment	High	Medium	Low
Disclosure	High	Medium	Low
Ambivalence	High	Medium	Low
Conflict	High	Low	High

Source: Based on data in Ting-Toomey, 1991.

orientation with extended kinship, neighborhood, and work groups. The investigator chose the United States, France, and Japan for comparison because research has shown them to represent high, medium, and low individualism, respectively. It was hypothesized that the higher a society's individualism, the greater would be all four types of intimacy expression.

University students in the three nations responded to a scale measuring the expression of intimacy in relationships. As shown in Table 8.4, the hypothesis was supported with respect to love commitment, disclosure maintenance, and relational ambivalence. But the expression of conflict did not follow the expected pattern, being high in both the United States and Japan

and low in France (possibly because of the high level of selfless love found among French women). Apparently, conflict is equally likely in individualistic and collectivist societies.

All together, these studies suggest the important role cultural influences play in determining the meaning of love and the expression of intimate feelings.

Summary and Review

A crucial aspect of our lives is the establishment of close, loving *relationships*.

Interdependent Relationships

Interdependence occurs when two people influence one another's lives and engage in many joint activities over an extended time period. This kind of relationship often involves relatives such as parents and siblings and also *close friends,*

but most people report that they feel closest to a romantic partner. The basis for romantic relationships is often *passionate love,* an intense, overpowering emotional experience. A close, caring friendship with a romantic partner is labeled *companionate love*—a less intense and more lasting state than passionate love. Additional elements and types of love have been described by Hendrick and Hendrick and by Sternberg. Those who want a close relationship but fail to establish one express feelings of *loneliness*. With more effective social skills and cognitive restructuring, loneliness can be overcome.

Intimate Relationships

Premarital sexual experience has become normative in the United States and in many other nations in the second half of the twentieth century, despite the threats posed by unwanted pregnancies and *sexually transmissible diseases*. Despite a high divorce rate, most people marry. Couples develop a variety of relationship patterns in dealing with jobs, household duties, leisure activities, and parenthood. Though most surveys indicate that married individuals are happier than single ones, the difference is less today than in the past.

Troubled Relationships

Problems and conflicts arise in long-term relationships. Among the common difficulties are dissimilarities between the partners, boredom, increasingly negative interactions, and *jealousy*. When the problems become sufficiently intense, the relationship sometimes can be restored, but breakups often occur. Whether the relationship is maintained or dissolved depends on such factors as personality, the meaning of the relationship to each partner, and the availability of alternate partners.

Social Diversity: Cultural Differences in Love and Intimacy

Cross-cultural research has shown how the specific expression of romantic love differs in different countries. For example, love is perceived differently in Japan, the United States, Germany, and France. Also, the expression of intimacy is greater in societies high in individualism (such as the United States) than in more collectivist societies (such as Japan).

Key Terms

Acquired Immune Deficiency Syndrome (AIDS) A viral STD that causes a breakdown of the body's immune system resulting in death.

Chlamydia A common bacterial STD that can be treated with antibiotics. Untreated, it can cause female infertility.

Close Friends Friends who spend a great deal of time together, interact in varied situations, exclude others from the relationship, and provide one another with emotional support.

Cognitive Therapy An interpersonal therapy stressing the importance of altering the client's maladaptive beliefs and thought processes.

Companionate Love Feelings of love that are based on friendship, mutual attraction, common interests, mutual respect, and concern for each other's happiness and welfare.

Decision/Commitment In Sternberg's triangular model of love, the cognitive elements involved in deciding to form a relationship and in being committed to it.

Dependence Model of Breakups A formulation proposing that an individual's decision to end a relationship is more likely the less the individual is dependent on that relationship.

Genital Herpes A viral STD resulting in periodic outbreaks resembling cold sores on the genitals and elsewhere. No cure has yet been found, but medication can alleviate the symptoms.

Gonorrhea A bacterial STD characterized by a mucous discharge and painful urination. The symptoms are more noticeable in males than in females.

Hopelessness A feeling of despair in which an individual gives up on life. Sometimes hopelessness leads to suicide.

Human Immunodeficiency Virus (HIV) A sexually transmissible virus; HIV infection develops into AIDS.

Inclusion of Other in the Self (IOS) Scale A measure of closeness developed by Aron and colleagues; consists of pairs of circles labeled "self" and "other" depicting a series of possible relationships, ranging from nonoverlapping pairs to almost completely overlapping pairs. The person taking the test selects the pair that best represents his or her relationships with another individual. The greater the overlap, the closer the relationship.

Interdependence The characteristic common to

all close relationships; means that two people influence one another's lives and engage in many joint activities over an extended period of time.

Intimacy In Sternberg's triangular model of love, the closeness or bondedness of two partners.

Jealousy The thoughts, feelings, and actions that arise when a relationship is threatened by a real or imagined rival for a partner's affection.

Loneliness The emotional state of a person who wants to be in a relationship but is not. Can also be a personality disposition. The lonely person feels unhappy and isolated but lacks the necessary social skills and cognitive awareness to overcome the problem.

Passion In Sternberg's triangular model of love, the sexual drives and sexual arousal associated with an interpersonal relationship.

Passionate Love An intense and often unrealistic emotional response to another person. When two individuals respond to one another in this way, they interpret their feelings as "true love," while observers often label their response as "infatuation."

Relationship Awareness Consciousness of the pros and cons of an existing relationship; occurs when at least one member of a romantic couple begins to think about how the two of them interact and to compare and contrast their respective roles.

Relationship Closeness Inventory A scale developed by Berscheid and her colleagues to measure the closeness of two individuals in a romantic, friendly, or family relationship.

Sexually Transmissible Disease (STD) An infection that can be transmitted through sexual contact.

Social Skills Training A therapeutic process that teaches individuals what to do and say in interpersonal interactions.

Sociosexuality A personality dimension that ranges from an "unrestricted" sexual orientation (willingness to engage in casual, emotionally uninvolved sexual interactions) to a "restricted" orientation (willingness to engage in sexual interactions only if there is closeness, commitment, and emotional bonding).

Sociosexual Orientation Inventory (SOI) A scale that measures individual differences in sociosexuality; high scores indicate an unrestricted orientation and low scores indicate a restricted orientation.

Triangular Model of Love Sternberg's formulation that conceptualizes love relationships in terms of the relative emphasis placed on intimacy, passion, and decision/commitment.

UCLA Loneliness Scale A personality test that assesses the extent to which an individual feels lonely and isolated from others.

For More Information

Brehm, S. S. (1992). *Intimate relationships.* New York: McGraw-Hill.

In this second edition of a book aimed at undergraduate readers, Professor Brehm covers the primary topics relevant to relationships including attraction, love and romance, sexual interactions, equity, jealousy, loneliness, and the dissolution of relationships.

Duck, S. (1991). *Human relationships.* Newbury Park, CA: Sage.

A very readable summary of social psychological work on interpersonal relationships. Among the many topics covered are love, long-term relationships, family interactions, and the effects of divorce on children.

Hatfield, E., & Rapson, R. L. (1993). *Love, sex, and intimacy: Their psychology, biology, and history.* New York: Harper Collins.

This unique book was coauthored by a social psychologist and her historian husband, and it covers a wide range of material relevant to love, sex, intimacy, and relationships in an interesting, readable fashion. In discussing these topics, the authors draw on psychology, biology, history, literature, arts, and their personal observations.

Hendrick, S. S., & Hendrick, C. (1992). *Romantic love.* Newbury Park, CA: Sage.

Two psychologists who are at the forefront in investigating the phenomenon of love bring together what is known on the subject. They combine material from psychologists, sociologists, historians, and philosophers in dealing with the history of love, love in close relationships, love styles, and the way love affects our everyday lives.

Social Influence:
Changing Others' Behavior

Conformity: Group Influence in Action

Factors Affecting Conformity: Cohesiveness, Group Size, and Social Support / The Bases of Conformity: Why We Often Choose to "Go Along" / The Need for Individuation and the Need for Control: Why, Sometimes, We Choose *Not* to Go Along / Minority Influence: One More Reason Why the Majority Doesn't Always Rule

Compliance: To Ask—Sometimes—Is to Receive

Ingratiation: Liking As a Basis for Influence / Multiple Requests: Two Steps to Compliance / Sweetening the Deal: the "That's Not All!" Technique / Complaints: Griping One's Way to Compliance

Obedience: Social Influence by Demand

Destructive Obedience: Some Basic Findings / Destructive Obedience: Why Does It Occur? / Destructive Obedience: Resisting Its Effects

SOCIAL DIVERSITY ▼ A Critical Analysis
Gender Differences and Conformity: The Vanishing Myth of Female Submissiveness

---

Special Sections

FOCUS ON RESEARCH: CLASSIC CONTRIBUTIONS—Group Pressure: The Irresistible Social Force?

WORK IN PROGRESS—Resisting Implicit Social Pressure: Threats to Personal Control in Everyday Interactions

WORK IN PROGRESS—Complaining in Close Relationships: Evidence for Some Intriguing Gender Differences

FOCUS ON RESEARCH: THE CUTTING EDGE—Social Influence in Everyday Life: Which Tactics Do People Use Most, When Do They Use Them, and with What Effect?

INDIVIDUAL DIVERSITY—Personality and Obedience: Who Resists and Who Obeys?

It was the summer of 1958. Eisenhower was president, Elvis was wiggling away on television screens across the nation, and I was fifteen years old. My family was spending the summer in the country, and I had quickly formed friendships with the teenagers in the area. Most of the time I hung out with three of them—Ron Stein, Bobby Montero, and Lonny Bier. They were good guys, and we played ball together, fished together, and even went to parties together. Yet despite all these diversions, we sometimes got bored.

It was during one sultry July afternoon, when time hung especially heavy on our hands, that Ron had his great brainstorm. "Hey!" he shouted, leaping to his feet. (Ron often jumped around like a puppy when he got excited.) "Remember that old wagon we found?" He was referring to a rusty old relic we had discovered in a nearby barn. "Why don't we drag it to the top of the hill and ride it down? Wouldn't that be great?" The others agreed instantly,. "Wow! That's cool!" Bobby exclaimed. "Yeah, what a ride!" said Lonny. But I had my doubts. "How are we going to steer it?" I asked. "And what about stopping once we get started? I don't think it has any brakes." My concerns had little impact on my friends. At first they just laughed, calling me a worrier. But when I persisted, they began to get annoyed. "What do you want to do, sit around all day?" Ron asked. "Yeah, get with it!" Bobby chimed in. "Stop worrying." Gradually our discussion grew more heated, until finally Bobby lost his temper. "Look," he said, turning red, "Either you're in or you're out. But if you're out, find yourself some other guys to hang around with. We don't like chickens!" That did it; I was defeated. Plans for the Big Ride, as we began to call it, moved ahead.

The next day it rained, but the following morning dawned bright and clear. At the chosen hour we assembled at the barn and pulled the wagon outside. It was in terrible shape. The wheels were rusty; the axle groaned; and, as I had suspected, there were no brakes. But it was too late to back out now, so I joined the others in getting it up the hill.

Once we got there, the road down looked even longer and steeper than I imagined. *What if we can't stop and hit that wall?* I thought to myself. And once again I began to wonder about taking part in this potential disaster. Bobby quickly noticed my hesitation and began to cackle like a chicken to remind me of where things stood. In the face of this derision, my resolve crumbled once again. Crossing my fingers, I climbed into the wagon with the others. And then . . . a miracle happened! Mr. Kaitz, who owned the land on both sides of the road, pulled up in his truck. He took one look at the scene on the hilltop and began to shout. "What are you crazy kids up to? You trying to get yourselves killed? I knew you were dumb, but I didn't realize you were *this* dumb. Of all the stupid, lamebrained ideas. . . ." He broke off,

shaking his head. "Put that wagon back where you found it, *right now!* And just wait until I tell your fathers. . . . They'll know how to handle jerks like you!"

Slowly and carefully we moved the wagon back down the hill. When we finally had it inside the barn we were all hot, dirty, and exhausted; so much for our thrilling ride. And Aaron Kaitz was a man of his word; he went to see our parents that very day. What a tongue-lashing I got from my dad! But that night, mixed with my embarrassment and regret, was the following question: What made me do it? I knew all along that it was a dumb idea. So why did I give in and go along with my friends? Somewhere, there was a lesson in all this. But what was it? I wasn't quite sure.

Everyone's life is unique, so you have probably never had an experience precisely like this one. But we're equally certain that you *have* encountered many situations in which you found yourself doing or saying things you would not have said or done in the absence of pressure from others. In short, you have often been on the receiving end of attempts by other persons to alter your behavior in various ways. And turning the situation around, you have probably also engaged in such efforts yourself on many occasions. In a practical sense, therefore, you already know quite a lot about the topic on which we'll focus in this chapter—**social influence**: efforts on the part of one person to alter the behavior or attitudes of one or more others.

As suggested by Figure 9.1, social influence takes many different forms, some blatant and obvious, others more subtle or disguised. There can be little doubt, however, that this is an important process. Every day we are subjected to many attempts by others to influence us in some manner; and we in turn often engage in efforts to influence *them*. Thus, from the standpoint of sheer frequency, social influence is an important form of social behavior—one worthy of careful attention. In addition, as we'll note in later chapters, success in changing others' behavior also plays a key role in many other aspects of social

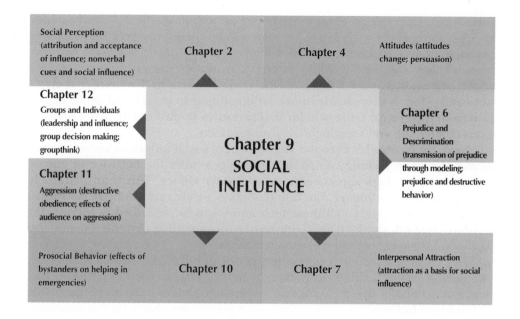

	Chapter 2	Chapter 4	
Social Perception (attribution and acceptance of influence; nonverbal cues and social influence)			Attitudes (attitudes change; persuasion)

Chapter 12

Groups and Individuals (leadership and influence; group decision making; groupthink)

Chapter 11

Aggression (destructive obedience; effects of audience on aggression)

Chapter 9 SOCIAL INFLUENCE

Chapter 6

Prejudice and Descrimination (transmission of prejudice through modeling; prejudice and destructive behavior)

	Chapter 10	Chapter 7	
Prosocial Behavior (effects of bystanders on helping in emergencies)			Interpersonal Attraction (attraction as a basis for social influence)

interaction, ranging from *leadership* on the one hand through *bargaining* or *negotiation* on the other (see, especially, chapter 12). Social influence is an important topic for this reason, too.

In a sense, we began the discussion of social influence in chapter 4, where we examined the nature of *persuasion* and other forms of *attitude change* (Judd et al., 1991). Here, we'll expand the scope of this earlier discussion by examining several additional forms of social influence. We'll start by focusing on **con-**

"I like it"

The many faces of social influence

FIGURE 9.1 Efforts to exert *social influence* take many different forms. Some of these are blatant and obvious, while others, like the one shown here, are much more subtle.

Source: The New Yorker.

formity: Pressures to go along with the crowd, to behave in the same manner as other persons in one's group or society. Such pressures toward conformity probably played an important role in my own decision to go along with my friends' plans for the Big Ride. After all, as part of the group, how could I resist their enthusiasm for this senseless and risky action? The answer is clear: not easily—for, as they clearly informed me, doing so would lead to my expulsion from the group! Little wonder that pressures toward conformity can often exert compelling and seemingly irresistible effects.

Next, we'll consider a second major form of social influence known as *compliance*. A person seeking compliance attempts to alter the behavior of one or more others through direct requests or similar tactics. This is an extremely common form of influence, but one that takes a wide variety of specific forms. The guiding principle in all these techniques can be described as follows: Do anything that will tip the balance in your favor—anything that will increase the likelihood that others will say yes to your requests.

Critical Thinking Question 1

Finally, we'll examine a third form of social influence—**obedience.** Here, one person simply orders one or more others to change their behavior in specific ways. Usually the persons who issue such orders have some means of enforcing submission to them: They have *power* over those on the receiving end (Yukl & Falbe, 1991). Research findings indicate, however, that direct orders can often be effective in inducing obedience even in situations where the persons who issue these commands have little or no means for backing them up.

As we consider each of these major forms of social influence, we'll address two crucial questions: (1) Why do they succeed—why are they effective in changing others' behavior? and (2) What factors or conditions determine their degree of success in this regard?

CONFORMITY: GROUP INFLUENCE IN ACTION

Have you ever found yourself in a situation in which you felt that you stuck out like the proverbial sore thumb? If so, you have already had direct experience with pressures toward *conformity*. In such situations, you probably experienced a strong desire to "get back into line"—to fit in with the other people around you. Such pressures toward conformity stem from the fact that in many contexts, there are spoken or unspoken rules indicating how we *should* or *ought to* behave. These rules are known as **social norms.** In some instances, norms can be both detailed and precise. For example, governments generally function through constitutions and written laws; athletic contests are usually regulated by written rules; and signs in many public places (e.g., along highways, in parks, and at airports) frequently describe expected behavior in considerable detail.

Discussion Question 2

In contrast, other norms are unspoken or implicit. Most of us obey such unwritten rules as "Don't stand too close to strangers on elevators if you can help it" and "Don't arrive at parties or other social gatherings exactly on time." Similarly, we are often strongly influenced by current and rapidly changing standards of dress, speech, and personal grooming. Regardless of whether social norms are explicit or implicit, one fact is clear: *Most people obey them most of the time.* For example, few persons visit restaurants without leaving a tip for their server. And virtually everyone, regardless of personal political beliefs, stands when the national anthem of their country is played at sports events or other public gatherings.

 Pressures to conform: Sometimes they are objectionable

FIGURE 9.2 When pressures to conform force individuals to behave in ways that cause discomfort, these pressures can be viewed as objectionable.

At first glance, this strong tendency toward conformity—toward going along with society's expectations about how we should behave in various situations—may strike you as objectionable. After all, it does prevent people from "doing their own thing." Actually, though, there is a strong basis for the existence of so much conformity: Without conformity we would quickly find ourselves facing social chaos. Imagine what would happen outside movie theaters or voting booths or at supermarket checkout counters if people did not follow the simple rule, "Form a line and wait your turn." And consider the danger to both drivers and pedestrians if there were not clear and widely followed traffic regulations. In many situations, then, conformity serves a useful function. But this in no way implies that it is always helpful. Some norms governing individual behavior appear to have no obvious purpose; they simply exist. For example, even today many companies require that their male employees wear neckties and that their female employees wear skirts or dresses, despite the facts that (1) such clothing is not directly related to performance of their jobs, and (2) it may cause them considerable personal discomfort when temperatures are very high (neckties) or very low (short skirts; see Figure 9.2). In cases such as these, the existence of strong pressures toward conformity can seem quite unacceptable.

Given that strong pressures toward conformity do exist in many settings, it is surprising to learn that conformity, as a social process, was not the subject of systematic investigation by social psychologists until the 1950s. At that time Solomon Asch (1951) carried out a series of experiments that added much to our knowledge of this important form of social influence. For a description of his research, please see the **Classic Contributions** section that follows.

Transparency 9.1

Focus on Research: Classic Contributions

GROUP PRESSURE: THE IRRESISTIBLE SOCIAL FORCE?

Suppose that just before an important exam, you discover that your answer to a homework problem is different from that obtained by another member of the class. How do you react? Probably with mild concern. Now imagine that you learn that a second person's answer, too, is different from yours. Moreover, to make matters worse, it agrees with the answer reported by the first person. How do you feel *now*? The chances are good that your anxiety will rise to high levels. Next you discover that a third person agrees with the other two. At this point you know that you are in big trouble. Which answer should you accept? Yours or the one obtained by your three friends? There's no time to find out, for at this moment the exam starts. Sure enough, the first question on the exam relates to this specific problem. Which answer should you choose? Can all three of your friends be wrong while you are right?

Life is filled with such dilemmas—instances in which we discover that our own judgments, actions, or conclusions are different from those reached by other persons. What do we, and others, do in such cases?

Exercise 1

The answer is provided by a series of studies conducted by Asch (1951) that are considered to be true classics in social psychology. In his research Asch asked participants to respond to a series of simple perceptual problems such as the one in Figure 9.3. On each problem they indicated which of three comparison lines matched a standard line in length. Several other persons (usually six to eight) were also present during the session; but, unknown to the real participant, all were accomplices of the experimenter. On certain occasions (twelve out of eighteen problems) the accomplices offered answers that were clearly wrong (e.g., they unanimously stated that line A matched the standard line in Figure 9.3). Moreover, they gave their answers before the participant responded. Thus, on such trials, the participants faced the type of dilemma described above. Should they go along with the other persons present or stick to their own judgments? A large majority of the participants in Asch's research opted for conformity. Indeed, fully 76 percent of those tested in several different studies went along with the group's false answers at least once. In contrast, only 5 percent of the subjects in a control group, who responded to the same problems in the absence of any accomplices, made such errors.

Video: The Power of the Situation

 Asch's line judgment task: An example

FIGURE 9.3 Participants in Asch's research were asked to report their judgments on problems such as this one. On each problem, they indicated which of the comparison lines (A, B, or C) best matched the standard line in terms of length.

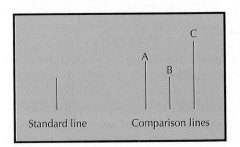

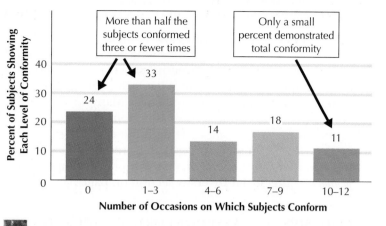

Asch's key results: Most people conform, but only part of the time

FIGURE 9.4 While most participants in Asch's research yielded to the false group judgments at least once, most resisted group pressure on most occasions. For example, fully 58 percent conformed three times or less during the twelve critical trials (occasions when the accomplices gave false answers).

Source: Based on data from Asch, 1957.

While most persons conformed at least once, however, it is important to note that they also *resisted* such influence on many other occasions. As shown in Figure 9.4, almost 24 percent never conformed, and many others yielded on only a few of the trials on which the accomplices gave wrong answers. Yet a large majority did conform to the accomplices' false answers, and the implicit norm these generated, at least part of the time. These results, and those obtained in many later studies (Tanford & Penrod, 1984) point to an unsettling conclusion: Many persons find it easier publicly to contradict the evidence of their own senses than to disagree openly with the unanimous judgments of other persons—even those of total strangers.

In later research, Asch (1957) repeated the above procedures with one important change: Instead of stating their answers out loud, participants wrote them down on a piece of paper. As you might guess, conformity dropped sharply. This finding points to the importance of distinguishing between *public compliance*—doing or saying what others around us say or do—and *private acceptance*—actually coming to feel or think as they do. Often, it appears, we overtly adhere to social norms or yield to group pressure without changing our private views or interpretations of the social world (Maas & Clark, 1984). Thus, in Asch's research, and in many real-life situations too, individuals may modify their overt actions so as to get into line with others while at the same time maintaining their attitudes and personal views largely intact. We will return to this distinction between public compliance and private acceptance at several points in this chapter.

FACTORS AFFECTING CONFORMITY: COHESIVENESS, GROUP SIZE, AND SOCIAL SUPPORT

Asch's research demonstrated the existence of powerful pressures toward conformity. Even a moment's reflection, however, indicates that conformity does not occur to the same degree in all settings or among all persons. This fact raises an intriguing question: What factors determine the extent to which individuals yield to conformity pressure? Many variables play a role, but among them three have received most attention: (1) *cohesiveness*—degree of attraction to the group or persons exerting influence; (2) *group size*—how many persons are exerting influence; and (3) the presence or absence of *social support*. We will consider another factor that can play an important role in conformity—*gender*—in the **Social Diversity** section on page 385.

Critical Thinking
Question 2

COHESIVENESS AND CONFORMITY: ACCEPTING INFLUENCE FROM THOSE WE LIKE.   Consider the following situation. After graduation from college, you go to work for a large corporation. You like your job very much and feel that you have a bright future with the company. There's only one minor problem. In the past, you have considered yourself to be a political moderate with a slight preference for Democratic candidates. Now, however, you discover that most of the people with whom you work are relatively conservative. They repeatedly voice their opposition to various government programs and criticize judges who, in their opinion, are too lenient toward criminals. Will your own views change as a result of exposure to these statements? Perhaps. You may find yourself agreeing with your new friends more and more as time passes. And even if you do not, you may demonstrate the kind of public compliance noted above: Sometimes you may voice agreement with your coworkers even if you don't really share their views.

Now, in contrast, imagine that you have signed up for an evening course in personal self-defense. During the sessions you hear other members of the class express extremely conservative views about law and order, the right to own guns, and punishing criminals. Will you be influenced by these statements? Probably not. In fact, the chances are good that you will pay little if any attention to them. Why do you react so differently in these two contexts? Partly because of contrasting levels of attraction to these different groups of persons. You are fairly neutral toward the persons in your self-defense class, but you like your coworkers very much and want to gain their acceptance. Thus, while you have little motivation for adopting the views of persons in your evening class, you have strong motivation for agreeing with people where you work.

In social psychology, this kind of attraction toward a particular group or its individual members is usually described by the term **cohesiveness,** and there is little doubt about its impact on conformity. When cohesiveness is high (i.e., when we are strongly attracted to a group and want badly to be accepted by it), pressures toward conformity are generally much greater than when cohesiveness is low (Forsyth, 1992). This is one basic reason why most persons are much more willing to accept social influence from friends or persons they admire than from others.

A compelling illustration of the impact of cohesiveness on conformity is provided by a study by Crandall (1988). In this investigation, members of two different sororities completed two questionnaires: one designed to measure patterns of friendship within these social organizations (i.e., who was friends with whom), the other to measure tendencies toward the potentially serious health problem of *binge eating,* in which individuals report uncontrollable urges to eat and actually consume tremendous amounts of food (see Figure 9.5). Both questionnaires were completed by members of the two sororities on two occasions: at the start of the academic year and again when it was nearly over. The purpose was to allow Crandall to determine whether shifts in friendship patterns over time would be related to changes in tendencies toward binge eating. Specifically, Crandall hypothesized that the young women who participated in the study would report becoming more like their friends with respect to binge eating as time passed and bonds of friendship (cohesiveness) deepened. Results offered strong support for this prediction. Groups of friends become increasingly like one another over time in terms of binge eating. Initially, friends were no more similar to one another in this respect than they were to other members of the sorority. After approximately seven months had passed, however, their patterns of binge eating grew increasingly similar. Additional findings indicated that relatively clear social norms concerning binge eating had emerged and were operating in both sororities. The nature of these norms, however, differed in the two organizations. In one sorority, the more individuals binged, the more popular they were. In the other, women were most popular when they engaged in binge eating with moderate frequency; binging too often or not often enough reduced their popularity.

These findings provide a clear illustration of the fact that the more we like others and wish to gain their approval, the more we tend to be influenced by them. Moreover, they also underscore the fact that pressures toward conformity can affect virtually any aspect of behavior—even something as basic as eating habits.

 Binge eating: Is it influenced by social pressure?

FIGURE 9.5 In *binge eating* individuals report uncontrollable urges to eat and consume incredibly large amounts of food. Growing evidence suggests that this potentially harmful disorder is sometimes influenced by pressures to conform to the norms of specific social groups.

CONFORMITY AND GROUP SIZE. WHY "MORE" ISN'T ALWAYS "BETTER" WITH RESPECT TO SOCIAL INFLUENCE. A second factor that exerts important effects upon the tendency to conform is the size of the influencing group. Studies designed to investigate this relationship indicate that up to a point—about three or four members—rising group size does increase conformity. Beyond this level, however, further increments in group size produce less and less additional effect (e.g., Gerard, Wilhelmy, & Conolley, 1968). It's important to note, by the way, that these findings were obtained in short-term laboratory studies; informal observation suggests that under natural conditions conformity may increase with increments in group size up to a somewhat larger number than three or four. But it still seems likely that at some point further increments in group size exert little or no effect on conformity.

Why is this the case? One reason seems to involve the fact that as group size rises beyond three or four members, individuals exposed to social pressure begin to suspect *collusion*. They conclude that group members are not expressing individual views or behaving in accordance with individual preferences but working together to exert influence (Wilder, 1977). This makes a great deal of sense; after all, it is rare to find all the people around us agreeing unanimously with one another. Usually people hold varying opinions and engage in a wide range of behaviors reflecting different preferences. When too many people agree, therefore, this may be a signal that it is time to be on guard.

Critical Thinking Question 3

Regardless of the reason for this leveling off in conformity pressure as group size mounts, there is another complication in the picture. Groups do not always seek to exert influence upon a single, holdout member. On the contrary, conformity pressure may be directed to several persons rather than to only one. How does this factor affect the picture? One answer is provided by a theory known as the **social influence model** (or **SIM** for short; Tanford & Penrod, 1984). This model suggests that the function relating group size to conformity or social influence is as follows. At first, each person added to the group (each additional source of influence) produces a larger increment in conformity pressure than the one before. Soon however, this function levels off so that each additional person adds *less* to the total amount of influence than did the preceding ones. The SIM model also suggests that as the number of targets of social influence increases, the impact of group size on conformity decreases. This is because the impact of the influencing group is now spread over several target persons rather than a single holdout.

Transparency 9.5

Is the SIM model accurate? Some evidence suggests that it is. When Tanford and Penrod (1984) applied their model to the findings of many previous studies dealing with the impact of group size on conformity, they found that this model predicted the obtained results quite accurately. Thus, the SIM model appears to provide a useful description of how pressures toward conformity vary both with group size and with the number of persons who are the target of such influence.

THE EFFECTS OF SUPPORT FROM OTHERS: WHEN HAVING AN ALLY HELPS. In Asch's research, and in many later studies of conformity, subjects were exposed to social pressure from a unanimous group: All the other persons present seemed to hold views different from their own. Under those conditions it is hardly surprising that most persons yielded to social pressure. What would happen if persons facing pressure to conform discovered that they had an *ally*—someone who shared their views or at least failed to accept the position of the majority? Under such conditions, perhaps, conformity might be reduced. That this is actually so is indicated by the results of several experiments (e.g., Allen & Levine, 1971; Morris & Miller, 1975). In these studies subjects provided with an ally or partner showed much less conformity than ones who did not receive such social support.

Perhaps the importance of such support in reducing conformity is best illustrated by two additional facts. First, conformity is reduced even when the partner or ally is someone not competent in the present situation. For example, in one study involving visual judgments, conformity was reduced even by a partner who wore thick glasses and could not see the relevant stimuli (Allen & Levine, 1971). Second, it is not crucial that the ally even share the subject's views. Conformity is reduced even if this person merely differs from the other group members—breaks their united front in some manner.

These and other findings suggest that almost any form of social support can help a person resist social pressure. As you might guess, though, certain types of support are more effective than others. For example, it appears that support received early—before pressures toward conformity are in place—is more effective than support received later (Morris, Miller, & Spangenberg, 1977). Apparently, learning that someone else shares their views can help strengthen individuals' ability to resist group pressure as it grows. This fact has important implications for many real-life settings. If you ever find yourself in a situation in which pressures toward conformity are rising and you feel that they should be resisted, try to speak out as quickly as possible. The sooner you do, the greater your chances of rallying others to your side and resisting the majority.

THE BASES OF CONFORMITY: WHY WE OFTEN CHOOSE TO "GO ALONG"

As we have just seen, several factors determine whether and to what extent conformity occurs. Yet this does not alter the essential point: Conformity is a basic fact of social life. Most people conform to the norms of their groups or societies most of the time. Why is this the case? Why do people so often choose to go along with these social rules or expectations instead of combating them? The answer seems to center primarily on two powerful needs possessed by all human beings: the desire to be liked or accepted by others and the desire to be right (Insko, 1985).

THE DESIRE TO BE LIKED: NORMATIVE SOCIAL INFLUENCE.   How can we get others to like us? This is one of the eternal puzzles of social life. As we noted in chapter 7, many tactics can prove effective in this regard. One of the most successful, though, is to appear to be as similar to others as possible. From our earliest days, we learn that agreeing with the persons around us and behaving much as they do causes them to like us. Parents, teachers, friends, and others often heap praise and approval on us for demonstrating such similarity (refer to our discussion of attitude formation in chapter 4). One important reason we conform, therefore, is simple: We have learned that doing so can yield the approval and acceptance we strongly crave. This source of social influence—and especially of conformity—is known as **normative social influence,** since it involves altering our behavior to meet others' expectations. Clearly, it is a common aspect of daily life.

THE DESIRE TO BE RIGHT: INFORMATIONAL SOCIAL INFLUENCE. If you want to know your weight, you can step onto a scale. Similarly, if you want to know the dimensions of a room, you can measure them directly. But how can you establish the "accuracy" of your own political or social views or decide which hairstyle suits you best? There are no simple physical tests or measuring devices for answering these questions. Yet most of us have just as strong a desire to be correct about such matters as about questions relating to the physical world. The solution is obvious: To answer these questions, or at least to obtain information about them, we must turn to other people. We use *their* opinions and *their* actions as guides for our own. Obviously, such reliance on others can be another source of conformity, for in an important sense, other people's actions and opinions define social reality for us. This source of social influence is known as **informational social influence,** since it is based on our tendency to depend upon others as a source of information about many aspects of the social world.

Critical Thinking
Question 5
Direct evidence for the operation of such informational social influence is provided by a field study conducted by Weenig and Midden (1991) in the Netherlands. These investigators reasoned that individuals obtain much of their information about new government programs from other persons in their neighborhoods. Thus, the greater the number of communication ties people have with friends, neighbors, and relatives, the greater their awareness of such programs should be and the greater the amount of attention they will direct to them. In short, the researchers predicted that *information diffusion*—the spread of information about new programs or initiatives—would be greater in neighborhoods where many communication links existed among residents than in neighborhoods where relatively few links existed.

To test this hypothesis, they studied the spread of information about a new energy conservation program in two neighborhoods that were similar in all major respects except one: In one neighborhood residents had many informal friendly contacts (cohesiveness was high), while in the other residents had relatively few social contacts (cohesiveness was low). The program was designed to induce residents to adopt such practices as putting insulation into the walls of their homes and adding storm windows (double glazing). The investigators measured awareness of the new program by asking neighborhood residents whether they had heard of the program and then asking them to mention as many program activities (newsletters, information meetings, booklets, and so on) as they could remember. The researchers also measured attention to the program by asking residents to rate the extent to which they had taken notice of the information provided in each aspect of the program. As predicted, persons in the cohesiveness neighborhood did discuss the program with others more frequently than those in the less cohesive neighborhood. In addition, they reported receiving more advice on the various options than persons in the less-cohesive neighborhood (see Figure 9.6). Further, and of even greater importance, both awareness of the program and attention to it increased with the number of communication ties between residents. So, in sum, persons in these neighborhoods did seem to rely on one another for information about new and potentially important programs: Neighbors served as sources of *informational social influence* about energy conservation.

Together, normative and informational social influence provide a strong basis for our tendency to conform—to act in accordance with existing social norms. In short, there is nothing mysterious about the compelling and

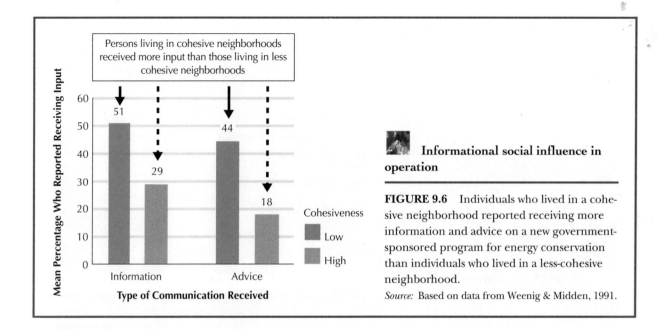

Informational social influence in operation

FIGURE 9.6 Individuals who lived in a cohesive neighborhood reported receiving more information and advice on a new government-sponsored program for energy conservation than individuals who lived in a less-cohesive neighborhood.

Source: Based on data from Weenig & Midden, 1991.

pervasive occurrence of conformity; it stems directly from basic needs and motives that can be fulfilled only when we do indeed decide to "go along" with others.

THE NEED FOR INDIVIDUATION AND THE NEED FOR CONTROL: WHY, SOMETIMES, WE CHOOSE *NOT* TO GO ALONG

Having read this discussion of normative and informational social influence, you may now have the distinct impression that pressures toward conformity are all but impossible to resist. If that's so, take heart. While such pressures are indeed powerful, they are definitely *not* irresistible. In many cases, individuals—or groups of individuals—decide to dig in their heels and say *no*. This was certainly true in Asch's research, where, as you may recall, most of the subjects yielded to social pressure, but only part of the time. On many occasions they stuck to their own judgments, even in the face of a disagreeing, unanimous majority. What accounts for this ability to resist even powerful pressures toward conformity? Research findings point to two key factors.

First, as you probably already realize, most of us have a strong desire to maintain our uniqueness or individuality. We want to be like others, but not to the extent that we lose our personal identity. In other words, along with the needs to be right and to be liked, most of us possess a desire for **individuation**—for being distinguished in some respects from others (e.g., Maslach, Santee, & Wade, 1987; Snyder & Fromkin, 1980). The result is that most people want to be similar to others *generally*, but don't want to be *exactly* like the people around them. In short, they want to hold on to at least a modicum of individuality (e.g., Snyder & Endelman, 1979). It is partly because of this motive that individuals sometimes choose to disagree with others or to act in unusual or even bizarre ways (see Figure 9.7, p. 362). They realize that such

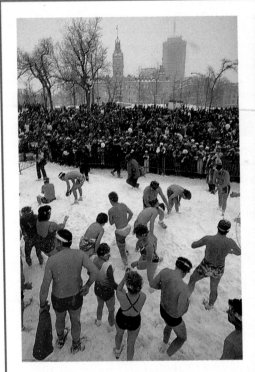

The need to be unique

FIGURE 9.7 Most people seem to have a need for *individuation*—a need to establish their unique identity. This is one factor that sometimes operates against yielding to conformity pressures.

behavior may be costly in terms of gaining the approval or acceptance of others, but their desire to maintain a unique identity is simply stronger than various inducements to conformity.

A second reason why individuals often choose to resist group pressure involves the desire to maintain control over the events in their lives (e.g., Burger, 1992; Burger & Cooper, 1979). Most persons want to believe that they can determine what happens to them, and yielding to social pressure sometimes runs counter to this desire. After all, going along with a group implies behaving in ways one might not ordinarily choose, and this can be interpreted as a restriction of personal freedom and control.

Direct evidence for the powerful impact of this factor has been reported by Burger (1987) in several related studies. In one of these experiments, male and female students were asked to rate each of ten cartoons in terms of how funny they found them to be. Half of the participants rated these cartoons while alone; the others rated them after hearing the ratings provided by several other persons. As in Asch's research, these other persons were all accomplices of the researcher. The accomplices rated the cartoons as being quite funny (an average rating of almost seventy on a one-hundred-point scale), despite the fact that other evaluators had previously rated them as quite dull. Before rating the cartoons, all participants had completed a questionnaire designed to measure the strength of their desire for personal control (the *Desirability of Control Scale;* Burger & Cooper, 1979). It was predicted that those high in the desire for personal control would show less yielding to the accomplices' influence than those low in desire for personal control, and this prediction was confirmed. In the absence of the accomplices, subjects high and low in desire for personal control did not differ in their ratings of the cartoons; both groups rated them as not very funny. In the presence of social influence from the accomplices, however, subjects low in desire for personal control rated the cartoons as funnier than those high in desire for personal control. They yielded to pressures toward conformity to a greater extent.

In sum, while pressures toward conformity often win out and induce individuals to behave in ways they would not otherwise choose, this is not always the case. On some occasions, at least, our desires to maintain our uniqueness and to exert control over our lives help us to resist even strong social influence.

Work in Progress

Resisting Implicit Social Pressure: Threats to Personal Control in Everyday Interactions

In many situations other persons try to change our attitudes and our behavior in fairly direct ways: They call attention to the fact that we are somehow out of line with others, or they try to persuade us directly (see chapter 4). But in many other cases their actions are more ambiguous: It is uncertain whether these behaviors are designed to influence us, and so reduce our personal control, or not. How do we react in such situations? Burger (1992) suggests that persons high in the desire for personal control may be especially sensitive to ambiguous behaviors and may find them highly unsettling. After all, they want very much to shape their own destinies; thus, they resent subtle attempts by others to influence them to a much greater extent than persons lower in the desire for control.

One situation in which such effects might be visible involves reactions to help from others. While many people are grateful for such assistance, some people tend to react negatively. Such reactions are understandable: Help from another person may constitute a subtle form of social influence, for the help creates an obligation to repay this person in some manner. Do persons high in the desire for control react more negatively to help from others than persons low in desire for control? Research by Daubman (1993) suggests that they do. In her study Daubman had pairs of participants work independently on a set of puzzles. Each participant then received feedback suggesting that he or she had done only average work, while the other person in the pair had done quite well. (Both persons received this same information.) At this point, participants either did or did not receive a helpful hint from the other person on how to solve the problems. Daubman found that persons low in desire for control reported feeling better after receiving help but reported slightly lower motivation to do well on the next task. In contrast, persons high in desire for control reported feeling *worse* after receiving help, and indicated that they now had even higher motivation to succeed. Finally, fully half of the high desire for control participants said that receiving help was irritating; only 22 percent of the low desire for control participants had such reactions.

These findings, and those of related research (e.g., Schonbach, 1990) lend support to Burger's (1992) contentions. Persons high in the desire for control do tend to perceive others' behavior as threatening to their personal freedom and often take active steps to resist such incursions. In short, they tend to go about their daily lives all too ready to say, to real or imagined influence attempts, "Oh, yeah?"

MINORITY INFLUENCE: ONE MORE REASON WHY THE MAJORITY DOESN'T ALWAYS RULE

As we have just noted, individuals can—and often do—resist group pressure (Wolfe, 1985). Lone dissenters or small minorities can dig in their heels and refuse to go along. Yet even this is not the total story; in addition, there are cases in which such persons or groups can turn the tables on the majority and *exert* rather than merely receive social influence. History provides numerous examples of such events. Such giants of the scientific world as Galileo, Pasteur, and Freud faced virtually unanimous majorities who rejected their views in harsh terms. Yet over time they won growing numbers of colleagues to their side until, ultimately, their opinions prevailed. More recent examples of minorities influencing majorities are provided by the success of environmentalists. Initially such persons were viewed as wild-eyed radicals operating at the fringes of society. Over time, however, they have succeeded in changing strongly held attitudes and laws, with the result that society itself has been altered through their efforts.

When do minorities succeed in exerting social influence on majorities? Research findings suggest that they are most likely to be successful under certain conditions (Moscovici, 1985).

Critical Thinking
Question 6

First, the members of such groups must be *consistent* in their opposition to majority opinions. If they waffle or show signs of yielding to the majority view, their impact is reduced. Second, in order for a minority to affect a larger majority, its members must avoid appearing rigid and dogmatic (Mugny, 1975). A minority that merely repeats the same position over and over again is less persuasive than one that demonstrates a degree of flexibility in its stance. Third, the general social context in which a minority operates is important. If a minority argues for a position that is consistent with current social trends (e.g., conservative views at a time of growing conservatism), its chances of influencing a majority are greater than if it argues for a position that is out of step with such trends. Finally, *single minorities,* minorities that differ from the majority only with respect to beliefs or attitudes, are more effective in exerting influence than *double minorities*—ones that differ both in attitudes and in their group membership. For example, in the United States, members of a black radical group holding extreme political views would constitute a double minority; members of a white radical group holding similar views would represent a single minority.

Even when minorities are consistent and flexible and promote views consonant with current social trends, however, they may fail to exert much influence. The power of majorities to evoke conformity is great, so most people may continue to comply with established norms even in the presence of eloquent vocal minorities. While minorities may fail to change overt behavior in many cases, they can still produce important effects. For example, they may induce large numbers of persons to think more deeply or carefully about the issues in question (Nemeth, 1986). "How can they [the vocal minority] be wrong and yet be so sure of themselves?" "Why are they willing to go to so much trouble for such a ridiculous cause?" These are the kind of questions observers may ask themselves when confronted with an unpopular but highly committed minority. And the minority may lead some persons to consider ideas and alternatives they would otherwise have ignored. As we noted in chapter 4, such cognitive effort can often serve as an initial step to attitude change, placing individuals on the *central route* to persuasion. In sum, even when minorities fail to sway majorities initially, they may launch processes that lead eventually to social change. In this respect, at least, there is much truth to the phrase "Long live the loyal opposition!"

COMPLIANCE: TO ASK—
SOMETIMES—IS TO RECEIVE

How many times each day do you receive requests from others? If you kept a record, you'd probably be surprised by the total; for friends, coworkers, acquaintances, family members, lovers, and roommates frequently ask us to change various aspects of our behavior. Advertisers, politicians, and many others also get into the act, so that finally, the list of people attempting to exert such influence upon us is large indeed.

Social psychologists term efforts to influence us through direct requests **compliance,** and in its most basic form, it is quite straightforward: Persons seeking compliance state their wishes and hope these will be granted. In many instances, however, the workings of this type of influence are somewhat more complex. Rather than presenting their requests cold, persons seeking compliance begin with preliminary steps designed to tip the balance in their favor— tactics they hope will increase the likelihood of the targets' saying yes. Persons seeking compliance use many different procedures for this purpose, but here we'll concentrate on the ones that appear to be most successful.

INGRATIATION: LIKING AS A BASIS FOR INFLUENCE

Earlier we noted that most people have a strong desire to be liked by others. While this motive probably stems from several different sources, one of the most important of these is this: We realize that if others like us, they are more willing to do things for us. They are more likely to help us with various tasks, to evaluate us favorably, and to say yes to our requests. Recognition of this basic fact lies behind a common technique for gaining compliance: **ingratiation** (Jones, 1964). What this involves, in essence, is efforts by individuals to enhance their attractiveness to a target so that this person will then be more susceptible to their requests (Liden & Mitchell, 1988; Wortman & Linsenmeier, 1977).

What ingratiation techniques are effective? As noted in our discussion of *impression management* (see chapter 2), several can be useful. First, individuals seeking to ingratiate themselves to others can employ *target-directed* tactics (Liden & Mitchell, 1988). These concentrate on inducing positive feelings in the target person. Presumably, such feelings will transfer to the ingratiator and

Discussion Question 4

will increase liking for him or her (refer to our discussion of attraction in chapter 7). Included among target-directed tactics are *flattery*, expressing *agreement* with the target person's views, showing *interest* in the target (e.g., appearing to hang on their every word), and directing many positive nonverbal cues toward them (e.g., smiling, leaning in their direction; Wortman & Linsenmeier, 1977). As suggested by Figure 9.8, such tactics often work—they increase the likelihood that target persons will say yes to various requests (e.g., Godfrey, Jones, & Lord, 1986; Kacmar, Delery, & Ferris, 1993). As you probably know from your own experience, however, such techniques can be overdone; and when they are, they can sometimes backfire. For example, recent evidence suggests that *excessive flattery*—flattery that is recognized as undeserved praise by the recipient—can increase rather than reduce interpersonal conflict (Baron et al., 1990).

Critical Thinking Question 7

Other tactics include efforts by would-be ingratiators to enhance their personal appeal to target persons—techniques sometimes described as involving *self-enhancement*. As we noted in chapter 2, the goal is to make a favorable impression on the target person (Schlenker, 1980). This can involve trying to improve one's personal appearance through dress or grooming; presenting information that suggests that one possesses desirable characteristics (e.g., sincerity, competence, intelligence, friendliness); or merely associating oneself with positive events or people the target already likes. In this latter category, ingratiators can name-drop, thus linking themselves to important or respected persons, and can casually introduce evidence of their past accomplishments into the conversation. Additional tactics include *self-deprecation*—providing negative information about oneself as a means of promoting the image of modesty—and *self-disclosure*, or offering personal information about oneself even if it is not requested. This latter tactic fosters the impression that the ingratiator is honest and likes the target person (Tedeschi & Melburg, 1984).

Do such tactics work? A growing body of evidence suggests that, if used with skill and care, they do. For example, in one laboratory study on this topic, Godfrey, Jones, and Lord (1986) asked pairs of unacquainted subjects to carry

Flattery: Often, it succeeds

FIGURE 9.8 Flattery is sometimes a highly effective technique for obtaining compliance.
Source: King Features Syndicate, Inc., 1986.

on two brief conversations with one another. After the first conversation, one individual in each pair was asked to try to make the other person like him or her as much as possible. The others were not given such instructions. After the conversations, subjects rated one another on a number of dimensions. In addition, videotapes of their conversations were carefully coded and analyzed by two trained raters. Results indicated that subjects told to ingratiate themselves with their partners succeeded in this task: They were indeed rated as more likable after the second conversation than after the first. In contrast, subjects in the control group did not show such gains. Further, some of the factors behind this success were apparent in the tapes. The ingratiating subjects reduced the amount of time they spoke and showed more agreement with their partners in the second conversation. Again, control subjects failed to show such changes.

Other studies point to the success of ingratiation in applied contexts. It is now well established that job applicants who dress and groom appropriately and who emit positive nonverbal cues (e.g., smile frequently, maintain eye contact with the interviewer) receive higher ratings than applicants who do not engage in such actions (e.g., Arvey & Campion, 1982). However, additional evidence suggests that as is true in other contexts involving ingratiation, these tactics can be overdone. And if overdone they result in lower rather than higher ratings. For example, Rasmussen (1984) found that when applicants with poor credentials emit many nonverbal cues, they are down-rated relative to applicants who do not engage in such behavior. This may happen because interviewers think such applicants are trying to distract them and shift their attention away from their poor credentials. In short, the use of too many ingratiatory tactics seems to backfire and worsen rather than enhance reactions to the applicants.

MULTIPLE REQUESTS: TWO STEPS TO COMPLIANCE

Suppose you wanted a fairly large favor from one of your friends. Would you simply approach this person and make your request? Perhaps, but it is more likely that you would try to prepare the ground before seeking compliance. One way in which you might do this would be to begin with an initial request—asking for something different from what you really wanted. Then you would somehow use this as an entering wedge for gaining the compliance you really seek, and you would follow up with your actual request. Several variations on this *multiple request* strategy exist, and under appropriate circumstances, all can be effective.

THE FOOT IN THE DOOR: SMALL REQUEST FIRST, LARGE REQUEST SECOND. Experts in gaining compliance—skilled salespersons, confidence artists—often start their campaigns for gaining compliance with a trivial request. They ask potential customers to accept a free sample, or potential victims to do something that seems totally without risk (e.g., hold a receipt or the key to a safe deposit box). Only after these small requests are granted do they move on to the requests they really want—ones that can prove quite costly to the target persons. In all such instances, the basic strategy is much the same: Somehow induce another person to comply with a small initial request and thereby increase the chances that he or she will agree to a much larger one. Is this technique—often known as the **foot-in-the-door technique**—really successful? Evidence from many different studies suggests that it is (Beaman et al., 1983).

Discussion Question 3

In what is perhaps the most famous study concerned with this topic (Freedman & Fraser, 1966), a male experimenter phoned homemakers and identified himself as a member of a consumers' group. During this initial contact, he asked subjects to answer a few simple questions about the kinds of soap they used at home. Several days later, the same person called again and made a much larger request: Could he send a crew of five or six persons to the subject's home to conduct a thorough inventory of all the products he or she had on hand? It was explained that this survey would take about two hours, and that the crew would require freedom to search in all closets, cabinets, and drawers. As you can see, this was a truly huge request! In contrast, subjects in a one-contact control group were called only once and were presented with the large, second request "cold." Results were impressive: While only 22.2 percent of those in the one-contact condition agreed, fully 52.8 percent of those in the two-contact "foot-in-the-door" group complied. While results have not been as strong in several later studies (Beaman et al., 1983), existing evidence suggests that the foot-in-the-door tactic *is* effective in producing enhanced compliance in many settings, and in response to a wide range of requests—everything from signing a petition (Baron, 1973) through contributing to charity (Pliner et al., 1974). But how, precisely, does it operate? Why does agreeing to an initial small request increase one's likelihood of saying yes to a later and much larger one? Two possibilities exist.

Exercise 4   First, it may be that after consenting to a small request, individuals come to hold a more positive view of helping situations generally. They now perceive such situations as less threatening or costly than would otherwise be the case. As a result, they are more willing to comply with later—and larger—requests (Rittle, 1981).

Second, once individuals agree to a small initial request, they may experience subtle shifts in their own self-perceptions. Once they have agreed to an initial request, they may come to view themselves as the kind of person who does that sort of thing—one who offers help to people who need it. Thus, when contacted again and presented with a much larger request, they agree in order to be consistent with their enhanced self-image.

Both of these explanations have received some support from research findings (DeJong & Musilli, 1982; Rittle, 1981). A study conducted by Eisenberg, Cialdini, and their colleagues (1987), however, offers impressive and convincing evidence for the accuracy of the second (the self-perception view). This study was based on the fact that before age seven, children do not possess sufficient cognitive capacity to use their past behavior, and inferences about it, as predictors of their future behavior. That is, they are not capable of reasoning, "I was helpful before; therefore, I will probably be helpful again." Since they lack the capacity for such reasoning, they experience few, if any, pressures to be consistent in their behavior.

On the basis of these facts, Eisenberg and her colleagues reasoned that children younger than age seven would not demonstrate susceptibility to the foot-in-the-door effect. Children seven and above, however, would indeed be affected by it. To test this prediction, the investigators exposed children in three age groups (five to six, seven to eight, and ten to eleven) to an initial small request, or to no initial request. This request involved donating coupons that could be used to win prizes to poor children described as having no toys. Subjects received six coupons apiece, and virtually all complied with the experimenter's request that they donate one of these to the poor youngsters.

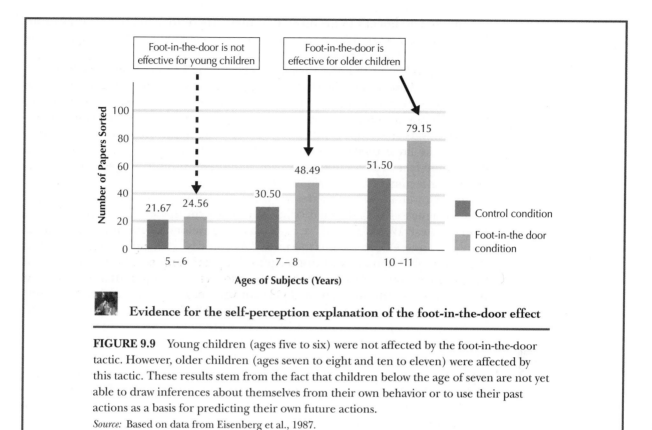

Foot-in-the-door is not effective for young children

Foot-in-the-door is effective for older children

Evidence for the self-perception explanation of the foot-in-the-door effect

FIGURE 9.9 Young children (ages five to six) were not affected by the foot-in-the-door tactic. However, older children (ages seven to eight and ten to eleven) were affected by this tactic. These results stem from the fact that children below the age of seven are not yet able to draw inferences about themselves from their own behavior or to use their past actions as a basis for predicting their own future actions.

Source: Based on data from Eisenberg et al., 1987.

Transparency 9.3

In a second session one or two days later, children were given a choice of either playing with an array of attractive toys or helping "sick children in the hospital" by sorting colored paper into four color-coded piles. Doing this rather than playing with the toys constituted the second, larger request. (It involved considerable effort and giving up the opportunity to play with the attractive toys.)

Results offered support for the hypothesis that the foot-in-the-door effect would not occur among the youngest children. For the five- to six-year-olds, there was no difference between the foot-in-the-door group and the control condition (children who were not exposed to the initial request) in terms of willingness to expend effort for the "sick children." Among the older children, in contrast, those in the foot-in-the-door group sorted more papers than those in the control condition. This difference was significant for the ten- to eleven-year-olds, and approached significance for the seven- to eight-year-olds (see Figure 9.9).

The findings reported by Eisenberg and her colleagues support the self-perception interpretation of the foot-in-the-door effect. Apparently, exposing individuals to small initial requests they are unlikely to refuse leads them to view themselves as *helpful* persons. This, coupled with strong internal pressures to be consistent (to live up to their enhanced self-image), then produces greater compliance with subsequent, larger requests. In a sense, therefore, the foot-in-the-door technique works because target persons help it to work: Their desire to be consistent is stronger than their desire to avoid the costs associated with saying yes.

THE DOOR IN THE FACE: LARGE REQUEST FIRST, SMALL REQUEST SECOND.   Another strategy for gaining compliance that is also based on multiple requests is, in a sense, opposite to that behind the foot in the door. Here, persons seeking compliance start by asking for a very large favor—one the target is almost certain to refuse. Then, when refusal occurs, they shift to a smaller request, the favor they really wanted all along. This approach is known as the **door-in-the-face technique** or the *rejection-then-retreat tactic* and also appears to be quite effective.

In one well-known study designed to investigate this strategy, Cialdini and his colleagues (1975) stopped college students on the street and presented a huge request: Would they serve as unpaid counselors for juvenile delinquents two hours a week for the next *two years!* As you can guess, none agreed to this proposition. When the experimenters then scaled down their request to a much smaller one—would the same students take a group of delinquents on a two-hour trip to the zoo—fully 50 percent agreed. In contrast, less than 17 percent of those in a control group agreed to this smaller request when it was presented alone rather than after an initial giant request.

The use of this technique can be observed in many real-life situations. Negotiators often begin with a position that is extremely favorable to themselves but very unfavorable to their opponents. When this initial proposal is rejected, they back down to a position much closer to the one they really hope to obtain. Similarly, television writers who wish to get certain lines or scenes past the network censors often sprinkle throughout their scripts words or situations they know will be cut. Then they agree to the elimination of many of these while still retaining the key lines they wanted all along (Cialdini, 1988).

Why does this tactic sometimes succeed? Two explanations have been proposed. The first relates to the notion of *reciprocal concessions*. When individuals who start with a very large request back down to a smaller one, target persons may view this as a concession. Such persons then feel obligated to make a matching concession themselves. As a result, they become more willing to comply with the requester's second, scaled-down proposal.

Another possibility involves our concern over *self-presentation*—our wish to present ourselves in a favorable light to others. If we refuse a large and unreasonable request, this appears justifiable and our image doesn't suffer. If we then also refuse a much smaller request from the same source, however, we may appear unreasonable. Thus, we may often yield to the rejection-then-retreat tactic because of our concern that failing to do so will cause us to look rigid or intransigent (Pendleton & Batson, 1979).

COMPARING THE FOOT-IN-THE-DOOR AND DOOR-IN-THE-FACE TACTICS: THE ROLE OF SOURCE LEGITIMACY.   Research findings, as well as informal observations of daily life, indicate that both the foot-in-the-door and the door-in-the-face techniques sometimes succeed. Is one of these tactics preferable to the other? In general, the answer seems to be no. Neither has a clear overall advantage over the other. Several factors do suggest, however, that the foot-in-the-door tactic may operate successfully in a somewhat wider range of situations.

First, consider the issue of time between the first and second requests. Since shifts in self-perception tend to persist, the foot-in-the-door technique should succeed even when the first and second requests are separated by substantial periods of time (several hours or more). In contrast, the door-in-the-face procedure may fail under such conditions, because the tendency to make a reciprocal concession to the requester after he or she backs down may quickly dissipate. Existing evidence suggests that this is indeed the case (e.g., Cann, Sherman, & Elkes, 1975).

Second, it appears that the foot-in-the-door tactic can succeed even when the first and second requests are made by two different persons. Again, this is due to the fact that shifts in self-perception, once induced, tend to persist. Thus, internal pressure toward being consistent (i.e., toward helping others) may enhance compliance even when the second request is made by a different person. In contrast, target persons should feel little or no obligation to make concessions to a person different from the one who proposed the initial large request. This technique, therefore, may succeed only when the two requests are made by the same individual.

Critical Thinking
Question 8

Third, the foot-in-the-door technique may succeed regardless of the legitimacy of the requester, while the door-in-the-face tactic may work only when the requester is judged to be high on this dimension. This would be the case because pressures to be consistent by agreeing to a second, larger request should operate regardless of source legitimacy. In contrast, individuals might feel little obligation to reciprocate for concessions by a source of influence that is low in legitimacy. This prediction has been confirmed by several studies (e.g., Patch, 1986).

In sum, while both techniques are useful in gaining compliance, existing evidence suggests that the foot-in-the-door tactic is applicable in a somewhat broader range of contexts than the door-in-the-face tactic. For this reason, it may often—though certainly not always—prove more effective as a means of exerting social influence.

SWEETENING THE DEAL: THE "THAT'S NOT ALL!" TECHNIQUE

One television program popular during the 1950s ("The Milton Berle Show"), contained a segment that many people found highly amusing. A man would come out onto the stage and set up a small platform. He would then roll up his sleeves and begin to offer members of the audience what he described as "incredible deals" (see Figure 9.10, p. 372). During this comedy routine he would mention a deal and then immediately indicate how he would sweeten it by throwing in something extra. "Tell you what I'm gonna do," he'd comment. "You say that's not enough? You say you want more for your money? Tell you what I'm gonna do . . ."

The deals offered in this comic routine were preposterous, but the technique itself is an intriguing one. Have you ever been in a situation where someone tried to sell you something and then, before you could answer yes or no, offered to add some bonus to the deal? Auto dealers sometimes do this, offering to add an option to the car in question as a "closer." Similar techniques are used in many other settings, too. Does this approach, sometimes termed the **that's not all (TNA) technique,** really work? Evidence gathered by Burger (1986) suggests that it does.

Critical Thinking
Question 9

In an initial study on this tactic, Burger conducted a bake sale on a college campus. Cupcakes were displayed on a table, but no price was indicated. In one condition of the study (the *that's not all* condition), when potential buyers

The "that's not all!" technique in operation

FIGURE 9.10 In order to close a deal, persons like the one shown here often throw something extra in before the potential customer has made her or his decision. This is the essence of the *that's not all* technique for gaining compliance.

asked the price for the cupcakes, they were given this information and then, before they could respond, were also shown a bag containing two cookies. The seller noted that the price included the cookies. In a second (control) condition, in contrast, subjects were shown the cookies and told that these were included in the deal before being given the price. Results indicated that the TNA technique worked. 73 percent of subjects in the TNA group bought the cupcakes, while only 40 percent of those in the control condition did so.

In a follow-up study, the seller told subjects in the TNA condition that the cupcakes were priced at $1.25. Then, before they could respond, the seller indicated that he would lower the price to $1.00 since he was planning to close his booth very soon. In a control condition, in contrast, subjects were simply told that the cupcakes were priced at $1.00. Finally, in a third (*bargain*) condition, the experimenter indicated that the cupcakes were now $1.00, although formerly they had been $1.25. This group was included to determine if any increased tendency to buy the cupcakes in the TNA condition was due merely to the fact that these items were now a bargain (their price had been reduced).

Results indicated that the TNA technique was effective once again. More than 50 percent of subjects in this condition bought the cupcakes; the corresponding percentages were much lower in both the control and bargain conditions. This latter finding suggests that the TNA technique is not effective merely because it offers items at a bargain price; rather, there is something about sweetening the deal in midstream that generates increased compliance.

Why does the TNA technique work? One possibility involves the *norm of reciprocity*. As we noted in our discussion of the door-in-the-face technique, we often feel obligated to reciprocate when another person makes a concession.

In view of the norm of reciprocity, persons who are the target of the that's not all technique may feel an increased obligation to say yes when the requester lowers the price, throws in a bonus, or takes some similar action. Support for this view is provided by the fact that the TNA technique succeeds only when subjects perceive the requester's addition of a bonus as a personal gesture; if it is viewed as something the requester had to do, this tactic fails.

Whatever its precise basis, the that's not all technique can be quite effective. Moreover, as we noted previously, it appears to be in widespread current use. For this reason you should definitely be on guard whenever someone attempts to induce you to say yes by offering more than they did initially. The chances are good that in such situations, the new, "improved" deal is the one the requester had in mind all along.

COMPLAINING: GRIPING ONE'S WAY TO COMPLIANCE

How many times a day do you *complain*—express discontent or dissatisfaction with yourself or some aspect of the external world? If you are like most people, you probably complain several times each day. Most of these complaints concern your personal states ("I feel really rotten today"), the external world ("What lousy weather!"), or simple frustration or annoyance ("I can't stand this traffic jam any longer!"). Sometimes, however, **complaining** is used as a tactic of social influence: "Why didn't you take out the garbage? It was your turn"; "We always go to see the movie you want; it's not fair"; or the classic *"You don't love me anymore!"* Statements such as these are directed toward the goal of getting the recipient to change his or her behavior in some manner. Are complaints effective in this respect? Research conducted by Alicke et al. (1992) sheds revealing light on this issue.

These researchers asked college students to keep diaries in which they recorded their daily complaints over a three-day period. Each time they complained, participants recorded the complaint and indicated when and where it occurred, the reason for the complaint, and the response of the other person or persons present. Results indicated that most complaints fell into several distinct categories. The first group were global statements expressing attitudes or feelings about a person, object, or event ("Those fraternity brothers are so vain," "The guy next to me on the bus is a dork"). The second group were specific complaints about others' behavior or one's own actions ("You forgot to pay the phone bill," "I ate like a pig at lunch today"). The third category included complaints about one's physical state ("If I don't eat soon, I'll collapse," "My head is really pounding"); falling below achievement expectations ("I'll probably fail my chemistry class," "My roommate thinks I let him down last night"); obligations ("I hate this psychology experiment I agreed to do," "I wish I didn't have to pick up my sister after work"); and obstacles to goal achievement ("I am getting really sick of school," "I wish I had more time to spend with my girlfriend").

Stated reasons for complaining varied widely, with the desire to vent or express frustration being by far the most common (50.0 percent). Seeking advice (9.6 percent), sympathy (6.1 percent), or information (3.8 percent), and making direct efforts to change others' attitudes or behavior (7.5 percent) were also relatively frequent. Perhaps the most interesting findings of this research from the point of view of social influence relate to others' reactions to participants' complaints. As shown in Figure 9.11, p. 374, efforts to change others' behavior or attitudes through complaints were moderately successful:

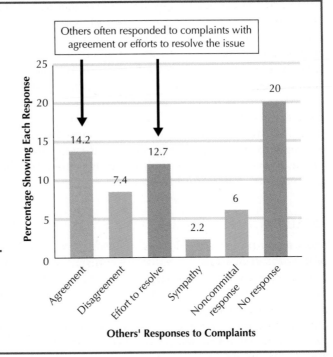

Others often responded to complaints with agreement or efforts to resolve the issue

Complaints as a technique for gaining compliance

FIGURE 9.11 Individuals who kept a diary of the complaints they made reported that their efforts to change others' behavior through complaints were often successful.

Source: Based on data from Alicke et al., 1992.

Others agreed with the complaint or tried to resolve it more than 25 percent of the time. Complaints that were less direct in nature but that still sought to change others' behavior or attitudes—complaints that requested information or involved attempts to coordinate behavior—were even more successful in this regard, perhaps because they did not trigger *reactance* (recall chapter 4) on the part of recipients.

In sum, complaining to others does seem to be a moderately effective technique for gaining compliance in some situations. Of course, chronic complainers may find that this tactic quickly loses its impact if it is repeated too frequently, just as those who engage in excessive flattery and related techniques find that these procedures gradually lose their punch.

Work in Progress

Complaining in Close Relationships: Evidence for Some Intriguing Gender Differences

No one likes a "chronic complainer," but as the research by Alicke and his colleagues (1992) suggests, complaining is a basic fact of social life: People do a lot of it, and their complaints focus on a wide range of topics. But to whom, precisely, do they complain? Common sense suggests that in most cases the answer is: to others whom they know quite well. In other words, to family, friends, and romantic partners. In order to investigate the nature of complaining in such relationships, Klotz and Alicke (1993) have recently conducted a

follow-up study in which same-sex friends, opposite-sex friends, and dating couples reported on the frequency and content of complaints in their relationships. Participants came to the study in pairs, and they each completed a questionnaire on which they listed the types of things they complained about most frequently to their partner and the complaints that their partner typically made to them. The researchers then used the data provided by participants to assess several intriguing hypotheses about complaining in close relationships.

Obedience to authority: Sometimes the results are tragic

FIGURE 9.13 Soldiers, members of secret police forces, and others often obey orders directing them to inflict serious harm on innocent victims. Such tragic instances of *destructive obedience* are all-too-common events in recent history. Shown here is a refugee camp for Kurds—victims of ruthless oppression by the troops of Saddam Hussein.

participants in his studies (all males) that they were participating in an investigation of the effects of punishment on learning. Their task was to deliver electric shocks to another person (actually an accomplice) each time he made an error in a simple learning task. These shocks were to be delivered by means of thirty switches on the equipment shown in Figure 9.14, p. 380. Participants were told to move to the next higher switch each time the learner made an error. Since the first switch supposedly delivered a shock of 15 volts, it was clear that if the learner made many errors, he would soon be receiving powerful jolts. Indeed, according to the labels on the equipment, the final shock would be 450 volts! In reality, of course, the accomplice (the learner) *never received any shocks* during the experiment. The only real shock ever used was a mild demonstration pulse from one button (number three) to convince subjects that the equipment was real.

During the session the "learner" (following prearranged instructions) made many errors. Thus, subjects soon found themselves facing a dilemma: Should they continue punishing this person with what seemed to be increasingly painful shocks? Or should they refuse to go on? The experimenter pressured them to continue, for whenever they hesitated or protested, he made one of a series of graded remarks. These began with "Please go on," escalated to "It is absolutely essential that you continue," and finally shifted to "You have no other choice; you *must* go on."

Since subjects were all volunteers and were paid in advance, you might predict that they would quickly refuse the experimenter's orders. Yet, in reality, fully *65 percent showed total obedience* to the experimenter's commands, proceeding through the entire series to the final 450-volt level (see Figure 9.15). In contrast, subjects in a control group who were not given such commands generally used only very mild shocks during the session. Many persons, of course, protested and asked that the session be ended. When ordered to proceed, however, a majority yielded to the experimenter's social influence and contin-

Critical Thinking Question 10

Reading: Lesko (26), Behaviorial Study of Obedience

 Studying obedience in the laboratory

FIGURE 9.14   Left: Stanley Milgram with the apparatus he used in his famous experiments on obedience. (It has recently been displayed in a special exhibit at the Smithsonian Institution in Washington, D.C.) Right: The experimenter (right front) and a participant (rear) attaching electrodes to the learner's (accomplice's) wrists.

Source: From the film *Obedience*, distributed by the New York University Film Library, Copyright 1965 by Stanley Milgram. Reprinted by permission of the copyright holder.

ued to obey. Indeed, they continued to do so even when the victim pounded on the wall as if in protest against the painful treatment he was receiving (refer to Figure 9.15).

In further experiments, Milgram (1965a, 1974) found that similar results could be obtained even under conditions that might be expected to reduce such obedience. When the study was moved from its original location on the campus of Yale University to a run-down office building in a nearby city, subjects' level of obedience remained virtually unchanged. Similarly, a large proportion continued to obey even when the accomplice complained about the painfulness of the shocks and begged to be released. Most surprising of all, many (about 30 percent) continued to obey even when they were required to grasp the victim's hand and force it down upon the "shock" plate! That these chilling results were not due to special conditions present in Milgram's laboratory is indicated by the fact that similar findings were soon reported in studies conducted in several different nations (e.g., Jordan, West Germany, Australia) and with children as well as adults (e.g., Kilham & Mann, 1974; Shanab & Yahya, 1977). Thus, these findings seemed to be alarmingly general in scope.

In Milgram's research, not all individuals obeyed repeated commands from the stern experimenter. Why not? Was the ability to resist related to the personal characteristics of these individuals? For information on this possibility, please see the **Individual Diversity** section on the next page.

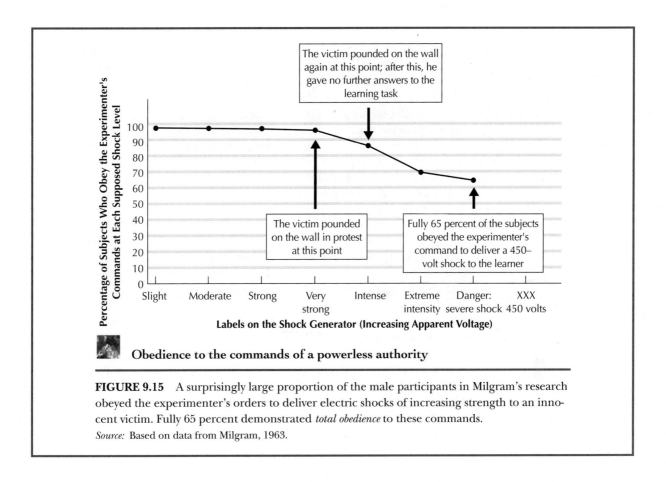

The victim pounded on the wall again at this point; after this, he gave no further answers to the learning task

The victim pounded on the wall in protest at this point

Fully 65 percent of the subjects obeyed the experimenter's command to deliver a 450–volt shock to the learner

Percentage of Subjects Who Obey the Experimenter's Commands at Each Supposed Shock Level

Labels on the Shock Generator (Increasing Apparent Voltage)

Slight   Moderate   Strong   Very strong   Intense   Extreme intensity   Danger: severe shock   XXX 450 volts

Obedience to the commands of a powerless authority

FIGURE 9.15 A surprisingly large proportion of the male participants in Milgram's research obeyed the experimenter's orders to deliver electric shocks of increasing strength to an innocent victim. Fully 65 percent demonstrated *total obedience* to these commands.
Source: Based on data from Milgram, 1963.

Individual Diversity

PERSONALITY AND OBEDIENCE: WHO RESISTS AND WHO OBEYS?

What would *you* do if you were ordered by an imposing experimenter to hurt an innocent stranger—someone who had never done you any wrong? When asked to make such a prediction, an overwhelming majority of individuals say "Not me!" But, as we have already seen, research findings indicate that in fact, large proportions do actually obey. Are there any personal characteristics that predispose specific persons to obey or to resist such social influence? The Milgram paradigm is often presented as demonstrating that strong situational pressures can overwhelm personality; but the fact that some people, at least, do resist suggests that this is not entirely accurate. And in fact, a growing body of research findings suggest that certain personal characteristics are related to whether, and to what extent, specific individuals obey the experimenter's commands.

One such characteristic is **authoritarian submission**—the tendency to adopt a submissive, uncritical attitude toward authority figures (Adorno, et al., 1950). The results of several studies suggest that persons high on this characteristic tend to be more obedient in the Milgram situation than those relatively low on this characteristic (Elms, 1972; Elms & Milgram, 1966). Further, individuals who score high on authoritarian submission are also more obedient to commands that they deliver painful electric shocks to *themselves* than those who score lower on this dimension (Miller, 1975).

Exercise 3

Another personal characteristic related to such obedience is the **internal–external locus of control dimension** (Rotter, 1971). Persons who score at the *internal* end of this dimension believe that their fate is largely in their own hands—the actions they perform determine their outcomes. In contrast, those who score at the *external* end believe that they have little control over their own outcomes; rather, they perceive themselves largely as chips in the winds of fate or as ruled by forces beyond their control. The results of several studies (e.g., Miller, 1975) indicate that externals are more likely to obey commands from authority figures, at least under some conditions, than internals. In one of these studies (Holland, 1967), participants either were exposed to conditions very much like those in Milgram's original research, or were informed that they were not regular subjects but controls, who were to watch carefully and try to figure out what the experiment was really about. As might be expected, those in the second condition were less obedient than those in the first (which generally replicated Milgram's procedures). In addition, when participants' scores on the I–E dimension were considered, an interesting pattern of findings emerged. The drop in obedience in the second condition was due almost entirely to reduced obedience among internals; externals, in contrast, showed obedience even when they were informed that they were not actual subjects! This suggests that persons scoring at the external end of the I–E dimension are indeed more likely to obey commands from authority figures than those scoring at the internal end.

Finally, there is some indication that deeply religious persons—or at least those who strongly accept the role of divine influence in human affairs—tend to be more obedient than those who are less religious in orientation (Bock, 1972).

So, in sum, it appears that certain personal characteristics do indeed predispose some persons toward—or away from—obedience. In general, persons who are willing to cede control over their outcomes and fate to external forces seem to be more willing to accept commands from sources of authority than persons who believe that their fate is largely under their own control. We should hasten to add that the magnitude of such differences is relatively small, especially when compared with the impact of various situational factors (e.g., in a situation like Milgram's, the proximity of the victim and this person's behavior; or the apparent status of the authority figure). Still, as noted by Blass (1991), it appears that personal characteristics as well as situational factors influence behavior in the Milgram situation. As is true of virtually all aspects of social behavior, therefore, a greater understanding of the nature of obedience can be gained through attention to both sets of variables than through exclusive focus on either one.

DESTRUCTIVE OBEDIENCE: WHY DOES IT OCCUR?

The results obtained by Milgram and others are disturbing. The parallels between the behavior of subjects in these studies and atrocities against civilians during time of war or civil uprising seem clear. (For example, consider the willingness of Chinese troops to fire upon civilians during the Tiananmen Square demonstrations of spring 1989.) But why, precisely, do such effects occur? Why were subjects in these experiments—and many persons in tragic situations outside the laboratory—so willing to yield to the commands of authority figures? Several factors appear to play a role.

Reading: Lesko (25), *The Education of a Torturer*

First, in many situations, the persons in authority relieve those who obey of the responsibility for their own actions. "I was only carrying out orders," is the defense many offer after obeying harsh or cruel directives. In life situations this transfer of responsibility may be implicit. In Milgram's experiments, in contrast, it was quite explicit. Subjects were told at the start that the experimenter (the authority figure), not they, would be responsible for the victim's well-being. Given this fact, it is not surprising that many tended to obey.

Second, persons in authority often possess visible badges or signs of their status and power. These consist of special uniforms, insignia, titles, and similar factors. Faced with such obvious reminders of who's in charge, most people find it difficult to resist. The powerful impact of such cues has been demonstrated by Bushman (1984, 1988) in several similar experiments. For example, in one of these investigations, a female accomplice of the researcher ordered pedestrians to give a nickel to a young man who needed it for a parking meter. In one condition the accomplice was dressed in a uniform (although its precise nature was ambiguous). In a second condition she was dressed as a business executive, and in a third she was dressed as a panhandler. Not surprisingly, a higher percentage of subjects obeyed in the first condition (72 percent) than in the others (48 and 52 percent respectively). Other data, which the researcher collected by asking subjects who obeyed why they did so, indicated that the uniform had the expected effect: Subjects in this condition reported that they obeyed simply because they had been ordered to do so by someone with authority. These findings, and those in related studies, suggest that the possession of outward signs of authority, even if they are largely irrelevant to the present situation, play an important role in the ability of authority figures to induce high levels of obedience to their commands.

Transparency 9.4

A third reason for obedience in many situations where the targets of such influence might resist involves its gradual nature. Initial commands are often relatively small and innocuous. Only later do they increase in scope and come to require behavior that is dangerous or objectionable. For example, police or military personnel may at first be ordered to question, arrest, or threaten potential victims. Gradually, demands are increased to the point where they are commanded to beat, torture, or even kill unarmed civilians. In a similar manner, subjects in the laboratory research on obedience were first required to deliver only mild and harmless shocks to the victim. Only as this person continued to make errors on the learning task did the intensity of these "punishments" rise to harmful levels.

In sum, several factors contribute to the high levels of obedience witnessed in laboratory studies and in a wide range of real-life contexts. Together these merge into a powerful force—one that most persons find difficult to resist. Unfortunately, the consequences of this compelling form of social influence can be disastrous for many innocent and largely defenseless victims.

DESTRUCTIVE OBEDIENCE: RESISTING ITS EFFECTS

Now that we have considered some of the factors responsible for the strong tendency to obey sources of authority, we will turn to a related question: How can this type of social influence be resisted? Several strategies seem to be effective in helping reduce the tendency to obey.

Reading: Lesko (27), *Understanding Behavior in the Milgram Obedience Experiment*

First, individuals exposed to commands from authority figures can be reminded that they—not the authorities—are responsible for any harm produced. Under these conditions sharp reductions in the tendency to obey have been observed (e.g., Hamilton, 1978; Kilham & Mann, 1974).

Second, individuals can be provided with an indication that beyond some point, unquestioning submission to destructive commands is inappropriate. For example, they can be exposed to the actions of *disobedient models*—persons who refuse to obey an authority figure's commands. Research findings suggest that this strategy, too, is quite effective in reducing obedience (Milgram, 1965b; Powers & Geen, 1972).

Third, individuals may find it easier to resist influence from authority figures if they question the expertise and motives of the authority figures. Are such persons really in a better position to judge what is appropriate and what is inappropriate? What motives lie behind their commands—socially beneficial goals or selfish gain? By asking such questions, persons who might otherwise obey may find support for independence rather than submission.

Finally, simply knowing about the power of authority figures to command blind obedience may be helpful in itself. Growing evidence (e.g., Sherman, 1980) suggests that when individuals learn about the findings of social psychological research, they may change their behavior to take account of this knowledge. With respect to destructive obedience, there is some hope that knowing about this process can enhance individuals' ability to resist. To the extent this is the case, then even exposure to findings as disturbing as those reported by Milgram can have positive social value. As they become widely known, they may produce desirable shifts within society.

To conclude: The power of authority figures to command obedience is certainly great, but it is definitely *not* irresistible. Under appropriate conditions it can be countered and reduced (see Figure 9.16). As in many other spheres

Resisting sources of authority: The potential benefits are great

FIGURE 9.16 Pressure to obey from sources of authority is *not* irresistible. When large numbers of persons decide to disobey, the results can be dramatic. (Shown here are German students dismantling the Berlin Wall in 1989.)

life, there *is* a choice. Deciding to resist the dictates of authority can, of course, be dangerous. Those holding power wield tremendous advantages in terms of weapons and technology. Yet, as recent events in Eastern Europe, the former Soviet Union, and elsewhere demonstrate, the outcome is by no means certain when committed groups of citizens choose to resist. Ultimately, victory may go to those on the side of freedom and decency rather than to those who possess the guns, tanks, and planes. The human spirit, in short, is not so easily controlled or extinguished as many dictators would like to believe.

Social Diversity ▼ A Critical Analysis

Gender Differences and Conformity: The Vanishing Myth of Female Submissiveness

Transparency 9.2

Suppose that you approached one hundred people at random in some public place (e.g., a large shopping mall) and asked them the following question: "Do women and men differ in terms of their tendencies to conform?" What would you find? Even today, the chances are good that more individuals would identify females as higher in conformity than the reverse. In support of this supposed difference, they might note that women are more likely than men to obey the changing dictates of fashion. Or they might comment that women are more concerned with being liked or being pleasing to others. In short, they would call attention to contrasting gender-role stereotypes for males and females.

Are such views accurate? Are women really more susceptible to conformity pressure or to other forms of social influence than men? Early studies on this issue seemed to indicate that they are (e.g., Crutchfield, 1955). The results of these investigations suggested that women

do indeed show greater conformity or yielding to social pressure than men. More recent studies, however, point to very different conclusions (e.g., Eagly & Carli, 1981). They suggest that in fact there are no significant differences between males and females in this respect. What accounts for the sharply contrasting findings in these two groups of studies? Several factors seem to play a role.

One of these involves the nature of the tasks and materials used in the early experiments (those conducted during the 1950s and 1960s). In many of these studies, the tasks employed were ones more familiar to males than to females. Since individuals of both genders yield more readily to social influence when they are uncertain about how to behave than when they are more confident, it is hardly surprising that females demonstrated higher levels of conformity. After all, the dice were strongly loaded against them.

That this factor was indeed responsible for the gender dif-

ferences obtained in early research is indicated by the findings of an experiment performed by Sistrunk and McDavid (1971). These researchers found that when females were less familiar with the items used than males, they did in fact show greater yielding to group pressure. However, when the tables were turned so that the items used were less familiar to males, it was *they* who showed greater conformity. So in efforts to compare the sexes in terms of susceptibility to social pressure, we must be on guard against confounding gender with an additional, unrelated factor—familiarity with the items or tasks used in the research.

Another reason for the disagreement between early and more recent studies on susceptibility to conformity pressure (Steffen & Eagly, 1985) involves major shifts in gender roles and gender-role stereotypes during the 1970s and 1980s. An ever-increasing number of women have moved into jobs and fields once occupied solely by males;

and stereotypes suggesting that women are less ambitious, less competent, and less independent than males have weakened. It seems reasonable to suggest that one result of such changes has been a fading of any tendency for females either to be, or simply to be perceived as being, more susceptible to social influence than males (Maupin & Fisher, 1989).

Critical Thinking
Question 4

Additional Evidence Indicating that Gender Differences in Conformity Are More Illusory than Real

Several other lines of research also point to the conclusion that males and females do not actually differ with respect to conformity. One of these has focused on the following possibility: One reason why many persons continue to believe that females are easier to influence than males lies in the fact that in general, females have lower status (Eagly, 1987). Since persons holding low status *are* often easier to influence than those holding higher status, this difference between the sexes may account, at least in part, for the popularity of the view that females are more susceptible to conformity pressure. Support for this reasoning has been obtained in several studies conducted by Eagly and her colleagues (e.g., Steffen & Eagly, 1985). For example, in one such investigation, Eagly and Wood (1982) asked men and women to read a brief story in which one employee of a business attempted to influence the views of another employee of the opposite sex. In half the cases, the would-be influencer was male and the target was female; in the remainder, the reverse was

true. In half of the stories, job titles were included, thus informing subjects of the status of the persons involved. In the remaining instances, information of this type was omitted.

After reading the story, subjects were asked to indicate the extent to which the target person would be influenced. It was predicted that when no information on status was provided, participants would tend to assume that females would be lower in this regard than males. Thus, they would predict greater compliance by female targets than by male targets. When information on status was provided, however, this factor—not gender—would affect their judgments. Both predictions were confirmed. In the absence of any information about relative status, subjects predicted greater yielding by females. When information on status was present, they predicted greater yielding by low-status than by high-status targets, regardless of their gender.

Still another line of investigation indicates that when females have demonstrated their competence on a task or in a specific situation, they are no more likely to yield to social influence than are males. In fact, under conditions where females have shown superior knowledge or expertise on a given task, males are more likely to yield to *their* judgments than vice versa. This fact has been demonstrated quite convincingly in a study conducted by Maupin and Fisher (1989). These researchers provided pairs of participants (one male, one female) with information suggesting either that the female had performed better than her partner on a task related to intellectual ability or that

the two persons had performed equally. Then both participants completed a questionnaire on which they expressed their opinions on a number of different issues. The participants then received information indicating that their partner disagreed with them on several of these items. Finally, they completed the same questionnaire once again.

Yielding was measured in terms of the number of items on which participants changed their initial responses in order to agree with those of their partner. As shown in Figure 9.17, males confronted with a female who had outperformed them on the initial task changed more items in order to agree with her than did males faced with a partner who had performed equally to themselves. Similarly, and as expected, females who learned that their performance was superior on the initial task showed *less* yielding to their partner than those who learned that their scores had been about equal. Additional findings confirmed the results of previous studies with respect to the nature of the items on which yielding occurred (Sistrunk & McDavid, 1971). That is, males showed more yielding to their partner's opinions on items more familiar to females and females showed more yielding on items more familiar to males.

Why an Absence of Gender Differences in Conformity Does Not Imply that Full Equality Has Arrived

To sum up, contrary to popular belief, females do *not* demonstrate greater tendencies to yield to social influence or conformity pressure than do males. This

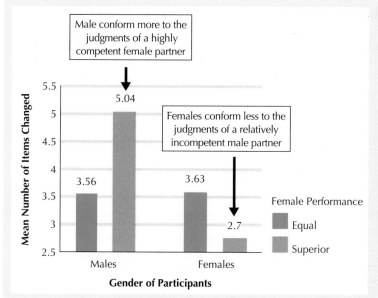

FIGURE 9.17 Males confronted with a female partner who had outperformed them on an initial task were more likely to conform to her opinions than were males faced with a partner whose performance equaled their own. These findings suggest that *demonstrated competence*—not gender—is a key factor determining who conforms to whom.

Source: Based on data from Maupin & Fisher, 1989.

does not mean, however, that females currently experience no disadvantages whatsoever when interacting with males. In fact, recent evidence suggests that even today females must still contend with what might well be termed efforts at *male domination*. For example, when interacting in mixed-gender groups, females often take a less active role in the group's activities as their proportion within the group decreases (Johnson & Schulman, 1989). In contrast, males do not show a similar drop in participa-tion. In fact, males who initially play little role in a group's activities actually demonstrate *increasing* participation as the proportion of females rises—almost as if they feel that it is their duty to take charge when surrounded mostly by females! These and related findings have important negative implications for females entering workplaces and occupations that until recently were the sole domain of males. Unless they prevent the males already present from dominating group activities, such females may have less opportunity to influence these activities and hence less chance to advance their own careers. As we noted in chapter 6, this and other barriers to female achievement must be overcome if women are to have full equality of opportunity in all areas of life. But at least we can report that the battle appears to have been won where suscepti-bility to

conformity is concerned: Differences between males and females in this respect no longer exist, if in fact they ever did!

Summary and Review

Conformity

Conformity occurs when individuals change their attitudes or behavior to comply with *social norms*—rules or expectations about how they should be-have in various situations. Conformity increases with *cohesiveness*—liking for the sources of such influence—and with the number of persons exert-ing conformity pressure; but only up to a point. Conformity is reduced by the presence of *social support*—one or more individuals who share the target persons's views, or who at least depart from the majority's position in some manner. One reason individuals sometimes resist conformity pressure is that they wish to maintain their unique identity as individuals. Minorities can sometimes influence larger majorities, especially when they appear to be deeply committed to the views they support.

Compliance

Compliance involves direct efforts by individuals to change the behavior of others. Many techniques can be used to increase the likelihood that target persons will say yes. *Ingratiation* involves efforts by requesters to increase their attractiveness to target persons, and may include flattery, expressing agreement with the target persons, and self-deprecation. Other techniques are based on the use of *multiple requests*. Here the *foot-in-the-door* and the *door-in-the-face* techniques are most prevalent. Another tactic for gaining compliance is the *that's not all* technique. Here, target persons are offered something extra before they decide to accept or reject a request.

Complaints are sometimes an effective way to gain compliance from others. Among the most common tactics used for gaining compliance are *rational persuasion, ingratiation,* and *inspirational appeals.*

Obedience

The most direct form of social influence is *obedience*—direct orders from one person to another. Research findings indicate that many persons obey commands from an authority figure even when such persons have little power to enforce their orders. These tendencies toward obedience stem from several causes (e.g., authority figures gradually escalate the scope of their orders; they have visible signs of power). Obedience can be reduced or resisted through several procedures, such as reminding individuals that they, not the authority figures, will be responsible for any harmful outcomes and exposing the targets of obedience to disobedience models.

Social Diversity: The Myth of Gender Differences in Conformity

Early investigations seemed to suggest that females are more susceptible to conformity and other forms of social influence than males. More recent investigations, however, have called these conclusions into question. It now appears that early studies used materials and tasks more familiar to males than to females and so placed females at a disadvantage in terms of susceptibility to conformity pressure. Many persons continue to believe that females are more conforming than males, because females generally occupy lower-status positions in society, and low-status persons tend to conform to a greater degree than high-status persons. Recent findings suggest that when faced with a female who has previously demonstrated her competence, males are willing to defer to this person and accept influence from her. Thus, *competence*, not gender, appears to be the crucial factor in conformity.

Key Terms

Authoritarian Submission The tendency to submit in an unquestioning manner to the directives of authority figures.

Cohesiveness In the context of social influence, the degree to which individuals like or are attracted to other members of a group or to persons who attempt to influence them.

Complaining Expressing discontent, dissatisfaction, resentment, or regret. On some occasions complaints are used to exert social influence on others, to change their behavior or attitudes in some manner.

Compliance A form of social influence in which one or more persons attempts to influence one or more others through direct requests.

Conformity A type of social influence in which individuals change their attitudes or behavior in order to adhere to existing social norms.

Door-in-the-Face Technique A procedure for gaining compliance in which requesters begin with a large request and then, when this is refused, retreat to a smaller one (the one they actually desired all along).

Foot-in-the-Door A procedure for gaining compliance in which requesters begin with a small request and then, when this is granted, escalate to a larger one (the one they actually desired all along).

Individuation Differentiation of oneself from others by emphasis on one's uniqueness or individuality.

Informational Social Influence Social influence based on the desire to be correct (i.e., to possess accurate perceptions of the social world).

Ingratiation A technique for gaining compliance in which requesters first induce target persons to like them, then attempt to change their behavior in some desired manner.

Internal–External Locus of Control Dimension A dimension relating to the extent to which individuals believe that their outcomes are under their own (internal) control or are determined by forces outside (external) their control.

Normative Social Influence Social influence based on the individual's desire to be liked or accepted by other persons.

Obedience A form of social influence in which one person simply orders one or more others to perform some action(s).

Social Influence Efforts on the part of one person to alter the behavior or attitudes of one or more others.

Social Influence Model (SIM) A general model of social influence designed to account for the impact of group size, number of targets, and several other factors upon the acceptance of influence in a wide range of settings.

Social Norms Rules indicating how individuals are expected to behave in specific situations.

That's Not All (TNA) Technique A technique for gaining compliance in which requesters offer additional benefits to target persons before the target persons have decided whether to comply with or reject specific requests.

For More Information

Cialdini, R. B. (1988). *Influence: Science and practice* (2nd ed.). Glenview Ill.: Scott-Foresman.

An insightful account of the major techniques people use to influence others. The book draws both on the findings of systematic research and on informal observations made by the author in a wide range of practical settings (e.g., sales, public relations, fund-raising agencies, organizations). This is the most readable and informative account of knowledge about influence currently available.

Hendrick, C. (Ed.). (1987). *Group processes.* Newbury Park, CA: Sage.

Contains chapters dealing with several of the topics covered in this chapter (e.g., majority and minority influence, how groups affect the behavior of their members). Each chapter is written by experts on the lines of research and concepts covered. This is a useful source to consult if you'd like to know more about key aspects of social influence.

Milgram, S. (1974). *Obedience to authority.* New York: Harper & Row.

This book remains the definitive work on obedience as a social psychological process. The untimely death of its author only added to its value as a lasting contribution to our field.

Milgram, S., Sabini, J., & Silver, M. (1992). *The individual in a social world.* New York: McGraw-Hill.

Presents a collection of essays written by Stanley Milgram, whose research on obedience is a classic in social psychology. Several of the chapters included deal with obedience, conformity, and other aspects of social influence. The style is very readable, and the content is thought-provoking, to say the least.

Prosocial Behavior:
Providing Help to Others

In the spring of 1966, I was in my office at the University of Texas, attempting to finish an article I was writing. Two of my colleagues came by on their way to lunch, but instead of joining them I decided to skip a meal and keep on with my work. One of my graduate students, Maitland Huffman, stopped in for a few minutes with some questions about his dissertation, and then he left for the student union. Expecting no further interruptions, I went back to my typewriter (remember those?).

My desk was next to a window in Mezes Hall, and I was dimly aware of the trees outside and the bright Austin sunshine. Over the next half hour or so, unusual sounds came through the window from time to time. I wasn't really paying attention to them, but afterwards was aware that there had been some unidentifiable noises.

At some point I stopped what I was doing and listened more closely. It sounded as though someone were setting off a firecracker every now and then. I didn't think about it very seriously, but I wondered if there were some sort of celebration going on. It didn't seem particularly important, so I continued with the manuscript. Then the sounds became more persistent and more puzzling, especially when sirens could also be heard.

Special Sections

Eventually my curiosity was aroused, and it seemed sensible to find out just what was going on. In the hallway people were talking excitedly. They explained what was happening on the campus—something I probably never would have been able to guess. A student named Whitman was on the balcony that ran along the four sides of the library tower, near the top. He appeared from time to time, rising above the railing to aim his rifle at the lunch-hour crowds below. At each appearance he randomly shot whoever happened to pass within range.

What next? A few people went cautiously out the front door of the building to get a better look. Gardner Lindzey rushed to his convertible, circled around to another building elsewhere on campus, and picked up his daughter, who was potentially in danger.

Several people (not psychologists) produced guns and began shooting in the general direction of the sniper. My own unheroic response to this emergency was to join Jerry Clore in a windowless room next to Elliot Aronson's office. We listened in safety to the radio account of this appalling event until a much braver soul went to the top of the tower, took Mr. Whitman by surprise, and killed him.

Dozens of bodies of dead and wounded students, faculty, staff members, and others lay on sidewalks and lawns in the area surrounding the tower. Ambulances, medical workers, and police officers swarmed over the campus. I then discovered that after Maitland left my office earlier, he was one of the early victims. But he had the "good fortune" to be shot in the arm; he was hospital-

ized and treated and eventually was able to return to school.

A few years after this terrible incident, two social psychologists, Bibb Latane and John Darley, began publishing research on analogous emergency situations, and their work represented a major step in explaining why bystanders respond to unexpected events as they do. Specifically, some respond by taking an active role in attempting to help others; for example, those who began firing at the sniper or Gardner Lindzey risking his life to protect his offspring. Some venture close to the scene but take no active steps to alter the situation; for example, those who left the building to view the carnage. And some essentially hold back and do nothing; for example, me.

Exercise 1 This chapter will examine some of what is known about the variables that predict who does and does not engage in *prosocial behavior* when emergency situations arise. By **prosocial behavior,** we mean actions that provide benefit to others but that have no obvious benefits for the person who carries them out. A very similar term, **altruistic behavior,** refers to acts that suggest an unselfish concern for the welfare of others. Sometimes prosocial and altruistic behaviors even involve risk for the one who helps. Still other labels, such as *helping behavior* and *charitable behavior,* are also used to describe the "good" things that some people do to provide needed assistance to other people. In this chapter we begin with the story of how an important research program began with efforts to explain why *response to an emergency* sometimes consists of tremendous effort, risk-taking, and sacrifice—and sometimes consists of doing little or nothing. We then examine some of the specific variables that increase or decrease the likelihood that *helping behavior* will occur, as well as its effect on the recipient. Next we describe alternative *motivational explanations of altruism* along with the kinds of research evidence that support these competing formulations.

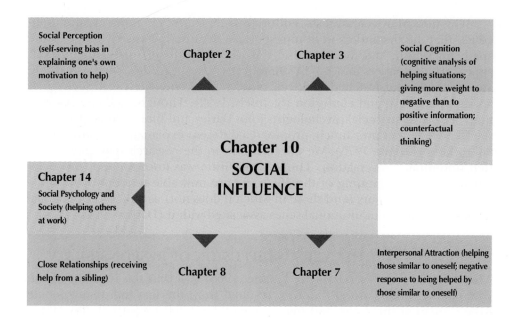

Social Perception (self-serving bias in explaining one's own motivation to help)

Chapter 2

Chapter 3

Social Cognition (cognitive analysis of helping situations; giving more weight to negative than to positive information; counterfactual thinking)

Chapter 14

Social Psychology and Society (helping others at work)

Chapter 10
SOCIAL INFLUENCE

Close Relationships (receiving help from a sibling)

Chapter 8

Chapter 7

Interpersonal Attraction (helping those similar to oneself; negative response to being helped by those similar to oneself)

RESPONDING TO AN EMERGENCY: WHAT DO BYSTANDERS DO?

The daily news provides many examples of people helping one another, even risking their lives to provide aid to strangers in distress. The following story is not an uncommon one. Two men who happened to live in the same building heard a woman (a stranger to them) screaming in the parking lot. Independently, they rushed out to provide help:

> The two "good Samaritans" . . . said screams awakened them. Both said they could see what appeared to be an attack from their windows. As one ran out the door, his wife said she'd call the police, but he said there wasn't time. When he reached the parking lot, the man was sitting on the woman's back, hitting her on the head, and telling her he was going to rape her. The attacker pretended he was her boyfriend, but the rescuer said, "I don't care, get off of her." He pulled the woman to her feet, and the second rescuer ran up, saying the police were on their way. The assailant ran off, but was later caught and arrested. (De Mare, 1992)

Despite these dramatic incidents, we seem to pay more attention to the opposite extreme: **bystander apathy,** when witnesses seem to ignore the problem and fail to provide help. An extreme example of such seeming indifference occurred in New York about two years before the sniper opened fire on innocent passersby in Texas. On March 13, 1964, at 3:20 A.M., Kitty Genovese was returning from her job as manager of a bar. She had parked her car and was about to enter her apartment building. Suddenly a man ran up to her brandishing a knife. She ran, but he chased after her, caught up, and stabbed her. Ms. Genovese screamed for help, and lights came on in many of the apartment windows that overlooked the scene. The attacker started to leave but then came back to resume his assault on the screaming victim. Almost forty-five minutes after the initial attack, Kitty Genovese lay dead as the result of multiple stab wounds. Afterward, thirty-eight people reported that they had heard her screams, but not one had offered assistance or even placed a call to the police (Rosenthal, 1964).

Why not? Many columnists, editorial writers, and TV commentators suggested that the bystanders were unresponsive because our society had become apathetic, selfish, and indifferent to the plight of others. Similar themes still appear in newspapers and on TV: Americans have been described as turning away from the outstretched hands of those who are homeless with feelings of apathy, numbness, and confusion (Steinfels, 1992). Though such characterizations are plausible, social psychologists John Darley and Bibb Latané, discussing the Genovese story over lunch, proposed a different explanation of why people fail to help (Krupat, 1975). We will turn now to the research that grew out of that noontime conversation. Though very little was known about prosocial behavior at the beginning of the 1960s, we are now able to identify the situations in which it occurs (and those in which it does not) as well as the personality dispositions and motivational states associated with it (Darley, 1991).

BYSTANDER "APATHY" VERSUS DIFFUSION OF RESPONSIBILITY

Reading: Lesko (28), When Will People Help in a Crisis?

The initial hypothesis (Darley & Latané, 1968) was that the inaction of the bystanders in the Genovese murder resulted from the fact that many people were present at the scene and that no one person felt responsible for taking action. Thus, there was **diffusion of responsibility.** Darley and Latané tested the hypothesis that as the number of bystanders increases, the diffused responsibility results in a decrease in prosocial behavior. Each subject in their initial experiment was exposed to a bogus medical emergency and believed himself or herself to be either the only one who knew about the problem, one of two bystanders, or one of five bystanders. The basic question was whether helpfulness would decrease as the number of bystanders increased.

When undergraduate subjects arrived at the laboratory to take part in a psychological experiment, the instructions indicated that they would discuss with fellow students some of the problems involved in attending college in a high-pressure urban setting. The participants were told that each of them would be assigned to a separate room and could communicate only by an intercom system; they could hear each other, but the experimenter would not be listening. This arrangement was supposedly designed to avoid any embarrassment about discussing personal matters.

Some subjects were told that they were one of two discussants, others that they were part of a group of three, and still others that six students were participating. Each participant was supposed to talk for two minutes, after which the listener or listeners would comment on what the others had said. In reality, only one subject took part in each session, and the other participant or participants were simply tape recordings. Thus, the stage was set for a controlled emergency apparently overheard by varying numbers of bystanders.

In each session the first person to speak was the tape-recorded individual who was to be the "victim". He said, sounding embarrassed, that he sometimes had seizures, especially when facing a stressful situation such as exams. After the participant (and, in two of the conditions, other "participants") had given a two-minute talk about college problems, the victim spoke again.

> I er I think I need er if if could er er somebody er er help because I er I'm er h-h-having a a a real problem er right now and I er if somebody could help me out it would er er s-s-sure be good . . . because er there er er a thing's coming on and and I could really er use some help so if somebody here er help er uh uh uh (choking sounds) . . . I'm gonna die er er I'm gonna die er help er er seizure (chokes, then is quiet). (Darley & Latané, 1968, p. 379)

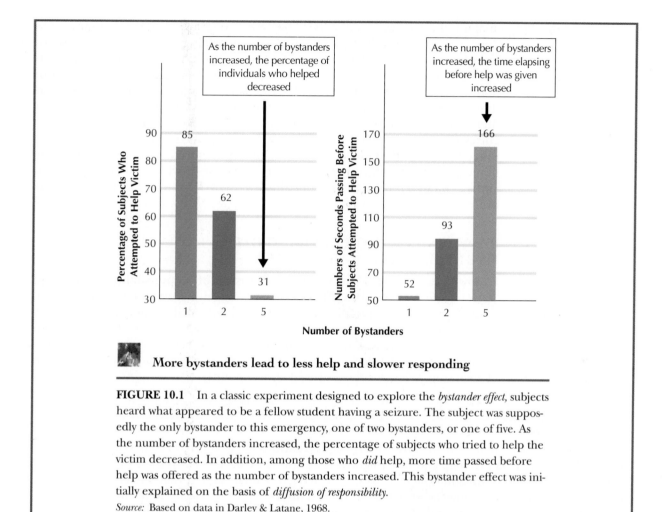

As the number of bystanders increased, the percentage of individuals who helped decreased

As the number of bystanders increased, the time elapsing before help was given increased

More bystanders lead to less help and slower responding

FIGURE 10.1 In a classic experiment designed to explore the *bystander effect*, subjects heard what appeared to be a fellow student having a seizure. The subject was supposedly the only bystander to this emergency, one of two bystanders, or one of five. As the number of bystanders increased, the percentage of subjects who tried to help the victim decreased. In addition, among those who *did* help, more time passed before help was offered as the number of bystanders increased. This bystander effect was initially explained on the basis of *diffusion of responsibility*.

Source: Based on data in Darley & Latane, 1968.

Two aspects of bystander responsiveness were measured, and the results are shown in Figure 10.1. A helpful response consisted of leaving the experimental room to look for the imaginary victim. As the number of apparent bystanders increased, the percentage of subjects attempting to help decreased. Further, among those who did respond, an increase in the number of bystanders led to increased delay in taking action. Such findings are consistent with Darley and Latane's hypothesis that the presence of others leads to diffused responsibility and makes helpfulness less probable.

Beyond demonstrating the **bystander effect**, this experiment also called into question the idea of the "apathetic bystander." For example, among those who thought they were the only witness, 85 percent tried to help, and did so within the first minute. Such responsiveness decreased and slowed down as more bystanders were present. But the subjects who failed to respond were not indifferent. Instead, they seemed emotionally upset, confused, and uncomfortable.

Discussion Question 1

As this line of research has progressed, additional insights have added to our understanding of the psychological factors contributing to or interfering with a prosocial response to an emergency. For example, Lang (1987) has conceptualized the helping response itself in greater detail. He asked subjects to

Transparency 10.3imagine the following situation. They are sitting in a hotel lobby, waiting to meet a friend, when they overhear a woman talking on a pay phone, out of sight in a hallway nearby. In one of several conditions, the caller says she is feeling physically ill and dizzy; her anxiety increases throughout the conversation. Lang asked the subjects to describe what they would do, if anything, as they listened to her talk—in other words, to provide self-report data about their potentially helpful or unhelpful actions. Their responses fell into six categories (four helpful and two not), as shown in Table 10.1, and these categories ranged from helpful-involved to unhelpful-uninvolved. The investigator proposed that identifying *degrees* of helping behavior provides much more useful and less limited information about altruism than the simple fact that help is or is not provided.

PROVIDING OR NOT PROVIDING HELP: FIVE NECESSARY COGNITIVE STEPS

Critical Thinking
Question 2Following the initial experiment on diffusion of responsibility, Latane and Darley (1970)—as well as others—carried out numerous interrelated experiments, and they eventually formulated a theoretical model to explain why bystanders sometimes do and sometimes do not help a victim. They described a helping response as the end point of a series of cognitive decisions, as outlined in Figure 10.2. Help is provided only if the appropriate decision is made at each step. What are these crucial choice-points?

Analysis of responses to specific emergency situations suggests that the extent to which bystanders help or fail to help can be categorized as falling at six levels. In the example here, subjects were asked to imagine themselves overhearing a woman saying that she is feeling ill, dizzy, and anxious. The subjects were asked what, if anything, they would do in this situation. Their responses ranged from a direct intervention with a plan about what to do on one extreme to a refusal to help based on attributions about the woman and a rationalization for not doing anything.

TABLE 10.1 Six levels of helpfulness–unhelpfulness

Helpful Responses

1. Direct Intervention with a Plan for Helping	"I'll give her my seat, and offer to get her a glass of water or wait with her."
2. General Help	"I'll go over and ask if she's okay."
3. Indirect Help or Reporting the Incident	"I'll tell someone at the hotel desk that the woman on the phone needs assistance."
4. Conditional Help	"If she walks around where I'm sitting and if she looks really sick and wants my help, then I guess I'll help her."

Unhelpful Responses

5. No Help or Interaction	"I think I'll read this magazine."
6. Refusal to Help Along with an Attribution or Rationalization	"I'm not going to help her. The information probably isn't important anyway."

Source: Based on data in Lang, 1987.

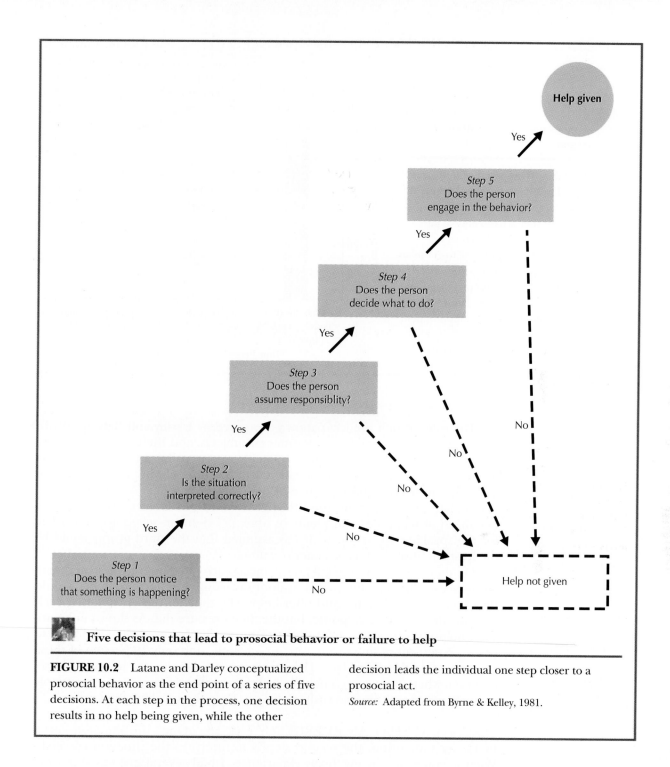

Five decisions that lead to prosocial behavior or failure to help

FIGURE 10.2 Latane and Darley conceptualized prosocial behavior as the end point of a series of five decisions. At each step in the process, one decision results in no help being given, while the other decision leads the individual one step closer to a prosocial act.

Source: Adapted from Byrne & Kelley, 1981.

ATTENDING TO THE EMERGENCY. The first decision is whether to shift one's attention from whatever one is doing to the unexpected emergency—to *notice* that something is wrong. As I worked in my office at the University of Texas, the gunshots from the library tower had been going on for at least fifteen or twenty minutes before I paid any attention to them. If, instead of working, I had simply been sitting by the window and looking out, I would probably have noticed the sounds much more quickly.

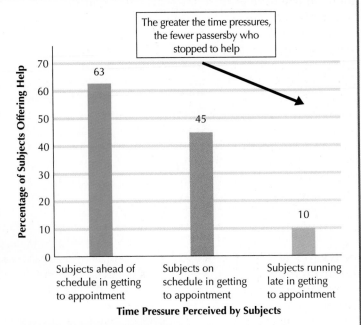

Too preoccupied to attend to an emergency

FIGURE 10.3 When potential helpers are preoccupied by other concerns, they are much less likely to help a person in need—in part because they are too busy to pay attention to the victim. Subjects who believed they had plenty of time to get to an appointment were most likely to stop and help a stranger who was slumped in a door-way, coughing and groaning. Those who believed they were late for the appointment were least likely to help.

Source: Based on data in Darley & Batson, 1973.

Reading: Lesko (29), *From Jerusalem to Jerico*

The role of such preoccupation was studied by Darley and Batson (1973). Seminary students served as experimental subjects, and their task was to go to a nearby building to present a talk. In an attempt to prime a helping response, the researchers specified that the talk was to be either about providing help to a stranger in need (Luke's parable of the Good Samaritan) or about jobs. To manipulate preoccupation, the investigators told the subjects that they were (1) ahead of schedule, with plenty of time; (2) right on schedule; or (3) late for the speaking engagement. It was assumed that the third group would be the least attentive to an emergency situation.

Discussion Question 2

On their way to give the talk, the subjects each encountered an experimental assistant who was slumped in a doorway, coughing and groaning. Would they notice this individual and offer help? The topic of the upcoming speech had no effect on their response, but the time pressure did. As shown in Figure 10.3, help was offered by 63 percent of those who believed they had time to spare, 45 percent of those who were on schedule, and only 10 percent of those who were told they were late. The preoccupied subjects were in such a hurry that even when they were going to talk about the Good Samaritan, some simply stepped over the victim and rushed along to keep the speaking appointment.

PERCEIVING THAT AN EMERGENCY EXISTS.   Once the situation gets a bystander's attention, the second step is to interpret the situation correctly. What is going on? In my Texas experience, I had several guesses about the meaning of the sounds, but none of my ideas involved the possibility of someone firing a rifle at innocent strangers. In general, it is easier to imagine a routine, everyday explanation of events than a highly unusual and unlikely one (Macrae & Milne, 1992). And a problem with interpreting an everyday situation as an emergency is that you can end up looking foolish (see Figure 10.4). Imagine how others would have reacted if I had run out of my office shouting about murderous gunfire and the truth had been that someone was simply lighting firecrackers on the lawn.

To avoid being embarrassed about being incorrect and behaving in an inappropriate way, most people fail to engage in any drastic action until the evidence is clear and convincing that an emergency is actually occurring. Often there is some degree of ambiguity in emergency situations, so potential helpers hold back and wait for additional information in order to be sure about what is going on. The more ambiguous the situation, the less likely people are to offer help (Bickman, 1972). Because it is easier *not* to help than to take an active helping role, and because we tend to give more weight to negative than to positive information (see chapter 3), people are especially attentive to any information that suggests there is no reason to be concerned (Wilson & Petruska, 1984).

When more than one bystander witnesses an emergency, each interprets the event in part on the basis of what the others do or say—each relies on *social comparison* (see chapter 7). If fellow witnesses fail to react, helping behavior is strongly inhibited. A special problem is that in our culture we are taught to remain calm in an emergency; it isn't socially acceptable to begin screaming when we see a stranger slip on an icy path, for example. As a result, most bystanders pretend to be calm, and this cool response is perceived by other bystanders as evidence that nothing serious is occurring. In an actual emergency, therefore, multiple bystanders can inadvertently and incorrectly inform one another that everything is all right.

This phenomenon is known as **pluralistic ignorance,** and an experiment by Latane and Darley (1968) demonstrates how it operates. The investigators asked subjects to fill out questionnaires in a room either alone or in groups of

Exercise 2

 Fear of looking foolish

FIGURE 10.4 Most people are very concerned about the reactions of others and feel that it is best not to stand out from the crowd by doing something that may elicit ridicule. Engaging in an overt act when you are alone is safe, because there is no one to evaluate your actions as foolish. For this reason, a bystander who is the sole witness to what appears to be a stranger in distress is more likely to help than a bystander who is one of several witnesses.
Source: Universal Press Syndicate, May 31, 1978.

three. Shortly after they began, smoke was pumped into the room through a vent. The experimenters waited for the subjects to respond (but terminated the experimental session after six minutes if the subjects remained in their seats and failed to act). When subjects were in the room alone, 75 percent went out to report the smoke, and half of those who responded did so within two minutes. When three people were in the room, only one person reacted in the first four minutes—the majority (62 percent) did nothing for the entire six minutes even though the smoke became thick enough to make it difficult to see.

Ambiguity and social acceptability also inhibit the tendency to help when a man is hurting a woman. Suppose you heard the sounds of a fight in a neighboring apartment, and the woman yelled, "I hate you! I don't ever want to see you again!" Would you do anything? Most people would decide that it was simply a lovers' quarrel and none of their business. Bystanders would probably be likely to respond, however, if the woman shouted, "Whoever you are, just get out of my apartment!" In an experimental version of such interactions, Shotland and Strau (1976) found that three times as many interventions took place when a fight was between a man and woman who were strangers than when it involved a married couple.

Ambiguity sometimes includes indecision as to whether a victim does or does not *want* to be helped. That is one reason why people are hesitant to respond to a domestic quarrel; sometimes the victim of domestic aggression resents an outsider's interference as much as the aggressor does.

IS IT MY RESPONSIBILITY TO HELP?   At the third decision point in the model, the bystander either does or does not assume responsibility to act. When the sniper was firing from the university tower, not only did I lack the bravery to assume responsibility, but it made little sense for a college professor to rush out the front door to take charge. This was a situation that police officers could handle, not a social psychologist. Even though you notice that an emergency exists and correctly interpret what is going on, you are not likely to do anything about it unless you decide that it's your responsibility to help. For example, you see an elderly person lying on the sidewalk—moaning in pain— and an ambulance has just pulled up (see Figure 10.5). Will you dash over to help or will you assume that in this situation responsibility for providing aid belongs to the trained medical personnel? When the responsibility is reasonably clear, you will probably do nothing.

Transparency 10.1 Many situations are not that clear, of course. If you are in a classroom and a fellow student falls to the floor and lies there with his eyes closed, you will probably expect your instructor to take some appropriate action. That is, the leader of a given group is perceived to be responsible for taking charge and deciding what to do (Baumeister et al., 1988). In that same classroom, if the instructor collapses on the floor, what will you do? Because none of the students has any clear responsibility, this is the kind of situation in which everyone may very well stand back and fail to do anything.

The direct link between the number of bystanders and perceived responsibility was tested by Schwartz and Gottlieb (1980). These investigators arranged for participants to witness an "emergency" either alone or with a second person. As in many other studies, helping behavior was less likely to occur when there were two bystanders than when there was one. The investigators determined perceived responsibility by asking participants afterward why they

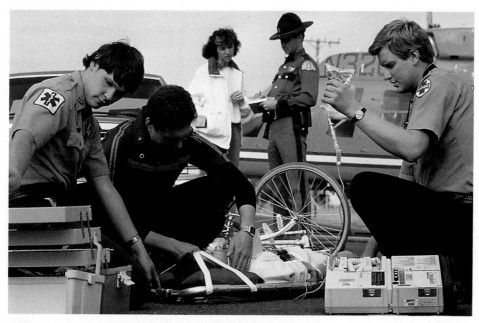

 Whose responsibility? Leave it to the experts

FIGURE 10.5   If one of the bystanders witnessing an emergency has special skills and training that are relevant to providing help, other bystanders are much less likely to offer assistance to a victim. For example, a medical emergency is best handled by medical personnel.

helped or failed to help. Of those who were alone, 80 percent said that they felt personally responsible for offering help; only 17 percent of those who had a fellow bystander mentioned any feelings of responsibility.

HOW TO HELP? KNOWING WHAT TO DO.   Once a bystander assumes responsibility, there is a fourth decision point. *How* can the victim be helped? As suggested in Figure 10.6, p. 402, in an emergency situation, it seldom makes sense to take time to consult with others about what to do. In some emergencies, almost anyone is able to provide the necessary aid—by telephoning the police, helping a victim stand up on a slippery sidewalk, and so forth. Other emergencies call for special skills, and useful help can be provided only by those who have the required training. For example, a bystander who could not swim would be unable to rescue someone who was having difficulty in the water. In the Texas incident, armed law enforcement personnel were much more competent to act than unarmed professors and students.

When a bystander is able to help, he or she is likely to act even though other bystanders are present and unresponsive. Cramer et al. (1988) found that when another bystander was present, registered nurses were more likely than college students to offer assistance to an accident victim. When no other bystanders were present, however, a college student was as likely to offer assistance as was a nurse.

Deciding what to do in an emergency situation

FIGURE 10.6 A necessary step in the prosocial sequence is deciding how to provide help. If the bystander doesn't know what to do, there obviously isn't time to turn the matter over to a committee.
Source: The New Yorker, July 16, 1990, p. 37.

"Under new business: Peterson, at Hammond Point Beach, reports that a person in the water is flailing about and calling for help. Peterson wants to know what action, if any, he should take."

Video: Helping and Prosocial Behavior*

DECIDING TO HELP. The final decision in the model is whether or not to act. Among the factors influencing this behavior are the possible costs involved—being rejected by the victim or getting one's clothes dirty, for example. When others are present, additional costs arise, such as making a mistake and appearing foolish. Social blunders can be avoided if the bystanders are able to communicate about what is going on and what to do about it. For this reason, prosocial behavior is less inhibited by the bystander effect if the bystanders are acquainted than if they are strangers (Rutkowski, Gruder, & Romer, 1983).

Another factor that reduces the fear of making a blunder and also increases the tendency to communicate with strangers is the consumption of alcohol. Even a modest amount of alcohol increases the tendency to help, and additional drinking leads to still more prosocial actions (Steele, Critchlow, & Liu, 1985). Steele and his colleagues hypothesized that intoxication causes "cognitive myopia." The inebriated person perceives the victim's need and is unaware of the ambiguities of the situation or of possible negative consequences of providing aid. Steele notes, "Now you may not want the help of a drunk . . . I don't know about the quality of the help you'd get, but they're more likely to do it" (quoted in Kent, 1990, p. 13).

In the research discussed so far, we have emphasized work indicating that helping behavior is affected by aspects of the situation (for example, number of bystanders, ambiguity); temporary influences on the bystander (for example, time pressures, intoxication); and learned skills (for example, medical training, ability to swim). In addition to such variables, individuals differ in more basic personality characteristics that affect the tendency to behave in a prosocial way, as we will discuss in the following **Individual Diversity** section.

THE ALTRUISTIC PERSONALITY: DISPOSITIONAL FACTORS ASSOCIATED WITH HELPING OTHERS

Over the years, despite the demonstrated importance of situational variables, numerous investigations have suggested that some individuals are more altruistic than others. In some instances, altruistic behavior seems to be motivated by other concerns. Certain individuals, for example, have a strong *need for approval,* and they are more likely to provide help *if* they have previously received positive interpersonal feedback for this kind of behavior (Deutsch & Lamberti, 1986). Other research indicates that altruistic motives are important predictors of who will help (Clary & Orenstein, 1991) and that an individual's altruism is probably based on his or her socialization experiences (Grusec, 1991). What exactly are the components of the **altruistic personality?**

Bierhoff, Klein, and Kramp (1991) reviewed the literature and identified a number of possible variables that had been found to be relevant in previous research. The investigators selected several of these personality variables and administered measures to assess their levels in two groups of German citizens. The first group consisted of men and women who had been at the scene of an accident and administered first aid before an ambulance arrived. To obtain such a sample, the investigators asked members of an ambulance team for names and addresses of individuals who had been administering first aid at the scene of an accident when the ambulance arrived. These "first aiders" were sent a questionnaire. They ranged in age from 13 to 65, with a mean of 37.8. The second group consisted of control subjects who reported witnessing an automobile accident but providing no help to the victims. The researchers matched these nonhelpers to the helpers with respect to sex, age, and social

---

In an attempt to identify the factors that make up the *altruistic personality,* investigators compared citizens who witnessed a traffic accident and provided first aid to the victim with citizens who witnessed such an accident and did not provide first aid. As indicated here, five personality characteristics were found to differentiate the two groups. Together these characteristics identify altruistic individuals.

TABLE 10.2 Components of the altruistic personality

Individuals Who Administered First Aid after a Traffic Accident	Individuals Who Failed to Administer First Aid
Were higher in internal locus of control	Were lower in internal locus of control
Believed more strongly in a just world	Believed less strongly in a just world
Felt more socially responsible (were interested in public matters and involved in the community; felt a sense of duty)	Felt less socially responsible
Had higher empathy component in self-concept	Had lower empathy component in self-concept
Were less egocentric	Were more egocentric

Source: Based on data in Bierhoff, Klein, & Kramp, 1991.

---

status. Five of the measures administered to the subjects significantly differentiated these two groups, as summarized in Table 10.2. Social psychologists see the characteristics identified in this study as major components of the altruistic personality. Each characteristic is described below.

First, the altruistic sample scored higher than the control group on a measure of **self-concept encompassing empathy.** A high score on this measure indicates that an individual has rated himself or herself as being responsible and socialized, having self-control, wanting to make a good impression, achieving goals by means of conformity, and being tolerant.

Those who had given first aid to accident victims also scored higher than control subjects in the tendency called **belief in a just world.** Those who hold this belief perceive the world as a fair and predictable place in which good behavior is rewarded and bad behavior punished. In other words, everybody gets what they deserve. The person giving first aid is doing the right thing and will benefit from doing so.

A third variable differentiating the two groups was **social responsibility.** Those who accept the norm of social responsibility—the idea that we should all do our best to help others—are more helpful than those who deny responsibility, believing that it doesn't apply to them.

The fourth characteristic of those who provided first aid was **internal locus of control**—the assumption that you can behave in such a way as to maximize good outcomes and minimize bad ones; in other words, that you are not a helpless pawn at the mercy of luck, fate, and other uncontrollable forces.

 Altruistic individuals: Saving Jews from Nazi persecution

FIGURE 10.7   Current studies of those who provide first aide to accident victims and studies of those who helped protect Jews from Nazi persecution during World War II reveal very similar personality characteristics. Those who are altruistic have an internal locus of control, believe in a just world, feel socially responsible, feel empathic, and are not egocentric.

The altruistic group was *lower* than the control group on a measure of **egocentrism**, or self-absorption. People who are primarily concerned with themselves are often found to be high in competitiveness and less willing to help others. Other research is consistent in finding that people whose social values place an emphasis on cooperation are more helpful than those who stress individualistic or competitive values (McClintock & Allison, 1989).

These five characteristics of the altruistic personality were confirmed in another study of people who helped a quite different kind of victim. Oliner and Oliner (1988) obtained personality data on people throughout Europe who were actively involved in rescuing Jews from the Nazis during World War II (see Figure 10.7). Those who bravely defied the authorities and protected Jews were found to be remarkably similar to those who provided first aid to accident victims.

Altogether, people with an altruistic personality have a strong sense of internal control, a high belief in a just world, a sense of duty, a self-concept involving empathy, and a concern for others rather than an egocentric concern for self. How would you rate yourself on these five dimensions?

INTERNAL AND EXTERNAL FACTORS THAT INFLUENCE ALTRUISTIC BEHAVIOR

We have discussed several variables that affect altruism, including the number of bystanders who witness an emergency, cognitive appraisal and decision making, and dispositional differences in help-related characteristics. Additional factors also affect whether or not altruistic responses will occur: the presence of *role models,* the *emotional state* of potential helpers, and various *victim characteristics.*

ROLE MODELS: PROVIDING HELPFUL CUES

If you are out shopping and pass someone collecting money to help the homeless, provide warm coats for needy children, buy food for those in poverty, or whatever, do you reach in your pocket or purse to make a contribution? One determinant of your behavior is whether you see someone else contribute. People are much more likely to give money if they observe others do so (Macauley, 1970). Even the presence of paper money and coins in the collection box acts as an encouragement to a charitable response.

The presence of fellow bystanders who fail to respond to an emergency inhibits helpfulness, as we have seen. In an analogous way, the presence of a helpful bystander provides a role model and encourages helpfulness. This modeling effect was shown in a field experiment in which a female confederate was parked by the side of a road with a flat tire. Male motorists were much more likely to stop and help if (several minutes earlier) they had observed another woman with car trouble receiving help (Bryan & Test, 1967).

The positive effect of models is not limited to real-life encounters. Television is found to influence viewers in a variety of ways, and altruism is one of them (see Figure 10.8, p. 406). In a study of the effects of TV, investigators showed six-year-olds an episode of "Lassie" that contained a rescue scene, an episode of the same program unrelated to prosocial behavior, or a humorous segment of "The Brady Bunch" (Sprafkin, Liebert, & Poulous, 1975). Afterward, while the sub-

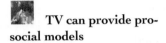

TV can provide pro-social models

FIGURE 10.8 Though television often provides models for undesirable behavior such as aggression, some programs depict prosocial models and are found to increase the likelihood of helpful behavior.

Critical Thinking
Question 10
jects were playing a game in which the winner would receive a prize, they came in contact with some puppies who were whining unhappily. Despite the fact that helping the puppies would decrease their chance of winning, the children who had watched the "Lassie" rescue scene spent much more time trying to comfort the animals than did those in the other two TV conditions.

Other investigators have found that when preschool children are exposed to prosocial programs such as "Mister Rogers' Neighborhood" or "Sesame Street," they are more likely to behave in an altruistic way than children who have not watched such shows (Forge & Phemister, 1987). These studies consistently indicate that television can exert a very positive influence on the development of prosocial responses.

EMOTIONS: EFFECTS OF POSITIVE VERSUS NEGATIVE MOODS

Critical Thinking
Question 6
It might seem obvious that being in a good mood would make an individual more likely to provide help to someone in need and that a bad mood would interfere with altruistic behavior. Research indicates, however, that the effects of mood on helping are somewhat more complicated than that. Other variables must be taken into account before we can predict how mood operates in specific situations (Salovey, Mayer, & Rosenhan, 1991).

POSITIVE EMOTIONS.   Children sometimes wait for their parents to be in an especially good mood before asking for something. They assume that a happy parent is more likely to do something for them than an unhappy one. Research has identified many instances supporting this underlying assumption. When a pleasant mood is created by experiences such as listening to Steve Martin on a comedy album (Wilson, 1981), finding money or being given cookies (Isen & Levin, 1972), or going out on a day when the sun is shining (Cunningham, 1979), the result is an increase in the tendency to assist others in need. Even the presence of a pleasing fragrance in the room increases helping behavior (Baron & Thomley, 1992).

Despite these findings, other investigations have reported *less* prosocial behavior among individuals in a positive mood (Shaffer & Graziano, 1983)—especially when helping is potentially too embarrassing or risky (Rosenhan, Salovey, & Hargis, 1981). An individual experiencing positive emotions is more likely than a less happy person to engage in helpful acts only if these acts are rewarding rather than costly (Cunningham, Steinberg, & Grev, 1980) or if others are present to encourage helpfulness (Cunningham et al., 1990).

The explanation for the inhibition of costly prosocial behavior is that happy people are reluctant to do anything that might spoil their present mood (Isen, 1984). Another factor is that a good mood leads the person to feel powerful (*I can do anything*), and this includes the power to say no to a person requesting help. Figure 10.9 summarizes the findings on the effects of positive emotions on helping behavior.

 Positive emotions can help, or hinder, prosocial behavior

FIGURE 10.9 A positive emotional state sometimes increases and sometimes decreases the likelihood of engaging in prosocial actions. Positive feelings lead to greater helpfulness if social concerns are involved, the consequences of helping are pleasant rather than unpleasant, and the need for help is not ambiguous. Positive emotions result in less helpfulness if the need is ambiguous or if the consequences of helping are unpleasant; under such circumstances, the happy bystander feels sufficiently powerful that he or she can refuse to help.

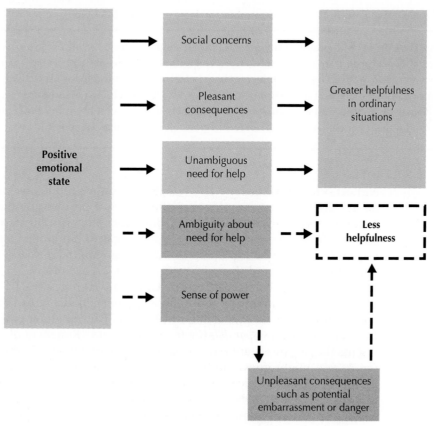

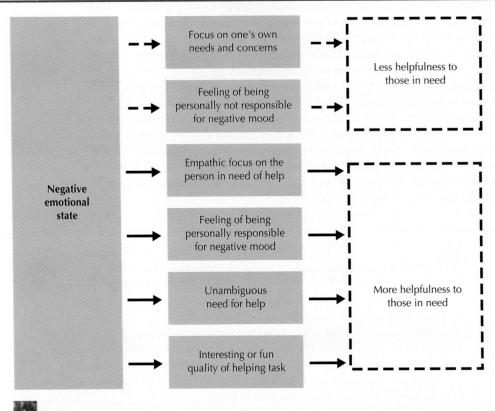

Negative emotions can lead to more, or less, prosocial behavior

FIGURE 10.10 As with positive emotions, negative feelings can foster or inhibit prosocial behavior, depending on specific circumstances. Helpfulness increases if there is an empathic focus on the person needing help, if the potential helper feels responsible for his or her own negative mood, if the need for help is not ambiguous, and if the helping task is interesting or fun. Negative emotions lead to less helpfulness if the person focuses on his or her own concerns and if the potential helper does not feel responsible for the negative mood.

NEGATIVE EMOTIONS.   The effects of negative moods on prosocial behavior are slightly more complex than the effects of positive emotions. Sometimes negative moods increase helping, sometimes they inhibit it, and sometimes they are found to have no effect. When negative emotions increase prosocial responding, it can be explained by the *negative state relief model*—helping makes people feel good, and those in a negative mood are motivated to do anything to make themselves feel better (Cialdini, Kenrick, & Bauman, 1982). Depressed individuals, for example, are especially likely to help if what they have to do to help is interesting or pleasant (Cunningham et al., 1990) and if they feel *personally responsible* for their bad mood (Rogers et al., 1982). We will discuss the negative state relief model in more detail later in the chapter.

As you might guess, helping others is not always a remedy for a negative mood. If you are sufficiently angry or depressed, no amount of helping will make you feel better. Helping as a way to relieve negative feelings is most likely to occur if (1) the required behavior is perceived as relatively easy and effective, (2) it seems clear that the helpful act will lead to more positive feelings, and (3) the negative feelings are not too intense (Berkowitz, 1987).

The effects of negative emotions also have to do with the focus of those emotions. When the potential helper is concentrating on his or her own unhappy circumstances, helping is less likely to occur; helping increases when the focus is on the other person's problems (Thompson, Cowan, & Rosenhan, 1980). These investigators suggested that when attention is directed toward the misfortunes of others, empathy is aroused, and this motivates a prosocial response. This hypothesis was supported by an Australian study of the extent to which help was provided in a real-life emergency. When a destructive bushfire occurred near the city of Melbourne, a sample of the residents described their emotional reactions when they first heard about the fire and about their subsequent helping behavior (Amato, 1986). Those who were upset by the news reports of the plight of the victims (shocked, horrified, sick, etc.) and who felt sympathy for them donated significantly more money to the relief efforts than did those whose reactions were more self-centered (angry at authorities, indifferent, etc.).

The various factors that determine the effect of negative emotions on helping behavior are summarized in Figure 10.10.

Much of the research on prosocial behavior and much of our discussion in this chapter deal with responses to an acute emergency. Eagly and Crowley (1986) point out that in such situations, helping involves short-term encounters with strangers. Because this type of helpfulness is part of the male gender role (see chapter 5), men are found to provide more help than women—and women to receive more help than men. If one assumes, however, that an appropriate female helping role is expressed in long-term, close relationships, this kind of prosocial behavior has *not* been overlooked in the primarily male-oriented research on altruism.

We will now turn, therefore, to research on helping in the context of a long-term commitment to socially responsible activities (Clary & Snyder, 1991). In the following **On the Applied Side** section, we examine prosocial involvement that extends beyond an acute emergency.

Social Psychology: On the Applied Side

AIDS VOLUNTEERISM:
MOTIVATION, HELPING EXPERIENCES, AND CONSEQUENCES

In response to the plight of others, many people regularly contribute their time, skills, and/or money to help those in need (Radley & Kennedy, 1992). Whether in emergencies or in long-term prosocial behavior, the five cognitive steps are relevant. For example, consider a situation in which innocent men, women, and children in a distant country are facing starvation, lack of adequate medical care, and homelessness as the result of civil war or a natural disaster. In order for you to provide any sort of help, you must become aware of the problem (TV, newspapers); make a correct interpretation of the difficulty (the victims need food supplies, money, etc.); decide that you are responsible for helping your fellow human beings; decide what to do (volunteer your time, make a donation);

Critical Thinking
Question 9

and then actually engage in the necessary behaviors. And indeed, according to a Gallup Poll estimate, almost one hundred million Americans engage in some sort of voluntary helping behavior on a regular basis.

An example of a continuing problem requiring help is the HIV epidemic that has developed since 1981, the year in which the Centers for Disease Control reported the first case of a disease that would soon become known as AIDS. In chapter 8 we discussed the extent of the problem and its spread throughout the world. Because there is as yet no effective immunization and no effective cure, society is faced with a tremendous number of people living with AIDS who are in need of immediate help. Volunteers can provide emotional and social support to patients and their families, help with household chores and transportation needs, staff hotlines, raise funds, and become politically active in advocacy groups (see Figure 10.11).

Why do people volunteer to provide such help? Snyder and Omoto (1992a, 1992b) have identified five different basic motivations that lead individuals to engage in this kind of prosocial response to the HIV epidemic. These five underlying factors (listed in Table 10.3) include personal values, the need to understand, community concern, the desire for personal growth,

 Volunteerism: Helping those with AIDS

FIGURE 10.11 Prosocial behavior takes many forms besides responding to a victim in an emergency. Long-term commitment to helping others often takes the form of volunteering to provide needed assistance to those in distress, providing care for those forced to live with the frightening reality of AIDS.

Those who volunteer to help in the AIDS epidemic do so on the basis of five different motivations. Thus, the same overt behavior can satisfy quite different needs. Those who recruit volunteers do best to aim different kinds of recruiting messages to those whose motives differ. Interestingly, recruits who continue such work over time are more likely than those who quit to be motivated by the "self-centered" motives—enhancement of self-esteem or desire for personal development.

TABLE 10.3   Motivations underlying AIDS volunteerism

Motivation for Volunteering to Help in the AIDS Epidemic

1. Personal Values	"Because of my humanitarian obligation to help others"
2. Desire to Increase Understanding	"Because I want to learn how people cope with AIDS"
3. Community Concern	"Because of my concern and worry about the gay community"
4. Personal Development	"I want to challenge myself and test my skills"
5. Enhancement of Self-Esteem	"I want to feel better about myself"

Source: Based on data in Snyder & Omoto, 1992.

and attempts to enhance one's own self-esteem. Thus, people may volunteer to help and engage in identical helping behaviors in response to quite different motives. This also means that those who work to recruit volunteers are more successful when they employ different kinds of messages designed to appeal to each type of motivation.

Transparency 10.5

Though recruitment of volunteers is often difficult, retention is much more difficult—the dropout rate is high. Why do some volunteers continue a pattern of helpful behavior while others do not? Snyder and Omoto (1992) contacted a set of AIDS volunteers, asked them about the details of their work, and then recontacted them a year later. About half had quit during this period. The researchers then interviewed both the continuing volunteers and those who had dropped out. Both groups were satisfied with the work they had done, and both remained committed to the purposes of the organizations with which they worked. One differentiating factor was their original motivation. Those who continued volunteer work were more likely to be motivated by self-esteem enhancement or personal development than those who quit. These "selfish" needs to raise their self-esteem and help their personal development turned out to predict continued helping better than the "selfless" motives.

Discussion Question 3

Another major difference was that those who quit simply perceived the costs as being too high. That is, it took too much of their time *and* they felt embarrassed and uncomfortable about working with AIDS patients. These volunteers seemed to feel that the stigma of the disease might rub off on them. Social rejection based on mere association with stigmatized individuals is known as responding to a *courtesy stigma* (Goffman, 1963). That is, it is as if a sympathetic outsider (the volunteer) becomes a "courtesy member" of the stigmatized group and hence becomes the target of whatever negative stereotypes may be associated with that group.

The findings of research on volunteerism can now be used to make recruiting more efficient. The following **Work in Progress** section describes the ways in which organizations may be able to use these research findings. (Snyder, 1993).

Work in Progress

Practical Implications of Research on Volunteerism

On the basis of their research on AIDS volunteers, Omoto and Snyder (1993) next addressed the practical concerns of organizations that rely on volunteerism. These investigators point out that the research has implications beyond AIDS volunteerism and should be applicable to any volunteer work involving sustained ongoing assistance, emotional cost to the volunteers, the development of committed helping relationships, and beneficial outcomes to both the volunteers and the recipients of their efforts. Examples include working with terminally ill patients in hospices, children in foster homes, elderly individuals with infirmities, and those who are physically or mentally disabled. What does the AIDS research suggest for organizations specializing in such work? Omoto and Snyder (1993) list five basic implications:

1. Recruitment strategies should be targeted to the specific motivations of particular people. For example, a stress on humanitarian obligation should be most successful in recruiting those motivated by value-oriented concerns.

2. Because the volunteers who worked the longest were motivated by self-esteem enhancement and personal development, it might be most efficient to concentrate recruitment efforts on these individuals. Further, such volunteers should be most satisfied with a work environment that provides esteem enhancement along with counseling, feedback, problem solving, and emotional support.

3. An alternative strategy would be to seek people motivated to help specific ethnic or age groups or those motivated by specific humanitarian values and community concerns. Because this kind of volunteer seems to meet his or her needs quickly and then move on, however, a high rate of volunteer turnover could be expected.

4. Organizations should be sensitive in assigning volunteers to activities that match their underlying motivations. A crucial step would be to assess the motives of each individual, using the measures developed by Omoto and Snyder.

5. Motivations sometimes change. Periodic reassessments of volunteers could reveal such changes and suggest ways for the organization to satisfy the newly emerging motivations and thus maintain the commitment of volunteers to continue working.

Altogether, this research suggests that volunteer organizations can strengthen their programs by paying attention to the psychological costs and benefits associated with the work of volunteers.

WHO NEEDS HELP? CHARACTERISTICS OF THE VICTIM

If you were walking down the sidewalk in a large city and noticed a man passed out next to the curb, would you be more likely to stop and help if he wore filthy clothes and clutched a wine bottle next to his stained shirt or if he were neatly dressed and had a dark, swollen bruise on his forehead? The odds are you would be more strongly motivated to help the victim in the second case. Why?

VICTIM RESPONSIBILITY.   A generally accepted social norm is that when anyone runs into difficulties because of his or her own irresponsibility or carelessness, it's up to that person to solve the problem (Schmidt & Weiner, 1988). "You've made your bed, now lie in it." That is one reason why most people would help an unconscious stranger who apparently has been injured but not one who drank enough alcohol to pass out.

As shown in Figure 10.12, a model formulated by Weiner (1980) proposes that we respond with disgust to a victim who is responsible for the problem, and that this reaction does not motivate helping. When the victim is not responsible for the problem, we respond with empathy, which does motivate a helpful response.

Exercise 3

Individuals differ in the readiness with which they assign blame and responsibility to a victim. Thornton (1992) hypothesized that when we encounter a victim, we feel threatened, because we realize that the same misfortune could happen to us. Two characteristic defenses for dealing with this threat are **repression,** in which one avoids or denies the threat, and **sensitization,** in which one thinks, worries, and intellectualizes about the threat (Byrne, 1964). Thornton predicted that those who use sensitizing defenses would be more likely to blame the victim than those who repress. He reasoned that repressors can easily reduce the threat by denying that the problem is serious, forgetting about it, and suppressing their uncomfortable feelings. Sensitizers, in contrast, tend not to deny, forget, or suppress, so they can most easily reduce the threat by blaming the victim.

Critical Thinking Question 3

To test this hypothesis, Thornton (1992) used a questionnaire to categorize undergraduate women with respect to whether they generally responded to threat by repressing or sensitizing. The participants then read about an event in the life of a twenty-year-old unmarried fellow student at their university. One evening she encountered a young man in the campus library and had

 Who is responsible for the victim's plight?

FIGURE 10.12   Weiner's (1980) attributional analysis of helping behavior suggests that perceptions of the cause of the victim's problems have different effects on the emotions aroused by the situation. If the victim is believed to be responsible for the problem, disgust is aroused and help is not given. If, in contrast, the problem is attributed to external circumstances, empathy is aroused and help *is* given.

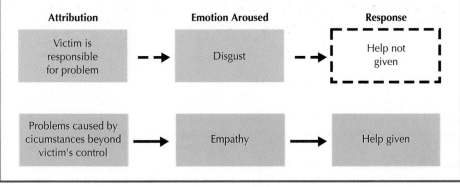

a casual conversation with him. Then—as she was returning to her dorm—the man followed the young student, caught up to her, and raped her. After reading about the assault, participants were asked whether they agreed with statements involving behavioral responsibility ("She shouldn't have walked alone at night," "She shouldn't have talked to a stranger," etc.) and characterological responsibility ("She's the type to get into predicaments she can't handle," "She's too open and trusting," etc.—see chapter 3 for a discussion of such counterfactual thinking). This distinction between behavioral and characterological blame was originally proposed by Janoff-Bulman (1979). In any event, did the sensitizers blame the victim, as predicted?

As shown in Figure 10.13, high sensitizers were most likely to blame the victim in terms of both her behavior and her character, while high repressors

 Blaming the rape victim: Repressors versus sensitizers

FIGURE 10.13 Undergraduate women were asked to read about a fellow student who was the victim of rape. Responsibility was most likely to be attributed to the victim's behavior and character by subjects who usually responded to threat with sensitizing defenses, because those subjects felt threatened and could reduce the threat by blaming the victim. Such victim-blaming attributions were least likely to be made by subjects who responded to threat with repressing defenses (denial, forgetting), because these defenses reduce the threat and make victim-blaming unnecessary.

Source: Based on data in Thornton, 1992.

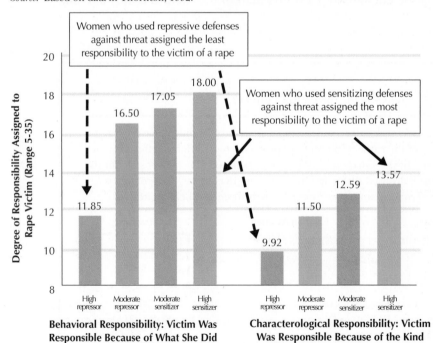

were least likely to assign such blame. The same patterns were evident when the rape victim was an aspiring actress in New York City who talked to a young man in a department store and was raped on her way to a subway; but this actress victim was blamed more than the college student, presumably because it is more threatening to read about a fellow college student who is raped than about a victim less similar to oneself. Consistent with other studies of repression, a follow-up study conducted four weeks later found that repressors remembered less about the rape story than did the sensitizers.

ATTRACTION.   On the basis of the material presented in chapter 7, you might assume that the more we like a person, the stronger our tendency to provide assistance, and you would be correct (Clark et al., 1987; Schoenrade et al., 1986). The variables that increase attraction also increase prosocial responses. For example, help is provided more often for an attractive victim than for an unattractive one (Benson, Karabenick, & Lerner, 1976), and more often for a victim who is similar to the helper than for a dissimilar one (Dovidio, 1984).

WHO ASKS FOR HELP AND HOW DOES IT FEEL TO BE HELPED?

Research on prosocial behavior has focused primarily on the person who provides or fails to provide help, but the victim can also play a central role in an emergency situation.

ASKING FOR HELP.   Earlier in this chapter we saw how ambiguity can inhibit a prosocial response. One way to resolve ambiguity is for the victim to *ask* for help; this makes the need quite clear. But some people find it difficult to ask and thus are less likely to be helped. For example, shy individuals are very reluctant to seek help from a member of the opposite sex (DePaulo et al., 1989). Whether or not a person who needs help actually seeks it also depends on demographic factors—women seek help more than men, the elderly seek help less than young adults, and those high in socioeconomic status make more requests for help than those low in socioeconomic status (Nadler, 1991).

Critical Thinking
Question 4

One reason that some people are reluctant to ask for help is the belief that they will be viewed as less competent if they do so (DePaulo & Fisher, 1980). Interestingly enough, the more the potential helper resembles the person needing help, the greater the reluctance to seek help (Nadler, 1987; Nadler & Fisher, 1986), in part because the similarity emphasizes the incompetence of the one who needs help.

In somewhat more general terms, Nadler (1993) finds that help-seeking can be stigmatizing. He suggests that the act of asking for help touches on a basic human dilemma—the conflict between dependence and independence. Western culture values independence and self-reliance as indicators of personal strength and adequacy. To seek help is to violate those values. An experiment examined people's perceptions of the person who asks for help. Compared to those of high socioeconomic status, an individual from a low socioeconomic background "loses" more by seeking help, because this request seems to confirm the stereotype that such a person is dependent, incompe-

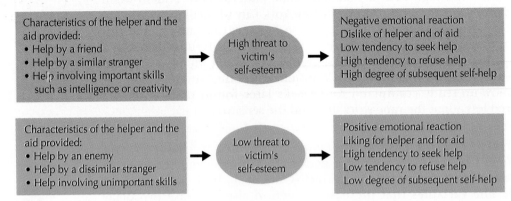

 How do victims respond to being helped? It depends on who helps

FIGURE 10.14 When a victim is helped, he or she sometimes responds negatively and sometimes positively. According to Fisher, Nadler, and Whitcher-Alagna (1982), being helped by a friend on important tasks is threatening, lowers one's self-esteem, and evokes negative emotions, but leads to more self-help afterward. Being helped by a non-friend on an unimportant task is not threatening, does not lower self-esteem, and evokes positive emotions, but leads to less self-help afterward.

tent, and unsuccessful. That effect is moderated by requests that imply independence ("help me because I want to understand what to do") rather than dependence ("help me because I can't do it by myself").

A related reason not to request aid is the realistic assumption that potential helpers may view the victim's emotional response as inappropriate. For example, if a natural disaster occurs but the victim suffers only minor property damage, indications of distress and the need for help are viewed as inappropriate behavior caused by character faults (Yates, 1992).

REACTIONS TO BEING HELPED. Because needing help and receiving it implies a lack of competence, the victim's self-esteem decreases when help is provided, especially if the help comes from a friend or a similar person and suggests that the victim is lacking in important skills and abilities (DePaulo et al., 1981; Nadler, Fisher, & Itzhak, 1983). And when the victim's self-esteem is threatened, the victim responds with negative feelings and dislikes the helper. The only positive result is that the victim is motivated to provide self-help in the future (Fisher, Nadler, & Whitcher-Alagna, 1982). Help by someone who is a dissimilar or disliked other does not threaten self-esteem or evoke negative feelings (Cook & Pelfrey, 1985), but the victim is also not motivated to help him- or herself in the future. These various reactions are outlined in Figure 10.14.

If help from someone like yourself is threatening, how do you suppose people react to receiving aid from a brother or sister? The following **Cutting Edge** section offers evidence relevant to that question.

RESPONDING TO AID FROM A SIBLING

Laboratory research has provided considerable support for the threatening aspects of being helped by similar others, but there has been only limited evidence about the real-life effects of being helped by someone who is actually very much like oneself. Searcy and Eisenberg (1992) obtained just such data with a sample of college students and their siblings.

Because age differences among siblings are perceived as crucial during childhood and adolescence, age tends to be equated with status even after the siblings reach adulthood. Older siblings have higher status, more power in the family, more knowledge while growing up, and so on. So when an older sibling offers help (either in childhood or in adulthood), such behavior is expected; but similar help is threatening if it comes from a younger sibling. Gender is also a crucial variable, in that older sisters tend to help siblings much more than older brothers do, and younger brothers rarely provide help (Brody et al., 1985).

On the basis of such findings, Searcy and Eisenberg (1992) hypothesized that the least-threatening and most-preferred helpers would be older sisters, while the most-threatening and least-preferred helpers would be younger brothers. College undergraduates were asked how they would respond if one of their actual siblings (older or younger, male or female) offered advice, gave emotional support, provided a loan or gift, or acted in some other helpful way. The degree to which the students perceived help from a sibling as threatening was assessed by a measure of defensiveness that included refusal to accept help from a specific sibling and negative attributions about the sibling's motivation in offering help.

The results indicated that help from a sibling often elicited a negative emotional response and defensiveness, especially among those whose self-esteem was low. As hypothesized, help from a sister was less threatening than help from a brother. Also consistent with expectations, the least threat was posed by help from older sisters, whereas help from younger brothers was the most threatening. These reactions were strongly related to the frequency with which an individual would seek help from a given sibling—the greater the threat, the less frequently help was requested.

EXPLANATIONS OF PROSOCIAL BEHAVIOR

As you may have noticed, the study of prosocial behavior repeatedly has raised the question of *why* people help others or fail to do so. Among the many possibilities raised so far are apathy, diffusion of responsibility, altruistic motives, and selfish motives. These concepts have led to detailed theories of prosocial behavior, and we will now summarize some of these contrasting views and the research evidence that provides support for each. To some extent, these different explanations are based on assumptions as to whether human nature is basically selfish or basically selfless (Campbell & Specht, 1985).

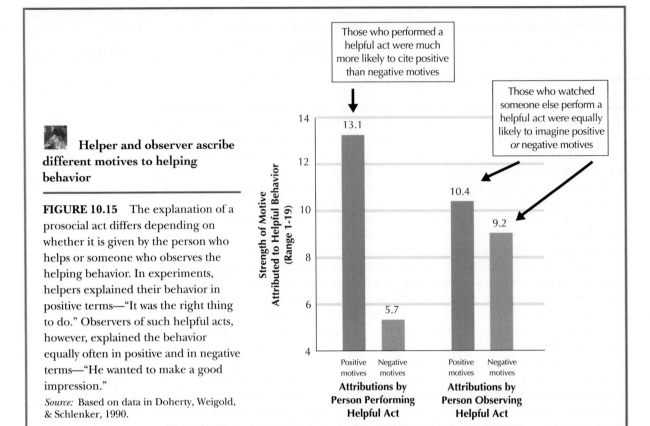

Helper and observer ascribe different motives to helping behavior

FIGURE 10.15 The explanation of a prosocial act differs depending on whether it is given by the person who helps or someone who observes the helping behavior. In experiments, helpers explained their behavior in positive terms—"It was the right thing to do." Observers of such helpful acts, however, explained the behavior equally often in positive and in negative terms—"He wanted to make a good impression."

Source: Based on data in Doherty, Weigold, & Schlenker, 1990.

You might expect people who provide help to attribute their prosocial acts to positive motives ("It was the right thing to do")—and people who observe such helping to be equally likely to assume either positive or negative motives ("He wanted to make a good impression"). To determine whether this difference occurs, Doherty, Weigold, and Schlenker (1990) placed subjects in an experimental situation in which they either helped another subject by sharing some of their winnings or observed someone else provide such help. And in fact, as shown in Figure 10.15, those who helped attributed their own actions to positive motives, while those who observed were equally likely to attribute such behavior to positive or negative motivation. You may remember our discussion of the self-serving bias and other attribution variations in chapter 2. Once again, actors and observers are found to make different attributions.

EMPATHY-ALTRUISM THEORY: UNSELFISH HELPING

Empathy is defined as responding to another person's emotional state with a vicarious emotional reaction that resembles what the other person is experiencing (Eisenberg & Fabes, 1991). For example, an individual experiences distress in response to the distress of others. This appears to be an evolutionarily useful response, and it has been observed in monkeys and apes (Brothers, 1990) and in some children as young as twelve months of age (Ungerer et al., 1990). By the time we reach adulthood, this capacity for empathic concern is a common one, especially if we have grown up in a supportive family in which such reactions are encouraged (Zahn-Waxler & Radke-Yarrow, 1990).

The **empathy-altruism hypothesis,** proposed by Batson and his colleagues (1981), suggests that at least some prosocial behavior is motivated solely by the desire to help the recipient (Batson & Oleson, 1991). Empathy includes feeling sympathetic and compassionate toward the victim (Betancourt, 1990). The individual who expresses sympathy or empathic concern very much wants to have control over the emergency situation and to be able to provide help (Smith, 1992). As outlined in Figure 10.16, when a person perceives an emergency in which help is needed, empathy is aroused, and then helping occurs. If empathy is not aroused and if the person can find a way out of the situation, helping will not occur; if it is difficult or impossible to escape the scene, the person may provide help even in the absence of empathy.

Transparency 10.2

To test this model, Batson and others (Batson et al., 1983; Toi & Batson, 1982) devised an experimental procedure in which they manipulated empathic concern for the victim and ease of escape from the situation. Each participant was informed that he or she would either have to perform a task while receiving random electric shocks while an observer watched on closed-circuit TV, or be the observer while another participant received the shocks. A "chance" drawing was then conducted. The real subject always drew the role of observer, while the other subject (in fact, an accomplice of the experimenter) was to perform the task and be shocked.

Reading: Lesko (30), *Noncompliance with Persuasive Appeals*

As the observation began, the accomplice (who actually was on videotape) pretended to be in pain when shock was given. But she announced that despite having had a traumatic experience with electricity as a child, she could continue with the experiment. At this point the experimenter hesitated and then asked the real subject if he or she was willing to take the victim's place. The experimenter manipulated empathic concern by informing the subject that the

 Empathy-altruism as the motive for prosocial behavior

FIGURE 10.16 According to the *empathy-altruism hypothesis* (Batson et al., 1981, 1983; Toi & Batson, 1982), some prosocial acts are motivated purely by concern about the welfare of the victim. Without feelings of empathy, the bystander escapes from the scene if this can be done easily.

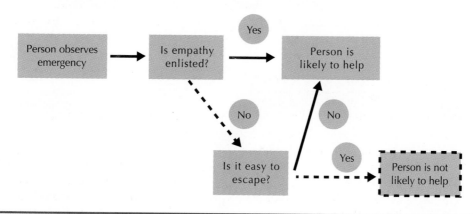

victim had values that were similar to his or her own (high empathy) or very dissimilar (low empathy). The experimenter also manipulated the ease with which the subjects could escape from the situation by informing them either that they could leave after watching only two random shock trials (easy escape) or that they had to watch ten such trials before leaving (difficult escape).

What did the subjects do? When empathy was low and escape was easy, subjects tended to leave rather than engage in prosocial behavior. When empathy was high, subjects volunteered to take the victim's place, regardless of how easy it was to escape. Thus, empathic concern fostered prosocial behavior even when participants could easily have left the situation.

Critical Thinking
Question 5
It is possible, of course, that the altruistic behavior in this experiment was *not* based on empathy. Perhaps the subjects took the victim's place in order to avoid being evaluated negatively by the experimenter and/or the victim (Archer, 1984). But this alternate explanation was rejected on the basis of additional findings by Batson and his colleagues indicating that subjects volunteered to change places with the victim even when they believed that neither the experimenter nor the victim would ever know that they had declined to help.

EGOISTIC THEORY: HELPING OTHERS REDUCES UNCOMFORTABLE FEELINGS

As we indicated earlier, negative moods sometimes increase the likelihood of helping behavior. One explanation for such findings is based on the proposition that altruism may in fact be based on the selfish desire to make yourself feel better (Cialdini, Baumann, & Kenrick, 1981). These investigators offered the **negative state relief model,** as outlined in Figure 10.17. The basic idea is

 Negative state relief as the motive for prosocial behavior

FIGURE 10.17 According to the *negative state relief model* (Cialdini et al., 1973, 1981), prosocial behavior is motivated by a desire to reduce negative feelings (either preexisting or aroused by the victim's problem). Help is given only if the bystander experiences negative emotions, if there is no other way to eliminate such feelings, and if helping *will* eliminate them.

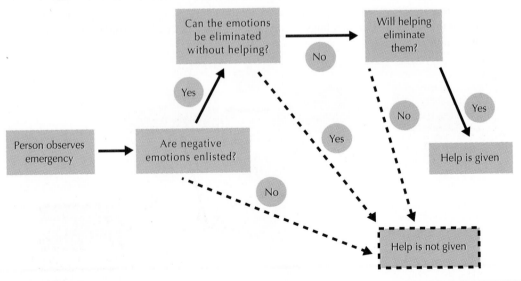

that individuals who are experiencing negative emotions are motivated to help a victim as a way to relieve themselves of such feelings. Also note that it doesn't matter whether the negative emotions are already present when the emergency arises or if they are aroused by the emergency itself. Either way, helping is motivated by desire to make oneself feel better (Fultz, Schaller, & Cialdini, 1988).

In support of this model, Cialdini and his colleagues (1987) provided evidence that when empathy occurs, sadness is also aroused. When these researchers examined the effects of empathy and sadness separately, they found that helping increases when sadness increases, but not when feelings of empathy increase.

The empathy-altruism theorists counterattacked with additional research designed to show that sad feelings were irrelevant. They were able to demonstrate that empathy leads to helping even when study participants know that their unpleasant mood will be relieved by other means—that is, when researchers have told them that they will be engaging in a mood-enhancing experience very shortly (Batson et al., 1989). As is often true with such controversies, the final, conclusive answer is still a matter of debate. To add additional complications, two other models have been proposed.

EMPATHIC JOY:
AN ALTERNATIVE EGOISTIC THEORY

According to Smith, Keating, and Stotland (1989), empathy leads to helping—but not because of a selfless concern for the welfare of others or because helping reduces uncomfortable emotions. Instead, prosocial behavior is motivated by the joy one experiences when observing that someone else's needs have been met. As outlined in Figure 10.18, the **empathic joy hypothesis** states that

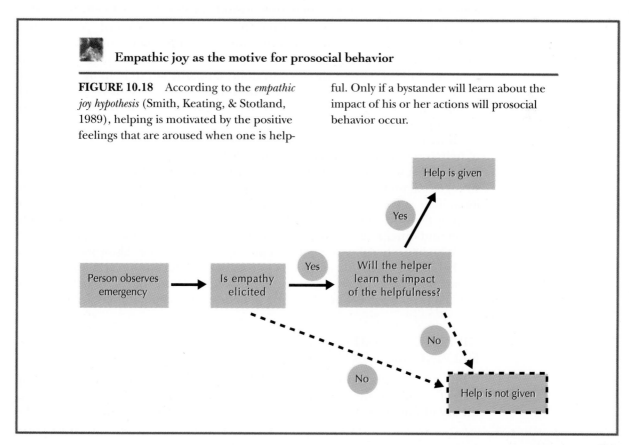

Empathic joy as the motive for prosocial behavior

FIGURE 10.18 According to the *empathic joy hypothesis* (Smith, Keating, & Stotland, 1989), helping is motivated by the positive feelings that are aroused when one is helpful. Only if a bystander will learn about the impact of his or her actions will prosocial behavior occur.

empathy leads to helping, but only if the helper can learn about the results of his or her helpfulness. Without that egoistic reward, empathy doesn't lead to prosocial behavior.

Research indicates clearly that when an individual offers to help someone in need, his or her mood becomes more positive (Yinon & Landau, 1987). In fact, under many conditions, even if an individual is *required* to provide help, positive affect increases and negative affect decreases (Williamson & Clark, 1992). When a person engages in a helpful act, he or she may feel a surge of positive emotion that is known as *helper's high,* and this includes calmness, feelings of self-worth, and a physical sensation of warmth (Luks, 1988). In other words, prosocial activity makes you feel good (Williamson & Clark, 1989).

To compare the predictive powers of explanations based on empathy-altruism, negative state relief, and empathic joy, Smith, Keating, and Stotland (1989) designed an experiment in which they manipulated whether or not the subjects would receive feedback about their helping. The reasoning was that such feedback about the positive effects of helping is necessary for the helper to experience joy; such feedback should be irrelevant if the motivation is purely altruistic or if helping is motivated by the need to reduce negative feelings. These somewhat complicated experimental predictions are outlined in Figure 10.19.

The investigators showed subjects a videotape of a female college student who said that she might withdraw from school because she felt isolated and stressed. The experimental subjects were told that they could offer her advice on how to cope with college life. Half were told that if they gave advice, they would be able to see a follow-up tape on which the unhappy student would provide feedback about how helpful the advice had been; the other half were informed that they would receive no further information about the young woman, whether they gave advice or not. As in other research, the experimenters manipulated empathy by giving each subject information indicating that the young woman was similar to or dissimilar from the subject. Under these conditions, empathy led to helping only when subjects believed that they would find out about the results of their advice giving. The investigators concluded that empathic joy is a necessary component of prosocial action.

If helping others leads to positive feelings, what is the result when an offer of help is rejected? Cheuk and Rosen (1992) designed an experiment in which each subject was assigned the role of "tutor"; after watching a close friend or a stranger fail on two easy tasks, the subject was to offer help. For half of the subjects, help was accepted, and for half it was refused. As expected, rejection of help by the person in need results not only in no help being given but also to anger and other negative reactions on the part of the potential helper.

Whether other theorists will accept empathic joy as the "last word" on prosocial behavior is doubtful, and we can probably look forward to additional experiments designed to test alternative explanations. Meanwhile, a fourth explanation has been offered—one based on genetic factors and natural selection.

GENETIC SELFISHNESS: HELPING SIMILAR OTHERS

While other explanations of prosocial behavior are based on the motivating role of emotions, the **genetic determinism model** is based on a more general theory of human behavior. Rushton (1989) and other evolutionary psycholo-

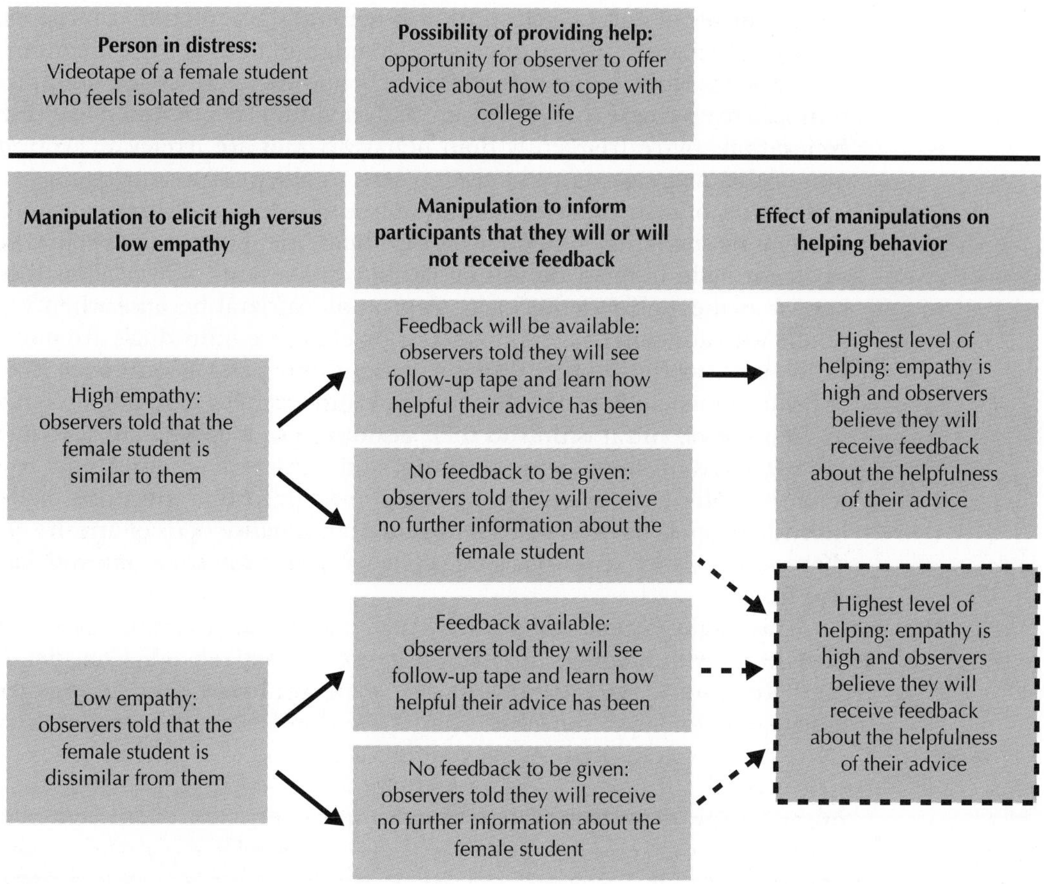

Person in distress: Videotape of a female student who feels isolated and stressed	Possibility of providing help: opportunity for observer to offer advice about how to cope with college life

Manipulation to elicit high versus low empathy	Manipulation to inform participants that they will or will not receive feedback	Effect of manipulations on helping behavior
High empathy: observers told that the female student is similar to them	Feedback will be available: observers told they will see follow-up tape and learn how helpful their advice has been	Highest level of helping: empathy is high and observers believe they will receive feedback about the helpfulness of their advice
	No feedback to be given: observers told they will receive no further information about the female student	
Low empathy: observers told that the female student is dissimilar from them	Feedback available: observers told they will see follow-up tape and learn how helpful their advice has been	Highest level of helping: empathy is high and observers believe they will receive feedback about the helpfulness of their advice
	No feedback to be given: observers told they will receive no further information about the female student	

Comparing empathy-altruism, negative state relief, and empathic joy explanations of prosocial behavior

FIGURE 10.19 To test competing models of altruism, Smith, Keating, and Stotland (1989) created an experimental situation in which an observer had the opportunity to help an unhappy stranger by offering her advice. The experimenters created feelings of high or low empathy by providing information that the stranger was very similar to or very dissimilar from the observer. In addition, some participants were told that feedback about the effects of the advice would be given; others were told that they would receive no feedback. According to the *empathic joy* theory, feedback would be necessary for helping to occur; but feedback would *not* be essential according to the *empathy-altruism* or *negative state relief* models. As the experimenters hypothesized, the highest level of helping occurred in the high empathy plus feedback condition, thus providing support for the *empathic joy* model.

gists propose that many aspects of our behavior are genetically determined and that we are generally unaware of why we do what we do. You may remember that various aspects of this formulation were noted earlier in discussions of prejudice (chapter 6), attraction (chapter 7), and mate selection (chapter 8); and this topic will come up again when we consider aggression (chapter 11).

Critical Thinking Question 7

Exercise 4

As Archer (1991) points out, all such sociobiological concepts are based on the theory of natural selection. It is generally accepted that physical attributes are "selected" for their successful adaptation to the environment in which they have evolved. In an analogous way, behaviors that increase an individual's reproductive success (or **fitness**) are assumed to be represented in subsequent generations more frequently than behaviors that are irrelevant to reproduction or that decrease reproductive success.

Studies of other species such as ants and aphids indicate that the greater the genetic similarity between two individuals, the more likely it is that one will act to provide help to the other (Ridley & Dawkins, 1981). This tendency, known as the "selfish gene," acts to promote survival because when you help others who are genetically similar to yourself, those individuals are more likely to live and to reproduce, thus preserving and passing on genes like yours (Rushton, Russell, & Wells, 1984). For example, siblings are 50 percent similar in their genes, and it is thus to their advantage to help one another survive in order to pass on these genes to future generations. Each individual is unconsciously motivated not only to live long enough to reproduce his or her own individual genes but also to enhance the reproductive odds of anyone else who shares those genes (Browne, 1992). This process is known as **maximizing inclusive fitness.**

This might explain why we are likely to help our relatives, but what does it have to do with helping those to whom we are not related? Consider an analogy. Rushton (1989) argues that we seek out lovers and spouses who are genetically similar to ourselves; that is, we don't mate with random strangers

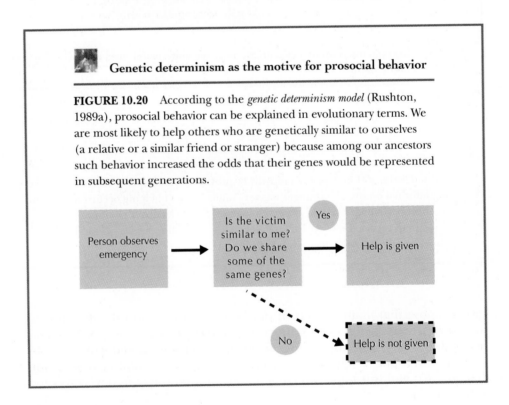

Genetic determinism as the motive for prosocial behavior

FIGURE 10.20   According to the *genetic determinism model* (Rushton, 1989a), prosocial behavior can be explained in evolutionary terms. We are most likely to help others who are genetically similar to ourselves (a relative or a similar friend or stranger) because among our ancestors such behavior increased the odds that their genes would be represented in subsequent generations.

but with a partner who has genes that overlap with our own. As a result, our offspring are more similar to ourselves genetically than if we mated with a genetically dissimilar partner. The same argument holds with respect to a stranger in distress (see Figure 10.20). By helping people like ourselves, we are acting to preserve the genes we have in common.

You may wonder how it is that people can determine who is and who is not genetically similar to themselves. Rushton concedes that there is no clear answer to this question, but he suggests interesting possibilities. First, we are familiar with the appearance and the behavior of our relatives, so we may react positively to anyone who looks and acts like them; if such similarities are genetically based, we probably share some genes with these other individuals. Second, a study of several thousand British and Australian twins indicated that attitudes may in part be genetically determined (Martin et al., 1986). This finding raises the possibility that attitude similarity leads to attraction (see chapter 7) because of genetic similarity; thus, when we help those we like, we are helping to preserve our portion of the gene pool.

Such ideas are intriguing, but they are also quite difficult to test and the subject of considerable controversy. It is usually impossible to provide convincing data that clearly indicate a genetic basis for attraction, mate selection, altruism, and so forth. The argument that we respond to strangers on the basis of genetic similarity is the target of much criticism, because superficial similarities are not necessarily based on common genes (Anderson, 1989; Dunbar, 1989). Some critics make a Freudian argument that we are attracted to those who resemble our parents and that genetic similarity is simply a byproduct of this attraction and not the basic reason for it (Daly, 1989; Gangstad, 1989). A more general problem with evolutionary psychology is that no one can study the behavior of our distant ancestors. Instead, sociobiologists engage in "storytelling" in which past behavior is necessarily imagined on the basis of present behavior—and the resulting accounts of how primitive humans might have behaved is highly influenced by current ideology and current cultural characteristics (Brewer & Caporael, 1990; Caporael & Brewer, 1990). These are all reasonable arguments. A totally unfair criticism, in contrast, is that which denounces all genetic theorizing as racist and politically unacceptable (Gross, 1990).

In reviewing the literature on altruism, Buck and Ginsburg (1991) conclude that there is no evidence of a gene that determines prosocial behavior. Among humans, however, there *is* a genetically based capacity to communicate one's emotional state and to form social bonds. These inherited aspects of social behavior make it possible for us to help one another when the need arises. In other words, people are inherently sociable, and when people interact in social relationships, "they are always prosocial, usually helpful, and often altruistic" (Fiske, 1991, p. 209).

Once again we are left with alternative hypotheses, and there is as yet no final agreement about how best to explain the motivation that underlies prosocial behavior. At the moment, the authors of this book lean toward the negative state relief model, but additional future experiments may well change our minds.

We have discussed several aspects of help-seeking, but it should be added that cultural values also influence whether or not an individual seeks help from others. In the following **Social Diversity** section, we examine societal differences in such behavior.

Help-Seeking in Communal and Individualistic Cultures: Israel and Hong Kong

Cross-cultural comparisons often focus on societies that differ in their emphasis on individual versus communal behavior. At the individualistic extreme on the spectrum, each person strives to be a self-contained unit and seeks success and recognition on the basis of individual achievement. It's every man for himself, every woman for herself. In contrast, communal societies stress interlocking familylike connections in which individuals depend on one another, sharing both hardship and success. It's one for all and all for one. These differences in individualism versus collectivism are also discussed in the **Social Diversity** sections of chapters 8 and 12. Given such differences in outlook, differences in help-seeking behavior might well be expected.

City Dwellers and Kibbutz Dwellers in Israel

Comparisons of behavior in different parts of the world often focus on cultures that differ in a specific way; behavioral differences may be attributed to that particular difference (although the cultures may differ in other ways that may also affect behavior). Nadler (1986) was able to concentrate on citizens of a single nation, Israel, and yet examine the effect of individualistic versus communal living on help-seeking behavior. He points out that his country provides a

unique opportunity for such comparisons because there are both urban dwellers whose environment stresses typical Western attitudes such as self-reliance and individual achievement and kibbutz dwellers whose environment stresses egalitarian-communal ideology (see Figure 10.21).

Based on these cultural differences, Nadler predicted that those living in a kibbutz would expect to be dependent on one another and thus should be willing to seek help when it is needed. This should be an expected and normative way to cope with problems. Those living in a city, however, should view self-reliance as all-important and thus should be reluctant to turn to others for help; as in the studies described earlier in the chapter, these individuals should feel uncomfortable about seeking help.

Nadler asked study participants from kibbutzim and urban settings to imagine a series of everyday situations in which they faced a problem and a potential helper was available; for each situation the participants were to indicate the likelihood that they would actually seek help from the other person. As predicted, kibbutz dwellers indicated more help-seeking than did city dwellers.

Nadler further hypothesized that the type of situation requiring help would also influence help-seeking by the two cultural

subgroups. Some high school students were placed in a situation that involved a group, while others were supposed to be working only for themselves. In other words, they were given a communal task or an individual task. Specifically, subjects worked on anagrams that were supposedly a measure of success at the university; a score would be assigned either to the person's group or to the individual. They were allowed to ask for hints on those anagrams for which they needed help. Again, kibbutz and city dwellers differed. Those raised on a kibbutz were more likely to seek help when the task involved the success of the group, while city dwellers sought help primarily when individual success was at stake.

Thus, it appeared that socialization in different subcultures within Israel resulted in differences in help-seeking behavior. The generality of this finding was further tested, however, as described in the **Work in Progress** discussion that follows this section.

Internal versus External Coping in Hong Kong: Reliance on Self or Others

Though the Chinese culture is often identified as a communal one, Shek and Cheung (1990) have demonstrated that individual differences among Chinese may be as great as differences

Individualistic versus communal cultures affect helping behavior

FIGURE 10.21 In Israel both communal and individualistic cultures are represented (kibbutz dwellers versus city dwellers). Nadler (1986) found that those raised communally in a kibbutz are more likely to seek help than those raised individualistically in a city, especially when the help benefits the group rather than the individual.

across cultures. For example, previous research has found that coping strategies among Chinese citizens include both self-reliance and help-seeking.

Shek and Cheung developed a scale to measure these two different coping strategies in a large sample of Chinese working parents in Hong Kong. The research was conducted through child-care centers, and the subjects were drawn from a wide array of geographic areas and socioeconomic levels within Hong Kong. The investigators asked subjects about their typical responses to various types of stress, including marital stress, family-related stress, interpersonal stress, and work-related stress. Among the possible responses, two basic approaches were to face the problem and devise a solution or to seek help (from spouse, friends, superiors, professionals, fortune-tellers).

The findings indicated wide differences within this "communal culture." The two major subgroups were characterized as differing in *locus of coping*. That is, those who coped with stress by relying on themselves differed markedly from those who coped by seeking help from others. Such results suggest that we sometimes go too far in identifying cultures as representing a particular ideology or set of values when, in fact, each culture contains subgroups of individuals who differ greatly from one another.

As discussed in the **Social Diversity** section, help-seeking behavior appeared to differ in different Israeli subcultures. But could this finding be generalized further? The following **Work in Progress** section addresses that question.

Work in Progress

Help-Seeking by Immigrants from the United States and the Soviet Union

Nadler (1993) points out that different help-seeking tendencies for those raised in a kibbutz versus a city *may* be the result of individualistic versus collectivist social contexts, but that (as in all cross-cultural comparisons) the difference may also rest on other factors. To explore this issue in depth, Nadler decided to extend the research to recent immigrants to Israel from the United States (an individualistic society) and from the former Soviet Union (a collectivist society) and to compare their help-seeking with that of longtime Israeli residents from a kibbutz or from a city.

Consistent with the earlier research, the kibbutz participants were the highest in help-seeking among the four groups. As predicted, those from individualistic cultures (U.S. immigrants and Israeli city dwellers) were significantly lower in help-seeking and not different from one another. The surprise, however, was the fact that immigrants from the collectivist Soviet Union were *lowest* in help-seeking among the four groups.

Why? To answer that question, Nadler and his colleagues turned to Hollander's (1978) study of Soviet citizens. In this study interpersonal trust was found to be a cherished but rare commodity in the Soviet Union. Perhaps people socialized in this society would trust and seek help only from those to whom they felt close and intimate, avoiding such interactions with those outside the small circle of trusted family and friends. Nadler and one of his graduate students are now in the process of testing the hypothesis that former Soviet citizens will show the predicted high level of help-seeking, but only when the assistance would be provided by someone they trust.

This research is an excellent example of the fact that while a hypothesis can be wrong in its original form, unexpected findings can lead to a new and more inclusive formulation.

Summary and Review

Prosocial behavior refers to acts of helping that have no obvious benefit to the person who helps.

Responding and Not Responding to Emergencies

Latane and Darley proposed a decision-making model to predict helping responses in emergency situations. Individuals must make the appropriate decision at each of five steps in order to engage in a prosocial act: attending to the emergency, perceiving that it is an emergency, assuming responsibility, determining what needs to be done, and deciding to provide help. Other research indicates that dispositional factors are also involved, and a combination of characteristics constitutes the *altruistic personality*.

Factors Influencing Altruistic Behavior

Helping behavior is influenced by the presence of helpful models, the potential helper's emotional state, feelings of attraction toward the recipient, and the degree to which the victim is perceived to be responsible for the problem. Not all help involves emergency situations, and long-term volunteering is motivated by both selfless and selfish needs; the latter motivation is a better predictor of who will stick with the hard work of volunteer aid. Some people are more likely to seek help than others. Though receiving help may seem to be a positive experience, it is often uncomfortable and threatening to one's self-esteem. Within families, help-seeking is least threatening when the helper is one's older sister and most threatening when a younger brother provides aid.

Theories of Helpfulness

Several quite different theories have been proposed to explain prosocial behavior, but none has been conclusively demonstrated to be the best predictor. The *empathy-altruism model* is based on the arousal of empathic concern that leads to helping. The *negative state relief model* states that helping is based on the desire to relieve uncomfortable feelings. The *empathic joy model* proposes that helping occurs because it makes us feel good. The *genetic determinism model* explains prosocial behavior on the basis of natural selection.

Social Diversity: Help-Seeking Behavior

Studies in Israel indicate that help-seeking is more likely among individuals familiar with a communal experience (living in a kibbutz) than among those with an individualistic background (living in a city). Also, those raised on a kibbutz were most likely to seek help when the group needed it, while city dwellers were most likely to seek help when they needed it as individuals. Even within a generally homogeneous, communal culture such as Hong Kong, subgroups can be identified who differ in the way they cope with stress. In some people the "locus of coping" engenders self-reliance, while in others it promotes help-seeking.

Key Terms

Altruistic Behavior Acts that suggest an unselfish concern for the welfare of others, sometimes involving risk for the individual who behaves altruistically.

Altruistic Personality The combination of dispositional variables that make an individual more likely to engage in altruistic behavior. Included are an empathic self-concept, belief in a just world, feelings of social responsibility, internal locus of control, and low egocentrism.

Belief in a Just World The tendency to believe that the world is a predictable and fair place in which good behavior is rewarded and bad behavior punished.

Bystander Apathy Indifference on the part of witnesses to an emergency; formerly assumed to explain bystanders' failure to help a stranger in distress. Research indicates, however, that bystanders are often quite concerned by the distress of a stranger; their failure to help is based on quite different factors.

Bystander Effect The finding that as the number of bystanders witnessing an emergency increases, the likelihood of each bystander's responding, and the speed of responding, decrease.

Diffusion of Responsibility The presence of multiple bystanders at the scene of an emergency, resulting in the responsibility for taking action being shared among all members of the group. As a result of diffusion of responsibility, each individual feels less responsible and is less likely to act than if he or she were alone.

Egocentrism The tendency to be primarily concerned with oneself and to hold individualistic and competitive values.

Empathic Joy Hypothesis The proposal that prosocial behavior is motivated by the positive feelings that are aroused when a person helps someone in need.

Empathy The tendency to respond to another person's emotional state with a vicarious emotional reaction that resembles what the other person is experiencing. For example, a person who observes someone in distress may also feel distressed.

Empathy-Altruism Hypothesis The proposal that at least some prosocial behavior is motivated solely by a desire to help the person in need.

Fitness In evolutionary theory, reproductive success and the attributes associated with it.

Genetic Determinism Model The proposal that prosocial behavior is motivated by genetic factors that evolved because they enhanced the ability of our ancestors to survive and reproduce.

Internal Locus of Control The belief that you are not at the mercy of outside forces but can behave in such a way as to make a difference—to maximize good outcomes and minimize bad ones.

Maximizing Inclusive Fitness In evolutionary theory, helping and supporting siblings and other kin; that is, enhancing the reproductive odds of all who share common genes.

Negative State Relief Model The proposal that prosocial behavior is motivated by the desire to relieve uncomfortable negative emotions.

Pluralistic Ignorance A phenomenon that can occur when multiple bystanders witness an emergency: Each interprets the event in part on the basis of what the others do or say, but when none of them is sure about what is happening, all hold back and pretend that everything is all right. Each then uses this "information" to justify not responding.

Prosocial Behavior Acts that benefit others but have no obvious benefits for the person who carries them out, sometimes involving risk for the individual who behaves in a prosocial way.

Repression A characteristic response to threat that attempts to control anxiety by mechanisms such as avoidance, denial, and forgetting.

Self-Concept Encompassing Empathy An individual's perception of himself or herself as responsible, socialized, self-controlled, interested in making a good impression, conforming in order to achieve, and tolerant.

Sensitization A characteristic response to threat that attempts to control anxiety by mechanisms such as approach, rumination, and intellectualization.

Social Responsibility A social norm to the effect that each of us has a responsibility to do our best to help others, taking care of those in need.

For More Information

Clark, M. S. (Ed.). (1991). *Prosocial behavior.* Newbury Park, CA: Sage.

    A review of the current status of research on prosocial behavior, with individual chapters written by those most active in this field of inquiry. Included are such topics as empathy, volunteerism, mood, and help-seeking.

Eisenberg, N. (1985). *Altruistic emotion, cognition, and behavior.* Hillsdale, NJ: Erlbaum.

    Two of the crucial factors determining altruism—emotions and cognitions—are the central focus of this book. Specific topics sinclude sympathy, conceptions of altruism, and moral decision making.

Spacapan, S., & Oskamp, S. (Eds.). (1992). *Helping and being helped.* Newbury Park, CA: Sage.

    This collection of chapters grew out of a symposium at which investigators presented research and theories on helping behavior in daily life. Included are studies of people who donate kidneys, self-help groups, the support of stroke patients by their spouses, and family help for relatives with Alzheimer's disease.

Chapter ELEVEN

Aggression: Its Nature, Causes, and Control

23 questions

Theoretical Perspectives on Aggression: In Search of the Roots of Violence

Aggression As an Innate Tendency / Aggression As an Elicited Drive: The Motive to Harm or Injure Others / Aggression As a Reaction to Aversive Events: The Role of Negative Affect Aggression As Learned Social Behavior

Social Determinants of Aggression: How Others' Actions, or Our Understanding of Them, Influence Aggression

Frustration: Why Not Getting What You Want (and What You Expect) Can Sometimes Lead to Aggression / Direct Provocation: When Aggression Breeds Aggression / Exposure to Media Violence: The Effects of Witnessing Aggression / Heightened Arousal: Emotion, Cognition, and Aggression / Sexual Arousal and Aggression: Are Love and Hate Really Two Sides of the Same Behavioral Coin? / The Effects of Violent Pornography: Aggressive Actions, Hardened Attitudes / Alcohol and Aggression: A Potentially—but Not Necessarily—Dangerous Mix

Personal Causes of Aggression

The Type A Behavior Pattern / Perceiving Evil Intent in Others: Hostile Attributional Bias / Shame-Proneness and Aggression: From Self-Rejection to Hostility and Anger / Gender Differences in Aggression: Are They Real?

The Prevention and Control of Aggression: Some Useful Techniques

Punishment: An Effective Deterrent to Violence? / Catharsis: Does Getting It Out of Your System Really Help? / Cognitive Interventions: The Role of Apologies and Accounts / Other Techniques for Reducing Aggression: Nonaggressive Models, Training in Social Skills, and Incompatible Responses

SOCIAL DIVERSITY ▼ A Critical Analysis
Culture and Aggression: The Social Context of Violence

Special Sections

FOCUS ON RESEARCH: CLASSIC CONTRIBUTIONS—Resolving the Experimenter's Dilemma: Methods for Studying Aggression in the Laboratory

FOCUS ON RESEARCH: CLASSIC CONTRIBUTIONS—The Role of Aggressive Cues: Does the Trigger Sometimes Pull the Finger?

FOCUS ON RESEARCH: THE CUTTING EDGE—Gender Differences in Aggression: The Potential Role of Hormones and Sexual Orientation

WORK IN PROGRESS—Where Hormones and Personality Meet: Effects of Testosterone and Type A Behavior Pattern on Aggression by Males

WORK IN PROGRESS—Training in Social Skills: Maximizing Its Effectiveness

I don't remember how the feud started, but I do vividly recall how much unpleasantness it caused me. I was eleven years old and, for reasons I couldn't fathom, I had a real enemy: Nancy Gordon. Nancy was the smartest girl in the fifth grade, perhaps in the entire school. But she wasn't very popular. Nancy knew she was bright and never missed an opportunity to let other people know it. Further, she was a teacher's pet of the worst kind. She was constantly being held up as a model we should emulate; and she seemed to go out of her way to make the rest of us look bad. No, Nancy wasn't popular. But for some reason she singled *me* out as the chief object of her disfavor. She was always watching me in class so she could report any misdeeds to our teacher, Ms. Kavouti. And she goaded me every chance she got. If I couldn't answer a question in class, she'd remark, voice dripping with sarcasm: *"What's the matter, Bobby, no brain today?"* And because I was one of the shortest boys in the class—much shorter than Nancy—she never missed a chance to rub salt into this sore point. "Maybe you'd better bring along a ladder next time," she'd comment as I returned to my seat after working a math problem on the blackboard at the front of the room. Worst of all, Nancy lived in my apartment building, and she was constantly making fun of my younger brother, who was more than a little clumsy and, because of this, also painfully shy.

One day the situation reached the boiling point. My brother was playing a game with some of the other kids in the building, and for the tenth time that day, he tripped and fell down. Nancy was standing nearby on roller skates with her friend Evelyn and they both began to laugh loudly. "Hey Richard," she shouted with glee, "if you like the ground so much, why don't you go around on all fours like the other monkeys!" When I heard this, I rushed to his defense. Richard was bleeding from bad scrapes on his knees, and tears of frustration were trickling down his face. How could she be so cruel? I ran over and shouted at her: *"Leave him alone, you jerk! Pick on someone your own age!"* Now I was in for it. Nancy turned the full force of her high IQ and biting tongue on me. "Oh look," she said,

laughing cruelly, "they've brought out the midget brigade. I'm so scared I'm shaking!" And then she shook herself in mock fright. I responded as best I could, but as usual she was much quicker than I was and made me look sillier and sillier. But finally I said something that really got through to her: I accused her of being a little Ms. Reynolds. Ms. Reynolds was the principal of our school. She repeatedly showed her disdain for "You bunch of riff-raff," as she described us; she was roundly hated by all the students. That did it: Nancy screeched something incoherent, skated in my direction, and actually spit at me. When she did that, I really saw red. Without thinking, I pushed her—hard. I had forgotten that she was on skates, and never counted on what happened next. Her legs flew out from under her and she fell on her arm. When she got up, she was crying, and she rushed back into

the building. The next day I learned that she had broken her arm.

Oh the shame of it! *I had actually broken a girl's arm!* My friends were merciless: "Here comes Baron the lady-killer," they would shout, or "Hey Baron, beat up any girls yet today?" I was humiliated. Worst of all, my parents took Nancy's part and wouldn't even listen to my explanations about what had happened. They made me go with them to her apartment and apologize to Nancy and her parents— abjectly. And they punished me severely, too. The next six weeks, while she wore the cast on her arm, were among the worst I ever experienced. Even today, almost forty years later, I can still feel a twinge as I recall this incident— my first and only experience with inflicting serious physical harm on a female . . .

The incident described above had a major impact on my life, but it certainly pales into insignificance when compared with events that appear every day on the evening news. Chilling accounts of assault, murder, child abuse, rape; the torture and execution of civilians by armed soldiers in Bosnia, Iraq, and many other locations; ethnic violence in South Africa, several regions of the former Soviet Union, and other locations—the list of human inhumanity seems almost endless (see Figure 11.1). In view of such events, it is clear that **aggression,** the intentional infliction of some form of harm on others, is an important and all-too-common form of social behavior (Geen, 1991). It is hardly surprising, therefore, that it has been an important topic of research in social psychology for several decades (Baron & Richardson, 1994).

Such research has added significantly to our current understanding of human aggression—what it is, why it occurs, and how it can be prevented. In fact, in our view, the social psychological perspective on aggression has been

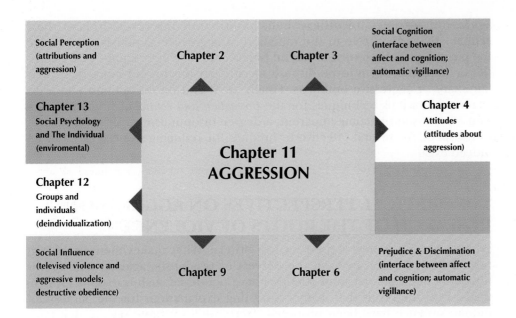

| Social Perception (attributions and aggression) | Chapter 2 | Chapter 3 | Social Cognition (interface between affect and cognition; automatic vigillance) |

Chapter 13
Social Psychology and The Individual (enviromental)

Chapter 11
AGGRESSION

Chapter 4
Attitudes (attitudes about aggression)

Chapter 12
Groups and individuals (deindividualization)

| Social Influence (televised violence and aggressive models; destructive obedience) | Chapter 9 | Chapter 6 | Prejudice & Discimination (interface between affect and cognition; automatic vigillance) |

proven to be a uniquely revealing and, in several important respects, uniquely encouraging one. In order to provide you with an overview of what social psychologists have discovered about human aggression, we'll proceed as follows. First, we'll describe several different *theoretical perspectives* on aggression—contrasting views about the nature and origins of such behavior. Some of these views are mainly of historical interest, but others represent the cutting edge of our current knowledge about aggression and draw heavily on recent advances in other areas of social psychology. Next, we'll review important *social causes* of

Exercise 3

Aggression: An all-too-common form of behavior

FIGURE 11.1 Aggression is disturbingly common. As we'll note in this chapter, however, it is *not* inevitable.

aggression—aspects of others' behavior (or our interpretations of their actions) that play a role in the initiation of aggressive outbursts. To balance the picture, we'll then turn to several *personal causes* of aggression—characteristics or traits that seem to predispose specific persons toward more than their fair share of aggressive outbursts. Finally, we'll end on an optimistic note by examining various techniques for the *prevention and control* of human aggression. As will soon become apparent, a degree of optimism really is justified in this respect, for several effective techniques for reducing overt aggression do indeed exist.

THEORETICAL PERSPECTIVES ON AGGRESSION: IN SEARCH OF THE ROOTS OF VIOLENCE

Why do human beings aggress against others? What makes them turn, with brutality unmatched by even the fiercest of predators, against their fellow human beings? Scholars and scientists have pondered such questions for centuries, with the result that many contrasting explanations for the paradox of human violence have been proposed. Here, we'll examine several that have been especially influential.

AGGRESSION AS AN INNATE TENDENCY

Transparency 11.2

Critical Thinking
Question 1

The oldest and probably best known explanation for human aggression centers on the view that human beings are somehow "programmed" for violence by their biological nature. According to this **instinct theory** of aggression, people aggress because, quite simply, it is part of their essential human nature to do so. The most famous early supporter of this perspective was Sigmund Freud, who held that aggression stems mainly from a powerful *death wish* or instinct (thanatos) possessed by all persons. According to Freud, this instinct is initially aimed at self-destruction but is soon redirected outward, toward others. Freud believed that the hostile impulses it generates increase over time and, if not released periodically, soon reach high levels capable of generating dangerous acts of violence. It is interesting to note that a death instinct was not originally part of Freud's theories. Rather, he added it after witnessing the atrocities and wholesale slaughter of World War I. Freud also suggested that directly opposed to this death wish is another instinct, *eros,* which is focused on pleasure, love, and procreation. The complex relationship between these two powerful forces fascinated Freud, and is reflected in modern research on the potential links between sex and aggression discussed later in this chapter.

A related view was proposed by Konrad Lorenz, a Nobel Prize–winning scientist. Lorenz (1966, 1974) proposed that aggression springs mainly from an inherited *fighting instinct* that human beings share with many other species. Presumably, this instinct developed during the course of evolution because it yielded important benefits. For example, fighting serves to disperse populations over a wide area, thus ensuring maximum use of available natural resources. Further, because it is often closely related to mating, fighting helps assure that only the strongest and most vigorous individuals will pass their genes on to the next generation. Very similar views have been proposed by Ardrey (1976), who contends that because early in the development of our species "we either attacked or starved" (1976, p. 337), our ancestors quickly evolved into a species of hunters. It is our anatomical, physiological, and psychological adaptations to a life as hunters, Ardrey suggests, that underlie our strong and innate aggressive tendencies.

A third perspective suggesting that aggression is at least partly innate is provided by the field of *sociobiology* (Barash, 1977; Buss, 1991; Rushton, 1989). According to sociobiologists all aspects of social behavior, including aggression, can be understood in terms of evolution. Briefly, behaviors that help individuals get their genes into the next generation will become increasingly prevalent in the species' population. Since aggression aids the males of many species in obtaining mates, principles of natural selection will, over time, favor increasing levels of aggression, at least among males. Sociobiologists further contend that since human beings, too, evolved in the context of natural selection, our strong tendencies toward aggression behavior can be understood in this context. Thus, they are now part of our inherited biological nature.

Is there any basis for the views just described? Do biologically inherited tendencies toward aggression actually exist among human beings? Most social psychologists doubt that they do, primarily for two important reasons. First, they note that proponents of instinct views such as those of Freud and Lorenz use somewhat circular thinking. These theorists begin by observing that aggression is a common form of behavior. On the basis of this fact, they then reason that such behavior must stem from universal, built-in urges or tendencies. Finally, they use the high incidence of aggression as support for the presence of such instances and impulses! As you can see, this is questionable logic.

Second, and perhaps more important, several findings argue against the existence of universal, innate human tendencies toward aggression. Comparisons among various societies indicate that the level of at least some forms of aggression varies tremendously. For example, in Norway murder is a very rare event: Fewer than one person per 100,000 is a victim of homicide each year. In the United States this figure is more than eight times higher; but in part of New Guinea, it is almost *eight hundred* times higher! (Please see Figure 11.2.) Such huge differences in the incidence of aggression suggest that aggression is strongly influenced by social and cultural factors, and that even if it is based on innate tendencies, these are literally overwhelmed by other

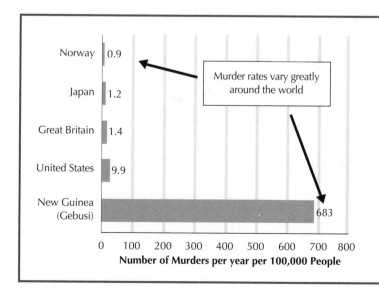

Murder rates vary greatly around the world

	Number
Norway	0.9
Japan	1.2
Great Britain	1.4
United States	9.9
New Guinea (Gebusi)	683

Number of Murders per year per 100,000 People

 Violence: Its rate varies greatly around the world

FIGURE 11.2   As shown here, murder is much more common in some nations than in others.

Source: Based on data in Scott, 1992.

determinants of such behavior. (Please see the **Social Diversity** section at the end of this chapter for further discussion of this issue.)

For these and other reasons, an overwhelming majority of social psychologists reject instinct theories of aggression. This does not imply, however, that they also reject any role of biological factors in such behavior. On the contrary, there is increasing awareness among social psychologists of the importance of biological factors in a wide range of social behavior (Nisbett, 1990). Further, evidence points to the conclusion that some biological factors do indeed predispose specific individuals toward aggression (Gladue, 1991; Mednick, Brennan, & Kandel, 1988). For example, several studies suggest that individuals arrested for violent crimes are considerably more likely than persons not arrested for such crimes to have suffered mild neurological damage during the prenatal period (Denno, 1982; Baker & Mendick, 1984). These and related findings indicate that biological factors do indeed play a significant role in at least some instances of aggression. However, this is still a far cry from the suggestion that human beings possess a universal, inherited instinct toward aggression. Theories such as those offered by Freud, Lorenz, and others, therefore, should be viewed as intriguing but largely unverified proposals concerning the origins of human violence.

AGGRESSION AS AN ELICITED DRIVE:
THE MOTIVE TO HARM OR INJURE OTHERS

An alternative view concerning the nature of aggression, and one that continues to enjoy more support among psychologists, suggests that such behavior stems mainly from an externally elicited *drive* to harm or injure others. This approach is reflected in several different **drive theories** of aggression (e.g., Berkowitz, 1988, 1989; Feshbach, 1984). Such theories propose that external conditions (e.g., frustration, loss of face) arouse a strong motive to engage in harm-producing behaviors. This aggressive drive, in turn, leads to the performance of overt assaults against others. By far the most famous of these theories is the well-known *frustration-aggression hypothesis*. According to this view frustration leads to the arousal of a drive whose primary goal is that of harming some person or object. This drive, in turn, leads to attacks against various targets—especially the source of frustration. Berkowitz (1989) has recently offered a sophisticated revision of this hypothesis; we'll consider it in detail in a later section.

Because they suggest that external conditions rather than innate tendencies are crucial in the occurrence of aggression, drive theories seem somewhat more optimistic about the possibility of preventing such behavior than instinct theories. Since being frustrated or thwarted in various ways is a common aspect of everyday life, however, drive theories, too, seem to leave us facing continuous—and often unavoidable—sources of aggressive impulses.

AGGRESSION AS A REACTION TO AVERSIVE EVENTS:
THE ROLE OF NEGATIVE AFFECT

Transparency 11.5

Think back over occasions when you have behaved in an aggressive manner. Now, try to remember how you felt at those times. The chances are good that you will recall feeling upset or annoyed. In short, you probably were experiencing some type of *negative affect* in situations where you aggressed against others. This relationship between negative, unpleasant feelings and overt aggression serves as the basis for a third theoretical perspective on aggression, sometimes known as the **cognitive neoassociationist** view (Berkowitz, 1984, 1988). According to this theory, exposure to aversive events (ones we prefer to avoid) generates negative affect (unpleasant feelings). These feelings, in turn, automatically activate tendencies toward both aggression and flight (efforts to escape from the unpleasant situation), as well as physiological reactions and thoughts or memories related to such experiences. Whether overt aggression then follows depends on several factors, such as higher levels of thought and cognition. For example, consider a woman shopping in a supermarket who is bumped by another shopper's cart. This experience is painful, and the shopper reacts with tendencies toward aggression, plus thoughts and memories related to similar unpleasant events. Then the other shopper apologizes profusely, explaining that she lost her footing on a wet spot on the floor. At this point the angry shopper reappraises the situation and decides that the incident was truly an accident. As a result her anger subsides, and aggression is unlikely.

Considerable evidence offers support for the accuracy of this theory. Individuals exposed to a wide range of unpleasant, aversive events do tend to behave more aggressively than persons not exposed to such conditions, even when their aggression cannot possibly eliminate the causes of such negative affect (Berkowitz, 1989). Further, negative affect, induced in several different ways, encourages aggressive thoughts and memories (e.g., Rule, Taylor, & Dobbs, 1987). Thus, the cognitive neoassociationist theory seems to offer important insights into the origins and nature of aggressive behavior. Unfortunately, unpleasant events, and the negative affect they generate, are an all-too-common part of daily life. Thus, this modern approach is similar to earlier ones in at least one respect: It too suggests that instigations to aggression, if not aggression itself, are an ever-present fact of life.

AGGRESSION AS LEARNED SOCIAL BEHAVIOR

Yet another important perspective on aggression, the **social learning view,** is more of a general framework than a fully developed theory. This approach (Bandura, 1973; Baron & Richardson, 1994) emphasizes the fact that aggression, like other complex forms of social behavior, is largely *learned*. Human beings, this perspective contends, are *not* born with a large array of aggressive responses at their disposal. Rather, they must acquire these in much the same way that they acquire other complex forms of social behavior: through direct experience or by observing the behavior of others (i.e., social models; Bandura, 1973). Thus, depending on their past experience, people in different cultures learn to attack others in contrasting ways—by means of kung fu, blowguns, machetes, or revolvers. But this is not all that is learned where aggression is concerned. Through direct and vicarious experience, individuals also learn (1) which persons or groups are appropriate targets for aggression, (2) what actions by others either justify or actually require aggressive retaliation, and (3) what situations or contexts are ones in which aggression is either appropriate or inappropriate.

In short, the social learning perspective suggests that whether a specific person will aggress in a given situation depends on a vast array of factors, including that person's past experience, the current reinforcements associated with aggression, and many variables that shape the person's thoughts and perceptions concerning the appropriateness and potential effects of such behavior (refer to Figure 11.3, p. 440). Since most if not all of these factors are open

Video: *Aggression**

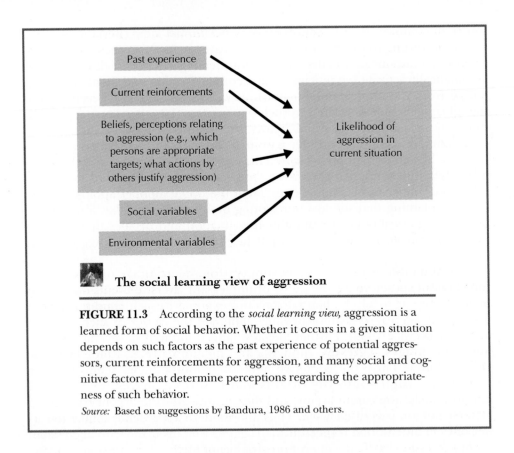

The social learning view of aggression

FIGURE 11.3 According to the *social learning view,* aggression is a learned form of social behavior. Whether it occurs in a given situation depends on such factors as the past experience of potential aggressors, current reinforcements for aggression, and many social and cognitive factors that determine perceptions regarding the appropriateness of such behavior.

Source: Based on suggestions by Bandura, 1986 and others.

to change, the social learning approach is quite positive with respect to the possibility of preventing or controlling overt aggression. Indeed, it is more encouraging in this respect than any of the other views we have considered.

SOCIAL DETERMINANTS OF AGGRESSION: HOW OTHERS' ACTIONS, OR OUR UNDERSTANDING OF THEM, INFLUENCE AGGRESSION

Think back to the last time you lost your temper. What made you "lose your cool?" The chances are quite good that your anger, and any subsequent aggression, stemmed from the actions of another person. In fact, when asked to describe situations that made them angry, most persons refer to something another person said or did—something that caused them to become upset and to view aggression against this person as justified (Torestad, 1990). They are much less likely to mention purely physical events, such as a flat tire, bad weather, or the like. In short, aggression often stems from various *social* conditions that either initiate its occurrence or increase its intensity. As you can probably guess, many factors play a role in this regard. We'll examine several of these below.

Before doing so, however, we will first consider a closely related question: *How can human aggression—especially physical aggression—be studied in a systematic manner without the risk of harm to the persons involved?* We will consider this question in the **Classic Contributions** section below, for from this point on, we'll be discussing specific studies designed to investigate various aspects of aggression. In order to understand the findings of these studies, it is crucial that you know something about the methods they employ and the ethical issues involved in their use.

Focus on Research: Classic Contributions

RESOLVING THE EXPERIMENTER'S DILEMMA: METHODS FOR STUDYING AGGRESSION IN THE LABORATORY

Researchers wishing to investigate human aggression under carefully controlled conditions face the following paradox. On the one hand they wish to study a form of behavior that is by definition potentially dangerous. On the other, they cannot expose the participants in their research to the risk of harm. How can this dilemma be resolved? Methods for doing so emerged in the 1960s. The basic reasoning behind these techniques was as follows: Why not inform research participants that they can harm another person in some manner when in fact they cannot? To the extent that participants accept such information, their intentions to inflict harm on others can then be studied without any risk of actual harm to the supposed victim. Since aggression is generally defined as involving intentional harm to others, these procedures may well capture the essence, if not the precise form, of aggression in many real contexts. Several different variations on this basic approach were soon developed (e.g., Berkowitz, 1962). The two that quickly gained widest use, however, were procedures devised by Arnold Buss (1961) and Stuart Taylor (1967).

Critical Thinking Question 2

In the approach devised by Buss, participants are informed that they are taking part, along with another person, in a study concerned with the effects of punishment on learning. They are further told that one of the two persons present will serve as a *teacher* and the other as a *learner*. The teacher (always the actual subject) will present various materials to the learner (who is actually an accomplice). On occasions when the learner makes a correct response, the teacher is to reward him or her by indicating that this person's response has been correct. Whenever the learner makes an error, however, the teacher will punish this person by means of electric shock. These shocks are delivered by means of a device similar to the one shown in Figure 11.4, p. 442 (often known in social psychology as an **aggression machine**) and can vary in strength from very mild to quite intense. The higher the number on each button, the stronger the supposed shock to the learner. To convince subjects that the apparatus actually works, the experimenter then lets them feel mild sample shocks from several of the buttons.

During the course of the session, the learner (accomplice) makes many errors, thus providing participants with numerous opportunities on which to deliver electric shocks (or, in more recent studies, other unpleasant stimuli such as loud noises or heat; Baron, Russell, & Arms, 1985; Gustafson, 1989). Since any shock, even the mildest one, is sufficient to inform the learner that he or she has made an error, the strength of the shocks subjects actually

The aggression machine: One technique for studying aggression in the laboratory

FIGURE 11.4 Equipment such as this is often used to study aggression under controlled—and relatively safe—laboratory conditions. Researchers inform participants that they can deliver electric shocks (or some other form of aversive stimuli) to another person by pushing buttons on the apparatus. The higher the number on the button, the stronger the supposed shocks. In fact, the "victim" is an accomplice who never receives any unpleasant stimuli.

choose to deliver provides a measure of aggression—their willingness to inflict harm or injury on the accomplice. A second index of aggression is the length of time subjects depress each button—the duration of their assault against the victim. Please note: The *accomplice never actually receives any shocks.* Rather, subjects are simply led to believe that shocks are being delivered.

If these procedures remind you of the ones used by Milgram to study destructive obedience (see chapter 9), you are correct: The two approaches are quite similar. There is one crucial difference, however. In Milgram's research, subjects were *ordered* to push buttons of increasing "shock" strength. Thus, their actions reflected their willingness to obey such orders. In research using Buss's procedures, in contrast, subjects are free to select any buttons they wish. Thus, their actions reflect (presumably) their own desire to harm the learner.

A second popular technique for studying human aggression under controlled laboratory conditions was devised by Taylor (1967). In this procedure, participants are told that they will be competing with another person in a *competitive reaction time task.* On each trial, participants and another person (who is generally an accomplice of the researcher) set the level of shock their opponent will receive if she or he loses in the competition—that is, if she or he responds more slowly. There are generally ten levels of shock, and the highest one is set equal to the participant's pain threshold, the level of shock they find to be definitely unpleasant. During the competition, participants are informed that they have lost on a number of occasions (usually 50 percent of the trials); thus, they actually receive shocks ostensibly set for them by their opponent. Aggression is measured in terms of the level of shock participants set for their opponent—the level *this* person will receive if she or he loses on a given trial. A key advantage of the Taylor procedure is that in contrast to conditions in the Buss approach, the participant's victim (the accomplice) is not a helpless target: This person can retaliate if he or she is attacked by participants. On the other hand, a serious drawback is that in these procedures, participants actually receive unpleasant (though harmless) electric shocks from their opponent.

Both the Buss and Taylor procedures are relatively safe—they minimize the potential risk to research participants. But do they really provide a valid means for studying aggression? Some critics have argued that most participants don't accept the notion that they can really hurt the victim. Consequently, all that is measured by these procedures is their tendency to push various buttons on the apparatus; aggressive intent is totally missing from their actions. In response to their suggestions, researchers who use these procedures call attention to several points. First, they mention studies indicating that people with a prior history of violent behavior often choose stronger levels of shock (or heat or noise) than persons without such a history (e.g., Gully & Dengerink, 1983; Wolfe & Baron, 1971). Second, they note that subjects participating in such studies often *do* believe that they can harm the supposed victim in some manner (Berkowitz & Donnerstein, 1982). To the extent this is so, subjects' behavior can be viewed as aggressive in nature: It stems from conscious intentions to inflict discomfort on another person. Third, researchers note that subjects who have been angered or frustrated by the accomplice generally deliver stronger attacks against this person than those who have not (e.g., Baron & Richardson, 1994).

Together, these arguments provide some basis for assuming that the methods described above do measure aggression or aggressive intent. Certainly they are far from perfect; a great deal of "noise" can enter the picture and distort (or even potentially invalidate) experimental results. Still, if used with care, caution, and numerous safeguards, they do seem to provide at least a rough index of the central concept we wish to measure: people's willingness to inflict harm—physical or otherwise—on another human being.

Transparency 11.3

FRUSTRATION: WHY NOT GETTING WHAT YOU WANT (AND WHAT YOU EXPECT) CAN SOMETIMES LEAD TO AGGRESSION

Suppose that you asked twenty people you know to name the single most important cause of aggression. How would they reply? The chances are good that a majority would answer, *frustration*. And if asked to define frustration, many would state, "The way I feel when something prevents me from getting what I want to get and expect to get in some situation." In short, many persons would indicate that in their experience, aggression often stems from interference with their efforts to reach various goals.

The widespread acceptance of such views stems, at least in part, from the famous **frustration-aggression hypothesis,** first proposed by Dollard and his colleagues more than fifty years ago (Dollard et al., 1939). In its original form, this hypothesis made the following sweeping assertions: (1) Frustration *always* leads to some form of aggression, and (2) aggression *always* stems from frustration (Dollard et al., 1939). In short, the theory held that frustrated persons always engage in some type of aggression and that all acts of aggression, in turn, result from frustration. Bold statements like these are always appealing—they are intellectually stimulating if nothing else. But growing evidence suggests that both portions are also far too sweeping in scope to be accurate.

First, it is now clear that frustrated individuals do not always respond with aggressive thoughts, words, or deeds. On the contrary, they show a wide variety of reactions to frustration, ranging from resignation and despair on the one hand to attempts to overcome the source of their frustration on the other.

Second, it is also apparent that *not* all aggression results from frustration. People aggress for many different reasons and in response to many different factors. For example, professional boxers hit and sometimes seriously injure others because it is their role to do so and because they wish to win valued prizes—not because of frustration. Similarly, during time of war, many pilots report that flying their planes is a source of intense pleasure, and that they bomb and strafe enemy targets while feeling elated, not frustrated. In these and many other cases, aggression definitely stems from factors other than frustration.

In view of these considerations, few social psychologists now accept the idea that frustration is the only, or even the most important, cause of aggression. Instead, most believe that it is simply one of a host of different factors that can potentially lead to aggression. Along these lines, Berkowitz (1989) has recently proposed a revised version of the frustration-aggression hypothesis that seems consistent with a large amount of existing evidence. According to this view, frustration is an aversive, unpleasant experience, and frustration leads to aggression because of this fact. In short, frustration sometimes produces aggression because of the basic relationship between negative feelings and aggressive behavior we described earlier in this chapter.

These suggestions seem to be quite straightforward, and they contribute much to our understanding the role of frustration in aggression. In particular, they help explain why *unexpected* frustration and frustration that is viewed as *illegitimate* (e.g., the result of someone's whims or hostile motives) produce stronger aggression than frustration that is expected or viewed as legitimate. Presumably this is so because unexpected and illegitimate frustration generates stronger negative feelings than that which is expected or legitimate.

Critical Thinking
Question 3
Going farther, Berkowitz (1989) also explains why frustration, even when strong, unexpected, and illegitimate, does not always lead to aggression. He notes that the negative feelings generated by frustration do initially produce tendencies toward aggression; but these tendencies are soon modified by higher-level cognitive processes. Individuals who have been frustrated may examine the nature of their feelings, attempt to understand *why* they have experienced frustration, consider the relative appropriateness of aggression and other possible reactions, and engage in efforts to control their anger or annoyance. Given the unpredictable outcome of these processes, it is hardly surprising that frustration does not always lead to aggression.

In sum, frustration is indeed one potential cause of overt aggression (Gustafson, 1989). It is certainly not the only cause behind such behavior, however, and is not necessarily the strongest or most important cause. Thus, it does not play the very central role in human aggression that many people seem to assume.

DIRECT PROVOCATION: WHEN AGGRESSION BREEDS AGGRESSION

Imagine the following scene: One morning you hand in an important report that your boss had asked you to write. That afternoon she storms into your office, throws the report onto your desk, and says, "Where did you ever learn to write? I've seen better from my eight-year-old son!" After this she continues, disparaging your report in every conceivable way. How do you react? If you are like most people, you probably make excuses or just stand there sullenly; after all, she's the boss, and there's not much else you can do. But all the while she is attacking your work, you are thinking such thoughts as "Who does she think she is?" "How dare she speak to me like that?" and "Just wait—I'll get even for this!"

This incident illustrates an important point about aggression: Often, it is the result of verbal or physical **provocation** from others. That is, when we are the victims of some form of aggression from others, we rarely "turn the other cheek"—at least not if we can help it. Instead, we tend to reciprocate, returning as much aggression as we have received, or perhaps slightly more. Many studies have provided evidence for such effects (Dengerink, Schnedler, & Covey, 1978; Ohbuchi and Ogura, 1984). In all these investigations, individuals provoked either verbally or physically by others tended to retaliate in kind. In fact, as we just noted, their reactions to such provocation were often stronger than the provocations themselves. This finding helps explain why aggression often spirals upward from mild taunts to stronger insults, and from pushing or shoving to kicks, blows—or worse (see Figure 11.5).

Exercise 1

 Aggression: The dangerous spiral upward

FIGURE 11.5 Aggression often begins with the trading of verbal provocations—taunts, insults. But it may quickly escalate into physical violence.
Source: King Features Syndicate, 1990.

But what actions by others, precisely, serve as direct provocation? A study by Torestad (1990) provides some intriguing answers. Torestad asked teenagers to describe situations in which they became angry, then analyzed the more than 900 situations described to determine whether basic patterns could be uncovered. In fact, these were readily apparent. As shown in Table 11.1, participants in the study indicated that they were frequently angered by certain kinds of actions by others. At the top of the list was what might be described as *unreasonable* or *opinionated* behavior by others: instances in which other persons disagreed with participants' views and would not listen to reason in this respect. A close second was actions by others in which they unfairly *blamed* or *slandered* the participant. Among other types of behaviors that participants found to be anger- and aggression-provoking were direct insults, thoughtless or inconsiderate actions by others, teasing, nagging, and physical assault or harassment. Examples of these potential causes of anger and aggression are presented in Table 11.1

COGNITIVE FACTORS AND REACTIONS TO PROVOCATION.   While reactions to direct provocation from others generally follow the rule of *reciprocity,* it is important to note that this is not always the case. Several factors seem to determine whether, and to what extent, individuals choose to overlook provocation or to respond to it in kind. Perhaps the most important of these factors is the *perceived intentionality* of such provocation. When individuals conclude that provocation from another person was *intended*—purposely performed—they generally become quite angry and engage in strenuous efforts to reciprocate. If, instead, they conclude that provocation was *unintended*—the result of accident or factors beyond others' control—they are much less likely to lose their temper and behave aggressively. In short, *attributions* concerning

When asked to describe events that make them angry, individuals generally list ones that fall into the major categories shown here.

TABLE 11.1   Causes of anger

Category of Anger-Provoking Events	Example
Unreasonable Behavior	I say something I know is true but nobody believes me.
Unfair Blame, Slander	I am blamed for doing something I haven't done.
Direct Insults	Someone insults me and it is unjustified.
Thoughtless Behavior	People in high positions abuse their power.
Teasing	I am teased about my appearance.
Thwarted Plans	My parents don't allow me to go out in the evening.
Nagging, Yelling	Somebody takes his bad mood out on me.
Physical Harassment	My brother hits me without cause.
Frustration (Environmental)	I go to see a film listed in the paper, but when I get there it isn't playing.
Assaults on Belongings	Something I own is stolen or damaged.

Source: Based on data from Torestad, 1990.

the causes behind provocative actions by others play a key role in determining our reactions to them.

Evidence for the importance of attributions in determining response to provocation is provided by several experiments (e.g., Kremer and Stephens, 1983). The results of these studies suggest that when provoked or angered by another person, we do not always automatically dish out what we have received; Sometimes this is the case, but often our reactions reflect our interpretations of the *causes* behind provocative actions. As is true in many other contexts, therefore, our behavior toward others is strongly determined by our thoughts about them.

Transparency 11.4

Exercise 2

EXPOSURE TO MEDIA VIOLENCE:
THE EFFECTS OF WITNESSING AGGRESSION

List five films you have seen in recent months. Once you have formulated this list, answer the following question: How much aggression or violence did each of these films contain? How often did characters in these movies hit, shoot at, or otherwise attempt to harm others? Unless your moviegoing habits are somewhat unusual, you probably recognize that many popular films contain a great deal of violence—much more, we hope, than you will ever see in your real life. The fact that many films, television shows, and even televised sports events have a great deal of aggressive content has led social psychologists and others to pose the following question: Does exposure to a steady diet of such materials have any effect upon behavior of viewers? This is an important question, so it is not surprising that it has been the subject of literally hundreds of research projects. The findings of these studies have not been entirely consistent; indeed, given the complexity of the issues addressed, this is only to be expected. However, taken together, they point to the following conclusion: *Exposure to media violence may in fact be one factor contributing to high and rising levels of violence in the United States and elsewhere.*

EVIDENCE FOR THE EFFECTS ON AGGRESSION OF MEDIA VIOLENCE. Several different lines of research, conducted in very different ways, are consistent with the interpretation stated above. First, this interpretation is supported by many short-term laboratory studies. In the earliest of these investigations, Bandura, Ross, and Ross (1963) exposed young children to one of two short films. In one film, an adult model aggressed in various ways against an inflated toy clown known as a Bobo doll (e.g., she sat on the toy and punched it repeatedly in the nose). In the other, the same model behaved in a quiet and nonaggressive manner. Later the children in both groups were allowed to play freely in a room containing many toys, including a Bobo doll and other toys used by the model. Observations of the children's behavior revealed that those who had seen the model behave aggressively were much more likely to attack the Bobo doll than those who had not witnessed such behavior. These findings suggest that even very young children can acquire new ways of aggressing against others through exposure to filmed or televised violence.

In subsequent laboratory studies, subjects viewed actual television programs or films and were then given an opportunity to attack (supposedly) a real victim rather than an inflated toy (e.g., Liebert & Baron, 1972). Once again, results were the same: Participants in such studies (both children and adults) who witnessed media violence later demonstrated higher levels of

Reading; Lesko (32), *Transmission of Aggression*

aggression than participants who were not exposed to such materials (Josephson, 1987; Liebert, Sprafkin, & Davidson, 1989).

Additional and in some ways even more convincing evidence for the aggression-enhancing impact of media violence has emerged from a wide range of *field studies* conducted under more realistic conditions. Some of these investigations have used experimentation to examine the effects of prolonged exposure to media violence (e.g., Leyens et al, 1975; Parke et al., 1977). In these studies investigators exposed groups of children to contrasting amounts of media violence, and then observed the children's overt levels of aggression in natural situations (e.g., Leyens et al., 1975; Parke et al., 1977). Again, results indicated that youngsters exposed to violent movies or programs demonstrate higher levels of aggression than those exposed to nonviolent materials.

Other field studies, in contrast, have employed *systematic observation* (the correlational method) to study this issue. For example, consider a study conducted by Black and Bevan (1992). These researchers approached persons waiting on line to see either violent movies or ones lacking in violent content and asked them to complete a brief questionnaire designed to measure the tendency to engage in aggressive behavior. Other moviegoers were asked to complete the same questionnaire as they left the theater. Results were both revealing and unsettling. First, they indicated that, as the researchers predicted, scores on the aggression scale were higher among those who had just seen a violent movie than they were among persons waiting to see such films. In contrast, a similar increase in reported aggression did *not* occur among persons who watched nonaggressive movies (see Figure 11.6). Second, individuals waiting to see the violent films scored higher on the aggression scale than

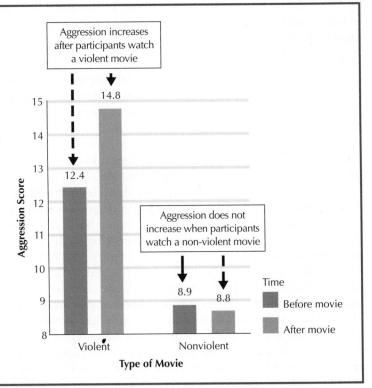

The effects of media violence: A field study

FIGURE 11.6 Persons who had just seen a violent film scored higher on a measure of aggressive tendencies than those who had just seen a nonviolent film. In addition, those waiting to see a violent film scored higher than those waiting to see a nonviolent one.
Source: Based on data from Black & Bevan, 1992.

those waiting to see the nonviolent films. As noted by Black and Bevan (1992, pp. 42–43), these findings, taken together, suggest "not only that films featuring violence attract an audience with a propensity for aggression, but that viewing the film further heightens this tendency."

At this point we should note that similar effects have also been observed among people who view aggressive sports events (Russell, 1981). Many sports involve actions by players that can be described as aggressive in nature—sports such as football, hockey, and boxing, to name just a few. And exposure to such sports does seem to increase aggression among viewers and fans (e.g., Russell, 1981). Indeed, growing evidence suggests that even sentences or words that bring aggressive sports to mind may serve to *prime* aggressive cognitions and so increase individuals' tendencies to perceive others as hostile (e.g., Wann & Branscombe, 1990).

Finally, other investigators have conducted long-term studies in which the amount of media violence watched by individuals as children is related statistically to their rated levels of aggression several years—or even decades—later (e.g., Eron, 1982; Huesmann, 1982). Once again, results indicate that these two variables are indeed related: The more media violence individuals watch as children, the higher their rated levels of aggression as adults.

At this point we should insert an additional note of caution: Not all findings obtained to date have been consistent with the view that exposure to media violence (or participation in aggressive video games) increases actual aggression (Freedman, 1984). Further, the evidence for relatively short-term effects of viewing violence are more firmly established by research evidence than the potential long-term effects of such experience. Still, taken as a whole, existing evidence does seem to offer at least moderately strong support for the conclusion that exposure to media violence can contribute, along with many other factors, to the occurrence of aggressive behavior (Wood, Wong, & Chachere, 1991).

Critical Thinking Question 4

The fact that exposure to media violence can facilitate similar behavior among viewers is, by itself, somewhat unsettling. Perhaps even more disturbing, however, is evidence pointing to the conclusion that even inanimate objects can sometimes encourage dangerous instances of aggression. For a discussion of such possibilities, please see the **Classic Contributions** section below.

Focus on Research: Classic Contributions

THE ROLE OF AGGRESSIVE CUES: DOES THE TRIGGER SOMETIMES PULL THE FINGER?

Suppose that someone you knew owned a large collection of guns, and that one evening you got into an argument with this person while sitting in the room containing the personal arsenal. Would you be more likely to lose your temper and behave aggressively in this setting than elsewhere? In other words, would the presence of racks of weapons on the walls actually facilitate the likelihood of aggression? (Assume, by the way, that all the guns are unloaded!)

According to one noted authority on aggression, Leonard Berkowitz (1969, 1974), this might well be the case. He has proposed that one important determinant of aggression is the presence of what he terms **aggressive cues.** These are stimuli that have been associated or linked with aggression in the past. Berkowitz suggests that such aggressive cues serve to elicit aggressive responses from persons who have been angered or otherwise made ready to aggress. Thus, the greater the presence of such cues on the scene, the higher the level of aggression that is likely to occur.

Reading: Lesko (31), *Why Violent Toys Are Good for Kids*

What does this have to do with the gun collection example presented above? According to Berkowitz, the objects in this collection (guns) have been intimately associated with aggression on numerous occasions. As a result, they

 Weapons as aggressive cues

FIGURE 11.7 Participants delivered more shocks to a person who had annoyed them when weapons were present near the shock button than when these weapons were absent. These findings lend support to the view that weapons, because of their previous association with aggression, can serve as *aggressive cues.*
Source: Based on data from Berkowitz & LePage, 1967.

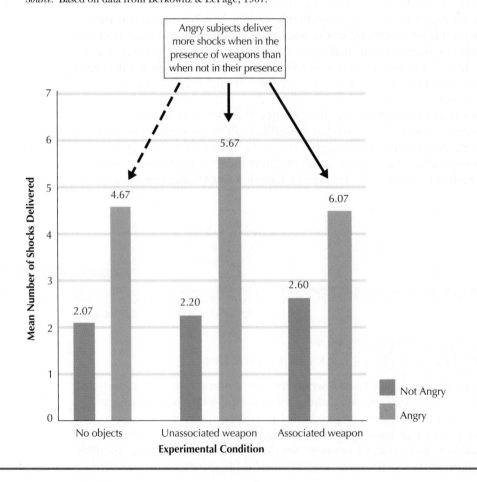

become aggressive cues, and their mere presence on the scene may facilitate aggressive behavior *even if they are not themselves used in such actions*. Support for this reasoning comes from a famous experiment by Berkowitz and LePage (1967). In this study, male participants were first angered or not angered by an accomplice and were then provided with an opportunity to aggress against this person by means of electric shock. (Participants were given an opportunity to evaluate the accomplice's work by giving him from one to nine "shocks". The lower their evaluation, the higher the number of shocks.) In the control condition (*no-objects condition*), only the equipment used by subjects ostensibly to deliver shocks to the accomplice was present. In two other conditions, in contrast, a .38 caliber revolver and a 12-gauge shotgun were lying on the table near the shock button. In one of these groups, it was explained that the weapons were being used in another study and had no connection with the present experiment (*unassociated-weapons* condition). In the other, participants were told that the weapons were being used by the accomplice in another study that he was conducting (*associated-weapons* condition). Berkowitz and LePage (1967) predicted that the mere physical presence of the weapons would facilitate aggression by the angry subjects, but would fail to enhance aggression by those who had not been angered. As you can see from Figure 11.7, this is precisely what occurred. Individuals who had previously been angered by the victim delivered more shocks to the accomplice in the presence of weapons than in their absence. There was no difference between the associated- and unassociated-weapons conditions, however.

These findings seem to suggest that the presence of weapons can indeed facilitate aggression, even if the weapons themselves are not used in the subsequent assaults. As Berkowitz himself has put it (1968, p. 22): *"Guns not only permit violence, they can stimulate it as well. The finger pulls the trigger, but the trigger may also be pulling the finger."*

Unfortunately, the relatively neat picture provided by this initial study has been somewhat complicated by subsequent research (Buss, Booker, & Buss, 1972; Turner and Simon, 1974). These later studies suggest that the **weapons effect** reported by Berkowitz and LePage (1967) may occur only under relatively restricted conditions (e.g., when participants have no suspicions concerning the presence of these unusual items in a research laboratory; Carlson, Marcus-Newhall, & Miller, 1990). Regardless of the ultimate validity of the weapons effect, however, there can be little doubt that Berkowitz's more general suggestion that aggression is *pulled* from without rather than merely *pushed* from within has gained widespread acceptance among social psychologists. In this respect, certainly, his research on the impact of aggressive cues has been highly influential.

THE IMPACT OF MEDIA VIOLENCE: WHY DOES IT OCCUR?   The finding that exposure to violence on television or in the movies can encourage similar behavior among viewers has important implications. It suggests that steps designed to limit such exposure, or to reduce the violent content in TV and Hollywood offerings, might help to lessen one potential cause of aggression. But assuming that such effects occur, another question arises: *How*, precisely, does exposure to media violence stimulate increased aggression among viewers? Several processes seem to play a role.

First, exposure to media violence weakens the *inhibitions* of viewers against engaging in such behavior. After watching many characters—including heroes and heroines—handle many situations through aggression, some viewers feel less restrained about engaging in similar actions themselves. "If *they* can do it," such persons seem to reason, "then so can I."

Second, exposure to media violence provides viewers with new techniques for attacking and harming others not previously at their disposal. And such behaviors, once acquired, tend to be used when individuals are angered or annoyed by others.

Third, watching others engage in aggressive actions can influence viewers' cognitions in several different ways (e.g., Berkowitz, 1984, 1988). Violent materials can serve to *prime* aggressive thoughts and memories, making these more readily available in viewers' cognitive systems. (See our discussion of priming in chapter 3.) Such thoughts and memories may then serve to pave the way for overt aggressive actions. Interestingly, priming can influence the impact of media violence in another way. When individuals have been exposed to aggressive words—words such as *insult, stab, anger*—the aggressive schema activated may increase their interest in watching violent films or television programs. Precisely such effects have been reported by Langley, O'Neal, Craig, and Yost (1992). They exposed three groups of participants to three different lists of words: Words that were related to aggression, words that were inconsistent with aggression (e.g., praise, smile, jolly), or words that were totally irrelevant to aggression (hold, zone, move). The researchers then asked persons in all three groups to write stories using these words. Exposure to the words and writing the stories constituted the manipulation of priming. Next, all participants were asked to rate their interest in seeing each of twenty-nine different film clips, each of which was described in a brief paragraph as being violent, hostile comedy, nonhostile comedy, erotic, or neutral in content. As shown in Figure 11.8, those participants primed with aggressive words expressed greatest interest in seeing the violent films and hostile comedy films; they did *not*, however, express greater interest than participants primed with irrelevant or nonaggressive words in seeing the erotic or neutral films.

Finally, repeated exposure to media violence may reduce emotional sensitivity to violence and its harmful consequences. That is, after watching countless murders, fights, and assaults, viewers may become *desensitized* to such materials and show lessened emotional reaction to them (Geen, 1981). Then they may find real-life aggression, too, less disturbing; and they may demonstrate reduced empathy toward its victims, even when the victims evidence signs of considerable pain and suffering (Baron, 1971, 1979). As we will soon see, such effects may be especially damaging when they occur as a result of exposure to scenes involving sexual violence (Linz, Donnerstein, & Penrod, 1988).

In sum, media violence seems to enhance the occurrence of overt aggression for several different reasons, and through several different mechanisms. Given this fact, it is not at all surprising that such materials influence the behavior of children and adults alike.

HEIGHTENED AROUSAL: EMOTION, COGNITION, AND AGGRESSION

Imagine that you encounter the following chain of events. You are on the way to the airport to meet a friend. There is a slow-moving truck in the lane ahead of you, so you begin to pull out to pass. As you do, you hear prolonged honking. You ram on your brakes and just barely avoid colliding with a car which

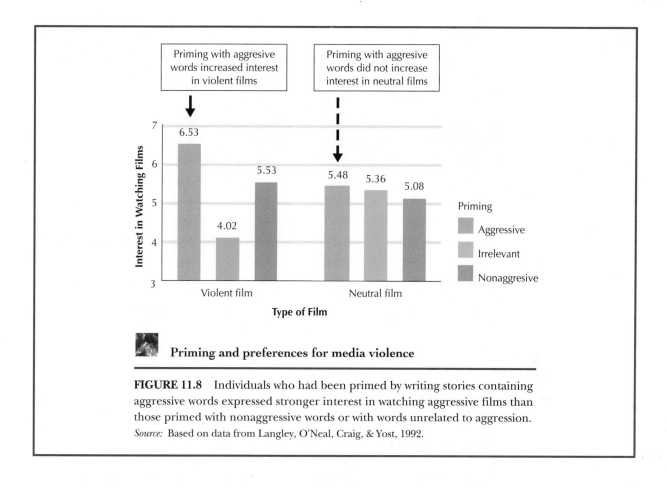

Priming and preferences for media violence

FIGURE 11.8   Individuals who had been primed by writing stories containing aggressive words expressed stronger interest in watching aggressive films than those primed with nonaggressive words or with words unrelated to aggression.
Source: Based on data from Langley, O'Neal, Craig, & Yost, 1992.

Critical Thinking Questkion 5

was about to pass *you* on your left. You are very embarrassed and can feel your heart pounding wildly. Now you arrive at the airport. It's almost time for your friend's flight, so you park hurriedly and rush through the terminal. When you get to the security check, there is an elderly man in front of you. As he walks through, the buzzer sounds and he becomes confused. The security guard can't make him understand that he must empty his pockets and walk through again. You are irritated by the delay. In fact, you feel yourself growing unbearably angry. "What's wrong with him?" you think to yourself. "Can't he follow simple directions?" You begin to mutter under your breath and shake your head in disbelief. "One more minute," you imagine, "and I'll just shove him out of the way."

What's going on in this situation? Do you think that your recent near miss in traffic is playing any role in your excessive anger? In short, could the emotional arousal from that incident have somehow transferred to the totally unrelated situation at the security gate? Growing evidence suggests that it could (Zillmann, 1983, 1988). Under some circumstances, heightened arousal—whatever its original source—can enhance aggression in response to annoyance, frustration, or provocation. In different experiments, arousal stemming from participation in competitive games (Christy, Gelfand, & Hartmann, 1971), vigorous exercise (Zillmann, 1979), and even some types of music (Rogers & Ketcher, 1979) has been found to facilitate subsequent aggression. Why is this the case? A compelling explanation is offered by **excitation transfer theory** (Zillmann, 1983, 1988).

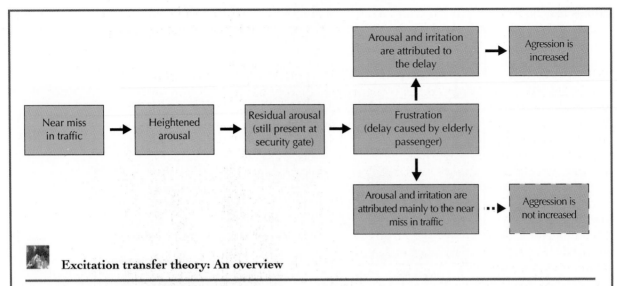

Excitation transfer theory: An overview

FIGURE 11.9 *Excitation transfer theory* suggests that arousal occurring in one situation can persist and can intensify emotional reactions in later, unrelated situations. Thus, the arousal generated by a near miss in traffic can intensify feelings of annoyance or frustration produced by later delays occurring at an airport security gate. Such effects are most likely to occur if the person involved is unaware of the residual arousal or attributes such arousal to events in the present (airport) situation.

Source: Based on suggestions by Zillmann, 1988.

Discussion Question 4 EXCITATION TRANSFER THEORY.   This framework begins by noting that physiological arousal, however produced, dissipates slowly over time. As a result, some portion of such arousal may persist as a person moves from one situation to another. In the example above, some portion of the arousal you experienced as a result of a near miss in traffic may still be present as you approach the security gate in the airport terminal. Now, when you encounter minor annoyance, such arousal intensifies your emotional reactions to it. The result: You become enraged rather than just mildly irritated. When are such effects most likely to occur? Excitation transfer theory offers two related answers. First, they are most likely to take place when the persons involved are relatively unaware of their residual arousal—a common occurrence, since small elevations in arousal are difficult to detect (Zillmann, 1988). Second, such effects are also most likely to occur when the persons involved recognize the presence of such arousal but attribute it to events occurring in the present situation (Taylor et al., 1991). Thus, in the incident we have been describing, if you attributed your residual feelings of arousal to the delay you were now experiencing, your anger would be intensified. (Please see Figure 11.9 for a summary of excitation transfer theory as it applies to this situation.)

Interestingly, recent findings suggest that excitation transfer effects are most likely to occur when individuals experience a state known as **deindividuation**—one in which they experience reduced self-awareness and reduced awareness of social norms in a given situation (e.g., Prentiss-Dunn & Rogers, 1982). Deindividuation often occurs when individuals feel that they are an anonymous part of a large crowd. When they experience deindividuation, individuals may be less aware of any residual arousal and more likely to attribute it to external causes (Taylor et al., 1991). The result: The likelihood of excitation transfer—and increased aggression—is enhanced.

EMOTION, COGNITION, AND AGGRESSION: COMPLEX INTERDEPEN-DENCIES. While excitation transfer theory offers important insights into the way in which arousal can influence aggression, it has recently been expanded in several important ways (Zillmann, 1988). The theory now considers how emotion (arousal) and cognition interact in shaping aggressive reactions. Let's consider the impact of cognition on emotion first. How can our thoughts influence arousal and so subsequent aggression? One answer involves the fact that our thoughts can lead us to *reappraise* various emotion-provoking events. Such reappraisal, in turn, can affect our reactions to them. A dramatic illustration of such effects is provided by a study conducted at a university by Zillmann and Cantor (1976). In this experiment, participants were severely annoyed by a rude experimenter and then provided with an opportunity to retaliate against this man by voting for or against his reappointment as a research fellow. Before retaliating, two groups of participants received mitigating information suggesting that the experimenter was under a lot of stress from important exams, and that he had acted in a rude fashion for this reason. One group received this information *before* being annoyed by the experimenter; the second received it only *after* he had acted in a rude fashion. (Persons in a control condition never received any mitigating information.) Results indicated that participants who received the mitigating information about the experimenter before he had annoyed them showed very little arousal after being provoked. Those who never received such information showed the highest level of arousal, while those who received mitigating information only after being annoyed showed an intermediate level. Similar findings were found with respect to retaliation against the accomplice: Participants who received mitigating information prior to being provoked showed the lowest level of retaliation, while those in the control group showed the highest. Interestingly, those who received mitigating information only after being provoked retaliated almost as strongly as those who received no information of this type. These findings, and those of other studies (Zillmann, 1988), suggest that cognitive processes can strongly affect arousal in response to various forms of annoyance or provocation, and in this manner can strongly affect aggression as well.

Now let's turn briefly to the impact of arousal on cognition. Do high levels of arousal affect our thoughts about others' behavior, and so our tendencies to aggress against them? Again, the answer appears to be yes. Several studies indicate that when individuals are strongly aroused—by exercise, a near miss in traffic, or virtually any other exciting event—their ability to process complex information about others, their intentions, and the reasons behind their behavior may be reduced. The result may then be an impulsive lashing out at others.

In sum, it appears that aggression, like many other forms of social behavior, is influenced by a complex interplay between emotion and cognition. As we noted in chapter 3, cognition frequently influences emotional reactions, and these in turn often shape cognition. In other words, what we think influences what and how we feel, and what we feel influences what, and how, we think. And together, the complex pattern of thoughts and emotions we experience determines whether, and to what degree, we aggress against others.

SEXUAL AROUSAL AND AGGRESSION: ARE LOVE AND HATE REALLY TWO SIDES OF THE SAME BEHAVIORAL COIN?

According to folklore, *love* and *hate* are closely linked; when one occurs, the other, it is contended, is not very far away. Are such suggestions actually true? If *love* is interpreted primarily in terms of sexual passion, social psychological research on aggression offers a basis for suspecting that there may be a substantial grain of truth in this age-old idea. Sexual passion certainly involves increased arousal; and as we have just seen, heightened arousal can sometimes influence aggression. Such reasoning aside, belief in a link between sex and aggression has a long history in psychology. For example, Freud (1933) suggested that desires to hurt or be hurt by one's lover are a normal part of sexual relations. Is there any direct evidence that sexual arousal affects aggression or vice versa? The answer, once again, is yes.

Critical Thinking
Question 6

The results of several studies indicate that mild levels of sexual arousal, such as those induced by exposure to pictures of attractive persons shown either nude or partially clothed, can reduce individuals' later aggression against those who have previously provoked them in some fashion (e.g., Baron, 1974, 1979; Baron & Bell, 1973; Ramirez, Bryant, & Zillmann, 1983). Stronger levels of sexual arousal, however, such as those induced by highly erotic reading matter or films of explicit lovemaking, has opposite effects: They actually seem to increase subsequent aggression (e.g., Jaffe et al., 1974; Zillmann, 1984). In short, the relationship between sexual arousal and overt aggression appears to be *curvilinear*. Mild levels of arousal reduce aggression below that shown in the absence of sexual arousal, while higher levels actually increase aggression above this point. What accounts for this curvilinear function? A *two-component model* proposed by Zillmann (1984) offers one useful answer.

According to this model, exposure to erotic stimuli produces two effects. First, it increases arousal. Second, it influences current *affective states*—positive and negative feelings. Whether sexual arousal will increase or reduce aggression, then, depends on the overall pattern of such effects. Mild erotic materials generate only weak levels of arousal but substantial levels of positive affect. As a result, exposure to such materials tends to reduce subsequent aggression. In contrast, explicit erotic materials generate stronger levels of arousal. Also, since many people find some of the acts demonstrated to be unpleasant or repulsive, such explicit materials also produce considerable amounts of negative affect. As a result, erotica of this type may increase aggression. The findings of several studies support this two-factor theory (e.g., Ramirez, Bryant, & Zillmann, 1983), so it appears to be helpful in understanding the relationship between sexual arousal and aggression.

To conclude: It seems that there is indeed a link between sexual arousal and aggression. However, the nature of this relationship is more complex than at first suspected and relates to the effects of both affect (emotions) and cognition.

THE EFFECTS OF VIOLENT PORNOGRAPHY: AGGRESSIVE ACTIONS, HARDENED ATTITUDES

In recent decades restrictions against the explicit depiction of sexual behavior in films and magazines have all but disappeared in many nations. This fact, coupled with the huge sale of videocassette recorders, has resulted in a situation where access to such materials is as close as the nearest shopping center.

Moreover, some of the X-rated tapes available (as well as other media sources such as magazines) contain scenes that offer a volatile mixture of sex and violence. In such materials, women are generally the victims, and they are shown being raped, tortured, and brutalized in many ways. Given that exposure to media violence can encourage aggressive behavior among viewers and that high levels of sexual arousal (coupled with negative affect) can also increase aggression, it seems possible that such **violent pornography,** as it is often termed, may be quite dangerous. Unfortunately, growing empirical evidence suggests that this is actually the case.

Transparency 11.6

First, several studies indicate that exposure to such materials increases the tendency of males to aggress against females (Malamuth & Briere, 1986). Second, exposure to violent pornography seems to encourage the development of callous attitudes toward sexual violence among both males and females (e.g., Linz, Donnerstein, & Penrod, 1984; Zillmann & Bryant, 1984). These callous attitudes, in turn, lead the viewers of violent pornography to perceive crimes such as rape as less serious and to report less sympathy toward rape victims. Further, these attitudes lead these people to report greater acceptance of false beliefs about rape (e.g., the myth that many women really want to be ravaged) and to become more accepting of various bizarre forms of pornography. These are disturbing findings, to say the least.

Finally, additional research (Linz, Donnerstein, & Penrod, 1988) suggests that such effects can occur as a result of watching films that contain violence but do not contain explicit sexual behavior. These findings suggest that it is the violent content—the aggression against women, not explicit sexual behavior—that is crucial. Support for this conclusion is provided by a study conducted by Demare, Briere, and Lips (1988). These researchers asked students at a Canadian university to indicate whether and how frequently they had watched both nonviolent pornography and violent pornography during the previous year. In addition, participants reported on the likelihood they would use force in sexual encounters and the likelihood that they would actually rape a woman if they thought they could get away with this serious crime. Results indicated that two variables predicted a high reported likelihood of engaging in sexual violence: acceptance of interpersonal violence generally and *the amount of sexually violent pornography viewed by participants.*

Transparency 11.1

Taken as a whole, research findings to date suggest that exposure to scenes of violence against women may well exert adverse effects upon viewers—and upon females with whom viewers come into contact. After watching such materials, males become desensitized both to the violent materials and to signs of pain and suffering on the part of victims of real crimes such as rape. Further, there is some indication that the willingness of some males to engage in actual sexual violence against women may be increased by exposure to violent pornography. Given the popularity of films depicting violence, and the fact that violence against women is an all-too-common theme in many pornographic films, it seems possible that long-term social costs associated with the ready availability of such materials may be very high indeed.

Discussion Question 1

ALCOHOL AND AGGRESSION:
A POTENTIALLY—BUT NOT NECESSARILY—DANGEROUS MIX

Common sense suggests that some people, at least, become more aggressive when they consume alcoholic beverages. Bars and nightclubs are notorious as the scenes of impulsive acts of violence (refer to Figure 11.10, p. 458). More formal evidence for an important link between alcohol and aggression is also provided by many laboratory studies. In such experiments, participants given substantial doses of alcohol—enough to make them legally drunk—often behave more aggressively in general (Gustafson, 1992) or respond more strongly to provocation than persons given drinks containing no alcohol, or doses so small that they have no appreciable effects (Taylor & Leonard, 1983). (*Please note:* Participants in such research are always warned that they may be receiving alcoholic beverages and take part in such studies as willing volunteers.)

Critical Thinking
Question 7

What accounts for such effects? One possibility is that alcohol acts directly on the brain, releasing relatively primitive areas that govern emotion and rage from control by the cerebral cortex. If this is indeed the case, then people who consume alcohol may find it extremely difficult, if not impossible, to control aggressive outbursts (Zeichner & Pihl, 1980). They are, quite simply, no longer capable of such restraint. Another and less disturbing possibility is that alcohol weakens restraints against aggressive (or sexual) behavior, but leaves people able to monitor and regulate their own actions to some degree.

 Alcohol and aggression: A dangerous combination

FIGURE 11.10 The fact that bars, nightclubs, and other places where alcohol is consumed by many persons are frequently the scene of violence constitutes informal evidence for a link between alcohol and aggression.

This latter conclusion is supported by a growing body of research evidence (Jeavons & Taylor, 1985). For example, in one interesting study on this topic (Taylor & Sears, 1988), male subjects consumed either a large dose of alcohol (1.5 ounces of 100 proof vodka per forty pounds of body weight) or no alcohol (they consumed drinks that smelled of alcohol, but actually had none in them). After this, they competed with another person (who was actually nonexistent) in the Taylor reaction time task (see the **Classic Contributions** section earlier in this chapter). As you may recall, in this task, the slower player on each trial received a shock set for him by his opponent. Thus, participants' willingness to aggress against the fictitious opponent could be measured in terms of the strength of the shocks they choose for this person. Two observers (accomplices of the researchers) were present during the session, and at first these persons exerted increasing social pressure on participants to use strong shocks. They commented that doing so would make the situation more exciting; moreover, they expressed approval when participants followed their recommendations (or disapproval when they did not). Near the end of the session, one of the accomplices suggested that their comments might be interfering with the session. After that they sat silently and exerted no pressure on the subject to behave aggressively.

It was predicted that the intoxicated participants would actually be *more* responsive than nonintoxicated participants to the accomplices' social pressure, increasing the strength of the shocks they delivered to a greater extent when urged to do so. However, when social pressure was removed, near the end of the session, they would reduce their level of aggression. This is precisely what happened. Intoxicated participants in the study first increased and then decreased their level of aggression in response to the accomplices' pressure. Nonintoxicated participants showed little change over the course of the study.

Additional support for the view that alcohol does not totally eliminate individuals' ability to regulate their own behavior—and so does not automatically increase aggression—is provided by other studies indicating that alcohol does *not* increase aggression in nonthreatening contexts, where individuals do not feel that they are at risk of harm from others (Taylor et al., 1976). However, at least one study (Gantner & Taylor, 1992) found that when they confront an opponent who cannot retaliate in any manner (this opponent cannot deliver shocks to them in the Taylor competitive reaction time task), persons who have consumed a high dose of alcohol (1.5 ounces of 100 proof vodka per forty pounds of body weight) are more aggressive initially, in the absence of prior provocation, than those who have not consumed alcohol. As shown in Figure 11.11, p. 460, such differences disappear over time and in the face of repeated provocation, but their initial existence suggests that alcohol may sometimes increase the likelihood that individuals will take advantage of a helpless victim.

While the picture is still far from complete, existing evidence concerning the effects of alcohol on aggression seems to point to the following conclusions: (1) Alcohol does *not* automatically increase aggression by individuals who consume it; such persons retain considerable ability to regulate their own behavior. (2) Alcohol is most likely to increase the likelihood or intensity of aggression in the presence of social or situational cues suggesting that such behavior is appropriate—for example, strong provocation from others, social pressures to behave aggressively). (3) Alcohol may, however, sometimes increase the tendency to attack potential victims who appear to have no means

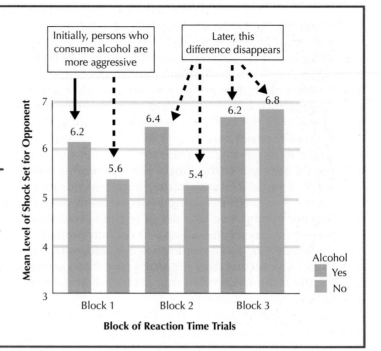

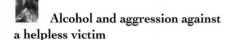 **Alcohol and aggression against a helpless victim**

FIGURE 11.11 Initially, persons who consumed alcohol showed higher levels of aggression against a helpless opponent— one powerless to retaliate against them— than persons who had not consumed alcohol. These findings suggest that alcohol can sometimes increase aggression, especially toward a helpless victim.

Source: Based on data from Gantner & Taylor, 1992.

to retaliate in kind. So, should the warnings placed on alcoholic beverages in several countries—warnings that focus on potential risks to health (see Figure 11.12)—be expanded to include a statement such as: *"Warning: Alcohol may promote dangerous instances of aggression"*? The answer suggested by existing evidence would appear to be "Probably not."

PERSONAL CAUSES OF AGGRESSION

Are some persons primed, by their personalities or by other characteristics, for aggression? Informal observation suggests that this is so. While some persons rarely lose their tempers or participate in aggressive encounters, others seem to be forever blowing their tops, often with serious consequences. Many personal factors play a role in such differences, and in this section we will consider three that appear to be of considerable importance.

THE TYPE A BEHAVIOR PATTERN

Critical Thinking Question 8

Do you know anyone you could describe as (1) extremely competitive, (2) always in a hurry, and (3) especially irritable and aggressive? If so, this person stands a good chance of being what psychologists term **Type A** (Glass, 1977). This set of characteristics (known as the *Type A Behavior pattern*) sets such persons apart from others who do not share such traits, who are described as **Type B**. As is true with virtually any individual difference, Types A and B represent extremes on a dimension. We should note, however, that research evidence suggests that the Type A/Type B distinction does seem to be a real

 Alcohol: Current warnings

FIGURE 11.12 In the United States all beverages containing alcohol must be labeled with the warning shown here. Should this warning be expanded to mention the potential aggression-enhancing effects of alcohol? Existing evidence does not seem to offer strong support for such action.

dichotomy: Most people tend to fall into one category or the other (Strube, 1989).

Given the characteristics mentioned above, it seems only reasonable that Type A's would tend to be more aggressive, in a wide range of situations, then Type B's. After all, they are highly competitive, easily irritated, and always in a hurry. The results of several experiments indicate that this is indeed the case (Baron, Russell, & Arms, 1985; Berman, Gladue, & Taylor, 1993; Carver & Glass, 1978). Moreover, other findings indicate that Type A's are truly hostile. They don't merely aggress against others because this is a useful means for reaching other goals, such as furthering their own careers or winning in athletic contests. (This is known as **instrumental aggression.**) On the contrary, they are more likely than B's to engage in **hostile aggression**—aggression whose prime purpose is to inflict pain and suffering on the victims (Strube et al., 1984). Additional evidence suggests that Type A's are more likely than Type B's to engage in such actions as child abuse or spouse abuse (Strube et al., 1984).

That the relationship between Type A behavior and aggression is not restricted to specific cultures is indicated by the findings of an ingenious field study conducted by Evans, Palsane, and Carrere (1987). These researchers compared the behavior and driving records of bus drivers in two countries—the United States and India—who were classified as being Type A or Type B. In order to obtain evidence about the drivers' on-the-job behavior, the researchers obtained records of the drivers' previous accidents from their employers. In addition, assistants boarded the drivers' buses and, unknown to them, observed their behavior during typical working days.

Results indicated that Type A drivers did in fact behave differently—and more aggressively—than Type B drivers. In both countries the rate of accidents

Exercise 4

was several times higher among Type A drivers than among Type B drivers. That this difference was due, at least in part, to differences in aggressive actions was suggested by observations of the drivers' daily behavior. In India Type A drivers passed other drivers more frequently, stepped on their brakes more often, and blew their horns almost twice as often as Type B drivers (see Figure 11.13). Similar differences were not observed among bus drivers in the United States, perhaps because they worked under much less hectic driving conditions. Thus, they rarely blew their horns or passed other vehicles. Recall that Type A and Type B drivers did differ in accident rates in both countries, however.

These findings suggest that the link between the Type A pattern and aggression is cross-cultural in nature: Type A's are more likely than Type B's to become involved in aggressive encounters regardless of where they happen to live. The findings also imply that it may be prudent to avoid hiring Type A individuals for jobs that involve considerable amounts of stress and frustration. Such persons, it appears, may be happier—and less dangerous to themselves and to others!—in less stressful occupations.

PERCEIVING EVIL INTENT IN OTHERS: HOSTILE ATTRIBUTIONAL BIAS

Earlier we noted that *attributions* about others' intentions often play an important role in aggression. When individuals perceive ambiguous actions by others as stemming from malicious intentions they are much more likely to retaliate

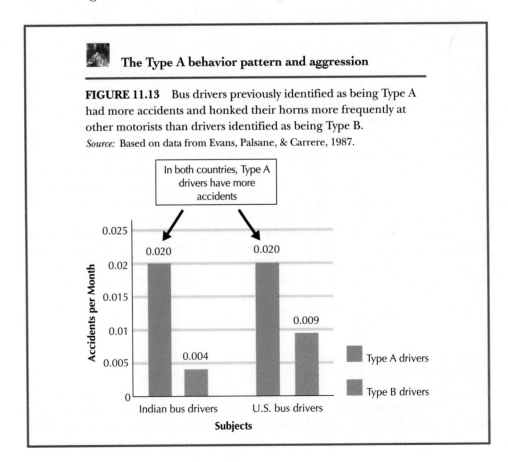

The Type A behavior pattern and aggression

FIGURE 11.13 Bus drivers previously identified as being Type A had more accidents and honked their horns more frequently at other motorists than drivers identified as being Type B.
Source: Based on data from Evans, Palsane, & Carrere, 1987.

than when they perceive the same actions as stemming from other motives (e.g., Johnson & Rule, 1986). This fact points to another personal characteristic that may potentially play an important role in the occurrence of aggression: the tendency to perceive hostile intent in others even when it is totally lacking. Presumably, the stronger this tendency—known as **hostile attributional bias**—the greater individuals' likelihood of engaging in reactive aggression in response to provocation from others.

Evidence that this is actually the case has been provided by several studies (Dodge, Murphy, & Buchsbaum, 1984). For example, in one revealing investigation, Dodge and Coie (1987) measured boys' tendency falsely to attribute hostile intentions to others and then observed these boys' behavior while playing with other children. Results supported the major prediction: The greater the boys' tendency to demonstrate hostile attributional bias, the greater their tendency to engage in aggression.

While much of the research concerned with the hostile attributional bias has focused on children, several recent investigations have extended these findings to adolescents and adults. For example, in one of these studies, Dodge et al. (1990) examined the relationship between hostile attributional bias and aggression among a group of male adolescents confined to a maximum security prison for juvenile offenders. These young men had been convicted of a wide range of violent crimes, including murder, sexual assault, kidnapping, and armed robbery. The researchers hypothesized that hostile attributional bias among these men would be related to the number of interpersonally violent crimes they had committed and to trained observers' ratings of the prisoners' tendencies to engage in reactive aggression in response to provocation. However, the researchers also predicted that the hostile attributional bias would *not* be related to observers' ratings of the young men's *proactive* aggression—aggressive acts performed in the absence of provocation for purposes of gaining dominance over others. In order to measure individual differences in hostile attributional bias, the researchers asked the prisoners to watch videotapes of incidents in which one person's actions toward another appeared to stem from hostile intent, appeared to stem from prosocial intent, or were ambiguous. After viewing each incident, participants indicated whether the actor's intent was hostile, helpful, ambiguous, or accidental in nature. Hostile attributional bias was measured in terms of the tendency to attribute hostile intent to others in situations where most observers would agree that it was *not* present. Results offered support for the major predictions: Hostile attributional bias was related to reactive but not to proactive aggression.

Taken as a whole, the findings reported by Dodge and other investigators indicate that hostile attributional bias is an important personal characteristic with respect to aggression. In short, the tendency to perceive malevolence or malice in the actions of others, even when it doesn't really exist, is an important trait—one that can involve individuals in a higher-than-average incidence of aggressive encounters with others.

Discussion Question 2

SHAME-PRONENESS AND AGGRESSION: FROM SELF-REJECTION TO HOSTILITY AND ANGER

Imagine that you promised to do a small favor for a friend. Then you failed to perform it, simply because it seemed like too much effort. How would you feel? Most people would experience some degree of *guilt* in this situation. They would feel regret or remorse over having failed to keep their word. Others, however, might experience an even stronger reaction—one most people would label *shame*. They would criticize themselves harshly, asking, for example, "Why am I so selfish?" or "Why am I so lazy?" Both guilt and shame are negative reactions, but shame appears to be much stronger, since it involves negative evaluations of one's *self* rather than merely of specific actions one has performed (Tangney, 1990).

Is there any relationship between the tendency to experience shame and the tendency to engage in aggression? A growing body of evidence suggests that there is. When individuals feel shame, it appears, they often also experience anger and hostility: They are angry with themselves for having behaved in a fashion that casts doubt on their own self-worth. Such feelings are then redirected outward toward others, who are seen as the cause of the shame: After all, it is *they* who will disapprove of the individual and cause her or him deep humiliation. Since shame is a powerful emotion, the negative affect it generates is often intense—out of proportion to the scope of the triggering events. Persons experiencing shame recognize this fact, and it increases their tendency to become angry at others and to blame them for the unpleasant feelings. (See Figure 11.14 for a summary of these suggestions.) Together, these considerations suggest that persons who are prone to experience shame may also be prone to aggression.

Direct evidence for such a link between shame-proneness and aggression has been reported in several studies (e.g., Harder & Lewis, 1986; Tangney, 1990). In what is perhaps the most revealing study to date, Tangney et al. (1992) asked participants to complete questionnaires designed to measure their tendency to experience guilt or shame in a wide range of situations, and questionnaires designed to measure their tendencies to experience anger or irritability as well as to engage in various forms of aggression. Results were clear: Shame-proneness was indeed positively related to the measures of anger and aggression. In other words, the greater individuals' tendencies to experience shame during the course of their social interactions with others, the greater their reported tendencies to become angry and engage in aggression.

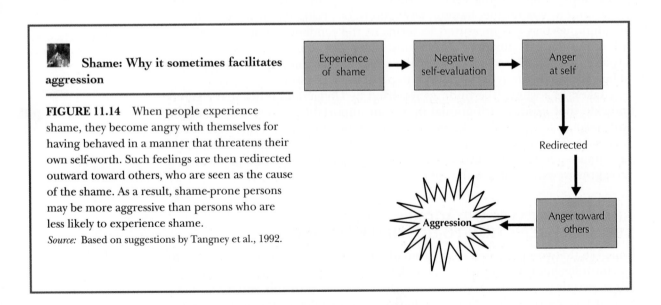

Shame: Why it sometimes facilitates aggression

FIGURE 11.14 When people experience shame, they become angry with themselves for having behaved in a manner that threatens their own self-worth. Such feelings are then redirected outward toward others, who are seen as the cause of the shame. As a result, shame-prone persons may be more aggressive than persons who are less likely to experience shame.
Source: Based on suggestions by Tangney et al., 1992.

Interestingly, similar relationships were *not* observed between the tendency to experience guilt and anger or aggression. Since both guilt and shame involve negative reactions to "bad" behavior, these findings suggest that the link between shame and aggression may well stem from the extension of such disapproval to one's self-image. In other words, it is the tendency of shame-prone persons to shred their own egos that underlies their greater proclivity for aggression. Whatever the precise origins of the relationship between shame and aggression, however, it is clear that the tendency to experience shame is potentially harmful not only to the persons who have such reactions, but to others around them as well.

GENDER DIFFERENCES IN AGGRESSION: ARE THEY REAL?

Are males more aggressive than females? Folklore suggests that this is the case. And crime statistics do indicate that males are much more likely than females to be arrested for violent acts. Does this mean that large and consistent differences exist between males and females with respect to the tendency to engage in overt aggression?

Research findings provide something of a mixed answer. On the one hand, existing evidence does indicate that males are more likely to both instigate and to serve as the target of various forms of aggression (e.g., Bogard, 1990; Harris, 1992; Eagly & Steffen, 1986). However, on closer inspection, the size of this difference appears to be relatively small—smaller than popular belief often suggests. Further, the tendency for males to engage in aggressive actions more frequently than females is larger with respect to *physical* forms of aggression (hitting, punching, kicking, use of weapons) than for other forms of aggression (yelling at someone, treating someone condescendingly; Harris, 1992). In fact, recent findings suggest that females may actually be *more* likely than males to engage in various *indirect* forms of aggression, such as spreading rumors or gossip about another person, rejecting this person as a friend, or ignoring or avoiding the target (Lagerspetz, Bjorkqvist, & Peltonen, 1988). Clear evidence for precisely such differences is provided by a series of studies conducted by Lagerspetz and her colleagues.

In the most recent of these investigations (Bjorkqvist, Lagerspetz, & Kaukinen, 1992), boys and girls in three age groups—eight, eleven, and fifteen years old—were asked to indicate how other members of their class in school reacted when angry. Responses were then divided into three categories: *direct aggression* (kicks or strikes others, uses profanity, delivers verbal abuse, pushes, shoves); *indirect aggression* (gossips, says "I'm not your friend," shuns the target person); or *withdrawal* (goes away, sulks). The researchers predicted that girls would be more likely than boys to use indirect aggression or withdrawal at all ages, but that such differences would strengthen with increasing age, as the cognitive skills needed for use of indirect forms of aggression developed. As shown in Figure 11.15, p. 466, results offered clear support for these predictions. Boys were more likely to use direct forms of aggression than girls at all ages. Similarly, girls were more likely to use indirect forms of aggression at all ages; however, this difference was smallest among eight-year-olds and larger among the eleven- and fifteen-year-olds. As noted by Bjorkqvist, Lagerspetz, and Kaukiainen (1992, p. 126), these findings lend support to popular beliefs suggesting that where aggression is concerned, girls often *manipulate* (use indirect forms) while boys *fight* (use more direct forms).

Critical Thinking
Question 10

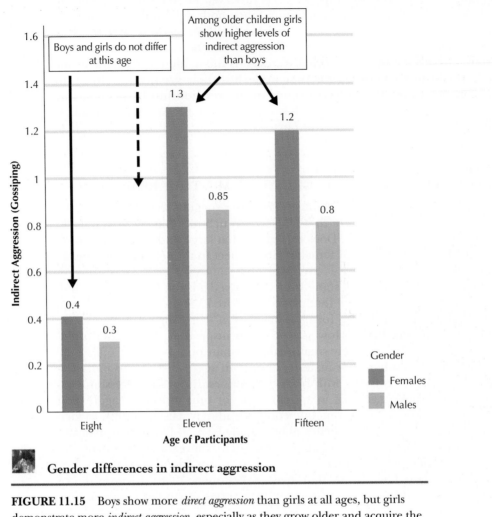

Gender differences in indirect aggression

FIGURE 11.15 Boys show more *direct aggression* than girls at all ages, but girls demonstrate more *indirect aggression*, especially as they grow older and acquire the cognitive skills needed for this type of aggression.

Source: Based on data from Bjorkqvist, Lagerspetz, & Kaukiainen, 1992.

Additional evidence suggests that males and females also differ to some extent in their attitudes toward aggression (Eagly & Steffen, 1986). Males generally report less guilt or anxiety about engaging in such behavior than females, while females report greater concern over the possibility that aggressing against others may pose a threat to their own safety (e.g., if the victim chose to retaliate).

In sum, existing evidence indicates that men and women do differ to a degree in their willingness to handle interpersonal relations through aggression. The next question, then, is obvious: What is the basis for such differences? Are men somehow programmed for violence by biological or genetic factors—such as possession of a Y chromosome or higher levels of male sexual hormones such as testosterone? Contrasting sex roles and socialization practices for boys and girls? For a discussion of recent evidence pertaining to the role of biological factors, please see the **Cutting Edge** section on the next page.

GENDER DIFFERENCES IN AGGRESSION: THE POTENTIAL ROLE OF HORMONES AND SEXUAL ORIENTATION

Do biological or genetic factors play a role in gender differences with respect to aggression? Many social psychologists reject this notion; they believe, instead, that gender roles and contrasting socialization experiences for males and females are the primary determinants of such differences. According to such arguments, males are more aggressive than females because they are taught from an early age that such behavior is appropriate for males, or even required as a demonstration of their masculinity. In contrast, females are taught that aggression is "unfeminine" and should be avoided—especially in its direct and obvious forms.

Such arguments are compelling and certainly valid to an important degree. Yet, as we noted earlier, some evidence points to the conclusion that biological or genetic factors play some role in the greater tendency of males to engage in many forms of aggression. Perhaps the most convincing evidence in this regard is that demonstrating a link between levels of testosterone (an important male sexual hormone) and the incidence of aggressive behavior. Several different studies indicate that higher concentrations of testosterone are associated with higher levels of self-reported aggression in males (Christiansen & Knussman, 1987; Olweus, 1986). A particularly clear example of such research is a study conducted by Gladue (1991).

In this investigation male and female participants completed a measure of sexual orientation (heterosexual or homosexual) and a measure of the incidence with which they engaged in various forms of aggression—physical, verbal, impulsive. Samples of their blood were also taken and were later analyzed for levels of various hormones, including testosterone. Results indicated that for males, the higher the concentrations of testosterone in their blood, the greater their self-reported tendencies to engage in physical, verbal, and impulsive aggression. For females, in contrast, the higher the levels of testosterone, the *lower* their tendencies to engage in various forms of aggression.

An additional aspect of the study involved a comparison between persons with heterosexual and homosexual orientations. Gladue reasoned that if social factors and gender roles play a dominant part in differences between males and females with respect to aggression, then perhaps such differences might be larger among heterosexuals. If biological factors play an important role, then the size of such differences should be the same for both groups. As shown in Figure 11.16, p. 468, results supported this latter prediction. For both homosexuals and heterosexuals, males reported higher levels of aggression than females; and for both genders, homosexuals and heterosexuals did not differ. Among females, however, lesbians reported being less likely than heterosexual women to engage in physical aggression. Finally, it was noted that while levels of testosterone were much higher among males than females, there were no differences between homosexual and heterosexual males or females in this respect.

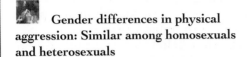

Gender differences in physical aggression: Similar among homosexuals and heterosexuals

FIGURE 11.16 Among both homosexuals and heterosexuals, males report engaging in higher levels of physical aggression than females. These findings suggest that being male is a better predictor of aggression than one's sexual preference. This, in turn, implicates biological factors in gender differences in aggression.

Source: Based on data from Gladue, 1991.

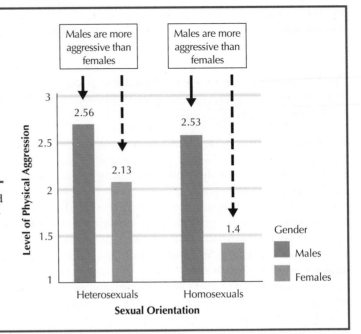

Taken together, these findings, and those of many other studies (e.g., Olweus, 1986) suggest that biological factors may indeed play a role in gender differences in aggression.

Males may be predisposed by hormonal and genetic factors to demonstrate somewhat higher levels of aggression than females. But please note: This in no way implies that they *must* demonstrate higher levels of aggression. On the contrary, as we'll note in the next section, all forms of aggression can be prevented or reduced by appropriate techniques. Thus, there is no reason why biologically based aggressive tendencies among males must be translated into overt instances of aggression. As is true of many other forms of social behavior, in short, biology is definitely *not* destiny. Perceiving males as somehow compelled to behave aggressively by factors beyond their control is both misleading and inappropriate.

Work in Progress

Where Hormones and Personality Meet: Effects of Testosterone and Type A Behavior Pattern on Aggression By Males

Gladue's (1991) study indicates that the higher males' level of testosterone, the greater the extent to which they *report* engaging in various forms of aggression. As we have seen at several points in this book, however, people are not always entirely accurate in describing their own behavior—especially behavior that occurred some time in the past. So the question remains: Is overt aggression in males related to their basal levels of testosterone? Gladue and his colleagues (Berman, Gladue, & Taylor,

1993) have investigated this issue in intriguing follow-up research.

In this study, males who had previously been identified as Type A's or Type B's competed with another person in the Taylor reaction time paradigm. As you may recall, in this method for measuring physical aggression, the slower person to respond on each reaction time trial receives a shock set by her or his opponent. In the study conducted by Berman, Gladue, and Taylor (1993), participants were informed that they had lost on 50 percent of the trials; moreover, the level of shock supposedly set for them by their opponent increased as the study proceeded. (In fact, there was no opponent; the experimenter controlled the levels of shock received by participants.) Half of the subjects in the study had previously been classified as being Type A's and half as Type B's. Participants' testosterone levels were measured at several points during the study through readings obtained from their saliva.

The researchers hypothesized that both testosterone levels and Type A behavior would influence aggression, and this was in fact the case. First, participants with high testosterone levels did in fact demonstrate higher levels of aggression than those with relatively low testosterone levels. Second, for Type A men, those with high testosterone levels demonstrated increasing levels of attack against their opponent during the study. In contrast, Type B men did not show this same pattern. Finally, the highest level of aggression was shown by Type A's who were also high in testosterone level.

Together, these findings expand the scope of the earlier research by Gladue (1991). Not only do males with high testosterone levels *report* engaging in more physical aggression; they actually engage in such behavior to a greater extent under controlled laboratory conditions. So hormones do seem to play some role in human aggression. Since these effects were stronger for Type A than Type B men, however, it is clear that hormones and biological factors are only part of the total picture. Where human aggression is concerned, learning, experience, cognitions, and individual differences all enter into the picture and can often make a crucial difference.

THE PREVENTION AND CONTROL OF AGGRESSION: SOME USEFUL TECHNIQUES

An underlying theme in this discussion of aggression—perhaps the most important theme—has been this: Aggression stems from the complex interplay between a variety of external events (e.g., provocation, frustration), cognitions concerning these events (e.g., attributions, memories), and individual differences along several key dimensions (e.g., the Type A behavior pattern). As such, aggression is definitely *not* a "programmed," automatic response. To the extent you accept this point of view, you will also find our next proposal to be a reasonable one: Aggression can be prevented or at least reduced. It is *not* an inevitable pattern, either for individuals or for our entire species. On the contrary, several techniques for controlling its occurrence or intensity exist and can be put to practical use (Baron & Richardson, 1994). In this final section, we'll consider several of these procedures.

Critical Thinking
Question 11

Reading: Lesko (33),
*The Control of
Human Aggression*

Transparency 11.3

PUNISHMENT: AN EFFECTIVE DETERRENT TO VIOLENCE?

Throughout history, most societies have used **punishment** as a means of deterring human violence. Nations have established harsh punishment for such crimes as murder, rape, and assault. Are such tactics actually effective? In one sense, of course, they are. Persons who are imprisoned or executed for performing violent acts cannot repeat these offenses. But what about deterrence:

Will the threat of severe punishment prevent individuals from engaging in aggressive acts in the first place? The pendulum of scientific opinion on this issue has swung back and forth for decades. At present, however, the weight of existing evidence seems to suggest that if used in an appropriate manner, punishment *can* be an effective deterrent to violence. In order for it to succeed, however, several conditions must be met (Bower & Hilgard, 1981).

First, punishment must be prompt—it must follow aggression as soon as possible. Second, it must be strong—it must be of sufficient magnitude to be highly aversive to potential recipients. Third, it must be very likely—the likelihood that it will follow aggressive actions must be quite high. Unfortunately, of course, these conditions are precisely the ones lacking from the criminal justice systems of many nations. In many societies, the delivery of punishment for aggressive actions is delayed for months or even years; the magnitude of punishment itself is variable from one locale to another; and it is well known that many violent crimes go unpunished—no one is ever apprehended, tried, or convicted of them. In view of these facts, it is hardly surprising that punishment has often seemed to fail as a deterrent to violent crime. The dice, so to speak, are heavily loaded against the possibility of its succeeding.

In sum, the fact that punishment does not currently seem to be successful in deterring the rising tide of violence in many nations does not necessarily mean that punishment itself is useless. Rather, it may simply stem from the fact that this procedure is being used in ways that virtually guarantee its failure. If these conditions were changed, we believe, the potential impact of punishment might well be enhanced. And then the safety and well-being of countless innocent victims might also be better protected.

CATHARSIS: DOES GETTING IT OUT OF YOUR SYSTEM REALLY HELP?

Are activities such as the one shown in Figure 11.17 of any use? In other words, does somehow blowing off steam really help individuals get rid of—or at least control—their aggressive impulses? The belief that such activities are effective in this respect is very widespread. Many persons accept some version of what psychologists describe as the **catharsis hypothesis** (Dollard et al., 1939)—the idea that participation in activities that allow individuals to vent their anger and hostility in some relatively safe way will actually reduce later aggression. Presumably, such activities yield two important benefits: (1) They help to reduce emotional tension; and (2) since they help eliminate anger, they reduce the likelihood of more dangerous forms of aggression.

Are these suggestions accurate? Existing evidence provides a mixed reply (Feshbach, 1984; Geen, 1991). First, consider the suggestion that participation in so-called cathartic activities can reduce the arousal stemming from frustration or provocation. Here, some findings do seem to indicate that physically exhausting activities can reduce arousal (Zillmann, 1979). Unfortunately, though, such effects appear to be temporary. Arousal stemming from provocation or frustration may reappear when individuals bring real or imagined wrongs at the hands of others to mind once again (Zillmann, 1988). Further, the most effective technique for reducing such arousal seems to be that of attacking the source of one's anger (Hokanson, Burgess, & Cohen, 1963). These facts suggest that the benefits of participation in "cathartic" activities may be quite minimal.

Critical Thinking
Question 9

 Catharsis: Is it really effective?

FIGURE 11.17 Can the tendency to aggress against others actually be reduced by activities designed to let people release their aggressive impulses? Existing evidence casts doubt on the widespread belief that such *catharsis* is effective for this purpose.

What about the idea that the performance of "safe" aggressive actions reduces the likelihood of more harmful forms of aggression? Here the picture is even more uncertain. Research on this topic indicates that overt aggression is _not_ reduced by (1) watching scenes of filmed or televised violence (Geen, 1978), (2) attacking inanimate objects (Mallick & McCandless, 1966), or (3) aggressing verbally against others. Indeed, there is some evidence that aggression may actually be increased by each of these conditions.

Contrary to popular belief, then, catharsis does not appear to be as effective a means for reducing aggression as is widely assumed. Participating in "safe" forms of aggression, or merely in vigorous, energy-draining activities, may produce temporary reductions in arousal and in this way may lower the tendency to aggress in some situations. But because of the strong impact of cognition upon arousal, feelings of anger and irritation may quickly reappear when individuals encounter or merely think about the persons who previously annoyed them. For this reason, catharsis may be less effective in producing long-term reductions in aggression than has often been assumed.

COGNITIVE INTERVENTIONS:
THE ROLE OF APOLOGIES AND ACCOUNTS

Discussion Question 3

Imagine the following scene: You are waiting for another person with whom you have an appointment. She is late, and as time passes, you become more and more upset. Finally, fully thirty minutes after the agreed-upon time, she shows up. Before you can say a word, she apologizes profusely: "I'm so sorry. My car wouldn't start. Then, I got stuck in a traffic jam on the highway. I'm really upset; please forgive me." Would you be angry and criticize this person severely? Probably you would not. Her apology—an admission of wrongdoing plus a request for your forgiveness—would go a long way toward defusing your annoyance. Of course, your reactions would depend strongly on the nature of her excuses. Research findings suggest that ones that make reference to causes beyond the excuse-giver's control are much more effective than ones that refer to events within this person's control (e.g., "Sorry . . . I just forgot"; Weiner et al., 1987).

In addition, excuses or explanations for provocative actions (sometimes termed *causal accounts*) that appear to be *sincere* and are *specific* in nature—provide a clear and detailed explanation of the factors involved—are much more effective in defusing anger and subsequent aggression than excuses that appear to be insincere or are lacking in detail (e.g., Shapiro, Buttner, & Barry, 1993).

In sum, systematic research on the effects of cognitive interventions such as apologies and reasonable explanations confirm informal observations about the effectiveness of such procedures: In many cases, they do go a long way toward reducing anger aroused by provocative actions and so also toward preventing overt aggression (e.g., Baron, 1988; Ohbuchi, Kameda, & Agarie, 1989). In short, while it is often difficult to admit wrongdoing and to say "I'm sorry," the value of doing so may well make this effort worthwhile.

OTHER TECHNIQUES FOR REDUCING AGGRESSION:
NONAGGRESSIVE MODELS, TRAINING IN SOCIAL SKILLS, AND INCOMPATIBLE RESPONSES

Many other techniques for reducing overt aggression have been suggested (e.g., Baron, 1983). Here, we'll briefly consider three that appear to be quite effective.

EXPOSURE TO NONAGGRESSIVE MODELS: IS RESTRAINT CONTAGIOUS?

As we noted previously, exposure to aggressive actions by others in films or on television can increase aggression among viewers. If this is so, then it seems only reasonable to expect parallel—but opposite—effects from exposure to persons who either demonstrate or urge *restraint* in the face of provocation. That exposure to such *nonaggressive models* actually produces such effects is indicated by the findings of several experiments (e.g., Baron, 1972; Donnerstein & Donnerstein, 1976). In these studies, persons exposed to the actions of nonaggressive models later demonstrated lower levels of aggression than persons not exposed to such models, even if they had been strongly provoked. These findings suggest that it may be useful to plant restrained, nonaggressive models in tense and threatening situations. Their presence may well serve to tip the balance against the occurrence of violence.

Lack of social skills: One factor behind many aggressive encounters

FIGURE 11.18 Inadequate social skills often contribute to the occurrence of dangerous instances of aggression.
Source: The New Yorker.

"Winthrop had the soft answer that turneth away wrath all ready on the tip of his tongue and then he forgot it."

TRAINING IN SOCIAL SKILLS: LEARNING TO GET ALONG WITH OTHERS. One reason why many persons become involved in aggressive encounters they would prefer to avoid is straightforward: Like Winthrop in Figure 11.18, they are sorely lacking in basic social skills that would enable them to avoid such events. For example, they do not know how to respond to provocations from others in a way that will soothe these persons rather than fan the flames of anger. Similarly, they do not know how to make their wishes known to others, and they grow increasingly frustrated when people don't respond as they desire. And they often have an abrasive style of self-expression coupled with insensitivity to signs of others' emotional states. As a result of these deficits, they experience severe, repeated frustration, and they say or do things that unnecessarily anger the people around them. Persons lacking in social skills seem to account for a high proportion of violence in many societies (Toch, 1985). Thus, equipping them with the social skills they so badly lack may go a long way toward reducing the incidence of aggression.

Fortunately, systematic procedures for teaching individuals precisely such skills exist. Moreover, when people master these skills, the likelihood that they will become involved in aggressive encounters with others seems to decrease dramatically (e.g., Schneider & Byrne, 1987). These benefits are clearly illustrated by a study conducted by Schneider (1991). In this investigation, boys and girls at a treatment center for children with conduct disorders underwent social skills training designed to reduce their very high levels of aggression. The sessions involved small groups of two to four children and lasted about thirty to forty minutes; they were continued for twelve weeks. During these sessions the children (ages seven to fourteen) were taught through a variety of exercises to handle situations that might otherwise escalate into aggression.

For example, they learned to respond to teasing in a nonaggressive manner, to avoid overreacting in frustrating situations, and to understand others' feelings and reactions more accurately.

After the training sessions were complete, the investigators observed participants' behavior during recess and free-play periods. Results indicated that the children showed a marked reduction in aggressive actions and a sharp increase in cooperative actions. These and related findings (see the **Work in Progress** section below) suggest that providing highly aggressive persons with improved social skills can often help them avoid dangerous encounters with others.

Work in Progress

Training in Social Skills: Maximizing Its Effectiveness

The findings reported by Schneider (1991) are encouraging: They suggest that equipping aggressive children with specific social skills can help them deal more effectively with many situations, and so can reduce their levels of aggression toward others. In follow-up research, Bienert and Schneider (1993) have taken this work several steps farther, focusing on the task of refining such training so that it is maximally successful. This research has identified a number of specific skills in which aggressive-disruptive children fall far below the average for their classmates. These turn out to include deficits in recognizing others' feelings, dealing with anger, using self-control, staying out of fights, dealing with embarrassment, and responding to teasing. In all these areas, children rated as aggressive and disruptive by peers and teachers show less effective patterns of behavior than other members of their classes.

Can such youngsters master improved skills in these areas? Data gathered by Bienert and Schneider (1993) suggest that they can, provided appropriate methods of training are employed. In this study, the researcher exposed highly aggressive children in the sixth grade (the final year of elementary school) to social skills training that was specifically focused on these problems. Small groups of youngsters (three to seven) practiced the ten most important skill deficits identified by their teachers and classmates. They did this by playing games, by watching videotapes in which models showed effective and ineffective actions, and by reading vignettes in which other children coped successfully or unsuccessfully with problem situations. There were ten training sessions lasting one hour each. Participants in two control groups of aggressive children either did not receive the training until a later time, or received training that was appropriate for other problems (e.g., social isolation). (Both of these control groups later received appropriate training.)

Results were clear: Children who received the social skills training showed significant improvements in the ratings they received from peers and teachers and also in their own self-perceptions. Moreover, they showed significantly lower levels of aggression than those in the control groups. Interestingly, such benefits were still present more than a year later, when the children moved to new schools (several different junior high schools). These findings serve to underscore the following optimistic conclusions: (1) Highly aggressive children are not "bad" persons who attack others because of uncontrollable hostile impulses. (2) Their aggression is certainly *not* an inevitable aspect of their personality; on the contrary, with appropriate short-term training, it can be sharply reduced.

INCOMPATIBLE RESPONSES: POSITIVE AFFECT AS A MEANS OF REDUC-
ING ANGER. The final technique for reducing aggression we will consider
rests upon the following basic principle: It is impossible to engage in two
incompatible responses or experience two incompatible emotional states at
once. If we apply this idea to aggression, it seems that we may be able to lessen
both anger and overt aggression by inducing reactions or emotional states
incompatible with them. That this is indeed the case is indicated by a large
body of research evidence. When angry persons are induced to experience
emotional states incompatible with anger or aggression, such as *empathy, mild
sexual arousal,* or *humor,* they do show reduced levels of aggression (Baron,
1983; Ramirez, Bryant, & Zillmann, 1983). This may occur because the positive
feelings produced by such reactions reduce the negative feelings stemming
from frustration or annoyance, and also because such positive affect tends to
lower the very high levels of arousal associated with extreme anger. As we
noted previously, high levels of arousal make it difficult for individuals to regulate their own behavior. Whatever the precise mechanisms involved, one fact
seems clear: People in a pleasant or happy frame of mind are usually much
less likely to aggress against others. Thus, steps designed to generate these
incompatible responses can be a useful strategy for the control of human
aggression.

Social Diversity ▼ *A Critical Analysis*

Culture and Aggression: The Social Context of Violence

Early in this chapter, we called
attention to the existence of
huge variations in the rate of violence around the world. For
example, murder rates in the
United States are ten to twenty
times higher than in other
industrialized nations; but in several tribal societies they are fifty
to eighty times higher (Scott,
1992). Perhaps a more concrete
example—one that places such
numbers in a specific context—
will prove helpful.

Aggression: The Role
of Microculture

In the Mexican state of Oaxaca,
there are two Zapotec villages
located less than four miles

apart. The two villages have
existed in their present locations
for at least 450 years, and in
terms of language, religion, economics, and virtually every other
aspect, they are identical. Yet the
murder rate in one is more than
six times higher than in the
other. Thus, while residents of
the nonviolent village might
expect to witness one murder
every fourteen years, those in
the violent village could expect
to see one every eighteen
months to two years (Fry, 1990).
What accounts for this difference? Careful comparison of the
villages suggests that the key difference lies in what sociologists
term *microculture*—cultural differences between groups within

a larger culture. In this case, it
appears that the nonviolent villagers view themselves as peace-
ful people who have a high
amount of respect for others. In
contrast, those in the violent village perceive themselves as
tough and aggressive; they have
a much higher rate of fist fights,
spouse abuse, and, of course,
homicides. What underlies these
differences? In attempting to
explain them, Scott (1992) calls
attention to what might be
termed *social inertia*—the tendency of a social system or culture to remain unchanged and
stable in certain dimensions
once it is established. Researchers
theorize that when these two villages were founded, they were

organized along different lines, perhaps by persons with different perspectives on aggression. The norms established in those long-gone days have persisted, and find expression in the sharply contrasting rates of violence we now observe.

In short, *culture* does seem to play an important role in aggression. Growing evidence suggests that it determines not only the rate of violence but the forms it generally takes and the targets selected. In this context, the relations between mountain villages in Northern Italy are also informative (Tak, 1990). To an outsider, these villages appear to be virtually identical: ethnically, economically, architecturally. Yet the persons living in them hold strong stereotypes about their neighbors. They label these outsiders with unpleasant and derisive nicknames (e.g., little frogs, charcoal burners, bean-heads); and they attribute negative traits or characteristics to outsiders, viewing them as promiscuous, untrustworthy, and *violent*. For example, in describing residents of a neighboring village, persons in one village often say: "They would as soon stick you with a knife as talk with you." Such attitudes, in turn, explain the fact that relations between the villages are sometimes strained and that feuds between them are not uncommon.

Culture and Reactions to Frustration

One especially important way in which culture influences aggression is by determining when and how reactions to frustration are expressed. In many cultures aggression is a strongly disapproved form of behavior, so persons subjected to frustration or provocation are urged to show restraint in the face of such events. For example, in Sri Lanka, *quiet-self-control* is highly

 Culture and reactions to frustration

FIGURE 11.19 When they were an ethnic minority in their schools, Hispanic children demonstrated increased moodiness but not more aggression. In contrast, when Anglo children were an ethnic minority, they demonstrated more aggression but not more moodiness. These findings indicate that culture plays an important role in the expression of frustration-induced aggression.

Source: Based on data from Kaufman, Gregory, & Stephan, 1990.

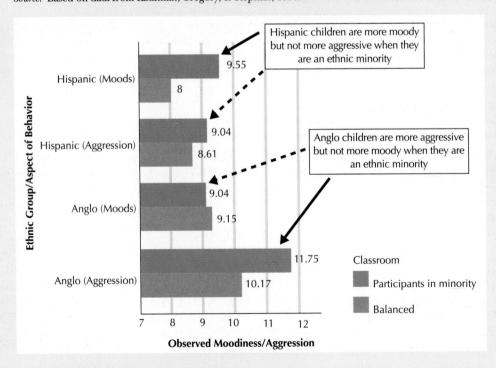

valued (Spencer, 1990). As a result, many persons refrain from aggressing in response to provocations that would evoke powerful retaliation from persons in other cultures.

A clear illustration of the role of cultural factors in shaping reactions to frustration is provided by a study conducted by Kaufman, Gregory, and Stephan (1990). These researchers examined the reactions of Anglo and Hispanic students in the United States to one important type of frustration: being an ethnic minority in their schools. Kaufman et al. (1990) predicted that because Hispanic culture strongly emphasizes *simpatia*—efforts by individuals to be likable, easygoing, and fun to be with—Hispanic children would demonstrate increased moodiness but *not* increased aggression in classrooms where they were an ethnic minority. In contrast, because

Anglo culture is more accepting of overt aggression, Kaufman et al. (1990) expected that Anglo children might demonstrate higher levels of aggression when they were an ethnic minority. As shown in Figure 11.19, p. 476, results offered support for these predictions. These findings illustrate the important role of culture in shaping the form and incidence of aggression in many contexts.

The Persistence of Cultural Differences in Aggression

One final point: Why do cultural differences in aggression persist? Why, in short, do the members of some cultures demonstrate rates of violence so much higher than those of other cultures? One answer seems to involve contrasting beliefs about aggression and the different child-rearing practices these encourage.

Various cultures hold contrasting views concerning the appropriateness of aggression and reasons for its occurrence. For example, a study by Osterwell and Nagano-Nakamura (1992) indicates that Japanese mothers view aggression as a natural part of their children's behavior but believe that it should be expressed *within* the family, where it can be regulated and so do little serious harm. In contrast, Israeli mothers believe that aggression is mainly a response to external provocations, and they believe that aggression should be expressed outside the family rather than within it. Such contrasting beliefs about aggression influence child-rearing practices in various cultures, and these, in turn, help explain why cultural differences in the rate and intensity of many forms of aggression tend to persist over time (Fraczek & Kirwil, 1992).

Summary and Review

Theoretical Perspectives on Aggression

Aggression—the intentional infliction of harm on others—has been attributed to many different causes. *Instinct theories,* such as the ones proposed by Freud and Lorenz, suggest that aggression stems from innate urges toward destructive actions. *Drive theories* suggest that aggression stems from externally generated motives to harm or injure others. In contrast, modern perspectives (the *neoassociationist* and *social learning* views) suggest that aggression stems from negative reactions to aversive experiences, memories, cognitions, learning, and present reinforcement or punishments for aggressive actions.

Social Determinants of Aggression

Many acts of aggression are triggered by the words or deeds of persons with whom the aggressor interacts, or by social conditions generally. *Frustration,* interference with goal-directed behavior, can facilitate aggression, perhaps because of the negative feelings it generates. *Direct provocations* from others are an important cause of aggression, especially when such actions appear to stem from malevolent intent. Considerable evidence suggests that exposure to *media violence* (in films or television shows) can increase aggression on the part of viewers.

Heightened arousal can increase aggression. However, the impact of arousal on aggression depends on the complex interplay between emotions and cognitions. Cognitions sometimes shape emotions and hence aggression. Conversely, emotions affect cognitions, and this, too, can influence aggressive behavior. *Alcohol* can facilitate aggression under some conditions, but persons who consume this drug remain responsive to social cues and will aggress only when this seems appropriate or justified. They may be more likely, however, to aggress against targets who cannot retaliate.

Personal Determinants of Aggression

Type A persons, because of their extreme competitiveness and hostility, are more aggressive in many situations than *Type B* persons. Individuals who perceive hostile intent behind others' actions even when this is lacking are more aggressive than those without such hostile *attributional bias*. Persons who are high in *shame-proneness* are more likely to engage in aggression than persons who are low in this tendency. Males appear to be somewhat more aggressive overall than females. However, females are more likely than males to engage in indirect forms of aggression. While such differences stem primarily from contrasting gender roles and socialization experiences, there is some indication that biological factors also play a role in this respect.

The Reduction of Aggression

Several techniques are effective in reducing aggression. *Punishment* can serve as an effective deterrent to aggression if it is delivered swiftly, it is intense, and its likelihood of occurrence is high. Participation in *cathartic activities* (e.g., vigorous nonaggressive behaviors) can sometimes lower arousal and anger. But such reductions appear to be temporary, and anger can readily reemerge when individuals bring thoughts and memories associated with aggression (or past sources of provocation) to mind.

Direct *apologies* and *reasonable explanations* for provocative actions are often highly effective in reducing anger and subsequent aggression. Additional techniques effective in reducing aggression include exposure to *nonaggressive models,* training in basic *social skills,* and the induction of responses *incompatible* with anger.

Key Terms

Aggression Behavior directed toward the goal of harming or injuring another living being who is motivated to avoid such treatment.

Aggression Machine Apparatus used to measure physical aggression under safe laboratory conditions.

Aggressive Cues Stimuli that, because of previous association with aggression, acquire for capacity to elicit such behavior.

Catharsis Hypothesis The view that providing angry persons with an opportunity to engage in vigorous but noninjurious activities will reduce their level of emotional arousal and lower their tendencies to aggress against others.

Cognitive Neoassociationist View A theory suggesting that aversive experiences generate negative affect, which in turn activates tendencies toward both aggression and flight. Which of these actions follows depends in part on higher-level cognitive processes.

Deindividuation A psychological state characterized by reduced self-awareness and major shifts in perception; encourages wild, impulsive forms of behavior, including aggression. Deindividuation is encouraged by external conditions such as anonymity.

Drive Theories Theories suggesting that aggression stems from external conditions that arouse the motive to harm or injure others. The most famous of these theories is the frustration-aggression hypothesis.

Excitation Transfer Theory A theory suggesting that arousal produced in one situation can persist and intensify emotional reactions occurring in subsequent situations.

Frustration-Aggression Hypothesis The suggestion that frustration is a very powerful determinant of aggression.

Hostile Aggression Aggression whose primary goal is harm or injury to the victim.

Hostile Attributional Bias The tendency to perceive others' actions as stemming from hostile intent even when this is not clearly the case.

Incompatible Responses In relation to aggression, responses that are incompatible with anger or overt aggressive actions against others.

Instinct Theory A view suggesting that specific forms of behavior (e.g., aggression) stem from innate tendencies that are universal among members of a given species.

Instrumental Aggression Aggression directed toward primary goals other than harm or injury to the victim.

Provocation Actions by others that are perceived as acts of aggression deriving from hostile intentions.

Punishment Procedures in which aversive consequences are delivered to individuals each time they engage in specific actions. Under appropriate conditions, punishment can serve as an effective deterrent to human aggression.

Social Learning View A perspective suggesting that aggression is a complex form of learned behavior.

Type A's Persons characterized by high levels of competitiveness, time urgency, and hostility.

Type B's Persons who do not show the pattern of characteristics demonstrated by Type As (i.e., they are relatively low in competitiveness, time urgency, and hostility).

Violent Pornography Pornographic materials that contain scenes of violence—especially violence toward women.

Weapons Effect The facilitation of aggression by the presence of weapons even when the weapons are not used in the aggressive actions performed.

For More Information

Baenninger, R. (Ed.). (1991). *Targets of violence and aggression.* Amsterdam: Elsevier/North-Holland.

    This book deals with aggression toward targets that are either helpless or unable to retaliate. Separate chapters (each written by a different expert) examine such important and timely topics as human aggression toward other species, child abuse, athletes as targets of aggression, aggression toward homosexuals, and aggression along roadways. A comprehensive overview of what we currently know about several especially distressing forms of violence.

Baron, R. A., & Richardson, D. R. (1994). *Human aggression* (2nd ed.). New York: Plenum.

    A broad introduction to current knowledge about human aggression. Separate chapters examine the biological, social, environmental, and personal determinants of aggression. Additional chapters examine the development of aggression and the occurrence of aggression in many natural settings.

Felson, R. B., & Tedeschi, J. T. (Eds.). (1993). *Aggression and violence: social interactionist perspectives.* American Psychological Association: Washington, D.C.

    Distinguished researchers from several fields (psychology, sociology, criminology) examine aggression from different perspectives. Intriguing hypotheses concerning the causes of aggression, and the potential role of such factors as social power and the self-serving effects of conflict, are examined.

Geen, R. G. (1991). *Human aggression.* Pacific Grove, CA: Brooks/Cole.

    A well-written and relatively brief overview of research findings concerning aggressive behavior. One unique chapter integrates laboratory research on aggression with findings in behavioral medicine concerning potential links between hostility and heart disease.

Chapter TWELVE

Groups and Individuals:
The Consequences of Belonging

20 questions

▬▬▬▬▬▬▬▬▬▬▬▬▬▬▬▬▬▬▬▬▬▬▬▬
▬▬▬▬▬▬▬▬▬▬▬

Special Sections

I'm not certain whether it's advancing age or a sign of the times, but if you asked me right now whether I have any heroes, I'd have to answer no. This wasn't always the case, however. If we could climb into a time machine and visit the late 1950s, the situation would be very different. At that time I had lots of heroes—famous athletes like Mickey Mantle (baseball) and Bob Cousey (basketball), plus one more who lived much closer to home: David Carlton. Dave was the uncontested leader of all the teenage boys who lived in our apartment building. He was the one who decided what game we'd play on a given day—baseball, stickball, handball, or basketball—and who would be on each of the opposing teams. Dave decided when it was time to quit and go for a snack, and whether it would be pizza or ice cream. And Dave definitely set the styles for the rest of us. When he began using a new expression we picked it up too. And when he switched from one brand of jeans or sneakers to another we all did the same. Dave took the lead in our discussions about all the topics that interested boys our age—sports, big exams, and girls—and he usually had the last word, too. No doubt about it: He was the leader and we all knew it.

Why did he hold this role? Even now, almost thirty-five years later, I know the answer: *Dave had our respect*. Somehow, he was a little quicker, sharper, and just plain better at most things than the rest of us. No, he wasn't at the top in every activity. I could run faster than he could and Marty Fogel could throw a football farther. But Dave was very good at virtually everything we cared about. In baseball he was an ace pitcher and a crack hitter; in basketball he could dribble circles around the rest of us. To top it all off, he always managed to look very graceful both on and off the field. Dave even shone at parties, where he always seemed to end up with the prettiest girl. Perhaps the best thing he had going for him was *confidence*. At a time in life when the rest of us were painfully insecure, Dave oozed self-assurance. Cool and collected, he was never at a loss for words, and he could charm his way out of almost anything, anywhere, anytime.

In 1959 my family moved to another neighborhood, so I didn't see Dave again for many years. But there's a sequel to the story: I ran into him once again at the thirtieth-year reunion for my high school class. It took only a couple of minutes for me to discover that despite some changes in outward appearance, Dave was still very much the same person—still cool, slightly aloof, and supremely self-assured. I wasn't surprised when he told me that he had graduated from an Ivy League school and was now a senior partner at a very prestigious law firm (where, I estimated, his income approached $1,000,000 a year). No, there was no basic change: Dave was still a leader and still, it seemed, a step or two ahead of his competition.

Did *your* group of teenage friends have a clear-cut leader like Dave? Whether it did or not, we're certain that at some point in your life, you have had direct experience with *leadership* and its effects. It is a basic fact of social life that within almost any group, some persons are more influential than others and exert a powerful effect upon virtually all activities. Indeed, the outcomes experienced by most groups, whether they are *informal* such as the one described above, or *formal* as in various organizations, depend to an important degree upon the skill, competence, and judgment of their leaders (see Figure 12.1, p. 483).

Yet leadership is only one of many ways in which belonging to a group can affect individuals. Once persons join various groups, they are subject to a wide variety of forces and processes—ones that can affect their behavior, attitudes, and values in many ways. It is on such *group influence*—the effects of group membership on individual behavior—that we will focus in this chapter. First, to set the stage for further discussion, we'll examine the basic nature of groups: what they are and how they function. Second, we'll consider the impact of groups on *task performance*. Here we'll examine the ways in which performance in various tasks can be affected by the presence of others or their potential evaluations—a process known as *social facilitation*. In addition, we'll address the complex question of whether groups or individuals are better at performing various tasks. Third, we'll turn to *decision making* in groups, examining both the process through which groups move toward consensus and various factors that can distort or bias the decisions they reach. Finally, we'll return to the topic of our opening story, *leadership*, considering the question of whether leaders are born or made, their style of exerting influence, and several factors that seem to determine their effectiveness.

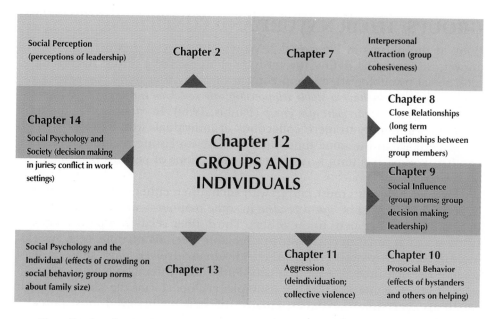

Social Perception (perceptions of leadership)	Chapter 2	Chapter 7	Interpersonal Attraction (group cohesiveness)

Chapter 14
Social Psychology and Society (decision making in juries; conflict in work settings)

Chapter 12 GROUPS AND INDIVIDUALS

Chapter 8
Close Relationships (long term relationships between group members)

Chapter 9
Social Influence (group norms; group decision making; leadership)

Social Psychology and the Individual (effects of crowding on social behavior; group norms about family size)

Chapter 13

Chapter 11
Aggression (deindividuation; collective violence)

Chapter 10
Prosocial Behavior (effects of bystanders and others on helping)

One final point before proceeding: While the emphasis in this chapter will be on the many ways in which groups influence their individual members, it is important to note that groups, in turn, are shaped *by* their members. Indeed, *group composition*—the background, gender, characteristics, and attitudes of group members—can strongly influence the nature and operation of groups (Moreland & Levine, 1992a). So, in a key sense, the relationship between individuals and groups is very much a two-way street.

 Leaders: A key ingredient in group performance

FIGURE 12.1 The success experienced by many groups depends to a major extent upon the effectiveness of their leaders.

GROUPS: THEIR NATURE AND FUNCTION

Exercise 1

Look at the photos in Figure 12.2. Which show social groups? In order to answer, we must first define the term *group* in concrete terms. According to most social psychologists, a **group** consists of *two or more interacting persons who share common goals, have a stable relationship, are somehow interdependent, and perceive that they are in fact part of a group* (Paulus, 1989). In other words, the term *group* does not apply to mere collections of individuals who happen to be in the same place at the same time but who have no lasting relationship to one another. Rather, this term is restricted to collections of persons that meet certain criteria.

First, such persons must *interact* with each other, either directly or indirectly. Second, they must be *interdependent* in some manner—what happens to one must affect what happens to the others. Third, their relationship must be relatively *stable;* it must persist over appreciable periods of time (e.g., weeks, months, or even years). Fourth, the individuals involved must share at least some goals that they all seek to attain. Fifth, their interactions must be *structured* in some manner, so that, for example, each performs the same or similar functions each time they meet. Finally, the persons involved must perceive themselves as members of a group—they must recognize the existence of a lasting relationship among them.

This is quite a lengthy list: Are all these conditions really necessary before it makes sense to describe several persons as belonging to a group? Opinion is split on this issue (e.g., Turner, 1985), but many feel that awareness of group membership may be the most important. In other words, people belong to a group when they perceive that they belong to it. In any case, it is also clear that groups do not spring into existence as fully formed entities. Rather, they emerge out a continuous process of *social integration* in which bonds between potential members strengthen gradually, as people develop shared feelings, beliefs, and behaviors (Moreland, 1987).

Applying this definition to the photos in Figure 12.2, it is easy to see that the people in the bottom picture are members of a group. In contrast, those in the top two photos are not; they are simply persons who happen to be in the same place at the same time but who have no real relationship to one another.

GROUP FORMATION: WHY DO PEOPLE JOIN?

Discussion Question 4

At present you probably belong to several different groups. Why did you join them in the first place? Existing evidence on this question suggests that individuals generally enter groups for several major reasons (Greenberg & Baron, 1993). First, groups help us to satisfy important psychological or social needs such as those for belonging and receiving attention and affection. Second, groups help us achieve goals that we could not attain as individuals. By working within groups we can perform tasks we could not perform alone. Third, group membership often provides us with knowledge and information that would otherwise not be available to us. For example, individuals are often denied access to sensitive or restricted information held by a group until they are admitted to full membership. Fourth, groups help meet our need for security; in many cases there is a degree of safety in numbers, and belonging to various groups can provide protection against common, external enemies.

Finally, group membership also contributes to establishment of a positive *social identity*—it becomes part of the self-concept (refer to chapter 5). Simply

Groups: More than just collections of individuals

FIGURE 12.2 Which of these photos show true social *groups?* According to the definition offered in the text, only the bottom.

put, the greater the number of prestigious, restrictive groups to which an individual is admitted, the more her or his self-concept is bolstered. In sum, there are many important reasons for joining groups, so it is not at all surprising that most persons seek entry to many over the course of their lives.

HOW GROUPS FUNCTION: ROLES, STATUS, NORMS, AND COHESIVENESS

That groups often exert powerful effects upon the behavior and cognitions of their members is obvious. Indeed, we will devote much of this chapter to the task of describing such effects. Before turning to specific types of *group influence,* however, we should address a more basic issue: How, precisely, do groups affect their members? A complete answer to this question involves many processes, including several we have examined in previous chapters (e.g., conformity, persuasion, attraction). However, there is general agreement that four aspects of groups play a crucial role in this regard. These are known, respectively, as *roles, status, norms,* and *cohesiveness* (Forsyth, 1983; Paulus, 1989).

ROLES: DIFFERENTIATION OF FUNCTION WITHIN GROUPS.   Think of a group to which you have belonged—anything from the scouts to a professional association relating to your occupation. Now consider the following question: Did everyone in the group act in the same way or perform the same functions? Your answer is probably no. On the contrary, a considerable degree of differentiation may well have existed. Specific persons worked at different tasks and were expected to accomplish different things for the group. In short, they fulfilled different **roles.** Sometimes roles are assigned in a formal and specific manner. For example, an individual may be chosen by a group to serve as its leader, secretary, or treasurer. In other cases individuals gradually acquire certain roles without being formally assigned to them. Leaders often emerge in this manner (Ellis, 1989). And within a given group, different persons gradually come to fulfill either *task-oriented roles* (focusing on getting the group's major jobs done), or *relations-oriented roles* (focusing on reducing interpersonal friction and maintaining good relations between members). However roles emerge, people often *internalize* them; they link their roles to key aspects of their self-concept or self-perceptions (see chapters 2 and 5). When this happens, roles may exert truly profound and general effects on behavior, even at times when individuals interact with other persons not in their group. For example, a high-powered attorney may find herself behaving toward her children in the same aggressive, confrontational ways she uses to good advantage in the courtroom; or a police officer may approach friends and neighbors with the swagger that says, "Look out—here comes authority!"

Roles help to clarify the responsibilities and obligations of the persons belonging to a group. In addition, roles constitute one key way in which groups shape the behavior and thoughts of their members. They do have a downside, however. First, group members sometimes experience *role conflict*— pressures stemming from the fact that they must play two or more roles concurrently, or from the fact that a single role requires competing forms of behavior. A very common example of role conflict involves the pressures experienced by new mothers and fathers who find the obligations of being a *parent* incompatible with the obligations of the role of *student* or *employee.*

Second, because they prescribe specific forms of behavior, roles tend to restrict individual freedom, and this in turn can lead to negative reactions on the part of group members. A clear illustration of such effects is provided by a study conducted by Worchel and Shackelford (1991). These researchers had groups of six to eight individuals perform a problem-solving task (determining which equipment was most valuable and important to a group of astronauts after an emergency crash landing) under either stressful or nonstressful conditions. In two *high-stress* conditions, participants performed this task either in the presence of high levels of noise or under very crowded conditions (a room only eight feet by eight feet in size). In two *low-stress* conditions participants performed the same task in a large and comfortable room. In one condition they were told that the room had been designed to provide a pleasant work environment; in another they were told that it was inadequate but was the best avilable. (The same room was used in both cases; only the experimenter's comments about it differed.) Within each environmental condition, half of the groups were given a clear structure involving *assigned roles* before working on the problem: One member was appointed as leader, and a specific procedure was instituted for assuring that each member contributed. The remaining groups were not provided with such structure before working on the task. After completing their work, group members rated their perceptions of the task, their liking for other members, their mood, and the process through which group decisions were made.

Results indicated that in the two nonstressful conditions, group structure (i.e., assigning specific roles) enhanced reactions to the group along most dimensions. In contrast, under high levels of stress, the opposite pattern emerged: Ratings were less favorable in the presence of structure than in its absence (see Figure 12.3). A similar (but nonsignificant) pattern was obtained for actual task performance; assigned roles enhanced performance in the non-stressful condition but reduced it in the presence of noise or crowding. Worchel and Shackelford (1991) interpreted these findings as stemming from the fact that under stressful conditions, an imposed group structure limited participants' flexibility in dealing with the problem and also their experienced sense of control. Whatever the precise mechanism involved, however, these results suggest that clearly defined roles are not always a plus where group process or performance is concerned, and may be detrimental when groups confront unpleasant or stressful conditions.

STATUS: THE PRESTIGE OF VARIOUS ROLES. Suppose you visited the office of the president of your university; would it be different in any respect

 Assigned group structure (roles): Some surprising effects

FIGURE 12.3 Contrary to what common sense might suggest, imposing an assigned structure—specific roles—on a task-performing group led to negative reactions (and reduced performance) under conditions of high stress. When conditions were less stressful, however, such assigned structure had a positive effect on participants' ratings of the task process.
Source: Based on data from Worchel & Shackelford, 1991.

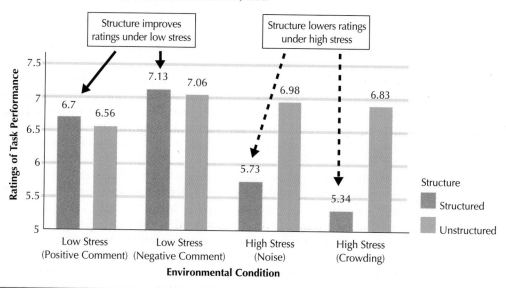

from the office of a new assistant professor? Absolutely! Unless your school is a very unusual one, the president's office would be much larger and much more luxurious. Such differences are hardly surprising—we view them as a normal part of social life. They reflect the fact that within any group (and organizations like colleges can be viewed as being large and complex groups), different roles (positions) are associated with different degrees of **status**—social standing or rank. And status, in turn, is related to a wide variety of outcomes, including the size and plushness of one's office, use of a reserved parking spot, and having or not having an expense account. So status is as important aspect of groups and the way they function.

NORMS: THE RULES OF THE GAME.   A third factor responsible for the powerful impact of groups upon their members is one we have already considered—*norms*. As you may recall from chapter 9, **norms** are rules—implicit or explicit—established by groups to regulate the behavior of their members. They tell group members how to behave (*prescriptive norms*) or how *not* to behave (*proscriptive norms*) in various situations. Most groups insist upon adherence to their norms as a basic requirement for membership. Thus, it is not surprising that individuals wishing to join or remain in specific groups generally follow these rules of the game quite closely. If they do not, they may soon find themselves on the outside looking in!

Norms develop in several different ways (Feldman, 1984). First, they can be established by leaders, who state them as explicit principles. Second, they may derive from critical events in the group's history. For example, a costly leak of information from a decision-making group may lead its members to adopt strict rules about secrecy. Third, norms are often carried over from past situations. Individul members know how they have behaved in other groups, and they may import such patterns—and the expectations that these are the correct or preferred ways of behaving—into a newly formed group. However they are formed, once group norms take shape, they often exert strong effects upon members and upon all activities that occur within the group.

COHESIVENESS: THE EFFECTS OF WANTING TO BELONG.   Consider two groups. In the first, members like one another very much, strongly desire the goals their group is seeking, and feel that they could not possibly find another group that would better satisfy their needs. In the second, the opposite is true: Members don't like one another, they do not share common goals, and they are actively seeking other groups that might offer them a better deal. Which group would exert stronger effects upon its members? The answer is obvious: the first. The reason for this difference lies in the fact that **cohesiveness**—all pressures or forces causing members to remain part of a group—is much higher in the first group than in the second. In other words, individuals in the first group want to retain their membership much more strongly than those in the second.

While cohesiveness has sometimes been viewed as a unitary dimension ranging from low to high, growing evidence suggests that it actually involves at least two distinct aspects (Zaccaro & McCoy, 1988). The first involves the degree to which members like each other—*interpersonal cohesiveness*. The second involves the extent to which group membership provides for the attainment of important personal goals—*task-based cohesiveness*. Interestingly, it appears that under some conditions, only groups that are high in both will be successful. Specifically, on tasks that require members to work together to generate and choose correct solutions, both high interpersonal cohesiveness and high task-based cohesiveness are necessary for good performance (Zaccaro & McCoy, 1988). This is because on such tasks members must be committed to the task *and* willing to expend effort for the group. When members can work alone and close coordination between them isn't needed, in contrast, only task-based cohesiveness is required. In fact, high levels of interpersonal cohesiveness may actually interfere with performance by generating social interactions that interfere with performance.

Additional factors that influence cohesiveness include (1) the amount of effort required to gain entry into the group (the greater the costs of joining the group in the first place, the higher members' attraction to it; as dissonance theory suggests—see chapter 4—the harder we must work to attain a goal, such as group membership, the higher our evaluation of it); (2) external threats or severe competition (Sherif et al., 1961); and (3) size—small groups tend to be more cohesive than large ones.

In sum, several aspects of groups determine the extent to which they can, and do, influence their members. Since these play an important role in group influence, keeping them in mind is well worthwhile as we consider some of the specific ways in which groups shape the behavior and thought of individuals.

GROUPS AND TASK PERFORMANCE: THE BENEFITS—AND COSTS— OF WORKING WITH OTHERS

Some activities, such as studying, balancing one's checkbook, or writing love letters, are best carried out alone. Most tasks we perform, however, are done either with others or in their presence. This raises an intriguing question: What impact, if any, do groups exert upon task performance? In order to answer this question, it is necessary to consider two separate but related issues: (1) What are the effects of the mere presence of others on individual performance; and (2) are groups more, or less, efficient than individuals in carrying out various tasks?

SOCIAL FACILITATION: PERFORMANCE IN THE PRESENCE OF OTHERS

Imagine that you must make a speech in front of a large audience. You have several weeks to prepare, so you write the speech and then practice it alone over and over again. Now, finally, the big day has arrived. You are introduced and begin to speak. How will you do? Better or worse than was true when you delivered it to the four walls of your own room? In short, will the presence of an audience facilitate or interfere with your performance? Early research concerned with this question (Triplett, 1898) yielded a confusing pattern of results. Sometimes performance was improved by the presence of an audience, and sometimes the opposite was true. How could this puzzle be resolved? An insightful answer was offered by Zajonc (1965).

THE DRIVE THEORY OF SOCIAL FACILITATION: OTHER PERSONS AS A SOURCE OF AROUSAL. Before describing Zajonc's theory, we should clarify a basic point. The term *social facilitation* is used by social psychologists to

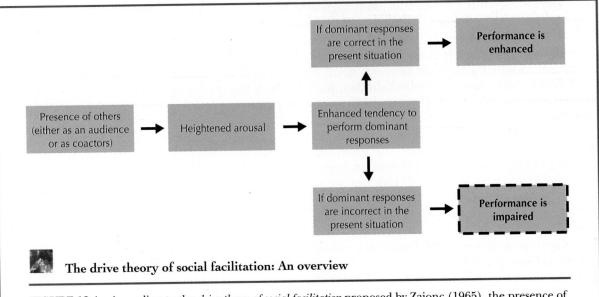

The drive theory of social facilitation: An overview

FIGURE 12.4 According to the *drive theory of social facilitation* proposed by Zajonc (1965), the presence of others increases arousal. This in turn enhances the performance of dominant responses. If these responses are correct in a given situation, performance is also enhanced. If they are incorrect, performance is reduced. *Source:* Based on suggestions by Zajonc, 1965.

Transparency 12.1

Critical Thinking
Question 1

refer to any effects on performance stemming from the presence of others. Thus, it includes decrements as well as improvements in task performance.

Now, back to Zajonc's theory. The basic idea behind his theory, now known as the **drive theory of social facilitation,** is that the presence of others produces increments in level of arousal. As you can readily see, this suggestion agrees closely with our informal experience. The presence of other persons—especially when they serve as an audience—does seem to generate signs of increased arousal (e.g., feelings of tension or excitement). But how do such increments in arousal then affect our performance? Zajonc suggests that the answer involves two facts.

First, it is a basic principle of psychology that increments in arousal enhance the occurrence of *dominant responses*—the responses an individual is most likely to make in a given situation. Thus, when arousal increases, the tendency to make dominant responses increases, too (Davis & Harvey, 1992). Second, such dominant responses can be either correct or incorrect for any task currently being performed.

When these two facts are combined with the suggestion that the presence of others is arousing, two predictions follow: (1) The presence of others will facilitate performance when an individual's dominant responses are the correct ones for the particular situation; (2) the presence of others will impair performance when a person's dominant responses are incorrect for the situation. (Please see Figure 12.4 for a summary of these suggestions.) Another implication of these predictions is that the presence of others will facilitate the performance of strong, well-learned responses, but may interfere with the performance of new and as yet unmastered ones.

Initial studies designed to test these predictions generally yielded positive results (e.g., Matlin & Zajonc, 1968: Zajonc & Sales, 1966). Individuals were in fact more likely to emit dominant responses when in the presence of others than when alone, and performance on various tasks was either enhanced or impaired depending on whether these responses were correct or incorrect in each situation (Geen, 1989; Geen & Gange, 1977). For example, in one ingenious investigation, Davis and Harvey (1992) found that the batting performance of major league baseball players declines in high-pressure situations (such as when there are runners on base during late innings or when there are already two outs). Since audience-induced arousal would be expected to be very high in such situations, and since batting is a difficult task (even most professionals fail to get a hit more than 70 percent of the time), these findings are consistent with the predictions based on Zajonc's theory.

Additional research, however, soon raised an important question: Does social facilitation stem from the mere physical presence of others (and, perhaps, the increased tendencies to monitor carefully what's happening); or do other factors (e.g., concern over others' possible evaluations) also play a role? Support for the latter possibility was provided by the results of several interesting studies suggesting that social facilitation occurred only when individuals believed that their performance could be observed and evaluated by others (e.g., Bond, 1982; Bray & Sugarman, 1980; Cottrell et al., 1968). Such findings led some researchers to propose that social facilitation actually stems either from **evaluation apprehension**—concern over being judged by others—or related concerns over *self-presentation*—looking good in front of others (Carver & Scheier, 1981). Thus, it may be these factors, not the mere physical presence of others, that are crucial in determining the impact of an audience or coactors upon task performance.

At first glance, such suggestions seem quite reasonable. Most of us are concerned with the impressions we make on others and care about others' evaluations of us. Further, such concerns might be motivating or arousing in many situations. Other evidence, however, points to the conclusion that social facilitation effects can sometimes occur even in situations where these factors do not seem to play a role (e.g., Markus, 1978; Schmitt et al., 1986). For example, it has been found that animals—even insects!—perform simple tasks better in the presence of an audience than when alone. Since it is difficult to assume that insects are concerned about the impression they are making on other insects (common roaches were actually used in one of these studies; Zajonc, Heingartner, & Herman, 1969), these findings raise serious questions about an interpretation of social facilitation based solely on evaluation apprehension.

Research conducted with humans raises similar questions. For example, in one carefully conducted study on this issue, Schmitt and his colleagues (Schmitt et al., 1986) had participants perform both a simple task and a more complex one under one of three conditions: alone in the room, in the presence of another person who wore a blindfold and earphones (the *mere presence* condition), or in the presence of another person who could directly observe their performance (*evaluation apprehension* condition). The simple task was that of typing their own names. The complex one involved typing their names backward and inserting ascending numbers between every two letters. If the mere presence of others is arousing, then social facilitation effects should occur in this condition. This was indeed the case. Participants in the mere presence condition performed the simple task faster, but the complex task more slowly, than those in the control (alone) condition. Moreover, those in the evaluation apprehension condition performed the simple task the most quickly of all. These findings suggest that the mere presence of others is arousing, and that the possibility of being evaluated increases such arousal still further—at least for the purposes of performing simple tasks.

ONE POTENTIAL RESOLUTION: DISTRACTION-CONFLICT THEORY.
How can the diverse and seemingly contradictory findings we have described
so far be explained? One answer is provided by **distraction-conflict theory,**
developed by R. S. Baron, Sanders, and Moore (e.g., R. S. Baron, 1986;
Sanders, 1983).

Like other explanations of social facilitation, this theory assumes that audiences and coactors (others performing the same task as subjects) heighten
arousal. In contrast to earlier views, however, distraction-conflict theory suggests that such arousal stems from conflict between two tendencies: (1) the
tendency to pay attention to the task being performed, and (2) the tendency
to direct attention to an audience or coactors. The conflict produced by these
competing tendencies is arousing, and such arousal in turn enhances the tendency to perform dominant responses. If these are correct, performance is
enhanced; if they are incorrect, performance is reduced (refer to Figure 12.5).

Several different findings support this theory. For example, audiences produce social facilitation effects only when directing attention to them conflicts
in some way with task demands (Groff, R. S. Baron, & Moore, 1983). When
paying attention to an audience does not conflict with task performance,
social facilitation fails to occur. Similarly, individuals experience greater distraction when they perform various tasks in front of an audience than when
they perform them alone (R. S. Baron, Moore, & Sanders, 1978). Finally, when
individuals have little reason to pay attention to others present on the scene
(e.g., these persons are performing a different task), social facilitation fails to
occur; when they have strong reasons for paying close attention to others,
social facilitation occurs (Sanders, 1983).

Distraction-conflict theory offers two additional advantages worth considering. First, since animals as well as people can experience the type of conflict

 Distraction-conflict theory: A summary

FIGURE 12.5 According to *distraction-conflict theory,*
the presence of others produces conflict between
tendencies to (1) pay attention to these others and
(2) pay attention to the task being performed. The

conflict generated by these competing tendencies increases arousal. This in turn accounts for the occurrence of social facilitation effects.

Source: Based on suggestions by R. S. Baron, 1986.

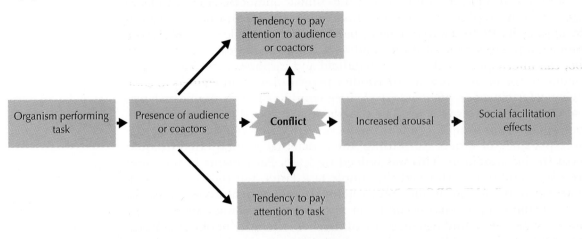

shown in Figure 12.5, this theory may account for the occurrence of social facilitation among animals. Second, with certain modifications (R. S. Baron, 1986), the theory can explain the occurrence of social facilitation without reference to the notion of arousal. The reasoning is as follows. The presence of an audience (or coactors) threatens the persons involved with *information overload*—they have more things demanding their attention than they can readily handle. As a result, they focus their attention primarily on those cues most central to the task at hand. Such focused attention can enhance performance on simple tasks, but may reduce it on complex ones that require attention to a wide range of stimuli. In short, a modified form of distraction-conflict theory can explain social facilitation effects in terms of our limited information-processing capacity.

To conclude: While distraction-conflict theory may not provide a final answer to the persistent puzzle of social facilitation, it is quite promising in this respect. In any case, it has added substantially to our understanding of what many social psychologists consider to be the simplest type of group effect.

GROUPS VERSUS INDIVIDUALS: WHICH HAS THE EDGE IN TASK PERFORMANCE?

At the start of this discussion, we called attention to the fact that many tasks people perform involve working with others. One reason why this is so involves the nature of the tasks themselves: Many simply cannot be performed by one person alone (refer to Figure 12.6, p. 494). Another basis for this reliance on groups where tasks are concerned is as follows: there is a general, widespread belief that people can accomplish more by working with others than by working alone. In one sense, this suggestion must be true; several people working together do generally accomplish more than any one of them in isolation. But more to the point, are groups really more *efficient* than individuals—do they accomplish more *per member*—than persons working alone?

PROS AND CONS OF WORKING IN GROUPS.   The answer, it turns out, is fairly complex (Stroebe, Diehl, & Abakoumkin, 1992). Working in groups does indeed offer certain advantages. It allows individuals to pool knowledge, skills, and equipment. Similarly, it allows for an efficient division of labor.

On the other hand, working in groups has important costs as well. When cohesiveness is high, members may spend a lot of time engaging in pleasant but nonproductive interactions. Further, strong pressures to adhere to existing norms may interfere with the development of new and better procedures for completing essential tasks. The likelihood of conflict between group members, too, can interfere with effective performance (e.g., Thomas, 1992). Finally, as group size increases, it may become increasingly difficult for members to coordinate their activities, with the result that output suffers. In sum, group settings offer a mixed bag of potential pluses and minuses where task performance is concerned. What determines the final balance between these factors? Research findings suggest that the most important single factor in this regard is the type of task being performed.

TYPE OF TASK AND GROUP PERFORMANCE.   One useful framework for understanding the different types of tasks performed by groups has been proposed by Steiner (1972, 1976). According to this perspective, most tasks fall into one of four different categories.

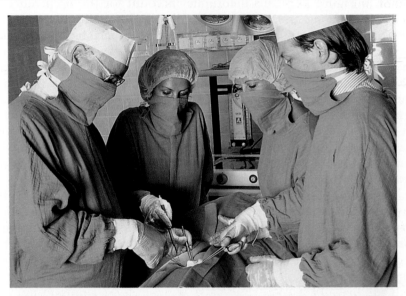

**Group effort:
Required for many tasks**

FIGURE 12.6 Many tasks, such as the ones shown here, can be successfully completed only by groups of individuals working together in a coordinated manner.

Discussion Question 3

First, there are **additive tasks.** These are ones in which the contributions of each member are combined into a single group product. For example, when several persons combine their efforts to lay the foundation for a house, move a heavy object, or pick up litter, the tasks being performed are additive ones. The group's output is based upon the sum of its members' individual efforts, and the extent to which these are coordinated in a useful way.

A second category is that of **compensatory tasks.** These are ones on which the contributions of the various members are averaged together to form a single group outcome. For example, consider a group of economic forecasters trying to predict next year's rate of inflation. The group outcome is the average of all their predictions. Presumably, since the rosy predictions of optimists in the group will be offset by the dire predictions of pessimists, the final prediction will tend to be more accurate than the judgments of any individual member.

Third, there are **disjunctive tasks.** Here, the group's product is determined by the performance of its best or most competent person. Many complex problem-solving tasks faced by groups are disjunctive in nature: The correct solution will be obtained only if one member discovers it and can then convince the others of its accuracy. For example, if a group of mathematicians is trying to solve a difficult equation, a solution will be obtained only if at least one member of the group can generate it and then gain the acceptance of the others.

Finally, there are **conjunctive tasks.** Here, the group's final product is determined by its weakest link—the poorest-performing member. A clear example of this type of task is a team of mountain climbers. The entire team can advance only as fast as its slowest member.

Now, to return to our basic question: How do groups and individuals compare with respect to each of these types of tasks? Many factors play a role in the performance of both individuals and groups, so a complete answer would require many pages. A useful rule-of-thumb reply, however, is as follows. On both additive and compensatory tasks, groups usually outperform individuals. (Please see Figure 12.7 for a summary of these conclusions.) In fact, they often do better than the best individual member. In such cases, then, the whole is indeed greater than the sum of its individual parts. (But see the next section for a discussion of one important exception to this conclusion, at least where additive tasks are concerned.) On disjunctive tasks, groups tend to do better than the average individual, because the final outcome is determined largely by the talents and contributions of the best (most effective) member. Finally

additive & compensatory
groups outperform
individuals

Critical Thinking
Question 2

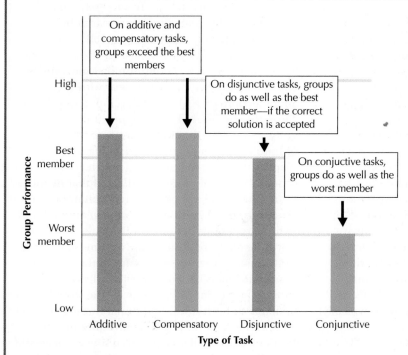

Groups, individuals, and task performance: Who has the edge?

FIGURE 12.7 Groups often outperform individuals on *additive* tasks, on which individual members' contributions are combined into a single group product, and on *compensatory* tasks, on which group performance is determined by the average performance of group members. Groups are about equal to individuals on *disjunctive* tasks, on which performance is determined by the best member. They are less productive than individuals on *conjunctive* tasks, where performance is determined by the weakest group member.

Figure labels: On additive and compensatory tasks, groups exceed the best members. On disjunctive tasks, groups do as well as the best member—if the correct solution is accepted. On conjuctive tasks, groups do as well as the worst member.

Group Performance (High, Best member, Worst member, Low) — Type of Task (Additive, Compensatory, Disjunctive, Conjunctive) on conjunctive tasks, groups generally perform more poorly than individuals, since overall performance is determined by the weakest member.

Discussion Question 1

One final point: As we suggested earlier, group output is also often strongly affected by group size (Kerr & Bruun, 1983). As group size increases, potential productivity increases, especially on additive tasks. But the possible occurrence of what Steiner terms *process losses*—reductions in productivity due to lack of coordination or reduced motivation—also rises. Recent findings indicate that as Steiner's model predicts, performance on additive tasks generally increases with group size; this is so because productivity gains exceed process losses. In contrast, performance on disjunctive tasks at first increases, but then declines, with increasing group size (Littlepage, 1991). This is because at some point, gains in potential productivity are more than offset by incoordination and other process losses. So, in sum, in answer to the question "Are groups or individuals more productive?" the most reasonable answer seems to be: It depends

Discussion Question 2

on several factors, including the nature of the task and the size of the group.

Work in Progress

Groups and Negotiation: Are Two Heads Better Than One?

While groups perform many important tasks, one of the most crucial of these is *negotiation*. When unions and management sit down to hammer out a contract, both sides send *negotiating teams* to perform this key function. Similarly, negotiations between countries over everything from arms limitation treaties to trade agreements generally involve discussions and bargaining between teams of diplomats. On the other hand, however, some negotiations do occur between individuals—for example, the classic face-off between the buyer and seller of a used car. So, which are more effective at negotiating—groups or individuals? There are several reason for predicting that groups may have an edge.

First, consider the fact that in order to be successful, complex negotiations require creative strategies by both sides. A simple win-lose approach, in which each side tries to defeat the other, tends to yield mediocre outcomes for both, or total deadlock. To the extent that creativity is needed, groups would be expected to have an edge because within Steiner's framework, negotiation can be viewed as a *disjunctive* task: In order for a successful strategy to be adopted, all that's needed is that one person uncover it. Since groups typically have an edge in disjunctive situations, we can predict that groups will do better in negotiations. Teams of negotiators may benefit from other advantages,

too: They may mutually reinforce one another's beliefs and so have higher commitment to a chosen strategy and higher confidence. And groups, when they show a united front, may be more successful in lowering the aspirations of opponents.

Are groups actually more successful in negotiations than individuals? Recent research by Thompson, Brodt, and Peterson (1993) suggests that in some—but by no means all—respects, they are. In her research, Thompson had individuals or teams bargain with other teams or with individuals about a complex real estate development project. The situation offered many opportunities for integrative strategies that would improve the outcomes of both sides; but of course, participants had to identify these strategies during the negotiations in order to use them. Results indicated that negotiations in which teams participated were more successful from the point of view of *joint* outcomes than negotiations between individuals. In other words, teams bargaining against teams or against individuals were more successful in this respect than individuals bargaining with individuals. In short, teams managed to increase the size of the pie available to both sides. Additional findings indicated that the reason was that teams were in fact better than single individuals at identifying successful negotiating strategies. Surprisingly, however, teams did *not* manage to claim or receive a larger share of the available rewards than individuals. Why was this the case? Apparently because in order to gain an advantage in this respect, team members must be able to closely coordinate their strategies. For example, they must agree on what information (including misleading information) to offer to the opponent. Here, in a sense, the situation becomes a conjunctive one: The team's success depends on the performance of the least-skilled member—the person least able to mislead or persuade the opponent.

So, in sum, groups or teams do better than individuals in negotiations in some respects, but not in others. Two heads are better than one in terms of increasing joint outcomes, but they do not necessarily provide larger gains for either of the parties involved. (By the way, we will consider negotiation in more detail in chapter 14.)

SOCIAL LOAFING: LETTING OTHERS DO THE WORK IN GROUP TASKS

Suppose that you and several other people are helping a friend to move. In order to lift the heaviest pieces of furniture, you join forces, with each person lending a hand. Will all of the people helping exert equal effort? Probably not. Some will take as much of the load as possible, while others will simply hang on, appearing to help without really doing much.

This pattern is quite common in situations where groups perform *additive tasks*. Some persons work hard while others engage in **social loafing,** doing as little as they can get away with. Why do such effects occur? Because it is difficult, in many additive tasks, to identify the contributions of each participant. The group outcome depends on the combined efforts of all members, and the efforts exerted by each cannot be separated or identified.

Direct evidence for the occurrence of social loafing has been obtained in many experiments. For example, in one of the first of these studies, Latane, Williams, and Harkins (1979) asked groups of male students to clap or cheer as loudly as possible at specific times, supposedly so that the experimenter could determine how much noise people make in social settings. Subjects engaged in clapping and cheering either alone or in groups of two, four, or six persons. Results were clear: The magnitude of the sounds made by each person decreased sharply as group size rose. In other words, each participant put out less and less effort as the number of other group members increased. And the experimenters were able to confirm that this was not due to an increasing lack of coordination between group members. Additional research suggests that such social loafing is quite general in scope; it occurs in both sexes, in several different cultures, and under a wide range of work conditions (e.g., Brickner, Harkins, & Ostrom, 1986; Harkins, 1987; Harkins & Petty, 1982). Moreover, it occurs with respect to cognitive tasks as well as ones involving physical effort (Weldon & Mustari, 1988).

REDUCING SOCIAL LOAFING: SOME USEFUL TECHNIQUES.   The fact that social loafing is so general in its occurrence is quite discouraging. It suggests that many persons will goof off and do less than their fair share when working in groups. Since so many important tasks are performed under group conditions, the implications for society are quite unsettling. Can anything be done to counter such tendencies? Fortunately, additional evidence points to several techniques that may prove useful in this respect.

The most obvious of these involves making the output or effort of each participant readily identifiable (e.g., Williams, Harkins, & Latane, 1981). Under these conditions, individuals cannot conceal minimal effort within the group, and the tendency to sit back and let others do the work is greatly reduced.

Second, groups can reeduce social loafing by increasing group members' commitment to successful task performance (Brickner et al., 1986; Zaccaro, 1984). Pressures toward working hard will then serve to offset temptations to engage in social loafing. Moreover, the larger the group, the stronger such pressures will be. Thus, output per group member may actually *increase* rather than decrease as group size rises.

Third, several recent studies suggest that social loafing can be reduced by conditions that provide individuals with an opportunity to evaluate their own contributions or those of the entire group relative to other groups (Harkins & Szymanski, 1988; Szymanski & Harkins, 1987). In other words, social loafing seems to occur not simply because individuals believe that their contributions cannot be identified, but also, at least in part, because they feel these cannot be evaluated, either by themselves or others. Conditions that afford the opportunity for such evaluation greatly reduce tendencies toward social loafing (Harkins & Szymanski, 1989).

Finally, social loafing can be reduced by strengthening of group cohesiveness. This increases the extent to which members care about the group's outcomes, and so too their level of individual effort.

Together, these findings suggest that tendencies toward social loafing are not an unavoidable part of task performance by groups. On the contrary, they *can* be reduced under appropriate circumstances. Further, in order to reduce social loafing it is not necessary to convince individuals that their outputs will be readily identifiable. Providing them with a standard against which to evaluate their contributions, or even those of the entire group, may be sufficient.

How do individuals react to evidence that other members of their group are engaging in social loafing or that these persons may soon be tempted to do so? For some surprising evidence on this important issue, please see the **Cutting Edge** section below.

Focus on Research: The Cutting Edge

REACTIONS TO SOCIAL LOAFING BY OTHERS: ANGER AND WITHDRAWAL OR SOCIAL COMPENSATION?

Nearly everyone has been in the situation of working with others and concluding, at some point, that these persons are not doing their fair share. Typical reactions to such perceptions include anger, resentment, and annoyance. And in some cases such feelings are so strong that they lead to actual withdrawal from the group (Messick & Brewer, 1986). Negative reactions to social loafing by others appear to be quite universal and have been observed in diverse cultures in North America, Asia, and elsewhere (Yamagishi, 1988). But they do not appear to constitute the entire story where responses to others' real or potential social loafing is concerned. Research findings suggest that in some instances a very different reaction known as **social compensation** may occur (Williams & Karau, 1991). Social compensation involves increased effort on the part of some group members in order to make up for a lack of effort on the part of others. Why would individuals attempt to pick up the slack, to so speak, for others who choose to goof off? According to Williams and Karau (1991), two investigators who have conducted careful studies of social compensation, several motives might play a role in such reactions.

First, individuals' self-identity may be linked to the outcomes of the group. Thus, they work hard to avoid negative results that might damage their own egos. Second, to the extent that they care about other members of their group, they may wish to save them from negative outcomes or evaluations. A third motive may involve the belief that if the group succeeds, their extra effort will enable these hard workers to take credit for its achievements. For all these reasons, individuals may attempt to compensate for social loafing by others. They would not be expected to do so under all conditions, however. Williams and Karau reason that social compensation is most likely to occur when individuals expect others to perform poorly because of a lack of ability or motivation and when they care about the task at hand—when it is meaningful and important to them.

To test these predictions the researchers conducted several related studies in which pairs of participants worked on a brainstorming task that involved generating as many uses as possible for a common object (a knife). In one condition the two persons worked independently (coaction), while in another, they worked together as a group (collective). The experimenters varied participants' expectations concerning possible social loafing by their partner in several different ways. In one study, they arranged for participants to hear their partner remark, before working on the task, either that she or he was going to work very hard on it (high effort) or that she or he would not work hard on it (low effort). In another, the partner informed the participant that she or he was very good at this type of task (high ability) or quite poor at it (low ability). It was predicted that when their partner expressed low motivation or ability, participants would engage in social compensation: They would actually work harder in the collective condition (where one would normally expect tendencies toward social loafing) than in the coaction condition. When their partner expressed high motivation or ability, however, the opposite would be true: Participants would actually work harder and generate more uses for a knife in the coaction condition than in the collective condition (where they would, indeed, show social loafing). As shown in Figure 12.8, p. 500, results offered support for these predictions.

In a third experiment, Williams and Karau (1991) varied the apparent importance or meaningfulness of the participants' task as well as their partner's apparent ability. The researchers varied task importance by describing the task to some participants as unimportant but to others as a measure of intelligence. It was expected that participants would be most likely to engage in social compensation when the task was important and their partner expressed low ability to perform it, and again these predictions were confirmed.

Considered as a whole, the findings reported by Williams and Karau 0suggest that social loafing by others is not always contagious. When confronted with *free-riders* in their groups, individuals do not necessarily engage in such behavior themselves. On the contrary, under some conditions, they may actually attempt to compensate for such behavior and increase their own effort. Such effects will not occur in all cases, however. Rather, they are most

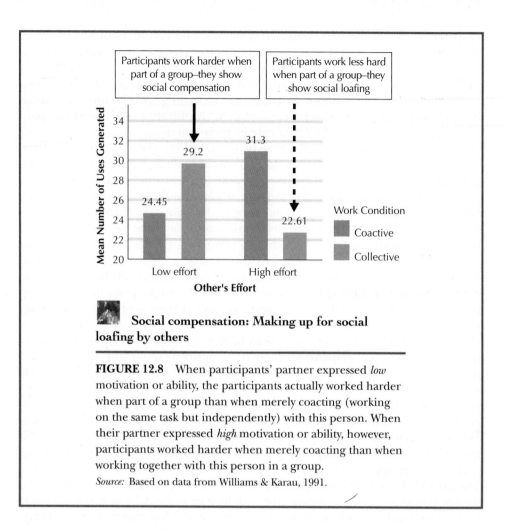

Social compensation: Making up for social loafing by others

FIGURE 12.8 When participants' partner expressed *low* motivation or ability, the participants actually worked harder when part of a group than when merely coacting (working on the same task but independently) with this person. When their partner expressed *high* motivation or ability, however, participants worked harder when merely coacting than when working together with this person in a group.
Source: Based on data from Williams & Karau, 1991.

likely to occur when individuals care about the evaluation their group will receive and when they expect to remain in the group. In addition, social compensation is probably not a permanent state of affairs: If individuals find that others continue to loaf despite their own best efforts, feelings of anger or resentment may become so strong that they give up and loaf themselves or actually leave the group. At least for a while, however, some persons do appear willing to "carry" other members of their groups toward shared group goals.

SOCIAL FACILITATION AND SOCIAL LOAFING: TWO SIDES OF THE SAME COIN?

Because they have been studied as distinct topics by social psychologists, we have discussed social facilitation and social loafing separately. Before concluding, though, we should note that they may actually be closely related. According to one investigator (Sanna, 1992), both social facilitation and social loafing can be understood within the context of **self-efficacy theory** (Bandura, 1986)—a theory proposing that an individual's motivation is determined by two types of expectancies: (1) *self-efficacy expectancy*—an individual's belief that she or he is capable of performing some task; and (2) *outcome expectancy*—the belief that a specific behavior or level of performance will yield certain outcomes (for example, praise and approval from others; desired rewards). What, precisely, do these expectations have to do with social facilitation and social loafing? According to Sanna (1992), quite a bit. He reasons as follows. High self-efficacy expectancies coupled with high outcome expectancies produce expectations of positive evaluations; improved performance should follow under these conditions. In other words, when individuals believe that they can perform a task well and also believe that doing so will yield desired outcomes, they tend to work very hard. In contrast, high self-efficacy expectancies coupled with *low* outcome expectancies yield expectations of negative evaluations; both effort and task performance should be low under these conditions.

Now let's apply these predictions to understanding both social facilitation and social loafing. With respect to social facilitation, it would be predicted that when self-efficacy expectancies are high, individuals will perform better in the presence of others than when alone. This is because in the presence of others, outcome expectancies, too, are high—after all, these persons may well notice and praise good performance. When self-efficacy expectancies are *low*, in contrast, individuals will perform better when working alone, because under these conditions outcome expectancies are low in the presence of others.

Turning to social loafing, it would be expected that when self-efficacy expectancies are high, persons working in groups (where their individual efforts cannot be identified and outcome expectancies are therefore low) will do worse than persons working alone or in the presence of others (coaction). However, when self-efficacy expectancies are low, persons working in groups will perform better than persons working alone or in the presence of others.

To test these predictions, Sanna (1992) conducted a study in which individuals worked on a visual vigilance task: They had to push a red button each time a square flashed on a computer screen. They worked on this task alone, in the presence of another person, or as part of a two-person group in which their individual performance could *not* be evaluated. Sanna reasoned that these three conditions would produce low, high, and low outcome expectancies, respectively. Before performing the main vigilance task, participants received feedback on a preliminary task; this feedback indicated either that they had scored very high or very low. This information was used to vary their self-efficacy expectancies.

As shown in Figure 12.9, p. 502, results offered clear support for predictions concerning the effect of self-efficacy and outcome expectancies upon performance. When self-efficacy expectancies were high, participants did better in the coaction condition than in the alone or group conditions. When self-efficacy expectancies were low, however, participants performed better in the group and alone conditions (where outcome expectancies were also low) than in the coaction condition. These findings suggest that social facilitation and social loafing can both be understood in the context of individuals' expectations concerning their capacity to perform a given task and future evaluations of their work. When individuals anticipate positive evaluations and believe that they can perform well, they will exert maximum effort and do their best work. Under other conditions, both effort and task performance will be lower. So, in a sense, social facilitation and social loafing represent two sides of the same coin—and this coin primarily involves individuals' expectations about the outcomes they can expect to attain.

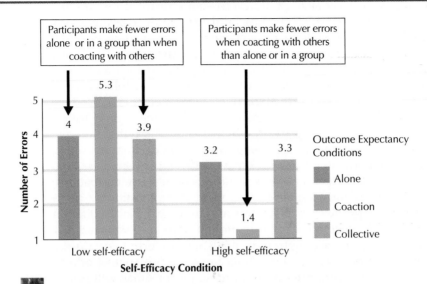

Participants make fewer errors alone or in a group than when coacting with others

Participants make fewer errors when coacting with others than alone or in a group

Self-efficacy and outcome expectancies: Their role in social loafing and social facilitation

FIGURE 12.9 When participants' self-efficacy expectancies were *high,* they performed better when coacting with others (where their individual efforts could be observed) than when working alone or when working in a group (where individual efforts could not be observed). In contrast, when participants' self-efficacy expectancies were *low,* they performed better when working in a group or alone than when working in the presence of others. These findings lend support to the view that both social facilitation and social loafing can be understood in terms of self-efficacy expectancies and outcome expectancies.

Source: Based on data from Sanna, 1992.

DECISION MAKING BY GROUPS: HOW IT OCCURS, THE OUTCOMES IT YIELDS, AND THE PITFALLS IT FACES

Groups are called upon to perform a wide range of tasks—everything from conducting delicate surgical operations through harvesting the world's crops. One of the most important activities they perform, however, is **decision making.** Governments, large corporations, military units, and virtually all other social entities entrust key decisions to groups. As a result, most of the laws, policies, and business practices that affect our daily lives are determined by committees, boards of directors, and similar groups—not by single individuals. There are several reasons for this fact, but perhaps the most important is this: Most people believe that groups, by pooling the expertise of their members and by avoiding extreme courses of action, can usually reach better decisions than individuals.

Are such assumptions accurate? Do groups actually make better (i.e., more accurate) decisions than individuals? In their efforts to deal with this practical question, social psychologists have focused on three major, and closely related, topics: (1) How do groups actually go about moving toward consensus and reaching decisions? (2) Do decisions reached by groups differ in any way from those reached by individuals? And (3) what accounts for the fact that groups sometimes make truly disastrous decisions—ones that are so bad they seem hard to explain?

THE DECISION-MAKING PROCESS: HOW GROUPS MOVE TOWARD CONSENSUS

When a group first begins to discuss an issue, its members rarely voice unanimous agreement. Rather, they support a wide range of views and favor competing courses of action. After some period of discussion, however, they usually reach a decision. This is not always the case—for example, juries become hung, and other decision-making groups, too, may deadlock. In most cases, though, *some* decision is reached. Is there any way of predicting this final outcome? In short, can we predict the decision a group is likely to reach from information about the views initially held by its members? Growing evidence suggests that we can (e.g., Kerr & MacCoun, 1985; Kaplan & Miller, 1987).

SOCIAL DECISION SCHEMES.   To summarize some very complex findings in simple terms, it appears that the final decisions reached by groups can often be predicted quite accurately by relatively simple rules known as **social decision schemes.** These rules relate the initial distribution of member views or preferences to the group's final decisions. For example, one scheme—the *majority-wins rule*—suggests that in many cases the group will opt for whatever position is initially supported by a majority of its members. According to this rule, discussion serves mainly to confirm or strengthen the most popular view. In contrast, a second decision scheme—the *truth-wins rule*—indicates that the correct solution or decision will ultimately come to the fore as its correctness is recognized by a growing number of members. A third decision scheme, adopted by many juries, is the *two-thirds majority rule.* Here, juries tend to convict defendants if two-thirds of the jurors initially favor this decision (Davis et al., 1984). Finally, some groups seem to follow a *first-shift rule.* They tend, ultimately, to adopt a decision consistent with the direction of the first shift in opinion shown by any member.

Surprising as it may seem, the results of many studies indicate that these straightforward rules are quite successful in predicting even complex group decisions. Indeed, they have been found to be accurate in this regard up to 80 percent of the time (e.g., Stasser, Taylor, & Hanna, 1989). Of course, different rules seem to be more successful under some conditions than others. Thus, the majority-wins scheme predicts decisions best in *judgmental tasks*—ones that are largely a matter of opinion. In contrast, the truth-supported rule seems best in predicting group decisions on *intellective tasks*—ones for which there *is* a correct answer (Kirchler & Davis, 1986).

PROCEDURAL PROCESSES: WHEN DECISIONS ARE INFLUENCED BY THE PROCEDURES USED TO REACH THEM.   While the decisions reached by groups can often be predicted from knowledge of members' initial positions, it is clear that many other factors play a role in this complex process. Among the most important of these are several aspects of the group's *procedures*—the rules it follows in addressing its agenda, managing the flow of interaction among members, and handling related issues (Stasser, Kerr, & Davis, 1989). One procedure adopted by many decision-making groups is the **straw**

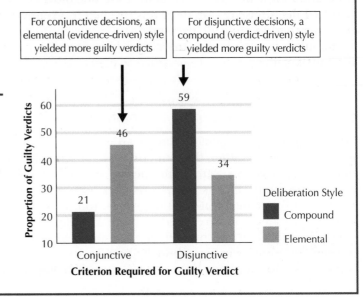

Deliberation style and group decisions

FIGURE 12.10 When the presence of both of two different criteria was required for a guilty verdict (a *conjunctive decision*), jurors were more likely to report a guilty verdict when using an evidence-driven deliberation style than when using a verdict-driven style. When either criterion was sufficient for a guilty verdict (a *disjunctive decision*), however, the opposite was true: A verdict-driven deliberation style yielded more guilty verdicts.

Source: Based on data from Kameda, 1991.

poll, in which members indicate their present positions or preferences in a nonbinding vote. While straw polls are non-binding and leave members free to change their views, it seems possible that simply learning about the current distribution of opinions within a group may have strong effects upon the individual members. That this is actually the case is confirmed by research findings (e.g., Davis et al., 1988; MacCoun & Kerr, 1988). Specifically, it appears that when a straw poll is held early in a group discussion, and especially when it involves each member reporting her or his views sequentially, the straw poll can lead to important shifts in the positions held by each member and so, ultimately, in the decision reached by the group.

A second procedural factor that can exert powerful effects on group decisions is what has been described as *deliberation style* (Hastie et al., 1983). This refers to the manner in which group members exchange information about their individual views. In one approach, known as *verdict-driven* (or *compound*) *deliberation,* members of a group first reach their personal decisions and then discuss these with other members. In another, known as *evidence-driven* (or *elemental*) *deliberation,* each piece of relevant information is examined by the group first, before individual decisions are made. In sum, in compound deliberation group members discuss their personal decisions, while in elemental deliberation they discuss the evidence or information before them. What effect does this procedure have on group decisions? A study by Kameda (1991) provides revealing information on this issue.

Kameda (1991) asked groups of six male and female students to act as mock juries and reach a decision concerning a case of fraud: A businessman was charged with serving as an accessory to a crime in which the businessman's friend cheated an old farmer. Groups were instructed to make their individual judgments first and then discuss them (compound deliberation), or to discuss the evidence first (elemental deliberation). Because Kameda reasoned that the effects of deliberation procedures would vary for two types of decisions, half of the participants in each condition were told that they could reach a guilty decision only if two criteria were met: The defendant knew of the intention of his friend to swindle the farmer, *and* he played an active role in perpetrating the fraud. This is called a *conjunctive decision*. The other half were told that they could reach a verdict of guilty if either of these two criteria were met; this is a *disjunctive decision*.

Results indicated that in the conjunctive situation, jurors were more likely to report a guilty verdict when using the elemental (evidence-driven) deliberation style than the compound (verdict-driven) style. However, in the disjunctive situation, the opposite was true: Jurors judged the defendant to be guilty more frequently in the compound condition (see Figure 12.10). These findings indicate that the procedures used by a decision-making group can play an important role in its final decision. The precise effects of various procedures may interact in complex ways, however, with the kind of decisions being reached. To repeat a comment we made in chapter 1: Who ever said that understanding people—and especially their relations with others—would be simple?!

THE NATURE OF GROUP DECISIONS: MODERATION OR POLARIZATION?

Truly important decisions are rarely entrusted to individuals. Instead, they are generally the responsibility of groups whose members' training, expertise, and background seem to qualify them for this crucial task. Indeed, even kings, queens, and dictators usually consult with groups of advisers before taking major action (see Figure 12.11). As we noted earlier, the major reason behind this strategy is the belief that groups are far less likely than individuals to make

 Group decision making: A fact of life in all forms of government

FIGURE 12.11   Most major decisions are reached in decision-making groups. Even kings, queens, and ruthless dictators seek the input of top-level advisors before making major policy decisions.

serious errors—to rush blindly over the edge. Is this really true? Are groups actually better at making wise decisions than individuals? Research conducted by social psychologists offers some surprising answers.

Exercise 2 GROUPS VERSUS INDIVIDUAL DECISIONS: A SHIFT TOWARD RISK OR A SHIFT TOWARD POLARIZATION?   Around 1960 a graduate student named James Stoner decided to examine this question in his master's thesis. In order to do so, he asked college students to play the role of advisers to imaginary persons supposedly facing decisions between two alternatives: one choice that was attractive but relatively high in risk, and another that was less appealing but quite conservative (Stoner, 1961). For example, in one of these situations, a character had to choose between a low-paying but secure job and a higher-paying but uncertain one.

During the first part of Stoner's study, each subject made individual recommendations about these situations. Then the subjects met in small groups and discussed each problem until a unanimous agreement was attained. Stoner expected that the decisions recommended by the groups would be more conservative than those offered by their individual members. Surprisingly, however, just the opposite was true: Groups actually recommended riskier decisions than individuals. The size of this difference was small, but it had important implications. After all, if groups make riskier decisions than individuals, the strategy of entrusting important decisions to committees, juries, and so on may be a poor one. In fact, it may be downright dangerous.

Impressed by these possibilities, many researchers conducted additional studies on this so-called **risky shift** (e.g., Burnstein, 1983; Lamm & Myers, 1978). At first these experiments seemed to confirm Stoner's initial findings. Gradually, however, a more mixed pattern of results emerged. In some cases group discussion actually seemed to produce shifts toward *caution* rather than risk (e.g., Knox & Safford, 1976). How could this be? How could group discussion produce both shifts toward caution and shifts toward risk? Eventually, a clear answer emerged. What had at first seemed to be a shift toward risk was actually a more general phenomenon—a *shift toward polarization*. Group discussion, it appeared, led individual members to become more extreme, not simply more risky or more cautious. In short, it enhanced or strengthened initial views. Thus, if an individual group member was mildly in favor of a course of action before the group discussion, he or she might come to favor it more strongly after the group deliberations. Similarly, if an individual was mildly opposed to some action before the discussion, he or she might come to oppose it even more strongly after the exchange of views. Since such shifts occur in the direction of greater extremity, this effect is known as **group polarization** (please see Figure 12.12.)

As we noted earlier, the tendency for groups to become increasingly extreme in their views has important—and unsettling—implications. Thus, it is not surprising that group polarization has been the subject of a considerable amount of research (Burnstein, 1983). Much of this research has focused on the following question: Why, precisely, does this polarization occur? What is it about group discussions that tends to intensify the initial beliefs of individual members?

GROUP POLARIZATION: WHY IT OCCURS.   Several different explanations for group polarization have been proposed, but two have received most support. These are known as the *social comparison* and *persuasive arguments* views.

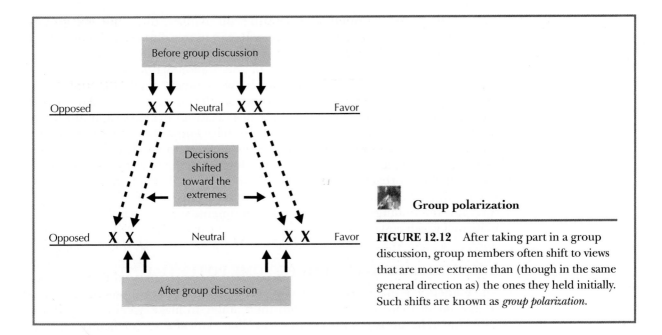

Group polarization

FIGURE 12.12   After taking part in a group discussion, group members often shift to views that are more extreme than (though in the same general direction as) the ones they held initially. Such shifts are known as *group polarization*.

Critical Thinking Question 4

The social comparison approach suggests that before group discussion, most persons assume that they hold "better" views than the other members. They assume that their views are more extreme in the right (valued) directions. Since it is impossible for everyone to be above average in this respect, many individuals experience a rude awakening during group discussion: They discover that their own views are not nearly as far above average as they assumed. The result: They shift to more extreme positions (Goethals & Zanna, 1979).

The persuasive arguments view offers a contrasting explanation for the occurrence of polarization. In essence, it suggests that group members gradually convince themselves of the correctness of their initial views, and so come to adopt these even more strongly. The result, of course, is a shift toward extremity. More specifically, this view suggests that during group discussion, most of the information presented by group members supports their own views. Thus, if even a slight majority of the members lean in a particular direction, most of the arguments tend to favor this view. Gradually, then, the view that predominated initially gains greater and greater support (Vinokur & Burnstein, 1974).

Both explanations are supported by research findings, but some recent evidence (Zuber, Crott, & Werner, 1992) seems to cast doubt upon the ability of the role of persuasive arguments in group polarization. Specifically, when all group members are provided with an extensive list of arguments concerning an issue, polarization effects still occur. According to the persuasive arguments hypothesis, this should not be true, since all members would already have full information about the various arguments. In view of these and related findings, several researchers have recently concluded that group polarization can be better understood in terms of social decision schemes, such as the ones discussed under "The Decision-Making Process," above (Zuber, Crott, & Werner, 1992). Specifically, it appears that the view that the median group member supports is the best predictor of the final group decision. To the extent this position leans toward one of the existing alternatives, then, this is the one most likely to be chosen, and the group will shift in this direction.

Regardless of the precise basis for group polarization, it definitely has important implications. The occurrence of polarization may lead many decision-making groups to adopt positions that are increasingly extreme—and therefore increasingly dangerous. In this context, it is interesting to speculate about the potential role of such shifts in disastrous decisions by political, military, or business groups who should, by all accounts, have known better—for example, the decision by President Johnson and his advisers to escalate U.S. involvement in Vietnam, and the decision by hard-liners in the Soviet government to arrest Mikhail Gorbachev—an action that soon led to dissolution of the Soviet Union. Did group polarization influence these events? It is difficult to say for sure. But the findings of many careful experiments suggest that this is a possibility well worth considering.

DECISION MAKING BY GROUPS: SOME POTENTIAL PITFALLS

The tendency of many decision-making groups to drift toward polarization is a serious factor that can interfere with their ability to make accurate decisions. Unfortunately, this is not the only process that can exert such negative effects. Several others, too, seem to emerge out of group discussions and can lead groups into disastrous courses of action. Among the most important of these are (1) *groupthink* and (2) the apparent inability of groups to pool expertise by discussing information not shared by all members.

Reading: Lesko (34), Groupthink

GROUPTHINK: WHEN TOO MUCH COHESIVENESS IS A DANGEROUS THING. Common sense suggests that a high level of cohesiveness among group members is beneficial. After all, if members are strongly attracted to a group, their motivation—and hence the group's performance—should be enhanced. Up to a point, this seems to be true. But when very high levels of cohesiveness are coupled with several other conditions (e.g., a *provocative situational context*—one in which a group is fighting for its survival against strong external adversaries—and *structural and procedural faults*—such as a lack of means for resolving internal conflicts), an unsettling process known as **groupthink** may emerge (Janis, 1982). Groupthink is a mode of thinking by group members in which concern with maintaining group consensus—*concurrence seeking,* in Janis's terms—overrides the motivation to evaluate all potential courses of action as accurately and realistically as possible. In short, groupthink involves a shift from primary concern with making the best decision to primary concern with reaching and maintaining consensus (see Figure 12.13).

Once groupthink develops, several trends—all potentially catastrophic from the point of view of effective decision making—soon follow. Members come to view their group as invulnerable—one that can't possibly make mistakes. Similarly, they engage in *collective rationalization,* discrediting or ignoring any information counter to the group's current views. Third, they conclude that their group is not only right, it is also morally superior, and that all others (especially those who do not share its views) are confused, evil, or worse. Once groupthink develops, pressures on members to go along with the group's stated views become intense. Members who have lingering doubts engage in self-censorship; and if they do not, they are quickly silenced by other group members. Finally, self-appointed "mind guards" shield the group from external sources of information that is inconsistent with the group's position. The final result: A powerful illusion takes hold that the group is correct and infallible and has no dissent—or need for it. (See Figure 12.14, p. 510, for an overview of the model of groupthink proposed by Janis.)

Reading: Lesko (36), *Group Decision Fiascoes Continue: Space Shuttle Challenger*

Is groupthink a real effect? And does it develop under the conditions proposed by Janis? Despite many efforts to answer these questions (e.g., Flowers, 1977; Moorhead & Montanari, 1986), the issue remains somewhat in doubt. Perhaps the most revealing evidence to date concerning the nature and occurrence of groupthink has been provided by Tetlock and his colleagues (Tetlock et al., 1992). These researchers asked participants to consider factual accounts of several historic decisions that potentially involved groupthink. These included the decision by President Carter and his cabinet to try to rescue the hostages in Iran and the decision by President Kennedy to launch the Bay of Pigs military operation. Participants then sorted various statements about how the decision-making groups involved in these situations operated. Participants

 Groupthink: An Extreme Example

FIGURE 12.13   Groups sometimes become more concerned with achieving and maintaining agreement (consensus) than with making good decisions. When they do, the results can be catastrophic.
Source: The New Yorker.

"The motion has been made and seconded that we stick our heads in the sand."

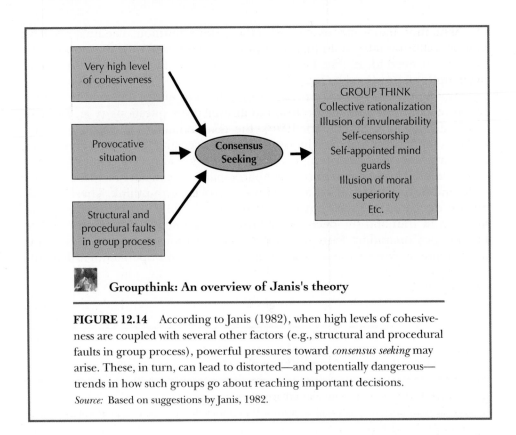

Groupthink: An overview of Janis's theory

FIGURE 12.14 According to Janis (1982), when high levels of cohesiveness are coupled with several other factors (e.g., structural and procedural faults in group process), powerful pressures toward *consensus seeking* may arise. These, in turn, can lead to distorted—and potentially dangerous—trends in how such groups go about reaching important decisions.
Source: Based on suggestions by Janis, 1982.

sorted the statements according to the extent to which they felt that these statements were or were not characteristic of the groups involved in each historic incident. On the basis of these data, Tetlock and his colleagues (1992) were able to test the accuracy of Janis's (1982) theory of groupthink. The results they obtained provided mixed support for the theory. On the one hand, it was found that historic events involving disastrous decisions were indeed described by participants as showing more characteristics of groupthink than events that led to successful decisions (e.g., the decision of President Truman and his cabinet to launch the Marshall Plan after the end of World War II). This finding offered support for the model. Further, participants also associated structural and procedural faults in the groups with increased tendencies toward concurrence seeking; this too was consistent with the groupthink model. However, contrary to what the theory proposes, Tetlock and his colleagues did not find that group cohesiveness or provocative situational context (i.e., emergency situations) were associated with concurrence seeking on the part of the groups.

Together, these findings, and those of several other studies (e.g., McCauley, 1989) seem to point to two conclusions. First, something like groupthink does exist, and it affects the decisions of important decision-making groups. However, the precise nature and form of groupthink may be somewhat different from what Janis (1982) initially proposed. In other words, Janis has called attention to an important aspect of group decision making, but the precise nature of this process remains to be determined.

Assuming that groupthink exists, an important question arises: What steps can be taken to counter its effects—which, as we have already noted, can be disastrous? Several procedures may prove helpful. First, groups wishing to avoid the development of groupthink should promote open inquiry and *skepticism* among their members. Group leaders should encourage careful questioning of each alternative or policy and should, if necessary, play the role of devil's advocate, intentionally finding fault with various options as they are discussed. Second, the use of *subgroups* can be helpful. Such groups consider different aspects of the problem, and any final decision is then based on discussion of their recommendations. Since the subgroups work independently, spirited disagreements among them are far from rare; and this, of course, can halt any drift toward premature consensus and groupthink. Third, once a decision is reached, *second-chance* meetings, in which group members are asked to express any lingering doubts, can be extremely helpful. Such meetings provide a setting in which pressures toward conformity and consensus are reduced; this gives new ideas and criticism a chance to emerge and may effectively counter tendencies toward groupthink.

In sum, groupthink is a real danger faced by decision-making groups, especially under certain conditions. However, through steps such as those outlined above, the drift toward such premature closure can be halted, or even reversed.

TO SHARE OR NOT TO SHARE INFORMATION: OR, WHY GROUP MEMBERS OFTEN TELL EACH OTHER WHAT THEY ALREADY KNOW.   As we noted earlier, one reason why many key decisions are entrusted to groups is the belief that members will pool their resources—share ideas and knowledge unique to each individual. In this way, the decisions they reach will be better informed, and presumably more accurate, than those that would be reached by individuals working in isolation. Is this actually the case? Do groups really share the knowledge and expertise brought to them by individual members? A series of sophisticated studies conducted by Stasser and his colleagues (Stasser, 1992; Stasser & Titus, 1985, 1987; Stasser, Taylor, & Hanna, 1989) suggests that in fact such pooling of resources may be the exception rather than the rule.

Exercise 3

These studies were undertaken to test the validity of a model of group discussion known as the **information sampling model** (Stasser & Titus, 1985). This model suggests that because information shared by many members is more likely to be mentioned during group discussion than information held by only a single member, decision-making groups are more likely to discuss—and discuss again—information shared by most members than information known to only a single member. More specifically, the model predicts that the larger the group, the greater the advantage of shared over unshared information. Further, and even more discouraging, the model also indicates that efforts to increase the pooling of resources by structuring group discussions will usually fail. This will happen because such efforts will enhance each member's recall of available information, and this in turn will actually increase the discussion of shared information.

Critical Thinking Question 3

In general, the results of studies undertaken to test this model have offered support for it (Stasser, 1992). Groups tend to discuss information shared by all members, and this tendency may actually be increased rather than reduced if groups are urged to review all information carefully before reaching a decision (Stasser, Taylor, & Hanna, 1989). There is some room for optimism, however: Some research findings indicate that group members can be encouraged to discuss *unshared* information, and so to discover "hidden profiles" in the available information, if they are convinced that there is a correct answer or decision. Under these conditions more extensive discussion may ensue, because if members perceive their task as uncovering the correct solution rather than simply reaching consensus, they may recognize the importance of unshared information to a greater extent and focus more attention on uncovering it.

Support for these predictions has recently been reported by Stasser and Stewart (1992). These researchers conducted a study in which six-person groups read evidence pertaining to a murder investigation involving three suspects. Half of the groups were led to believe that they could solve the case: They were simply asked to identify the guilty suspect. The remaining groups were told that they were to identify the most likely suspect, but that there might not be enough information available for them to determine who was actually guilty. Within these two conditions, in half the groups all members received all the critical clues (this information was shared), while in the remaining groups only some members received this information (it was not shared by all group members).

Stasser and Stewart (1992) predicted that groups faced with the *hidden profile* of information (all information was not shared) would be less successful in identifying the guilty culprit than those where all critical information was shared. However, they also predicted that those groups led to believe that they could solve the mystery would do better than those who felt that they might not have enough information to reach this goal. In addition, the investigators expected that telling the groups they could solve the mystery—that there was a correct answer—would lead to greater discussion of critical unshared informa-

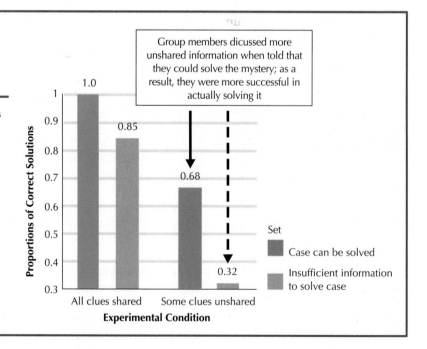

Countering the tendency of group members to tell each other what they already know

FIGURE 12.15 When participants believed that a correct solution to a murder mystery existed, they were more likely to discuss critical unshared information—and to reach a correct solution—than was true when they believed that a correct solution could not be obtained.

Source: Based on data from Stasser & Stewart, 1992.

Group members discussed more unshared information when told that they could solve the mystery; as a result, they were more successful in actually solving it

tion, and that this would help them succeed. As shown in Figure 12.15, all these predictions were confirmed.

The findings reported by Stasser and his colleagues have important implications for many decision-making groups. These findings suggest that in general such groups are much better at rehashing and repeating information already shared by most members than at bringing new, unshared information into focus. But such problems can be overcome—at least to a degree—if group members believe that there *is* a correct decision. This implies that the group may have enough information at its disposal to make the right choice. And this, in turn, increases the likelihood that group members will uncover, and discuss, unshared information.

Work in Progress

How Groups Overcome the Tendency to Discuss Shared Information: The Role of Expectations and Strategic Processing

While groups do seem to suffer from strong tendencies to discuss information already shared by all or most members, recent studies by Stasser and his colleagues (e.g., Stasser & Hinkle, 1993; Stewart, 1992; Wittenbaum et al., 1993) help to paint a somewhat optimistic picture of this process. Together, these studies suggest that as group members work together, they form expectations about what information each of them is likely to have and can contribute to the group's decisions. Then, depending on the task the group faces and various social forces, the group members may put this understanding of each other's knowledge to good use. In particular, it appears that when groups are focused on reaching consensus, they may choose to talk about shared information; after all, this is what they all know and will be most comfortable discussing. In contrast, if getting all information out on the table seems important in order to solve a problem, group members may choose to present the information they believe is *not* shared by other members.

The operation of such processes has been clearly observed by Hinkle and Stasser in research concerned with the sharing of information among ships' crews. These studies try to simulate some of the factors present under battle conditions. Different participants (who play the role of crew members) have different information at their disposal—for example, the location of enemy planes, other military operations in the vicinity, and so on. The information must be transmitted to the ship's commander, who will then decide whether to fire or not fire on the potentially threatening aircraft. Careful analysis of the ways group members share information and coordinate their communications indicates that as the groups gain experience in working together, they do come to understand which members have what type of information. And then they increasingly coordinate communication so that only essential unshared information is sent upward to the commander.

These and related findings indicate that groups are definitely *not* doomed to repeat and belabor information already shared by most members. On the contrary, as group members work together and become familiar with one another's expertise, they can actively *choose* whether to act in this fashion, and so enhance consensus and conformity, or to focus on *unshared* information and so, perhaps, enhance the quality of their decisions. To a degree, then, the fate of decision-making groups is in their own hands, and under some conditions members *can* avoid the trap of telling each other what they already know.

Can group decision making be improved by modern technology? For information on this timely issue, please see the **Applied Side** section below.

Social Psychology: On the Applied Side

GROUP DECISION MAKING: IS ELECTRONIC COMMUNICATION A PLUS?

We live at a time of exciting technological breakthroughs. Each year computers get faster, smaller, and less expensive. As a result, nearly every technical, professional, or white-collar worker now has one on her or his desk. This fact opens up intriguing possibilities with respect to group decision making. In the past, group decisions required the physical presence of group members. Now, technological advances such as *E-mail*, in which many computers are linked in a network permitting instant communication, allow for the exchange of information between group members without their face-to-face contact (see Figure 12.16).

Advocates of these electronic forms of communication suggest that they offer important advantages—ones that may enhance not only the speed and efficiency of communication but decision making too (e.g., Zuboff, 1988). Is this actually so? An increasing amount of research has focused on comparing decision making under traditional face-to-face conditions with decision making by means of electronic communication. Interestingly, the results of such research paint a mixed picture where the potential benefits of modern communication technology are concerned.

Research by Kiesler and her associates (e.g., Kiesler & Sproull, 1992) is especially revealing in this respect. These investigators have compared the performance of decision-making groups operating under traditional face-to-face conditions and by means of electronic communication. Results indicate that in fact the groups do function somewhat differently under these two sets of conditions. First, with respect to the amount of time needed to reach a decision, it is clear that face-to-face contact is more efficient. Indeed, groups using electronic communication often require four times as long to reach decisions. Why is this so? Apparently because when people communicate solely through words on a computer monitor, many valuable social cues are missing. According to Kiesler and Sproull (1992), these cues include *static cues*, such as where people sit and how they look, and *dynamic cues*, such as nonverbal behavior and other actions. When such cues are absent, the decision-making process slows down—appreciably. Balancing this apparent disadvantage, however, is the fact that more equal participation by all group members occurs under electronic conditions. Typically, face-to-face discussions are dominated by one or a few group members. This tendency seems to disappear when people communicate by electronic means. This, in turn, may stem from the fact that status cues are missing, and so people are less inhibited by such factors—and more willing to express their views (Dubrovsky, Kiesler & Sethna, 1991).

 Electronic communication: A plus or minus for group decision making?

FIGURE 12.16   Growing evidence suggests that groups function differently when attempting to reach decisions by means of electronic communication than when operating in the traditional face-to-face manner. Some of these effects are beneficial (e.g., more equal participation by all group members), while others seem to be detrimental (e.g., an increase in the intensity of conflicts; Kiesler & Sproull, 1992.)

On the other hand, the removal of such inhibitions also has a downside. Groups that communicate by electronic means tend to have more intense conflicts. When they disagree, in short, they *really* disagree. In fact, a phenomenon known as *flaming*—rude, impulsive behavior and the expression of extreme views—is much more common in electronic than in face-to-face groups (Dubrovsky et al., 1991).

So where does all this leave us? With the conclusion that group decision making via electronic means offers a very mixed bag of advantages and disadvantages. On the one hand, it can speed the exchange of information and permit the participation of people who could not previously take part in group discussions—for example, group members who work in geographically remote locations. And it seems to reduce the impact of status cues, a shift that enhances the free exchange of information among members. On the other hand, when individuals can communicate only by electronic means, many social cues present in face-to-face interactions are lost, with the result that decision making actually slows down and inhibitions that normally prevent conflict and rude behavior are reduced. Like any other tool, then, electronic means of communication do *not* constitute a panacea or magic bullet where group decision making is concerned. Rather, they may be helpful in some contexts but detrimental in others. It remains for future research to indicate precisely when and how electronic communication provides maximum benefits for groups.

LEADERSHIP: ITS NATURE AND IMPACT IN GROUPS

Video: *Group Decision Making and Leadership**

Suppose you surveyed persons belonging to a wide range of groups (businesses, sports teams, charities, social clubs) and asked them to name the single most important factor in determining the success of their group. What would you find? The chances are good that many—perhaps most—would reply "Effective leadership." This answer reflects the widespread belief that leadership is a key ingredient in group activities. Indeed, many people believe that a group without an effective leader is worse than no group at all—the members would do better, in terms of reaching key goals, on their own. But what, precisely, *is* leadership? Like love, it is something we all feel we can recognize but can't precisely define. For social psychologists, however, leadership does have a clear focus: *influence.* Thus, many experts on this topic agree that **leadership** is *the process through which one member of a group (its leader) influences other group members toward the attainment of specific group goals* (Yukl, 1989).

In the remainder of this section, we will consider several issues related to the leadership process. First, we'll consider the question of who, precisely, becomes a *leader*—why some persons but not others rise to positions of authority. Second, we'll examine evidence concerning the possibility of *gender differences* in leadership. Finally, we'll examine current views concerning the basis of leaders' *effectiveness,* and a new perspective that deals with the inspirational (*transformational*) aspect of leadership.

THE TRAIT APPROACH: ARE LEADERS BORN OR MADE?

Are some people born to lead? Common sense suggests that this is so. Eminent leaders of the past such as Alexander the Great, Queen Elizabeth I, and Abraham Lincoln do seem to differ from ordinary human beings in several respects. Such observations led early researchers to formulate the **great person theory** of leadership. According to this approach, great leaders possess key traits that set them apart from most human beings. Further, the theory contends that these traits remain stable over time and across different groups. Thus, it suggests that all great leaders share these characteristics regardless of when and where they live or the precise roles they fulfill.

Certainly, these are intriguing suggestions, and they seem to fit quite well with our own informal experience. You will probably be surprised to learn, therefore, that they have *not* been confirmed. Decades of research (most conducted before 1950) failed to yield a short, agreed-upon list of key traits shared by all leaders (Geier, 1969; Yukl, 1981). Although a few consistent findings did emerge (e.g., leaders are slightly taller and more intelligent than their followers), these were hardly dramatic in nature or in scope. Indeed, the overall results of this persistent search for traits associated with leadership were so disappointing that most investigators gave up in despair and reached the following conclusion: Leaders simply do not differ from followers in clear and consistent ways.

Until quite recently this conclusion was widely accepted as true. Now, however, it has been called into question by a growing body of evidence indicating that leaders *do* actually differ from other persons in several important—and measurable—respects. After reviewing a large number of studies concerned with this issue, Kirkpatrick and Locke (1991) have recently contended that in business settings, at least, traits do matter—that certain traits, together with other factors, contribute to leaders' success. What are these traits? Table 12.1 Exercise 4 presents a summary of the ones identified as most important by Kirkpatrick and Locke, plus descriptions of their basic nature. Most of these characteristics are ones you will readily recognize (drive, honesty and integrity, self-confidence). Others, however, seem to require further clarification.

Consider first what Kirkpatrick and Locke term *leadership motivation.* This refers to leaders' desire to influence others—in essence, to lead. Such motivation, however, can take two distinct forms. On the one hand, it may cause leaders to seek power as an end in itself. Leaders who demonstrate such *personalized power motivation* wish to dominate others, and their desire to do so is often reflected in an excessive concern with status. In contrast, leadership motivation can cause leaders to seek power as a means to achieve desired shared goals. Leaders who evidence such *socialized power motivation* cooperate with others, develop networks and coalitions, and generally work with subordinates rather than trying to dominate or control them. Needless to add, this type of leadership motivation is usually far more adaptive for organizations than personalized power motivation.

With respect to *cognitive ability,* it appears that to be effective, leaders must be intelligent and capable of integrating and interpreting large amounts of information. Mental genius, however, does not seem to be necessary and may, in some cases, prove detrimental (Lord, DeVader, & Alliger, 1986).

While the list of traits presented in Table 12.1 is quite comprehensive and provides a good overall summary of recent evidence concerning this issue, we

Research findings indicate that successful business leaders demonstrate the traits listed here.

TABLE 12.1 Characteristics of successful leaders

Trait	Description
Drive	Desire for achievement; ambition; high energy; tenacity; initiative
Honesty and Integrity	Trustworthiness; reliability; openness
Leadership Motivation	Desire to exercise influence over others to reach shared goals
Self-Confidence	Trust in own abilities
Cognitive Ability	Intelligence; ability to integrate and interpret large amounts of information
Expertise	Knowledge of the group's activities; knowledge of relevant technical matters
Creativity	Originality
Flexibility	Ability to adapt to needs of followers and to changing requirements of the situation

Source: Based on suggestions by Kirkpatrick & Locke, 1991.

should note that one particular characteristic seems to play an especially crucial role in effective leadership. This trait, *flexibility*, refers to the capacity of leaders to recognize what actions are required in a given situation and then to act accordingly.

Evidence for the importance of flexibility is provided by an ingenious laboratory simulation conducted by Zaccaro, Foti, and Kenny (1991). These researchers investigated the role of flexibility in leader emergence in small task-performing groups. They arranged for groups of students who were unacquainted with one another to work on several different tasks. The tasks chosen were ones known to require different styles of leadership, so it was possible to determine whether the persons who emerged as leaders in these groups actually adopted a style of leadership appropriate for each task. For example, one task employed involved brainstorming about the issue "Should children with AIDS be allowed to attend school?" Previous research indicated that this task required a leadership style focused on maintaining good interpersonal relations among group members. In contrast, another task involved constructing "moon tents" by folding paper. This task required a leadership style that emphasized production. It is important to note that the same persons did *not* work together on each task; rather, group members were rotated, so that new groups were formed for each task.

After completing a given task, group members rated each other's behaviors on several leadership dimensions (e.g., efforts at persuasion, emphasis on production, etc.). In addition, they rated each other in terms of acting as a leader. Results offered support for the view that flexibility plays a key role in leader emergence. First, there was a strong tendency for the same persons to be perceived as leaders across the four tasks used and across the many different groups. Second, these persons did show flexibility, matching their leadership style (as shown by specific behaviors) to the requirements of the task being performed. For example, they showed a high level of concern with interpersonal relations when this was required, but a high level of concern with production when this was necessary. And the greater a person's degree of flexibility, the higher the leadership ratings he or she received from other group members. In short, it appears that flexibility—the ability to match one's style and behavior to the needs of followers and the demands of the situation—may be an important trait where effective leadership is concerned.

In additional, follow-up research, Zaccaro and his colleagues (Mumford et al., in press) examined the relationship between a large number of personal characteristics and leadership activities among high school students and college freshmen. They found that several of these characteristics, including *achievement motivation, persuasiveness, good social skills, creativity,* and *good social adjustment* (i.e., popularity), were all significcant predictors of students' serving as leaders. Moreover, these characteristics were predictive of leadership behavior by both females and males.

In sum, recent evidence seems to require some revision in the widely accepted view that leaders do not differ from other persons with respect to specific traits. As noted by Kirkpatrick and Locke (1991, p. 58):

> Regardless of whether leaders are born or made . . . it is unequivocally clear that *leaders are not like other people.* Leaders do not have to be great men or women by being intellectual geniuses or omniscient prophets to succeed, but they do need to have the "right stuff" and this stuff is not equally present in all people. . . .

GENDER DIFFERENCES IN LEADERSHIP:
DO MALE AND FEMALE LEADERS DIFFER?

Do male leaders and female leaders differ in their style or approach to leadership? The authors of many popular books suggest that they do (e.g., Grant, 1988). Is there any validity to these claims? Do male and female leaders really differ? Systematic research on this issue suggests that, in general, *they do not* (Powell, 1990). While female and male leaders do appear to differ in a few respects, these differences are smaller in magnitude, and fewer in number, than widely held gender role stereotypes suggest. Perhaps the most comprehensive evidence on this issue is that reported by Eagly and Johnson (1990).

These researchers examined the results of more than 150 separate studies of leadership in which comparisons between females and males were possible. They performed this task by means of the highly sophisticated technique known as *meta-analysis,* a statistical procedure for evaluating the effects of one or more variables across many different studies. Eagly and Johnson included three types of investigations in the analysis: *laboratory studies* (in which participants interacted with a stranger), *assessment studies* (in which measures of subject's leadership style were obtained), and *organizational studies* (in which leadership behavior in actual organizations was assessed). The researchers reasoned that any differences between males and females would be more apparent in the first two types of studies than in the third type. This would be the case because in actual organizations, leadership roles would require similar behavior from males and females. As a result, any gender differences would tend to disappear. In laboratory and assessment studies, in contrast, differences between males and females would not be reduced by such role requirements.

The investigators examined potential differences between male and female leaders with respect to two key dimensions generally viewed as playing a crucial role in leader behavior or style: (1) concern with maintenance of good interpersonal relations (often known as *showing consideration*) versus concern with task performance (known as *initiating structure)* and (2) participative versus autocratic decision-making style. Gender role stereotypes suggest that female leaders might show more concern with interpersonal relations and tend to make decisions in a more participative manner than male leaders. Results, however, offered only weak support for such beliefs. With respect to showing consideration and initiating structure, there were few significant findings. In laboratory studies, females were slightly higher than males on *both* dimensions. In organizational studies, no differences on these dimensions were observed.

Turning to decision-making style, females did appear to adopt a more democratic or participative style than males; moreover, this was true across all three groups of studies (laboratory, assessment, and organizational studies). What accounts for this difference? One possibility is that female leaders *are* more concerned than males with interpersonal relations and realize that permitting subordinates to offer input to decisions is one way of maintaining good relations with them. Another possibility, suggested by Eagly and Johnson, involves the fact that women are higher than men in interpersonal skills. Such superiority, in turn, may make it easier for them to adopt a decision-making approach utilizing considerable give-and-take with subordinates. Whatever the precise basis for this difference, the overall findings of the meta-analysis conducted by Eagly and Johnson suggest that female and male leaders may indeed differ in some respects, but that these differences are smaller in magnitude and less consistent than gender role stereotypes suggest.

LEADER EFFECTIVENESS: TWO INFLUENTIAL VIEWS

Critical Thinking
Question 5

All leaders are definitely not equal. Some are effective and contribute to high levels of performance and satisfaction on the part of their followers. Others are much less successful in these respects. Why is this the case? What factors determine leaders' success in directing their groups? This has been a central issue in much research concerned with leadership (Kiesler, Reber, & Wunderer, 1987; Vecchio, 1987). As yet, no definitive answers have emerged. But the two theories described below—Fiedler's *contingency theory* (Fiedler, 1978; Fiedler & Garcia, 1987) and Vroom and Yetton's *normative theory* (Vroom & Yetton, 1973)—have added considerably to our understanding of this issue.

CONTINGENCY THEORY: MATCHING LEADERS AND TASKS.   Fiedler labels his approach the **contingency theory**, and this term is quite appropriate, for the theory's central assumption is this: A leader's contribution to successful performance by his or her group is determined both by the leader's traits and by various features of the situation. For a full understanding of leader effectiveness, both types of factors must be considered.

Transparency 12.3

With respect to characteristics possessed by leaders, Fiedler identifies *esteem* (liking) for *least-preferred coworker* (LPC for short) as most important. LPC refers to a leader's tendency to evaluate in a favorable or in an unfavorable manner the person with whom she or he has found it most difficult to work. Leaders who perceive this person in negative terms (low-LPC leaders) seem primarily concerned with successful task performance. In contrast, those who perceive their least-preferred coworker in a positive light (high-LPC leaders) seem mainly concerned with good relations with subordinates. Which of these types of leaders is more effective? Contingency theory's answer is: It depends. And what it depends on is several situational factors. Fiedler suggests that whether low-LPC or high-LPC leaders are more effective depends on the degree to which the situation is favorable to the leader—provides this person with control over subordinates. This, in turn, is determined largely by three factors: (1) the nature of the leader's relations with group members (the extent to which he or she enjoys their support); (2) the degree of structure in the task being performed (the extent to which task goals and subordinates' roles are clearly defined); and (3) the leader's position power (his or her ability to enforce compliance by subordinates). Combining these three factors, the leader's situational control can range from very high (positive relations with members, a highly structured task, high position power) to very low (negative relations, an unstructured task, low position power).

To return to the central question: When are different types of leaders most effective? Fiedler suggests that low-LPC leaders (ones who are task-oriented) are superior to high-LPC leaders (ones who are people-oriented) when situational control is either very low or very high. In contrast, high-LPC leaders have an edge when situational control falls within the moderate range (see Figure 12.17). The reasoning behind these predictions is as follows: Under conditions of low situational control, groups need considerable guidance to operate effectively. Since low-LPC leaders are more likely to provide firm guidance, they will usually be superior in such cases. Similarly, low-LPC leaders have an edge under conditions that offer leaders high situational control.

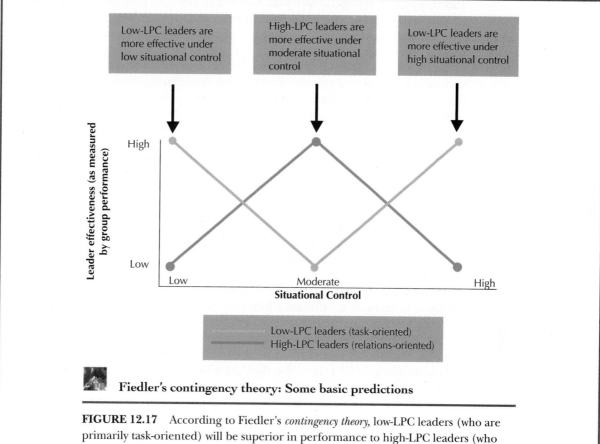

Low-LPC leaders are more effective under low situational control

High-LPC leaders are more effective under moderate situational control

Low-LPC leaders are more effective under high situational control

Leader effectiveness (as measured by group performance)

High

Low

Low   Moderate   High

Situational Control

Low-LPC leaders (task-oriented)
High-LPC leaders (relations-oriented)

Fiedler's contingency theory: Some basic predictions

FIGURE 12.17   According to Fiedler's *contingency theory,* low-LPC leaders (who are primarily task-oriented) will be superior in performance to high-LPC leaders (who are primarily person-oriented) when situational control is either very low or high. In contrast, high-LPC leaders are more effective when situational control is moderate.

Here such leaders realize that conditions are very favorable and that task performance is assured. As a result, they often adopt a relaxed hands-off style, which is appreciated by subordinates. In contrast, high-LPC leaders, feeling that they already enjoy good relations with subordinates, may shift their attention to task performance. Their attempts to provide guidance in this respect may then be perceived as needless meddling, with the result that performance suffers.

To repeat: Fiedler's theory predicts that low-LPC (task-oriented) leaders will be more effective than high-LPC (relations-oriented) leaders under conditions of either low or high situational control. In contrast, high-LPC leaders will have an edge under conditions in which situational control is moderate.

CONTINGENCY THEORY: ITS CURRENT STATUS.   Have these predictions been supported by research findings? Existing evidence presents something of a mixed picture. On the one hand, most laboratory studies performed to test various aspects of contingency theory have yielded positive results (Strube & Garcia, 1981). On the other, the results of studies conducted with naturally existing groups have not been as favorable (Peters, Hartke, & Pohlman,

1985). Such investigations have sometimes yielded results contrary to what contingency theory predicts. In addition, the theory has been criticized on several important grounds. A degree of ambiguity exists with respect to the placement of specific situations along the dimension of situational control (Ashour, 1973). Unless situations can be accurately classified as low, moderate, or high in situational control, predictions concerning leader effectiveness are difficult to make. Similarly, some critics have questioned the adequacy of the procedures used to measure leaders' standing along the LPC dimension, and even the validity of this dimension itself (e.g., Peters, Hartke, & Pohlman, 1985).

Taking such criticism plus existing evidence into account, the following tentative conclusions seem justified. Contingency theory has indeed added to our understanding of key aspects of leadership and leader effectiveness. Several questions about its accuracy remain, however, and require further careful attention. Therefore, this theory should be viewed as one still undergoing refinement rather than as one that offers a fully developed framework for understanding all aspects of leader effectiveness.

NORMATIVE THEORY: DECISION MAKING AND LEADER EFFECTIVE-NESS.   One of the key tasks performed by leaders is making decisions. Indeed, a defining characteristic of leadership positions is that they are places where "the buck stops" and concrete actions must be taken. Yet leaders do not operate in a social vacuum; even when they possess considerable power and authority, there is no guarantee that their decisions will be accepted or implemented by followers. Thus, leadership is always something of a two-way street, in which leaders influence followers and followers, in turn, exert some degree of influence over leaders.

Given this fact, an intriguing question arises: In making decisions, how much participation by followers should leaders permit? According to one theory of leadership, **normative theory,** this question is an important determinant of leader effectiveness (Vroom & Yetton, 1973). Leaders who permit an appropriate amount of participation by followers will generally be more effective, over the long haul, than leaders who permit either too much or too little. But how much participation is enough? Vroom and Yetton's theory suggests that this depends on several issues relating, primarily, to the importance of the decision's being high in quality and the importance of its being accepted by subordinates. For example, consider a situation in which a high-quality decision is crucial (the stakes are high), the leader has enough information or expertise to make the decision alone, and acceptance by subordinates is not crucial (the decision will work even without their support). Here, a relatively *autocratic* style of decision is best. It is efficient, and getting the decision implemented will cost very little. In contrast, consider a situation in which a high-quality decision is necessary, the leader has enough information to make the decision alone, but acceptance by subordinates *is* crucial—the decision won't work without their active support. Here, a more *participative* style would be preferable.

Vroom and Yetton's theory suggests that by answering a series of such questions, leaders can arrive at the appropriate decision style—one that affords subordinates just the right amount of participation to maintain their morale while retaining the highest degree of efficiency possible. In general, these guidelines and suggestions seem to work: Leaders who adapt their style of decision making to existing conditions are generally more successful than ones who are either uniformly autocratic or participative in style (Vroom & Jago, 1978). Additional evidence, however, suggests the need for certain adjustments in the theory.

First, it appears that most persons prefer a participative approach by their leader even under conditions where normative theory recommends an autocratic style (Heilman et al., 1984). Second, leaders and subordinates seem to differ in their reactions to various methods for reaching decisions. Leaders tend to prefer those methods suggested by the normative model in any given situation, while subordinates tend to prefer participative strategies in all cases (Heilman et al., 1984). Third, it appears that certain personal characteristics of a leader may play a key role in determining the relative effectiveness of various decision strategies (Crouch & Yetton, 1987). For example, in situations involving conflicting opinions, only managers who are relatively high in conflict-handling skills should use the kind of participative decision-making strategy recommended by the Vroom and Yetton model. Managers low in conflict-handling skills, in contrast, obtain better results with a relatively autocratic style, despite the fact that this is not predicted by the model.

Finally, evidence reported by Field and House (1990) indicates that the Vroom and Yetton model predicts the perceived effectiveness of decisions among managers, but not necessarily among their subordinates. Field and House asked both managers and their subordinates to report their reactions to a recent decision made by the managers. Participants described the process used by the managers to make the decision (the various decision strategies listed in the Vroom and Yetton model) as well as their own perceptions of the extent to which the decisions were accepted and were effective. Results indicated that managers and their subordinates generally agreed in their perceptions of the decision processes used by the managers, and also with respect to the effectiveness of these decisions. Turning to tests of the Vroom and Yetton model, it was found that when managers used one of the decision strategies identified as appropriate by the model, they rated these decisions as more effective than was true when they adopted a decision strategy not identified by the model. This finding offered support for the validity of the Vroom and Yetton model. Similar results were *not* obtained for subordinates, however. They did not rate their managers' decisions as more effective when they were made autocratically in accordance with strategies identified by the model (see Figure 12.18, p. 524).

Why did data from subordinates fail to confirm the Vroom and Yetton model? Field and House suggest that the contrasting roles of subordinates and managers may account, in part, for this finding. Subordinates, it appears, have a strong aversion to autocratic decision-making strategies, even when these are predicted by the model to be most effective. This, in turn, may reflect subordinates' strong desire to have a say in decisions affecting their jobs. Whatever the precise mechanism, it seems clear that the Vroom and Yetton model may be more applicable, in certain respects, to managers than to subordinates.

To conclude: Existing evidence suggests that the normative theory offers useful guidelines to leaders for choosing the most effective approach to decision making. However, adjustments in the model seem necessary, to take account of strong general preferences for participative procedures, differences in the perspectives of leaders and subordinates, and the personal skills or traits of leaders. With the addition of such modifications, the Vroom and Yetton model may prove very helpful in our efforts to understand this key aspect of leader effectiveness.

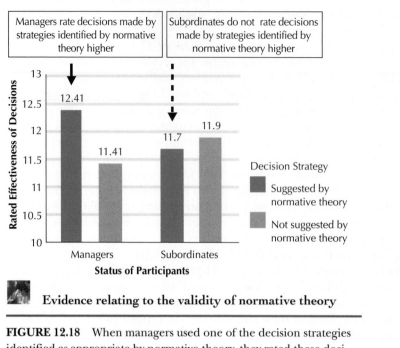

Managers rate decisions made by strategies identified by normative theory higher

Subordinates do not rate decisions made by strategies identified by normative theory higher

Decision Strategy

■ Suggested by normative theory

■ Not suggested by normative theory

Evidence relating to the validity of normative theory

FIGURE 12.18   When managers used one of the decision strategies identified as appropriate by normative theory, they rated these decisions as more effective than when they adopted a decision strategy not identified by the model. Subordinates did not demonstrate the same pattern, however. Instead, they indicated a strong aversion to autocratic approaches to decision making, even when these were identified as most effective by the model.

Source: Based on data from Field & House, 1990.

TRANSFORMATIONAL LEADERSHIP: LEADERSHIP THROUGH VISION AND CHARISMA

In the darkest days of the Depression, the United States seemed poised on the brink of social chaos. With millions out of work and the economy in a seemingly endless decline, despair was rampant. Through his inspiring speeches ("The only thing we have to fear is fear itself . . .") and vigorous actions, President Franklin Roosevelt pulled the nation back from the edge of violence and saved the grand American experiment in political democracy. . . .

World history is filled with similar examples. Down through the ages, some leaders have demonstrated extraordinary success in generating profound changes in the beliefs, perceptions, values, and actions of their followers (see Figure 12.19). Indeed, it is not extreme to suggest that such persons have often served as key agents of social change, transforming entire societies through their words and actions (Bass, 1985). Individuals who accomplish such feats are often described as being **transformational** or **charismatic leaders,** and the terms seem fitting. Such persons do indeed transform social, political, or economic reality; and they do seem to possess unusual and special skills that equip them for this task. (The word charisma means *gift* in Greek.) What personal charac-

 **Transformational (charismatic) leaders**

FIGURE 12.19 Throughout recorded history, some leaders have exerted a profound impact on their followers and on entire societies. Research findings have begun to shed much light on how such persons achieve these dramatic effects.

teristics make certain leaders charismatic? How do such leaders exert their profound effects upon many other persons? Systematic research on this issue has begun to yield some intriguing answers to these and related questions.

THE BASIC NATURE OF CHARISMA: TRAITS OR RELATIONSHIPS?   At first glance, it is tempting to assume that transformational or charismatic leaders are special by virtue of the possession of certain traits; in other words, such leadership might be understood as an extension of the *great person theory* described earlier in this chapter. While traits may well play a role in transformational leadership, there is growing consensus that it makes more sense to understand such leadership as involving a special type of *relationship* between leaders and their followers (House, 1977). Within this framework, charismatic leadership rests more on specific types of reactions by followers than on traits possessed by leaders. Such reactions include: (1) levels of performance beyond those that would normally be expected; (2) high levels of devotion, loyalty, and reverence toward the leader; (3) enthusiasm for and excitement with the leader and the leader's ideas; and (4) a willingness on the part of subordinates to sacrifice their own personal interests for the sake of a larger collective goal. In short, transformational or charismatic leadership involves a special kind of leader-follower relationship, one in which the leader can, in the words of one author, "make ordinary people do extraordinary things in the face of adversity."

THE BEHAVIOR OF TRANSFORMATIONAL LEADERS.   But what, precisely, do transformational or charismatic leaders do to generate this kind of relationship with their subordinates? Studies designed to answer this question point to the following general conclusion: Such leaders gain the capacity to exert profound influence over others through many different tactics.

First, and perhaps most important, transformational leaders propose a *vision* (Howell & Frost, 1989). They describe, usually in vivid, emotion-provoking terms, an image of what their nation, group, or organization could—and should—become. A dramatic example of such leadership is provided by the words of Martin Luther King, in his famous "I Have a Dream" speech:

> "So I say to you, my friends, that even though we must face the difficulties of today and tomorrow, I still have a dream. It is a dream deeply rooted in the American dream that one day this nation will rise up and live out the true meaning of its creed—we hold these truths to be self-evident, that all men are created equal. This will be the day when all of God's children will be able to sing with new meaning "My country, 'tis of thee, sweet land of liberty. . . ."

But transformational leaders do not simply describe a dream or vision; in addition, they offer a clear road map for attaining it; they tell their followers, in straightforward terms, how to get from here to there. This too seems to be crucial, for a vision that seems perpetually out of reach is unlikely to motivate people to try to attain it.

Third, transformational leaders engage in what Conger (1991) terms *framing*: they define the purpose of their movement or organization in a way that gives meaning and purpose to whatever actions they are requesting from followers. Perhaps the nature of framing is best illustrated by the well-known anecdote of two stonecutters working on a cathedral in the Middle Ages. When asked what they are doing, one replies, "Why, cutting this stone, of course." The other replies, "Building the world's most beautiful temple to the glory of God." Which person would be more likely to expend greater effort? The answer is obvious.

In addition, transformational leaders often show greater-than-average willingness to take risks and engage in unconventional actions in order to reach their stated goals. In order to help thwart the coup that threatened the budding democracy of his nation, Boris Yeltsin rushed to the Russian parliament building, where he stood on top of a tank and pleaded with troops sent there by the hard-liners to withdraw. In this manner he demonstrated his deep commitment to the forces of reform.

Other tactics shown by transformational leaders include high levels of self-confidence and confidence in their followers; a high degree of concern for their followers' needs; excellent communication skills, such as the ability to "read" others' reactions quickly and accurately; and a stirring personal style (House, Spangler, & Woycke, 1991). Finally, transformational leaders are often masters of *impression management,* engaging in many actions designed to enhance their attractiveness and appeal to others. When these forms of behavior are added to the captivating and exciting visions they propound, the tremendous impact of transformational or charismatic leaders begins to come sharply into focus. Their influence, it appears, does not stem from the possession of semimagical traits; rather, it is a logical result of a complex cluster of behaviors and techniques. In the final analysis, however, the essence of transformational leadership does appear to rest on the ability of such persons to inspire others, through their words, their vision, and their actions. As Conger puts it (1991, p. 44): "If you as a leader can make an appealing dream seem like tomorrow's reality, your subordinates will freely choose to follow you."

Are the kind of group processes we have described in this chapter universal—present in all cultures? Or do groups operate differently in different cultures? For information on this important issue, please see the **Social Diversity** section below.

Social Diversity ▼ *A Critical Analysis*

Cultural Differences in Group Processes: A Tale of Many Lands

People all over the world spend much of their time working together in groups. At work, in school, and at play, groups constitute an important fact of daily life. Do these groups function in the same manner everywhere? Or are the processes that take place within them influenced by cultural factors? A growing body of evidence points to the following conclusion: The events that occur within groups, and the relationships that develop among their members, are strongly affected by cultural forces. In order to provide you with some insight into the nature of such effects, we'll examine cultural differences with respect to two key aspects of group functioning: leadership and conflict-resolution techniques.

Leadership in American and Asian Corporations

While the term *leadership* generally conjures up images of politi-

cal or military leaders, it is clear that in these times of increasing economic competition a nation's fortunes rest to an important extent with its business leaders. And important differences have been noted in the style of such leaders in different countries (Kotter, 1982). Some of the most revealing information on this issue to date has been reported by Doktor (1990) in comparative studies of the heads of major companies in the United States, Japan, Korea, and Hong Kong. Doktor contends that cultural values strongly determine how people perceive the nature of their jobs, and this includes the chief executive officers (CEOs for short) of major companies. In Japan, he notes, business leaders perceive that what affects one part of society may well affect other parts as well. Thus, they view their corporate decisions in a broad context that takes account of the decisions' consequences for other segments of

society outside the business community. According to Doktor (1990), Korean culture is similar, but also places stronger emphasis on authority and a top-down decision-making process. Hong Kong presents a mixed picture, since in that culture traditional Chinese values emphasizing mutual influences between various aspects of society are combined with Western beliefs that place a high value on individuality and independence. In the United States, in contrast, decisions are viewed in a somewhat narrower context, focused on a company and its goals.

How do these contrasting cultural values influence the leadership style of Asian and American CEOs? To find out, Doktor compared the workdays of CEOs in Japan, Korea, Hong Kong, and the United States. These comparisons yielded some revealing findings. First, he found that CEOs in each country spent about the same proportions of their days working alone (25 percent) and working in groups (75 percent). However, the *duration* of each task they performed varied greatly. In the United States, almost 50 percent of all tasks were completed in only *nine minutes or less.* In contrast, the comparable percentages of short tasks in Japan and Korea were much lower—10 percent and 14 percent, respectively; as expected, Hong Kong was in between. The reverse pattern appeared for tasks requiring more than one hour. American business leaders spent only 10 percent of their time on such activities; Japanese and Korean managers spent 42 and 44 percent of their time on such tasks. In short, a clear pattern of differences emerged: American leaders spent their days performing a large number of tasks of brief duration; Japanese and Korean managers divided their days into a smaller number of longer segments.

Doktor contends that these differences are consistent with cultural differences among these countries. Because Japanese and Korean managers consider the broader context of their actions and decisions, they feel strongly that these should not be rushed. Thus, they spend more time on each task they perform. In contrast, American managers adopt a more restricted view of the impact of their decisions, so they are more willing to make them quickly. These differences are magnified by the contrasting status of business leaders in U.S. and Asian cultures. Asian cultures generally confer very high status on top business leaders. Thus, it is inappropriate to rush these people through an over-

crowded schedule. CEOs in the United States also enjoy high status and respect, but not, according to Doktor, quite as high as that in Japan and Korea. As a result, their subordinates are less reluctant to rush them through many brief meetings.

These findings suggest that even today, when modern technology dictates the form of many business practices, cultural differences can and do play a key role in shaping the actions and perceptions of business leaders. As T. Fujisawa, the cofounder of Honda Corporation, once put it, "Japanese and American management are 95 percent the same—and differ in all important respects." We might add: "And those differences can be traced, to an important degree, to specific cultural factors."

Conflict and "Saving Face" in Various Cultures

Cultures differ in many ways, but one that appears to be very important in its effects involves differences along an *individualistic-collectivistic dimension* (Hofstede, 1980; Smith & Bond, 1993). Individualistic cultures tend to value individual goals over group goals and individual rights and needs over collective responsibilities. This is true of the United States and many European countries. Collectivistic cultures, in contrast, tend to value group goals over individual ones and collective needs over individual rights. Cultures classified as collectivistic include Japan, Korea, and many other Asian countries.

Differences along this dimension are related to many aspects of group functioning,

from how groups handle *free-rider* effects (Yamagishi, 1988) through the extent to which leaders are held responsible for group failures (Takahashi, 1991). Perhaps the impact of such differences in cultural values is most visible, however, in group reactions to conflict. According to Ting-Toomey (1988), a researcher who has studied this issue in detail, people from collectivistic cultures show greater concern than people from individualistic cultures with saving *others' face*—with others' desire to maintain their self-respect and personal image. This implies that they would avoid humiliating their opponents in a conflict and would try to provide them with an out—a good excuse for a negative performance or a poor outcome. In contrast, people from individualistic cultures show much more concern with protecting or enhancing their own image and self-respect—what might be termed *self-face.*

A second difference between people from collectivistic and individualistic cultures proposed by Ting-Toomey involves specific strategies for resolving ongoing conflicts. Presumably, persons from individualistic cultures would tend to use more active strategies, such as direct competition or efforts to collaborate with opponents, while those from collectivistic cultures would tend to use such tactics as accommodating their opponents or avoiding conflict altogether.

Research conducted by Ting-Toomey and her colleagues (e.g., Ting-Toomey et al., 1991) provides support for these predictions. In these studies, thousands of persons in various cultures (the United States, Japan,

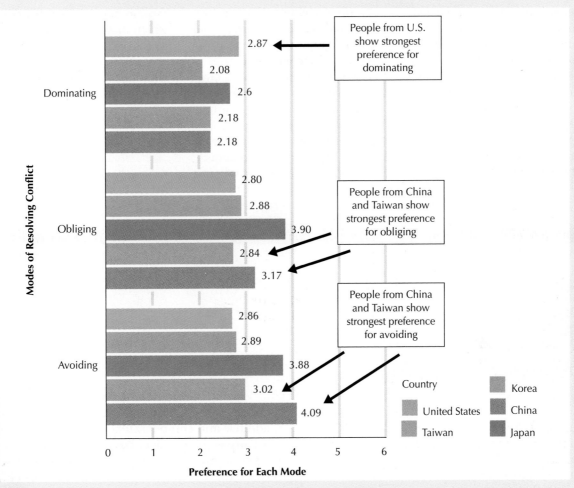

Cultural differences in preferred means of resolving conflicts

FIGURE 12.20 As shown here, people from *individualistic cultures* such as the United States showed a stronger preference than people from *collectivistic cultures* such as China and Taiwan for resolving conflicts through dominating. In contrast, people from collectivistic cultures showed stronger preferences for resolving conflicts through giving in to opponents and avoiding the situation.

Source: Based on data from Ting-Toomey et al., 1991.

China, Korea, Taiwan) completed questionnaires designed to measure their concern with maintaining their own face and their opponent's face in conflict situations, and other questionnaires designed to measure their preferred techniques for resolving conflicts with others (competition, accommodation, compromise, avoidance, etc.).

Results indicated that, as predicted, persons from China, Korea, and Taiwan all reported more concern with maintaining others' face than participants from the United States. With respect to maintaining their own face, participants from Japan reported the highest concern and those from Korea the lowest concern. Participants from the United States, China, and Taiwan fell in between in this respect.

Cultural differences in preferred modes of handling conflict also emerged. As expected, participants from the United States reported stronger preference for dominating others than did participants from Japan and Korea. In contrast, participants from Taiwan and China showed the strongest preference for giving in to their opponents and for avoiding conflict (see Figure 12.20, p. 529).

In sum, cultural factors do appear to play an important role where group processes are concerned. Leadership style, concern with others' and one's own face, preferred means of resolving conflict—these and many other aspects of behavior in group settings are affected by culture. In order fully to understand groups, therefore, we must take account of the cultures in which they operate; failure to do so is like trying to understand the growth of a beautiful plant without considering the soil that nurtures its roots.

Summary and Review

The Nature and Function of Groups

A *group* consists of two of more individuals who share common goals, whose fates are interdependent, who have a stable relationship, and who recognize the group's existence. Groups exert influence upon their members through *roles* (members' assigned functions within the group), *status* (their relative standing or influence), *norms* (rules concerning appropriate behavior), and *cohesiveness* (forces acting to keep members within the group, e.g., their attraction to it).

Groups and Task Performance

Individuals' performance of various tasks is often affected by the presence of others or by the potential evaluation of their work. Such effects are known as *social facilitation,* although they can involve reduced as well as enhanced task performance. Social facilitation appears to stem from arousal induced by the presence of others. *Distraction-conflict theory* suggests that such arousal stems from conflict between paying attention to others and paying attention to the task at hand.

Groups are more efficient in performing certain types of tasks than are individuals (e.g., additive and compensatory tasks). However, they are worse than individuals in performing other types of tasks (e.g., conjunctive ones). In some cases where groups might prove relatively efficient, their output is hindered by *social loafing*—the tendency of some members to take it easy and let others do most of the work. Social loafing stems from such persons' beliefs that their effort will be pooled with that of others, and from the fact that for various reasons their individual effort cannot be evaluated. Several techniques (e.g., making individuals' work identifiable, providing standards for self-evaluation) are effective in countering tendencies toward social loafing. When a task is important or meaningful to individuals, they may react to social loafing by others not solely with anger or withdrawal but with *social compensation*—an increase in their own effort.

Recent findings indicate that social facilitation and social loafing may both be related to, and involve, individuals' expectancies concerning their own self-efficacy and the likelihood that engaging in specific behaviors will yield desired outcomes (outcome expectancies).

Decision Making in Groups

Groups make many key decisions. These can sometimes be predicted by *social decision schemes*—simple rules relating the initial views of members to the group's final decision. Procedures such as *straw polls* can influence the views of individual members and hence the decisions reached by groups. In addition, group decision making is influenced by *deliberation style*—whether groups focus on information and evidence or on members' judgments.

As a result of their deliberations, groups often demonstrate *group polarization,* a tendency to shift toward more extreme views. Two other potential difficulties faced by decision-making groups are *groupthink,* a tendency to become concerned more with maintaining consensus than with choosing the best alternative, and an inability to pool unshared information.

Leadership

Leaders are group members who exert influence on other group members in the direction of specific goals. The *great person theory* of leadership suggests that specific persons become leaders because they possess crucial traits. Recent evidence suggests that there may be a grain of truth in this theory: Successful leaders do appear to differ from other persons in several respects. In particular, they demonstrate great *flexibility* in responding to the needs of group members and to changing external conditions.

Male and female leaders do not differ in their relative concern with task performance and interpersonal relations. However, female leaders tend to adopt a more democratic leadership style than do males.

According to Fiedler's *contingency theory,* leader effectiveness stems from a complex interplay between leaders' characteristics and the situations they confront. Vroom and Yetton's *normative theory* proposes that one important determinant of such effectiveness is decision-making style—the extent to which leaders permit participation by followers in key decisions. Leaders who permit the most appropriate level of participation by followers in a given situation are more effective than leaders who permit too little or too much participation.

Transformational or *charismatic leaders* exert profound effects on their followers. They do this by establishing a special kind of relationship with their followers, and by proposing an inspiring vision of where the group could be or ought to be.

Cultural Differences in Group Processes

Important cultural differences exist with respect to several group processes. American business leaders and Asian business leaders show several differences in style. In addition, persons from *collectivistic* and *individualistic* cultures differ appreciably in their preferred modes of resolving conflict.

Key Terms

Additive Tasks Tasks in which the group product is the sum or combination of the efforts of individual members.

Charismatic Leaders Leaders who induce high levels of loyalty, respect, and admiration for themselves among their followers. (See also *Transformational Leaders.*)

Cohesiveness All forces acting on group members to cause them to remain part of a group; including mutual attraction, interdependence, shared goals, and so on.

Compensatory Tasks Tasks in which the group product is the average of all members' contributions.

Conjunctive Tasks Tasks in which the performance of the poorest member determines the group product.

Contingency Theory A theory suggesting the leader effectiveness is determined by a complex interplay between the leader's characteristics and the favorability of the situation (situational control) for the leader.

Decision Making The processes through which groups move toward consensus and reach decisions.

Disjunctive Tasks Tasks in which the contribution of the best member determines the final group product.

Distraction-Conflict Theory A theory suggesting that social facilitation stems from the conflict produced when individuals attempt simultaneously to pay attention to other persons and to the task being performed.

Drive Theory of Social Facilitation A theory suggesting that the mere presence of others is arousing and increases the tendency to perform dominant responses.

Evaluation Apprehension Concern over being evaluated by others. Such concern can increase arousal and so contribute to social facilitation.

Great Person Theory A theory of leadership suggesting that all great leaders share key traits that suit them for positions of authority.

Group Polarization The tendency of group members to shift toward more extreme positions than those they initially held as a result of group discussion.

Groups Two or more persons who interact with one another, share common goals, are somehow interdependent, and recognize that they belong to a group.

Groupthink The tendency of members of highly cohesive groups to seek consensus so strongly that they ignore information inconsistent with their views and often make disastrous decisions.

Information Sampling Model A theory of group decision making suggesting that group members are more likely to discuss shared information than information not shared by all group members. This tendency increases with group size.

Leadership The process through which leaders influence other group members toward attainment of specific group goals.

Norms Rules within a group indicating how its members should (or should not) behave.

Normative Theory A theory suggesting that leaders are most effective when they adopt the style of decision making (from autocratic to participative) most appropriate in a given situation.

Risky Shift The tendency for groups to recommend riskier courses of action following group discussion than before its occurrence.

Roles The set of behaviors that individuals occupying specific positions within a group are expected to perform.

Social Compensation Increased effort on the part of one or more group members to compensate for social loafing on the part of one or more others.

Social Decision Schemes Rules relating the initial distribution of member views to final group decisions.

Social Facilitation Effects upon performance resulting from the presence of others.

Social Loafing The tendency of some group members to exert less effort on a task than they would if working on it alone.

Status Social standing or rank.

Straw Poll A procedure in which group members indicate their current preferences regarding a decision. These statements are not binding upon them, so they are free to shift to other positions.

Transformational Leaders Leaders who exert profound influence over followers by proposing an inspiring vision, among other techniques. (See also *Charismatic Leaders*.)

For More Information

Hendrick, C. (Ed.). (1987). *Group processes.* Newbury Park, CA: Sage.

A collection of chapters dealing with various aspects of group processes (e.g., group decision making, leadership, minority influence). Each chapter is quite up to date and was prepared by established experts in the field.

Paulus, P. B. (Ed.). (1989). *Psychology of group influence* (2nd ed.). Hillsdale, NJ: Erlbaum.

This book deals with many of the topics considered in this chapter (e.g., social facilitation, social loafing, leadership). If you'd like to know more about these aspects of behavior in group meetings, this is an excellent source to consult.

Social Psychology and the Individual: Population, Health, and Environmental Applications

Special Sections

When I was about six years old, I had my first experience with a serious illness and with being in a hospital. I had started the first grade at Matthews School, and I was beginning to enjoy the experience of going to elementary school. My teacher was great, and I had made several new friends. During that winter, however, I developed a cold that progressed into a more general upper respiratory illness, including a bad earache. I stayed home from school for about a week and clearly was not feeling any better.

Though the words didn't mean much to me at the time, Dr. Robinson said that I had mastoiditis, an infection of the bone that lies just behind the ear. Today such an infection is treated routinely with antibiotics, but in the late 1930s there were no sulfa, penicillin, or tetracycline drugs. My parents were told that an operation was necessary. Mastoidectomy is a somewhat crude procedure in which the surgeon chips or chisels away the bone in that part of the skull in order to drain the infection. In my case, if this were not done, the infection was likely to spread, and the possible consequences ranged from hearing loss to a fatal brain infection.

I didn't know all of those details at the time, and my real concerns centered on three aspects of the process. What was going to happen to me in the hospital? Would the operation hurt? Was it possible to live as I did at home (my mother nearby, toys to play with, food that I liked, and so forth)?

Today, many decades later, research in health psychology indicates that both young and old patients worry most about just such details. When medical personnel attend to these issues and provide comfort and reassurance, patients respond positively, find the experience less traumatic, and recover faster. As an example of such applications, I recently accompanied my young daughter and her classmates on a tour of the children's ward of a local hospital. The guide demonstrated one of the first experiences provided for each young patient—a session with a "robot," who shows the child videotapes depicting exactly what will happen in the hospital. Each child finds out what he or she will

wear, what the rooms look like, how the nurse measures temperature, how the patient is put to sleep so there will be no pain, and many other details of hospital life. The child is told to bring a favorite toy and that a parent can sleep in his or her room. Altogether, the hospital makes every effort to remove the fear of the unknown and to make the experience as comfortable as possible.

Back in my childhood, however, none of this was done. Every step from hospital gown to the administration of ether was an unexpected and frightening new event. My parents had to be unusually assertive to get the hospital to bend the rules and allow my mother to stay in my room at night. And, after the operation, a very kind nurse discovered I disliked the food and let me plan some of my own meals (such as toast with

catsup and a cup of hot chocolate) to be sneaked into my room. In any event, the operation was performed, I survived, and the efforts of my parents and others helped make the experience less traumatic than it ordinarily would have been.

Though I have been fortunate enough to avoid serious illnesses and surgery in recent decades, I suspect that even as an adult entering a hospital, I would raise the same questions as in my childhood. That is, the immediate concerns would not be about medical technology and possible outcomes nearly so much as about the precise details of what would happen to me, potential pain, and the possibility of finding some familiar comforts in an unfamiliar environment.

Some of the many applications of social psychology will be described in this chapter and the following one. By **applied social psychology** we mean the utilization of social psychological principles and research methods in real-world settings in efforts to solve a variety of individual and societal problems (Weyant, 1986). In the present chapter, we will focus on the ways in which each of us is affected by and can have an effect on world population growth, our health, and the physical environment that surrounds us.

We first examine *population psychology*, concentrating on the effects of the rapid expansion of the number of humans on this planet and on efforts to control this expansion. We then turn to *health psychology* and research that ranges from preventive medicine to the ways people cope with illness. The third major focus is on *environmental psychology*, research that deals with the interaction between the physical world and human behavior (Sanchez & Wiesenfeld, 1987).

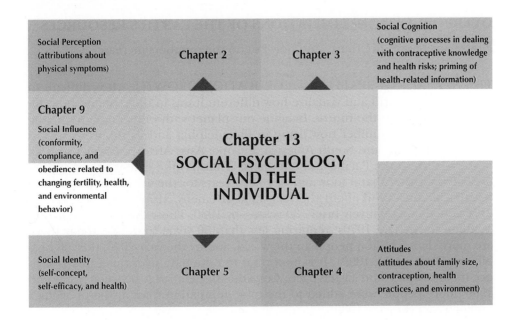

Social Perception
(attributions about
physical symptoms)

Chapter 2

Chapter 3

Social Cognition
(cognitive processes in dealing
with contraceptive knowledge
and health risks; priming of
health-related information)

Chapter 9

Social Influence
(conformity,
compliance, and
obedience related to
changing fertility, health,
and environmental
behavior)

**Chapter 13
SOCIAL PSYCHOLOGY
AND THE
INDIVIDUAL**

Social Identity
(self-concept,
self-efficacy, and health)

Chapter 5

Chapter 4

Attitudes
(attitudes about family size,
contraception, health
practices, and environment)

POPULATION PSYCHOLOGY:
UNLIMITED GROWTH VERSUS STABILIZATION

Throughout most of human history, including recent history, a constant factor has been the reality of population growth. In each century there are more human beings on this planet than ever before, as suggested by Figure 13.1. Throughout the world, people have welcomed such growth, and cities and nations often equate their progress and well-being with increases in the number of citizens residing there. By the end of the eighteenth century, however, some dissenting voices began to be raised (Malthus, 1798/1872). The problems associated with continued growth were gradually identified, and in recent decades the necessity for a stable world population has become increasingly clear. In this section we will outline the realities of population growth, point out the problems that are created by the presence of more and more human beings, and discuss possible solutions.

The Earth's population continues to grow

FIGURE 13.1   Though a population growth rate of about 2 percent per year does not sound very alarming, an exponential increase in the total number of people on our planet has begun to outstrip our resources. There are now more than five billion people to feed, house, clothe, educate, and provide with adequate health care. We need to find acceptable ways to persuade individuals to adopt the attitudes and behaviors that produce a stabilized population.

OVERPOPULATION? LIMITATIONS OF THE EARTH'S RESOURCES

How many people are there, and how fast do the numbers increase?

THE SURPRISING REALITY OF POPULATION GROWTH.   It is difficult to look at today's world and visualize how different it was in the past and how different it may be in the future. Imagine our planet with only 5 million inhabitants—about the number now living in Philadelphia and its suburbs—spread throughout North and South America, Europe, Asia, Africa, Australia, and all of the islands in the Pacific and elsewhere. That was the extent of our species in 8000 B.C. After that it took almost 10,000 years for the world's population to reach 1 billion—until about the year 1800 (Demeny, 1974). The next billion were added in a relatively brief 130 years—by 1930. Those 2 billion doubled to 4 billion in the late 1970s, requiring less than 50 years to do so. Today there are more than 5 billion people in the world, and by the year 2000, there'll be 6 billion (Dumanoski, 1990). It is important to note that, over time, this growth occurs at a faster and faster pace. Consider the fact that between 1950 and 1990, more people were added to the total population than in the previous 3 million years (Keyfitz, 1989).

Though such numbers are difficult to imagine, it is easier to visualize an addition of about 5 thousand people every 30 minutes (Haub, 1991). This is the present rate of growth, and as a result the world's population currently increases by about 24,000 people every day—equivalent to adding a new Columbus, Georgia, each twenty-four hours. In the nation with the fastest growing population, Kenya, the annual increase of about 4 percent means that the population there *doubles* every eighteen years (Kaplan, 1992).

How is it that the number of human beings has grown in this fashion? Sagan (1989) explains the mathematical phenomenon in terms of the "secret of the Persian chessboard." Legend has it that the grand vizier of Persia invented the game of chess, played on a board divided into sixty-four squares. The king was pleased by this new game, and he told the vizier to select whatever he wished as a reward. The clever inventor pretended to be a modest man who seemed to make only a small request. He asked the king to give him a few grains of wheat—just one grain on the first square of the board, doubling it to two grains on the second square, four grains on the third, and so on for all sixty-four squares. The king thought that this was a small reward, and he was relieved that so little had been requested.

Critical Thinking
Question 1
What was not obvious to the king, or to most of us, is that by the time the doubling continued to the sixty-fourth square, the reward would add up to 18.5 quintillion grains of wheat—about 75 billion metric tons—more than the contents of all the king's granaries. As Sagan (1989) pointed out, if the chessboard had contained one hundred squares, the resulting wheat would have weighed as much as the entire earth. How can that be? The secret is that each new chessboard square constitutes an **arithmetic progression,** in which the series adds a constant number (in this instance, one) each time. In contrast, the wheat grains were added in a **geometric progression,** in which the series represents a ratio increase each time (in this instance, doubling). The astonishing growth in the number of wheat grains is called an *exponential increase.* In a similar way, when time passes arithmetically (for example, one year, two years, etc.) and population grows geometrically each year (for example, a 2 percent increase), population growth over time is as spectacular as the growth in the number of wheat grains over sixty-four squares. Thus, you can start with very small numbers of anything (human beings, grains of wheat, or whatever),

and a geometric progression leads to an exponential increase in those numbers. To give another example, *compound interest* works the same way; ten dollars invested 200 years ago at 6 percent interest would be worth more than a million dollars today.

WHY EXPONENTIAL GROWTH COMES AS A SURPRISE.   The legendary king of Persia was surprised by the wheat, and we are surprised by population growth and by compound interest, in part because we ordinarily think in arithmetical rather than geometric terms. Our cognitive set is simply not adapted to thinking in terms of percentage increases.

A second reason is that with relatively low percentages of increase, noticeable growth requires the passage of large segments of time. For example, as I drive through downtown Albany, I see no evidence that the population is growing. If, however, Henry Hudson or the Mohicans who resided here could travel forward in time, they would be dumbfounded to see the growth that has occurred in the Albany area between Hudson's arrival aboard the *Half Moon* in September 1609 and the present time. The Native Americans who first settled in the area about 10,000 years ago would be even more impressed by the changes.

Consider the example in Figure 13.2. Think of a lake that consists of 128 square miles of sparkling blue water—with the minor exception of 1 square

 Exponential increase—a slow start and a rapid finish

FIGURE 13.2   As an illustration of the effects of a *geometric* progression, consider an imaginary lake with an area of 128 square miles, with just 1 of those square miles covered with algae. If the algae doubles each decade, its progress will follow the curve shown below. In the beginning, the growth seems slow and unimpressive. As time passes, the problem becomes much more obvious. In sixty years half of the lake will be covered; in seventy, the water will have totally disappeared.

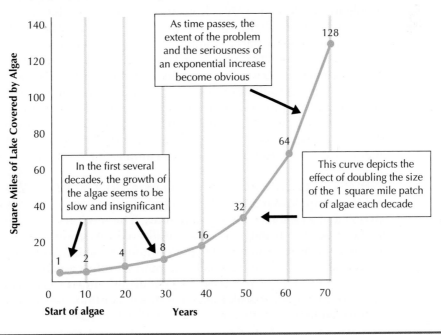

mile of green algae near the distant shore. Imagine that the patch of algae grows at a relatively modest rate, doubling every decade. You could return to the lake ten years later and still find a beautiful scene with 126 square miles of water and only 2 square miles of algae. Even forty years after your first visit, there would be 112 square miles of clear water and only 16 of algae. In fact, the green growth might take sixty years to get your attention as a problem—when half of the lake was covered with algae. It could well be too late to save the lake at that point, however, because in just one additional decade, the blue water would entirely disappear beneath the green scum.

ZERO POPULATION GROWTH: DECREASING THE BIRTH RATE

Some observers, known as "cornucopians," argue that continued population growth is essential; short-term misery is beneficial in the long run because it acts as an incentive, resulting in a rise in everyone's standard of living (Simon, 1989; Wattenberg, 1989). Umpleby (1990) and others point out that human intelligence and ingenuity is such that we can expand and improve resources. The opposite view is that human beings are equivalent to a malignant form of cancer on the earth's surface, a tumor that will continue to grow until it destroys its environment and itself (Hern, 1990).

Critical Thinking
Question 2
Most people agree that an infinite increase in the total number of human beings is not feasible. Consider that at the current growth rate, 95 million additional people must be fed each year, even though it is obviously impossible to increase the amount of topsoil or groundwater (Ehrlich, 1991). No one can specify the optimal world population, but one goal is to balance the number of people with the available resources so that everyone can have what he or she needs to live a good life (Daly, 1991), including affordable energy such as electricity (Holdren, 1991). Some believe that such a goal is impossible and that the only question is exactly at what point the world population will become sufficiently large to result in widespread famine, vicious wars over scarce resources such as water and land, and/or the spread of fatal diseases—any one of which will lead to fewer people on our planet and thus temporarily solve the problem (Heilbroner, 1974). Both the optimists and the pessimists agree that at some point population growth must and will stop, whether by choice or by catastrophe (Luten, 1991). Assuming that we prefer choice, Parsons (1991, p. 355) proposes that "This task is a problem of social control, the central process in all societies. If society's controllers and their institutions are aware, intelligent, flexible, and suitably motivated, there is no reason why most problems of population, development, and pollution should not be solved and then kept permanently in check." In other words, the theories and methods of social psychology can be applied to bring about changes in attitudes and behavior (see chapters 4 and 9). How is that to be accomplished?

INDIA AND CHINA: ATTEMPTS TO CONTROL FERTILITY.   In the world's two most populous nations, the governments have made serious efforts to halt growth and to stabilize their populations. The motivation for this interference in the lives of individual citizens is the rapid depletion of usable farmland, a growing shortage of water, and the economic inability to keep up with needs for housing, education, medical care, and all other aspects of even a minimal standard of living. Even if these two countries' efforts to control their populations are totally successful, their growth will continue well into the twenty-first century, adding more than one and a half billion humans to the world's total.

In India today a third of the population suffers from malnutrition, and India is home to almost half of the illiterate people in the world. India's population is growing faster (2.1 percent each year) than that of China (1.4 percent each year), and India is expected to become the world's most populous country early in the twenty-first century, with 2 billion citizens (Chaudhry, 1992). It is estimated that China's population will reach about 1.5 billion before growth can be stopped (Family planning . . ., 1992). These two nations both desire to stop population growth, but one has been more successful than the other in moving toward this goal. What has each done to bring about the necessary behavioral changes?

After some early attempts at the use of force (for example, involuntary sterilizations), India has primarily relied on making education and family planning available to those who are interested (Chaudhry, 1990). This approach has been less successful than the one utilized in China.

At least from the perspective of Western culture (Hardin, 1991a), China's efforts are perceived as coercive and hence have drawn criticism (Aird, 1990). Table 13.1, p. 542, outlines the evolution of the Chinese experience in fertility control. The process involved a combination of social psychological principles, including persuasion and attitude change, conformity pressures, compliance techniques, and coercive demands for obedience. Stycos (1991) points out that China began dealing with the population problem somewhat reluctantly, for ideological reasons, and its efforts were also delayed by shortages of medical personnel and contraceptives. Initially, in the early 1960s (when the IUD and vacuum pump abortion became available), China utilized promotional material that emphasized health and the doctrine that two children represent an ideal family. In urban areas this effort met with partial success—there was a drop by the end of the decade from about six children per mother to about three. In rural areas an additional ten years passed before family size began to decline. The next step was to stress the importance to the nation of voluntary delays in the age of marriage and in the utilization of family planning. In the 1970s coercion became a central part of the effort. For example, health workers went door to door each month to determine what form of contraception each family used, and the information was posted on the wall of the health center (Sidel, 1973). Population targets were set for each city and county, and community pressure was brought to bear in group settings featuring testimonials of "sinners" who had married too young or had too many offspring. Also, the names of those scheduled to give birth in the coming months were posted in public places.

By the late 1970s contraceptive pills were widely available in China, a simpler method of female sterilization was developed, and the abortion rate rose almost to the levels found in the United States. At this point the government redefined the "ideal number of children" as one. Among couples who had no children or one child, 57 percent signed "one-child certificates," meaning that the couple agreed to have no more than one offspring (Tien, 1983). In 1982 the Chinese constitution became the world's first to specify fertility control as a societal requirement. Individual decision making about parenthood was no longer legal, and family planning became a *duty* rather than a *right*. These legal changes led to an often heavy-handed program of enforced obedience (including involuntary abortions) and penalties for exceeding the one-child limit. However negatively you may evaluate the methods, the result has been a successful reduction in birthrates and a higher proportional use of family planning procedures than in the United States. There is continuing controversy

Discussion Question 3

In 1949 Chairman Mao of China proclaimed a classic Marxist theme: The problem of overpopulation simply could not occur in a communist society. Just four years later, a national census discovered that there were one hundred million more Chinese citizens than previously estimated. Despite zigzags in the official party line, the government gradually committed itself to a long-term and eventually successful campaign to alter attitudes and behavior relevant to family size and family planning.

TABLE 13.1 Stabilizing China's population: Attitude change and social influence

The Odyssey of Population Control in China

1949	• Communists defeat nationalists and take control of China • "Of all things in the world people are the most precious."—Mao • Party line: Under communism, problem of overpopulation cannot occur
1953–58	• Food shortages • Census indicates that China has 100,000,000 more people than had been assumed • Family planning clinics quietly set up and weakly promoted • Condoms, diaphragms, jellies in short supply; abortion and sterilization expensive and uncommon • Swallowing tadpoles and using acupuncture recommended to prevent conception • Public argument that birth control would stimulate promiscuity and undermine morals • Birth rate remains unchanged
1958	• "Great Leap Forward" • All promotion of family planning halted • Party line: People equal capital • Agricultural production drops; famine follows • Birth rate declines because marriages are delayed and disrupted
1962	• Government steps up birth control efforts • A mission is sent to Japan to study their success in lowering birth rates • IUDs and vacuum pump abortions become available • Party line: Birth control good for health of mothers and their children • "Two children is just right, three is too many, and four is a mistake"
1963–1969	• Urban fertility rate dropping—from 6 per woman to 3 by the late 1960s; rural fertility rate will show similar drop 10 years later • 1963 census indicates population of 900,000,000, but government claims it is 800,000,000 and suppresses the data for 20 years • In Cultural Revolution of late 1960s, birth control program is suspended *(continued)*

about whether these various forms of behavior control should be condemned as a violation of human rights; but the alternative, unrestricted population growth, would have disastrous consequences (Hardin, 1991b). In any event, educational efforts by the Chinese goverment seem to have convinced the majority of the Chinese citizens to adopt the goal of stopping population growth and to behave accordingly (Stycos, 1991). A similar approach may well be unworkable in a democratic society.

VOLUNTARY CHANGES BASED ON THE DECISIONS OF INDIVIDUALS. In contrast to India's slow progress by means of informational techniques and China's effective but totalitarian intervention in the lives of its married couples, some Asian nations—such as South Korea, Thailand, and Indonesia—have succeeded in accomplishing voluntary fertility reduction. The apparent

China's Population

TABLE 13.1   *continued*

The Odyssey of Population Control in China

Early 1970s
- Family planning and late marriages become national priorities
  - "To allow anarchy in human reproduction is not to be tolerated."—Mao
- *Control* of reproduction is the new goal
- Volunteer health workers undertake detailed supervision of contraception in neighborhoods; charts of contraceptive use posted in health centers
- Public charts of city and county goals, names of the pregnant, public testimonials of contraceptive "sinners" and heroes
- Families become convinced that limiting the number of children helps China, so they want to help
- Party line: Small families will hasten world revolution, consolidate the "dictatorship of the proletariat," and facilitate preparation for war

Late 1970s
- Contraceptive pills available
- Simpler female sterilization method introduced
- Family planning integrated with mother and child services
- 70% of all couples of childbearing age using contraceptives
- Abortion rate almost as high as in U.S.
- Government goal: population growth to stop by the year 2000
- Party line: Population growth hinders the accumulation of capital, interferes with science, culture, and standard of living

1980s
- Government policy: Each couple should have no more than one child
- 57% of all eligible couples sign contracts agreeing to limit offspring to a maximum of 1
- Constitutional additions: Fertility control a societal requirement; family planning a duty rather than a right
- Higher proportion of Chinese than of U.S. couples use modern family planning methods
- Surveys of high school students and older individuals indicate desired family size of two or less
- Fertility rate drops; end of population growth is predicted

Source: Based on information in Stycos, 1991.

key is the development of a strong industrial base; when couples become economically secure, they are motivated to control the size of their families. Thus, they become increasingly receptive to educational efforts that promote family planning. In highly developed and economically successful nations such as Japan, self-directed population control has been the rule for the last several decades (Stycos, 1991)—see Figure 13.3, p. 544. Many hope that economic improvement will eventually occur in every nation and automatically take care of the problem of overpopulation. But Culbertson (1989) and Hardin (1990) label this expectancy a myth that supports a do-nothing approach; they point out that no one can *guarantee* either economic growth or changes in fertility-related behavior.

Population size in the United States may already have reached a point where the number of people exceeds the "carrying capacity" of the country.

Economic security leads to smaller families

FIGURE 13.3 In some parts of the world, one of the results of economic development is a reduction in family size. Couples spontaneously decide to limit the number of offspring in order to maintain a rising standard of living. Such changes have been documented in the United States and Canada, in much of Western Europe, and in Japan and Korea. This kind of change provides an ideal solution to population problems, but no one can guarantee when and where economic growth will occur or whether such growth will automatically change fertility-related behavior.

Reading: Lesko (38), *Territorial Defense and the Good Neighbor*

When you travel, you may notice miles and miles of empty space and assume that there is still plenty of room for population growth. There are, however, environmental factors, such as the availability of water, that severely limit such expansion (Durham, 1991). Many observers believe that the physical, cultural, and social environment is steadily getting worse; they often point out California as an example of what can go wrong when population exceeds environmental capacity (McConnell, 1991, 1992). The American problem is different from that of India and China, however, in that the birthrate is now sufficiently low that the U.S. population would stabilize in forty years if it were not for immigration. About 880,000 legal and illegal immigrants arrive here each year (Kinsley, 1992). One result, as predicted by the U.S. Census Bureau, is that the country's population will grow from 255 million in 1992 to 275 million in the year 2000 and 383 million in 2050 (Pear, 1992). Any suggestion of limiting immigration seems incompatible with the nation's history and ideals, but Hardin (1992) argues persuasively that zero net immigration should be the goal. One aspect of the problem is that the greatest increases in terms of both immigration and high birthrates are among Hispanics, African-Americans and Asian-Americans; thus, many people are likely to perceive any efforts to limit fertility or restrict immigration as racist policies based on prejudice. What do you think? Should anything be done about population growth? If so, what can be done?

Moving from large-scale problems of world and national population issues, there is another area of concern that is relevant both to the population issue and to the health of individuals. As the following **Applied Side** section indicates, unwanted teenage pregnancies have been the focus of a considerable amount of research, theory, and application.

Social Psychology: On the Applied Side

CONTRACEPTIVE NEGLECT AMONG SEXUALLY ACTIVE ADOLESCENTS

Despite the many political and ideological controversies that surround issues of overpopulation and fertility control, there is much more agreement about the related problem of unwanted teenage pregnancies. That is, essentially no one argues in favor of adolescent males impregnating adolescent females when neither the potential mother nor the potential father wishes to become a parent. The only disagreement is whether to concentrate on encouraging chastity or on encouraging the use of contraception.

Primarily because the incidence of youthful premarital sexual activity continues to rise, most of the research interest in the United Sstates has centered on identifying the reasons for the nonuse of contraception among those who are sexually active. (A neglected issue is the fact that studies of teenage females who are pregnant, give birth, or contract an STD indicate that 70 percent of their male partners are over age twenty; Males, 1992.) At least 20 percent of the fifteen-year-olds in this country are sexually active (Moore, Nord, & Peterson, 1989). Despite fears of AIDS and widespread publicity about its dangers, teenage sexual activity rates continue to increase (Centers for Disease Control, 1991). Among American high school students, the increases are striking. In 1971, less than one-third of these teenagers engaged in intercourse; by 1990, 54 percent were sexually experienced, and this figure was 72 percent for high school seniors (Haber, 1993)—see Figure 13.4. However one evaluates youthful premarital sexuality, one aspect of this behavior is curiously maladaptive. For at least thirty years, the data have consistently indicated that large proportions of these couples fail to use contraceptives consistently, use ineffective methods of contraception, or avoid contraception altogether (Byrne, Kelley, & Fisher, 1993; Ingham, Woodcock, & Stenner, 1991).

With high rates of sexual intercourse and low rates of contraceptive use, the outcome is obvious. Each day in the United States, about 2,740 adolescents conceive, and this means approximately a million unplanned teenage pregnancies each year (National Center for Health Statistics, 1987). Despite high rates of abortion and miscarriage, half of these pregnancies result in the birth of an unplanned—and often unwanted—child (Brody, 1991).

For social psychologists and others, the primary questions center on why teenagers do not use contraception and what to do to change their behavior. The reasons for nonuse of contraception include lack of accurate information, widely held beliefs in subgroups of the population that conception is desirable, situational constraints on obtaining contraception, and personality dispositions that interfere with contraceptive use. Figure 13.5, p. 547, provides a summary of these factors.

To bring about change, it is obviously important for psychologists to help increase the quality and quantity of sex education, to bring about changes that reduce situational constraints, and either to modify dispositional variables or to modify educational messages and contraceptive availability to take account of individual differences. We will provide brief examples.

Clearly, young people need to acquire accurate information about conception and its prevention (Reis & Herz, 1989). Our culture's ambivalent attitudes about sexuality are reflected in the limitations placed on sex education in primary and secondary schools and often in its total absence from the curriculum (Reiss, 1990). One result is confusion about such details as the relationship between intercourse frequency and the odds of conceiving (Kelley, 1982). In addition, relevant connections between information and behavior are often missing. Consider the fact that the actual use of condoms is not related to knowledge about the risks of not using them (Roscoe & Kruger, 1990).

Cognitive processes are critical (see chapter 3). An individual must have ready access to his or her concerns about conception in order to behave appropriately to avoid risk (Norris & Devine, 1992). Further, even when knowledge is adequate and risks are clearly perceived, human decision-making processes are such that a person may be influenced more by the high probabil-

 Teenage sex + contraceptive neglect = teenage pregnancy

FIGURE 13.4   Since the "sexual revolution" that followed World War II, American teenagers have become increasingly active sexually; but a great many couples fail to use effective contraceptives on a regular basis. The result is approximately one million unplanned teenage pregnancies each year in the United States.

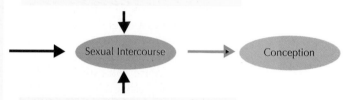

Situational Interferences
- Economic pressures
- Inconsistent messages from adults
- Embarrassing situations in which to obtain contraceptives
- Nonavailability of pruducts when intercourse is about to take place

Informational Deficits
- Lack of appropriate education
- Culture-specific encouragement to conceive
- Assumption that sex should be spontaneous and unplanned
- Lack of knowledge about where to go for products and services
- Absence of role models who communicate with partners about contraception
- Avoidance by educators of teaching details of contraceptive use

Sexual Intercourse → Conception

Dispositional Problems
- Sex guilt
- Erotophobia
- Belief in invulnerability
- Risk-taking behavior
- Chronic self-destructiveness
- Low self-efficacy
- Lack of perceived control
- Low self-esteem
- Feelings of low sexual self-worth
- Feelings of hopelessness
- Limited time-perspective
- Unrealistic assessment of consequences of pregnancy and childbirth
- Inadequate problem-solving skills

 Barriers to contraceptive use

FIGURE 13.5 Among the reasons for the high rate of adolescent conception are various barriers to the use of contraception. Successful intervention to overcome these barriers requires a combination of increased educational availability, removal of situational constraints, and modification of personality dispositions.

Source: Based on information in Byrne, Kelley, & Fisher, 1993.

ity of immediate sexual pleasure than by later difficulties with low or moderate probability (Pinkerton & Abramson, 1992). One necessity, then, is early, widespread, accurate, and relevant educational interventions. For those who believe that parenthood is a way to escape their own unhappy family life or a way to obtain economic security, convincing persuasion techniques and legislated changes in societal rewards are required (Males, 1992).

Perhaps the greatest change brought about by society's growing acceptance of contraceptive use has been the increased availability of contraceptives. Thus, condoms and spermicides are displayed on open shelves in drug stores, and information and contraceptive devices are widely available in family planning clinics, college health services, and other public sources. Perhaps more surprising is the increasing incidence of condom distribution through school programs and even the availability of contraceptive implants in public school clinics (Tifft, 1991; Lewin, 1992).

The most difficult problem seems to be the necessity of overcoming dispositional barriers to contraception. In order to deal with *erotophobic* (anxious and guilty) attitudes about sex (Byrne et al., 1993), the belief that one is personally invulnerable to consequences such as an unintended pregnancy (Moore & Rosenthal, 1991), the tendency to take risks (Breakwell, Fife-Schaw, & Clayden, 1991), a pattern of self-destructive behavior (Kelley & Dawson, 1991), low self-esteem (Blinn, 1987), and low self-efficacy (Rosenthal, Moor, & Flynn, 1991), our society needs to make high-intensity efforts to design and carry out a complex program of intervention.

The most effective intervention efforts are those that provide both education about sexuality and contraceptive products and services. These interventions also utilize procedures designed to make erotophobic attitudes less negative, increase self-esteem and self-efficacy, alter beliefs about invulnerability, and reduce risk-taking and self-destructive behaviors. Detailed descriptions of such programs are provided by Fisher (1989), Gerrard, McCann, and Fortini (1983), and Jaccard (1992). These applications of social psychological findings, theories, and methods can and do result in changes in contraceptive behavior and a decrease in the rate of teenage pregnancies.

HEALTH PSYCHOLOGY: MAINTAINING GOOD HEALTH, RESPONDING TO ILLNESS

Though you may think of health and illness in terms of physical processes and the field of medicine, we now know that psychological factors affect all aspects of our physical well-being (Rodin & Salovey, 1989). **Health psychology** is the speciality that studies the psychological processes affecting the development, prevention, and treatment of physical illness (Glass, 1989). Let's consider four examples of ways in which social psychological research has been applied to health.

ACCEPTING HEALTH-RELEVANT INFORMATION

A major obstacle to the prevention of many physical disorders is the reluctance of people to believe that some aspect of their lifestyle requires changing. Daily we are bombarded by health information and must decide whether to accept what we are told by newspapers and television about each newly identified threat (Thompson, 1992).

You might think that people would be most receptive to information that was personally relevant to them. But because we tend to defend ourselves against threat in ways that often are maladaptive, Liberman and Chaiken (1992) proposed that the more relevant the health threat is to an individual, the *less* likely that person is to accept the truth of the message. To test this hypothesis, they created a fictitious report, supposedly from the *New England Journal of Medicine,* that indicated a link between caffeine and fibrocystic breast disease. This "report" was either highly threatening (follow-up studies supported the finding) or low in threat (follow-up studies were inconsistent). Personal relevance to the participants in the study (all female) was defined in terms of their coffee-drinking habits. The researchers assumed low relevance for those women who didn't drink coffee, high relevance for those who drank two to seven cups a day.

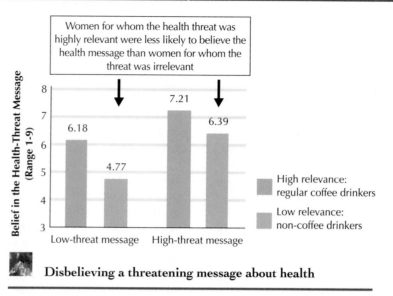

Women for whom the health threat was highly relevant were less likely to believe the health message than women for whom the threat was irrelevant

Disbelieving a threatening message about health

FIGURE 13.6 Because information about possible health threats arouses fear and anxiety, the more relevant such messages are to oneself, the less one believes them. Women were given bogus information about medical research that purportedly found a link between caffeine and a breast disorder. The threat was either high (follow-up studies supported the finding) or low (inconsistent findings in follow-up studies). Women for whom the threat was most relevant (regular coffee drinkers) were less likely to believe either the high-threat or the low-threat message than were women who did not drink coffee.
Source: Based on data in Liberman & Chaiken, 1992.

In response to both low- and high-threat health messages, women to whom the information was most relevant expressed less belief in the accuracy of the finding than did those for whom the message was irrelevant (see Figure 13.6). It seems that when a health threat is relevant to oneself, one processes the information in a biased way that defuses the threat, reduces anxiety, and therefore makes it unnecessary to change one's present behavior.

The rejection of a relevant, threatening message would seem to be extremely maladaptive, and the following **Work in Progress** section describes the next steps in understanding this reaction.

Work in Progress

Personal Relevance versus Threatening or Beneficial Self-Interest

Liberman and Chaiken (1993) raised the following question: Do people usually become defensive when a message concerns a personally relevant issue, or does personal relevance more typically motivate them to pay increased attention to the message so that they can form an accurate judgment? In the Liberman and Chaiken (1992) experiment, relevance was linked to self-interest in the form of threat. This led the experimenters to ask, "How do people respond to a personally relevant message that is *not* threatening?"

That question had been answered by research in which personal relevance involved a nonthreatening topic (Chaiken, 1980; Petty & Cacioppo, 1979). For example, students were asked to read about an academic policy change that had supposedly been proposed at their own school (high personal relevance) or at some other school (low personal relevance) and were then asked their opinions about the proposal. Under these conditions, personal relevance motivated increased attention to the message and open-mindedness about it.

The next question is whether the heightened attention (generally motivated by personal relevance) is objective or—as in the coffee experiment—biased. When threat is low (as in the academic policy change), personal relevance enhances attention and open-mindedness; but in the experiment the new policy was not only nonthreatening, it was also unrelated to the students' self-interest. They had nothing to lose or to gain by the change. So the next step will be to compare how people respond to threatening and beneficial messages that are or are not personally relevant.

For example, if you do well on multiple-choice exams but poorly on essay exams, then a proposal to require the use of essay exams would be threatening. Therefore, if you expected the proposal to be enacted at your school (high personal relevance), you would probably pay a great deal of attention to an informational message about this plan. But, because of the threat involved, would you stay open-minded, or would you become defensive, biased, and critical of any arguments favoring the proposal? In contrast, if you do well on essay exams and poorly on multiple-choice exams, would personal relevance lead you to be easily convinced by arguments favoring the proposal, which would be to your benefit? On the basis of such experimental comparisons, these investigators hope to gain a better understanding of how personal relevance and self-interest (based on threats or benefits) interact in affecting how people respond to informational messages.

low threat → ↑ personal relevance → enhanced attention

STRESS AND ILLNESS

At least since World War II, psychologists have been interested in **stress** and its effects on human behavior (Lazarus, 1993). For purposes of this discussion, *stress* refers to the responses elicited by physical or psychological events that an individual perceives to be harmful or emotionally upsetting. The original focus on the physical causes of stress (Selye, 1956) was soon broadened to include *psychological stress* (Lazarus, 1966). In response to either physical or psychological danger, the individual feels threatened and tries to **cope** with the situation; coping behavior is considered successful if it reduces or eliminates the threat (Taylor, Buunk, & Aspinwall, 1990). What is the connection between stress and illness?

Discussion Question 5

THE EFFECTS OF STRESS.   The most common sources of stress are occupational threats (such as pressure from a supervisor to work harder) and family threats (such as complaints from a spouse) (Hendrix, Steel, & Schultz, 1987). As stress increases, illness becomes more common. Among steel pipe mill workers, for example, increases in the work load are found to result in an increase in physical symptoms (Perrewe & Anthony, 1990). For college students, common sources of stress include low grades, the divorce of parents, or an unwanted pregnancy (Brody, 1989). For all of us, even such minor everyday hassles as driving in heavy traffic or having to interact with an annoying coworker can increase our likelihood of catching a cold or developing the flu (Weinberger, Hiner, & Tierney, 1987). With a more serious problem such as the death of a loved one, there is an even greater probability that illness will occur (Schleifer et al., 1983).

When several negative events occur in the same general time period, they Exercise 4 have a cumulative effect (Seta, Seta, & Wang, 1991); and as the total number of stressful experiences increases, the probability of illness increases. Scales have been developed to quantify stress. (For example, death of a spouse = 100, losing your job = 47, going on a vacation = 13, etc.) These values are sometimes simply added (Crandall, 1992) and sometimes combined according to a complex formula (Birnbaum & Sotoodeh, 1991). Either way, as the number of negative events increases, both perceived stress and susceptibility to the common cold increase (Cohen, Tyrrell, & Smith, 1993).

One reason that physical illness is likely to occur during times of stress is that the resulting anxiety and worry may interfere with such health-related behaviors as eating a balanced diet or exercising (Wiebe & McCallum, 1986). In addition to this indirect effect, the body's immune system functions less well when stress is high (Stone et al., 1987). This finding of a direct link between psychological responses and the body's defense against disease has led to the development of the field of **psychoneuroimmunology.** This interdisciplinary approach studies stress, emotional and behavioral reactions, and the immune system simultaneously (Ader & Cohen, 1993).

As an example of such work, consider the fact that college students are found to develop upper-respiratory infections at exam time (Dorian et al., 1982). How could that happen? Jemmott and Magloire (1988) did a study of college students in which they obtained samples of the students' saliva, which contains *secretory immunoglobulin A,* the body's primary defense against such infections. The level of this substance was found to drop during final exams and then to rise again when exams were over. Thus, the psychological stress of finals resulted in a change in body chemistry that facilitated the development of disease.

REDUCING THE HARMFUL EFFECTS OF STRESS. Stress is unavoidable in Transparency 13.3 our lives, so what can we do to reduce its harmful effects? A common recommendation is to stay as healthy as possible through a sensible pattern of diet, sleep, and regular exercise. The result is an increase in *fitness*—the maintenance of good physical condition as evidenced by endurance and strength. Fitness is associated with *hardiness,* or positive psychological characteristics such as self-confidence and self-discipline (Hogan, 1989; see below). Is there also evidence that simply being fit has any effect on whether a person gets sick?

The answer is yes, according to convincing data provided by Brown (1991). He studied over one hundred undergraduate students, obtaining self-reports about their physical exercise. In addition, the investigator obtained an objective indicator of fitness by measuring each student's heart rate before, during, and after he or she rode an exercise bike under standard conditions. Similarly, the investigator assessed illness episodes through students' self-reports and through the records of their visits to the college health center during two semesters. Stress was defined by the number and severity of negative events in the students' lives over the previous twelve months. The role of stress was quite clear. Students with little stress in their lives had very few illnesses, regardless of their physical fitness. When stress was high, however, fitness was of great importance. Among those who experienced high stress, the low-fitness students had significantly more health center visits to treat illnesses than did those high in fitness. As hypothesized, the health of those who are physically fit is found much less vulnerable to the negative effects of life stress.

Beyond one's physical condition, there is the psychological factor of **hardiness.** This involves a sense of commitment, a perception that difficulties represent a challenge that can be overcome, and a belief that you have control over your life (Kobasa, 1979). We'll look at further evidence about the importance of perceived control in the following section. Hardiness is found to be associated with a positive self-concept (Allred & Smith, 1989). Studies of adolescents indicate that individuals high in *either* commitment or control had fewer health problems than those low in both (Shepperd & Kashani, 1991). Zimmerman (1990) suggests that the term "learned hopefulness" (as contrasted with "learned helplessnes") be applied to individuals who know how to solve problems and who feel a sense of control.

Critical Thinking
Question 3
Together, exercise, fitness, and hardiness combine to protect against illness, as shown in a study of undergraduates by Roth et al. (1989). Kessler et al. (1992) present evidence indicating that genetic factors also play a role in determining how well an individual adjusts to stress.

HOW PERSONALITY DISPOSITIONS AFFECT HEALTH.   Several personality variables (in addition to hardiness) also predict who is likely to develop or not develop illness (Smith & Williams, 1992). For example, *neurotic* individuals react more negatively to stress than those who are not neurotic (Bolger & Schilling, 1991), and they are also more likely to become ill as a result (Larsen & Kasimatis, 1991).

An important reason for the negative effect of stressful events is the sense that we are powerless to prevent accidents, bad grades, failed love affairs, and so forth. When events appear to be beyond our control, we are more likely to become depressed (Brown & Siegel, 1988) and physically ill (McFarlane et al., 1983). Compas et al. (1991) propose a two-level process in our response to threat. As outlined in Figure 13.7, the first reponse is emotional distress and an attempt to cope with one's emotions. A second step is to examine the various contingencies and to assess one's competence in being able to deal with them; if the result is the perception of being in control, problem-focused coping takes place. There is a sex difference in coping styles, in that women more frequently use emotion-focused coping, while men tend to use problem-focused coping (Ptacek, Smith, & Zanas, 1992).

In some instances the only possibility is emotion-focused coping. A child about to undergo surgery can't do anything to avoid the threat or remove the need for an operation, but he or she can benefit from relaxation training and learning the techniques of cognitive distraction ("thinking about something else"). When the situation permits, a more satisfactory approach is to teach a child competence skills, provide a sense of control, and encourage problem-focused coping; for example, a child distressed about a math exam can be taught how to study and how to master the subject matter.

A widely studied aspect of personality, **locus of control** (see chapter 10), refers to our tendency to hold generalized beliefs that either external or internal factors control our lives. Those who express an *internal locus of control* seek more health-related information, remember the information better, and obtain medical examinations more readily than those with an external locus of control (Quadrel & Lau, 1989). Among patients who had recovered from a heart attack, "externals" were found to have higher serum cholesterol levels, to eat more fat, and to perceive themselves as less healthy than "internals" (Birkimer, Lucas, & Birkimer, 1991).

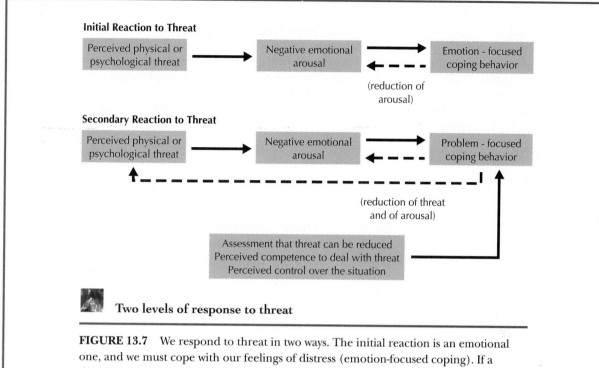

Initial Reaction to Threat

Perceived physical or psychological threat → Negative emotional arousal → Emotion - focused coping behavior

(reduction of arousal)

Secondary Reaction to Threat

Perceived physical or psychological threat → Negative emotional arousal → Problem - focused coping behavior

(reduction of threat and of arousal)

Assessment that threat can be reduced
Perceived competence to deal with threat
Perceived control over the situation

Two levels of response to threat

FIGURE 13.7   We respond to threat in two ways. The initial reaction is an emotional one, and we must cope with our feelings of distress (emotion-focused coping). If a situation is truly uncontrollable, this is the best anyone can do. Secondarily, if the situation can be modified, feelings of competence and the perception of control can relieve the emotional distress *and* result in attempts to solve the stressful difficulty (problem-focused coping). One developmental challenge is to learn to differentiate those threats that are controllable from those that are not.
Source: Based on proposals in Compas et al., 1991.

Related research indicates that health is also affected by the kind of goals for which we strive. Emmons (1992) identified undergraduates and older married couples in terms of their expressing high- or low-level strivings. Table 13.2 gives examples. Subjects who reported high-level strivings were found to experience more psychological distress but less physical illness. Low strivings were associated with less negative affect and more physical illness. The investigator suggested that in their everyday lives people have a trade-off between feeling depressed and getting sick. One explanation is that high, difficult goals require commitment and effort (thus increasing hardiness) but that in reality such goals are seldom met (thus increasing negative affect). Easy goals require little effort and commitment, but they are easy to reach.

One possible implication of research on striving for different kinds of goals is the possibility that those who express low-level strivings habitually avoid threatening emotions, as described in the following **Work in Progress** section.

Personal strivings are the characteristic recurring goals that a person is trying to accomplish in his or her life. People differ in whether they strive for relatively difficult, abstract goals or relatively easy, concrete ones. Those who emphasize high-level strivings experience more psychological stress (because they can't meet their goals) but less physical illness (because their commitment increases hardiness). Those who emphasize low-level strivings experience less emotional discomfort (because they can reach their goals) but more illness (because of a lack of commitment).

TABLE 13.2 High-level versus low-level goals in life

High-Level, Abstract Strivings	Low-Level, Concrete Strivings
I want to deepen my relationship with God.	I want to look well-groomed and clean-cut.
I want to be totally honest.	I want to be funny and make others laugh.
I want to be a fun person to be around.	I want to look attentive and not bored in class.
I want to compete against myself rather than against others.	I want to be organized and neat—clean my room and make my bed.
I want to increase my knowledge of the world.	I want to work hard or at least look like I'm working hard.

Source: Based on data in Emmons, 1992.

Work in Progress

Avoiding Emotion Leads to Illness

Emmons (1993) speculated that low-level strivers might use *repression* (see chapter 10) as a way of dealing with threat and anxiety. Low-level striving may simply represent one way of avoiding uncomfortable affect. To test this possibility, Emmons correlated striving level with several different measures of repressive defensiveness—but found *no* relationship.

Then what might explain the correlation between low-level strivings and physical illness? Emmons reasoned that whereas the striving level measure contains several dimensions, it would be necessary to examine only one dimension—*emotionality in strivings*—because that seemed to be the element most relevant for repression and for physical health. He then examined strivings with respect to specific reference to emotion or emotional avoidance. Examples include such goals as "Not be quick to anger because it is not a good feeling sometimes," "Think positively about myself," and "Not worry over little, insignificant things." Such statements *were* associated with measures of repression, and they were found to be responsible for the relationship between striving and health.

Emmons sees the prevalent theme as emotional avoidance. This appears to indicate that repressors are not using unconscious defenses; rather, they have insight into the fact that they are trying to avoid negative emotion. But why is such avoidance bad for one's physical health? One link involves social support (discussed in the following section). Emmons has new data suggesting that emotionally avoidant people receive less social support than emotionally aware individuals, and this lack of support may contribute to illness.

Once again, the links among stress, response to stress, and health are supported by empirical research.

People also differ in their characteristic feelings of **pessimism/optimism.** Those with a *pessimistic* outlook view events not only as uncontrollable but as likely to get worse; one result of this dark perception of life is that a given amount of stress causes more symptoms of illness than is true for optimistic individuals (Scheier & Carver, 1987). When asked about their experiences with episodes of flu, pessimists perceive that the illness lasted longer and caused more stress than was true for optimists; pessimists also expected to catch the flu in the future (Hamid, 1990). Some research, such as that by Smith et al. (1989), suggests that pessimism is not distinguishable from the combination of anxiety and depression that is labeled *neuroticism.* In a similar way, low self-esteem is associated with perceiving daily events in a more negative way (Campbell, Chew, & Scratchley, 1991).

The tangible benefits of *optimism* were demonstrated in a study of middle-aged men who had undergone heart bypass surgery. The more optimistic the patient, the faster his recovery and his return to a normal and active life (Scheier et al., 1989). Even more dramatic is the finding that pessimistic people die at an earlier age than optimistic ones (Peterson, Seligman, & Vaillant, 1988).

The *Type A* behavior pattern (competitiveness, anger, an urgency about time, and a workaholic life style) was discussed in chapter 11 as a personality variable associated with aggression. The original interest in Type A individuals (and their relaxed opposites—those who are *Type B*) centered on increased risk for heart disease. Research indicates that people classified as Type A, compared to Type B, have higher blood pressure (Contrada, 1989); produce smaller amounts of HDL—"good cholesterol" (Type A's lack . . ., 1992); and are twice as likely to suffer from heart disease (Weidner, Istvan, & McKnight, 1989). It appears that the anger component is a critical factor that leads to coronary problems (Smith & Pope, 1990). Thus, working hard to achieve does not cause heart disease, but failure to achieve elicits a hostile self-schema for the Type A person; this hostility in turn is detrimental to good health (Fekken & Jakubowski, 1990; Moser & Dyck, 1989).

Transparency 13.6

What exactly is the effect of anger on the heart? One study of patients with coronary disease monitored heart functioning while people talked about events in their lives that still make them mad (Goleman, 1992). As these patients talked about being a prisoner of war, having someone back into their car, and so on, the pumping efficiency of their hearts dropped by 5 percent. Revealing the importance of anger was the fact that in response to other stressors (riding a stationary bicycle, doing difficult arithmetic problems, giving a speech), pumping efficiency showed no change or even improved. Anger thus seems to be the key element.

Studies of Type A children suggest the importance of attempting to alter this pattern of behavior *before* coronary heart disease develops (Hunter et al., 1991). Even something as simple as an aerobic exercise program results in a decrease in Type A behavior (Jasnoski et al., 1987).

When a person is confronted by a stressful event, he or she is often advised to talk about it, to express feelings, to share the problem with a friend, and the like. Is that good or bad advice? In the following **Cutting Edge** section, we will examine evidence that indicates the advantages of disclosing versus concealing unpleasant aspects of one's life.

Focus on Research: The Cutting Edge

HEALTH EFFECTS OF SELF-CONCEALMENT VERSUS SELF-REPORTING

Reading: Lesko (39),
*Life Stage Differences
in Resident Coping
with Restart of
Three Mile Island*

A familiar concept in health psychology is the importance of **social support**—physical and psychological comfort from friends and family. The general finding is that people who interact closely with friends and relatives are better able to avoid illness than those who remain isolated from others; if illness does occur, those who receive social support recover more quickly. One of the reasons that natural disasters (such as a severe flood) are distressing is that they disrupt networks of social support (Kaniasty & Norris, 1993). It is even found that adolescents who experience stress but lack social support are more likely to receive sports injuries than those who do have the support of an interpersonal network (Smith, Smoll, & Ptacek, 1990). As aging progresses, social support has important positive effects on cardiovascular responses and thus decreases the risk of heart disease (Uchino, Kiecolt-Glaser, & Cacioppo, 1992). An interesting tie-in between Type A hostility and social support is the finding that not only do mistrusting and antagonistic individuals have more cardiovascular problems, but their interpersonal style also makes social support less available (Smith & Christensen, 1992).

A crucial question is *why* social support should be beneficial. One answer is simple: Friends and relatives can help you get through a bad experience by providing housing, meals, affection, and encouragement (Pilisuk, Boylan, & Acredolo, 1987). One proposition, known as the *fever model,* suggests that talking about fears and problems is like having a high temperature (Stiles, Shuster, & Harrigan, 1992). That is, with an infection, fever is an indication that something is wrong, and it is also useful in helping to fight the bacteria. With psychological distress, talking about what is wrong may have these same two functions. Some research has stressed the cognitive processes involved, in that people whose schemas (see chapter 3) include social support perceive such support as more helpful (Lakey, Moineau, & Drew, 1992).

Part of the explanation for the benefits of social support seems to be biological, as indicated by studies of animals. When researchers placed male monkeys under stressful, unstable social conditions for more than two years, their affiliative behavior increased (Cohen et al., 1992). Further, stress led to suppressed immune system responsiveness, but those animals who were most affiliative showed an enhanced immune response. Similarly, when a person talks to someone else about unpleasant and threatening life events, physiological stress decreases, and this is beneficial to health. Pennebaker, Hughes, and O'Heron (1987) found that people who never confide their traumatic experiences to others have more major and minor health problems than those who *do* talk about such stressful events. The greatest benefit occurs, however, when people talk about solving problems rather than simply venting their negative emotions (Costanza, Derlega, & Winstead, 1988).

Such findings led Larson and Chastain (1990) to examine individual differences in **self-concealment.** They point out that most people have secret feelings, embarrassing thoughts, and distressing information about themselves; this is the kind of information that most of us may share with only one or two others or with no one else. One example is the experience of being sexually abused as a child. Some individuals, however, are consistently more concerned than others with maintaining secrecy about themselves and their experiences, even about relatively minor difficulties. It follows that individual differences in self-concealment may predict who seeks social support and thus benefits from it.

Critical Thinking Question 10

The investigators developed a **Self-Concealment Scale** to measure the active tendency to maintain secrecy about information considered negative or distressing, as presented in Table 13.3. Research indicates that persons who score high on the scale report higher levels of anxiety and depression and indicate more bodily symptoms than those with low scores, even when such variables as the number of traumas experienced and the ease of access to a social network are held constant.

Experiments have shown that even in a laboratory setting, it is beneficial to let others know about one's negative experiences. Pennebaker and Beall (1986) asked subjects to write about a personal traumatic event for twenty minutes a day for four days. Compared with subjects who did not engage in this task, those who wrote about stressful events reported having fewer health problems in the months that followed. It seems that putting such experiences into words and communicating them acts to reduce stress.

Instead of relying on real-life communication patterns, Mendolin and Kleck (1993) exposed research participants to a stress-inducing video (accidents in a woodworking shop) and an emotionally neutral nature video. Some of the participants were instructed to talk to the experimenter about their subsequent emotional reactions, and they were more distressed than other participants who were instructed simply to *describe* either the accident or the nature video. When the stressful scenes were shown a second time, however, those

---

The Self-Concealment Scale measures the active tendency to conceal from others any personal information thought to be negative or embarrassing. Individuals high in self-concealment experience more anxiety, depression, and physical symptoms. Other research supports this suggestion that failure to communicate about stressful events results in health problems.

TABLE 13.3 The Self-Concealment Scale

Sample Items of the Self-Concealment Scale

Subjects respond to each of the following statements on a five-point scale ranging from "strongly disagree" to "strongly agree."

I have an important secret that I haven't shared with anyone.

If I shared all my secrets with my friends, they'd like me less.

When something bad happens to me, I tend to keep it to myself.

Telling a secret often backfires and I wish I hadn't told it.

I have negative thoughts about myself that I never share with anyone.

Source: Based on information in Larson & Chastain, 1990.

who had talked about their emotional reactions were the *least* disturbed, as shown by physiological measures of arousal and by self-ratings. Thus, it may be upsetting to communicate one's feelings, but the aftereffects are beneficial.

In a further study of the benefits of writing about secret traumas, Greenberg and Stone (1992) asked different groups of undergraduate men and women to spend some time each day for four days writing about trivial events (the day's activities, their shoes, a social function); about a traumatic and upsetting experience that *had* been discussed with others; or about the "most traumatic and upsetting experience of your entire life" that had not been talked about with anyone else in detail. Compared with other subjects, students who wrote about the most severe traumas reported fewer physical symptoms in the two months following the study. Again, there seem to be health benefits from disclosing severe traumatic events.

Altogether, this line of research supports the conclusion that confession is good not only for the soul but for the body as well.

RESPONDING TO HEALTH PROBLEMS

It might seem reasonable to assume that even though psychological factors affect the probability of becoming ill, only physiological factors are of importance once illness strikes. In fact, when illness strikes, physical symptoms must be noticed and interpreted, and then a series of critical decisions and choices must be made—whether to rely on self-diagnosis, seek informal or formal treatment, or do nothing, and how to cope with the symptoms or with the treatment. As a result, psychological processes affect each step of an illness episode.

Exercise 5   ATTENDING TO SYMPTOMS: YOU HAVE TO NOTICE THAT SOMETHING IS WRONG.   A sudden and dramatic symptom such as fainting or vomiting is unlikely to go unnoticed by anyone, but what about less-obvious changes in your physical state? Considerable time may pass before you notice a slight pain in your lower back, a rash on your chest, or a gradual change in the workings of your gastrointestinal system. Also, some people pay less attention to internal sensations than others, and they are less likely to notice changes or to interpret them as indicating a possible illness (Mechanic, 1983). At the opposite extreme are *hypochondriacs,* sometimes characterized as the "worried well"— who constantly overestimate the seriousness of every minor symptom that occurs and seek unneeded medical help (Wagner & Curran, 1984).

The number of symptoms an individual reports is affected by *priming* (see chapter 3). That is, when subjects take part in a task requiring them to respond to health-related words such as "pain" and "pill," they report having more symptoms than if they are asked about symptoms *before* being given the task (Skelton & Strohmetz, 1990). Such findings suggest the possibility that exposure to health-relevant material in newspapers or on television may also prime people to attend to and report their physical symptoms.

One's mood also affects how much attention one pays to symptoms. College students who watched a movie that made them feel sad or depressed reported more physical symptoms than those in a more positive emotional state (Croyle & Uretsky, 1987).

DECIDING WHAT IS WRONG. Once you notice a pain, a lump, a stiffness, or whatever, you must decide what, if anything, is wrong. If you conclude that nothing is wrong, you do nothing. As in the self-attribution process discussed in chapter 2, people tend to use a commonsense attributional model when engaging in self-diagnosis (Leventhal, Nerenz, & Steele, 1984). Let's say that you have a pain in your stomach, and you begin throwing up; it's easy to decide that you picked up an intestinal virus that will go away in a few hours. Though your virus assumption is quite likely true, should you be incorrect in your self-diagnosis, the mislabeling could be dangerous (Routh & Ernst, 1984). For example, if you actually have appendicitis, you have made a mistake that discourages you from seeing a doctor. One possible result is a ruptured appendix, a serious and sometimes fatal complication.

Transparency 13.4

Other common examples of mislabeling include the attributions made by elderly people who assume that every ache and pain is simply due to "old age." This assumption may convince them not to visit a physician (Prohaska et al., 1987). A related problem occurs when patients are taking drugs to control high blood pressure. Because this disorder has no symptoms, the patient may assume that the problem has been cured and thus stop taking the needed medication (Meyer, Leventhal, & Gutman, 1985).

TAKING ACTION. If a given symptom has been noticed and self-diagnosed, what is the next step? The person either ignores the problem, tries to treat it himself or herself, or seeks professional help.

According to Bishop (1987), four factors enter into most people's decision-making behavior: whether the person attributes the cause to a virus, whether the symptoms affect the upper or lower body, whether the problem is psychological or physiological, and whether it disrupts daily activities. The most common response to a supposed viral infection or a disruptive illness is self-care with over-the-counter remedies. A person is most likely to seek professional help if the symptom is interpreted as a nonviral physiological problem in the lower half of the body.

Critical Thinking Question 8

A personality disposition that affects decision making at this step is known as *monitoring* (being on the lookout for problems). High monitors are constantly on the alert for threatening information, and they are more likely to make a doctor's appointment in response to a mild problem than are low monitors (Miller, Brody, & Summerton, 1988).

MEDICAL CARE AS A SOURCE OF PROBLEMS

The process doesn't end when the individual decides to seek medical help. What is involved in interacting with a physician, undergoing necessary tests, and receiving treatment?

PATIENT-DOCTOR INTERACTIONS. After taking the major step of making an appointment, waiting to see the doctor, and then interacting with him or her, the patient is often sufficiently anxious and fearful that crucial symptoms go unreported or important questions are not asked. It helps to rehearse or even to write down what you want to say and what you need to find out (Roter, 1984). With this kind of preparation, patients say more and obtain more information than when they simply "play it by ear." A related problem arises when the physician is abrupt or disinterested or maintains control of the interaction by talking too much and interrupting; such behavior can discourage or prevent patients from describing and discussing their concerns (Goleman, 1991; Street & Buller, 1987). Again, coaching patients to focus on what they want to bring up is helpful, as is encouraging them to be assertive with medical personnel.

As you may have experienced, doctors differ in their ability to communicate. A patient is most satisfied and most likely to carry out the treatment plan if the physician is good at both sending and interpreting nonverbal messages (DiMatteo, Hays, & Prince, 1986). When a medical practitioner cannot control his or her nonverbal communications (for example, feelings of anxiety or uncertainty), the patient is likely to assume the worst: *My condition is so bad that the doctor won't tell me the truth!* When physicians are taught good communication skills, these problems can be averted (Hays & DiMatteo, 1984).

Physicians also need to learn how to present medical information. Consider the possible effects of **framing**—that is, influencing decisions by the way relevant information is presented. For example, an individual can be told that a pregnancy has a 50 percent chance of producing a normal offspring or that there is a 50 percent chance of producing an abnormal child. The information is the same, but the negative framing of the second wording leads to more decisions to seek an abortion than when the more positive wording is used (Wilson, Kaplan, & Schneiderman, 1987). In a similar way, information can be provided that the chances of dying are 10 percent or that the chances of surviving are 90 percent; intensive care is more likely to appear necessary in response to the former than to the latter information.

Reading: Lesko (37), *Private Passions and Public Health*

COPING WITH DIAGNOSIS AND TREATMENT.   Unlike the simple medical procedures on "Star Trek," the interventions we have to undergo in the twentieth century are often intrusive, painful, and even dangerous. Diagnostic tests and medical treatment are thus stressful, and patients must somehow cope with them. Is there any way to reduce these medical threats?

Though avoidance and denial may be dangerous at the self-diagnosis stage of an illness episode, they can be very useful techniques when treatment is actually under way (Suls & Fletcher, 1985). Sometime when you are in a dentist's office having your teeth cleaned or a cavity drilled, try concentrating on something else—past events, future plans, a movie you liked, seeking the solution of a difficult problem. To a surprising extent, these incompatible thoughts actually prevent or reduce pain or discomfort.

Distraction (e.g., thinking about one's room at home) is a helpful strategy in dealing with a painful experimental task such as cold-pressor, in which the volunteer's hand is placed in ice cold water and left there "as long as possible" (Cioffi & Holloway, 1993). These investigators found, however, that paying close attention to the painful sensations (*monitoring*) results in a more rapid recovery from the experience. The worst strategy is to suppress awareness ("empty your mind") of the painful experience. To test the aftereffects of these different strategies, the experimenters later exposed the participants to an innocuous vibration—and it was perceived as more unpleasant by those who had used suppression than by those using either distraction or monitoring.

Related research also indicates that when one's mood is incompatible with pain, self-reported pain decreases. Thus, when Stalling (1992) induced a positive mood in subjects, their self-reports of pain decreased.

Attributions also affect how people respond to a serious illness. Male heart attack patients in intensive care were asked their opinions as to *why* the coronary problem had occurred (Bar-On, 1987). Those who emphasized external, uncontrollable factors—such as bad luck—had more problems with recovery than those who stressed internal, controllable causes—such as being an angry person. During a six-month follow-up, those making external attributions took more time before returning to work and before resuming their sex life than did those making internal attributions.

As emphasized earlier in our discussion, perceived control is important in relation to stress, and this is equally true with respect to physical symptoms and pain (Affleck et al., 1987). For example, it hurts much less if you remove a painful splinter from your own finger than if another person does it for you. Even when a person does not have control, *belief* in personal control can be adaptive. Studies of patients with heart disease, cancer, and AIDS found that those who felt that they personally were in control of their symptoms, care, and treatment adjusted much better to their condition than those who did not feel in control (Taylor et al., 1991; Thompson et al., 1993).

There are, however, realistic boundaries to perceived control. In studying heart patients, Helgeson (1992) told them that some people believe that they can exert control over the course of their disease by adopting a positive attitude, changing their diets, or engaging in more exercise. Then the researcher asked the patients to rate their belief in their ability to control their health. High perceived control was found to be adaptive, but this was most true when the threat was high and the perception of control was based on reality. Even patients' belief that doctors and others could control their condition (**vicarious control**) resulted in better adjustment, but only if the physicians had actually *done* something such as angioplasty or bypass surgery.

A different kind of control has been introduced in some medical settings, where patients may make use of an interactive laser-disk player, a touch-screen terminal, and a keyboard (Freudenheim, 1992). For example, a doctor may tell a man that he has an enlarged prostate gland and that surgery is one option. Rather than simply following the physician's advice, the patient enters his own health data (age, weight, symptoms, etc.) on the system and then can ask for and receive information about the pros and cons of having the surgery, trying drug treatment, or simply waiting to find out if his condition gets worse. The program explains the pluses and minuses of each option, and the final decision is up to the patient.

As suggested at the beginning of this chapter and in the cartoon in Figure 13.8 with respect to children undergoing surgery, we also gain a sense of con-

"Relax, I'm just here to water your flowers."

 Fear of medical procedures

FIGURE 13.8 Medical procedures are often frightening and mysterious. The patient benefits both emotionally and physically from being given details about what is happening and what is going to happen. What a patient does *not* need is fear based on a lack of knowledge.

Source: North America Syndicate, Inc., September 30, 1990.

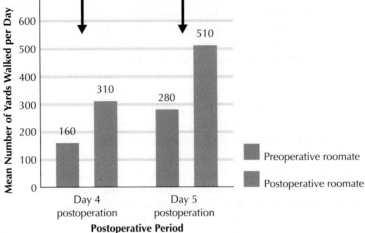

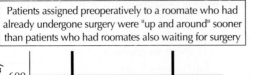

Patients assigned preoperatively to a roomate who had already undergone surgery were "up and around" sooner than patients who had roomates also waiting for surgery

A postoperative roommate is better than a preoperative roommate

FIGURE 13.9 When surgery patients are assigned roommates who have already undergone the same operation, recovery proceeds faster. One example is shown here: Those assigned a postoperative roommate were found to walk farther each day than those with a preoperative roommate. Other benefits of such a roommate included less anxiety, the need for less pain medication, and an earlier discharge from the hospital.

Source: Based on data in Kulik & Mahler, 1987.

trol through accurate information about what is happening and what is going to happen (Jay et al., 1983). Such knowledge is far less stressful than ignorance and fear of the unknown (Suls & Wan, 1989). Information provides a cognitive "road map" that permits a patient to interpret the experience without frightening surprises.

The importance and generality of this concept is shown by many research findings. One example: the effect of prior information on children in a new school setting. R. Cohen and his colleagues (1986) found improved adjustment to kindergarten among children who either walked around the school before beginning classes or simply viewed slides of other children taking such a tour; familiarity reduces anxiety and provides needed information.

In chapter 7 we reported that patients facing surgery prefer a roommate who has already successfully undergone the same kind of surgery rather than someone who has not yet had the operation. The effect of actually assigning roommates on this basis is startling. Kulik and Mahler (1987) compared patients who were assigned (randomly) to a room with someone who was about to have the same surgery or with someone who had already completed

it. As shown in Figure 13.9, patients with a postoperative roommate walked farther each day after surgery than did those with a preoperative roommate; they
also were less unhappy and anxious, needed less medication for their pain,
and were able to go home more quickly.

ENVIRONMENTAL PSYCHOLOGY: EFFECTS OF ENVIRONMENTAL FACTORS ON BEHAVIOR AND EFFECTS OF HUMAN BEHAVIOR ON THE ENVIRONMENT

In chapter 1 we identified five factors that influence social behavior and
thought, and one of these was *ecological variables*—the direct and indirect influence of the physical environment. The study of such effects led to the growth
of **environmental psychology.** In this section we will focus not only on how the
environment affects our behavior but also on how human behavior affects the
environment. Much of the initial research in this field dealt with how the presence of people influences each of us—studies of crowding, for example.
During the 1960s and 1970s, however, interest broadened to include various
environmental effects—such as air pollution, noise, and high temperature—
on behavior. In the 1980s and 1990s, there has been increasing interest in pin-
pointing the negative effects of human activity on the environment and in promoting positive changes in this behavior.

Exercise 1

HOW THE ENVIRONMENT AFFECTS HUMAN BEHAVIOR

To what extent are we adversely affected by environmental factors?
Environmental stress refers to our reaction to perceived threats in the world
around us. Throughout our existence, humans have faced such threats as
floods, earthquakes, and tornadoes, but technological advances have brought
us new dangers. For example, newspapers and television bring us stories of the
possible increased risk of cancer associated with living or working near power
lines (Brodeur, 1992; Gorman, 1992), using electrical appliances such as toast-
ers and computer terminals (Toufexis, 1989), talking on cellular telephones
(Angier, 1993), or being exposed to pesticides (Grieshop & Stiles, 1989). In
some people such information has given rise to **technophobia,** the fear of living in a technological society (Pilisuk & Acredolo, 1988). Some of the most
common specific concerns are shown in Table 13.4, p. 564, along with the
opinions of experts with respect to various hazardous risks. As you can see,
public concern and expert concern often diverge.

Discussion Question 2

Because environmental threats are a source of stress, people must find
ways to cope, as discussed earlier. Perhaps the least-effective coping strategy is
"wishful thinking," in which people simply hope that the problem will go away
(Hallman & Wandersman, 1992). Another way of coping is to assign responsibility for environmental problems. Though little research has concentrated on
this tendency, it seems likely that coordinated efforts to blame the actions of a
specific industry or to blame the government for failing to provide protection
may result in beneficial changes.

Exercise 3

NOISE: LOUD AND UNPREDICTABLE.   One of the notable aspects of life
in our increasingly crowded cities is the presence of noise both day and

Transparency 13.5

Surveys indicate that people are concerned about the dangerous effects of technology on our health and safety. Scientific experts at the Environmental Protection Agency agree that hazards exist, but their assessments tend not to match those of the general public. People in general seem to worry most about immediate, short-term problems, while the scientists are more concerned about future, long-term problems.

TABLE 13.4   Concerns about technological hazards: The public versus the experts

	Perceptions of the General Public	Perceptions of Experts
Highest Concerns	Contaminated drinking water Storage of toxic chemicals Cancer-causing chemicals	Global climate change Species extinction and loss of biological diversity Soil erosion and deforestation
Moderate Concerns	Pesticide residue in food Air pollution Nuclear power plant accidents	Herbicides and pesticides Pollution of surface water Acid rain
Low Concerns	Car accidents Transport of explosives Food preservatives	Oil spills Groundwater pollution Escape of radioactive materials

Source: Based on data in Pilisuk & Acredolo, 1988, and Stevens, 1991a.

Critical Thinking 6

night—moving traffic, horns, sirens, police whistles, construction work, squealing brakes (Cooke, 1992). Some years ago, Glass, Singer, and Friedman (1969) proposed that it is harder to adapt to unpredictable than to predictable noise, because unpredictability involves a loss of perceived control. Subjects were given a proofreading task to carry out while they were exposed to one or the other type of noise. The proofreading was completed in both conditions, but with unpredictable noise there were more errors and a decrease in the subjects' tolerance for frustration. In general, exposure to unpredictable, uncontrollable noise leads to changes in behavior *after* the noise is terminated (Cohen, 1980). There is some evidence of a physiological basis for such effects, in that *endogenous opioids* (bodily secretions that reduce pain) are produced in response to stress as a bodily coping mechanism, and the effects of these opioids may include performance deficits (Davidson, Hagmann, & Baum, 1990). See chapter 5 for a discussion of self-efficacy and physiological responses.

Critical Thinking 4

The negative effects of noise are reduced, researchers find, when subjects gain *perceived control* upon learning that they can press a switch and turn off the noise. Performance improves and subjects feel less upset, even though most individuals do not actually press the switch (Glass et al., 1969). Personality also determines how people react to noise. For example, on a comprehension task, noise impairs the performance of introverts but not that of extraverts (Standing, Lynn, & Moxness, 1990).

Noise diminishes behavioral effectiveness not only in the laboratory but in daily life as well. Compared to children living in relatively quiet environments, children who are regularly exposed to the noise of highway traffic or of airplanes taking off and landing are found to have lower reading ability (Cohen, Glass, & Singer, 1973) and perform more poorly on math achievement tests and problem-solving tasks (Cohen et al., 1986). Noise disrupts adult behavior, too (Smith & Stansfeld, 1986). For example, as a result of daily exposure to loud aircraft, people suffer effects such as confusion about left versus right when giving directions, difficulty in finding items in a supermarket, problems with memory, and the tendency to drop things.

Exposure to loud, unpredictable noise in everyday life is also found to be associated with health risks, presumably because such stimulation is arousing and stressful (Topf, 1989). For example, children living on the lower floors of an apartment building in New York City that was built over a busy highway showed evidence of lowered auditory discrimination (Cohen, Glass, & Singer, 1973). Other research shows that regular exposure to noise in a busy industrial plant or in housing near an airport is associated with numerous health problems—hypertension (Cohen et al., 1986), hospitalization in mental institutions (Meecham & Smith, 1977), and fatal strokes (Dellinger, 1979).

TEMPERATURE AND BEHAVIOR.   You often hear people say that climate and other meteorological factors affect behavior—that everyone seems more cheerful when there is a lot of sunshine or that they behave strangely when there is a full moon. Is behavior *really* affected by these aspects of the environment?

There is a large body of evidence that negative interpersonal responses increase and positive responses decrease when the temperature rises. When it is very hot, both interpersonal attraction and prosocial behavior are negatively affected (Bell et al., 1990). In a study of drivers in Phoenix, Arizona, the higher the temperature, the more they honked their horns at a car that failed to move when the light turned green (Kenrick & McFarlane, 1986).

Consistent with such findings is evidence linking temperature and serious interpersonal aggression (Anderson & DeNeve, 1992). For example, Anderson and Anderson (1984) examined the association between the number of aggressive crimes (murder and rape) and the daily temperature over a two-year period in two large American cities. The data indicate that criminal violence occurred more frequently as the temperature rose. Research in other cities shows similar effects; as the average monthly temperature rises, rapes and aggravated assaults become more frequent (Cohn, 1990; Simpson & Perry, 1990). It is also interesting to note that the relationship between temperature and *nonviolent* crimes such as burglary and car theft is much weaker (Anderson, 1987).

Beyond crime statistics, the effects of temperature on aggression are also evident in more "acceptable" kinds of human interaction. In major league baseball, it is not uncommon for a batter to be hit by the ball. Are such pitches accidents or evidence of aggression on the part of the pitchers? If aggression is the explanation, Reifman, Larrick, and Fein (1991) reasoned that more such hits would occur as the temperature rose. They analyzed data from 826 major league baseball games played during the 1986–1988 seasons. As shown in Figure 13.10, p. 566, the hypothesis was strongly confirmed. The higher the temperature, the greater the mean number of players hit by a pitch.

Despite general agreement that the frequency of many types of aggressive behavior increases as the temperature rises, there is some disagreement about the effect of extremely high temperatures. Some argue that the data indicate a steadily rising curve in which aggression goes up as the temperature goes up (Anderson, 1989). In contrast, the *negative affect escape model* (Baron & Bell,

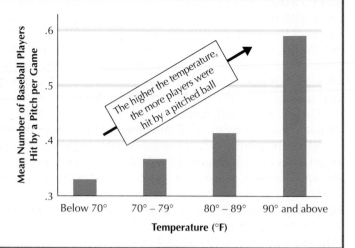

Temperature and aggression on the baseball diamond

FIGURE 13.10 The relationship between temperature and aggressive behavior has been extended to baseball. Data based on hundreds of major league baseball games revealed that as the temperature rose, the average number of times the man at bat was hit by the ball increased.

Source: Based on data in Reifman, Larrick, & Fein, 1991.

1976; Bell, 1992) proposes that when the discomfort caused by heat is sufficiently great, aggression actually begins to decline. The result is an inverted U-shaped curve. The explanation for this model is that the discomfort aroused by very high temperatures becomes so great that the individual is motivated to escape and seek relief by drinking a cold liquid, sitting under an air conditioner, going for a swim, or whatever. Proponents of both models agree that further research is needed to resolve the controversy.

AIR POLLUTION.   Because of numerous human activities (driving cars, burning coal, smoking tobacco, etc.), our air is increasingly full of particles and gases that can have negative effects on our health and our interpersonal interactions. Despite the physical and emotional dangers of pollution, people quickly accept its presence. For example, newcomers to a heavily polluted area such as southern California almost always complain about the smog, but those who live there seldom notice it and do not even judge it to be an important issue for the community (Evans, Jacobs, & Frager, 1982). Nevertheless, pollution arouses negative emotions; one effect is an increase in the frequency of family disturbances reported to the police (Rotton & Frey, 1985).

In general, air that smells bad elicits negative feelings and less friendly interpersonal behavior (Rotton et al., 1979). Air that has a pleasant smell has the opposite effect—positive emotions and friendly behavior. Baron (1990) found that subjects who worked on a clerical task set higher goals, used more efficient strategies, and engaged in more friendly interpersonal behavior when surrounded by a pleasant artificial scent than when no air freshener was present. Presumably, the addition of pleasant smells to a work setting could enhance both morale and performance.

A troublesome form of atmospheric pollution is cigarette smoke. Not only does smoke smell foul, but smokers face serious health risks—and nonsmokers who breathe smoke-filled air also are more likely to develop health problems. "Passive smokers," such as a nonsmoking woman married to a heavy-smoking man, are more likely to develop lung cancer than similar women whose husbands do not smoke; also, children exposed to secondhand smoke have an increased likelihood of developing respiratory illnesses (Kenworthy, 1993).

ELECTRICAL IONS IN THE ATMOSPHERE.   Some environmental effects are based on natural phenomena, including some that you may never have noticed. Because of the presence of lightning, strong winds, and other meteorological disturbances, air molecules frequently split into positively and negatively charged particles called *ions*. The result is **atmospheric electricity,** which affects social behavior in several ways. For example, it has long been known that as the ion level in the atmosphere rises, there is an increase in the frequency of suicides, industrial accidents, and several categories of crime (Muecher & Ungeheuer, 1961; Sulman et al., 1974). Why?

One promising explanation is that negative ions activate people. As a result, they become more likely to do something they were already inclined to do. In laboratory studies, experimenters use special equipment to generate high levels of atmospheric electricity. As negative ions increase, participants' general activation level rises, adding to the strength of whatever responses are dominant for a particular person in a given situation. For example, negative ions increase the aggressiveness of Type A individuals, presumably because they already possess a strong tendency to aggress (Baron, Russell, & Arms, 1985).

A similar activation can be shown in studies of similarity and attraction of the kind described in chapter 7. When negative ions are present, attraction increases toward a similar stranger and decreases toward a dissimilar one (Baron, 1987). As shown in Figure 13.11, the usual reactions are intensified.

There are a few situations that bring together all of the major issues discussed in this chapter. In the **Applied Side** section on the next page, we will describe the possible effects on nutrition, prescription medicines, and viral diseases resulting from the rapid destruction of part of our environment that is occurring because of the needs of a growing population.

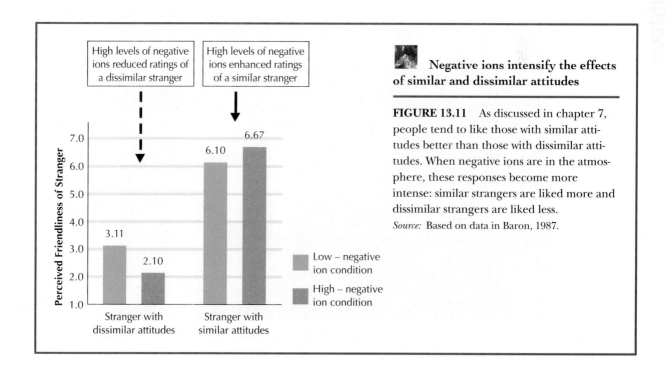

Negative ions intensify the effects of similar and dissimilar attitudes

FIGURE 13.11   As discussed in chapter 7, people tend to like those with similar attitudes better than those with dissimilar attitudes. When negative ions are in the atmosphere, these responses become more intense: similar strangers are liked more and dissimilar strangers are liked less.
Source: Based on data in Baron, 1987.

Social Psychology: On the Applied Side

AGRICULTURAL, PHARMACEUTICAL, AND VIRAL DISASTERS: THE ULTIMATE REVENGE OF THE TROPICAL RAIN FORESTS?

The links between our treatment of the environment and threats to our health can sometimes be surprising. When rain forests are cleared for seemingly good economic reasons, the consequences may ultimately be catastrophic. Most of us have seen news stories about the destruction of rain forests (Linden, 1992) as people cut or burn trees (Egan, 1992) and clear land to obtain lumber and make room for new settlements and farms (see Figure 13.12). You may have reacted with indifference or with concern, but most of us perceived no reason for acute fear and alarm simply because trees were being cut down and some exotic plants and animals ceasing to exist. Those opposed to the destruction of forests have often been viewed as extremists, and these individuals are often attacked and intimidated by business interests, government agents, and citizens whose jobs are threatened (Toufexis, 1992).

 Clearing a tropical rain forest: Perhaps more dangerous than we knew

FIGURE 13.12 Environmentalists and others have long been concerned about the effects of destroying forests because of the negative impact on the carbon dioxide level in the atmosphere and the destruction of plant and animal species. Recent evidence suggests that the spread of new and potentially deadly viruses may also result from such deforestation.

How many species are in danger? Even though biologists and other scientists have discovered about 1.4 million species of living organisms, extrapolation indicates that many more remain unknown as yet (Thernstrom, 1993). Conservative estimates indicate that another 4 million species exist, predominantly in tropical rain forests. When we destroy such habitats, we destroy undiscovered varieties of plants and animals.

Why should that matter? One reason is that many of the plants have agricultural potential. For example, a valuable disease-resistant perennial species of corn (Jalisco maize) grew only on a twenty-five-acre site in Mexico; it was discovered and saved from extinction by a graduate student just before the area was to be cleared for farming.

A second reason is that plant extracts are the basis of many of today's medicines (including aspirin). In the United States, 25 percent of all medical prescriptions involve drugs made from plants, as well as another 3 percent made from animals. Each unknown species that is exterminated is one less potential cure for human illnesses.

As important as improved agriculture and new medicine may be for our nutrition and health, there is yet a third reason to be deeply concerned about the fate of rain forests. By now we are all familiar with the mysterious outbreak of AIDS at the beginning of the 1980s and the spread of this fatal viral infection throughout the world. Speculations about the origins of this new plague ranged from secret germ warfare experiments that got out of control (Null, 1989) to a disease common to African green monkeys that somehow spread to humans (Kanki, Alroy, & Essex, 1985). Less well known but equally mysterious and almost as dangerous are a series of other viral infections that seem to have originated in tropical areas, transferring from one or more animal species to human beings and then spreading rapidly through the population. Besides HIV, there is the flulike dengue (or "break-bone") fever in the Caribbean and a little-known filovirus—meaning "thread virus" because such viruses look like spaghetti under an electron microscope—known as Ebola.

The name comes from the Ebola River in northern Zaire, where the virus first appeared in September 1976. The residents of fifty-five African villages near that river suddenly became ill, first complaining of a headache, then developing a fever, followed by blood clots, strokes, hemorrhaging, vomiting, and paralysis. These complications were usually deadly; and within a week, 88 percent of those who were infected died. Except for HIV and rabies, Ebola is the deadliest virus ever to infect humanity. Where did it come from, and why should this and other new diseases appear near the end of the twentieth century, seemingly from nowhere?

Preston (1992) presents evidence linking such viral invaders to the environmental disruption of tropical rain forests—because rain forests are also a reservoir for viruses. Each plant and animal species is host to one or more unique viruses. Humans, for example, carry around more than one hundred cold viruses—specific parasites that survive only because they have adapted to life in our bodies. If all humans were to die, the cold viruses would become extinct unless they could quickly adapt to life in another species. Viruses are, in fact, quite good at modifying themselves in response to necessity.

When an entire ecosystem, such as a rain forest, is destroyed, many species of mammals, insects, arthropods, fungi, and other living organisms cease to exist. What happens to their viruses? They jump ship and find a new host. The humans who are busy clearing the forests make convenient targets, and if the viruses can adapt, they will. Some are harmless, some cause mild diseases, and some—like Ebola Zaire—are deadly.

What happened to the Ebola virus that killed the villagers in Zaire? The area was sealed off, houses and bodies were burned, and the outbreak was thus isolated. Of course, no one believes that this deadly virus has ceased to exist. And, because jets carry people (and their new viruses) to and from all parts of the world, it is essentially impossible for diseases to remain isolated. In addition, tropical monkeys and other species are captured and sold to research laboratories all over the globe. To illustrate how easily viruses are transported, a closely related form of Ebola broke out among tropical monkeys in a facility in Reston, Virginia; this particular Ebola virus was deadly to the monkeys, but among the humans who worked there it had only mild effects or none at all. Another Ebola virus (the Marburg) appeared in Germany in 1967 in a laboratory that conducted medical research using green monkeys from Uganda. A technician in the laboratory contracted the virus and died two weeks later. Soon thirty-one other employees of the laboratory were ill. The Marburg filovirus has a death rate of 22 percent—extremely serious, though still not nearly as deadly as the Ebola Zaire.

If the source of such new diseases is in fact viruses spread by the destruction of tropical areas and of some of the creatures living there, the carelessness with which human beings treat their environment may have brought each of us a truly frightening problem. As Preston (1992) suggests, these diseases may represent the ultimate revenge of the rain forests.

HOW HUMAN BEHAVIOR AFFECTS THE ENVIRONMENT

Almost everything that humans do has a measurable effect on the environment. Whenever someone becomes a parent, drives a car, uses hair spray, buys a product made of plastic, sends garbage to a landfill, uses salt on icy sidewalks or streets, or engages in thousands of other seemingly small acts, the environmental problems grow. As with population growth, the effects are neither obvious nor immediate. Though anything that you personally may do probably has only a very small effect, what you plus a few billion other people do can and does bring about changes in the environment (Stern, 1992). What are the most dangerous of these changes?

Transparency 13.2 THE GREENHOUSE EFFECT: A WARMER, WETTER WORLD.   Though experts are far from unanimous in their conclusions (Stevens, 1991b), there is a great deal of evidence that the earth is growing warmer at a rate that is being accelerated by human activities (Elmer-Dewitt, 1992). If **global warming** is occurring, scientists say that it will hasten the melting of the ice caps; this will cause the seas to rise, and many low-lying areas of land will be submerged (Schneider, 1989). The most agreed-upon forecast is that the sea level will rise two to three feet during the next century. The only force available to stop this disaster would be a complementary disaster in which the onset of the next ice age acted to reverse this trend (Olivenstein, 1992).

Such predictions may seem like science fiction or, at most, a reason for minor adjustments in one's life (see Figure 13.13); but the 214,000 residents of the Republic of Maldives are easier to convince (Crossette, 1990). This is a nation composed of 1,190 islands in the Indian Ocean, and most of the land is less than three feet above sea level. The water level is rising about one inch every five years, and three of the Maldive islands are now under water. The rest are expected to disappear within the next hundred years. In other parts of the world, including Bermuda and several Caribbean islands, the gradual loss of land area is also clearly visible. The problem is sufficiently real that the nations meeting at the 1992 Earth Summit in Rio de Janeiro began to set goals and propose steps to try to keep our planet from slowly getting hotter without at the same time bringing economic development to a halt (Havel, 1992; Nasar, 1992).

Global warming will mean that many U.S. plants and animals, such as the sugar maple and the deer mouse, will survive only by migrating northward. Many other animal species, such as polar bears, monarch butterflies, tigers, and walruses may disappear entirely (Schneider, 1991; Stevens, 1992).

The cause of this climatic change is known as the **greenhouse effect:** the trapping of heat by rising levels of three gases in the earth's atmosphere, a rise that began around 1850. About half of the problem is attributable to *carbon dioxide.* Until the middle of the nineteenth century, this gas was produced almost entirely by the breath we and other animals exhaled and the natural decay of dead plants and animals. But when we began burning coal and oil to supply our need for energy, carbon dioxide production increased sharply, and there is now more of it in the atmosphere than at any time in the earth's

"Don't worry, when the greenhouse effect really sets in we'll start growing orchids!"

 Adapting to global warming

FIGURE 13.13 Though scientists are not in total agreement about the timing and the intensity, most agree that the atmospheric changes brought about by human activity will lead to gradual global warming through the *greenhouse effect.* Most people, however, do not take such threats seriously enough to change their present activities. *Source:* North America Syndicate, Inc., January 7, 1990.

existence (Fischer, 1989). Trees and other plants absorb carbon dioxide; but, paradoxically, excessive amounts of carbon dioxide also interfere with the health of plants and hence with crop growth (Browne, 1992b).

Discussion Question 4

The other two gases that act to trap heat in the atmosphere are *methane* and the *chlorofluorocarbons,* each being responsible for about 25 percent of global warming. Most of the methane is generated in rice paddies, forest fires, landfills, and the digestive tracts of the 3.3 billion domesticated cattle and other mammals that humans raise for milk, food, and hides. Each time one of these animals releases gas in a belch or in flatulence, methane is expelled into the atmosphere (Chesek, 1992). Methane from all these sources has doubled the atmospheric methane level in the past three hundred years, and the total amount is growing at the rate of 1 percent each year, (Remember the effects of exponential growth?) The remaining cause of the warming trend, chlorofluorocarbons (or CFCs), are the gases used in refrigerators, air conditioners, and many spray cans. CFCs have two negative effects; they help trap heat in the atmosphere like the other two gases, but they also act to create holes in the ozone layer. As a result, the earth's plants and animals are less and less protected from the most intense and dangerous of the sun's rays (Lemonick, 1992).

Can anything be done to reverse these trends? The answer is yes, but change is not easy. To reduce carbon dioxide emissions, we need to develop an energy technology that is not based on burning organic matter (solar power and wind power are examples), and we need to alter our behavior (using public rather than private transportation; buying reusable artificial Christmas trees). You can even help by planting new trees; each tree absorbs up to forty-eight pounds of carbon dioxide annually (Grondahl, 1989). You need not be a Scrooge to note that U.S. citizens cut down more than thirty-five million evergreen trees each December and discard them in January; these trees are thus prevented from absorbing carbon dioxide, while their decomposition over the next thirty years produces significant amounts of this gas (Cool, 1991).

The reduction of methane should be easy. One promising approach is to feed our cud-chewing animals (the *ruminants*—cattle, sheep, goats, buffalo, and camels) something other than the high-fiber diets they now eat. Chlorofluorocarbons must be banned completely and replaced with alternatives; fifty nations have agreed to do this. You may already have noted such changes as liquid deodorants that are sprayed out by a pump rather than by gas pressure. Such small changes can have major effects. More dramatically, new technology (such as refrigerators whose cooling is based on sound waves) is being developed to permit CFCs to be gradually phased out (Browne, 1992a).

A related, but often ignored, effect is urban warming. By the year 2035 most U.S. cities with a population of 200,000 or more can expect an increase in temperature (Viterito, 1991). Why? The concentration of people and the replacement of plants and open spaces with buildings are the major cause. Data indicate that between 1920 and 1977, a growing city such as Phoenix showed an increase in winter temperatures of almost four degrees Fahrenheit.

Exercise 2

GARBAGE, LITTER, AND OTHER WASTE PRODUCTS. It is possible to view our world as being buried in masses of trash and sewage, even though many individuals highly value a clean environment (Simmons et al., 1992). As the human population grows, we produce more and more waste. Where are we going to put it? The United States alone produces about 180 million tons of waste each year, and more than 70 percent of this trash is now being buried in

Critical Thinking Question 5

5,500 landfills across the country (Rathje, 1991). Most landfills are reaching capacity, however, and few new ones are being approved.

Rather than focusing on a problem of that magnitude, let's consider a simpler problem—litter. There is no reason for our sidewalks, parks, and other public places to be the final resting place for paper cups, candy wrappers, bottles, and so forth. How can you motivate people to avoid littering and also to pick up the litter of others? In university cafeterias, prominent reminders encouraging students to do what they know is right, or **prompts,** have been somewhat effective. An important element, however, is the tone of the prompt. Durdan, Reeder, and Hecht (1985) compared the effects of positive versus negative messages on cafeteria littering. Probably because they create a pleasant affective state, positive prompts ("Please be helpful!") resulted in less littering than mildly negative prompts ("Please don't litter!"). Before the prompts were used, over half of the students littered; when positive prompts were present, fewer than a third littered.

Several studies have focused on movie theaters and their attempts to change people's habit of throwing waste material under the seats. More than 80 percent of snack bar trash is simply dropped on the floor. Theaters have tried several prompting methods—making trash cans available, showing an antilittering cartoon on the screen, and passing out litter bags. Such techniques have an effect, but the reduction in littering is small. When Clark, Hendee, and Burgess (1972) provided rewards, however, a much greater effect was apparent. The investigators gave movie patrons litter bags; when these were filled and turned in, the customer received either a dime or a free movie ticket. This simple reward system reduced the percentage of litter discarded on the floor to 10 percent.

Discussion Question 1

Even if there is only the *possibility* of a reward, people litter less. Hayes, Johnson, and Cone (1975) used the *marked item technique.* With this technique, only a few rewards are given, so each can be reasonably valuable (as in a lottery). The researchers scattered marked items among the litter on the grounds of a penal institution. They told inmates that some of the litter was marked in such a way that it could be seen only under a special light; anyone who picked up litter should bring it to a collection station and hold it under the light. If a marked item was in the litter, the person would win an attractive prize. The result was an immediate increase in the amount of litter collected.

These and other studies suggest that reminders can help change behavior, that positive wording is preferable to negative demands, and that small rewards can strongly affect environmental behavior.

ENCOURAGING PEOPLE TO RECYCLE.   A major solution to the garbage problem is to recycle paper, glass, plastic, cans, and other products rather than to throw them away. Most of us indicate that we are in favor of recycling, but most of us don't actually recycle much without some form of extra encouragement, such as a series of persuasive communications (Burn & Oskamp, 1986). Even those who fail to recycle express concern for the environment, but they tend to be less knowledgeable about the process and more concerned about rewards for recycling than is true for more committed recyclers (Vining & Ebreo, 1990).

A surprisingly effective legislative approach to motivating people to recycle uses a combination of mild coercion and a small monetary reward—the *bottle bill.* In many states, customers who purchase beer, soft drinks, and other liquids in bottles or cans must pay a small deposit (usually five cents) for each

Legislation regulates one aspect
of environmental behavior:
The bottle bill

Compliance with the law is based
on monetary rewards and acceptance
of social norms

New behavior becomes habitual

Attitudes about the bottle bill
become more favorable, a shift
based on the desire for consistency

Attitudes generalize, resulting in
positive views about other
environmental issues

**Legislation leads to reluctant behavioral compliance; then attitudes shift
to reduce cognitive dissonance**

FIGURE 13.14 Legislation such as a bottle bill can help change environmental behavior by combining new social norms with monetary rewards. When the new behavior becomes habitual, attitudes about the legislation become more favorable. Then these new proenvironmental attitudes generalize to other, quite different issues.
Source: Based on suggestions in Kahle & Beatty, 1987.

item. The "reward" is a refund of the deposit when the customer returns the bottle or can to the store. Most people return their containers rather than lose the deposit money. Even when containers are thrown away, people who need the money often collect them from roadsides, parks, and other public places and turn them in.

Transparency 13.1   Though bottle bills reduce the amount of waste and conserve resources, many consumers are at least mildly negative at first because of the trouble involved. Over time, though, attitudes become very positive. Kahle and Beatty (1987) conducted a longitudinal study of public reaction in Oregon and discovered an interesting sequence of events (shown in Figure 13.14). When a bottle bill is enacted into law, recycling behavior changes despite feelings of reluctance. This new behavior becomes habitual, and then attitudes change to correspond with the altered behavior (see the discussion of cognitive dissonance in chapter 4). There are also changes in subjective norms about what is the "right" thing to do. Once these behaviors and attitudes change, there is also an interesting generalization to other environmental concerns and to other proenvironment actions.

A behavior that is relevant to both environmental quality and health is smoking cigarettes. Those who smoke are at much higher risk for lung and heart disease than nonsmokers, and smoke-filled air is unpleasant and health-threatening for nonsmokers, as we have discussed. There are, however, considerable differences across cultures in the incidence of smoking, societal encouragement or discouragement for smoking, and the reasons people give for quitting cigarettes. We will examine some of these differences in the following **Social Diversity** section.

Social Diversity ▼ *A Critical Analysis*

Differences in Smoking Behavior: Gender, Race, Ethnic Group, and Nationality

Critical Thinking Question 7

In the United States alone, about 1,200 people die each day as the result of cancer brought about by smoking tobacco (Sunstein, 1993). A momentous change in smoking behavior has taken place in the United States over the past several decades. According to the Centers for Disease Control, in 1955 42 percent of Americans smoked—but by 1992 that figure had dropped to about 25 percent. This change has been attributed to some combination of such factors as the warning labels printed on cigarette packages, antismoking campaigns that heighten awareness of the dangers, the ban on radio and television cigarette advertising, special taxes that increase the cost of cigarettes, and the prohibitions against smoking in many public places. Whatever the exact cause or causes, attitudes and behavior have shown a remarkable shift from prosmoking to antismoking.

The growing rejection of tobacco is largely an American phenomenon. Compared to U.S. citizens, those in most other nations continue to smoke at a rate as high as or higher than was true for Americans forty years ago. For example, the smoking rate is about 70 percent among males in China and in Indonesia. About 61 percent of adult males in Japan smoke (Smolowe, 1992), and smokers are still in the majority in the United Kingdom (Jarvis, 1991). The declining U.S. market has encouraged tobacco companies to emphasize foreign sales in Eastern Europe, the Middle East, Japan, Argentina, and the former Soviet republics. In 1992 Philip Morris, for example, showed a revenue increase of 5.4 percent in the United States but a 20.8 percent increase internationally (Miles & Murray, 1992). It should be noted, however, that many other nations are begin-

ning to take steps to discourage smoking. For example, new laws in France and in China restrict smoking in public places; China also bans all cigarette advertising (Smolowe, 1992). Singapore aspires to become the first smoke-free nation in the world, and its restrictive laws (e.g., no smoking in public, no vending machines) have reduced adult smoking to only 16 percent of the population. Hong Kong has been equally effective in reducing smoking by the use of high taxes; cigarettes there are now $2.60 a pack.

Despite the overall American success story, some subgroups of the U.S. population smoke much more heavily than others. Gender is one variable. Men are generally found to begin smoking at an earlier age, to have a higher percentage of smokers, and to smoke more heavily than women (Rogers, 1991; Santi et al., 1990–1991).

The incidence of smoking differs markedly across racial and ethnic groups in the United States, and the motivations for giving up cigarettes are also found to differ. Such findings suggest that antismoking interventions need to be tailored to meet the specific concerns of the target group.

TABLE 13.5   Why quit smoking?

Racial/Ethnic Group	Motivation to Quit Smoking
White	Smoking may be the cause of my current physical symptoms and illnesses.
African-American	Smoking doesn't give me much pleasure.
Hispanic-American	Smoking may set a bad example for my children, and I want them to be healthy.

Source: Based on data in Marin et. al., 1990, and Vander-Martin, Cummings, & Coates, 1990.

On the other hand, unlike men, the percentage of women smokers is *increasing* annually (Smoking rate . . ., 1993).

Ethnic and racial comparisons show even greater differences in smoking behavior, but not necessarily in ways that you might expect. For example, among Native Americans the smoking rate remains about as high today (38.1 percent) as was true for the general population in the mid-1950s (Heaviest smokers, 1992). These data for Native Americans might lead you to conclude that smoking would be higher among minority groups or among those who are economically disadvantaged. In fact, white Americans are the second heaviest smokers, with lower rates found for African-Americans, lower still for Hispanics, and lowest for Asian-Americans (Gillmore et al.,

1990; Gritz & Crane, 1991; Rogers, 1991).

The reasons for the differences are not at all clear. When one finds high rates of smoking in China and Japan but the lowest rates among Asian-Americans, neither genetics nor cultural background seem to be likely explanations. Attempts to identify differential social factors have not been successful (Wallace & Bachman, 1991). In all subgroups, smoking is more likely when family and peers smoke; and all groups seem equally aware of information about the detrimental effects on health.

Differences are found, however, in the reasons given by different racial/ethnic groups for wanting to *quit* smoking, as shown in Table 13.5. Whites tend to blame smoking as the cause of their current physical

symptoms and illnesses; African-Americans say they want to quit because smoking is not especially pleasurable; and Hispanic-Americans are motivated by the desire to provide a good example for their children and thus to protect their offspring (Marin et al., 1990; Vander-Martin, Cummings, & Coates, 1990).

Such differences suggest the possibility that intervention campaigns designed to help smokers give up the habit must be sensitive to cultural differences in motivation. Beyond that, it may be that different subgroups of the population begin smoking for different reasons. If those reasons can be identified, they can be used as a guide for programs that attempt to stop children and adolescents from ever acquiring the nicotine habit in the first place.

Critical Thinking Question 19

Summary and Review

Applied social psychology utilizes social psychological principles and research methods in real-world settings in efforts to solve a variety of individual and societal problems.

The Perils of Continued Population Growth

The *exponential* growth of the world population is beginning to reach a critical point with respect to the availability of resources. There is general agreement that such growth cannot continue indefinitely, but there is disagreement about how to go about changing attitudes and behavior. To date, the greatest success has occurred in economically developed countries, where couples have spontaneously decided to limit family size, and in China, where the government has directed massive efforts to bring about change. The desire to solve the related problem of unplanned adolescent pregnancies in the United States and Canada has led to intervention programs that combine education, availability of contraceptive products and services, and attempts to alter personality dispositions that interfere with contraception.

Psychology and Health

Health psychology is the speciality that studies how psychological processes affect the development, prevention, and treatment of physical illness. Considerable research has been directed at *stress* and the factors that make some individuals better able to *cope* with environmental and psychological threat. Factors such as *fitness, hardiness,* and numerous personality dispositions are associated with how well individuals deal with stress. *Social support* is helpful in preventing and helping a person cope with illness, in part because of the importance of having someone with whom to talk about unpleasant life events rather than engaging in *self-concealment*. When an illness does strike, the person has to make a series of critical choices and decisions—noticing and interpreting symptoms, deciding to take action, and coping with medical procedures.

The Environment

Environmental psychology is the field that deals with the interaction between the physical world and human behavior. Among the environmental factors that affect behavior are *environmental stress, noise, temperature, air pollution, atmospheric electricity,* and new *viruses* that have—possibly—emerged from the rapidly disappearing rain forests. The negative effects of human actions on the environment include *global warming* and the ever-mounting problem of *waste.* Studies designed to control littering suggest that pro-environmental behavior can be increased by the use of *prompts, rewards,* and legislation such as that requiring a deposit on cans and bottles.

Social Diversity: Cigarette Smoking

Educational, legal, and economic pressures have brought about a dramatic overall decrease in the use of cigarettes among Americans, while citizens in other countries continue to smoke at high levels. Within the United States, men smoke more than women, and members of different races and ethnic groups differ greatly in smoking behavior. The explanation for these differences does not seem to be related to socioeconomic factors. Racial/ethnic groups *are* found to differ in the reasons they wish to quit smoking, and intervention efforts need to be sensitive to these differences.

Key Terms

Applied Social Psychology Social psychological research and practice in real-world settings, directed toward the understanding of human social behavior and the attempted solution of social problems.

Arithmetic Progression A numerical series in which each number increases by a constant amount added to the previous number.

Atmospheric Electricity The presence of positive and negative ions in the atmosphere.

Higher numbers of ions create higher levels of atmospheric electricity.

Cope Respond to stress. Coping includes what a person does, feels, or thinks in order to master, tolerate, or decrease the negative effects of a stressful situation.

Environmental Psychology The field that deals with the interaction between the physical world and human behavior.

Environmental Stress A negative emotional reaction to perceived threats in the physical world.

Framing Affecting judgments or decisions by the way in which relevant information is presented.

Geometric Progression A numerical series in which each number increases by a ratio of the previous number.

Global Warming The gradual increase in the earth's atmospheric temperature brought about by various human activities.

Greenhouse Effect The basis of global warming—Gases released into the atmosphere (carbon dioxide, methane, and chlorofluorocarbons) trap the sun's heat, turning the earth into a "greenhouse."

Hardiness A cluster of characteristics that includes a sense of commitment, a perception of difficulties as representing challenges and opportunities, and a belief in one's ability to control one's own life.

Health Psychology The study and practice of the role of the psychological factors that affect the origin, prevention, and treatment of physical illness.

Locus of Control One's generalized belief that the control of one's life in terms of positive and negative outcomes rests either on con-trollable internal factors or on uncontrollable external factors.

Pessimism/Optimism Alternate outlooks on events of life in general: Either a negative view that one's life is bad and getting worse or a positive view that it is good and getting better.

Prompts Reminders that encourage a person to engage in behavior about which he or she already holds favorable attitudes.

Psychoneuroimmunology The study of the way one's responses to external events affect internal physiological states that are crucial to the immune system in defending the body against disease.

Self-Concealment The active tendency to maintain secrecy about personal information perceived by the individual as negative or distressing.

Self-Concealment Scale A test that measures the tendency to maintain secrecy about negative personal information.

Social Support The help provided by friends and relatives who give physical and psychological comfort to an individual facing stress. Those receiving social support tend to be in better physical health and to be better able to resist stress than those lacking such support.

Stress In social psychology, the responses elicited by physical or psychological events perceived by the individual to be harmful or emotionally upsetting.

Technophobia The fear that various aspects of a technological society are a source of danger.

Vicarious Control The generally beneficial belief that medical personnel are able to control one's physical condition.

For More Information

Ehrlich, P., & Ehrlich, A. (1990). *The population explosion*. New York: Simon and Schuster.

A very readable book intended to alarm and activate those who are not committed to the proposition that overpopulation is a critical problem for each of us. The environ-mentalist authors use dramatic terms to characterize population growth as a "bomb" or an "explosion." This may sound alarmist, in that nothing catastrophic seems to occur. The actual changes in population are, however, proceeding relentlessly, and the effects really are catastrophic. The authors suggest long-term solutions to this critical problem.

Gore, A. (1992). *Earth in the balance*. Boston: Houghton Mifflin.

U.S. Vice President Al Gore wrote this book while serving in the U.S. Senate, because he had become convinced of the global environmental crisis and wanted to try to convince others of the reality and the seriousness of the problem. He proposes a Global Marshall Plan with specific steps to begin bringing about the necessary alterations in behavior and in technology.

Shorter, E. (1992). *From paralysis to fatigue: A history of psychosomatic illness in the modern era*. New York: Free Press.

Interest in the relationship between psychological factors and physical health began with the identification of psychosomatic illnesses. This is a fascinating history of nineteenth-century cases such as "imaginary paralysis" and fainting fits and their modern counterparts such as chronic fatigue syndrome and environmental hypersensitivity. The most general point is that some genuinely excruciating physical ailments do not have a physical cause and that psychosomatic conditions tend to come suddenly into fashion and then eventually fade away.

Social Psychology and Society:
Legal, Political, and
Organizational Applications

Social Psychology and the Legal System

Before the Case Goes to Court: Police Interrogation and Pretrial Publicity
The Testimony of Eyewitnesses / Actions of Attorneys and of the Judge:
Effects on the Verdict / Characteristics of Defendants and Jurors

Social Psychology and Politics: Attitudes, Liking, and Leadership

Political Attitudes and Behavior / Voting for the Candidate You Like
Voting for the Candidate Who Appears to Be a Leader

Social Psychology in Work Settings: Job Satisfaction, Work Motivation, and Conflict

Work-Related Attitudes: Their Nature, Measurement, and Effects / Work
Motivation: Getting People to Do Their Best / Conflict in Work Settings:
A Social Psychological Perspective

SOCIAL DIVERSITY ▼ A Critical Analysis
**Voting Rights, Voter Apathy, and Voter Preferences: Effects of Sex, Class,
Race, and Age in the United States and the United Kingdom.**

Special Sections

WORK IN PROGRESS—Pretrial Publicity As Governmental Abuse: Is There
a Remedy?

FOCUS ON RESEARCH: THE CUTTING EDGE—Liability Cases: Evidence
Filtered through Cognitive Processes

WORK IN PROGRESS—Appearance-Based Inferences Regarding Character

FOCUS ON RESEARCH: CLASSIC CONTRIBUTIONS—The Bennington
Study: Political Attitudes in College and Afterward

WORK IN PROGRESS—How Did Bill Clinton Win the 1992 Presidential
Election?

WORK IN PROGRESS—The Appeal of Strong Candidates in Threatening
Times

FOCUS ON RESEARCH: THE CUTTING EDGE—Genetic Influences on
Job Satisfaction

WORK IN PROGRESS—Pleasant Working Conditions: Another Means for
Reducing Conflict?

College professors are usually
exempt from jury duty because of
the nature of their occupation. But
one summer vacation, after more
than three decades of such exemp-
tion, I received a summons to
report to the County Courthouse.
Because there was no excuse to do
otherwise, I ventured briefly into
the world of law.

After receiving general instructions and taking an oath, we
potential jurors were taken to a
courtroom in which the judge,
prosecutors, defense attorneys,
and the defendant were already
seated. The upcoming trial was a
criminal case in which a young
black man was accused of raping a
white college student. The indict-
ment was read, and then the
process of jury selection began.
My name was among those randomly called for the first panel to
be questioned by the defense
lawyer and by the district attorney. These opposing advocates ask
various questions in order to
determine which, if any, potential
jurors should be excused for any
reason—including possible bias
for or against the defendant—in a
procedure known as the *voir dire*
(to speak truthfully) examination.
Each side is allowed to reject persons they deem unsuitable, and
the judge then excuses these persons from serving on the jury in
this particular trial.

The defendant in our trial was
charged with luring the victim to

his apartment, keeping her there against her will for several hours, and forcing her to engage in various sexual acts.

As I sat there observing the process, it seemed to me that dozens of biases were almost certainly operating and that a totally objective jury could not be found in that room or anywhere else on the planet. For example, the defendant's race would be a negative factor for any individual juror (they were all white) who happened to be racially prejudiced. When questioned about prejudice, each man and woman vowed not to hold such views. Is it likely, however, that anyone would sit on a jury bench and announce to the assembled audience, "I hold many racist views and acknowledge that I am a bigot"?

I also felt that the defendant, regardless of his race, did not help his case as he spent that hot summer morning staring at each potential juror in turn. He seemed to be unpleasantly amused by this group of middle-aged and elderly white citizens; he periodically leaned over to whisper something to his attorney, who laughed quiet-

ly at what was said. I may be wrong, of course, but the defendant did not seem to me to fit the image of a person wrongfully accused of a criminal act but rather of an angry, and perhaps evil, man who heartily disliked those who were being asked to form a jury of his peers.

The questioning of the veniremen and venirewomen continued. We were asked whether any one of us would be upset to hear detailed testimony about several common and uncommon sexual practices that were part of the alleged crime, if we would identify with the young college student who said he raped her, if any of us had a close friend or relative who had been the victim or the perpetrator of the crime of rape, and so forth. Our group swore not only that we were racially unprejudiced but that sordid sexual details would elicit no emotional discomfort, no one would identify with the young white woman who was to testify about being brutalized, and no one had at any time ever had personal acquaintance with a rapist or a rape victim. Because I doubt that most of these citizens were telling the truth, I can only assume that

the opposing attorneys were having to guess about who was lying and who was not.

Some members of the panel were retained, and some were excused. I was excused because my wife is also a social psychologist; her work would not allow her to take care of our two children while I spent a week or more at the trial, which would require being sequestered each night in a hotel with eleven other jurors.

Even without my help, the trial was conducted, and it was reported on TV that the defendant was found guilty and sentenced to spend many years in prison. Quite possibly, justice was done. I talked to a lawyer friend soon afterward about the general problem of bias in the courtroom. He laughed and said that the biggest question in any trial is whether the jury likes and believes a given defendant, victim, or witness. Such things as evidence and factual details, he said, are generally of secondary importance. He may be right; but if he is, the point he makes is a disturbing one.

When social psychologists apply their theories and research skills in real-life settings such as the legal system, the political process, and the organizations in which we work, it becomes obvious that our field is applicable to many societal concerns. In this chapter, we first describe the relevance of social psychology to the *legal system,* one of the original topics to which applied research was directed by some of the founders of our profession. Research has focused on many factors, including the accuracy of eyewitness testimony and the way in

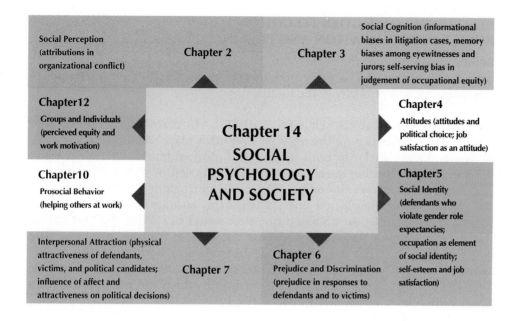

which judicial decisions are influenced by each participant in the legal process. The next aspect of society we'll consider is the *psychology of politics,* including the political attitudes and actions of citizens, media effects, and the variables that affect our choices of specific candidates. We then turn to the way social psychological factors and principles operate in *work settings.* The field of *industrial-organizational psychology* developed, in part, out of this applied interest, and seeks to investigate all aspects of behavior in work settings. Here, we'll focus on three lines of research that have been strongly influenced by the social psychological tradition: *Work-related attitudes*—employees' beliefs about and evaluations of their jobs and companies; *work motivation*—the level of effort individuals expend on performing their jobs; and *organizational conflict* among individuals and groups in work settings (Thomas, 1992).

SOCIAL PSYCHOLOGY AND THE LEGAL SYSTEM

Ideally, the judicial process should provide the fairest set of procedures ever devised to reach objective, unbiased decisions about violations of society's criminal and civil laws. Our legal and judicial professions ordinarily strive to live up to that ideal. Yet research in **forensic psychology** (psychology specifically concerned with legal issues) repeatedly indicates that the human participants in the process do not always function according to rational guidelines (Davis, 1989). Social psychologists have provided a considerable body of evidence indicating that when people interact, their behavior and their judgments are affected by attitudes, cognitions, and emotions that may be biased, irrational, and unfair. And those same factors are equally relevant when people interact in a courtroom.

BEFORE THE CASE GOES TO COURT:
POLICE INTERROGATION AND PRETRIAL PUBLICITY

Before a case reaches the courtroom, two major factors operate to influence both the testimony that is presented and the decisions that are made: police interrogation and publicity in the media.

INTERROGATION AND SUGGESTIBILITY.   In many instances the first interpersonal influence on the legal process takes place when police ask questions (see Figure 14.1). In both formal and informal questioning, police and others often ask **leading questions**—questions worded in such a way that they suggest what the answer should be. When the interrogator asks such questions, the person being questioned often accepts the assumptions underlying the inquiry. For example, an unbiased question would be, "What did you see on the afternoon of the accident?" A leading question, in contrast, would be "Did you see the car strike the pedestrian and toss her body onto the curb?" Whether or not a witness is influenced by such questions depends on specific personality characteristics and on the setting in which the questioning takes place (Schooler & Loftus, 1986).

 Interrogation: Leading questions suggest what to answer

FIGURE 14.1   When the police interrogate eyewitnesses or suspected criminals, the setting is controlled by someone with authority and special knowledge, which increases the suggestibility of the person being questioned. *Leading questions* tend subtly to persuade people to respond with what they think the officer wants to hear. Once individuals give such an answer, however inaccurate it may be, they tend to believe what they have just said.

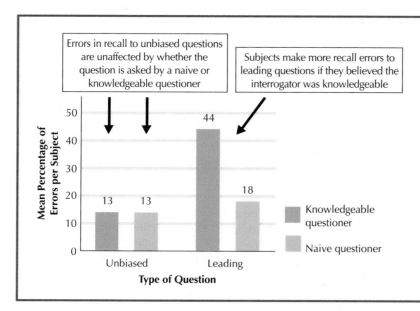

Errors in recall to unbiased questions are unaffected by whether the question is asked by a naive or knowledgeable questioner

Subjects make more recall errors to leading questions if they believed the interrogator was knowledgeable

Mistakes are made when experts ask leading questions

FIGURE 14.2 Research indicates that witnesses make more errors in responding to *leading questions* than to *unbiased questions* and that the most inaccurate answers are given when the questioner is identified as knowledgeable.

Source: Based on data from Smith & Ellsworth, 1987.

Transparency 14.1

Gudjonsson and Clark (1986) point out that the way the usual interrogation is structured tends to reinforce the citizen's assumption that the official asking the questions possesses special knowledge. This increases the suggestibility of the witness or suspect, who then is more likely to respond as directed. For example, in police interrogations the officer is usually in charge, interruptions are not permitted, and the person being questioned is discouraged from answering back. This situation involves three components that encourage suggestible responses. When a leading question is asked, the witness usually feels some *uncertainty* about the "right" answer, some degree of *trust* in the officer asking the question, and an *expectation* that one is supposed to know the answer and should be able to provide it. As a result, rather than saying "I don't know" or "I'm not sure," the person is subtly persuaded to give a positive answer. Having given that answer, the individual is inclined to believe whatever he or she has just said, especially if the interrogator indicates approval.

As you might guess, witnesses are more accurate when asked only unbiased questions (Sanders & Chiu, 1988). In a study of police interrogation, subjects saw a videotape of a bank robbery and afterward were questioned about the crime (Smith & Ellsworth, 1987). The questioner was a confederate who had been described either as being very *knowledgeable* about the robbery or as being *naive*. Half the subjects were asked unbiased questions such as "Was there a getaway car?" Half were asked leading questions such as "Where was the getaway car parked?" As shown in Figure 14.2, the unbiased questions resulted in the most accurate answers, no matter who asked them. With the leading questions, accuracy decreased, especially when the questioner was supposed to be knowledgeable.

PRETRIAL PUBLICITY.   On a regular basis, daily newspapers, radio and television news programs, and sometimes magazines and books devote a lot of space to information about crimes, accidents, and lawsuits, especially if they are dramatic or unusual or involve famous people (Barnes, 1989; Henry, 1991). One of the potentially negative aspects of a free press in this instance is that public opinion (including the opinion of individuals who might later be jurors) can be affected by how such news is presented. For example, in the rape trial described at the beginning of this chapter, local newspaper and television coverage strongly suggested that the defendant was guilty as charged. In the Rodney King case in Los Angeles, a videotape showing him being beaten and kicked by several policemen was broadcast repeatedly on television.

In research on two highly publicized cases involving defendants accused of distributing marijuana and a defendant charged with murdering a police officer, Moran and Cutler (1991) surveyed potential jurors. They found in each instance that the more knowledge people had about the details of the case, the more blame they placed on those arrested for the crimes. The investigators also found that knowledge of the crimes was unrelated to whether or not the respondents *believed* they could make impartial judgments. Given people's mistaken faith in their own lack of bias, Judge O'Connell (1988) suggests that asking potential jurors whether they can be fair and impartial is as useless as asking a man who is a practicing alcoholic if he has his drinking under control.

You may consider pretrial publicity and its effects as a minor problem caused by the media. As indicated in the following **Work in Progress** section, however, serious legal issues may be involved.

Work in Progress

Pretrial Publicity As Governmental Abuse: Is There a Remedy?

Moran's (1993) work in the Legal Psychology doctoral program at Florida International University suggests that government agencies (police, district attorneys, etc.) provide the pretrial crime information to newspapers and television stations for a very specific reason. Moran proposes that the goal is not simply to inform the public, but rather to create a negative impression of the defendant in the general population and, specifically, among potential jurors. Because people form impressions on the basis of such news items, it is important to note that in making judgments about morality such as good/bad or innocent/guilty we are especially affected by negative information (Skowronski & Carlston, 1989). If this analysis is correct, the purpose of pretrial publicity is to help the government win its case by predisposing the jury toward a guilty verdict. What can be done to lessen these effects and make trials more fair and impartial?

One possible remedy would be to attempt to educate the jurors after they reach the courtroom. Dexter, Cutler, and Moran (1992) tested one such procedure. Some research participants read

newspaper stories about a murder, and others did not. All were taken to a law school courtroom and exposed either to a minimal *voir dire* procedure ("Is there anyone on this jury panel who cannot try this case fairly and impartially . . ." etc.) or to an hour-long educational voir dire in which the mock jurors were asked about their exposure to the publicity, told that reporters sometimes write untrue or irrelevant stories, and warned about the prejudicial effects of prior information. Afterward, the participants watched a two-hour mock trial on videotape and then gave a verdict of guilty or not guilty. As in previous research, exposure to pretrial publicity resulted in a greater proportion of guilty verdicts. The extended voir dire procedure did *not*, however, reduce the impact of pretrial publicity.

Unless an effective procedure can be developed to undo the effects of biasing information, the only other remedy is to forbid the distribution of crime news until after defendants have gone to trial. What do you think? Would you prefer to suppress information about crime or to make jurors more likely to render guilty verdicts?

Not only does pretrial publicity affect people's judgment about a specific case, but media information also has more general effects. For example, when people are exposed to descriptions of very serious crimes, they then view other crimes and other offenders more harshly than if they have not had such exposure—even to the extent of recommending more severe prison sentences (Roberts & Edwards, 1989). Presumably, they overgeneralize on the basis of the selective information in the crime stories.

THE TESTIMONY OF EYEWITNESSES

When anyone witnesses a crime, an accident, or any other event relevant to a legal matter, he or she may later be called upon to testify about what was seen or heard, as shown in Figure 14.3. Each year in U.S. courtrooms, witnesses present crucial evidence concerning about 77,000 suspects (Goldstein, Chance, & Schneller, 1989). This testimony has a major impact on jurors—even though eyewitnesses are frequently wrong (Wolf & Bugaj, 1990). Jurors are most convinced by such testimony when a witness presents many details (Bell & Loftus, 1988) or speaks with confidence and without hesitation (Whitley & Greenberg, 1986).

EYEWITNESS INACCURACY. Because the events that are witnessed are almost always totally unexpected, of brief duration, and stressful (Hosch & Bothwell, 1990), even the most honest, intelligent, and well-meaning citizen

 What happened?

FIGURE 14.3 Please look at the photograph for just ten seconds, then turn to page 628 and answer a few questions about what you remember.

may be inaccurate when asked to recall the details of a past event or to identify a suspect—though witnesses are better with details than with identification (Yuille & Cutshall, 1986). A witness's certainty is found to be unrelated to his or her accuracy (Bothwell, Deffenbacher, & Brigham, 1987).

Reading: Lesko (42), *The Discrediting Effect of Eyewitness Testimony*

Many factors affect the accuracy of a witness (Wells & Luus, 1990). For example, accuracy decreases if there is a weapon in the suspect's hand (Tooley et al., 1987); if the suspect and the witness belong to different racial or ethnic groups (Platz & Hosch, 1988); and/or if misleading suggestions are made to the witness (Ryan & Geiselman, 1991). Eyewitnesses who had been drinking alcohol were less accurate than sober eyewitnesses in recalling the details of a staged theft, but they were equally able to recognize the thief's picture (Yuille & Tollestrup, 1990).

Before appearing in a lineup, guilty suspects may try to alter their appearance in an attempt to confuse witnesses, and this technique works. Also, if an innocent person is unlucky enough to wear the kind of clothing the criminal wore when committing the crime, witnesses are likely to identify him or her as the guilty party (Sanders, 1984).

INCREASING THE ACCURACY OF WITNESSES.   Correct identification of a criminal is improved when witnesses are first allowed to practice with a lineup containing only innocent volunteers. Any choice they make is wrong; they then receive information about the serious consequences of making such mistakes (Wells, 1984). As a result of this experience, their ability to recall crucial details about the suspect improves.

Another technique that bolsters memory and increases the accuracy of witnesses is to "reinstate the context" just before the identification is made; that is, first to show witnesses pictures of the crime scene and of the victim (Cutler, Penrod, & Martens, 1987). Witness reliability is also improved by exposure to just one suspect at a time, rather than to the usual lineup of several at once (Leary, 1988) and by instructions designed to improve witnesses' memory of an event (Yuille & McEwan, 1985).

BELIEVABILITY OF EYEWITNESSES.   Regardless of the accuracy of a witness, he or she must be believed if the testimony is to have any effect. What characteristics increase or decrease eyewitness believability?

To answer this question, Leippe, Manion, and Romanczyk (1992) conducted a laboratory experiment in which the "witnesses" were college students and children aged five to six and nine to ten. The experimenters told these individuals that the study dealt with skin sensitivity. Midway through the procedure, a female intruder entered the room, made an inquiry, and left. Afterward, each participant was asked to describe what had happened, the physical appearance of the experimenter and of the intruder, and what these two people had said and done. Participants were also asked to identify these two individuals from a group of photographs. The most and least accurate witnesses in each age group were thus identified.

A video camera recorded the participants' "testimony" from behind a one-way mirror. The researchers later asked other college students to view the tapes of accurate and inaccurate witnesses and to rate each one on several dimensions related to believability. The students perceived the most accurate witnesses as more accurate than the least accurate ones, but the difference was surprisingly small. One interesting finding was that the students rated the children as less believable and less accurate than the adults, even when they were equally accurate.

The student participants were most likely to believe a witness (regardless of age) if that person seemed confident. Ratings of witness confidence seemed to be based on the person's speaking without hesitation in long, elaborate sentences and not contradicting himself or herself. Altogether, believability was found to depend more on such characteristics as speaking style and age than on the accuracy of the testimony. Similarly, the more nervous the witness appears, the less accurate he or she is perceived to be (Bothwell & Jalil, 1992).

ACTIONS OF ATTORNEYS AND OF THE JUDGE: EFFECTS ON THE VERDICT

Trials can be shaped in part by what is said and done by the opposing attorneys and by the judge. Attorneys make judgments as to which jurors are acceptable, which witnesses will be asked to testify, what evidence to present and when, and how best to summarize the case to the jury. The judge presides over the interactions, rules on the admissibility of testimony and of exhibits presented as evidence, and explains the case and the legal ramifications to the jury. Each of these acts can influence what the jurors decide.

ATTORNEYS: ADVOCATES FOR ONE SIDE, FOES OF THE OTHER.

Lawyers obviously play a major role in a courtroom. Before the trial begins, jury selection takes place. Who does and does not serve on the jury can be critical, and some legal experts propose that the case has already been decided once the jury has been chosen (Hans & Vidmar, 1982).

Olczak, Kaplan, and Penrod (1991) conducted a series of investigations to determine how well the jury selection process operates. First, the researchers asked attorneys to react to a number of juror characteristics, in order to find out what information lawyers typically use. Most lawyers were found to utilize just one or two characteristics while ignoring the remainder; Table 14.1 gives

Discussion Question 1

Critical Thinking Question 1

Before a trial begins, attorneys take part in a jury selection process in which they look for certain positive and negative characteristics and ask various questions in an effort to decide which prospective jurors should be retained and which should be excused. When attorneys were asked to indicate the most important characteristics and the *voir dire* questions they most often ask, these were the results.

TABLE 14.1   What do attorneys seek in selecting a jury?

Characteristics Attorneys Say Are Important in Jury Selection	Voir Dire Questions Attorneys Say They Ask Most Often
Intelligence	What is your attitude about this kind of crime?
Age	What is your general reaction to police officers?
Appearance	How much have you heard about this case in the media?
Occupation	Were you ever the victim of this kind of crime?
Open-mindedness	How do you feel about someone who has been arrested?
Gender	Do you have any racial bias?
Attentiveness	Have any of your acquaintances ever been arrested or convicted
Impressibility	Do you have any relationship with any of the individuals connected with
Race	this case?

Source: Based on data from Olczak, Kaplan, & Penrod, 1991.

the characteristics thought most important and the questions most frequently asked in the voir dire process. Second, the researchers gave attorneys and introductory psychology students information about prospective jurors and asked the two groups to rate the jurors' desirability; these two groups responded to the characteristics in almost identical ways. Third, the attorneys and students were given information about individuals who really had served as jurors; the subjects were asked to decide how desirable each juror would be from the point of view of the defense. Both groups were wrong more often than right in their selections. The researchers concluded that even experienced attorneys use stereotypes in selecting jurors and that their choices are no better than those of college students.

The timing of opening statements turns out to be another important variable. Experimental evidence clearly shows that the defense is helped by presenting its opening statement early in the trial rather than after the prosecution presents evidence. Experimenters gave subjects the details of an actual trial, with variations in the timing of the defense opening statement. Early rather than delayed presentation affected the mock jurors' perceptions of the eyewitness testimony, the prosecutor's opening and closing statements, and the defense closing statement, as well as the perceived effectiveness of the attorneys—all in ways favoring the defense (Wells, Wrightsman, & Miene, 1985).

As in police interrogations, lawyers can ask leading questions of the person in the witness stand and thus bias the person's responses and the reactions of the jury. When questioning their own witnesses, attorneys tend to seek information by means of unbiased questions such as, "Can you tell me exactly what happened on the afternoon of the murder?" When cross-examining witnesses for the opposing side, however, they are more likely to ask leading questions such as, "You opened the door to the victim's apartment with your own key, didn't you?" Jurors perceive the witness as more competent and more credible when he or she is responding to unbiased questions (McGaughey & Stiles, 1983).

THE EFFECT OF THE JUDGE.   A judge's biases can affect the trial outcome. For example, when jurors are exposed to inadmissible evidence (Cox & Tanford, 1989) or to the judge's attack on the credibility of a witness (Cavoukian & Doob, 1980), the final verdict is swayed. Many of the cognitive processes described in chapter 3 (such as priming) obviously apply to how jurors respond to what the judge says and does.

People frequently express the view that some judges coddle criminals while others ("hanging judges") favor giving the maximum penalties. Carroll et al. (1987) found that judges actually do fall into one of two categories. Either they emphasize the social or economic causes of crime and the benefits of rehabilitation, or they blame the criminal for the crime and stress the importance of punishment and retribution. Whether you support "hard" or "soft" judges seems to depend on your views about what causes crime. Guimond and Palmer (1990) found that college students who major in social sciences usually blame society, while business and engineering majors blame the individual who committed the crime.

Judges have a great deal of leeway in making various decisions about defendants, including the amount of bail that is set and the monetary level of fines—within maximum limits set by law. Because of the pervasive importance of physical attractiveness in interpersonal evaluations (see chapter 7), Downs

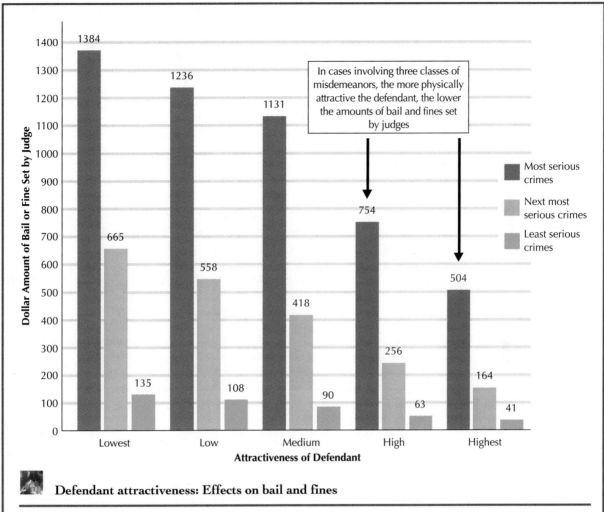

Defendant attractiveness: Effects on bail and fines

FIGURE 14.4 In a study of actual courtroom misdemeanor cases, policemen rated the physical attractiveness of defendants. Judges decided on bail amounts for those held in jail and on the amount of fines for those found guilty. For three classes of misdemeanors, the more attractive the defendant, the less the monetary amount set for bail and for fines.

Source: Based on data in Downs & Lyons, 1991.

and Lyons (1991) hypothesized that defendant attractivenss would affect the amounts of bail and fines. These researchers collected data on bail and fines assigned by forty actual judges in more than 1,500 court cases involving misdemeanors. The appearance of the defendant in each case was rated by police officers who were not involved in the arrest and who did not know what the study was about. The findings, presented in Figure 14.4, strongly indicate that the more attractive the defendant, the lower the amount of bail or fine set by the judge. A similar analysis of felony cases revealed no attractiveness effect, however, so these biased judgments appear to be limited to relatively minor offenses.

One option a judge has is to inform or not inform juries, before their deliberations, about **jury nullification rights:** the right of jurors to disregard all

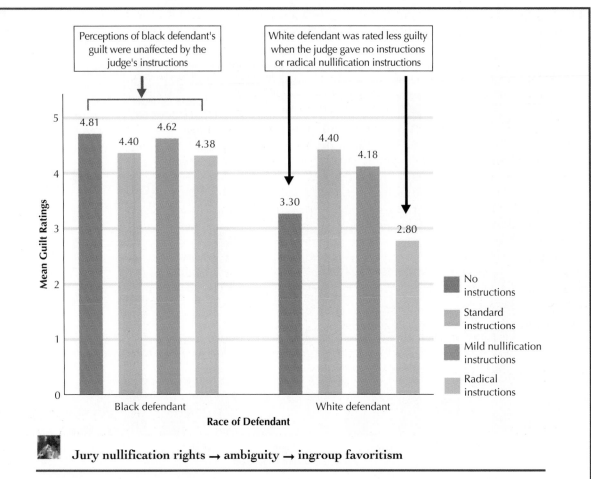

Perceptions of black defendant's guilt were unaffected by the judge's instructions

White defendant was rated less guilty when the judge gave no instructions or radical nullification instructions

No instructions

Standard instructions

Mild nullification instructions

Radical instructions

Black defendant

White defendant

Race of Defendant

Mean Guilt Ratings

Jury nullification rights → ambiguity → ingroup favoritism

FIGURE 14.5   In deciding the guilt of a defendant in a mock trial, jurors were given either no instructions, standard instructions, or mild or radical instructions about jury nullification rights. When no instructions or radical nullification instructions were given, the defendant was rated as less guilty when identified as white than when identified as black—an example of ingroup favoritism.
Source: Based on data in Hill & Pfeifer, 1992.

Discussion Question 3

instructions in a trial and to decide on the basis of their own judgments. Hill and Pfeifer (1992) proposed that nullification leads to greater ambiguity and may encourage a juror to be guided by his or her own attitudes rather than by legalities. If so, nullification could permit racism to operate whenever cases involved a defendant who was a member of a minority.

In an experiment, a male was accused of raping a white female at knifepoint. All subjects were given the same trial transcript, except that some were informed that the defendant was white and others that he was black. Subjects were given either no instructions or standard instructions about the law (the presumption that the accused is innocent, the requirement that the prosecutor prove guilt beyond a reasonable doubt, the legal definition of rape, etc.). Then the subjects heard either a mild or a radical (Horowitz, 1988) nullification statement from the judge. The mild statement contained such information as, ". . . whatever I have told you about the law, in the above instructions, while it is intended to be helpful to you . . ., it is not binding . . . and you may accept or reject it." The radical statement said such things as, ". . . you have the final authority to decide whether or not to apply a given law to the acts of the defendant . . . it is appropriate to bring into your deliberation . . . your own feelings based on conscience." As shown in Figure 14.5, ratings of guilt were not significantly different for the black and white defendants when either the standard instructions about the law were provided or such instructions were followed by a mild nullification statement. With no instructions, or with instructions followed by the radical nullification statement, however, the white defendant was judged to be less guilty than the black one. That is, the ambiguity did not lead to a more negative judgment about a black accused of rape but rather to a more positive judgment about a white accused of the same crime—*ingroup favoritism*. In any event, the ambiguity created either by no instructions or by a radical nullification statement allowed racial attitudes to affect the judicial outcome.

Most of us think of the courtroom primarily as a place in which criminal trials are held, and this function of the judicial system is most often emphasized by the news media, on television programs and in movies, and even in social psychological research. Though less dramatic, civil cases such as *liability* represent a large portion of the work of the courts, and the outcome of such cases is economically important. As you might suspect, the decisions made in civil suits are also affected by psychological factors. An example is provided in the following **Cutting Edge** section.

Focus on Research: The Cutting Edge

LIABILITY CASES: EVIDENCE FILTERED THROUGH COGNITIVE PROCESSES

We are most likely to hear about the outcome of a civil trial involving a suit in which a plaintiff wins and is awarded a large sum of money to be paid by the defendant, as suggested in Figure 14.6, p. 594. How are such decisions made?

Consider a fictional case of personal damage. The plaintiff is hit by a car as he crosses a street; he then sues the driver for damages to compensate for his loss of wages. Thomas and Parpal (1987) presented five such cases to subjects and manipulated the apparent *fault* of the plaintiff and of the defendant. For different subjects, the plaintiff (1) was in a crosswalk; (2) was not in a crosswalk but had looked both ways; or (3) was not in a crosswalk, did not look, and dashed across the street. In a similar way, the defendant driving the car (1) had sudden brake failure; (2) had bad brakes but was driving until a needed part came in; or (3) had bad brakes but had taken no steps to get them repaired and was driving ten miles per hour over the speed limit. The general finding across most of the cases was that the liability assessed against the defendant increased as the defendant's fault increased; the liability decreased as the plaintiff's fault increased. The outcomes were affected much more, however, by the mock jurors' subjective judgments of fault than by fault as indicated by the evidence. That is, each juror made attributions (see chapter 2) about the plaintiff and the defendant, reached conclusions about how bad the consequences were for the defendant, judged the degree to which the incident was

"We the jury award the plaintiff all the gold in Fort Knox."

 Liability cases: When a plaintiff sues a defendant

FIGURE 14.6 Though criminal cases receive most of the attention in news reports, dramatic presentations, and social psychological research, civil cases constitute a large portion of the legal process; and here too, psychological factors affect the decisions that are reached. This particular jury was obviously impressed by the plaintiff's case.

Source: The New Yorker, January 26, 1981, p. 41.

simply an accident, decided whether there was any intent to do harm, and apparently identified and sympathized more with defendants of the same sex than with those of the opposite sex in assigning responsibility. Altogether, these individual reactions by each juror predict outcome better than the evidence does.

In other liability studies, researchers found subjects to be somewhat inconsistent in dealing with statistical probabilities. Wells (1992) presented subjects with a fictional case in which—in the "standard version"—the Blue Bus Company was being sued by Mrs. Prob for having caused her dog's death. She was walking her dog on a country road, a passing bus swerved recklessly, she jumped to safety, but the bus hit and killed her dog. The only other buses that ever use that road are those of the Grey Bus Company, but Mrs. Prob is colorblind and so does not know the color of the bus. The Blue Bus Company is the target of the suit because it owns 80 percent of the buses in the area and accounts for 80 percent of the bus traffic on the country road. Half of the sub-

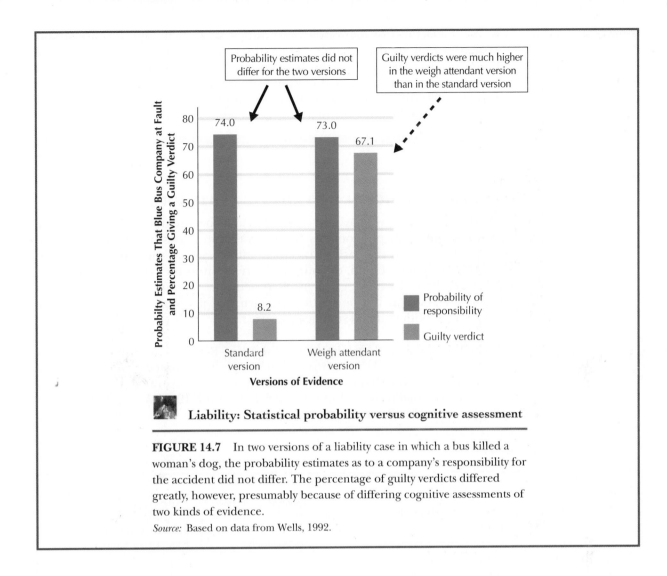

Liability: Statistical probability versus cognitive assessment

FIGURE 14.7 In two versions of a liability case in which a bus killed a woman's dog, the probability estimates as to a company's responsibility for the accident did not differ. The percentage of guilty verdicts differed greatly, however, presumably because of differing cognitive assessments of two kinds of evidence.

Source: Based on data from Wells, 1992.

jects were asked to estimate the probability that a bus from the Blue Bus Company killed the dog, and half were asked to render a verdict. Most (74 percent) judged that the bus company was responsible, but only 8.2 percent voted against the bus company in favor of Mrs. Prob.

In a second version of the case—the "weigh attendant version"—each of the two bus companies was described as accounting for 50 percent of the traffic on the road. The same probabilities applied here, but they were based on a different factor: An attendant at a nearby weigh station wrote in his log that a blue bus had been checked just ten minutes before the accident, but his log entries were correct 80 percent of the time and incorrect 20 percent of the time. Again, most (73 percent) thought the Blue Bus Company was responsible, but in this version 67.1 percent voted in favor of the plaintiff. The results are shown in Figure 14.7.

Thus, differences in the volume of traffic did not seem to be sufficient evidence to cause "jurors" to rule against the Blue Bus Company, but differences in the correctness of log entries *were* sufficient, even though the probability estimates remained the same. Interestingly, experienced trial judges were found to reach decisions in this hypothetical case almost identical to those of college undergraduates. In these and many other instances (Pennington & Hastie, 1992), the cognitions of the jurors are found to be of vital importance in determining the outcome of a legal proceeding.

CHARACTERISTICS OF DEFENDANTS AND JURORS

In earlier chapters we have described research on prejudice, attraction, attributions, and other phenomena—research that indicates how people respond to one another on the basis of race, sex, attractiveness, and other characteristics. These factors should, of course, be irrelevant in the courtroom. But, having read about the effect of physical attractiveness on the monetary decisions of judges, you may not be startled to learn that just such variables affect the outcome of both real and simulated trials (Dane, 1992).

DEFENDANTS: EQUAL UNDER THE LAW?   Research consistently indicates that attractive defendants are treated better than unattractive ones in gaining acquittals, receiving light sentencing, eliciting the sympathy of the jury, being considered dangerous, and so on (Esses & Webster, 1988; Wuensch, Castellow, & Moore, 1991). Because attorneys are aware of this attractiveness bias, they

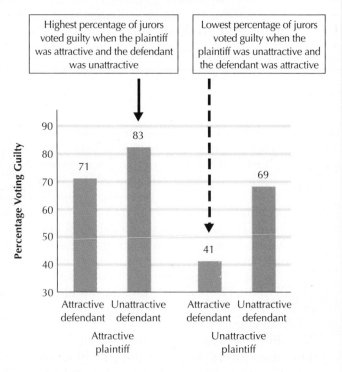

Sexual harassment: Attractiveness of plaintiff and defendant

FIGURE 14.8   Mock jurors were asked to decide on guilt and innocence with respect to charges of sexual harassment. They read a trial summary based on actual court cases and were shown photographs of the plaintiff and the defendant. The photographs were actually pictures of either an attractive or an unattractive man (identified as the defendant) and either an attractive or an unattractive woman (identified as the plaintiff). Judgments of guilt were clearly affected by the appearance of the two individuals. Both male and female jurors were most likely to give a guilty verdict when an attractive woman charged an unattractive man with harassment and least likely to vote guilty when an unattractive woman made that same charge against an attractive man.

Source: Based on data from Castellow, Wuensch, & Moore, 1990.

advise their clients to do everything possible to improve their appearance before entering the courtroom.

In a case involving sexual harassment, the attractiveness of both the plaintiff and the defendant can play a role (Castellow, Wuensch, & Moore, 1990). Study participants read the trial summary of a case in which a twenty-three-year-old secretary-receptionist accused her employer of repeatedly making suggestive remarks, attempting to kiss and fondle her, and providing detailed descriptions of the sexual activities he would enjoy sharing with her. Different groups of subjects also saw photographs purported to be of the two individuals; the photos showed (1) two attractive individuals, (2) two unattractive ones, or (3) and (4) the two possible attractive-unattractive combinations. As shown in Figure 14.8, attractiveness made a difference. Guilty judgments were most likely with an attractive plaintiff and an unattractive defendant (83 percent) and least likely with an unattractive plaintiff and an attractive defendant (41 percent).

As described in the following **Work in Progress** section, Castellow and his colleagues went a step farther in attempting to understand the effects of attractiveness in the courtroom.

Work in Progress

Appearance-Based Inferences Regarding Character

In the sexual harassment experiment just described, Castellow and his colleagues found not only that attractiveness influenced judgments about guilt, but that the physically attractive plaintiffs and defendants were also rated more favorably on personality characteristics. This led Castellow (1993) to ask whether the effects of attractiveness on the judgments of jurors might be related to appearance-based inferences about character rather than on attractiveness itself.

To follow up this possibility, Egbert et al. (1992) again used a case of alleged sexual harassment; but instead of being portrayed as attractive or unattractive in appearance, the female plaintiff and male defendant were described either positively or negatively by character witnesses. That is, the plaintiff was described either in such terms as friendly, likable, pleasant, and helpful or as grumpy, unpleasant, unhelpful, and unprofessional. In a similar way, the defendant was described either in positive (respected, honest, fair, churchgoing) or in negative (uncaring, low-achieving, perhaps dishonest, etc.) terms. Just as with the attractiveness manipulation, the highest percentage of guilty decisions were toward a defendent described negatively with a plaintiff described positively; the lowest percentage of guilty decisions were toward a positive defendant with a negative plaintiff. These findings are consistent with the hypothesis that attractiveness affected inferences about character and that the judicial decisions were based on assumed character.

That is not necessarily true, however; in the follow-up study, the participants rated those with positive character descriptions as being more physically attractive than those with negative descriptions, even though no photographs or information about appearance was provided. Thus, it seems that there are two stereotypes—"What is beautiful is good" and "What is good is beautiful." Because both of these stereotypes are present, we don't know whether jurors are responding primarily to appearance, to character, or to both factors.

The defendant's sex sometimes affects judicial decisions. In a mock trial, Cruse and Leigh (1987) presented jurors with testimony in an assault case. A couple was engaged in an argument about ending their relationship, and the defendant was alleged to have cut the victim with a kitchen knife. For half of the jurors, the defendant, "Jack Bailey," was accused of knifing "Lucy Hill," and 43 percent of the jurors found *him* guilty. The remaining jurors read the same evidence, except that Lucy was accused of knifing Jack; under these conditions, 69 percent found *her* guilty. The investigators suggested that the woman was more likely to be judged as guilty because stabbing someone with a knife was a masculine behavior—a woman "shouldn't act that way." In other words, she violated expectancies based on gender roles (see chapter 5).

Critical Thinking
Question 2

The defendant's ethnicity and race also influence the outcome. Defendants whose testimony is in another language that must be translated are judged more guilty than when the same testimony is originally given in English (Stephan & Stephan, 1986). In the United States, African-American defendants are more likely to be convicted than white defendants and more likely to receive a prison sentence (Stewart, 1980). Similarly, the death penalty is applied disproportionately to blacks. The 1990 census indicates that 12.1 percent of the U.S. population is black, but 40 percent of the prisoners awaiting execution on death row are black (Sniffen, 1991). The reasons for these findings may include racist bias, the possibility that blacks commit more crimes that directly result in someone's death, and/or the likelihood that economic differences permit white defendants to employ more skillful attorneys.

Racism may be the primary factor in another finding. A study of American trials indicated that 11.1 percent of criminals (regardless of race) who kill a white victim receive a death sentence, while only 4.5 percent of those who kill a black victim are sentenced to die (Henderson & Taylor, 1985).

AN UNBIASED JURY OF YOUR PEERS?   Criminal verdicts are found to be determined in part by such seemingly irrelevant factors as the proportion of jurors with previous jury experience—the more such jurors, the more likely is conviction (Werner et al., 1985).

Some general attitudes are common among jurors, including a bias in favor of the defendant, known as a **leniency bias** (MacCoun & Kerr, 1988). On the opposite side are juror attitudes that are associated with a tendency to vote for conviction. One example is *legal authoritarianism*—a tendency to ignore the defendant's civil liberties and rights, including the presumption that the accused is innocent unless proven guilty. Narby, Cutler, and Moran (1993) reported a clear tendency across a series of studies for legal authoritarians to favor conviction.

Some attitudes, such as opposition to the death penalty, are held only by some potential jurors, and those persons are routinely eliminated during the jury selection process of a murder trial. The result is bad for the defendant, because those who favor the death penalty are more likely to vote for conviction than those who do not (Bersoff, 1987). Other specific attitudes (such as how one evaluates psychiatrists) can affect the verdict in specific cases that require psychiatric testimony (such as those involving an insanity plea) (Cutler, Moran, & Narby, 1992).

Research on the legal system provides ample evidence that additional effort is needed to increase judicial fairness and objectivity. The elimination of all biases and inaccuracies is a difficult but important goal.

SOCIAL PSYCHOLOGY AND POLITICS: ATTITUDES, LIKING, AND LEADERSHIP

Social psychologists first became involved in political research by conducting surveys that asked voters to indicate their choices between candidates competing for political office. Such polls can be quite accurate predictors if the sample is sufficiently large and sufficiently representative of actual voters, and when the survey is carried out close to the time of the election. Political research has broadened over the years and now includes such questions as the role of attitudes in voter behavior and the bases on which electoral decisions are made.

POLITICAL ATTITUDES AND BEHAVIOR

Attitudes are crucial elements in political behavior, ranging from broad dimensions such as liberalism versus conservatism to narrowly defined topics such as pro-life versus pro-choice.

LIBERAL AND CONSERVATIVE VIEWS.   Though this somewhat oversimplifies a complex range of views, **conservatism** may be defined as the desire to preserve the social order in its present form or—if changes have been made—to return it to its previous state. The go-slow underpinning of conservative philosophy is exemplified by former President Bush's onetime chief of staff, John Sununu, who humorously suggested in 1990 that it would be best if the members of Congress just went home and did nothing for the next two years of the president's term of office (Pinkerton, 1992).

Liberalism includes the desire to modify political, social, and economic institutions to promote the rights of individuals and the assurance of civil liberties. The activist thrust of liberal philosophy is shown in a statement made by President Franklin Roosevelt: "It is common sense to take a method and try it; if it fails, admit it frankly and try another. But above all, try something" (Pinkerton, 1992, p. 27).

You might assume that these contrasting political attitudes would be related to positive versus negative evaluations of government functioning. Actually, in a study of politically active, economically successful individuals, both liberals and conservatives were found to hold negative views about the U.S. government (Sirgo & Eisenman, 1993). The two attitudinal groups may be displeased about different things (e.g., too much money being spent on welfare versus too much money being spent on the military), but both express unhappiness about what the government is doing.

Though many U.S. citizens prefer to call themselves "independents," those who express liberal views on most issues tend to be Democrats; Republicans are more likely to hold conservative views (Eisenman & Sirgo, 1991). Because neither conservatism nor liberalism can solve all of a nation's problems and make everyone happy, Arthur Schlesinger, Jr. (1986, 1992) proposes that politics in the United States alternate between liberal and conservative periods. Thus, private action, private enterprise, and private interest are emphasized for a couple of decades, and then public action and the public interest are the rule for the next couple of decades. Proponents of each philosophy tend to go too far in one direction, so the alternation is an essential feature that makes democracy work effectively.

As described in the following **Classic Contributions** section, students often acquire political attitudes during their college years and maintain or adapt those attitudes during the following decades as an integral part of their lives.

Focus on Research: Classic Contributions

THE BENNINGTON STUDY: POLITICAL ATTITUDES IN COLLEGE AND AFTERWARD

Theodore Newcomb was a social psychologist who joined the faculty at Bennington College in the 1930s, shortly after the institution was founded. At the time, the student body consisted of young women whose families were primarily wealthy and conservative. The faculty, in contrast, tended to be socially and politically liberal. Newcomb (1943) published a famous book documenting the shift in student political attitudes from conservatism when they

Research at Bennington College that began in the 1930s indicated that the political attitudes of students shifted in a liberal direction during their four years at this institution. Follow-up studies discovered that these liberal attitudes were maintained in the decades after graduation. As shown here, Bennington graduates consistently preferred the more liberal candidate in U.S. presidential elections over the years, while other women (matched in educational attainment and age) consistently preferred the more conservative candidate.

TABLE 14.2 The Bennington experience: Liberals for a lifetime

Voting Patterns (Percentages): Bennington Women versus Comparable Women

1952		*Eisenhower*	*Stevenson*
	Bennington Women	42.6	57.4
	Comparable Women	64.3	35.7
1960		*Nixon*	*Kennedy*
	Bennington Women	26.0	74.0
	Comparable Women	75.0	25.0
1968		*Nixon*	*Humphrey*
	Bennington Women	32.9	66.5
	Comparable Women	79.1	18.6
1976		*Ford*	*Carter*
	Bennington Women	31.2	68.8
	Comparable Women	54.9	45.1
1984		*Reagan*	*Mondale*
	Bennington Women	26.4	73.3
	Comparable Women	73.0	25.7

Source: Based on data from the Institute for Social Research, *National Election Studies, 1952–1984.*

entered college to liberalism by the time they graduated. He proposed the concept of *reference group* (the group to which a person compares himself or herself with respect to attitudes, beliefs, values, etc.) as the source of change. That is, the students' initially conservative reference group of family and friends was replaced by a liberal reference group of role models, professors, and classmates.

Whether you evaluate this effect on student attitudes as a positive or a negative one depends, of course, on your own political views. In any event, the question arose as to whether the liberalism of the college years would continue after these students left the Vermont campus and moved on to other influences in the outside world. This question was answered by a follow-up study in the 1960s (Newcomb et al., 1967) in which the original subjects, then in their forties, were studied all over again. The investigators found that the attitudes formed in college were remarkably stable over the years.

Another follow-up investigation was undertaken in the 1980s. Ted Newcomb died before it was completed, but the data have been published (Alwin, Cohen, & Newcomb, 1991). Again, the former students were found to express liberal views; rather than becoming more conservative as they grew older, they had become slightly more liberal. One index of the effect of the "Bennington experience" on political views is a comparison of the Bennington women's choice of candidates in various presidential elections with the choice of other college-educated women in their same age group (all born between 1910 and 1924). As shown in Table 14.2, the Bennington graduates consistently preferred the more liberal candidate in each election, while the sample of comparable women consistently preferred the more conservative candidate.

Transparency 14.2

One former Bennington student who had gradually become "very liberal," described some of the elements involved in her shift. She said that she was

> exposed to a whole lot of ideas that I hadn't been exposed to or even thought about. . . . The faculty was young and liberal. It was the time of the Depression and social upheaval. Those years I knew people who suffered from the Depression—it was appalling. (The Bennington Study, 1991–92, p. 6)

The "Bennington experience" was a lasting one.

MEDIA EFFECTS.   Among the many sources of information and persuasive messages are the media. Many people complain about this source because they perceive the presence of a general bias against whatever they believe (Vallone, Ross, & Lepper, 1985). Careful analyses of network news broadcasts and other outlets indicate a surprising degree of fairness toward opposing candidates and an equal presentation of liberal and conservative views (Mullen et al., 1986). What people seem to want is not fairness but the presentation of attitudes exactly like their own (Hentoff, 1992). Most people are also convinced that the media affect the views and the votes of others, but not of themselves (Innes & Zeitz, 1988).

It is sometimes suggested that television has altered the political process because it is a powerful tool for providing information and misinformation. Research suggests, however, that newspapers are better teaching devices than TV broadcasts (Gunter, Furnham, & Leese, 1986). This conclusion was

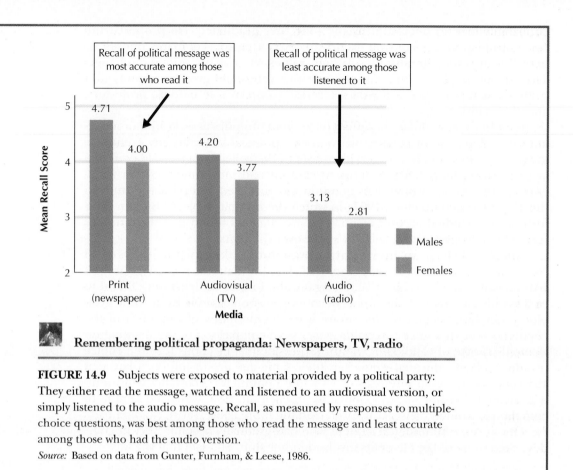

Recall of political message was most accurate among those who read it

Recall of political message was least accurate among those listened to it

Remembering political propaganda: Newspapers, TV, radio

FIGURE 14.9 Subjects were exposed to material provided by a political party: They either read the message, watched and listened to an audiovisual version, or simply listened to the audio message. Recall, as measured by responses to multiple-choice questions, was best among those who read the message and least accurate among those who had the audio version.

Source: Based on data from Gunter, Furnham, & Leese, 1986.

reached in an experiment in which undergraduates were exposed to political propaganda on TV, on radio, or in print for approximately five minutes. Afterward, the students' memory for the content of the political messages was tested. For both men and women, recall of the content was best for those who read the material, next for those who saw the television version, and least accurate for those who only listened to the broadcast (see Figure 14.9).

VOTING FOR THE CANDIDATE YOU LIKE

In a democracy the election process is often cluttered with irrelevant details—such as distorted campaign advertisements, the average of 9.8 seconds allotted to a given campaign on the evening news as a "sound bite" (Adatto, 1990), personal attacks, and endorsements by stars of the entertainment industry. Despite all this, the *intent* of most voters is to select candidates who meet two criteria. Voters want to vote for the individual they like best (Stengel, 1988) and for one who appears to have leadership qualities (Adler, 1988). What specifically is involved in each criterion?

In chapter 7 we discussed many of the variables that influence interpersonal attraction and friendship formation. Those same variables affect how much people like political candidates; and the greater the liking, the greater the probability of an individual's casting a vote for a candidate. We will provide a few examples. Note, however, that voter personality helps determine which variables are most important. For example, persons high in self-monitoring (see chapter 5) tend to respond to image-related variables such as appearance, while low self-monitors respond more to the issues (Young & Osborne, 1989).

Critical Thinking
Question 4

REPEATED EXPOSURE. Research on propinquity, as we've pointed out, shows that the more contacts you have with someone you don't know, the more you tend to like that person. The same rule works in politics. With TV appearances, billboards, handouts, and buttons, the name and the face become familiar with repeated exposure. And as exposure increases, the number of votes increases (Grush & McKeogh, 1975).

AFFECT. People generally like whoever or whatever is associated with positive affect; dislike results from association with negative affect; and differential emotional responses to candidates are excellent predictors of how an individual will vote (Christ, 1985). Though we have described the relative inefficiency of TV in providing political information, what about its role in creating positive and negative affect? After the 1988 U.S. presidential election, a poll reported that one-fourth of those voting said that TV spots affected their choice (Denton & Woodward, 1990). It is often assumed that the negative TV ads of George Bush helped him defeat Michael Dukakis. A content analysis of the two candidates' respective ads revealed, however, that the only significant difference between the two campaigns was in the emphasis on positive traits and the positive record of Bush versus the greater emphasis on a vision for a better nation by Dukakis (Hacker & Swan, 1992). The two sides used negative advertising equally, but Bush employed more *positive* affective appeals.

The power of a positive versus a negative message has been confirmed in research by Zullow et al. (1988). These investigators compared the level of optimism and pessimism in the convention speeches given each election year, beginning in 1948, by the two major U.S. presidential candidates after they were nominated. In all but one of the ten elections studied, the candidate with the more optimistic message won the general election.

Discussion Question 2

Keep in mind that affective manipulation is also involved in the use of bands, flags, balloons, and pictures of smiling candidates and their families—and in efforts to associate the opponent with negative words and deeds indicating that he or she is untrustworthy, unpatriotic, soft on crime, wishy-washy, and so forth (see Figure 14.10, p. 604). The classic example of associating the other candidate with negative affect occurred in the 1950 senatorial primary in Florida. The incumbent senator, Claude Pepper, was described by challenger George Smathers in terms that sounded very bad to poorly educated rural voters. In a popular speech, Smathers described Senator Pepper as a "shameless extrovert . . . whose sister was a thespian" and as a man who admitted that before his marriage he engaged in the practice of "celibacy." Smathers won the primary (Catchpole, 1992).

It is worth emphasizing that we are not really mindless creatures who must respond obediently to every attempt to manipulate our political decisions. Pratkanis and Aronson (1992) point out that people can inoculate themselves against such persuasion attempts (see chapter 4). When, for example, a political ad appeals to fear ("My opponent and his party will lead us down the road to economic ruin"), you can focus on your emotions and ask yourself, "What

Political conventions: Creating positive affect

FIGURE 14.10 In American political conventions it has become standard practice to create and maintain as much positive affect as possible by means of band music, flags, chanted slogans, balloons, and any other gimmicks that make the participants and the audience feel good. The relevance of all of this to the candidates or the issues is of secondary importance.

am I feeling and why?" If you decide that a given candidate is trying to make you unjustly fearful, turn off your television set or just remind yourself of the unreasonableness of what is being said.

Nevertheless, a skillful candidate can employ specific persuasion strategies and even influence the inoculation process by anticipating what the other side is going to say or do, as described in the following **Work in Progress** section.

Work in Progress

How Did Bill Clinton Win the 1992 Presidential Election?

Pratkanis and Aronson (1993) analyzed the 1992 election and concluded that Clinton won by using three common persuasion strategies—setting an agenda, providing an appealing image, and responding to negative attacks (Pratkanis, 1993).

Laboratory research has shown that repeated exposure to news about a specific public issue convinces viewers that the issue is of central importance; they also evaluate candidates who are strong on that issue most positively (Iyengar & Kinder, 1987). Polls showed that voters felt that Clinton was

stronger than Bush on the economy, while the reverse was true for foreign affairs. Clinton (with a little help from Perot) used *agenda setting* by focusing over and over on the economy. The famous sign in his campaign headquarters read: "The economy, stupid." Clinton linked the economy to other issues as well. Thus, education and welfare reform were called investments, affordable health care was described as a way to reduce the deficit, and so on.

In creating an *appealing image*, the Clinton campaign used a strategy like that of cigarette advertising, in which an image (e.g., a cowboy on a horse) is designed to appeal to a specific market (e.g., male smokers who want to be macho). Clinton created an image to reach young voters (appearing on MTV and playing the saxophone on the Arsenio Hall show), women voters (taking a firm pro-choice position on abortion), Southern voters (creating an all-Southern ticket with Al Gore), and working-class voters (taking a bus on the campaign trail and stopping at McDonald's instead of at the local country club).

Beginning in the primaries, Bill and Hillary Clinton were the targets of very strong negative campaigning and advertising. By *responding to negative attacks,* Clinton defused them. For example, he used inoculation to deal with possible criticisms about the Arkansas River being polluted with chicken droppings: He visited the site early in the presidential race and blamed the federal government for making a poor state choose between jobs and the environment. Another tactic was to create the expectation of a negative attack from Bush, thus boxing him in. If Bush then failed to attack, he looked weak; but if he did attack, he was just living up to the prediction by slinging mud.

Altogether, these strategies were extremely effective, and they quite possibly played a major role in determining who became president of the United States.

OVERT CHARACTERISTICS.   Physical attractiveness is as important in elections as in dating. In a study of candidates in a Canadian federal election, those who were physically attractive received almost three times as many votes as those who were unattractive (Efran & Patterson, 1974). Interestingly, in mayoral and county clerk contests in the United States, physical attractiveness has a more positive effect for male than for female candidates (Sigelman et al., 1986). That is, women were not discriminated against for being pretty, but they weren't helped by attractiveness as men were.

Exercise 1

Other aspects of appearance also have an effect on voters; in a contest between two male candidates, the taller one most often wins (Feldman, 1975; Gillis, 1982). In the absence of substantial amounts of relevant information, even the emotional response to a candidate's name can be a determining factor. Thus, voters are found to prefer a candidate with a "soap opera" name like *Fairchild* to a less familiar "ethnic" name like *Sangmeister* (O'Sullivan et al., 1988), unless the voter belongs to the ethnic group in question (Byrne & Pueschel, 1973).

Critical Thinking Question 7

SIMILARITY.   Of all the attraction variables that influence voting, similarity of attitudes is the most rational and defensible (Krosnick, 1988); and voters are surprisingly accurate in judging whether they agree or disagree with a given candidate (Krosnick, 1990). As a result, we vote for a candidate who is most like ourselves in his or her general liberal/conservative attitudes (Byrne & Przybyla, 1980) or stand on important issues (Ottati, Fishbein, & Middlestadt, 1988), or on the basis of specific attitudes about a given issue such as race (Eisenman, 1992). Similarity of attitudes about issues is even more important than voter self-interest (Young et al., 1991). Are there any problems with the similarity effect in politics?

One difficulty is that candidates have learned to avoid controversial issues or to distort their own views to get elected. They may express firm opinions only about topics that are generally popular; it is safe to be in favor of economic growth and against crime, for example. Also, when a candidate is communicating to an audience holding opposing views, his or her message tends to become simplistic (Suedfeld & Wallbaum, 1992). The other difficulty is that in voting we tend to extend our similarity preference beyond attitudes to a preference for someone like ourselves in age, race, and sex (Piliavin, 1987; Sigelman & Sigelman, 1982). The similarity effect, then, leads to preferences based on such prejudices as ageism, racism, and sexism.

VOTING FOR THE CANDIDATE WHO APPEARS TO BE A LEADER

Video: *Group Decision Making and Leadership**

For major political positions such as a governorship or the presidency, liking is not enough. Voters also want a *leader*. As we pointed out in chapter 12, a leader is someone who can influence other group members toward attaining agreed-upon goals. You may remember some of the traits associated with leadership: drive, leadership motivation, intelligence, honesty, self-confidence, expert knowledge, creativity, and flexibility. In part, voters make their choices on the basis of whether or not they attribute these characteristics to a given candidate. To the extent that nonverbal "display" behavior affects voters' perceptions, it is even possible that we respond in part to primitive cues developed by our species over millions of years that are now transmitted by television (Masters, 1991).

Critical Thinking Question 5

PERCEIVED LEADERSHIP CHARACTERISTICS AND VOTER PREFERENCES.   Drive and leadership motivation have been studied in terms of Type A behavior characteristics among actual political leaders, who are generally found to be hard-driving and competitive, impatient, and involved in their work (Wiegele & Oots, 1990).

Several of these leadership characteristics fit the masculine stereotype, and male candidates make every effort to sound tough and manly, leading to what has been called "macho-mouth rhetoric" (Kimmell, 1988). Research indicates, in fact, that men running for office benefit from being perceived as masculine (Sigelman et al., 1986).

Also, a self-confident, expert candidate is not expected to change his or her mind on issues. One who "waffles" is perceived to be weak (Hoffman & Carver, 1984).

The question of honesty is most often discussed in terms of character, leading to questions such as, "Would you trust this man to lead?" Thus, people discuss marital infidelity by a candidate as a character flaw in part because it often involves lying and deceit (Taylor, 1992). When responses to candidates are examined in detail, character weaknesses are found to have a much greater effect than character strengths (Klein, 1991). Perhaps this explains why political advertising most often concentrates on the alleged shortcomings of the opponent. Political scandals also result in a more negative view of politicians in general, though not of specific politicians not involved in the scandal (Schwarz & Bless, 1992). This may explain why general sentiment about the U.S. Congress often advocates "throwing all the rascals out of office," while at the same time the vast majority of incumbents in each district easily win reelection.

A candidate's own good qualities are best suggested indirectly by identification with a past, widely admired leader. For example, during the war in the Persian Gulf, Saddam Hussein was compared to Adolf Hitler. One result was that people completed the scenario by perceiving President Bush in the role of either Winston Churchill or Franklin Roosevelt during World War II (Spellman & Holyoak, 1992).

A question of continuing theoretical and practical importance involves the factors that determine assessments of presidential greatness (Simonton, 1986,

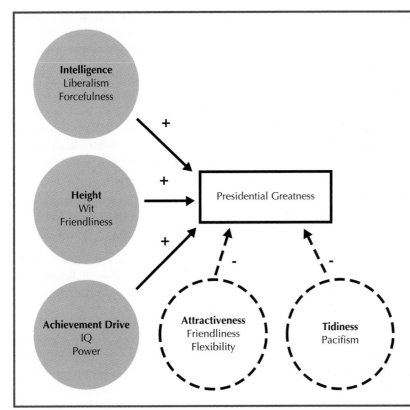

Presidential greatness

FIGURE 14.11 Perceived greatness of U.S. presidents is found to be a function of situational factors and personal characteristics. Situationally, greatness ratings increase as a function of the number of wartime years the individual spent as president, the total years in office, the fact that he was assassinated, and/or the absence of a major scandal. On the personal side, greatness ratings increase with intelligence, height, and achievement drive and decrease with attractiveness and tidiness. Shown with each factor are other variables that correlate with it.
Source: Based on data in McCann, 1992.

1992). One attempt to develop a formula to predict presidential greatness was that of McCann (1992), who discovered that ratings of past U.S. presidents (Washington to Johnson) were best predicted by a series of personality characteristics involving leadership qualities. As shown in Figure 14.11, greatness is predicted by such positive qualities as intelligence, achievement drive, forcefulness, height, flexibility, and strength that constitute many of the identified qualities of leadership.

McCann (1993c) has concentrated on how external events, in addition to personality factors, influence how voters respond to presidential candidates, as described in the following **Work in Progress** section.

Work in Progress

The Appeal of Strong Candidates in Threatening Times

McCann has been examining the private versus public phases of historian Arthur Schlesinger that were described earlier in this chapter. Those presidents who headed the United States during a public phase were more likely to be rated as "great" than those holding office during a private phase. Why? The investigator pursued the idea that Schlesinger's public phases are characterized by

national crisis and upheaval to a greater extent than are private phases; this difference was hypothesized to be the link to presidential greatness.

First, McCann established a relationship between periods of dominant public purpose and threats to America's social, economic, and political well-being. Among the correlates of threat are fluctuations in stock prices, number of housing starts, unemployment, and suicide rate (McCann & Stewin, 1990).

Second, McCann (1993a) substantiated a link between public/private phases and the occurrence of crises during the first terms of thirty-nine presidents from George Washington to Ronald Reagan. Crisis was clearly characteristic of the public purpose phase as opposed to the private interest phase. It was found that Americans show more interest in "powerful" presidential candidates during threatening periods and that the margin of victory is lower if the candidate's power does not match the degree of threat. In fact, the interaction of societal threat and a candidate's strength or forcefulness predicts success in the election.

The next step is to establish the relationship between the variables that lead to election success *and* to presidential greatness. The basic idea is that people turn to a strong leader in threatening times, such leaders stress public purpose more than private interest, and one result is that they are evaluated with labels such as "greatness."

STYLES OF LEADERSHIP.   Leaders behave in different ways, of course. Miroff (1993) identifies four major styles: heroic (Theodore Roosevelt), democratic (Abraham Lincoln), dissenting (Martin Luther King), and aristocratic (Alexander Hamilton).

Simonton (1988) has identified five distinct styles among the thirty-nine U.S. presidents from Washington to Reagan, basing his model on previous research, biographical information, and performance. In this model, the presidential styles are *interpersonal, charismatic, deliberative, creative,* and *neurotic.* Characteristics of each style, along with names of those presidents best fitting each category, appear in Table 14.3. The four most successful styles are either person-oriented (interpersonal and charismatic) or task-oriented (deliberative and creative). The least successful is the self-oriented neurotic style.

When people encounter extreme difficulties (war, economic problems, social unrest, etc.), they are likely to turn to *transformational leadership,* leadership with vision and charisma (see chapter 12). Among the U.S. presidents who were high on this dimension—Theodore and Franklin Roosevelt, John Kennedy, and Ronald Reagan—each was forceful, able to influence others, skillful, driven to achieve, and innovative (Simonton, 1988). These characteristics elicit enthusiastic emotional support and loyalty from the general public. This can be beneficial when the leader is someone like F.D.R., whom many historians regard as having led the United States out of economic despair and mobilized the population to defend itself against aggressors. But a transformational leader like Adolf Hitler is able to lead a nation to an offensive war, totalitarianism, and genocide.

SOCIAL PSYCHOLOGY IN WORK SETTINGS: JOB SATISFACTION, WORK MOTIVATION, AND CONFLICT

What single activity fills more of most adults' time than any other? The answer is simple: *work.* Unless they are fortunate enough to be born with or to acquire vast wealth, most people spend a majority of their waking hours doing some type of job. The single most important reason for this lifelong toil is obvious: We must work in order to earn a living. But this is certainly *not* the only reason why most adults hold a job or pursue a career. For many of us, work becomes an important part of our self-concept (see chapter 5). When asked, "Who are

The thirty-nine U.S. presidents from Washington to Reagan were analyzed, and five different leadership styles were identified. Shown here are the characteristics of the *interpersonal, charismatic, deliberative, creative,* and *neurotic* styles along with the presidents who were rated highest on each dimension.

TABLE 14.3 Leadership styles of U.S. presidents

Presidential Style

Interpersonal

Gives credit to others for work done	Millard Fillmore
Endears himself to staff through	George Washington
courtesy and consideration	Gerald Ford
Is willing to make compromises	
Is not impatient or abrupt in conferences	

Gerald Ford

Charismatic

Enjoys the ceremonial aspects of the office	Franklin Roosevelt
Has a flair for the dramatic	Andrew Jackson
Uses rhetoric effectively	Lyndon Johnson
Is a dynamo of energy and determination	John Kennedy
Keeps in contact with the American public and its moods	Theodore Roosevelt
Is rarely shy or awkward in public	Ronald Reagan

Ronald Reagan

Deliberative

Is able to visualize alternatives and weigh long-term	Millard Fillmore
consequences	George Washington
Keeps himself thoroughly informed	James Madison
Is cautious and conservative in action	
Avoids emotional outbursts	

George Washington

Creative

Initiates new legislation and programs	Andrew Jackson
Is innovative in his role as an executive	Thomas Jefferson
Is rarely a middle-of-the-roader	Franklin Roosevelt
	Richard Nixon

Franklin Roosevelt

Neurotic

Places political success over effective policy	James Polk
Suffers health problems during difficult and critical	Ulysses Grant
periods in office	Martin Van Buren
Avoids the direct, uncomplicated approach	Lyndon Johnson

Lyndon Johnson

Source: Based on data from Simonton, 1988.

you?" one usually gives a reply centered, at least in part, on one's job: "I'm a secretary," "I'm a doctor," "I'm a sales representative." Further, because of long-standing beliefs about the necessity—and the virtue!—of productive work, a large majority of people experience guilt if they do not participate in such activities (Riggio, 1990).

Given the importance of work in our lives, it is hardly surprising that it, and the settings in which it occurs, have long been the subjects of study in fields ranging from engineering and architecture on the one hand through psychology and management on the other. Does social psychology have anything specific to add to those efforts? Absolutely. In fact, as we noted earlier, **industrial-organizational psychology,** the branch of psychology that seeks to investigate all aspects of behavior in work settings, has important foundations in social psychology (Murnighan, 1993). To illustrate this point, we'll point out how social psychological principles, theories, and findings have contributed to our understanding of three major topics frequently investigated by industrial-organizational psychologists: *work-related attitudes* (for example, job satisfaction), *work motivation,* and *conflict* in work settings.

WORK-RELATED ATTITUDES:
THEIR NATURE, MEASUREMENT, AND EFFECTS

Have you ever purchased a product like the one shown in Figure 14.12? We hope not! But in all probability, you *have* purchased products that suffered from one or more defects. Why were these present? Part of the answer involves faulty equipment and materials: It is impossible to make a perfect product with poor tools and supplies. Another part of the answer involves **work-related attitudes**—individuals' attitudes toward their jobs and their organizations. In chapter 4 we defined attitudes as evaluations of various objects (aspects of the world around us) that are stored in memory (Judd et al., 1991). Applying this definition to jobs and work settings, work-related attitudes involve employees' evaluations of virtually any aspect of their jobs, the settings in which they work, or the organization itself (Greenberg & Baron, 1993; Locke, 1976). Those attitudes centering on jobs have received the most research attention. For example, **job satisfaction** includes a person's cognitive, affective, and evaluative reactions to his or her job. These attitudes are important because they affect important work-related behaviors such as performance, productivity, and the tendency to look for another job. It seems reasonable to suggest that the employee who inspected the sweater shown in the cartoon had low job satisfaction: He or she did not enjoy the work and did not feel committed to inspecting each garment carefully. But please note: as we indicated in chapter 4, atti-

Work-related attitudes in action

FIGURE 14.12   When individuals have negative attitudes toward their jobs or their organization, the work they do may turn out like this!
Source: The New Yorker, 1984.

> **The items shown here are similar to those used on two popular measures of job satisfaction. (Please note: the items shown are *not* identical to ones on the actual questionnaires.)**

TABLE 14.4   Questionnaires for measuring job satisfaction

Job Description Index (JDI)		Minnesota Satisfaction Questionnaire (MSQ)
	Enter "Yes," "No," or "?" for each description or word below.	Indicate the extent to which you are satisfied with each aspect of your present job. Enter one number next to each aspect.
Work itself:	_____Routine	1 = Not at all satisfied
	_____Satisfactory	2 = Not satisfied
	_____Good	3 = Neither satisfied nor dissatisfied
		4 = Satisfied
		5 = Extremely satisfied
Promotions:	_____Dead-end job	_____Utilization of your abilities
	_____Few promotions	_____Authority
	_____Good opportunity for promotion	_____Company policies and practices
		_____Independence
		_____Supervision, human relations

tudes do not *always* predict behavior very accurately. So be ready for some surprises where the relationship between job satisfaction and job performance is concerned.

JOB SATISFACTION: HOW IT'S MEASURED.   If we view job satisfaction as a special type of attitude, then we ought to be able to measure it in much the same way as we measure other attitudes—through the use of appropriate surveys or questionnaires. In fact, several useful questionnaires for measuring job satisfaction have been developed. One very popular measure is the **Job Descriptive Index** (or JDI for short). Persons completing the JDI indicate whether various adjectives describe or do not describe a particular aspect of their work (Smith, Kendall, & Hulin, 1969). They do this by placing a *Y* for *yes,* an *N* for *no,* or a *?* for *undecided* next to each adjective. Another widely used measure of job satisfaction is the **Minnesota Satisfaction Questionnaire** (MSQ). On this instrument individuals rate the extent to which they are satisfied with various aspects of their present job. Such ratings range from *not at all satisfied* to *extremely satisfied.* Table 14.4 shows sample items from both measures.

Transparency 14.5

Other techniques for measuring job satisfaction include interviews, in which employees discuss their reactions to various aspects of their work with the interviewer, and *confrontation meetings,* in which employees are invited to "lay it on the line" by telling others about their major complaints and concerns.

FACTORS AFFECTING JOB SATISFACTION.   Large-scale surveys employing the JDI and the MSQ indicate that employees differ greatly in terms of their reported levels of job satisfaction. While most say they are quite satisfied (Quinn & Staines, 1979), some report very negative attitudes and intentions to change jobs as soon as possible. What are the bases of these contrasting reac-

Critical Thinking Question 8

Exercise 4

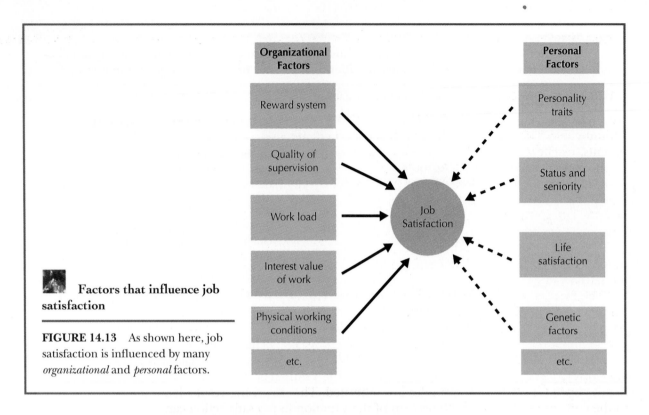

Factors that influence job satisfaction

FIGURE 14.13 As shown here, job satisfaction is influenced by many *organizational* and *personal* factors.

tions? Research indicates two major groups of factors: *organizational factors*—ones related to a company's practices and working conditions; and *personal factors*—ones related to the traits or characteristics of specific employees.

Among organizational factors, a very important one is the company's *reward system*—the way in which the company distributes raises, promotions, and other rewards. Not surprisingly, job satisfaction is higher when individuals believe that the reward system is fair and operates impartially than when they believe it is unfair and shows favoritism (Miceli & Lane, 1991). Another factor that plays an important role in job satisfaction is the *perceived quality of supervision*—the extent to which employees believe that their bosses are competent, have the employees' best interests at heart, and treat them with respect and consideration. A third organizational factor is the extent to which individuals feel that they can participate in decisions that affect them. The greater such participation, in general, the higher the reported job satisfaction.

Turning to personal factors, two important predictors of job satisfaction are status and seniority. Usually, the higher a person's position within the company, the greater the reported satisfaction. Also, the longer an individual has been on the job, the greater the satisfaction (Zeitz, 1990). In addition, certain personality traits seem to predispose individuals toward high or low levels of job satisfaction. Persons high in self-esteem (see chapter 5) report higher levels of satisfaction than those low in self-esteem. And, as you might expect, *optimists* generally report higher levels of satisfaction than *pessimists* (Greenberg & Baron, 1993).

As shown in Figure 14.13, organizational and personal factors that affect job satisfaction include most of the variables you might expect—with one exception: *genetic factors*. If you find this surprising—and we're sure that you do—please see the following **Cutting Edge** section for a further explanation.

GENETIC INFLUENCES ON JOB SATISFACTION

Do we inherit tendencies to be relatively satisfied or dissatisfied with our work? Attitudes, we pointed out in chapter 4, are learned. Depending on what our parents, teachers, and friends say and do, and depending on the preferences of our particular culture or subgroup, we acquire specific attitudes toward virtually all aspects of the social and physical world. Work-related attitudes, too, are clearly learned. They reflect our experiences at work, the views expressed by other persons in our organizations, and many other factors (Kanfer, 1993). Unexpectedly, recent evidence suggests that job satisfaction can also be affected by genetic factors. In other words, each of us may also have genetically influenced tendencies to experience relatively high or relatively low levels of job satisfaction.

The first evidence for this relationship was reported by Arvey et al. (1989). These researchers assessed the current job satisfaction reported by thirty-four pairs of identical (monozygotic) twins who had been separated at an early age and then reared apart. Because such pairs have identical genetic makeups but have undergone different life experiences (being raised in different homes), any correlation between twins' current levels of job satisfaction provides evidence suggesting that such attitudes are inherited. The surprising results led to the conclusion that about 30 percent of the variation in job satisfaction can be attributed to genetic factors.

These findings have been questioned by other investigators (e.g., Cropanzano & James, 1990), who call attention to several potential flaws in the research conducted by Arvey and his colleagues (1989). For example, identical twins represent a special sample, and it may be inappropriate to generalize results from twins to people in general. Similarly, it seems possible that the separated twins were raised in fairly similar environments. If so, estimates of the impact of genetic factors reported by Arvey et al. (1989) may be somewhat inflated. Finally, contact between the twin pairs in adulthood, as they underwent the emotion-charged experience of being reunited with a long-lost brother or sister, may have increased their attitudinal similarity.

While such criticisms can be answered only by additional research, other findings also point to the conclusion that there is in fact a genetic component in job satisfaction and other work-related attitudes. In particular, Keller and her colleagues (1992) have recently reported an investigation focused on the possible role of genetic influences on *work values*. Work values refer to the importance individuals attach to various job outcomes, and many researchers consider these values to be a key component of job satisfaction (Locke, 1969). Work values involve preferences for specific outcomes, and job satisfaction may reflect the size of the gap between what people prefer to receive from their jobs and what they are actually receiving (Kanfer, 1993).

To determine the effect of genes on work values, the Keller group asked identical and nonidentical (dizygotic) twins who had been raised apart to complete a standard measure of job values: the Minnesota Importance Questionnaire. This test measures preferences for different job-related outcomes such as achievement, status, safety, autonomy, and comfort. As shown in Figure 14.14, p. 614, the results again offered support for genetic influences in

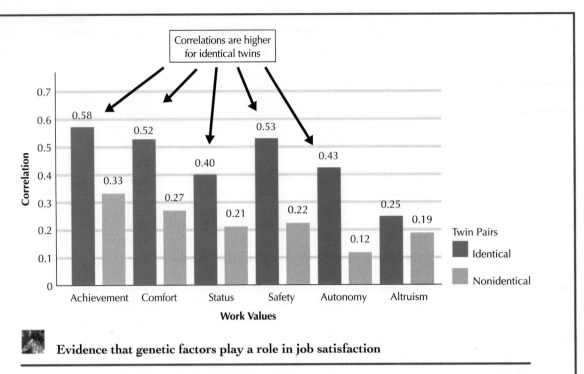

Correlations are higher
for identical twins

Evidence that genetic factors play a role in job satisfaction

FIGURE 14.14   The work values of identical twins separated early in life are more highly correlated than the work values of nonidentical twins. These findings suggest that genetic factors play a role in job satisfaction and other work-related attitudes.

Source: Based on data from Keller et al., 1992.

job satisfaction (in this instance, through work values). The correlations between the work values of identical twins were much higher than those for nonidentical twins (whose genetic makeup is not identical) on five of the six values measured; only for altruism did the difference fail to attain significance. In fact, it appeared that about 40 percent of the variance in work values could be accounted for by genetic factors.

In view of these and related findings, it seems reasonable to conclude that job satisfaction and other work-related attitudes are indeed influenced by genetics. But please note two points: (1) This influence is far from dominant; in fact, environmental factors appear to be stronger. And (2) the presence of a genetic influence does not in any sense imply that such attitudes cannot be altered. What is suggested is that genetic influences may be one of many different factors affecting job satisfaction among their employees.

JOB SATISFACTION: ITS MAJOR EFFECTS.   Attitudes often are reflected in overt actions; thus, we might expect job satisfaction to influence work-related behavior. In fact, it does; but the relationship is not a perfect one, and additional variables play a crucial role. What aspects of on-the-job behavior are influenced by job satisfaction? *Task performance,* for one. Though the relationship is weak, high levels of job satisfaction facilitate performance on many tasks to a modest degree (e.g., Miller & Monge, 1986). But we emphasize the word *modest*.

Why isn't the relationship a strong one? Shouldn't people who are happy with their jobs be more productive? Not necessarily. One reason is that many jobs actually leave little room for individual variation in performance. Individuals cannot fall below a minimum level and still retain their jobs. They also cannot exceed this minimum by much, because their work depends on what others do. Because of this limited range of possible performance, job satisfaction cannot exert a strong influence.

Another explanation for the modest role of job satisfaction is that many other factors also determine task performance; examples include working conditions, the availability of required tools and materials, and the extent to which the task is structured. For these and other reasons, job satisfaction is not always directly related to performance. Note, however, that this conclusion may hold true only for standard measures of performance such as total output or quality. Job satisfaction may be more closely linked to other aspects of work-related behavior such as helping coworkers, protecting the organization and its resources, making constructive suggestions, or praising the company to outsiders (e.g., Bateman & Organ, 1983). Together, such actions (and others) have been described as **organizational spontaneity** (George & Brief, 1992) or **organizational citizenship behavior** (Organ, 1988). These actions may contribute to the smooth and effective functioning of organizations without showing up directly in monthly summaries of output or sales.

Job satisfaction is also modestly related to employees' absenteeism from work and voluntary turnover (quitting their jobs). Again, these relationships are weak because many other factors affect these behaviors. For example, consider voluntary turnover. All things being equal, low levels of job satisfaction will, indeed, lead employees to seek another job. But consider the impact of economic conditions on this relationship. If the economy is weak and few other jobs are available, even highly dissatisfied workers will think twice about quitting their current jobs. In such instances, the relationship between job satisfaction and turnover will be very weak or even nonexistent. The findings of a study conducted by Carsten and Spector (1987) confirm this prediction. These researchers found that when unemployment rates were low, the correlation between job satisfaction and turnover was relatively high; with high unemployment, however, the relationship was much lower.

In sum, job satisfaction and other work-related attitudes do predict behavior in work settings, but the strength of this relationship depends on many other influences.

WORK MOTIVATION: GETTING PEOPLE TO DO THEIR BEST

What is the key difference between a highly successful organization and a mediocre one? Along with many other factors, one crucial difference is the **work motivation** of employees—their willingness to expend sustained effort on their jobs, carrying out their responsibilities as well and carefully as possible (Kanfer, 1990, 1993; Steers & Porter, 1989). Psychologists interested in human behavior in work settings have long been aware of this basic fact. Thus, efforts to understand the nature of work motivation, and to develop techniques for increasing it among employees, have been central to industrial-organizational psychology and related fields (Alliger & Williams, in press).

Reading: Lesko (41), *One More Time: How Do You Motivate Employees?*

Critical Thinking Question 9

On the basis of such research, several theories of work motivation have been developed. One of these—**expectancy theory**—adopts a largely cognitive approach, suggesting that people will work hard at a given job only when three conditions prevail: (1) They believe that working hard (effort) will lead to better performance (this is termed *expectancy* in the theory); (2) they believe that good performance will be recognized and rewarded (this is termed *instrumentality*); and (3) they view the rewards that can be obtained through performance to be desirable ones (termed *valence*). Many studies have tested expectancy theory (e.g., Miceli & Lane, 1991); and, in general, they confirm that the three conditions listed above are important in maintaining high levels of work motivation.

Another view, known as **goal-setting theory** (Locke & Latham, 1990), suggests that high levels of motivation occur when individuals have specific goals with respect to their jobs. The basic idea is that a goal increases motivation because it causes people to compare their present performance with the levels needed to attain the goal. If there is a gap, workers increase their effort in order to reach the levels needed for goal attainment. The theory also suggests that specific goals help to increase performance by clarifying just what levels of performance are required in a given situation. Do you set specific goals for yourself when you perform various tasks? Almost certainly you do. And you probably realize that once such goals are set, they guide your behavior and provide you with incentives for expending the effort needed to reach them. So goal-setting theory fits well with our own personal experience. A large body of research also supports the theory. This research also indicates, however, that goal setting is most effective when it follows certain guidelines, such as "set specific rather than general goals" and "set challenging goals"—goals that are difficult but still attainable. Table 14.5 gives a summary of these basic guidelines for effective goal setting.

Both expectancy theory and goal-setting theory provide valuable insights into the nature of work motivation, and both suggest techniques for increasing it. Neither, however, is directly concerned with social factors. In contrast, a

The benefits of goal setting can be maximized by adherence to the guidelines listed here.

TABLE 14.5   Goal setting: Some basic guidelines

Guidelines	Rationale
Set specific goals	General goals do *not* clarify desired levels of performance
Set difficult but attainable goals	Easy goals are not challenging; goals that are impossible to attain produce discouragement
Provide feedback about goal attainment	People want to know whether they are making progress toward their goals
Allow individuals to participate in setting goals for their work	This increases goal acceptance
Use goal setting with relatively simple tasks or ones that have clearly defined objectives	Goal setting is more effective with such tasks; it is less effective with respect to tasks where performance cannot be readily assessed (e.g., complex decisions)

third formulation, **equity theory,** focuses directly on such factors (Adams, 1965; Greenberg, 1992). In fact, this theory was developed by social psychologists interested in interpersonal relations (see chapter 8) and was applied to work motivation only after it had been studied in other settings for many years. Because of this fact, we will now discuss it in more detail.

EQUITY THEORY: PERCEIVED FAIRNESS IN WORK SETTINGS.   The central issue in equity theory is *fairness*. Briefly, the theory suggests that most people are deeply concerned with being treated fairly by others. In order to determine whether this is or is not the case, they engage in *social comparison*—they compare themselves with others. Specifically, equity theory states that people compare the ratio of their own *inputs* and *outcomes*—what they contribute to a relationship and what they receive from it—with the ratio of the inputs and outcomes of others. They perceive that the relationship is fair when these ratios are approximately equal. In other words, they perceive fairness or equity when what *they* contribute and receive is roughly in balance with what *other persons* contribute and receive. Perhaps a concrete example will help clarify this point.

Consider two employees who work in adjoining offices. One receives an annual salary of $100,000 and has a private secretary, a plush office, and a reserved parking space in the company garage. The other receives an annual salary of $40,000, shares a secretary with five other persons, and has a small, plain office and no reserved parking spot. Will the second person perceive his or her treatment as fair? According to equity theory, this depends on the person's views concerning the relative size of his or her inputs as compared to those of the coworker. If the first person has many more years' experience, has earned more degrees, and works longer hours than the second, this latter individual may conclude that fairness exists despite quite different outcomes. After all, the coworker's contributions are greater. If, instead, the first person has only a few more years' experience, possesses no additional degrees, and actually works fewer hours (or less hard), the second person will perceive that *inequity* exists—the treatment will seem unfair (refer to Figure 14.15).

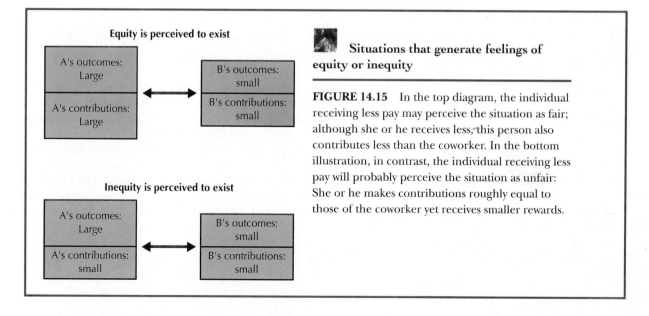

Equity is perceived to exist

A's outcomes: Large

A's contributions: Large

B's outcomes: small

B's contributions: small

Inequity is perceived to exist

A's outcomes: Large

A's contributions: small

B's outcomes: small

B's contributions: small

Situations that generate feelings of equity or inequity

FIGURE 14.15   In the top diagram, the individual receiving less pay may perceive the situation as fair; although she or he receives less, this person also contributes less than the coworker. In the bottom illustration, in contrast, the individual receiving less pay will probably perceive the situation as unfair: She or he makes contributions roughly equal to those of the coworker yet receives smaller rewards.

Please note that equity (or inequity) is largely in the eye of the beholder. Each individual makes his or her own judgment about the relative size of the outcomes and inputs of each person being compared. Thus, one person may perceive fairness where another perceives gross inequity. Unfortunately, the *self-serving bias* (see chapter 2) often leads individuals to exaggerate their own inputs while underestimating those of others. The result can be considerable friction and conflict.

As you probably know from your own experience, the feeling that one is being treated unfairly is an uncomfortable one. In such situations, equity theory predicts that individuals will attempt to eliminate these negative feelings in one of several ways. First, they can alter their inputs. If they feel *underrewarded,* they can reduce their effort. In contrast, if they feel *overrewarded* (an exceedingly rare event!), they can work harder or take over tasks from others—ones outside their job description (George & Brief, 1992). Alternatively, they can attempt to alter their outcomes. If they feel they are getting less than they deserve, it is possible to request a raise, go on strike, or seek a higher-paying job. Third, they can adopt various *psychological strategies* for dealing with feelings of inequity. These do not change the actual situation but rather alter perceptions of it. For example, they can convince themselves that others' inputs are actually greater than they initially believed or that their own outcomes are actually more valuable. This latter type of reaction is illustrated in a study by Greenberg (1989) in which employees who received a 6 percent pay cut dealt with the resulting feelings of inequity by raising their evaluation of their work environments. In other words, they convinced themselves that despite the lower pay, the situation was still fair because they worked in such pleasant surroundings. Such alterations in perceptions or beliefs permit individuals to reduce feelings of inequity without actually making concrete changes in the situation.

EQUITY THEORY AND WORK MOTIVATION.   Now that we have explained the basic nature of equity theory, we can return to the central point of this discussion: its role in work motivation. In fact, this role appears to be crucial; many studies indicate that high levels of motivation depend on the belief that one is being treated fairly. To the extent that this belief or perception is lacking, motivation will decrease. When an individual concludes that he or she is being treated very unfairly, motivation may vanish entirely (Cropanzano, 1992). A dramatic illustration of the effects of perceived unfairness is provided by a field study conducted by Greenberg (1990).

This investigation involved three different manufacturing plants. In two of the plants, poor economic conditions made it necessary to reduce employees' pay by 15 percent; in the third plant business was better, so no pay cut was necessary. In one of the two plants where a pay cut was required, employees were provided with a very complete explanation of why this serious step had to be taken (the *adequate explanation* condition), and management showed a considerable amount of concern over the cut and sympathy for the employees. In contrast, in the second plant where there was a cut in pay, employees were given only a very brief explanation of why it was done (the *inadequate explanation* condition), and management showed little concern for the hardships this would cause. Greenberg reasoned that employees in the inadequate explanation plant would experience much stronger feelings of inequity than those in the adequate explanation plant. Thus, employees in the former plant would be more likely to engage in efforts to reduce their feelings of unfairness.

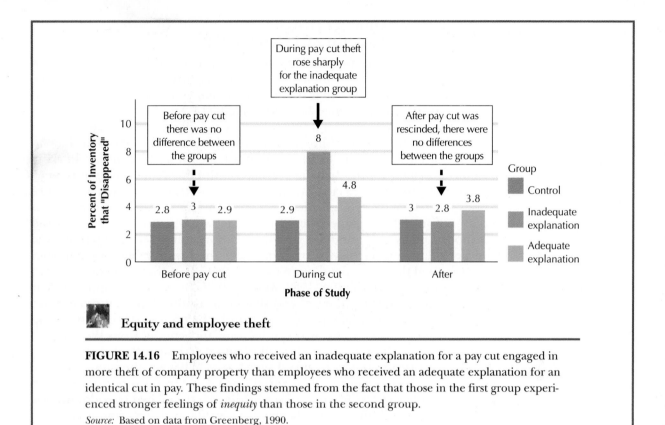

Equity and employee theft

FIGURE 14.16 Employees who received an inadequate explanation for a pay cut engaged in more theft of company property than employees who received an adequate explanation for an identical cut in pay. These findings stemmed from the fact that those in the first group experienced stronger feelings of *inequity* than those in the second group.
Source: Based on data from Greenberg, 1990.

(Those in the control plant, the plant with no pay cut, of course, would have no reason for experiencing inequity.) While efforts to reduce the discomfort of inequity can take many different forms, Greenberg used an unusual and ingenious measure in this research: the amount of theft of company tools, supplies, equipment, and products by employees. It was predicted that such theft would be greater in the plant getting an inadequate explanation than in the other two plants. As shown in Figure 14.16, this is precisely what happened. After the pay cut was instituted, theft rates (the percentage of inventory that simply disappeared) rose dramatically at the inadequate explanation plant. They rose much less at the adequate explanation plant and did not rise at all at the control (no pay cut) plant. Later, when economic conditions improved, the pay cuts were rescinded. As you can see in the figure, this led to a reduction in thefts.

These findings and those of many other studies (Greenberg, 1989, 1992) suggest that feelings of inequity produce large decrements in work motivation. Indeed, such effects have even been observed among major league baseball players (Bretz & Thomas, 1992): Those who lose when salary disputes go to arbitration experience stronger feelings of inequity and show larger declines in performance than those who win in arbitration. In sum, it appears that equity theory is a very useful framework for understanding work motivation. Because this framework was first developed by social psychologists, it is clear that this is one way in which the field of social psychology has provided important insights into the factors affecting human behavior in work settings.

CONFLICT IN WORK SETTINGS:
A SOCIAL PSYCHOLOGICAL PERSPECTIVE

Critical Thinking
Question 10

In several important respects, all employees working in the same organization are interdependent. They often must depend on each other in order to be able to perform their jobs; they frequently share information, equipment, and materials; and their individual fates are linked, at least to a degree, to the fortunes of their organization. If it prospers, they can all share in a growing pie. If it fails, their individual outcomes may be sharply reduced or may even come to an end. Given these basic facts, one might expect that *cooperation*—working together to attain various benefits—would be the dominant mode of interaction in work settings. In fact, however, this is often not the case. Instead of working together in a coordinated fashion, individuals and groups in a given organization often engage in **conflict**—they work against each other and attempt to block one another's interests. Unfortunately, such **organizational conflict** is far from rare. In surveys managers in a wide range of companies have reported that they spend more than 20 percent of their time dealing with conflict and its effects (Baron, 1989; Kilmann & Thomas, 1977). And it is clear that the smoldering resentments and shattered relationships that often result from intense conflicts may persist for months or even years, continuing to exact a major toll in terms of precious time and energy from the persons involved. At the present time, when international competition in business is intense, few organizations can afford such losses. What are the causes of these conflicts? And what steps can organizations take to reduce both the occurrence of conflict and its harmful effects? Research stimulated by social psychological theories and findings has begun to provide intriguing—and practical—answers to these questions (e.g., Rahim, 1990; Thomas, 1992).

THE CAUSES OF CONFLICT AT WORK: ORGANIZATIONAL AND INTERPERSONAL.   If we asked a large number of executives to describe the factors that contribute to conflict in their organizations, the chances are good that most would cite what have been described as *organizational causes* of conflict (e.g., Baron, 1993). That is, they would describe factors such as the ones summarized on the left side of Figure 14.17—causes relating to the structure and functioning of their companies, such as *competition over scarce resources* or *ambiguity over responsibility or jurisdiction* (uncertainty about who's in charge and who is responsible for various actions or outcomes). Such answers reflect a traditional approach to organizational conflict, the approach that dominated the study of this topic in the past.

Discussion Question 4

More recently, however, another perspective—one deriving directly from social psychology—has emerged. According to this point of view, conflict in work settings, like conflict in many other contexts, stems at least in part from *interpersonal factors*—factors related to individuals, their social relationships, and the ways in which they think about others (e.g., Baron, 1990; Hammock & Richardson, 1992; Kabanoff, 1991). As shown on the right side of Figure 14.17, such factors include anger, stereotypes, prejudice, the belief that one has been treated unfairly, faulty styles of interpersonal communication, lasting grudges produced by "loss of face," and many others.

As an example of such research, consider several studies concerned with the possibility that conflict often stems from or is intensified by *faulty attributions*—errors about the causes of other people's behavior. When individuals find that their interests are being thwarted by another person—in other words,

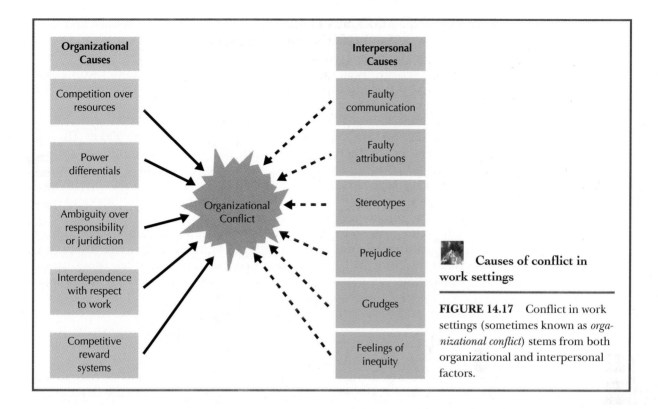

Organizational Causes		Interpersonal Causes
Competition over resources		Faulty communication
Power differentials		Faulty attributions
Ambiguity over responsibility or juridiction	Organizational Conflict	Stereotypes
Interdependence with respect to work		Prejudice
Competitive reward systems		Grudges
		Feelings of inequity

Causes of conflict in work settings

FIGURE 14.17 Conflict in work settings (sometimes known as *organizational conflict*) stems from both organizational and interpersonal factors.

when conditions are ripe for conflict—they generally try to determine *why* this person acted in a provocative manner. Was it malevolence—a desire to harm them? Or did the provoker's actions stem from factors beyond his or her control? A growing body of evidence suggests that when people reach the former conclusion, anger and subsequent conflict are more likely and more intense than when they reach the latter conclusion (e.g., Bies, Shapiro, & Cummings, 1988; Shapiro, Buttner, & Barry, 1993). For example, in one study on this issue, Baron (1988) had students engage in simulated negotiations with another person (actually an accomplice). Both individuals played the role of executives representing different departments within a large organization: They bargained over the division of $1,000,000 in surplus funds. The accomplice adopted a very confrontational stance, demanding fully $800,000 out of the $1,000,000 for his or her own department, and offered only two small concessions during the negotiations. As the bargaining proceeded, the accomplice made several statements indicating that he or she had either chosen to behave in this "tough" manner simply because this was a personal preference (an *internal* cause) or been ordered to act in this manner by his or her constituents (an *external* cause). Another aspect of the study involved apparent sincerity; half of the subjects who heard the accomplice claim that he or she had been "ordered" to adopt a tough bargaining stance received information suggesting that these statements were accurate (the accomplice appeared sincere), and the others received information suggesting that the accomplice had lied.

Results indicated that information about the causes behind the accomplice's behavior exerted strong effects on the participants' reactions to this person. As expected, the most favorable reactions to the accomplice and more conciliatory responses occurred when the accomplice's provocative actions appeared to stem from direct orders. In contrast, negative reactions and non-conciliatory responses were elicited by an accomplice whose behavior stemmed from his or her own preferences or when that person had apparently lied about receiving tough orders. These and related findings offer strong support for the view that interpersonal factors such as attributions often play a key role in the occurrence and intensity of organizational conflict.

ORGANIZATIONAL CONFLICT: REDUCING ITS ADVERSE EFFECTS.   As we noted earlier, conflict is often a costly process for both individuals and organizations. Thus, it seems important to develop practical techniques for reducing its negative effects. Many different procedures for attaining this goal have been developed, and several of them rest firmly on the findings and principles of social psychology.

Perhaps the most widely used procedure for resolving conflicts, and therefore for heading off their adverse effects, is **bargaining** (e.g., Sheppard, Bazerman, & Lewicki, 1990). In this process opposing sides to a dispute exchange offers, counteroffers, and concessions, either directly or through representatives. If the process is successful, a solution acceptable to both sides is attained, and the conflict is effectively resolved. If, instead, bargaining is unsuccessful, a costly deadlock may result, intensifying the conflict. What factors or conditions help tip the balance toward favorable outcomes? Several decades of research on this issue have yielded some interesting results.

One group of factors that strongly affects the outcomes of bargaining involves the tactics adopted by each side. Many of these tactics are designed to reduce opponents' aspirations—to convince them that they have little chance of reaching their goals and should instead accept offers that are quite favorable to the side proposing them. Among the specific strategies used for this purpose are the suggestion by one side that it has an "out" (another potential partner with whom to make a deal) and the *big lie* technique—claims that one's break-even point is much lower than it really is. A third tactic often used by bargainers to tip the balance in their favor involves "tough" or extreme initial offers. Relatively extreme offers seem to put strong pressure on opponents to make concessions and, as we noted in chapter 12, may serve as cognitive anchors for counteroffers by the opposing side. (This is another form of the door-in-the-face technique descriped in chapter 9.)

A second group of factors that determine the nature and outcomes of bargaining involves the perceptions of the persons involved in the process. Studies by Thompson and her colleagues reveal that negotiators often enter bargaining situations with important misperceptions about the situation (Thompson, 1990; Thompson & Hastie, 1990). In particular, they seem to begin with the view that their own interests and those of the other side are totally incompatible—the **incompatibility error.** This causes them to overlook interests that are actually compatible. Recent findings suggest that the incompatibility error stems from the tendency of negotiators to perceive falsely that the quantity of available outcomes is fixed and that they must seize the largest possible share of this amount (Thompson, 1993).

Another common misperception in bargaining is the belief by each side that the other party places the same importance or priority on each issue. Such assumptions prevent the negotiators from engaging in *logrolling,* a process in which each side makes concessions on the issues of less importance to it, with the result that a mutually satisfactory agreement emerges.

Fortunately, these misperceptions concerning interests and priorities tend to fade over the course of negotiations—often within the first few minutes (Thompson & Hastie, 1990). Also, experienced negotiators are less likely to fall prey to such errors than inexperienced ones (Thompson, 1990). Finally, these perceptual errors can also be overcome by feedback about an opponent's interests and outcomes, although such feedback must be quite complete to be helpful (Thompson & DeHarpport, 1993). Still, many negotiators retain these false perceptions even over prolonged periods of bargaining, with the result that both sides obtain outcomes less favorable than would otherwise be true. These findings suggest that steps designed to increase the accuracy of negotiators' perceptions could go a long way toward improving the process. Such steps might include training negotiators to seek information from each other during negotiations (instead of clinging to their initial assumptions) and increasing negotiators' awareness of perceptual errors.

Perhaps the single most important factor determining the success of negotiations involves participants' overall orientation toward this process. As noted by many negotiation experts, one can approach bargaining either from the perspective of a "win-lose" (*distributive*) situation, in which gains by one side mean losses for the other—or from the perspective of a "win-win" (*integrative*) situation, in which the potential gains of both sides can be maximized (Pruitt et al., 1983). Not all situations offer the potential for win-win agreements; but even when direct head-on clashes seem inevitable, more positive possibilities may exist. If participants are willing to explore all options carefully and exert the effort required to identify creative potential solutions, they can frequently obtain greater benefits than those yielded by simple compromise.

Two other techniques for resolving conflicts rest firmly on social psychological foundations. One involves the induction of **superordinate goals**—goals that tie the interests of the two sides together. As we noted in chapter 6, one important basis for prejudice (and, often, of conflict) is the tendency to divide the world into two opposing camps: *us* and *them*. One means of countering this tendency is to identify goals shared by the two groups. Once two parties focus on common goals and objectives, the barriers between them tend to dissolve, enhancing the chances of cooperation rather than conflict (Sherif et al., 1961).

Another technique for reducing conflict employs procedures found to be effective in reducing aggression (e.g., Baron, 1984; Baron et al., 1990). As noted by Hammock and Richardson (1992), aggression and conflict are related; in fact, aggression represents one specific reaction to intense conflicts. One technique that reduces aggression is the *incompatible response strategy* (Baron & Richardson, 1994). As you may recall from chapter 11, the incompatible response strategy involves exposing angry individuals to conditions that create reactions or emotional states incompatible with anger and overt aggression. Examples include empathy, mild sexual arousal, or feelings of amusement (Baron, 1983, 1993). Applying this strategy to conflict reduction, Baron et al. (1990) exposed individuals who had previously been angered by an accomplice either to no additional manipulation (the control group) or to various treatments designed to induce positive feelings. In three different conditions, participants either received a small gift (cherry Life Savers), were flattered by the accomplice, or heard the accomplice make mildly self-disparaging remarks.

Following these events, participants rated their preferences for resolving future conflicts with the accomplice in each of five different ways: through

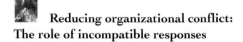
**Reducing organizational conflict:
The role of incompatible responses**

FIGURE 14.18 Male subjects exposed to treatments designed to induce positive reactions incompatible with anger and annoyance expressed stronger preferences for resolving future conflicts through collaboration (active problem solving) than males not exposed to such incompatible response–generating treatments.

Source: Baron et al., 1990.

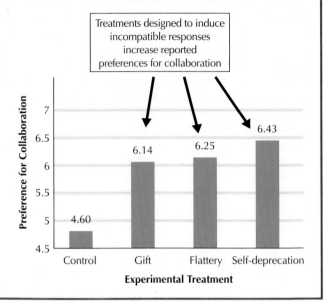

avoidance, compromise, collaboration, competition, or *accommodation.* Results indicated that male participants exposed to a gift, flattery, or self-deprecation from the accomplice reported stronger preferences for resolving conflict through collaboration than those in the control condition (see Figure 14.18). Similar findings were not obtained for female participants, because they preferred conciliatory approaches to resolve conflicts in all conditions.

In sum, the findings, principles, and theories of social psychology have suggested several useful techniques for reducing or resolving conflicts. In this respect, as in many others, our field has made valuable contributions to understanding human behavior in organizational settings and to making such environments more pleasant and more productive places in which to work.

Work in Progress

Pleasant Working Conditions: Another Means for Reducing Conflict?

Nearly everyone wants to work in pleasant surroundings. Comfortable temperatures, good lighting, clean air, attractive furnishings: These are conditions most white-collar employees—and many blue-collar workers, too—expect at work. And most companies do try to provide such conditions, at least to the extent this is economically feasible. The main reason behind companies' efforts to make employees comfortable is clear: A large body of evidence indicates that *unpleasant* working conditions can reduce performance and productivity (e.g.,

Baron, in press; Sundstrom & Sundstrom, 1986). But recent findings suggest that there may be another benefit to such conditions, as well: Comfortable physical working conditions may also help to reduce organizational conflict!

Several studies demonstrating such effects have been reported. For example, in one of these (Baron, Rea, & Daniels, 1992), participants reported stronger tendencies to resolve conflicts with others through compromise or collaboration, and weaker tendencies to resolve conflicts through competition or avoidance, when they worked in the presence of low levels of warm-white light than when they worked under levels of cool-white light. (Warm-white light is shifted toward the red/yellow end of the spectrum; cool-white light is shifted toward the blue/green end.) In another recent investigation (Baron & Thomley, 1993), individuals expressed greater willingness to work cooperatively with others and were actually more helpful in the presence of pleasant fragrances (lemon or light floral) than in the absence of such fragrances.

How can pleasant physical conditions in work environments help to reduce conflict? One possibility involves the fact that such conditions induce *positive affect* among the persons involved. As we have noted in numerous other chapters, positive feelings often exert strong effects on aspects of cognition and behavior. For example, they can reduce anger, help bring positive thoughts to mind, induce attraction, and increase helpfulness. In view of these findings, it is not surprising that pleasant working conditions can also contribute to the reduction of organizational conflict. To put it simply, when people feel good—happy, comfortable, relaxed—they often adopt a cooperative, conciliatory approach to others. The result? The likelihood of conflict drops sharply.

The democratic goal is to permit each citizen to have a voice in government on the basis of being able to vote on candidates and, in many instances, on specific issues. Though people have literally fought and died for this right, many individuals who have the vote fail to exercise it, as discussed in the following **Social Diversity** section.

Critical Thinking
Question 6

Exercise 5

Social Diversity ▼ *A Critical Analysis*

Voting Rights, Voter Apathy, and Voter Preferences: Effects of Sex, Class, Race, and Age in the United States and the United Kingdom

Even when the general goal of democracy is embraced by government, there are usually restrictions on who can vote. For example, in the United States the original voters were white men (age twenty-one or older) who owned property. Other groups—women, slaves, non-landowners—were excluded. The struggle to broaden the franchise has included such historic steps as women's suffrage, the emancipation of slaves, federal protection of civil rights, the abolition of class-based restric-

tions such as the poll tax, and the lowering of the voting age from twenty-one to eighteen.

Once the right to vote has been obtained, however, not everyone votes. Why are some individuals politically active while others are not? In general elections in the United Kingdom, almost a third of the electorate do not vote. Fife-Schaw and Breakwell (1990) compared voters and nonvoters from samples in England and Scotland. One of their findings was that women were less likely

to vote than men. The best predictors of nonvoting, however, were cynicism about politics and politicians and a lack of educational attainment. The investigators concluded that the typical nonvoter does not trust politicians *and* has difficulty in comprehending political issues, finding them to be too abstract and difficult.

In the United States, only about half of those who can vote actually do so. Among eighteen-to twenty-one-year-olds, two-thirds did not participate in the

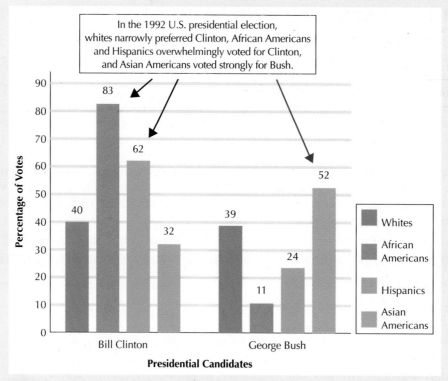

In the 1992 U.S. presidential election, whites narrowly preferred Clinton, African Americans and Hispanics overwhelmingly voted for Clinton, and Asian Americans voted strongly for Bush.

Presidential choices in 1992 as a function of ethnic group

FIGURE 14.19   In the U.S. presidential election in 1992, preferences differed greatly on the basis of ethnic group. Whites split almost evenly between George Bush and Bill Clinton, African-Americans and Hispanics gave Clinton a large majority, and Asian-Americans clearly preferred Bush. Among voters whose racial/ethnic group did not fit any of those four categories, Clinton was preferred by 60 percent to 26 percent. For each group, H. Ross Perot was third in the number of votes received.
Source: Based on data in Barrett, 1992.

1988 presidential election (Simpson, 1992). The importance of such figures becomes clear when you realize that the outcome of an election can be greatly affected by who participates. In the 1992 presidential election, for example, women favored Clinton over Bush more strongly than men did, and Clinton's strongest support was among voters aged twenty-four and under *and* those aged sixty and over (Barrett, 1992). In addition, socioeconomic differences in voting preferences were also apparent. In 1992 Clinton received just 38 percent of the vote among those whose annual earnings were $100,000 or more, but 53 percent of the vote among those making $20,000 or less (McLeod, 1993).

Even more striking is the fact that different racial/ethnic subgroups vote quite differently, as shown in Figure 14.19. Among white voters, Bill Clinton and George Bush ran about even. Among African-American and Hispanic voters, Clinton was an overwhelming winner, but among Asian-Americans Bush won easily. Thus, when any segment of the population (based on sex, age, income, or ethnicity) actively participates or fails to do so, the final electoral decision is potentially at stake.

Summary and Review

The findings and principles of social psychology have been applied to many of our social institutions and have provided a better understanding of how these institutions function and how they can be improved.

The Legal System

Forensic psychology has produced ample evidence that the reality of our legal system often does not live up to its ideals. Witnesses and defendants are influenced by interrogation procedures and pretrial media publicity. Eyewitness testimony is often inaccurate, and the behavior of attorneys and judges can influence verdicts. Jurors respond in part on the basis of cognitive reinterpretations of the evidence and on emotional biases for and against specific defendants.

The Political Process

The electoral process is a crucial aspect of a democratic society, but political behavior is determined by psychological factors. Political attitudes often fall along a continuum ranging from *liberalism* to *conservatism,* and we tend to develop such attitudes in response to whatever constitutes our reference group. Research has concentrated on the effects of the media and on the determinants of political activism. Political choices are affected by one's attraction toward the competing candidates, and voting is influenced by such familiar variables as *repeated exposure, affect, overt characteristics,* and *similarity.* In addition to liking, voters make electoral choices on the basis of their perceptions as to who possesses the best qualities of *leadership.* These include drive, intelligence, honesty, and self-confidence. *Leadership style* is also important, especially in difficult times when *transformational leadership* is highly valued.

Work Settings

The principles of social psychology have been applied to the understanding of behavior in work settings, especially within the field of *industrial-organizational psychology. Work-related attitudes* include employees' evaluations of their jobs (job satisfaction) and of their organizations. Research has emphasized the determinants and the consequences of these attitudes. *Work motivation* is influenced by cognitive factors, the outcomes of performance, and the perception of *inequity.* A common problem in organizations is *conflict,* and psychologists have identified both organizational causes, such as competition over scarce resources, and interpersonal causes, such as stereotypes, prejudices, grudges, and ineffective communication styles. Organizational conflicts can be reduced or resolved by such techniques as *bargaining, superordinate goals,* and the induction of responses *incompatible* with anger and conflict.

Social Diversity: Voting Preferences

The right to vote is essential to democracy, but many people do not take part in the election process for reasons ranging from apathy to distrust of politicians. Because different subgroups of the population (based on factors such as sex, age, socioeconomic class, and ethnicity) differ in their voting preferences, differential participation in elections by such groups can clearly affect the final decision.

Key Terms

Bargaining A process in which two or more parties in a dispute exchange offers, counteroffers, and concessions in an effort to attain a mutually acceptable agreement.

Conflict The process set in motion when individuals or groups perceive that others have taken or will soon take actions incompatible with their own interests. Conflict involves awareness of opposing interests, the thoughts and emotions of all involved parties, and the parties' strategies, intentions, and overt actions.

Conservatism A political philosophy based on the desire to preserve the social order in its present form or (if changes have occurred) to return it to its previous state.

Equity Theory A theory suggesting that individuals strive to maintain rough equivalence between the ratio of their own contributions and outcomes in a relationship and the ratio of others' contributions and outcomes.

Expectancy Theory A theory suggesting that work motivation is based on people's beliefs about the probability that effort will lead to improved performance, that good performance will be recognized and rewarded, and that the rewards offered are ones they want.

Forensic Psychology Psychology as it relates to aspects of legal proceedings and the law, including eyewitness reliability and issues involving the police, the media, attorneys, judges, defendants, victims, plaintiffs, and jurors.

Goal-Setting Theory A theory suggesting that motivation is enhanced if individuals are provided with specific, challenging goals.

Incompatibility Error the perception on the part of bargainers that their own interests and those of the other side are completely incompatible.

Industrial-Organizational Psychology The branch of psychology that investigates all aspects of behavior in work settings.

Job Satisfaction The attitudes held by individuals about their jobs, ranging from extremely positive to extremely negative.

Job Description Index A popular questionnaire for measuring job satisfaction (JDI for short).

Jury Nullification Rights Information provided by the judge letting jurors know of their right to disregard all instructions and to use their own judgments as the basis for making decisions.

Leading Questions Questions (asked of witnesses by the police or by attorneys) that are worded so as to suggest answers. These questions can provide information that is inconsistent with what the witness actually observed.

Leniency Bias A general bias among jurors that leads them to tend to sympathize with and favor the defendant.

Liberalism A political philosophy based on the desire to modify political, social, and economic institutions to promote the rights of individuals and the assurance of civil liberties.

Minnesota Satisfaction Questionnaire A widely used questionnaire for measuring job satisfaction (MSQ for short).

Organizational Citizenship Behavior Voluntary behaviors by individuals that aid their organizations and that are not related to the formal reward system or their formal job descriptions.

Organizational Conflict Conflict occurring in work settings. (See also *Conflict*.)

Organizational Spontaneity Voluntary acts by individuals that facilitate the accomplishment of organizational goals. These actions include ones that are recognized by the formal reward system as well as actions that fall outside this system.

Superordinate Goals Goals shared by the parties in a conflict or dispute.

Work Motivation Willingness to expend sustained effort on a task or job.

Work-Related Attitudes Attitudes pertaining to jobs or organizations

Questions from page 587:

What do you think happened? How many vehicles were at the scene? Were there people present? Male or female? What were the road conditions? What type of rescue apparatus was available? What color vehicles were in the photo? What directions were the vehicles facing?

For More Information

Greenberg, J., & Baron, R. A. (1993). *Behavior in organizations* (4th ed.). Boston: Allyn & Bacon.

A broad introduction to many aspects of behavior in work settings. Many of the topics covered are closely related to the topics covered in this chapter and to the interests of social psychologists.

Hentoff, N. (1992). *Free speech for me—but not for thee.* New York: HarperCollins.

In this readable and often amusing book about political censorship, the author provides abundant evidence that conservatives, liberals, and just about everyone else favor free speech, as long as they agree with what is being said. Most people seem to feel that views dissimilar to their own should not be given free expression.

Milburn, M.A. (1991). *The social psychology of public opinion.* Pacific Grove, CA: Brooks/Cole.

The author applies theories and research from various areas of psychology (particularly social psychology) to questions of how and why people hold opinions about politics and about specific political issues. Also examined is the role of the mass media in influencing political opinions and reasoning.

Wrightsman, L. S. (1991). *Psychology and the legal system.* Pacific Grove, CA: Brooks/Cole.

This volume uses psychological concepts to examine the legal system and is useful for students of law and psychology. It is meant to serve as a bridge between social science issues and methods on the one hand and the law and criminal justice system on the other. Topics include moral judgment, children's rights, and psychologists' role in the legal system.

References

Abramson, L. Y., Metasky, G. I., & Alloy, L. B. (1990). The hopelessness theory of depression: Does the research test the theory? In L. Y. Abramson (Ed.), *Social cognition and clinical psychology: A synthesis*. New York: Guilford Press.

Acitelli, L. HI (1992). Gender differences in relationship awareness and marital satisfaction among young married couples. *Personality and Social Psychology Bulletin, 18,* 102–110.

Adams, J. S. (1965). Inequity in social exchange. In L. Berkowitz (Ed.), *Advances in experimental social psychology* (Vol. 2, pp. 267–299). New York: Academic Press.

Adatto, K. (1990). The incredible shrinking sound bite. *New Republic, 202*(22), 20–23.

Ader, R., & Cohen, N. (1993). Psychoneuroimmunology: Conditioning and stress. In L. W. Porter & M. R. Rosenzweig (Eds.), *Annual review of psychology* (Vol. 44, pp. 53–85). Palo Alto, CA: Annual Reviews, Inc.

Adler, V. (1988, November). Heart votes. *Psychology Today,* pp. 61, 64.

Adorno, T. W., Frenkel–Brunswick, E., Levinson, D. J., & Sanford, R. H. (1950). *The authoritarian personality*. New York: Harper & Row.

Affleck, G., Tennen, H., Pfeiffer, C., & Fifield, J. (1987). Appraisals of control and predictability in adapting to a chronic disease. *Journal of Personality and Social Psychology,* 53, 273–279.

AIDS will claim 330,000 by 1995, U. S. projects. (1993, January 15). *Albany Times Union,* p. A–12.

Aird, J. S. (1990). Slaughter of the innocents: Coercive birth control in China. Washington, DC: AEI Press.

Alagna, F. J., Whitcher, S. J., & Fisher, J. D. (1979). Evaluative reactions to interpersonal touch in a counseling interview. *Journal of Counseling Psychology, 26,* 465–472.

Alberts, J. K. (1988). An analysis of couples' conversational complaints. *Communication Monographs, 55,* 184–197.

Albright, L., Kenny, D. A., & Malloy, T. E. (1988). Consensus in personality judgments at zero acquaintance. *Journal of Personality and Social Psychology, 55,* 387–395.

Alden, L. (1986). Self–efficacy and causal attributions for social feedback. *Journal of Research in Personality,* 20, 460–473.

Alicke, M. D., Braun, J. C., Glor, J. E., Klotz, N. L., Nagee, J., Sederhold, H., & Siegel, R. (1992). Complaining behavior in social interaction. *Personality and Social Psychology Bulletin, 18,* 286–29S.

Allen, V. L., & Levine, J. M. (1971). Social support and conformity: The role of independent assessment of reality. *Journal of Experimental Social Psychology, 4,* 48–58.

Alliger, G. M., & Williams, K. J. (1991). Affective congruence and the employment interview. *Advances in Information Processing in Organizations, 4,* 31–43.

Allison, S. T., Worth, L. T., & King, M. C. (1990). Group deci-

sions as social inference heuristics. *Journal of Personality and Social Psychology, 58,* 801–811.

Alloy, L. B., & Abramson, L. Y., & Dykman, B. M. (1990). Depressive realism and nondepressive optimistic illusions: The role of the self. In R. E. Ingram (Ed.), *Contemporary psychological approaches to depression: Treatment, research and theory*. New York: Plenum Press.

Allport, G. W. (1985). Attitudes. In C. Murchison (Ed.), *Handbook of social psychology*. Worcester, MA: Clark University Press.

Allport, T. N. (1924). *Social psychology*. Boston: Houghton Mifflin.

Allred, K. D., & Smith, T. W. (1989). The hardy personality: Cognitive and physiological responses to evaluative threat. *Journal of Personality and Social Psychology, 56,* 257–266.

Alwin, D. F., Cohen, R. L., & Newcomb, T. N. (1991). *Personality and social change: Attitude persistence and changes over the lifespan*. Madison: University of Wisconsin Press.

Ambrosio, A. L., & Sheehan, E. P. (1991). The just world belief and the AIDS epidemic. *Journal of Social Behavior and Personality, 6,* 163–170.

Anderson, C. A. (1987). Temperature and aggression: Effects on quarterly, yearly, and city rates of violent and nonviolent crime. *Journal of Personality and Social Psychology, 46,* 91–97.

Anderson, C. A. (1989). Temperature and aggression: The ubiquitous effects of heat on the occurrence of human violence. *Psychological Bulletin, 106,* 74–96.

Anderson, C. A., & Anderson, D. C. (1984). Ambient temperature and violent crime: Tests of the linear and curvilinear hypotheses. *Journal of Personality and Social Psychology, 46,* 91–97.

Anderson, C. A., & DeNeve, K. M. (1992). Temperature, aggression, and the negative affect escape model. *Psychological Bulletin, 111,* 347–351.

Anderson, C. A., & Sedikides, C. (1991). Thinking about people: Contributions of a topological alternative to associationistic and dimensional models of person perception. *Journal of Personality and Social Psychology, 60,* 203–217.

Anderson, J. L. (1989). A methodological critique of the evidence for genetic similarity detection. *Behavioral and Brain Sciences, 12,* 518–519.

Anderson, N. H. (1981). *Foundations of information interaction theory*. New York: Academic Press.

Angier, N. (1993, February 2). Cellular phone scare discounted. *New York Times,* pp. C1, C3.

Anstett, P. (1992, December 8). Why is it harder for women to quit smoking, scientists ask. *Albany Times Union,* p. B–1.

Anthony, T., Cooper, C., & Mullen, B. (1992). Cross–racial identification: A social cognitive integration. *Personality and Social Psychology Bulletin, 18,* 296–301.

Archer, J. (1991). Human sociobiology: Basic concepts and limitations. *Journal of Social Issues, 47*(3), 11–26.

Archer, R. L. (1984). The farmer and the cowman should be friends: An attempt at reconciliation with Batson, Coke, and Psych. J*ournal of Personality and Social Psychology, 46,* 709–711.

Ardrey, R. (1976). *The hunting hypothesis.* New York: Atheneum.

Arkin, R. M., Lake, E. A., & Baumgardner, A. B. (1986). Shyness and self–presentation In W. H. Jones, J. M. Cheek, & R. Briggs (Eds.), *Shyness: Perspective on research and treatment* (pp. 189–203). New York: Plenum.

Arkin, R. M., & Baumgardner, A. H. (1985). Self–handicapping. In J. H. Harvey & G. W. Weary (Eds.), *Attribution: Basic issues and applications* (pp. 169–202). Orlando, FL: Academic Press.

Aron, A. (1993, February). Personal communication.

Aron, A., Aron, E. N., & Smollan, D. (1992). Inclusion of other in the Self Scale and the structure of interpersonal closeness. *Journal of Personality and Social Psychology, 63,* 596–612.

Aron, A., Dutton, D. G., Aron, E. N., & Iverson, A. (1989). Experiences of falling in love. *Journal of Social and Personal Relationships, 6,* 243–257.

Aronoff, J., Woike, B. A., & Hyman, L. M. (1992). Which are the stimuli in facial displays of anger and happiness? Configurational bases of emotion recognition. *Journal of Personality and Social Psychology, 62,* 1050–1066.

Aronson, E., Bridgeman, D. L., & Oeffner, R. (1978). Interdependent interactions and prosocial behavior. *Journal of Research and Development in Education, 12,* 16–27.

Aronson, E., Fried, C. T., & Stone, J. (1991). Overcoming denial: Increasing the intention to use condoms through the induction of hypocrisy. *American Journal of Public Health, 18,* 1636–1640.

Aronson, E., & O'Leary, M. (1983). The relative effectiveness of models and prompts on energy conservation: A field experiment in a shower room. *Journal of Environmental Systems, 12,* 219–224.

Arvey, R. D., Bouchard, T. J., Jr., Segal, N. L., & Abraham, L. M. (1989). Job satisfaction: Genetic and environmental components. *Journal of Applied Psychology, 74,* 187–192.

Arvey, R. D., & Campion, J. E. (1982). The employment interview: A summary and review of recent research. *Personnel Psychology, 35,* 281–322.

Asante, M. K. (1980). *Afrocentricity: The theory of social change.* Buffalo, NY: Amulefi Publishing Company.

Asch, S. E. (1946). Forming impressions of personality. *Journal of Abnormal and Social Psychology, 41,* 258–290.

Asch, S. E. (1951). Effects of group pressure upon the modification and distortion of judgment. In H. Guetzkow (Ed.), *Groups, leadership, and men.* Pittsburgh, PA: Carnegie.

Asch, S. E. (1957). An experimental investigation of group influence. In *Symposium on preventive and social psychiatry,* 15–17. Walter Reed Army Institute of Research, Washington, DC: U. S. Government Printing Office.

Asendorpf, J. B. (1989). Shyness as a final common pathway for two different kinds of inhibition. *Journal of Personality and Social Psychology, 57,* 481–492.

Asendorpf, J. B. (1992). A Brunswickean approach to trait continuity: Application to shyness. *Journal of Personality, 60,* 55–77.

Averill, J. R., & Boothroyd, P. (1977). On falling in love: Conformance with romantic ideal. *Motivation and Emotion, 1,* 235–247.

Axsom, D., Yates, S., & Chaiken, S. (1987). Audience response to a heuristic cue in persuasion. *Journal of Personality and Social Psychology, 53,* 30–40.

Baker, R. L., & Mednick, B. R. (1984). *Influences on human development: A longitudinal perspective.* Boston: Kluwer–Hijhofff Publishing

Bandura, A. (1973). *Aggression: A social learning analysis.* Englewood Cliffs, NJ: Prentice–Hall.

Bandura, A. (1977). Self–efficacy: Toward a unifying theory of behavior change. *Psychological Review, 84,* 191–215.

Bandura, A. (1986). *Social foundations of thought and action: A social cognitive theory.* Englewood Cliffs, NJ: Prentice–Hall.

Bandura, A. (1986). The explanatory and predictive scope of self–efficacy theory. *Journal of Social and Clinical Psychology, 4,* 359–373.

Bandura, A., & Adams, N. E. (1977). Analysis of self–efficacy theory of behavioral change. *Cognitive Therapy and Research, 1,* 287–310.

Bandura, A., Adams, N. E., & Hardy, A. B. (1980). Tests of the generality of self–efficacy theory. *Cognitive Theory and Research, 4,* 39–66.

Bandura, A., Cioffi, D., Taylor, C. B., & Brouillard, M. E. (1988). Perceived self–efficacy in coping with cognitive stressors and opioid activation. *Journal of Personality and Social Psychology, 55,* 479–488.

Bandura, A., Ross, D., & Ross, S. (1963). Imitation of film–mediated aggressive models. *Journal of Abnormal and Social Psychology, 66,* 3–11.

Banner, L. W. (1983). *American beauty.* New York: Knopf.

Bargh, J. A. (1989). Conditional automaticity: Varieties of automatic inference in social perception and cognition. In J. S. Uleman & J. A. Bargh (Eds.), *Unintended thought* (pp. 3–51). New York: Guilford.

Bargh, J. A., Chaiken, S., Covender, R., & Pratto, F. (1992). The generality of the automatic attitude activation effect. *Journal of Personality and Social Psychology, 62,* 893–912.

Bargh, J. A., & Pietromonaco, P. (1982). Automatic information processing and social perception: The influence of trait information presented outside of conscious awareness on impression formation. *Journal of Personality and Social Psychology, 43,* 437–449.

Barnes, F. (1989). Fearless leader. *New Republic, 201*(22), 11–13.

Barnett, R. C., Marshall, N. L., & Singer, J. D. (1992). Job experiences over time, multiple roles, and women's mental health: A longitudinal study. *Journal of Personality and Social Psychology, 62,* 634–644.

Bar–On, D. (1987). Causal attributions and the rehabilitation of myocardial infarction victims. *Journal of Social and Clinical Psychology, 5,* 114–122.

Baron, R. A., & Bell, P. A. (1976). Aggression and heat: The influence of ambient temperature, negative affect, and a cooling drink in physical aggression. J*ournal of Personality and Social Psychology, 33,* 245–255.

Baron, R. A. (1971). Magnitude of victim's pain cues and level of prior anger arousal as determinants of adult aggressive behavior. *Journal of Personality and Social Psychology, 17,* 236–243.

Baron, R. A. (1972). Reducing the influence of an aggressive model: The restraining effects of peer censure. *Journal of Experimental Social Psychology, 8,* 266–275.

Baron, R. A. (1973). The "foot–in–the–door" phenomenon: Mediating effects of size of first request and sex of requester. *Bulletin of the Psychonomic Society, 2,* 113–114.

Baron, R. A. (1974). The aggression: inhibiting influence of heightened sexual arousal. *Journal of Personality and Social Psychology, 30,* 318–322.

Baron, R. A. (1976). The reduction of human aggression: A field study of the influence of incompatible responses. *Journal of Applied Social Psychology, 6,* 95–104.

Baron, R. A. (1977). *Human aggression.* New York: Plenum.

Baron, R. A. (1979). Aggression, empathy, and race: Effects of victim's pain cues, victim's race, and level of instigation on physical aggression. *Journal of Applied Social Psychology, 9,* 103–114.

Baron, R. A. (1981). The "costs of deception" revisited: An openly optimistic rejoinder. *IRB: A Review of Human Subjects Research, 3,* 8–10.

Baron, R. A. (1983). The control of human aggression: A strategy based on incompatible responses. In R. G. Geen & E. I. Donnerstein (Eds.), *Aggression: Theoretical and empirical reviews.* New York: Academic Press.

Baron, R. A. (1984). Reducing organizational conflict: An incompatible response approach. *Journal of Applied Psychology, 69,* 272–279.

Baron, R. A. (1987a). Effects of negative air ions on interpersonal attraction: Evidence for intensification. *Journal of Personality and Social Psychology, 52,* 547–553.

Baron, R. A. (1987). Interviewer's moods and reactions to job applicants: The influence of affective states on applied social judgments. *Journal of Applied Social Psychology, 16,* 16–28.

Baron, R. A. (1988a). Attributions and organizational conflict: The mediating role of apparent sincerity. *Organizational Behavior and Human Decision Processes, 41,* 111–127.

Baron, R. A. (1988b). Negative effects of destructive criticism: Impact on conflict, self–efficacy, and task performance. *Journal of Applied Psychology, 73,* 199–207.

Baron, R. A. (1989a). Applicant strategies during job interviews. In G. R. Ferris & R. W. Eder (Eds.), *The employment interview: Theory, research, and practice* (pp. 204–216). Newbury Park, CA: Sage.

Baron, R. A. (1989b). Personality and organizational conflict: The Type A behavior pattern and self–monitoring. *Organizational Behavior and Human Decision Processes.*

Baron, R. A. (1990). Attributions and organizational conflict. In S. Graham & V. Folkes (Eds.), *Attribution theory: Applications to achievement, mental health, and interpersonal conflict* (pp. 185–204). Hillsdale, NJ: Erlbaum.

Baron, R. A. (1990b). Conflict in organizations. In K. R. Murphy & F. E. Saal (Eds.), *Psychology in organizations: Integrating science and practice* (pp. 197–216). Hillsdale, NJ: Erlbaum.

Baron, R. A. (1990). Environmentally induced positive affect: Its impact on self–efficacy, task performance, negotiation, and conflict. *Journal of Applied Social Psychology, 20,* 368–384.

Baron, R. A. (1993a). Criticism (informal negative feedback) as a source of perceived unfairness in organizations: Effects, mechanisms, and countermeasures. In R. Cropanzano (Ed.), Justice in the workplace: Approaching fairness in human resource management. Hillsdale, NJ: Erlbaum.

Baron, R. A. (1993). Effects of interviewers' moods and applicant qualifications on ratings of job applicants. Manuscript submitted for publication.

Baron, R. A., Fortin, S. P., Frei, R. L., Haver, L. A., & Shack, M. L. (1990). Reducing organizational conflict: The potential role of socially–induced positive affect. *International Journal of Conflict Management, 1,* 133–152.

Baron, R. A., Rea, M. S., and Daniels, S. G., & (1992). Lighting as a source of environmentally-generated positive affect in work settings: Impact on cognitive tasks and interpersonal behaviors. *Motivation and Emotion, 14,* 1–34.

Baron, R. A., Rea, M. S., & Daniels, S. G. (1992). Effects of indoor lighting (illuminance and spectral distribution) on the performance of cognitive tasks and interpersonal behaviors: The potential mediating role of positive affect. *Motivation and Emotion, 16,* 1–33.

Baron, R. A., & Richardson, D. R. (1994). *Human aggression* (2nd ed.). New York: Plenum.

Baron, R. A., Russell, G. W., & Arms, R. I. (1985). Negative ions and behavior: Impact on mood, memory, and aggression among Type A and Type B persons. *Journal of Personality and Social Psychology, 48,* 746–754.

Baron, R. A., & Bell, P. A. (1973). Effects of heightened sexual arousal on physical aggression. *Proceedings of the American Psychological Association,* 81st Annual Convention, 171–72.

Baron, R. S., Moore, D., & Sanders, G. S. (1978). Distraction as a source of drive in social facilitation research. Journal of Personality and Social Psychology, 36, 816–824.

Baron, R. S. (1986). Distraction–conflict theory: Progress and problems. In L. Berkowitz (Ed.), Advances in experimental social psychology, Vol. 20. New York: Academic Press.

Barrett, L. I. (1992). A new coalition for the 1990s. Time, 140(20), 47–48.

Bass, B. M. (1985). *Leadership and performance and expectations.* New York: Free Press.

Bateman, T. S., & Morgan, D. W. (1983). Job satisfaction and the good soldier: The relationships between affect and employee "citizenship." *Academy of Management Journal, 26,* 587–595.

Batista, S. M., & Berte, R. (1992). Maternal behavior and feminine work: Study with Belgian mothers with infants. *Interamerican Journal of Psychology, 26,* 143–157.

Batson, C. D., Batson, J. G., Griffitt, C. A., Carrientos, S., Brandt, J. R., Sprengelmeyer, P., & Bayly, M. J. (1989). Negative state relief and the empathy–altruism hypothesis. *Journal of Personality and Social Psychology, 56,* 922–933.

Batson, C. D., Duncan, B. D., Ackerman, P., Buckley, T., & Birch, K. (1981). Is empathic emotion a source of altruistic motivation? *Journal of Personality and Social Psychology, 40,* 290–302.

Batson, C. D., & Olson, k. C. (1991). Current status of the empathy–altruism hypothesis. In M. S. Clark (Ed.), *Prosocial behavior* (pp. 62–85). Newbury Park, CA: Sage.

Batson, C. D., O'Quin, K., Fultz, J., Vanderplas, M., & Isen, A. M. (1983). Influence of self–reported distress and empathy on egoistic versus altruistic motivation to help. *Journal of Personality and Social Psychology, 45,* 706–718.

Baugh, S. G., & Parry, L. E. (1991). The relationship between physical attractiveness and grade point average among college women. *Journal of Social Behavior and Personality, 6,* 219–228.

Baumeister, R. F. (1986). *Identity.* New York: Oxford University Press.

Baumeister, R. F., Chesner, S. P., Sanders, P. S., & Tice, D. M. (1988). Who's in charge here? Group leaders do lend help in emergencies. *Personality and Social Psychology*

Bulletin, 14, 17–22.

Baumeister, R. F., & Covington, N. V. (1985). Self–esteem, persuasion, and retrospective distortion of initial attitudes. *Electronic Social Psychology, 1*, 1–22.

Baumeister, R. F., Heatherton, T. F., & Tice, D. M. (1993). When ego threats lead to self–regulation failure: Negative consequences of high self–esteem. *Journal of Personality and Social Psychology, 64*, 141–156.

Baumeister, R. F., Stillwell, A., & Wotman, S. R. (1990). Victim and perpetrator accounts of interpersonal conflict: Autobiographical narratives about anger. *Journal of Personality and Social Psychology, 59*, 994–1003.

Baumeister, R. F., Wotman, S. R., & Stillwell, A. M. (1993). Unrequited love: On heartbreak, anger, guilt, scriptlessness, and humiliation. *Journal of Personality and Social Psychology, 64*, 377–394.

Baxter, L. A. (1990). Dialectical contradictions in relationship development. *Journal of Social and Personal Relationships, 7*, 69–88.

Beaman, A. L. (1991). An empirical comparison of meta–analytic and traditional reviews. *Personality and Social Psychology Bulletin, 17*, 252–257.

Beaman, A. L., Cole, . N., Preston, M., Glentz, B., & Steblay, N. M. (1983). Fifteen years of the foot–in–the–door research: A meta–analysis. *Personality and Social Psychology Bulletin, 9*, 181–186.

Beauvois, J. L., & Dubois, N. (1988). The norm of internality in the explanation of psychological events. *European Journal of Social Psychology, 18*, 299–316.

Beauvois, J. L., & Le Poultier, F. (1986). Norme d'internalite et pouvoir social en psychologie quotidienne. *Psychologie Francaise, 31*, 100–108.

Beckwith, J. B. (1992). Stereotypes and reality in the division of household labor. *Social Behavior and Personality, 20*, 283–288.

Beggan, J. K. (1992). On the social nature of nonsocial perception: The mere ownership effect. *Journal of Personality and Social Psychology, 62*, 229–237.

Belcastro, P. A. (1985). Sexual behavior differences between black and white students. *Journal of Sex Research, 21*, 56–67.

Bell, B. (1991). Loneliness and values. *Journal of Social Behavior and Personality, 6*, 771–778.

Bell, B. E., & Loftus, E. F. (1988). Degree of detail of eyewitness testimony and mock juror judgments. *Journal of Applied Social Psychology, 18*, 1171–1192.

Bell, P. A. (1991). Gender, friendship network density, and loneliness. *Journal of Social Behavior and Personality, 6*, 45–56.

Bell, P. A. (1992). In defense of the negative affect escape model of heat and aggression. *Psychological Bulletin, 111*, 342–346.

Bell, P. A., Fisher, J. D., Baum, A., & Green, T. E. (1990). *Environmental psychology* (3rd ed.). New York: Holt, Rinehart, & Winston.

Belmore, S. M., & Hubbard, M. L. (1987). The role of advance expectancies in person memory. *Journal of Personality and Social Psychology, 53*, 61–70.

Bem, S. L. (1974). The measurement of psychological androgyny. *Journal of Consulting and Clinical Psychology, 42*, 155–162.

Bem, S. L. (1983). Gender schema theory and its implications for child development: Raising gender–aschematic children in a gender–schematic society. *Science: Journal of

Women in Culture and Society, 8*, 598–616.

Bem, S. L. (1984). Androgyny and gender–schema theory: A conceptual and empirical integration. In *Nebraska symposium on motivation: Psychology and gender* (pp. 179–226). Lincoln: University of Nebraska Press.

Benson, P. L., Xarabenick, S. A., & Lerner, R. M. (1976). Pretty pleases: The effects of physical attractiveness, race, and sex on receiving help. *Journal of Experimental Social Psychology, 12*, 409–415.

Berg, J. H., & McQuinn, R. D. (1989). Loneliness and aspects of social support networks. *Journal of Social and Personal Relationships, 6*, 359–372.

Bergos, H., Diaz, M., & Volands, I. (1988). An exploration of human sexuality in the Puerto Rican. *Journal of Social Work and Human Sexuality, 4*, 135–150.

Berkowitz, L. (1962). *Aggression: A social psychological analysis.* New York: McGraw-Hill.

Berkowitz, L. (1968, September). Impulse, aggression, and the gun. *Psychology Today*, pp. 18–22.

Berkowitz, L. (1974). Some determinants of impulsive aggression: The role of mediated associations with reinforcements for aggression. *Psychological Review, 81*, 165–176.

Berkowitz, L. (1984). Some effects of thought on anti- and pro-social influence of media events: A cognitive-neoassociation analysis. *Psychological Bulletin, 95*, 410–427.

Berkowitz, L. (1987). Mood, self–awareness, and willingness to help. *Journal of Personality and Social Psychology, 52*, 721–724.

Berkowitz, L. (1988). Frustrations, appraisals, and aversively stimulated aggression. *Aggressive Behavior, 14*, 3–11.

Berkowitz, L. (1989). Frustration-aggression hypothesis: Examination and reformulation. *Psychological Bulletin, 106*, 59–73.

Berkowitz, L. (Ed.) (1969). *Roots of aggression.* New York: Atherton.

Berkowitz, L., & Donnerstein, E. (1982). External validity is more than skin deep: Some answers to criticism of laboratory experiments. *American Psychologist, 37*, 245–257.

Berkowitz, L., & LePage, A. (1967). Weapons as aggression-eliciting stimuli. *Journal of Personality and Social Psychology, 11*, 202–207.

Berman, M., Gladue, B., & Taylor, S. (1993). The effects of hormones, Type A behavior pattern and provocation on aggression in men. *Journal of Applied Social Psychology, in press.*

Berndt, T. J. (1992). Friendship and friends' influence in adolescence. *Current Directions in Psychological Science, 1*, 156–159.

Bernhardt, P. C., & Dabbs, J. M. (1993). *Vicarious experiences and testosterone changes: Spectators at basketball games.* Manuscript submitted for publication.

Bernstein, W. M., Stephenson, B. O., Snyder, M. L., & Wicklund, R. A. (1983). Causal ambiguity and heterosexual affiliation. *Journal of Experimental Social Psychology, 19*, 78–92.

Berry, D. S. (1991). Attractive faces are not all created equal: Joint effects of facial babyishness and attractiveness on social perception. *Personality and Social Psychology Bulletin, 17*, 523–531.

Berry, D. S., & Brownlow, S. (1989). Were the physiognomists right? Personality correlates of facial babyishness. *Personality and Social Psychology Bulletin, 15*, 266–279.

Berry, D. S., & Zebrowitz-McArthur, L. (1988). What's in a face?

Facial maturity and the attribution of legal responsibility. *Personality and Social Psychology Bulletin, 14,* 23–33.

Berscheid, E., Dion, K. K., Walster, E., & Walster, G. W. (1971). Physical attractiveness and dating choice: A test of the matching hypothesis. *Journal of Experimental Social Psychology, 7,* 173–189.

Berscheid, E., Snyder, M., & Omoto, A. M. (1989). The Relationship Closeness Inventory: Assessing the closeness of interpersonal relationships. *Journal of Personality and Social psychology, 57,* 792–807.

Bersoff, D. (1987). Social science data and the Supreme Court: Lockhart as a case in point. *American Psychologist, 42,* 52–58.

Betancourt, H. (1990). An attribution–empathy model of helping behavior: Behavioral intentions and judgments of help–giving. *Personality and Social Psychology Bulletin, 16,* 573–591.

Betz, A. I., & Krosnick, J. A. (1993). *A test of the primacy effect: Does detection of the affective tone of a stimulus precede detection of stimulus presence or content?* Unpublished Manuscript, 0hio State University.

Bickman, L. (1972). Social influence and diffusion of responsibility in an emergency. *Journal of Experimental Social Psychology, 8,* 438–445.

Bienert, H., & Schneider, B. H. (1993). Diagnosis-specific social skill is training with peer-nominated aggressive-disruptive and sensitive-isolated preadolescents. *Journal of Applied Developmental Psychology,* in press.

Bierhoff, H. W., Klein, R., & Kramp, P. (1991). Evidence for the altruistic personality from data on accident research. *Journal of Personality, 59,* 263–280.

Birkimer, J. C., Lucas, M., & Birkimer, S. J. (1991). Health locus of control and status of cardiac rehabilitation graduates. *Journal of Social Behavior and Personality, 6,* 629–640.

Birnbaum, M. H., & Sotoodeh, Y. (1991). Measurement of stress: Scaling the magnitudes of life changes. *Psychological Science, 2,* 236–243.

Bishop, G. D. (1987). Lay conceptions in physical symptoms. *Journal of Applied Social Psychology, 17,* 127–146.

Bjorkqvist, K., Lagerspetz, K. M. J., & Kaukiainen, A. (1992). Do girls manipulate and boys fight? Developmental trends in regard to direct and indirect aggression. *Aggressive Behavior, 18,* 117–127.

Black, S. L., & Bevan, S. (1992). At the movies with Buss and Durkee: A natural experiment on film violence. *Aggressive Behavior, 18,* 37–45.

Blankenship, V., Hnat, S. M., Hess, T. G., & Brown, D. R. (1984). Reciprocal interaction and similarity of personality attributes. *Journal of Social and Personal Relationships.*

Blass, T. (1991). Understanding behavior in the Milgram obedience experiment: The role of personality, situations, and their interactions. *Journal of Personality and Social Psychology, 60,* 398–413.

Bless, H., Bohner, G., Schwarz, N., & Strack, F. (1990). Mood and persuasion: A Cognitive response analysis. *Personality and Social Psychology Bulletin, 16,* 331–345.

Blinn, L. M. (1987). Prototherapeutic intervention to improve self–concept and prevent repeat pregnancies among adolescents. *Family Relations: Journal of Applied Family and Child Studies, 36,* 252–257.

Bobo, L. (1983). Whites' opposition to busing: Symbolic racism or realistic group conflict? *Journal of Personality and Social Psychology, 45,* 1196–1210.

Bochner, A. P. (1991). On the paradigm that would not die. In J. A. Anderson (Ed.), *Communication yearbook 14* (pp. 44–491). Newbury Park, CA: Sage.

Bock, D. C. (1972). Obedience: A response to authority and Christian commitment. *Disseration Abstracts International, 33,* 3278B–3279B. (University Microfilms No. 72–31,651)

Bodenhausen, G. V. (1988). Stereotypic biases in social decision making and memory: Testing process models of stereotype use. *Journal of Personality and Social Psychology, 55,* 726–737.

Bogard, N. (1990). Why we need gender to understand human violence. *Journal of Interpersonal Violence, 5,* 132–135.

Bolger, N., & Schilling, E. A. (1991). Personality and the problems of everyday life: The role of neuroticism in exposure and reactivity to daily stressors. *Journal of Personality, 59,* 355–386.

Bolig, R., Stein, P. I. J., & Mckenry, P. C. (1984). The self-advertisement approach to dating: Male-female differences. *Family Relations, 33,* 587–592.

Bond, C. F. (1982). Social facilitation: A self–presentational view. *Journal of Personality and Social Psychology, 42,* 1042–1050.

Bond, S., & Cash, T. F. (1992). Black beauty: Skin color and body images among African-American college women. *Journal of Applied Social Psychology, 22,* 874–888.

Bornstein, R. F. (1989). Subliminal techniques as propaganda tools: Review and critique. *Journal of Mind and Behavior, 10,* 231–262.

Bornstein, R. F. (1992). Subliminal mere exposure effects. In R. F. Bornstein & T. S. Pittman (Eds.), *Perception without awareness: Cognitive, clinical and social perspectives* (pp. 191–210). New York: Guildford.

Bornstein, R. F. (1993, February). Personal communication.

Bornstein, R. F., & D'Agostino, P. R. (1992). Stimulus recognition and the mere exposure effect. *Journal of Personality and Social Psychology, 63,* 545–552.

Borrello, G. M., & Thompson, G. (1990). An hierarchical analysis of the Hendrick-Hendrick measure of Lee's typology of love. *Journal of Social Behavior and Personality, 5,* 327–342.

Bossard, J. H. S. (1932). Residential propinquity as a factor in marriage selection. *American Journal of Sociology, 38,* 219–224.

Bothwell, R. K., Brigham, J. C., & Malpass, R. S. (1989). Cross–racial identification. *Personality and Social Psychology Bulletin, 15,* 19–25.

Bothwell, R. K., Deffenbacher, K. A., & Brigham, J. C. (1987). Correlation of eyewitness accuracy and confidence: Optimality hypothesis revisited. *Journal of Applied Psychology, 72,* 691–695.

Bothwell, R. K., & Jalil, M. (1992). The credibility of nervous witnesses. *Journal of Social Behavior and Personality, 7,* 581–586.

Bower, G. H., & Hilgard, E. R. (1981). *Theories of learning* (5th ed.). Englewood Cliffs, NJ: Prentice-Hall.

Bradbury, T. N., & Fincham, F. D. (1992). Attributions and behavior in marital interaction. *Journal of Personality and Social Psychology, 63,* 613–628.

Branscombe, N. R., & Wann, D. L. (1993). Collective self-esteem consequences of outgroup derogation under identity-threatening and identity-bolstering conditions. *European Journal of Social Psychology,* in press.

Bray, R. M., & Sugarman, R. (1980). Social facilitation among interaction groups: Evidence for the evaluation apprehension hypothesis. *Personality and Social Psychology Bulletin, 6,* 137–142.

Breakwell, G. M., Fife–Schaw, C., & Clayden, K. (1991). Risk-taking, control over partner choice and intended use of condoms by virgins. *Journal of Community and Applied Social Psychology, 1,* 173–187.

Brehm, J. W. (1966). *A theory of psychological reactance.* New York: Academic Press.

Brennan, T. (1982). Loneliness at adolescence. In L. A. Peplau & P. Perlman (Eds.), *Loneliness: A sourcebook of current theory, research, and therapy.* New York: Wiley.

Bretz, R. D., Jr., & Thomas, S. L. (1992). Perceived equity, motivation, and final-offer arbitration in major league baseball. *Journal of Applied Psychology, 77,* 280–287.

Brewer, M. B. (1989). A dual process model of impression formation. In R. S. Wyer & T. K. Srull (Eds.), *Advances in social cognition* (Vol. 1, pp. 1–36). Hillsdale, NJ: Erlbaum.

Brewer, M. B. (1991). The social self: On being the same and different at the same time. *Personality and Social Psychology Bulletin, 17,* 475–482.

Brewer, M. B., & Caporael, L. R. (1990). Selfish genes vs. selfish people: Sociobiology as origin myth. *Motivation and Emotion, 14,* 237–243.

Brewer, M. B., Ho, H., Lee, J., & Miller, M. (1987). Social identity and social distance among Hong Kong school children. *Personality and Social Psychology Bulletin, 13,* 156–165.

Brickner, M., Harkins, S., & Ostrom, T. (1986). Personal involvement: Thought-provoking implications for social loafing. *Journal of Personality and Social Psychology, 51,* 763–769.

Briggs, S. R., & Cheek, J. M. (1988). On the nature of self–monitoring: Problems with assessment, problems with validity. *Journal of Personality and Social Psychology, 54,* 663–678.

Bringle, R. G. (1993, February). Parent-child estrangement. Personal communication.

Bringle, R. G., & Bagby, G. J. (1992). Self–esteem and perceived quality of romantic and family relationships in young adults. *Journal of Research in Personality, 26,* 340–356.

Bringle, R. G., & Winnick, T. A. (1992, October). *The nature of unrequited love.* Paper presented at the first Asian Conference in Psychology, Singapore.

Broadstock, M., Borland, R., & Gason, R. (1991). Effects of suntan on judgments of healthiness and attractiveness by adolescents. *Journal of Applied Social Psychology, 22,* 157–172.

Brockner, J., & Guare, J. (1983). Improving the performance of low self-esteem individuals: An attributional approach. *Academy of Management Journal, 26,* 642–656.

Brodeur, P. (1992, December 7). The cancer at Slater School. *New Yorker,* pp. 86–94, 96–106, 108–119.

Brody, G. H., Neubaum, E., & Forehand, R. (1988). Serial marriage: A heuristic analysis of an emerging family form. *Psychological Bulletin, 103,* 211–222.

Brody, G. H., Stoneman, Z., MacKinnon, C. E., & MacKinnon, R. (1985). Role relationships and behavior between preschool-aged and school-aged sibling pairs. *Developmental Psychology, 21,* 124–129.

Brody, J. E. (1989, August 24). Boning up on possible mental and physical health needs of children who are bound for college. *New York Times,* p. 912.

Brody, J. E. (1991, October 2). Helping teen–agers avoid pregnancy. *New York Times,* p. A14.

Brooks-Gunn, J., & Lewis, M. (1981). Infant social perception: Responses to pictures of parents and strangers. *Developmental Psychology,* 647–649.

Brothers, L. (1990). The neural basis of primate social communication. *Motivation and Emotion, 14,* 81–91.

Broude, G. J. (1992). The May-September algorithm meets the 20th century actuarial table. *Behavioral and Brain Sciences, 15,* 94–95.

Brown, C. (1991, September 28). Teen sex study renews education issue. *Albany Times Union,* pp. B–1 – B–2.

Brown, J. D. (1991). Staying fit and staying well: Physical fitness as a moderator of life stress. *Journal of Personality and Social Psychology, 60,* 555–561.

Brown, J. D., & Mankowski, T. A. (1993). Self–esteem, mood, and self–evaluation: Changes in mood and the way you see you. *Journal of Personality and Social Psychology, 64,* 421–430.

Brown, J. D., Novick, N. J., Lord, K. A., & Richards, J. M. (1992). When Gulliver travels: Social context, psychological closeness, and self–appraisals. *Journal of Personality and Social Psychology, 62,* 717–727.

Brown, J. D., & Rogers, R. J. (1991). Self–serving attributions: The role of physiological arousal. *Personality and Social Psychology Bulletin, 17,* 501–506.

Brown, J. D., & Siegel, J. M. (1988). Attributions for negative life events and depression: The role of perceived control. *Journal of Personality and Social Psychology, 54,* 316–322.

Browne, M. W. (1992a, April 14). Biologists tally generosity's rewards. *New York Times,* pp. C1, C8.

Browne, M. W. (1992b, February 25). Cooling with sound: An effort to save ozone shield. *New York Times,* pp. C1, C7.

Browne, M. W. (1992c, September 18). Report says carbon dioxide rise may hurt plants. *New York Times,* p. A14.

Bryan, J. H., & Test, M. A. (1967). Models and helping: Naturalistic studies in aiding behavior. *Journal of Personality and Social Psychology, 6,* 400–407.

Buck, R., & Ginsburg, B. (1991). Spontaneous communication and altrusim: The communicative gene hypothesis. In M. S. Clark (Ed.), *Prosocial behavior* (pp. 149–175). Newbury Park, CA: Sage.

Buckhout, R. (1980). Nearly 2000 witnesses can be wrong. *Bulletin of the Psychonomic Society, 16,* 307–310.

Bumpass, L. (1984). Children and marital disruption: A replication and update. *Demography, 21,* 71–82.

Burger, J. M. (1986a). Increasing compliance by improving the deal: The that's-not-all technique. *Journal of Personality and Social Psychology, 51,* 277–283.

Burger, J. M. (1986). Temporal effects on attributions: Actor and observer differences. *Social Cognition, 4,* 377–387.

Burger, J. M. (1987). Desire for control and conformity to a perceived norm. *Journal of Personality and Social Psychology 53,* 355–360.

Burger, J. M. (1991). Changes in attributions over time: The ephemeral fundamental attribution error. *Social Cognition, 9,* 182–193.

Burger, J. M. (1992). *Desire for control: Personality, social, and clinical perspectives.* New York: Plenum.

Burger, J. M., & Cooper, H. N. (1979). The desirability of control. *Motivation and Emotion, 3,* 381–393.

Burger, J. M., & Palmer, M. L. (1992). Changes in and generalization of unrealistic optimism following experiences with stressful events: Reactions to the 1989 California earthquake. *Personality and Social Psychology Bulletin, 18,* 39–43.

Burger, J. M., & Pavelich, J. L. (1993). *Attributions for presidential elections: The situational shift over time.* Unpublished manuscript, Santa Clara University.

Burke, J. P., Hunt, J. P., & Bickford, R. L. (1985). Causal internalization of academic performance as a function of self–esteem and performance satisfaction. *Journal of Research in Personality, 19,* 321–329.

Burn, S. M., & Oskamp, S. (1986). Increasing community recycling with persuasive communication and public commitment. *Journal of Applied Social Psychology, 16,* 29–41.

Burnstein, E. (1983). Persuasion as argument processing. In M. Brandstatter, J. H. Davis, & G. Stocker-Kriechgauer (Eds.), *Human decision processes.* London: Academic Press.

Burnstein, E., & Schul, Y. (1982). The informational basis of social judgments: Operations in forming an impression of another person. *Journal of Experimental Social Psychology, 18,* 217–234.

Buss, A. H., Booker, A., & Buss, E. (1972). Firing a weapon and aggression. *Journal of Personality and Social Psychology, 22,* 196–302.

Bushman, B. J. (1984). Perceived symbols of authority and their influence on compliance. *Journal of Applied Social Psychology, 14,* 501–508.

Bushman, B. J. (1988). The effects of apparel on compliance: A field experiment with a female authority figure. *Personality and Social Psychology Bulletin, 14,* 459–467.

Buss, A. H. (1961). *The psychology of aggression.* New York: Wiley.

Buss, D. M. (1987). Sex differences in human mate selection criteria: An evolutionary perspective. In C. Crawford, M. Smith, & D. Hrebs (Eds.), *Sociobiology and psychology.* Hillsdale, NJ: Erlbaum.

Buss, D. M. (1988). Love acts: The evolutionary biology of love. In R. J. Sternberg & M. L. Barnes (Eds.), *The psychology of love* (pp. 100–118). New Haven, CT: Yale University Press.

Buss, D. M. (1989a). Conflict between the sexes: Strategic interference and the evocation of anger and upset. *Journal of Personality and Social Psychology, 56,* 735–747.

Buss, D. M. (1989b). Sex differences in human mate preferences: Evolutionary hypotheses tested in 37 cultures. *Behavioral and Brain Sciences, 12,* 1–49.

Buss, D. M. (1990). Evolutionary social psychology: Prospects and pitfalls. *Motivation and Emotion, 14,* 265–286.

Buss, D. M. (1991). Evolutionary personality psychology. *Annual Review of Psychology.* Palo Alto, CA: Annual Reviews.

Buss, D. M. (1991b). Conflict in married couples: Personality predictors of anger and upset. *Journal of Personality, 59,* 663–688.

Buss, D. M., Larsen, R. J., Westen, D., & Semmelroth, J. (1992). Sex differences in jealousy: Evolution, physiology, and psychology. *Psychological Science, 3,* 251–255.

Butler, D., & Geis, F. L. (1990). Nonverbal affect responses to male and female leaders: Implications for leadership evaluations. *Journal of Personality and Social Psychology, 58,* 48–59.

Butler, J. M., & Haigh, G. V. (1954). Changes in the relation between self-concepts and ideal concepts consequent upon client-centered counseling. In C. R. Rogers & R. Diamond (Eds.), *Psychotherapy and personality change* (pp. 55–75). Chicago: University of Chicago Press.

Buunk, B., & Hupka, R. B. (1987). Cross-cultural differences in the elicitation of sexual jealousy. *Journal of Sex Research, 23,* 12–22.

Byrne, D. (1961). The influence of propinquity and opportunities for interaction on classroom relationships. *Human Relations, 4,* 63–69.

Byrne, D. (1964). Repression sensitization as a dimension of personality. In B. A. Maher (Ed.), *Progress in experimental personality research* (Vol. 1, pp. 169–220). New York: Academic Press.

Byrne D. (1991). Perspectives on research classics: This ugly duckling has yet to become a swan. *Contemporary Social Psychology, 15,* 84–85.

Byrne, D. (1992). The transition from controlled laboratory experimentation to less controlled settings: Surprise! Additional variables are operative. *Communication Monographs,* 190–198.

Byrne, D., & Buehler, R. A. (1955). A note on the influence of propinquity upon acquaintanceships. *Journal of Abnormal and Social Psychology, 51,* 147–148.

Byrne, D., & Clore, G. L. (1970). A reinforcement–affect model of evaluative responses. *Personality: An International Journal, 1,* 103–128.

Byrne, D., Clore, G. L., & Smeaton, G. (1986). The attraction hypothesis: Do similar attitudes affect anything? *Journal of Personality and Social Psychology, 51,* 1167–1170.

Byrne, D., & Kelley, K. (1981). *An introduction to personality* (3rd ed.). Englewood Cliffs, NJ: Prentice-Hall.

Byrne, D., & Kelley, K. (1992). Differential age preferences: The need to test evolutionary versus alternative conceptualizations. *Behavioral and Brain Sciences, 15,* 96.

Byrne, D., Kelley, K., & Fisher, W. A. (1993). Unwanted teenage pregnancies: Incidence, interpretation, and intervention. *Applied & Preventive Psychology, 2,* 101–113.

Byrne, D., & Murnen, S. K. (1988). Maintaining loving relationships. In R. J. Sternberg & M. L. Barnes (Eds.), *The psychology of love* (pp. 293–310). New Haven, CT: Yale University Press.

Byrne, D., & Nelson, D. (1965). Attraction as a linear function of proportion of positive reinforcements. *Journal of Personality and Social Psychology, 1,* 659–663.

Byrne, D., & Przybyla, D. P. J. (1980). Authoritarianism and political preferences in 1980. *Bulletin of the Psychonomic Society, 16,* 471–472.

Byrne, G. C., & Pueschel, J. K. (1973). But who shall I vote for county coroner? *Journal of Politics, 36,* 778–784.

Cacioppo, J. T. Martzke, J. S., Petty, R. E., & Tassinary, L. G. (1988). Specific forms of facial EMG response index emotions during an interview: From Darwin to the continuous flow hypothesis of affect-laden information processing. *Journal of Personality and Social Psychology, 54,* 602–604.

Cahoon, D. D., & Edmonds, E. M. (1989). Male-female estimates of opposite-sex first impressions concerning females' clothing styles. *Bulletin of the Psychonomic Society, 27,* 280–281.

Callaci, D. (1993, March 3). The glass is half full. *New York Teacher,* pp. 9–11.

Calvert, J. D. (1988). Physical attractiveness: A review and reevaluation of its role in social skill research. *Behavioral Assessment, 10,* 29–42.

Campbell, D. T., & Specht, J. C. (1985). Altruism: Biology, culture, and religion. *Journal of Social and Clinical Psychology, 3,* 33–42.

Campbell, J. D. (1986). Similarity and uniqueness: The effects of attribute type, relevance, and individual differences in self–esteem and depression. *Journal of Personality and Social Psychology, 50,* 281–294.

Campbell, J. D., Chew, B., & Scratchley, L. S. (1991). Cognitive and emotional reactions to daily events: The effects of self–esteem and self–complexity. *Journal of Personality, 59,* 473–505.

Cann, A., Sherman, S. J., & Elkes, R. (1975). Effects of initial request size and timing of a second request on compliance: The foot-in-the-door and the door-in-the-face. *Journal of Personality and Social Psychology, 32,* 774–782.

Cantor, N. (1990). Social psychology and sociobiology: What can we leave to evolution? *Motivation and Emotion, 14,* 245–254.

Caplow, T., & Forman, R. (1950). Neighborhood interaction in a homogeneous community. *American Sociological Review, 15,* 357–366.

Caporael, L., & Brewer, M. (1990). We ARE Darwinians, and this is what the fuss is all about. *Motivation and Emotion, 14,* 287–293.

Cappella, J. N., & Palmer, M. T. (1990). Attitude similarity, relational history, and attraction: The mediating effects of kinesic and vocal behaviors. *Communication Monographs, 57,* 161–183.

Carli, L. L. (1989). Gender differences in interaction style and influence. *Journal of Personality and Social Psychology, 56,* 565–576.

Carli, L. L., Ganley, R., & Pierce-Otay, A. (1991). Similarity and satisfaction in roommate relationships. *Personality and Social Psychology Bulletin, 17,* 419–426.

Carlson, N., Marcus-Newhall, & Miller, H. (1990). Effects of situational aggression cues: A quantitative review. *Journal of Personality and Social Psychology, 58,* 622–633.

Carroll, J. L., Yolk, K. D., & Hyde, J. S. (1985). Differences between males and females in motives for engaging in sexual intercourse. *Archives of Sexual Behavior, 14,* 131–139.

Carroll, S. J., Perkowitz, W. T., Lurigio, A. J., & Waver, F. M. (1987). Sentencing goals, causal attributions, ideology, and personality. *Journal of Personality and Social Psychology, 36,* 107–118.

Carsten, J. M., & Spector, P. E. (1987). Unemployment, job satisfaction, and employee turnover: A meta-analytic test of the Muchinsky model. *Journal of Applied Psychology, 72,* 75–80.

Carter, D. B., & McCloskey, L. A. (1984). Peers and the maintenance of sex–typed behavior: The development of children's conceptions of cross–gender behavior in their peers. *Social Cognition, 2,* 294–314.

Carver, C. S., & Scheier, M. F. (1981). *Attention and self-regulation: A control–theory approach to human behavior.* New York: Springer-Verlag.

Carver, C. S., & Scheier, M. F. (1982). *Perspectives on personality* (2nd ed.). Boston: Allyn & Bacon.

Cash, T. F., & Derlega, V. J. (1978). The matching hypothesis: Physical attractiveness among same–sexed friends. *Personality and Social Psychology Bulletin, 4,* 240–243.

Cash, T. F., & Duncan, N. C. (1984). Physical attractiveness stereotyping among black American college students. *Journal of Social Psychology, 122,* 71–77.

Cash, T. F., & Jacobi, L. (1992). Looks aren't everything (to everybody): The strength of ideals of physical appearance. *Journal of Scoial Behavior and Personality, 7,* 621–630.

Cash, T. F., & Kilcullen, R. N. ((1985). The aye of the beholder: Susceptibility to sexism and beautyism in the evaluation of

managerial applicants. *Journal of Applied Social Psychology, 15,* 591–605.

Cash, T. F., & Trimer, C. A. (1984). Sexism and beautyism in women's evaluation of peer performance. *Sex Roles, 10,* 87–98.

Caspi, A., & Herbener, E. S. (1990). Continuity and change: Assortative marriage and the consistency of personality in adulthood. *Journal of Personality and Social Psychology, 58,* 250–258.

Caspi, A., Herbener, E. S., & Ozer, D. J. (1992). Shared experiences and the similarity of personalities: A longitudinal study of married couples. *Journal of Personality and Social Psychology, 62,* 281–291.

Castellow, W. A. (1993, March 2). Personal communication.

Castellow, W. A., Wuensch, K. L., & Moore, C. H. (1990). Effects of physical attractiveness of the plaintiff and defendant in sexual harassment judgments. *Journal of Social Behavior and Personality, 5,* 547–562.

Catchpole, T. (1992). A short history of political dirty tricks. *Playboy, 39*(11), 86–87, 169–170.

Cavoukian, A., & Doob, A. N. (1980). The effect of a judge's charge and subsequent recharge on judgments of guilt. *Basic and Applied Psychology, 1,* 103–114.

Centers for Disease Control. (1991). *Morbidity and Mortality Weekly Report, 29,* 929–932.

Chacko, T. I. (1982). Women and equal employment opportunity: Some unintended effects. *Journal of Applied Psychology, 57,* 119–123.

Chaiken, S. (1980). Heuristic versus systematic information processing and the use of sources versus message cues in persuasion. *Journal of Personality and Social Psychology, 39,* 752–766.

Chaiken, S. (1987). The heuristic model of persuasion. In N. P. Zanna, J. N. Olson, and C. P. Herman (Eds.), *Social influence: The Ontario symposium* (Vol. 5, pp. 3–39). Hillsdale, HJ: Erlbaum

Chaiken, S., & Stagnor, C. (1987). Attitudes and attitude change. *Annual Review of Psychology, 38,* 575–630.

Chapman, B. (1992). T*he attraction paradigm revisited: The additional effect of the number of dissimilar attitudes.* Unpublished manuscript, University at Albany, State University of New York.

Chatterjee, J., & McCarrey, M. (1991). Sex–role attitudes, values, and instrumental-expressive traits of women trainees in traditional vs. non-traditional programmes. *Applied Psychology: An International Review, 40,* 281–297.

Chaudhry, M. D. (1990). Role of the social and cultural factors in human fertility in India. *Population and Environment, 72,* 117–137.

Chaudhry, M. D. (1992). Population growth trends in India: 1991 census. *Population and Environment, 14,* 31–48.

Chesek, C. (1992, August). At the American Museum. *Natural History,* p. 64.

Chester-Taxin, S. (1993, March). Longevity. *Penthouse,* p. 12.

Cheuk, W. H., & Rosen, S. (1992). Helper reactions: When help is rejected by friends or strangers. *Journal of Social Behavior and Personality, 7,* 445–458.

Chidester, T. R. (1986). Problems in the study of interracial aggression: Pseudo-interracial dyad paradigm. *Journal of Personality and Social Psychology, 50,* 74–79.

Christ, W. G. (1985). Voter preference and emotion: Using emotional response to classify decided and undecided voters. *Journal of Applied Social Psychology, 15,* 237–254.

Christiansen, K., & Knussman, R. (1987). Androgen levels and components of aggressive behavior in men. *Hormones and Behavior,* 170–180.

Christopher, F. S., & Cate, R. M. (1985). Premarital sexual pathways and relationship development. *Journal of Social and Personal Relationships, 2,* 271–288.

Christy, P. R., Gelfand, D. N., & Hartmann, D. P. (1971). Effects of competition-induced frustration on two classes of modeled behavior. *Developmental Psychology, 5,* 104–111.

Cialdini, R. B. (1988). *Influence: Science and practice,* (2nd ed.). Glenview, IL: Scott, Foresman.

Cialdini, R. B., Baumann, D. J., & Kenrick, D. T. (1981). Insights from sadness: A three–step model of the development of altruism as hedonism. *Developmental Review, 1,* 207–223.

Cialdini, R. B., Darby, B. L., & Vincent, J. E. (1973). Transgression and altruism: A case for hedonism. *Journal of Experimental Social Psychology, 9,* 502–516.

Cialdini, R. B., Green, B. L., & Rusch, A. J. (1992). When tactical pronouncements of change become real change: The case of reciprocal persuasion. *Journal of Personality and Social Psychology, 6,* 30–40.

Cialdini, R. B., Kenrick, D. T., & Bauman, D. J. (1982). Effects of mood on prosocial behavior in children and adults. In N. Eisenberg-Berg (Ed.), *Development of prosocial behavior.* New York: Academic Press.

Cialdini, R. B., & Petty, R. (1979). Anticipatory opinion effects. In R. B. Petty, T. Ostrom, & T. Brock (Eds.), *Cognitive responses in persuasion.* Hillsdale, NJ: Erlbaum.

Cialdini, R. B., Schaller, M., Houlainhan, D., Arps, H., Fultz, J., & Beaman, A. L. (1987). Empathy-based helping: Is it selflessly or selfishly motivated? *Journal of Personality and Social Psychology, 52,* 749–758.

Cioffi, D., & Holoway, J. (1993). Delayed costs of suppressed pain. *Journal of Personality and Social Psychology, 64,* 274–282.

Clark, K., & Clark, M. (1947). Racial identification and racial preferences in Negro children. In T. M. Newcomb & E. L. Hartley, *Readings in social psychology* (pp. 169–178). New York: Holt.

Clark, L. A., & Watson, D. (1988). Mood and the mundane: Relations between daily life events and self–reported mood. *Journal of Personality and Social Psychology, 54,* 296–308.

Clark, M. S., Ouellette, R., Powel, M. C., & Milberg, S. (1987). Recipient's mood, relationship type, and helping. *Journal of Personality and Social Psychology, 53,* 94–103.

Clark, M. S., & Reis, H. T. (1988). Interpersonal processes in close relationships. *Annual Review of Psychology, 39,* 609–672.

Clark, R. N., Hendee, J. C., & Burgess, R. L. (1972). The experimental control of littering. *Journal of Environmental Education, 4,* 22–28.

Clary, E. G., & Orenstein, L. (1991). The amount and effectiveness of help: The relationship of motives and abilities to helping behavior. *Personality and Social Psychology Bulletin, 17,* 58–64.

Clary, E. G., & Snyder, M. (1991). A functional analysis of altrusim and prosocial behavior: The case of volunteerism. In M. S. Clark (Ed.), *Prosocial behavior* (pp. 119–148). Newbury Park, CA: Sage.

Clement, U., Schmidt, G., & Kruse, M. (1984). Changes in sex differences in sexual behavior: A replication of a study on West German students (1966–1981). *Archives of Sexual Behavior, 13,* 99–120.

Clore, G. L., & Byrne, D. (1974). A reinforcement–affect model of attraction. In T. L. Huston (Ed.), *Foundations of interpersonal attraction* (pp. 143–170). New York: Academic Press.

Cohen, R., Goodnight, J. A., Poag, C. K., Cohen, S., Nichol, G. T., & Worley, P. (1986). Easing the transition to kindergarten: The affective and cognitive effects of different spatial familiarization experiences. *Environment and Behavior, 13,* 330–345.

Cohen, S. (1980). Aftereffects of stress on human performance and social behavior: A review of research and theory. *Psychological Bulletin, 81,* 82–108.

Cohen, S., Evans, G. W., Stokols, D., & Krantz, D. (1986). *Behavior, health and environmental stress.* New York: Plenum.

Cohen, S., Glass, D. C., & Singer, J. E. (1973). Apartment noise, auditory discrimination, and reading ability in children. *Journal of Experimental Social Psychology, 9,* 407–422.

Cohen, S., Kaplan, J. R., Cunnick, J. E., Manuck, S. G., & Rabin, G. S. (1992). Chronic social stress, affiliation, and cellular immune response in nonhuman primates. *Psychological Science, 3,* 301–304.

Cohen, S., Tyrrell, D. A. J., & Smith, A. P. (1993). Negative life events, perceived stress, negative affect, and susceptibility to the common cold. *Journal of Personality and Social Psychology, 64,* 131–140.

Cohn, E. G. (1990). Weather and violent crime: A reply to Perry and Simpson, 1987. *Environment and Behavior, 22,* 280–294.

Coleman, D. (1991, November 13). All too often, the doctor isn't listening, studies show. *New York Times,* pp. Cl, C15.

Coleman, D. (1992, September 2). Study blames anger for reducing heart's efficiency. *Albany Times Union,* pp. A–I, A–9.

Coleman, L. M., & Antonucci, T. C. (1983). Impact of work on women at midlife. *Developmental Psychology, 19,* 290–294.

Coleman, L. M., Jussim, L., & Abraham, J. (1987). Students' reactions to teachers' evaluations: The unique impact of negative feedback. *Journal of Applied Social Psychology,* 1051–1070.

Compas, G., Banez, G. A., Malcarne, V., & Worsham, N. (1991). *Journal of Social Issues, 47*(4), 23–34.

Condon, J. W., & Crano, W. D. (1988). Inferred evaluation and the relation between attitude similarity and interpersonal attraction. *Journal of Personality and Social Psychology, 54,* 789–797.

Conger, J. A. (1991). Inspiring others: The language of leadership. *Academy of Management Executives 5*(1), 31–45.

Connell, E. B. (1983). What practical advice can physicians give patients on avoiding genital herpes? *Medical Aspects of Human Sexuality, 17*(8), 157–158, 160, 163–164, 169, 173, 176–177.

Connelly, M. S., Zaccaro, S. J., & Mumford, M. D. (1992). *Evidence for trait-based leadership: Social intelligence and cognitive ability as determinants of multi-situational leadership.* Paper presented at the Annual Convention of the American Psychological Association, Washington, DC.

Contrada, R. J. (1989). Type A behavior, personality hardiness, and cardiovascular responses to stress. *Journal of Personality and Social Psychology, 57,* 895–903.

Cook, S. W. (1984). Cooperative interaction in multiethnic contexts. In N. Miller & M. Brewer (Eds.), *Groups in contact: The psychology of desegregation* (pp. 155–185). New York: Academic Press.

Cook, S. W. (1985). Experimenting on social issues: The case of school desegregation. *American Psychologist, 40*, 452–460.

Cook, S. W., & Pelfrey, M. (1985). Reactions to being helped in cooperating interracial groups: A context effect. *Journal of Personality and Social Psychology, 49*, 1231–1245.

Cooke, P. (1992). Noises out: What it's doing to you. *New York ,25*(4), 28–33.

Cool, L. C. (1991, January). Getting wasted. *Penthouse*, pp. 139, 192.

Coontz, S. (1992). *The way we never were: American families and the nostalgia trap.* New York: Basic Books.

Cooper, J., & Fazio, R. H. (1984). A new look at dissonance theory. In L. Berkowitz (Ed.), *Advances in experimental social psychology* (Vol. 17, pp. 229–266). New York: Academic press.

Cooper, J., & Scher, S. J. (1992). Actions and attitudes: The role of responsibility and aversive consequences in persuasion. In T. Brock & S. Shavitt (Eds.), *The psychology of persuasion.* San Francisco: Freeman.

Costanza, R. S., Derlega, V. J., & Winstead, G. A. (1988). Positive and negative forms of social support: Effects of conversation topics on coping with stress among same–sex friends. *Journal of Experimental Social Psychology, 24*, 182–193.

Cotterell, N., Eisenberger, R., & Speicher, H. (1992). Inhibiting effects of reciprocation wariness on interpersonal relationships. *Journal of Personality and Social Psychology, 62*, 658–668.

Cottrell, H. B., Wack, K. L., Sekerak, G. J., & Rittle, R. (1968). Social facilitation of dominant responses by the presence of an audience and the mere presence of others. *Journal of Personality and Social Psychology, 51*, 245–250.

Cox, M., & Tanford, S. (1989). Effects of evidence and instructions in civil trials: An experimental investigation of rules of admissibility. *Social Behavior, 4*, 31–55.

Cramer, R. E., McMaster, M. R., Bartell, P. A., & Dragna, M. (1988). Subject competence and minimization of the bystander effect. *Journal of Applied Social Psychology, 18*, 1133–1148.

Crandall, C. S. (1992). Psychophysical scaling of stressful life events. *Psychological Science, 3*, 256–258.

Crandall, C. S., & Coleman, R. (1992). AIDS–related stigmatization and the disruption of social relationships. *Journal of Social and Personal Relationships, 9*, 163–177.

Crawford, D. W., & Huston, T. L. (1993). The impact of the transition to parenthood on marital leisure. *Personality and Social Psychology Bulletin, 19*, 39–46.

Crocker, J. (1993, February). Personal communication.

Crocker, J., Cornwell, B., & Major, B. (1993). The stigma of being overweight: Affective consequences of attributional ambiguity. *Journal of Personality and Social Psychology, 64*, 60–70.

Crocker, J., & Major, B. (1989). Social stigma and self-esteem: The self-protective properties of stigma. *Psychological Review, 96*, 609–630.

Crocker, J., & Major, B. (1991, June). *Reactions to stigma: The moderating role of justification.* Paper presented at the Ontario Symposium on Personality and Social Psychology: The Psychology of Prejudice, Waterloo, Ontario.

Crocker, J., & Major, B. (1993). *When bad things happen to bad people: The perceived justifiability of negative outcomes based on stigma.* Manuscript submitted for publication,.

Cropanzano, R. (Ed.). (1993). *Justice in the workplace: Approaching fairness in human resource management.* Hillsdale, NJ: Erlbaum.

Cropanzano, R., & James, K. (1990). Some methodological considerations for the behavioral–genetic analysis of work attitudes. *Journal of Applied Psychology, 21*, 433–439.

Crossette, G. (1990, November 26). 1,190 islands in danger: Sea could drown them. *New York Times,* p. A4.

Crouch, A., & Yetton, P. (1987). Manager behavior, leadership style, and subordinate performance: An empirical extension of the Vroom–Yetton conflict rule. *Organizational Behavior and Human Decision Processes, 39*, 384–396.

Crouse, B. B., & Mehrabian, A. (1977). Affiliation of opposite–sexed strangers. *Journal of Research in Personality, 11*, 38–47.

Croyle, R., & Uretsky, M. B. (1987). Effects of mood on self–appraisal of health status. *Health Psychology, 6*, 239–254.

Crusco, A. H., & Wetzel, C. G. (1984). The Midas touch: The effects of interpersonal touch on restaurant tipping. *Personality and Social Psychology Bulletin, 10*, 512–517.

Cruse, D., & Leigh, B. S. (1987). "Adam's Rib" revisited: Legal and non–legal influences on the processing of trial testimony. *Social Behavior, 2*, 221–230.

Culbertson, J. M. (1989). "Economic growth," population, and the environment. *Population and Environment, 11*, 83–100.

Cunningham, M. R., Shaffer, D. R., Barbee, A. P., Wolff, P. L., & Kelley, D. J. (1990). Separate processes in the relation of elation and depression to helping: Social versus personal concerns. *Journal of Experimental Social Psychology, 26*, 13–33.

Cunningham, M. R. (1979). Weather, mood, and helping behavior: Quasi–experiments with the sunshine samaritan. *Journal of Personality and Social Psychology, 37*, 1947–1956.

Cunningham, M. R. (1986). Measuring the physical in physical attractiveness: Quasi–experiments on the sociobiology of female facial beauty. *Journal of Personality and Social Psychology, 50*, 925–935.

Cunningham, M. R. (1988). Does happiness mean friendliness? Induced mood and heterosexual self–disclosure. *Personality and Social Psychology Bulletin, 14*, 283–297.

Cunningham, M. R. (1989). Reactions to heterosexual opening gambits: Female selectivity and male responsiveness. *Personality and Social Psychology Bulletin, 15*, 27–41.

Cunningham, M. R., Steinberg, J., & Grev, R. (1980). Wanting to and having to help: Separate motivations for positive mood and guilt–induced helping. *Journal of Personality and Social Psychology, 38*, 181–192.

Curtis, R. S., & Miller, K. (1986). Believing another likes or dislikes you: Behavior making the beliefs come true. *Journal of Personality and Social Psychology, 50*, 284–290.

Cutler, B. L., Moran, G., & Narby, D. J. (1992). Jury selection in insanity defense cases. *Journal of Research in Personality, 26*, 165–182.

Cutler, B. L., Penrod, S. D., & Martens, T. K. (1987). Improving the reliability of eyewitness identification: Putting content into context. *Journal of Applied Psychology, 72*, 629–637.

Cutler, B. L., & Wolfe, R. N. (1989). Self–monitoring and the association between confidence and accuracy. *Journal of Research in Personality, 23*, 410–420.

Dabbs, J. M., Jr. (1992). Testosterone measurements in social and clinical psychology. *Journal of Social and Clinical Psychology, 10,* 302–321.

Dabbs, J. M. (1993, February). Update on testosterone research. Personal communication.

Daley, S. (1983, February 13). Tales of the giant storm: Camaraderie and misery. *New York Times,* I35.

Daly, H. E. (1991). Population and economics: A bioeconomic analysis. *Population and Environment, 12,* 257–263.

Daly, M. (1989). On distinguishing evolved adaptation from epiphenomena. *Behavioral and Brain Sciences, 12,* 520.

Dane, F. C. (1992). Applying social psychology in the courtroom: Understanding stereotypes in jury decision making. *Contemporary Social Psychology, 16,* 33–36.

Darkness with no dawn. (1992, June 15). *Time,* p. 27.

Darley, J. M. (1991). Altruism and prosocial behavior research: Reflections and prospects. In M. S. Clark (Ed.), *Prosocial Behavior* (pp. 312–327). Newbury Park, CA: Sage.

Darley, J. M., & Batson, C. D. (1973). From Jerusalem to Jericho: A study of sitautional and dispositional variables in helping behavior. *Journal of Personality and Social Psychology, 27,* 100–108.

Daubman, K. A. (1993). *The self-threat of receiving help: A comparison of the threat-to-self-esteem model and the threat-to-interpersonal-power model.* Unpublished mansucript, Gettysburg College, Gettysburg, PA.

Davidson, L. M., Hagmann, J., & Baum, A. (1990). An exploration of a possible physiological explanation for stressor aftereffects. *Journal of Applied Social Psychology, 20,* 869–880.

Davie, M. R., & Reeves, R. J. (1939). Propinquity of residence before marriage. *American Journal of Sociology, 44,* 510–517.

Davis, J. H., Tindale, R. S., Naggao, D. H., Hinsz, V. B., & Robertson, B. (1984). Order effects in multiple decisions by gruops: A demonstration with mock juries and trial procedures. *Journal of Personality and Social Psychology, 47,* 1003–1012.

Davis, J. H., Stasson, M., Ono, K., & Zimmerman, S. (1988). Effects of straw polls on group decision making, sequential voting pattern, timing, and local majorities. *Journal of Personality and Social Psychology, 55,* 918–926.

Davis, J. H. (1989). Psychology and the law: The last 15 years. *Journal of Applied Social Psychology, 19,* 119–230.

Davis, M. H., & Harvey, J. C. (1992). Declines in major league batting performance as a function of game pressure: A drive theory analysis. *Journal of Applied Social Psychology, 22,* 714–735.

Davis, M. H., & Kraus, L. A. (1989). Social contact, loneliness, and mass media use: A test of two hypotheses. *Journal of Applied Social Psychology, 19,* 1100–1124.

Davis, S. F., Miller, K. M., Johnson, D., McAuley, H., & Dinges, D. (1992). The relationship between optimism–pessimism, loneliness, and death anxiety. *Bulletin of the Psychonomic Society, 30,* 135–136.

Dawes, R. M. (1989). Statistical criteria for establishing a truly false consensus effect. *Journal of Experimental Social Psychology, 25,* 1–17.

Deaux, K. (1982). *Sex as a social category: Evidence for gender stereotypes.* Invited address, American Psychological Association, Washington, DC

Deaux, K. (1993). Reconstructing social identity. *Personality and Social Psychology Bulletin, 19,* 4–12.

Deaux, K., & Lewis, L. L. (1984). The structure of gender stereotypes: Interrelationships among components and

gender label. *Journal of Personality and Social Psychology, 46,* 991–1004.

Deaux, K., & Major, B. (1987). Putting gender into context: An interactive model of gender–related behavior. *Psychological Review, 94,* 369–389.

DeBono, K. G., & Harnish, R. J. (1988). Source expertise, source attractiveness, and the processing of persuasive information: A functional approach. *Journal of Personality and Social Psychology, 55,* 541–546.

DeBono, K. G., & Packer, M. (1991). The effects of advertising appeal on perceptions of product quality. *Personality and Social Psychology Bulletin, 17,* 194–200.

DeBono, K. G. (1992). Pleasant scents and persuasion: An information processing approach. *Journal of Applied Social Psychology, 22,* 910–919.

DeJong, W., & Musilli, L. (1982). External pressure to comply: Handicapped versus nonhandicapped requesters and the foot–in–the–door phenomenon. *Personality and Social Psychology Bulletin, 8,* 522–527.

DeLamater, J. (1981). The social control of sexuality. *Annual Review of Sociology, 7,* 263–290.

Dellinger, R. W. (1979). Jet roar: Health problems take off near airports. *Human Behavior, 8,* 50–51.

Demare, D., Briere, J., & Lips, H. M. (1988). Violent pornography and self-reported likelihood of sexual aggression. *Journal of Research in Personality, 22,* 140–153.

Demeny, P. (1974). The populations of underdeveloped countries. *Scientific American, 231*(3), 148–159.

Dengerink, H. A., Schnedler, R. W., & Covey, M. X. (1978). Role of avoidance in aggressive responses to attack and no attack. *Journal of Personality and Social Psychology, 36,* 1044–1053.

Denno, D. J. (1982). *Sex differences in cognition and crime: Early developmental, biological, and social correlates.* Unpublished doctoral dissertation, University of Pennsylvania.

DePaulo, B. M., Dull, W. R., Greenberg, J. M., & Swaim, G. W. (1989). *Journal of Personality and Social Psychology, 56,* 834–844.

DePaulo, B. M. (1992). Nonverbal behavior and self–presentation. *Psychological Bulletin, 111,* 230–243.

DePaulo, B. M., & Fisher, J. D. (1980). The costs of asking for help. *Basic and Applied Social Psychology, 1,* 23–35.

DePaulo, B. M., Kirkendol, S. E., Tang, J., & O'Brien, T. (1988). The motivational impairment effect in the communication of deception: Replications and extensions. *Journal of Nonverbal Behavior, 12,* 177–202.

DePaulo, B. M., Stone, J. L., & Lassiter, G. D. (1985). Deceiving and detecting deceit. In B. R. Schlenker (Ed.), *The self and social life* (pp. 323–370). New York: McGraw–Hill.

Deutsch, F. M., Sullivan, L., Sage, C., & Basile, N. (1991). The relations among talking, liking, and similarity between friends. *Personality and Social Psychology Bulletin, 17,* 406–411.

Deutsch, F. M., & Lamberti, D. M. (1986). Does social approval increase helping? *Personality and Social Psychology Bulletin, 12,* 149–157.

Deutsch, F. M., Zalenski, C. M., & Clark, M. E. (1986). Is there a double standard of aging? *Journal of Applied Social psychology, 16,* 771–785.

Deutsch, M., & Collins, M. E. (1951). *Interracial housing.* Minneapolis: University of Minnesota Press.

de Waal, F. (1989). *Peacemaking in primates.* Cambridge, MA:

Harvard University Press.

Devine, P. O. (1989). Stereotypes and prejudice: Their automatic and controlled components. *Journal of Personality and Social Psychology, 56,* 5–18.

Devine, P. O., Monteith, M. J., Zuwerink, R. J., & Elliot, A. J. (1991). Prejudice with and without compunction. *Journal of Personality and Social Psychology, 60,* 817–830.

Dexter, H. R., Cutler, B. L., & Moran, G. (1992). A test of voir dire as a rememdy for the prejudicial effects of pretrial publicity. *Journal of Applied Social Psychology, 22,* 819–832.

Dickerson, C. A., Thibodeau, R., Aronson, E., & Miller, D. (1992). Using cognitive dissonance to encourage water conservation. *Journal of Applied Social Psychology, 22,* 841–854.

Dillard, J. P. (1991). The current status of research on sequential request compliance techniques. *Personality and Social Psychology Bulletin, 17,* 283–288.

DiMatteo, M. R., Hays, R. B., & Prince, L. M. (1986). Relationships of physicians' nonverbal communication skill to patient satisfaction, appointment noncompliance, and physician workload. *Health Psychology, 5,* 581–594.

Dion, H. H., & Dion, H. L. (1991). Psychological individualism and romantic love. *Journal of Social Behavior and Personality, 6,* 17–33.

Dion, H. L., & Dion, H. H. (1988). Romantic love: Individual and cultural perspectives. In R. J. Sternberg & M. L. Barnes (Eds.), *The psychology of love* (pp. 264–289). New Haven, CT: Yale University press.

Dion, K. K., Berscheid, E., & Walster, E. (1972). What is beautiful is good. *Journal of Personality and Social Psychology, 24,* 285–290.

Dion, K. L. (1993, March). Personal communication.

Dion, K. L., & Dion, K. K. (1987). Belief in a just world and physical attractiveness stereotyping. *Journal of Personality and Social Psychology, 52,* 775–780.

Dion, K. L., Dion, K. K., & Keelan, J. P. (1990). Appearance anxiety as a dimension of social–evaluative anxiety: Exploring the ugly duckling syndrome. *Contemporary Social Psychology, 14,* 220–224.

Ditto, P. H., Jemmot, J. B., III, & Darley, J. M. (1988). Appraising the threat of illness: A mental representational approach. *Health Psychology, 7,* 183–200.

Ditto, P. H., & Lopez, D. F. (1992) Motivated skepticism: Use of differential decision criteria for preferred and nonpreferred conclusions. *Journal of Personality and Social Psychology, 63,* 568–584.

Ditto, P. H., & Skobelsk. A. M. (1993). Research in progress, Kent State University, Kent, Ohio.

Dixon, J. G., & Swann, W. B., Jr. (1993). When does introspection bear fruit? Self-reflection, self–insight, and interpersonal choices. *Journal of Personality and Social Psychology, 64,* 35–43.

Dixon, T. M., & Baumeister, R. F. (1991). Escaping the self: The moderating effect of self–complexity. *Personality and Social Psychology Bulletin, 17,* 363–368.

Dodge, K. A., & Coie, J. D. (1987). Social–information–processing factors in reactive and proactive aggression in children's peer groups. *Journal of Personality and Social Psychology, 53,* 1146–1158.

Dodge, K. A., Murphy, R. R., & Buchsbaum, K. (1984). The assessment of intention–cue detection skills in children: Implications for developmental psychopathology. *Child Development, 55,* 163–173.

Dodge, K. A., Price, J. N., Bachorowski, J. A., & Newman, J. P. (1990). Hostile attributional biases in severely aggressive adolescents. *Journal of Abnormal Psychology, 99,* 385–392.

Doherty, K., Weigold, M. F., & Schlenker, B. R. (1990). Self–serving interpretations of motives. *Personality and Social Psychology Bulletin, 16,* 485–495.

Doktor, R. H. (1990). Asian and American CEOs: A comparative study. *Organizational Dynamics. 18*(3), 46–56.

Dollard, J., Doob, L., Miller, N., Mowrer, O. H., & Sears, R. R. (1939). *Frustration and aggression.* New Haven: Yale University Press.

Donnerstein, E., & Donnerstein, M. (1976). Research in the control of interracial aggression. In R. G. Geen & E. C. O'Heal (Eds.), *Perspectives on aggression.* New York: Academic Press.

Donnerstein, M., Donnerstein, E., Berkowitz, L., & Linz, D. (1987). In E. Donnerstein, D. Linz, & S. Penrod (Eds.), *The question of pornography: Research findings and implications.* New York: Free Press.

Dorian, B. J., Keystone, E., Garfinkel, P. E., & Brown, J. M. (1982). Aberrations in lymphocyte subpopulations and function during psychological stress. *Clinical and Experimental Immunology, 50,* 132–138.

Dovidio, J. F., Evans, N., & Tyler, R. B. (1986). Racial stereotypes: The contents of their cognitive representations. *Journal of Experimental Social Psychology, 22,* 22–37.

Dovidio, J. F., & Gaertner, S. L. (1993). Stereotypes and evaluative intergroup bias. In D. M. Mackie & D. L. Hamilton (Eds.), *Affect, cognition, and stereotyping: Interactive processes in perception.* Orlando, FL: Academic Press.

Downey, J. L., & Damhave, K. W. (1991). The effects of place, type of comment, and effort expended on the perception of flirtation. *Journal of Social Behavior and Personality, 6,* 35–43.

Downs, A. C., & Lyons, P. M. (1991). Natural observations of the links between attractiveness and initial legal judgments. *Personality and Social Psychology Bulletin, 17,* 541–547.

Drachman, D., DeCarufel, A., & Insko, C. A. (1978). The extra credit effect in interpersonal attraction. *Journal of Experimental Social Psychology, 14,* 458–465.

Drigotas, S. M., & Rusbult, C. E. (1992). Should I stay or should I go? A dependence model of breakups. *Journal of Personality and Social Psychology, 62,* 62–87.

Driscoll, R., Davis, H. E., & Lipetz, M. E. (1972). Parental interference and romantic love: The Romeo and Juliet effect. *Journal of Personality and Social Psychology, 24,* 1–10.

Dubrovsky, V., Kiesler, S., & Sethna, B. (1991). The equalization phenomenon: Status effects in computer–mediated and face–to–face decision making groups. *Human Computer Interaction, 6,* 119–146.

Duck, S., & Barnes, M. H. (1992). Disagreeing about agreement: Reconciling differences about similarity. *Communication Monographs, 59,* 199–208.

Dumanoski, D. (1990, February 13). Population growth seen as major force in our global environmental problems. *Albany Times Union,* pp. C–1, C–4.

Dunbar, R. I. M. (1989). Genetic similarity theory needs more development. *Behavioral and Brain Sciences, 12,* 520–521.

Dunn, J. (1992). Siblings and development. *Current Directions in Psychological Science, 1,* 6–11.

Dupre, J. (1992). Arbitrariness and bias in evolutionary speculation. *Behavioral and Brain Sciences, 15,* 98–99.

Durdan, C. A., Reeder, G. D., & Hecht, P. R. (1985). Litter in a university cafeteria: Demographic data and the use of prompts as an intervention strategy. *Environment and Behavior, 17,* 387–404.

Durham, D. F. (1991). Notes on "carrying capacity." *Population and Environment, 13,* 119–120.

Dutton, D. G., & Aron, A. P. (1974). Some evidence for heightened sexual attraction under conditions of high anxiety. *Journal of Personality and Social Psychology, 30,* 510–517.

Dutton, D. G., & Lake, R. A. (1973). Threat of own prejudice and reverse discrimination in interracial situations. *Journal of Personality and Social Psychology, 28,* 94–100.

Duval, S., & Wicklund, R. A. (1972). A theory of objective self–awareness. New York: Academic Press.

Eagly, A. H. (1987). *Sex differences in social behavior: A social–role interpretation.* Hillsdale, NJ: Erlbaum.

Eagly, A. H., & Carli, L. (1981). Sex of researchers and sex–typed communications as determinants of sex differences in influence ability: A meta–analysis of social influence studies. *Psychological Bulletin, 90,* 1–20.

Eagly, A. H., & Chaiken, S. (1984). Cognitive theories of persuasion. In L. Berkowitz (Ed.), *Advances in experimental social psychology.* (Vol. 17, pp. 267–359). New York: Academic Press.

Eagly, A. H., & Crowley, M. (1986). Gender and aggressive behavior: A meta–analytic review of the social psychological literature. *Psychological Bulletin, 100,* 309–330.

Eagly, A. H., & Crowley, M. (1986). Gender and helping behavior: A meta-analytic review of the social psychological literature. *Psychological Bulletin, 100,* 283–308.

Eagly, A. H., & Johnson, B. T. (1990). Gender and leadership style: A meta–analysis. *Psychological Bulletin, 108,* 233–256.

Eagly, A. H., & Steffen, V. J. (1986). Gender and aggressive behavior: A meta–analytic review of the social psychological literature. *Psychological Bulletin, 100,* 309–330.

Eagly, A. H., & Wood, W. (1991). Explaining sex differences in social behavior: A meta-analytic perspective. *Personality and Social Psychology Bulletin, 17,* 306–315.

Ebbeson, E. B., Kjos, G. L., & Konecni, V. J. (1976). Spatial ecology: Its effects on the choice of friends and enemies. *Journal of Experimental Social Psychology, 12,* 508–518.

Efran, M. G., & Patterson, E. W. J. (1974). Voters vote beautiful: The effect of physical appearance on a national election. *Canadian Journal of Behavioral Science, 6,* 352–356.

Egan, T. (1992, June 14). Forest damage, north and south. *New York Times,* p. E6.

Egbert, J. M. Jr., Moore, C. H., Wuensch, K. L., & Castellow, W. A. (1992). The effect of litigant social desirability on judgments regarding a sexual harassment case. *Journal of Social Behavior and Personality, 7,* 569–579.

Ehrhardt, A. A., Yingling, S., & Warne, P. A. (1991). Sexual behavior in the era of AIDS: What has changed in the United States? In J. Bancroft, C. M. Davis, & H. J. Ruppel, Jr. (Eds.), *Annual review of sex research.* (Vol. 2, pp. 25–47). Mt. Vernon, IA: Society for the Scientific Study of Sex.

Ehrlich, A. H. (1991). People and food. *Population and Environment, 72,* 221–229.

Eisenberg, N., Cialdini, R. B., McCreath, H., & Shell, R. (1987). Consistency based compliance: When and why do children become vulnerable? *Journal of Personality and Social Psychology, 52,* 1174–1181.

Eisenberg, N., & Fabes, R. A. (1991). Prosocial behavior and empathy: A multimethod developmental perspective. In M. S. Clark (Ed.), *Prosocial behavior* (pp. 34–61). Newbury Park, CA: Sage.

Eisenberg, N., Roth, K., Bryniarski, K. A., & Murray, E. (1984). Sex differences in the relationship of height to children's actual and attributed social and cognitive competencies. *Sex Roles, 11,* 719–734.

Eisenman, R. (1985). Marijuana use and attraction: Support for Byrne's similarity-attraction concept. *Perceptual and Motor Skills, 61,* 582.

Eisenman, R. (1992). Creativity, social and political attitudes, and liking or disliking David Duke. *Bulletin of the Psychonomic Society, 30,* 19–22.

Eisenman, R., & Sirgo, H. (1991). Liberals versus conservatives: Personality, child-rearing attitudes, and birth order/sex differences. *Bulletin of the Psychonomic Society, 29,* 240–242.

Ekman, P. (1973). Cross–cultural studies of facial expression. In P. Ekman (Ed.), *Darwin and facial expression.* New York: Academic Press.

Ekman, P. (1985). *Telling lies.* New York: Norton.

Ekman, P. (1989). The argument and evidence about universals in facial expressions of emotion. In H. Wagner & A. Manstead (Eds.), *Handbook of psychophysiology: Emotion and social behavior* (pp. 143–164). New York: Wiley.

Ekman, P. (1992). Are there basic emotions? *Psychological Review, 99,* 550–553.

Ekman, P. (in press). An argument for basic emotions. *Cognition and Emotion.*

Ekman, P., Davidson, R. J., & Friesen, W. V. (1990). The Duchenne smile: Emotional expression and brain physiology II. *Journal of Personality and Social Psychology, 58,* 342–353.

Ekman, P., & Friesen, W. V. (1975). *Unmasking the face.* Englewood Cliffs, NJ: Prentice–Hall.

Ellis, R. J. (1988). Self–monitoring and leadership emergence in groups. *Personality and Social Psychology Bulletin, 14,* 681–693.

Ellis, S., Rogoff, B., & Cramer, C. C. (1981). Age segregation in children's social interactions. *Developmental Psychology, 17,* 399–407.

Ellsworth, P. C., & Carlsmith, J. M. (1973). Eye contact and gaze aversion in aggressive encounter. *Journal of Personality and Social Psychology, 33,* 117–122.

Elmer–Dewitt, P. (1992). What's wrong with the weather? *Time, 139*(24), 60–61.

Elms, A. C. (1972). *Social psychology and social relevance.* Boston: Little, Brown.

Elms, A. C., & Milgram, S. (1966). Personality characteristics associated with obedience and defiance toward authoritative command. *Journal of Experimental Research in Personality, 1,* 282–289.

Emmons, R. A. (1992). Abstract versus concrete goals: personal striving level, physical illness, and psychological well–being. *Journal of Personality and Social Psychology, 62,* 292–300.

Emmons, R. A. (1993, March 2). Personal communication.

Epstein, S. (1983). The unconscious, the preconscious, and the self–concept. In J. Suls & A. Greenwald (Eds.), *Psychological perspectives on the self* (Vol. 2, pp. 220–247). Hillsdale, NJ: Erlbaum.

Erber, R. (1991). Affective and semantic priming: Effects of mood on category accessibility and inference. *Journal of*

Experimental Social Psychology, 27, 480–498.

Erber, R., & Fiske, S. T. (1984). Outcome dependency and attention to inconsistent information. *Journal of Personality and Social Psychology, 47,* 709–726.

Erdley, C. A., & D'Agostino, P. R. (1989). Cognitive and affective components of automatic priming effects. *Journal of Personality and Social Psychology, 54,* 741–747.

Eron, L. B. (1982). Parent–child interaction, television violence, and aggression of children. *American Psychologist, 37,* 197–211.

Esses, V. M. (1989). Mood as a moderator of acceptance of interpersonal feedback. *Journal of Personality and Social Psychology, 57,* 769–781.

Esses, V. M., & Webster, C. D. (1988). Physical attractiveness, dangerousness, and the Canadian criminal code. *Journal of Applied Social Psychology, 18,* 1017–1031.

Evans, G. W., Jacobs, S. V., & Frager, N. (1982). Behavioral responses to air pollution. In A. Baum & J. E. Singer (Eds.), *Advances in environmental psychology* (Vol. 4). Hillsdale, NJ: Erlbaum.

Evans, G. W., Palsane, M. N., & Carrere, S. (1987). Type A behavior and occupational stress: A cross–cultural study of blue–collar workers. *Journal of Personality and Social Psychology, 52,* 1002–1007.

Evans, M. C., & Wilson, M. (1949). Friendship choices of university women students. *Educational and Psychological Measurement, 9,* 307–312.

Fajardo, D. M. (1985). Author race, essay quality, and reverse discrimination. *Journal of Applied Social Psychology, 16,* 255–268.

Family planning mishandled in China and India, study says. (1992, September 16). *Albany Times Union,* p. A–12.

Fandt, P. M., & Ferris, G. R. (1990). The management of information and impressions: When employees behave opportunistically. *Organizational Behavior and Human Decision Processes, 45,* 140–158.

Farina, A., Wheeler, D. S., & Mehta, S. (1991). The impact of an unpleasant and demeaning social interaction. *Journal of Social and Clinical Psychology, 10,* 351–371.

Fazio, R. H. (1989). On the power and functionality of attitudes: The role of attitude accessibility. In A. R. Pratkanis, S. J. Breckler, & A. G. Greenwald (Eds.), *Attitude structure and function* (pp. 153–179). Hillsdale, NJ: Erlbaum.

Fazio, R. H., Chen, J., McDonel, E. C., & Sherman, S. J. (1982). Attitude accessibility and the strength of the object–evaluation association. *Journal of Experimental Social Psychology, 18,* 339–357.

Fazio, R. H., Sanbonmatsu, D. M., Powell, N. C., & Kardes, F. F. (1986). On the automatic activation of attitudes. *Journal of Personality and Social Psychology, 50,* 229–238.

Fazio, R. H., & Williams, C. J. (1986). Attitude accessibility as a moderator of the attitude–perception and attitude–behavior relations: An investigation of the 1984 presidential election. *Journal of Personality and Social Psychology, 51,* 505–514.

Fazio, R. H., & Zanna, N. P. (1981). Direct experience and attitude–behavior consistency. In L. Berkowitz (Ed.), *Advances in experimental social psychology* (vol. 14, pp. 161–202). New York: Academic Press.

Feingold, A. (1990). Gender differences in the effects of physical attractiveness on romantic attraction: A comparison across five research paradigms. *Journal of Personality and Social Psychology, 59,* 981–993.

Feingold, A. (1992a). Good–looking people are not what we think. *Psychological Bulletin, 111,* 304–341.

Feingold, A. (1992b). Gender differences in mate selection preferences: A test of the parental investment model. *Psychological Bulletin, 112,* 125–139.

Feingold, A. J. (1992). *Sex differences in personality: A quantitative analysis of personality inventory norms and gender–stereotyping experiments.* Unpublished doctoral dissertation, Yale University, New Haven, CT.

Fekken, G. C., & Jakubowski, I. (1990). Effects of stress on the health of Type A students. *Journal of Social Behavior and Personality, 5,* 473–480.

Feldman, D. C. (1984). The development and enforcement of group norms. *Academy of Management Review, 9,* 47–53.

Feldman, S. D. (1975). The presentation of shortness in everyday life—height and heightism in American society: Toward a sociology of stature. In S. D. Feldman & G. W. Thielbar (Eds.), *Life styles: Diversity in American society.* Boston: Little, Brown.

Feldman, S. S., & Nash, S. C. (1984). The transition from expectancy to parenthood: Impact of the firstborn child on men and women. *Sex Roles, 11,* 61–78.

Felson, R. B. (1989). Parents and the reflected appraisal process: A longitudinal analysis. *Journal of Personality and Social Psychology, 56,* 965–971.

Feltz, D. L. (1982). Path analysis of the causal elements in Bandura's theory of self-efficacy and an anxiety based model of avoidance behavior. *Journal of Personality and Social Psychology, 42,* 764–781.

Feshbach, S. (1984). The catharsis hypothesis, aggressive drive, and the reduction of aggression. *Aggressive Behavior, 10,* 91–101.

Festinger, L. (1954). A theory of social comparison processes. *Human Relations, 7,* 117–140.

Festinger, L. (1957). *A theory of cognitive dissonance.* Evanston, IL: Row, Peterson.

Festinger, L., & Carlsmith, J. M. (1959). Cognitive consequences of forced compliance. *Journal of Abnormal and Social Psychology, 38,* 203–210.

Festinger, L., Schachter, S., & Back, K. (1950). *Social pressures in informal groups: A study of a housing community.* New York: Harper.

Fichten, C. S., & Amsel, R. (1986). Trait attributions about college students with a physical disability: Circumplex analyses and methodological issues. *Journal of Applied Social Psychology, 16,* 410–427.

Fiedler, F. E. (1978). Contingency model and the leadership process. In L. Berkowitz (Ed.), *Advances in experimental social psychology* (Vol. 11). New York: Academic Press.

Fiedler, F. E., & Forgas, J. P. (Eds.). (1988). *Affect, cognition, and social behavior.* Toronto: Hogrefe.

Fiedler, F. E., & Garcia, J. E. (1987). *Leadership: Cognitive resources and performance.* New York: Wiley.

Field, R. H. G., & House, R. J. (1990). A test of the Vroom–Yetton model using manager and subordinate reports. *Journal of Applied Psychology, 75,* 362–366.

Fife-Schaw, C., & Breakwell, G. M. (1990). Predicting the intention not to vote in late teenage: A U. K. study of 17- and 18-year-olds. *Political Psychology, 11,* 739–755.

Fincham, F. D., & Bradbury, T. N. (1992). Assessing attributions in marriage: The relationship attribution measure. *Journal of Personality and Social Psychology, 62,* 457–468.

Fincham, F. D., & Bradbury, T. N. (1993). Marital satisfaction, depression, and attributions: A longitudinal analysis. *Journal of Personality and Social Psychology, 64,* 442–452.

Finn, J. (1986). The relationship between sex role attitudes and attitudes supporting marital violence. *Sex Roles, 14,* 235–244.

Fischer, G. (1989). Atmospheric lifetime of carbon dioxide. *Population and Environment, 13,* 177–181.

Fischman, J. (1986, January). Women and divorce: Ten years after. *Psychology Today,* p. 15.

Fisher, H. (1992). Anatomy of love. New York: W. W. Norton.

Fisher, J. D., & Fisher, WI A. (1992). Changing AIDS–risk behavior. *Psychological Bulletin, 111,* 455–474.

Fisher, J. D., Nadler, A., & Whitcher–Alagna, S. (1982). Recipient reactions to aid. *Psychological Bulletin, 91,* 27–54.

Fisher, W. A. (1989). Understanding and preventing adolescent pregnancy and sexually transmissible disease—AIDS. In J. Edwards et al. (Eds.), *Applying social influence processes in preventing social problems.* Beverly Hills, CA: Plenum.

Fisher, W. A., & Fisher, J. D. (1993). A general social psychological model for changing AIDS risk behavior. In J. Pryor & G. Reeder (Eds.), *The social psychology of HIV infection* (pp. 127–153). Hillsdale, NJ: Erlbaum.

Fiske, A. P. (1991). The cultural relativity of selfish individualism: Anthropological evidence that humans are inherently sociable. In M. S. Clark (Ed.), Prosocial behavior (pp. 176–214). Newbury Park, CA: Sage.

Fiske, S. T. (1980). Attention and weight in person perception: The impact of negative and extreme behavior. *Journal of Personality and Social Psychology, 33,* 889–906.

Fiske, S. T. (1989). *Interdependence and stereotyping: From the laboratory to the Supreme Court (and back).* Invited address, American Psychological Association, New Orleans.

Fiske, S. T., & Neuberg, S. L. (1990). A continuum model of impression formation, from category–based to individuating processes: Influence of information and motivation on attention and interpretation. In M. P. Zanna (Ed.), *Advances in experimental social psychology* (Vo1. 23). New York: Academic Press.

Fiske, S. T., & Taylor, S. E. (1991). *Social cognition* (2nd ed.). New York: Random House.

Fletcher, G. J. O., & Kininmonth, L. A. (1992). Measuring relationship beliefs: An individual differences scale. *Journal of Research in Personality, 26,* 371–397.

Flowers, M. (1977). A laboratory test of some implications of Janis's group think hypothesis. *Journal of Personality and Social Psychology, 55,* 888–896.

Folkman, S., & Lazarus, R. S. (1980). An analysis of coping in a middle–aged community sample. *Journal of Health and Social Behavior, 21,* 219–239.

Forgas, J. P. (1991a). Affective influences on partner choice: Role of mood in social decisions. *Journal of Personality and Social Psychology, 61,* 708–720.

Forgas, J. P. (1991b). Affect and social perception: Research evidence and an integrative theory. In W. Stroebe & M. Newstone (Eds.), *European review of social psychology.* New York: Wiley.

Forgas, J. P. (1992a, in press). Mood and the perception of atypical people: Affect and prototypicality in person memory and impressions. *Journal of Personality and Social Psychology,* in press.

Forgas, J. P. (l993b,). Mood and the perception of unusual people: Affective asymmetry in memory and social judgments.

European Journal of Social Psychology, in press.

Forgas, J. P. (1993c). On making sense of odd couples: Mood effects on the perception of mismatched relationships. *Personality and Social Psychology Bulletin, 19,* 59–70.

Forgas, J. P., & Bower, G. H. (1988). Affect in social and personal judgments. In K. Fiedler & J. P. Forgas (Eds.), *Affect, cognition, and social behavior.* Toronto: Hogrefe.

Forge, K. L., & Phemister, S. (1987). The effect of prosocial cartoons on preschool children. *Child Development Journal, 17,* 83–88.

Forrest, J. D., & Singh, S. (1990). The sexual and reproductive behavior of American women, 1982–1988. *Family Planning Perspectives, 22,* 206–214.

Forston, M. T., & Stanton, A. L. (1992). Self–discrepancy theory as a framework for understanding bulimic symptomatology and associated distress. *Journal of Social and Clinical Psychology, 11,* 103–118.

Forsyth, D. R. (1983). *An introduction to dynamics.* Monterey, CA: Brooks/Cole.

Forsyth, D. R. (1990). *An introduction to dynamics,* (2nd ed.). Monterey, CA: Brooks/Cole.

Forsyth, D. R. (1992). *An introduction to group dynamics,* (2nd ed.). Monterey, CA: Brooks/Cole.

Forsythe, S., Drake, M. F., & Cox, C. E. (1985). Influence of applicant's dress on interviewer's selection decisions. *Journal of Applied Psychology, 70,* 374–378.

Fraczek, A., & Kirwil, L. (1992). Living in the family and child aggression: Studies on some socialization conditions of development of aggression. In A. Fraczek & H. Zumkey (Eds.), *Socialization and aggression.* Berlin: Springer–Verlag.

Frank, M. G., & Gilovich, T. (1988). The dark side of self and social perception: Black uniforms and aggression in professional sports. *Journal of Personality and Social Psychology, 54,* 74–85.

Frankel, A., & Prentice–Dunn, S. (1990). Loneliness and the processing of self–relevant information. *Journal of Social and Clinical Psychology, 9,* 303–315.

Franzoi, S. L., & Herzog, M. E. (1987). Judging physical attractiveness: What body aspects do we use? *Personality and Social Psychology Bulletin, 13,* 19–33.

Freedman, J. L., Cunninghman, J. A., & Krismer, K. (1992). Inferred values and the reverse–incentive effect in induced compliance. *Journal of Personality and Social Psychology, 62,* 357–368.

Freedman, J. L., & Fraser, S. C. (1966). Compliance without pressure: The foot–in–the–door technique. *Journal of Personality and Social Psychology, 4,* 195–202.

Freedman, J. L. (1984). Effects of television violence on aggressiveness. *Psychological Bulletin, 96,* 227–246.

Freud, S. (1933). *New introductory lectures on psycho–analysis.* New York: Horton.

Freud, S. (1963). *The sexual enlightenment of children.* New York: Collier.

Freudenheim, M. (1992, October 14). Software helps patients make crucial choices. *New York Times,* p. D6.

Friedman, H. S., & Miller–Herringer, T. (1991). Nonverbal display of emotion in public and private: Self–monitoring, personality, and expressive cues. *Journal of Personality and Social Psychology, 61,* 766–775.

Friedman, H. S., Riggio, R. E., & Casella, D. F. (1988). Nonverbal skill, personal charisma, and initial attraction. *Personality and Social Psychology Bulletin, 14,* 203–211.

Fry, D. P. (1990). Aggressive interaction among Zapotec children in two different microcultural environments. *Proceedings of the Ninth World Meeting of the International Society for Research on Aggression,* Banff, Canada.

Fultz, J., Shaller, M., & Cialdini, R. B. (1988). Empathy, sadness, and distress: Three related but distinct vicarious affective responses to another's suffering. *Personality and Social Psychology Bulletin, 14,* 312–325.

Funder, D. C., & Colvin, C. R. (1988). Friends and strangers: Acquaintanceship, agreement, and the accuracy of personality judgment. *Journal of Personality and Social Psychology, 55,* 149–158.

Fussell, S. R., & Krauss, R. M. (1989). Understanding friends and strangers: The effects of audience design on message comprehension. *European Journal of Social Psychology, 19,* 509–525.

Gaertner, S. L., & Dovidio, J. F. (1986). Prejudice, discrimination, and racism: Problems, progress, and promise. In J. F. Dovidio & S. L. Gaertner (Eds.), *Prejudice, discrimination, and racism* (pp. 315–332). Orlando, FL: Academic Press.

Gaertner, S. L., Dovidio, J. F., Anastasio, P. A., Bachman, B. A., & Rust, M. C. (1993). The common ingroup identity model: Recategorization and the reduction of intergroup bias. In W. Stroebe & H. Hewstone (Eds.), *European Review of Social Psychology, 4,* in press.

Gaertner, S. L., Mann, J., Murrell, A., & Dovidio, J. F. (1989). Reducing intergroup bias: The benefits of recategorization. *Journal of Personality and Social Psychology, 57,* 239–249.

Gaertner, S. L., Rust, M. C., Dovidio, J. F., Bachman, B. A., & Anastasio, P. A. (1993). The contact hypothesis: The role of a common ingroup identity on reducing intergroup bias. *Small Business Research,* in press.

Gaertner, S. L., & Dovidio, J. F. (1976). The aversive form of racism. In J. F. Dovidio & S. L. Gaertner (Eds.), *Prejudice, discrimination, and racism* (pp. 61–89). San Diego, CA: Academic Press.

Galambos, N. I., (1992). Parent–adolescent relations. *Current Directions in Psychological Science, 1,* 146–149.

Gangestad, S., & Snyder, M. (1985). On the nature of self–monitoring: An examination of latent causal structure. In P. Shaver (Ed.), *Review of personality and Social Psychology (Vol. 6,* pp. 65–85). Beverly Hills, CA: Sage.

Gangestad, S. W. (1989). Uncompelling theory, uncompelling data. *Behavioral and Brain Sciences, 12,* 525–526.

Gantner, A. B., & Taylor, S. P. (1991). Human physical aggression as a function of alcohol and threat of harm. *Aggressive Behavior, 18,* 29–36.

Garcia, L. T. (1982). Sex role orientation and stereotypes about male–female sexuality. *Sex Roles, 8,* 863–876.

Geen, R. G. (1978). Some effects of observing violence upon the behavior of the observer. In B. A. Maher (Ed.), *Progress in experimental personality research,* (Vol. 8). New York: Academic Press.

Geen, R. G. (1981). Behavioral and physiological reactions to observed violence: Effects of prior exposure to aggressive stimuli. *Journal of Personality and Social Psychology, 40,* 868–875.

Geen, R. G., & Gange, J. J. (1977). Drive theory of social facilitation: Twelve years of theory and research. *Psychological Bulletin, 8*(3), 1267–1288.

Geen, R. G. (1989). Alternative conceptions of social facilitation. In P. B. Paulus (Ed.), *Psychology of group influence* (2nd ed., pp. 1–37). New York: Academic Press.

Geen, R. G. (1991). *Human aggression.* Pacific Grove, CA: Brooks/Cole.

Geier, J. G. (1969). A trait approach to the study of leadership in small groups. *Journal of Communication, 17,* 316–323.

Genovese, M. A. (1993). *Women as national leaders.* Newbury Park, CA: Sage.

George, J., & Brief, A. P. (1992). Feeling good—doing good: A conceptual analysis of the mood at work–organizational spontaneity relationship. *Psychological Bulletin, 112,* 310–329.

George, J. M. (1991). State or trait: Effects of positive mood on prosocial behaviors at work. Journal of Applied Psychology, 76, 299–307.

Gerard, H. B., Wilhelmy, R. A., & Conolley, E. S. (1968). Conformity and group size. *Journal of Personality and Social Psychology, 8,* 79–82.

Gerrard, M. (1986). Are men and women really different? In K. Kelley (Ed.), *Females, males, and sexuality* (pp. 213–242). Albany, NY: SUNY Press.

Gerrard, M., McCann, L., & Fortini, M. E. (1983). Prevention of unwanted pregnancy: *American Journal of Community Psychology, 11,* 153–167.

Gilbert, D., & Booker, C. (1993). *The automatization of correction.* Research in progress, University of Texas, Austin.

Gilbert, D., & Jones, E. E. (1986). Perceiver–induced constraint: Interpretations of self–generated reality. *Journal of Personality and Social Psychology, 50,* 269–280.

Gilbert, D. T., & Hixon, J. O. (1991). The trouble of thinking: Activation and application of stereotypic beliefs. *Journal of Personality and Social Psychology, 6,* 509–517.

Gilbert, D. T., McNulty, S. E., Giuliano, T. A., & Benson, J. E. (1992). Blurry words and fuzzy deeds: The attribution of obscure behavior. *Journal of Personality and Social Psychology, 62,* 18–25.

Gilbert, D. T., & Osborne, R. E. (1989). Thinking backward: Some curable and incurable consequences of cognitive busyness. *Journal of Personality and Social Psychology, 57,* 685–694.

Gilbert, D. T., Pelham, B. W., & Rrull, D. S. (1988). On cognitive busyness: When person perceivers meet persons perceived. *Journal of Personality and Social Psychology, 54,* 733–740.

Gilbert, L. A. (1993). *Two careers/one family.* Newbury Park, CA: Sage.

Gillen, B. (1981). Physical attractiveness: A determinant of two types of goodness. *Personality and Social Psychology Bulletin, 7,* 277–281.

Gillis, J. S. (1982). *Too small, too tall.* Champaign, IL: Institute for Personality and Ability Testing.

Gillmore, M. R., Catalano, R. F., Morrison, D. M., Wells, E. A., Iritani, G., & Hawkins, J. D. (1990). Racial differences in acceptability and availability of drugs and early initiation of substance use. *American Journal of Drug and Alcohol Abuse, 16,* 185–206.

Gladue, B. A. (1991). Aggressive behavioral characteristics, hormones, and sexual orientation in men and women. *Aggressive Behavior, 17,* 313–326.

Gladue, B. A., & Delaney, H. J. (1990). Gender differences in perception of attractiveness of men and women in bars. *Personality and Social Psychology Bulletin, 16,* 378–391.

Glass, D. C. (1977). *Behavior patterns, stress, and coronary disease.* Hillsdale, NJ: Erlbaum.

Glass, D. C. (1989). Psychology and health: Obstacles and

opportunities. *Journal of Applied Social Psychology, 19,* 1145–1163.

Glass, D. C., Singer, J. E., & Friedman, L. N. (1969). Psychic cost of adaptation to an environmental stressor. *Journal of Personality and Social Psychology, 12,* 200–210.

Glass, S. P., & Wright, T. L. (1992). Justifications for extramarital relationships: The association between attitudes, behaviors, and gender. *Journal of Sex Research, 29,* 361–387.

Glenn, N. D., & Weaver, C. N. (1988). The changing relationship of marital status to reported happiness. Journal of Marriage and the Family, 50, 317–324.

Glick, P. C. (1983). Seventh–year itch. *Medical Aspects of Human Sexuality, 17*(5), 103.

Godfrey, D. R., Jones, E. E., & Lord, C. C. (1986). Self–promotion is not ingratiating. *Journal of Personality and Social Psychology, 50,* 106–115.

Goethals, G. R. (1986a). Fabricating and ignoring social reality: Self–serving estimates of consensus. In J. Olson, C. P. Herman, & N. P. Zanna (Eds.), *Relative deprivation and social comparison: The Ontario symposium on social cognition IV.* Hillsdale, NJ: Erlbaum.

Goethals, G. R. (1986b). Social comparison theory: Psychology from the lost and found. *Personality and Social Psychology Bulletin, 12,* 261–278.

Goethals, G. R., Cooper, J., & Naficy, A. (1979). Role of foreseen, foreseeable, and unforeseeable behavioral consequences in the arousal of cognitive dissonance. *Journal of Personality and Social Psychology, 37,* 1179–1185.

Goethals, G. R., & Zanna, M. P. (1979). The role of social comparison in choice shifts. *Journal of Personality and Social Psychology, 37,* 1469–1476.

Goffman, E. (1963). *Stigma: Notes on the management of spoiled identity.* Englewood Cliffs, NJ: Prentice–Hall.

Gold, J. A., Ryckman, R. M., & Mosley, N. R. (1984). Romantic mood induction and attraction to a dissimilar other: Is love blind? *Personality and Social Psychology Bulletin, 10,* 358–368.

Goldstein, A. G., Chance, J. E., & Schneller, G. R. (1989). Frequency of eyewitness identification in criminal cases: A survey of prosecutors. *Bulletin of the Psychonomic Society, 27,* 71–74.

Goleman, D. (1991, October 15). Happy or sad, a mood can prove contagious. *New York Times,* pp. C1, C8.

Gooren, L., & Cohen–Kettenis, P. T. (1991). Development of male gender identity/role and a sexual orientation towards women in a 46, XY subject with an incomplete form of the androgen insensitivity syndrome. *Archives of Sexual Behavior, 20,* 459–470.

Gordin, F. M., Willoughby, A. D., Levine, L. A., Ourel, L., & Neill, K. M. (1987). Knowledge of AIDS among hospital workers: Behavioral correlates and consequences. *AIDS, 1,* 183–188.

Gorman, C. (1992). Danger overhead. *Time, 140*(7), 70.

Gouaux, C. (1971). Induced affective states and interpersonal attraction. *Journal of Personality and Social Psychology, 30,* 37–43.

Gould, D., & Weiss, M. (1981). Effect of model similarity and model self–talk on self–efficacy in muscular endurance. *Journal of Personality Psychology, 3,* 17–29.

Grabielcik, A., & Fazio, R. H. (1984). Priming and frequency estimation: A strict test of the availability heuristic. *Personality and Social Psychology Bulletin, 10,* 85–89.

Graham, B., & Folkes, V. (Eds.). *Attribution theory: Applications to achievement, mental health, and interpersonal conflict.* Hillsdale, NJ: Erlbaum.

Graham, J. A., & Argyle, M. (1975). A cross–cultural study of the communication of extra–verbal meaning by gestures. *International Journal of Psychology, 10,* 57–67.

Grant, J. (1988, Winter). Women as managers: What they can offer to organizations. *Organizational Dynamics,* pp. 56–63.

Gray, P. (1993). What is love? Time, 141(7), 46–49.

Green, S. K., Buchanan, D. R., & Heuer, S. K. (1984). Winners, losers, and choosers: A field investigation of dating initiation. *Personality and Social Psychology Bulletin, 10,* 502–511.

Greenbaum, P., & Rosenfield, H. W. (1978). Patterns of avoidance in responses to interpersonal staring and proximity: Effects of bystanders on drivers at a traffic intersection. *Journal of Personality and Social Psychology, 36,* 575–587.

Greenberg, J. (1989). Cognitive re–evaluation of outcomes in response to underpayment inequity. Academy of Management Journal, 32, 174–184.

Greenberg, J. (1989). Cognitive re–evaluation of outcomes in response to underpayment inequity. *Academy of Management Journal, 32,* 174–184.

Greenberg, J. (1990). Employee theft as a reaction to underpayment inequity: The hidden cost of pay cuts. *Journal of Applied Psychology, 75,* 561–568.

Greenberg, J. (1992). The social side of fairness: Interpersonal and informational classes of organizational justice. In R. Cropanzano (Ed.), *Justice in the workplace: Approaching fairness in human resource management.* Hillsdale, NJ: Erlbaum.

Greenberg, J., & Baron, R. A. (1993). *Behavior in organizations,* (4th ed.). Boston: Allyn & Bacon.

Greenberg, J., Pyszcynski, T., & Solomon, S. (1982). The self–serving attributional bias: Beyond self–presentation. *Journal of Experimental Social Psychology, 18,* 56–67.

Greenberg, J., Solomon, S., Pyszczynski, T., Rosenblatt, A., Burling, J., Lyon, D., Simon, L., & Pinel, E. (1992). Why do people need self–esteem? Converging evidence that self–esteem serves an anxiety–buffering function. *Journal of Personality and Social Psychology, 63,* 913–922.

Greenberg, M. A., & Stone, A. A. (1992). Emotional disclosure about traumas and its relation to health: Effects of previous disclosure and trauma severity. *Journal of Personality and Social Psychology, 63,* 75–84.

Greenwald, A. G., Bellazza, F. S., & Banaji, M. R. (1988). Is self–esteem a central ingredient of the self–concept? *Personality and Social Psychology Bulletin, 14,* 34–45.

Grieshop, J. I., & Stiles, M. C. (1989). Risk and home pesticide users. *Environment and Behavior, 21,* 699–716.

Griffin, E., & Sparks, G. G. (1990). Friends forever: A longitudinal exploration of intimacy in same–sex friends and platonic pairs. *Journal of Social and Personal Relationships, 7,* 29–46.

Gritz, E. R., & Crane, L. A. (1991). Use of diet pills and amphetamines to lose weight among smoking and nonsmoking high school seniors. *Health Psychology, 10,* 330–335.

Groff, D. B., Baron, R. S., & Moore, D. L. (1983). Distraction, attentional conflict, and drive like behavior. *Journal of Experimental Social Psychology, 19,* 359–380.

Grondahl, P. (1989, December 5). Trees of life: Reforestation begins in the backyard. *Albany Times Union,* pp. C–l, C–12.

Gross, B. R. (1990). The case of Phillipe Rushton. *Academic Questions, 3*(4), 35–46.

Grover, S. L., & Brockner, J. (1989). Empathy and the relationship between attitudinal similarity and attraction. *Journal of Research in Personality, 23,* 469–479.

Grusec, J. E. (1991). The socialization of altruism. In M. S. Clark (Ed.), *Prosocial behavior* (pp. 9–33). Newbury Park, CA: Sage.

Grush, J. E., & McKeogh, K. L. (1975, May). *The finest representation that money can buy: Exposure effects in the 1972 congressional primaries.* Paper presented at the meeting of the Midwestern Psychological Association, Chicago.

Gudjonsson, G. H., & Clark, N. K. (1986). Suggestibility in police interrogation: A social psychological model. *Social Behaviour, 1,* 83–104.

Guidubaldi, J., Perry, J. D., & Nastasi, B. H. (1987). Growing up in a divorced family: Initial and long–term perspectives on children's adjustment. In S. Oskamp (Ed.), *Family processes and problems: Social psychological aspects* (pp. 202–237). Beverly Hills, CA: Sage.

Guimond, S., & Palmer, D. L. (1990). Type of academic training and causal attributions for social problems. *European Journal of Social Psychology, 20,* 61–75.

Gully, K. J., & Dengerink, H. A. (1983). The dyadic interaction of persons with violent and nonviolent histories. *Aggressive Behavior, 9,* 13–20.

Gunter, B. G., & Gunter, N. C. (1991). Inequities in household labor: Sex role orientation and the need for cleanliness and responsibility as predictors. *Journal of Social Behavior and Personality, 6,* 559–572.

Gunter, G., Furnham, A., & Leese, J. (1986). Memory for information from a party political broadcast as a function of the channel of communication. *Social Behaviour, 1,* 135–142.

Gustafson, R. (1989). Frustration and successful vs. unsuccessful aggression: A test of Berkowitz' completion hypothesis. *Aggressive Behavior, 15,* 5–12.

Gustafson, R. (1992). Alcohol and aggression: A replication study controlling for potential confounding variables. *Aggressive Behavior, 18,* 21–28.

Haber, B. (1993, Spring). Women today: Sexually active teens. *Radcliffe News.*

Hackel, L. S., & Ruble, D. N. (1992). Changes in the marital relationship after the first baby is born: Predicting the impact of expectancy disconfirmation. *Journal of Personality and Social Psychology, 62,* 944–957.

Hacker, K. L., & Swan, W. O. (1992). Content analysis of the Bush and Dukakis 1988 presidential election campaign television commercials. *Journal of Social Behavior and Personality, 7,* 367–374.

Halford, W. K., & Sanders, M. R. (1990). The relationship of cognition and behavior during marital interaction. *Journal of Social and Clinical Psychology, 9,* 489–510.

Hall, J. A. (1984). *Nonverbal sex difference: Communication accuracy and expressive style.* Baltimore: Johns Hopkins University Press.

Hall, J. A., & Veccia, E. M. (1990). More "touching" observations: New insights on men, women, and interpersonal touch. *Journal of Personality and Social Psychology, 59,* 1155–1162.

Hallman, W. K., & Wandersman, A. (1992). Attribution of responsibility and individual and collective coping with environmental threats. *Journal of Social Issues, 48*(4), 101–118.

Hamid, P. N. (1990). Optimism and the reporting of flu

episodes. *Social Behavior and Personality, 13,* 225–234.

Hamilton, D. L., & Sherman, S. J. (1989). Illusory correlations: Implications for stereotype theory and research. In D. Bar-Tal, C. F. Graumann, A. W. Kruglanski, & W. Stroebe (Eds.), *Stereotyping and prejudice: Changing conceptions* (pp. 59–82). New York: Springer-Verlag.

Hamilton, D. L., Sherman, S. J., & Ruvolo, C. (1990). Stereotype–based expectancies: Effects on information processing and social behavior. *Journal of Social Issues, 46*(2), 35–60.

Hamilton, G. V. (1978). Obedience and responsibility: A jury simulation. *Journal of Personality and Social Psychology, 36,* 126–146.

Hamilton, J. C., Falconer, J. J., & Greenberg, M. D. (1992). The relationship between self–consciousness and dietary restraint. *Journal of Social and Clinical Psychology, 11,* 158–166.

Hammock, D. S., & Richardson, D. B. (1992). Aggression as one response to conflict. *Journal of Applied Social Psychology, 22,* 298–311.

Hans, V., & Vidmar, N. (1982). Jury selection. In N. L. Kerr & R. M. Bray (Eds.), *The psychology of the courtroom* (pp. 39–82). New York: Academic Press.

Hansen, C. H, & Hansen, R. D. (1988). Finding the face in the crowd: An anger superiority effect. *Journal of Personality and Social Psychology, 54,* 917–924.

Hansen, R. D. (1980). Common sense attribution. *Journal of Personality and Social Psychology, 17,* 398–411.

Hansen, R. D., & O'Leary, V. E. (1985). Sex–determined attributions. In V. E. O'Leary, R. B., Kesler Unger, & B. Strudler Wallston (Eds.), *Women, gender, and social psychology* (pp. 67–99). Hillsdale, NJ: Erlbaum.

Harder, D. W., & Lewis, S. J. (1986). The assessment of shame and guilt. In J. N. Butcher & C. D. Spielberger (Eds.), *Advances in personality assessment* (Vol. 6, pp. 89–114). Hillsdale, NJ: Erlbaum.

Hardin, G. (1990). Mythic aspects of the demographic transition. *Population and Environment, 12,* 41–58.

Hardin, G. (1991a). Book review. *Population and Environment, 12,* 417–418.

Hardin, G. (1991b). From shortage to longage: Forty years in the population vineyards. *Population and Environment, 12,* 339–349.

Hardin, G. (1992). Zero net immigration as the goal. *Population and Environment, 14,* 197–200.

Harkins, S. (1987). Social loafing and social facilitation. *Journal of Experimental Social Psychology, 23,* 1–18.

Harkins, S., & Petty, R. (1982). Effects of task difficulty and task uniqueness on social loafing. *Journal of Personality and Social Psychology, 43,* 1214–1229.

Harkins, S., & Szymanski, K. (1988). Social loafing and self–evaluation with an objective standard. *Journal of Experimental Social Psychology, 24,* 354–365.

Harkins, S., & Szymanski, K. (1989). Social loafing and group evaluation. *Journal of Personality and Social Psychology, 56,* 934–941.

Harpending, H. (1992). Age differences between mates in southern African pastoralists. *Behavioral and Brain Sciences, 15,* 102–103.

Harrell, W. A. (1990). Husband's masculinity, wife's power, and marital conflict. *Social Behavior and Personality, 18,* 207–216.

Harrigan, J. A. (1985). Self touching as an indicator of underlying affect and language processing. *Social Science and Medicine, 20,* 1161–1168.

Harrigan, J. A., Lucic, K. S., Kay, D., McLaney, A., & Rosenthal, R. (1991). Effect of expresser role and type of self–touching on observers' perceptions. *Journal of Applied Social Psychology, 21,* 585–609.

Harris, M. B., Harris, R. J., & Bochner, S. (1982). Fat, foureyed, and female: Stereotypes of obesity, glasses, and gender. *Journal of Applied Social Psychology, 12,* 503–516.

Harris, M. J., Milich, R., Corbitt, E. M., Hoover, D. W., & Brady, M. (1992). Self–fulfilling effects of stigmatizing information on children's social interactions. *Journal of Personality and Social Psychology, 63,* 41–50.

Harris, N. B. (1992). Sex, race, and experiences of aggression. *Aggressive Behavior, 18,* 201–217.

Harris, R. N., Snyder, R. L., Higgins, R. L., & Schrag, J. L. (1986). Enhancing the prediction of self–handicapping. *Journal of Personality and Social Psychology, 51,* 451–458.

Harvey, J. H., & Weary, G. (Eds.). (1989). *Attribution: Basic issues and applications.* San Diego: Academic Press.

Hastie, R., Penrod, S., & Pennington, N. (1983). *Inside the jury.* Cambridge, MA: Harvard University Press.

Hatfield, E., & Rapson, R. L. (1987). Passionate love/sexual desire: Can the same paradigm explain both? *Archives of Sexual Behavior, 16,* 259–278.

Hatfield, E. (1988). Passionate and companionate love. In R. L. Sternberg & M. I. Barnes (Eds.), *The psychology of love* (pp. 191–217). New Haven, CT: Yale University Press.

Hatfield, E., & Rapson, R. L. (1992a). Similarity and attraction in close relationships. *Communication Monographs, 59,* 209–212.

Hatfield, E., & Rapson, R. L. (1992b, November). *Culture and passionate love.* Paper presented at the meeting of the Society for the Scientific Study of Sex, San Diego.

Hatfield, E., & Rapson, R. L. (1992c). Similarity and attraction in close relationships. *Communication Monographs, 59,* 209–212.

Hatfield, E., & Rapson, R. L. (1993). *Love, sex, and intimacy: Their psychology, biology, and history.* New York: Harper Collins.

Hatfield, E., & Sprecher, S. (1986a). Measuring passionate love in intimate relations. *Journal of Adolescence, 9,* 383–410.

Hatfield, E., & Sprecher, S. (1986). *Mirror, mirror. . . The importance of looks in everyday life.* Albany, NY: SUNY Press.

Hatfield, E., Sprecher, S., Pillemer, J. T., Greenberger, D., & Wexler, P. (1989). Gender differences in what is desired in the sexual relationship. *Journal of Psychology and Human Sexuality, 1,* 39–52.

Hatfield, E., & Walster, G. W. (1981). A new look at love. Reading, MA: Addison–Wesley.

Haub, C. (1991). World and United States population prospects. *Population and Environment, 12,* 297–310.

Havel, V. (1992, June 3). Rio and the new millennium. *New York Times,* p. A21.

Hayes, S. C., Johnson, S. V., & Cone, J. D. (1975). *The marked item technique: A practical procedure for litter control.* Unpublished manuscript, West Virginia University, Morgantown.

Hays, R. B. (1989). The day–to–day functioning of close versus casual friendships. *Journal of Social and Personal Relationships, 6,* 21–37.

Hays, R. B., & DiMatteo, M. R. (1984). Toward a more thera-

peutic physician–patient relationship. In S. Duck (Ed.), *Personal relationships: Vol. 5. Repairing personal relationships* (pp. 1–20). New York: Academic Press.

Hazan, C., & Shaver, P. R. (1990). Love and work: An attachment–theoretical perspective. *Journal of Personality and Social Psychology, 59,* 270–280.

Heaviest smokers. (1992, June 1). *Time,* p. 26.

Heider, F. (1958). *The psychology of interpersonal relations.* New York: Wiley.

Heilbroner, R. L. (1974). *An inquiry into the human prospect.* New York: Norton.

Heilman, M. E. (1984). Information as a deterrent against sex discrimination: The effects of applicant sex and information type on preliminary employment decisions. *Organizational Behavior and Human Performance, 33,* 174–186.

Heilman, M. E., & Herlihy, J. M. (1984). Affirmative action, negative reaction? Some moderating conditions. *Organizational Behavior and Human Performance, 33,* 204–213.

Heilman, M. E., Hornstein, H. A., Cage, J. H., & Herschlag, J. X. (1984). Reactions to prescribed leader behavior as a function of role perspective: The case of the Vroom–Yetton model. *Journal of Applied Psychology, 69,* 50–60.

Heilman, M. E., & Martell, R. F. (1986). Exposure to successful women: Antidote to sex discrimination in applicant screening decisions? *Organizational Behavior and Human Decision Processes, 37,* 376–390.

Heilman, M. E., Martell, R. F., & Simon, M. C. (1988). The vagaries of sex bias: Conditions regulating the undervaluation, equivalation, and overvaluation of female job applicants. *Organizational Behavior and Human Decision Processes, 41,* 98–110.

Heinberg, L. J., & Thompson, J. K. (1992). Social comparison: Gender, target importance ratings, and relation to body image disturbance. *Journal of Social Behavior and Personality, 7,* 335–344.

Helgeson, V. S. (1992). Moderators of the relation between perceived control and ajustment to chronic illness. *Journal of Personality and Social Psychology, 63,* 656–666.

Helman, D., & Bookspan, P. (1992, February 8). In Big Bird's world, females are secondary. *Albany Times Union,* p. E–2.

Helson, R., & Roberts, B. (1992). The personality of young adult couples and wives' work patterns. *Journal of Personality, 60,* 575–597.

Henderson, J., & Taylor, J. (1985, November 17). Study finds bias in death sentence: Killers of whites risk execution. *Albany Times Union,* p. A–19.

Hendrick, C., & Hendrick, S. S. (1986). A theory and method of love. *Journal of Personality and Social Psychology, 50,* 392–402.

Hendrick, S. S., Hendrick, C., & Adler, N. L. (1988). Romantic relationships: Love, satisfaction, and staying together. *Journal of Personality and Social Psychology, 54,* 980–988.

Hendrix, W. H., Steel, R. P., & Schultz, S. A. (1987). Job stress and life stress: Their causes and consequences. *Journal of Social Behavior and Personality, 2,* 291–302.

Henley, N. (1973). Status and sex: Some touching observations. *Bulletin of the Psychonomic Society, 2,* 91–93.

Henry, W. A., III. (1991). The journalist and the murder. *Time 138*(15), 86.

Hentoff, N. (1992). *Free speech for me—but not for thee*. New York: Harper Collins.

Hepworth, J. T., & West, S. O. (1988). Lynchings and the economy: A time–series reanalysis of Hovland and Sears (1940). *Journal of Personality and Social Psychology, 55*, 239–247.

Herni ,W. M. (1990). Why are there so many of us? Description and diagnosis of a planetary ecopathological process. *Population and Environment, 12*, 9–39.

Hewstone, M., Bond, N. . H., & Wan, K. C. (1983). Social factors and social attributions: The explanation of intergroup differences in Hong Kong. *Social Cognition, 2*, 142–157.

Hewstone, M., & Jaspars, J. (1982). Explanations for racial discrimination: The effect of group discussion on intergroup attributions. *European Journal of Social Psychology, 12*, 1–16.

Hg, N., & Lau, R. R. (1990). Sexual attitudes in the Chinese. *Archives of Sexual Behavior, 19*, 373–398.

Hieva, V. F., & Gutek, B. A. (1981). *Women and work: A psychological perspective*. New York: Praeger.

Higgins, E. T. (1987). Self–discrepancy: A theory relating self and affect. *Psychological Review, 94*, 319–340.

Higgins, E. T., & Bargh, J. A. (1987). Social cognition and social perception. In M. R. Rosenszweig & L. W. Porter (Eds.), *Annual review of psychology* (Vol. 38, pp. 369–425). Palo Alto, CA: Annual Reviews Inc.

Higgins, E. T., & King, G. (1981). Accessibility of social constructs: Information processing consequences of individual and contextual variability. In N. Cantor & J. Kihlstrom (Eds.), *Personality, cognition, and social interaction* (pp. 69–121). Hillsdale, NJ: Erlbaum.

Higgins, E. T., Rohles, W. S., & Jones, C. R. (1977). Category accessibility and impression formation. *Journal of Experimental Social Psychology, 13*, 141–154.

Hill, C. A. (1987). Affiliation motivation: People who need people but in different ways. *Journal of Personality and Social Psychology, 52*, 1008–1018.

Hill, C. T., Rubin, Z., & Peplau, L. A. (1976). Breakups before marriage: The end of 103 affairs. *Journal of Social Issues, 32*, 147–168.

Hill, E. L., & Pfeifer, J. E. (1992). Nullification instructions and juror guilt ratings: An examination of modern racism. *Contemporary Social Psychology, 16*, 6–10.

Hilliard, A. (1985). *Parameters affecting the African-American child*. Paper presented at the Black Psychology Seminar, Duke Unviersity, Durham, NC.

Hilton, J. L., Klein, J. G., & von Hippel, W. (1991). Attention allocation and impression formation. *Personality and Social Psychology Bulletin, 17*, 548–559.

Hinsz, V. B., & Tomhave, J. A. (1991). Smile and (half) the world smiles with you; frown and you frown alone. *Personality and Social Psychology Bulletin, 17*, 586–592.

Hirt, E. R., Zillmann, D., Erickson, G. A., & Kennedy, C. (1992). Costs and benefits of allegiance: Changes in fans' self–ascribed competencies after team victory versus defeat. *Journal of Personality and Social Psychology, 61*, 724–738.

Hoffman, H. S., & Carver, C. S. (1984). Political waffling: Its effect on the evaluations of observers. *Journal of Applied Social Psychology, 14*, 375–385.

Hofstede, G. (1980). *Culture's consequences: International differences in work–related values*. Beverly Hills, CA: Sage

Hogan, J. (1989). Personality correlates of physical fitness. *Journal of Personality and Social Psychology, 56*, 284–288.

Hokanson, J. E., Burgess, M., & Cohen, M. E. (1963). Effects of displaced aggression on systolic blood pressure. *Journal of Abnormal and Social Psychology, 67*, 214–218.

Holdren, J. p. (1991). Population and the energy problem. *Population and Environment, 12*, 231–255.

Holland, C. D. (1967). Sources of variance in the experimental investigation of behavioral obedience. *Dissertation Abstracts International, 29*, 2802A. (University Microfilms No. 69–2146.)

Hollander, P. (1978). *Soviet and American society: A comparison*. Chicago: University of Chicago Press.

Holowaty, L. S., Pliner, P., & Flett, G. L. (1990). Social responses to justified and unjustified depression: Evidence for a depression prototype. *Journal of Social Behavior and Personality, 5*, 29–44.

Holtzworth–Munroe, A., & Jacobson, N. S. (1985). Causal attributions of married couples: When do they search for causes? What do they conclude when they do? *Journal of Personality and Social Psychology, 48*, 1398–1412.

Horowitz, I. A. (1988). Jury nullification: The impact of judicial instructions, arguments, and challenges on jury decision making. *Law and Human Behavior. 12*, 439–453.

Hosch, H. M., & Bothwell, R. K. (1990). Arousal, description and identification accuracy of victims and bystanders. *Journal of Social Behavior and Personality, 5*, 481–488.

House, R. J. (1977). A theory of charismatic leadership. In J. G. Hunt & L. L. Larson (Eds.), *Leadership: The cutting edge* (pp. 189–207). Carbondale, IL: Southern Illinois University Press.

House, R. J., Spangler, W. D., & Woycke, J. (1991). Personality and charisma in the U. S. presidency: A psychological theory of leader effectiveness. *Administrative Science Quarterly, 36*, 364–396.

Hovland, C. I., Janis, I. L., & Kelley, H. H. (1953). *Communication and persuasion: Psychological studies of one on one*. New Haven, CT: Yale University Press.

Hovland, C. I., Lumsdaine, A. A., & Sheffield, F. D. (1949). *Experiments on mass communications*. Princeton, NJ: Princeton University Press.

Hovland, C. I., & Sears, R. R. (1940). Minor studies in aggression: VI. Correlation of lynchings with economic indices. *Journal of Psychology, 9*, 301–310.

Hovland, C. I., & Weiss, W. (1951). The influence of source credibility on communication effectiveness. *Public Opinion Quarterly, 1*, 635–650.

Howard, G. S. (1985). The role of values in the science of psychology. *American Psychologist, 40*, 255–265.

Howell, J. M., & Frost, P. J. (1989). A laboratory study of charismatic leadership. *Organizational Behavior and Human Decision Processes, 43*, 243–269.

Hsee, C. K., Hatfield, E., & Chemtob, C. (1992). Assessments of the emotional states of others: Conscious judgments versus emotional contagion. *Journal of Social and Clinical Psychology, 11*, 119–128.

Huesmann, L. R. (1982). Television violence and aggressive behavior. In D. Pearl, L. Bouthilet, & J. Lazar (Eds.), *Television and behavior: Vol., 2. Technical reviews* (pp. 220–256). Washington, DC: National Institute of Mental Health.

Hummert, M. L., Crockett, W. H., & Kemper, S. (1990). Processing mechanisms underlying use of the balance schema. *Journal of Personality and Social Psychology, 58*, 5–21.

Humphriss, N. (1989, November 20). Letters. *Time*, p. 12.

Hunter, C. E., & Ross, M. W. (1991). Determinants of health–care workers' attitudes toward people with AIDS. *Journal of Applied Social Psychology, 21,* 947–956.

Hunter, S. MacD., Johnson, C. C., Vizelber, I. A., Webber, L. S., & Berenson, G. S. (1991). Tracking of Type A behavior in children and young adults: The Bogalusa heart study. *Journal of Social Behavior and Personality, 6,* 71–84.

Hutton, D. C., & Baumeister, R. F. (1992). Self–awareness and attitude change: Seeing oneself on the central route to persuasion. *Personality and Social Psychology Bulletin, 18,* 68–75.

Ickes, W., Reidhead, S., & Patterson, M. (1986). Machiavellianism and self-monitoring: As different as "me" and "you." *Social Cognition, 4,* 58–74.

Ickes, W., & Turner, M. (1983). On the social advantages of having an older, opposite–sex sibling: Birth order influences in mixed–sex dyads. *Journal of Personality and Social Psychology, 45,* 210–222.

Ingham, R., Woodcock, A., & Stenner, K. (1991). Getting to know you. . . Young people's knowledge of their partners at first intercourse. *Journal of Community & Applied Social Psychology, 1,* 117–132.

Innes, J. M., & Zeitz, H. (1988). The public's view of the impact of the mass media: A test of the "third person" effect. *European Journal of Social Psychology, 18,* 457–463.

Insko, C. A., Hoyle, R. H., Pinkley, R. L., Hong, G. Y., Slim, R. M., Dalton, B., Lin, Y. H. W., Ruffin, P. P., Dardis, G. J., Brenthal, P. R., & Schopler, J. (1988). Individual–group discontinuity: The role of a consensus rule. *Journal of Experimental Social Psychology, 24,* 505–519.

Insko, C. A. (1985). Balance theory, the Jordan paradigm, and the West tetrahedron. In L. Berkowitz (Ed.), *Advances in experimental social psychology.* New York: Academic Press.

Isen, A. M. (1984). Toward understanding the role of affect in cognition. In S. R. Wyer & T. K. Srull (Eds.), *Handbook of social cognition* (Vol. 3, pp. 179–236). Hillsdale, NJ: Erlbaum.

Isen, A. M. (1987). Positive affect, cognitive processes, and social behavior. In L. Berkowitz (Ed.), *Advances in experimental social psychology* (Vol. 20, pp. 203–253. New York: Academic Press.

Isen, A. M., & Baron, R. A. (1991). Affect and organizational behavior. In B. M. Staw & L. L. Cummings (Eds.), *Research in organizational behavior* (vol. 15, pp. 1–53). Greenwich CT: JAI Press.

Isen, A. M., & Daubman, K. A. (1984). The influence of affect on categorization. *Journal of Personality and Social Psychology, 47,* 1206–1217.

Isen, A. M., Daubman, K. A., & Howicki, G. P. (1987). Positive affect facilitates creative problem solving. *Journal of Personality and Social Psychology, 52,* 1122–1131.

Isen, A. N., Johnson, N. M. S., Merz, E., & Robinson, G. (1985). The influence of positive affect on the unusualness of work association. *Journal of Personality and Social Psychology, 48,* 1413–1426.

Isen, A. M., & Levin, P. A. (1972). Effect of feeling good on helping: Cookies and kindness. *Journal of Personality and Social Psychology, 21,* 384–388.

Isen, A. M., & Shalker, T. E. (1982). Do you "accentuate the positive, eliminate the negative" when you are in a good mood? *Social Psychology Quarterly, 41,* 345–349.

Israeli, D. N., Israeli, D., & Eden, D. (1985). Giving credit where credit is due: A case of no sex bias in attribution. *Journal of Applied Social Psychology, 15,* 516–530.

Istvan, J., & Griffitt, W. (1980). Effects of sexual experience on dating desirability and marriage desirability. *Journal of Marriage and the Family, 43,* 377–385.

Istvan, J., Griffitt, W., & Weidner, G. (1983). Sexual arousal and the polarization of perceived sexual attractiveness. *Basic and Applied Social Psychology, 4,* 307–318.

Iyengar, S., & Kinder, D. R. (1987). *News that matters.* Chicago: University of Chicago Press.

Izard, C. (1991). *Human emotions* (2nd ed.). New York: Plenum.

Izard, C. (1992). Basic emotions, relations among emotions, and emotion–cognition relations. *Psychological Review, 99,* 561–565.

Jaccard, J. (1992, November). *Women and AIDS.* Paper presented at the meeting of the Society for the Scientific Study of Sex, San Diego.

Jackson, L. A., Gardner, P., & Sullivan, L. (1992). Explaining gender differences in self–pay expectations: Social comparison standards and perceptions of fair pay. *Journal of Applied Psychology, 77,* 651–663.

Jackson, L. A., & Grabski, S. V. (1988). Perceptions of fair play and the gender wage gap. *Journal of Applied Social Psychology, 18,* 606–625.

Jacobs, J. R. (1992). Facilitators of romantic attraction and their relation to lovestyle. *Social Behavior and Personality, 20,* 227–234.

Jaffe, Y., Malamuth, N., Feingold, J., & Feshbach, S. (1974). Sexual arousal and behavioral aggression. *Journal of Personality and Social Psychology, 30,* 759–764.

James, K. (1993). Conceptualizing self with in–group stereotypes: Context and esteem precursors. *Personality and Social Psychology Bulletin, 19,* 117–121.

Janis, I. L. (1954). Personality correlates of susceptablity to persuasion. *Journal of Personality, 22,* 504–518.

Janis, I. L. (1982). *Victims of groupthink* (2nd ed.). Boston: Houghton Mifflin.

Janoff–Bulman, R. (1979). Characterlogical versus behavioral self–blame: Inquiries into depression and rape. *Journal of Personality and Social Psychology, 37,* 1798–1809.

Jarvis, M. J. (1991). A time for conceptual stock taking. Special issue: Future directions in tobacco research. *British Journal of Addiction, 86,* 632–647.

Jasnoski, M. L., Cordray, D. S., Houston, G. K., & Osness, W. H. (1987). Modification of Type A behavior through aerobic exercise. *Motivation and Emotion, 111,* 1–17.

Jaspars, J. (1983). The process of attribution. In M. R. C. Hewstone (Ed.), *Attribution theory: Social and functional extensions* (pp. 28–44). Oxford, England: Blackwell.

Jay, S. M., Ozolins, M., Elliott, C. H., & Caldwell, S. (1983). Assessment of children's distress during painful medical procedures. *Health Psychology, 2,* 133–147.

Jeavons, C. M., & Taylor, S. P. (1985). The control of alcohol–related aggression: Redirecting the inebriate's attention to socially appropriate conduct. *Aggressive Behavior, 11,* 93–101.

Jeffries, V. (1987). Love: The five virtues of St. Thomas Aquinas. A factor analysis of love of parents among university students. *Sociology and Social Research, 71,* 174–182.

Jeffries, V. (1990). Adolescent love, perception of parental love, and relationship quality. *Family Perspective, 24,* 175–196.

Jeffries, V. (1993, in press). Virtue and attraction: Validation of a measure of love. *Journal of Social and Personal Relationships, 10,* in press.

Jemmott, J. B., III, Ashby, K. L., & Lindenfield, K. (1989). Romantic commitment and the perceived availability of opposite–sex persons: On loving the one you're with. *Journal of Applied Social Psychology, 19,* 1198–1211.

Jemmott, J. B., III, & Magloire, K. (1988). Academic stress, social support, and secretory immunoglobulin. *Journal of Personality and Social Psychology, 55,* 803–810.

Jennings, S. R. (1985). *The relationship of personality factors to social anxiety and disaffiliation.* Unpublished doctoral dissertation, University of Texas, Austin.

Johnson, B. T., & Eagly, A. H. (1989). Effects of involvement on persuasion: A meta–analysis. *Psychological Bulletin, 106,* 290–314.

Johnson, D. F., & Pittenger, J. B. (1984). Attribution, the attractiveness stereotype, and the elderly. *Developmental Psychology, 20,* 1168–1172.

Johnson, D. J., & Rusbult, C. E. (1989). Resisting temptation: Devaluation of alternative partners as a means of maintaining commitment in close relationships. *Journal of Personality and Social Psychology, 57,* 967–980.

Johnson, H. P., Huston, T. I., Gaines, S. O., Jr., & Levinger, G. (1992). Patterns of married life among young couples. *Journal of Social and Personal Relationships, 9,* 343–364.

Johnson, J. T. (1987). The heart on the sleeve and the secret self: Estimations of hidden emotion in self and acquaintances. *Journal of Personality, 55,* 563–581.

Johnson, K. A., Johnson, J. E., & Petzel, T. P. (1992). Social anxiety, depression, and distorted cognitions in college students. *Journal of Social and Clinical Psychology, 11,* 181–195.

Johnson, R. A., & Schulman, G. I. (1989). Gender–role composition and role entrapment in decision–making groups. *Gender & Society, 3,* 355–372.

Johnson, R. D. (1991). The influence of time–frame for achieving gender neutrality on evaluations of a male–dominated profession. *Journal of Social Behavior and Personality, 6,* 833–842.

Johnson, R. D., & Downing, L. L. (1979). Deindividuation and valence of cues: Effects on prosocial and antisocial behavior. *Journal of Personality and Social Psychology, 37,* 1532–1538.

Johnson, T. E., & Rule, B. G. (1986). Mitigating circumstance information, censure, and aggression. *Journal of Personality and Social Psychology, 50,* 537–542.

Johnstone, B., Frame, C. L., & Bouman, D. (1992). Physical attractiveness and athletic and academic ability in controversial–aggressive and rejected–aggressive children. *Journal of Social and Clinical Psychology, 11,* 71–79.

Jones, E. E. (1964). *Ingratiation: A social psychological analysis.* New York: Appleton–Century Crofts

Jones, E. E. (1990). *Interpersonal perception.* New York: W. H. Freeman.

Jones, E. E., & Davis, K. E. (1965). From acts to disposition: The attribution process in person perception. In L. Berkowitz (Ed.), *Advances in experimental social psychology.* (Vol. 2, pp. 219–266). New York: Academic Press.

Jones, E. E., & McGillis, D. (1976). Corresponding inferences and the attribution cube: A comparative reappraisal. In J. H. Harvey, W. J. Ickes, & R. F. Kidd (Eds.), *New directions in attribution research* (Vol. 1). Morristown, NJ: Erlbaum.

Jones, E. E., & Nisbett, R. E. (1971). *The actor and the observer: Divergent perceptions of the causes of behavior.* Morristown, NJ:

General Learning Press.

Jones, E. E., & Pittman, T. S. (1982). Toward a general theory of strategic self presentation. In J. Suls (Ed.), *Psychological perspective on the self.* Hillsdale, NJ: Erlbaum.

Jones, W. H., Carpenter, B. N., & Quintana, D. (1985). Personality and interpersonal predictors of loneliness in two cultures. *Journal of Personality and Social Psychology, 48,* 1503–1511.

Jones, W. H., Hobbs, S. A., & Hockenbury, D. (1982). Loneliness and social skill deficits. *Journal of Personality and Social Psychology, 42,* 682–689.

Josephs, R. A., Markus, H. R., & Tafarodi, R. W. (1992). Gender and self–esteem. *Journal of Personality and Social Psychology, 63,* 391–402.

Josephson, W. D. (1987). Television violence and children's aggression: Testing the priming, social script, and disinhibition predictions. *Journal of Personality and Social Psychology, 55,* 882–890.

Judd, C. M., Drake, R. A., Downing, J. W., & Krosnick, J. A. (1991). Some dynamic properties of attitude structures: Context–induced response facilitation and polarization. *Journal of Personality and Social Psychology, 60,* 193–202.

Judd, C. M., & Krosnick, J. A. (1989). The structural bases of consistency among political attitudes: Effect of political expertise and attitude importance. IN A. R. Pratkanis, S. J. Breckler, & A. G. Greenwald (Eds.), *Attitude structure and function* (pp. 99–128). Hillsdale, NJ: Erlbaum.

Judd, C. M., Ryan, C. N., & Parke, B. (1991). Accuracy in the judgment of in–group and out–group variability. *Journal of Personality and Social Psychology, 61,* 366–379.

Jussim, L. (1991). Interpersonal expectations and social reality: A reflection–construction model and reinterpretation of evidence. *Psychological Review, 98,* 54–73.

Kabanoff, B. (1991). Equity, equality, power, and conflict. *Academy of Management Review, 12,* 9–22.

Kacmar, K. M., Delery, J. E., & Ferris, G. R. (1992). Differential effectiveness of applicant impression management tactics on employment interview decisions. *Journal of Applied Social Psychology, 22,* 1250–1272.

Kahle, L. R., & Beatty, S. E. (1987). Cognitive consequences of legislating post–purchase behavior: Growing up with the bottle bill. *Journal of Applied Social Psychology, 17,* 828–843.

Kahneman, D., & Miller, D. T. (1986). Norm theory: comparing reality to its alternatives. *Psychological Review, 93,* 136–153.

Kahneman, D., & Tversky, A. (1982). The simulation heuristic. In D. Kahneman, P. Slovic, & Tversky, A. (Eds.), *Judgments under uncertainty: Heuristics and biases* (pp. 201–208). New York: Cambridge University Press.

Kalick, S. M. (1988). Physical attractiveness as a status cue. *Journal of Experimental Social Psychology, 24,* 469–489.

Kalick, S. M., & Hamilton, T. E. (1986). The matching hypothesis reexamined. *Journal of Personality and Social Psychology, 51,* 673–682.

Kameda, T. (1991). Procedural influence in small–group decision making: Deliberation style and assigned decision rule. *Journal of Personality and Social Psychology, 61,* 245–256.

Kandel, D. B. (1978). Similarity in real–life adolescent friendship pairs. *Journal of Personality and Social Psychology, 36,* 306–312.

Kanekar, S., Kolsawalla, M. B., & Nazareth, T. (1988). Occupational prestige as a function of occupant's gender. *Journal of Applied Social Psychology, 19,* 681–688.

Kanfer, R. (1990). Motivational theory and industrial and organizational psychology. In M. D. Dunnette & L. M. Hough (Eds.), *Handbook of industrial and organizational psychology* (2nd ed., Vol. 1, pp. 75–170). Palo Alto, CA: Consulting Psychologists Press.

Kanfer, R. (1993). Work motivation: New directions in theory and research. In C. L. Cooper & I. T. Robertson (Eds.), *International review of industrial and organizational psychology*. (Vol. 7). New York: Wiley.

Kaniasty, K., & Norris, F. H. (1993). A test of the social support deterioration model in the context of natural disaster. *Journal of Personality and Social Psychology, 64,* 395–408.

Kanki, P. J, Alroy, J., & Essex, M. (1985). Isolation of T–lymphotropic retrovirus related to HTLV–III/LAV from wild–caught African green monkeys. *Science, 230,* 951–954.

Kaplan, H. B., & Pokorny, A. D. (1971). Self–derogation and childhood broken home. *Journal of Marriage and the Family, 33,* 328–337.

Kaplan, M. F. (1981). State dispositions in social judgment. *Bulletin of the Psychonomic Society, 18,* 27–29.

Kaplan, M. F., & Miller, C. E. (1987). Group decision making and normative versus informational influence: Effects of type of issue and assigned decision rule. *Journal of Personality and Social Psychology, 59,* 306–313.

Kaplan, R. D. (1992). Continental drift. *New Republic, 207*(27), 15–16, 18, 20.

Karraker, K. H., Vogel, D. A., & Evans, S. (1987, August). *Responses of students and pregnant women to newborn physical attractiveness.* Paper presented at the meeting of the American Psychological Association, New York.

Kaufman, K., Gregory, W. L., & Stephan, W. G (1990). Maladjustment in statistical minorities within ethnically unbalanced classrooms. *American Journal of Community Psychology, 18,* 757–765.

Keiman, H. C., & Hovland, C. I. (1953). "Reinstatement" of the communicator in delayed measurement of opinion change. *Journal of Abnormal and Social Psychology, 48,* 327–33S.

Keller, L. M., Bouchard, T. J., Jr., Arvey, R. D., Segal, N. L., & Dawis, R. V. (1992). Work values: Genetic and environmental influences. *Journal of Applied Psychology, 77,* 79–88.

Kellerman, J., Lewis, J., & Laird, J. D. (1989). Looking and loving: The effects of mutual gaze on feelings of romantic love. *Journal of Research in Personality, 23,* 145–161.

Kelley, H. H. (1972). Attribution in social interaction. In E. E. Jones et al. (Eds.), *Attribution: Perceiving the causes of behavior.* Morristown, NJ: General Learning Press.

Kelley, H. H., & Michela, J. L. (1980). Attribution theory and research. *Annual Review of Psychology, 31,* 457–501.

Kelley, K. (1982). Playing roulette with pregnancy. In L. H. Gross (Ed.), *The parents' ode to teenagers* (pp. 309–310). New York: McGraw–Hill.

Kelley, K., & Byrne, D. (1992). *Exploring human sexuality.* Englewood Cliffs, NJ: Prentice–Hall.

Kelley, K., & Dawson, L. J. (1991). The role of chronic self–destructiveness in adolescence. In R. M. Lerner, A. C. Petersen, & J. Brooks-Gunn (Eds.), *The encyclopedia of adolescence.* New York: Garland.

Kelley, K., & Harvan, A. (1993, in press). Sexual behavior: Affect and attribution. In A. S. R. Manstead & M. Hewstone (Eds.), *The Blackwell dictionary of social psychology.* Oxford, U. K. : Blackwell.

Kelley, K., & Streeter, D. (1992). The role of gender in organizations. In K. Kelley (Ed.), *Issues, theory, and research in industrial/organizational psychology* (pp. 285–337). Amsterdam: North–Holland.

Kelman, H. C. (1967). Human use of human subjects: The problem of deception in social psychological experiments. *Psychological Bulletin, 67,* 1–11.

Kenealy, P., Gleeson, K., Frude, N., & Shaw, W. (1991). The importance of the individual in the "causal" relationship between attractiveness and self–esteem. *Journal of Community and Applied Social Psychology, 1,* 45–56.

Kennedy, G. E. (1991). Grandchildren's reasons for closeness with grandparents. *Journal of Social Behavior and Personality, 6,* 697–712.

Kenrick, D. T., & Keefe, R. C. (1992). Age preferences in mates reflect sex differences in human reproductive strategies. *Behavioral and Brain Sciences, 15,* 75–133.

Kenrick, D. T., Sadalla, E. K., Groth, G., & Trost, M. R. (1990). Evolution, traits, and the stages of human courtship: Qualifying the parental investment model. *Journal of Personality, 58,* 97–116.

Kent, D. (1990). A conversation with Claude Steele. *APS Observer, 3*(3), 11–15, 17.

Kent, G. G., Davis, J. D., & Shapiro, D. A. (1981). Effect of mutual acquaintance on the construction of conversation. *Journal of Experimental Social Psychology, 17,* 197–209.

Kenworthy, T. (1993, January 6). Secondhand smoke makes EPA blacklist. *Albany Times Union,* pp. A–I, A–6.

Kerr, H. L., & Bruun, S. E. (1983). Dispensability of member effort and group motivation losses: Free–rider effects. *Journal of Personality and Social Psychology, 45,* 78–94.

Kerr, H. L., & MacCoun, R. J. (1985). The effects of jury size and polling method on the process and product of jury deliberations. *Journal of Personality and Social Psychology, 48,* 349–363.

Kessler, R. C., Kendler, K. S., Heath, A., Neale, M. C., & Eaves, L. J. (1992). Social support, depressed mood, and adjustment to stress: A genetic epidemiologic investigation. *Journal of Personality and Social Psychology, 62,* 257–272.

Keyfritz, N. (1989). The growing human population. *Scientific American, 261*(3), 119–126.

Kidwell, J. S. (1982). The neglected birth order: Middleborns. *Journal of Marriage and the Family, 44,* 225.

Kiesler, A., Reber, G., & Wunderer, R. (Eds.), *Encyclopedia of leadership* (pp. 378–390). Kernerstrasse, FRG: C. E. Paeschel Verlag.

Kiesler, C. A., & Kiesler, S. B. (1969). *Conformity.* Reading, MA: Addison–Wesley.

Kiesler, S., & Sproull, L. (1992). Group decision making and communication technology. *Organizational Behavior and Human Decision Processes, 52,* 96–123.

Kilham, W., & Mann, L. (1974). Level of destructive obedience as a function of transmitter and executant roles in the Milgram obedience paradigm. *Journal of Personality and Social Psychology, 29,* 696–702.

Kimmell, M. S. (1988, October). Macho mouth on the campaign trail. The winning strategy in '88: Talk like a man. *Psychology Today,* p. 27.

Killmann, R. H., & Thomas, K. W. (1977). Developing a forced-choice measure of conflict-handling behavior. The "MODE" instrument. *Educational and Psychological Measurement, 37,* 309–325.

Kinsey, A. C., Pomeroy, W., & Martin, C. (1948). Sexual behavior in the human male. Philadelphia: W. B. Saunders.

Kinsey, A. C., Pomeroy, W., Martin, C., & Gebhard, P. (1953). *Sexual behavior in the human female*. Philadelphia: W. B. Saunders.

Kinsley, M. (1992). Gatecrashers. *New Republic, 207*(27), 6.

Kipnis, D., & Schmidt, S. M. (1988). Upward influence styles: Relationship with performance evaluation, salary, and stress. *Administrative Science Quarterly, 33,* 528–542.

Kirchler, E., & Davis, J. H. (1986). The influence of member status differences and task type on group consensus and member position change. *Journal of Personality and Social Psychology, 51,* 83–91.

Kirkpatrick, S. A., & Locke, E. A. (1991). Leadership: Do traits matter? *Academy of Management Executive, 5*(2), 48–60.

Klagsbrun, F. (1992). *Mixed feelings: Love, hate, rivalry, and reconciliation in brothers and sisters*. New York: Bantam.

Klein, J. G. (1991). Negativity effects in impression formation: A test in the political arena. *Personality and Social Psychology Bulletin, 17,* 412–418.

Klein, S. B., & Loftus, J. (1988). The nature of self–referent encoding: The contributions of elaborative and organizational processes. *Journal of Personality and Social Psychology, 55,* 5–11.

Klein, S. B., Loftus, J., & Burton, H. A. (1989). Two self–reference effects: The importance of distinguishing between self–descriptiveness judgments and autobiographical retrieval in self–referent encoding. *Journal of Personality and Social Psychology, 56,* 853–865.

Kleinke, C. L. (1986). Gaze and eye contact: A research review. *Psychological Bulletin, 100,* 78–lOO.

Kleinke, C. L., & Dean, G. D. (1990). Evaluation of men and women receiving positive and negative responses with various acquaintance strategies. *Journal of Social Behavior and Personality, 5,* 369–377.

Kleinke, C. L., Meeker, F. B., & Staneski, R. A. (1986). Preference for opening lines: Comparing ratings by men and women. *Sex Roles, 15,* 585–600.

Kleinke, C. L., & Staneski, R. A. (1980). First impressions of female bust size. *Journal of Social Psychology, 110,* 123–134.

Klotz, M. L., & Alicke, M. D. (1993). *Complaining in close relationships*. Manuscript under review.

Knapp, M. L. (1978). *Nonverbal communication in human interaction*. New York: Holt, Rinehart, & Winston.

Knox, R. E., & Safford, R. K. (1976). Group caution at the race track. *Journal of Experimental Social Psychology, 12,* 317–324.

Kobasa, S. C. (1979). Stressful life events, personality, and health: An inquiry into hardiness. *Journal of Personality and Social Psychology, 37,* 1–11.

Koestner, R., Bernieri, F., & Zuckerman, M. (1992). Self–regulation and consistency between attitudes, traits, and behaviors. *Personality and Social Psychology Bulletin, 18,* 52–59.

Kolbert, E. (1991, October 10). Sexual harassment at work is pervasive. *New York Times*, pp. 1, 22.

Kondracke, M. (1992). Washington diarist: Blenders. *The New Republic, 207*(13), 501.

Kotter, J. (1982). *The general managers*. New York: Free Press.

Krauss, R. M., Morrel–Samuels, P., & Colasante, C. (1991). Do conversational hand gestures communicate? *Journal of Personality and Social Psychology, 61,* 743–754.

Kremer, J. F., & Stephens, L. (1983). Attributions and arousal as mediators of mitigation's effects on retaliation. *Journal of Personality and Social Psychology, 45,* 335–343.

Krosnick, J. A., & Alwin, D. F. (1989). Aging and susceptibility to attitude change. *Journal of Personality and Social Psychology, 57,* 416–425.

Krosnick, J. A. (1989). Attitude importance and attitude accessibility. *Personality and Social Psychology Bulletin, 15,* 297–308.

Krosnick, J. A. (1990). Americans' perceptions of presidential candidates: A test of the projection hypothesis. *Journal of Social Issues, 46,* 159–182.

Krosnick, J. A., Betz, A. L., Jussim, L. J., & Lynn, A. R. (1992). Subliminal conditioning of attitudes. *Personality and Social Psychology Bulletin, 18,* 152–162.

Kruglanski, A. W. (1990). Motivations for judging and knowing: Implications for causal attribution. In E. T. Higgins & R. M. Sorrentino (Eds.), *The handbook of motivation and cognition: Foundations of social behavior* (Vol. 2, pp. 333–368). New York: Guildford Press.

Krupat, E. (1975). *Psychology is social*. Glenview, IL: Scott, Foresman.

Kulik, J. A., & Mahler, H. I. M. (1987). Effects of preoperative roommate assigment on preoperative anxiety and recovery from coronary–bypass surgery. *Health Psychology, 6,* 525–544.

Kulik, J. A., & Mahler, H. I. M. (1989). Stress and affiliation in a hospital setting: Preoperative roommate preferences. *Personality and Social Psychology Bulletin, 15,* 183–193.

Kunda, Z., Fong, G. T., Sanitioso, R., & Reber, E. (1993). Directional questions direct self–conceptions. *Journal of Experimental Social Psychology, 29,* 63–86.

Kurdek, L. A. (1993). Predicting marital dissolution: A 5–year longitudinal study of newlywed couples. *Journal of Personality and Social Psychology, 64,* 221–242.

La Fromboise, T. D., Heyle, A. M., & Ozer, E. J. (1990). Gender and ethnicity: Perspectives on dual status. *Sex Roles, 22,* 455–476.

Lakey, G., Moineau, S., & Drew, J. (1992). Perceived social support and individual differences in the interpretation and recall of supportive behaviors. *Journal of Social and Clinical Psychology, 11,* 336– 348.

Lamm, H. & Myers, D. C. (1978). Group–induced polarization of attitudes and behavior. In L. Berkowitz (Ed.), *Advances in experimental social psychology*. New York: Academic Press.

Lang, E. L. (1987). Associations among different levels of helping, speed, and situational constraints. *Journal of Social Behavior and Personality, 2,* 419–436.

Langley, T., O'Neal, E. C., Craig, K. M., & Yost, E. A. (1992). Aggression–consistent, –inconsistent, and –irrelevant priming effects on selective exposure to media violence. *Aggressive Behavior, 18,* 349–356.

Langlois, J. H., Ritter, J. M., Roggman, L. A., & Vaughn, L. S. (1991). Facial diversity and infant preferences for attractive faces. *Developmental Psychology, 27,* 79–84.

Langlois, J. H., & Roggman, L. A. (1990). Attractive faces are only average. *Psychological Science, 1,* 115–121.

Langlois, J. H., Roggman, L. A., & Rieser–Danner, L. A. (1990). Infants' differential social responses to attractive and unattractive faces. *Developmental Psychology, 26,* 153–159.

Langston, C. A., & Cantor, N. (1989). Social anxiety and social constraint: When making friends is hard. *Journal of Personality and Social Psychology, 56,* 649–661.

LaPiere, R. T. (1934). Attitude and actions. *Social Forces, 13,* 230–237.

LaPrelle, J., Hoyle, R. H., Insko, C. A., & Bernthal, P. (1990). Interpersonal attraction and descriptions of the traits of others: Ideal similarity, self similarity, and liking. *Journal of Research in Personality, 24,* 216–240.

Larkin, J. C., & Pines, H. A. (1982). No fat persons need apply. *Sociology of Work and Occupations, 6,* 312–327.

Larsen, R. J., & Kasimatis, M. (1991). Day–to–day physical symptoms: Individual differences in the occurrence, duration, and emotional concomitants of minor daily illnesses. *Journal of Personality, 59,* 387–423.

Larson, D. G., & Chastain, R. L. (1990). Self–concealment: Conceptualization, measurement, and health implications. *Journal of Social and Clinical Psychology, 9,* 439–455.

Larson, J. H., & Bell, N. J. (1988). Need for privacy and its effects upon interpersonal attraction and interaction. *Journal of Social and Clinical Psychology, 6,* 1–10.

Lassiter, G. D., Briggs, M. A., & Bowman, R. E. (1991). Need for cognition and the perception of ongoing behavior. *Personality and Social Psychology Bulletin, 17,* 156–160.

Lassiter, G. D., Briggs, M. A., & Slaw, R. D. (1991). Need for cognition, causal processing, and memory for behavior. *Personality and Social Psychology Bulletin, 17,* 694–700.

Lasswell, M. E., & Lobsenz, N. M. (1980). *Styles of loving.* New York: Ballantine.

Latane, B., & Darley, J. M. (1968). Group inhibition of bystander intervention in emergencies. *Journal of Personality and Social Psychology, 10,* 215–221.

Latane, B., & Darley, J. M. (1970). *The unresponsive bystander: Why doesn't he help?* New York: Appleton–Century–Crofts.

Latane, B., Williams, K., & Harkins, S. (1979). Many hands make light the work: The causes and consequences of social loafing. *Journal of Personality and Social Psychology, 37,* 822–832.

Lau, S. (1989). Sex role orientation and domains of self esteem. *Sex Roles, 21,* 415–422.

Lau, S., & Gruen, G. E. (1992). The social stigma of loneliness: Effect of target person's and perceiver's sex. *Personality and Social Psychology Bulletin, 18,* 182–189.

Lauer, J., & Lauer, R. (1985, June). Marriages made to last. *Psychology Today,* pp. 22–26.

Lavrakas, P. J. (1975). Female preferences for male physiques. *Journal of Research in Personality, 9,* 324–334.

Lazarus, R. S. (1966). *Psychological stress and the coping process.* New York: McGraw–Hill.

Lazarus, R. S. (1993). From psychological stress to the emotions: A history of changing outlooks. In L. W. Porter & M. R. Rosenzweig (Eds.), *Annual review of psychology* (Vol. 44, pp. 1–21). Palo Alto, CA: Annual Reviews, Inc.

Leary, M. R., Kowalski, R. M., & Bergen, D. J. (1988). Interpersonal information acquisition and confidence in first encounters. *Personality and Social Psychology Bulletin, 14,* 68–77.

Leary, W. E. (1988, November 15). Novel methods unlock witnesses' memories. *New York Times,* pp. C1, C15.

Leippe, M. R., Manion, A. P., & Romanczyk, A. (1992). Eyewitness persuasion: How and how well do fact finders judge the accuracy of adults' and children's memory reports? *Journal of Personality and Social Psychology, 63,* 181–197.

Lemonick, M. D. (1992). The ozone vanishes. *Time, 139*(7), 60–63.

Levenson, R. W., Ekman, P., & Friesen, W. V. (1990). Voluntary facial action generates emotion–specific autonomic nervous system activity. *Psychophysiology, 27,* 363–384.

Levenson, R. W., Ekman, P., Heider, K., & Friesen, W. V. (1992). Emotion and autonomic nervous system activity in the Minangkabau of West Sumatra. *Journal of Personality and Social Psychology, 62,* 972–988.

Leventhal, A., Nerenz, D. R., & Steele, D. J. (1984). Illness representations and coping with health threats. In A. Baum & J. Singer (Eds.), *Handbook of psychology and health* (pp. 219–252). Hillsdale, NJ: Erlbaum.

Leventhal, H., Singer, R., & Jones, S. (1965). The effects of fear and specificity of recommendation upon attitudes and behavior. *Journal of Personality and Social Psychology, 2,* 20–29.

Leventhal, G. S., & Anderson, D. (1970). Self–interest and the maintenance of equity. *Journal of Personality and Social Psychology, 15,* 57–62.

Levinger, G. (1980). Toward the analysis of close relationships. *Journal of Experimental Social Psychology, 16,* 510–544.

Levinger, G. (1988). Can we picture "love"? In R. J. Sternberg & M. L. Barnes (Eds.), *The psychology of love* (pp. 139–158). New Haven, CT: Yale University Press.

Lewin, K., Lippitt, R., & White, R. R. (1939). Patterns of aggressive behavior in experimentally created "social climates." *Journal of Social Psychology, 10,* 271–299.

Lewin, T. (1992, December 4). Baltimore school clinics to offer birth control by surgical implant. *New York Times,* pp. Al, A28.

Leyens, J. P., Camino, L., Parke, R. D., & Berkowitz, L. (1975). Effects of movie violence on aggression in a field setting as a function of group dominance and cohesion. *Journal of Personality and Social Psychology, 32,* 346–360.

Liberman, A. (1993, March 16). Personal communication.

Liberman, A., & Chaiken, S. (1992). Defensive processing of personally relevant health messages. *Personality and Social Psychology Bulletin, 18,* 669–679.

Liden, R. C., & Mitchell, T. R. (1988). Ingratiatory behaviors in organizational settings. *Academy of Management Review, 13,* 572–587.

Liebert, R. N., & Baron, R. A. (1972). Some immediate effects of televised violence on children's behavior. *Developmental Psychology, 6,* 469–47S.

Liebert, R. N., Sprafkin, J. H., & Davidson, E. S. (1989). *The early window: Effects of television on children and youth,* (3rd ed.). New York: Pergamon.

Linden, E. (1992). Rio's legacy. *Time, 139*(25), 44–45.

Linville, P. W., Fischer, O. W., & Salovey, P. (1989). Perceived distributions of the characteristics of in–group and out–group members: Empirical evidence and a computer simulation. *Journal of Personality and Social Psychology, 57,* 165–188.

Linz, D., Donnerstein, E., & Penrod, S. (1984). The effects of multiple exposure to filmed violence against women. *Journal of Communication, 34,* 130–137.

Linz, D., Donnerstein, E., & Penrod, S. (1988). Effects of long–term exposure to violent and sexually degrading depictions of women. *Journal of Personality and Social Psychology, 55,* 758–768.

Lipman–Blumen, J. (1988, August). *Connective leadership: A female perspective for an interdependent world.* Paper presented at the meeting of the American Psychological Association, Atlanta, GA.

Lippa, R., & Donaldson, S. I. (1990). Self–monitoring and idiographic measures of behavioral variability across interpersonal relationships. *Journal of Personality, 58,* 465–479.

Lipson, M. (1983). The influence of religious affiliation on children's memory for text information. *Reading Research Quarterly, 18,* 448–457.

Littlepage, G. E. (1991). Effects of group size and task characteristics on group performance: A test of Steiner's model. *Personality and Social Psychology Bulletin, 17,* 449–456.

Living memorial. (1992, October 26). Time, p. 21.

Locke, E. A. (1969). What is job satisfaction? *Organizational Behavior and Human Performance, 4,* 309–336.

Locke, E. A. (1976). The nature and causes of job satisfaction. In M. D. Dunnette (Ed.), *Handbook of industrial and organizational psychology* (pp. 1297–1350). Chicago: Rand McNally.

Locke, E. A., & Latham, G. P. (1990). *A theory of setting and task performance.* Englewood Cliffs, NJ: Prentice–Hall.

Lord, R. G., DeVader, C. L., & Alliger, G. M. (1986). A meta–analysis of the relationship between personality traits and leadership perceptions: An application of validity generalization procedures. *Journal of Applied Psychology, 17,* 401–410.

Lorenz, K. (1966). *On aggression.* New York: Harcourt, Brace, & World.

Lorenz, K. (1974). *Civilized man's eight deadly sins.* New York: Harcourt, Brace, Jovanovich.

Luginbuhl, J., & Palmer, R. (1991). Impression management aspects of self–handicapping: Positive and negative effects. *Personality and Social Psychology Bulletin, 17,* 655–662.

Luhtanen, R., & Crocker, J. (1992). A collective self–esteem scale: Self–evaluation of one's social identity. *Personality and Social Psychology Bulletin, 18,* 302–318.

Luks, A. (1988, October). Helper's high. *Psychology Today,* pp. 39–40.

Lundberg, G. A., & Beazley, V. (1948). "Consciousness of kind" in a college population. *Sociometry, 11,* 59–74.

Lundberg, G. A., Hertzler, V. B., & 0ickson, L. (1949). Attraction patterns in a university. *Sociometry, 12,* 158–159.

Lupfer, M. B., Clark, L. F., & Hutcherson, H. W. (1990). Impact of context on spontaneous trait and situational attributions. *Journal of Personality and Social Psychology, 58,* 239–249.

Luten, D. B., Jr. (1991). Population and resources. *Population and Environment, 12,* 311–329.

Lynn, M., & Shurgot, B. A. (1984). Responses to lonely hearts advertisements: Effects of reported physical attractiveness, physique, and coloration. *Personality and Social Psychology Bulletin, 10,* 349–357.

Maas, A., & Clark, R. D. III. (1984). Hidden impact of minorities: Fifteen years of minority influence research. *Psychological Bulletin, 95,* 233–243.

Maas, A., & Volpato, C. (1989). Gender differences in self–serving attributions about sexual experiences. *Journal of Applied Social Psychology, 19,* 517–542.

Macaulay, J. (1970). A shill for charity. In J. Macaulay & L. Berkowitz (Eds.), *Altruism and helping behavior* (pp. 43–59). New York: Academic Press.

Mack, D., & Rainey, D. (1990). Female applicants' grooming and personnel selection. *Journal of Social Behavior and Personality, 5,* 399–407.

Mackie, D. M. (1986). Social identification effects in group polarization. *Journal of Personality and Social Psychology, 40,* 720–728.

Mackie, D. M., Allison, S. T., Worth, L. T., & Asuncion, A. G.

(1992). The impact of outcome biases on counterstereotypic inferences about groups. *Personality and Social Psychology Bulletin, 18,* 44–51.

Mackie, D. M., Allison, S. T., Worth, L. T., & Asuncion, A. G. (1993). Research in progress, University of California, Santa Barbara.

Mackie, D. M., & Worth, L. T. (1989). Processing deficits and the mediation of positive affect in persuasion. *Journal of Personality and Social Psychology, 57,* 27–40.

Macrae, C. N., & Milne, A. B. (1992). A curry for your thoughts: Empathic effects on counterfactual thinking. *Personality and Social Psychology Bulletin, 18,* 625–630.

Macrae, C. N. (1992). A tale of two curries: Counterfactual thinking and accident–related judgments. *Personality and Social Psychology Bulletin, 18,* 84–87.

Madden, M. E. (1987). Perceived control and power in marriage: A study of marital decision making and task performance. *Personality and Social Psychology Bulletin, 13,* 73–82.

Maisonneuve, J., Palmade, G., & Fourment, C. (1952). Selective choices and propinquity. *Sociometry, 15,* 135–140.

Major, B., & Adams, J. B. (1983). Roles of gender, interpersonal orientation, and self–presentation in distributive justice behavior. *Journal of Personality and Social Psychology, 45,* 598–608.

Major, B., Carnevale, P. J. D., & Deaux, K. (1981). A different perspective on androgyny: Evaluations of masculine and feminine personality characteristics. *Journal of Personality and Social Psychology, 41,* 988–1001.

Major, B., Carrington, P. I., & Carnevale, P. J. D. (1984). Physical attractiveness and self–esteem: Attributions for praise from an other–sex evaluator. *Personality and Social Psychology Bulletin, 10,* 43–50.

Major, B., & Deaux, K. (1982). Individual differences in justice behavior. In J. Greenberg & R. L. Cohen (Eds.), *Equity and justice in social behavior.* New York: Academic Press.

Major, B., & Konar, E. (1984). An investigation of sex differences in pay expectations and their possible causes. *Academy of Management Journal, 27,* 777–792.

Major, B., Schmidlin, A. M., & Williams, L. (1990). Gender patterns in social touch: The impact of setting and age. *Journal of Personality and Social Psychology, 58,* 634–643.

Malamuth, H. N., & Briere, J. (1986). Sexual arousal in response to aggression: Ideological, aggressive, and sexual correlates. *Journal of Personality and Social Psychology, 49,* 330–350.

Males, M. (1992). Adult liaison in the "epidemic" of "teenage" birth, pregnancy, and venereal disease. *Journal of Sex Research, 29,* 525–545.

Mallick, S. K., & McCandless, B. R. (1966). A study of catharsis of aggression. *Journal of Personality and Social Psychology, 4,* 591–596.

Malthus, T. R. (1798/1872). *An essay on the principle of population.* London: Reeves and Turner.

Manes, A. I., & Melynk, P. (1974). Televised models of female achievement. *Journal of Applied Social Psychology, 4,* 365–374.

Marangoni, C., & Ickes, W. (1989). Loneliness: A theoretical review with implications for measurement. *Journal of Social and Personal Relationships, 6,* 93–128.

Marasch, M. J. (1992). *Student attitudes toward the threat of nuclear war: Friends as influential reference persons.* Unpublished doctoral dissertation, University of North Dakota, Grand Forks, ND.

Margalit, M., & Eysenck, S. (1990). Prediction of coherence in adolescence: Gender differences in social skills, personality, and family climate. *Journal of Research in Personality, 24,* 510–521.

Margolin, G., John, R. S., & O'Brien, M. (1989). Sequential affective patterns as a function of marital conflict style. *Journal of Social and Clinical Psychology, 8,* 45–61.

Marin, G., Marin, B. V., Perez, S., Eliseo, J., & Sabogal, F. (1990). Cultural differences in attitudes and expectancies between Hispanic and non–Hispanic white smokers. *Hispanic Journal of Behavioral Sciences, 12,* 422–436.

Markman, H. J. (1981). Prediction of marital distress: A 5–year follow–up. *Journal of Consulting and Clinical Psychology, 49,* 760–762.

Marks, G., Graham, J. W., & Hansen, W. B. (1992). Social projection and social conformity in adolescent alcohol use: A longitudinal analysis. *Personality and Social Psychology Bulletin, 18,* 96–101.

Marks, G., & Miller, N. (1982). Target attractiveness as a mediator of assumed attitude similarity. *Personality and Social Psychology Bulletin, 8,* 728–735.

Marks, N. L., & Miller, H. (1987). Ten years of research on the false–consensus effect: An empirical and theoretical review. *Psychological Bulletin, 8,* 728–735.

Markus, H. (1978). The effects of mere presence on social facilitation: An unobtrusive test. *Journal of Experimental Social Psychology, 14,* 389–397.

Markus, H., & Nurius, P. (1986). Possible selves. *American Psychologist, 41,* 954–969.

Markus, H., & Wurf, E. (1987). The dynamic self–concept: A social psychological perspective. In M. R. Rosenszweig & L. W. Porter (Eds.), *Annual review of psychology* (Vol. 38, pp. 299–377). Palo Alto, CA: Annual Reviews Inc.

Marshall, G. D., & Zimbardo, P. (1979). Affective consequences of inadequately explained physiological arousal. *Journal of Personality and Social Psychology, 37,* 970–988.

Marsiglio, W. (1987). Adolescent fathers in the United States: Their initial living arrangements, marital experience, and educational outcomes. *Family Planning Perspectives, 19,* 240–256.

Martin, C. L. (1987). A ratio measure of sex stereotyping. *Journal of Personality and Social Psychology, 52,* 489–499.

Martin, J. A. (1990). Motherhood and power: The production of a woman's culture of politics in a Mexican community. *American Ethnologist, 17,* 470–490.

Martin, N. G., Eaves, L. J., Heath, A. C., Jardine, R., Feingold, L. M., & Eysenck, H. J. (1986). The transmission of social attitudes. *Proceedings of the National Academy of Sciences of the United States of America, 83,* 4365–4368.

Maslach, C., Santee, R. T., & Wade, C. (1987). Individuation, gender role, and dissent: Personality mediators of situational forces. *Journal of Personality and Social Psychology, 53,* 1088–1094.

Masters, R. D. (1991). Individual and cultural differences in response to leaders' nonverbal displays. *Journal of Social Issues, 47,* 151–165.

Mathes, E. W., Adams, H. E., & Davies, R. M. (1985). Jealousy: Loss of relationship rewards, loss of self–esteem, depression, anxiety, and anger. *Journal of Personality and Social Psychology, 48,* 1552–1561.

Matlin, M. W., & Zajonc, R. B. (1968). Social facilitation of word associations. *Journal of Personality and Social Psychology,* 10, 455–460.

Matsumoto, D. (1987). The role of facial response in the experience of emotion: More methodological problems and a meta–analysis. *Journal of Personality and Social Psychology, 52,* 769–774.

Maupin, H. E., & Fisher, R. J. (1989). The effects of superior female performance and sex–role orientation on gender conformity. *Canadian Journal of Behavioral Science, 21,* 55–69.

May, J. L., & Hamilton, P. A. (1980). Effects of musically evoked affect on women's interpersonal attraction and perceptual judgments of physical attractiveness of men. *Motivation and Emotion, 4,* 217–228.

McAdams, D. P., & Constantian, C. A. (1983). Intimacy and affiliation motives in daily living: An experience sampling analysis. *Journal of Personality and Social Psychology, 45,* 851–861.

McAdams, D. P., & Losoff, M. (1984). Friendship motivation in fourth and sixth graders: A thematic analysis. *Journal of Social and Persnal Relationships, 1,* 11–27.

McArthur, L. A. (1972). The how and what of why: Some determinants and consequences of causal attribution. *Journal of Personality and Social Psychology, 22,* 171–193.

McArthur, L. Z., & Eisen, S. V. (1976). Achievements of male and female storybook characters as determinants of achievement behavior by boys and girls. *Journal of Personality and Social Psychology, 33,* 467–473.

McCabe, M. P. (1987). Desired and experienced levels of premarital affection and sexual intercourse during dating. *Journal of Sex Research, 23,* 23–33.

McCann, S. J. H. (1992). Alternative formulas to predict the greatness of U. S. presidents: Personological, situational, and zeitgeist factors. *Journal of Personality and Social Psychology, 62,* 469–479.

McCann, S. J. H. (1993a). *Threatening times and the success of "strong" candidates in U. S. presidential elections 1824–1984.* Manuscript submitted for publication, University College of Cape Breton.

McCann, S. J. H. (1993b, May). *Charismatic candidates, turbulent times, and the margin of victory in U. S. presidential elections (1824–1984).* Paper presented at the meeting of the Canadian Psychological Association, Montreal.

McCann, S. J. H. (1993c, March 2). Personal communication.

McCann, S. J. H., & Stewin, L. L. (1990). Good and bad years: An index of American social, economic, and political threat (1920–1986). *Psychological Reports, 69,* 121–122.

McCanne, T. R., & Anderson, J. A. (1987). Emotional responding following experimental manipulation of facial electromyographic activity. *Journal of Personality and Social Psychology, 52,* 759–768.

McCarthy, J., & Radish, E. S. (1982). Education and childbearing among teenagers. *Family Planning Perspectives.* 14, 154–155.

McCarty, P. A. (1986). Effects of feedback on the self–confidence of men and women. *Academy of Management Journal, 29,* 840–847.

McCauley, C. (1989). The nature of social influence in groupthink: Compliance and internalization. *Journal of Personality and Social Psychology, 57,* 250–260.

McClintock, C. G., & Allison, S. T. (1989). Social value orientation and helping behavior. *Journal of Applied Social Psychology, 19,* 353–362.

McConnell, R. (1992). Population growth and environmental quality in California: An American laboratory. *Population and Environment, 14,* 9–29.

McConnell, R. L. (1991). The real environmental crisis, or what happened to government by the people, for the people? *Population and Environment, 12,* 407–416.

McDougall, W. (1908). *Introduction to social psychology.* London: Methuen.

McFarland, C., & Miller, D. T. (1990). Judgments of self–other similarity: Just like other people, only more so. *Personality and Social Psychology Bulletin, 6,* 475–484.

McFarland, C., & Ross, N. (1987). The relation between current impressions and memories of self and dating partners. *Personality and Social Psychology Bulletin, 13,* 228–238.

McFarland, C., Ross, M., & DeCourville, H. (1989). Women's theories of menstruation and biases in recall of menstrual symptoms. *Journal of Personality and Social Psychology, 57,* 522–531.

McFarlane, A. H., Norman, G. R., Streiner, D. L., & Roy, R. G. (1983). The process of social stress: Stable, reciprocal, and mediating relationships. *Journal of Health and Social Behavior, 24,* 160–173.

McGaughey, K. J., & Stiles, W. B. (1983). Courtroom interrogation of rape victims: Verbal response mode use by attorneys and witnesses during direct examination vs. cross–examination. *Journal of Applied Social Psychology, 13,* 78–87.

McGonagle, K. A., Kessler, R. C., & Schilling, E. A. (1992). The frequency and determinants of marital disagreements in a community sample. *Journal of Social and Personal Relationships, 9,* 507–524.

McGue, M., & Lykken, D. T. (1992). Genetic influence on risk of divorce. *Psychological Science, 3,* 368–373.

McIntyre, C. W., Watson, D., Clark, L. A., & Cross, S. A. (1991). The effect of induced social interaction on positive and negative affect. *Bulletin of the Psychonomic Society, 29,* 67–70.

McIntyre, C. W., Watson, D., & Cunningham, A. C. (1990). The effects of social interaction, exercise, and test stress on positive and negative affect. *Bulletin of the Psychonomic Society, 28,* 141–143.

McKillip, J., & Reidel, S. L. (1983). External validity of matching on physical attractiveness for same and opposite sex couples. *Journal of Applied Social Psychology, 13,* 328–337.

McLeod, R. G. (1993, February 19). Wealth's in wallet of the beholder. *Albany Times Union,* p. A–5.

McMillan, M. (1988). The doll test studies—from cabbage patch to self–concept. *Journal of Black Psychology, 25,* 69–72.

Mealey, L. (1985). The relationship between social status and biological success: A case study of the Mormon religious hierarchy. *Ethology and Sociobiology, 6,* 249–257.

Mechanic, D. (1983). Adolescent health and illness behavior: Hypotheses for the study of distress in youth. *Journal of Human Stress, 9,* 4–13.

Mednick, S. A., Brennan, P., & Kandel, E. (1988). Predispositions to violence. *Aggressive Behavior, 14,* 25–33.

Meecham, W. C., & Smith, H. G. (1977, June). (*British Journal of Audiology.*) Quoted in N. Napp, Noise drives you crazy—jets and mental hospitals. *Psychology Today,* p. 33.

Meindl, J. R., & Lerner, M. J. (1985). Exacerlation of extreme responses to an out-group. *Journal of Personality and Social Psychology, 47,* 71–84.

Mellers, B. A., Richards, V., & Birnbaum, M. H. (1992). Distributional theories of impression formation.

Organizational Behavior and Human Decision Processes, 51, 313–343.

Mendolia, M., & Kleck, R. E. (1993). Effects of talking about a stressful event on arousal: Does what we talk about make a difference? *Journal of Personality and Social Psychology, 64,* 283–292.

Meyer, D., Leventhal, H., & Gutman, M. (1985). Common–sense models of illness: The example of hypertension. *Health Psychology, 4,* 115–135.

Miceli, M. P., & Lane, M. C. (1991). Antecedents of pay satisfaction: A review and extension. In K. Rowland & O. R. Ferris (Eds.), *Research in personnel and human resources management* (Vol. 9, pp. 235–309). Greenwich, CT: JAI Press.

Michelini, R. L., & Snodgrass, S. S. (1980). Defendant characteristics and juridic decisions. *Journal of Research in Personality, 14,* 340–350.

Miles, M. A., & Murray, W. (1992, Third Quarter Report). Report to stockholders. *PM/Quarterly,* p. 11.

Milestones. (1989, September 18). *Time,* p. 75.

Milgram, S. (1963). Behavioral study of obedience. *Journal of Abnormal and Social Psychology, 67,* 371–378.

Milgram, S. (1965a). Liberating effects of group pressure. *Journal of Personality and Social Psychology, 1,* 127–134.

Milgram, S. (1965b). Some conditions of obedience and disobedience to authority. *Human Relations, 18,* 57–76.

Milgram, S. (1974). *Obedience to authority.* New York: Harper.

Millar, M. G., & Tesser, A. (1989). The effects of affective–cognitive consistency and thought on the attitude–behavior relation. *Journal of Experimental Social Psychology, 25,* 189–202.

Miller, C. T., Rothblum, E. D., Barbour, L., Brand, P. A., & Felicio, D. (1990). Social interactions of obese and nonobese women. *Journal of Personality, 58,* 365–380.

Miller, D. T., & McFarland, C. (1986). Counterfactual thinking and victim compensation: A test of norm theory. *Personality and Social Psychology Bulletin, 12,* 513–519.

Miller, D. T., & Ross, M. (1975). Self–serving biases in attribution of causality: Fact or fiction? *Psychological Bulletin, 82,* 313–325.

Miller, D. T., Turnbull, W., & McFarland, C. (1989). When a coincidence is suspicious: The role of mental simulation. *Journal of Personality and Social Psychology, 57,* 581–589.

Miller, D. T., Turnbull, W., & McFarland, C. (1990). Counterfactual thinking and social perception: Thinking about what might have been. In M. P. Zanna (Ed.), *Advances in experimental social psychology* (Vol. 23, pp. 305–331). Orlando FL: Academic Press.

Miller, F. D. (1975). *An experimental study of obedience to authorities of varying legitimacy.* Unpublished doctoral dissertation, Harvard University.

Miller, K. I., & Monge, P. R. (1986). Participation, satisfaction, and productivity: A meta–analytic review. *Academy of Management Journal, 29,* 727–753.

Miller, M. L., & Thayer, J. F. (1989). On the existence of discrete classes in personality: Is self–monitoring the correct joint to carve? *Journal of Personality and Social Psychology, 57,* 143–155.

Miller, N., Maruyama, G., Beaber, R. J., & Valone, K. (1976). Speed of speech and persuasion. *Journal of Personality and Social Psychology, 34,* 615–624.

Miller, R. S. (1991). On decorum in close relationships: Why aren't we polite to those we love? *Contemporary Social Psychology, 15,* 63–65.

Miller, S. N., Brody, D. S., & Summerton, J. (1988). Styles of coping with threat: Implications for health. *Journal of Personality and Social Psychology, 54*, 142–148.

Miller, T. Q., Heath, L., Molcan, J. R., & Dugoni, B. L. (1991). Imitative violence in the real world: A reanalysis of homicide rates following championship prize fights. *Aggressive Behavior, 17*, 121–134.

Milliman, R. (1982). Using background music to affect the behavior of supermarket shoppers. *Journal of Marketing, 46*, 86–91.

Miroff, B. (1993). *Icons of democracy: American leaders as heroes, aristocrats, dissenters. and democrats.* New York: Basic Books.

Monsour, M. (1992). Meanings of intimacy in cross– and same–sex friendships. *Journal of Social and Personal Relationships, 9*, 277–295.

Montag, I., & Levin, J. (1990). The location of the Self–Monitoring Scale in the factor space of the EPQ and the IGPF. *Journal of Research in Personality, 24*, 45–56.

Montepare, J. M., & Zebrowitz–McArthur, L. (1987). Perceptions of adults with childlike voices in two cultures. *Journal of Experimental Social Psychology, 23*, 331–349.

Montepare, J. M., & Zebrowitz–McArthur, L. (1988). Impressions of people created by age–related qualities of their gaits. *Journal of Personality and Social Psychology, 54*, 547–556.

Moore, J. S., Graziano, W. G., Miller, M. G. (1987). Physical attractiveness, sex role orientation, and the evaluation of adults and children. *Personality and Social Psychology Bulletin, 13*, 95–102.

Moore, S., & Rosenthal, D. (1991a). Adolescent invulnerability and perceptions of AIDS risk. *Journal of Adolescent Research, 6*, 164–180.

Moore, S., & Rosenthal, D. (1991). Adolescents' perceptions of friends' and parents' attitudes to sex and sexual risk–taking. *Journal of Community & Applied Social Psychology, 1*, 189–200.

Moorhead, G., & Montanari, J. R. (1986). An empirical investigation of the groupthink phenomenon. *Human Relations, 39*, 399–410.

Moran, G. (1993, February 23). Personal communication.

Moran, G., & Cutler, B. L. (1991). The prejudicial impact of pretrial publicity. *Journal of Applied Social Psychology, 21*, 345–367.

Morell, M. A., Twillman, R. K., & Sullaway, M. E. (1989). Would a Type A date another Type A?: Influence of behavior type and personal attributes in the selection of dating partners. Journal of Applied Social Psychology, 19, 918–931.

Moreland, R. L. (1987). The formation of small groups. In C. Hendrick (Ed.), *Review of personality and social psychology*, (Vol. 8, pp. 80–110). Newbury Park, CA: Sage.

Moreland, R. L., & Beach, S. R. (1992). Exposure effects in the classroom: The development of affinity among students. *Journal of Experimental Social Psychology, 28*, 255–276.

Moreland, R. L., & Zajonc, R. B. (1982). Exposure effects in person perception: Familiarity, similarity, and attraction. *Journal of Experimental Social Psychology, 18*, 395–415.

Moreland, R. L., & Levine, J. M. (1992a). The composition of small groups. *Advances in Group Processes, 9*, 237–280.

Moreland, R. L., & Levine, J. M. (1992b). Problem identification by groups. In S. Worchel, W. Wood, & J. A. Simpson (Eds.), *Group processes and productivity* (pp. 17–47). Newbury Park, CA: Sage.

Morgan, D. L., & White, R. L. (1993). The structure of the field of personal relationships: Part I. Disciplines. *Personal Relationships Issues, 1*, 2–5.

Morgan, D. W. (1988). *Organizational citizenship behavior: the good soldier syndrome.* Lexington, MA: Lexington Books.

Mori, D. A., Chaiken, S., & Pliner, P. (1987). "Eating lightly" and the self–presentation of femininity, *Journal of Personality and Social Psychology, 53*, 693–702.

Mori, D. L., & Morey, L. (1991). The vulnerable body image of females with feelings of depression. *Journal of Research in Personality, 25*, 343–354.

Morris, K. J. (1985). *Discriminating depression and social anxiety: Self–efficacy analysis.* Unpublished master's thesis, Texas Tech University, Lubbock.

Morris, W. N., & Miller, R. S. (1975). The effects of consensus–breaking and consensus–preempting partners on reduction of conformity. *Journal of Personality and Social Psychology, 11*, 215–223.

Morris, W. N., Miller, R. S., & Spangenberg, S. (1977). The effects of dissenter position and task difficulty on conformity and response to conflict. *Journal of Personality, 45*, 251–266.

Morris, W. N., Worchel, S., Bois, J. L., Pearson, J. A., Rountree, C. A., Samaha, G. M., Wachtler, J., & Wright, S. I. (1976). Collective coping with stress: Group reactions to fear, anxiety, and ambiguity. *Journal of Personality and Social Psychology, 33*, 674–679.

Morrison, E. W., & Bies, R. J. (1991). Impression management in the feedback–seeking process: A literature review and research agenda. *Academy of Management Review, 16*, 322–341.

Moscovici, S. (1985). Social influence and conformity. In G. Lindzey & E. Aronson (Eds.), *Handbook of social psychology.* 3rd ed. New York: Random House.

Moser, C. G., & Dyck, D. G. (1989). Type A behavior, uncontrollability, and the activation of hostile self–schema. *Journal of Research in Personality, 23*, 248–267.

Moskowitz, G. B., & Roman, R. J. (1992). Spontaneous trait inferences as self–generated primes: Implications for conscious social judgment. *Journal of Personality and Social Psychology, 62*, 728–738.

Muecher, H., & Ungeheuer, H. (1961). Meterological influence on reaction time, flicker–fusion frequency, job accidents, and medical treatment. *Perceptual and Motor Skills, 12*, 163–168.

Mugny, G. (1975). Negotiations, image of the other and the process of minority influence. *European Journal of Social Psychology, 5*, 209–229.

Mullen, B., Futrell, D., Stairs, D., Tice, D., Baumeister, R., Dawson, K., Riordan, C., Radloff, C., Kennedy, J., & Rosenfield, P. (1986). Newscasters' facial expressions and voting behavior of viewers: Can a smile elect a president? *Journal of Personality and Social Psychology, 51*, 291–295.

Mullen, B., & Johnson, C. (1990). Distinctiveness-based illusory correlations and stereotyping: A meta-analytic integration. *British Journal of Social Psychology, 29*, 11–28.

Mumford, M. D., O'Connor, J., Clifton, T. C., Connelly, M. S., & Zaccaro, S. D. (in press). Background data constructs as predictors of leadership behavior. *Human Performance.*

Murnighan, K. (Ed.). (1993). *Handbook of social psychology in organizations.* Englewood Cliffs, NJ: Prentice–Hall.

Murray, D. M., & Wells, G. I. (1982). Does knowledge that a

crime was staged affect eyewitness performance? *Journal of Applied Social Psychology, 72,* 42–53.

Murray, H. A. (1938/1962). *Explorations in personality.* New York: Science Editions.

Murstein, B. I., Merighi, J. R., & Vyse, S. A. (1991). Love styles in the United States and France: A cross–cultural comparison. *Journal of Social and Clinical Psychology, 10,* 37–46.

Myers, D. G. (1991). Union is strength: A consumer's view of meta–analysis. *Personality and Social Psychology Bulletin, 17,* 265–266.

Nadkarni, D. V., Lundgren, D., & Burlew, A. K. (1991). Gender differences in self–depriving behavior as a reaction to extreme inequity. *Journal of Social Behavior and Personality, 6,* 105–117.

Nadler, A. (1986). Help seeking as a cultural phenomenon: Differences between city and kibbutz dwellers. *Journal of Personality and Social Psychology, 51,* 976–982.

Nadler, A. (1987). Determinants of help-seeking behaviour: The effects of helper's similarity, task centrality and recipient's self esteem. *European Journal of Social Psychology, 17,* 57–67.

Nadler, A. (1991). Help-seeking behavior: Psychological costs and instrumental benefits. In M. S. Clark (Ed.), *Prosocial behavior* (pp. 290–311). Newbury Park, CA: Sage.

Nadler, A. (1993, March). Personal communication.

Nadler, A., & Fisher, J. D. (1986). The role of threat to self-esteem and perceived control in recipient reactions to aid: Theory development and empirical validation. In L. Berkowitz (Ed.), *Advances in experimental social psychology* (Vol. 17, pp. 81–123). New York: Academic Press.

Nadler, A., Fisher, J. D., & Itzhak, S. B. (1983). With a little help from my friend: Effect of a single or multiple act of aid as a function of donor and task characteristics. *Journal of Personality and Social Psychology, 44,* 310–321.

Nahemow, L., & Lawton, M. P. (1975). Similarity and propinquity in friendship formation. *Journal of Personality and Social Psychology, 32,* 205–213.

Nakao, K. (1987). Analyzing sociometric preferences: An example of Japanese and U. S. business groups. Journal of *Social Behavior and Personality, 2,* 523–534.

Narby, D. J., Cutler, B. L., & Moran, G. (1993). A meta–analysis of the association between authoritarianism and jurors' perceptions of defendant culpability. *Journal of Applied Psychology, 78,* 34–42.

Nasar, S. (1992, May 31). Cooling the globe would be nice, but saving lives now may cost less. *New York Times,* p. E6.

National Center for Health Statistics. (1987, June 26). Birth in America: A fact sheet. *New York Times,* p. C3.

Neale, M. A., & Bazerman, N. H. (1985). The effects of framing and negotiator overconfidence on bargaining behaviors and outcomes. *Academy of Management Journal, 28,* 34–49.

Nemeth, C. J. (1986). Differential contributions of majority and minority influence. *Psychological Review, 93,* 23–32.

Neto, F. (1992). Loneliness among Portuguese adolescents. *Social Behavior and Personality, 20,* 15–22.

Neuberg, S. L. (1989). The goal of forming accurate impressions during social interactions: Attenuating the impact of negative expectancies. *Journal of Personality and Social Psychology, 56,* 374–386.

Newcomb, M. D., Rabow, J., & Hernandez, A. C. R. (1992). A cross–national study of nuclear attitudes, normative support, and activist behavior: Additive and interactive effects. *Journal of Applied Social Psychology, 22,* 780–800.

Newcomb, P. R. (1979). Cohabitation in America: An assessment of consequences. *Journal of Marriage and the Family, 41,* 597–603.

Newcomb, T. M. (1943). *Personality and social change: Attitude formation in a student community.* New York: Dryden; Holt, Rinehart, and Winston.

Newcomb, T. M. (1961). *The acquaintance process.* New York: Holt, Rinehart, & Winston.

Newcomb, T. M., Koenig, K. E., Flacks, R., & Warwick, D. P. (1967). *Persistence and change: Bennington College and its students after twenty–five years.* New York: Wiley.

Newman, P. J., & Cochrane, R. (1987). Wives' employment and husbands' depression. *Social Behavior, 2,* 211–219.

Nicola, J. A. S., & Hawkes, G. R. (1986). Marital satisfaction of dual–career couples: Does sharing increase happiness? *Journal of Social Behavior and Personality, 1,* 47–60.

Nida, S. A., & Koon J. (1983). They get better looking at closing time around here, too. *Psychological Reports, 52,* 657–658.

Niedenthal, P. M., Setterlund, M. B., & Wherry, M. B. (1992). Possible self–complexity and affective reactions to goal–relevant evaluation. *Journal of Personality and Social Psychology, 63,* 5–16.

Nieva, V. F., & Outek, B. A. (1981). *Women and work: A psychological perspective.* New York: Praeger Publishers.

Nisbett, R. E. (1990). Evolutionary psychology, biology, and cultural evolution. *Motivation and Emotion, 14,* 255–264.

Norris, A. E., & Devine, P. G. (1992). Linking pregnancy concerns to pregnancy risk avoidant action: The role of construct accessibility. *Personality and Social Psychology Bulletin, 18,* 118–127.

Norwood, J. L. (1992). Working women: Where have we been? Where are we going? *Population and Environment, 14,* 95–103.

Nowicki, S., Jr. (1992). Interpersonal complementarity, gender of interactants, and performance on puzzle and word tasks. *Personality and Social Psychology Bulletin, 18,* 351–356.

Nowicki, S., Jr., & Manheim, S. (1991). Interpersonal complementarity and time of interaction in female relationships. *Journal of Research in Personality, 25,* 322–333.

Null, G. (1989, January). AIDS: A man–made plague? *Penthouse,* pp. 160–162, 164–165, 200.

Nuttin, J. M., Jr. (1987). Affective consequences of mere ownership: The name letter effect in twelve European languages. *European Journal of Social Psychology, 17,* 381–402.

Nyquist, L., Slivken, K., Spence, J. T., & Helmreich, R. I. (1985). Household responsibilities in middle–class couples: The contribution of demographic and personality variables. *Sex Roles, 12,* 15–34.

O'Connell, P. D. (1988). Pretrial publicity, change of venue, public opinion polls—A theory of procedural justice. *University of Detroit Law Review, 65,* 169–197.

O'Grady, K. E. (1989). Physical attractiveness, need for approval, social self–esteem, and maladjustment. *Journal of Social and Clinical Psychology, 8,* 62–69.

Ohbuchi, K., & Kambara, T. (1985). Attacker's intent and awareness of outcome, impression management, and retaliation. *Journal of Experimental Social Psychology, 21,* 321–330.

Ohbuchi, K. I., Kameda, M., & Agarie, N. (1989). Apology as aggression control: Its role in mediating appraisal of and response to harm. *Journal of Personality and Social Psychology, 56,* 219–227.

Ohbuchi, K. I., & Ogura, S. (1984). The experience of anger (1): The survey for adults and university students with

Averill's questionnaire (Japanese). *Japanese Journal of Criminal Psychology, 22,* 15–35.

Olczak, P. V., Kaplan, M. F., & Penrod, S. (1991). Attorneys' lay psychology and its effectiveness in selecting jurors: Three empirical studies. *Journal of Social Behavior and Personality, 6,* 431–452.

Oliner, S. P., & Oliner, P. M. (1988). *The altruistic personality: Rescuers of Jews in Nazi Europe.* New York: Free Press.

Olivenstein, L. (1992). Cold comfort. *Discover, 13*(8), 18, 20–21.

Olmstead, R. E., Guy, S. M., O'Malley, P. M., & Bentler, P. M. (1991). Longitudinal assessment of the relationship between self–esteem, fatalism, loneliness, and substance use. *Journal of Social Behavior and Personality, 6,* 749–770.

Olson, J. N., & Ross, N. (1988). False feedback about placebo effectiveness: Consequences for the misattribution of speech anxiety. *Journal of Experimental Social Psychology, 24,* 275–291.

Olweus, D. (1986). Aggression and hormones: Behavioral relationship with testosterone and adrenaline. In Olweus D., Block, J., Radke–Yarrows, M. (Eds.), *Development of antisocial and prosocial behavior* (pp. 51–72.) New York: Academic Press.

Omoto, A. M., & Snyder, M. (1993). AIDS volunteers and their motivations: Theoretical issues and practical concerns. *Nonprofit Management and Leadership,* in press.

Organ, D. W. (1988). *Organizational citizenship behavior: The soldier syndrome.* Lexington, MA: Lexington Books.

Orive, R. (1988). Social projection and social comparison of opinions. *Journal of Personality and Social Psychology, 54,* 953–964.

Orlofsky, J. L., & O'Heron, C. A. (1987). Stereotypic and nonstereotypic sex role trait and behavior orientations: Implications for personal adjustment. *Journal of Personality and Social Psychology, 52,* 1034–1042.

Oskamp, S., & Costanzo, M. (Eds.) (1993). *Gender issues in social psychology.* Newbury Park, CA: Sage.

Osterwell, Z., & Nagano–Hakamura, K. (1992). Maternal views on aggression: Japan and Israel. *Aggressive Behavior, 18,* 263–270.

O'Sullivan, C. S., Chen, A., Mohapatra, S., Sigelman, L., & Lewis, E. (1988). Voting in ignorance: The politics of smooth–sounding names. *Journal of Applied Social Psychology, 18,* 1094–1106.

O'Sullivan, C. S., & Durso, F. T. (1984). Effects of schema–incongruent information on memory for stereotypical attributes. *Journal of Personality and Social Psychology, 47,* 55–70.

O'Sullivan, L. F., & Byers, E. S. (1992). College students' incorporation of initiator and restrictor roles in sexual dating interactions. *Journal of Sex Research, 29,* 435–446.

Ottati, V., Fishbein, M., & Middlestadt, S. E. (1988). Determinants of voters' beliefs about the candidates' stands on the issues: The role of evaluative bias heuristics and the candidates' expressed message. *Journal of Personality and Social Psychology, 55,* 517–529.

Padilla, E. R., & O'Grady, K. E. (1983). *Sexuality among Mexican–Americans: An empirical approach.* Unpublished manuscript, University of New Mexico.

Page, D. C., Mosher, R., Simpson, E. M., Fisher, E. M. C., Mardon, G., Polloch, J., McGillivray, B., de la Chapelle, A., & Brown, L. G. (1987). The sex-determining region of the human Y chromosome encodes a finger protein. *Cell, 51,* 1091–1104.

Page, N. M., & Kahle, L. R. (1976). Demand characteristics in the satiation–deprivation effect on attitude conditioning. *Journal of Personality and Social Psychology, 33,* 553–562.

Page, R. M. (1991). Loneliness as a risk factor in adolescent hopelessness. *Journal of Research in Personality, 25,* 189–195.

Pan, S. (1993). China: Acceptability and effect of three kinds of sexual publication. *Archives of Sexual Behavior, 22,* 59–71.

Parke, R. D., Berkowitz, L., Leyens, J. P., West, S. G., & Sebastian, R. J. (1977). Some effects of violent and nonviolent movies on the behavior of juvenile delinquents. In L. Berkowitz (Ed.), *Advances in experimental social psychology* (Vol. 10). New York: Academic Press.

Parsons, J. (1991). Population control and politics. *Population and Environment, 12,* 355–377.

Patch, M. E. (1986). The role of source legitimacy in sequential request strategies of compliance. *Personality and Social Psychology Bulletin, 12,* 199–205.

Paulhus, D. L., & Bruce, M. N. (1992). The effect of acquaintanceship on the validity of personality impressions: A longitudinal study. *Journal of Personality and Social Psychology, 63,* 816–824.

Paulus, P. B. (ed.) (1989). *Psychology of influence* (2nd ed.). Hillsdale, NJ: Erlbaum.

Pear, R. (1992, December 4). New look at the U. S. in 2050: Bigger, older and less white. *New York Times,* pp. A1, D18.

Pear, R. (1993, January 15). Poverty erodes family, study finds. *Albany Times Union,* pp. A–I, A–8.

Pearson, K., & Lee, A. (1903). On the laws of inheritance in man: I. Inheritance of physical characters. *Biometrika, 2,* 357–462.

Pendleton, M. G., & Batson, C. D. (1979). Self– presentation and the door–in–the–face technique for inducing compliance. *Personality and Social Psychology Bulletin, 5,* 77–81.

Pennebaker, J. W., & Beall, S. (1986). Confronting a traumatic event: Toward an understanding of inhibition and disease. *Journal of Abnormal Psychology, 95,* 274–281.

Pennebaker, J. W., Dyer, M. A., Caulkins, R. S., Litowicz, D. L., Ackerman, P. L., & Anderson, D. B. (1979). Don't the girls all get prettier at closing time: A country and western application to psychology. *Personality and Social Psychology Bulletin, 5,* 122–125.

Pennebaker, J. W., Hughes, C. F., & O'Heron, R. C. (1987). The psychophysiology of confession: Linking inhibitory and psychosomatic processes. *Journal of Personality and Social Psychology, 52,* 781–793.

Pennington, N., & Hastie, R. (1992). Explaining the evidence: Tests of the story model for juror decision making. *Journal of Personality and Social Psychology, 62,* 189–206.

Peplau, L. A., & Perlman, D. (1982). Perspective on loneliness. In L. A. Peplau & D. Perlman (Eds.), *Loneliness: A sourcebook of current theory, research, and therapy.* New York: Wiley.

Perdue, C. W., & Gurtman, M. B. (1990). Evidence for the automaticity of ageism. *Journal of Experimental Social Psychology, 26,* 199–216.

Perrewe, P. L., & Anthony, W. P. (1990). Stress in a steel pipe mill: The impact of job demands, personal control, and employee age on somatic complaints. *Journal of Social Behavior and Personality, 5,* 77–90.

Peters, L. H., Hartke, D. D., & Pohlman, J. R. (1985). Fiedler's contingency theory of leadership: An application of the meta–analysis procedures of Schmidt and Hunter.

Psychological Bulletin, 97, 274–285.

Petersen, & JBrooks–Gunn, Jr. (Eds.). T*he encyclopedia of adolescence.* New York: Garland.

Peterson, C., & Seligman, M. (1984). Causal explanations as a risk factor for depression: Theory and evidence. *Psychological Review, 91,* 147–174.

Peterson, C., Seligman, M. E. P., & Vaillant, G. (1988). Pessimistic explanatory style as a risk factor for physical illness: A thirty–five–year longitudinal study. *Journal of Personality and Social Psychology, 55,* 23–27.

Pettigrew, M. (1987, May 12). "Useful" modes of thought contribute to prejudice. *New York Times,* pp. 17–20.

Pettigrew, T. F. (1969). Racially separate or together? *Journal of Social Issues, 25,* 43–69.

Pettigrew, T. F. (1979). The ultimate attribution error: Extending Allport's cognitive analysis of prejudice. *Personality and Social Psychology Bulletin, 5,* 461–476.

Pettigrew, T. F. (1981). Extending the stereotype concept. In D. L. Hamilton (Ed.), *Coganitive processes in stereotyping and intergroup behavior* (pp. 303–331). Hillsdale, NJ: Erlbaum.

Petty, R. E., & Cacioppo, J. P. (1979). Issue involvement can increase or decrease persuasion by enhancing message–relevant cognitive responses. *Journal of Personality and Social Psychology, 37,* 1915–1926.

Petty, R. E., & Cacioppo, J. T. (1985). *Communication and persuasion: Central and peripheral routes to attitude one.* New York: Springer–Verlag.

Petty, R. E., & Cacioppo, J. T. (1986). The elaboration likelihood model of persuasion. In L. Berkowitz (Ed.), *Advances in experimental social psychology* (Vol. 19, pp. 123–205). New York: Academic Press.

Petty, R. E., Ostrom, T. N., & Brock, T. C. (Eds.). (1981). *Cognitive responses in persuasion.* Hillsdale, NJ: Erlbaum.

Petty, R. E., Wells, G. L., & Brock, T. C. (1976). Distraction can enhance or reduce yielding to propaganda: Thought disruption versus effort justification. *Journal of Personality and Social Psychology, 34,* 874–884.

Phelps, E. J. (1981). *The maid of the North.* New York: Holt, Rinehart, & Winston.

Piaget, J. (1965). *The moral judgement of the child.* New York: Free Press.

Pierce, C. A. (1992). *The effects of physical attractiveness and height on dating choice: A meta–analysis.* Unpublished masters thesis, University at Albany, State University of New York.

Piliavin, J. A. (1987). Age, race, and sex similarity to candidates and voting preference. *Journal of Applied Social Psychology, 17,* 351–368.

Pilisuk, M., & Acredolo, C. (1988). Fear of technological hazards: One concern or many? *Social Behavior, 3,* 17–24.

Pilisuk, M., Boylan, R., & Acredolo, C. (1987). Social support, life stress, and subsequent medical care utilization. *Health Psychology, 6,* 273–288.

Pillow, D. R., West, S. G., & Reich, J. W. (1991). Attributional style in relation to self-esteem and depression: Mediational and interactive models. *Journal of Research in Personality, 25,* 57–69.

Pines, A., & Aronson, E. (1983). Antecedents, correlates, and consequences of sexual jealousy. *Journal of Personality, 51,* 108–136.

Pinkerton, J. (1992). Life in Bush hell. *New Republic, 207*(25), 22–23, 26–27.

Pinkerton, S. D., & Abramson, P. R. (1992). Is risky sex rational? *Journal of Sex Research, 29,* 561–568.

Pittenger, J. B., Mark, L. S., & Johnson, D. F. (1989). Longitudinal stability of facial attractiveness. *Bulletin of the Psychonomic Society, 27,* 171–174.

Planalp, S., & Benson, A. (1992). Friends' and acquaintances' conversations I: Perceived differences. *Journal of Social and Personal Relationships, 9,* 483–506.

Platz, S. G., & Hosch, H. M. (1988). Cross–racial/ethnic eyewitness identification: A field study. *Journal of Applied Social Psychology, 13,* 972–984.

Pliner, P., & Chaiken, S. (1990). Eating, social motives, and self–presentation in women and men. *Journal of Experimental Social Psychology, 26,* 240–254.

Pliner, P., Chaiken, S., & Flett, G. L. (1990). Gender differences in concern with body weight and physical appearance over the life span. *Personality and Social Psychology Bulletin, 16,* 263–273.

Pliner, P., Hart, H., Kohl, J., & Saari, D. (1974). Compliance without pressure: Some further data on the foot–in–the–door technique. *Journal of Experimental Social Psychology, 10,* 17–22.

Polivy, J. (1990). Inhibition of internally cued behavior. In E. T. Higgins & R. Sorrentino (Eds.), *Handbook of motivation and cognition* (Vol. 2, pp. 131–150). New York: Guilford.

Popper, K. (1959). *The logic of scientific discovery.* London: Hutchinson.

Porter, C., Markus, H., & Nurius, P. S. (1984). *Conceptions of possibility among people in crisis.* Unpublished manuscript, University of Michigan, Ann Arbor.

Powell, G. N. (1990). One more time: Do female and male managers differ? *Academy of Management Executive, 4*(3), 68–7S.

Powers, P. C., & Geen, R. G. (1972). Effects of the behavior and perceived arousal of a model on instrumental aggression. *Journal of Personality and Social Psychology, 23,* 175–184.

Prager, K. J., & Bailey, J. M. (1985). Androgyny, ego development, and psychosocial crisis. *Sex Roles, 13,* 525–536.

Pratkanis, A. R. (1993). Propaganda and persuasion in the 1992 U. S. presidential election: What are the implications for a world democracy? *Current World Leaders,* in press.

Pratkanis, A., & Aronson, E. (1992). *Age of propaganda: Uses and misuses of persuasion.* New York: W. H. Freeman.

Pratkanis, A. R., & Aronson, E. (1993, March 22). Personal communication.

Pratkanis, A. R., Breckler S. J., & Greenwald, A. G. (Eds.). (1989). *Attitude structure and function.* Hillsdale, NJ: Erlbaum.

Pratto, F., & John, O. P. (1991). Automatic vigilance: The attention–grabbing power of negative social information. *Journal of Personality and Social Psychology, 51,* 380–391.

Prentice-Dunn, S., & Rogers, R. (1983). Deindividuation in aggression. In R. G. Geen & E. I. Donnerstein (Eds.), *Aggression: Theoretical and empirical reviews* (Vol. 2, pp. 155–171). New York: Academic Press.

Preston, R. (1992, October 26). Crisis in the hot zone. *New Yorker,* pp. 58–62, 64–76, 78–81.

Price, K. H., & Vandenberg, S. G. (1979). Matching for physical attractiveness in married couples. *Personality and Social Psychology Bulletin, 5,* 398–400.

Pritchard, R. (1991). The effects of cultural schemata on reading processing strategies. *Reading Research Quarterly, 24,* 273–29S.

Prohaska, T. R., Keller, M. L., Leventhal, E. A., & Leventhal, H. (1987). Impact of symptoms and aging attribution on emotions and coping. *Health Psychology, 6,* 495–514.

Provine, R. R. (1992). Contagious laughter: Laughter is a sufficient stimulus for laughs and smiles. *Bulletin of the Psychonomic Society, 30,* 1–4.

Pruitt, D. G., Carnevale, J. D., Ben–Yoav, O., Nochajski, T. H., & Van Slyck, M. R. (1983). Incentives for cooperation in integrative bargaining. In R. Tietz (Ed.), *Aspiration levels in bargaining and economic decision making.* Berlin: Springer–Verlag.

Pryor, J. B., Biggons, F. X., Wicklund, R. A., Fazio, R. H., & Hood, R. (1977). Self–focused attention and self–report validity. *Journal of Personality, 45,* 514–527.

Ptacek, J. T., Smith, R. E., & Zanas, J. (1992). Gender, appraisal, and coping: A longitudinal analysis. *Journal of Personality, 60,* 747–770.

Quadrel, M. J., & Lau, R. R. (1989). Health promotion, health locus of control, and health behavior: Two field experiments. *Journal of Applied Social Psychology, 19,* 1497–1521.

Queen Victoria. (1981, January). *Medical Aspects of Human Sexuality,* p. 86.

Quinn, R. P., & Staines, G. L. (1979). *The 1977 quality of employment survey.* Ann Arbor, MI: Institute for Social Research.

Radley, A., & Kennedy, M. (1992). Reflections upon charitable giving: A comparison of individuals from business, "manual" and professional backgrounds. *Journal of Community & Applied Social Psychology, 2,* 113–129.

Rahim, A. (Ed.). (1990). *Theory and research in conflict management.* New York: Praeger.

Ramirez, E., Maldonado, A., & Martos, R. (1992). Attributions modulate immunization against learned helplessness in humans. *Journal of Personality and Social Psychology, 62,* 139–146.

Ramirez, J., Bryant, J., & Zillmann, D. (1983). Effects of erotica on retaliatory behavior as a function of level of prior provocation. *Journal of Personality and Social Psychology, 43,* 971–978.

Rathje, W. L. (1991). Once and future landfills. *National Geographic, 179*(5), 116–134.

Raty, H., & Snellman, L. (1992). Does gender make any difference? Common–sense conceptions of intelligence. *Social Behavior and Personality, 20,* 23–34.

Reed, D., & Weinberg, M. S. (1984). Premarital coitus: Developing and establishing sexual scripts. *Social Psychology Quarterly, 47,* 129–138.

Reifman, A. S., Larrick, R. P., & Fein, S. (1991). Temper and temperature on the diamond: The heat–aggression relationship in major league baseball. *Personality and Social Psychology Bulletin, 17,* 580–585.

Reis, H. T., Nezlek, J., & Wheeler, L. (1980). Physical attractiveness in social interaction. *Journal of Personality and Social Psychology, 38,* 604–617.

Reis, J., & Herz, E. J. (1989). An examination of young adolescents' knowledge of and attitude toward sexuality according to perceived contraceptive responsibility. *Journal of Applied Social Psychology, 19,* 231–250.

Reis, T. J., Gerrard, M. & Gibbons, F. X. (1993). Social comparison and the pill: Reactions to upward and downward comparison of contraceptive behavior. *Personality and Social Psychology Bulletin, 19,* 13–20.

Reisenzein, R. (1983). The Schachter theory of emotion: Two decades later. *Psychological Bulletin, 94,* 239–264.

Reisman, J. M. (1984). Friendliness and its correlates. *Journal of Social and Clinical Psychology, 2,* 143–155.

Reiss, I. L. (1990). *An end to shame: Shaping our next sexual revolution.* Buffalo, NY: Prometheus.

Revenson, T. A. (1981). Coping with loneliness: The impact of causal attributions. *Personality and Social Psychology Bulletin, 7,* 565–571.

Rhodewalt, F., & Davison, J., Jr. (1983). Reactance and the coronary–prone behavior pattern: The role of self–attribution in response to reduced behavioral freedom. *Journal of Personality and Social Psychology, 44,* 220–228.

Ridley, M., & Dawkins, R. (1981). The natural selection of altruism. In J. P. Rushton & R. M. Sorrentino (Eds.), *Altruism and helping behavior.* Hillsdale, NJ: Erlbaum.

Riess, M., & Schlenker, B. R. (1977). Attitude change and responsibility avoidance as modes of dilemma resolution in forced–compliance situations. *Journal of Personality and Social Psychology, 35,* 21–30.

Riggio, R. E. (1990). *Industrial and organizational psychology.* New York: Harcourt Brace Jovanovich.

Riordan, C. A. (1978). Equal–status interracial contact: A review and revision of a concept. *International Journal of Intercultural Relations, 2,* 161–185.

Rittle, R. H. (1981). Changes in helping behavior: Self–versus situational perceptions as mediators of the foot–in–the–door effect. *Personality and Social Psychology Bulletin, 7,* 431–437.

Roballey, T. C., McGreevy, C., Rongo, R. R., Schwantes, M. L., Steger, P. J., Wininger, M. A., & Gardner, E. B. (1985). The effect of music on eating behavior. *Bulletin of the Psychonomic Society, 23,* 221–222.

Robberson, N. R., & Rogers, R. W. (1988). Beyond fear appeals: Negative and positive persuasive appeals to health and self–esteem. *Journal of Applied Social Psychology, 18,* 277–287.

Roberts, J. E., & Monroe, S. M. (1992). Vulnerable self–esteem and depressive symptoms: Prospective findings comparing three alternative conceptualizations. *Journal of Personality and Social Psychology, 62,* 804–812.

Roberts, J. V., & Edwards, D. (1989). Contextual effects in judgments of crimes, criminals, and the purposes of sentencing. *Journal of Applied Social Psychology, 19,* 902–917.

Robinson, W. L. V., & Calhoun, K. S. (1983). Sexual fantasies, attitudes, and behavior as a funciton of race, gender, and religiosity. *Imagination, Cognition, and Personality, 2,* 281–290.

Rodgers, J. L., Billy, J. O. B., & Udry, J. R. (1984). A model of friendship similarity in mildly deviant behaviors. *Journal of Applied Social Psychology, 14,* 413–425.

Rodin, J., & Salovey, P. (1989). Health psychology. In M. R. Rosenzweig & L. W. Porter (Eds.), *Annual review of psychology* (Vol. 40, pp. 533–579). Palo Alto, CA: Annual Reviews.

Rodin, M. J. (1987). Who is memorable to whom: A study of cognitive disregard. *Social Cognition, 5,* 144–165.

Rogers, M., Miller, N., Mayer, F. S., & Duvall, S. (1982). Personal responsibility and salience of the request for help: Determinants of the relations between negative affect and helping behavior. *Journal of Personality and Social Psychology, 43,* 956–970.

Rogers, R. G. (1991). Demographic characteristics of cigarette smokers in the United States. *Social Biology, 38,* 1–12.

Rogers, R. W. (1980). *Subjects' reactions to experimental deception.* Unpublished manuscript, University of Alabama,

Tuscaloosa.

Rogers, R. W., & Ketcher, C. M. (1979). Effects of anonymity and arousal on aggression. *Journal of Psychology, 102,* 13–19.

Roscoe, B., & Kruger, T. L. (1990). AIDS, late adolescents' knowledge and its influence on sexual behaviour. *Adolescence, 25,* 39–48.

Rose, S. M. (1984). How friendships end: Patterns among young adults. *Journal of Social and Personal Relationships, 1,* 267–277.

Rosenbaum, M. E. (1986). The repulsion hypothesis: On the nondevelopment of relationships. *Journal of Personality and Social Psychology, 51,* 1156–1166.

Rosenbaum, M. E., & Levin, I. P. (1969). Impression formation as a function of source credibility and the polarity of information. *Journal of Personality and Social Psychology, 12,* 34–37.

Rosenberg, M. (1965). *Society and the adolescent self-image.* Princeton, NJ: Princeton University Press.

Rosenblatt, A., & Greenberg, J. (1988). Depression and interpersonal attraction: The role of perceived similarity. *Journal of Personality and Social Psychology, 54,* 112–119.

Rosener, J. B. (1990). Ways women lead. *Harvard Business Review, 68*(6), 202.

Rosenfield, D., Greenberg, J., Folger, R., & Borys, R. (1982). Effect of an encounter with a black panhandler on subsequent helping for blacks: Tokenism or conforming to a negative stereotype? *Personality and Social Psychology Bulletin, 8,* 664–671.

Rosenhan, D. L., Salovey, P., & Hargis, K. (1981). The joys of helping: Focus of attention mediates the impact of positive affect on altruism. *Journal of Personality and Social Psychology, 40,* 899–905.

Rosenthal, A. M. (1964). *Thirty–eight witnesses.* New York: McGraw–Hill.

Rosenthal, D., Moore, S., & Flynn, I. (1991). Adolescent self–efficacy, self–esteem, and sexual risk–taking. *Journal of Community & Applied Social Psychology, 1,* 77–78.

Rosenthal, E. (1992, August 18). Troubled marriage? Sibling relations may be at fault. *New York Times,* pp. C1, C9.

Rosenzweig, J. M., & Daley, D. M. (1989). Dyadic adjustment/sexual satisfaction in women and men as a function of psychological sex role self–perception. *Journal of Sex and Marital Therapy, 15,* 42–56.

Roskos–Ewoldsen, D. R., & Fazio, R. H. (1992). The accessibility of source likability as a determinant of persuasion. *Personality and Social Psychology Bulletin, 18,* 19–25.

Ross, L. D. (1977). Problems in the interpretation of 'self–serving' assymetries in causal attribution: Comments on the Stephan et al. paper. *Sociometry, 40,* 112–114.

Ross, N. (1989). Relation of implicit theories to the construction of personal histories. *Psychological Review, 96,* 341–357.

Rotenberg, K. J., & Kmill, J (1992). Perception of lonely and non–lonely persons as a function of individual differences in loneliness. *Journal of Social and Personal Relationships, 9,* 325–330.

Roter, D. L. (1984). Patient question asking in physician–patient interaction. *Health Psychology, 3,* 395–409.

Roth, D. L., Wiebe, D. J., Fillingim, R. G., & Shay, K. A. (1989). Life events, fitness, hardiness, and health: A simultaneous analysis of proposed stress–resistance effects. *Journal of Personality and Social Psychology, 57,* 136–142.

Rotter, J. B. (1971). Generalized expectancies for interpersonal trust. *American Psychologist, 26,* 443–452.

Rotton, J., & Frey, J. (1985). Psychological costs of air pollution: Atmospheric conditions, seasonal trends, and psychiatric emergencies. *Population and Environment, 7,* 3–16.

Rotton, J., Frey, J., Barry, T., Milligan, M., & Fitzpatrick, M. (1979). The air pollution experience and physical aggression. *Journal of Applied Social Psychology, 9,* 397–412.

Rotton, J., & Kelley, I. W. (1985). Much ado about the full moon: A meta-analysis of lunar-lunacy research. *Psychological Bulletin, 97,* 286–306.

Routh, D. K., & Ernst, A. R. (1984). Somatization disorder in relatives of children and adolescents with functional abdominal pain. *Journal of Pediatric Psychology, 50,* 427–437.

Rozin, P., Millman, L., & Nemeroff, C. (1986). Operation of the laws of sympathetic magic in disgust and other domains. *Journal of Personality and Social Psychology, 50,* 703–712.

Rubin, J. Z. (1985). Deceiving ourselves about deception: Comment on Smith and Richardson's "Amelioration of deception and harm in psychological research." *Journal of Personality and Social Psychology, 48,* 252–253.

Rubin, Z. (1982). Children without friends. In L. A. Peplau & D. Perlman (Eds.), *Loneliness: A sourcebook of current theory, research, and therapy.* New York: Wiley.

Rule, B. G., Bisanz, G. L., & Kohn, M. (1985). Anatomy of a persuasion schema: Targets, goals, and strategies. *Journal of Personality and Social Psychology, 48,* 1127–1140.

Rule, B. G., Taylor, B. R., & Dobbs, A. R. (1987). Priming effects of heat on aggressive thoughts. *Social Cognition, 5,* 131–143.

Rusbult, C. E. (1983). A longitudinal test of the investment model: The development (and deterioration) of satisfaction and commitment in heterosexual involvements. *Journal of Personality and Social Psychology, 45,* 101–117.

Rusbult, C. E., Morrow, G. D., & Johnson, D. J. (1990). Self–esteem and problem–solving behavior in close relationships. *British Journal of Social Psychology.*

Rusbult, C. E., & Zembrodt, I. M. (1983). Responses to dissatisfaction in romantic involvements: A multidimensional scaling analysis. *Journal of Experimental Social Psychology, 19,* 274–293.

Rushton, J. P. (1988a). Epigenetic rules in moral development: Distal–proximal approaches to altruism and aggression. *Aggressive Behavior, 14,* 35–50.

Rushton, J. P. (1988b). Genetic similarity, mate choice, and fecundity in humans. *Ethology and Sociobiology, 9,* 329–333.

Rushton, J. P. (1989a). Genetic similarity, human altruism, and group selection. *Behavioral and Brain Sciences, 12,* 503–559.

Rushton, J. P. (1989b). Genetic similarity in male friendships. *Ethology and Sociobiology, 10,* 361–373

Rushton, J. P. (1990). Sir Francis Galton, epigenetic rules, genetic similarity theory, and human life–history analysis. *Journal of Personality, 58,* 117–140.

Rushton, J. P., & Nicholson, I. R. (1988). Genetic similarity theory, intelligence, and human mate choice. *Ethology and Sociobiology, 9,* 45–57.

Rushton, J. P., Russell, R. J. H., & Wells, P. A. (1984). Genetic similarity theory: Beyond kin selection. *Behavior Genetics, 14,* 179–193.

Russell, D., Peplau, L. A., & Cutrona, C. E. (1980). The revised UCLA Loneliness Scale: Concurrent and discriminant validity evidence. *Journal of Personality and Social Psychology, 39,* 472–480.

Russell, G. W. (1981). Aggression in sport. In P. F. Brain & D. Benton (Eds.), *Multidisciplinary approaches to aggression research* (pp. 431–446). Amsterdam: Elsevier/North Holland.

Russell, J. A., Weiss, A., & Mendelsohn, C. A. (1989). Affect grid: A single-item scale of pleasure and arousal. *Journal of Personality and Social Psychology, 57,* 493–502.

Russell, P. A. (1992). The evolutionary model is synthetic not heuristic. *Behavioral and Brain Sciences, 15,* 108–109.

Rutkowski, G. K., Gruder, C. L., & Romer, D. (1983). Group cohesiveness, social norms, and bystander intervention. *Journal of Personality and Social Psychology, 44,* 545–552.

Ryan, R. H., & Geiselman, R. E. (1991). Effects of biased information on the relationship between eyewitness confidence and accuracy. *Bulletin of the Psychonomic Society, 29,* 7–9.

Ryckman, R. M., Robbins, M. A., Kaczor, L. M., & Gold, J. A. (1989). Male and female raters' stereotyping of male and female physiques. *Personality and Social Psychology Bulletin, 15,* 244–251.

Ryff, C. D., & Essex, M. J. (1992). The interpretation of life experience and well-being: The sample case of relocation. *Psychology and Aging, 7,* 507–517.

Saarni, C. (1988). Children's understanding of the interpersonal consequences of dissemblance of nonverbal emotional–expressive behavior. *Journal of Nonverbal Behavior, 12,* 275–294.

Sadalla, E. K., Kenrick, D. T., & Vershure, B. (1987). Dominance and heterosexual attraction. *Journal of Personality and Social Psychology, 52,* 730–738.

Sagan, C. (1989, February 5). The secret of the Persian chessboard. *Parade,* pp. 14–15.

Salovey, P. (1992). Mood-induced self–focused attention. *Journal of Personality and Social Psychology, 62,* 699–707.

Salovey, P., Mayer, J. D., & Rosenhan, D. L. (1991). Mood and helping: Mood as a motivator of helping and helping as a regulator of mood. In M. S. Clark (Ed.), *Prosocial behavior* (pp. 215–237). Newbury Park, CA: Sage.

Salovey, P., & Rodin, J. (1991). Provoking jealousy and envy: Domain relevance and self–esteem threat. *Journal of Social and Clinical Psychology, 10,* 395–413.

Sanbonmatsu, D. M., Shavitt, S., & Sherman, S. J. (1991). The role of personal relevance in the formation of distinctiveness–based illusory correlations. *Personality and Social Psychology Bulletin, 17,* 124–132.

Sanchez, E., & Wiesenfeld, E. (1987). Environmental psychology: A new field of application in psychology and a new professional role for the psychologist. *Interamerican Journal of Psychology, 21,* 90–100.

Sanchez–Bernardos, M. L., & Sanz, J. (1992). Effects of the discrepancy between self–concepts on emotional adjustment. *Journal of Research in Personality, 26,* 303–318.

Sanders, G. S. (1983). An attentional process model of social facilitation. In A. Hare, H. Blumberg, V. Kent, and M. Davies (Eds.), *Small groups.* London: Wiley.

Sanders, G. S. (1984). Effects of context cues on eyewitness identification responses. *Journal of Applied Social Psychology, 14,* 386–397.

Sanders, G. S., & Chiu, W. (1988). Eyewitness errors in the free recall of actions. *Journal of Applied Social Psychology, 18,* 1241–1259.

Sanders Thompson, V. L. (1988). *A multi–faceted approach to racial identification.* Unpublished doctoral dissertation, Duke University, Durham, NC.

Sanders Thompson, V. L. (1990). Factors affecting the level of African American identification. *Journal of Black Psychology, 17,* 14–23.

Sanders Thompson, V. L. (1991). Perceptions of race and race relations which affect African American identification. *Journal of Applied Social Psychology, 21,* 1502–1516.

Sanna, L. J. (1992). Self–efficacy theory: Implications for social facilitation and social loafing. *Journal of Personality and Social Psychology, 62,* 774–786.

Santi, S., Best, J. A., Brown, K. S., & Cargo, M. (1990–1991). Social environment and smoking initiation. *International Journal of the Addictions, 25,* 881–903.

Schachter, S. (1951). Deviation, rejection, and communication. *Journal of Abnormal and Social Psychology, 46,* 190–207.

Schachter, S. (1959). *The psychology of affiliation.* Stanford, CA: Stanford University Press.

Schachter, S. (1964). The interaction of cognitive and physiological determinants of emotional state. In L. Berkowitz (Ed.), *Advances in experimental social psychology* (Vol. 1, pp. 48–81). New York: Academic Press.

Schachter, S., & Singer, J. E. (1962). Cognitive, social and physiological determinants of emotional states. *Psychological Review, 69,* 379–399.

Schaller, M. (1992). In–group favoritism and statistical reasoning in social inference: Implications for formation and maintenance of group stereotypes. *Journal of Personality and Social Psychology, 63,* 61–74.

Schaller, M., & Maas, A. (1989). Illusory correlation and social categorization: Toward an integration of motivational and cognitive factors in stereotype formation. *Journal of Personality and Social Psychology, 56,* 709–721.

Scheier, M. F., & Carver, C. S. (1987). Dispositional optimism and physical well–being: The influence of generalized outcome expectancies in health. *Journal of Personality, 55,* 169–210.

Scheier, M. F., Matthews, K. A., Owens, J. F., Magovern, G. J., Sr., Lefebvre, R. C., Abbott, R. A., & Carver, C. S. (1989). Dispositional optimism and recovery from coronary artery bypass surgery: The beneficial effects on physical and psychological well–being. *Journal of Personality and Social Psychology, 57,* 1024–1040.

Scher, S. J., & Cooper, J. (1989). Motivational basis of dissonance: The singular role of behavioral consequences. *Journal of Personality and Social Psychology, 56,* 899–906.

Schiaffino, K. M., & Revenson, T. A. (1992). The role of perceived self–efficacy, perceived control, and causal attributions in adaptation to rheumatoid arthritis: Distinguishing mediator from moderator effects. *Personality and Social Psychology Bulletin, 18,* 709–718.

Schiller, B. (1932). A quantitative analysis of marriage selection in a small group. *Journal of Social Psychology, 3,* 297–319.

Schleifer, S. J., Keller, S. E., Camerino, M., Thornton, J. C., & Stein, M. (1983). Suppression of lymphocyte function following bereavement. *Journal of the American Medical Association, 250,* 374–377.

Schlenker, B. R. (1980). *Impression management: The self–concept, social identity, and interpersonal relations.* Belmont, CA: Brooks/Cole.

Schlenker, B. R., & Weigold, M. F. (1989). Goals and the self–identification process: Constructing desired identities. In L. Pervin (Ed.), *Goal concepts in personality and social psy-*

chology (pp. 243–290). Hillsdale, NJ: Erlbaum.

Schlesinger, A. M. Jr. (1986). *The cycles of American history*. Boston: Houghton Mifflin.

Schlesinger, A. M., Jr. (1992, November 16). The turn of the cycle. *New Yorker*, pp. 46, 48, 50, 52–54.

Schmidt, G., & Weiner, B. (1988). An attributional affectation theory of behavior: Replications of judgments of helping. *Personality and Social Psychology Bulletin, 14*, 610–621.

Schmitt, B., Gilovich, T., Goore, H., & Joseph, L. (1986). Mere presence and social facilitation: One more time. *Journal of Experimental Social Psychology, 22*, 242–248.

Schneider, B. H. (1991). A comparison of skill–building and desensitization strategies for intervention with aggressive children. *Aggressive Behavior, 17*, 301–311.

Schneider, B. H., & Byrne, B. M. (1987). Individualizing social skills training for behaviour–disordered children. *Journal of Consulting and Clinical Psychology, 55*, 444–445.

Schneider, K. (1991, August 13). Ranges of animals and plants head north. *New York Times*, pp. C1, C9.

Schneider, S. H. (1989). *Global warming*. San Francisco: Sierra Club.

Schoenrade, P. A., Batson, C. D., Brandt, J. R., & Loud, R. E. (1986). Attachment, accountability, and motivation to benefit another not in distress. *Journal of Personality and Social Psychology, 51*, 557–563.

Schonbach, P. (1990). *Account episodes: The management of escalation of conflict*. Cambridge: Cambridge University Press.

Schooler, J. W., & Engstler–Schooler, T. Y. (1990). Verbal overshadowing of visual memories: Some things are better left unsaid. *Cognitive Psychology, 22*, 36–71.

Schooler, J. W., & Loftus, E. F. (1986). Individual differences and experimentation: Complementary approaches to interrogative suggestibility. *Social Behaviour, 1*, 105–112.

Schullo, S. A., & Alperson, B. I. (1984). Interpersonal phenomenology as a function of sexual orientation, sex, sentiment, and trait categories in long–term dyadic relationships. *Journal of Personality and Social Psychology, 47*, 983–1002.

Schuster, E., & Elderton, E. M. (1906). The inheritance of psychical characters. *Biometrika, 5*, 460–469.

Schwalbe, M. L. (1991). Role–taking, self–monitoring, and the alignment of conduct with others. *Personality and Social Psychology Bulletin, 17*, 51–57.

Schwartz, S. H., & Gottlieb, A. (1980). Bystander anonymity and reaction to emergencies. *Journal of Personality and Social Psychology, 39*, 418–430.

Schwarz, N. (1990). Feelings as information: Informational and motivational functions of affective states. In R. Sorrentino & E. T. Higgins (Eds.), *Handbook of motivation and cognition: Foundations of social behavior* (Vol. 2, pp. 527–561). New York: Guilford.

Schwarz, N., & Bless, H. (1992). Scandals and the public's trust in politicians: Assimilation and contrast effects. *Personality and Social Psychology Bulletin, 13*, 574–579.

Schwarz, N., Bless, H., Strack, F., Klumpp, G., Rittenauer–Schatka, G., & Simons, A. (1991). Ease of retrieval as information: Another look at the availability heuristic. *Journal of Personality and Social Psychology, 61*, 195–202.

Schwarzwald, J., Amir, Y,., & Crain, R. L. (1992). Long–term effects of school desegregation experiences on interpersonal relations in the Israeli defense forces. *Personality and Social Psychology Bulletin, 18*, 357–368.

Scott, J. P. (1992). Aggression: Functions and control in social systems. *Aggressive Behavior, 18*, 1–20.

Scott, K. P., & Feldman–Summers, S. (1979). Children's reactions to textbook stories in which females are portrayed in traditionally male roles. *Journal of Educational Psychology, 71*, 396–402.

Searcy, E., & Eisenberg, N. (1992). Defensiveness in response to aid from a sibling. *Journal of Personality and Social Psychology, 62*, 422–433.

Sears, D. O., & Allen, H. M., Jr. (1984). The trajectory of local desegregation controversies and whites' opposition to busing. In N. Miller & M. Brewer (Eds.), *Groups in contact: The psychology of desegregation*. (pp. 123–151). Orlando, FL: Academic Press.

Sears, D. O., & Kinder, D. R. (1985). Whites' opposition to busing: On conceptualizing and operationalizing group conflict. *Journal of Personality and Social Psychology, 48*, 1141–1147.

Sedikides, C. (1992). Attentional effects on mood are moderated by chronic self–conception valence. *Personality and Social Psychology Bulletin, 18*, 580–584.

Segal, M. M. (1974). Alphabet and attraction: An unobtrusive measure of the effect of propinquity in a field setting. *Journal of Personality and Social Psychology, 30*, 654–657.

Seligman, M. E. P. (1975). *On depression, development, and death*. San Francisco: Freeman.

Selye, H. (1956). *The stress of life*. New York: McGraw–Hill.

Seta, J. J., Seta, C. E., & Wang, M. A. (1991). Feelings of negativity and stress: An averaging summation analysis of impressions of negative life experiences. *Personality and Social Psychology Bulletin, 17*, 376–384.

Shaffer, D. R., & Graziano, W. G. (1983). Effects of positive and negative moods on helping tasks having pleasant or unpleasant consequences. *Motivation and Emotion, 7*, 269–278.

Shanab, N. E., & Yahya, K. A. (1977). A behavioral study of obedience in children. *Journal of Personality and Social Psychology, 35*, 530–536.

Shapiro, D. L., Buttner, E. H., & Barry, B. (1992). Explanations: What factors enhance their perceived adequacy? *Organizational Behavior and Human Decision Processes*.

Shapiro, J. P. (1988). Relationships between dimensions of depressive experience and evaluative beliefs about people in general. *Personality and Social Psychology Bulletin, 14*, 388–400.

Shapiro, J. P., Baumeister, R. F., & Kessler, J. W. (1991). A three–component model of children's teasing: Aggression, humor, and ambiguity. *Journal of Social and Clinical Psychology, 10*, 459–472.

Shaver, P. R., & Brennan, K. A. (1992). Attachment styles and the "big five" personality traits: Their connections with each other and with romantic relationship outcomes. *Personality and Social Psychology Bulletin, 18*, 536–545.

Shavitt, S. (1989). Operationalizing functional theories of attitudes. In A. R. Pratkanis, S. J. Breckler, & A. G. Greenwald (Eds.), *Attitude structure and function* (pp. 311–337). Hillsdale, NJ: Erlbaum.

Shavitt, S. (1990). the role of attitude objects in attitude functions. Journal of Experimental Social Psychology, 26, 124–148.

Shavitt, S., Swan, S., & Lowrey, T. N. (1993). The interaction of endorser attractiveness and involvement in persuasion depends on the goal that guides message processing.

Shaw, M. E. (1981). *Group dynamics: The psychology of small group behavior* (3rd ed.). New York: McGraw-Hill.

Shek, D. T. L., & Cheung, C. –K. (1990). Locus of coping in a sample of Chinese working parents: Reliance on self or seeking help from others. *Social Behavior and Personality, 18,* 327–346.

Sheldon, W. H., Stevens, S. S., & Tucker, W. B. (1940). *The varieties of human physique.* New York: Harper.

Sheppard, B. H., Bazerman, M. H., & Lewicki, R. J. (Eds.). (1990). *Research in negotiation in organizations* (Vol. 2). Greenwich, CT: JAI Press.

Sheppard, J. A., & Strathman, A. J. (1989). Attractiveness and height: The role of stature in dating preference, frequency of dating, and perceptions of attractiveness. *Personality and Social Psychology Bulletin, 15,* 617–627.

Shepperd, J. A., & Kashani, J. H. (1991). The relationship of hardiness, gender, and stress to health outcomes in adolescents. *Journal of Personality, 59,* 747–768.

Sherif, M. (1935). A study of some social factors in perception. *Archives of Psychology,* No. 187.

Sherif, M., Harvey, O. J., White, B. J., Hood, W. E., & Sherif, C. W. (1961). *Intergroup conflict and cooperation: The Robbers Cave experiment.* Norman, OK: Institute of Group Relations.

Sherman, S. J., Presson, C. C., & Chassin, L. (1984). Mechanisms underlying the false consensus effect: The special role of threats to the self. *Personality and Social Psychology Bulletin, 10,* 127–138.

Sherman, S. S. (1980). On the self–erasing nature of errors of prediction. *Journal of Personality and Social Psychology, 16,* 388–403.

Shiffrin, R. M. (1988). Attention. In R. C. Atkinson, R. J. Herrnstein, G. Lindzey, & R. D. Luce (Eds.), *Stevens' handbook of experimental psychology: Vol. 2. Learning and cognition* (pp. 739–811). New York: Wiley.

Shore, B. (1991). Twice–born, once conceived: Meaning construction and cultural cognition. *American Anthropologist, 32,* 9–23.

Shotland, R. I., & Strau, M. K. (1976). Bystander response to an assault: When a man attacks a woman. *Journal of Personality and Social Psychology, 34,* 990–999.

Showers, C. (1992a). Compartmentalization of positive and negative self–knowledge: Keeping bad apples out of the bunch. *Journal of Personality and Social Psychology, 62,* 1036–1049.

Showers, C. (1992b). Evaluative integrative thinking about characteristics of the self. *Personality and Social Psychology Bulletin, 18,* 719–729.

Showers, C., & Ryff, C. D. (1993). *Self–differentiation and well–being in a life transition.* Manuscript submitted for publication.

Shupe, L. M. (1954). Alcohol and crimes: A study of the urine alcohol concentration found in 882 persons arrested during or immediately after the commission of a felony. *Journal of Criminal Law and Criminology, 33,* 661–665.

Sidel, R. (1973). *Women and child care in China: A firsthand report.* New York: Penguin Books.

Sigelman, L., & Sigelman, C. K. (1982). Sexism, racism, and ageism in voting behavior: An experimental analysis. *Social Psychology Quarterly, 45,* 263–269.

Sigelman, C. K., Thomas, D. B., Sigelman, L., & Ribich, F. D. (1986). Gender, physical attractiveness, and electability: An experimental invesigation of voter biases. *Journal of Applied Social Psychology, 16,* 229–248.

Simmons, C. H., vom Kolke, A., & Shimizu, H. (1986). Attitudes toward romantic love among American, German, and Japanese students. *Journal of Social Psychology, 126,* 327–336.

Simmons, D. D., Binney, S. E., & Dodd, B. (1992). Valuing "a clean environment": Factor location, norms, and relation to risks. *Journal of Social Behavior and Personality, 7,* 649–658.

Simon, J. (1989). *The economic consequences of immigration.* New York: Basil Blackwell.

Simonton, D. K. (1986). Presidential greatness: The historical consensus and its psychological significance. *Political Psychology, 7,* 259–283.

Simonton, D. K. (1988). Presidential style: Personality, biography, and performance. *Journal of Personality and Social Psychology, 55,* 928–936.

Simonton, D. K. (1992). Presidential greatness and personality: A response to McCann (1992). *Journal of Personality and Social Psychology, 63,* 676–679.

Simpson, J. A. (1987). The dissolution of romantic relationships: Factors involved in relationship stability and emotional stress. *Journal of Personality and Social Psychology, 53,* 683–692.

Simpson, J. A., & Gangestad, S. W. (1991). Individual differences in sociosexuality: Evidence for convergent and discriminant validity. *Journal of Personality and Social Psychology, 60,* 870–883.

Simpson, J. A., & Gangestad, S. W. (1992). Sociosexuality and romantic partner choice. *Journal of Personality, 60,* 31–51.

Simpson, J. C. (1992). Rock the vote. *Time, 139*(24), 66–67.

Simpson, M., & Perry, J. D. (1990). Crime and climate: A reconsideration. *Environment and Behavior, 22,* 295–300.

Singh, R., & Tan, L. S. C. (1992). Attitudes and attraction: A test of the similarity-repulsion hypotheses. *British Journal of Social Psychology, 31,* 227–238.

Sirgo, H. B., & Eisenman, R. (1993). Liberals versus conservatives: Are attitudes toward government related to experiences with government? *Bulletin of the Psychonomic Society, 31,* 155–157.

Sistrunk, F., & McDavid, J. W. (1971). Sex variable in conforming behavior. *Journal of Personality and Social Psychology, 29,* 200–207.

Sivacek, J., & Crano, W. D. (1982). Vested interest as a moderator of attitude–behavior consistency. *Journal of Personality and Social Psychology, 43,* 210–221.

Skelton, J. A., & Strohmetz, D. (1990). Priming symptom reports with health–related cognitive activity. *Personality and Social Psychology Bulletin, 16,* 449–464.

Skinner, B. F. (1986). What is wrong with daily life in the Western world? *American Psychologist, 41,* 568–574.

Skowronski, J. J., & Carlston, D. E. (1989). Negativity and extremity biases in impression formation: A review of explanations. *Psychological Bulletin, 105,* 131–142.

Slater, E. J., & Calhoun, K. S. (1988). Familial conflict and marital dissolution: Effects on the social functioning of college students. *Journal of Social and Clinical Psychology. 65,* 118–126.

Smeaton, G., Byrne, D., & Murnen, S. K. (1989). The repulsion hypothesis revisited: Similarity irrelevance or dissimilarity bias? *Journal of Personality and Social Psychology, 56,* 54–59.

Smeaton, G., Rupp, D., Vig, C., & Byrne, D. (1992). *The mediating role of similarity assumptions on the effects of attitude similarity and dissimilarity on attraction and repulsion.* Manuscript submitted for publication.

Smith, A., & Stansfeld, S. (1986). Aircraft noise exposure, noise sensitivity, and everyday errors. *Environment and Behavior, 18,* 214–226.

Smith, D. E., Gier, J. A., & Willis, F. N. (1982). Interpersonal touch and compliance with a marketing request. *Basic and Applied Social Psychology, 3,* 35–38.

Smith, E. R. (1989). *Interpersonal attraction as a function of similarity and assumed similarity in traditional gender role adherence.* Unpublished doctoral dissertation, University at Albany, State University of New York.

Smith, K. D. (1992). Trait sympathy and perceived control as predictors of entering sympathy–arousing situations. *Personality and Social Psychology Bulletin, 18,* 207–216.

Smith, K. D., Keating, J. P., & Stotland, E. (1989). Altruism reconsidered: The effect of denying feedback on a victim's status to empathetic witnesses. *Journal of Personality and Social Psychology, 57,* 641–650.

Smith, P. B., & Bond, N. H. (1993). *Social psychology across cultures.* Boston: Allyn & Bacon.

Smith, P. C., Kendall, L. M., & Hulin, C. L. (1969). *The measurement of satisfaction in work and retirement.* Chicago: Rand McNally.

Smith, R. E., Smoll, F. L., & Ptacek, J. T. (1990). Conjunctive moderator variables in vulnerability and resiliency research: Life stress, social support and coping skills, and adolescent sport injuries. *Journal of Personality and Social Psychology, 58,* 360–370.

Smith, R. H., Kim, S. H., & Parrott, W. G. (1988). Envy and jealousy: Semantic problems and experiential distinctions. *Personality and Social Psychology Bulletin, 14,* 401–409.

Smith, S. M., & Shaffer, D. R. (1991). Celerity and cajolery: Rapid speech may promote or inhibit persuasion through its impact on message elaboration. *Personality and Social Psychology Bulletin, 17,* 663–669.

Smith, S. S., & Richardson, D. (1985). On deceiving ourselves about deception: Reply to Rubin. *Journal of Personality and Social Psychology, 48,* 254–255.

Smith, T. W., & Christensen, A. J. (1992). Cardiovascular reactivity and interpersonal relations: Psychosomatic processes in social context. *Journal of Social and Clinical Psychology, 11,* 279–301.

Smith, T. W., & Pope, M. K. (1990). Cynical hostility as a health risk: Current status and future directions. *Journal of Social Behavior and Personality, 5,* 77–88.

Smith, T. W., Pope, M. K., Rhodewalt, F., & Poulton, J. L. (1989). Optimism, neuroticism, coping, and symptom reports: An alternative interpretation of the Life Orientation Test. *Journal of Personality and Social Psychology, 56,* 640–648.

Smith, T. W., & Williams, P. G. (1992). Personality and health: Advantages and limitations of the five–factor model. *Journal of Personality, 60,* 395–423.

Smith, V. I., & Ellsworth, P. C. (1987). The social psychology of eyewitness accuracy: Misleading questions and communicator expertise. *Journal of Applied Psychology, 72,* 294–300.

Smoking rate up for blacks, women. (1993, April 2). *Albany Times–Union,* p. A–9.

Smolowe, J. (1992). Where there's smoke. *Time,* 140(21), 59.

Sniffen, M. J. (1991, September 30). Blacks make up 40% of death row. *Albany Times Union,* p. A–3.

Snyder, C. R., & Endelman, J. R. (1979). Effects of degree of interpersonal similarity on physical distance and self–reported attraction: A comparison of uniqueness and reinforcement theory predictions. *Journal of Personality, 47,* 492–505.

Snyder, C. R., & Fromkin, H. L. (1980). *Uniqueness: The human pursuit of difference.* New York: Plenum.

Snyder, M. (1974). Self-monitoring of expressive behavior. *Journal of Personality and Social Psychology, 30,* 526–537.

Snyder, M. (1993, March). Personal communication.

Snyder, M., Gangestad, S., & Simpson, J. A. (1983). Choosing friends as activity partners: The role of self–monitoring. *Journal of Personality and Social Psychology, 45,* 1061–1072.

Snyder, M., & Ickes, W. (1985). Personality and social behavior. In G. Lindzey & E. Aronson (Eds.), *The handbook of social psychology* (Vol. 1, 3rd ed., pp. 883–947). New York: Random House.

Snyder, M., & Omoto, A. M. (1992a). Volunteerism and society's response to the HIV epidemic. *Current Directions in Psychological Science, 1,* 113–116.

Snyder, M., & Omoto, A. M. (1992b). Who helps and why? The psychology of AIDS volunteerism. In S. Spacapan & S. Oskamp (Eds.), *Helping and being helped: Naturalistic studies.* Newbury Park, CA: Sage.

Snyder, M., & Simpson, J. A. (1984). Self–monitoring and dating relationships. *Journal of Personality and Social Psychology, 47,* 1281–1291.

Snyder, M., & Swann, W. B., Jr. (1978) Behavioral confirmation in social interaction: From social perception to social reality. *Journal of Experimental Social Psychology, 14,* 148–162.

Sogin, S. R., & Pallak, M. S. (1976). Bad decisions, responsibility, and attitude change: Effects of violation, foreseeability, and locus of causality of negative consequences. *Journal of Personality and Social Psychology, 33,* 300–306.

Solano, C. H., Barren, P. G., & Parish, E. A. (1982). Loneliness and patterns of self–disclosure. *Journal of Personality and Social Psychology, 43,* 524–531.

Solano, C. H., & Koester, N. H. (1989). Loneliness and communication problems: Subjective anxiety or objective skills? *Personality and Social Psychology Bulletin, 15,* 126–133.

Solomon, R. C. (1981, October). The love lost in cliches. *Psychology Today,* pp. 83–85, 87–88.

Solomon, S., Greenberg, J., & Pyszczynski, T. (1991). Terror management theory of self–esteem. In C. R. Snyder & D. Forsyth (Eds.), *Handbook of social and clinical psychology: The health perspective* (pp. 21–40). New York: Pergamon.

Spellman, B. A., & Holyoak, K. J. (1992). If Saddam is Hitler then who is George Bush? Analogical mapping between systems of social roles. *Journal of Personality and Social Psychology, 62,* 913–933.

Spencer, J. (1990). Collective violence and everyday practice in Sri Lanka. *Journal of Asian Studies, 24,* 603–623.

Sprafkin, J. N., Liebert, R. M., & Poulous, R. W. (1975). Effects of a prosocial televised example on children's helping. *Journal of Personality and Social Psychology, 48,* 35–46.

Srull, T. K., Lichtenstein, M., & Rothbart, M. (1985). Associative storage and retrieval process in person memory. *Journal of Experimental Psychology: Learning, Memory, and Cognition,* 11, 316–345.

Srull, T. K., & Wyer, R. S. (1989). Person memory and judgment. *Psychological Review, 96,* 58–83.

Staats, A. W., & Staats, C. K. (1958). Attitudes established by classical conditioning. *Journal of Abnormal and Social Psychology, 15,* 37–40.

Staats, A. W., Staats, C. K., & Crawford, H. L. (1962). First–order conditioning of meaning and the parallel conditioning of GSR. *Journal of General Psychology, 67,* 159–167.

Stalling, R. (1992). Mood and pain: The influence of positive and negative affect on reported body aches. *Journal of Social Behavior and Personality, 7,* 323–334.

Standing, L., Lynn, D., & Moxness, K. (1990). Effects of noise upon introverts and extraverts. *Bulletin of the Psychonomic Society, 28,* 138–140.

Stangor, C., Lynch, L. H., Duan, C., & Glass, B. (1992). Categorization of individuals on the basis of multiple social features. *Journal of Personality and Social Psychology, 62,* 207–218.

Stangor, C., & Ruble, D. H. (1989). Strength of expectancies and memory for social information: What we remember depends on how much we know. *Journal of Experimental Social Psychology, 25,* 18–35.

Stasser, G. (1992). Pooling of unshared information during group discussion. In S. Worchel, W. Wood, & J. H. Simpson (Eds.), *Process and productivity* (pp. 48–67). Newbury Park, CA: Sage.

Stasser, G., Kerr, N. L., & Davis, J. H. (1989). Influence processes and consensus models in decision–making groups. In P. B. Paulus (Ed.), *Psychology of influence* (2nd ed.). Hillsdale, NJ: Erlbaum.

Stasser, G., & Hinkle, S. (1993). Research in progress, Miami University, Oxford, Ohio.

Stasser, G., & Stewart, D. (1992). Discovery of hidden profiles by decision–making groups: Solving a problem versus making a judgment. *Journal of Personality and Social Psychology, 63,* 426–434.

Stasser, G., Taylor, L. A., & Hanna, C. (1989). Information sampling in structured and unstructured discussions of three- and six-person groups. *Journal of Personality and Social Psychology, 57,* 67–78.

Stasser, G., & Titus, W. (1985). Pooling of unshared information in group decision making: Biased information sampling during discussion. *Journal of Personality and Social Psychology, 48,* 1467–1478.

Stasser, G., & Titus, W. (1987). Effects of information load and percentage of shared information on the dissemination of unshared information during group discussion. *Journal of Personality and Social Psychology, 55,* 81–93.

Steele, C. M., Critchlow, B., & Liu, T. J. (1985). Alcohol and social behavior: The helpful drunkard. *Journal of Personality and Social Psychology, 48,* 35–46.

Steers, R. M., & Porter, L. W. (Eds.). (1989). *Motivation and work behavior* (5th ed.). New York: McGraw–Hill.

Steffen, V. J., & Eagly, A. H. (1985). Implicit theories about influence style: The effects of status and sex. *Personality and Social Psychology Bulletin, 11,* 191–205.

Steinberg, R., & Shapiro, S. (1982). Sex differences in personality traits of female and male master of business administration students. *Journal of Applied Psychology, 67,* 306–310.

Steiner, I. D. (1972). *Process and productivity.* New York: Academic Press.

Steiner, I. D. (1976). Task–performing groups. In J. W. Thibaut, J. T. Spence, & R. C. Carson (Eds.), *Contemporary topics in social psychology.* Morristown, NJ: General Learning Press.

Steinfels, P. (1992, January 20). Apathy is seen toward agony of the homeless. *New York Times,* pp. Al, B7.

Stengel, R. (1988, October 24). The likability sweepstakes. *Time,* p. 20.

Stephan, C. W., & Stephan, W. G. (1986). Habla Ingles? The effects of language translation on simulated juror decisions. *Journal of Applied Social Psychology, 16,* 577–589.

Stephan, W. G. (1985). Intergroup relations. In G. Lindzey & E. Aronson (Eds.), *Handbook of social psychology* (Vol. 2, pp. 599–658). New York: Random House.

Stephan, W. G. (1992). Sexual motivation, patriarchy, and compatibility. *Behavioral and Brain Sciences, 15,* 111–112.

Stephan, W. G., & Stephan, C. W. (1988). Emotional reactions to interracial achievement outcomes. *Journal of Applied Social Psychology, 19,* 608–621.

Stern, P. C. (1992). Psychological dimensions of global environmental change. In M. R. Rosenzweig & L. W. Porter (Eds.), *Annual review of psychology* (Vol. 43, pp. 269–302). Palo Alto, CA: Annual Reviews, Inc.

Sternberg, R. J. (1986). A triangular theory of love. *Psychological Review, 93,* 119–135.

Sternberg, R. J. (1988). Triangulating love. In R. J. Sternberg & M. L. Barnes (Eds.), *The psychology of love* (pp. 119–138). New Haven, CT: Yale University Press.

Stevens, W. K. (1991a, January 29). What really threatens the environment? *New York Times,* p. C4.

Stevens, W. K. (l991b, February l9). Warming of globe could build on itself, some scientists say. *New York Times,* p. C4.

Stevens, W. K. (1992, February 25). Global warming threatens to undo decades of conservation efforts. *New York Times,* p. C4.

Stewart, D. D. (1992). *Expertise, collective recall, and consensus.* Unpublished doctoral dissertation, Miami University, Oxford, OH.

Stewart, J. E. (1980). Defendant's attractiveness as a factor in the outcome of criminal trials: An observational study. *Journal of Applied Social Psychology, 10,* 348–361.

Stewart, J. E. (1985). Appearance and punishment: The attraction–leniency effect. *Journal of Social Psychology, 125,* 373–378.

Stier, D. S., & Hall, J. A. (1984). Gender differences in touch: An empirical and theoretical review. *Journal of Personality and Social Psychology, 47,* 440–459.

Stiff, J. B., Miller, G. R., Sleight, C., Mongeau, P. I., Gardelick, R., & Rogan, R. (1989). Explanations for visual cue primacy in judgments of honesty and deceit. *Journal of Personality and Social Psychology, 56,* 555–564.

Stifter, C. A., & Fox, N. A. (1987). Preschool children's ability to identify and label emotions. *Journal of Nonverbal Behavior, 11,* 43–54.

Stiles, W. B., Shuster, P. L., & Harrigan, J. A. (1992). Disclosure and anxiety: A test of the fever model. *Journal of Personality and Social Psychology, 63,* 980–988.

Stinson, I., & Ickes, W. (1992). Empathic accuracy in the interactions of male friends versus male strangers. *Journal of Personality and Social Psychology, 62,* 787–797.

Stone, A. A., Cox, D., Valdimarsdotti, H., Jandorf, L., & Neale, J. M. (1987). Evidence that secretory IGA antibody is associated with daily mood. *Journal of Personality and Social Psychology, 52,* 988–993.

Stone, J., Aronson, E., Crain, L., Winslow, N., & Fried, C. (1992). *Creating hypocrisy as a means of inducing adults to purchase condoms.* Unpublished manuscript, University of California at Santa Cruz.

Stoner, J. A. F. (1961). *A comparison of individual and group decisions involving risk.* Unpublished master's thesis, School of Industrial Management, MIT.

Strack, F., Martin, L. L., & Stepper, S. (1988). Inhibiting and facilitating conditions of facial expressions: A non–obtrusive test of the facial feedback hypothesis. *Journal of Personality and Social Psychology, 54,* 768–777.

Street, R. L., Jr., & Buller, D. G. (1987). Nonverbal response patterns in physician–patient interactions: A functional analysis. *Journal of Nonverbal Behavior, 11,* 234–253.

Strentz, T., & Auerbach, S. M. (1988). Adjustment to the stress of simulated captivity: Effects of emotion–focused versus problem–focused preparation on hostages differing in locus of control. *Journal of Personality and Social Psychology, 55,* 652–660.

Strickland, B. R. (1992). Women and depression. *Current Directions in Psychological Science, 1,* 132–135.

Stroessner, S. J., Hamilton, D. L., & Mackie, D. M. (1992). Affect and stereotyping: The effect of induced mood on distinctiveness–based illusory correlations. *Journal of Personality and Social Psychology, 62,* 564–576.

Strom, S. (1991, October 20). Harassment rules often not pushed. *New York Times,* pp. A1, A22.

Strube, M., Turner, C. W., Cerro, D., Stevens, J., & Hinchey, F. (1984). Interpersonal aggression and the Type A coronary–prone behavior pattern: A theoretical distinction and practical implications. *Journal of Personality and Social Psychology, 47,* 839–847.

Strube, M. J. (1989). Evidence for the Type in Type A behavior: A taxonometric analysis. *Journal of Personality and Social Psychology, 56,* 972–987.

Strube, M. J., & Garcia, J. E. (1981). A meta-analytic investigation of Fiedler's contingency model of leadership effectiveness. *Psychological Bulletin, 90,* 307–321.

Stycos, J. M. (1991). The second great wall of China: Evolution of a successful policy of population control. *Population and Environment, 12,* 389–406.

Subich, L. M., Cooper, E. A., Barrett, G. V., & Arthur, W. (1986). Occupational perceptions of males and females as a function of sex ratios, salary, and availability. *Journal of Vocational Behavior, 28,* 123–134.

Suedfeld, P., & Wallbaum, A. B. C. (1992). Modifying integrative complexity in political thought: Value conflict and audience disagreement. *Interamerican Journal of Psychology, 26,* 19–36.

Sullins, E. S. (1991). Emotional contagion revisited: Effects of social comparison and expressive style on mood convergence. *Personality and Social Psychology Bulletin, 17,* 166–174.

Sulman, F. G., Levy, D., Levy, A., Pfeifer, Y., Saperstein, E., & Tal, E. (1974). Ionometry of hot, dry desert winds (*sharav*) and application of ionizing treatment to weather–sensitive patients. *International Journal of Biometeorology, 13,* 393.

Suls, J., & Fletcher, B. (1985). The relative efficacy of avoidant and nonavoidant coping strategies: A meta–analysis. *Health Psychology, 4,* 249–288.

Suls, J., & Greenwald, A. G. (Eds.). (1986). *Psychological perspectives on the self* (Vol. 3). Hillsdale, NJ: Erlbaum.

Suls, J., & Rosnow, J. (1988). Concerns about artifacts in behavioral research. In M. Morawski (Ed.), *The rise of experimentation in American psychology* (pp. 163–187). New Haven, CT: Yale University Press.

Suls, J., & Wan, C. K. (1987). In search of the false uniqueness phenomenon: Fear and estimates of social consensus. *Journal of Personality and Social Psychology, 52,* 211–217.

Suls, J., & Wan, C. K. (1989). The effects of sensory and procedural information on coping with stressful medical procedures and pain: A meta–analysis. *Journal of Consulting and Clinical Psychology, 57,* 372–379.

Suls, J., Wan, C. K., & Sanders, G. S. (1988). False consensus and false uniqueness in estimating the prevalence of health–protective behaviors. *Journal of Applied Social Psychology, 19,* 66–79.

Summers, R. J. (1991). The influence of affirmative action on perceptions of a beneficiary's qualifications. *Journal of Applied Social Psychology, 21,* 1265–1276.

Sunnafrank, M. (1992). On debunking the attitude similarity myth. *Communication Monographs, 59,* 165–179.

Sunstein, C. R. (1993). Valuing life. *New Republic, 208*(7), 36–40.

Swallow, S. R., & Kuiper, N. A. (1987). The effects of depression and cognitive vulnerability to depression on judgments of similarity between self and other. *Motivation and Emotion, 11,* 157–167.

Swann, W. B., Jr. (1993, February). Personal communication.

Swann, W. B., Jr., De La Ronde, C., & Hixon, J. G. (1993). *Authenticity and positivity strivings in marriage and courtship.* Manuscript submitted for publication.

Swann, W. B., Jr., Griffin, J. J., Jr., Predmore, S. C., & Gaines, B. (1987). Cognitive-affective crossfire: When self-consistency meets self–enhancement. *Journal of Personality and Social Psychology, 52,* 881–889.

Swann, W. B., Jr., Hixon, J. G., & De La Ronde, C. (1992). Embracing the bitter "truth": Negative self-concepts and marital commitment. *Psychological Science, 3,* 118–121.

Swann, W. B., Jr., Stein–Seroussi, A., & Giesler, R. B. (1992). Why people self–verify. *Journal of Personality and Social Psychology, 62,* 392–401.

Swap, W. C. (1977). Interpersonal attraction and repeated exposure to rewarders and punishers. *Personality and Social Psychology Bulletin, 3,* 248–251.

Szymanski, K., & Harkins, S. (1987). Social loafing and self–evaluation with a social standard. *Journal of Personality and Social Psychology, 55,* 891–897.

Tajfel, H. (1982). *Social identity and intergroup relations.* Cambridge: Cambridge University Press.

Tak, H. (1990). Longing for local identity: Intervillage relations in Italian mountain area. *Anthropological Quarterly, 63,* 90–100.

Takahashi, T. (1991). A comparative study of Japanese and American group dynamics. *Psychoanalytic Review, 78*(1), 49–62.

Tanford, S., & Penrod, S. (1984). Social influence model: A formal integration of research on majority and minority influence processes. *Psychological Bulletin, 95,* 189–225.

Tangney, J. P. (1990). Assessing individual differences in proneness to shame and guilt: Development of the self–conscious affect and attribution inventory. *Journal of Personality and Social Psychology, 59,* 102–111.

Tangney, J. P., Wagner, P., Fletcher, C., & Gramzow, R. (1992). Shamed into anger? The relation of shame and guilt to anger and self–reported aggression. *Journal of Personality and Social Psychology, 62,* 669–675.

Taylor, J. (1992). What characters. Reconstructing the big "C" issue. *New York, 25*(15), 48–50.

Taylor, M. S., Locke, E. A., Lee, C., & Gist, M. E. (1984). Type A behavior and faculty research productivity: What are the mechanisms? *Organizational Behavior and Human Performance, 34,* 402–418.

Taylor, S. E., Buunk, B. P., & Aspinwall, L. G. (1990). Social comparison, stress, and coping. *Personality and Social Psychology Bulletin, 16,* 74–89.

Taylor, S. E., Helgeson, V. S., Reed, G. M., & Skokan, L. A. (1991). Self–generated feelings of control and adjustment to physical illness. *Journal of Social Issues, 47,* 91–109.

Taylor, S. L., O'Neal, E. C., Langley, T., & Butcher, A. H. (1991). Anger arousal, deindividuation, and aggression. *Aggressive Behavior, 17,* 193–206.

Taylor, S. P. (1967). Aggressive behavior and physiological arousal as a function of provocation and the tendency to inhibit aggression. *Journal of Personality, 35,* 297–310.

Taylor, S. P., Gammon, C. B., & Capasso, D. R. (1976). Aggression as a function of the interaction of alcohol and threat. *Journal of Personality and Social Psychology, 34,* 938–991.

Taylor, S. P., & Leonard, K. E. (1983). Alcohol and human physical aggression. In R. Geen & E. Donnerstein (Eds.), *Aggression: Theoretical and empirical reviews.* New York: Academic Press.

Taylor, S. P., & Sears, J. D. (1988). The effects of alcohol and persuasive social pressure on human physical aggression. *Aggressive Behavior, 14,* 237–243.

Tedeschi, J. T., & Melburg, V. (1984). Impression management and influence in organizations. In S. B. Bacharach & E. J. Lawler (Eds.), *Research in the sociology of organizations* (Vol 3., pp. 31–58). Greenwich, CT: JAI Press.

Terry, R. L., & Macy, R. J. (1991). Children's social judgments of other children who wear eyeglasses. *Journal of Social Behavior and Personality, 6,* 965–974.

Tesser, A., Campbell, J., & Smith, M. (1984). Friendship choice and performance: Self-evaluation maintenance in children. *Journal of Personality and Social Psychology, 46,* 561–574.

Tetlock, P. E., & Boettger, R. (1989). Accountability: A social magnifier of the dilution effect. *Journal of Personality and Social Psychology, 57,* 388–398.

Tetlock, P. E., Peterson, R. S., McGuire, C., Change, S., & Feld, P. (1992). Assessing political group dynamics: A test of the groupthink model. *Journal of Personality and Social Psychology, 63,* 403–425.

Thayer, S., & Saarni, C. (1975). Demand characteristics are everywhere (anyway): A comment on the Stanford prison experiment. *American Psychologist, 30,* 1015–1016.

The anti–smoking trend. (1993, January 4). *Time,* p. 60.

The Bennington study. (1991–92). *ISR Newsletter, 17*(2), 4–7.

Thernstrom, S. (1933). Jungle fever. *New Repulic, 208*(16), 12, 14.

Thomas, E. A. C., & Parpal, M. (1987). Liability as a function of plaintiff and defendant fault. *Journal of Personality and Social Psychology, 53,* 843–857.

Thomas, W. K. (1992). Conflict and negotiation processes. In M. Dunnette (Ed.), *Handbook of industrial and organizational psychology* (2nd ed.). Chicago: Rand McNally.

Thompson, D. (1992). The danger in doomsaying. *Time, 139*(10), 61.

Thompson, J. K., & Tantleff, S. (1992). Female and male ratings of upper torso: Actual, ideal, and stereotypical conceptions. *Journal of Social Behavior and Personality, 7,* 345–354.

Thompson, L. (1990). An examination of naive and experienced negotiators. *Journal of Personality and Social Psychology, 59,* 82–90.

Thompson, L., Brodt, S. E., & Peterson, E. (1993). *Team versus solo negotiations: Are two heads better than one?* Unpublished manuscript, University of Washington, Seattle, WA.

Thompson, L., & Hastie, R. (1990). Social perception in negotiation. *Organizational Behavior and Human Decision Processes, 40,* 136–147.

Thompson, L. L. (1993). *Biases in negotiation: An examination of reception and transmission processes.* Unpublished manuscript, University of Washington, Seattle, WA.

Thompson, L. L., & DeHarpport, T. (1993). Social judgment, feedback, and interpersonal learning in negotiation. *Organizational Behavior and Human Decision Processes,* in press.

Thompson, S. C., Sobolew–Shubin, A., Galbraith, M. E., Schwankovsky, L., & Cruzen, D. (1993). Maintaining perceptions of control: Finding perceived control in low–control circumstances. *Journal of Personality and Social Psychology, 64,* 293–304.

Thompson, W. C., Cowan, C. L., & Rosenhan, D. L. (1980). Focus of attention mediates the impact of negative affect on altruism. *Journal of Personality and Social Psychology, 38,* 291–300.

Thorne, A. (1987). The press of personality: A study of conversations between introverts and extraverts. *Journal of Personality and Social Psychology, 53,* 718–726.

Thornton, A., & Freedman, D. (1982). Changing attitudes toward married and single life. *Family Planning Perspectives, 14*(6), 297–303.

Thornton, B. (1992). Repression and its mediating influence on the defensive attribution of responsibility. *Journal of Research in Personality, 26,* 44–57.

Tien, H. Y. (1983). China: Demographic billionaire. *Population Bulletin, 38*(2).

Tifft, S. (1991). Better safe than sorry? *Time, 137*(3), 66.

Ting–Toomey, S. (1988). Intercultural conflict styles: A face–negotiation theory. In Y. Kim & W. Gudykunst (Eds.), *Theories in intercultural communication* (pp. 313–235). Newbury Park, Ca: Sage.

Ting–Toomey, S. (1991). Intimacy expressions in three cultures: France, Japan, and the United States. *International Journal of Intercultural Relations, 15,* 29–46.

Ting–Toomey, S., Gao, G., Trubisky, P., Yang, Z., Kim, H. S., Lin, S. L., & Nishida, T. (1991). Culture, face maintenance, and styles of handling interpersonal conflict: A study in five cultures. *International Journal of Conflict Management, 2,* 275–296.

Toch, H. (1985). *Violent men* (rev. ed.). Cambridge, MA: Schenkman.

Toch, H. (1980). The catalytic situation in the violence equation. *Journal of Applied Social Psychology, 15,* 105–123.

Toi, M., & Batson, C. D. (1982). More evidence that empathy is a source of altruistic motivation. *Journal of Personality and Social Psychology, 43,* 281–292.

Tooley, V., Brigham, J. C., Maass, A., & Bothwell, R. K. (1987). Facial recognition: Weapon effect and attentional focus. *Journal of Applied Social Psychology, 17,* 845–859.

Topf, M. (1989). Sensitivity to noise, personality hardiness, and noise–induced stress in critical care nurses. *Environment and Behavior, 21,* 717–733.

Torestad, B. (1990). What is anger provoking: A psychophysical study of perceived causes of anger. *Aggressive Behavior, 16,* 9–26.

Tornstam, I. (1992). Loneliness in marriage. *Journal of Social and Personal Relationships, 9,* 197–217.

Toufexis, A. (1989, July 17). Panic over power lines. *Time,* p. 71.

Toufexis, A. (1992). Endangered species. *Time, 139*(17), 48–50.

Toufexis, A. (1993). The right chemistry. *Time, 141*(7), 49–51.

Traeen, B., Lewin, B., & Sundet, J. M. (1992). The real and the ideal: Gender differences in heterosexual behaviour among Norwegian adolescents. *Journal of Community & Applied Social Psychology, 2,* 227–237.

Triplett, H. (1898). The dynamogenic factors in pace making and competition. *American Journal of Psychology, 9,* 507–533.

Trope, Y. (1986). Identification and inferential processes in dispositional attribution. *Psychological Review, 93,* 239–257.

Tucker, J. S., & Riggio, R. E. (1988). The role of social skills in encoding of posed and spontaneous facial expressions. *Journal of Nonverbal Behavior, 12,* 87–97.

Tuckman, B. W., & Sexton, T. L. (1990). The relation between self–beliefs and self–regulated performance. *Journal of Social Behavior and Personality, 5,* 465–472.

Turner, C. W., & Simons, L. S. (1974). Effects of subject sophistication and evaluation apprehension on aggressive responses to weapons. *Journal of Personality and Social Psychology, 30,* 341–348.

Turner, J. C., Hogg, M. A., Oakes, P. J., Reicher, S. D., & Wetherell, M. S. (1987). *Rediscovering the social group: A self–categorization theory.* Oxford, England: Blackwell.

Turner, M. E., Pratkanis, A. R., & Hardaway, T. J. (1991). Sex differences in reaction to preferential selection: Towards a model of preferential selection as help. *Journal of Social Behavior and Personality, 6,* 797–814.

Tversky, A., & Kahneman, D. (1973). Availability: A heuristic for judging frequency and probability. *Cognitive Psychology, 5,* 207–232.

Tversky, A., & Kahneman, D. (1982). Judgment under uncertainty: Heuristics and biases. In D. Kahnamen, P. Slovic, & A. Tversky (Eds.), *Judgment under uncertainty* (pp. 3–20). New York: Cambridge University Press.

Tyler, T. R., & Schuller, R. A. (1991). Aging and attitude change. *Journal of Personality and Social Psychology, 61,* 689–697.

Type A's lack cholesterol aid, study says. (1992, November 18). *Albany Times Union,* p. A–5.

Uchino, G. N., Kiecolt–Glaser, J. K., & Cacioppo, J. T. (1992). Age–related changes in cardiovascular response as a function of a chronic stressor and social support. *Journal of Personality and Social Psychology, 63,* 839–846.

Udry, J. R. (1980). Changes in the frequency of marital intercourse from panel data. *Archives of Sexual Behavior, 9,* 319–325.

Ullman, C. (1987). From sincerity to authenticity: Adolescents' view of the "true self. " *Journal of Personality, 55,* 583–595.

Umpleby, S. A. (1990). The scientific revolution in demography. *Population and Environment, 11,* 159–174.

Ungerer, J. A., Dolby, R., Waters, B., Barnett, B., Kelk, N., & Lewin, V. (1990). The early development of empathy: Self–regulation and individual differences in the first year. *Motivation and Emotion, 14,* 93–106.

Urbanski, L. (1992, May 21). Study uncovers traits people seek in friends. *The Evangelist,* p. 41

Vallacher, R. R., & Wegner, D. M. (1987). What do people think they're doing? Action identification and human behavior. *Psychological Review, 94,* 3–1S.

Vallone, R., Ross, L., & Lepper, M. R. (1985). The hostile media phenomenon: Biased perception and perceptions of media bias in coverage of the Beirut massacre. *Journal of Personality and Social Psychology, 49,* 577–585.

Vanbeselaere, N. (1987). The effects of dichotomous and crossed social categorization upon intergroup discrimination. *European Journal of Social Psychology, 17,* 143–156.

Vander–Martin, R., Cummings, S. R., & Coates, T. J. (1990). Ethnicity and smoking: Differences in white, black, Hispanic, and Asian medical patients who smoke. *American Journal of Preventive Medicine, 6,* 194–199.

Van Hook, E., & Higgins, E. T. (1988). Self–related problems beyond the self–concept: Motivational consequences of discrepant self–guides. *Journal of Personality and Social Psychology, 55,* 625–633.

Van Vianen, A. E. M., & Willemsen, T. M. (1992). The employment interview: The role of sex stereotypes in the evaluation of male and female job applicants in the Netherlands. *Journal of Applied Social Psychology, 22,* 471–491.

Vecchio, R. P. (1987). Situational leadership theory: An examination of a prescriptive theory. *Journal of Applied Psychology, 72,* 444–451.

Vig, P. S. (1985). Respiration, nasal airway, and orthodontics: A review of current clinical concepts and research. In L. E. Johnston (Ed.), *New vistas in orthodontics* (pp. 76–102). Philadelphia: Lea & Febiger.

Vining, J., & Ebreo, A. (1990). What makes a recycler? A comparison of recyclers and nonrecyclers. *Environment and Behavior, 22,* 55–73.

Vinokur, A., & Burnstein, E. (1974). Effects of partially shared persuasive arguments on group–induced shifts: A group problem–solving approach. *Journal of Personality and Social Psychology, 29,* 305–315.

Vitaliano, P. P. (1985). The Ways of Coping Checklist: Revision and psychometric properties. *Multivariate Behavioral Research, 20,* 3–26.

Viterito, A. (1991). Future warming for U. S. cities. *Population and Environment, 13,* 101–111. Vox pop. (1993, February 15). *Time,* p. 13.

Vroom, V. H., & Jago, A. G. (1978). On the validity of the Vroom–Yetton model. *Journal of Applied Psychology, 63,* 151–26.

Vroom, V. H., & Yetton, P. W. (1973). *Leadership and decision–making.* Pittsburgh: University of Pittsburgh Press.

Wagner, P. J., & Curran, P. (1984). Health beliefs and physician identified "worried well. : *Health Psychology, 3,* 459–474.

Wallace, J. M., & Bachman, J. G. (1991). Explaining racial/ethnic differences in adolescent drug use: The impact of background and lifestyle. *Social Problems, 33,* 333–357.

Wallen, K. (1992). Evolutionary hypothesis testing: Consistency is not enough. *Behavioral and Brain Sciences, 15,* 118–119.

Waller, N. G., Koietin, B. A., Bouchard, T. J., Jr., Lykken, D. T., & Tellegen, A. (1990). Genetic and environmental influences on religious interests, attitudes, and values: A study of twins reared apart and together. *Psychological Science, 1,* 138–142.

Walster, E., & Festinger, L. (1962). The effectiveness of "overheard" persuasive communication. *Journal of Abnormal and Social Psychology, 65,* 395–402.

Wann, D. L., & Branscombe, N. R. (1990). Person perception when aggressive or nonaggressive sports are primed. *Aggressive Behavior, 16,* 27–32.

Watson, D., & Clark, L. A. (1992). Affects separable and inseparable: On the hierarchical arrangement of the negative affects. *Journal of Personality and Social Psychology, 62,* 489–505.

Wattenberg, B. J. (1989, February 13). The case for more immigrants. *U. S. News and World Report,* pp. 29–31.

Watts, B. L. (1982). Individual differences in circadian activity rhythms and their effects on roommate relationships. *Journal of Personality, 50,* 374–384.

Waynbaum, I. (1907). *La physionomie humaine: Son mecnisme et son role social (The human face: Its mechanisms and social function).* Paris: Alcan.

Wayne, S. J., & Kacmar, K. M. (1991). The effects of impression management on the performance appraisal process. *Organizational Behavior and Human Decision Processes, 48,* 70–88.

Wedell, D. H., Parducci, A., & Geiselman, R. E. (1987). A formal analysis of ratings of physical attractiveness: Successive contrast and simultaneous assimilation. *Journal of Experimental Social Psychology, 23,* 230–249.

Weeks, M. O., & Gage, B. A. (1984). A comparison of the marriage–role expectations of college women enrolled in a functional marriage course. *Sex Roles, 11,* 377–388.

Weenig, M. W. H., & Midden, C. J. H. (1991). Communication network influences on information diffusion and persuasion. *Journal of Personality and Social Psychology, 54,* 734–742.

Wegner, D. M., Short, J. W., Blake, A. W., & Page, M. S. (1990). The suppression of exciting thoughts. *Journal of Personality and Social Psychology, 58,* 409–418.

Weidner, G., Istvan, J., & McKnight, J. D. (1989). Clusters of behavioral coronary risk factors in employed women and men. *Journal of Applied Social Psychology, 19,* 468–480.

Weinberg, P. C., & Wiulliams, C. J. (1988). Black sexuality: A test of two theories. *Journal of Sex Research, 25,* 197–218.

Weinberger, M., Hiner, S. L., & Tierney, W. M. (1987). In support of hassles as a measure of stress in predicting health outcomes. *Journal of Behavioral Medicine, 16,* 19–32.

Weiner, B. (1980). A cognitive (attribution) emotion–action model of motivated behavior: An analysis of judgments of helpgiving. *Journal of Personality and Social Psychology, 39,* 186–200.

Weiner, B., Amirkhan, J., Folkes, V. S., & Verette, J. A. (1987). An attributional analysis of excuse giving: Studies of a naive theory of emotion. *Journal of Personality and Social Psychology, 52,* 316–324.

Weis, D. L. (1983). Affective reactions of women to their initial experience of coitus. *Journal of Sex Research, 19,* 209–237.

Weitzman, L., Eifler, D., Hokada, E., & Ross, C. (1972). Sex–role socialization in picture books for preschool children. *American Journal of Sociology, 77,* 1125–1150.

Weldon, E., & Mustari, L. (1988). Felt dispensability in groups of coactors: The effects of shared responsibility and explicit anonymity on cognitive effort. *Organizational Behavior and Human Decision Processes, 41,* 330–351.

Wells, G. L. (1984). The psychology of lineup identification. *Journal of Applied Social Psychology, 14,* 89–103.

Wells, G. L. (1992). Naked statistical evidence of liability: Is subjective probability enough? *Journal of Personality and Social Psychology, 63,* 739–752.

Wells, G. L., & Gavanski, I. (1989). Mental simulation of causality. *Journal of Personality and Social Psychology, 56,* 161–169.

Wells, G. L., & Luus C. A. E. (1990). Police lineups as experiments: Social methodology as a framework for properly conducted lineups. *Personality and Social Psychology Bulletin, 16,* 106–117.

Wells, G. L., Wrightsman, L. S., & Miene, P. K. (1985). The timing of the defense opening statement: Don't wait until the evidence is in. *Journal of Applied Social Psychology, 15,* 758–772.

Wenzlaff, R. N., Wegner, D. N., & Klein, S. B. (1991). The role of thought suppression in the bonding of thought and mood. *Journal of Personality and Social Psychology, 60,* 500–508.

Werner, C. M., Altman, I., & Brown, B. B. (1992). A transactional approach to interpersonal relations: Physical environment, social context, and temporal qualities. *Journal of Social and Personal Relationships, 9,* 297–323.

Werner, C. M., Strube, M. J., Cole, A. M., & Kagehiro, D. K. (1985). The impact of case characteristics and prior jury experience on jury verdicts. *Journal of Applied Social Psychology, 15,* 409–427.

Weyant, J. M. (1986). *Applied social psychology.* New York: Oxford University Press.

White, G. L. (1980). Inducing jealousy: A power perspective. *Personality and Social Psychology Bulletin, 6,* 222–227.

White, G. L., & Mullen, P. E. (1990). *Jealousy: Theory, research, and clinical strategies.* New York: Guilford.

White, J. L. & Parham, T. (1990). *The psychology of blacks: An African-American perspective.* Englewood Cliffs, NJ: Prentice Hall.

White, R. K. (1977). Misperception in the Arab-Israeli conflict. *Journal of Social Issues, 33,* 190–221.

Whitley, G. E., & Greenberg, M. S. (1986). The role of eyewitness confidence in juror perceptions of credibility. *Journal of Applied Social Psychology, 16,* 387–409.

Whyte, W. W., Jr. (1956). *The organization man.* New York: Simon and Schuster.

Wicker, A. W. (1969). Attitudes versus actions: The relationship of verbal and overt behavioral responses to attitude obiects. *Journal of Social Issues, 25,* 41–78.

Wiebe, D. J., & McCallum, D. M. (1986). Health practices and hardiness as mediators in the stress–illness relationship. *Health Psychology, 5,* 425–438.

Wiederman, M. W., & Allgeier, E. R. (1992). Gender differences in mate selection criteria: Sociobiological or socioeconomic explanation. *Ethnology and Sociobiology, 13,* 115–124.

Wiegele, T. C., & Oots, K. L. (1990). Type A behavior and local government elites. *Political Psychology, 11,* 721–737.

Wilder, D. A. (1977). Perception of groups, size of opposition, and social influence. *Journal of Experimental Social Psychology, 13,* 253–268.

Wilder, D. A. (1984). Intergroup contact: The typical member and the exception to the rule. *Journal of Experimental Social Psychology, 20,* 177–194.

Williams, J. G., & Solano, C. H. (1983). The social reality of feeling lonely: Friendship and reciprocation. *Personality and Social Psychology Bulletin, 9,* 237–242.

Williams, K., & Alliger, G. (in press). *Industrial–organizational psychology.* Boston: Allyn & Bacon.

Williams, K., Harkins, S., & Latane, B. (1981). Identifiability as a deterrent to social loafing: Two cheering experiments. *Journal of Personality and Social Psychology, 40,* 303–311.

Williams, K. D., & Karau, S. J. (1991). Social loafing and social compensation: The effects of expectations of co–worker performance. *Journal of Personality and Social Psychology, 61,* 570–581.

Williams, R. L. (1976). *Manual of directions for Williams awareness sentence completion.* St. Louis, MO: Robert L. Williams & Associates, Inc.

Williamson, G. M., & Clark, M. S. (1989). Providing help and desired relationship type as determinants of changes in moods and self–evaluations. *Journal of Personality and Social Psychology, 56,* 722–734.

Williamson, G. M., & Clark, M. S. (1992). Impact of desired relationship type on affective reactions to choosing and being required to help. *Personality and Social Psychology Bulletin, 18,* 10–18.

Wilson, D. K., Kaplan, R. M., & Schneiderman, L. J. (1987). Framing of decisions and selections of alternatives in health care. *Social Behavior, 2,* 51–59.

Wilson, D. W. (1981). Is helping a laughing matter? *Psychology, 18,* 6–9.

Wilson, J. P., & Petruska, R. (1984). Motivation, model attributes, and prosocial behavior. *Journal of Personality and Social Psychology, 46,* 458–468.

Wilson, P. M. (1986). Black culture and sexuality. *Journal of Social Work and Human Sexuality, 4,* 29–44.

Wilson, T. D. (1990). Self–persuasion via self–reflection. In M. Olson & M. P. Zanna (Eds.), *Self–inference processes: The Ontario symposium* (Vol. 6, pp. 43–67). Hillsdale, NJ: Erlbaum.

Wilson, T. D., & Klaaren, K. J. (1992). Effects of affective expectations on willingness to relive pleasant and unpleasant events. Unpublished data. Cited in Wilson, T. D., & Klaaren, K. J., "Expectation whirl me round": The role of affective expectations in affective experience. In M. S. Clark (Ed.), *Emotion and social behavior* (pp. 1–31). Newbury Park, CA: Sage.

Wilson, T. D., & Linville, P. W. (1982). Improving the academic performance of college freshmen: Attribution therapy revisited. *Journal of Personality and Social Psychology, 42,* 367–376.

Wilson, T. D., Lisle, D. J., Kraft, D., & Wetzel, C. G. (1989). Preferences as expectation-driven inferences: Effects of affective expectations on affective experience. *Journal of Personality and Social Psychology, 56,* 519–530.

Wilson, T. D., & Schooler, J. (1991). Thinking too much: Introspection can reduce the quality of preferences and decisions. *Journal of Personality and Social Psychology, 60,* 181–192.

Winn, K. I., Crawford, D. W., & Fischer, J. (1991). Equity and commitment in romance versus friendship. *Journal of Social Behavior and Personality, 6,* 301–314.

Wittenbaum, G., Vaughan, S., Merry, C., & Stasser, G. (1993). Research in progress. Miami University, Oxford, OH.

Wolf, N. (1992). Father figures. *New Republic, 207*(15), 22, 24–25.

Wolf, S., & Bugaj, A. M. (1990). The social impact of courtroom witnesses. *Social Behaviour, 5,* 1–13.

Wolfe, B. M., & Baron, R. A. (1971). Laboratory aggression related to aggression in naturalistic social situations: Effects of an aggressive model on the behavior of college student and prisoner doservers. *Psychonomic Science, 24,* 193–194.

Wolfe, S. (1985). Manifest and latent influence of majorities and minorities. *Journal of Personality and Social Psychology, 48,* 899–908.

Wood, W. (1982). Retrieval of attitude–relevant information from memory: Effects on susceptibility to persuasion on intrinsic motivation. *Journal of Personality and Social Psychology, 42,* 798–810.

Wood, W., Wong, F. Y., & Chachere, J. G. (1991). Effects of media violence on viewers' aggression in unconstrained social interaction. *Psychological Bulletin, 109,* 371–383.

Woodall, W. G., & Burgoon, J. R. (1984). Talking fast and changing attitudes: A critique and clarification. *Journal of Nonverbal Behavior, 8,* 126–142.

Worchel, S., & Shackelford, S. L. (1991). Groups under stress: The influence of group structure and environment on process and performance. *Personality and Social Psychology Bulletin, 17,* 640–647.

Wortman, C. B., & Linsenmeier, J. A. W. (1977). Interpersonal attraction and techniques of ingratiation in organizational settings. In B. N. Staw & G. R. Salancik (Eds.), *New directions in organizational behavior* (pp. 133–178). Chicago: St. Clair Press.

Wright, P. H. (1984). Selfreferent motivation and the intrinsic quality of friendship. *Journal of Social and Personal Relationships, 1,* 115–130.

Wu, C., & Shaffer, D. R. (1987). Susceptibility to persuasive appeals as a function of source credibility and prior experience with the attitude object. *Journal of Personality and Social Psychology, 52,* 677–688.

Wuensch, K. L., Castellow, W. A., & Moore, C. H. (1991). Effects of defendant attractiveness and type of crime on juridic judgment. *Journal of Social Behavior and Personality, 6,* 713–724.

Wyer, R. S. (1988). Social memory and social judgment. In P. R. Solomon, G. R. Goethals, C. M. Kelley, & B. R. Stephens (Eds.), *Perspectives on the research.* New York: Springer–Verlag.

Wyer, R. W., & Srull, T. X. (1980). Category accessibility and social perception: Some implications for the study of person memory and interpersonal judgments. *Journal of Personality and Social Psychology, 28,* 841–856.

Wyer, R. W., & Srull, T. K. (1984). Human cognition in its social context. *Psychological Review, 93,* 322–359.

Yamagishi, T. (1988). Exit from the group as an individualistic solution to free rider problem in the United States and Japan. *Journal of Experimental Social Psychology, 24,* 530–542.

Yates, S. (1992). Lay attributions about distress after a natural disaster. *Personality and Social Psychology Bulletin, 18,* 217–222.

Young, J., & Osborne, R. (1989, June). *"Aim vs. shrimp": Individual differences in the use of political issues and images.* Paper presented at the meeting of the American Psychological Society, Alexandria, VA.

Young, J., Thomsen, C. J., Borgida, E., Sullivan, J. L., & Aldrich, J. H. (1991). When self–interest makes a difference: The role of construct accessibility in political reasoning. *Journal of Experimental Social Psychology, 27,* 271–296.

Young, J. E. (1982). Loneliness, depression, and cognitive therapy: Theory and application. In L. A. Peplau & D. Perlman (Eds.), *Loneliness: A sourcebook of current theory, research, and therapy.* New York: Wiley.

Yuen, E. C., & Lim, H. L. (1990). The interaction of biases in the evaluation of managers in Singapore. *International Journal of Psychology, 25,* 491–508.

Yuille, J. C., & Cutshall, J. L. (1986). A case study of eyewitness memory of a crime. *Journal of Applied Psychology, 71,* 291–301.

Yuille, J. C., & McEwan, N. H. (1985). Use of hypnosis as an aid to eyewitness memory. *Journal of Applied Psychology, 70,* 389–400.

Yuille, J. C., & Tollestrup, P. A. (1990). Some effects of alcohol on eyewitness memory. *Journal of Applied Psychology, 75,* 268–273.

Yukl, G. (1981). *Leadership in organizations.* Englewood Cliffs, NJ: Prentice–Hall.

Yukl, G. (1989). *Leadership in organizations* (2nd ed.). Englewood Cliffs, NJ: Prentice–Hall.

Yukl, G., & Falbe, C. M. (1990). Influence tactics and objectives in upward, downward, and lateral influence attempts. *Journal of Applied Psychology, 75,* 132–140.

Yukl, G., & Falbe, C. M. (1991). Importance of different power sources in downward and lateral relations. *Journal of Applied Psychology, 76,* 416–423.

Yukl, G., & Tracey, J. B. (1992). Consequences of influence tactics used with subordinates, peers, and the boss. *Journal of Applied Psychology, 77,* 525–535

Zaccaro, S. J., Foti, R. J., & Kenny, D. A. (1991). Self–monitoring and trait–based variance in leadership: An investigation of leader flexibility across multiple group situations. *Journal of Applied Psychology, 76,* 308–315.

Zaccaro, S. J., & McCoy, M. C. (1988). The effects of task and interpersonal cohesiveness on performance of a disjunctive group task. *Journal of Applied Social Psychology, 18,* 837–851.

Zajonc, R. B. (1965). Social facilitation. *Science, 149,* 269–274.

Zajonc, R. B. (1968). Attitudinal effects of mere exposure. *Journal of Personality and Social Psychology Monograph Supplement, 9,* 1–27.

Zajonc, R. B. (1980). Feeling and thinking: Preferences need no inferences. *American Psychologist, 35,* 151–175.

Zajonc, R. B. (1982). Exposure effects in person perception: Familiarity, similarity, and attraction. *Journal of Experimental Social Psychology, 18,* 395–415.

Zajonc, R. B. (1984). On the primacy of affect. *American Psychologist, 39,* 117–123.

Zajonc, R. B. (1985). Emotion and facial difference: A theory reclaimed. *Science, 228,* 15–21.

Zajonc, R. B., Adelmann, P. K., Murphy, S. T., & Niedenthal, P. M. (1987). Convergence in the physical appearance of spouses. *Motivation and Emotion, 11,* 335–346.

Zajonc, R. B., Heingartner, A., & Herman, E. M. (1969). Social enhancement and impairment of performance in the cockroach. *Journal of Personality and Social Psychology, 13,* 83–92.

Zajonc, R. B., & McIntosh, D. N. (1992). Emotions research: Some promising questions and some questionable promises. *Psychological Science, 3,* 70–74.

Zajonc, R. B., Murphy, S. T., & Inglehart, M. (1989). Feeling and facial inference: Implications of the vascular theory of emotion. *Psychological Review, 96,* 395–416.

Zajonc, R. B., & Sales, S. H. (1966). Social facilitation of dominant and subordinate responses. *Journal of Experimental Social Psychology, 2,* 160–168.

Zammichieli, M. E., Gilroy, F. D., & Sherman, M. F. (1988). Relation between sex–role orientation and marital satisfaction. *Personality and Social Psychology Bulletin, 14,* 747–754.

Zebrowitz, L. A., Olson, K., & Hoffman, K. (1993). Stability of babyfacedness and attractiveness across the lifespan. *Journal of Personality and Social Psychology, 64,* 453–466.

Zeichner, A., & Phil, R. O. (1980). Effects of alcohol and instigator intent on human aggression. *Journal of Studies on Alcohol, 41,* 265–276.

Zeitz, G. (1990). Age and work satisfaction in a government agency: A situational perspective. *Human Relations, 43,* 419–438.

Zillmann, D. (1979). *Hostility and aggression.* Hillsdale, NJ: Erlbaum.

Zillmann, D. (1983). Transfer of excitation in emotional behavior. In J. T. Cacioppo & R. E. Petty (Eds.), *Social psychophysiology: A sourcebook* (pp. 215–240). New York: Guilford Press.

Zillmann, D. (1984). *Connections between sex and aggression.* Hillsdale, NJ: Erlbaum.

Zillmann, D. (1988). Cognition–excitation interdependencies in aggressive behavior. *Aggressive Behavior, 14,* 51–64.

Zillmann, D., & Bryant, J. (1984). Effects of massive exposure to pornography. In N. M. Malamuth and E. Donnerstein (Eds.), *Pornography and sexual aggression.* New York: Academic Press.

Zillmann, D., & Cantor, J. R. (1976). Effects of timing of information about mitigating circumstances on emotional responses to provocation and retaliatory behavior. *Journal of Experimental Social Psychology, 12,* 38–55.

Zimbardo, P. G. (1977). *Shyness: What it is and what we can do about it.* Reading, MA: Addison–Wesley.

Zimmerman, M. A. (1990). Toward a theory of learned hopefulness: A structural model and analysis of participation and empowerment. *Journal of Research in Personality, 24,* 71–86.

Zuber, J. A., Crott, H. W., & Werner, J. (1992). Choice shift and group polarization: An analysis of the status of arguments and social decision schemes. *Journal of Personality and Social Psychology, 62,* 50–61.

Zuboff, S. (1988). *In the realm of the smart machine.* New York: Basic Books.

Zuckerman, M. (1991). *Psychology of personality.* New York: Cambridge University Press.

Zuckerman, M., DePaulo, B. M., & Rosenthal, R. (1981). Verbal and nonverbal communication of deception. In L. Berkowitz (Ed.), *Advances in experimental social psychology* (Vol. 14, pp. 1–59). New York: Academic Press.

Zuckerman, M., & Driver, R. E. (1989). What sounds beautiful is good: The vocal attractiveness stereotype. *Journal of Nonverbal Behavior, 13,* 67–82.

Zullow, H. M., Oettingen, G., Peterson, C., & Seligman, M. E. P. (1988). Pessimistic explanatory style in the historical record: CAVing LBJ, presidential candidates, and East ver-

Name Index

Cool, L.C., 572
Coontz, S., 324, 328
Cooper, C., 238
Cooper, H.N., 362, 363
Cooper, J., 163, 165, 166
Cornwell, B., 207
Costanza, R.S., 556
Cotterell, N., 337
Cousteau, J., 146
Covey, M.X., 445
Covington, N.V., 144
Cowan, C.L., 409
Cox, C.E., 73
Cox, M., 590
Craig, K.M., 452
Crain, R.L., 243
Cramer, C.C., 298
Cramer, R.E., 401
Crandall, C.S., 329, 356, 357, 551
Crane, L.A., 576
Crano, W.D., 139, 298
Crawford, D.W., 309, 333
Crawford, H.L., 132
Critchlow, B., 402
Crocker, J., 184, 207, 208, 253
Crockett, W.H., 294
Cropanzano, R., 613, 618
Crossette, G., 570
Crott, H.W., 507
Crouch, A., 523
Crouse, B.B., 277
Crowley, M., 409
Croyle, R., 558
Crusco, A.H., 48
Cruse, D., 17, 598
Crutchfield, R.A., 385
Culbertson, J.M., 543
Cummings, L.L., 621
Cummings, S.R., 576
Cunningham, A.C., 273, 274
Cunningham, J.A., 164
Cunningham, M.R., 190, 273, 406, 407, 408
Curran, P., 558
Curtis, R.C., 298
Cutler, B.L., 190, 586, 588, 598
Cutrona, C.E., 322
Cutshall, J.L., 588

Dabbs, J.M., 206, 207
D'Agostino, P.R., 90, 270
Daley, D.M., 201
Daley, H.E., 279, 540
Daly, M., 425
Damhave, K.W., 273
Dane, F.C., 596
Daniels, S.G., 116, 272, 624
Darley, J., 394, 395, 396, 399
Darley, J.M., 398
Daubman, K.A., 116, 363
Davidson, E.S., 448
Davidson, L.M., 564
Davidson, R.J., 112
Davie, M.R., 268
Davies, R.M., 340
Davis, H.E., 314
Davis, J.D., 293
Davis, J.H., 503, 504, 503583

Davis, K.E., 54, 55
Davis, M.H., 323, 490, 491
Davison, J., Jr., 154
Dawes, R.M., 295
Dawkins, R., 424
Dawson, L.J., 548
Dean, G.D., 273
Deaux, K., 174, 201, 206, 209, 249, 253
DeBono, K.G., 146, 148, 190
DeCarufel, A., 298
Deffenbacher, K.A., 588
DeHarpport, T., 623
DeJong, W., 368
DeLamater, J., 327
Delaney, H.J., 291
De La Ronde, C., 331, 332
Delery, J.E., 73, 74, 75, 366
Dellinger, R.W., 565
Demeny, P., 538
DeNeve, K.M., 565
Dengerink, H.A., 443, 445
Denno, D.J., 438
Denton, R.E., 603
Depaulo, B.M., 42, 43, 45, 50, 51, 53, 415, 416
Derlega, V.J., 288, 556
Deutsch, F.M., 208, 298, 403
Deutsch, M., 14, 269
DeVader, C.L., 517
Devine, P.G., 546
Devine, P.O., 218, 220, 223, 224, 225, 233
de Waal, F., 276
Dexter, H.R., 586
Diaz, M., 168
Dickson, L., 268
Diehl, M., 493
Dillard, J.P., 29
DiMatteo, M.R., 560
Dion, H.H., 313, 319
Dion, H.L., 313, 319
Dion, K.K., 284, 286, 287
Dion, K.L., 284, 286
Ditto, P.H., 86, 99, 100, 101
Dixon, T.M., 192
Dobbs, A.R., 439
Dodge, K.A., 463
Doherty, K., 418
Doktor, R.H., 527, 528
Dollard, J., 444, 470
Donaldson, S.I., 189
Donnerstein, E., 443, 452, 457, 472
Donnerstein, M., 472
Doob, A.N., 590
Dorian, B.J., 551
Dovidio, J.F., 218, 221, 225, 240, 415
Dovidio, J.H., 231
Downey, J.L., 273
Downing, L.L., 283
Downs, A.C., 17, 590, 591
Drachman, D., 298
Drake, M.F., 73
Drew, J., 556
Drigotas, S.M., 342
Driscoll, R., 314
Driver, R.E., 285
Dubois, N., 192
Dubrovsky, V., 514, 515

Duck, S., 294, 306
Dukakis, M., 603
Dumanoski, D., 538
Dunbar, R.I.M., 425
Duncan, N.C., 287
Dunn, J., 308
Dupre, J., 317
Durdan, C.A., 573
Durham, D.F., 544
Durso, F.T., 231
Dutton, D.G., 221, 314
Duval, S., 192
Dyck, D.G., 555

Eagly, A.H., 146, 147, 205, 209, 385, 386
Ebbesen, E.B., 269
Ebreo, A., 573
Eden, D., 254
Edmonds, E.M., 280
Edwards, D., 587
Efran, M.G., 605
Egan, T., 568
Egbert, J.M., Jr., 597
Ehrhardt, A.A., 329
Ehrlich, A.H., 540
Eisen, S.V., 204
Eisenberg, N., 291, 368, 369, 417, 418
Eisenberger, R., 337
Eisenman, R., 298, 599, 605
Ekman, P., 43, 44, 51, 76, 77, 110, 112
Elderton, E.M., 330
Elizabeth I, Queen, 516
Ellis, R.J., 486
Ellis, S., 298
Ellsworth, P.C., 46, 585
Elmer-Dewitt, P., 570
Elms, A.C., 382
Emerson, R.W., 8
Emmons, R.A., 553, 554
Endelman, J.R., 361
Engstler-Schooler, T.Y., 102
Epstein, S., 194
Erber, R., 246, 271
Erdley, C.A., 92
Ernst, A.R., 559
Eron, L.B., 449
Esses, V.M., 182, 596
Essex, M., 569
Essex, M.J., 193
Evans, G.W., 461, 566
Evans, M.C., 268
Evans, N., 231
Evans, S., 285
Eysenck, S., 209

Fabes, R.A., 418
Fajardo, D.M., 222
Falbe, C.M., 352, 376, 377
Falconer, J.J., 207
Farina, A., 273
Fazio, R.H., 89, 129, 136, 139, 140, 141, 142, 146, 165
Fein, S., 565
Feingold, A., 209, 284, 287, 316
Fekken, G.C., 555
Feldman, D.C., 488
Feldman, S.D., 605

Subject Index